Handbook of Research on Sustainable Tourism and Hotel Operations in Global Hypercompetition

Hakan Sezerel
Anadolu University, Turkey

Bryan Christiansen
Global Research Society, LLC, USA

A volume in the Advances in Hospitality, Tourism, and the Services Industry (AHTSI) Book Series

Published in the United States of America by
IGI Global
Business Science Reference (an imprint of IGI Global)
701 E. Chocolate Avenue
Hershey PA, USA 17033
Tel: 717-533-8845
Fax: 717-533-8661
E-mail: cust@igi-global.com
Web site: http://www.igi-global.com

Copyright © 2023 by IGI Global. All rights reserved. No part of this publication may be reproduced, stored or distributed in any form or by any means, electronic or mechanical, including photocopying, without written permission from the publisher. Product or company names used in this set are for identification purposes only. Inclusion of the names of the products or companies does not indicate a claim of ownership by IGI Global of the trademark or registered trademark.

Library of Congress Cataloging-in-Publication Data

Names: Sezerel, Hakan, 1981- editor. | Christiansen, Bryan, 1960- editor.
Title: Handbook of research on sustainable tourism and hotel operations in
   global hypercompetition / Hakan Sezerel, and Bryan Christiansen,
   editors.
Description: Hershey, PA : Business Science Reference, an imprint of IGI
   Global, [2023] | Includes bibliographical references and index. |
   Summary: "This publication will add value to the hospitality,
   recreation, and tourism industry via empirical research, theoretical
   development, and current best practices, especially considering the
   increased global hypercompetition following the recent pandemic"--
   Provided by publisher.
Identifiers: LCCN 2022018640 (print) | LCCN 2022018641 (ebook) | ISBN
   9781668446454 (h/c) | ISBN 9781668446461 (ebook)
Subjects: LCSH: Hospitality industry. | Sustainable tourism. |
   Globalization.
Classification: LCC TX911 .H363 2023 (print) | LCC TX911 (ebook) | DDC
   647.94--dc23/eng/20220714
LC record available at https://lccn.loc.gov/2022018640
LC ebook record available at https://lccn.loc.gov/2022018641

This book is published in the IGI Global book series Advances in Hospitality, Tourism, and the Services Industry (AHTSI) (ISSN: 2475-6547; eISSN: 2475-6555)

British Cataloguing in Publication Data
A Cataloguing in Publication record for this book is available from the British Library.

All work contributed to this book is new, previously-unpublished material. The views expressed in this book are those of the authors, but not necessarily of the publisher.

For electronic access to this publication, please contact: eresources@igi-global.com.

Advances in Hospitality, Tourism, and the Services Industry (AHTSI) Book Series

Maximiliano Korstanje
University of Palermo, Argentina

ISSN:2475-6547
EISSN:2475-6555

Mission

Globally, the hospitality, travel, tourism, and services industries generate a significant percentage of revenue and represent a large portion of the business world. Even in tough economic times, these industries thrive as individuals continue to spend on leisure and recreation activities as well as services.

The Advances in Hospitality, Tourism, and the Services Industry (AHTSI) book series offers diverse publications relating to the management, promotion, and profitability of the leisure, recreation, and services industries. Highlighting current research pertaining to various topics within the realm of hospitality, travel, tourism, and services management, the titles found within the AHTSI book series are pertinent to the research and professional needs of managers, business practitioners, researchers, and upper-level students studying in the field.

Coverage

- Casino Management
- Food and Beverage Management
- International Tourism
- Travel Agency Management
- Customer Service Issues
- Hotel Management
- Destination Marketing and Management
- Cruise Marketing and Sales
- Sustainable Tourism
- Leisure & Business Travel

IGI Global is currently accepting manuscripts for publication within this series. To submit a proposal for a volume in this series, please contact our Acquisition Editors at Acquisitions@igi-global.com or visit: http://www.igi-global.com/publish/.

The Advances in Hospitality, Tourism, and the Services Industry (AHTSI) Book Series (ISSN 2475-6547) is published by IGI Global, 701 E. Chocolate Avenue, Hershey, PA 17033-1240, USA, www.igi-global.com. This series is composed of titles available for purchase individually; each title is edited to be contextually exclusive from any other title within the series. For pricing and ordering information please visit http://www.igi-global.com/book-series/advances-hospitality-tourism-services-industry/121014. Postmaster: Send all address changes to above address. Copyright © 2023 IGI Global. All rights, including translation in other languages reserved by the publisher. No part of this series may be reproduced or used in any form or by any means – graphics, electronic, or mechanical, including photocopying, recording, taping, or information and retrieval systems – without written permission from the publisher, except for non commercial, educational use, including classroom teaching purposes. The views expressed in this series are those of the authors, but not necessarily of IGI Global.

Titles in this Series

For a list of additional titles in this series, please visit: www.igi-global.com/book-series

Handbook of Research on Urban Tourism, Viral Society, and the Impact of the COVID-19 Pandemic
Pedro Andrade (University of Minho, Portugal) and Moisés de Lemos Martins (University of Minho, Portugal)
Business Science Reference • © 2022 • 721pp • H/C (ISBN: 9781668433690) • US $315.00

Employability and Skills Development in the Sports, Events, and Hospitality Industry
Vipin Nadda (University of Sunderland in London, UK) Ian Arnott (Westminster University, UK) Wendy Sealy (University of Chichester, UK) and Emma Delaney (University of Surrey, UK)
Business Science Reference • © 2022 • 260pp • H/C (ISBN: 9781799877813) • US $215.00

Entrepreneurship Education in Tourism and Hospitality Management
Satish Chandra Bagri (Hemvati Nandan Bahuguna Garhwal University, India) R.K. Dhodi (Hemvati Nandan Bahuguna Garhwal University, India) and K.C. Junaid (Hemvati Nandan Bahuguna Garhwal University, India)
Business Science Reference • © 2022 • 313pp • H/C (ISBN: 9781799895107) • US $230.00

Global Perspectives on Strategic Storytelling in Destination Marketing
Ana Cláudia Campos (CinTurs, University of Algarve, Portugal) and Sofia Almeida (Faculty of Tourism and Hospitality, Universidade Europeia, Portugal)
Business Science Reference • © 2022 • 313pp • H/C (ISBN: 9781668434369) • US $240.00

Promoting Social and Cultural Equity in the Tourism Sector
Priscila Cembranel (Universidade Sociedade Educacional de Santa Catarina, Brazil) Jakson Renner Rodrigues Soares (Universidad da Coruña, Spain) and André Riani Costa Perinotto (Parnaíba Delta Federal University, Brazil)
Business Science Reference • © 2022 • 302pp • H/C (ISBN: 9781668441947) • US $240.00

Challenges and Opportunities for Transportation Services in the Post-COVID-19 Era
Giuseppe Catenazzo (ICN Business School, France)
Business Science Reference • © 2022 • 268pp • H/C (ISBN: 9781799888406) • US $250.00

Handbook of Research on Cultural Tourism and Sustainability
Claudia Ribeiro de Almeida (University of the Algarve, Portugal) Joao Carlos Martins (University of the Algarve, Portugal) Alexandra R. Gonçalves (University of the Algarve, Portugal) Silvia Quinteiro (University of the Algarve, Portugal) and Maria Laura Gasparini (University of Bologna, Italy)
Business Science Reference • © 2022 • 482pp • H/C (ISBN: 9781799892175) • US $315.00

701 East Chocolate Avenue, Hershey, PA 17033, USA
Tel: 717-533-8845 x100 • Fax: 717-533-8661
E-Mail: cust@igi-global.com • www.igi-global.com

List of Contributors

Akgiş Ilhan, Öznur / *Kırşehir Ahi Evran University, Turkey* 163
Akın, Mehmet Halit / *Erciyes University, Turkey* 118
Amin, Sakib Bin / *North South University, Bangladesh* 451
Avan, Ali / *Afyon Kocatepe University, Turkey* 362
Aydınlı, Feridun / *Selcuk University, Turkey* 451
Babadağ, Gonca / *Anadolu University, Turkey* 433
Barakazi, Mahmut / *Harran University, Turkey* 517
Baran, Günseli Güçlütürk / *Isparta University of Applied Sciences, Turkey & Isparta Vocational School, Turkey* 82
Barbini, Francesco / *Campus of Rimini, Italy* 344
Baytok, Ahmet / *Afyon Kocatepe University, Turkey* 362
Bulut Solak, Birsen / *Selcuk University, Turkey* 451
Cankül, Duran / *Eskişehir Osmangazi University, Turkey* 220
Carvalho, Fatima L. / *Cinturs, University of Algarve, Portugal* 535
Cattabiani, Jessica / *Campus of Rimini, Italy* 344
Chelliah, Shankar / *Universiti Sains Malaysia, Malaysia* 277
Cohendet, Patrick / *HEC Montreal, Canada* 137
Deliormanli, Ayse / *Beykent University, Turkey* 203
Devkota, Niranjan / *Quest International College, Pokhara University, Nepal* 235
Drakulevski, Ljubomir / *Faculty of Economics, University "Ss. Cyril and Methodius" in Skopje, Macedonia* 549
Eide, Dorthe / *Nord University, Norway* 1
Ekincek, Sema / *Anadolu University, Turkey* 433
Ferdinandi, Massimo / *Campus of Rimini, Italy* 344
Fernandes, Silvia C. / *Faculty of Economics, Cinturs, University of Algarve, Portugal* 535
Fredendall, Lawrence D. / *Department of Management, Clemson University, USA* 255
Godwin, Eun Sun / *University of Wolverhampton, UK* 490
Göktekin, Zekiye / *Faculty of Health Sciences, Gümüşhane University, Turkey* 413
Hanes, Emanuela / *Independent Researcher, Austria* 298
Høegh-Guldberg, Olga / *Nord University, Norway* 1
Jatav, Sunita / *School of Management (PG), Dr.Vishwanath Karad, MIT World Peace University, Pune, India* 391
John, Suja / *Christ University, India* 475
Josimovski, Sasho / *Faculty of Economics, University "Ss. Cyril and Methodius" in Skopje, Macedonia* 549

Name	Page
Kama, Selin / *Bitlis Eren University, Turkey*	181
Karatas-Ozkan, Mine / *University of Southampton, UK*	490
Khamcha, Shreedhar / *Quest International College, Pokhara University, Nepal*	235
Kiziltaş, Mustafa Çağatay / *Sivas Cumhuriyet University, Turkey*	220
Kjiroski, Kiril / *Faculty of Computer Science and Engineering, University "Ss. Cyril and Methodius" in Skopje, Macedonia*	549
Laohavichien, Tipparat / *Department of Technology and Operations Management, Kasetsart University, Thailand*	255
Mahato, Surendra / *Nepal Commerce Campus, Tribhuvan University, Nepal*	235
Mahendran, Ramya / *Independent Researcher, India*	26
Mahmood, Samia / *University of Wolverhampton, UK*	490
Mallika Sankar M. / *Christ University, India*	100
Michael, Priyanka / *Christ University, India*	475
Özgür Göde, Merve / *Anadolu University, Turkey*	65
Özoğul Balyali, Tuğçe / *Van Yüzüncü Yıl University, Turkey*	163
Pattano, Duangthida / *Universiti Sains Malaysia, Malaysia*	277
Paudel, Udaya Raj / *Quest International College, Pokhara University, Nepal*	235
Presutti, Manuela / *University of Bologna, Italy*	344
Rahimi, Roya / *University of Wolverhampton, UK*	490
Raj, Lakshmi / *Christ University, India*	100
Sankar, Mallika / *Christ University, India*	475
Sarkanjac, Branislav / *Faculty of Philosophy, University "Ss. Cyril and Methodius" in Skopje, Macedonia*	549
Sarkanjac, Smilka Janeska / *Faculty of Computer Science and Engineering, University "Ss. Cyril and Methodius" in Skopje, Macedonia*	549
Sezer, Erdeniz / *Independet Researcher, Turkey*	82
Şimşek, Ahmet Bahadır / *Faculty of Health Sciences, Gümüşhane University, Turkey*	413
Sultana, Nasrin / *HEC Montreal, Canada*	137
Turkina, Ekaterina / *HEC Montreal, Canada*	137
Upretee, Sahadeb / *Central Washington University, USA*	235
Wang, Heyun / *Independent Researcher, China*	26
Wang, YuHan / *Independent Researcher, China*	298
Yamak, Sibel / *University of Wolverhampton, UK*	490
Yu, Poshan / *Soochow University, China & Australian Studies Centre, Shanghai University, China*	26, 298
Zorlu, Özcan / *Afyon Kocatepe University, Turkey*	362

Table of Contents

Foreword xxi

Preface xxiii

Chapter 1
Innovation for Sustainability by Smaller Organizations: Strategies and Sustainability Impacts
During the Pandemic 1
    Dorthe Eide, Nord University, Norway
    Olga Høegh-Guldberg, Nord University, Norway

Chapter 2
Australian Wine, Tourism, and Culture: Using Digital Methods via Social Media to Promote
Wine Tourism to Chinese Tourists 26
    Poshan Yu, Soochow University, China & Australian Studies Centre, Shanghai University, China
    Heyun Wang, Independent Researcher, China
    Ramya Mahendran, Independent Researcher, India

Chapter 3
"Green" Fine Dining Restaurants 65
    Merve Özgür Göde, Anadolu University, Turkey

Chapter 4
Effects of the COVID-19 Pandemic on Restaurants and Menus 82
    Günseli Güçlütürk Baran, Isparta University of Applied Sciences, Turkey & Isparta
        Vocational School, Turkey
    Erdeniz Sezer, Independedt Researcher, Turkey

Chapter 5
Exploring the Role of Social Media Influencer Marketing in the Tourism Sector 100
    Lakshmi Raj, Christ University, India
    Mallika Sankar M., Christ University, India

Chapter 6
"Green Computing" in Hospitality 118
    Mehmet Halit Akın, Erciyes University, Turkey

Chapter 7
Innovation Environment for Sustainable Medical Tourism in a Country 137
    Nasrin Sultana, HEC Montreal, Canada
    Ekaterina Turkina, HEC Montreal, Canada
    Patrick Cohendet, HEC Montreal, Canada

Chapter 8
Plan, Do, Watch: Making Tourism Sustainable Through Geographical Information Systems (GIS) 163
    Tuğçe Özoğul Balyali, Van Yüzüncü Yıl University, Turkey
    Öznur Akgiş Ilhan, Kırşehir Ahi Evran University, Turkey

Chapter 9
Sustainability as a Consequence of Memory and Memorable Experience 181
    Selin Kama, Bitlis Eren University, Turkey

Chapter 10
Tourism and Women 203
    Ayse Deliormanli, Beykent University, Turkey

Chapter 11
Use of Blockchain in the Context of Sustainable Gastronomy 220
    Mustafa Çağatay Kiziltaş, Sivas Cumhuriyet University, Turkey
    Duran Cankül, Eskişehir Osmangazi University, Turkey

Chapter 12
Visitors' Perceptions of Homestay Management in Nepal: Evidence From Structural Equation Modelling 235
    Niranjan Devkota, Quest International College, Pokhara University, Nepal
    Shreedhar Khamcha, Quest International College, Pokhara University, Nepal
    Sahadeb Upretee, Central Washington University, USA
    Udaya Raj Paudel, Quest International College, Pokhara University, Nepal
    Surendra Mahato, Nepal Commerce Campus, Tribhuvan University, Nepal

Chapter 13
Sustainable Inventory Management in Hotels 255
    Tipparat Laohavichien, Department of Technology and Operations Management, Kasetsart University, Thailand
    Lawrence D. Fredendall, Department of Management, Clemson University, USA

Chapter 14
Revitalization of Creative Tourism in Post-Pandemic Environment in Thailand 277
    Duangthida Pattano, Universiti Sains Malaysia, Malaysia
    Shankar Chelliah, Universiti Sains Malaysia, Malaysia

Chapter 15
Does Brand Equity Matter? How Chinese Tourists View Wine Brand Equity When Making Wine Tourism Decisions – A Case Study of European Wine Tourism From the Perspective of the Chinese Market 298

    Poshan Yu, Soochow University, China & Australian Studies Centre, Shanghai University, China
    YuHan Wang, Independent Researcher, China
    Emanuela Hanes, Independent Researcher, Austria

Chapter 16
Culture as a Critical Enabler for Tourism Destination Development 344

    Manuela Presutti, University of Bologna, Italy
    Francesco Barbini, Campus of Rimini, Italy
    Massimo Ferdinandi, Campus of Rimini, Italy
    Jessica Cattabiani, Campus of Rimini, Italy

Chapter 17
Accessibility of Thermal Hotels for Disabled and Elderly Tourists: The Case of Afyonkarahisar, Turkey 362

    Özcan Zorlu, Afyon Kocatepe University, Turkey
    Ahmet Baytok, Afyon Kocatepe University, Turkey
    Ali Avan, Afyon Kocatepe University, Turkey

Chapter 18
Current Trends in Sustainable Tourism in the Indian Context 391

    Sunita Jatav, School of Management (PG), Dr.Vishwanath Karad, MIT World Peace University, Pune, India

Chapter 19
Evaluation of the Disaster Tourism Potential of Countries 413

    Zekiye Göktekin, Faculty of Health Sciences, Gümüşhane University, Turkey
    Ahmet Bahadır Şimşek, Faculty of Health Sciences, Gümüşhane University, Turkey

Chapter 20
Eco-Gastronomy, Sustainability, and Art: A Design Study With the Chefs of the Future 433

    Gonca Babadağ, Anadolu University, Turkey
    Sema Ekincek, Anadolu University, Turkey

Chapter 21
Food and Beverage Operations and Safety: The Global Scenario 451

    Birsen Bulut Solak, Selcuk University, Turkey
    Feridun Aydınlı, Selcuk University, Turkey
    Sakib Bin Amin, North South University, Bangladesh

Chapter 22
Sustainable Practices in Indian Aviation 475
    Mallika Sankar, Christ University, India
    Priyanka Michael, Christ University, India
    Suja John, Christ University, India

Chapter 23
Transformation or Retaining the Status Quo: Multinational Hospitality Companies and SME
Collaboration on Sustainability in Emerging Countries 490
    Sibel Yamak, University of Wolverhampton, UK
    Mine Karatas-Ozkan, University of Southampton, UK
    Eun Sun Godwin, University of Wolverhampton, UK
    Samia Mahmood, University of Wolverhampton, UK
    Roya Rahimi, University of Wolverhampton, UK

Chapter 24
Using the Technology Acceptance Model in Tourism Businesses 517
    Mahmut Barakazi, Harran University, Turkey

Chapter 25
Sustainable Tourism and an Analysis of Opportunities for and Challenges to Researchers and
Professionals 535
    Fatima L. Carvalho, Cinturs, University of Algarve, Portugal
    Silvia C. Fernandes, Faculty of Economics, Cinturs, University of Algarve, Portugal

Chapter 26
Adoption of the Sharing Economy in the Tourism and Hospitality Industry in Developing
Countries 549
    Kiril Kjiroski, Faculty of Computer Science and Engineering, University "Ss. Cyril and
        Methodius" in Skopje, Macedonia
    Smilka Janeska Sarkanjac, Faculty of Computer Science and Engineering, University "Ss.
        Cyril and Methodius" in Skopje, Macedonia
    Sasho Josimovski, Faculty of Economics, University "Ss. Cyril and Methodius" in Skopje,
        Macedonia
    Ljubomir Drakulevski, Faculty of Economics, University "Ss. Cyril and Methodius" in
        Skopje, Macedonia
    Branislav Sarkanjac, Faculty of Philosophy, University "Ss. Cyril and Methodius" in Skopje,
        Macedonia

Compilation of References 572

About the Contributors 665

Index 674

Detailed Table of Contents

Foreword xxi

Preface xxiii

Chapter 1
Innovation for Sustainability by Smaller Organizations: Strategies and Sustainability Impacts
During the Pandemic 1
    Dorthe Eide, Nord University, Norway
    Olga Høegh-Guldberg, Nord University, Norway

In the conditions of growing sustainability challenges, organizations are increasingly expected to take action and report sustainability. However, many organizations and local communities struggle with concretizing and balancing sustainability goals and actions. Drawing upon parts of a larger qualitative case study, six innovation pilots within the experience-based tourism industry are elaborated and compared. All cases got financial support within a program taking an overall strategy of getting visitors to stay longer. The chapter contributes knowledge to the field of innovation for sustainability in tourism and experiences by concretizing strategies and sustainability impacts, and discusses them related to the concepts of weak and strong sustainability. The cases illustrate different ways of how tourism industry and other collaborators can work toward achieving the sustainability development goals (SDGs) by avoiding negative impacts and increasing positive impacts within economic, environmental, and social sustainability dimensions.

Chapter 2
Australian Wine, Tourism, and Culture: Using Digital Methods via Social Media to Promote
Wine Tourism to Chinese Tourists 26
    Poshan Yu, Soochow University, China & Australian Studies Centre, Shanghai University, China
    Heyun Wang, Independent Researcher, China
    Ramya Mahendran, Independent Researcher, India

In this chapter, the authors explore social media as a tool for promoting products and services. The industry of application is wine tourism in which the authors investigate whether and how digital methods can help local businesses in Australia in the wine tourism sector gain a better perspective among Chinese tourists. They analyze the characteristics of different wine tourism regions in Australia and assess how these regions are competing against each other and shaping their social media strategies to promote the hospitality and tourism of said region to Chinese tourists. The main goal is to explore how social media is influencing the travel decisions, choice of destination, and wine consumption of Chinese tourists and empowering the tourists on the Australia's wine heritage is going to convey meaning, culture, and traditions to aid them in these decisions. Recommendations will be provided on using digital social media to promote wine tourism to different stakeholders.

Chapter 3
"Green" Fine Dining Restaurants 65
    Merve Özgür Göde, Anadolu University, Turkey

Food and beverage businesses have recently started to use sustainable practices. The "green restaurant" is an eco-label that restaurants receive as a result of these practices. Today, almost any type of restaurant can become a green restaurant. This study examines the processes of fine dining restaurants to become "green restaurants" and to determine which criteria are prominent in them. The study revealed that fine dining "green restaurants" received fewer points in the transparency and education and building categories in the process of becoming green restaurants.

Chapter 4
Effects of the COVID-19 Pandemic on Restaurants and Menus 82
    Günseli Güçlütürk Baran, Isparta University of Applied Sciences, Turkey & Isparta
        Vocational School, Turkey
    Erdeniz Sezer, Independet Researcher, Turkey

The aim of this research is to reveal the impact of the COVID-19 pandemic in Turkey in terms of the restaurants and menu planning. The authors believe it is possible for people's attitudes to shape their consumer behavior, which are considered in food and beverage preferences. In this respect, it is important to examine the effects of the COVID-19 pandemic on restaurants and menu planning within the scope of gastronomy in Turkey. This research is based on a case study. Primary and secondary data sources were used among the data collection techniques. Secondary data consists of data such as studies, reports, and statistical information in the relevant literature. The primary data of the research consists of qualitative data. Accordingly, the semi-structured in-depth interview technique was used. The sampling method was used in the research and interviews were conducted with a total of 12 participants in Istanbul, Turkey.

Chapter 5
Exploring the Role of Social Media Influencer Marketing in the Tourism Sector 100
    Lakshmi Raj, Christ University, India
    Mallika Sankar M., Christ University, India

The growing popularity of social media influencers (SMI) increasingly encourages destinations to use social media influencer marketing (SMIM) for their promotional campaigns. SMIs demonstrate the power of an individual based on certain factors employed to influence a broad segment of audience, and when it is used for marketing purposes, it is known as SMIM. SMIM is a part of the social media marketing that exercises all the commercial marketing techniques via social media channels. SMIM has impacted many industries including tourism, but looking at the progressive growth of SMIM today, it is surprising that such little attention had been paid to this area. However, while there is increasing use of SMIM by tourism organizations, there is a lack of research and limited knowledge on the roles of SMIM in travel and tourism. This chapter sheds light on the use of SMIM in the tourism sector where existing literature on the SMIM, its factors, and the influence of SMIM on the tourism sector by distinct authors are reviewed to identify the effectiveness of SMIM in the travel and tourism industry.

Chapter 6
"Green Computing" in Hospitality 118
    Mehmet Halit Akın, Erciyes University, Turkey

"Green computing" is an approach adopted to ensure the technological devices and byproducts used by businesses in their business processes cause the least harm to the environment. Green computing, which is a new concept for hospitality as well as for other sectors, increasingly attracts attention by researchers—especially due to the increase in the destruction of environmental factors in recent years and the importance of these factors for hospitality. However, in the body of knowledge, it is seen there is scant research on hospitality with green computing. Therefore, green computing that emerges with sustainability should be further researched, and green computing practices in hospitality should be evaluated. In light of this information, this chapter aimed to create a conceptual framework that is expected to have a widespread impact on the body of knowledge based on the current literature on the concepts of green computing.

Chapter 7
Innovation Environment for Sustainable Medical Tourism in a Country 137
    Nasrin Sultana, HEC Montreal, Canada
    Ekaterina Turkina, HEC Montreal, Canada
    Patrick Cohendet, HEC Montreal, Canada

Medical tourism has become one of the fastest-growing service industries in the 21st century. The purpose of this chapter is to advance the idea that the growth of medical tourism is influenced not only by the innovation in medical technology but also by the overall innovation environment in a country. Conducting a fixed effect regression analysis, the authors find empirical evidence in support of the argument. Because of the inter-sectoral nature of the medical tourism industry, the findings imply a plethora of opportunities for all related industries to realize the full potential of the resources available for innovation in a country. The most important implication of the findings is that strengthening the innovation environment in a country is momentous for sustainable medical tourism. The findings show a way to achieve sustainable medical tourism by integrating different stakeholders through collaboration and innovation.

Chapter 8
Plan, Do, Watch: Making Tourism Sustainable Through Geographical Information
Systems (GIS) 163
    Tuğçe Özoğul Balyali, Van Yüzüncü Yıl University, Turkey
    Öznur Akgiş Ilhan, Kırşehir Ahi Evran University, Turkey

In the tourism industry, the use of digital tools has been becoming increasingly common due to the development of alternative movements, such as smart tourism. One of these digital tools is geographic information systems (GIS), which is an information system used for the processing, analysis, and storage of spatial data. Within this context, this chapter focuses on the role of GIS use in ensuring the sustainability of tourism activities. In the chapter, the use of GIS in the planning, doing, and watching processes of tourism is discussed with examples. This chapter will provide information on how to benefit from GIS in the context of sustainable tourism.

Chapter 9
Sustainability as a Consequence of Memory and Memorable Experience 181
    Selin Kama, Bitlis Eren University, Turkey

The degree of remembrance of an experience can affect an individual's contribution to social, cultural, economic, and environmental sustainability by transforming their behavior. In other words, memory and memorability are important predictors of sustainable behavior. Therefore, the focus of this study is to evaluate the memory and memorable experiences from the macro-sustainability perspective. Within this study, the impact of visitors' memorable experiences on sustainability and how sustainability shapes memorable experiences are evaluated conceptually. The results show that emotional and cognitive essence that makes tourism experiences memorable provides a competitive advantage for destinations by influencing the sustainability behaviors of visitors. In line with this study, the relationship between memory and sustainability behaviors of visitors must be evaluated via qualitative and quantitative methods.

Chapter 10
Tourism and Women 203
    Ayse Deliormanli, Beykent University, Turkey

Gender-related issues have not lost their importance from the past to the present and are being carefully emphasized. As one of the important subjects of sociology, gender and gender discrimination continues to exist in the tourism sector as well. There are basic predispositions for both employment in tourism and the participation of women as consumers in tourism activities. The roles socially determined for women can create an obstacle for women to participate in working life. The same attitude is observed at the stage of women's participation in tourism activities. In particular, the risks and concerns faced by women traveling as a group or alone indicate the perspective on women has not changed. Based on this point of view, this study aims to present the relationship between gender and tourism, the experiences of women both in working life and in tourism activities as a tourist in a theoretical framework.

Chapter 11
Use of Blockchain in the Context of Sustainable Gastronomy 220
    Mustafa Çağatay Kiziltaş, Sivas Cumhuriyet University, Turkey
    Duran Cankül, Eskişehir Osmangazi University, Turkey

Global food systems, from agricultural production to processing, distribution, retail sale, food processing, and the resulting waste in the entire process in the supply chain, create greenhouse gas emissions that cause climate change. At the same time, some negative environmental effects such as misuse of spring water, environmental pollution, and loss of biodiversity may occur during the production of food. While access to food is a major problem in underdeveloped countries, food waste is a concern in developed countries. In addition, people want to trust the food they consume, and they want to know under what conditions the food they consume is produced and whether it comes to their table as promised. Especially in the field of gastronomy, many people are curious about the adventure of food. Issues such as traceability, transparency, reliability, and efficiency offered by blockchain technology ensure that waste can be prevented; on the other hand, it also provides the opportunity for consumers to monitor their food from field to table and provides a more sustainable food system.

Chapter 12
Visitors' Perceptions of Homestay Management in Nepal: Evidence From Structural Equation Modelling 235

    Niranjan Devkota, Quest International College, Pokhara University, Nepal
    Shreedhar Khamcha, Quest International College, Pokhara University, Nepal
    Sahadeb Upretee, Central Washington University, USA
    Udaya Raj Paudel, Quest International College, Pokhara University, Nepal
    Surendra Mahato, Nepal Commerce Campus, Tribhuvan University, Nepal

Tourists' visits to rural areas are increasingly experiencing growth; however, there is no literature available to reveal how the Nepalese community has taken advantage of tourism as an opportunity to increase income. The study assesses the visitors' perception of homestay management in one of the indigenous homestay areas: Gabhar Valley, Nepal. Based on an explanatory research design, primary data was collected from 285 tourist guests using the structural equation modelling (SEM) technique which was applied to find the visitors perceptions about homestay management. This study found there is positive and significant influence on visitors' intension to visit using homestay. Variables such as environmental concerns indeed exert a positive influence on their subjective norms and perceived moral obligation, which in turn influence their intention to visit homestay as expected. This study concludes that as homestay programs contribute significantly towards environmental concern and rural livelihood, it is an effective tourism tool for economic sustainability.

Chapter 13
Sustainable Inventory Management in Hotels 255

    Tipparat Laohavichien, Department of Technology and Operations Management, Kasetsart University, Thailand
    Lawrence D. Fredendall, Department of Management, Clemson University, USA

The objectives of this chapter are to present inventory planning and control systems in the hotel industry and to examine how to use the existing inventory management practices in the hotel industry to promote sustainability based on the concept of a triple bottom line (i.e., economic, social, and environmental sustainability). Yield or revenue management is the method most hotels use to manage their perishable inventory (rooms). The basic principle of yield management is that hotels achieve maximum revenue by matching customer needs with the right room rate and the right time of sale. Yield management directly promotes economic and social sustainability but indirectly fosters environmental sustainability. In addition, techniques and models for managing nonperishable hotel inventory are discussed, including the EOQ model, JIT and Lean systems, and the ABC classification. Moreover, radio-frequency identification (RFID), the technology used to support the effectiveness of a sustainable inventory management system, is discussed, and finally, further research is provided.

Chapter 14
Revitalization of Creative Tourism in Post-Pandemic Environment in Thailand 277

    Duangthida Pattano, Universiti Sains Malaysia, Malaysia
    Shankar Chelliah, Universiti Sains Malaysia, Malaysia

The spread of the COVID-19 pandemic has had a significant negative impact on many tourist destinations around the world, including Thailand. A shift in typical vacation behavior has emerged as a major issue in the global tourism industry as a result of travel restriction and social distancing issues. In the new normal scenario of COVID-19 pandemic, creative tourism, which focuses on participating in onsite activities and interacting with people, is facing challenges. It is important to pay attention to what tourists consider when making decisions about future travel plans, especially in creative tourism. This chapter focuses on tourist motivation, travel decisions, and travel practices for service providers, all of which are discussed in terms of how Thailand's creative tourism potential can be revitalized. Furthermore, an integrated model of creative tourism is proposed in predicting future travel behavior related to health risk concerns. Several potential implications and concerns for managerial decision-making in service and marketing contexts are discussed.

Chapter 15
Does Brand Equity Matter? How Chinese Tourists View Wine Brand Equity When Making Wine Tourism Decisions – A Case Study of European Wine Tourism From the Perspective of the Chinese Market 298
    Poshan Yu, Soochow University, China & Australian Studies Centre, Shanghai University, China
    YuHan Wang, Independent Researcher, China
    Emanuela Hanes, Independent Researcher, Austria

This chapter examines how tourism in the hypercompetitive world can create a flexible mean to generate advantages and maintain advantages to achieve sustainable development. This chapter reflects the international wine business and global wine tourism by studying the wine tourism in the tourism industry, and studies the driving forces and factors of the sustainable development of tourism economy with wine tourism as the core. This work also reflects the demands and preferences of Chinese consumers on global wine business and wine tourism from the perspective of consumers through a Chinese case study and a questionnaire survey. After nearly 2 years of COVID-19 lockdown, the authors investigate which international wine tourism region(s) Chinese tourists most want to go after the COVID-19 lockdown and why. This study attempts to measure the wine brand equity (WBE) on travel intention based upon surveying Chinese travelers' data.

Chapter 16
Culture as a Critical Enabler for Tourism Destination Development 344
    Manuela Presutti, University of Bologna, Italy
    Francesco Barbini, Campus of Rimini, Italy
    Massimo Ferdinandi, Campus of Rimini, Italy
    Jessica Cattabiani, Campus of Rimini, Italy

The relationship between cultural heritage and tourism has stimulated the theoretical debate for many years. While it is evident that cultural attractions have the potential to be critical assets for tourism policymakers and destinations, tourist behaviors are often seen as potential harm to both the preservation of cultural heritage and the development of a profound cultural experience. Nevertheless, a growing number of experiences show that a sound management of cultural tourism can generate substantial social, economic, and even environmental benefits. This chapter aims to investigate the trajectories and strategies tourism destinations can adopt to leverage their (material and immaterial) cultural assets, improve their brand, and eventually, enhance their competitive position in the tourism markets, with particular reference to the case of Parma Italian Capital of Culture 2020.

Chapter 17
Accessibility of Thermal Hotels for Disabled and Elderly Tourists: The Case of Afyonkarahisar, Turkey 362
    Özcan Zorlu, Afyon Kocatepe University, Turkey
    Ahmet Baytok, Afyon Kocatepe University, Turkey
    Ali Avan, Afyon Kocatepe University, Turkey

This study explores how thermal hotels are considering the accessibility of facilities and adjustments for disabled and elderly tourists during service production. Within this scope, observations were made in thermal hotels and semi-structured interviews were held with the senior managers of thermal hotels in Afyonkarahisar, Turkey. Thermal hotels were chosen as research areas because their potential guests are generally elderly and disabled tourists, and there may be more arrangements for disabled people in these hotels. As a powerful method of analyzing qualitative data, a thematic analysis was conducted on the data set. Results show no specific arrangement was made for the visually impaired guests, and participants think that physical regulations regarding accessibility may adversely affect the functionality of the service delivery process. In addition, arrangements for disabled people are focused on legal requirements.

Chapter 18
Current Trends in Sustainable Tourism in the Indian Context 391
    Sunita Jatav, School of Management (PG), Dr.Vishwanath Karad, MIT World Peace University, Pune, India

Indian tourism is rich with culture, heritage, ecology, and natural beauty across the country. The tourism sector plays a vital role for foreign exchange earnings and gross domestic product (GDP) in India. India's travel and tourism business ranks 7th internationally, contributing almost 9.6% to GDP, and is expected to rise 6.9% annually over the next decade to rank 4th. This will have a multiplier effect on India's socio-economic progress via improved infrastructure, job creation, and skill development. India was ranked 10th among 185 countries in 2019. India is a globally and digitally advanced nation in term of planning, booking, and positive experience for travel and tour. Indian middle class people's disposable income is increasing, which creates a positive impact on outbound tourism. The Indian travel market is projected to grow to US$125 billion by 2027. This study identifies best practices and the need for sustainable tourism in India's growth.

Chapter 19
Evaluation of the Disaster Tourism Potential of Countries 413
    Zekiye Göktekin, Faculty of Health Sciences, Gümüşhane University, Turkey
    Ahmet Bahadır Şimşek, Faculty of Health Sciences, Gümüşhane University, Turkey

Disasters are tragic events that cause losses. The curiosity of people to feel sadness and pain motivates disaster tourism. Each disaster region has the potential for disaster tourism, which offers various benefits. This chapter covers the evaluation of the disaster tourism potential of countries with the fuzzy-TOPSIS method. The criteria affecting the disaster tourism potential as the number of dead, injured, affected, and homeless people were weighted according to the evaluations of the decision-makers. Disasters that occurred worldwide between 1980-2022 were analyzed with the criteria weights based on the countries where they occurred. Decision-makers mostly evaluated the number of deaths and homeless as more effective in affecting the desire to visit a disaster area and the attractiveness of the region. Among 90 countries, it has been determined that Sri Lanka and the Russian Federation are the two countries with the highest disaster tourism potential as to the number of losses/disasters, while Ethiopia is the country with the lowest disaster tourism potential.

Chapter 20
Eco-Gastronomy, Sustainability, and Art: A Design Study With the Chefs of the Future 433
    Gonca Babadağ, Anadolu University, Turkey
    Sema Ekincek, Anadolu University, Turkey

Sustainability refers to the careful use of natural resources by considering future generations. Especially in the food sector, the sustainability of resources and the reduction of environmental impacts are very important. The relationship between gastronomy and sustainability might be described using the term "eco-gastronomy." As practitioners of gastronomy, it is very important that chefs recognize the ecosystem, protect natural resources, and respect the natural environment. In this context, the aim of the study is to provide potential chef candidates with the opportunity to express their emotions via creative design by incorporating sustainability, eco-gastronomy, and art. A total of 21 students were included in the study. With these students, designs related to both sustainability and gastronomy were realized, and they were enabled to design and present sustainable green restaurant logos and slogans in accordance with the concept they determined. Consequently, it was seen that the design stages and creativity stages of the students were exactly the same.

Chapter 21
Food and Beverage Operations and Safety: The Global Scenario 451
    Birsen Bulut Solak, Selcuk University, Turkey
    Feridun Aydınlı, Selcuk University, Turkey
    Sakib Bin Amin, North South University, Bangladesh

For the past three years the COVID-19 pandemic has received much global attention due to the high risk of fatality and human-to-human transmission. This pandemic has forced changes in every sector as well as in different aspects of everyone's daily lives. Travelling has had a critical role in contributing to its transmission by negatively influencing the majority of public health. The hospitality and tourism industry is subject to being immediately influenced by the external environment. This chapter explains how COVID-19 has affected food and beverage operations and safety in the sector and the global economy. New rules and regulations are described in detail. The future of food and beverage operations has changed by integrating technology, touchless contact, social distancing, and hygiene precautions, focusing on domestic travel, virtual tourism, and luxury travel.

Chapter 22
Sustainable Practices in Indian Aviation.. 475
    Mallika Sankar, Christ University, India
    Priyanka Michael, Christ University, India
    Suja John, Christ University, India

Air travel produces about three percent of carbon dioxide emissions worldwide. The air travel industry requires an enduring vision that focuses on sustainable practices in the entire aviation sector, which will be a significant aspect of the future of civil aviation. The study adopts a systematic review to portray significant challenges, issues, and best practices in the worldwide aviation industry, highlighting the Indian scenario to establish future exploration in India. The chapter extensively investigates the latest sustainable developments in the airline business, the logical agreement on its ecological effects, and steps taken for sustainability.

Chapter 23
Transformation or Retaining the Status Quo: Multinational Hospitality Companies and SME Collaboration on Sustainability in Emerging Countries 490

Sibel Yamak, University of Wolverhampton, UK
Mine Karatas-Ozkan, University of Southampton, UK
Eun Sun Godwin, University of Wolverhampton, UK
Samia Mahmood, University of Wolverhampton, UK
Roya Rahimi, University of Wolverhampton, UK

This chapter focuses on the dynamics of MHC-SME collaboration on sustainability in an emerging country context. The findings show that MHC sustainability policy is generally driven from headquarters and that economic sustainability has priority over environmental and social sustainability. By contrast, SMEs appear to be able to initiate fully sustainable strategies based on the culture, tradition, family history, industry, and ethical standing of the owners. The interaction of MHCs and SMEs in relation to sustainability involves varying factors at the macro, meso, and micro levels. However, the micro level factor (i.e., human agency) seems to be the determining factor of the relationship. The authors provide rich contextual data by adopting a qualitative research method (case study) based on primary data, which is rare in international business literature.

Chapter 24
Using the Technology Acceptance Model in Tourism Businesses 517

Mahmut Barakazi, Harran University, Turkey

It is seen that technological elements are frequently used to provide a better quality tourism experience and to expand the comfort zone. It is understood that many tourism businesses, especially in the fields of accommodation, travel, and gastronomy, have gained a more competitive structure by developing their technological infrastructure. In this direction, the suitability of the technology acceptance model (TAM), which was first developed by Davis and based on two basic elements, in terms of tourism enterprises is associated with examples. It is understood that the perceived convenience and usefulness within the scope of the research is met positively in terms of tourism services. In addition, it is thought the quality-of-service perception will be increased by better using the opportunities brought by technology in tourism. The goal is to contribute to the relevant literature by evaluating the effect of the TAM model on the tourism sectors from a general perspective.

Chapter 25
Sustainable Tourism and an Analysis of Opportunities for and Challenges to Researchers and Professionals 535

Fatima L. Carvalho, Cinturs, University of Algarve, Portugal
Silvia C. Fernandes, Faculty of Economics, Cinturs, University of Algarve, Portugal

This work analyzes academic work from 2004 to 2020 with an influence on the blueprint for sustainable tourism innovation strategies. Criteria used include verifying which are the main concerns, the contribution of sustainability indices, and implications to practitioners and high educational institutions in the area. This is increasingly important due to present and future challenges undermining the existence of a sustainable tourism industry. Accurate metrics can empower destinations, and higher education and its inner research must have a key role in the development of effective instruments. The challenge comprises selecting and monitoring them for sustainable tourism policy. Educational and research institutes with tourism studies should include in their syllabuses real cases and tools for developing key sustainability models and metrics to integrate and respond more promptly to critical challenges and trends.

Chapter 26
Adoption of the Sharing Economy in the Tourism and Hospitality Industry in Developing Countries 549

> *Kiril Kjiroski, Faculty of Computer Science and Engineering, University "Ss. Cyril and Methodius" in Skopje, Macedonia*
> *Smilka Janeska Sarkanjac, Faculty of Computer Science and Engineering, University "Ss. Cyril and Methodius" in Skopje, Macedonia*
> *Sasho Josimovski, Faculty of Economics, University "Ss. Cyril and Methodius" in Skopje, Macedonia*
> *Ljubomir Drakulevski, Faculty of Economics, University "Ss. Cyril and Methodius" in Skopje, Macedonia*
> *Branislav Sarkanjac, Faculty of Philosophy, University "Ss. Cyril and Methodius" in Skopje, Macedonia*

The tourism and hospitality industry has been affected by sharing economy platforms and eco-systems, which constitute disruptive innovations (i.e., innovations that create new markets and value networks while disrupting existing ones and displacing industry incumbents). As the third-largest socioeconomic activity within the European Union (EU), tourism can be considered an engine for economic development, accounting for about 8% between 2007 and 2016, while it has been close to 10% worldwide. This chapter examines the potential of the sharing economy in the tourism and hospitality sectors to disrupt the incumbent tourist regions and proposes sharing economy platforms for the introduction of new destinations in developing countries such as the Republic of Macedonia. It is crucial to examine the issue of the sharing economy from a governance perspective. The authors contend that sharing economy should be a part of a comprehensive national tourism policy based on contemporary governance principles and on experiences of other countries.

Compilation of References 572

About the Contributors 665

Index 674

Foreword

Extraordinary situations such as economic crises and epidemics devastate many economic systems. Although the crises experienced increase the skills of the enterprises in dealing with the crisis, each new crisis that occurs in a different structure can catch the enterprises unprepared. Moreover, the extraordinary situation experienced, as in the COVID-19 pandemic, showed that the sustainability of businesses is not predominantly dependent on economic sustainability and that the antecedent effect of environmental sustainability was severe, even shocking. Another factor that multiplies the complicating effect of crisis environments is the point reached by global competition. Socio-cultural sustainability in global competition is also the central pillar of the struggle for existence and even the strategy of making a difference. With the awareness of the editors of this book, the existence and development of tourism businesses and destinations in hyper-competition will only be possible with the acceptability of change. Being sustainable against shocks such as epidemics and crises, ups and downs, political slippage, and disorder, in other words being antifragile, is a subject that must be studied and considered seriously. Macro results can be reached as a result of scrutinizing on a micro-scale.

Sustainability is at the forefront of the issues discussed to be antifragile. In this book, one can find studies such as on sustainability innovation, innovation for medical tourism, inventory management, green/sustainable practices in both food and beverage businesses and hotel businesses, in addition to aviation, transformation and collaborations in hotel businesses, sharing economy, the emphasis of experience on sustainability, sustainability analysis for researchers and professionals, art, and eco-gastronomy.

In our age, in the tourism industry, where the Z generation, which has been raised with technology, has started to make itself felt, the sections that focus on technology such as digitalization, use of Blockchain, technology acceptance model in tourism businesses, and geographic information systems as a decision support system in achieving sustainability in the tourism industry will also attract your attention.

In addition to the effects of COVID-19 on restaurants, you can also get an idea of the effects on the revival of creative tourism. In this inclusive book, you can encounter the epidemic environment, which is the scene of the change and transformation of tourism, and then homestay accommodation, the role of culture in tourism destination development, and studies that look from the unexpected corner, such as disaster tourism as well as social media, the current state of marketing. Studies on growing markets and emerging tourism destinations such as India, Thailand, China, and Turkey will provide an opportunity to look from the national to the global. For a significant part of the world, women, the disabled, and the elderly can still be considered vulnerable groups. Examining tourism from the perspective of these groups is an issue that can open doors for innovation and inclusion.

I believe this book will contribute to students who are trying to make progress in all fields of tourism, which is an interdisciplinary subject, researchers who want to add value to tourism with their disciplines, and professionals and managers who demonstrate sustainability. I wish the book to reach a broad audience, and I congratulate the editors and authors who have contributed.

Semra Günay Aktaş
Faculty of Tourism, Anadolu University, Turkey

Preface

There is no doubt the COVID-19 pandemic has deeply disrupted every aspect of business and life worldwide, and tourism is no exception. In the post-pandemic era, the effects of global hypercompetition have only increased the speed and intensity of business activity in every corner of the planet. Competitiveness has been a subject of study in the manufacturing and related sectors since the early 1990s, but fairly recently researchers have begun examining the tourism and hospitality industry in more depth, both conceptually and empirically. The purpose of this publication is to do exactly that by providing current and relevant research via 26 chapters on sustainable tourism and hotel operations which can act as a catalyst for further research and effective practice.

Chapter 1 explores how tourism organizations in northern Norway are conducting innovations for sustainability during the pandemic. This is a qualitative multi-case study focusing on the experience-based innovation pilots tested during the Summer of 2021, all partly financed by a regional fund aiming to facilitate economic value creation and reduce climate footprints through prolonged visitors' stay. The chapter contributes new knowledge about different ways tourism organizations and their collaborating partners innovate for sustainability. Essentially, the chapter concretizes sustainability impacts and collaborating practices demonstrated by the participants of the "One day more" program.

Chapter 2 studies social media as a tool for promoting products and services. The industry of application is wine tourism in which we will investigate whether and how digital methods can help local businesses in Australia in the wine tourism sector gain a better perspective among Chinese tourists. The authors analyze the characteristics of different wine tourism regions in Australia and assess how these regions are competing against each other and shaping their social media strategies to promote the hospitality and tourism of said region to Chinese tourists. The main goal is to explore how social media is influencing the travel decisions, choice of destination, and wine consumption of Chinese tourists and empowering the tourists on the Australia's wine heritage is going to convey meaning, culture, and traditions to aide them in these decisions. Recommendations will be provided on using digital social media to promote wine tourism to different stakeholders.

Chapter 3 examines food and beverage businesses which have recently started to use sustainable practices. The "green restaurant" is an eco-label that restaurants receive as a result of these practices. Today, almost any type of restaurant can become a green restaurant. This study examines the processes of fine dining restaurants to become "green restaurants" and to determine which criteria are prominent in them. The study reveals that fine dining "green restaurants" received fewer points in the transparency and education and building categories in the process of becoming green restaurants.

Chapter 4 reveals the impact of the COVID-19 pandemic in Turkey in terms of the restaurants and menu planning. We believe it is possible for people's attitudes to shape their consumer behavior which are considered in food and beverage preferences. In this respect, it is important to examine the effects of the COVID-19 pandemic on restaurants and menu planning within the scope of gastronomy in Turkey. This research is based on a case study. Primary and secondary data sources were used among the data collection techniques. Secondary data consists of data such as studies, reports, and statistical information in the relevant literature. The primary data of the research consists of qualitative data. Accordingly, the semi-structured in-depth interview technique was used. The sampling method was used in the research and interviews were conducted with a total of 12 participants in Istanbul, Turkey.

Chapter 5 discusses how the growing popularity of social media influencers (SMI) increasingly encourages destinations to use social media influencer marketing (SMIM) for their promotional campaigns. SMI demonstrates the power of an individual based on certain factors employed to influence a broad segment of audience, and when it is used for marketing purposes it is known as SMIM. SMIM is a part of the social media marketing that exercises all the commercial marketing techniques via social media channels. SMIM has impacted many industries including tourism but looking at the progressive growth of SMIM today, it is surprising that such little attention had been paid to this area. However, while there is increasing use of SMIM by tourism organizations there is a lack of research and limited knowledge on the roles of SMIM in travel and tourism. This chapter sheds light on the use of SMIM in the tourism sector where existing literature on the SMIM, its factors, and the influence of SMIM on the tourism sector by distinct authors are reviewed to identify the effectiveness of SMIM in the travel and tourism industry.

Chapter 6 covers the subject of "Green computing", which is an approach adopted to ensure the technological devices and by-products used by businesses in their business processes cause the least harm to the environment. Green computing, which is a new concept for hospitality as well as for other sectors, increasingly attracts attention by researchers--especially due to the increase in the destruction of environmental factors in recent years and the importance of these factors for hospitality. However, in the body of knowledge, it is seen there is scant research on hospitality with green computing. Therefore, green computing that emerges with sustainability should be further researched and green computing practices in hospitality should be evaluated. This chapter creates a conceptual framework that is expected to have a widespread impact on the body of knowledge based on the current literature on the concepts of green computing.

Chapter 7 investigates medical tourism which has become one of the fastest-growing service industries in the 21st century. The purpose of this chapter is to advance the idea that the growth of medical tourism is influenced not only by the innovation in medical technology but also by the overall innovation environment in a country. Conducting a fixed effect regression analysis, the authors find empirical evidence in support of the argument. Because of the inter-sectoral nature of the medical tourism industry, the findings imply a plethora of opportunities for all related industries to realize the full potential of the resources available for innovation in a country. The most important implication of the findings is that strengthening the innovation environment in a country is momentous for sustainable medical tourism. The findings show a way to achieve sustainable medical tourism by integrating different stakeholders through collaboration and innovation.

Chapter 8 covers the subject of Geographic Information Systems (GIS). In the tourism industry, the use of digital tools has been becoming increasingly common due to the development of alternative movements, such as smart tourism. One of these digital tools is GIS, which is an information system used for the processing, analysis, and storage of spatial data. Within this context, this chapter focuses

Preface

on the role of GIS use in ensuring the sustainability of tourism activities. In the chapter, the use of GIS in the planning, doing, and watching processes of tourism is discussed with examples. This chapter will provide information on how to benefit from GIS in the context of sustainable tourism.

Chapter 9 encompasses how the degree of remembrance of an experience can affect an individual's contribution to social, cultural, economic, and environmental sustainability by transforming their behavior. In other words, memory and memorability are important predictors of sustainable behavior. Therefore, the focus of this study is to evaluate the memory and memorable experiences from the macro-sustainability perspective. Within this study the impact of visitors' memorable experiences on sustainability and how sustainability shapes memorable experiences are evaluated conceptually. The results show that emotional and cognitive essence that makes tourism experiences memorable provides a competitive advantage for destinations by influencing the sustainability behaviors of visitors'. In line with this study, the relationship between memory and sustainability behaviors of visitors must be evaluated via qualitative and quantitative methods.

Chapter 10 researches why gender-related issues have not lost their importance from the past to the present and are being carefully emphasized. As one of the important subjects of sociology, gender and gender discrimination continues to exist in the tourism sector as well. There are basic predispositions for both employment in tourism and the participation of women as a consumer in tourism activities. The roles socially determined for women can create an obstacle for women to participate in working life. The same attitude is observed at the stage of women's participation in tourism activities. In particular, the risks and concerns faced by women traveling as a group or alone indicate the perspective on women has not changed. Based on this point of view, this study aims to present the relationship between gender and tourism, the experiences of women both in working life and in tourism activities as a tourist in a theoretical framework.

Chapter 11 investigates global food systems, from agricultural production to processing, distribution, retail sale, food processing and the resulting waste in the entire process in the supply chain that create greenhouse gas emissions that cause climate change. At the same time, some negative environmental effects such as misuse of spring water, environmental pollution, and loss of biodiversity may occur during the production of food. While access to food is a major problem in underdeveloped countries, food waste is a concern in developed countries. In addition, people want to trust the food they consume, and they want to know under what conditions the food they consume is produced and whether it comes to their table as promised. Especially in the field of gastronomy, many people are curious about the adventure of food. Issues such as traceability, transparency, reliability and efficiency offered by blockchain technology ensure that waste can be prevented; on the other hand, it also provides the opportunity for consumers to monitor their food from field to table and provides a more sustainable food system.

Chapter 12 examines visitors' perception of Homestay tourism in Nepal. Tourist visits to rural areas are increasingly experiencing growth; however, literature is not available to reveal how the Nepalese community has taken advantage of tourism as an opportunity to increase income. The study assesses the visitors' perception of homestay management in one of the indigenous Homestay areas: Gabhar Valley, Nepal. Based on an explanatory research design, primary data was collected from 285 tourist guests using the Structural Equation Modelling (SEM) technique which was applied to find the visitors perception about homestay management. This study found there is positive and significant influence on visitors' intension to visit using Homestay. Variables such as environmental concerns indeed exert a positive influence on their subjective norms, and perceived moral obligation, which in turn influence their intention to visit homestay as expected. This study concludes that as Homestay programs contributing significantly towards environmental concern and rural livelihood, it is an effective tourism tool for economic sustainability.

Chapter 13 presents inventory planning and control systems in the hotel industry and examine how to use the existing inventory management practices in the hotel industry promote sustainability based on the concept of a triple bottom line (i.e., economic, social, and environmental sustainability). Yield or revenue management is the method most hotels use to manage their perishable inventory (rooms). The basic principle of yield management is that hotels achieve maximum revenue by matching customer needs with the right room rate and the right time of sale. Yield management directly promotes economic and social sustainability but indirectly fosters environmental sustainability. In addition, techniques and models for managing nonperishable hotel inventory are discussed, including the EOQ model, JIT and Lean systems, and the ABC classification. Moreover, radio-frequency identification (RFID), the technology used to support the effectiveness of a sustainable inventory management system, is discussed, and finally, a further research direction is provided.

Chapter 14 focuses on tourist motivation, travel decisions, and travel practices for service providers, all of which are discussed in terms of how Thailand's creative tourism potential can be revitalized. Furthermore, an integrated model of creative tourism is proposed in predicting future travel behavior related to health risk concerns. Several potential implications and concerns for managerial decision-making in service and marketing contexts are discussed. The spread of the Covid-19 pandemic has had a significant negative impact on many tourist destinations around the world, including Thailand. A shift in typical vacation behavior has emerged as a major issue in the global tourism industry as a result of travel restriction and social distancing issues. In the new normal scenario of COVID-19 pandemic, creative tourism, which focuses on participating in onsite activities and interacting with people, is facing challenges. It is important to pay attention to what tourists consider when making decisions about future travel plans, especially in creative tourism.

Chapter 15 examines how tourism in the hypercompetitive world can create a flexible mean to generate advantages and maintain advantages to achieve sustainable development. This chapter reflects the international wine business and global wine tourism by studying the wine tourism in the tourism industry, and studies the driving forces and factors of the sustainable development of tourism economy with wine tourism as the core. This work also reflects the demands and preferences of Chinese consumers on global wine business and wine tourism from the perspective of consumers through a Chinese case study and a questionnaire survey. After nearly 2 years of Covid-19 lockdown, we will investigate which international wine tourism region(s) Chinese tourists most want to go after the Covid-19 lockdown and why. This study will attempt to measure the wine brand equity (WBE) on travel intention based upon surveying Chinese travelers' data.

Chapter 16 postulates that the relationship between cultural heritage and tourism has stimulated theoretical debate for many years. While it is evident that cultural attractions have the potential to be critical assets for tourism policymakers and destinations, tourist behaviors are often seen as potential harm to both the preservation of cultural heritage and the development of a profound cultural experience. Nevertheless, a growing number of experiences show that a sound management of cultural tourism can generate substantial social, economic, and even environmental benefits. This chapter aims to investigate the trajectories and strategies tourism destinations can adopt to leverage their (material and immaterial) cultural assets, improve their brand and, eventually, enhance their competitive position in the tourism markets, with particular reference to the case of Parma Italian Capital of Culture 2020.

Preface

Chapter 17 discusses how thermal hotels are considering the accessibility of facilities and adjustments for disabled and elderly tourists during service production. Within this scope, observations were made in thermal hotels and semi-structured interviews were held with the senior managers of thermal hotels in Afyonkarahisar, Turkey. Thermal hotels were chosen as research areas because their potential guests are generally elderly and disabled tourists, and there may be more arrangements for disabled people in these hotels. As a powerful method of analyzing qualitative data, a thematic analysis was conducted on the data set. Results show no specific arrangement was made for the visually impaired guests, and participants think that physical regulations regarding accessibility may adversely affect the functionality of the service delivery process. In addition, arrangements for disabled people are focused on legal requirements.

Chapter 18 acknowledges that Indian tourism is rich with culture, heritage, ecology, and natural beauty across the country. The tourism sector plays vital role for foreign exchange earnings and Gross Domestic Product (GDP) in India. India's travel and tourism business ranks 7th internationally, contributing almost 9.6% to GDP, and is expected to rise 6.9% annually over the next decade to rank 4th. This will have a multiplier effect on India's socio-economic progress via improved infrastructure, job creation, and skill development. India was ranked 10th among 185 countries in 2019. India is a globally, digital advanced nation in term of planning, booking, and positive experience for travel and tour. Indian middle class people disposable income is increasing, which creates a positive impact on outbound tourism. The Indian travel market is projected to grow to US$125 billion by 2027. This study identifies best practices and the need for sustainable tourism in India's growth.

Chapter 19 recognizes that disasters are tragic events which cause losses. The curiosity of people to feel sadness and pain motivates disaster tourism. Each disaster region has the potential for disaster tourism, which offers various benefits. This chapter covers the evaluation of the disaster tourism potential of countries with the Fuzzy-TOPSIS method. The criteria affecting the disaster tourism potential as the number of dead, injured, affected, and homeless people, were weighted according to the evaluations of the decision-makers. Disasters that occurred worldwide between 1980-2022 were analyzed with the criteria weights based on the countries where they occurred. Decision-makers mostly evaluated the number of deaths and homeless as more effective in affecting the desire to visit a disaster area and the attractiveness of the region. Among 90 countries, it has been determined that Sri Lanka and the Russian Federation are the two countries with the highest disaster tourism potential as to the number of losses/disasters, while Ethiopia is the country with the lowest disaster tourism potential.

Chapter 20 contends that sustainability refers to the careful use of natural resources by considering future generations. Especially in the food sector, the sustainability of resources and the reduction of environmental impacts are very important. The relationship between gastronomy and sustainability might be described using the term "eco-gastronomy". As practitioners of gastronomy, it is very important that chefs recognize the ecosystem, protect natural resources, and respect the natural environment. In this context, the aim of the study is to provide potential chef candidates with the opportunity to express their emotions via creative design by incorporating sustainability, eco gastronomy, and art. A total of 21 students were included in the study. With these students, designs related to both sustainability and gastronomy were realized, and they were enabled to design and present sustainable green restaurant logos and slogans in accordance with the concept they determined. Consequently, it was seen that the design stages and creativity stages of the students were exactly the same.

Chapter 21 notes that over the past three years the COVID-19 pandemic has received much global attention due to the high risk of fatality and human-to-human transmission. This pandemic has forced changes in every sector as well as in different aspects of everyone's daily lives. Travelling has had a critical role in contributing to its transmission by negatively influencing the majority of public health. The hospitality and tourism industry is subject to being immediately influenced by the external environment. This chapter explains how COVID-19 has affected food and beverage operations and safety in the sector and the global economy. New rules and regulations are described in detail. The future of food and beverage operations has changed by integrating technology, touchless contact, social distancing, and hygiene precautions, focusing on domestic travel, virtual tourism, and luxury travel.

Chapter 22 states that air travel produces about three percent of carbon dioxide emissions worldwide. The air travel industry requires an enduring vision that focuses on sustainable practices in the entire aviation sector, which will be a significant aspect of the future of civil aviation. The study adopts a systematic review to portray significant challenges, issues, and best practices in the worldwide aviation industry, highlighting the Indian scenario to establish future exploration in India. The chapter extensively investigates the latest sustainable developments in the airline business, the logical agreement on its ecological effects, and steps taken for sustainability.

Chapter 23 focuses on the dynamics of MHC-SME collaboration on sustainability in an emerging country context. Our findings show that MHC sustainability policy is generally driven from headquarters and that economic sustainability has priority over environmental and social sustainability. By contrast, SMEs appear to be able to initiate fully sustainable strategies based on the culture, tradition, family history, industry, and ethical standing of the owners. The interaction of MHCs and SMEs in relation to sustainability involves varying factors at the macro, meso, and micro levels. However, the micro level factor (i.e., human agency) seems to be the determining factor of the relationship. The authors provide rich contextual data by adopting a qualitative research method (case study) based on primary data, which is rare in international business literature.

Chapter 24 contributes to the relevant literature by evaluating the effect of the Technology Acceptance Model (TAM) model on the tourism sectors from a general perspective. It is seen that technological elements are frequently used to provide a better quality tourism experience and to expand the comfort zone. It is understood that many tourism businesses, especially in the fields of accommodation, travel and gastronomy, have gained a more competitive structure by developing their technological infrastructure. In this direction, the suitability of the TAM, which was first developed by Davis and based on two basic elements, in terms of tourism enterprises is associated with examples. It is understood the perceived convenience and usefulness within the scope of the research is met positively in terms of tourism services. In addition, it is thought the quality of service perception will be increased by better using the opportunities brought by technology in tourism.

Chapter 25 analyzes academic work from 2004 to 2020 with an influence on the blueprint for sustainable tourism innovation strategies. Criteria used include verifying which are the main concerns, the contribution of sustainability indices, and implications to practitioners and high educational institutions in the area. This is increasingly important due to present and future challenges undermining the existence of a sustainable tourism industry. Accurate metrics can empower destinations, and higher education and its inner research must have a key role in the development of effective instruments. The challenge comprises selecting and monitoring them for sustainable tourism policy. Educational and research institutes with tourism studies should include in their syllabuses real cases and tools for developing key sustainability models and metrics to integrate and respond more promptly to critical challenges and trends.

Preface

Chapter 26 examines the potential of the sharing economy in the tourism and hospitality sectors to disrupt the incumbent tourist regions and proposes sharing economy platforms for the introduction of new destinations in developing countries such as the Republic of Macedonia. It is crucial to examine the issue of the sharing economy from a governance perspective. The authors contend that sharing economy should be a part of a comprehensive national tourism policy based on contemporary governance principles and on experiences of other countries. The tourism and hospitality industry have been affected by sharing economy platforms and eco-systems, which constitute disruptive innovations (i.e., innovations that create new markets and value networks while disrupting existing ones and displacing industry incumbents). As the third largest socioeconomic activity within the European Union (EU), tourism can be considered an engine for economic development, accounting for about 8% between 2007 and 2016, while it has been close to 10% worldwide.

We trust these works will inspire additional research into sustainable tourism and hotel operations on a global scale which, in practice, can further enhance these two important aspects of national economic wealth and stability.

Hakan Sezerel
Anadolu University, Turkey

Bryan Christiansen
Global Research Society, LLC, USA

Chapter 1
Innovation for Sustainability by Smaller Organizations:
Strategies and Sustainability Impacts During the Pandemic

Dorthe Eide
Nord University, Norway

Olga Høegh-Guldberg
Nord University, Norway

ABSTRACT

In the context of growing sustainability challenges, organizations are increasingly expected to take action and report on sustainability. However, many organizations and local communities struggle with concretizing and balancing sustainability goals and actions. The present study, which draws upon parts of a larger qualitative case study, examines and compares six innovation pilots within the experience-based tourism industry. All cases received financial support within a program promoting an overall strategy of getting visitors to stay longer in tourist destinations. The chapter contributes knowledge to the field of innovation for sustainability in tourism and experiences by concretizing strategies and sustainability impacts and discussing them in relation to the concepts of weak and strong sustainability. The cases illustrate different ways the tourism industry and other collaborators can work toward achieving the sustainability development goals (SDGs) by avoiding negative impacts and increasing positive impacts within economic, environmental, and social sustainability dimensions.

INTRODUCTION

The aim of this chapter is to concretize and discuss how to carry out innovations for sustainability (IFS) with a focus on strategies adopted and their impacts on sustainability during the Covid-19 pandemic. Much effort has been made over the last four decades to conceptualize sustainability, including the development of a range of tools and approaches to help organizations improve sustainability. One such

DOI: 10.4018/978-1-6684-4645-4.ch001

approach involves certifications at the organizational and destination levels (Eide et al., 2021; Eide & Hoarau-Heemstra, 2022). Another approach is to increase regulation. A third involves raising expectations regarding documenting and reporting sustainability—seen particularly when organizations interact with financial institutions and investors, as suggested in the Environmental, Social Responsibility, Governance (ESG) framework proposed by the UN, for example, through the EU's Corporate Sustainability Reporting Directive (European Commission, n.d.). However, expectations about sustainability come from a range of stakeholders, including customers, destination management organizations (DMOs), tour operators, municipalities, and other collaborators. Before Covid-19, UNWTO (2019) described tourism as one of the fastest-growing industries, carrying the potential for job creation, income, and revitalizing of communities. On the dark side, the growth resulted in overtourism, creating pressures on infrastructure, nature, and local communities in an increasing number of destinations and adding strength to the call for stronger sustainability and even systemic changes (Epler Wood et al., 2019; Høegh-Guldberg et al., 2021). The neo-classical worldview, with its mantras of growth and competition, was questioned (Hall, 2018, 2019; Torkington et al., 2020). The Agenda 2030 United Nations Sustainability Development Goals (UN SDGs) are holistic since the three main value dimensions—economic, environmental, and social—must be integrated. Focusing on only a single SDG, or even on only one of the three sustainability dimensions, can be argued to be an approach that is fragmented and weak.

Coping with sustainability challenges and pursuing the SDGs is a dynamic ongoing phenomenon, and often depends on innovations and interdisciplinary collaboration. Different terms and approaches exist within research on this topic; this chapter uses "innovation for sustainability" (IFS), which is a rather new umbrella concept. The concept is used at different levels and needs further conceptualizing. IFS can be defined as "the intentional introduction of (radically) new or (incrementally) improved products and services or entire systems, which, based on traceable comparative analysis, lead to environmental and (or) social benefits that surpass those of the prior products, services, or systems" (Bocken et al., 2019, p. 6). Many organizations and local communities find it challenging to concretize and balance the sustainability dimensions and UN SDGs in practice (Albareda & Hajikhani, 2019; Skirbekk, 2019; Oftedahl et al., 2021). The research field is still in an early phase with several knowledge gaps regarding how IFS can be achieved. The literature is lacking in discussion of contextual strategies, tools, and examples of IFS at local levels for different stakeholder types (Nordregio, n.d.) and of IFS on the part of smaller organizations, given that larger firms have generally been studied (Tura et al., 2019).

This empirical study concretizes IFS strategies adopted by smaller organizations within the experience-based sectors of tourism. The remaining chapter first presents the theoretical framework, focused on perspectives on sustainability and innovation for sustainability, including the concepts of weak and strong sustainability. The methodology is briefly elaborated before the findings are presented and discussed. The empirical research was conducted in Northern Norway during the Covid-19 pandemic. In spring 2020, during the pandemic, regional DMOs in Norway, as in many countries, searched for alternative business strategies by focusing on domestic market segments and exploring other opportunities for change. For example, nature-based firms had earlier noted that Norwegians seldom were willing to pay for guided tours, which suggested the need for product innovations. Destinations and firms operating throughout the year, previously seen as most economically sustainable, were often the hardest hit as they were dependent on international and conference markets. At the same time, other destinations traditionally focused on domestic markets experienced growth in the number of visitors during the pandemic summers (NHO Reiseliv, 2020, 2021). Sustainability is complex and one of the main challenges of our time; increasingly, the tourism and experience sectors need to address and cope with sustainability issues in the context of changing conditions, including hyper-competitiveness nationally and internationally. Balancing different sustainability impacts by reducing negative impacts and increasing positive impacts becomes a must.

THEORETICAL FRAMEWORK

Sustainability

There are different perspectives on sustainability. Although it has become common to conceptualize sustainability by addressing three main dimensions, i.e. economy, environment (nature), and social. It can be unclear what the three dimensions include, how they interplay, and how to balance them. Differences in understandings and priorities can be explained by different disciplinary interpretations and different basic ontological assumptions (Temesgen et al., 2019).

The discussion of renewable and non-renewable resources goes back to the 1970s without explicit using the sustainability terminology (Dietz & Neumayer, 2007). Researchers often refer to Eric Neumayer and his first 1999 edition of *Weak versus Strong Sustainability* as the first labeling of the two extreme views on sustainability. The only point, seemingly, that the two views share is the Brundtland Commission's definition of sustainable development as "meeting the needs of the present without compromising the ability of future generations to meet their needs" (Brundtland, 1987, p. 16). Otherwise, the two viewpoints disagree on both the definition of "needs" and trajectories for achieving the stated goal; that is, they have different ontologies. The weak view of sustainability, most typically attributed to neoclassical economic theory, emphasizes the importance of economic values and prosperity. In essence, proponents of weak sustainability argue that at least one of the following conditions apply: "natural resources are super-abundant; or the elasticity of substitution between natural and produced capital is greater than or equal to unity…; or technological progress can increase the productivity of the natural capital stock faster than it is being depleted" (Dietz & Neumayer, 2007, p. 5). According to this view, the environmental impacts of economic growth can be remedied by instruments of economic policy. In other words, natural resources are treated as substitutable by other kinds of capital, opening the possibility of infinite economic growth and affirming the superiority of the economic system.

In the 1990s, a more critical environmental or ecological economic view emerged (Barbier et al., 1994; Turner et al., 1993). It aimed first at opening a cross-disciplinary dialogue between economists and ecologists (Barbier et al., 2019) and later at taking a cross-disciplinary account of all three sustainability dimensions, where none is considered superior to another. Originally, the main point upon which environmental economists disagreed with neoclassical economists was on the matter of natural capital, which, as the provider of basic systems and functions on which both human life and the economic system depend, is impossible to substitute (Dietz & Neumayer, 2007). As argued by Ott (2003, p. 62): "The human sphere is embedded in a natural system ("biosphere") and assumes that natural limits ought to constrain our actions." Further, it was argued that economic, environmental, and social capitals have their own inherent values. The three dimensions are interwoven and dependent on each other; therefore, reaching holistic sustainability requires the integration of different values, balancing, and compromise. A way for organizations to address all three dimensions is often defined as Elkington's (1994) triple bottom line (TBL). Elkington (1998, p. 397) defines the TBL as "the simultaneous pursuit of economic prosperity, environmental quality, and social equity. Companies aiming for sustainability need to perform not against a single, financial bottom line but against the triple bottom line." Thus, the TBL can be seen as a way of measuring corporate sustainability beyond short-term financial performance and corporate social responsibility towards long-term outcomes. However, according to Nilsen (2010), there are different approaches to the TBL, such as the simple TBL, in which one dimension can be substituted, and the balanced approach argued for by Elkington.

In essence, weak sustainability denotes a resource-exploitative position, while strong sustainability often denotes extreme preservationist positions (Cotterell et al., 2019). Although the scholarly discussion of sustainability is witnessing unprecedented interest and has matured over the years, Neumayer (2013) argues in his later editions of *Weak versus Strong Sustainability* that there are few strong sustainability solutions beyond "technical" work. Cotterell et al. (2019) summarize the continuum from "weak" to "strong" sustainability as indicated in Table 1, arguing that weaker approaches to sustainability are common in all economic sectors, not least tourism.

Table 1. Conceptualizations of sustainability. Adapted from Cotterell et al. (2019, p. 886)

Very weak	Weak	Moderate	Strong	Very strong
Economic growth: Business as usual	**Sustainable growth:** Focus on the environmental dimension in addition to economic considerations	**Sustainable development:** Economics, society, and environment (triple bottom line)	**New ecological paradigm:** Strong sustainability based on integrity and systems thinking	**Anti-economic growth:** Complex system of adaptive management and systems thinking

Other debates about weak versus strong sustainability address the difference between merely seeking to reduce or avoid negative impacts and seeking to create positive values, viewing the former as weak and the latter as strong (Dyllick & Muff, 2016). More recently, the concept of "regenerative" has been suggested as an alternative to "sustainability" in different industries, including tourism. In this view, past approaches to sustainability are seen as too reactive and focused on reducing negative "footprints," whereas industries should be more proactive and aim for value creation, transformation, and thriving (Pollock, 2019).

Within tourism, there are different perspectives and foci regarding sustainability, some of which are in line with the more general debates addressed above and some more contextually specified. For example, Saarinen (2006, 2014) argues that studies within tourism have been conducted from three main perspectives: (1) the resource-based perspective that focuses on environmental or cultural sustainability, often in the form of governance protection implemented mainly by public organizations; (2) the activity-based perspective, which focuses on the economic activity performed by enterprises; and (3) the perspective of community-based tourism (CBT), which aims to involve local communities in tourism planning and development to secure their "control over the uses and benefits of (common) resources used in tourism" (Saarinen, 2014, p. 5). In focus, the three perspectives overlap with the three main sustainability dimensions. If applied separately, they can be argued to lead to weak approaches as each focuses mainly on one sustainability dimension, although the CBT perspective overlaps with community-based sustainability (CBS) (Høegh-Guldberg et al., 2022; Saarinen, 2019) and can be argued to entail a local, bottom-up approach which potentially can prioritize or balance the economic, environmental and society dimensions in weak or strong ways depending on local decisions. Spenceley and Rylance (2019) use the UN SDGs to discuss the positive and negative impacts of tourism on sustainability, claiming that positive impacts on local communities often are missing since outsiders use local resources and obtain benefits.

Given that it is often argued that tourism can be a tool to revitalize communities (Jørgensen et al., 2021), a lack of positive impact is problematic and can be partly due to the approaches used by the actors in charge of development but also due to a lack of involvement of those influenced by tourism (Heslina et al., 2019). For this reason, scholars (e.g. (Saarinen, 2019) increasingly call for more bottom-up involvement, as in CBT/CBS, and more radical systemic change in terms of ontology and the perspective taken on sustainability, as proposed in CBS, ecological economy, and regenerative tourism. Spenceley and Rylance (2019) also claim that the tourism literature seldom addresses the climate challenge. Transport using fossil energy contributes mostly to h negative impact of tourism on the climate (Chatti, 2021), suggesting the need for innovations that can reduce this negative impact. One such approach is nudging, which can be used to change tourists' transport behavior (Nikolova, 2020).

Innovation for Sustainability

The research fields of sustainability and innovation have become increasingly merged (Bocken et al., 2019), as innovations are central when coping with sustainability challenges. Different terms have been suggested to conceptualize these combinations. We choose "innovation for sustainability" (IFS) since it emphasizes that innovation is used to improve sustainability. However, that does not mean that there are no negative impacts of such innovations. The positive and negative impacts largely depend on the sustainability focus and the approaches taken in the innovations. Generic literature reviews show different approaches within IFS that can be grouped within three main paradigms (Albareda & Hajikhani, 2019; Ritala, 2019): (1) the skeptical one, focusing on a single dimension, often economic considerations; (2) the pragmatic one, with a focus on two dimensions, as in "the green turn" addressing economic considerations and, to some extent, the environment; (3) the idealistic paradigm, which is holistic and ambitious, addressing all three dimensions. Traditionally, most studies of innovation focus on firms and are situated within the skeptical paradigm based on neo-liberalism, which prioritizes increasing economic value through growth, competition, and often internationalization. As organizations are increasingly expected to care not only for monetary value and shareholders but also for non-monetary value and different stakeholders within and outside the organization, more holistic sustainability must be addressed and reported (Evans et al., 2017). This makes innovation not only more diverse in terms of value creation (monetary and non-monetary value, short- and long-term perspectives) but also more open in terms of the knowledge and partners involved (Boons & Lüdeke-Freund, 2013). The skeptical paradigm is found not only in economic perspectives but also in other disciplines focused on only one dimension, such as traditional environmental preservation, cultural preservation, and social perspectives (Bocken et al., 2019; Lee & Thapa, 2017). The idealistic IFS paradigm overlaps with Cotterells' "strong" and "very strong" continuum types and probably the "moderate" type as well. The research field of IFS is still in its early phase and has so far mainly offered insight into the skeptical paradigm, and within that mostly related to larger organizations and business model innovations for sustainability (Bocken et al., 2019; Ritala, 2019). The traditional typologies of innovation types, such as the Oslo Manual (OECD, 2005), which focus on product, process, market, and organizational innovations, originate from the skeptical paradigm focused on the entrepreneur or larger organizations in manufacturing industries. Over time, other innovation types have been added, such as business model or value chain/network innovations and social innovations. Previous studies have shown that tourism enterprises have different motivations and values shaping their perspectives on sustainability (Lindberg et al., 2019) as well as in IFS (Hoarau-Heemstra & Eide, 2016). For example, studies of whale-watching firms show that they are motivated by multiple values, which lead to different strategies; for example, care for culture leads to boat preservation, while care for whales spurs the development and dissemination of knowledge about whales.

METHODOLOGY

This interpretive study was conducted through a hermeneutical multi-case design (Alvesson & Sköldberg, 2009). The cases are innovation pilots, developed and tested during 2021. Tourism-related organizations in Northern Norway were invited by a regional bank fund to apply for funding as a single enterprise or in collaboration with other organizations to develop and test one or more pilots during the summer of 2021. The fund acknowledged that tourism and culture-based sectors had been hit hard by the pandemic and wanted to stimulate innovations to provide income and also contribute to other sustainability areas and particularly environmental challenges. They introduced an overall strategy of encouraging visitors to "stay one day more" or longer in the local destination. Ninety-one applications were funded from the population of 219. We strategically selected 21 of the supported projects based on variation in the following criteria: type of subsectors and innovations, SDGs addressed, geographic situatedness of the organizations, and participation of one or more formal partners. The 21 projects involved 36 pilots, as the numbers of pilots in projects varied from one to five. It is these pilots that are the cases, not the projects or the contact enterprises. This chapter focuses on six of these pilots.

The main method of data gathering was semi-structured interviews, which were done in two rounds: the first one in June 2021 to cover the plans and organizational histories, and the second one after the summer (September–October, mainly) to cover their experiences and self-reported results. Usually, one informant from each project was interviewed. Interviews were conducted via Zoom video conferencing due to the pandemic and the long distances involved (travel would have been very resource-demanding). There are limitations that arise from not meeting project participants face to face. However, these limitations were largely mitigated by the video interview technology, which allowed us to see and interpret the body language of our informants and establish effective dialogues. Interviews normally lasted about 1 hour, and they were recorded and transcribed. Combinations of methods and data contribute to triangulation, which can increase study quality; therefore, we supplemented our data with documents in the form of applications and reports to the bank fund, as well as information about enterprises and their pilots from social media and organizational websites.

Analysis of the interviews was conducted using qualitative thematized content analysis, searching for meaning patterns. A hermeneutical coding approach, partly inspired by the literature and partly open, was used in within- and cross-case analysis, involving meaning calibrations and meaning condensations (Kvale & Brinkman, 2009). In the within- and cross-case analyses, analytical tables were used to maintain an overview and record interpretations (Miles & Huberman, 1984). Both authors did interviews and analyses, and multiple rounds of calibration took place. Different IFS strategies and sustainability sub-impacts were localized and categorized. The sustainability impacts of pilots were not measured by exact tools; rather, they are our suggested constructions based on informants' first-order concepts when self-reporting in interviews and project reports. In interviews, we asked how they tested and/or documented their work, and almost all argued that it is difficult to systematically test and document experiences and sustainability impacts for various reasons, often due to the lack of time and tools.

FINDINGS

This section first addresses innovation types and innovation for sustainability (IFS) strategies. Then, six pilots are elaborated to concretize the sustainability continuum. Finally, the six pilots are compared.

Main Types of Innovations and IFS Strategies

Five of the six pilots were *product innovations* involving new or significantly improved experience products (non-functional services); one was a marketing pilot. However, most pilots also involved other innovation types, not least process innovations (new ways of producing) and some degree of market innovation due to new domestic segments forced by the pandemic (i.e., market innovations were not involved only in the specific market pilot). There are also examples of new collaborations in or for production (i.e.,

Table 2. IFS strategies and sustainability impacts

Strategies (what)	Sustainability impacts (why)
1. Use *fossil-free transport in products*: biking, boat, walking, el-car.	Reduce pressure on nature (climate, animals). Reduce noise for visitors and perhaps residents.
2. Use new *technology* in experience products.	Create value for visitors by increasing sensual experiences (visualizing, hearing), become attractive.
3. *Visitor management* to distribute visitors to other paths and places, new signs and information.	Reduce pressure on nature, locals, and/or social infrastructure.
4. *Renewal harvesting* of local natural resources in careful ways, both on land (plants) and/or in water (e.g., seaweed, crabs), combined with knowledge dissemination, cooking and/or followed by eating. Interactive and multi-sensing design.	Increase visitor value and attractiveness of products/place, learn (about plants, harvesting, use of the resources in cooking, inspire sustainable transformation.
5. Use and disseminate *local nature (e.g., wildlife, geology)* in new ways, often involving interactive, multi-sensing design.	Create value for visitors and firms, but in careful ways to avoid negative impact on nature. May involve environmental improvements (e.g., garbage picking).
6. Use and disseminate *local culture* (tangible, intangible, traditions) in new ways, often involving interactive, multi-sensing design.	Create value for visitors and firms, but in careful ways to avoid negative impact on the locals and other social dimensions. May increase social sustainability in the form of residents' knowledge, pride, identity, etc.
7. Develop new/prolonged *seasons* toward year-round activity through attractive differentiated products and market development.	Create more year-round work to attract and keep competence (often challenging), and create positive impact on economy and the social dimension (local community, taxes, residents).
8. Improve *marketing* (materials, methods of promotion, e.g., events,) of firm and destination *by storytelling* (pictures, video, texts) about place, local producers, local produce, experiential marketing.	Become more known and attractive in responsible ways for segments. Potentially positive impact also on residents (social dimensions like identity, pride, locals as internal marketers).
9. *Collaborate locally* in innovation, production, and marketing, including inviting new partners.	Increase competitiveness nationally and internationally through local partnership (e.g., networks, packages).
10. Use *local produce made by others*, e.g., local food, handcrafts, harvesting equipment, visit other firms, etc.	Increase quality of own product (economic) by others' local products can avoid negative pressure on nature, increase local thematizing (educational, social), contribute income for other sectors (e.g., agriculture, fishing, art and handcrafts).
11. *Small scale* (numbers of customers), *high value*.	Retain same economic income or increase it while hosting fewer visitors. Avoid negative impact on nature and/or locals/social infrastructure due to mass tourism. Can be less wearing on staff. Can give higher value for visitors.

value chain innovations, organizational innovations) and marketing, as well as new ways to increase the competence of personnel or other changes to improve working conditions (i.e., organizational innovations). Some of these included technological innovations (e.g., the use of electric bikes, drones). In the larger study of 36 pilots, a few informants explicitly describe how a new offering is part of their larger process of innovation-for-sustainable business model since it involves a radical change in the logic of doing business—for example, greater care for nature, employees, and locals, combined with co-creating value for visitors by encouraging them to stay longer, engage in fossil-free activities, and partake of local food. It seems reasonable that more organizations have started a business model innovation by taking small steps towards a long-term transformation.

The overall aim of the pilots was to increase the value creation of the organization, and sometimes also the destination, by adding new or changed services and, in particular, experience-based offerings for guests. The pandemic led to changed overall market segmentation practices focused on domestic tourists and sometimes also locals. Reducing financial losses and improving economic value creation can be argued to be the main motivation for participating in the project. However, the participants' use of innovation strategies and reported sustainability impacts are far more nuanced than the imperative to economic survival alone would dictate. The project stimulated strategies for becoming climate-friendly and prolonging visitors' stays; the incentives influenced the strategies chosen by the participants. Table 2 presents the main innovation strategies and sustainability impacts. It shows that most strategies try both to reduce or avoid negative impacts *and* increase positive values, not just one or the other.

The larger study involving all pilots revealed additional strategies, such as n*ew booking routines* with minimums of 2–3 days in accommodation, sometimes combined with total experiences, which can keep visitors longer in a destination, reduce the number of visitors, reduce the use of fossil transport, reduce resource use and repetitive work tasks, reduce pressure on locals and local infrastructure, and increase value creation for visitors and firms. *Extended opening hours* were another strategy used to increase customer value.

From Weak to Strong Sustainability

Indications of sustainability impacts linked to the strategies were presented above. An array of sub-impacts within the three main sustainability dimensions were revealed. When all the pilots were re-coded with the relevant sub-categories, each pilot was related to a smaller or larger set of sub-impacts. Then all pilots were compared and grouped according to similarities in sub-impacts as well as total impact

Figure 1. A continuum from weak to strong and cases within it

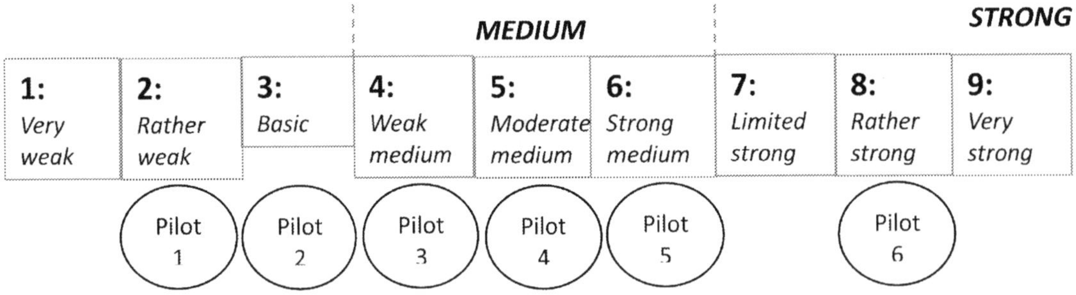

(our summative interpretation) and ordered. Based on the empirical findings and inspiration from the literature, a continuum from weak via medium to strong was constructed using a scale from one to nine, as shown in Figure 1.

Below, the six chosen pilots are elaborated with a focus on innovation type, innovation strategy, and sustainability impacts, ordered from weaker to stronger sustainability.

Rather Weak (type 2)

Pilot 1 is a marketing (M) pilot realized as an event. The project owner had applied for two marketing pilots, realized together by the project participants on a somewhat reduced scale. The project participants are situated in a popular Northern city destination that attracts many international visitors in summer and winter alike.

Innovation: The pilot is a summer backyard arrangement for local and visiting guests designed to promote a group of local actors and invite other local actors to collaborate (IFS 8 and 9, see Table 2). The focus is on authentic local experiences in the historic quarter of the city, particularly on showing/selling local design, local products, and local food experiences associated with music and a good atmosphere (IFS 6), that is, experiential marketing. To realize both pilots, a part-time project manager was hired to ensure planning, bring partners to events in the backyard, coordinate, and do marketing. In addition to marketing expenses, the project funding was used to rent various pieces of equipment and decorate the venue. The pilot was successful, although not without external challenges, such as bad weather shortening visitors' stays. Many people went through the big tent during the day. The project participants and invited firms were content: although the sales numbers varied among the firms, "they got a lot of phone numbers and made contacts and got to show themselves" under the arrangement.

Sustainability impacts: The pilot has a strong focus on economic sustainability. In addition to emphasizing the importance of high-quality, durable products by all project participants, the pilot stresses the importance of 100% local ownership, job creation, and promotion of local brands in the regional and national contexts. The pilot also has some positive impact on socio-cultural sustainability due to the focus on the authenticity of and pride in the products produced locally. However, the one-time nature of the event makes it inferior to the second marketing pilot in terms of environmental impacts, including the promotion of reuse and recycling practices in the project participants' production lines. Among the SDGs relevant to the pilot, the following are listed by the project owners: 4 (Education), 8 (Decent work and economic growth), 11 (Sustainable cities and communities), 12 (Responsible consumption and production), and 17 (Collaboration).

Partnership: The project owner is a small, informal network of companies that had collaborated before they applied for the current pilot. The network consists of three local companies located in the city center: a goldsmith, a brewery, and a glass-blowing studio. In addition to being retailers, the firms are classified as experience providers since they represent local history, promote local production and innovation, and offer experiences and activities related to their products. They target both the local market and tourists, who participate in their activities and buy products to take home.

Further development: The project owners want to continue working with similar arrangements given their marketing effect and contribution to joint marketing efforts: "There is a wish to keep this up and going." The only limitation is that such arrangements require resources that are not always available internally in the participating firms. There is also an interest from other local actors in future joint events and establishing collaboration with the project participants. In the future, the project participants want to create a joint platform to sell offerings and to become even more visible, in addition to Facebook and Instagram accounts that they have worked on in the other marketing pilot. They are considering extending the arrangement for international guests when the Covid situation improves: "I think everything that is interesting and exciting for Norwegians is the same for foreigners. The real, the unique experience is what they are looking for." With their unique and authentic experiences, the project participants also want to contribute to the ongoing debate about the future of the city center.

Basic

Pilot 2 is a nature-based (NB) experience by boat. The project owner applied for three pilots, this one being the weakest in its sustainability impacts. The firm is situated in a well-known tourism region, although the local destination is less developed. Recently, a tourism chain invested in the firm to develop more year-round activity and put the local destination "on the map." The chain contributed with competent new staff and management.

Innovation: The pilot, termed "rib tour with crab harvesting," was open for individuals to book. The experience lasted about four hours, including dressing, introduction, boating with nature-watching, harvesting, and a light meal. A rib boat was used, offering the potential to travel long distances and reach high speeds. The boat driver also served as nature guide, pointing out animals and features of the landscape, storytelling (IFS 5), and crabbing (IFS 4). After the boat trip, guests were served crab soup in a restaurant: "There is good access to crabs in this area, but crabs are seldom used as food here, and we wanted to explore harvesting. The harvesting was only one part of the tour; the largest part was nature-watching. We saw many sea eagles and seals, in addition to the coastal landscape." Three to twelve guests participated in each tour.

Sustainability impacts: Regarding economic sustainability, the new experience product makes the firm and local destination more attractive for visitors to come and stay longer as there are more interesting activities to engage in. It creates value for the firm and guests and creates additional jobs. Guests are educated through the guided tour. Regarding environmental sustainability, the careful harvesting of little-used local food resources food is seen as the strategy with the largest potential for positive impact in the future and a potential contributor to the development of new seasons (IFS 7). New, nature-friendly harvesting equipment developed by a local producer (IFS 10) puts less pressure on animals: "We used two different pieces of harvest equipment during the season. During the first part, we used traditional equipment. During the second half, we used a new type, developed by a local producer, which makes it possible for the small crabs and fish to escape. In the old type, they could not escape, and fish died unnecessarily if the equipment was not checked sufficiently often. The new design reflects a more cautious approach to what lives in the ocean." The harvesting activity is thus involved in both reducing negative impacts and increasing positive ones. Most challenging, however, is the use of a rib boat with a fossil fuel–powered motor, which has a negative impact through increasing pressure on the environment (climate footprints) and animals (disturbing birds, noise pollution). All the same, most visitors seem to enjoy the speed (fun) and the opportunity to see larger stretches of the local coast beyond the crab harvesting area. The SDGs involved are 4 (Education), 8 (Decent work and economic growth), 9 (Innovation) to some degree, 11 (Community), 12 (Production & consumption), and 14 (Below water).

Partnership: There was no direct partnership in this pilot, as a single firm served as the main developer and producer of the new approach. Indirectly, however, two types of stakeholders were involved: the local producer of the new crab-fishing equipment and local crab-fishers contacted before the start and during the testing of the pilot: "We had dialogue with crab-fishers, asking their opinions on where to put out the harvesting equipment. It was important not to compete with them, that they found it okay. Also, we talked with them during the season; they have shared knowledge."

Further development: The increasing focus on sustainability in society has made them start looking for non-fossil-fueled engines for the boats. However, the el-motors available are too small: "The problem is that electric engines are not as strong as the ones driven by fossil fuels, unfortunately... If using them, the tour would be less focused on high speed and more on nature experiences and harvesting. It might work, but many like the thrill of speed. It would mean a change in the type of people towards more modern hippies." Electric engines are expected to improve and become an alternative in coming years, which could make the firm's new nature-based products more environmentally sustainable, more consistent with the harvesting arguments, and a better match for segments with strong sustainability values. Fossil energy can then be replaced with more green energy (SDG 13). The corresponding reduction of sound pollution would not only reduce some negative pressure on animals (SDG 14-15) but also increase the experience quality and value for customer segments appreciating it (SDG 12). Other potential improvements include more education about harvesting, including instruction on how to cook with crabs. Social sustainability was not mentioned. This firm also developed a pilot termed "seaweed harvesting." However, according to our informant, the testing of these two pilots had been limited due to some boat problems and a lack of international customers. Both pilots are assumed to have stronger potential for international markets. The domestic guests seemed most interested in the boat trip with nature guiding. The firm is therefore planning to make the pilots shorter and less costly, taking out the served meal—although there is ambivalence about this change, as harvesting is a rising trend both nationally and internationally.

Weak Medium

Pilot 3 is a nature and partly culture-based experience (NC) innovation, with guiding taking place mainly during hiking. It was one of three pilots in the project carried out through a collaboration between two firms. One of the firms had, for years, on a part-time basis, run a lodge for salmon fishers by a river on the edge of a national park. More recently, they had also become a service center connecting visitors and experience providers. The other firm was an experience provider specializing in nature-based adventures. They have several plans of innovation for sustainability: "We want to keep the guests longer. If looking at the whole year, we want to offer so many activities that guests do not want to leave us." The pandemic gave an extra push for the lodge owner since he lost access to his main market of international salmon fishers and needed a new existential fundament in the form of new products and visitors.

Innovation: Riverboat trips have been offered for decades by different providers in this area, with little differentiation and product development. Firms take guests in a riverboat up the river and point the way to a waterfall that guests can then reach on their own; afterward, guests are driven back downriver in the boat. Drivers often use hearing protection due to the noise. The owners of this innovation pilot wanted to develop internationally high-value products by using knowledge about nature and culture in guiding. The experience in the pilot lasts four hours, in addition to the boat ride. Most of the time is spent hiking to attractions, eating lunch, and storytelling about nature and culture (IFS 5-6), all organized by a guide: "One walks to X, one of North Europe's largest waterfalls. Then one enjoys a light lunch, and coffee is made on the bonfire. One looks at petroglyphs and a large pine tree, and there is guiding about culture in the valley.... The idea is to convey genuine experiences. The nature-based experience is intended to be real, without much modern technology. Local produce is served on a white cloth." The boat ride was not new, but the other parts of the offering were.

Sustainability impacts: That most visitors arrive by plane is the largest negative environmental impact. This changed during Covid-19, when most visitors were domestic, and many came from the local region, meaning the negative impact was reduced. Another negative factor is the fossil-fueled boat motor, which has some negative impact on the environment, including noise pollution (for animals, guests, and employees on short parts of the tour). However, most of the product involves hiking (IFS 1). The product takes place in a national park in which there are many regulations (e.g., one must not pick flowers, not leave garbage) to protect against negative impacts on nature (environmental sustainability). The firms do not want mass tourism; they pursue a small-scale strategy (IFS 11): "We do not want to overuse the national park and end up like, for example, Lofoten, where the tracks become as big as motorways, damaging the natural setting. The guests do not have to be many, but they should spend a lot of money. We think it can be done sustainably." They avoid negative pressures by taking care of the landscape and animals (e.g., the fish). For example, they will not use speed motors during the salmon's spawning periods: "I have to take care of the delivery room in the river." The new product contributes to economic sustainability by improving the firms' existential fundament (new markets), generating income, and providing some work. In addition, it makes the firm and destination more attractive, which is important when seeking year-round activity (IFS 7). These economic impacts also spur some positive impacts on society sustainability by making the local community an attractive place to live and work. Most people, including children, can participate in the product as the hike is rather short. Still, it has some positive health impacts for guests due to the physical activity, some learning, and being in nature. The guiding with storytelling has educational and experience quality impacts for visitors (economic sustainability), mainly, and can have some positive impact on cultural and environmental sustainability. What is more, the use of local produce in the lunch (IFS 10) contributes some to work and income for stakeholders in other sectors (society sustainability). The main SDGs involved are 3 (Health/well-being), 4 (Education), and 8 (Work and economy), along with some 9 (Innovation), 12 (Production and consumption), 13 (Climate main parts of the tour), and 17 (Collaboration). A negative impact is seen in relation to 13 (Climate) when using the boat and potentially also 14 (Water) and 15 (Land), although the enterprise is conducted with some care.

Partnership: The two formal partners exclusively developed and produced the pilot. There was some collaboration with local food producers supplying the lunches. Development of a site into a more attractive year-round destination cannot be done by a single party alone; rather, the firms involved generally must work with other firms in the local destination network. For example, one of their other pilots is about marketing on social media with storytelling using pictures and videos filmed with drones during productions of the two "river & hiking" experience pilots in good weather conditions. This will give visibility and attention not only to the products and firms but also to the destination.

Further development: This and a longer "river & hiking" pilot received good feedback, and new marketing (the third pilot) will be used to attract guests in the future. This pilot will be tested on international markets when the borders open, and the price will be increased. The pilots were part of the larger development processes of becoming attractive and providing year-round activity for the firms and destination. Year-round activity (IFS 11) depends on collaboration (IFS 9); both are argued to be vital if economic sustainability is to increase: "To create year-round work in the destination so that providers can hire more people and external guides will not go home and not come back.... My impression is that before, there was little collaboration.... It is important that we make each other better and develop pride."

Year-round work can help firms attract and retain qualified staff, which is a challenge now. In addition, they see the need to obtain fossil-free motors for the boats to reduce environmental impacts. However, like pilot 2, they argue that el-motors are not yet good enough. The silence of electric motors, when the technology improves, will contribute positively to experience quality (i.e., economic sustainability) and reduce noise pressure on animals (environmental), employees (economic), and other locals (society).

Moderate Medium

Pilot 4 is a nature- and culture-based (NC) experience with digital guiding focused on culture to accompany cycling along a planned route, mainly in rural parts of the municipalities.

Innovation: This project owner had, prior to the pilot, established bicycle rental as a bookable activity. Originally, there were two companies that ran bicycle rentals, but the project participants were rather flexible in customizing bicycle pickup and delivery to other project participants during the pilot (IFS 1). The bicycles can be booked online through the common platform connecting the project participants. The pilot aims to contribute to developing activities along the path, which runs throughout the whole municipality, with a large part being on a nature trail. The path was planned to be tested for disseminating local history with the help of QR codes and apps: "We used the funding to build a platform for digital storytelling…. It contains the history of X" (IFS 2, 6). The platform, which is a web page, links stories to specific stops along the path to make it interesting for guests to visit and read on their own devices. The pilot included 12–15 such stops. The project owner got the inspiration for the platform development from a local hiking app in another Norwegian city and outsourced technical help to realize the project. There is a link to each project participant in the digital platform with storytelling: "The idea was to divert traffic to each player based on where the cyclist was on the map. Because it is also a digital map where the cyclist can track his position on the trail and see where the next restaurant or accommodation is located" (IFS 9). Other IFS strategies, such as the use of a local natural path (IFS 5) and improved marketing (by placing participating firms on the route map, IFS 8) were employed as preconditions and/or intentions (prolonged season, IFS 7) for the pilot.

Sustainability impacts: The pilot is meant to create more activity, interactions, and learning for different age groups of visitors with the help of sustainable transportation, that is, by bicycle or on foot. The latter not only contributes to better public health but attracts new customer groups: "The bicycle path runs along this river, so many of the fishermen who come visiting, they rent bikes and bike along the river to find their fishing spots." The applicant argues that the pilot could also contribute to extending the high season. The offer began to be used by locals as well as visitors. The bicycle path contributes to increased collaboration between project participants by creating packages and a platform for firms to recommend one another to visitors. The following global sustainability goals are prioritized as central for the pilot: 3 (Health and quality of life), 4 (Education), 11 (Communities), and 17 (Collaboration).

Partnership: The project owner is a tourism business network that had formalized collaborations for three years before participating in the current project. The network includes six different firms working with accommodation, food, and activities. As one of the outcomes of the project, they have established a common platform with descriptions of their offers and contact information for the member firms. In addition, for the purposes of the project, the network established collaboration with a history association: "We connected with X History Association, who many years ago published X book containing local history from the old days. So we entered into a collaboration with them, where they shared these stories that have previously been published in book form." Technically, the project was realized by an external firm.

Further development: The project owner has considered a number of options for further development of the bicycle path, given that "it is agreed [by the network members] that the bicycle path and history dissemination will be developed further and be a type of main product for the business network." The project owner applied for a second round of project funding but was rejected; in the second phase, the project was to be extended to include art dissemination with a broader partnership (e.g., including an art gallery). The network intends to work further on diversifying activities along the path (including during shoulder and potentially winter seasons) with the help of the platform established during the pilot as well as by inviting new collaborating partners. This would help the network to build the foundation for designing experience packages with the offers from the actors along the path. Technically, the platform may be extended to include "oral retelling, so that you can have a plug in your ear and hear the story" and, perhaps, become available in languages other than Norwegian once international guests are able to travel again.

Strong Medium

Pilot 5 is a culture-based (CB) experience. It was one of two pilots that the firm applied for, both using electric bikes and guiding. The rather newly established firm was situated in a city providing experience offerings for both tourists and locals. Due to the pandemic, most guests have been locals, either business groups, groups of friends, or individuals.

Innovation: The pilot is an electric bike tour (IFS 1) in the city area, devoted to the history of the Second World War (IFS 6). The tour was offered one evening every week during the summer but could also be done in the Spring and Fall (IFS 7). It is dependent on the participation of a war museum (IFS 9). The museum (an old war bunker) is run by enthusiasts doing voluntary work, showing pictures while storytelling, guiding visitors around the building, and offering them coffee. The guiding with storytelling in other parts of the tour, that is, while biking and visiting other war attractions, was done by the firm: "The product is attractive because of the visit to the bunker museum, there is no doubt about that. Our contribution is the round trip with visits to several of the places discussed in the museums' presentation and pictures... Our guided tours in the city are mainly storytelling about history; the bike is simply a tool to make it easier and less physically straining. The distance covered is about 16 km, 2–3 hours."

Sustainability impacts: The electric bike tour in fresh air involves exercise and can contribute to health and quality of life (social sustainability). The fossil-free transport is argued to be climate-friendly and create no noise. It does not take place in natural landscapes (therefore causing no negative impact on nature). The use of bikes can be seen as placing less pressure on roads and locals than cars or buses would. The visit to cultural attractions and storytelling contributes to education and experience quality for guests and to more attractive products for the firm and destination, or economic sustainability. It also contributes to cultural sustainability (education, dissemination, pride). The new product provides some income for both organizations. The SDGs involved are 3 (Health), 4 (Education), 8 (Work and economic growth), 12 (Production & consumption), 13 (Climate), and 17 (Partnership), as well as some 9 (Innovation) and 11 (City & community).

Partnership: The firm was the main developer and producer, although its work could not be done without the participation of the museum. The museum is a voluntary organization, with members very interested in war history and caring for the buildings taking full responsibility for the storytelling and educational element in the museum. In addition, the local DMO helped with marketing and a booking platform. The pilot also got help from a local media outlet that tested the product and published an informative newspaper article.

Further development: The firm is still in an early phase of establishing itself, and developing activity in seasons other than summer is argued to be the greatest sustainability challenge. Much investment in equipment has been and will continue to be necessary; income to cover investment and wages are a must for the project to keep going. The firm is exploring the possibility of collaborating with coastal cruise firms on new versions of the product tailored to cruise guests, first for the fall season (IFS 7). This would mean more guests from a segment that often is less physically fit and would require the purchase of bikes that are easier to get onto. In addition, it would create a need for more tour guides. Testing the pilot on international markets is another potential development, which would mean that guiding must be done in English, which might be challenging for the museum. Larger organizations like cruise firms often ask about certifications related to sustainability; their requests for documentation have motivated the firm into a certification process. The firm intends to develop more nature-based biking for the winter season using fat bikes, as well as themed adventures, for example, hunting the polar light by bike. In addition, there is potential to develop comprehensive packages in collaboration with others in the region outside the city: "Biking tourism, including mountain biking, is increasing substantially in Norway. To lead cycle trips in natural settings, we need permission from the landlords. A variety of such permissions are often necessary. Commercial tours require permission, but for individual cyclists, the general public access law guarantees access… It has been more usual for Norwegians to go abroad in Europe on biking holidays." A moose-watching cycle trip is among the many other ideas in circulation.

Rather Strong

Pilot 6 is a nature- and culture-based (NC) experience involving hiking. The project owner applied for five related pilots, two combined nature- and culture-based experiences, one meal- and one nature-based experience, and a marketing pilot. The latter was an umbrella for experiences in the destination, including the pilots, during the summer season. The project participants are situated in a popular island sub-destination that attracts many international visitors, especially during the summer months.

Innovation: The pilot is a new activity trail (IFS 1, 3) consisting of different points of interest where guests must answer questions, find or count particular objects, and complete other assignments. The main purpose of the trail was to create a "fun and educational activity for families connected to nature, culture, and history in X" (IFS 5, 6). The trail was suitable for different customer groups, but families were particularly prioritized in the planning process. Upon fulfilling the tour and completing the assignments, participants received a certificate. The trail was very engaging and became popular. "They had to stop by many different places—indeed, the whole of X [sub-destination]—to get this award…in the old shop." Participants' forms were reviewed when they got to the old shop, and those who had managed to complete a set number of items were awarded the X Certificate. The certificate was signed by the leader of the business network and carried the logos of partners supporting the sub-destinations' sustainability initiatives. Thus, the activity trail connected many actors within the sub-destination, including some not directly participating in the project (IFS 9, 8).

Sustainability impacts: The pilot has a strong, holistic sustainability focus, contributing to all three dimensions. It integrates previous work towards becoming a more sustainable destination and community (SDG 11) and contributes to the synergies of the other four pilots that the project includes (IFS 8, 9, 10). "What we have worked for during the summer is to have an awareness of what sustainability means in X. We think this is very important to experience both when you get here as a guest and also when living your life here…that you have quality in your life." Developing additional economic activity and enhancing the visibility of participating partners were, thus, elements of the dialogue with the local population. "The pressure on people who live their lives in X is great during the summer season. The working hours for those who work…are extreme, and the challenges associated with infrastructure are enormous when guest traffic increases." The pilot also aimed to educate and distribute visitors to other natural areas than those traditionally used (IFS 1, 3, 5, 6). The pilot "should in a way engage people, and they should learn something along the way." At the same time, additional activities encouraged guests to stay longer and released some of the pressure on tourism employees. In addition to 11 (Community), the project contributes to 3 (Health and quality of life) and 14 (Life in the sea) due to the path's proximity to the sea.

Partnership: The project owner is a business network consisting of 15 small and micro firms involved primarily in tourism. The companies have collaborated prior to participating in the current project and stand together in the ongoing dialogue on sustainability within the destination, working together on, among other projects, active engagement of the local population, particularly youth: "Alone, it is difficult to bring about change and development, and therefore the corporate network is an important, unifying player for the business community here. The majority of the companies in X are owned and operated by the local population."

Further development: The pilot was the result of innovation and collaboration synergies and stimulated further developments. The assignments developed for the activity trail have been used for other social initiatives in the community: "It was great, and we have also used it afterwards in other ways. We have used it as a quiz when it starts to get very dark in the evenings or if the weather is bad. Then it is nice to sit inside and do it." The pilot also has synergies with other innovation pilots developed by the network, including podcasts narrating the history of the area for those traveling to the destination by car. The network aims to continue working with this and the podcast pilot, which not only contribute to the destination's visibility and promote its history but also have a great potential to inform visitors about expected behaviors and distribute them around the destination in a more sustainable way. It is considered that the pilot could be adapted to the needs of international tourists if the Covid-19 situation becomes better in the summer of 2022.

Cross-Case Comparison

Table 3 and the text below summarize and compare the six in-depth pilot cases regarding pilot type, innovation type, strategy, sustainability strength, sustainability sub-impacts, and SDGs addressed.

The most frequently used *strategy* (in five out of six pilots) was to "collaborate locally" (9); four pilots aimed to "use and disseminate culture in new ways" (6). Two of the strategies, to "use fossil-free transport" (1) and "use and disseminate nature" (5), are seen as central by three of the six pilots. Strategies 2 ("new technology"), 4 ("harvesting"), 7 ("new seasons/year-round"), 8 ("improve marketing"), 10 ("use local produce"), and 11 ("small scale, high value") were each argued to be central in only one of the six pilots, although some mentioned these as supplementary strategies. Strategy 3 ("visitor management") was referenced only as a supplementary strategy and in only one pilot; arguably, this is a strategy more commonly used by destination management or networks. Strategy 8 is little used in the pilots studied in-depth since only one was a marketing pilot, although often it supplemented other strategies due to new market segments being targeted. All six pilots combine strategies.

Regarding *sustainability impacts,* the pilots have been presented in Table 3 in order from the weakest type ("rather weak") to the strongest ("rather strong"). The *weak* categories (illustrated by pilots 1 and 2) involve only or mainly one sustainability dimension, which in our pilots was typically economic con-

Table 3. Cross-case comparison

Case ->	Pilot 1 (M)	Pilot 2 (NB)	Pilot 3 (NC)	Pilot 4 (NC)	Pilot 5 (CB)	Pilot 6 (NC)
INNOVATION TYPE(S)	Marketing	Product, process, and organizational	Product and process	Product, process, and organizational	Product, process, and organizational	Product, process, organizational, and marketing
INNOVATION STRATEGIES	6, 8, 9	4-5, (7, 10)	5-7, 9, 11, (1, 8, 10)	1, 2, 6, 9, (5, 7, 8)	1, 6, 9, (7)	1, 5, 6, 9, (3, 8)
SUSTAINABILITY STRONGNESS	Rather weak	Basic	Weak medium	Moderate medium	Strong medium	Rather strong
Economy dimension:	3 (4)	4 (1), -	4 (3)	4 (1)	4 (2)	3 (1)
Firm level:						
Economic income	(x)	X	X	X	X	
Existential fundament	X		X		X	X
Employment and employee wellbeing		(x)	(x)	(x)	(x)	
Visibility and attractiveness of firm/products	X	X				
Customer value	(x)	X	X	X	X	X
Destination level:						
Visibility and image	(x)			X		
Content attractiveness of destination	(x)	X	X	X	X	X
Contribution to other tourism firms	X		(x)		(x)	(x)
Industry image and attractiveness			(x)			
Environmental dimension:	0	1 (2)-	1 (2) (-)	2	1	2 (1)
Careful harvesting		X				
Fossil-free transport used in product		-	X, (-)	X	X	X
Resource use and other pollution					(x)	(x)
Avoiding/reducing pressure on natural landscape and water			(x)	X	X	X
Avoiding/reducing pressure on animals		(x)	(x)	X	X	
Social dimension:	1	(2)	(3)	2	3 (1)	2
Reducing/avoiding pressure on social infrastructure					(x)	
Impacts for other sectors		(x)	(x)		X	
Cultural sustainability		(x)	(x)	X	X	X
Offers for locals	X		(x)	X	X	X
UN SDGs *(all involve 9; others are listed)*	4, 11-12, 17	8, 4, (11-12, 14)	3-4, 8, (12-13, 17)	3, 4, 11, 17	3-4, 8, 12-13, 17, (11)	3, 11, 14

X = main impact, (x) = some impact, - = negative impact; no symbol indicates there is neither positive nor negative impact siderations. *Medium* sustainability (illustrated with pilots 3–5) involves two sustainability dimensions, or one main dimension along with some (one or two) sub-impacts from one or two other dimensions. The *strong* category of sustainability impact (illustrated with pilot 6) involves attention to all three dimensions, with at least two (and usually more) sub-categories within each sustainability dimension, addressed in a more balanced way. The main similarity is that all pilots are reported to have the most impacts within sub-categories that we have situated within the economic dimension. None of the pilots were focused only on profit for shareholders, nor on only one of the other single sub-impacts within the economic or any other main dimension; such a narrow focus would have been interpreted as the weakest type of innovation ("very weak"). Pilot 1 is considered not that weak but still "rather weak," with no impact on the environmental dimension and one sub-impact on the social. Pilots 4 and 6 report the most impacts within the dimension of nature, and pilot 5 most impacts the social dimension. Only pilot 6 is reported to address two or more sub-categories as main rather than merely supplementary concerns within all three dimensions; it is therefore the most balanced pilot and the one that, we argue, demonstrates the strongest sustainability. Nevertheless, none of the pilots reported an equally balanced impact on all three main dimensions. Pilots 4 and 5 both have some impacts on all three main dimensions and can be argued, in sum, to demonstrate rather similar levels of sustainability, although they do so differently, as one is stronger in relation to the dimension of nature and the other in relation to the social dimension. This shows that different combinations of sub-impacts can be involved in pilots situated at approximately the same place on the continuum. The type of innovation seems to exert some influence on the sustainability impacts. Pilots 3, 4, and 6 are nature- and culture-based experience innovations, using both nature and culture as central resources, which opens the possibility of both positive and negative impacts on these two dimensions. However, an indoor or outdoor cultural experience not situated in nature would have had less potential impact on nature. The sub-impacts shown in the table are those found in the six pilots, while the larger study revealed additional ones, such as "productivity" and "employee education."

The UN SDGs that are most frequently addressed by the innovation pilots (discussed in at least four of the six pilots) are good health and well-being (SDG 3), quality education (SDG 4), sustainable cities and communities (SDG 11), responsible consumption and production (SDG 12), and partnerships for meeting the goals (SDG 17). Decent work and economic growth (SDG 8), climate action (SDG 13), and life under water (SDG 14) are also mentioned by three, two, and two pilots, respectively. Interestingly, the majority of the pilots have social impacts, reflected in SDGs 3, 4, and 11, and some natural impacts (SDGs 13 and 14); a few mention economic impacts (SDGs 12 and 8).

DISCUSSION AND CONCLUSION

This chapter explores and elaborates on how small organizations can carry out innovations for sustainability (IFS) and how strong their sustainability impacts are. The empirical study can be summarized into five main claims.

Firstly, *the pandemic situation stimulated innovations*. Earlier studies have demonstrated the vulnerability of many small experience-based organizations and their dependence on governmental support (Seeler et al., 2021). Already in the first months of the pandemic, rapid assessments of the industry called for rethinking economic activity with a stronger focus on holistic sustainability (Hall & Seyfi, 2020; Higgins-Desbiolles, 2020). While some publications demonstrate firms' focus on rebuilding their economic fundament in the new conditions (Arbulú et al., 2021; Breier et al., 2021), fewer publications discuss business diversification that helps firms come out of the crisis stronger and more resilient (Kraus et al., 2020; Sahebalzamani et al., 2022), and even fewer concretize how firms can close the gap between desired advances in tourism sustainability and innovation strategies adopted by firms under the pandemic. This chapter illustrates some ways that experience-based organizations can innovate for sustainability during the pandemic and thereby contributes new knowledge about crisis management.

Secondly, rather *modest funding coupled with an overall strategy of "one day more" and reporting on SDGs nudged organizations to make innovations for sustainability:* Nikolova (2020) elaborates on different ways tourism firms and others can use nudging as a way to stimulate sustainability, particularly regarding visitors. Our study confirms that nudging organizations can work and contributes new knowledge about, and examples of, how external funding and being part of a larger program in which organizations must report on their progress towards SDGs can motivate them to IFS.

Thirdly, the empirical study demonstrates that *IFS can be undertaken with different innovation strategies and impacts, even when the market situation and trends are rather similar.* This chapter focused on six of the pilots; still, it revealed 11 strategies and that a pilot often combines strategies. When these strategies are compared to strategies found in other studies, there are interesting overlaps both with adventure tourism trends (ATTA, 2018) and with the new Norwegian National Tourism Strategy (Innovasjon Norge, 2021). Similarly to our study, ATTA (2018) describes the trend of slow travel—that is, staying and experiencing a destination over a longer time—which is in line with the "one day more" strategy. Slow travel creates space for transformative experiences and mental health benefits that were developed by other pilots in the project. The projects and illustrated pilots also demonstrate ways of working towards the 2030 goals of The Norwegian National Tourism Strategy, which sees the green shift, digitalization, and overcoming the pandemic as the main prerequisites. These goals include projects such as growing value creation in tourism and ripple effects in other industries, growing guest value, and increasing the attractiveness of local communities while minimizing the climate footprint (Innovasjon Norge, 2021).

Fourthly, *different combinations of innovation strategies contributed to different sustainability impacts and sub-impacts, as well as sustainability strength:* The pilots have been categorized as representing weak and moderate sustainability. All six pilots had an impact within the economic dimension and, to varying degrees, within the environmental and social dimensions. One pilot stood out as being more balanced in its impacts and is categorized as offering stronger sustainability (Cotterell et al., 2019). None of the innovation pilots in this study represent the *very strong* end of the sustainability continuum with anti-economic growth strategies (Cotterell et al., 2019), which can be explained by the limited scale of production and scant organizational resources, a situation aggravated by the pandemic, on the one hand, and growth policy expectations and polemics of funding institutions on the other. However, some of the project participants have discussed anti-growth strategies in terms of sustaining (as opposed to increasing) customer numbers and being content with the same level of income in a long-term perspective, which can be interpreted as a version of the anti-economic strategies and thereby be in line with very strong eco-centric sustainability, where the utilization of natural resources is minimized (Cotterell et al., 2019), and economic considerations are seen as subordinate to both the social dimension and nature (Temesgen et al., 2019). Comparing the sustainability impacts revealed in the pilot descriptions and Table 3 with the skeptical, pragmatic, and idealist IFS paradigms (Ritala, 2019), one can argue that the six innovation pilots are mainly situated within the skeptical and pragmatic paradigms; only pilot 6 overlaps with the idealistic paradigm.

Fifthly, most of the 11 individual *IFS strategies focus on both reducing or avoiding negative impacts and creating positive impacts*. The fact that strategies tend to be combined increases the relevance of this claim. This is an interesting observation, relevant to the discussion on reactive (weaker) versus proactive (stronger) approaches to sustainability (Dyllick & Muff, 2016), as well as the debates about regenerative approaches (Pollock, 2019) and the role of ontology (including value systems) (Temesgen et al., 2019). It confirms that the tourism and experience sectors are diverse in their value priorities and not focused only on economic considerations (Lindberg et al., 2019). This might be partly due to the nature of experience-based innovations, being fuzzier than in manufacturing (Hjalager, 2010) and often very dependent on local resources. Another reason could be that the theorizing in the literature is oversimplified, being less in line with the practical complexity and nuances of particular cases. Addressing the scant empirical research on practicing stronger sustainability and confronting the prevailing neo-liberal mindset of international policymakers and global competition (Dwyer, 2018), this study has illustrated variety across firms' sustainability initiatives from weak to strong. While Norway ranks rather high in its implementation of the UN SDGs (Ministries, 2016), the work toward these goals is rather demanding. The state must prioritize and follow up on international ambitions and the SDGs, and so must the counties and municipalities, including when it comes to tourism. Lundberg et al. (2020) have demonstrated how demanding it can be for the regional and local levels to prioritize and implement SDGs while at the same time needing to follow national policies. The six innovation pilots demonstrate the potential of sustainability impacts going beyond the project objectives due to the fuzziness and social significance of experience-based innovation, which can contribute to local communities in non-economic terms. Beyond pursuing preservationist environmental strategies, experience-based innovation can contribute to a more active population and healthier lifestyles (SDG 3), learning, pride, and other sociocultural impacts (SDG 4), revitalizing local communities (SDG 11). Thus, the innovation pilots demonstrate both moderate and stronger sustainability beyond the weaker economic (SDG 8 and 12) and environmental sustainability (SDG 13, 14) foci of the projects.

Practical Implications and Policy Implications

Given that tourism prior to Covid-19 had been a fast-growing (and often referred to as a "hypercompetitive") industry (Alcalde-Giraudo et al., 2021; Lindskov, 2021), small and micro experience-based tourism firms were forced to respond to continuously growing tourist expectations and changing technology while finding other ways to increase customer value, as part of *hyper-competitiveness*. On top of these demands comes the demand for sustainability, not only as part of increasing formal industry regulations but also to create a competitive advantage with the increasing number of sustainability-aware customers and cooperators. This cocktail of pressures leaves small experience-based firms most vulnerable in the dual need for organizational stability and flexibility in their strategic responses to change (Volberda, 1996). It makes them dependent on destination structures, marketing and management organizations, and additional external resources. The response of the tourism sector to Covid-19 has also demonstrated that only a small percent of tourism stakeholders were able to promptly adjust their operations to the new circumstances (Seeler et al., 2021). Further, Covid-19 has revealed tourism's overreliance on international markets to be unsustainable, while some of the "one day more" participants focusing on national and Nordic markets had a better tourism season than before Covid-19 as restrictions began to ease. Madhok (2021) claims that the damage wrought by the pandemic demonstrates the negative effects of hyper-globalizing and shareholder power and calls for approaches more focused on local stakeholders.

The pandemic, and the "one day more" program, have boosted the development of ideas for innovation, some new and some that smaller organizations had begun to develop prior to the launch of the program. Innovation was undertaken with a more substantial sustainability agenda and ingrained in the firms' practices and long-term destination development rather than focusing on increasing marketing to push sales.

The IFS strategies of developing attractive new products and cultivating domestic guests and other visitor segments with less distance to travel can be argued to be important to consider even after the pandemic when striving for stronger sustainability. Furthermore, since products and practices should be sustainable in more than economic terms, it becomes important to use more specific segmentation strategies that help in finding customers with values matching the products and sustainability practices on offer. The suggested innovation strategies and related sustainability impacts contribute by providing examples and concrete "tools" for how to work with some of the sustainability challenges as part of the recovery and the reduction of negative impacts (Ritchie & Jiang, 2019), but also for more proactive exploring and exploiting of the potential to create positive impacts as aimed for in stronger sustainability and regenerative approaches. Given that coping with IFS and documenting sustainability increasingly becomes a must—part of hyper-competitiveness and a prerequisite to access to financing on the international level—relevant strategies and tools become vital. Within these six pilots, innovation was attempted mainly through new types of offerings and, to some extent, through marketing. However, there are also indications of business model innovations and more radical transformations, which need further study. Some informants suggest that the pilots (e.g., harvesting) might be more relevant for international market segments, or just as relevant, an assumption that needs to be studied further. Finally, there is a need for relevant and practical tools and taxonomies for testing, documenting, and reporting the nuances of the sustainability impacts potentially involved for experience-based sectors, including smaller organizations.

REFERENCES

Albareda, L., & Hajikhani, A. (2019). Innovation for Sustainability: Literature Review and Bibliometric Analysis. In N. Bocken, P. Ritala, L. Albareda, & R. Verburg (Eds.), *Innovation for Sustainability: Business Transformations Towards a Better World* (pp. 35–58). Palgrave Macmillan. doi:10.1007/978-3-319-97385-2_3

Alcalde-Giraudo, A., Fernández-Hernández, R., Paradinas-Márquez, C., Sánchez-González, P., & García-Muiña, F. E. (2021). Marketing approach to Nordic tourism. *Technological Forecasting and Social Change*, *163*, 120441. doi:10.1016/j.techfore.2020.120441

Alvesson, M., & Sköldberg, K. (2009). *Reflexive methodology: New vistas for qualitative research* (2nd ed.). Sage.

Arbulú, I., Razumova, M., Rey-Maquieira, J., & Sastre, F. (2021). Can domestic tourism relieve the COVID-19 tourist industry crisis? The case of Spain. *Journal of Destination Marketing & Management*, *20*, 100568. doi:10.1016/j.jdmm.2021.100568

ATTA. (2018). *2018 Trends Report: Continued Growth, Innovative Marketing Technology*. Retrieved on May 9, 2020, from: https://www.adventuretravelnews.com/2018-trends-report-continued-growth-innovative-marketing-technology

Barbier, E. B., Burgess, J., & Folke, C. (1994). *Paradise Lost? The Ecological Economics of Biodiversity*. Earthscan Publication Limited.

Barbier, E. B., Burgess, J., & Folke, C. (2019). *Paradise Lost? The ecological economics of biodiversity* (Vol. 2). Routledge. doi:10.4324/9780429342219

Bocken, N., Ritala, P., Albareda, L., & Verburg, R. (2019). Introduction: Innovaion for Sustainability. In N. Bocken, P. Ritala, L. Albareda, & R. Verburg (Eds.), *Innovation for Sustainability: Business Transformations Towards a Better World* (pp. 1–20). Palgrave Macmillan. doi:10.1007/978-3-319-97385-2_1

Boons, F., & Lüdeke-Freund, F. (2013). Business models for sustainable innovation: State-of-the-art and steps towards a research agenda. *Journal of Cleaner Production*, *45*, 9–19. doi:10.1016/j.jclepro.2012.07.007

Breier, M., Kallmuenzer, A., Clauss, T., Gast, J., Kraus, S., & Tiberius, V. (2021). The role of business model innovation in the hospitality industry during the COVID-19 crisis. *International Journal of Hospitality Management*, *92*, 102723. doi:10.1016/j.ijhm.2020.102723

Brundtland, G. (1987). *Report of the World Commission on Environment and Development: Our Common Future*. Academic Press.

Chatti, W. (2021). Moving towards environmental sustainability: Information and communication technology (ICT), freight transport, and CO2 emissions. *Heliyon*, *7*(10), e08190. doi:10.1016/j.heliyon.2021.e08190 PMID:34729432

Cotterell, D., Hales, R., Arcodia, C., & Ferreira, J.-A. (2019). Overcommitted to tourism and under committed to sustainability: The urgency of teaching "strong sustainability" in tourism courses. *Journal of Sustainable Tourism*, *27*(7), 882–902. doi:10.1080/09669582.2018.1545777

Dietz, S., & Neumayer, E. (2007). Weak and strong sustainability in the SEEA: Concepts and measurement. *Ecological Economics*, *61*(4), 617–626. doi:10.1016/j.ecolecon.2006.09.007

Dwyer, L. (2018). Saluting while the ship sinks: The necessity for tourism paradigm change. *Journal of Sustainable Tourism*, *26*(1), 29–48. doi:10.1080/09669582.2017.1308372

Dyllick, T., & Muff, K. (2016). Clarifying the meaning of sustainable business: Introducing a typology from business-as-usual to true business sustainability. *Organization & Environment*, *29*(2), 156–174. doi:10.1177/1086026615575176

Eide, D., & Hoarau-Heemstra, H. (2022). Innovation for sustainable destinations: The role of certification and partnership. In I. Booyens & O. Brouder (Eds.), *Handbook of Innovation for Sustainable Tourism* (pp. 112–139). Edward Elgar Publishing.

Elkington, J. (1994). Towards the Sustainable Corporation: Win-Win-Win Business Strategies for Sustainable Development. *California Management Review*, *36*(2), 90–100. doi:10.2307/41165746

Elkington, J. (1998). *Cannibals with Forks: The Triple Bottom Line of 21st Century Business*. New Society Publishers.

Epler Wood, M., Milstein, M., & Ahamed-Broadhurst, K. (2019). *Destinations at Risk: The Invisible Burden of Tourism*. Retrieved on September 22, 2020, from: www.thetravelfoundation.org.uk

European Commission. (n.d.). *Corporate Sustainability Reporting*. Retrieved on June 2, 2020, from: https://ec.europa.eu/info/business-economy-euro/company-reporting-and-auditing/company-reporting/corporate-sustainability-reporting_en

Evans, S., Vladimirova, D., Holgado, M., Van Fossen, K., Yang, M., Silva, E. A., & Barlow, C. Y. (2017). Business model innovation for sustainability: Towards a unified perspective for creation of sustainable business models. *Business Strategy and the Environment*, 26(5), 597–608. doi:10.1002/bse.1939

Hall, C. M. (2018). Resilience theory and tourism. In J. Saarinen & A. M. Gill (Eds.), *Resilient Destinations and Tourism* (pp. 34–47). Routledge. doi:10.4324/9781315162157-3

Hall, C. M., & Seyfi, S. (2020). COVID-19 pandemic, tourism and degrowth. In C. M. Hall, L. Lundmark, & J. J. Zhang (Eds.), *Degrowth and Tourism* (pp. 220–238). Routledge. doi:10.4324/9780429320590-17

Heslinga, J., Groote, P., & Vanclay, F. (2019). Strengthening governance processes to improve benefit-sharing from tourism in protected areas by using stakeholder analysis. *Journal of Sustainable Tourism*, 27(6), 773–787.

Higgins-Desbiolles, F. (2020). Socialising tourism for social and ecological justice after COVID-19. *Tourism Geographies*, 22(3), 610–623. doi:10.1080/14616688.2020.1757748

Hoarau-Heemstra, H., & Eide, D. (2016). Values and concern: Drivers of innovation in experience-based tourism. *Tourism and Hospitality Research*, 19(1), 15–26. doi:10.1177/1467358416683768

Høegh-Guldberg, O., Maziliauske, E., Eide, D., & Ryan, A. W. (2022). Innovation for Sustainability in World Heritage Destinations: Opportunities and Challenges of the Idealistic Paradigm. In C. Ribeiro de Almeida, J. C. Martins, A. R. Gonçalves, S. Quinteiro, & M. L. Gasparini (Eds.), *Handbook of Research on Cultural Tourism and Sustainability* (pp. 56–83). IGI Global. doi:10.4018/978-1-7998-9217-5.ch004

Høegh-Guldberg, O., Seeler, S., & Eide, D. (2021). Sustainable Visitor Management to Mitigate Overtourism – What, Who, and How. In A. Sharma & H. Azizul (Eds.), *Over-tourism as Destination Risk: Impacts and Solutions* (pp. 167–186). Emerald Publishing Limited. doi:10.1108/978-1-83909-706-520211012

InnovasjonNorge. (2021). *Nasjonal reiselivsstrategi 2030 – Sterke inntrykk med små avtrykk*. Retrieved on July 4, 2021, from: https://www.regjeringen.no/no/tema/naringsliv/reiseliv/nasjonal-reiselivsstrategi-2030-sterke-inntrykk-med-sma-avtrykk/id2893884/

Jørgensen, M. T., Hansen, A. V., Sørensen, F., Fuglsang, L., Sundbo, J., & Jensen, J. F. (2021). Collective tourism social entrepreneurship: A means for community mobilization and social transformation. *Annals of Tourism Research*, 88, 103171. doi:10.1016/j.annals.2021.103171

Kraus, S., Clauss, T., Breier, M., Gast, J., Zardini, A., & Tiberius, V. (2020). The economics of COVID-19: initial empirical evidence on how family firms in five European countries cope with the corona crisis. *International Journal of Entrepreneurial Behavior & Research*.

Kvale, S., & Brinkman, S. (2009). Interview quality. *Interviews: Learning the craft of qualitative research interviewing*, 161-175.

Lindberg, F., Fitchett, J., & Martin, D. (2019). Investigating sustainable tourism heterogeneity: Competing orders of worth among stakeholders of a Nordic destination. *Journal of Sustainable Tourism, 27*(8), 1277–1294. doi:10.1080/09669582.2019.1614188

Lindskov, A. (2021). Hypercompetition: a review and agenda for future research. *Competitiveness Review: An International Business Journal.* doi:10.1108/CR-06-2021-0097

Lundberg, A. K., Granås Bardal, K., Vangelsten, B. V., Brynildsen, M., Bjørkan, R., Bjørkan, M., & Richardson, T. K. (2020). *Strekk i laget. En kartlegging av hvordan FNs bærekraftsmål implementeres i regional og kommunal planlegging.* Academic Press.

Madhok, A. (2021). Globalization, de-globalization, and re-globalization: Some historical context and the impact of the COVID pandemic. *Business Research Quarterly, 24*(3), 199–203. doi:10.1177/23409444211008904

Miles, M. B., & Huberman, A. M. (1984). *Qualitative data analysis.* SAGE Publications.

Ministries. (2016). *Norway's follow-up of Agenda 2030 and the Sustainable Development Goals.* Ministry of Foreign Affairs. Retrieved on February 14, 2020, from: https://www.regjeringen.no/en/dokumenter/follow-up-sdg2/id2507259/

Neumayer, E. (2013). *Weak versus Strong Sustainability: Exploring the Limits of Two Opposing Paradigms* (4th ed.). Edward Elgar Publishing. doi:10.4337/9781781007082

NHO Reiseliv/The Norwegian Hospitality Association. (2020). *Koronavirus.* https://www.nhoreiseliv.no/vi-mener/koronavirus/

Nikolova, M. S. (2020). *Behavioral Economics for Tourism: Perspectives on Business and Policy in the Travel Industry.* Academic Press.

Nilsen, H. R. (2010). The joint discourse 'reflexive sustainable development'—From weak towards strong sustainable development. *Ecological Economics, 69*(3), 495–501. doi:10.1016/j.ecolecon.2009.11.011

Nordregio. (n.d.). *Welcome to Agenda 2030 at the local level.* https://nordregioprojects.org/agenda2030local/

OECD. (2005). Oslo manual: guidelines for collecting and interpreting innovation data (3rd ed.). Paris: OECD.

Oftedal, E. M., Bertella, G., Lanka, S., Grzegorczyk, M., & Molthan-Hill, P. (2021). Perspectives of Sustainability. *Revista de Administração Contemporânea, 25*(3), 1–8.

Ott, K. (2003). The case for strong sustainability. *Greifswald's environmental ethics,* 59-64.

Pollock, A. (2019). *Regenerative Tourism: The Natural Maturation of Sustainability.* Retrieved on August 22, 2020, from: https://medium.com/activate-the-future/regenerative-tourism-the-natural-maturation-of-sustainability-26e6507d0fcb

Ritala, P. (2019). Innovation for Sustainability: Sceptical, Pragmatic, and Idealist Perspectives on the Role of Business as a Driver for Change. In N. Bocken, P. Ritala, L. Albareda, & R. Verburg (Eds.), *Innovation for Sustainability: Business Transformations Towards a Better World* (pp. 21–34). Palgrave Macmillan. doi:10.1007/978-3-319-97385-2_2

Ritchie, B. W., & Jiang, Y. (2019). A review of research on tourism risk, crisis and disaster management: Launching the annals of tourism research curated collection on tourism risk, crisis and disaster management. *Annals of Tourism Research*, *79*, 102812. doi:10.1016/j.annals.2019.102812

Saarinen, J. (2006). Traditions of sustainability in tourism studies. *Annals of Tourism Research*, *33*(4), 1121–1140. doi:10.1016/j.annals.2006.06.007

Saarinen, J. (2014). Critical Sustainability: Setting the Limits to Growth and Responsibility in Tourism. *Sustainability*, *6*(1), 1–17. doi:10.3390u6010001

Saarinen, J. (2019). Communities and sustainable tourism development: Community impacts and local benefit creation in tourism. In S. McCool & K. Bosak (Eds.), *A research agenda for sustainable tourism* (pp. 206–222). Edward Elgar Publishing. doi:10.4337/9781788117104.00020

Sahebalzamani, S., Jørgensen, E. J. B., Bertella, G., & Nilsen, E. R. (2022). A Dynamic Capabilities Approach to Business Model Innovation in Times of Crisis. *Tourism Planning & Development*, 1–24. doi:10.1080/21568316.2022.2107560

Seeler, S., Høegh-Guldberg, O., & Eide, D. (2021). Impacts on and Responses of Tourism SMEs and MEs on the COVID-19 Pandemic–The Case of Norway. In S. K. Kulshreshtha (Ed.), *Virus Outbreaks and Tourism Mobility* (pp. 177–193). Emerald Publishing Limited. doi:10.1108/978-1-80071-334-520211016

Spenceley, A., & Rylance, A. (2019). The contribution of tourism to achieving the United Nations Sustainable Development Goals. In S. F. McCool & K. Bosak (Eds.), *A research agenda for sustainable tourism* (pp. 107–125). Edward Elgar Publishing. doi:10.4337/9781788117104.00015

Temesgen, A., Storsletten, V., & Jakobsen, O. (2019). Circular Economy – Reducing Symptoms or Radical Change? *Philosophy of Management*. Advance online publication. doi:10.100740926-019-00112-1

Torkington, K., Stanford, D., & Guiver, J. (2020). Discourse (s) of growth and sustainability in national tourism policy documents. *Journal of Sustainable Tourism*, *28*(7), 1041–1062. doi:10.1080/09669582.2020.1720695

Tura, N., Mortimer, G., & Kutvonen, A. (2019). Exploring the Pitfalls of Systemic Innovations for Sustainability. In N. Bocken, P. Ritala, L. Albareda, & R. Verburg (Eds.), *Innovation for Sustainability: Business Transformations Towards a Better World* (pp. 157–175). Palgrave Macmillan. doi:10.1007/978-3-319-97385-2_9

Turner, R. K., Turner, R. K., Pearce, D. W., & Bateman, I. (1993). *Environmental economics: an elementary introduction*. Johns Hopkins University Press.

UNWTO. (2019). *International Tourism Highlights, 2019 Edition*. UNWTO.

Volberda, H. W. (1996). Toward the flexible form: How to remain vital in hypercompetitive environments. *Organization Science*, *7*(4), 359–374. doi:10.1287/orsc.7.4.359

Chapter 2
Australian Wine, Tourism, and Culture:
Using Digital Methods via Social Media to Promote Wine Tourism to Chinese Tourists

Poshan Yu
https://orcid.org/0000-0003-1069-3675
Soochow University, China & Australian Studies Centre, Shanghai University, China

Heyun Wang
Independent Researcher, China

Ramya Mahendran
https://orcid.org/0000-0001-9585-9077
Independent Researcher, India

ABSTRACT

In this chapter, the authors explore social media as a tool for promoting products and services. The industry of application is wine tourism in which the authors investigate whether and how digital methods can help local businesses in Australia in the wine tourism sector gain a better perspective among Chinese tourists. They analyze the characteristics of different wine tourism regions in Australia and assess how these regions are competing against each other and shaping their social media strategies to promote the hospitality and tourism of said region to Chinese tourists. The main goal is to explore how social media is influencing the travel decisions, choice of destination, and wine consumption of Chinese tourists and empowering the tourists on the Australia's wine heritage is going to convey meaning, culture, and traditions to aid them in these decisions. Recommendations will be provided on using digital social media to promote wine tourism to different stakeholders.

DOI: 10.4018/978-1-6684-4645-4.ch002

INTRODUCTION

With the rapid phase of development across the globe, the business environment has become hyper competitive across industries. Over the last decade, maintaining and improving the world's ecological environment has become an important issue (Perkumienė et al., 2020). Sustainable development has become more than a trend, it is one of the key focus areas across industries. With clear sustainable development goals enterprises can survive the ever-growing global competition. Though sustainable development has been a highly discussed and practiced topic, sustainable tourism is a new arena. Today there are many trending topics in tourism like ecotourism, agrotourism, culture tourism, volunteer tourism, food tourism and so on. Irrespective of the type of tourism that is being explored the sustainability aspect of it is becoming a hot topic for both researchers and tourists.

Post the COVID-19 pandemic, travel has become more of a luxury, imposing global travel restrictions. The tourism industry is trying to reshape and redefine itself to recover from the crisis. The internet and social media-based channels have been playing a significant role in the development of tourism industry and has helped to establish and grow the e-tourism space. The promotion and development of online tourism have become the choice of tourism lovers (Vázquez et al., 2021). Social media has become the digital carrier of sustainable tourism. The main idea is to explore how social media is influencing the travel decisions, choice of destination and wine consumption of Chinese tourists and how the Australia's wine heritage empowered is going to convey meaning, culture, and traditions to aide them in these decisions. It will use social media as digital methods to analyze the situation and publicity methods of Australian wine tourism and culture. While conducting a study for online publicity, we will also discuss the current situation and future situation of offline publicity.

In this chapter, we will investigate the different wine regions of Australia and explore the distinctive tourism experience and travel itineraries according to the environmental characteristics of each city. We will also see how each of these regions promote themselves to Chinese tourists. Among them, the wine culture of each region is the focus of discussion, and the wine characteristics of different regions are also different (Lacorde, 2019). While promoting wine culture, the characteristics of different wines and representative wineries in various regions are worth understanding.

This chapter analyzes the tourism and cultural characteristics of Australian States and discusses how to formulate strategies to attract tourists and give full play to their respective advantages. It focuses on tourism, wine, culture, and information regarding entertainment in each region using digital tools to collect and summarize the literature about social media, cultural heritage, wine tourism, and entertainment. It describes the different forms of offline publicity that is leveraged and showcases the main contents on promoting offline and the needs that cannot be met by online (digital) methods.

After summarizing the key information of the literature, this chapter discusses the relationship between the aforementioned and the publicity effect after mutual influence of said methodologies. It also explores, how to display relevant content on social media to attract Chinese tourists by using different formats. Using the CiteSpace tool to cross analyze the literature data on Australian wine tourism and social media content and display similar data of the overall content through data visualization. After developing the relevant content, we issue an online questionnaire for a survey which targeted Chinese tourists to understand the current situation and future development of Australian wine tourism culture, and Chinese social media content are counted and analyzed (Gu & Huang, 2018). We explore how to use these publicity methods to effectively show Australian wine tourism and culture to Chinese tourists.

Finally, the chapter analyzes the promotion effect and current situation, and suggests how to improve opinions of social media in Australian wine tourism and culture.

THE CHARACTERISTICS OF WINE TOURISM & HOSPITALITY REGIONS ACROSS AUSTRALIA

Australia is a tourist-friendly country from a global tourism and hospitality perspective. As a developed country in the southern hemisphere, Australia is mainly known for its wine industry, tourism, and hotel industry. These industries have been the lifeblood of their economy. The entertainment, dining, and hotel industry are integral elements of the country for tourists and locals alike (Son et al., 2021).

Figure 1. The map of Australia. Source: Touropia, 2021

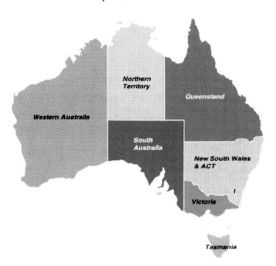

The entertainment industry includes regional tourism development, and each state has its unique tourism model and culture. New South Wales is famous for its featured performance-based events and event venues, Kangaroo Island in South Australia, and more. As tourism is very well-developed in Australia, the closely related hotel industry is also performing well. In Australia, tourists can choose different types of accommodation like hostels, private rooms, budget hotels, chain hotels, and even camping (Dhirasasna et al., 2020). Additionally, Australia has been trying to integrate the hotel industry with other entertainment industries to create integrated hotels, where tourists can enjoy dining and entertainment activities. The catering industry is one of the most important industries in Australia and is famous for barbecue (Kortt et al., 2018).

In addition, statistics demonstrate the national consumption expenditure of Australia, expenditure pertaining food types and food places constitute more than that of other industries. The catering industry includes wine, and Australia produces more than one billion liters of wine a year, which accounts for four percent of the world's total, two-thirds of which are exported (Strickland et al., 2016). Australians drink 23 liters of wine per person per year, twice as much as France, another famous wine destination.

One of the biggest factors in wine production is the climate. Australian continent spans three climatic zones - arid, tropical, and temperate - which are fairly favorable for viticulture. The north is tropical and the south temperate. Due to the difference in temperature between day and night, different regions in Australia have different flavors of wine (Ristic et al., 2019). In addition, Australian wines are more inclusive than other countries, and age has little influence on wines.

This chapter mainly examines the characteristics and current situation of wine tourism and hotel entertainment in Western Australia, South Australia, Queensland, Victoria, New South Wales, Northern Territory, and Tasmania (Figure 1).

Western Australia (WA)

Western Australia borders the Indian Ocean, and its area is equal to that of all western Europe. This state is the largest in the country and accounts for one-third of the total area of Australia. Western Australia has many deserts and salt lakes, a large area, a small population, rich mineral resources, natural scenery, and a unique ecological environment. Many areas remain pristine, making them western Australia's most desired tourist attractions. The main geographical characteristics of Western Australia are drought, vast territory, primitive soil, and other factors (DeLorenzo & Techera, 2018). A popular tourist destination, Western Australia offers beaches, cliffs, and mountains, quite unlike the big cities. One of the world's most famous heritage sites, Ningaloo Reef, faces the world's largest coral reef and is a must-see in Western Australia. Located on the coast of the Ningaloo coral Reef, the Sarsalis Hotel is a paradise for diving enthusiasts (Jones, 2021). It is possible to swim with whale sharks, turtles, and humpback whales, or to find ancient mountains in national parks. In the evening, one can enjoy the view and food on the beach.

In terms of wine in Western Australia, the Margaret River is known for its mild maritime climate and its cabernet sauvignon and Bordeaux wines (Firth et al., 2017). However, due to issues with the soil the wines produced in this region are not special; therefore, it is difficult to stand out among the many Australian wine categories (Bruwer & Rueger-Muck, 2018). The wines from this region are characterized by aromas and a long finish.

South Australia (SA)

South Australia is Australia's fourth-largest state with Adelaide as its capital. The northwestern part of the Western Australian plateau is a desert and semi-desert region which is sparsely populated. The Southeast region's fertile soil is an important grape production area, and wine resources are very rich. South Australia is as important to Australia as California is to the United States as a famous wine-producing region. Australia's annual wine export sales account for 40% of the total wine sales, which is enough to prove that wine export is very important for Australia. Of all the Australian states and territories, South Australia's economy is the most export-dependent. Among them, wine export is extensive, thus driving the economic development of South Australia.

South Australia's average wine exports account for 60% of Australia's total wine exports. However, due to the current impact of the COVID-19 pandemic, industry revenue is expected to decline by another 1.2% in 2022 compared to 2021. As of December 2021, the export volume of Australian wine fell by 30% to US$2.03 billion, and the export volume fell by 17% to 619 million liters (69 million 9 liters equivalent). This resulted in a 15% decline in the average to just US$3.27 per liter (Mileham, 2022).

South Australia also has many interesting places to visit, including the village of Hahndorf near Adelaide. The Flinders Ranges, located in South Australia, has some of the most spectacular and beautiful scenery in the country. The sheer cliffs and ancient mountains combine the spirit of adventure and is a must visit place for adventure tourists. One of these, the Akaba Reserve, offers exclusive mountain views and the perfect experience of the wild bush of the Australian outback. Australia is famous for its ecological environment, and its wildlife is one of the rarest in the world. One can experience a great stay at a restored 1850s estate where kangaroos and koalas can be spotted in the woods nearby and it is possible to enjoy some of South Australia's finest wines.

South Australia's rich wine resources are an essential experience for tourists, accounting for 50% of Australia's total wine production (Overton et al., 2019). The famous wine variety Syrah arrived in the 19th century and has developed into South Australia's most iconic grape variety, and the old Syrah vine is still producing grapes despite its age. South Australian wine is characterized by its stable quality, natural sweetness, fruity flavor, and rich and full taste (Ristic et al., 2019). At the same time, the natural conditions and climate here are very suitable for viticulture. The terrain is a host to mountains, rivers, and river valleys, which makes it an ideal place for a rich variety of wine. It is also worth noting that South Australian wine is cheap.

Before the COVID-19 pandemic, South Australian wine was a necessary companion gift. Although South Australia accounts for half of Australia's total wine production, it has another wine region that is different from the rest. The famous Barossa Valley produces only 9.1% of Australia's total wine production, as it is the quintessential fine wine region and the pride of Australia (Lacorde, 2019). Another popular wine-making trend in South Australia is the fermentation of Syrah with the Viognier white grape variety, which is used to add flavor and stabilize the color. While this method is used throughout Australia, it is most common and prominent in the Barossa Valley.

Queensland (QLD)

Queensland, located in the northeast of Australia, is Australia's second-largest state. Its name is in honor of Queen Victoria of England. About 54% of Queensland lies north of the Tropic of Capricorn. Most areas have low rainfall and a warm and sunny climate, so Queensland is also known as the Sunshine State (Richardson et al., 2015). Queensland has many famous attractions such as the Great Barrier Reef, the largest collection of coral reefs in the world, and many national parks. Brisbane, the capital of Queensland, is one of Australia's best cities to visit.

Tourism in Queensland is famous for its sun and sand beaches. Surfing is a must for all ocean lovers (Flew & Kirkwood, 2020). Therefore, for Queensland, the tourism industry is an essential economic lifeline. Tourism in Queensland has been extremely depressed in recent years due to the COVID-19 pandemic (Dhirasasna et al., 2020). In Queensland, the Great Barrier Reef can be called one of the most famous tourist attractions in the world. Diving, sea fishing, and swimming can be enjoyed here, not to mention the scenic beauty and food. One of the attractions, famous for its rock shape, looks like a heart when viewed from the sky (Genç, 2018). Hence its name, the Heart-shaped Reef, it is one of the must-see attractions for honeymooners and couples visiting Queensland. One can take a seaplane arranged through the hotel to see the combination of Queensland's mountains and sea and enjoy some visitors from the sea.

For wine tourism, Queensland is a large wine region in its own right alongside two other regions: the Granite Belt and South Burnett. Queensland spans 20 latitudes and has a diverse climate. However, most areas are too dry or wet to grow grapes. Only the east coast has a mild climate that is more suitable for growing grapes, so Queensland's vineyards are concentrated in this area (Bamberry & Wickramasekara, 2012). Queensland's wines are arguably the least well-known in Australia, but its wine industry is growing rapidly. The growth can be attributed to its tourism.

In addition to the development of the wine industry driven by tourism, Australia's export wine production increased year by year before the COVID-19 epidemic, which is also an important reason for the rapid development of the Queensland wine industry (Flew & Kirkwood, 2020). Queensland wine is mostly made of locally grown fruits, which also represents to help the development of local planting industry.

Victoria (VIC)

While Victoria is Australia's smallest mainland state, it holds an important economic status within the country. There are mountains, forests, caves, and lakes in the east and hills and grasslands in the west. Melbourne, the capital of Victoria, is a commercial center of culture, arts, and industry (Abram et al., 2021). It is responsible for major economic development and dissemination of Victoria's cultural heritage. Melbourne is also a must see for Chinese tourists to experience Australia's prosperity and unique heritage (Boroujeni et al., 2021). Victoria is also known as Australia's proudest state, although Victorian wine is not very famous. The state possesses a typical continental climate with hot summers and large temperature differences between day and night. Victoria, a relatively famous wine region located in the Yarra Valley north of Melbourne, is the first wine region in Victoria with a wine production history of about 170 years. Due to climate reasons, the Yarra Valley has become recognized as one of the coolest areas in Australia, mainly producing sparkling wine, Chardonnay, Pinot Noir, and other wine varieties.

New South Wales (NSW)

New South Wales is Australia's most populous state. Founded in 1788, it was the first British colony in Australia and included the entire continent except for the west coast. Later, New South Wales was divided into the states of modern Australia (Wen & Huang, 2021). The capital of New South Wales is Sydney and, together with the ciy of Melbourne, account for almost half of Australia's population. Sydney is a famous metropolis with a world-class museum and opera house, and is the country's major financial center with the largest foreign population (Menacer & Becherair, 2019). Although it is not the most famous brand of wine, the wine-growing industry in New South Wales is very important in the history of Australian wine. Wine tasting is one of the most popular tourist activities in the state. The most famous wine region in New South Wales is the Hunter Valley (Maghradze et al., 2019). Although the climate is hot, there is plenty of rain, thus resulting in a wine with a long fruity and earthy finish. The Hunter Valley region is one of the most important wine regions in the world, and the region has both large and small family wineries with long histories.

Northern Territory (NT)

The Northern Territory is one of Australia's two inland territories and is known for its natural and cultural attractions including Kings Canyon located in Wanaka National Park. The canyon is more than 1,000 meters long with a drop of 270 meters. It is one of the deepest, steepest, and most spectacular canyons in Australia. The rock color of the canyon is primarily red and yellow, bright, and distinctive. Kings

Canyon is also a favorite summer resort for Aboriginal Australians and a top choice for hikers (Carson & Carson, 2019). As for the Northern Territory, Minister McCarthy has said: "Tourism is a very important industry for the Northern Territory Government, contributing about A$1.7 billion a year to the local economy." This comment demonstrates that tourism is a top priority for the Northern Territory and its economy is dependent on the industry (Genç, 2018).

According to the development data of Australian wine, China has become the leading importer of Australian wine in 2018, with an export amount of about US$1.04 billion. The overall export value of wine in Australia is about US$2.65 billion. Both the price and sales volume have increased to varying degrees (Young, 2021). Minister McCarthy mentioned on many occasions the importance of China to Australian wine and tourism industry and hoped that Chinese tourists would know more about Australia's unique Northern Territory.

Among them, as an important factor of tourism, the climate of the Northern Territory is hot and dry, and the situation in different regions is very extreme, which is not suitable for grape planting (Taylor et al., 2021). Although the climate type is not suitable for growing grapes, there are vineyards, but the wine industry is not active (Maghradze et al., 2019). In the south-central part of the Northern Territory, right in the heart of mainland Australia, is the famous town of Alice Springs. Vineyards in the north tend to be located here because of a slight rise in elevation and a correspondingly cool climate. Careful vineyard management and irrigation make the hot, dry climate around Alice Springs home for suitable vines.

Tasmania (TAS)

Tasmania is Australia's only island state and is the country's smallest. Further south is the South Pole; therefore, it is called "the end of the world". Hobart, Tasmania's capital, is backed by Mount Wellington, its ancient streets are peaceful, and its Derwent River has a Mediterranean feel. Tasmania has also been called the "Nature State", the "Holiday State", and the "Australian version of New Zealand". Tasmania is characterized by beautiful scenery and simple people. Resources are abundant and diverse. Tasmania has a mild and pleasant climate all year round, with snowy winters and pleasant summers (Abram et al., 2021). The mild maritime climate and cool South Sea winds make Tasmanian wines attractive.

Tasmania is one of the coolest wine regions in the world. Due to its proximity to the South Pole, it is Australia's most exciting wine region. Tasmania's harvest season runs mainly from April to June and Tasmania is highly regarded for its top sparkling wines, extraordinary Pinot Noir, and Chardonnay (Gatti et al., 2018). These wines demonstrate exquisite elegance and exceptional quality. Subtle natural acidity is characteristic of Tasmanian wines.

Most Tasmanian vineyards are located on the lower slopes and in the surrounding valleys. Most vineyards are concentrated around Launceston on the north of the island, Hobart on the south, and Bicheno on the east coast (Walker et al., 2021). Tasmania is an often-overlooked wine region in the world, perhaps because of its geographical location. Tasmania itself is a regional wine region, but there is not a single production region on the island that can be recognized. Later, Tasmania became more famous for its diverse terroir conditions, which led to an increase in wine development.

This section mainly covers the major tourism and entertainment activities in each Australian state, as well as the wine specialties of each region. Due to terrain, climate, and other factors, each state has different tourism priorities, especially wine tourism. There are many wine regions in Australia, while not very different are very important. It is these nuances that keep the Australian wine industry diverse (Raftery, 2017). Australia has put a lot of effort into investment and marketing to maintain this distinction. Both Australian tourism and wine tourism contribute greatly to Australia's economy and culture. Despite the downturn in Australia's entertainment and wine tourism industry during the COVID-19 pandemic (Boroujeni et al., 2021). The irreplaceable nature of Australian tourism and the heritage of Australian wine, there is still something to look forward to post-COVID-19.

LITERATURE REVIEW ON DIGITIZATION, CULTURAL HERITAGE, WINE TOURISM & HOSPITALITY

This section discusses the literature and academic discussion reports related to cultural heritage, wine tourism, and hotels, and provides data analysis according to their contents. Through the collection, analysis, and summary, the section describes their respective meanings and specific forms of existence. Then, it discusses the impact on Australian tourism and how it is related to Australian tourism. Finally, through data analysis results and literature content, the relationship between the three is determined, and the current situation of developing wine tourism utilizing digital stories is analyzed.

In recent years, digitization has been a hot topic in various industries. With the development of science and technology around the world, digitization has gradually changed from single-sided text to vivid 3D presentation effect, and from some simple numbers and symbols to tools to help people improve their quality of life (Sujová et al., 2019). Social media is a development in the new media era under the current social situation, which leverages different formats and combines numbers, human stories, emotions, and visuals in a meaningful manner to convey stories that appeal to the audience. Through social media platforms, Australian wine tourism and culture can effectively publicize to Chinese audiences. This part will focus on the digital tools analysis results and the combination of digital tourism.

Figure 2. Vocabulary distribution timeline of content related to tourism, wine culture and social media in Australia. Source: Web of Science

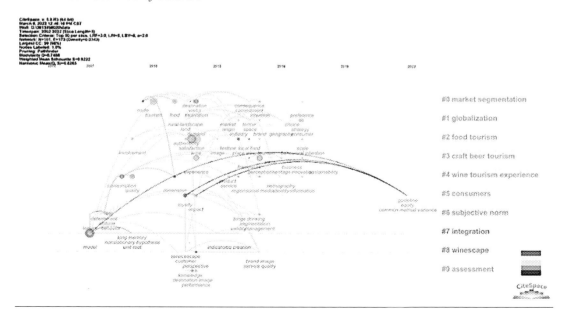

The digital tool of choice is CiteSpace in which its time chart is employed to show the specific links between tourism and digitization in Australia. The time distribution chart is used to observe the frequently discussed contents in the literature, summarize the keywords, and associate them with the main contents according to the year distribution. The main purpose is to explore the focus of Australian tourism and digital literature in different years. The specific trend of tourism and digital content in Australia under the development of the times. The chart is based on an analysis of digital, cultural, and wine tourism literature.

Between 2005 to 2022 the analysis is divided into different parts by year. The right side shows the main discussion directions with high frequency in thousands of literature data, and the keywords and all link lines on the left side show the relationship between these words and the literature of the same period. It can show an obvious time point. From 2019 to now, there is little literature on wine tourism in Australia due to the impact of the COVID-19. Among them, the main contents of wine tourism literature in Australia focuses on market segmentation, globalization, and food tourism. As this work is written during 2022, the authors who published relevant literature will focus more on tourist service and experience (Figure 2).

Simultaneously, the focus of each literature author also represents that Australian tourism has paid more attention to tourists in recent years. The data results show that under the influence of the COVID-19, Australian tourism was limited to online promotions, it has also challenged traditional view on marketing and pushed businesses to explore new methods. It is extremely difficult to implement the offline method. This digital tool uses specific algorithms to classify documents, extract keywords, and finally to summarize and analyze them. In comparison to manual statistics and analysis, digital tools, helps saves time and money.

The following are some manifestations of online and offline digital technology in Australian tourism. Digital applications may sound inappropriate in daily life, but they are everywhere. For example, from credit cards to social identity numbers and tourist information are kept track via digital means and identifiers. Many countries even created passports for COVID-19 vaccinations providing people special access to spaces after they have been vaccinated. Digital tools and means make the world fast, convenient, and simple. Digitization is more innovative fo Australia's tourism industry. In recent years, the corona pandemic has brought the global tourism industry to a standstill, but it has also spawned a new form of online cloud tourism. Cloud tourism refers to watching travel videos live through streaming media at home, rather than the actual travel experience (Xie et al., 2022).

The emergence of cloud tourism has triggered a heated debate on the Internet. Some people claim that cloud tourism can alleviate boredom at home and provide the same feeling of travel. But more people think cloud tourism is unnecessary (Sun & Drakeman, 2021). Because it only meets the visceral experience, cloud tourism is quite different from the physical experience. The previous generation is not yet comfortable with cloud tourism. Although the emergence and development of cloud tourism are not acceptable to all consumers, the combination of digital technology and tourism forms a meaningful "cooperation".

From the extant literature, the description of Australia's cultural heritage is mainly about Australia's original inhabitants, natural landscapes, and historic buildings. The representative words of Australian culture are rich and colorful, diverse cultural customs, and tolerance of foreign cultures (Furlong & Finnie, 2020). Due to the influence of European and American countries, Australia as we know it has only existed for around 100 years. Therefore, Australia is host to multiculturism and difference races. People from different cultures communicate and influence each other to form a new Australian culture, called derivation of foreign culture. Accordingly, many Australians believe these cultural contents cannot belong to their cultural heritage, which also causes them to believe that Australia has no independent culture.

For Australia, culture is not just foreign. The Aborigines can easily be called the oldest indigenous culture of Australia. The indigenous people, known as Yolngu, live in small communities made up of 13 different ethnic groups. After the development of Australia in the new era, most of the aboriginal people still live in this land. They are the traditional owners of the land, having inhabited it for at least 50,000 years (Leonard et al., 2013). Time is not the only reason. There is a lot of pressure on indigenous people in modern society to adapt to the western lifestyle and behavioral characteristics, even learn newer languages to integrate with the rest of the country. However, aborigines have maintained their cultural roots as much as possible and are proud that their culture goes back thousands of years.

In addition to the aborigines, Australia also has famous natural scenery and historic buildings known as Australia's cultural heritage. In June, 2004, the Royal Melbourne Exhibition Hall was added to the United Nations World Heritage List. It is currently the only building in Australia on the list (Zhang et al., 2012). For a tourist-oriented nation like Australia, buildings with historical and cultural significance are by no means a minority. There are world-class universities, beautiful and spectacular tourist resorts, and abundant natural species, which are also part of Australia's cultural heritage. These historical buildings and their heritage are creating a culture of their own. As a diversified country, Australia has a wide variety of cultural heritage and corresponding histories. Australia's integration and innovation of these diverse cultures have become an important reason for tourists to choose to visit Australia.

Wine tourism and hospitality can be said to be an important part of Australia's tourism industry. After all, when tourists travel, food and lodging are often a must (Okumus, 2020). Also experiencing local activities is a necessary tourism goal. The main attraction of hotels in Australia is the beautiful scenery, and as a country surrounded by the sea, the coastline and beaches are natural advantages for the marketing the hospitality industry.

In addition, the natural environment of Australia is very good, and the characteristic accommodation derived from this is also the focus of the tour. For example, a treehouse in a forest, a tent on a beach, or a habitat in a canyon are natural habitability features that many countries cannot emulate (Carson & Carson, 2019). In many ways, its tourism is an exploration of its rich natural landscape. Australia being a developed country, is host to many luxury hotels. Before the COVID-19 pandemic, any hotel chain would have definitely worked towards establishing their presence in Australia given its elite status as tourist destination.

The local food culture also acts as one of Australia's natural strengths. Australian cuisine uses a lot of local produce, which is unique to the region, from meats, to vegetables. Given that it is surrounded by seas on all sides, seafood is plentiful. Wine is a great accompaniment to food and an integral part of the culture, and an iconic way to socialize with others. Considering all wineries as the sample set, a total of 66% of them pair wine tasting with local food, bread, cheese, or other local delicacies. Some restaurants offer simple snacks and wine tasting, while others offer full meals. The local food is paired with wine. The restaurants hope to extend the dine-in time of tourists, where wine and other spirits are used to create a more relaxing food experience.

Additionally, the combination of Australia's tourism and wine industry can not only meet the wine sales market but also improve the tourism experience in Australia. Along the way, attending wine tastings at a local winery, helping pick grapes, or even making a bottle of wine at the winery (Ristic et al., 2019) have become activities that tourists engage in. 95% of wineries choose to offer the opportunity to visit facilities, vineyards, cellars, production lines, wine tasting rooms, other tourist attractions, such as agricultural tools folk museum or olive oil and honey production facilities (Vázquez et al., 2021). The combination of wine and other industries can drive the economy of both sides at the same time and can better meet the needs of consumers.

Combining storytelling and culture is a different use of digital tools. For example, a wine from Australia called *19 Crimes* combined storytelling and digital techniques in 2012. There are six bottles in the collection which includes one bottle of white wine and five bottles of red wine. Deep red, full and elegant, with dark fruit and vanilla aromas. The wine is not best known for its name or taste, but for its use of digital innovation through Augmented Reality (AR) technology (Dahlstrom, 2014). Every bottle of wine has a label on the package. Scan the label, a 3D story scene narrates the wine's back story and history.

19 Crime Wine takes its name from 19 crimes in which criminals were deprived of their liberty and sent to Australia as the first immigrants. One bottle of wine tells the story of John Boyle O'Reilly's arrest by the British government in 1867 for his involvement in the Irish independence movement. He was sentenced to death and later exiled to Australia. John, however, was no ordinary prisoner. After many difficult experiences, he wrote poems about his trip to Australia (Fullerton & Kendrick, 2011). Therefore, the wine uses AR technology to display each prisoner's story in three dimensions. This new form of presentation method is more influential than mere words.

The application of this digital means attracts more consumers to buy the wine and learn a story or get some new information during a wine tasting event, creating an immersive and transformative experience. By combining digital storytelling into the wine consuming experience, *19 Crime* wine aims to provide knowledge and information thereby differentiating it from other wine consuming experiences. Storytelling is more than knowledge and information sharing; it is about creating unique and unforgettable memories. *19 Crimes Wines* not only tells the brand story of its wine but also deploys an impulsive buying behavior by aiding the decision making not just through the product but by the experience that surround it, which is another innovation in the wine industry.

AR technology can be applied in various other industries to promote their products and services. *19 Crimes* wines are also beneficial to tourism as well as to the wine industry (Brabazon et al., 2014). The sales of wine and the emergence of wine tourism are the reasons why tourists who are interested in wine choose to travel to Australia. In addition to the wine itself, the combination of this digital technology is also worth discussing. If technologies like AR can be combined with Australian wine tourism, and social media can be leveraged for online promotion and publicity to attract consumer attention, it opens up the desire to explore new technologies and mediums. AR technology has the potential to help Australian tourism to enter a new phase. Once the outbreak is over, tourists familiar and unfamiliar with Australia are likely to be attracted again.

In addition to using digital technology, the wineries combine wine with brand storytelling to enhance their wine tourism. A brand story talks about history, values, behind the scenes of the business, and brings in transparency about the raw materials, making process and the people behind it. With the improvement of economic status and people's shifting focus to their spiritual needs, renders simple wine tasting too simple, and does not make it stand out in the industry.

By adding a layer of atmosphere or chateau history, every bottle of wine can bring a collectible value. People can be interested in the wineries, producers and even Australia through wine. If this approach can be implemented, consumers can learn about the concept of the winery and the brewing of wine through wine. Turning it into a meaningful experience.

This chapter is mainly about the offline form of Australian wine tourism and cultural content. Among them, the specific tourism activities and hotels in Australia can only be briefly introduced online, and the most important thing is to use offline publicity means. Wine culture can be publicized and sold online, but it is far less effective than the offline experience. However, Chinese tourists cannot choose to travel to Australia at present, which leads to the content of wine tourism and culture in Australia can only publicized through online means, and the offline publicity is limited. Among them, publicity through social media can be said to be the main online publicity method for Audrey wine tourism and cultural choice.

SOCIAL MEDIA STRATEGIES ON AUSTRALIAN WINE TOURISM

As states above, Australian tourism is an indispensable part of the Australian economy, and wine tourism occupies a very important position in the tourism industry. Social media platforms are currently driving a lot of traffic across the globe. Especially during COVID-19, people's mobility was restricted due to various governmental quarantines and lockdowns. The status of social media is more obvious, becoming people's indispensable daily entertainment items (Flew & Kirkwood, 2020).

Therefore, this section will discuss if social media is helpful to Australian tourism. Does social media play a big role in wine tourism? What is the relationship between tourism, wine, and social media in Australia? What is the status of Australian wine and social media in Australia's tourism industry? This part will use data analysis to cross-analyze wine and tourism information using CiteSpace analysis tools, and then cross-analyze social media and tourism information. The results are merged into the CiteSpace analysis tool. Therefore, this paper analyzes the contents of WOS literature based on CiteSpace analysis results.

Figure 3. Keywords co-occurrence of Australian tourism, wine culture and social media related content. Source: Web of Science

The results obtained from the CiteSpace tool show the keywords with high frequency in the literature will be reflected in the figure which shows the core words of the content in the literature. The higher the frequency of words, the higher the degree of discussion in the literature of related content. In addition to the main research directions of the article, experience, loyalty, and satisfaction are high frequency (Figure 3). The purpose of this chapter is to discuss the relationship between these keywords and the content of the literature analyzed.

Experience is a keyword that shows up throughout the research. It brings together the experience of travelling and wine tourism. It brings both the online and offline experience. It also concentrates on the social media based digital experience of the social media content creators, managers, and consumers. One should personally experience it to truly understand it. For example, Australia has a well-developed tourism industry, among which kangaroos and koalas watching a very popular tourist attraction. It is possible to be interested in appreciating the experience of others, but it cannot be truly felt by merely observing the experience of others. They can only feel it for themselves by experiencing it (Gu et al,.2019). Merely seeing kangaroos and koalas from a distance, and closely interacting with them, like touching and petting can shape one's experience.

Presently, the development of offline channels is limited, and online means can be used as much as possible. Therefore, social media can also be called the main way to attract tourists to travel or entice them back into planning their trips and vacations. People often see the experience of others to trigger their desire to go. With wine, the experience is more intuitive. Different wine regions in Australia have different tastes, which are described by other people's experiences. No matter how much others express their love for wine, only when everyone has experienced it, will they realize whether the wine, its taste, and its region are suitable for them. This kind of experience is not only about wine tasting, but is also about experiencing the winery and immersing in the unique and historical atmosphere of the wineries.

Spend quality time with friends and family, or other circles and create special memories. If one simply purchases a bottle of wine, all the experience will become monotonous (Knight et al., 2018). Therefore, the word experience does often appear. For travel and wine, experiences are paramount, and social media is there to document and showcase said experiences. This also means that offline channels are indispensable for tourism and wine.

Other keywords with high frequency were loyalty and satisfaction. Among them, loyalty is mainly reflected in wine and social media. Everyone has their own favorite social media application, thus forming a brand loyalty. It shows their preferred modes and mediums of data consumption. Given people are loyal to social media apps, it brings in a steady stream of traffic and their likes and dislikes are more discernable and targetable. Now, short videos and advertorials have become a preferred way of getting bits and pieces of information and combining them with travel proves that posting a travel story is the equivalent of talking about it to loyal users of social media apps.

For wine loyalty, every wine connoisseur will have their unique hobbies and tendencies. A person may prefer wine from a certain region, or prefer wine of a certain kind, say Pinot Noir from the Tasmanian region. A loyal customer is the most important thing in the wine industry, tourism, or any industry. Because there's no limit to what they can bring (Okumus, 2020). What every company needs most is to maintain their loyal customers.

As for the other keyword, satisfaction, the word appears in three main parts of the discussion with the subject. Among them, social media and platforms have their content direction and marketing strategy. For users, the most intuitive way to express love through software and platforms is satisfaction. In the tourism industry, a tourism project that is loved by many people is worth promoting. For example, before the COVID-19 outbreak, winery grape picking, and wine-making experiences were among the most satisfying activities for visitors in Australia. This has led to the emergence and development of wine tourism. Wine travel satisfaction is equally important. As a product, the wine will have good sales only when it satisfies customers. Satisfaction should be the main evaluation standard to judge whether things are good or bad, while the tourism experience is a very subjective idea. Only those who have experienced it can have high satisfaction and attract more people to experience and consume.

Therefore, the whole CiteSpace analysis chart can also show very important content; that is, whether social media is related to wine tourism, which is the focus of this research. From this analysis, social media does play a very important role in wine tourism in Australia. As an important means of communication in the current COVID-19 pandemic, the tourism industry has been active on various social media platforms, with wineries focusing on selling their brands while reducing the publicity of previous popular winery experience events. Almost all wineries have their own social media accounts and use social media platforms to display their wineries and wines online to attract consumers and stay connected with the community.

The large consumption capacity that Chinese market brings is an opportunity no manufacturer would want to give up. As a result, wineries have their product and targeted social media content on China's well-known social media platforms. This is leveraging what is left to develop post-COVID-19 customer resources (Olsen et al., 2020). With such marketing, these wineries and the Australian wine industry will grow rapidly again if COVID-19 passes. Until then, the winery will continue to promote its wine culture to attract visitors to experience it on the ground (Furlong & Finnie, 2020). Packaging and telling wine region stories are a great way to engage people on today's social media platforms.

Now people no longer focus only on the quality and taste of products, but they have started paying attention to the meaning behind products when the basic conditions are met. For example, if a winery has a touching story, the winery makes a wine to commemorate this story, and it is limited. So that means the story is what gets people to buy things. Australia's wineries all have beautiful scenery; besides wine, the country is also a great place to visit. Beautiful scenery and interesting experience will be few of the reasons why tourists choose to visit Australia. So now both the travel industry and the wine industry are taking advantage of the COVID-19 pandemic to try to build their brand stories and corporate cultures and make those stories a symbol that reminds people of the wine brand and its origins. This is enough to prove that Australia's tourism and wine industries need social media as a means of promotion (Bu et al., 2020).

According to CiteSpace, consumer is also an important keyword. The most important player in tourism is obviously the consumer. Although the tourism situation of various countries is grim, they still pay attention to the publicity of their national characteristics, and the publicity of the Australian wine tourism industry is still in progress (Galati et al., 2017). Before COVID-19, the biggest spenders in Australia were Chinese tourists. Tourism websites and social media of major Australian wineries provide multi-language switching options to help the audience choose the language of their preference, focusing on promoting their own brand culture and stories, and building their corporate brands. Offline development channels are not allowed for promotion, and only online channels can be constructed for publicity to maintain the sense of the presence of Australian wine tourism in Chinese tourists. Online promotions have also kept Australia's tourism, entertainment, and alcohol culture alive, ensuring that Australia's tourism industry will continue to attract large numbers of foreign visitors once the pandemic is over.

QUESTIONNAIRE

It is important to collect and understand Chinese tourists' understanding of Australian tourism and wine culture, as well as the situation of Chinese social media platforms. Combined with the current social situation, online questionnaires were selected for data collection. The online questionnaire is to use digital technology to make statistics and analysis on the selection results of respondents. This part conducts a questionnaire survey through WeChat. The questionnaire is used to investigate Chinese tourists and consumers. Study the results of questions related to Australian tourism and wine culture and Chinese social media platforms. The results of the questionnaire will show the attitudes and current situation of Chinese tourists and consumer groups towards Chinese social media and tourism, wine, and culture-related content in Australia.

Figure 4. Thought map of Australian tourism, wine culture, and Chinese social media questionnaire. Source: Data collected from a survey

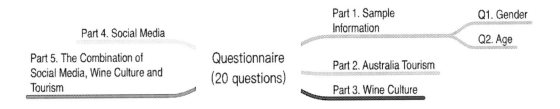

Figure 5. Flow chart of Australian tourism, wine culture, and Chinese social media questionnaire. Source: Data collected from a survey

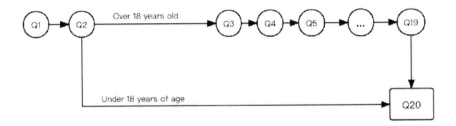

The questionnaire consists of 20 questions that includes the specific contents of each category in the questionnaire, starting with the basic information of the respondents. The text is divided into four parts: Australian tourism, wine culture, social media, and a combination of the three. The first part of the mind map is the basic personal information of the interviewee, which aims to determine whether the interviewee meets the answer conditions through the age and gender of the interviewee (Figure 4).

The specific process of the questionnaire is divided into two response processes according to the basic personal information. Respondents were divided into over 18 years old and under 18 years old by age. The reason why 18 years old is chosen as the distinguishing criterion is that the content category of the questionnaire contains questions related to wine (Figure 4 & 5). To meet China's legal requirements, teenagers under the age of 18 are prohibited from drinking. Therefore, the questionnaire identifies respondents under the age of 18 as not meeting the answer conditions and progresses to the end of the questionnaire.

Figure 6. Age distribution chart of respondents of different genders. Source: Data collected from a survey

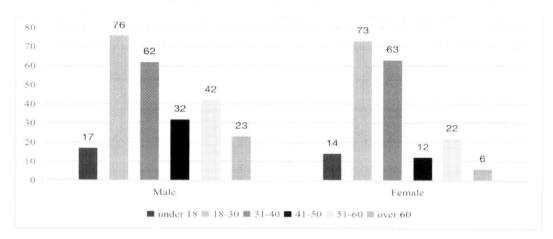

The results include the respondents' basic personal information, a cross-analysis of the respondents' age, and gender data. The data results are divided into five age ranges: those who are between 18-30 of age and between 31-40 of age constitute the main age distribution of respondents, which account for over 50% of the total respondents. A total of 149 respondents aged 18-30 accounted for 33.71% of the total respondents. There are 125 respondents aged 31-40, thus accounting for 28.28% of the total respondents. From different gender perspectives, the age group with the largest distribution of men and women is also 18-30 years old: a total of 76 men and 73 women (Figure 6). According to the histogram distribution, the distribution of age stages participating in the survey is relatively uniform. Respondents of different ages can ensure the authenticity and fairness of the information results, and there will be no single and absolute results due to their similar ages (Sujová et al., 2019).

Australia Tourism

1. Survey Questions
   a. Choice tendency of cloud travel and field travel experience
   b. Types of tourist destinations in Australia and characteristic tourism activities in various regions
   c. Content setting types and main information of the Australian tourism platform
2. Data and Results Analysis

The first part of the questionnaire takes Australian tourism as the main direction and sets up relevant questions to investigate Chinese respondents. Because of the worldwide spread of COVID-19, cloud tourism has gradually become a new tourism model. Cloud tourism refers to the use of Internet technology to enable consumers to simulate scenic spots online through video, live broadcast, VR experiences, and other ways (Sottini et al., 2021).

The questionnaire takes cloud tourism-related issues as the starting point to investigate the share of cloud tourism in the hearts of Chinese tourists under the current pandemic situation, and whether it can replace on-site tourism to meet the tourism expectations. The survey results show that Chinese tourists prefer to travel over online tourism. The total number of questionnaire samples answering this question is 411, of which 183 people prefer cloud tourism, thus accounting for 44.53% of the total respondents. A total of 228 people prefer field travel experience, which accounts for 55.47% of the total respondents.

The data difference between the two is about 10%, which proves that although the number of Chinese tourists choosing cloud tourism is less than that of field tourism, they have a good degree of acceptance and there is no exclusion. The emergence of cloud tourism is a better choice under the current situation that the society cannot travel abroad (Yang & Chen, 2020).

The questions about Australian tourism in the questionnaire mainly focuses on the city selection tendency of Australian tourism and related tourism activities. The survey asked the respondents who have never been to Australia and are interested in tourism in Australia to choose their first tourism destination. Those who have been to Australia in the survey will skip this question. Those who are not interested in Australian tourism will skip all the contents related to Australian Tourism in the questionnaire (Table 1). After selecting the destination, all respondents will make multiple choices on the travel itinerary and specific tourism activities (Figure 7).

Table 1. Whether respondents have been to Australia and the choice and distribution of first-time tourist destinations. Source: Data collected from a survey

Categories	Response		Tourist destination (state)	Response	
	n	Response rate		n	Response rate
Have been to Australia	72	17.52%	None		
Never been to Australia But interested	321	78.10%	New South Wales (University of Sydney, Sydney Opera House, etc.)	51	15.89%
			South Australia (Kangaroo Island, vineyard, zoo, etc.)	56	17.45%
			Western Australia (botanical garden, Pink Lake, etc.)	50	15.58%
			Northern Territory (nature, wildlife, etc.)	51	15.89%
			Tasmania (ancient buildings, leisure towns, etc.)	27	8.41%
			Queensland (Great Barrier Reef, Gold Coast, etc.)	39	12.15%
			Victoria (University of Melbourne, CBD financial center, etc.)	47	14.64%
Never been to Australia and uninterested	18	4.38%	None		
Total	411	100.00%	Total	321	100.00%

Source: Data collected from a survey

Figure 7. Distribution of respondents' favorite tourism activities and experiences. Source: Data collected from a survey

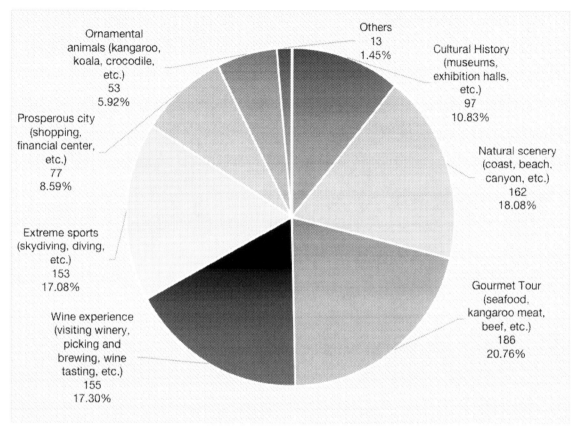

We divide the respondents who are interested in tourism in Australia, and then assume the preference of destination selection for first-time travel to Australia. Among them, a total of 72 people has been to Australia, thus accounting for 17.52% of the total respondents. A total of 321 people who have not been to Australia but are interested in going there in the future accounted for 78.10% of the total respondents, and 18 people who are completely not interested in tourism in Australia accounted for 4.38% of the total respondents. Fewer than 5% of tourists are not interested, which is enough to prove that Australian tourism is very attractive to Chinese tourists (Table 1).

Among the 321 interested people, the number of people selected by the seven states in Australia is close, and the most popular first-time tourist destination is South Australia. A total of 56 people is chosen, thus accounting for 17.45% of the total. Tasmania has the lowest number of people choosing among the seven states in which a total of 27 people chose that state, thus accounting for 8.41% of the total (Table 1). The fan-shaped statistical chart is used to summarize the data of the respondents' favorite tourism activities selected via a multiple-choice question. We can see the tourists' most favorite activities and travel itineraries. The tourism activities with a similar proportion are food tours, natural scenery, wine experience, and extreme sports.

Among them, the most popular is the Gourmet Tour chosen by 186 people, accounting for 20.76% of the total. The number of wine experience activities related to the research content of this chapter is also popular, with 155 people accounting for a total of 17.30% (Figure 7).

Table 2. Types of information that Australian tourism platforms need to provide to tourists. Source: Data collected from a survey

Categories	Response	
	n	Response rate
Introduction to tourist attractions	100	25.45%
Tourism characteristics of each city	172	43.77%
Catering, traffic information	185	47.07%
Travel itinerary introduction	160	40.71%
Travel expenses	123	31.3%
Accommodation hotel information	102	25.95%
Free mobile charging station, WiFi point layout	66	16.79%
Others	9	2.29%

Source: Data collected from a survey

The activities and itineraries desired by Chinese tourists are unique to Australian tourism. For example, some foods and ingredients used in Australia are unique and only available locally such as kangaroo and wallaby meat. Australia is also a place of interest for adventurers due to the countless number of extreme sports (Belias et al., 2017). To improve the attraction of Australian tourism to Chinese tourists, the country needs to collect the tourism needs of Chinese tourists. All respondents believed that the types of information that Australia's tourism platform should be provided to foreign tourists (Table 2).

Investigating the information that needs to be included in the Australian Tourism platform and conduct data statistics to determine the needs of Chinese tourists. The data shows the types of information that Chinese tourists hope the Australian Tourism platform can provide, including expenses, location of scenic spots, and traffic conditions. It is clear the tourists expect travel and hospitality platforms to provide rich context and diverse sets of information. The local tourist point of view is quite different from foreign tourist point of view.

There is little difference in the number of people selected for each information and each accounts for a high proportion. Respondents tend that the tourism platform can include as many rich information types as possible, not focus on just one format or platform. This is necessary to meet the needs of tourists of different kind, from age, to culture, food preference, socio-economic background, to type of travel and accommodation they choose. Every aspect paves way to their needs once they land in their destination. The most selected category is catering and traffic information.

Free mobile charging station and WiFi point layout have the lowest number of people, but a total of 66 people still chose it (Table 2). This means that Chinese tourists need to obtain rich types of tourism-related information for foreign tourism. Any type of information cannot be missing. Only when the tourism platform covers the information needed by tourists as much as possible can it ensure that tourists can fully understand Australia through the tourism platform (Wang et al., 2012).

Figure 8. Respondents' familiarity with wine countries in the world. Source: Data collected from a survey

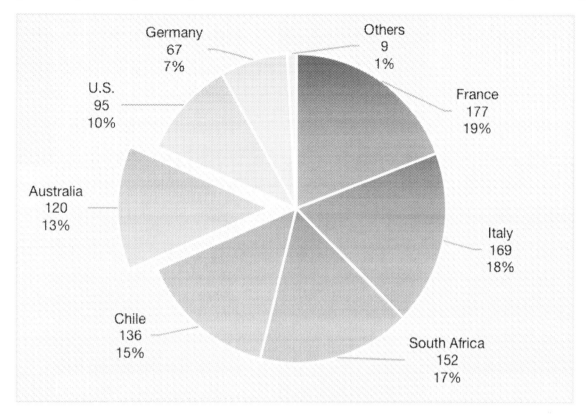

Figure 9. Reasons affecting consumers' purchase of wine. Source: Data collected from a survey

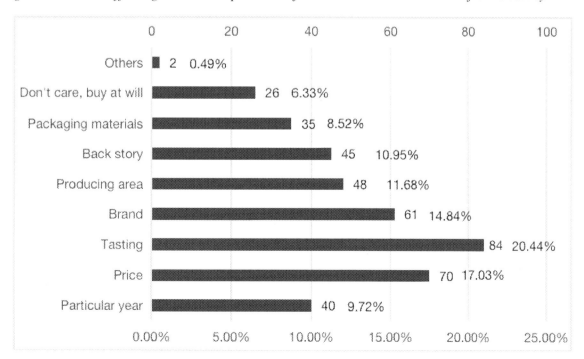

Wine Culture

1. *Survey Questions*
    a. World wine culture countries known to Chinese consumers
    b. Factors affecting consumers' choice of wine and understanding consumers' purchase demand
    c. Get feedback on the way of wine culture and the effect of online wine tourism promotion
2. *Data and Results Analysis*

The second part of the main body of the questionnaire is about the relevant contents of wine culture, mainly discussing the Chinese consumer's understanding of Australian wine and wine in general. Count the familiarity of Chinese consumers with the world's wine countries and analyze the specific data and proportion of the countries selected by the respondents. Among them, Australian wine is less well-known in the Chinese consumer market than in France (Bruwer & Rueger-Muck, 2018). Even in the result statistics, familiarity does not exist in the first three. Among them, France is the most familiar wine country for Chinese tourists, accounting for 19% and 13% choosing Australian wine (Figure 8).

Chinese consumers for Australian wine are comparatively less, and the number of choices of wines are also low. Summarize the data results and analyze the proportion of Australian wine in the current Chinese market and the influence of wine countries. The most important factor for Chinese consumers to buy wine is taste. The number of people who selected taste included 84 persons, thus accounting for 20.44% of the total survey takers. Second, the standard for purchasing wine is price of wine which accounts for 17.03% of the total survey takers, and the brand of wine accounts for 14.84% of the total survey takers. The region, year, and raw materials of wine will also affect Chinese consumers' purchase of wine (Figure 8 & 9).

This chapter aims to promote Australian tourism, wine, and culture to China through social media. Its main purpose is to enable Chinese tourists to deepen their understanding of Australian tourism, wine, and culture. At present, Chinese tourists are not familiar with Australian wine knowledge, so the way to spread wine knowledge to Chinese tourists is particularly important (Table 3).

Table 3. Ways for Chinese tourists and consumers to obtain wine-related knowledge. Source: Data collected from a survey

Categories	Response	
	n	Response rate
Search information online	114	27.74%
Recommended by friends	233	56.69%
Field visit to winery and experience	214	52.07%
Attend wine tasting	218	53.04%
Watch wine knowledge popularization video	106	25.79%
Others	17	4.14%

Investigate the ways for Chinese tourists to understand and learn wine-related knowledge. According to the data, recommendation by friends, field visits to winery and experience and attending wine tasting are the three most popular choices, accounting for more than 50%, respectively. The insights from this show that Chinese tourists, as previously seen, prefer more in-person and familial sources of recommendations with regards to wine. Using these methods will be effective ways to promote and publicize wine businesses. Field visit to winery and experience and attend wine tasting are more suitable publicity methods for Australian wine (Table 3). Besides, Australian wine tourism had already become a necessary tourism experience before the COVID-19 pandemic. This is enough to prove that Australian wine publicity is closely linked to Australian tourism (Sigala & Haller, 2018).

At present, Chinese tourists cannot choose to travel to Australia. Then, online Australia promotes wine tourism is a good choice in China. It can attract Chinese tourists to join the Australia wine tourism after the COVID-19 is finished. According to the statistics of the questionnaire results, the method of online promotion of wine tourism is loved by most Chinese tourists. A total of 265 people chose to be interested and will consider participating in the future, accounting for 64.48% of the total respondents in the survey. According to statistics, from January 2020 to October 2020, the online sales of food accounted for 86% of the total. It is estimated that more than 55% of consumers will become permanent online consumers. The specific reason is that the current development of offline tourism is limited by the epidemic, so Chinese tourists have a high degree of acceptance of online tourism promotion.

Figure 10. The specific usage of popular social media platforms in China. Source: Data collected from a survey

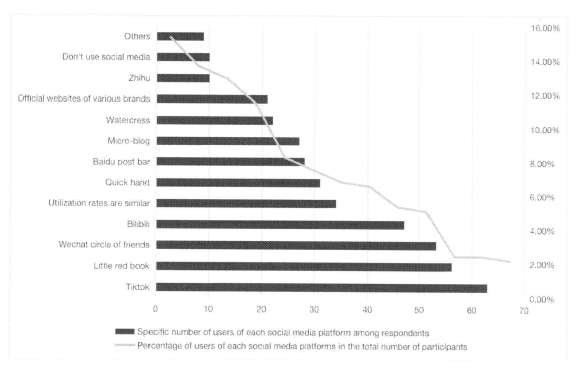

Social Media

1. *Survey Questions*
   a. Specific situation and frequency of respondents using social media platform
   b. Current Chinese consumers' acceptance of using social media for online promotion of goods
   c. Share and display the frequency of Australian wine tourism cultural content on social media
2. *Data and Results Analysis*

Figure 11. The frequency range of publishing content using social media platforms. Source: Data collected from a survey

Frequency (from low to high)	Once a month (1)					Once a day (7)	
Section	1-1.85	1.86-2.71	2.72-3.57	3.58-4.42	4.43-5.28	5.29-6.14	6.15-7
Number of participants	36	33	55	56	58	69	94

Total number of participants = 401

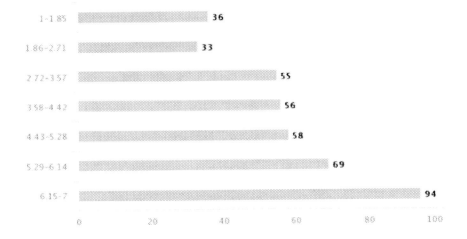

The third part of the questionnaire is connected to social media usage. As the respondents are Chinese tourists and consumers, the choice of social media platforms focuses on China. List the social media platforms frequently used by Chinese tourists and consumers and provide respondents with choices. The significance of this problem is to select social media platforms for promotion through data collection. TikTok is the most used social media platform, accounting for 15.33% of the total. Then, the number of users of Little Red Book accounted for 13.63% of the total (Figure 10). Combined with the age information of respondents, the higher proportion of these two social media platforms is due to the largest number of people aged 18-40 in the questionnaire (Figure 6). However, the age range of 18-40 years old is a group with a high frequency of use and high consumption of social media platforms.

In the questionnaire, the frequency of respondents using social media platforms to publish content was statistically analyzed. The fixed value range chosen by respondents is 1-7. The closer the value is to number 1, the lower the frequency of publishing content. It is usually published once a month. The higher the frequency of content release, the closer it is to number 7 which is usually published once a day. According to the data, a total of 401 respondents responded. The largest number of respondents in the range of 6.15-7 is 94, accounting for 34.44% of the total. This means that 34.44% of respondents publish content frequency nearly number 7. It stands for these respondents maybe share content every day (Figure 11). Using social media has gradually become a habit (Li & Liu, 2020).

Therefore, the publicity method of using social media platforms can be accepted by Chinese tourists and consumers. The attitudes and thoughts of respondents in the face of online promotion (Figure 12).

Figure 12. Distribution of users' attitudes towards online promotion on social media platforms. Source: Data collected from a survey

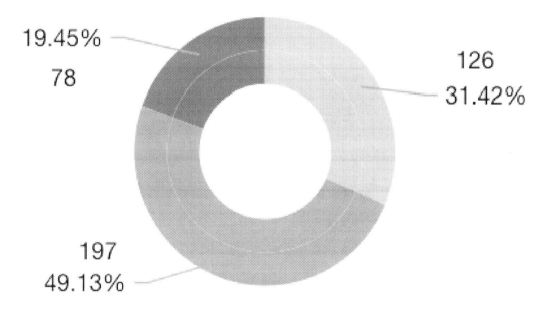

Statistics of respondents' attitudes and thoughts on online product promotion and online brand advertising. The data results clearly show that 49.13% of the respondents accept the online promotion and do not mind browsing the promotion content. A total of 31.42% of the respondents said they accepted the online promotion, were willing to understand the products, and chose to buy through online promotion. A total of 19.45% of the respondents said they did not accept the online promotion and hate when social media platforms are used for brand promotions. However, more than 80% of respondents accepted the promotion and intended to buy, which is enough to prove that the online promotion method is effective (Figure 12).

Online promotion is not limited to simple advertising sales but also includes brand story publicity, creating a unique brand image, and promoting the brand spirit (Sigala & Haller, 2018). According to the browsing of Australian tourism and wine culture content on social media platforms, a total of 39.15% of respondents said they often browse relevant content. A total of 37.66% of the respondents said they had browsed relevant content, but not often, and a total of 23.19% of the respondents said they had never seen anything about Australian tourism and wine culture.

In the whole social media platform, the push of relevant content in Australia also belongs to the scope of online promotion, but the promotion content is different (Li & Liu, 2020). Online promotion will also allow consumers to obtain more convenient and affordable purchase methods. Compared with offline promotion, online promotion using social media platforms also has more advantages (Table 4).

The Combination of Social Media, Wine Culture, and Australia Tourism

1. *Survey Questions*
    a. Advantages of using Chinese social media to promote Australian wine, tourism, and culture
    b. Provide charging piles and free Wi-Fi for tourists in the tourist area to meet their needs, and the frequency of use of social media platforms will be affected after providing them
    c. Acceptance of Australian wine tourism by Chinese consumers and tourists and specific suggestions on using social media to promote Australian tourism, wine, and culture
2. *Data and Results Analysis*

Table 4. Use social media platforms to promote the advantages of Australian tourism and wine culture online. Source: Data collected from a survey

Categories	Response	
	n	Response rate
Low cost	134	33.42%
Good interaction	203	50.62%
Rich content	211	52.62%
Targeted content	123	30.67%
Others	13	3.24%

Table 5. Chinese tourists' opinions on the behavior of providing charging piles and free Wi-Fi in touristic hot spots. Source: Data collected from a survey

Categories	Response	
	n	Response rate
Yes, it's important	203	49.39%
Yes, but not important	178	43.31%
No, I use my own mobile traffic	22	5.35%
No, I don't surf the Internet during the trip	8	1.95%
Total	411	100%

Source: Data collected from a survey

The fourth part of the questionnaire comprehensively discusses and analyzes the relevant contents of Australian tourism, wine culture, and social media. Questions using joint content can be accurately analyzed through the results of respondents.

The rapid adoption of internet and e-commerce means buying goods is becoming more easier, affordable, and convenient. Many users in China are also mobile first internet users, making internet access available anywhere, anytime for anyone. Compared with offline promotion, online promotion using social media platforms also has more advantages (Khan, 2021). Exploring the advantages of using social media to promote tourism, wine, and cultural content in Australia from the perspective of businesses show there are four main choices: low cost, good interaction, rich content, and targeted content. The data results show that the most popular option is rich in content, accounting for 52.62% of the total.

The second is good interaction, accounting for 50.62% of the total (Table 4). Among them, rich content is most preferred response from the survey takers. The promotion methods and forms of using social media are diverse, and the update cycles are faster. It meets the needs of a contemporary fast-paced lifestyle. Then, good interactivity is also an important reason for the rapid development of social media (Quadros, 2022). Viewers can interact with businesses through comments or likes and direct messages and enquiries. This is also the reason why network promotion can flourish. Businesses can timely supplement and change according to the needs of consumers and strengthen their connect with the audience.

The link between Australian tourism and social media lies not only in publishing tourism content through social media, but also in helping social media through tourism (Fullerton & Kendrick, 2011). The statistical results show that 203 people think that charging stations can convert electricity on the grid into electricity standards that can be used to charge electric vehicles. Charging piles generally provide two charging methods, slow charging and fast charging, and free Wi-Fi should exist and are very important, accounting for 49.39% of all respondents. A total of 178 people think there is a need, but it is not important, accounting for 43.31% of the total. The remaining 5.35% said they will use their own mobile data plans and 1.95% said they will not use the Internet in the process of tourism. More than 90% of Chinese tourists believe that charging piles and free Wi-Fi are needed (Table 5).

We assume the tourist area providing charging piles and free Wi-Fi will affect the frequency of visitors using social media to publish content. According to the summary data, a total of 48% and 34% of respondents believe they will increase and may increase the frequency of publishing. A total of 69 people believe this will not affect their release frequency, accounting for 18% of the total (Figure 13).

Figure 13. Impact of providing charging points and free Wi-Fi on the frequency of use of social media platforms. Source: Data collected from a survey

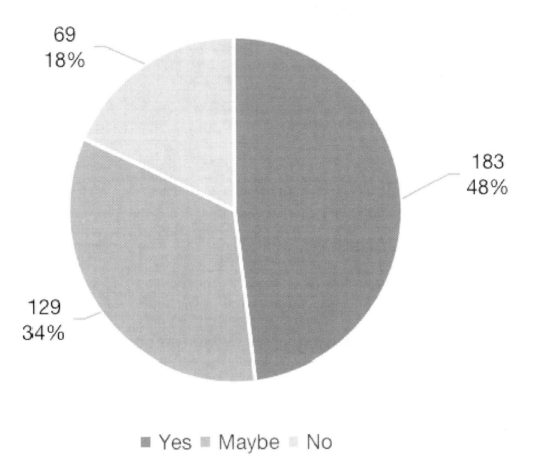

Increasing the frequency of visitors using social media to publish content is equivalent to helping Australian attractions promote online. This way of providing charging piles and free Wi-Fi is good cooperation between tourism and social media to achieve a win-win situation. Wine tourism highlights the combination of the Australian wine industry and tourism. Wine tourism already become a complete tourism activity in Australia. Through wine tourism, the wine sales of Australian wineries have also increased (Knight et al., 2018).

According to the statistical results of the questionnaire, for Chinese tourists who choose to travel to Australia in the future a total of 43.07% are willing to add wine tourism to the itinerary, and 36.98% will consider joining the itinerary. This shows that Australian wine tourism is attractive to Chinese tourists, and Australian tourism and wine culture will become popular tourism projects after COVID-19.

Finally, Chinese tourists put forward suggestions on using social media to promote tourism and wine culture in Australia. It is suggested to strengthen the publicity of Australian wine culture on social media. At present, the content of Australian wine contents on social media is not rich, and tourists cannot understand the relevant knowledge of Australian wine through social media. The Australian winery environment and wine tasting activities are displayed on social media platforms to enhance the interest of Chinese tourists.

In conclusion, the questionnaire can be used to directly understand the intuitive thoughts of Chinese tourists on Australian wine tourism culture and Chinese social media platforms. Based on the data statistics and the analysis of the problem results, the conclusion is that the promoting content on social media is a good choice for Australian wine tourism. However, the promotion and display of Australian wine needs to be strengthened (Sottini et al., 2021). Chinese tourists have a high acceptance of Australian wine tourism culture and social media-related content in form of online promotions.

At the same time, the method of using social media to publicize Australian wine tourism culture to Chinese tourists is effective and high-cost performance. It is imperative to collect and understand Chinese tourists' understanding of Australian tourism and wine culture, as well as the situation of Chinese social media platforms. Combined with the current social situation, online questionnaires were selected for data collection. This part conducts a questionnaire survey through WeChat. The questionnaire is used to investigate Chinese tourists and consumers and study the results of questions related to Australian tourism and wine culture and Chinese social media platforms. The results of the questionnaire will show the attitudes and current situation of Chinese tourists and consumer groups towards Chinese social media and tourism, wine, and culture-related content in Australia.

THE CASES ABOUT THE USE OF SOCIAL MEDIA TO PROMOTE AUSTRALIAN TOURISM, WINE, AND CULTURE

This section will discuss how social media can promote tourism, wine, and culture in Australia to foreign tourists. This section will analyze and summarize the forms and publicity strategies of social media. From the start of two main forms of social media to introduce and analyze, and then from the two aspects of online and offline of specific analysis and examples. Discuss how Australian tourism, wine, and culture are presented to consumers through social media promotion from the perspective of social media users. Each approach uses a real case to show content direction and how social media platforms relate to and impact tourism, wine, and culture in Australia.

Display Ways on Social Media

In social media, images, texts, and videos are the most common and basic formats of expression. Images and texts are arguably the first manifestations of social media. For users browsing images and texts, it is easy to understand what is expressed, and there is no time limit for each image and texts to be viewed as far as the content is not archived or deleted. In contrast to video, there is no need to pause and fast forward to view specific part or seek out a specific information, given its non-static nature.

In addition, most images and texts are presented very simply, which means that the main information can be captured faster (Patel et al., 2019). The presentation of image and texts formats are also easier for social media content creators. They need comparatively less editing and processing than videos. Images and texts require less design and production time than other forms, which means that publishing this form of content requires a lower cost time. In addition to not requiring complicated manipulation techniques, this presentation method can also satisfy some publishers who are not used to presenting themselves and are shy to consider it.

As far as pictures and texts are concerned, the contents about tourism, wine, and culture in Australia published on social media tend to focus on the listing and introduction of products or categories of things. For example, users search about travel to Australia content on social media, images and texts show about tourist attractions introduction or list places worth visiting in Australia (Sigala, 2019). With regards to Australian wine, the images and texts are mainly about Australian wine brand introductions and recommendations. Images and texts show the sights and types of wines worth visiting in Australia, but there is no specific explanation or introduction for each paragraph.

Therefore, if tourists choose to travel to Australia, they can quickly understand the general information about Australian tourism and wine culture through the display of images and texts on the social platform. Images and texts are suitable for displaying accurate information and high-definition image quality. This information is similar to presenting the user with a framework through which the user can retrieve specific information.

After images and texts, video is the most common form of presentation. In recent years, video has gradually overtaken images and texts. Especially the short format videos like reels and stories. This is mainly due to the rapid development of science and technology and the popularity of the Internet. People no longer must spend much time waiting for videos to load, and faster Internet speeds have made video more palatable as a method of presentation. In contrast to images and texts, video can add tools such as sound, special effects, and animation, thus making the content presented and displayed by the video richer and more interesting (Roth, 2020).

In terms of content, video can cover more information. If video, images, and texts need to show the same information content, images and texts are more likely to lose users' interest. A video can bring a better practical experience than boring text and exquisite freeze-frame pictures. In the case of Australian wine, videos on social media are mainly made up of wine lovers' detailed recommendations of wine types and explanations of wine knowledge, as well as winery posts about the viticulture environment and wine-making process.

For recommendations of similar content, videos are more vivid and persuasive. In videos, people will combine their emotions with information, making the content more accessible to the general audience. The video can also clearly show the texture, color, and packaging of each bottle of wine, which is harder if static images were used. In the category of Australian wine videos on social media, wine knowledge videos are also very popular with viewers (Strickland et al., 2016). In the video, the publisher uses simple oral language to replace complex wine book knowledge, so that many non-professional audiences can understand the Australian wine culture.

From the perspective of user experiences and emotions, people tend to prefer the rich sensory impact of videos. Video is easier to immerse in and enjoy the content through sound and visuals. Therefore, the effect of propagating through video will also be strengthened. For example, videos on social media are often used to show beautiful landscapes, attractions, or real-life experiences in the tourism process (Minazzi, 2014). It can also capture feedback from tourists and their stories. Videos about the content creator's actual travel experience and play-through are the most popular.

Because the real experience is usually more engaging to viewers, the atmosphere of such videos will enhance their interest, and viewers will be more easily attracted to the content. The content presented by the video will be more comprehensive and real than the images & texts, and the multi-angle presentation will also make the audience better understand and appreciate it.

Overall, images with texts, and videos are the two main forms of social media display about tourism, wine, and culture in Australia. Images and texts are usually shown information structure surface knowledge, with contents introductions, lists, and recommendations. The type of video content mainly includes the real experience of the content creator and publisher, the recommendation of scenic spots, and the explanation of characters. The content of the video is also more complete than the content of images & texts. Social media help the promotion of Australian tourism, wine, and culture is mainly presented to the audience in these two ways.

Publicity Strategy and Situation

Online

With the rapid development of the Internet era, the proportion of the network economy is gradually increasing. As a result, the variety of online transactions is increasing, even surpassing the well-established, offline sales model of "We-media" accounts which refer to online news sources operated by individuals or collectives who are often amateurs. offline sales model. The rapid rise of the new sales model also makes the network publicity gradually diversified (Schaffer, 2017). This part mainly discusses the online promotion methods and actual development of Australian tourism, wine, and culture on social media.

In recent years, we-media industry has risen rapidly, and many we-media people have emerged, who obtain traffic and income by publishing content on social platforms. We-media people have become a profession, and they are often called bloggers (Storm, 2022). With the rapid development of short videos, businesses choose to partner with bloggers who meet their needs. By partnering with these social media influencers, businesses can tap into their large number of followers to thereby targeting relevant consumer segment for their publicity needs and is becoming a popular tool for social media mangers.

Bloggers' paid partnerships and co-created promotion are low-cost and high return promotion method in the development of media. Partnering with bloggers has become the preferred method of promoting Australian tourism, wine, and culture on social media. Bloggers are selected based on the type of content they post and the number of followers they have (Quadros, 2022). Choose a travel expert, wine lover, or daily life vlogger (Video bloggers are also known as vloggers) to promote tourism, wine, and culture in Australia on social media platforms. These bloggers often use video to create content. Among them, bloggers' real travel experience is the content category that attracts the most viewers, so this kind of content has the best promotion effect. The advantages of working with bloggers are mainly the number of followers and promotional influence of bloggers.

Followers of social media influencers and blogger usually share their interest areas, and hence we can assume they are creating relevant content that are preferred by their follower base. A blogger's fan base can become a potential customer base. Through the blogger's promotion, followers can become tourists or consumers. There are many ways to collaborate with bloggers. For example, for the promotion of Australian wine, merchants can choose to send the wine to the blogger to taste or provide exclusive knowledge and give the blogger a commission according to the sales volume of the wine. Therefore, bloggers' cooperative promotion is a new publicity method after the progress of social media platforms.

The next type of publicity is a product of the rapid development of the Internet age, which is live streaming (Xie et al., 2022). Thanks to the popularity of 4G networks and the emergence of 5G networks in recent years, people can afford the bandwidth they need to be online in real-time. The main reason why live broadcast has become a very important way of publicity is that it allows the audience to interact with the host. A well-shot video is edited and shot by the content creator, but the content and technique may not meet the audience's psychological expectations. Live broadcasting can compensate for this.

The audience can let the host know their needs by posting comments, and the host can modify the live broadcast content at any time (Storm, 2022).

At present, the promotion content related to Australian tourism, wine, and culture mainly includes sales live broadcast and promotion live broadcast. Sales live streaming is to sell specific products through a live streaming platform and explanation. During the live broadcast, the host usually interacts with the audience through comments on the product to help consumers solve their queries about the product and try to meet their needs. Before the outbreak of COVID-19, many live broadcast rooms introduced and sold hotel rooms and tourism features for Australian tourists.

One of the reasons why the live broadcast for sale is popular among consumers is that the price of the live broadcast room is usually lower than the price when consumers buy it themselves. The businesses offer exclusion promotion codes and offers for immediate purchase decisions and are provided when promoting their brand through paid partnerships. In addition, to sell the product, anchors will also give a complete explanation and publicity to the product itself and its use background (Roggio, 2018). This approach has also boosted Australia's tourism and hospitality industry. After all, buying a night in a hotel room and experiencing local activities means visiting Australia at the same time.

The other type of live content is usually broadcast to promote something. Use live broadcasts to grasp consumers' interest points at any time and change the content of live broadcasts at any time. Promote by meeting the needs of the audience. This type of live broadcast usually uses the host to show the audience around or share their experience with the audience. For example, the wine culture of Australia is not very famous, or the effect is not obvious due to insufficient publicity. Before the COVID-19 pandemic, Australian wine culture made Australian wines known to more and more consumers through the promotion of Australian tourism (He & Zhu, 2020).

Due to the impact of the COVID-19 pandemic, Australian wine culture has also been introduced to Chinese audiences through promotional live broadcasts. Although the number of people and flow of Australian wine radio rooms are very small, the current wineries in Australia are more suitable for this kind of promotion. Because they need to spend a lot of time getting consumers to understand and get interested. Take Auscess winery in Australia as an example, the winery will show the wine tasting meeting to the online audience through live broadcast and also meet the audience's requirements to visit the winery environment.

At other times, the host of the live broadcast will regularly explain wine knowledge. This approach has helped Auscess winery accumulate a large number of consumers and visitors. This audience is not only a customer group accumulated by Auscess winery but also helps Australian wine culture improve development during this process.

This section briefly outlines two types of online promotion, but there are many other ways in which social media can help promote tourism, wine, and culture in Australia. Although offline promotion methods have limited, the offline promotion mode is still indispensable in consumers' minds.

Offline

From the current consumer market in various countries, the emergence of social media platforms enables consumers to discuss with each other and help answer questions. Online sales are booming, but offline channels are still essential. Back to the promotion itself, the product is richer and richer, more and more cost-effective, blind publicity doesn't achieve good results. Many industries choose to cooperate with other industries to promote and help each other. It is also an effective strategy to raise awareness of tourism, wine, and culture in Australia.

For example, prior to the COVID-19 pandemic, Australia's local wine industry was influenced by tourism, resulting in wine tourism. Visitors can learn about and buy Australian wines on their tour of Australia (Sigala, 2019). However, Australia's tourism industry has been hit hard by the COVID-19 pandemic. The development of the offline wine industry has also opened up cooperation models. The export wine selection is promoted and sold jointly with different industries in other countries. In restaurants, hotels, and other places where wine is needed, it can use wine with dishes and used in tasting meetings (Strickland et al., 2016). The advantage of offline promotion is that consumers can directly taste and appreciate the real product, and consumers may be interested in Australian wine because of taste, texture, and other factors. As well as selling wine, it helps to raise awareness of Australian wine culture.

Offline promotion can also make up for the deficiency of online channels and make use of offline advantages to help improve the promotion of Australian tourism and wine culture. For consumers, virtual description and viewing are still no substitute for real-world use. Consumers prefer real-world experiences and feelings, which is why offline channels exist. The strategy for improving publicity is to encourage consumers to make suggestions after playing (Flew & Kirkwood, 2020). Only according to the suggestions of consumers to improve, and then advertising can better meet the needs of consumers. Blind advertising should not exist.

For example, before the COVID-19 pandemic, many attractions in Australia conducted visitor satisfaction surveys after offline visits and events. After receiving feedback, the scenic spot offers rewards, such as a raffle or a reward like a custom-made doll after completing a questionnaire. But for some products that can be sold, consumers just need to complete the experience through online mails and feedback forms. On some social media platforms in China where Australian wines can be sold, merchants will offer preferential policies to encourage consumers to give feedback after using them. After feedback, merchants give product coupons or red cash envelopes.

Offline publicity means and development are far sparse and expensive than online. But to promote Australia's tourism and wine culture to Chinese tourists, offline channels must exist. At present, offline channel publicity is a supplementary and auxiliary promotion channel.

After discussion and summary, Chinese social media usually use images with texts, and videos to show Australian tourism, wine, and cultural content, and Chinese tourists also have a preliminary understanding and interest in relevant content through social media. The promotion of tourism, wine, and culture in Australia on social media has already had an impact on Chinese tourists. The social media content to promote Australia's tourism, wine, and culture is very comprehensive, and the content covered also reflects Australia's strengths and characteristics in various fields. It can be seen that social media is an indispensable media method for social development at present, and each social media platform carries a huge customer base. Not only does it help publishers who need publicity get noticed, but it also helps users organize various types of content.

CONCLUSION AND RECOMMENDATIONS

This chapter discusses the characteristics of Australian cities and specifically recommends and publicizes the uniqueness of each city to Chinese tourists. When introducing the characteristics of each city, focusing on tourism, wine, and culture. The results show that the publicity priorities of various regions in Australia are different, and the tour itinerary of various regions is varied and rich in their own regard. This chapter deals with the needs and ideas of Chinese tourists when discussing the relevant contents of digitization, cultural heritage, and wine tourism.

In terms of digitization, the CiteSpace tool is used to analyze the timeline of Australian wine tourism. In terms of cultural heritage, it mainly describes the unique cultural connotation of Australia. The results show that Australian culture is a specific display of comprehensive culture (Pavithra, 2021). In the future, the combination of digitalization and tourism can improve the tourism experience of tourists and help businesses improve efficiency. At the same time, digital tourism is not limited to offline. The development of online tourism is the choice in the future. Australian tourism and wine culture belong to the category of cultural heritage. We discussed specific online and offline ways of promotion for Australian wine tourism and culture to attract Chinese tourists.

This chapter also uses online survey tools to conduct a questionnaire survey for Chinese tourists and understand the promotion content of Australian wine tourism and culture through social media platforms. According to the analysis results, this chapter summarizes the attitudes and ideas of Chinese tourists on using social media to promote content. Show the specific presentation advantages of online and offline methods and how to use online methods to meet the limitations of offline publicity. This chapter discusses specific presentation forms of digital stories in social media and gives specific examples according to the actual situation. At the same time, it discusses the specific methods to promote the content of Australian wine tourism culture to Chinese tourists under the current social situation.

As a future direction we can explore if social media and wine tourism can promote the development of a sustainable tourism economy. The use of digital technology is in line with the concept of sustainable development. However, due to the defects of current digital technology, the concept of sustainable development cannot be presented perfectly (Vázquez et al., 2021). In the future of global competitive environment, the realization of sustainable tourism needs the continuous improvement of digital technology. The promotion of digital means that the realization of sustainable development of the global economy is just around the corner.

However, only the progress of digital technology cannot achieve sustainable economic development. This also requires the intervention of relevant national and government policies to put forward and implement the concept of sustainable economic development in enterprises (Factor et al., 2021). Digital tourism helps realize online tourism and reduce the burden on the local environment when meeting the tourism needs of consumers. Social media is an important expression method under the current sustainable development. Social media platform can not only meet the daily entertainment needs of people in the current society, but also cause lesser burden on the environment, nature, and other aspects. Tourism is responsible for roughly 8% of the world's carbon emissions. From plane flights and boat rides to souvenirs and lodging, numerous travel and stay activities contribute to tourism's carbon footprint[1].

Everything people do leaves a carbon footprint. When we are in the digital sphere, we still have an environmental footprint. This is largely the emissions from energy consumed to power the internet and the various devices we use. Furthermore, manufacturing, repairs, and disposal of these devices accumulates 'e-waste', creating significant impact on the environment, as many of the components in e-waste are not recovered, recycles and reused. When considering online and streamed events we should also consider any real-world production emissions. Social media, websites, online streaming of music and video, and storing data in a cloud all require the use of energy.

The reader of this chapter is using energy[2]. Another focus of discussion is the sustainability of wine tourism which is also very important. Sustainable wine tourism is a conscious development form integrating environmental, economic, and social forms. In the future, tourists can feel the power of nature again through unique tourism experience and taste wine in a sustainable environment. This is the significance of sustainable development of wine tourism. Finally, social media and wine tourism have the ability of sustainable development that cannot be ignored. In the global competitive environment, sustainable development is the best choice for future.

ACKNOWLEDGMENT

The authors extend sincere gratitude to:
- Our colleagues from Soochow University, the Australian Studies Centre of Shanghai University and Krirk University as well as the independent research colleagues who provided insight and expertise that greatly assisted the research, although they may not agree with all of the interpretations/conclusions of this chapter.
- China Knowledge for supporting our research.
- The Editor and the International Editorial Advisory Board (IEAB) of this book who initially desk reviewed, arranged a rigorous double/triple blind review process and conducted a thorough, minute and critical final review before accepting the chapter for publication.
- All anonymous reviewers who provided very constructive feedbacks for thorough revision, improvement and fine tuning of the chapter.

REFERENCES

Abram, N. J., Henley, B. J., Sen Gupta, A., Lippmann, T. J., Clarke, H., Dowdy, A. J., Sharples, J. J., Nolan, R. H., Zhang, T., Wooster, M. J., Wurtzel, J. B., Meissner, K. J., Pitman, A. J., Ukkola, A. M., Murphy, B. P., Tapper, N. J., & Boer, M. M. (2021). Connections of climate change and variability to large and extreme forest fires in Southeast Australia. *Communications Earth & Environment*, *2*(1), 8. Advance online publication. doi:10.103843247-020-00065-8

Bamberry, G., & Wickramasekara, R. (2012). Domestic and international strategies in the Queensland Wine Industry. *International Journal of Wine Business Research*, *24*(4), 302–318. doi:10.1108/17511061211280347

Belias, D., Velissariou, E., Kyriakou, D., Vasiliadis, L., Mantas, C., Sdrolias, L., Aspridis, G., & Kakkos, N. (2017). The importance of Customer Relationship Management and social media in the Greek wine tourism industry. *Innovative Approaches to Tourism and Leisure*, 249–259. doi:10.1007/978-3-319-67603-6_19

Boroujeni, M., Saberian, M., & Li, J. (2021). Environmental impacts of COVID-19 on Victoria, Australia, witnessed two waves of coronavirus. *Environmental Science and Pollution Research International*, *28*(11), 14182–14191. doi:10.100711356-021-12556-y PMID:33506421

Brabazon, T., Winter, M., & Gandy, B. (2014). Mark(ET)ing the bottle: Using QR codes to build new wine regions. *SpringerBriefs in Business*, 87–96. doi:10.1007/978-981-287-059-9_8

Bruwer, J., & Rueger-Muck, E. (2018). Wine tourism and hedonic experience: A motivation-based experiential view. *Tourism and Hospitality Research*, *19*(4), 488–502. doi:10.1177/1467358418781444

Bu, Y., Parkinson, J., & Thaichon, P. (2020). Digital Content Marketing as a catalyst for e-WOM in food tourism. *Australasian Marketing Journal*, *29*(2), 142–154. doi:10.1016/j.ausmj.2020.01.001

Carson, D. B., & Carson, D. A. (2019). *Disasters, market changes and 'the big smoke': Understanding the decline of remote tourism in Katherine*. Perspectives on Rural Tourism Geographies. doi:10.1007/978-3-030-11950-8_6

Dahlstrom, M. F. (2014). Using narratives and storytelling to communicate science with nonexpert audiences. *Proceedings of the National Academy of Sciences of the United States of America*, *111*(supplement_4), 13614–13620. doi:10.1073/pnas.1320645111 PMID:25225368

DeLorenzo, J., & Techera, E. J. (2018). Ensuring good governance of marine wildlife tourism: A case study of ray-based tourism at Hamelin Bay, Western Australia. *Asia Pacific Journal of Tourism Research*, *24*(2), 121–135. doi:10.1080/10941665.2018.1541186

Dhirasasna, N. N., Becken, S., & Sahin, O. (2020). A systems approach to examining the drivers and barriers of renewable energy technology adoption in the hotel sector in Queensland, Australia. *Journal of Hospitality and Tourism Management*, *42*, 153–172. doi:10.1016/j.jhtm.2020.01.001

Factor, A., Ulhøi, J. P., & Romm, N. (2021). Research on small and medium-sized enterprises and Sustainability. *Sustainability and Small and Medium-Sized Enterprises*, 26–47. doi:10.4324/9780429426377-2-2

Firth, R., Kala, J., Lyons, T. J., & Andrys, J. (2017). An analysis of regional climate simulations for Western Australia's wine regions—Model evaluation and future climate projections. *Journal of Applied Meteorology and Climatology*, *56*(7), 2113–2138. doi:10.1175/JAMC-D-16-0333.1

Flew, T., & Kirkwood, K. (2020). The impact of COVID-19 on cultural tourism: Art, culture and communication in four regional sites of Queensland, Australia. *Media International Australia*, *178*(1), 16–20. doi:10.1177/1329878X20952529

Fullerton, J. A., & Kendrick, A. (2011). Australia tourism advertising: A test of the bleed-over effect among us travelers. *Place Branding and Public Diplomacy*, *7*(4), 244–256. doi:10.1057/pb.2011.17

Furlong, Y., & Finnie, T. (2020). Culture counts: The diverse effects of culture and society on mental health amidst COVID-19 outbreak in Australia. *Irish Journal of Psychological Medicine*, *37*(3), 237–242. doi:10.1017/ipm.2020.37 PMID:32406358

Galati, A., Crescimanno, M., Tinervia, S., & Fagnani, F. (2017). Social media as a strategic marketing tool in the Sicilian wine industry: Evidence from Facebook. *Wine Economics and Policy*, *6*(1), 40–47. doi:10.1016/j.wep.2017.03.003

Gatti, M., Pirez, F. J., Frioni, T., Squeri, C., & Poni, S. (2018). Calibrated, delayed-cane winter pruning controls yield and significantly postpones berry ripening parameters in *vitis vinifera* L. cv. Pinot Noir. *Australian Journal of Grape and Wine Research*, *24*(3), 305–316. doi:10.1111/ajgw.12330

Genç, R. (2018). Catastrophe of environment: The impact of natural disasters on tourism industry. *Journal of Tourism & Adventure*, *1*(1), 86–94. doi:10.3126/jota.v1i1.22753

Gu, Q., & Huang, S. (2018). Profiling Chinese wine tourists by wine tourism constraints: A comparison of Chinese Australians and long-haul Chinese tourists in Australia. *International Journal of Tourism Research, 21*(2), 206–220. doi:10.1002/jtr.2255

Gu, Q., Qiu, H., King, B. E. M., & Huang, S. (2019). Understanding the wine tourism experience: The roles of facilitators, constraints, and involvement. *Journal of Vacation Marketing, 26*(2), 211–229. doi:10.1177/1356766719880253

He, H., & Zhu, L. (2020). Online shopping green product quality supervision strategy with consumer feedback and collusion behavior. *PLoS One, 15*(3), e0229471. Advance online publication. doi:10.1371/journal.pone.0229471 PMID:32126092

Jones, P. J. S. (2021). A governance analysis of Ningaloo and Shark Bay Marine Parks, Western Australia: Putting the 'eco' in tourism to build resilience but threatened in long-term by climate change? *Marine Policy, 127*, 103636. doi:10.1016/j.marpol.2019.103636

Khan, H. (2021). Buying behavior of online consumers during COVID-19 – buying behavior, payment mode, and critical factors affecting consumers buying behavior during the pandemic. *Journal of Management and Training for Industries, 8*(2), 1–23. doi:10.12792/JMTI.8.2.1

Knight, H., Megicks, P., Agarwal, S., & Leenders, M. A. A. M. (2018). Firm Resources and the development of environmental sustainability among small and medium-sized enterprises: Evidence from the Australian wine industry. *Business Strategy and the Environment, 28*(1), 25–39. doi:10.1002/bse.2178

Kortt, M. A., Sinnewe, E., & Pervan, S. J. (2018). The gender wage gap in the tourism industry: Evidence from Australia. *Tourism Analysis, 23*(1), 137–149. doi:10.3727/108354217X15143857878697

Lacorde, M. (2019). Assessing the environmental characteristics of the Margaret River Wine Region, Australia. *International Journal of Applied Geospatial Research, 10*(3), 1–24. doi:10.4018/IJAGR.2019070101

Leonard, S., Parsons, M., Olawsky, K., & Kofod, F. (2013). The role of culture and traditional knowledge in climate change adaptation: Insights from East Kimberley, Australia. *Global Environmental Change, 23*(3), 623–632. doi:10.1016/j.gloenvcha.2013.02.012

Li, X., & Liu, Q. (2020). Social media use, eHealth Literacy, disease knowledge, and preventive behaviors in the COVID-19 pandemic: Cross-sectional study on Chinese netizens. *Journal of Medical Internet Research, 22*(10), e19684. Advance online publication. doi:10.2196/19684 PMID:33006940

Maghradze, D., Aslanishvili, A., Mdinaradze, I., Tkemaladze, D., Mekhuzla, L., Lordkipanidze, D., Jalabadze, M., Kvavadze, E., Rusishvili, N., McGovern, P., This, P., Bacilieri, R., Failla, O., Cola, G., Mariani, L., Toffolatti, S. L., Lorenzis, G. D., Bianco, P. A., Quaglino, F., ... Davitashvili, L. (2019). Progress for research of grape and wine culture in Georgia, the South Caucasus. *BIO Web of Conferences, 12*, 03003. 10.1051/bioconf/20191203003

Menacer, R., & Becherair, A. (2019). The impact of the tourism sector on economic growth in Algeria: An analytical and econometric study (1990-2014). *Management & Economics Research Journal, 1*(1), 174–189. doi:10.48100/merj.v1i1.21

Mileham, A. (2022, February 3). *Chinese tariffs cost Australian exports AUS$1BN as overall exports plummet.* The Drinks Business. Retrieved July 20, 2022, from https://www.thedrinksbusiness.com/2022/02/chinese-tariffs-cost-australian-exports-1-billion-as-overall-value-of-exports-plummet-by-30/

Minazzi, R. (2014). Social media impacts on travel suppliers: Social media marketing. *Social Media Marketing in Tourism and Hospitality*, 77–126. doi:10.1007/978-3-319-05182-6_4

Okumus, B. (2020). Food Tourism Research: A perspective article. *Tourism Review*, 76(1), 38–42. doi:10.1108/TR-11-2019-0450

Olsen, S. J., Azziz-Baumgartner, E., Budd, A. P., Brammer, L., Sullivan, S., Pineda, R. F., Cohen, C., & Fry, A. M. (2020). Decreased influenza activity during the COVID-19 pandemic—United States, Australia, Chile, and South Africa, 2020. *American Journal of Transplantation*, 20(12), 3681–3685. doi:10.1111/ajt.16381 PMID:33264506

Overton, J., Murray, W. E., & Howson, K. (2019). Doing good by drinking wine? Ethical value networks and upscaling of wine production in Australia, New Zealand and South Africa. *European Planning Studies*, 27(12), 2431–2449. doi:10.1080/09654313.2019.1628181

Patel, S. B., Umar, R., Patel, N., & Chugh, R. (2019). Likes, comments and shares on social media: Exploring user engagement with a state tourism facebook page. *International Journal of Web Based Communities*, 15(2), 1. doi:10.1504/IJWBC.2019.10020618

Pavithra, A. (2021). Towards developing a comprehensive conceptual understanding of positive hospital culture and approaches to healthcare organisational culture change in Australia. *Journal of Health Organization and Management*, 36(1), 105–120. doi:10.1108/JHOM-10-2020-0385 PMID:33837683

Perkumienė, D., Pranskūnienė, R., Vienažindienė, M., & Grigienė, J. (2020). The right to a clean environment: Considering Green Logistics and sustainable tourism. *International Journal of Environmental Research and Public Health*, 17(9), 3254. doi:10.3390/ijerph17093254 PMID:32392737

Quadros, M. X. (2022, February 3). 12 tried-and-true ways to promote your blog posts. *HubSpot Blog*. Retrieved April 5, 2022, from https://blog.hubspot.com/marketing/blog-promotion-tactics

Raftery, D. (2017). Producing value from Australia's vineyards: An ethnographic approach to 'The quality turn' in the Australian Wine Industry. *Journal of Political Ecology*, 24(1). Advance online publication. doi:10.2458/v24i1.20877

Richardson, S., March, R., Lewis, J., & Radel, K. (2015). Analysing the impact of the 2011 natural disasters on the Central Queensland tourism industry. *Tourism Crisis and Disaster Management in the Asia-Pacific*, 149–160. doi:10.1079/9781780643250.0149

Ristic, R., Danner, L., Johnson, T. E., Meiselman, H. L., Hoek, A. C., Jiranek, V., & Bastian, S. E. P. (2019). Wine-related aromas for different seasons and occasions: Hedonic and emotional responses of wine consumers from Australia, UK and USA. *Food Quality and Preference*, 71, 250–260. doi:10.1016/j.foodqual.2018.07.011

Roggio, A. (2018, January 2). Live streaming can promote ecommerce products. *Practical Ecommerce*. Retrieved April 5, 2022, from https://www.practicalecommerce.com/live-streaming-can-promote-ecommerce-products

Roth, R. E. (2020). Cartographic design as visual storytelling: Synthesis and review of map-based narratives, genres, and tropes. *The Cartographic Journal*, 58(1), 83–114. doi:10.1080/00087041.2019.1633103

Schaffer, N. (2017, September 7). Social Media Promotion - 11 effective ways to boost your content. *11 Effective Ways to Use Social Media to Promote Your Content*. Retrieved April 5, 2022, from http://www.curata.com/blog/11-effective-ways-to-use-social-media-to-promote-your-content/

Sigala, M. (2019). The transformational power of wine tourism experiences: The socio-cultural profile of Wine Tourism in South Australia. *Social Sustainability in the Global Wine Industry*, 57–73. doi:10.1007/978-3-030-30413-3_5

Sigala, M., & Haller, C. (2018). The impact of social media on the behavior of wine tourists: A typology of power sources. *Management and Marketing of Wine Tourism Business*, 139–154. doi:10.1007/978-3-319-75462-8_8

Son, I. S., Huang, S., & Padovan, D. (2021). Realising the goals of event leveraging: The tourism and hospitality SME Perspective. *Journal of Hospitality and Tourism Management*, 49, 253–259. doi:10.1016/j.jhtm.2021.09.018

Sottini, V. A., Barbierato, E., Bernetti, I., & Capecchi, I. (2021). Impact of climate change on wine tourism: An approach through social media data. *Sustainability*, 13(13), 7489. doi:10.3390u13137489

Storm, M. (2022, March 18). 5 types of social media for growing your business strategy. *WebFX*. Retrieved April 5, 2022, from https://www.webfx.com/blog/social-media/types-of-social-media/

Strickland, P., Williams, K. M., Laing, J., & Frost, W. (2016). The use of social media in the wine event industry: A case study of the high country harvest in Australia. *Successful Social Media and Ecommerce Strategies in the Wine Industry*, 74–92. doi:10.1057/9781137602985_5

Sujová, E., Čierna, H., & Żabińska, I. (2019). Application of digitization procedures of production in practice. *Management Systems in Production Engineering*, 27(1), 23–28. doi:10.1515/mspe-2019-0004

Sun, Y.-Y., & Drakeman, D. (2021). The double-edged sword of wine tourism: The economic and environmental impacts of wine tourism in Australia. *Journal of Sustainable Tourism*, 30(4), 932–949. doi:10.1080/09669582.2021.1903018

Taylor, N., Miller, P., Coomber, K., Livingston, M., Scott, D., Buykx, P., & Chikritzhs, T. (2021). The impact of a minimum unit price on wholesale alcohol supply trends in the Northern Territory, Australia. *Australian and New Zealand Journal of Public Health*, 45(1), 26–33. doi:10.1111/1753-6405.13055 PMID:33559964

Travel Guides. (2021, December 18). *7 most beautiful regions in Australia*. Touropia. Retrieved April 24, 2022, from https://www.touropia.com/regions-in-australia-map/

Vázquez Vicente, G., Martín Barroso, V., & Blanco Jiménez, F. J. (2021). Sustainable tourism, economic growth and employment—The case of the wine routes of Spain. *Sustainability*, *13*(13), 7164. doi:10.3390u13137164

Walker, H. V., Jones, J. E., Swarts, N. D., & Kerslake, F. (2021). Manipulating nitrogen and water resources for improved cool climate vine to wine quality. *American Journal of Enology and Viticulture*, *73*(1), 11–25. doi:10.5344/ajev.2021.21004

Wang, X., Huang, S., Zou, T., & Yan, H. (2012). Effects of the high speed rail network on China's Regional Tourism Development. *Tourism Management Perspectives*, *1*, 34–38. doi:10.1016/j.tmp.2011.10.001

Ward, M. P., Xiao, S., & Zhang, Z. (2020). The role of climate during the COVID-19 epidemic in New South Wales, Australia. *Transboundary and Emerging Diseases*, *67*(6), 2313–2317. doi:10.1111/tbed.13631 PMID:32438520

Wen, J., & Huang, S. (2021). The effects of fashion lifestyle, perceived value of luxury consumption, and tourist–destination identification on visit intention: A study of Chinese cigar aficionados. *Journal of Destination Marketing & Management*, *22*, 100664. doi:10.1016/j.jdmm.2021.100664

Xie, C., Yu, J., Huang, S., & Zhang, J. (2022). Tourism e-commerce live streaming: Identifying and testing a value-based marketing framework from the Live Streamer Perspective. *Tourism Management*, *91*, 104513. doi:10.1016/j.tourman.2022.104513

Yang, S.-Y., & Chen, K.-Y. (2020). Development of a cloud tourism supported platform with friendly interfaces based on linked open data and Big Data Analysis Techniques. *2020 International Symposium on Computer, Consumer and Control (IS3C)*. 10.1109/IS3C50286.2020.00102

Young, A. (2021, May 6). *Premiumisation of Australia's wine exports continues*. National Liquor News. Retrieved July 20, 2022, from https://theshout.com.au/national-liquor-news/premiumisation-of-australias-wine-exports-continues/

Zhang, H. F., Cheng, X. J., & Shi, Y. T. (2012). Study on 3D modeling for history building and precision analyzing. *Advanced Materials Research*, *443-444*, 471–476. doi:10.4028/www.scientific.net/AMR.443-444.471

Chapter 3
"Green" Fine Dining Restaurants

Merve Özgür Göde
Anadolu University, Turkey

ABSTRACT

Food and beverage businesses have recently started to use sustainable practices. The "green restaurant" is an eco-label that restaurants receive as a result of these practices. Today, almost any type of restaurant can become a green restaurant. This study examines the processes of fine dining restaurants to become "green restaurants" and to determine which criteria are prominent in them. The study revealed that fine dining "green restaurants" received fewer points in the transparency and education and building categories in the process of becoming green restaurants.

INTRODUCTION

Due to the increase in sustainable practices in all sectors, food and beverage businesses have also started to implement sustainable activities. Food and beverage businesses affect the sustainability of the natural environment in which they operate by the consumption of significant amounts of natural resources. The sustainable and efficient use of natural resources in the food and beverage sector reduces the undesirable environmental impacts of the sector. Therefore, food and beverage businesses should turn to sustainable practices. Sustainable restaurants have developed from the need to meet even higher number of consumers who want sustainable healthy food and who are aware that having certain lifestyle habits decreases environmental impact (Güneş, 2019).

Recently, with the increasing environmental awareness of consumers and businesses, the green restaurant trend has been a growing trend (Hu, Parsa, & Self, 2010). Food and beverage businesses that adopt green practices can receive the "green restaurant" eco-label. Consumers who care about the environment, care about sustainability and act with sensitivity pay attention to these factors in restaurant selection. In this context, the green restaurant eco label makes a difference for restaurants. With the increase of conscious consumers, food and beverage businesses have started to focus on being environmentally friendly to meet their expectations. In this respect, restaurants need to adopt green practices in terms of sustainability and profitability (Namkung & Jang, 2013: 86).

DOI: 10.4018/978-1-6684-4645-4.ch003

Green restaurant practices can be listed as using biodegradable products, actively conserving energy and natural resources, purchasing energy-efficient equipment, reducing and recycling waste, and participating in environmental protection programs (Schubert, 2008).

Fine dining generally is a luxury restaurant that is usually for people who seek high quality, extravagant menu, affordable food, and unique ambiance (Rozeki et al., 2016). Furthermore, most of the luxury restaurants are considered to be at the top level of the restaurant types, not only regarding price but also food and beverage quality, decoration, style, influence, and service (Kiatkawsin & Sutherland, 2020). Luxury restaurants sometimes over-consume in order to give their customers the luxury they promise. This situation brings with it excessive energy and water use, and waste.

Therefore, fine dining restaurants must be becoming green restaurants. This study aims to examine the processes of fine dining restaurants to become green restaurants and to determine which criteria are prominent in green restaurants.

CONCEPTUAL FRAMEWORK

In this section, the concept of the "green restaurant" is mentioned and then information about the two most known green restaurant establishments is provided.

Green Restaurants

Food and beverage businesses are service organizations which form a significant part of the service industry which is considered an intangible concept. However, food and beverage businesses use some tangible components while providing their services. The tangible components of food and beverage businesses influence the environment (Ismail, Kassim, & Zahari, 2010). These businesses use high energy as they are open most of the day during each day of the year. Restaurant businesses, which are growing in number daily, have a large share of the increasing greenhouse gas emissions and waste around the world (Kozak, Keser, Büken, & Zaimoğlu, 2019). Restaurants must diminish the damage they cause to the environment.

The effects of food and beverage businesses on nature can be listed as follows:

- Energy consumption required for food preparation and cooling
- Water consumption for food and environment cleaning
- Food supply
- Use of chemical
- Waste food

Lorenzini (1994) defines green restaurants as new or reconstructed buildings designed to be environmentally friendly and energy efficient. Green restaurants have advantages with regards to cost management, market differentiation, and environmental protection (Schubert, 2008; Hu et al., 2010). It is significant to reduce, reuse and recycle (reduce-reuse-recycle), which is valid for green restaurants and consists of 3R's (Gilg, Barr, & Ford, 2005). At the same time, energy efficiency, which consists of 2E's, should also be considered for green generation restaurants (Gilg, Barr, & Ford, 2005). Green restaurants should adopt a green marketing approach in their businesses. Green marketing can be defined as the processes and activities carried out by companies by offering environmentally friendly products or services to create customer satisfaction (Tan & Yeap, 2012; Soonthonsmai, 2007).

When the studies related to the green restaurants in general are examined, it is seen that the studies mostly cover the topics such as marketing, consumer behavior, purchasing behavior, and restaurant preference (Wang et al., 2013; DiPietro & Partlow, 2013; Dipietro, Gregry, & Jackson, 2013; Namkung & Jang, 2014; Chen, Cheng, & Hsu, 2015; Kwok, Huang, & Hu, 2016; Xu & Jeon, 2019; Karagiannis & Andrinos, 2021; Băltescu et al., 2022; Mejia et al., 2022; Nyamogosa & Obonyo, 2022).

Wang et al. (2013) suggested that green restaurant management standards consist three facets (green foods; green environment and equipment; and green management and social responsibility), nine sub-facets, and 81 indicators. DiPietro and Partlow (2013) suggested in their study that green restaurant managers should choose more specific marketing strategies in their marketing activities. They also emphasized the provision of employee training on green practices in restaurants. Dipietro, Gregory, and Jackson (2013) suggested green practices should be implemented by restaurants to increase awareness of such practices to the general public.

Dewald, Bruin, and Jang (2014) indicated that more than half of consumers were willing to pay more for the "green" restaurant experience. In addition, authors found that consumers' decision to dine at a "green" restaurant in the following order of importance: fresh ingredients, healthy aspects, good value, easy access, and good for the environment. Namkung and Jang (2014) revealed that more than two-thirds of restaurant customers would be willing to pay extra money for green restaurant practices. Age, previous experience, involvement, and self-perception were found to be significant in accessing consumers' willingness to pay more for green practices in restaurants.

Chen, Cheng, and Hsu, (2015) suggested in their study that green restaurants should refer to restaurants that provide green food on their menus, such as organic, local and sustainable food, and restaurants that integrate green practices into their service processes to implement the idea of environmental conservation and ecological care. Kwok, Huang, and Hu (2016) investigated which of a restaurant's green attributes consumers deem most important and how consumers' attitudes toward various green attributes affect their behavioral intentions. Their findings indicate women were inclined to rate higher than men in all three categories of green attributes.

Xu and Jeon (2019) demonstrated that benefit-based messages are generally more persuasive than attribute-based messages in green restaurant advertisements. For fine dining restaurants, a green advertisement with benefit-based information would be more convincing than attribute-based information. Karagiannis and Andrinos (2021) identified the role that restaurant sustainability practices play on tourists' choices and specifically on city branding. As a result of the study, it was found that sustainable restaurant practices play in customer satisfaction as it relates to a potential re-visit of a destination.

Băltescu et al. (2022) discussed that sustainability in restaurants and the Covid 19 pandemic exist together. The study found five topics of discussion highlighting the managers' growing interest in finding solutions to counteract negative effects on the environment, ensure the wellbeing of customers and employees, and increase the profitability of their company.

Mejia et al. (2022) determined that U.S. restaurants' social sustainability practices. In the study, both theoretical and practical suggestions were provided. Theoretical implications exposed emphasis on individual justice in a highly specific temporal context. The practical contributions of the study are about community-based social sustainability initiatives. Nyamogosa and Obonyo (2022) investigated that sustainable business strategies for fast-food restaurant growth. This study revealed that three dimensions of sustainability should be applied in fast food restaurants.

Green Restaurant Establishments

There are organizations related to the green restaurant business in the world. One of the most prominent of these is the Sustainable Restaurant Association (SRA). The SRA is a community of food service businesses, suppliers, and discerning diners working together to create a sustainable food service industry for people and the planet. Their vision is to be the intersection of the foodservice industry and the sustainable food movement. As well as membership, the SRA rewards and celebrates restaurants that are leading the field with a 'sustainability rating' based on an independent accreditation covering all the different aspects of the restaurant's operations.

The SRA also highlights issues such as declining fish stocks, food waste, and animal welfare through consumer campaigns designed to engage the public and encourage them to make more sustainable choices whether dining out or in. The SRA was founded with the idea emphasizing that everyone has the right to eat out, but what is eaten and served is vital. It also advocates that food and beverage businesses should have an environmentally remedial effect (Sustainable Restaurants Association, 2022).

The SRA provides consultancy services focused on society, resources (supply), and the environment (Sustainable Restaurant Association, 2022). The working areas of the SRA are listed as follows:

- local and seasonal products
- serve more veg and better meat
- support global farmers
- sustainable fishing
- fair trade
- employee training
- healthy eating
- responsibility in marketing
- be with the local community
- ensuring the supply chain by considering the environment and collection impact
- waste management energy use
- water use

The SRA gives some suggestions to restaurants to be sustainable such as:

- Rebuild your menu
- Find new suppliers
- Make and share a to-do list
- Plot your path to higher public benefit
- Promote your sustainability successes to colleagues, investors, partners, and customers

One Planet Plate is a global restaurant campaign to put sustainability on the menu. In this way, chefs around the world can show their customers how they are contributing to the future of food (Sustainable Restaurant Association, 2022). Another organization is the Green Restaurant Association (GRA) which provides green restaurant recommendations for manufacturers, restaurants, and suppliers. The GRA is a non-profit organization established in 1990 that sets guidelines and certifies restaurants to make them more environmentally responsible and operates in 47 US states and Canada.

There are seven training courses on the web page of the association: "Energy, water, recycling, waste, chemicals, construction, and food". In addition, the association also issues employee certificates to employees who want to benefit individually. The association, which has been working actively for 29 years, gives a "green restaurant" certificate to restaurants.

The standards of this certificate consist of eight environmental categories that include the following (GRA, 2021):

1. Water Efficiency and Use: In this standard, it is emphasized to increase the efficiency of water use in toilets, taps, laundry, and garden.
2. Waste Reduction and Recycling: This section highlights the need to switch to recycled products with non-wood fiber paper products. These are napkins, paper towels, toilet paper, office paper, takeaway containers, coffee jackets, plates, and bowls.
3. Green Buildings: Green design and construction practices significantly reduce or eliminate the harmful effects of buildings on the environment, occupants, and the local community.
4. Sustainable Food: Sustainable food products support the long-term maintenance of ecosystems and agriculture for future generations. Organic farming prohibits the use of toxic synthetic pesticides and fertilizers, irradiation, sewage, and genetic engineering. Locally grown foods primarily reduce the amount of pollution carried by fossil fuels. Plant-based foods require fewer natural resources and create less pollution per product consumed. In this context, the imperative emphasis under this title is supporting organic agriculture and emphasizing locality.
5. Energy Efficiency and Utilization: This standard emphasizes increasing the energy efficiency of lighting, cooling, air conditioning, and gas appliances.
6. Renewable Energy: Electricity and energy can be obtained from renewable sources such as wind, solar, geothermal, and biomass. These energy sources cause significantly less air pollution and environmental damage compared to fossil fuel, nuclear and large-scale hydroelectric energy sources.
7. Reducing Chemicals and Pollution: It is emphasized to avoid the use of chemicals in dishwashing detergents, germ killers, disinfectants, toilet bowl cleaners, drains cleaner, floor washing, floor polish, glass cleaners, degreasers, and laundry detergents.
8. Transparency and Education. All employees, managers, and business owners should be trained on green practices. This training should explain storage areas, water pollution, air pollution and global warming, and the effects of the restaurant on the environment.

The GRA standards reflect 29 years of research in the field of restaurants and the environment. Thousands of restaurants and hundreds of thousands of restaurant personnel have provided the living laboratory for the continued evolution of the GRA Standards. The purpose of the GRA standards is to provide a transparent way to measure each restaurant's environmental accomplishments while providing a pathway for the next steps each restaurant can take towards increased environmental sustainability (GRA, 2019).

METHODOLOGY

Approach and Research Design

Qualitative research methods were used in this study to examine the processes of fine dining restaurants to become green restaurants and to determine which criteria are prominent in green restaurants. Qualitative research uses qualitative data collection methods such as observation, interview, and document analysis, and reveals perceptions and events realistically and holistically in the natural environment (Yıldırım & Şimşek, 2013). In the research, the qualitative research design was used to reveal the fine dining restaurant's process of becoming a green restaurant.

In the study, restaurants that have received certificates according to GRA criteria were examined. First, the official website of GRA was examined through content analysis method. Then, the total green points of fine dining restaurants that have received GRA certificate and which criteria are more important for this restaurant was described in detail.

Data Collection

In this study, data were collected using the document analysis method which includes the analysis of written materials containing information about the case or cases that are to be studied (Yıldırım & Şimşek, 2008). The data of the research were obtained by examining the official page of the GRA. When the website is examined, it is seen that the association gives certificates to many types of restaurants. In addition, the association classifies green restaurants. There is five classifications of the green restaurant: Level 1, 2 stars, 3 stars, 4 star, and sustainable badge (GRA, 2022). Among the food and beverage businesses on the website, those with fine dining restaurants were selected.

Data Analysis

The data collected by the document analysis method were analyzed with descriptive analysis. The main purpose of descriptive analysis is to reach concepts and relationships that can explain the collected data. The descriptive analysis consists of four stages (Yıldırım & Şimşek, 2013):

- Creating a framework for descriptive analysis
- Processing of data according to the thematic framework
- Description of findings
- Interpretation of the findings

FINDINGS

According to the findings obtained from the document analysis, there are 21 restaurants in the fine dining restaurant category. Six of these restaurants are Level 1, nine are 2-star, and six are three-star green restaurants. There is no four-star fine dining restaurants. All 21 restaurants are located in the United States. There is no restaurant in the fine dining restaurant category that has received a green restaurant certificate (GRA) from Canada other than America. Each restaurant examined was given a code as R1, R2…

The findings obtained from the document analysis were analyzed under eight themes. All of the factors in the green restaurant certificate issued by GRA were taken as a theme. The themes are listed as follows:

- Energy standards
- Water standards
- Waste standards
- Disposables standards
- Chemicals standards
- Food standards
- Building standards
- Transparency and education standards

1. Findings regarding energy standards

In the energy category, points are taken from 10 parts including the following:

- Healing, Cooling, and Ventilation
- Water heating
- Miscellaneous
- Lighting
- Kitchen Equipment-Cooking
- Kitchen Equipment-Refrigeration
- Annual Maintenance
- Official Equipment
- On-site energy production
- Renewable energy credits

Table 1 shows the energy scores of the restaurants.

The average energy score of Level 1 restaurants is 21.30, the average energy score of 2-star restaurants is 36.47, and the energy average of 3-star restaurants is 56.53. The average energy score of 21 restaurants is 37.87. Accordingly, the energy score of level 1 restaurants remains below the general average. The restaurant with the highest energy score is R17 and the restaurant with the lowest energy score is R3.

2. Findings regarding water efficiency standards

In the water efficiency category, points are taken from four parts which are the following:

- Landscaping
- Kitchen
- Restrooms
- Other

Table 2 shows the water efficiency scores of the restaurants.

Table 1. The energy scores of the restaurants

Restaurant	Level 1	2 Star	3 star
R1	25,45		
R2	21,48		
R3	**8,88**		
R4	20,5		
R5	41,03		
R6	10,5		
R7		17,49	
R8		41,78	
R9		38,65	
R10		16,75	
R11		50,12	
R12		32,61	
R13		34,74	
R14		29,96	
R15		66,16	
R16			41
R17			**77,86**
R18			43,69
R19			61,99
R20			57,95
R21			56,7
Average of classifications	21,30	36,47	56,53
Total Average		37,87	

Table 2. The water efficiency scores of the restaurants

Restaurant	Level 1	2 Star	3 Star
R1	**0**		
R2	14,28		
R3	2		
R4	**0**		
R5	14,13		
R6	5,17		
R7		10,25	
R8		12,5	
R9		15,5	
R10		12	
R11		11,41	
R12		12,6	
R13		11,75	
R14		12,6	
R15		16,16	
R16			10,25
R17			24,11
R18			16
R19			12,75
R20			12,75
R21			17
Average of classifications	5,93	12,75	15,47
Total Average		11,58	

The average water efficiency score of level 1 restaurants is 5,93, the average water efficiency score of 2-star restaurants is 12,75, and the water efficiency average of 3-star restaurants is 15,47. The average water efficiency score of 21 restaurants is 37.87. Accordingly, the water efficiency score of level 1 restaurants remains below the total average. The restaurant with the highest water efficiency score is R21 and the restaurant with the lowest water efficiency score is R1 and R4.

3. Findings regarding waste standards

In the waste category, points are taken from the following six parts:

- Recycling and composting
- Construction recycling
- Hazardous waste
- Waste reduction-office

"Green" Fine Dining Restaurants

- Waste reduction - disposable products and packaging
- Waste reduction- food

Table 3 shows the waste scores of the restaurants.

Table 3. The waste scores of the restaurants

Restaurant	Level 1	2 Star	3 Star
R1	54,5		
R2	**61,25**		
R3	52		
R4	**20**		
R5	37,5		
R6	30,75		
R7		54	
R8		22	
R9		51,5	
R10		51,5	
R11		52,5	
R12		31,88	
R13		27,88	
R14		27,38	
R15		28	
R16			35,75
R17			57,5
R18			49,25
R19			51,30
R20			53,95
R21			48,5
Average of classifications	42,66	38,51	49,37
Total Average	42,80		

The average waste score of level 1 restaurants is 42,66, the average waste score of 2-star restaurants is 36.47, and the energy average of 3-star restaurants is 49,37. The average waste score of 21 restaurants is 42,80. Accordingly, the waste score of 2-star restaurants remains below the general average. The restaurant with the highest waste score is R2 and the restaurant with the lowest waste score is R4.

4. Findings regarding disposables standards

In the disposable category, points are taken from the following three parts:

- Reusability
- Food service disposables and packaging
- Other recycled paper items

Table 4 shows the disposable scores of the restaurants.

Table 4. The disposable scores of the restaurants

Restaurant	Level 1	2 Star	3 Star
R1	8,75		
R2	10,35		
R3	12		
R4	**3,63**		
R5	4,35		
R6	7,74		
R7		20,5	
R8		20	
R9		14,21	
R10		11	
R11		12,94	
R12		14,5	
R13		11,25	
R14		14,5	
R15		10,58	
R16			10,88
R17			**25,97**
R18			23,15
R19			13,09
R20			16,32
R21			20,58
Average of classifications	7,80	14,38	18,33
Total Average		13,63	

The average disposable score of level 1 restaurants is 7,80, the average disposable score of 2-star restaurants is 14,38, and the average disposable score of 3-star restaurants is 18,33. The average disposable score of 21 restaurants is 13,63. Accordingly, the disposable score of level 1 restaurants remains below the total average. The restaurant with the highest waste score is R17 and the restaurant with the lowest waste score is R4.

5. Findings regarding chemical standards

In the chemical category, points are taken from the following nine parts:

- Transportation
- Site selection
- Stormwater management
- Transportation, petroleum reduction
- Chemical reduction
- Pest management
- Light pollution
- Chemicals
- Building Materials

Table 5 shows the chemical scores of the restaurants

Table 5. The chemical scores of the restaurants

Restaurant	Level 1	2 Star	3 Star
R1	20		
R2	12		
R3	3,75		
R4	5,5		
R5	4,35		
R6	**3,25**		
R7		11	
R8		12,88	
R9		14,21	
R10		13,18	
R11		15,1	
R12		17,68	
R13		10,3	
R14		17,83	
R15		16,16	
R16			12,25
R17			27,18
R18			29,29
R19			**32,31**
R20			12,68
R21			10,84
Average of classifications	**8,14**	**14,26**	**20,75**
Total Average	**14,36**		

The average chemical score of level 1 restaurants is 8,14, the average chemical score of 2-star restaurants is 14,26, and the average chemical score of 3-star restaurants is 20,75. The average chemical score of 21 restaurants is 14,36. Accordingly, the chemical score of level 1 restaurants remains below the total average. The restaurant with the highest waste score is R19 and the restaurant with the lowest waste score is R6.

6. Findings regarding food standards

Foods are evaluated in five different categories (GRA, 2022):

1. Local: Food transported 100 miles or less from farm/orchard to your plate, using the most direct transportation route
2. Regional: Food transported 300 miles or less from farm/orchard to your plate, using the most direct transportation route
3. 400-Mile Radius: Food sourced, processed and delivered from farm /orchard to plate within 400-mile radius of your restaurant
4. Certified humanely raised and handled: Certified Humane, Animal Welfare Approved, American Grass-fed, American Humane Certified, Global Animal Partnership 4, 5 and 5+
5. Sustainable Seafood: Favorably listed by Monterey Bay Aquarium, ASC, OceanWise, or MSC Certified

In the food category, points are taken from the following two parts:

- Items
- Based on % of Purchases

Table 6 shows the food scores of the restaurants

The average food score of level 1 restaurants is 35,04, the average food score of 2-star restaurants is 25,46, and the average food score of 3-star restaurants is 44,27. The average food score of 21 restaurants is 33,11. Accordingly, the food score of 2-star restaurants remains below the total average. The restaurant with the highest food score is R4 and the restaurant with the lowest waste score is R12.

7. Findings regarding building standards

In the building category, points are taken from the following three parts:

- Furnishings
- Building materials
- Other (equipment, cookware, uniforms, merchandise.)

Table 7 shows the building scores of the restaurants

The building score average of Level 1 restaurants is 3,6, the building score average of 2-star restaurants is 0,8, and the building average of 3-star restaurants is 3,83. The average building score of 21 restaurants is 2,33. Accordingly, the building score of 2-star restaurants remains below the total average. Most of the restaurants did not get points from the building standards. R18 received the highest building score.

Table 6. The food scores of the restaurants

Restaurant	Level 1	2 Star	3 Star
R1	25		
R2	16,85		
R3	13,85		
R4	**100**		
R5	19,53		
R6		26,85	
R7		37,45	
R8		30,5	
R9		31,45	
R10		37,65	
R11		16,4	
R12		**13**	
R13		15,5	
R14		21,5	
R15		24,31	
R16			67,3
R17			34
R18			49,25
R19			15,23
R20			47,88
R21			52
Average of classifications	35,04	25,46	44,27
Total Average		33,11	

Table 7. The building scores of the restaurants

Restaurant	Level 1	2 Star	3 Star
R1	0		
R2	2		
R3	0		
R4	16		
R5	0		
R6		0	
R7		4	
R8		0	
R9		0	
R10		0	
R11		0	
R12		0	
R13		0	
R14		0	
R15		4	
R16			0
R17			3
R18			**20**
R19			0
R20			0
R21			0
Average of classifications	3,6	0,8	3,83
Total Average		2,33	

8. Findings regarding transparency and education standards

In the transparency and education category, points are taken from these two parts:

- Transparency
- Education

Table 8 shows the transparency and education scores of the restaurants

The average transparency and education score of level 1 restaurants are 0,66, the average transparency and education score of 2-star restaurants is 0,66, and the average transparency and education score of 3-star restaurants is 0,16. The average transparency and education score of 21 restaurants is 0,52. Accordingly, the transparency and education score of 3-star restaurants remains below the total average. The restaurant with the highest food score is R8.

9. Findings regarding total green points of the restaurant

Table 9 shows the total green scores of all restaurants

When the total green scores of 21 restaurants are examined, it has the highest score of R17 (250,62). R17 is a three-star green restaurant. The restaurant with the lowest score is R6 with 93.13 points. R6 is a level 1 green restaurant.

Table 8. The transparency and education scores of the restaurants

Restaurant	Level 1	2 Star	3 Star
R1	0		
R2	1		
R3	1		
R4	2		
R5	0		
R6	0		
R7		0	
R8		4	
R9		0	
R10		0	
R11		2	
R12		0	
R13		0	
R14		0	
R15		0	
R16			0
R17			1
R18			0
R19			0
R20			0
R21			0
Average of classifications	0,66	0,66	0,16
Total Average		0,52	

Table 9. Total Green Points of Restaurants

Restaurants	Total Green Points
R1	133,7
R2	139,21
R3	93,13
R4	167,63
R5	116,54
R6	**84,26**
R7	154,69
R8	143,66
R9	162,56
R10	142,08
R11	158,47
R12	122,27
R13	111,42
R14	123,77
R15	165,37
R16	177,43
R17	**250,62**
R18	192,46
R19	186,67
R20	201,53
R21	205,62
Average of Total Green Points	153,95

CONCLUSION AND RECOMMENDATIONS

The study aims to reveal the process of becoming a green restaurant in fine dining restaurants and to determine in which category they are better and in which category they are worse. Fine dining restaurants use high-quality ingredients and has predetermined eating habits, including a dress code. Fine dining restaurants are expensive restaurants. These high-end restaurants are luxury restaurants. The purpose of the establishment of fine dining restaurants is to make customers feel special. Considering all these features, fine dining restaurants bring some extreme practices. Fine dining restaurants must be also sustainable, as restaurants have recently adopted the sustainability trend. For this reason, fine dining restaurants should get the green restaurant label.

The research shows there are 21 fine dining restaurants in total. The restaurant with the lowest total green point is level 1 fine dining restaurant. Fine dining restaurant which has the highest score is 3-star fine dining restaurant. There is no 4-star fine dining restaurants. All certified fine dining restaurants are located in the USA. The green restaurant standard which has the lowest average is transparency and education. This result is normal as it is not mandatory to score points in this category. On the other hand, this result contradicts with the result of the study by DiPietro and Partlow (2013).

In their study, the authors recommend employee training to restaurant managers in the process of becoming a green restaurant. The category with the lowest average after Transparency and education is building. It is not mandatory to get a score from the building category, such as transparency and education (GRA, 2022). In the categories of energy, water, waste, disposables, chemicals, and food, it is mandatory to get a minimum of 10 points from any of the three for level 1 level. For 2-star and 3-star restaurants, a minimum of 10 points must be obtained from all these categories (GRA, 2022). Three-star restaurants received the highest scores in the energy, water, disposables, chemical, and building categories. Two-star restaurants received the highest score in the food and waste category. Two-star restaurants only got the highest score in the education category. This result of the study is similar to the studies of Chen, Cheng, and Hsu (2015).

The lowest score for Level 1 restaurants is 62, the lowest score is 100 for two-star restaurants, and 175 for three-star restaurants. Level 1 restaurants are required to obtain five green points every three years. Two- and three-star restaurants are required to obtain 130 green points at the end of 3 years and 160 green points at the end of six years (GRA, 2022). When Level 1 fine dining restaurants are examined, it is seen that most of them have more than 100 points. The reason why these restaurants are not two-star restaurants with their current ratings is interpreted as they have not completed three years.

It will be good for the sustainability of restaurants if more fine dining restaurants adopt green practices. It is a shortcoming that there are no four-star fine dining restaurants. In case the managers work on education and building, which are among the categories of being a green restaurant, more restaurants will be formed into 4-star green restaurants.

This study has some limitations. Only fine dining restaurants were considered in the study. Another limitation of the study is that it only examines restaurants according to GRA criteria. It is possible to obtain different results by looking at more than one restaurant type in future studies. In addition, it is possible to examine restaurants according to the criteria of more than one green restaurant establishment in future studies. In future studies, green restaurant criteria can also be studied with the consumer dimension.

REFERENCES

Băltescu, C. A., Neacşu, N. A., Madar, A., Boşcor, D., & Zamfirache, A. (2022). Sustainable Development Practices of Restaurants in Romania and Changes during the COVID-19 Pandemic. *Sustainability*, *14*(7), 3798. doi:10.3390u14073798

Chen, C. T., Cheng, C. C., & Hsu, F. S. (2015). GRSERV scale: An effective tool for measuring consumer perceptions of service quality in green restaurants. *Total Quality Management and Business Excellence, 26*(3-4), 355-367.

Dewald, B., Bruin, B. J., & Jang, Y. J. (2014). US consumer attitudes towards "green" restaurants. *Anatolia, 25*(2), 171–180. doi:10.1080/13032917.2013.839457

DiPietro, B., R., C. Y., & Partlow, C. (2013). Green practices in upscale foodservice operations: Customer perceptions and purchase intentions. *International Journal of Contemporary Hospitality Management, 25*(5), 779–796. doi:10.1108/IJCHM-May-2012-0082

Gilg, A., Barr, S., & Ford, N. (2005). Green consumption or sustainable lifestyles? Identifying the sustainable consumer. *Futures, 37*(6), 481–504. doi:10.1016/j.futures.2004.10.016

Güneş, S. G. (2019). Eco-gastronomy, Tourism and Sustainability: The Rise of Sustainable Restaurants in the World. *Erasmus International Academic Research Symposium on Educational and Social Sciences*, 67-84.

Hu, H. H., Parsa, H. G., & Self, J. (2010). The dynamics of green restaurant patronage. *Cornell Hospitality Quarterly, 51*(3), 344–362. doi:10.1177/1938965510370564

Ismail, A., Kassim, A., & Zahari, M. S. (2010). Responsiveness of restaurateurs towards the implementation of environmentally-friendly practices. *South Asian Journal of Tourism and Heritage, 3*(2), 1–10.

Karagiannis, D., & Andrinos, M. (2021). The role of sustainable restaurant practices in city branding: The case of Athens. *Sustainability, 13*(4), 2271. doi:10.3390u13042271

Kiatkawsin, K., & Sutherland, I. (2020). Examining luxury restaurant dining experience towards sustainable reputation of the Michelin restaurant guide. *Sustainability, 12*(5), 2134. doi:10.3390u12052134

Kozak, M., Keser, D., Büken, M. E., & Zaimoğlu, Z. (2019). İklim Değişikliği İle Mücadelede Soframızdaki Yiyeceklerin Karbon Ayak İzi [The Carbon Footprint of the Food on Our Table in Combating Climate Change]. *International Symposium on Advanced Engineering Technologies,* 920-925.

Lorenzini, B. (1994). The green restaurant, part II: Systems and service. *Restaurants & Institutions,* (104), 119–136.

Nyamogosa, H. M., & Obonyo, G. O. (2022). Sustainable business strategies for fast-food restaurant growth: Fast-food restaurant managers' perspectives in lake region economic block, Kenya. *Journal of Hospitality and Tourism, 2*(1), 1–15. doi:10.47672/jht.958

Schubert, F. (2008). *Exploring and predicting consumers' attitudes and behaviours towards green restaurants*. The Degree Master's of Science in the Graduate School of The Ohio State University.

Soonthonsmai, V. (2007). Environmental or Green Marketing as Global Competitive Edge: Concept, Synthesis, and Implication. *EABR (Business) and ETLC (Teaching) Conference Proceeding*.

Tan, B. C., & Yeap, P. F. (2012). What drives green restaurant patronage intention? *International Journal of Business and Management, 7*(2), 215. doi:10.5539/ijbm.v7n2p215

Wang, Y. F., Chen, S. P., Lee, Y. C., & Tsai, C. T. S. (2013). Developing green management standards for restaurants: An application of green supply chain management. *International Journal of Hospitality Management, 34*, 263–273. doi:10.1016/j.ijhm.2013.04.001

Xu, Y., & Jeong, E. (2019). The effect of message framings and green practices on customers' attitudes and behavior intentions toward green restaurants. *International Journal of Contemporary Hospitality Management, 31*(6), 2270–2296. doi:10.1108/IJCHM-05-2018-0386

Yıldırım, A., & Şimşek, H. (2013). *Sosyal Bilimlerde Nitel Araştırma Yöntemleri* [Qualitative research methods in the social sciences]. Seçkin Yayıncılık.

ADDITIONAL READING

Başfırıncı Ç. (2008). Bir Pazarlama İletişim Medyası Olarak Web Ortamında İçerik Analizi Yapmanın Güçlükleri ve Olası Çözüm Önerileri [The Challenges of Content Analysis on the Web as a Marketing Communication Media and Possible Solutions]. *Yönetim Dergisi, 53*.

Büyüköztürk, Ş., Çakmak, E. K., Akgün, Ö. E., Karadeniz, Ş., & Demirel, F. (2008). Bilimsel araştırma yöntemleri [Scientific research methods] (2nd ed.). Ankara: Pegem Akademi.

Rozekhi, N. A., Hussin, S., Siddiqe, A. S. K. A. R., Rashid, P. D. A., & Salmi, N. S. (2016). The influence of food quality on customer satisfaction in fine dining restaurant: Case in Penang. *International Academic Research Journal of Business and Technology, 2*(2), 45–50.

Chapter 4
Effects of the COVID-19 Pandemic on Restaurants and Menus

Günseli Güçlütürk Baran
Isparta University of Applied Sciences, Turkey & Isparta Vocational School, Turkey

Erdeniz Sezer
Independet Researcher, Turkey

ABSTRACT

The aim of this research is to reveal the impact of the COVID-19 pandemic in Turkey in terms of the restaurants and menu planning. The authors believe it is possible for people's attitudes to shape their consumer behavior, which are considered in food and beverage preferences. In this respect, it is important to examine the effects of the COVID-19 pandemic on restaurants and menu planning within the scope of gastronomy in Turkey. This research is based on a case study. Primary and secondary data sources were used among the data collection techniques. Secondary data consists of data such as studies, reports, and statistical information in the relevant literature. The primary data of the research consists of qualitative data. Accordingly, the semi-structured in-depth interview technique was used. The sampling method was used in the research and interviews were conducted with a total of 12 participants in Istanbul, Turkey.

INTRODUCTION

Eating and drinking, which are described as one of the most basic needs and greatest pleasures of human beings, have been accepted as an important phenomenon in all areas of life, from cultural formation to economic structure, from sociological initiatives to political events, and have been evaluated as a status indicator throughout history. Today, in addition to the effort to produce to meet the mass nutritional needs of mass production, it is inevitable for restaurants to develop themselves according to the requirements of the day in their physical environment, production, business processes or menus. Like the concepts applied in food and beverage businesses, the menus also differ from each other. The factors affecting the

DOI: 10.4018/978-1-6684-4645-4.ch004

net income such as the location of the business, being in a province or district, and rent are reflected in the menu pricing. Considering the waste, profitability and popularity within the scope of menu products, menu engineering plays an important role at this point (Doğdubay, & Saatçi, 2014). Expenses such as employee salary payments, insurance, electricity, water, gas, wholesaler, supplier, and other purchases for the enterprise appear, and accordingly, all expenses and profit margin are determined and pricing is set. Cost information alone is not sufficient for menu pricing. Menu analysis allows the manager of the food and beverage business to evaluate the costs and sales systematically. Instead of comparing total revenue from the menu to total costs, it is possible to determine which menu items are profitable or harmful, which menu item(s) should be removed, and whether a new item should be added.

At this point, the menus, the quality of service they provide, and customer preferences used by restaurants can provide a significant advantage in competition with other restaurants. Today, many companies tend to use seasonal menus once every six months in relation to agricultural production. One of the main reasons for using this alternating menu is not to repeat itself but to differentiate itself from its competitors by offering healthier and newer products to its customers and to try to meet consumer expectations. In addition, restaurants specializing in one or a few products or specialty restaurants differ only in these products compared to their competitors. An example of this is fixed menus (fast food, pizza etc.) (Doğdubay, & Saatçi, 2014).

The COVID-19 pandemic has created a butterfly effect (Lacroix, & Milliot, 2021). Especially in 2020 and 2021, international tourism travels have been suspended. People have been tried to be transported from destinations to their homes. Then, according to the measures taken by the states, studies, and the number of cases, tourism mobility has started again with national travels. In addition, the behavior of traveling according to COVID-19 has begun to be made more individually and in small groups. These behaviors can be shown as adapting to the moment, such as the chameleon's changing color for self-protection. For example, the closure of accommodation and food and beverage establishments for a specific time has stimulated caravan tourism. Minibuses began to be converted into caravans. There was a significant decline of 100% in reservations. Although there is dynamism with the reopening of the businesses, the crisis is still being felt today. Many countries published guidance for food businesses to manage food safety risks and hygiene practices. Restaurants were allowed to reopen their doors, albeit with restrictions in place. First of all, in some businesses that had not provided takeaway services before, managerial decisions played an active role in the implementing takeaway services. This step shows the operational alternative in places where restaurants are allowed to stay open for takeaway service (Gössling, Scott, & Hall, 2020, p. 12). Restaurants lost billions of dollars, millions experienced severe employment changes, and numerous small restaurants closed. For those remaining in business, converting to online food ordering was essential. Unique to the food ordering setting, a study extended the Stimulus-Organism-Response model to predict the purchase intentions of participants in an online food ordering context, and it was revealed that the causal relationship was significantly mediated by consumers' desire for food and their perceived convenience of online food ordering (Brewer, & Sebby, 2021). However, as the effects of COVID-19 begin to decrease in many countries in 2022, it is critical for tourism businesses to reopen their doors so that real information about these businesses can be accessed. Well, what kind of process did/are cafes and restaurants go/going through in the COVID-19 crisis? Especially in crisis processes, businesses need to see their shortcomings and evaluate what they are doing. According to the social and economic decisions applied depending on the changing conditions of the global epidemic, the food and beverage industry requires a production process and menu structuring under these conditions.

Crises that cause negative effects can be defined as unexpected events. Global epidemics involved in such crises also disrupt all other sectors as well as the health sector. The restrictions and the number of cases and deaths in the press have affected people's well-being and socialization. On the other hand, the prolongation of the stay at home provides evidence that people engage in rational hoarding and unnecessary spending. Excessive purchases and waste are observed during the quarantine period owing to the insufficiency of the resources they have in their homes and the assumption that the existing products at home would be consumed. Consumers raising vegetables and other plants in pots or gardens acquired importance during COVID-19. On the other hand, contactless delivery (door-hanging orders) was among the measures that have been implemented.

The study aims to determine the impact of the COVID-19 epidemic in Turkey on restaurants and menu planning. In fact, it is possible that people's attitudes shape their behavior. These consumer behaviors are taken into account in food and beverage preferences. In this respect, it is important to examine the effects of the COVID-19 epidemic on restaurants, and menu planning within the scope of gastronomy in Turkey.

In this regard, this research is based on a case study. Case studies are useful for explaining processes and changes in situations involving individuals, groups, businesses, and institutions. In this context, the qualitative research approach was taken as the basis. Qualitative research is important because it examines a subject in depth in a certain social environment.

Among the data collection techniques, primary and secondary data sources were used. Secondary data consists of data such as studies, reports, and statistical information in the relevant literature. The primary data of the research consists of qualitative data. Accordingly, semi-structured in-depth interview technique was used. In this direction, the critical case sampling method was used in the research.

According to the findings of the study, the economic crisis caused by the global pandemic came to the fore. Cost and hygiene were identified as prominent concepts. It has been revealed that in menu planning, cost, customer demands, seasonal products, and healthy products are taken into consideration. Although it is allowed to open businesses from time to time during the pandemic, it has been determined that businesses mostly prefer to stay closed. Unemployment within the scope of the hospitality industry and tourism, which is a labor-intensive sector, has also affected cafe and restaurant workers. But, among the businesses, there are those who receive support from the short-time working allowance. According to the findings of this study, the pandemic had a negative economic effect on gastronomy. Production deficiencies during the global epidemic period arise within the scope of menu planning. Failure to implement the sufficient import of raw materials and agricultural products is among the important results. In this respect, it is recommended to adapt solutions such as extraordinary production acceleration and domestic and national production and development of agriculture to the crisis process. These difficult days for food and beverage businesses, whose capacities have been halved as a result of social distancing during the COVID-19 pandemic, businesses that can survive have reopened. Despite that, cafes and restaurants should review their business processes during the crisis.

LITERATURE REVIEW

Food is among the essential nutrients for survival. The behavior of finding food, which started with hunting in history, has drawn a different direction with the transition to settled life and agricultural production process. In the first example that stands out regarding the menu, it is seen that dates, meat, pears, apples, and figs consumed with wine in feasts in the Babylonian Kingdoms in 3000 BC. (Türksoy, 2002).

Collective food systems, which started with feudal fiefdoms within the scope of food and beverage, developed and entered the palaces. One of the reasons for this is that the food services provided to the notables of other societies who come as guests gain importance. At the same time, depending on the interaction of people from different countries as a result of this experience, cuisines have used various dishes for different meanings. These can be specified as prestige, status, show of power, and role in promotion (Bilgin, 2003).

In addition, soup kitchens and small-scale restaurants were opened for working people and slaves. Increasing interest and other developments required the restaurants, which are among the food and beverage businesses, to adapt to the changes. The word "restaurant" was used for the first time in 1765, when Parisian soup seller Boulanger opened his shop with the name "restaurer", which means a miracle, repairing and renewing his customers for soups. Restaurants, whose number has increased in line with demand, are among the important actors in the food and beverage industry today (Robert, 1996). It has been revealed that the opening of the first restaurant examples in Paris, France, may be caused not only by the need for nutrition and health, but also by the influence of sociological and psychological factors such as socialization and enjoyment. In this respect, people have started to adopt the behavior of eating in restaurants in their daily lives (Denizer, 2005).

In this historical development process, food and beverage businesses have been accepted as social, economic, and disciplined businesses with physical elements such as structure, comfort, and technical equipment, as well as qualitative elements such as service quality and social value (Kılıç, & Babat, 2011). Depending on the development of technology and the desire to have the relevant equipment, many fields of activity in the food and beverage industry have turned to mass production. In this respect, the developments in technology and communication tools since the 2000s have gained a different dimension to meet the increasing demand, expectation and consumption. In this context, many businesses in the food and beverage industry, such as banquet organization businesses, ready-to-eat businesses, and mass nutrition companies, have started to play an important role in the development of the country.

Today, the food and beverage industry is among the industries that contain important business lines due to the business volume of billions of dollars and the employment it creates. The food and beverage industry refers to a detailed process of activity, starting with agricultural production, from packaging to sales. Therefore, the production process includes different stages, and is complex. In addition, the use of a food product by turning it into an eating and drinking product requires careful consideration of consumer research, since the demand structure for these products is different. At this point, the geographical region where people live, social structure, eating habits, tastes, etc. factors have an important place in the development of countries and communities (Roberts, 1999). However, in line with the emerging war, global epidemic and economic crises, some important problems such as decreases in agricultural production, food intake restrictions, famine, temporary closure of enterprises, increase in unemployment, inability of consumers to access food or increase in product prices may occur. For example, the closure of cafeterias and canteens due to the closure of schools and areas such as dormitories in 2019-2020 during the COVID-19 crisis; the fact that food and beverage businesses only offer take-away services, banquet organizations cannot serve a large group, and the trade and transportation network has come to a standstill due to the closure of the borders or the restriction of crossings, and the associated with it problems the trade activities of the businesses, the wound inflicted in the food and beverage industry also reveals. Considering that crises are an experience, and a learning process in terms of minimizing the effects of crises, it can be stated that the importance of crisis management emerges at this point (United

Nations[UN], 2021). For example, it is an important crisis doctrine that businesses create additional savings opportunities instead of relying solely on government assistance (Alves, Lok, Luo, & Hao, 2021).

The spread of microorganisms in such a way as to cause contagion can lead to devastating results such as some diseases and deaths. Such situations are described as a global epidemic. Examples of these are the plague of Amvas, black plague, bird flu (World Health Organization [WHO], 2020a), cholera (Kruk, 2017), Spanish flu (WHO, 2020b), and swine flu (influanza) (Kara, 2010), and in addition, the global epidemic COVID-19, whose effects are still felt today, can be specified. Starting from the city of Wuhan in China, COVID-19, which has shown its effect almost all over the world, has led to many deaths and health problems. In light of these events, countries have taken certain measures. In light of these measures, first of all, restrictions started. After that, the flexibility on restrictions has led to an increase in the number of cases (Collins, 2020) (for example, closures still continued in Shanghai in 2022). As a matter of fact, the world order has changed due to the COVID-19 global epidemic. For example, face-to-face educational activities and sports competitions were suspended in the world. Although there are measures taken by governments against the epidemic, the virus has changed with different mutations (South African Mutation, England Mutation, etc.) in the world (Sequira, 2021; McGarty, 2021); therefore, with the emergence of mutations, different vaccine studies gained momentum.

Food and beverage businesses have also been adversely affected, as have many businesses that have been adversely affected by the COVID-19 pandemic. As a result of the closure/restriction in restaurants, there were -100% reservations in March and April, while a -32% reservation trend was observed on September 3, after the conditions were made more flexible (OpenTable, 2020). With the COVID-19 restrictions, allowing restaurants and cafes to only offer take-out service has led consumers to order take away or online. The prominence of take-out service due to the epidemic has led to the emergence of new trends. Milör (2021), related to this issue, states that the "Ghost/Dark Kitchen" application, which was established to serve meals with a takeaway method, will increase even more. In this regard, many restaurants and cafes that provide service in the sitting area have turned to takeaway service during their activities. As a result of the flexibility on the restrictions within the scope of food and beverage businesses, when other implemented measures, and activities are examined, minimizing human contact with food and beverage has found a priority application area. Examples of this are that the bread is in the bag, the open food products and service equipment (spoons, tongs, etc.) are not touched without gloves, or the employee transfers that customer's selected product from the back of the buffet to the plate in the establishments that provide open buffet service, and also disinfecting the areas where the food comes into touch contact (Oğur, Hayta, & Bekmezci, 2021).

Consumer behavior due to COVID-19; consumers have started to show behavioral changes in their preferences. For example, important information was obtained according to the results of the research conducted by the Sabri Ülker Foundation (2021) on the nutritional behaviors of the COVID-19 period with 600 people in 12 provinces in Turkey. These can be listed as follows:

- 1.6% increase in the rate of people procuring basic food items from public or municipal aid institutions,
- Decrease in purchasing behavior of fresh cheese, milk and bread,
- While the rate of people who prepared and consumed lunch at home before COVID-19 was 75%, this rate increased to 90% after COVID-19, the consumption of packaged products decreased and the consumption of snacks increased,
- Increasing frequency of consumption of fruit, vegetables, sugar, fresh meat and fish,

- The decrease in the frequency of eating and drinking in restaurants and cafes as a result of the fact that places such as restaurants and cafes are mostly closed for service,
- Increasing expenditure on food consumption,
- Increasing of interest in organic products by approximately 40%,
- Mostly stocking up on pasta, pulses and flour by the people,
- Within the scope of behavior change, disinfection of food packages and good cleaning of food.

There are other prominent issues regarding consumers in the COVID-19 pandemic. For example, the prolongation of staying at home due to restrictions provides evidence that people rationally hoard but spend unnecessarily. During the quarantine period in their homes, there is a shortage of materials in their possession and the thought that the existing products in the house will be consumed, and accordingly, waste is observed in purchases (Baker, 2020). On the other hand during the COVID-19 pandemic, consumers can grow vegetables, etc., in pots or in the garden, and it has also gained importance. In addition, consumers have generally searched words such as "mukbang" which is one of the eating practice, "vitamin D," "thermometer, "body mass index," and "diet" (Tolay, & Sinclair, 2020). Due to the emphasis on the importance of hygiene during the global epidemic period, there is also an attitude towards shopping online (Wang, & Hao, 2020). It has also been observed that consumers return to domestic goods in food and beverage products in terms of hygiene (Hassen, Bilali, & Allahyari, 2020).

In addition, practices such as contactless delivery (orders hung on the door) were introduced among the measures introduced, and thanks to the development of consumer databases, suitable products could be offered to the consumer (Tekin Çevik, 2020). Harford (2017) mentioned that with the different needs arise and increase in consumption, the deficiencies increase and that's why inventions are started to be developed. In this epidemic, it is important to increase other applications such as virtual menu applications in food and beverage businesses, the use of robots in terms of hygiene in the kitchen and service, virtual entrepreneurship, and boutique patisseries that produce less or according to order.

According to all this information, it is understood that food and beverage businesses should understand consumer behavior, and plan their products accordingly in the new order of COVID-19 that occurs with stretching. Considering the increase in food prices, the continuation of restrictions on some products in accessing food, and considering the number of employees, especially in the fixed cost calculation, determining how food and beverage businesses, such as restaurants and cafes, follow in their business processes and menu planning, will provide important information to enterprises to learn important lessons or to give some clues.

It can be stated that menus are an indispensable element in that they contain product prices, content, allergen information, product brands used, and other explanatory information offered by food and beverage businesses. In menu planning, some important studies need to be done, from menu type selection to recipe creation, from menu pricing to ranking products on the menu. Besides that issues such as food safety are the practices that food and beverage businesses should always pay attention to, and it can be stated that food safety education has increased during the COVID-19 pandemic (Pai, & Thomas, 2008). As a matter of fact, Arbeláez-Campillo, Bahamón-Rojas, and Arbeláez-Encarnación (2018) stated that the inadequacies in food safety in the food and beverage businesses are due to the fact that the workers have no idea about this issue. As a result of study, it was also reported that three out of five workers were inadequate in terms of food safety and hygiene. Against it today, it can be underlined that food technology has come to the fore, and technological applications such as machines and, robots that produce without human touch have become important. However, these developments are limited in the service production process, and the importance of human communication in service, and its power in production have an important place in food and beverage businesses.

In summary, the effects of the COVID-19 pandemic, the COVID-19 pandemic has created a butterfly effect. It can be stated that this effect caused a different reaction in the food and beverage industry. The fact that food and beverage activities draw a different direction on out-of-home consumption made it necessary for businesses to change color like a chameleon. At the same time, global research data was followed more frequently and the situation of competitors was also the subject of comparisons. At this point, it can be mentioned that businesses, like consumers, are under the influence of chameleon. For example, stocking products such as pulses, flour, pasta; increased interest in organic products; The steps taken by the businesses in line with the results such as the increase in the frequency of meat and fish consumption and virtual menu applications were shaped according to consumer behaviors and highlighted in terms of marketing. In this context, businesses have started to imitate each other with the effect of chameleon.

Based on all this information, it can be emphasized that it is important to conduct a situation analysis for eating and drinking behaviors and food and beverage businesses, especially during the COVID-19 pandemic. In this direction, the aim of the research is to determine how the COVID-19 crisis has effects on food and beverage businesses, how these businesses perceive and evaluate consumer demands, and what route they follow in menu planning.

RESEARCH METHOD

The research is aimed at examining the situation, business processes, menu planning and pricing situations and approaches of restaurants in Turkey's Istanbul province during the crisis caused by the COVID-19 global epidemic. The study is based on a case study. A case study is an important approach to explaining processes and changes in situations such as individuals, groups, businesses, and institutions (Yıldırım, & Şimşek, 2016). In this context, the qualitative research approach was taken as the basis. According to quantitative research, qualitative research examines a subject in depth by seeking answers to questions such as why and how in a particular social setting (Baltacı, 2017).

In this direction, the critical case sampling method was used in the research and interviews were conducted with a total of 12 participants in Istanbul. Two of the interviewed participants are restaurant managers, and ten are executive chefs. A descriptive analysis was applied in the research.

Among the data collection techniques, primary and secondary data sources were used. Secondary data consists of data such as studies, reports and statistical information in the relevant literature. The primary data of the research consists of qualitative data. Accordingly, a semi-structured in-depth interview technique was used. It is important to obtain more comprehensive information through interviews. In addition, its positive aspects are that it is more flexible compared to the survey technique and allows the participants to express themselves. Therefore, data about the experiences, and opinions of the participants can be obtained (Türnüklü, 2000; Gegez, 2007; Arıkan, 2011).

In this direction, the critical case sampling method was used in the research and interviews were made with a total of 12 participants in Istanbul in February 2021. Two of the interviewed participants are restaurant managers and 10 are executive chefs. Interviews were held online due to the global epidemic.

In the interview questionnaire, there were 11 questions to be asked to the managers. There are four about revealing situations due to COVID-19, and four about the menu and menu planning, and one each about the economic impact, employees, and competitors due to the epidemic. The researchers created the survey questions. Seven questions were included in the questionnaire in order to obtain information about the demographic characteristics of the participants and about the businesses, they work for. The questionnaire was sent to the participants for prior examination. Meeting dates and appointment times were determined by making an appointment with them. The interviews were recorded via video chat. The interviews lasted approximately 30 minutes. A descriptive analysis was applied in the research. The purpose of the descriptive analysis method is to organize and interpret the findings and present them. In this process, direct quotations from the interviews are included in order to present the findings more strikingly (Yıldırım & Şimşek, 2016).

Population, Sample and Sampling Method

The research population includes food and beverage business managers and executive chefs. However, as a result of the frequent closure of food and beverage businesses during the COVID-19 pandemic, sampling was required. Indeed, it is difficult to reach the whole universe. In this respect, it was aimed to obtain more detailed information in a more limited sample in the interviews. The sampling method of the research is the critical sampling method. In this study, a purposeful sampling method was used for critical cases. In critical-case sampling, cases that can be used to understand a previously justified point particularly well are selected for in-depth study (Johnson, & Christensen, 2012). The most important reason for choosing the critical case sampling is the COVID-19 pandemic. According to the data of the Union of Chambers and Commodity Exchanges of Turkey Information Access Directorate, 85 thousand 263 new enterprises were opened in Turkey in 2019, while 14 thousand 50 enterprises were closed. In 2019, there were approximately 35 thousand food and beverage businesses in Istanbul. It is important to note that Turkey's densest population is in Istanbul and according to the information given by the Istanbul Chamber of Commerce; 20 thousand businesses in Istanbul closed their shutters due to the measures taken within the scope of the Covid-19 outbreak (Öztürk, 2020; Oğuz, 2021). In this direction, it is important to conduct research on food and beverage businesses that remain open. It should be noted that it was difficult to reach the sample due to closures imposed during the pandemic in the sampling process. In this context, the interviews were made with 12 participants in Istanbul. Two of the interviewed participants are restaurant managers and 10 are executive chefs. Descriptive analysis was applied in the research.

The reason for this is that the decision makers in the business processes, and menu planning of a food and beverage business are the food and beverage business managers and chefs, and in this context, the criteria are the managers who are the decision makers in the COVID-19 pandemic, and accordingly, the managers will report their opinions on the crisis situation from a professional perspective. In this regard, Baltacı (2018) emphasizes the importance of obtaining as much in-depth information as possible in order to obtain the necessary benefit from the sample, and choosing the participants who are experienced in the relevant field objectively in the selection of the participants to be included in the sample. The place where the research was conducted are the restaurants with a "Tourism Business Certificate" operating in the city center of Istanbul. The types of businesses in which 12 participants in the research sample work are in the form of cafes and restaurants.

Limitations of the Research

The research is limited to the food and beverage businesses located in the city center of Istanbul. Within the scope of the research purpose, the opinions of the managers related to the subject were obtained. In this respect, the research is limited to the information provided by the participants who volunteered to participate in the interview. In addition, it was assumed that the participants gave correct information in the study. Furthermore, considering the continuation of the COVID-19 pandemic, the activities of the restaurants in the sample are limited.

Validity and Reliability of the Research

The interview technique was used in the research, and the main purpose of this is usually not to test a hypothesis, but rather to try to understand other people's experiences and how they make sense of those experiences. Therefore, the focus is on other people's descriptions and thoughts (Seidman, 1991). Therefore, the accuracy and precision of the verbal information transferred to the written text, depending on the acquisition of direct participant statements, forms the basis for the whole research. For this reason, in obtaining valid and correct information about social reality, primarily focusing on this process provides evidence in terms of validity and reliability (Türnüklü, 2000). In addition, the obtained data were analyzed by two researchers, and no guidance was given during the interview process. The questions were asked to the participants in the same way. Observation was also important in terms of reaching real data. At the point where the obtained information started to be repeated, the interviews were terminated in the sampling.

FINDINGS

Within the scope of the findings, the type of business and characteristics of the participants, demographic and sector experience information of the participants are given below. Then, within the scope of the findings obtained from the interviews, menu planning findings regarding the COVID-19 pandemic are presented below.

Types of Businesses, Demographic and Business İnformation of Participants

First of all, coding (such as Kitchen Chef1, Kitchen Chef2, Restaurant1, Restaurant2) was carried out for the interviewed participants. As can be seen in Table 1, while a total of 11 participants work in cafes and restaurants, one participant works in a fish and appetizer (meze) restaurant (traditional restaurant as meyhane) type of business.

Among the people participating in the research, two participants are restaurant managers, while a total of 10 participants are chefs. According to gender, the participants consisted of three women and nine men in total. According to the information obtained, it is perceived positively that female chefs take part in the kitchen. According to the age distribution of the participants, it was determined that the age situation changed between the ages of 25 and 42.

Table 1. Type of business, demographic and job information of the participants

Participants Code	Business Number (Code)	Type of Business	Jobs	Gender	Age	Education Degree	Working Time in the Business (Year)	Working Time in the Sector (Year)
Manager 1	Restaurant 1	Cafe, Restaurant	Manager	Female	35	Undergraduate	6	6
Manager 2	Restaurant 2	Cafe, Restaurant	Manager	Female	37	High School	12	17
Chef 1	Restaurant 3	Cafe, Restaurant	Executive Chef	Male	42	Associate Degree College	12	24
Chef 2	Restaurant 4	Cafe, Restaurant	Executive Chef	Male	42	High School	10	25
Chef 3	Restaurant 5	Cafe, Restaurant	Executive Chef	Male	35	Master's Degree	7	16
Chef 4	Restaurant 6	Cafe, Restaurant	Executive Chef	Male	30	High School	2	13
Chef 5	Restaurant 7	Cafe, Restaurant	Executive Chef	Male	32	Primary Education	12	14
Chef 6	Restaurant 8	Cafe, Restaurant	Executive Chef	Male	26	Undergraduate Education	10	10
Chef 7	Restaurant 9	Cafe, Restaurant	Executive Chef	Male	33	Undergraduate Education	9	15
Chef 8	Restaurant 10	Cafe, Restaurant	Executive Chef	Female	33	High School	11	13
Chef 9	Restaurant 11	Cafe, Restaurant	Executive Chef	Male	28	Primary Education	4	9
Chef 10	Restaurant 12	Seafood Restaurant/ Traditional Restaurant	Executive Chef	Female	25	Undergraduate Education	3	8

Findings Obtained from the Interviews

In the study, the menus of the businesses were examined before and after COVID-19. Within the scope of the data obtained from a total of 12 participants interviewed, it was determined that restaurant menus are generally fixed, but they removed some products from the menu due to the COVID-19 outbreak and included different products on the menu. As a result of the global epidemic, restaurants and cafes are closed or they turn to takeaway, all businesses also stated that they reduced their menu items. At the same time, it has been revealed that the menus are renewed alternately, on average every six months, summer and winter.

When the menu types are examined, it is understood that 10 restaurants offer Ala Carte menu, one restaurant offers a banquet type, and one restaurant offers only appetizers and grills. Among the prominent findings of the research, there is no special menu study for individuals or groups. Only one business has pricing studies for special days. All but one of the interviewed food and beverage businesses include alcoholic beverages in their menus. It has been explained by the participants that the businesses they work for provide take-out services (three businesses) or that the businesses they work for are closed (nine businesses) when restriction measures are taken. On the other hand, it has been determined that changes have been made in the menus due to the COVID-19 global epidemic. It is also among the important findings that more immune-boosting products are added to the menus in the COVID-19 global epidemic.

As a result of the interviews, it was determined that for economic impact of COVID-19, 11 enterprises among a total of 12 enterprises benefited from the Short Working Allowance provided by the state. Only one enterprise stated that it did not receive state aid. Stating that there are employees who have had a COVID-19 disease in the pandemic, businesses also stated that sent their staff to rest, if they show any signs of illness.

It has been determined that all businesses have lost their income-expenditure balance in the COVID-19 global epidemic. As a result of the interviews, it was also announced that the food and beverage industry is experiencing a great job loss.

The statements of the managers of food and beverage businesses within the scope of the findings are given below. Some of the factors they consider in menu planning are stated as follows:

"Customer demands are on healthy and organic foods. We are working on menu planning in line with customer satisfaction and demands." ~(Chef 1)

"Trendy products are preferred, with a priority on low-cost and high-profit products." ~(Chef 4)

"We have a desire to steer healthy food in line with customer demand. Making sense of healthy foods with different flavors in an enjoyable way is a factor in menu planning." ~(Manager 2)

"The freshness of the product, its durability and the type of products that we can easily access in the season are some of our important factors in menu planning." ~(Chef 10)

There is no answer that differs from the above, besides the cost and profitability situation in general, menu planning is in question according to accessible products.

In addition, a content analysis was carried out by determining the keywords for menu planning. The words in question are: cost, customer demands, seasonal products, healthy products. The word cost was specified by eight businesses, customer demands by five businesses, seasonal products by three businesses, and healthy products by three businesses. It is seen that the least used answers about menu planning are seasonal products and healthy products. It is among the important findings that kitchen chefs and their assistants in the food and beverage business, restaurant managers, bar managers, business owners and "Research and Development Chefs", if any, and take part in creating the menu. It has also been reported that in some businesses, professional support was obtained by using external resources (outsourcing) only for menu making and writing.

Due to the global epidemic COVID-19, some food and beverage businesses in Turkey have closed their doors or had to return to takeaway. In the interviews related to this, the question "What are the effects of the restrictions on their businesses and menu planning?" was also asked to the food and beverage managers and chefs. Below are statements for this:

"We did not change the menu, we switched to takeaway due to restrictions. The intensity of our work has increased even more. We think that the reason for this is that we are preferred because we make products that people who are at home cannot make at home." ~(Chef 6)

"Due to the pandemic, we had to downsize the menu. For this reason, we have shaped a menu for products that we do not have a shortage of supply. Normally, honey is a product that we only give in the morning breakfast plate, but now we have used it more in our menu because it increases immunity. In other products, we preferred more products for immune-boosting and healthy food. As a result of the restrictions, we had to return to the package service. We continue our business as a package service." ~(Chef 7)

"We gave priority to grilled varieties that are less oily in our menu. We also have a business in organic products. Due to the global epidemic, we are doing takeaway, but we can say that our business is going at the same rate right now." ~(Manager 1)

"We are closed due to restrictions. Since we are a fish restaurant (traditional fish and meze restaurant), we cannot do it in takeaway. We have menu studies for post-restrictions." ~(Chef 10)

It was determined that a business within the scope of the sample did not change the menu. The reason for this is stated as follows:

"We, as a business, did not change the menu, we have a very diverse menu, we have our own products that appeal to everyone and that they love to eat. Our system, which we adopted before the COVID-19 global epidemic, was in this direction. That's why we didn't make any changes." ~(Chef 9)

In addition, an important teaching of the global epidemic period was stated as showing more sensitivity to hygiene, and cleaning compared to previous practices. In response to the question posed to reveal whether there are changing attitudes, behaviors and habits in food and beverage businesses during the COVID-19 pandemic, the following statements were made:

"The highest level of hygiene rules have been put in place in all these cycles, including the kitchen, common areas of the personnel. Companies, including wholesalers and supply chains, were provided with training on hygiene and cleaning. In addition, we are constantly checked by food engineers and technicians appointed by the state." ~(Manager 2)

"There are measures such as keeping hand sanitizer and social distance, especially in terms of hygiene. We think that such measures will continue for a longer period of time." ~(Chef 3)

Managers stated for their situation before and after the global epidemic was a decrease in their jobs. Below are some statements about it:

"While the intensity of our work was around 80% before the global epidemic, it dropped to 35%-40% in the period after the news of the epidemic and restrictions." ~(Chef 5)

"In the pre-pandemic period, our workload was moderate. We are closed because we do not have a product suitable for takeaway in the pandemic." ~(Chef 3)

"We have become a surviving business, and we believe that we can get through this pandemic with the least injury. I can say that we are in a better position compared to other businesses." ~(Manager 2)

"When we look at the target tables and expense-income account balances in previous years, there is a really big decrease." ~(Chef 7)

The answers of the managers to the question about their status compared to their competitors during the global epidemic period are given below:

".......I think we are the sector most affected by the restrictions." ~(Chef 9)

"We can say that it is the best of the worst." ~(Chef 1)

"We did not lay off staff, but we are closed. We paid employees' wages from the state with the Short Working Allowance. I can't get into the benchmarking with our competitors because many businesses like us are closed." ~(Chef 10)

As a result of the above findings, food and beverage business managers stated that their business has deteriorated due to the global epidemic and the whole sector has been affected by the situation. On the other hand, it is important to start to include healthy products in menu planning. Based on the findings, the results of the research are given below. In addition, according to the results of the study, some suggestions were presented to practitioners and the literature for the COVID-19 crisis and menu planning.

CONCLUSION AND RECOMMENDATIONS

COVID-19, which started in Wuhan, China in December 2019 and showed its effects all over the world, caused an economic crisis, malnutrition, difficulties in businesses due to restrictions, and an increase in the unemployment rate. COVID-19 resulted in restricted food trade policies, and financial pressures on the food supply chain (Aday, & Aday, 2020). It seems that COVID-19 will remain in our lives. The fact that the COVID-19 virus continues as an important epidemic from the moment it emerged shows the importance of renewing the measures taken over time, studies in the fields of nutrition, medicine, and knowledge.

The economic destructiveness of the COVID-19 has been felt by Small and Medium Enterprises (SMEs) and many large-scale enterprises in Turkey as well. The Turkish government, along with the economic activities it carried out in the pandemic, relieved its insured employees a little more. For business owners, new payment terms, tax refunds, tax deductions or tax deferrals, and working allowances, as well as long-term loans, have been developed (Atkeson, 2020). However, although the effects of the economic crisis were tried to be alleviated to a certain extent, the businesses were adversely affected as a result of the closures, as they could not produce as in the past. Among these businesses are also the food and beverage businesses that are important both for being areas where socialization is provided and working to meet the nutritional needs of people.

This researh aim to determine the effects of the COVID-19 global epidemic on food and beverage businesses and their menus. Interviews were held with a total of 12 managers in Istanbul. The results of the research show that the businesses in the food and beverage sector either temporarily closed their workplaces or returned to takeaway due to restrictions. At the same time, as the participants stated, the majority of the enterprises are supported by the state. Due to COVID-19, the menu planning and implementation processes of food and beverage businesses are interrupted. In this study, it was concluded that access to many imported products was blocked as a result of restrictions, and this practice led to the removal of many products from the menus of food and beverage businesses. Therefore, it has been determined that some changes have been made in menu planning. Among these changes, low-cost products, and the inclusion of healthy foods and beverages in the menus are among the important results of this research. It can be stated that there is a tendency towards immune-boosting natural products for COVID-19 in nutrition. It is important to include such products in food and beverage businesses. However, it was also revealed that the menu planning activities could not be fully addressed within the scope of the sample. Therefore, it can be stated that a better understanding of post-epidemic consumer demands for menu planning is required, especially since the closures and restrictions of food and beverage businesses in Turkey continue in April-May 2021, and because businesses switch to more takeaway systems. Despite the increasing food costs of restaurants in COVID-19, according to the results of a study shows that a chain restaurant in Bulgaria served with takeaway, added new dishes to the menu for the summer season, and made the plate design more attractive in 2020 (Karaca, & Nergis Güçlü, 2021). In addition, in terms of marketing, it is emphasized that not displaying a restaurant menu on a resort hotel website is a lost opportunity (Baiomy et al., 2013). It can be stated that this implementation is also valid for any restaurants.

Pueyo (2020), in parallel with the results of this study, revealed the decrease in revenues of businesses that were closed due to the global epidemic, compared to previous years. At this point, it is an important step to provide state support as a Short Working Allowance in Turkey since the beginning of the crisis.

In addition, since the beginning of the crisis in Turkey, customers have been aware that cleaning and hygiene trainings are especially tailored to people working in the food sector, and that businesses provide and routinely inspect hygiene and sanitation environments. As a basis for this, it can be stated that people show eating behavior from outside, even with takeaway service, during the pandemic. At the same time, it is predicted that the attitudes of enterprises towards concepts such as social distance and disinfection are positive and that these practices will not be completely removed in the future. Thanks to vaccinations and other measures, businesses were opened in Turkey in 2022. Although an economic recovery process starts locally, the effects of the ongoing crisis in the world affect all countries.

Based on the results of the study, it would be appropriate to present some suggestions to practitioners and other researchers. These recommendations are listed below.

Suggestions to practitioners:

- In the menu planning, innovative recipes can be offered that differ in the production process, or a specialist area can be created on some products are identified. Thus, a difference can be shown from competitors.
- Consumers with chronic diseases should be provided with diet menu alternatives.
- The fact that food and beverage businesses fully comply with the hygiene and sanitation rules and demonstrate this will affect their preference.

Suggestions to researchers:

- Conducting studies on product contents and which foods and beverages are perceived as healthy in restaurants in menu planning, comparing them with expert opinions,
- Revealing the package service quality,

- Researching the practices of businesses such as cleaning and social distance through participatory observation,
- Depending on the economic crisis, it is recommended to compare the changes in product supply, product costs and product prices. Thus, an important contribution will be made to the literature.

Some suggestions regarding business strategies and economic development plans are given below:

- Money-value relationship should be developed with economic reforms. Turkish lira should be strengthened with permanent and sustainable policies.
- Regarding food production, support should be provided to farmers in the agricultural production process and local production should be given importance.

In the literature, studies on the impact of the COVID-19 global epidemic on food and beverage businesses are limited. Therefore, this research is important in terms of determining how food and beverage businesses are affected by the COVID-19 global epidemic by obtaining in-depth information. In this respect, the research makes a different contribution to the literature.

ETHICS COMMITTEE DECLARATION

Istanbul Ayvansaray University Academic Research and Publication Ethics Committee dated 09/02/2021, and numbered 2021/01 has decided that this study is in compliance with ethical principles. E-31675095-100-2100001386.

ACKNOWLEDGMENT

This research received no specific grant from any funding agency in the public, commercial, or not-for-profit sectors.

REFERENCES

Aday, S., & Aday, M. S. (2020). Impact of COVID-19 on the food supply chain. *Food Quality and Safety*, 4(4), 167–180. doi:10.1093/fqsafe/fyaa024

Alves, C. J., Lok, T. C., Luo, Y. B., & Hao, W. (2021). *Crisis management for small business during the COVID-19 outbreak: Survival, resilience and renewal strategies of firms in Macau*. www.researchsquare.com/article/rs-34541/v1

Arbeláez-Campillo, D., Rojas-Bahamón, M. J., & Arbeláez-Encarnación, T. (2018). Apuntes para el debate de las categorías ciudadanía universal, derechos humanos y globalización. Notes for the debate of the categories universal citizenship, human rights and globalization. *Cuestiones Políticas*, 34(61), 139–160.

Arıkan, R. (2011). *Research Methods and Techniques* [Araştırma Yöntem ve Teknikleri]. Nobel Akademi Publishing.

Atkeson, A. (2020). What will be the economic impact of COVID-19 in the US? Rough estimates of disease scenarios. *National Bureu of Economic Research, 26*, 21–25. doi:10.3386/w26867

Baiomy, M. A. E. A., Jones, E., Elias, A. N. E., & Dinana, T. R. (2013). Menus as Marketing Tools: Developing a Resort Hotel Restaurant Menu Typology. *Journal of Tourism Research & Hospitality, 2*(2), 1–10. doi:10.4172/2324-8807.1000116

Baker, S. R., Farrokhnia, R. A., Meyer, S., Pagel, M., & Yannelis, C. (2020). How does household spending respond to an epidemic? Consumption during the 2020 COVID-19 pandemic. *Review of Asset Pricing Studies, 10*(4), 834–862. doi:10.1093/rapstu/raaa009

Baltacı, A. (2017). Miles-Huberman Model in Qualitative Data Analysis [Nitel veri analizinde Miles-Huberman modeli]. *A Journal of Ahi Evran University Institute of Social Sciences, 3*(1), 1-15.

Baltacı, A. (2018). A Conceptual Review of Sampling Methods and Sample Size Problems in Qualitative Research [Nitel araştırmalarda örnekleme yöntemleri ve örnek hacmi sorunsalı üzerine kavramsal bir inceleme]. *Journal of Bitlis Eren University Institute of Social Sciences., 7*(1), 231–274.

Bilgin, A. (2003). Turkish Religious Foundation Encyclopedia of Islam [Türkiye Diyanet Vakfı İslam Ansiklopedisi]. Academic Press.

Brewer, P., & Sebby, G. A. (2021). The effect of online restaurant menus on consumers' purchase intentions during the COVID-19 pandemic. *Int J Hosp Manag., 94.* . doi:10.1016/j.ijhm.2020.102777

Collins, C. (2020). 08, 07). Productivity in a pandemic. *Science, 369*(6504), 603. doi:10.1126cience.abe1163 PMID:32764040

Denizer, D. (2005). *Food and Beverage Management in Hospitality Businesses* [Konaklama İşletmelerinde Yiyecek ve İçecek Yönetimi]. Detay Publishing.

Doğdubay, M., & Saatçi, G. (2014). *Menu Engineering* [Menü Mühendisliği]. Detay Publishing.

Gegez, A. E. (2007). *Marketing Research* [Pazarlama Araştırmaları]. Beta Publishing.

Gössling, S., Scott, D., & Hall, C. M. (2020). Pandemics, tourism and global change: A rapid assessment of COVID-19. *Journal of Sustainable Tourism, 29*(1), 1–20. doi:10.1080/09669582.2020.1758708

Harford, T. (2017). *Fifty Inventions That Shaped the Modern Economy* [Modern Ekonomiyi Şekillendiren Elli İcat]. Pegasus Publishing.

Hassen, T.B., Bilali, E. H., & Allahyari, M. (2020). Impact of COVID-19 on food behavior and consumption in Qatar. *Sustainability, 12*(17), 6973.

Johnson, B., & Christensen, L. (2012). *Educational Research, Quantitative, Qualitative, and Mixed Approaches.* SAGE Pub. Inc.

Kara, A. (2010). Swine flu [Domuz gribi]. *Journal of Child Health and Diseases, 53*, 21–25. PMID:21140890

Karaca, E., & Nergiz Güçlü, H. (2021). Examination of Menu Designs of Restaurants During COVID 19 Pandemic: Examples of Restaurant A (Bulgaria) and Restaurant B (Turkey) [COVID-19 Salgın Sürecinde Restoranların Menü Tasarımlarının İncelenmesi: Restoran A (Bulgaristan) ve Restoran B (Türkiye) Örneği]. *Journal of Social Sciences of Mus Alparslan University, 9*(3), 703-713.

Kılıç, Y., & Babat, B. V. (2000). *Quality Function Deployment: A Hypothetical Approach on Food and Beverage Establishment* [Kalite Fonksiyon Göçerimi: Yiyecek-İçecek İşletmelerine Yönelik Kuramsal Bir Yaklaşım]. Karamanoğlu Mehmetbey University Journal of Social and Economic Research.

Kruk, M. E., Pate, M., & Mullan, Z. (2017). Introducing the Lancet Global Health Commission on high-quality health systems in the SDG era. *The Lancet. Global Health, 5*(5), 480–481. doi:10.1016/S2214-109X(17)30101-8 PMID:28302563

Lacroix, L., & Milliot, E. (2021). The Butterfly Effect of COVID-19: Toward an Adapted Model of Commodity Supply. In M. A. Marinov & S. T. Marinova (Eds.), *COVID-19 and International Business* (pp. 192–204). Routledge.

McGarty, T. (2021). COVID-19: Mutations and Infectivity. Massachusetts Institute of Technology.

Milör, V. (2021, 04, 0). *The "Ghost kitchen" application has been on the rise during the pandemic period* ["Ghost kitchen" uygulaması pandemi döneminde yükselişe geçti]. Gastro Table. https://www.gastromasa.com/ghost-kitchen-uygulamasi-pandemi-doneminde-yukselise-gecti/

Oğur, S., Hayta, Ş., & Bekmezci, D. H. (2021). Food safety risks and precautions during the COVID-19 pandemic. epidemic. In Epidemic, agriculture and food [COVID-19 pandemisi sürecinde gıda güvenliği riskleri ve önlemleri]. Tasav, 91-100.

Oğuz, M. (2021). *The Number of Restaurants in Istanbul Has Dropped to 20 Thousand* [İstanbul'da Restoran Sayısı 20 Binlere Düştü]. Tourism Diary, Tourism and Travel Newspaper. https://www.turizmgunlugu.com/2021/02/13/istanbulda-restoran-sayisi-20-binlere-dustu/

OpenTable. (2020). *The state of the restaurant industry*. https://www.opentable.com/state-of-industry#:~:text=In%20March%202020%2C%20OpenTable%20launched,%2C%20states%2C%20and%20countries%20reopen

Öztürk, F. (2020). *Thousands of Businesses Shut Down During the Pandemic Process* [Pandemi Sürecinde Binlerce İşletme Kepenk İndirdi]. BBC News/Türkçe. https://www.bbc.com/turkce/haberler-dunya-55258396

Pai, S., & Thomas, R. (2008). Immune deficiency or hyperactivity-Nfkappa b illuminates autoimmunity. *Journal of Autoimmunity, 31*(3), 245–251. doi:10.1016/j.jaut.2008.04.012 PMID:18539434

Pueyo, T. (2020). *Coronavirus: Why You Must Act Now*. https://tomaspueyo.medium.com/coronavirus-act-today-or-people-will-die-f4d3d9cd99ca

Robert, I. (1996). Alexandrie 1830-1930: Historie d'une communaute citadine. Institut Fran‚ais d'Archéologie Orientale.

Roberts, P. (1999). Product innovation, product-market competition and persistent profitability in the US pharmaceutical industry. *Strategic Management Journal, 20*(7), 655–670. doi:10.1002/(SICI)1097-0266(199907)20:7<655::AID-SMJ44>3.0.CO;2-P

Sabri Ülker Foundation. (2021). *COVID-19 nutritional behavior research from the Sabri Ülker Foundation* [Sabri Ülker Vakfı'ndan COVID-19 dönemi beslenme davranışları araştırması]. www.sabriulkerfoundation.org/tr/sabri-ulker-vakfından-covid-19-donemi-beslenme-davranıslari-arastirmasi

Seidman, İ. E. (1991). *Interviewing as qualitative research: A guide for researchers in education and the social sciences.* Teachers College Press.

Sequira, T. (2021). *New COVID variant found in Finland may not shop up in test.* Helsinki Times. https://www.helsinkitimes.fi/finland/news-in-brief/18735-new-covid-variant-found-in-finland-may-not-show-up-in-tests.html

Tekin Çevik, İ. (2020). Changing Consumer Behavior In The Pandemic Process [Pandemi Sürecinde Değişen Tüketici Davranışları]. *BMIIJ, 8*(2), 2331–2347.

Tolay, İ., & Sinclair, L. (2020). *Instincts to help you understand consumer need in uncertain times* [Belirsiz zamanlarda tüketici ihtiyacını anlamanıza yardımcı olacak içgüdüler]. https://www.thinkwithgoogle.com/intl/tr-tr/icgoruler/t%C3%BCketici-trendleri/belirsiz-zamanlarda-tuketici-ihtiyacini-anlamaniza-yardimci-olacak-icgoruler-11-mayis-2020/

Türnüklü, A. (2000). A Qualitative Research Technique That Can Be Used Effectively in Educational Research: Interview [Eğitimbilim Araştırmalarında Etkin Olarak Kullanılabilecek Nitel Bir Araştırma Tekniği: Görüşme]. *Educational Management in Theory and Practice, 24*, 543–559.

United Nations. (2021). *The global food crises.* www.un.org/esa/socdev/rwss/docs/2011/chapter4.pdf

Wang, H., & Hao, N. (2020). Panic buying? Food hoarding during the pandemic period with city lockdown. *Journal of Integrative Agriculture, 9*(12), 2916–2925. doi:10.1016/S2095-3119(20)63448-7

World Health Organizastion (WHO). (2020a). *Resources Publications.* https://www.who.int/csr/resources/publications/WHO_CDS_EPR_GIP_2007_2c.pdf

World Health Organization (WHO). (2020b). *Sars Country Table.* https://www.who.int/csr/sars/country/table2004_04_21/en/

Yıldırım, A., & Şimsek, H. (2016). *Qualitative Research Methods in the Social Sciences* [Sosyal Bilimlerde Nitel Araştırma Yöntemleri]. Seçkin Publishing.

Chapter 5
Exploring the Role of Social Media Influencer Marketing in the Tourism Sector

Lakshmi Raj
https://orcid.org/0000-0002-4735-7539
Christ University, India

Mallika Sankar M.
Christ University, India

ABSTRACT

The growing popularity of social media influencers (SMI) increasingly encourages destinations to use social media influencer marketing (SMIM) for their promotional campaigns. SMIs demonstrate the power of an individual based on certain factors employed to influence a broad segment of audience, and when it is used for marketing purposes, it is known as SMIM. SMIM is a part of the social media marketing that exercises all the commercial marketing techniques via social media channels. SMIM has impacted many industries including tourism, but looking at the progressive growth of SMIM today, it is surprising that such little attention had been paid to this area. However, while there is increasing use of SMIM by tourism organizations, there is a lack of research and limited knowledge on the roles of SMIM in travel and tourism. This chapter sheds light on the use of SMIM in the tourism sector where existing literature on the SMIM, its factors, and the influence of SMIM on the tourism sector by distinct authors are reviewed to identify the effectiveness of SMIM in the travel and tourism industry.

INTRODUCTION

Tourism demonstrates positive impacts on individuals, society and global economy as a whole. For an individual it opens the gate to the outside world where they encounter experiences with different people, customs and traditions contributing to the pathway of knowledge enrichment. It plays a huge role in preserving local culture and heritage, commercialisation of art and culture, and revitalisations of differ-

DOI: 10.4018/978-1-6684-4645-4.ch005

ent customs and art forms. For enhancing economic growth, it plays an important role by improving the tax revenue, increasing the standard of living and employment opportunities. The travel and tourism's total contribution to the global economy is US$5.81 trillion, number of international tourists' arrival is 426.9 million and the global leisure travel spend is US$2.37 trillion (Lock,2022b). The recent pandemic has adversely effected tourism industry where the global revenue for the travel and tourism industry was estimated US$396.37 billion in 2020 - a decrease of around 42.1 percent from 2019 which is significantly lower than the original 2020 forecast of around US$712 billion dollars (Lock,2022a).

Technological progression has been a boon to tourism industry where the evolution of internet especially social media is playing a significant role in many aspects of tourism such as information search, tourism marketing and promotion, interactions with customers, and so forth. Consumers engage themselves in social networking sites such as Instagram, Facebook, Twitter and YouTube for research trips to gather information about the destination, airline, hotels etc so as to make an informed decision and to also share their personal experiences.

Global social networking user's penetration has escalated from 42 percent in 2018 to 60 percent in 2022 and by 2027 it is expected to reach 74 percent (Dixon,2022a). As the pace of social media users are escalating, the tourism industry must make a good use of social media to reach and cater the needs of their market segment. Social media marketing (SMM) is a concept where social media acts as a marketing tool to promote the brand of a product or service, to engage and retain the consumers with an ultimate objective to sell the product or service (Saravanakumar & SuganthaLakshmi, 2012; Constantinides,2014; Pourkhani et al., 2019).

However, inclusion of social media influencers (SMI) has become one of the most prominent communication and marketing strategies by different industries. SMIs exhibit the power of an individual who can influence a broad market segment, and when SMI posts about a product or service on social media in exchange of compensation, it is known as social media influencer marketing (SMIM) (Glucksman, 2017; Campbell & Grimm, 2019; Campbell & Farrell, 2020). SMIM was limited to fashion, beauty and style, but now it has spread to almost every industry, with tourism being one of the sectors where SMIs have become crucial.

The purpose of this study is to propose an enhanced view on the role of SMI marketing in the tourism industry by integrating the contribution by different authors (Xu & Pratt, 2018; Gretzel, 2018; Vassakis et al., 2019; Lalangan,2020; Femenia-Serra & Gretzel, 2020; Cholprasertsuk, 2020; Jang et al., 2020; Yaagoubi & Machrafi,2021; Kusumadewi et al., 2021; Sesar et al., 2021; Asan, 2021; Seçilmiş et al., 2021; Georgea et al., 2021; Femenia-Serra et al., 2022) along with different factors of SMIM (i.e., appearance, content production, credibility, genuine self-sharing, and expertise) (Glucksman, 2017; Isyanto et al., 2020; Tsen & Cheng, 2021) to identify the effectiveness of SMIM in influencing the travel choice decisions of the followers.

Significance of the Study

The relevance of this study stems from the fact that how SMI marketing and its elements influence customers and inspire them in making their travel choices. SMI marketing has become a revolutionary change in the business world. It can also make a major contribution to tourism sector development. Destination marketers can make very good use of SMIs in promoting the quality, track record, and reliability of the destination. It will also become directly or indirectly a source of livelihood for many people related to the tourism industry and industry associated with tourism. Given the scale of the influencer market nowadays, it is surprising that such little attention had been paid to this area. However, while there is increasing use of influencer marketing by tourism organizations there is a lack of research and limited knowledge on the roles of social media influencers marketing in travel and tourism (Gretzel, 2018; Femenia-Serra & Gretzel, 2020).

Research Questions

1. What is the role of social media influencer marketing (SMIM) in tourism sector?
2. What are the different factors of SMIM in promoting tourism?

Research Objectives

1. To study the role of social media influencer marketing (SMIM) in tourism sector.
2. To explore various factors of SMIM in promoting tourism.

Research Methodology

The study follows an exploratory design using theory synthesis approach where existing literature on SMIM and its influence on tourism sector along with different factors of SMIM by distinct authors are reviewed to achieve the conceptual integration across multiple theories to propose an enhanced view of the role of SMIM in tourism which contributes in identifying the effectiveness of SMIM in influencing the travel choice decisions.

Social Media Marketing in the Tourism Sector

The Internet is one of the most predominant technologies that have changed travellers' behaviour and the way people plan for and consume travel (Buhalis & Law, 2008), of which diffusion of social media has made a tremendous impact on travel and tourism (Dwityas & Briandana, 2017). Social media is reckoned as a platform for interaction among people by sharing information, experiences, perspectives, and to collaborate through community-oriented websites (Weinberg, 2009; Grosseck, 2009) that promotes a company's brand, product, or services. It has transformed society by providing "a platform, where users can jointly investigate, network content, share their experience and build up a relationship for different purposes, e.g., social or educational" (Jiao et al., 2015).

It plays both passive and active role by receiving all kinds of information, and sharing recommendations and advice with each other, acting as influencers themselves. Social media is defined as "a group of Internet-based applications that build on the ideological and technical foundations of Web 2.0, and that allow the creation and exchange of user-generated content" (Kaplan & Haenlein, 2010).

Over the last decade, the escalated growth of social media users from 2.86 billion in 2017 to 3.78 billion in 2021(Dixon, 2022c) along with the introduction of smartphones has significantly changed people's attitude towards information search on anything around the world which incorporates choosing a touristic destination to selecting a restaurant, from food to fashion, from religion to ethical issues. Electronic word of-mouth (eWoM) is the supreme aspect of social media in sharing data (Ingrassia et al., 2022). Social media plays a crucial role as a source of information (Xiang & Gretzel, 2009; Dwityas & Briandana, 2017) to guide the traveller in every stage of travel decision making, and at each step, the traveller is using the information in carrying out all activities to be undertaken (Dwityas & Briandana, 2017). The most important role of social media is to promote travellers to post and share their travel experiences, comments, and opinions, by having them serve as a source of information for other users (Zivkovic et al., 2014).

Information shared on social media sites is recognized as an important information source that may influence travel decision-making for potential travellers (Kang and Schuett,2013). Social media is quite expressive, where consumers can influence other consumers with their own opinions and experiences (Zivkovic et al., 2014). As the matter of fact, social media has become a predominant feature in marketing where marketing by means of social media is called "social media marketing". Felix et al. (2017) defined social media marketing as:

"An interdisciplinary and cross-functional concept that uses social media (often in combination with other communications channels) to achieve organizational goals by creating value for stakeholders."

The social media domain gives businesses new opportunities to improve their competitive position and to create new forms of customer value that attract new customers and builds strong relationships with them (Constantinides, 2014). Through social media marketing, individuals or firms can tap a much larger community by promoting the products, or services through their websites via online social channels (Barefoot & Szabo, 2010; Weinberg & Pehlivan, 2011). The basic objective of social media marketing is to stimulate sales, increase brand awareness, improve brand image, generate traffic to online platforms, reduce marketing costs, and create user interactivity on platforms by stimulating users to post or share content. The marketing framework relies on commercial marketing's conceptual framework, or the marketing mix, which includes eight components involved in the exchange process (i.e., the product, price, place, promotion, public partnership, policy, productivity, and quality) (Thorat et al., 2013).

In the tourism sector, social media marketing is considered a powerful tool in empowering, engaging and educating people about the tourist destination and many tourism businesses have recognized this and have invested in social media marketing to reach customers and engage with them in 'real time' (O'Connor et al., 2016); hence, tourism businesses have a strategy in place to successfully use it as a promotional tool (O'Connor et al., 2016). The typology of social media used for tourism marketing purposes is classified as follows (Sharma & Verma, 2018; Hysa et al., 2021):

- Blogs (e.g., Blogger, WordPress): "These are personal journals on the Internet arranged in reverse chronological order that facilitates interactive computer-mediated communication through text, images, and audio, video objects" (Huang et al., 2007).
- Microblogs (e.g., Twitter): "Microblogs are online social networks where the updates or content are limited by characters. It is basically used for sharing information and reporting news. There are Character limitations" (Sharma & Verma, 2018).
- Social networking sites (e.g., Facebook, Instagram, Google+): Web-based services where individuals create a public or semi-public profile within a bounded system including a list of other users with whom they share a connection (Boyd & Ellison, 2007).
- Professional social networking sites (e.g., LinkedIn): This social networking site is used for business purposes, job opportunities, etc where it can be employed by tourism companies in Business to the business storefront for destination marketing.

- Collaboration platforms/Cooperation networks/Shared projects (e.g., Wikipedia): The feature of crowdsourcing allows users to coordinate their efforts toward a common goal or task by collaborating ideas (Sharma & Verma,2018).
- Internet forums (e.g., Globetrotter, Fly4Free, Lonely Planet travel forums): Online exchange of information on tourism through these forums guides customers to make their travel decisions.
- Social bookmarking (e.g., Delicious): Sites that allow users to tag online content (Sharma and Verma,2018). It is a technique of tagging a website page with a browser-based tool so that users can easily visit it again later.
- Content communities/Content or media sharing services (e.g., YouTube, Vimeo, Pinterest): Sites that allow users to share videos, presentations, documents, audio, pictures, and other media with other users and are notified of regular updates by subscribing to the particular channel (Sharma & Verma,2018).
- Rating services and portals (e.g., TripAdvisor, Booking, Holiday Check): Rating services and portals guides customers in taking a precise decision on making travel choice by providing user-generated content and comparison-shopping website.
- Virtual worlds, social (e.g., Second Life): It is a three-dimensional computer-generated environment designed to simulate real-life situations (Utomo et al., 2022). The travel and tourism industry has also embraced Second Life as a collaborative and commercial platform for connecting with travellers, marketing tourism locations, and managing businesses (Utomo et al., 2022).

To attain maximum benefit from social media, marketers must select appropriate social media platforms to reach and engage their target audience (Kaur & Kumar,2020). According to Ryan Robinson (2020) in his paper, "The 7 Top Social Media Sites You Need to Care About in 2020", for marketing activities: Instagram is followed by YouTube which is then followed by Facebook, Twitter, TikTok, Pinterest, and Snapchat. Instagram launched in 2010, enables users to share their photos and videos enabling them to exploit the business ventures (Alkhowaiter, 2016), and has a professional dashboard, a central destination to track performance, access and discover professional tools, and explore educational information curated by Instagram (Instagram-Business-Team,2021).

Facebook is launched in 2004, and formerly Facebook for business is now known as Meta for business (October 28, 2021), it discovers tools, insights, and resources to reach and connect with the customers (Anonymous, n.d).YouTube was launched in 2005, where vloggers promote travel experiences, products, services, brands, and so forth via YouTube videos. Additionally, there is YouTube endorsement marketing, referred to as native advertising, it is a form of marketing where advertisements are included in the video content unlike traditional commercials (Wu,2016). Twitter was launched in 2006 which offers a microblogging service where customers can put opinions on the products or services, on which companies respond proactively to customer issues and, for marketing activities. Twitter has developed Twitter marketing services where social media strategists and content creators drive brand awareness, follower engagement and influencer relations (Anonymous, n.d.).

The active social media users of different networking sites include Facebook (2,910 million), YouTube (2,562 million), WhatsApp (2000 million), and Instagram (1,478 million) (Dixon,2022b). Social Media has become one of the elements of the promotional mix that helps marketers talk to their customers and assists them to talk directly to one another (Pourkhani et al., 2019).

Social Media Influencer Marketing in the Tourism Sector

Marketers are transferring some control out of the agency into the hands of influencers who posts product or service details on social media in exchange for compensation (Campbell and Grimm, 2019), leveraging their skill sets and close connections to the target audience and this concept is called Influencer marketing or social media influencer marketing (SMIM), a practice of compensating individuals for posting about a product or service on social media (Campbell and Farrell, 2020). According to Morgan Glucksman (2017), Influencer marketing is,

"the process of identifying, engaging, and supporting individuals who create conversations with a brand's customers, is a growing trend used in public relations initiatives. In recent years, this strategy has become predominantly centered around social media, creating an opportunity for brands to market through social media influencers".

SMIM involves a form of marketing activities in which influencers identify and build relationships with their followers (Ingrassia et al., 2022). It is also considered as a cost-effective marketing instrument (Femenia-Serral & Gretzel, 2020; Ingrassia et al., 2022). This study focuses on identifying the role of social media influencer marketing in tourism sector. The supporting literature that substantiates the role of social media influencer marketing in tourism sector are as follows:

Table 1.

Sr. no	Author & Year	Title	Role of social media influencer marketing on tourism industry
1	Femenia-Serra et al., 2022	Instagram travel influencers in #quarantine: Communicative practices and roles during COVID-19	The findings contribute to the crisis communication literature by illustrating that influencers constitute important allies for organisations when communicating during a crisis and have played a critical role in tourism recovery.
2	Georgea et al., 2021	Word-of-Mouth Redefined: A Profile of Influencers in the Travel and Tourism Industry	The research demonstrates how the new influencers have a strong role in generating travel urge and desire.
3	Seçilmiş et al., 2021	How travel influencers affect visit intention? The roles of cognitive response, trust, COVID-19 fear and confidence in vaccine	This study demonstrates that SMIs affect the travel intention and therefore it is necessary for tourism businesses and destination managers to give importance to influencers who can directly affect people in a competitive environment
4	Asan, 2021	Measuring the impacts of travel influencers on bicycle travellers	The findings showed four effects of followers that traveller influencers can influence; informative effects, motivating effects, effects as a role model, and communal effects.
5	Sesar et al., 2021	Influencer marketing in Travel and Tourism: Literature review	The results of the research indicate that there is a growing interest in the use of influencer marketing as a strategy tool to promote destination tourism and to induce customers travel intention.
6	Kusumadewi et al., 2021	Persuasion Mechanism of Social Media Influencers in Tourism	Travelers chose travel destinations, hotels, airlines and agencies based on the advice of influencers.

continues on following page

Table 1. Continued

Sr. no	Author & Year	Title	Role of social media influencer marketing on tourism industry
7	Yaagoubi and Machrafi, 2021	Social media influencers, Digital marketing and tourism in Morocco	Working with SMI will benefit tourism brands in extending the content reach of brand where they can target existing as well as new audiences.
8	Jang et al., 2020	The role of engagement in travel influencer marketing: the perspectives of dual process theory and the source credibility model	The results suggest that engagement becomes an important characteristic of SMIs that determines the effectiveness of advertising messages delivered by them, and their perceived attractiveness when consumers are skeptical about influencer messages.
9	Cholprasertsuk, 2020	Social Media Influencers and Thai Tourism Industry: Tourists' Behavior, Travel Motivation, and Influencing Factors	The findings suggest that social media influencers create significant impacts on consumers' decision-making in the tourism sector, in which most tourists tend to search for reviews or useful information from SMIs regarding travel plans in order to avoid terrible travel experiences.
10	Femenia-Serra and Gretzel, 2020	Influencer Marketing for Tourism Destinations: Lessons from a Mature Destination	The findings reveal that influencer marketing provides DMOs with an opportunity to gain back control over branding and promoting a destination while taking full advantage of the power of social media-based eWOM
11	Lalangan, 2020	Social Media in Tourism: The Impacts of Travel Content on YouTube and Instagram	Based on the findings, travel content impacts the follower by providing entertainment, travel education, tips from experts, and inspiration from travel role models.
12	Vassakis et al., 2019	Location-Based Social Network Data for Tourism Destinations	Influencer marketing can contribute to enhance destination attractiveness or destination branding since influencers can spread messages affecting communities in the digital world.
13	Gretzel, 2018	Influencer Marketing in Travel and Tourism	Destination marketers can take advantage of these influencers and their ability to reach large/targeted audiences with engaging contents by building mutually beneficial relationships with social media influencers that align with their brands.
14	Xu and Pratt, 2018	Social media influencers as endorsers to promote travel destinations: an application of self-congruence theory to the Chinese Generation Y	The congruence between SMIs' perceived images and consumers' ideal self-images is found to significantly positively impact visit intentions toward the endorsed destinations. Therefore, destination marketers should consider employing SMIs to promote tourism-related products and destinations.

According to the state of influencer marketing 2020: Benchmark report, the growth in influencer marketing witnessed an estimated market size increase from US$6.6 billion in 2019 to US$9.7 billion in 2020(Geyser,2022). In 2020, over 380 new influencer marketing-focused platforms and agencies entered the market. In 2015, there were 190 influencer platforms and agencies and now it has grown to 1120 in 2019. The market potential of influencer marketing as of 2022 is 16.4 billion dollars (Statista-Research-Department,2022). SMI is a third-party endorser who shapes audience attitudes through blogs, tweets, and videos using social media (Freberg, et al., 2010). It is also defined as,

"a person, a group, an organization who has the ability to influence the decisions of a target audience on a digital platform because of their popularity, credibility, expertise, status, or connection with their viewers" (Bansal & Saini, 2022).

The types of SMIs depend upon the size of the followers (i.e., nano, micro, macro, mega and celebrity influencers) (Campbell & Farrell,2020; Bansal & Saini,2022). Traditionally, these influencers were celebrities and they were used in advertising to endorse products (Gretzel, 2018); however, now they are "vocational, sustained and highly branded social media stars who exert influence over a large pool of potential customers" (Mokhare et al., 2021) and are also known as online opinion leaders (especially in China) (Gretzel, 2018). SMIs are also considered brand endorsers who are trusted individuals with great power to influence their followers by offering advice and opinions on a particular product or service (Gretzel, 2018; Mokhare et al., 2021).

Selecting the right SMI that represents the values of the brand or a destination is an important task and this can be achieved when the SMI's profile matches with the brand's target, advertisers values, when the personality of the SMI matches with the values of the company, when the content created by the SMI is of high quality in terms of pictures, writings, and stories and the most important is the destination knowledge SMI has on food, history, culture, and so forth (Yaagoubi & Machrafi, 2021). The correct SMIs help in increasing brand awareness, building trust, drive participation and sales (Huang & Copeland, 2020).

The major motive behind using these SMIs by the companies is to shift the company's goals from customer acquisition to retention and commitment (Manero & Navarro, 2020). The usage of appropriate social media platforms, designing the right message, and engaging the right users to spread the information is crucial in SMIM (Jashi,2013). SMIs have the capability to influence the decisions of followers in choosing travel destinations, hotels, airlines and agencies (Kusumadewi et al., 2021). SMIM provides destination marketing organizations with full advantage of social media based eWOM (electronic word of mouth) (Femenia-Serra & Gretzel,2020). They are highly capable of creating original, appealing, brand-friendly content rather than following the advertising model and, with a large base audience, they are more effective than celebrity endorsements (Huang & Copeland, 2020).

SMIM was applied to fashion, beauty and style, but now it has become highly prominent in travel and tourism (Femenia-Serra & Gretzel, 2020). In tourism, SMI is also known as a travel influencer who promotes a product, service, particular destination, or a brand by distributing electronic word of mouth through their online digital channels and presence (Georgea et al., 2021). To boost and stimulate travel desire, many international hotel firms are making use of SMIM (Gretzel, 2018) and marketers are advised to use social media influencers (Pop et al.,2021). Social media influencers improve the reputation of that particular destination by driving awareness and soliciting followers' comments and feedback which enhances the relationship with followers (Booth & Matic, 2011; Campbell & Farrell, 2020). Tourism practitioners select social media influencers as endorsers who construct great engagement with their followers (Jang et al., 2020).

Grassroots influencers or micro-influencers engage customers through their relevant content (Gretzel, 2018), they make up for their smaller reach through higher relevance and resonance, leading to much higher engagement rates and are increasingly used by marketers to spread messages to targeted audiences on social media (Gretzel, 2018). SMIM can enhance destination attractiveness or destination branding (Vassakis et al., 2019) and is treated by the practitioners as an accessible and affordable practice that has higher credibility, reflects authentic opinions, elicits deeper engagement with potential visitors, and adapts to current preferences of audiences (Femenia-Serra & Gretzel,2020). Xu and Pratt (2018) gave empirical evidence in their study implying that SMIs can be acknowledged as endorsers for destination marketing and a good fit between endorser and destination is important for converting their prospective customers to potential customers. Working with SMI will benefit tourism brands in extending the content reach of brand where they can target existing as well as new audiences (Yaagoubi & Machrafi, 2021).

The credibility of the SMI will push the follower to take actions such as sharing the message in their respective circle (Yaagoubi & Machrafi, 2021). The most affected industry at the time of the crisis COVID-19 was travel and tourism. SMIs have played a crucial role in shaping the online conversations on tourism communication and marketing which has played a pivotal position in the recovery phase (Femenia-Serra et al., 2022). They have also integrated safety measures and rules in their content, adding humour to their content to convey the campaign message to the audience (Femenia-Serra et al., 2022).

During this crisis, SMIs are recommending plans and alternatives for recovery and brands have asked for advice and support from the influencer community (Femenia-Serra et al., 2022). Despite the pandemic process, the current results prove that the cooperation between SMIs and tourism businesses has increased the market share of the tourism sector confirming SMIM as an effective marketing tool (Secilmis et al., 2021). Since 2020, the SMIs are focused on traveling domestically avoiding international and long trips with an objective to collaborate with local firms so that they can appeal to national followers and work with DMOs seeking to attract domestic visitors (Femenia-Serra et al., 2022).

SMIs can be categorized into different groups where they focus on specific experiences such as sustainability, family travel, solo travel, and outdoor adventures and, they post their personal experiences and personal tips such as travel budget details, places to shop/eat/visit and linguistics, etc which serves as a travel guide to their viewers (Lalangan, 2020). Some SMIs also create content on unique subjects like traveling on a low budget and visiting less known or less desirable destinations (Lalangan, 2020). SMIM is used as a strategy tool to promote customer travel intention and boost destination tourism (Sesar et al., 2021).

The appropriate influencer strategy can deliver many benefits to destination marketing organisations (Femenia-Serra & Gretzel, 2020). It is beneficial in a way that consumers seek SMIs who have real experience in their travel journey instead of companies publishing positive comments on their own products (Lalangan, 2020). According to Asan (2021), there are four effects of followers that SMIs can influence: informative effects, motivating effects, effects as a role model, and communal effects, and these effects are significant to managers and public leaders so that they can efficiently use it in SMIM approach for promoting tourism (Sesar et al., 2021).

Since SMIs affect the travel intention of followers, it is important for tourism businesses and destination managers to give importance to the influencers and select them on the basis of their expertise and attractive content (Secilmis et al., 2021). The expertise of SMIs in their respective field generates trust among followers which directly increases the visit intentions of potential customers (Secilmis et al., 2021). Influencer agencies play a huge part in encouraging tourism by acting as mediators between SMIs and businesses or destination managers which brings together the suitable influencers and destinations by considering the factors that affect visit intention (Secilmis et al., 2021).

Georgea et al. (2021) contributes to the wider academic literature that SMIs have an increasingly specialized role in tourism and hospitality marketing and perform a strong role in generating travel urge and desires. SMIs attract millions of followers with their shared content on platforms like Instagram and YouTube, and marketers have considered these SMIs as their brand's spokesperson and advertisers due to which a large budget is invested in SMI's endorsement (Ingrassia et al., 2022). In travel and tourism, SMIs are also considered opinion leaders who are recognized for giving advice to their followers (Ingrassia et al., 2022).

SMIs have the capability that brands and governments do not, that is to appear as authentic, independent, and trustable sources (Serra et al., 2022). Investment in traditional marketing is more compared to SMIs marketing and the effectiveness of SMIs is more compared to traditional marketing since SMI's target is more focused and reachable (Ingrassia et al., 2022). Tourism brands must communicate their requirements with SMI in following ways: by setting a timeline of all the posts and their content and at the same time giving freedom to the SMI since SMI knows better to talk to the community, SMI should be well versed with the idea, goals and objectives on what the brand needs (Yaagoubi & Machrafi, 2021).

While selecting SMIs as endorsers, their values and characteristics must align with the one that target customers admire and tend to pursue (Xu & Pratt, 2018). The future of SMIM is promising but also highly volatile, which makes it necessary for tourism companies and destination marketing organisation to keep their SMIM techniques and decisions updated (Femenia-Serra & Gretzel, 2020). The factors of social media influencers that guide marketing activities in the tourism industry are appearance, content production, credibility, genuine self-sharing, and expertise (Glucksman, 2017; Isyanto et al.,2020; Tsen & Cheng, 2021).

- *Appearance (500)*: Appearance is basically how the influencer is presenting herself or himself which also plays a major role in seeking the attention of the customers (Tsen & Cheng, 2021). The appearance of SMI can be classified as attractiveness (Tsen & Cheng, 2021; Ingrassia et al., 2022) and confidence (Glucksman,2017). According to Erdogan (1999), attractiveness is "a stereotype of positive associations to a person and entails not only physical attractiveness but also other characteristics such as personality and athletic ability". SMIs attractiveness engages his / her followers (Jang et al., 2020) and higher level of attractiveness is more likely to shape follower's purchase intention (Van der Waldt et al., 2009), in terms of tourism shapes follower's travel choice decisions. SMIs attractiveness not only help in increasing follower's trust in content but also accelerate brand awareness (Loua & Yuan, 2019). The attribute confidence in SMI is entailed when they trust themselves and assure their followers of their abilities (Glucksman, 2017). Destination marketing organisation will approach SMIs who are confident enough to capture the interest of their followers with their appearance.
- *Content production (500)*: Content production is an SMI's ability to produce attention-seeking videos, having good writing skills, photo-shooting skills, and photo editing skills (Tsen & Cheng,2021). Content production is the most significant aspect of SMI's role (Campbell & Farrell, 2020). Content is delivered in the form of videos, images, stories, blog post, podcast including embedded content and text descriptions (Huang & Copeland, 2020). Ong et al. (2022) highlights follower's interaction with SMI destination marketing campaign giving importance to the content product by the SMI which is to be considered as a significant tool in destination marketing. SMIs and their teams are skilled and qualified at directing, producing and editing social media content for their brand partners (Campbell & Farrell, 2020). Some brands give complete freedom to SMIs on producing the content, to show their creativity and some may prefer to give SMIs less autonomy or creative control (Campbell & Farrell, 2020). Brands may supply influencers with detailed guidelines on how a brand and product should be depicted, and SMI may have to undergo their content checked out before posting (Campbell & Farrell,2020). According to Shahbaznezhad et al., (2020), social media content can be classified into three main categories of "rational (also referred to as informational, functional, educational, or current event), interactional (e.g., experiential, personal, employee, brand community, customer relationship, cause-related),

and transactional (also referred to as remunerative, brand resonance, sales promotion)". Content accuracy and authenticity is an important factor in SMIM which increases trust in SMI and may positively influence follower's travel choice decisions (Secilmis, 2021), Therefore the up-to-date content, its relevance and how much informative and entertaining it is also plays an important role in content production.

- *Credibility (500)*: Credibility answers the question of whether the individual is believable (Wiedmann & Mettenheim,2020). A credible SMI is the one whom the followers can trust, who provides true information, and is able to provide professional advice to answer the inquiries of followers (Tsen & Cheng, 2021). An SMI must possess credibility or can be believed by consumers or followers of social media, accounts to generate confidence in prospective customers (Isyanto et al., 2020). Credibility of SMI has a significant positive influence on the intention of users to visit the endorsed destination (Han & Chen,2021). The total number of followers predicts the levels of expertise and source credibility the SMI possesses, the personality is expressed through social media activities presented using photos, videos and posts (Chatzigeorgiou, 2017; Jang et al., 2020). SMIs having more followers reflects their network size and leads to higher perception of popularity which ascribes their credibility (De Veirman et al., 2017). Trustworthiness is an important factor which validates credibility and is defined as "the honesty, integrity and believability the endorser possesses" (Van der Waldt et al., 2009). It concerns the follower's perception of a source as honest, sincere, or truthful (Ingrassia et al., 2022). It is when the SMI is genuine and relatable with their followers (Glucksman,2017). Followers trust SMI's propositions over brand advertisements and believe that SMIs are reliable/credible sources of information, are trustworthy, and provide authentic content (Chopra et al., 2021). The degree to which trust and loyalty between the followers and their SMIs have affects the sustainability of the relationships between the followers and the SMIs, the sales, and the brand (AlFarraj et al., 2021). Ethics of authenticity in SMI also suffices credibility where the decision-making is premised on two central tenets "(1) being true to oneself, and by extension, one's brand; (2) being true to one's audience by providing it with the content it seeks" (Wellman et al., 2020). SMIs use their "understanding of "authenticity" as an ethical principle when producing sponsored/paid content" (Wellman et al., 2020). The number of followers, trustworthiness and authenticity, in turn, confirm the critical role of credibility of social media influencers.
- *Genuine self-sharing (500)*: SMIs share their genuine life experience with their followers via vlog or blog and are willing to share their own privacy (e.g., relationship status, education qualifications, family status, etc.) weaknesses, daily life pictures, etc (Tsen & Cheng, 2021) which builds trust among their followers to believe in their opinions and the companies makes use of this trust in SMIs to promote their brand. Genuine sharing helps SMI to be positively identified by the followers (Tsen & Cheng, 2021). Genuine self-sharing of private information is a strategy to create intimacy among followers (Marwick, 2015).
- *Expertise (500)*: Expertise is mainly defined as "the degree to which the endorser is perceived to have the adequate knowledge, experience or skills to promote the product" (Van der Waldt et al., 2009). An SMI will be an expert in a particular area (Tsen & Cheng, 2021) and expertise describes SMI's level of knowledge who is endorsing a particular brand. An expert is capable of performing in a domain at a high level that can be achieved by a few others (perhaps by only a small percentage of the general population) (Wiedmann & Mettenheim, 2020). It is defined in terms of peak or at least high levels of knowledge, experience, and problem-solving skills within

a given domain. Experts are meant to provide plausible information in their domain compared to those who are not familiar with that field (AlFarraj et al., 2021). An SMI who has expertise in his/her domain is identified as an expert with immense persuasive quality and highly engaged with the brand (Erdogan, 1999). Followers or consumers seek for expert opinion and want to engage themselves with SMIs who are knowledgeable, so marketers wish to leverage expert SMIs who include abundant information conveyed via blog posts, videos on YouTube, and Instagram stories (Mudambi & Schuff, 2010). SMIs will not be considered as having expertise in a particular area unless his/her followers believe in him/her as skilful, proficient and having adequate knowledge (Schouten et al., 2019). Expert SMIs prove their credibility by presenting both the positive and negative attributes of products they review, and this has been shown to make reviews more persuasive (Mudambi & Schuff, 2010). With the expertise that SMIs possess, they could strongly shape the level of credibility, level of customer engagement, and accordingly, their intention to purchase as well (Schouten et al., 2019; AlFarraj et al., 2021). An effective SMI should be knowledgeable about the new products and trends (Tsen & Cheng, 2021). Including knowledge and experience, it is important for SMIs to have passion in that particular domain which is reflected in their work leading their followers to make the purchase decision.

Travel choice decisions of a traveller is motivated by cultural and historical exploration, socializing with different people, togetherness (family and friends), adventures sports attraction, local special event, savour different cuisines, recreational activities, enhancement of knowledge from particular destination, budget meals and accommodation, security and hygiene of a particular destination, natural sites, spiritual fulfilment and so forth. SMIs can work on their factors along with these motivating factors to come with a strategy to administer assistance to SMIM.

DISCUSSION

The immense growth of bloggers and vloggers and their power to influence people has resulted in many companies utilizing SMIs in marketing their brand through social media platforms. SMIs have a personal approach and engage a broad segment of customers via social media. This helps firms in promoting their business and creating a pragmatic view among consumers. It constructs heuristics in consumers' minds directing them to make travel choices. In this technologically progressed scenario where digital mobility and social media practices are making an enormous development, people turn to online sources for making their travel choices.

Companies make use of SMIs in promoting the quality, track record, and reliability of their brand. This study provides conclusive evidence and relevant contribution to the literature supporting that SMIM has an enormous power over the tourism industry whereby it can influence followers in making decisions on a particular travel choice. Tourism sector is one of the industries that are heavily affected by SMIM and has seized interest of both SMIs and destination marketing organizations. SMIs are a promotional medium that positively improves the image of a brand and tourist destination.

This positive image will create a high perceived value to enhance tourist satisfaction, their return visits and word-of-mouth promotion. They make use of multimedia features such as posts, videos, stories, live and IGTV etc to come up with a high-resolution social appearance. Their travel content inspires followers to travel where they suggest and this is harnessed by tourist companies and destination marketing organisations to collaborate with SMIs to improve their profile. Literature by different authors is reviewed in this study inclusive of different factors of SMI (i.e., appearance, content production, credibility, genuine self-sharing, and expertise with an objective to explore the role of SMIM in the tourism sector).

FUTURE TRENDS AND CONCLUSION

Technological progression has enhanced digital mobility and social media practices providing a pathway for the tourism industry. This research focuses on the capability and power of an influencer in promoting tourism. It gives a deeper understanding of the role and factors of social media influencer marketing (SMIM) in the tourism sector. The congruity between SMIs and followers plays a significant role in creating an influence (i.e., the SMIs must establish the values and characteristics through their factors such as appearance, content production, credibility, genuine self-sharing, and expertise that the followers admire). This research will not only promote the selection of the finest policies and long-term strategies prioritizing the development of value and enhancing the functioning and integration of the tourism industry but also recommend travel influencers incorporate important elements in their content to be more beneficial for their followers. And for scholars, it provides a pathway to conduct an empirical study to analyse which SMI factors have more influence on the travel choice decision of the followers so as to come up with a refined model of SMIM.

REFERENCES

AlFarraj, O., Alalwan, A. A., Obeidat, Z. M., Baabdullah, A., Aldmour, R., & Al-Haddad, S. (2021). Examining the impact of influencers' credibility dimensions: attractiveness, trustworthiness and expertise on the purchase intention in the aesthetic dermatology industry. *Review of International Business and Strategy*. doi:10.1108/RIBS-07-2020-0089

Alkhowaiter, W. (2016). The Power of Instagram in Building Small Businesses. *Social Media: The Good, the Bad, and the Ugly, 9844*, 59-64. doi:10.1007/978-3-319-45234-0_6

Asan, K. (2022). Measuring the impacts of travel influencers on bicycle travellers. *Current Issues in Tourism*, *25*(6), 978–994. doi:10.1080/13683500.2021.1914004

Bansal, R., & Saini, S. (2022). Leveraging Role of Social Media Influences in Corporate World—An Overview. *Journal of Global Marketing*, *5*(1), 1–5.

Barefoot, D., & Szabo, J. (2010). *Friends with benefits: A social media-marketing handbook*. William Pollock.

Berne-Manero, C., & Marzo-Navarro, M. (2020). Exploring how influencer and relationship marketing serve corporate sustainability. *Sustainability*, *12*(11), 4392. doi:10.3390u12114392

Booth, N., & Matic, J. A. (2011). Mapping and leveraging influencers in social media to shape corporate brand perceptions. *Corporate Communications*, *16*(3), 184–191. doi:10.1108/13563281111156853

Boyd, D. M., & Ellison, N. B. (2008). Social Network Sites: Definition, History, and Scholarship. *Journal of Computer-Mediated Communication*, *13*(1), 210–230. doi:10.1111/j.1083-6101.2007.00393.x

Buhalis, D., & Law, R. (2008). Progress in information technology and tourism management: 20 years on and 10 years after the Internet—The state of eTourism research. *Tourism Management, 29*(4), 609-623. doi:10.1016/j.tourman.2008.01.005

Campbell, C., & Farrell, J. R. (2020). More than meets the eye: The functional components underlying influencer marketing. *Business Horizons*, *63*(4), 469–479. doi:10.1016/j.bushor.2020.03.003

Campbell, C., & Grimm, P. E. (2019). The Challenges Native Advertising Poses: Exploring Potential Federal Trade Commission Responses and Identifying Research Needs. *Journal of Public Policy & Marketing*, *38*(1), 110–123. doi:10.1177/0743915618818576

Chatzigeorgiou, C. (2017). Modelling the impact of social media influencers on behavioural intentions of millennials: The case of tourism in rural areas in Greece. *Journal of Tourism, Heritage & Services Marketing, 3*(2), 25-29. doi:10.5281/zenodo.1209125

Chopra, A., Avhad, V., & Jaju, A. S. (2021). Influencer marketing: An exploratory study to identify antecedents of consumer behavior of millennial. *Business Perspectives and Research*, *9*(1), 77–91. doi:10.1177/2278533720923486

Constantinides, E. (2014). Foundations of Social Media Marketing. *Procedia: Social and Behavioral Sciences*, *148*(1), 40–57. doi:10.1016/j.sbspro.2014.07.016

De Veirman, M., Cauberghe, V., & Hudders, L. (2017). Marketing through Instagram influencers: The impact of number of followers and product divergence on brand attitude. *International Journal of Advertising*, *36*(5), 798–828. doi:10.1080/02650487.2017.1348035

Dixon, S. (2022a, June 15). *Social network penetration worldwide from 2018 to 2027*. https://www.statista.com/statistics/260811/social-network-penetration-worldwide/#:~:text=In%202021%2C%20approximately%2056%20percent,amounted%20to%204.59%20billion%20users

Dixon, S. (2022b, July 26). *Most popular social networks worldwide as of January 2022, ranked by number of monthly active users*. https://www.statista.com/statistics/272014/global-social-networks-ranked-by-number-of-users/

Dixon, S. (2022c, September 16). *Number of social media users worldwide from 2018 to 2027*. https://www.statista.com/statistics/278414/number-of-worldwide-social-network-users/

Dwityas, N. A., & Briandana, R. (2017). Social media in travel decision making process. *International Journal of Humanities and Social Science*, *7*(7), 193–201.

El Yaagoubi, W. L., & Machrafi, M. (2021). Social Media Influencers, Digital Marketing, and Tourism in Morocco. *Economic and Social Development: Book of Proceedings*, 145-152.

Erdogan, B. Z. (1999). Celebrity endorsement: A literature review. *Journal of Marketing Management*, *15*(4), 291–314. doi:10.1362/026725799784870379

Felix, R., Rauschnabel, P. A., & Hinsch, C. (2017). Elements of strategic social media marketing: A holistic framework. *Journal of Business Research, 70*(1), 118–126. doi:10.1016/j.jbusres.2016.05.001

Femenia-Serra, F., & Gretzel, U. (2020). Influencer Marketing for Tourism Destinations: Lessons from a Mature Destination. *Information and Communication Technologies in Tourism*, 65-78.

Femenia-Serra, F., Gretzel, U., & Alzua-Sorzabal, A. (2022). Instagram travel influencers in #quarantine: Communicative practices and roles during COVID-19. *Tourism Management, 89*, 104454. Advance online publication. doi:10.1016/j.tourman.2021.104454

Freberg, K., Graham, K., McGaughey, K., & Freberg, L. A. (2011). Who are the social media influencers? A study of public perceptions of personality. *Public Relations Review, 37*(1), 90–92. doi:10.1016/j.pubrev.2010.11.001

Georgea, R., Stainton, H., & Adu-Ampong, E. (2021). Word-of-Mouth Redefined: A Profile of Influencers in the Travel and Tourism Industry. *Journal of Smart Tourism, 1*(3), 31–44. doi:10.52255marttourism.2021.1.3.6

Geyser, W. (2022, February 8). *The State of Influencer Marketing 2020: Benchmark Report*. https://influencermarketinghub.com/influencer-marketing-benchmark-report-2020/

Glucksman, M. (2017). The rise of social media influencer marketing on lifestyle branding: A case study of Lucie Fink. *Elon Journal of Undergraduate Research in Communications, 8*(2), 77-87.

Gretzel, U. (2018). Influencer Marketing in Travel and Tourism. *Advances in Social Media for Travel, Tourism and Hospitality: New Perspectives, Practice and Cases*, 147-156.

Grosseck, G. (2009). To use or not to use web 2.0 in higher education? *Procedia: Social and Behavioral Sciences, 1*(1), 478–482. doi:10.1016/j.sbspro.2009.01.087

Han, J., & Chen, H. (2021). *Millennial social media users' intention to travel: the moderating role of social media influencer following behavior*. International Hospitality Review.

Huang, C. Y., Shen, Y. Z., Lin, H. X., & Chang, S. S. (2007). Bloggers' motivations and behaviors: A model. *Journal of Advertising Research, 47*(4), 472–484. doi:10.2501/S0021849907070493

Huang, O., & Copeland, L. (2020). GEN Z, Instagram Influences, and Hashtags' Influence on Purchase Intention of Apparel. *Academy of Marketing Studies Journal, 24*(3), 1–14.

Hysa, B., Karasek, A., & Zdonek, I. (2021). Social media usage by different generations as a tool for sustainable tourism marketing in society 5.0 idea. *Sustainability, 13*(3), 1018. doi:10.3390/su13031018

Ingrassia, M., Bellia, C., Giurdanella, C., Columba, P., & Chironi, S. (2022). Digital Influencers, Food and Tourism—A New Model of Open Innovation for Businesses in the Ho. Re. Ca. Sector. *Journal of Open Innovation: Technology, Market, and Complexity, 8*(1), 50. doi:10.3390/joitmc8010050

Instagram Business Team. (2021, January 25). *Introducing Professional Dashboard*. https://business.instagram.com/blog/announcing-instagram-professional-dashboard?locale=en_GB

Isyanto, P., Sapitri, R. G., & Sinaga, O. (2020). Micro Influencers Marketing and Brand Image to Purchase Intention of Cosmetic Products Focallure. *Systematic Review Pharmacy, 11*(1), 601–605.

Jang, W., Kim, J., Kim, S., & Chun, J. W. (2020). The role of engagement in travel influencer marketing: The perspectives of dual process theory and the source credibility model. *Current Issues in Tourism*. Advance online publication. doi:10.1080/13683500.2020.1845126

Jashi, C. (2013). Significance of Social Media Marketing in Tourism. *8th Silk Road International Conference "Development of Tourism in Black and Caspian Seas Regions*, 37-40.

Jiao, Y., Gao, J., & Yang, J. (2015, December). Social Value and Content Value in Social Media: Two Ways to Flow. *Journal of Advanced Management Science, 3*(4), 299–306. doi:10.12720/joams.3.4.299-306

Kang, M., & Schuett, M. A. (2013). Determinants of sharing travel experiences in social media. *Journal of Travel & Tourism Marketing, 30*(1-2), 93–107. doi:10.1080/10548408.2013.751237

Kaplan, A. M., & Haenlein, M. (2010). Users of the world, unite! The challenges and opportunities of Social Media. *Business Horizons, 53*(1), 59–68. doi:10.1016/j.bushor.2009.09.003

Kaur, K., & Kumar, P. (2020). Social media usage in Indian beauty and wellness industry: A qualitative study. *The TQM Journal, 33*(1), 17–32. doi:10.1108/TQM-09-2019-0216

Kusumadewi, N. M. W. (2021). Persuasion Mechanism of Social Media Influencers in Tourism. *IJISET - International Journal of Innovative Science, Engineering & Technology, 8*(8), 76–79.

Lalangan, K. (2020). *Social Media in Tourism: The Impacts of Travel Content on YouTube and Instagram*. Academic Press.

Lock, S. (2022a, January 7). *Forecasted change in revenue from the travel and tourism industry due to the coronavirus (COVID-19) pandemic worldwide from 2019 to 2020*. https://www.statista.com/forecasts/1103426/covid-19-revenue-travel-tourism-industry-forecast

Lock, S. (2022b, August 22). *Global tourism industry-statistics and facts*. https://www.statista.com/topics/962/global-tourism/#topicHeader__wrapper

Lou, C., & Yuan, S. (2019). Influencer marketing: How message value and credibility affect consumer trust of branded content on social media. *Journal of Interactive Advertising, 19*(1), 58–73. doi:10.1080/15252019.2018.1533501

Marwick, A. E. (2015). *You May Know Me from YouTube: (Micro-) Celebrity in Social Media*. https://en-gb.facebook.com/business

Mokhare, K., Satpute, A., Pal, V., & Badwaik, P. (2021). Impact of influencer marketing on travel and tourism. *International Journal of Advance Research and Innovative Ideas in Education, 7*(1), 1098–1105.

Mudambi, S. M., & Schuff, D. (2010). Research note: What makes a helpful online review? A study of customer reviews on Amazon. com. *MIS Quarterly*, 185-200.

O'Connor, N., Cowhey, A., & O'Leary, S. (2016). Social media and the Irish tourism and hospitality industry: The customer experience. *Ereview of Tourism Research*, 13.

Ong, Y. X., Sun, T., & Ito, N. (2022). Beyond Influencer Credibility: The Power of Content and Parasocial Relationship on Processing Social Media Influencer Destination Marketing Campaigns. *Information and Communication Technologies in Tourism, 2022*, 110–122. doi:10.1007/978-3-030-94751-4_11

Pop, R.-A., Săplăcan, Z., Dabija, D.-C., & Alt, M.-A. (2021). The impact of social media influencers on travel decisions: The role of trust in consumer decision journey. *Current Issues in Tourism*. Advance online publication. doi:10.1080/13683500.2021.1895729

Pourkhani, A., Abdipour, K., Baher, B., & Moslehpour, M. (2019). The impact of social media in business growth and performance: A scientometrics analysis. *International Journal of Data and Network Science*, *3*(3), 223–244. doi:10.5267/j.ijdns.2019.2.003

Robinson, R. (2020). *The 7 top social media sites you need to care about in 2020*. Preuzeto.

Saravanakumar, M., & SuganthaLakshmi, T. (2012). Social Media Marketing. *Life Science Journal, 9*(4), 4444-4451. http://www.lifesciencesite.com/lsj/life0904/670_13061life0904_4444_4451.pdf

Schouten, A. P., Janssen, L., & Verspaget, M. (2020). Celebrity vs. Influencer endorsements in advertising: The role of identification, credibility, and Product-Endorser fit. *International Journal of Advertising*, *39*(2), 258–281. doi:10.1080/02650487.2019.1634898

Secilmis, C., Ozdemir, C., & Kılıc, İ. (2021). How travel influencers affect visit intention? The roles of cognitive response, trust, COVID-19 fear and confidence in vaccine. *Current Issues in Tourism*, 1–16.

Sesar, V., Hunjet, A., & Kozina, G. (2021). Influencer marketing in travel and tourism: Literature review. *Economic and Social Development: Book of Proceedings*, 182-192.

Shahbaznezhad, H., Dolan, R., & Rashidirad, M. (2021). The role of social media content format and platform in Users' engagement behavior. *Journal of Interactive Marketing, 53*, 47-65. doi:10.1016/j.intmar.2020.05.001

Sharma, S., & Verma, H. V. (2018). *Social Media Marketing: Evolution and Change*. Springer Nature. doi:10.1007/978-981-10-5323-8_2

Statista Research Department. (2022, August 19). *Influencer marketing market size worldwide from 2016 to 2022*. https://www.statista.com/statistics/1092819/global-influencer-market-size/

Thorat, S. B., Kishor, S. B., & Meghe, B. (2013). Social media marketing mix: Applicability review for marketing in education. *International Proceedings of Economics Development and Research, 59*(4), 16-20. DOI: .2013.V59.4 doi:10.7763/IPEDR

Tsen, W. S., & Cheng, B. K. L. (2021). Who to find to endorse? Evaluation of online influencers among young consumers and its implications for effective influencer marketing. *Young Consumers*, *22*(2), 237–253. doi:10.1108/YC-10-2020-1226

Twitter Marketing Services. (n.d.). https://www.brafton.com/services/twitter-marketing-services/

Utomo, S. B., Triyonowati, & Mildawati, T. (2022). *Virtual tour as an alternative for destination marketing during the pandemic of COVID-19*. International Conference on Government Education Management and Tourism.

Van der Waldt, D. L. R., Van Loggerenberg, M., & Wehmeyer, L. (2009). Celebrity endorsements versus created spokespersons in advertising: A survey among students. *Suid-Afrikaanse Tydskrif vir Ekonomiese en Bestuurswetenskappe*, *12*(1), 100–114. doi:10.4102ajems.v12i1.263

Vassakis, K., Petrakis, E., Kopanakis, I., Makridis, J., & Mastorakis, G. (2019). Location-Based Social Network Data for Tourism Destinations. *Big Data and Innovation in Tourism, Travel, and Hospitality*, 105-114. doi:10.1007/978-981-13-6339-9_7

Weinberg, B. D., & Pehlivan, E. (2011). Social spending: Managing the social media mix. *Business Horizons, 54*(3), 275–282. doi:10.1016/j.bushor.2011.01.008

Weinberg, T. (2009). *The New Community Rules: Marketing on the Social Web*. Emerald Group Publishing Limited. doi:10.1108/dlo.2011.08125cae.002

Wellman, M. L., Stoldt, R., Tully, M., & Ekdale, B. (2020). Ethics of authenticity: Social media influencers and the production of sponsored content. *Journal of Media Ethics, 35*(2), 68-82. doi:10.1080/23736992.2020.1736078

Wiedmann, K. P., & Mettenheim, W. (2021). Attractiveness, trustworthiness and expertise – social influencers' winning formula? *Journal of Product and Brand Management, 30*(5), 707–725. doi:10.1108/JPBM-06-2019-2442

Wu, K. (2016). *YouTube Marketing: Legality of Sponsorship and Endorsement in Advertising*. Academic Press.

Xiang, Z., & Gretzel, U. (2010). Role of social media in online travel information search. *Tourism Management, 31*(2), 179-188. doi:10.1016/j.tourman.2009.02.016

Xu, X., & Pratt, S. (2018). Social media influencers as endorsers to promote travel destinations: An application of self-congruence theory to the Chinese Generation Y. *Journal of Travel & Tourism Marketing, 35*(7), 958–972. doi:10.1080/10548408.2018.1468851

Zivkovic, R., Gajic, J., & Brdar, I. (2014). The impact of social media on tourism. *Singidunum Journal of Applied Sciences*, 758-761. doi:10.15308/sinteza-2014-758-761

Chapter 6
"Green Computing" in Hospitality

Mehmet Halit Akın
https://orcid.org/0000-0002-9455-0323
Erciyes University, Turkey

ABSTRACT

"Green computing" is an approach adopted to ensure the technological devices and byproducts used by businesses in their business processes cause the least harm to the environment. Green computing, which is a new concept for hospitality as well as for other sectors, increasingly attracts attention by researchers—especially due to the increase in the destruction of environmental factors in recent years and the importance of these factors for hospitality. However, in the body of knowledge, it is seen there is scant research on hospitality with green computing. Therefore, green computing that emerges with sustainability should be further researched, and green computing practices in hospitality should be evaluated. In light of this information, this chapter aimed to create a conceptual framework that is expected to have a widespread impact on the body of knowledge based on the current literature on the concepts of green computing.

INTRODUCTION

The concept of travel, which is considered to have a past as much as the history of humanity, has moved away from the approach of people's change of location and has become a concept used with tourism (Çallı, 2015). The fact that travel is a concept used with tourism is based on factors such as, especially after the industrial revolution, the development of the understanding that not only the nobility but all people have the right to leisure and tourism, spread of the right to paid vacation, the diverse needs of people, and the development of technology in recent times. Several services needed by people, who move away from their homes with their travels, have led to the emergence of the concept of hospitality (Barrows & Power, 2008, p. 4). Consequently, hospitality has reached the position of a comprehensive sector that meets the accommodation, food and beverage, travel, and leisure needs for tourists during

DOI: 10.4018/978-1-6684-4645-4.ch006

their travels (Ionel, 2016). In other words, hospitality has reached a broad structure consisting of sectors and sectorial services, not a single sector (Hudson, p. 147). Therefore, such a development in hospitality has serious effects on the ecosystem and it is critical to adopt a sustainability approach in hospitality.

The hospitality industry, which is one of the largest sectors in the world, as human activities have been affecting the ecosystem for thousands of years, increases the severity of the effects on the ecosystem (Sloan, Legrand, & Chen, 2013, p. 1). In this direction, one of the main approaches that should be adopted and implemented in terms of hospitality businesses has been sustainability, with the understanding that the resources in the world will not be sufficient due to the increase in costs, the increasingly sensitive demand, as well as the decrease in resources (Arjona, 2020). Because one of the most important factors that increase the environmental effect of the hospitality industry is the information and communication technologies used by businesses to facilitate the production, dissemination and distribution of information (Iyer, Chakraborty, & Dey, 2015, p. 45), it is undoubtedly one of the basic approaches that should be adopted by businesses within the scope of sustainability.

One such approach is green computing. Green computing refers to using computing resources more efficiently to have less impact on the environment while maintaining or increasing the overall performance of the business (Harmon & Auseklis, 2009). Therefore, the green computing approach is very important for the hospitality business to maintain their existence in the global competitive environment by protecting the environmental resources that constitute an important component.

In this chapter, a conceptual framework will be created for the accommodation sector, the food and beverage sector, the travel sector, and the leisure sectors, and in this context, issues such as definitions, classifications, and characteristics of related concepts will be evaluated. Afterwards, green computing is examined, which is what makes this section original. Finally, applicable green computing practices related to hospitality and its sub-titles (e.g., the accommodation sector, the food and beverage sector, the travel sector, and the leisure sector), which is another issue that makes this section original and important, will be evaluated and sample practices will be presented.

LITERATURE REVIEW

The Hospitality Sector

The history of hospitality is based on the relationships between hosts and guests, which have existed since the first human societies arose (Clarke & Chen, 2009, p. 5). The fact that hospitality has many different sub-titles in addition to its structure based on human relations for many years shows that hospitality is a complex social phenomenon (Olsen, 2001, p. 98). This is also reflected in the definition of hospitality, which has been defined in many different ways based on focal points, such as services offered, mutual relations, and diversity of services (Burgess, 1982; Barrows & Power, 2008; Hsu & Powers, 2008; Reid & Bojanic, 2009). Hospitality is defined as a process that supports new or existing relationships while making both material and symbolic exchanges between the host and guest by focusing on the relations between people (Selwyn, 2000, p. 19). In terms of the services offered and the diversity of services, it is defined as a whole of services that includes many different components, such as accommodation, food and beverage, entertainment, travel services for needs such as rest, relaxation, eating, as well as the physical structure, design, decor, location, and security of the facilities (Burgess, 1982). Therefore, hospitality is a large scaled, open to improvement, popular and important sector that includes not only accommodation, food and beverage, leisure, and travel, but also many different sub-titles of each these sectors, such as public, health, communication, entertainment, and security services.

The fact that the sub-titles of hospitality are quite diverse is reflected in the elements of the hospitality offered by the researchers, and the elements of hospitality are discussed in quite a variety. Clarke and Chen (2009, p. 58) indicated the elements of hospitality as accommodation and food services based on people's basic needs, Woods and Deegan (2006, p. 32) indicated it as accommodation, food and beverage, transportation, leisure activities, and 64 other associated sections. However, Ionel (2016) indicated the elements of hospitality as travel, accommodation, food and beverage, and leisure and entertainment activities offered to meet the needs of tourists; Müller (2001, p. 62) indicated it as transportation, accommodation, adventure and amusement parks, sports facilities and amusement parks; Ottenbacher, Harrington, and Parsa (2009) basically indicated it as accommodation, food and beverage, travel, and leisure services. In this section, the elements of hospitality are discussed under the main and inclusive titles of accommodation, food and beverage, travel, and leisure. In addition, green computing practices in hospitality are evaluated in these titles.

The Accommodation Sector

Developments in information and communication technologies enable easier access to accurate and exact information and easier global communication by bringing distances closer together. In addition, it allows the accommodation, food and beverage, travel, and leisure sectors to develop faster in a global competitive environment. Therefore, the hospitality sector and its elements have a brighter future with correspondingly technological developments. It is obvious that the accommodation sector, which has an important attractive potential in tourism, has a very diverse and complex structure, similar to hospitality, since it is a sector that provides services for many different purposes, such as business, vacation, health, and personal development in today's world. Accommodation is one of the basic services offered in hospitality (Ionel, 2016) and refers to all types of accommodation facilities offered within hospitality (Brotherton, 1999). The accommodation sector refers to businesses, such as hotels, hostels, and holiday villages, with different characteristics that provide services for commercial purposes in order to meet the needs of people, such as accommodation, rest and nutrition, as well as other needs, such as entertainment, motivation, and sports, which they need during their travels for various reasons (Usta, 2014, p. 41).

In addition to the needs of people, the fact that their economic levels differ, causes a wide variety of classification of accommodation businesses. In other words, the needs and economic levels of people have a significant impact on the preferences for meeting the accommodation needs in travels for business, vacation, health, and other purposes. While the need determines the reason for the travel, the economic level determines the variables, such as the quality, price, and features of the accommodation business. Barrows and Power (2008, p. 271-283) discussed the classification of accommodation businesses based on criteria, such as price, function, location, a specific market segment, and other distinguishing features. Accommodation businesses are categorized as limited-service, full-service, and luxury according to price; as convention and commercial according to function; and as downtown hotels, suburban hotels, highway/interstate hotels, and airport hotels according to location. While accommodation businesses are categorized as executive conference centers, resort, casino, health spa, and vacation ownership according to a specific market segment, they are categorized as all-suite, extended-stay, historic conversions, bed-and-breakfast inns, and boutique according to other distinguishing features. As a result, the needs and economic levels of people have a determinant effect on the classification of accommodation businesses.

The fact that it is one of the most needed and demanded basic service sectors ensures that the tourism sector has its own characteristics (Karaca, 2021, p. 216). This structure of the tourism sector has enabled the characteristics of the accommodation sector to be unique. In addition, the typical characteristics of the accommodation sector are revealed depending on different variables. Özel (2012, p. 12-16) explained the characteristics of accommodation businesses on the basis of production, employees, accounting, marketing, and investment variables. The characteristics of the accommodation businesses on the basis of production, which include the basic features of accommodation, are explained as the spread of production to different times of the day, the perishability of the goods and services produced, simultaneous production and consumption. Although production is predominantly labor-intensive, it also shows techno-intensive characteristics and service-oriented production in general.

The Food and Beverage Sector

Nutrition, which is one of the basic needs that must be met in order for people to survive, also emerges as a basic need in travels. In order to meet the nutritional needs of people traveling for various reasons, the food and beverage sector has emerged as another sub-title in the hospitality sector. The food and beverage sector, which is offered as a service that provides added value to people in hospitality and serves not only in accommodation business, includes businesses that produce goods and services both to create attraction and to meet the nutritional needs of the travelers (Clarke & Chen, 2009, p. 62). Similar to accommodation businesses, food and beverage businesses can be classified in many different ways. Yılmaz (2007, p. 10) classified food and beverage businesses based on three different variables: size, ownership, and geographical location.

According to the size of business, food and beverage businesses are classified as small, medium, and large businesses. However, food and beverage businesses classified as private, public, or mixed businesses according to the ownership status, are classified as local, regional, national, and international businesses according to geographical location. Food and beverage businesses that meet one of the most basic and important needs in the hospitality sector have their own characteristics as well as features that reflect the basic features of the service. These characteristics are explained as having physical, non-durable, and heterogeneous products, differences in organizational structure, wide variety of inputs used in product production, simultaneous production and consumption, and diversity in terms of product and customer types (Baysal & Küçükaslan 2007: p. 18-19; Yavuz, 2007: p, 25; Sarıışık, Çavuş & Karamustafa, 2010: p. 10; Memiş, 2017, p. 5).

Travel Sector

Another basic sub-title of the hospitality sector is the travel sector, which includes sea, air, and land transportation (Jafari, 1983). The travel sector is a sector that includes commercial businesses that provide transportation services to people traveling for various purposes from tourism markets to touristic destinations (Gürdal, 2015, p. 9). There are some businesses that create the structure of the travel industry and have an important and basic role in the provision of travel services. At the same time, these businesses, which are the operators of the travel service, generally consist of travel agencies, tour operators, agent wholesalers, and online agencies, which have different functions (Mengü, 2018, p. 89). Although there is no comprehensive classification of travel businesses as a whole, Erkol, Bayram, and Bayram (2017) evaluated the classification of travel agencies based on various variables in different studies and presented the classification of travel agencies with structural, activity-oriented, and functionality approaches. Accordingly, while travel agencies are structurally classified as large, specialized for industrial businesses, incoming, and independent agencies; they are classified in terms of activity-oriented as retailer, agent wholesalers, and chain agents; and in terms of functionality as incoming, outgoing, and ingoing agencies. (Erkol Bayram & Bayram, 2017, p. 42-44).

In addition, this research presents that travel agencies can be classified according to their target market and travel agencies are classified as A, B, and C group agencies within the legal framework in Turkey. Another important issue in hospitality is the characteristics of travel businesses. Gürdal (2015, p. 9-10) focused on the structural features of travel businesses and listed the characteristics as follows: Providing time utility to people with low prices; being a rational sector that must fulfill the requirements of the modern age and technology; requires effective coordination between all operators providing transportation; providing and consuming as a service when and where needed.

The Leisure Sector

Undoubtedly, people have leisure time in tourism activities as well as in their daily lives. In hospitality, leisure activities are organized by both tourism and leisure businesses based on activities such as animation, sports, and entertainment in order to make use of people's leisure time. Therefore, at this point, the leisure sector emerges as another sector that provides services to people and takes place in the hospitality industry. The leisure sector, which has a significant impact on the quality and attractiveness of the hospitality sector (Costa et al., 2004), consists of businesses that provide services to meet the physical, mental and emotional rest, renewal, and development needs of people (Akat, 2000, p. 85).

Leisure businesses, which generally provide services in private and high-capacity facilities, are generally classified according to the type of leisure activities (Hsu & Powers, 2008, p. 88). The activities that people, who want to spend their leisure time in their travels, want to participate in, in other words, in the classification of the leisure sector, there are categories of simple entertainment, mental activity/contemplation and self-awareness, games, relaxation, social activities, nature activities/outdoor recreation, music and art, and sports and exercise (Leitner & Leitner, 2012, p. 14-15).

As a service sector, the leisure sector has many characteristics that make it different from other sectors, which are offered in line with the characteristics of recreation as well as the basic characteristics of the service. Karakuş and Gürbüz (2007, p. 36-37) evaluated the characteristics of the leisure industry as follows: Providing services that provide a sense of joy, pleasure, satisfaction, and freedom in leisure time; providing services of personal and social benefit, from which participants can voluntarily choose activities; providing personalized services in a way that will change the daily routines of life and add meaning; and provide physical, mental, and emotional mobility.

GREEN COMPUTING

Considering the other components directly or indirectly related to hospitality and its sub-titles, it is understood how big a sector hospitality is. However, the above-mentioned information shows that hospitality is a sector with a complex structure as well as being a rapidly developing sector. Therefore, the activities carried out in such a large, open to development, and complex sector require some tools to facilitate the processes. In hospitality, which provides global mobility, some of the main tools used to meet the diverse demands of people, as well as to increase productivity and guest satisfaction, and to help employees fully carry out their duties (Law, Buhalis, & Cobanoglu, 2014) are developments, especially in information and communication technologies.

The increasing dependence on information and communication technologies in hospitality provides the opportunity to see many developments in the sectoral basis, while also preparing the environment for natural, economic, and socio-cultural resources to be damaged within the large, open, and complex sector structure. Therefore, the development and growth of hospitality depends not only on the adoption of smart tourism applications with new technologies, but also on ensuring the sustainability of the resources that constitute the basic components of hospitality (Gavrilović & Maksimović, 2018).

In other words, in order to effectively manage the processes based on information and communication technologies in hospitality and to eliminate or minimize the negative effects on resources, operations related to information and communication technologies should be carried out on the basis of a sustainability approach (Arjona, 2020, p. 28). One of the basic approaches used to eliminate or minimize the negative effects of technologies that facilitate information and communication on resources is green computing applications.

Increases in global warming, energy consumption and e-waste increase the importance given to green computing and its applications, especially by businesses to provide sustainable improvement (Mohammed, Muhammed & Abdullah, 2015). Green computing is one of the important tools that offers viable economic solutions to protect natural resources and the environment, and includes the design, production, use, and disposal of computers and hardware as environmentally friendly products in order to minimize the effects on the environment (Sagar & Pradhan, 2020, p. 21).

Green computing is the definition of computers, servers, monitors, printers, storage devices, network and communication systems, and other similar hardware as environmentally friendly computing (Murugesan & Gangadharan, 2012; Sarkar & Gul, 2020, p. 40). In addition to the environmentally friendly product, there are three other critical components used in green computing: virtualization, dematerialization, and cloud computing (Baral & Verma, 2021, p. 110). The application of five critical components and the design, production, use, and disposal of environmentally friendly products on the basis of green computing will ensure that the possible environmental effects of information and communication technologies are eliminated or minimized.

Green computing, which allows to use information and communication technology resources more efficiently while maintaining or improving overall performance (Kumar et al., 2021, p. 9), transforms the negative effects of information and communication technologies into benefits. In other words, green computing is an important tool in minimizing the possible negative effects of information and communication technologies and transforming them into positive effects. Negative effects of information and communication technologies are (Adamson et al., 2005; ITU, 2008; ÇevreOnline, 2015; EAGD, 2016; Damar & Gökşen, 2018);

- The increase in *electronic waste*, which constitutes 1% of solid waste in the world
- The increase in *energy use* caused by computers and hardware, which causes the most CO_2 emissions in information and communication technologies
- The increase in *electromagnetic pollution*, which occurs in the living areas of people and other creatures and causes various diseases
- Intensive *consumption of natural resources,* such as fossil fuels and water, which are rare in nature and used in computer production

The multiplier effect of the negativities caused by information and communication technologies such as the increase of electronic waste, the increase in energy use, the increase of electromagnetic pollution, and the intense consumption of natural resources are minimized by green computing applications such as designs for energy efficiency, software that allows multiple use, renewable energy sources, and remote computerized systems (Ozturk et al., 2011). As mentioned above, in hospitality, which is complex, large, and one of the sectors that uses information and communication technologies most intensively, the implementation of such applications will both turn the negative effects of information and communication technologies into benefits and make significant contributions to the sustainability of the hospitality sector, one of the main components of which is natural resources. In this direction, the benefits of green computing applications to a hospitality business can be listed as follows (Murugesan, 2008; Jindal & Gupta, 2012; Damar & Gökşen, 2018);

- Saving up to 75% in energy use
- Saving up to 75% in energy, technology and other costs
- Reducing the environmental effects of information and communication technologies by 56%
- Gaining 47% of space in the physical areas where business processes are carried out,
- Significant improvement of business performance
- Achieving close to 2130 million tons of CO_2 savings with remote teleworking and online conferences
- With the electronic bill, both the protection of environmental resources and the saving of approximately 1.3 million tons of CO_2
- Ensuring the sustainability of natural resources by using environmentally friendly resources

The benefits of green computing actually reveal the reasons why hospitality businesses adopt and implement green computing applications. In addition to these benefits, which constitute the primary factor for hospitality businesses to adopt green computing, there are many different factors that lead to the emergence of green computing applications and the adoption of green computing by businesses. Harmon and Auseklis (2009) listed these factors as follows:

- Increases in internet use and energy costs
- Increasing awareness of the effects of information and communication technologies on environmental resources
- Increasing equipment, power density, and cooling requirements
- Restrictions on energy supply and access to energy
- Low utilization rate of the central server system

The hospitality sector is developing day after day, depending on the differing human needs as well as globalization, the effect of social media and developments in communication and transportation technologies. In parallel with the development of the hospitality, developments in technology lead businesses to use information and communication technologies more intensively with the vision of smart tourism (Gavrilović & Maksimović, 2018). Therefore, the increasing interest in the hospitality allows serious socio-cultural and economic developments to be seen in the destinations, while the information and communication technologies used extensively in the hospitality cause some destruction in energy and natural resources and hazardous chemical waste.

In hospitality, one of the most basic components, of which is natural resources, the negative effects of information and communication technologies are more important. In this direction, the sustainability of both natural resources and the hospitality will be ensured with green information computing being carried out by adopting a sustainability approach. As mentioned before, there are applications, such as virtualization, dematerialization, and cloud computing, as well as environmentally friendly products that include design, production, use, and disposal processes that can be used as green computing applications.

Green Computing in Hospitality

Information and communication technologies (ICTs), which facilitate access to information, enable people to reach objective information reflecting the truth about both hospitality businesses and destinations, while providing an opportunity for hospitality businesses to transmit information and promotions to more people globally. Therefore, ICTs are of vital importance for the hospitality in today's technological world. To minimize or eliminate the negative effects of such intensive use of information and communication technologies, some green computing applications are recommended. In this section, environmentally friendly products, virtualization, dematerialization, cloud, and computing applications are evaluated on the basis of the hospitality and sample applications are presented.

Environmentally Friendly Products

Environmentally friendly products are products that are produced based on renewable resources, do not contain chemical toxins, and can be recycled when the product completes its life cycle or can be destroyed in a way that does not harm nature or people (TBD, 2012). According to another definition, an environmentally friendly product is a process that focuses on energy efficiency in all production processes and includes products produced with green computing strategies, as well as productivity and raising awareness of users about environmentally friendly products (Jindal & Gupta, 2012).

When the environmentally friendly product is evaluated in terms of hospitality, it can be defined as a process that includes design, production, use, and destruction practices for the production of touristic products with materials that can be reused, recycled, destroyed, and chemical-free in a way that does not harm all resources. Replacing old coffee machines with energy-saving machines that can be recycled after use, or using solar energy to meet hot water needs, is an important example of an environmentally friendly product.

With this green computing application, the use of renewable resources is encouraged and an important support is provided in reducing the consumption of other energy resources. The fact that the touristic product is a combined product containing many different variables necessitates the adoption of the environmentally friendly product approach throughout the entire touristic experience. Therefore, it is important to carry out the environmentally friendly product approach in a planned manner within the design, production, use, and disposal processes.

Product Design

Product design refers to the consideration of efficiency in terms of energy/material use in production, consumption, and secondary consumption, as well as product performance and aesthetics (UNEPIE, 1996). In practice, product design is the design of power-saving environmentally friendly products and equipment that will increase environmental quality while providing economic development (Pazowski, 2015). In hospitality, product design can be defined as the design of touristic products that will increase overall performance and efficiency, and that will not have negative effects or minimal effects on the environment.

For example, it is a hospitality product design that a travel agency, which designs a thematic office visually and aesthetically, is also designed with reusable resources in a way that allows the office to be ventilated more ergonomically in order to prevent computer systems and other equipment from overheating and wasting energy. With this green computing application, it will be seen that the performance, aesthetics, consumption, and secondary consumption processes expressed in the definition of product design are fulfilled effectively.

Product Production

Production of environmentally-friendly products is the implementation of protective and preventive environmental strategies with a holistic and sustainable approach and the production to minimize or eliminate risks on the environment and people (Yücel & Ekmekçiler, 2008). The production of environmentally friendly products, which provides economic benefits, such as improvements in business processes as well as long-term cost savings (Pazowski, 2015), gains a different dimension in hospitality in that touristic products are a combined product. In other words, the production of environmentally friendly products in hospitality includes many different variables, not only the service offered, but also the intermediaries-suppliers that have an impact on the delivery of this service. It is an environmentally friendly product for a food and beverage business to prefer a QR code menu instead of a printed menu. It is also a component of the environmentally friendly product that a local greengrocer, that supplies the raw materials of the products offered in the relevant food and beverage business, distributes with eco-friendly vehicles. It is obvious that with this application, besides the protection of natural resources, the negative effects on nature are minimized.

Product Use

Product use aims to reduce the consumption of energy and other resources of computers and hardware, as well as other technological systems in the usage processes, and to minimize the negative effects on the environment (Sarkar & Gul, 2020, p. 42). In short, it refers to the use of products in an environmentally friendly way, while minimizing energy consumption (Sagar & Pradhan, 2020, p. 21). There are two dimensions of product use in terms of hospitality. The first is that a leisure business that produces services prefers energy-saving technological equipment and systems in its production processes. The second is that people, who receive service from the leisure business, adopt a sustainability approach and put the equipment and systems in power saving mode or turn them off completely when they are not using them. Therefore, whether both supply and demand adopt or do not adopt green computing applications while using the product has a determining effect on the direction of the effects on nature, humans, and other resources.

Product Disposal

Product destruction, which refers to the reuse of old machinery-equipment or its use in different products by recycling (Sagar & Pradhan, 2020, p. 21), also includes the responsibility of companies selling information and communication technologies to take their products back when the product life cycle is completed (Pazowski, 2015). The priority is the reuse of obsolete products, but it is important to recycle the products that are not suitable for reuse, to use them as raw materials or to use them as parts for other machinery-equipment.

In addition to computers and hardware in hospitality, there are many different technological systems used in other processes. For example, air conditioners used in rooms are one of the basic needs of a holiday village, which provides services, especially for sea-sand-sun tourism. Choosing energy-saving air conditioners will be an environmentally friendly product choice. Furthermore, in the event that the holiday village undergoes modernization, its old air conditioners, if they are in working condition, are evaluated elsewhere, donated, or sold for secondary use; if they are not in working condition, recycling and using it as both raw materials and parts will set an important example for the destruction of products in a way that will not harm the environment.

VIRTUALIZATION

Virtualization, which enables the operation of one physical server and multiple virtual servers, is an important strategy that enables less energy consumption, simplification of the data center, and strengthening the physical infrastructure of the data center (Saha, 2014). Virtualization, also called a green data center (Sharma et al., 2020, p. 152), is a technology move that is used to distribute cloud-based infrastructure that enables a single physical server to run multiple operating systems at the same time, and reduce the total physical footprint, with serious effects on the nature (Franca et al., 2020, p. 74). The sharing of a physical resource by multiple hardware and systems in virtualization (Raja, 2021) is very important, especially for chain hospitality businesses.

For example, the use of virtualization technology by a restaurant chain operating at a global level will make significant economic contributions to the business, as well as ensuring data security and protecting resources. Instead of running separate virtual servers in each business of the restaurant chain, establishing a green data center in a central location and operating it with a single server to which all businesses in different parts of the world are connected will save on energy, personnel, physical space, maintenance, and hardware. Therefore, positive effects of virtualization technology in hospitality will emerge for all resources.

DEMATERIALIZATION

Developments in information and communication technologies facilitate the replacement of physical products and processes with digital products and processes (Mickoleit, 2010, p. 9). This process of change, called dematerialization, refers to the reduction in the number of materials used in the production of goods or services (Heiskanen & Jalas, 2000). Dematerialization is the reduction of the amount of waste generated per product, the rate of physically consumed materials, or the density of raw materials used in economic activities (Sun, 2000).

Considering the effects of dematerialization, which can be used in different areas, such as economic and social life, on resources and costs, such as paper, energy, and physical space, it is understood that it is an important application for hospitality. The online travel agency, which emerged with the development of the internet in economic and social life, is the most basic example of dematerialization. A travel agency that operates online rather than in a physical business will provide savings in terms of resources, such as physical workspace, electricity, and water, and provide savings with applications, such as e-ticket, e-bill, and e-complaint. Another positive effect seen at this point is that the employees of the online travel agency will be able to work remotely as an e-office or home office, which will reduce energy consumption, especially regarding transportation. Therefore, a dematerialized online travel agency, as a green computing application, will provide the opportunity to provide savings and protect many different resources.

CLOUD COMPUTING

Another green computing application that has emerged with the developments in information and communication technologies and is utilized in both economic and social life is cloud computing. Cloud computing consists of a central and virtual computing repository that can be deployed and used faster and safer by making minimal use of management performance, and that can provide access to desired users anywhere (Mell & Grance, 2011).

Although cloud computing has negative effects, such as slowing down the response process, deficiencies in terms of customizability, price disadvantage, changes in user experiences (Smith, 2013, p. 71), cloud computing has benefits, such as on-demand user accessibility, wide network access, flexibility, scalable service, and also provides significant benefits in terms of resource conservation compared to physical storage (Mell & Grance, 2011). Cloud computing, which is an internet-based management process (Patra et al., 2021, p. 266), is an important green computing application that should be evaluated in hospitality. Gavrilović and Maksimović (2018) suggest applications, such as virtual tours, e-demonstrator, e-tour guide as cloud computing applications in hospitality.

When evaluated in this context, since hospitality services cannot be experienced beforehand, people, who intend to choose a destination, an accommodation business, or other services can be guided by taking virtual tours. In addition, storing information about a cultural property in the cloud computing system and transferring this information to visitors via a device will be an important example of an e-tour guide. With these applications, both economic resources will be protected and protective measures will be taken for natural resources in terms of issues, such as carrying capacity and energy consumption.

SOLUTIONS AND RECOMMENDATIONS

Sustainability is a process that requires the participation of all relevant stakeholders, such as the public institutions, local people and businesses. Particularly, it is important to ensure the participation of all stakeholders in the decision-making processes, and the participation and interaction of the stakeholders in the production processes together is the basic requirement for the success of sustainability. Therefore, on the basis of the sustainability approach, the success of green computing applications in hospitality is related to the sustainability awareness of all stakeholders, their adoption of the sustainability approach, and their participation in all processes. It is necessary to ensure these issues before all sustainability-related practices. However, the point to be considered is to ensure balance in green computing applications. In all processes of life, when the interest in a product, service, habits, values, and all similar elements increases excessively, negative effects occur in return. Similarly, it is important to maintain the balance in green computing applications, which have positive effects in the short term, and to consider the rebounds that may cause further destruction of resources (van Hoorik, Bomhof & Meulenhoff, 2010).

The interest in green computing, which is accepted as a new application in hospitality, has been increasing, especially in recent years, with the increase in the destruction of people and businesses towards the environment. It is said that people and businesses with sustainability awareness are willing to pay more for environmentally friendly products (Mostafa, 2007). In particular, businesses in the hospitality sector, one of the main components of which are natural, cultural, and social resources, show interest in green computing applications in order to create a positive perception in consumers and to ensure the continuity of hospitality by ensuring the sustainability of resources.

Hospitality businesses should focus on environmentally friendly service, which basically includes all processes from the design of the service to its disposal, as a green computing application. In addition, these processes should be supported by other applications such as virtualization, dematerialization, and cloud computing. In addition to the conceptual knowledge and examples given about green computing applications, the development of hospitality-specific suggestions is within the scope of this research. Accordingly, suggestions specific to hospitality can be listed as follows (Mohammed, Muhammed, & Abdullah, 2015; Gökşen, Damar, & Doğan, 2016; Gavrilović & Maksimović, 2018; Önaçan, 2019; Akın, 2021):

- Using ICTs in power mode and turning them off when not in use
- Duplex printing of documents other than official correspondence
- Preferring equipment and systems that consume less energy or do not consume fossil fuels
- Increasing the awareness of personnel about sustainability and green computing, and supporting their adoption as a lifestyle
- Policymaking about energy in hospitality businesses and informing users about energy consumption
- Establishing a central server room and using cloud computing applications
- Renewal of obsolete or outdated information and communication technologies, donating old ones, putting them into secondary use, and sending them for recycling
- Preferring energy efficient technologies in the preference of new ICTs
- Making software updates that improve ICTs
- Development of mobile applications that offer self-check-in
- Dematerialization of physical menus via QR code or tablet menus
- Providing e-tour guide, e-information service with information, and details stored in cloud computing
- Development of e-office application in departments suitable for remote working
- Storing people's personal information and preferences in cloud computing as a safer environment
- Implementation of applications such as e-invoice, e-complaint form, and e-ticket
- Development of smart rooms integrated with mobile phones
- Development of smart buildings for hospitality businesses

FUTURE RESEARCH DIRECTIONS

In this chapter, a conceptual framework has been created and examples are presented based on the relevant literature for green computing applications in hospitality. Therefore, although this constitutes the main limitation of the research, it presents an important suggestion for future research in terms of determining the practical applications of hospitality businesses related to green computing. However, conducting research on the evaluation of the beliefs and attitudes of the hospitality staff regarding green computing applications will enable to reveal the level of awareness and adoption of the sustainability approach. In particular, carrying out this research on different sub-titles of hospitality and in different populations and samples will contribute to the formation of important knowledge about green computing. Finally, conducting research to identify different green computing applications that can be used in hospitality will provide important contributions to businesses as well as protecting resources.

CONCLUSION

Green computing is a sustainability approach that aims to minimize or eliminate the negative effects that may occur on resources and the environment during the use of individual or corporate information and communication technologies. The negative effects of information and communication technologies vary according to the intended use of both people and businesses. Especially by determining the negative effects of information and communication technologies in different business, green computing applications that can be used for these negative effects have been put forward. However, the negative effects of information and communication technologies and the green computing applications that can be used have been very limited in hospitality, which makes the most use of information and communication technologies.

In general, it is obvious that information and communication technologies have negative effects in many different ways, from energy to nature, from natural resources to human health in hospitality, which includes accommodation, food and beverage, travel, and leisure sectors. However, it is important to reveal these negativities, especially to activate practices into action and to increase people's awareness. Based on the relevant literature, in this chapter, many different green computing applications, such as green data center, virtual tour, energy-saving equipment and systems, donation, recycling, QR code menu, e-ticket, e-tour guide, and e- invoice have been released. The last step that needs to be taken at this point is to raise people's awareness!

REFERENCES

Adamson, M., Hamilton, R., Hutchison, K., Kazmierowski, K., Lau, J., Madejski, D., & Macdonald, N. (2005). *Environmental impact of computer information technology in an institutional setting: A case study at The University Of Guelph*. Retrieved on April 22, 2021, from: https://www.uoguelph.ca/isc/documents/050602environcs_000.pdf

Akat, Ö. (2000). *Pazarlama ağırlıklı turizm işletmeciliği*. Ekin Kitabevi.

Akın, M. H. (2021). Yeşil bilişim uygulamalarının turizm sektörü açısından değerlendirilmesi: Kavramsal bir inceleme [Evaluation of green computing practices in terms of tourism: A conceptual evaluation]. In *2021 III. International Sustainable Tourism Congress* (pp. 319-325). ISTC.

Arjona, M. F. (2020). *Sustainability in hospitality and tourism sector*. Society Publishing.

Baral, M. M., & Verma, A. (2021). Analysing factors impacting the adoption of green computing in Indian universities. In S. Kumar, R. Raja, A. K. S. Kuswaha, S. Kumar, & R. K. Patra (Eds.), *Green computing and its applications* (pp. 109–130). Nova Science Publishers.

Barrows, C. W., & Powers, T. (2008). *Introduction to in the hospitality industry*. John Wiley & Sons.

Baysal, A., & Küçükaslan, N. (2007). *Beslenme ilkeleri ve menü planlaması*. Ekin Yayınları.

Brotherton, B. (1999). Towards a definitive view of the nature of hospitality and hospitality management. *International Journal of Contemporary Hospitality Management, 11*(4), 165–173. doi:10.1108/09596119910263568

Burgess, J. (1982). Perspectives on gift exchange and hospitable behavior. *International Journal of Hospitality Management, 1*(1), 49–57. doi:10.1016/0278-4319(82)90023-8

Çallı, D. S. (2015). Uluslararası seyahatlerin tarihi gelişimi ve son seyahat trendleri doğrultusunda Türkiye'nin konumu. *Turar Turizm ve Araştırma Dergisi, 4*(1), 4–28.

ÇevreOnline. (2015). *Elektromanyetik kirlilik*. https://cevreonline.com/elektromanyetik-kirlilik/

Clarke, A., & Chen, W. (2009). *International Hospitality Management*. Routledge. doi:10.4324/9780080547312

Costa, G., Glinia, E., Goudas, M., & Antoniou, P. (2004). Recreational services in resort hotels: Customer satisfaction aspects. *Journal of Sport & Tourism, 9*(2), 117–126. doi:10.1080/14775080410001732541

Damar, M., & Gökşen, Y. (2018). Yeşil bilişim yaklaşımıyla kullanıcı ve kurum odaklı enerji yönetim sistemi. *Dokuz Eylül Üniversitesi Mühendislik Fakültesi Fen ve Mühendislik Dergisi, 20*(58), 259–274. doi:10.21205/deufmd.2018205821

Elektronik Atıkların Geri Dönüşümü (EAGD). (2016). *Türkiye'de ve Dünya'da e-atık*. https://www.eagd.org.tr/turkiyede-ve-dunyada-e-atik/

Erkol Bayram, G., & Bayram, A. T. (2017). Uluslararası seyahat işletmelerinin türleri, görev, yetki ve sorumlulukları. In B. Zengin, M. Sarıışık, & C. Avcıkurt (Eds.), *Uluslararası seyahat işletmeciliği* (pp. 41–66). Detay Yayıncılık.

Franca, R. P., Iano, Y., Monteiro, A. C. B., & Arthur, R. (2020). Better transmission of information focused on green computing through data transmission channels in cloud environments with rayleigh fading. In B. Balusamy, N. Chilamkurti, & S. Kadry (Eds.), *Green Computing in Smart Cities: Simulation and Techniques* (pp. 71–94). Springer Nature.

Gavrilović, Z., & Maksimović, M. (2018). Green innovations in the tourism sector. *Strategic Management, 23*(1), 36–42. doi:10.5937/StraMan1801036G

Gökşen, Y., Damar, M., & Doğan, O. (2016). Yeşil bilişim: Bir kamu kurumu örneği ve politika önerileri. *Ege Academic Review, 16*(4).

Gürdal, M. (2015). *Turizm ulaştırması – Paket tur organizasyonu ve yönetimi*. Nobel Yayıncılık.

Harmon, R. R., & Auseklis, N. (2009). Sustainable IT services: Assessing the impact of green computing practices. In *PICMET'09-2009 Portland International Conference on Management of Engineering & Technology* (pp. 1707-1717). IEEE.

Heiskanen, E., & Jalas, M. (2000). *Dematerialization through services-A review and evaluation of the debate*. The Ministry of the Environment.

Hsu, C. H., & Powers, T. (2008). *Marketing Hospitality*. John Wiley and Sons.

Hudson, S. (2008). *Tourism and Hospitality Marketing: a global perspective*. Sage. doi:10.4135/9781446280140

Ionel, M. (2016). Hospitality industry. *Ovidius University Annals: Economic Sciences Series, 1*(1), 187–191.

ITU. (2008). *ITU and climate change, international telecommunication union*. https://www.itu.int/dms_pub/itu-t/oth/23/01/T23010000030002PDFE.pdf

Iyer, V. R., Chakraborty, S., & Dey, N. (2015). Advent of information technology in the world of tourism. In N. Ray (Ed.), *Emerging Innovative Marketing Strategies in the Tourism Industry* (pp. 44–53). IGI Global. doi:10.4018/978-1-4666-8699-1.ch003

Jafari, J. (1983). Anatomy of the travel industry. *The Cornell Hotel and Restaurant Administration Quarterly, 24*(1), 71–81. doi:10.1177/001088048302400112

Jindal, G., & Gupta, M. (2012). Green computing "future of computers". *International Journal of Emerging Research in Management &Technology*, 14-18.

Karaca, Ş. (2021). Sağlık turizminde pazarlama. In Ş. Karaca (Ed.), *Multidisipliner yaklaşımla sağlık turizmi* (pp. 215–238). Nobel Yayıncılık.

Karaküçük, S., & Gürbüz, B. (2007). *Rekreasyon ve kent(li)leşme*. Gazi Kitapevi.

Kumar, S., Raja, R., Kuswaha, A. K. S., Kumar, S., & Patra, R. K. (2021). *Green computing and its applications*. Nova Science Publishers. doi:10.52305/ENYH6923

Law, R., Buhalis, D., & Cobanoglu, C. (2014). Progress on information and communication technologies in hospitality and tourism. *International Journal of Contemporary Hospitality Management, 26*(5), 727–750. doi:10.1108/IJCHM-08-2013-0367

Leitner, M. J., & Leitner, S. F. (2012). *Leisure enhancement*. Sagamore Publishing LLC.

Mell, P., & Grance, T. (2011). The NIST definition of cloud computing. *NIST SPECIAL Publication*, 800-145.

Memiş, H. (2017). *Yiyecek ve içecek işletmelerinde hizmet kalitesinin DINESERV modeli ile ölçümü: Çanakkale ili örneği* [Unpublished master's thesis]. University of Çanakkale Onsekiz Mart, Çanakkale, Turkey.

Mengü, C. (2018). *Seyahat işletmelerinde yönetim ve operasyon stratejileri*. Detay Yayıncılık.

Mickoleit, A. (2010). *Greener and smarter: ICTs, the environment and climate change. OECD Green Growth Papers, No. 2010-01*. OECD Publishing. doi:10.1787/5k9h3635kdbt-

Mohammed, M. A., Muhammed, D. A., & Abdullah, J. M. (2015). Green computing beyond the traditional ways. *Int. J. of Multidisciplinary and Current Research, 3*.

Mostafa, M. (2007). A hierarchical analysis of the green consciousness of the Egyptian consumer. *Psychology and Marketing, 24*(5), 445–473. doi:10.1002/mar.20168

Müller, H. (2001). Tourism and Hospitality in the 21st Century. In S. Medlik & A. Lockwood (Eds.), *Tourism and Hospitality in the 21st Century* (pp. 61–70). Routledge. doi:10.1016/B978-0-7506-5627-6.50008-0

Murugesan, S. (2008). Harnessing Green IT: Principles and Practices. *IT Professional, 10*(1), 24–33. doi:10.1109/MITP.2008.10

Murugesan, S., & Gangadharan, G. R. (2012). *Harnessing green IT: Principles and practices*. Wiley. doi:10.1002/9781118305393

Önaçan, M. B. K. (2019). Küresel ısınmaya karşı yeşil bilişim kapsamında alınabilecek bireysel önlemler. *Turkish Studies-Social Sciences, 14*(6), 3283–3302. doi:10.29228/TurkishStudies.39715

Ottenbacher, M., Harrington, R., & Parsa, H. G. (2009). Defining the hospitality discipline: A discussion of pedagogical and research implications. *Journal of Hospitality & Tourism Research (Washington, D.C.), 33*(3), 263–283. doi:10.1177/1096348009338675

Özel, Ç. H. (2012). Otelcilik endüstrisi. In M. Akoğlan Kozak (Ed.), *Otel işletmeciliği* (pp. 1–28). Detay Yayıncılık.

Ozturk, A., Umit, K., Medeni, I. T., Ucuncu, B., Caylan, M., Akba, F., & Medeni, T. D. (2011). Green ICT (Information and communication technologies): A review of academic and practitioner perspectives. *International Journal of e-Business and eGovernment Studies, 3*(1), 1-16.

Patra, R. J., Rao, M. V., Balmuri, K., Konda, S., & Chande, M. K. (2021). High-performance computing and fault tolerance technique implementation in cloud computing. In S. Kumar, R. Raja, A. K. S. Kuswaha, S. Kumar, & R. K. Patra (Eds.), *Green computing and its applications* (pp. 255–310). Nova Science Publishers.

Pazowski, P. (2015). Green computing: latest practices and technologies for ICT sustainability. In *Managing Intellectual Capital and Innovation for Sustainable and Inclusive Society, Joint International Conference* (pp. 1853-1860). Academic Press.

Raja, S. P. (2021). Green computing: A future perspective and the operational analysis of a data center. *IEEE Transactions on Computational Social Systems*.

Reid, R. D., & Bojanic, D. C. (2009). *Hospitality marketing management*. John Wiley and Sons.

Sagar, S., & Pradhan, N. (2020). A review: Recent trends in green computing. In B. Balusamy, N. Chilamkurti, & S. Kadry (Eds.), *Green Computing in Smart Cities: Simulation and Techniques* (pp. 19–34). Springer Nature.

Saha, B. (2014). Green computing. *International Journal of Computer Trends and Technology, 14*(2), 46–50. doi:10.14445/22312803/IJCTT-V14P112

Sarıışık, M., Çavuş, Ş., & Karamustafa, K. (2010). *Profosyonel restoran yönetimi, ilkeler, uygulamalar ve örnek olaylar*. Detay Yayıncılık.

Sarkar, N. I., & Gul, S. (2020). Green Computing and internet of things for smart cities: Technologies, challenges, and implementation. In B. Balusamy, N. Chilamkurti, & S. Kadry (Eds.), *Green Computing in Smart Cities: Simulation and Techniques* (pp. 35–50). Springer Nature.

Selwyn, T. (2013). Hospitality. In M. Smith & G. Richards (Eds.), *The Routledge Handbook of Cultural Tourism*. Routledge.

Sharma, S. K., Gayathri, N., Rakesh Kumar, S., Ramesh, C., Kumar, A., & Modanval, R. K. (2020). Green ICT, communication, networking, and data processing. In B. Balusamy, N. Chilamkurti, & S. Kadry (Eds.), *Green Computing in Smart Cities: Simulation and Techniques* (pp. 151–170). Springer Nature.

Sloan, P., Legrand, W., & Chen, J. S. (2013). Sustainability in the hospitality industry: Principles of sustainable operations (2nd ed.). New York: Routledge.

Smith, B. E. (2013). *Green computing: Tools and techniques for saving energy, money, and resources*. CRC Press. doi:10.1201/b15098

Sun, J. W. (2000). Dematerialization and sustainable development. *Sustainable Development, 8*(3), 142–145. doi:10.1002/1099-1719(200008)8:3<142::AID-SD139>3.0.CO;2-H

Türkiye Bilişim Derneği – TBD. (2010). *Belge Grubu Raporu – Çevreci Bilişim*. TBD/Kamu-BIB/2010-BG.

UNEPIE. (1996). Eco-efficiency and cleaner production, charting the course to sustainability. UNEPIE.

Usta, Ö. (2014). *Turizm genel ve yapısal yaklaşım*. Detay Yayıncılık.

van Hoorik, P., Bomhof, F., & Meulenhoff, P. (2010). Assessing the positive and negative impacts of ICT on people, planet and profit. In *International Conference on Green Computing* (pp. 45-50), SCITEPRESS.

Woods, M., & Deegan, J. (2006). The impact of training on interfirm dynamics within a destination quality network: The Case of the Fuchsia Brand, Ireland. In J. S. Chen (Ed.), *Advances in Hospitality and Leisure* (pp. 25–50). Emerald Group Publishing Limited. doi:10.1016/S1745-3542(05)02002-3

Yavuz, H. (2007). *Yiyecek-içecek hizmetlerinde nitelikli işgören istihdamını etkileyen faktörler: Sakarya örneği* [Unpublished master's thesis]. University of Sakarya, Sakarya, Turkey.

Yılmaz, Y. (2007). *Otel ve yiyecek içecek işletmelerinde ziyafet organizasyonu ve yönetimi*. Detay Yayıncılık.

Yücel, M., & Ekmekçiler, Ü. S. (2008). Çevre dostu ürün kavramına bütünsel yaklaşım; Temiz üretim sistemi, eko-etiket, yeşil pazarlama. *Elektronik Sosyal Bilimler Dergisi, 7*(26), 320–333.

ADDITIONAL READING

Arjona, M. F. (2020). *Sustainability in hospitality and tourism sector*. Society Publishing.

Forés, B., Puig-Denia, A., & Fernández-Yáñez, J. M. (2020). On how to leverage green technologies for sustainability performance in the tourism sector. In *Adapting to Environmental Challenges: New Research in Strategy and International Business*. Emerald Publishing Limited. doi:10.1108/978-1-83982-476-020200008

Gavrilović, Z., & Maksimović, M. (2018). Green innovations in the tourism sector. *Strategic Management*, 23(1), 36–42. doi:10.5937/StraMan1801036G

Girau, R., Ferrara, E., Pintor, M., Sole, M., & Giusto, D. (2018, July). Be right Beach: A social IoT system for sustainable tourism based on beach overcrowding avoidance. In *2018 IEEE International Conference on Internet of Things (iThings) and IEEE Green Computing and Communications (GreenCom) and IEEE Cyber, Physical and Social Computing (CPSCom) and IEEE Smart Data (SmartData)* (pp. 9-14). IEEE. 10.1109/Cybermatics_2018.2018.00036

Iyer, V. R., Chakraborty, S., & Dey, N. (2015). Advent of information technology in the world of tourism. In N. Ray (Ed.), *Emerging Innovative Marketing Strategies in the Tourism Industry* (pp. 44–53). IGI Global. doi:10.4018/978-1-4666-8699-1.ch003

Kasemsap, K. (2018). Cloud computing, green computing, and green ICT. In *Cloud computing technologies for green enterprises* (pp. 28–50). IGI Global. doi:10.4018/978-1-5225-3038-1.ch002

Law, R., Buhalis, D., & Cobanoglu, C. (2014). Progress on information and communication technologies in hospitality and tourism. *International Journal of Contemporary Hospitality Management*, 26(5), 727–750. doi:10.1108/IJCHM-08-2013-0367

KEY TERMS AND DEFINITIONS

Dematerializatied: It is the transfer of materials that damage to nature, cause the consumption of resources, and can be converted into electronic format to electronic media. For example, e-bill, e-complaint form, e-ticket, e-book.

E-Bill: It is the converted form of the physical invoice into electronic format.

E-Office: It is an application that does not require a physical working environment, provides the opportunity to work remotely, and saves especially on resources such as paper, energy, water and personnel.

E-Tour Guide: It is a digital guide application that accompanies tourists on travels, provides information about the area to visit and is installed on technological devices.

Environmentally Touristic Product: These are environmentally friendly products such as destinations, food, souvenirs, and transportation that are designed and consumed in a way that does not harm nature and resources.

Green Data Center: It is a green computing application that is designed not to damage nature and provides data storage and flow in the center rather than in different locations.

Green Hotel: It is the title given to environmentally friendly hotels that protect nature by adopting a sustainability approach, consume all their resources at an ergonomic level, encourage the use of renewable energy and recycle their waste.

Power Mode: It is a function used in information and communication technologies to save energy by reducing power consumption.

Virtual Tour: It is a virtual reality application that consists of various videos and photos of the areas you want to travel and visit, and offers the opportunity to experience beforehand.

Chapter 7
Innovation Environment for Sustainable Medical Tourism in a Country

Nasrin Sultana
https://orcid.org/0000-0003-1203-426X
HEC Montreal, Canada

Ekaterina Turkina
HEC Montreal, Canada

Patrick Cohendet
HEC Montreal, Canada

ABSTRACT

Medical tourism has become one of the fastest-growing service industries in the 21st century. The purpose of this chapter is to advance the idea that the growth of medical tourism is influenced not only by the innovation in medical technology but also by the overall innovation environment in a country. Conducting a fixed effect regression analysis, the authors find empirical evidence in support of the argument. Because of the inter-sectoral nature of the medical tourism industry, the findings imply a plethora of opportunities for all related industries to realize the full potential of the resources available for innovation in a country. The most important implication of the findings is that strengthening the innovation environment in a country is momentous for sustainable medical tourism. The findings show a way to achieve sustainable medical tourism by integrating different stakeholders through collaboration and innovation.

DOI: 10.4018/978-1-6684-4645-4.ch007

INTRODUCTION

The medical tourism industry has become one of the fastest-growing service industries in the 21st century with the emergence of new technologies and globalization of the healthcare industry. Medical tourism typically refers to the movement of people from one country to another to receive medical services. Due to the improvements in communication technologies, people can now easily access information about medical treatments in other countries. For example, people can consult doctors and travel to get medical care whenever necessary. The global medical tourism market size was valued at US$54.4 billion in 2020 and is expected to grow annually at 21.1% from 2016 to 2027 (Medical Tourism Market Size, Industry Report, 2020-2027).

Although the medical tourism industry might see the ripple effect of the COVID-19 pandemic due to border closure and other restrictions, there has also been a radical shift toward remote and more affordable healthcare services that will attenuate the effect. Technological adaptations during the pandemic have become opportune for medical tourism. While in-person services have been impacted, remote medical consultation has significantly increased during the pandemic (Chhabra et al., 2021). Scholars and practitioners have often described medical tourism as the future of health services and assessed its impact from economic, technological, and social perspectives (Darwazeh et al., 2021; Sandberg, 2017). Medical tourism is about healthcare, technology, tourism, and other related industries at the same time, and therefore, innovation in these industries is as important as innovation in medical technology for the medical tourism industry to remain sustainable. Thereby, medical tourism has significant implications for global public health and might impact the future of how and where healthcare is delivered (Ratnasari et al., 2021; Sandberg, 2017).

However, the extant literature on medical tourism either discusses the role of medical tourism in the economic development of a country or, predominantly, emphasizes that advanced medical technology is one of the main drivers behind the growth of medical tourism (Ganguli & Ebrahim, 2017; Gupta et al., 2015; Weidenfeld, 2018). Earlier studies on medical tourism are country-specific case studies based on the top medical tourism destinations. All such studies mainly explore the reasons behind the popularity of the destination countries and the contribution of medical tourism to the economic development of a country (Ebrahim & Ganguli, 2019; Gupta et al., 2015; Hopkins et al., 2010; Richards, 2018).

In the absence of common features between countries, it is difficult to generalize the findings to other countries. Although the medical tourism industry is at the crossroads of multiple related industries, earlier studies do not necessarily consider the impact of such relationships or the relationship between medical tourism and the overall innovation environment in a country. Because of the limited research on medical tourism from the perspective of collaboration, the growth of medical tourism entails new challenges and opportunities for both destination and source countries (Hall, 2011; Ormond & Mainil, 2015; Sandberg, 2017; Upadhyay, 2011).

For example, the growing demand for medical tourism is creating both demand and opportunities for the development of medical technology (Szymanska, 2016). Furthermore, although tourism is increasingly becoming an important platform for knowledge-based activities and has great potential for innovation by combining diverse knowledge and cultural and natural resources, the literature on innovation tends to focus on the sectors related to advanced technology (Weidenfeld, 2018). Therefore, there is still a lack of a clear understanding of how the innovation environment affects the volume of medical tourism in a given country. Since the medical tourism industry is linked to both an advanced technology industry – the healthcare industry – and low technology industry – the tourism industry, innovations in these industries and other related industries will affect the sustainability of the medical tourism industry in a country. Therefore, in this chapter, the authors aim to understand *the association between medical tourism and the innovation environment in a country.*

The purpose of this chapter is to investigate the association between medical tourism and the innovation environment in a country in order to realize the full potential of this rapidly growing industry. A successful innovation environment, a set-up that facilitates collaboration and interaction at the group and individual levels to meet changing conditions, focuses on communication activities to support changes (Hiatt, 2006; Kliewe et al., 2013). Following the relevant literature, the authors consider the innovation environment in a country in terms of the knowledge intensity and the innovation capability in the country. With the globalization of healthcare, the interest is growing in moving healthcare out of facilities into communities, which creates opportunities for collaboration among different industries (Bhatti et al., 2017; Sandberg, 2017). Since the medical tourism industry is at the crossroad of the technology and tourism industries, the industry is affected by changes in related industries (Hjalager, 2009; Ormond & Mainil, 2015).

On the one hand, advanced medical technology is considered one of the drivers of medical tourism. On the other hand, innovation in medical tourism can be an indicator of the activities of different industries operating in the tourism market (Hjalager, 2002; Szmansky, 2016). Besides, innovation systems are cross-functional and require collective efforts and effective technology strategies as well as capturing the unmet needs for strong idea generation (Gardner et al., 2007; Kanagal, 2015). It requires a close connection between different stakeholders – in tourism and healthcare industries and in governments – to bring diverse knowledge together for the industry to be competitive.

The implementation of medical tourism will be effective and sustainable when the interests of all stakeholders are aligned, and they are involved in the process of innovation. The stakeholders of medical tourism include but are not limited to medical practitioners, private and public hospitals, tour operators, hotels, transportation services, and policymakers. The development of sustainable medical tourism is relevant to more than one sustainable development goal adopted by the United Nations and can contribute to achieving sustainable development in a country. For example, sustainable medical tourism will help a country to reduce inequality and ensure good health and well-being for all. Similarly, promoting sustainable medical tourism will also facilitate the sustainable development of industries related to medical tourism and investment in scientific research and innovation. Sustainable medical tourism practices will lead to reduction and standardization of costs, positive public relations, improved image, increased satisfaction, and a rise in demand (Perkumiene et al., 2019).

The theoretical definition of sustainable tourism also involves economic, social, and environmental protection dimensions (Streimikiene et al., 2020). A strong innovation environment in a country will create possibilities to achieve all three dimensions of sustainability. To the best of the authors' knowledge, this study is the first quantitative study, involving all the top medical tourism destinations and most of the OECD countries, to understand the relationship between medical tourism and the innovation environment of a country. The COVID-19 outbreak is affecting the medical tourism industry and causing new challenges for sustainable tourism development. A supportive and strong innovation environment will allow medical tourism stakeholders to innovate fast and deal with challenges in the future.

The findings of this chapter have multifaceted contributions. Theoretically, the findings will contribute to the limited literature on medical tourism by discussing the importance of innovation in sustainable medical tourism. Practically, the findings will help policymakers in medical tourism and other related industries to make proper policies and to build a better innovation environment that will not only support medical tourism and other related industries but also enhance economic development in a country. Understanding the association between medical tourism, knowledge intensity, and innovation capability in a country will be rewarding for all stakeholders in the tourism and healthcare industries and governments since such connections help them to access knowledge, to facilitate the learning process, and to foster knowledge creation (Rodriguez et al., 2017). The medical tourism industry will benefit from the overall innovation environment because of the industry's inter-sectoral nature (Shriedeh, 2019; Weidenfeld, 2018). In this COVID-19 era, the findings are particularly important for different stakeholders to understand their strengths and challenges to provide remote and affordable healthcare services.

The remainder of the chapter is structured as follows: in the next two sections, the authors review the literature on the association of medical tourism with the knowledge intensity and innovation capability of a country to develop relevant hypotheses. In the subsequent section, data and research methodology are described. In the following section, findings are presented and discussed. Directions for future research are also provided in this section. Finally, the authors conclude the chapter by shedding light on the limitations of the current analysis and highlighting the contributions made to the literature.

LITERATURE REVIEW & HYPOTHESES DEVELOPMENT

Medical tourism has grown extensively in the last decades as healthcare has become global and an interesting topic of research. The common terms used to discuss medical tourism are international medical tourism, domestic medical tourism, and employer-sponsored medical tourism. Medical tourism can simply be defined as the act of traveling to foreign countries to receive medical treatments (Balaban & Marano, 2010; Horowitz, 2007). According to the Centers for Disease Control and Prevention (CDC), medical tourism refers to traveling to another country for medical care. Carrera and Bridges (2006) define medical tourism as "the organized travel outside one's natural healthcare jurisdiction for the enhancement or restoration of the individual's health through medical intervention (p. 447)".

Later, Iordache et al. (2013) extend the definition of medical tourism by revealing that medical tourism has a wider and general scope that includes healthcare and wellness tourism. In the end, the most popular understanding of medical tourism is traveling to another country for getting medical care. Traveling for healthcare creates an opportunity to bring a vast range of resources that could be used for health, medical, and wellness-related issues (Smith & Puczko, 2014). Thereby, the growing popularity of medical tourism is creating new business opportunities and challenges for stakeholders in different industries and bringing the issues of sustainability to the fore (Foley et al., 2019; Ormond & Mainil, 2015; Streimikiene et al., 2020).

Sustainability plays a key role in promoting tourism destinations since tourists are becoming more focused on the quality of products and services to satisfy their physical, social, or spiritual needs (Goffi et al., 2019; Harrera et al., 2018). According to the World Tourism Organization (UNWTO), sustainable tourism is the tourism "that takes full account of its current and future economic, social and environmental impacts, addressing the needs of visitors, the industry, the environment, and host communities". Sustainable tourism development is closely connected to competitiveness (Streimikiene et al., 2020).

Because of the intersectoral nature of the medical tourism industry, the innovation environment in a country will enable the stakeholders of medical tourism to align their operations with global and local realities and innovate continuously to maintain competitive advantages. For example, technology plays a significant role in establishing an effective communication system that allows for the provision of services in a convenient manner and a continuation of care as patients and their medical information can be smoothly transitioned across countries (Mayakul et al., 2018). Developing a network of hospitals and digitalization of services also improves the quality of healthcare services up to international standards (Ratnasari et al., 2021).

In the end, there seem to be two streams of studies related to medical tourism: one stream discusses the role of medical tourism in the economic development of a country, and the other stream discusses the key drivers behind the prosperity of the medical tourism industry in destination countries. The authors discuss literature from both streams to understand the context regarding the association between medical tourism and the innovation environment of a country and to develop relevant hypotheses.

Knowledge Intensity and Medical Tourism

With the emergence of new technologies and an increased tendency for globalization, stakeholders of different industries are coming together along with their diversified knowledge. The extent to which an actor depends on knowledge to enhance competitive advantage or has the potential to utilize knowledge is known as the knowledge intensity of the actor (Autio et al., 2000; Otcenaskova & Mikulecka, 2012; Willoughby & Galvin, 2005). Knowledge intensity leads to growth through knowledge creation and utilization. Although knowledge intensity is attributed to the creation of new technologies, the scope of knowledge intensity is not necessarily limited to high-technology industries (Gifford & Mckelvey, 2019).

Knowledge intensity increases all knowledge processes, and all knowledge processes have a beneficial impact on innovation (Andreeva & Kianto, 2011). Besides, innovation is not only about discovering new knowledge or developing new products and services but also about the process of integrating new knowledge into the development of new products and services (Adner & Kapoor, 2016). Knowledge management is the key to successful innovation, and it requires effective strategies for external knowledge sourcing (Ghashemi et al., 2021; Moaniba et al., 2020). Hence, knowledge intensity depends on the types of actors and relationships between different actors as well as on their external environment and innovation system (Li & Gao, 2021).

Medical tourism involves both the technology and tourism industries, and therefore, it requires close connections between different stakeholders to bring diverse knowledge in these industries together and is affected by changes in different related industries (Hjalager, 2009; Ormond & Mainil, 2015). Key factors of medical tourism market growth include better healthcare, the latest technologies, innovative medicines, modern devices, better hospitality, and personalized care (Draghici et al., 2016; Ebrahim & Ganguli, 2019; Ganguli & Ebrahim, 2017; Gupta et al., 2015; Hopkins et al., 2010; Szymanska, 2016). Thus, the availability of experts and advanced knowledge in these areas is crucial for maintaining quality healthcare services in a country. Medical tourism is also becoming increasingly linked with tourist activities to ease their stay in a different environment and provide them with a comprehensive service (Hopkins et al., 2010).

Though a medical tourist's primary reason for traveling is to get better treatment than that is available at home, medical tourists expect the holistic experience to be better during their stay. Since medical tourism is part of the service industry, the overall experience of the patients or medical tourists is highly important for the sustainability and growth of this industry (Darwazeh et al., 2021). The availability of only better treatment opportunities will not be appealing to patients if there is no convenient transport to commute or an affordable place to stay, for instance.

The core competencies in the medical tourism industry range from the ability to offer holistic medical services to the ability to maintain efficient collaboration between the health and tourism industries (Darwazeh et al., 2021; Ebrahim & Ganguli, 2019). Therefore, medical tourism has a close connection to the knowledge accumulated in all related industries. For example, Draghici et al. (2016) study the role of health tourism in developing the territorial systems in Romania from 2000 to 2012 and find that tourism plays a preeminent role in the local economy by generating an increase in functional complexities of the territorial system. The idea of medical tourism and the resulting economic contribution to the economic development of a country work because even though information can easily be transferred from one place to another, the producers of knowledge still require specific spaces or locations to work (Evans, 2009; Pisano & Shih, 2009).

For example, in India, foreign companies have started to invest in the healthcare market to exploit the opportunities of government support and the availability of necessary structure, world-class medical professionals, and human capital and to conduct profitable international business (Ebrahim & Ganguli, 2019; Ganguli & Ebrahim, 2017; Gupta et al., 2015). Therefore, stakeholders of medical tourism need to take strategic decisions to improve medical technology by investing in research and development. Medical tourism also attracts foreign investment in different related sectors since governments in destination countries offer different benefits to foreign investors.

The differentiation in the tourism industry usually depends on natural and cultural resources, but the context changes to a great extent when we think about medical tourism; medical tourism brings technology and other related industries into the context. The presence of a cross-functional and complex set of strategic resources increases the competitiveness of medical tourism destinations and is responsible for the growth of the medical tourism industry in a country (Ebrahim & Ganguli 2019). The complex nature of the tourism industry and its inter-sectoral relationship with other industries create challenges and opportunities for innovation because the features and sources of knowledge differ from sector to sector (Malerba, 2004; Rodriguez et al., 2017; Weidenfeld, 2018).

For example, knowledge could be particular to a community when that knowledge emerges through situated activity and is constructed within a particular context (Bechky, 2003; Cohendet & Simon, 2017). Similarly, employees belonging to an industry reflect that significant knowledge about some economic activities is accumulated and is a sign of sectoral specialization (Perugini et.al., 2008; Pisano & Shih 2009). Sectoral specialization is also considered an important factor in industrial development and plays an important role in getting benefits from foreign investments (Hidalgo et al. 2007; Kinoshita, 2000; Perugini et al., 2008). Therefore, the availability of specialized knowledge, skilled labor, and a favorable environment is particularly important in the context of medical tourism.

The connection between different industries and innovation has been explored by researchers from different perspectives such as technology, culture, and entrepreneurship, in which creativity is considered fundamental in the innovation process (Bakhshi et al., 2008; Cooke & Schwartz, 2007). Certain industries require the presence of other industries in the vicinity to realize their full potential and to foster innovation and growth although the boundaries between knowledge in different sectors change over time (Bakhshi et al., 2008; Malerba, 2004). Similarly, successful communication between actors is important to stimulate innovation since a substantial part of the knowledge produced in different industries is tacit (Bakhshi et al., 2008).

The approach to knowledge management of actors is an important deciding factor in its innovation process (Bakhshi et al., 2008; Nonaka & Takeuchi, 1995). Countries tend to move towards products that are closer to their current specialization and need to use their existing knowledge base to improve the quality of production (Hiatt, 2006; Hidalgo et al., 2007). Hausmann et al. (2014) point out that the aggregate knowledge of a society does not depend on the knowledge of each individual living in that society but on the diversity of knowledge of each individual and the efficiency of the communication among them to make use of that knowledge.

The existing knowledge base and the capability to access the required knowledge are crucial in the context of medical tourism. For example, links with firms and clusters near ICT, biotech, health, medical, manufacturing, and tourism can enhance growth in relevant industries (Delgado, 2010; Turkina et al., 2019). Different types of knowledge and learning processes are essential for understanding a sector (Malerba, 2004). In the end, the knowledge intensity of an actor depends on the availability of knowledge in the external environment and the knowledge-seeking activity of the actor (Caloghirou & Protogerou, 2015; Gifford & Mckelvey, 2019). Therefore, the authors argue that the availability of diverse knowledge plays a role in the growth of medical tourism in a country and summarize this discussion in the following hypothesis:

Hypothesis One: *Medical tourism is positively associated with the knowledge intensity in a country.*

Innovation Capability and Medical Tourism

Innovation plays an important role in providing healthcare services. The variety in knowledge sourcing influences the degree of innovation, and innovation is the key to survival and sustainability (Caloghirou et al., 2004; Rodriguez et al., 2017). With the globalization of healthcare, the interest is growing in moving healthcare out of facilities into communities that create opportunities for collaboration among different industries (Bhatti et al., 2017; Gronroos, 1999). There is also rapid growth of various tourist programs that offer visitors to participate in different activities and make a positive impact in different areas of social life such as cultural, environmental, welfare, or health-related (De Bruin & Jelincic, 2016). Similarly, consumer-producer interactions are increasingly becoming an important way of value creation (Potts et al., 2008; Von Hippel, 2005; Weidenfeld, 2018).

Since medical tourists come from diverse backgrounds, they bring diversified knowledge; seeking regular feedback from them can enhance cooperation among different stakeholders of medical tourism and enhance the growth of the industry, eventually (Lee et al., 2012; Potts et al., 2008). For example, companies in health tourism services that introduce the participation of consumers in the process of innovation represent a higher level of innovation than the others who do not (Szymanska, 2016). Innovation in medical tourism can be an indicator of the activities of different industries operating in the tourism market, and advanced medical technology is considered one of the drivers of medical tourism (Hjalager, 2002; Szmansky, 2016). However, the lack of innovation capability hinders the process of innovation (Ghazinoory et al., 2020).

To develop sustainable medical tourism, it is important to understand the culture and behavior of patients to understand their expectations in order to provide quality healthcare (Liu & Chen, 2013). A truly sustainable means of fostering the growth of the medical tourism industry could be the one that connects different stakeholders in the process of relevant innovation. Innovation systems are cross-functional and require effective technology strategies, and capturing the unmet needs is required for strong idea generation (Gardner et al., 2007; Kanagal, 2015). Innovation is linked with co-creation that focuses on the identification and creation of values by involving different actors (Kanagal, 2015; Nonaka & Takeuchi, 1995).

For example, managing long-term relationships with medical tourists has a positive relationship with all types of innovation including product, service, and process innovation (Shriedeh, 2019). Creating sustainable medical tourism requires maintaining a strong relationship between different stakeholders for achieving competitive advantages through enhancing the experiences of the patients (Darwazeh et al., 2021). Similarly, technological adaptations are also important to make medical services available to people in need (Chhabra et al., 2021). Currently, an innovative approach through interactive and collective learning is gaining popularity.

Therefore, a shift of mindset towards the innovation process is important for successful innovation (Govindarajan & Trimble, 2012). Notably, an open and interactive model of innovation requires supporting different communities and knowledge bases to identify needs and facilitate collaborative creation (Cohendet & Simon, 2017; Zobel et al., 2017). The open innovation approach emphasizes the capability of actors to access new knowledge available in the environment and to produce something different by using the obtained knowledge (Chesbrough, 2006). Von Hippel (2005) also explains how different sources of information provide necessary complements to the innovation process. Patients can also play an important role in the process of innovation in medical tourism by bringing their experiences, expectations, and insights (Campos et al., 2018).

Medical tourist relationship management is positively associated with all types of innovation (Shriedeh, 2019). The link between tourism and culture as well as the survival and development of culture depends on technology, and tourism can be considered an innovative alternative (Wattanacharoensil & Schuckert, 2016; Weidenfeld, 2018). The stakeholders of medical tourism from different industries can collaborate to redefine problems and find innovative solutions to foster growth in this industry (Campos et al., 2018; Nonaka & Takeuchi, 1995). Therefore, the idea of involving different stakeholders in the process of innovation applies well to medical tourism.

Effective collaboration between public and private medical tourism stakeholders is one of the core competencies of medical tourism destinations (Ebrahim & Ganguli, 2019; Campos et al., 2018). For instance, Mattson et al. (2005) propose a model of innovation for understanding tourism that highlights the integration of knowledge available in different industries. By adopting a collaborative strategy, medical tourism stakeholders can share valuable information about the medical tourism market and credible statistics on the impact of medical tourism on the local economy (Darwazeh et al., 2021). Firms from one industry can acquire substantial knowledge by collaborating with firms in other industries (Hernández-Espallardo, 2011). The distinctive partnerships between stakeholders in healthcare, financing, hospitality, and a variety of reputable tourism services are the driving factors behind the prosperity of the medical tourism industry in India, Singapore, and Thailand (Ebrahim & Ganguli, 2019).

Furthermore, sources of outside knowledge are important for different stakeholders to access and exploit external knowledge, which contributes to the improvement of local innovation systems (Cockburn & Henderson, 1998; Kostopoulos et al., 2011; Mowery & Oxley, 1995; Powell et al., 1996; Rodriguez et al., 2017). Therefore, partnerships between different stakeholders bring together diverse knowledge, facilitate the innovation process, and contribute to the growth of the medical tourism industry.

The demand for better medical services has become a global phenomenon that results in opportunities for different industries because the healthcare industry is becoming a marketable industry day by day (Arunanondchai & Fink, 2007; Chhabra et al., 2021; Szymanska, 2016). For instance, countries are moving towards medical outsourcing by providing services to the overburdened medical care systems in western countries (Gupta et al., 2015; Sandberg, 2017). Those countries often offer different advantages such as reduced tax rates, special economic zones, medical research and development centers, etc. to attract FDI in the medical tourism sector and to build strength in the industry (Ormond & Mainil, 2015).

The situation also creates business opportunities for the local people and encourages startups to enter the healthcare industry. In the same way advancement in medical technology is considered infrastructure in the medical tourism industry (Caballero-Danell & Mugomba, 2007), the advancement in media and technology facilitates patients from other countries to benefit from a service available in a country (Gronroos, 1999). For example, India's renowned IT industry and the availability of state-of-the-art technology is a competitive advantage for the country to attract medical tourists (Gupta et al., 2015). Similarly, superior technology and a history of accomplishment of 'firsts' are competitive advantages for the medical tourism industry in Singapore (Connell, 2013). Therefore, the development of sustainable medical tourism is linked to changes and innovation in other related industries (Shriedeh, 2019).

In the end, achieving sustainability in medical tourism requires appropriate innovation strategies (Darwazeh et al., 2021). The innovativeness of tourism firms is an important determinant of competitiveness and is often a condition for survival (Sundbo et al., 2007). Accordingly, the authors argue that innovations in other related industries have a significant role in the growth of the medical tourism industry in a country and summarize this discussion in the following hypothesis:

Hypothesis Two: *Medical tourism is positively associated with the innovation capability of a country.*

METHODOLOGY

To understand the association between medical tourism and technology, the authors conduct a longitudinal regression analysis by considering medical tourism, measured in millions of US dollars, as the dependent variable and the knowledge intensity and innovation capability as the independent variables. Longitudinal studies provide us with a better understanding of the changes over time (Volberda et al., 2010). The study is conducted by using information of 51 countries, including all the top medical tourism destination countries and most of the OECD countries, for a period of 10 years from 2008 to 2017.

Dependent Variable

The authors measure medical tourism by using the revenue earned from medical tourism in a country. Medical tourism revenue concerns all domestic and inbound trips made with the purpose of some kind of medical treatment regardless of complexity including aesthetic or cosmetic surgery. The expenses for travel and tourism services such as hotel charges, travel costs to the destination, car rental, intermediaries, and so forth in the country are included to calculate the revenue from medical tourism. Travel services expenses of both the patient and any accompanying people are included. For inbound trips for medical purposes, transport tickets bought in the country of departure are excluded. The data on medical tourism come from the Euromonitor International database.

Independent Variables

The authors measure the innovation environment by using two indicators: knowledge intensity and innovation capability of a country. Following the available definitions of knowledge intensity at the organizational level (Autio et al., 2000; Otcenaskova & Mikulecka, 2012), the knowledge intensity of a country is defined as the aggregate knowledge available to a country and the country's ability to make use of such knowledge. To measure knowledge intensity, the authors use the economic complexity index data, extracted from the Economics Complexity Observatory (Simoes & Hidalgo, 2011). Economic complexity reflects the amount of knowledge that is embedded in the productive structure of an economy. Hausmann et al. (2014) point out that productive knowledge is necessary for a society to hold and enhance knowledge and propose a way to measure the amount of diverse productive knowledge of a country based on the types of products produced in a country. Countries that can generate greater knowledge accumulation and that offer better collaborative or interdisciplinary opportunities tend to have more capacity to generate innovative ideas and new business models that are widely considered the engines of economic growth (Hausmann et al., 2014).

The innovation capability of a country is measured by using the data obtained from the global competitiveness index. The innovation capability of a country is one of the twelve pillars of the global competitiveness index (highest score = best). The innovation capability is calculated based on ten different components of innovation including diversity of the workforce and the state of cluster development. Innovation capability is a suitable indicator to measure the technological environment of a country because it takes into account the quantity and quality of formal research and development: the extent to which a country's environment encourages collaboration, connectivity, creativity, diversity, and confrontation across different visions and angles and the capacity to turn ideas into new goods and services (The Global Competitiveness Report – the World Economic Forum).

Control Variables

The authors control for infrastructure, government expenditure on health, GDP, exchange rate, and availability of doctors and hospitals in a country to maintain consistency with the existing literature. In the context of medical tourism, it is important to develop the need-based infrastructure, especially in terms of connectivity, safety, and security. Well-developed infrastructure lowers transportation and transaction costs and facilitates the movement of goods and people and the transfer of information within a country and across borders (Gupta et al., 2015). It also ensures access to power and water – necessary conditions for modern economic activity. Infrastructure measures the quality and extension of transport infrastructure – road, rail, water, and air – and utility infrastructure. It is important to take infrastructure into account because better-connected geographic areas have generally been more prosperous.

Government supports and public policies play a major role in the development of the medical tourism industry in a country. There is a significant positive relationship between government expenditure on research and development and the development of the medical tourism market (Gupta et al., 2015). Therefore, government expenditure on health is controlled. Government expenditure on health includes expenditures such as research and development (R&D) expenditure on health, medical products, appliances and equipment, outpatient services, hospital services, and public health services.

The authors also control for GDP and exchange rate. GDP is an important variable that influences a country's industrial structure and is related to economic development. GDP per capita (USD Thousand) used in this study is measured at the purchasing power parity approach. The exchange rate is controlled since the exchange rate is an influencing variable in choosing a medical tourism destination (Lee et al., 2012; Smith & Forgione, 2007). The exchange rate is defined as the price in a given currency at which bills drawn in another currency may be bought. All exchange rates are against the US dollar.

Finally, the availability of doctors and hospitals in a country is controlled since the presence of high-quality medical is a key factor of international competitive advantage in medical tourism (Ebrahim & Ganguli, 2019). Doctors are measured as the number of physicians, general practitioners, and specialists who are actively practicing medicine in public and private institutions. Foreign physicians who are licensed to practice and are actively practicing medicine in the country are included, but qualified physicians who are working abroad, working in administration, research, and industry positions are excluded.

The number of hospitals and clinics refers to organizations with residential establishments equipped with inpatient facilities for 24-hour medical and nursing care, diagnosis, treatment, and rehabilitation of the sick and injured, usually for both medical and surgical conditions, and staffed with professionally trained medical practitioners, including at least one physician. The data on control variables come from the Euromonitor International database.

RESULTS & DISCUSSION

To understand the relationship between medical tourism and the innovation environment of a country, the authors conduct a longitudinal regression analysis with the dependent variable – medical tourism – and two independent variables – knowledge intensity and innovation capability of a country. Medical tourism is measured using the revenue earned from medical tourism (million US dollars); the data come from the Euromonitor International database. The knowledge intensity of a country is measured using the economic complexity index of countries; the data is extracted from the Economic Complexity Observatory. Innovation capability is one of the twelve pillars of the global competitiveness index; the data is obtained from the global competitiveness index (highest score = best). The STATA statistical software is used to conduct all analyses.

Results

At first, the authors conduct the Hausman test to specify the appropriate model, between the fixed effect model and the random effect model, for regression analysis since they are interested in analyzing the relationship between medical tourism and the innovation environment of a country during the period from 2008 to 2017. The Hausman test is conducted to specify the proper model to maintain the consistency of the findings. As per the results of the Hausman test, with the p-value<0.01, the findings of the fixed effect regression analysis are reported. Table 1 reports descriptive statistics of the variables used in this study.

A positive association between medical tourism and the innovation environment of a country is expected. In other words, the authors expect medical tourism to be positively associated with knowledge intensity and innovation capacity. The correlation statistics presented in Table 2 show the positive relationships as expected. Specifically, the positive and significant correlations (at a 10% significance level) of medical tourism with knowledge intensity (coef. 0.2636) and innovation capacity (coef. 0.2813) suggest a positive association between medical tourism and the innovation environment of a country. This correlation statistics provide preliminary support to conduct the regression analysis.

Table 1. Descriptive statistics

Variable	Mean	Standard Deviation	Observations
Medical Tourism	421.571	911.6209	510
Knowledge intensity	0.6755294	0.790619	510
Innovation Capacity	53.52412	16.69998	510
GDP (per capita)	1453517	2548592	510
Govt. healthcare expenditure	60355.26	193135.1	510
Infrastructure	74.46902	13.29277	510
Exchange rate	314.5598	1611.662	510
Doctors	125555.2	187261.6	510
Hospitals	2605.586	5900.531	510

Table 2. Correlation statistics (star at 10% significance level)

Variables	1	2	3	4	5	6	7	8	9
1. Medical Tourism	1.0000								
2. Knowledge intensity	0.2636*	1.0000							
3. Innovation Capacity	0.2813*	0.6755*	1.0000						
4. GDP (per capita)	0.7578*	0.2243*	0.3373*	1.0000					
5. Govt-Healthcare	0.7962*	0.3109*	0.4140*	0.8989*	1.0000				
6. Infrastructure	0.2427*	0.6380*	0.8094*	0.1467*	0.2752*	1.0000			
7. Exchange rate	-0.0799*	-0.1598*	-0.1719*	0.0472	-0.0517	-0.2105*	1.0000		
8. Doctors	0.5310*	0.1009*	0.1735*	0.8269*	0.5613*	-0.0222	-0.0619	1.0000	
9. Hospitals	0.6582	-0.0828*	0.1208*	0.4120*	0.0902*	-0.1060*	-0.0337	0.6528*	1.0000

Table 3. Regression statistics (fixed-effect model)

Medical Tourism	Coefficient	Standard Error	P-value	95% Confidence Interval	
Knowledge intensity	87.58292	35.38198	0.014	18.04892	157.1169
Innovation capacity	14.30829	3.369621	0.000	7.686186	20.9304
GDP	0.0000683	0.000036	0.058	-2.40e-06	0.000139
Govt-Healthcare	0.0010723	0.0003837	0.005	0.0003183	0.0018263
Infrustructure	4.064461	1.756823	0.021	0.6118859	7.517035
Exchange rate	-0.0404756	0.026206	0.123	-0.0919767	0.0110256
Doctors	0.0017103	0.0005833	0.004	0.0005639	0.0028567
Hospitals	-0.019368	0.0335088	0.564	-0.0852207	0.0464847
Constant	-1021.625	195.4408	0.000	-1405.713	-637.5372
Number of observations	510				
Fixed effect: prob>F	0.0000				
Hausman: prob>chi2	0.0011				

Next, the fixed effect regression analysis is conducted by using the dependent variable, medical tourism, and the independent variables, knowledge capacity and innovation capacity. Controlling for GDP, infrastructure, exchange rate, and availability of doctors and hospitals in a country, the authors find that medical tourism is positively and significantly associated with knowledge intensity (coef. 87.58292) and innovation capacity (coef. 14.30829) of a country. Table 3 reports the results.

The fixed effect regression analysis provides us with the evidence that, ceteris paribas, medical tourism is positively associated with the knowledge intensity and innovation capability in a country. The coefficients of control variables from the correlation analysis and regression analysis also indicate their relevance to the medical tourism industry, suggesting the importance of traditional determinants of medical tourism. However, the purpose of this chapter is to broaden the scope of our understanding and to advance the idea that the traditional determinants of medical tourism such as advanced medical technology is necessary but not sufficient for the growth of medical tourism in a country. The findings, therefore, support the idea that the innovation environment positively influences the growth of the medical tourism industry in a given country.

Discussion

In this chapter, the authors investigate the association between medical tourism and the innovation environment in a country and find that medical tourism is significantly and positively associated with the innovation environment, in terms of knowledge intensity and innovation capability, in a given country. The finding of the positive and significant association of medical tourism with knowledge intensity and innovation capability provides empirical evidence that the close connection between related industries is rewarding for all stakeholders of medical tourism. Such connection helps them to access knowledge, facilitate the learning process, and foster knowledge creation (Granstrand & Holgersson, 2020; Rodriguez et al., 2017; Volberda et al., 2010).

Furthermore, the connection and interaction between different actors will improve the capabilities of the actors in different industries and enhance the regional innovation system (Braczyk et al., 2003; Turkina et al., 2019; Wang & Hu, 2020). Because of the industry's inter-sectoral nature of the medical tourism industry, a strong innovation environment will benefit the stakeholders to innovate and maintain competitive advantages and be sustainable (Shriedeh, 2019; Wattanacharoensil & Schuckert, 2016; Weidenfeld, 2018). The most important point that can be inferred from the connection of medical tourism with knowledge intensity and innovation capacity is that there is a common ground between the healthcare, technology, innovation, and tourism industries.

Stakeholders and Innovation in Medical Tourism

Stakeholders of medical tourism include but are not limited to the actors in tourism and healthcare industries and governments. Different stakeholders in medical tourism can act as different communities of innovation that feed back to the process of developing medical technology. They can exchange knowledge and combine resources to form an active knowledge system required for innovation. For example, to attract foreign patients, medical tourism stakeholders can collaborate to offer packages including airfare, accommodations for the medical tourist and travel companion, local ground travel, coordination of medical itinerary, post-surgical care, travel site seeing, and entertainment. Although quality healthcare and affordability do not always go hand in hand, it is possible to adopt a lean process in healthcare and provide quality healthcare at much less cost compared to many countries (Kanagal, 2015).

For instance, Narayana Health in India is delivering healthcare through the lean process and is a successful model of innovation that brings different stakeholders together (Bhatti et al., 2017). India is now moving towards the area of "medical outsourcing" to provide healthcare services to overburdened countries on a contract basis (Gupta et al., 2015). Narayana Health provides heart surgery for less than 10% of the average cost in the United States. With strategic and effective planning, the practices can be replicated in the United States and other countries.

In medical tourism, stakeholders from different industries bring firsthand insights that are crucial for the relevant actors to be at a competitive edge in the industry (Chhabra et al., 2021). The collective learning of stakeholders in different industries will provide rewarding ideas for innovation and promote growth in the medical tourism industry (De Bruin & Jelincic, 2016; Radu-Daniel et al., 2014; Richards, 2016; Shriedeh 2019). On the one hand, advancements in technology can create numerous opportunities for medical tourism. On the other hand, the firsthand knowledge and ideas of the stakeholders in the related industries contribute to the creation of new products and services by using different technologies to support the industry.

Therefore, it is important to coordinate different communities and knowledge bases to identify needs and facilitate collaboration (Cohendet & Simon, 2017); a similar trend of collaboration is also noticed in medical tourism (Draghici et al., 2016; Ormond & Mainil, 2015; Richards, 2018). Quality of care, affordable medical fees, trained physicians, and international accreditation are important cornerstones for attracting foreign patients to a country (Darwazeh et al., 2021; Sandberg, 2017). Since medical tourism requires quality medical care at par with international standards, the stakeholders are now integrating more and more technological components to standardize the quality of service (Gupta et al., 2015). Consequently, the collaboration between different stakeholders such as consumers, service providers, researchers, and institutions can promote regional innovation (Romao & Nijkamp, 2019).

In the innovation process, knowledge at the beginning of the process is different than the knowledge at the end of the process, and different stakeholders can use the same knowledge in different ways (Nonaka & Takeuchi, 1995). The features and sources of knowledge differ from sector to sector (Malerba, 2004; Rodriguez et al, 2017). As a result, the complex nature of the medical tourism industry and its intersectoral relationship with other industries create challenges for innovation (Hjalager, 2009; Weidenfeld, 2018). The need to innovate is becoming stronger than ever in order to survive and prosper in competitive and globalized economies (Granstrand & Holgersson, 2020). A wide range of high-quality medical services and technology is required to meet the increasing demand for the global healthcare industry.

Since it is possible to produce user-developed innovations to offer custom manufacturing to specific users or for general commercial purposes (Von Hippel, 2005), sources of outside knowledge are important for different stakeholders to access and exploit external knowledge which contributes to the improvement of local innovation systems (Kostopoulos et al., 2011; Rodriguez et al., 2017). For example, to promote sustainability, stakeholders of medical tourism need to focus on different strategies such as energy consumption reduction, minimizing water contamination, and participating in community development projects (Darwazeh et al., 2021). Thus, the availability of experts and advanced knowledge in these areas is crucial for maintaining quality healthcare services in a country.

Involving feedback and ideas from medical tourism in the process of innovation will bring different industries together in addition to the technology industry (Shriedeh, 2019). The connection between different actors in medical tourism can be illustrated by looking at the top medical tourism destinations. For example, medical tourism is a major growth factor in the expansion of the Indian economy. India has become one of the top destinations of medical tourism by providing quality medical services at an affordable cost.

Government support and public policies along with the presence of world-class hospitals, skilled medical professionals, the high success rate in treatment, less waiting periods in the hospitals played a major role to promote the industry in India (Gupta et al., 2015). The Ministry of Tourism and the Ministry of Health in India are working together to support the industry by modernizing and expanding airports, introducing different visa systems to ease medical tourists' arrivals, and offering incentives and tax rebates to pharmaceutical industries (ibid). To maximize the potential of innovation in global health, product development partnerships between the public and private sectors are important in addition to health policy and systematic research (Gardner et al., 2007). Therefore, medical tourism stakeholders can gain competitiveness through innovation (Sundbo et al., 2007).

In terms of knowledge and innovation, the stakeholders of medical tourism need to act collaboratively. Organizational performance, in most cases, depends on the knowledge coming from external sources (Braczyk et al., 2003; Caloghirou et al., 2004; Chesborough, 2006; Rodriguez et al., 2017). For instance, Szymanska (2016) finds that when medical tourism service providers work with other stakeholders while creating innovation, they perform significantly better than those who do not involve the stakeholders in the process. There are different factors in medical tourism destinations that reflect the strength and competitiveness of a destination country compared to other countries.

Factors such as highly advanced infrastructure equipped with facilities and services such as transportation networks, banks, hotels, malls, and food establishments are also highly important for developing medical tourism in a country (Darwazeh et al., 2021; Sandberg, 2017). The intrinsic value of medical tourism is closely connected to other sectors such as healthcare, tourism, and urban development (Gupta et al., 2015; Hjalager, 2009; Shriedeh, 2019). For instance, the investment in a proper institutional framework, as well as research and development, played a significant role in the development of advanced medical tourism services in Israel, while the superior technology and history of accomplishment of "firsts" are competitive advantages for Singapore (Connell, 2013; Ebrahim & Ganguli, 2019).

As the stakeholders of medical tourism are not limited to the actors in the healthcare and tourism industries, the findings have implications beyond these industries. For example, technology and tourism are two drivers of creative industries (UN creative economy report, 2008). According to the literature, developing creative industries has a multiplier effect since creative industries attract other industries (Radu-Daniel et al., 2014). Besides, medical tourism is usually creative in focus (Hall, 2011). Liu and Chen (2013) suggest that it is important to understand the culture and behavior of patients to understand their expectations and provide quality healthcare; specifically, they suggest that cultural competencies be integrated into healthcare systems, medical organizations, and individuals by improving the communication systems among all stakeholders. Therefore, on the one hand, there are opportunities to develop medical tourism by improving healthcare and medical technology, and on the other hand, there are opportunities to involve stakeholders from different industries in the innovation process, which will enhance growth in medical tourism over time.

Innovation and Sustainable Medical Tourism

Tourism might also create some serious problems such as excessive energy consumption and increasing negative environmental effects including negative effects on the nature and quality of life of the local people (Streimikiene et al., 2020). By taking the negative effect of medical tourism into account, Beladi et al., (2019) find that an expansion in medical tourism increases the economic growth rate. In the case of medical tourism, although there are concerns about patient safety and the ethics of specific care, medical tourism has positive economic and development impacts on destination countries (Beladi et al., 2019; Hopkins et al., 2010). In reality, medical tourism can be a way to solve the shortage of medical care professionals in a country and provide access to healthcare services in another country (Sandberg, 2017). Therefore, it is important that the authorities and policymakers, knowing that the medical tourism industry is growing despite the negative effects, realize the need to engage all stakeholders in medical tourism in the process of creating their offers or organizational process (Szymanska, 2016).

The development of sustainable medical tourism emphasizes meeting the needs of existing tourists and host regions while safeguarding opportunities for the future. Therefore, to develop and maintain sustainable medical tourism, policies considering the interests of both medical tourists and local communities are important. For example, respecting the capacities and specificities of destinations will preserve local infrastructures, satisfy the tourists, and improve the image of the destination. Sustainable medical tourism can be achieved by integrating different stakeholders through collaboration and innovation. For example, private medical facilities could collaborate with governmental institutions to put forward the ideas of incentive services for foreign patients, including post-operation services, medical consultation, and other related activities (Darwazeh et al., 2021). Long-term strategies are necessary for sustainable tourism. The focus of sustainable tourism development is on retaining a high degree of satisfaction for tourists, assuring significant experience for consumers, and propagating practices of sustainable tourism among them (Streimikiene et al., 2020). Sustainable medical tourism can be attained when the principles of sustainability are integrated into the strategic planning of the related industries.

The ideal use of environmental resources and respecting the socio-cultural characteristics of host communities while ensuring viable long-term economic growth and providing socio-economic benefits to all stakeholders are important for developing sustainable medical tourism. For example, in medical tourism, quality control is not only about the completeness of facilities but also about the aspects of the accuracy of using sophisticated equipment and the efficiency and accuracy of patient handling. Thereby, sustainable medical tourism is closely linked to increasing innovations involving all stakeholders related to medical tourism. Aligning the interests of different stakeholders while promoting the innovation environment in a country will increase their motivations for providing sustainable tourism services and dealing with environmental challenges.

A strong innovation environment will encourage innovations to conserve natural heritage, biodiversity, and traditional values, will ensure viable, long-term economic operations, and will provide socio-economic benefits to all stakeholders including stable employment and income-earning opportunities and social services to host communities. A strong innovation environment will also increase the competitiveness of destination countries because the creation of innovative products and services as innovations and the application of innovations are seen as the key source of competitive advantage in an industry. Therefore, supports for sustainable tourism is closely linked to innovations.

The sustainability of medical tourism can be improved in different ways including communication and contact development, coordination and organization of work, and sharing of knowledge and experience between stakeholders, whereas insufficient cooperation between stakeholders to support sustainable practices can hamper a country's attempt to move towards sustainability. Cooperation is the most important factor for the medical tourism industry to move toward sustainability and is highly beneficial for all stakeholders. (Perkumiene et al., 2019). Medical tourism provides benefits to the government, businesses, and residents in a destination country. Sustainable medical tourism will ensure the inflow of tourists, stability of new jobs and income, and economic growth in a country. The development of sustainable medical tourism is relevant for all stakeholders.

For instance, advanced medical technologies and the professionalism of doctors are not enough to compete in the field of medical tourism. Sustainable medical tourism will not only encourage advancement in medical technologies and healthcare services but also increase the demand for accommodation, catering, transport, communication, recreation, and other tourist services. The UNWTO has launched initiatives to foster collaboration between partners that strives toward creating healthy places for both visitors and the host communities while ensuring resilient destinations for future generations. Developing policies and strategic plans for sustainable medical tourism necessitates collaboration between stakeholders and innovation to realize sustainability goals. Therefore, it is important to align the diverse interests of different stakeholders and develop a common sense of understanding for sustainable medical tourism.

FUTURE RESEARCH DIRECTIONS

Medical tourism is about healthcare, technology, tourism, and other related industries at the same time, but the scope of medical tourism stakeholders goes beyond these industries. As a result, innovations in all other industries are as important as innovations in medical technology for the medical tourism industry to grow. The key factors of medical tourism market growth include better healthcare, the latest technologies, innovative medicines, modern devices, better hospitality, and personalized care. The implementation of medical tourism will be effective and sustainable when the interests of all stakeholders are aligned and managed properly and professionally. Sustainable medical tourism depends mainly on the experience of tourists and necessitates the participation of all related stakeholders to maintain a high quality of the products and services offered.

For example, the implementation of new technologies in tourism services has positive impacts on the environment and local communities (Streimikiene et al., 2020). To anticipate, address, and overcome challenges in the Tourism sector, the UNWTO emphasizes investments in innovation, education, and digital transformation. Therefore, stakeholders of medical tourism need to reassess their abilities and realign operations with global and local realities in order to compete effectively today and to remain sustainable over the long term; they need to integrate the principles of sustainability into their strategic plans.

To achieve sustainable medical tourism, the stakeholders should aim not only to provide advanced medical treatments to medical tourists but also to integrate sustainability practices and maintain a long-term relationship with internal and external stakeholders. The authors believe that the findings of this paper will increase the awareness and desire of stakeholders of medical tourism to take appropriate steps and reinforce relevant policies in order to develop sustainable medical tourism. Earlier studies focus either on the role of medical tourism on the economic development of a country or on medical technology as one of the drivers of medical tourism. Those studies rarely consider that innovation in other related industries may also influence the growth of the medical tourism industry.

The purpose of this chapter is to broaden the scope of our understanding of medical tourism by connecting it to the innovation environment in a country. However, the authors are conscious that this study is limited by the availability of information on medical tourism destinations and activities. Further research with more information about medical tourism and specific industries would be helpful to cope with the challenges of global healthcare.

Developing policies and strategic plans for the development of sustainable medical tourism necessitates collaboration between stakeholders to innovate and realize sustainability goals. Therefore, it will be interesting to do a network analysis of medical tourism and study how the stakeholders of medical tourism in different industries are connected. For example, medical tourism is becoming increasingly linked with tourist activities to ease their stay in a different environment and provide them with a comprehensive service (Hopkins et al., 2010). In addition to receiving healthcare at affordable prices, medical tourists might also want to visit the local heritage sites, participate in cultural activities, taste local foods, etc. Technologies and communication channels such as social media can play important roles in making information about local activities and events available to medical tourists. Mapping the network of medical tourism stakeholders will help them better understand their challenges and opportunities and take necessary initiatives.

In the end, the main implication of the findings of this chapter is that the innovation environment in a country is not about the high-tech industries only; the innovation environment in a given country connects and fosters both high-tech and low-tech industries. Such connections bring on a multitude of challenges and opportunities for stakeholders of medical tourism to collaborate and innovate in order to maintain competitive advantages and be sustainable.

CONCLUSION

The medical tourism industry has grown significantly and become a global industry due to the globalization and rapid growth of international trading in tourism products. The authors find that medical tourism in a country is positively and significantly associated with the innovation environment, measured by the knowledge intensity and innovative capability, in a given country. The most important implication of the findings is that the innovation environment in a country connects and supports both high-tech and low-tech industries. Since the stakeholders of medical tourism come from different industries, the development of the medical tourism industry is related not only to the innovation in the medical technology or tourism industry but also to the overall innovation environment of a country. Emphasizing only advanced healthcare and medical technologies as drivers of medical tourism creates the potential of overlooking the innovative linkages among related industries, which will affect the policymaking regarding innovation and other capacity building (Evans, 2009). Similarly, focusing only on high-tech industries for innovation may limit the scope of external knowledge sources, which will affect the innovation performance of firms.

Currently, medical tourism is becoming an emerging industry in both developed and developing countries. An increase in healthcare costs and difficulties in accessing quality medical services in many countries contribute to the development of medical tourism (Chhabra et al., 2021). As a result, medical tourism is an answer for the patients who are in immediate need to get medical treatment but must wait long periods before getting quality care at affordable prices (Sandberg, 2017). Since medical tourism is at the crossroad of the medical and tourism industry and is significantly and positively associated with the knowledge intensity and innovation capability of a country, there is a multiplier effect – challenges and opportunities for all stakeholders of medical tourism. For countries with limited resources, medical tourism also offers an opportunity to transition to a knowledge-based economy (Ormond & Mainil, 2015; Turner, 2007). It is, therefore, important to understand and build on the relationships between medical tourism and the overall innovation environment, including all other related industries, in a country in order to realize the full potential of the resources available for innovation in a country

In the end, medical tourism can be a way to deal with the shortage of medical care in a country and can create a social impact by giving people access to improved healthcare at an affordable price. The findings of this study have both theoretical and practical implications for medical tourism stakeholders such as medical practitioners, private and public hospitals, policymakers, hotels, transportation services, and tour operators to deliver high-quality services. Theoretically, the positive and significant relationship between the medical tourism industry and the innovation system signifies the importance of medical tourism as well as the innovation performance at the firm, industry, and regional levels.

Practically, different stakeholders of tourism can bring firsthand insights through formal and informal interaction and contribute to innovation to provide quality services (Richards, 2016; Szymanska, 2016). The findings also pave the way for opportunities in creative industries since tourism and innovation are the two drivers of creative industries. Considering the contribution of medical tourism stakeholders to the innovation process and the resulting impact on the medical tourism industry will ensure delivering superior value to the customer as well as achieving organizational goals.

ACKNOWLEDGMENT

This research received no specific grant from any funding agency in the public, commercial, or not-for-profit sectors.

REFERENCES

Adner, R., & Kapoor, R. (2016). Innovation ecosystems and the pace of substitution: Re-examining technology S-curves. *Strategic Management Journal*, *37*(4), 625–648. doi:10.1002mj.2363

Andreeva, T., & Kianto, A. (2011). Knowledge processes, knowledge-intensity and innovation: A moderated mediation analysis. *Journal of Knowledge Management*, *15*(6), 1016–1034. doi:10.1108/13673271111179343

Arunanondchai, J., & Fink, C. (2006). Trade in health services in the ASEAN region. *Health Promotion International*, *21*(suppl_1), 59–66. doi:10.1093/heapro/dal052 PMID:17307958

Autio, E., Sapienza, H. J., & Almeida, J. G. (2000). Effects of age at entry, knowledge intensity, and imitability on international growth. *Academy of Management Journal*, *43*(5), 909–924.

Bakhshi, H., McVittie, E., & Simmie, J. (2008). *Creating Innovation: Do the creative industries support innovation in the wider economy?* Nesta.

Balaban, V., & Marano, C. (2010). Medical tourism research: A systematic review. *International Journal of Infectious Diseases*, *14*, e135. doi:10.1016/j.ijid.2010.02.1784

Bathelt, H., Cohendet, P., Henn, S., & Simon, L. (Eds.). (2017). *The Elgar companion to innovation and knowledge creation*. Edward Elgar Publishing. doi:10.4337/9781782548522

Bechky, B. A. (2003). Sharing meaning across occupational communities: The transformation of understanding on a production floor. *Organization Science*, *14*(3), 312–330. doi:10.1287/orsc.14.3.312.15162

Beladi, H., Chao, C. C., Ee, M. S., & Hollas, D. (2019). Does medical tourism promote economic growth? A cross-country analysis. *Journal of Travel Research*, *58*(1), 121–135. doi:10.1177/0047287517735909

Bhatti, Y., Taylor, A., Harris, M., Wadge, H., Escobar, E., Prime, M., Patel, H., Carter, A. W., Parston, G., Darzi, A. W., & Udayakumar, K. (2017). Global lessons in Frugal innovation to improve health care delivery in the United States. *Health Affairs*, *36*(11), 1912–1919. doi:10.1377/hlthaff.2017.0480 PMID:29137503

Braczyk, H. J., Cooke, P., & Heidenreich, M. (Eds.). (2003). *Regional innovation systems: the role of governances in a globalized world*. Routledge. doi:10.4324/9780203330234

Brix, J. (2017). Exploring knowledge creation processes as a source of organizational learning: A longitudinal case study of a public innovation project. *Scandinavian Journal of Management*, *33*(2), 113–127. doi:10.1016/j.scaman.2017.05.001

Caballero-Danell, S., & Mugomba, C. (2007). Medical Tourism and its Entrepreneurial Opportunities-A conceptual framework for entry into the industry. *rapport nr.: Master Thesis 2006: 91*.

Caloghirou, Y., Kastelli, I., & Tsakanikas, A. (2004). Internal capabilities and external knowledge sources: Complements or substitutes for innovative performance? *Technovation*, *24*(1), 29–39. doi:10.1016/S0166-4972(02)00051-2

Caloghirou, Y., & Protogerou, A. (2015). Knowledge-intensive entrepreneurship: Exploring a taxonomy based on the AEGIS survey. In *Dynamics of Knowledge Intensive Entrepreneurship* (pp. 119–144). Routledge.

Campos, A. C., Mendes, J., Valle, P. O. D., & Scott, N. (2018). Co-creation of tourist experiences: A literature review. *Current Issues in Tourism*, *21*(4), 369–400. doi:10.1080/13683500.2015.1081158

Carrera, P. M., & Bridges, J. F. (2006). Globalization and healthcare: Understanding health and medical tourism. *Expert Review of Pharmacoeconomics & Outcomes Research*, *6*(4), 447–454. doi:10.1586/14737167.6.4.447 PMID:20528514

Chesbrough, H. (2006). Open innovation: a new paradigm for understanding industrial innovation. *Open innovation: Researching a new paradigm*, *400*, 0-19.

Chhabra, A., Munjal, M., Mishra, P. C., Singh, K., Das, D., Kuhar, N., & Vats, M. (2021). Medical tourism in the Covid-19 era: Opportunities, challenges and the way ahead. *Worldwide Hospitality and Tourism Themes*, *13*(5), 660–665. doi:10.1108/WHATT-05-2021-0078

Cockburn, I. M., & Henderson, R. M. (1998). Absorptive capacity, coauthoring behavior, and the organization of research in drug discovery. *The Journal of Industrial Economics*, *46*(2), 157–182. doi:10.1111/1467-6451.00067

Connell, J. (2013). Medical tourism in the Caribbean islands: A cure for economies in crisis? *Island Studies Journal*, *8*(1), 115–130. doi:10.24043/isj.280

Cooke, P., & Schwartz, D. (2007). Key drivers of contemporary innovation and creativity. *European Planning Studies*, *15*(9), 1139–1141. doi:10.1080/09654310701528997

Darwazeh, D., Clarke, A., & Wilson, J. (2021). Framework for Establishing a Sustainable Medical Facility: A Case Study of Medical Tourism in Jordan. *WORLD (Oakland, Calif.)*, *2*(3), 351–373. doi:10.3390/world2030022

De Bruin, A., & Jelinčić, D. A. (2016). Toward extending creative tourism: Participatory experience tourism. *Tourism Review*, *71*(1), 57–66. doi:10.1108/TR-05-2015-0018

Delgado, M. (2020). The co-location of innovation and production in clusters. *Industry and Innovation*, *27*(8), 842–870. doi:10.1080/13662716.2019.1709419

Drăghici, C. C., Diaconu, D., Teodorescu, C., Pintilii, R. D., & Ciobotaru, A. M. (2016). Health tourism contribution to the structural dynamics of the territorial systems with tourism functionality. *Procedia Environmental Sciences*, *32*, 386–393. doi:10.1016/j.proenv.2016.03.044

Dziallas, M., & Blind, K. (2019). Innovation indicators throughout the innovation process: An extensive literature analysis. *Technovation*, *80*, 3–29. doi:10.1016/j.technovation.2018.05.005

Ebrahim, A. H., & Ganguli, S. (2019). A comparative analysis of medical tourism competitiveness of India, Thailand and Singapore. *Tourism: An International Interdisciplinary Journal*, *67*(2), 102–115.

Evans, G. (2009). *From cultural quarters to creative clusters–creative spaces in the new city economy*. Institute of Urban History.

Fisher, C., & Sood, K. (2014). What is driving the growth in medical tourism? *Health Marketing Quarterly*, *31*(3), 246–262. doi:10.1080/07359683.2014.936293 PMID:25120045

Ganguli, S., & Ebrahim, A. H. (2017). A qualitative analysis of Singapore's medical tourism competitiveness. *Tourism Management Perspectives*, *21*, 74–84. doi:10.1016/j.tmp.2016.12.002

Gardner, C. A., Acharya, T., & Yach, D. (2007). Technological and social innovation: A unifying new paradigm for global health. *Health Affairs*, *26*(4), 1052–1061. doi:10.1377/hlthaff.26.4.1052 PMID:17630448

Ghasemi, B., Khalijian, S., Daim, T. U., & Mohammadipirlar, E. (2021). Knowledge management performance measurement based on World-Class Competitive Advantages to develop strategic-oriented projects: Case of Iranian oil industry. *Technology in Society*, *67*, 101691. doi:10.1016/j.techsoc.2021.101691

Ghazinoory, S., Sarkissian, A., Farhanchi, M., & Saghafi, F. (2020). Renewing a dysfunctional innovation ecosystem: The case of the Lalejin ceramics and pottery. *Technovation*, *96*, 102122. doi:10.1016/j.technovation.2020.102122

Gifford, E., & McKelvey, M. (2019). Knowledge-intensive entrepreneurship and S3: Conceptualizing strategies for sustainability. *Sustainability*, *11*(18), 4824. doi:10.3390u11184824

Goffi, G., Cucculelli, M., & Masiero, L. (2019). Fostering tourism destination competitiveness in developing countries: The role of sustainability. *Journal of Cleaner Production*, *209*, 101–115. doi:10.1016/j.jclepro.2018.10.208

Granstrand, O., & Holgersson, M. (2020). Innovation ecosystems: A conceptual review and a new definition. *Technovation*, *90*, 102098. doi:10.1016/j.technovation.2019.102098

Grönroos, C. (1999). Internationalization strategies for services. *Journal of Services Marketing*, *13*(4/5), 290–297. doi:10.1108/08876049910282547

Gupta, M. K., Rajachar, V., & Prabha, C. (2015). Medical tourism: A new growth factor for Indian healthcare industry. *International Journal of Research in Medical Sciences*, *3*(9), 2161–2163. doi:10.18203/2320-6012.ijrms20150597

Hall, C. M. (2011). Health and medical tourism: A kill or cure for global public health? *Tourism Review*, *66*(1/2), 4–15. doi:10.1108/16605371111127198

Hausmann, R., Hidalgo, C. A., Bustos, S., Coscia, M., & Simoes, A. (2014). *The atlas of economic complexity: Mapping paths to prosperity*. MIT Press. doi:10.7551/mitpress/9647.001.0001

Hernández-Espallardo, M., Sánchez-Pérez, M., & Segovia-López, C. (2011). Exploitation-and exploration-based innovations: The role of knowledge in inter-firm relationships with distributors. *Technovation*, *31*(5-6), 203–215. doi:10.1016/j.technovation.2011.01.007

Herrera, M. R. G., Sasidharan, V., Hernández, J. A. Á., & Herrera, L. D. A. (2018). Quality and sustainability of tourism development in Copper Canyon, Mexico: Perceptions of community stakeholders and visitors. *Tourism Management Perspectives*, *27*, 91–103. doi:10.1016/j.tmp.2018.05.003

Hiatt, J. (2006). *ADKAR: a model for change in business, government, and our community*. Prosci.

Hidalgo, C. A., Klinger, B., Barabási, A. L., & Hausmann, R. (2007). The product space conditions the development of nations. *Science*, *317*(5837), 482–487. doi:10.1126cience.1144581 PMID:17656717

Hjalager, A. M. (2002). Repairing innovation defectiveness in tourism. *Tourism Management*, *23*(5), 465–474. doi:10.1016/S0261-5177(02)00013-4

Hjalager, A. M. (2009). Innovations in travel medicine and the progress of tourism—Selected narratives. *Technovation*, *29*(9), 596–601. doi:10.1016/j.technovation.2009.05.012

Hopkins, L., Labonté, R., Runnels, V., & Packer, C. (2010). Medical tourism today: What is the state of existing knowledge? *Journal of Public Health Policy*, *31*(2), 185–198. doi:10.1057/jphp.2010.10 PMID:20535101

Horowitz, M. D. (2007). Medical tourism-health care in the global economy. *Physician Executive*, *33*(6), 24. PMID:18092615

Iordache, C., Ciochină, I., & Roxana, P. (2013). Medical tourism–between the content and socio-economic development goals. Development strategies. *Romanian Journal of Marketing*, (1).

Jolly, D., & Dimanche, F. (2009). Investing in technology for tourism activities: Perspectives and challenges. *Technovation*, *9*(29), 576–579. doi:10.1016/j.technovation.2009.05.004

Kanagal, N. B. (2015). Innovation and product innovation in marketing strategy. *Journal of Management and Marketing Research*, *18*(4).

Käpylä, J., Laihonen, H., Lönnqvist, A., & Carlucci, D. (2011). Knowledge-intensity as an organisational characteristic. *Knowledge Management Research and Practice*, *9*(4), 315–326. doi:10.1057/kmrp.2011.23

Kliewe, T., Davey, T., & Baaken, T. (2013). Creating a sustainable innovation environment within large enterprises: A case study on a professional services firm. *Journal of Innovation Management*, *1*(1), 55–84. doi:10.24840/2183-0606_001.001_0006

Kostopoulos, K., Papalexandris, A., Papachroni, M., & Ioannou, G. (2011). Absorptive capacity, innovation, and financial performance. *Journal of Business Research*, *64*(12), 1335–1343. doi:10.1016/j.jbusres.2010.12.005

Lee, M., Han, H., & Lockyer, T. (2012). Medical tourism—Attracting Japanese tourists for medical tourism experience. *Journal of Travel & Tourism Marketing*, *29*(1), 69–86. doi:10.1080/10548408.2012.638564

Li, Z., & Gao, X. (2021). Makers' relationship network, knowledge acquisition and innovation performance: An empirical analysis from china. *Technology in Society*, *66*, 101684. doi:10.1016/j.techsoc.2021.101684

Liu, I. C., & Chen, C. C. (2013). Cultural issues in medical tourism. *American Journal of Tourism Research*, *2*(1), 78–83. doi:10.11634/216837861302318

Makedon, V., Drobyazko, S., Shevtsova, H., Maslosh, O., & Kasatkina, M. (2019). Providing security for the development of high-technology organizations. *Journal of Security & Sustainability Issues*, *8*(4), 757–772. doi:10.9770/jssi.2019.8.4(18)

Malerba, F. (Ed.). (2004). *Sectoral systems of innovation: concepts, issues and analyses of six major sectors in Europe*. Cambridge University Press. doi:10.1017/CBO9780511493270

Mattsson, J., Sundbo, J., & Fussing-Jensen, C. (2005). Innovation systems in tourism: The roles of attractors and scene-takers. *Industry and Innovation*, *12*(3), 357–381. doi:10.1080/13662710500195967

Mayakul, T., Kiattisin, S., & Prasad, R. (2018). A sustainable medical tourism framework based on the enterprise architecture design: The case in Thailand. *Journal of Green Engineering*, *8*(3), 359–388. doi:10.13052/jge1904-4720.838

Mikalef, P., Boura, M., Lekakos, G., & Krogstie, J. (2019). Big data analytics capabilities and innovation: The mediating role of dynamic capabilities and moderating effect of the environment. *British Journal of Management*, *30*(2), 272–298. doi:10.1111/1467-8551.12343

Moaniba, I. M., Lee, P. C., & Su, H. N. (2020). How does external knowledge sourcing enhance product development? Evidence from drug commercialization. *Technology in Society*, *63*, 101414. doi:10.1016/j.techsoc.2020.101414

Mowery, D. C., & Oxley, J. E. (1995). Inward technology transfer and competitiveness: The role of national innovation systems. *Cambridge Journal of Economics*, *19*(1), 67–93.

Nonaka, I., & Takeuchi, H. (1995). *The Knowledge-creating Company: How Japanese companies create the dynamics of innovation*. Oxford University Press.

Ormond, M., & Mainil, T. (2015). Government and governance strategies in medical tourism. In *Handbook on medical tourism and patient mobility* (pp. 154–163). Edward Elgar Publishing. doi:10.4337/9781783471195.00025

Otcenásková, T., Bures, V., & Mikulecká, J. (2012). Principal Starting Points of Organisational Knowledge Intensity Modelling. *Journal of Organizational Knowledge Management*, *2012*, 1.

Perkumienė, D., Vienažindienė, M., & Švagždienė, B. (2019). Cooperation perspectives in sustainable medical tourism: The case of Lithuania. *Sustainability*, *11*(13), 3584. doi:10.3390u11133584

Pisano, G. P., & Shih, W. C. (2009). Restoring american competitiveness. *Harvard Business Review*, *87*(7/8), 114–125.

Potts, J., Hartley, J., Banks, J., Burgess, J., Cobcroft, R., Cunningham, S., & Montgomery, L. (2008). Consumer co-creation and situated creativity. *Industry and Innovation*, *15*(5), 459–474. doi:10.1080/13662710802373783

Powell, W. W., Koput, K. W., & Smith-Doerr, L. (1996). Interorganizational collaboration and the locus of innovation: Networks of learning in biotechnology. *Administrative Science Quarterly*, *41*(1), 116–145. doi:10.2307/2393988

Radu-Daniel, P., Cristian, B., Constantin, D. C., & Irina, S. (2014). Territorial imbalances in the distribution of creative industries in the North-Eastern Development Region. *Procedia: Social and Behavioral Sciences*, *122*, 179–183. doi:10.1016/j.sbspro.2014.01.1323

Ratnasari, R. T., Gunawan, S., Pitchay, A. A., & Mohd Salleh, M. C. (2021). Sustainable medical tourism: Investigating health-care travel in Indonesia and Malaysia. *International Journal of Healthcare Management*, •••, 1–10.

Richards, G. (2016). The challenge of creative tourism. *Ethnologies (Québec)*, *38*(1-2), 31–45. doi:10.7202/1041585ar

Richards, G. (2018). Tourism, an underestimated driving force for the creative economy. *Revista Turismo em Análise*, *29*(3), 387–395. doi:10.11606/issn.1984-4867.v29i3p387-395

Rodriguez, M., Doloreux, D., & Shearmur, R. (2017). Variety in external knowledge sourcing and innovation novelty: Evidence from the KIBS sector in Spain. *Technovation*, *68*, 35–43. doi:10.1016/j.technovation.2017.06.003

Romão, J., & Nijkamp, P. (2019). Impacts of innovation, productivity and specialization on tourism competitiveness–a spatial econometric analysis on European regions. *Current Issues in Tourism*, *22*(10), 1150–1169. doi:10.1080/13683500.2017.1366434

Sandberg, D. S. (2017). Medical tourism: An emerging global healthcare industry. *International Journal of Healthcare Management*, *10*(4), 281–288. doi:10.1080/20479700.2017.1296213

Shriedeh, F. (2019). The impact of medical tourist relationship management dimensions on innovation capabilities. *Business and Economic Review*, *9*(3), 70–86. doi:10.5296/ber.v9i3.14955

Simoes, A. J. G., & Hidalgo, C. A. (2011, August). The economic complexity observatory: An analytical tool for understanding the dynamics of economic development. *Workshops at the twenty-fifth AAAI conference on artificial intelligence*.

Smith, M., & Puczkó, L. (2014). *Health, tourism and hospitality: Spas, wellness and medical travel*. Routledge. doi:10.4324/9780203083772

Smith, P. C., & Forgione, D. A. (2007). Global outsourcing of healthcare: A medical tourism decision model. *Journal of Information Technology Case and Application Research*, *9*(3), 19–30. doi:10.1080/15228053.2007.10856117

Streimikiene, D., Svagzdiene, B., Jasinskas, E., & Simanavicius, A. (2021). Sustainable tourism development and competitiveness: The systematic literature review. *Sustainable Development*, *29*(1), 259–271. doi:10.1002d.2133

Sundbo, J., Orfila-Sintes, F., & Sørensen, F. (2007). The innovative behaviour of tourism firms—Comparative studies of Denmark and Spain. *Research Policy*, *36*(1), 88–106. doi:10.1016/j.respol.2006.08.004

Szymańska, E. (2016). *Consumer participation in the health tourism innovation process. Ekonomia i Zarządzanie*, *8(4)*.

Turkina, E., Oreshkin, B., & Kali, R. (2019). Regional innovation clusters and firm innovation performance: An interactionist approach. *Regional Studies*, *53*(8), 1193–1206. doi:10.1080/00343404.2019.1566697

Turner, L. (2007). 'First world health care at third world prices': Globalization, bioethics and medical tourism. *Biosocieties*, *2*(3), 303–325. doi:10.1017/S1745855207005765

Upadhyay, P. (2011). Comparative and competitive advantages of globalised India as a medical tourism destination. *International Journal of Engineering and Management Sciences*, *2*(1), 26–34.

Volberda, H. W., Foss, N. J., & Lyles, M. A. (2010). Perspective—Absorbing the concept of absorptive capacity: How to realize its potential in the organization field. *Organization Science*, *21*(4), 931–951. doi:10.1287/orsc.1090.0503

Von Hippel, E. (2005). Democratizing innovation: The evolving phenomenon of user innovation. *Journal für Betriebswirtschaft*, *55*(1), 63–78. doi:10.100711301-004-0002-8

Wang, C., & Hu, Q. (2020). Knowledge sharing in supply chain networks: Effects of collaborative innovation activities and capability on innovation performance. *Technovation*, *94*, 102010. doi:10.1016/j.technovation.2017.12.002

Wattanacharoensil, W., & Schuckert, M. (2016). Reviewing Thailand's master plans and policies: Implications for creative tourism? *Current Issues in Tourism*, *19*(10), 1045–1070. doi:10.1080/13683500.2014.882295

Weidenfeld, A. (2018). Tourism diversification and its implications for smart specialisation. *Sustainability*, *10*(2), 319. doi:10.3390u10020319

Willoughby, K., & Galvin, P. (2005). Inter-organizational collaboration, knowledge intensity, and the sources of innovation in the bioscience-technology industries. *Knowledge, Technology & Policy, 18*(3), 56–73. doi:10.100712130-005-1005-z

World Tourism Organization. UNWTO. (n.d.). https://www.unwto.org/sustainable-development

Zobel, A. K., Lokshin, B., & Hagedoorn, J. (2017). Formal and informal appropriation mechanisms: The role of openness and innovativeness. *Technovation, 59*, 44–54. doi:10.1016/j.technovation.2016.10.001

Chapter 8
Plan, Do, Watch:
Making Tourism Sustainable Through Geographical Information Systems (GIS)

Tuğçe Özoğul Balyali
https://orcid.org/0000-0002-2263-4122
Van Yüzüncü Yıl University, Turkey

Öznur Akgiş Ilhan
https://orcid.org/0000-0001-7224-8353
Kırşehir Ahi Evran University, Turkey

ABSTRACT

In the tourism industry, the use of digital tools has been becoming increasingly common due to the development of alternative movements, such as smart tourism. One of these digital tools is geographic information systems (GIS), which is an information system used for the processing, analysis, and storage of spatial data. Within this context, this chapter focuses on the role of GIS use in ensuring the sustainability of tourism activities. In the chapter, the use of GIS in the planning, doing, and watching processes of tourism is discussed with examples. This chapter will provide information on how to benefit from GIS in the context of sustainable tourism.

INTRODUCTION

Problems and processes, such as rapid population growth, urbanization, inequality, and environmental degradation, raise concerns for the future. Increasing concern about the future has led to the emergence of alternative philosophies and policies. One of the most effective one is the sustainability approach. Sustainability and sustainable development can be expressed in interdisciplinary terms. Since the 1980s, especially before the United Nations Conference on Environment and Development (UNCED) held in Rio de Janeiro, in 1992, global academic and policy debates on these issues have gained momentum (Scoones, 2007). This world summit was designed to combine the wise management and protection of the natural environment with economic equality and access to basic needs for all people (MacDonald, 2002).

DOI: 10.4018/978-1-6684-4645-4.ch008

Many definitions have been proposed for sustainable development in this sense, but one of the most widely accepted can be found in the Brundtland Report. Accordingly, sustainable development is a development that meets the needs of the present without compromising the ability of future generations to meet their own needs (World Commission on Environment and Development, 1987). Within this context, sustainability can be defined as an approach that prioritizes the rational use of resources and, accordingly, makes it possible to reach a qualified future in terms of social, environmental, and economic aspects. In addition to guaranteeing rationality, it is one of the most widely accepted philosophies on a global scale, due to its spatial, historical, and social inclusiveness. Because of these characteristics, sustainability is an integral part of international development plans today.

Undoubtedly, a sustainable plan brings along a transformation process from daily life to politics. In this context, sectoral transformation and restructuring are among the main targets for a sustainable future. In this process, practices that are compatible with the main objectives of sustainability, in both industry and agriculture as well as the service sectors, have been introduced and are being introduced. One of the sectors that this transformation can be seen most clearly is tourism.

Although tourism is an economic sector, it represents social and spatial mobility, as well as a process that enables the production and reproduction of the environment. In this sense, it is closely related to all dimensions of sustainability, including economic, environmental, and social. This mutual and multidimensional relationship is one of the main challenges in the development of sustainable tourism policies. However, it is possible to discuss many successful policies. The development of alternative tourism types, such as ecotourism, camping tourism, nature tourism, and cave tourism, which prioritize harmony with the environment, are practices that make tourism environmentally sustainable.

Practices and tools that enable and improve the communication of local people and tourists make tourism socially sustainable, while efforts to ensure that local people benefit from tourism revenues can be shown as an example of the economic sustainability of tourism. In addition, tourism provides employment opportunities for women in many countries, and is aligned with sustainable policies in terms of gender equality. Similarly, it provides opportunities for disadvantaged groups, such as the elderly or the disabled, to participate in public life. Accordingly, it can be stated that sustainable tourism is on the way to becoming a reality rather than merely being a dream.

Digital tools are being used more and more to make tourism sustainable. This has led to the emergence of the concept of smart tourism. Smart tourism can be conceptualized as a term that allows large amounts of data regarding tourism destinations, industries, and tourists to be converted into value propositions. In this context, smart tourism also enables the integration of physical, digital and human systems with the environment to ensure a sustainable future. For example, the smart tourism approach aims to provide long-term social benefit by using resources in a smarter way with online governance systems in city management by supporting data sharing and participation of local people. While ensuring the sustainability of nature with digital tools, it allows control of all resources. Smart tourism practices are also reflected in transportation systems.

For example, it is possible to reduce the main problems of cities such as traffic congestion and air pollution, thanks to the optimal use of public transportation infrastructure with mobile applications that enable people to be directed to public transportation vehicles (Cohen, 2014). The Internet of Things, Blockchain, Image Recognition Systems, and Big Data are examples of the most widely used technologies within the scope of smart tourism applications (Xiang, 2018; Lampropoulos et al., 2021; Rolando & Scandiffio, 2021; Waleghwa et al., 2021). One of these is Geographical Information Systems (GIS), which is one of the spatial information technologies. GIS is a digital tool that enables the collection, storage, and processing of spatial information. GIS software generally consists of five sub-systems; data entry, data preprocessing, data storage and management, spatial analysis, and data output (Wei, 2012).

Decision-making in tourism has become complex. Despite this, GIS can be considered a tool of broadly applicable techniques and technologies for achieving sustainable tourism development (Bahaire & Elliott-White, 1999). In this context, it is possible to ensure that all stakeholders establish smarter, meaningful and sustainable connections in resource management with GIS in the context of sustainability. The most important point of sustainability is the use of resources. Optimal resource use to be provided with all tourism-related data to be processed with GIS contributes to the sustainability of tourism. Therefore, this section aims to clarify the areas where GIS is used to ensure sustainability.

This chapter will provide information on how to benefit from GIS in the context of sustainable tourism. First of all, the concepts of smart tourism, digitalization, and sustainability will be conceptualized. In the following, the potential usage areas of GIS in sustainable tourism will be explained. Finally, examples of the use of GIS in sustainable tourism will be evaluated.

BACKGROUND

Smart Tourism, Digitalization and Sustainability

Globalization and communication technologies that facilitate global flows have brought about a transformation in tourism policies and research. This transformation is characterized by the increasingly widespread use of information technologies in tourism research. Today, information technologies are considered one of the competitive elements of a destination, and tourism companies have been investing more and more in smart system initiatives (Lu et al., 2021). Therefore, information and communication technologies reproduce the way tourism organizations conduct business and interact with their stakeholders (Shafiee et al., 2019).

Similarly, information technologies support tourists in searching for first information regarding travel and destination, comparing information, decision-making processes, and affecting the tourist experience (Neuhofer et al., 2012). Information technologies contribute to the development of environmentally, economically, and socially sustainable tourism by combating climate change, protecting cultural heritage and protecting natural resources, as well as reducing dangerous pollutants and energy use (Lu et al., 2021). Therefore, at the beginning of the design process of digitalization, it requires adopting a perspective that includes sustainability, with comprehensive thinking from the beginning on how to reduce environmental impacts and achieve greater social justice (Hilty and Aebischer 2015).

Tourism is one of the multidimensional sectors by its nature. For this reason, current changes cause an increase in alternative tourism types. Smart tourism is one of the emerging and attractive tourism types. Smart tourism can be expressed as a tourism model that supports the accessible and sustainable development of tourist areas designed to provide better higher quality of life and tourism experiences (Gretzel, Sigala, Xiang, & Koo, 2015). In a broader sense, smart tourism is the type of tourism that is built on the infrastructure of the latest technology that guarantees the sustainable development of tourism destinations. In this type of tourism, destinations are accessible to everyone and facilitate the interaction of visitors with their surroundings (Lopez de Avila, 2015).

Smart tourism is discussed by Bulchand-Gidumal (2022) in a framework consisting of six areas. These are smart economy, smart governance, smart tourists, smart residents, smart mobility, and smart sustainability. The smart economy has been associated with the dimensions of promotion and marketing, innovation and entrepreneurship, as well as ancillary services. Smart governance can be characterized by its subcomponents of modernization, transparency, political strategies, participation, public participation, and data openness. Smart tourists are conceptualized as those who use technology to interact at the destination, and smart residents are expressed as an educated population with strong integration with tourists. Smart mobility, which is one of the most important infrastructure components of tourism, corresponds to the existence of modern transportation systems that increase accessibility within the destination. Finally, smart sustainability includes concepts such as the circular economy, environmental protection, and sustainable resource management (Bulchand-Gidumal, 2022).

Accordingly, smart tourism can be defined as a tourism model that prioritizes cooperation and integration between tourists in the destination, local people, and local governments requiring the use of modern technologies in infrastructure systems, and which aims for the rational use of social, economic, and environmental resources. Smart tourism facilitates the integration of online and physical infrastructure in a destination (Gretzel, Reino, Kopera, & Koo, 2015).

In order for smart tourism destinations to become sustainable, a technology-coordinated tourism and entertainment production and consumption system that regulates three basic dimensions in these destinations is required: 1) Social and economic equality and efficiency and reduction in energy consumption; 2) governance and knowledge management; and 3) satisfaction of the tourism experience (González-Reverté, 2019). Approaching smart tourism through sustainability places destinations in the context of social relations characterized by the convergence of technology and tourism experience (Hunter, Chung, Gretzel, & Koo, 2015).

Smart tourism promotes sustainable economic growth from an environmental, economic, and social perspective by integrating the philosophy of sustainability with information technologies. It also enables the development of new methods for tourism management through rational and competitive approaches (Vargas-Sánchez, 2016). The emphasis on smart tourism is increasing. In related studies, it can be seen that smart tourism is discussed in the context of certain topics (Table 1).

Eichelberger et al. (2020) has proven that the entrepreneurial ecosystem approach helps to strengthen smart destinations in promoting the development of urban sustainability. Lu et al. (2021) presented a data-driven sustainable smart city framework for sustainable green tourism strategies and policies to protect climate, cultural heritage and natural resources, and reduce hazardous pollutants and energy use. Ma et al. (2021) emphasizes that travel agencies using big data marketing technology can personalize lower carbon travel plans for tourists and increase environmental awareness of tourists.In this context, it attracts attention as an important research topic related to environmental sustainability and smart tourism (Table 1). The role of smart tourism policies in issues such as increasing efficiency in energy use, monitoring the impact of tourism on the environment, and reducing environmental pressure are noteworthy topics. Accordingly, the application of the smart concept in tourism destinations will add value to tourism stakeholders by creating an interaction between the destination and tourists and may improve the achievement of sustainability goals (Neuhofer et al., 2012).

Another issue addressed in the context of sustainability and smart tourism is the tourist experience (Table 1). Tourists are increasingly choosing smart tourism attractions (Wang et al., 2016). In addition, there is an emphasis on smart tourism destinations that provide information resources that meet the needs and preferences of tourists in their shopping journey with digital tools (García-Milon et al., 2020). Kim et al. (2021) determined that the perceived quality of the mobility application, which includes usability, trust, and interaction, positively affects the unforgettable tourism experiences and the re-use intention of the mobility application by reducing the stress caused by mobility.

Table 1. Dimensions of smart tourism considered in tourism research

Scholar (s)	Energy and Environment	Tourist Experience	Data and Analysis	COVID-19
Lu et al., 2021	X			
Ma et al., 2021	X			
Eichelberger et al., 2020	X			
García-Milon et al., 2020		X		
Kim et al., 2021		X		
Wang et al., 2016		X		
Tavitiyaman et al., 2021			X	
Balasaraswathi et al., 2020			X	
Guizzardi et al., 2021			X	
Bulchand-Gidumal, 2022				X
Akgiş-İlhan, 2021				X
Wassler and Fan, 2021				X

Tourist behavior is becoming increasingly digital in both the planning of the travel, the experience, and the recall processes of the tourist experience. Tourists are increasingly making their reservations online and using chatbots more and more to register their entrance at facilities. They are more commonly using online tools to control room temperature and reserve a place at the pool or restaurant. This digital transformation is one of the reasons for the increase in emphasis on smart tourism.

The transformation in the tourist experience has become much more visible with the COVID-19 pandemic (Akgiş-İlhan, 2021). This is because the pandemic has clearly demonstrated the necessity of digitization, not only in the tourist experience, but also in the tourism industry as a whole. In this context, smart tourism is also discussed in the context of its relationship with the pandemic. Studies for the post-COVID-19 recovery of tourism using a smart tourism destination framework have come to the fore (Bulchand-Gidumal, 2022).

The need for data is increasing daily in the development of successful tourism policies and in understanding the transformation in the tourism sector. Accordingly, the processes of collecting, storing, and analyzing data related to the sector are also affected by digital transformation. This makes data and methodology an important research topic in research on smart tourism. Örneğin, Balasaraswathi et al. (2020) leveraged Big Data Analytics to help transform cities into a smarter and more sustainable location. Guizzardi et al. (2021) used big data to forecast tourism demand in their research. In addition, it has been proven that smart tourism applications are effective on perceived destination image and behavioral intention (Tavitiyaman et al., 2021) (Table 1).

To obtain maximum efficiency from the tourism resources of any destination, and to develop more planned, livable, and sustainable destinations, decision parameters in smart tourism management should be handled rationally with an integrated geographical perspective. Therefore, with GIS, which allows for the analysis of different parameters, it may be possible to deal with the sustainability philosophy from a comprehensive perspective. In the context of smart tourism, there is a large amount of data usage related to destinations. Many different criteria within the scope of sustainability involve processes that normally require a long period of decision-making.

Large amounts of data can be used effectively with GIS for more objective and sustainable development of destinations in a shorter time. For example, processing of data such as a destination's terrain information, coverage data (land use, land cover, geology and soils), network-oriented data (streams, water distribution systems and sewer systems), and groundwater information (groundwater modelling) is possible with GIS. With GIS, many operations can be performed from simple inventory and management analysis to complex analysis and modeling of spatial data (Fonseca & Gouveia, 2005).

All economic, social and environmental processes that are considered in the context of sustainability are naturally spatial. They cannot be fully understood without considering their spatial dimensions. The relationship between man and the environment cannot be represented without reference to a specific place, in other words, without considering it on a particular piece of land. Because the environment is defined by topological relationships between physical objects (e.g. soil or air composition, solar radiation at a particular space-time location), and human activities have spatial effects on the environment (Campagna, 2005). Decision criteria for the environmental, economic, and social dimensions of sustainability and detailed geographical operations can be carried out in a short time period with the designed models.

GEOGRAPHICAL INFORMATION SYSTEM (GIS) IN SUSTAINABLE TOURISM

GIS is defined in different ways by different researchers. It is possible to collect these definitions under five categories:

- GIS as a process: The collection and storage of spatial data. For example, it was decided to survey the local population to learn how tourism can be developed on the island of Tioman in Malaysia. GIS was used to store survey respondents' location data and their responses (Lechner et al., 2010).
- GIS as a tool: It is the collection and storage of spatial data, as well as its transformation and visualization. There are tourist towns in the state of Georgia in the United States that are highly susceptible to flooding. The three-dimensional imaging feature of GIS is used to increase public awareness about the possible dangerous scenarios that may occur in the event of a flood in these settlements (Yang, 2016).
- GIS as a database: It is the storage of spatial data. For example, Portugal's Aveiro region is seen as one of the areas that has tourism potential, but which cannot make use of it adequately. A database or tourism resource inventory was created using GIS to determine the tourism wealth of the region (Albuquerque, 2018).
- GIS as an application: It is the use of spatial data in marketing and planning processes. For example, in the Czech Republic, cycling is an important area of leisure activities. GIS is used to develop the bicycle road network, locate traffic markers and plan new routes (Bíl et al., 2012).

- GIS as a decision support mechanism: It is the inclusion and use of spatial data in the problem-solving process. For example, the policies implemented in the management of nature-based tourism resources in the Indonesian city of Bogor differ according to the institutions. Data was collected and analyzed from various stakeholders for the development of a common tourism policy. As a result, an agreed nature-based tourism resource management plan was prepared using GIS (Rahayuningsih et al., 2016).

Based on the definitions expressed categorically above, Geographic Information Systems in the context of tourism can be defined as follows: GIS is an information technology that provides the collection, storage, and display of spatial data in tourism, is used in the creation of tourism and tourist databases on an international or national scale, and is used as a decision support mechanism in the development of tourism policies, in addition to tourism management, marketing, and planning processes.

GIS has great potential for planning more sustainable tourism infrastructure (Beedasy & Whyatt 1999). In practice, managers can test many scenarios with GIS as a tool to help identify who or what may be affected by certain decisions (Landres et al., 2001). Determining an ideal tourism model for a potential tourism region includes a complex set of criteria (Chen, 2007). Regarding GIS applications in tourism, especially within the scope of sustainable tourism planning:

- Identifying suitable places for tourism development
- Creating tourism resource inventories
- Measuring the impact of tourism
- Analyzing relationships related to resource use
- Performing visitor management
- Creating tourist maps.
- Forecasting potential impact of tourism development

Accordingly, the functional capabilities of GIS related to the tourism sector, namely tourism resource inventories, are used to identify the most suitable places for sustainable tourism, relationships associated with resource use, measuring the impact of tourism, analyzing visitor management and visitor flows, and evaluating the potential impact of sustainable tourism development (Albuquerque et al., 2018).

OPERATIONALIZATION OF GIS IN SUSTAINABLE TOURISM

The use of GIS in tourism activities is quite diverse. However, it is possible to collect these areas under three headings concerning their functions. These are plan, do, and watch. Accordingly, in this section, how GIS is operationalized in sustainable tourism will be discussed.

Plan: Tourism Resource Inventory and Information System

Tourism planning is a multi-dimensional process that involves the inclusion of several factors in the decision-making process. The need for any rational tourism planning to be compatible with the principles of sustainable development, which means preserving the socio-geographical and physical qualities of a destination, but at the same time striking a balance with the interests of local communities, has made the use of GIS in the private and public sectors a necessity in this process (Pobrić & Sivac, 2022). Tourism resource inventories and information systems created through GIS can guide sustainable tourism studies.

Tourism resource inventories are made to consider land use and activities, manage and control tourism development, natural resources, and existing infrastructure, where the current situation and capacity of a region are defined (Bahaire & Elliott-White, 1999). Some of the information in the tourism resource inventories are as follows:

- Natural tourism resources (mountains, caves, canyons, geoparks, streams, waterfalls, lakes, hot waters, forests, protected areas, monumental trees, and biodiversity)
- Historical tourism resources (mounds, ancient cities, historical buildings, castles, historical settlements, historical cities, and towers)
- Cultural tourism resources (folk dances, traditional clothes, folk songs, and handicrafts)
- Gastronomy-based tourism resources (food and beverage businesses, geographically indicated products, local dishes, and food festivals)
- Religious tourism resources (mosques, tombs, churches, and cemeteries)
- Health tourism resources (thermal and spas, baths, and hospitals)
- Battlefield tourism resources (monuments and cemeteries)
- Sports tourism resources (sports halls and fields)
- City tourism resources (accommodation facilities, museums, cinemas, culture and convention centers, theater and concert halls, libraries, social facilities, zoos, recreation/picnic areas, city parks, bus stations and parking lots)

The inventory and information system of tourism resources primarily involves the creation of a database of the social-geographic, geographical, and physical tourism resources of a destination. At the same time, a database containing tourism infrastructure and demographic information can be created and integrated into an interactive map. This database has a detailed description of basic data regarding the attraction, possible visit times, ticket price, and may contain various other information. This system allows the user to learn more about the location and features of certain places of interest, thereby making it easier to select the desired route and places of interest. This option can be used to create routes and present them to visitors in the management of destinations (Pobrić & Sivac, 2022).

Mango et al. (2021) emphasizes that a Web-based Geographic Information System (GIS) model with interactive and dynamic maps is necessary to manage and promote tourism resources in Tanzania. A well-known example of this practice is the identification of areas suitable for tourism development. With GIS, it is possible to determine the ecotourism potential areas of a destination, define suitable areas for tourism development, develop the spatial information system (accommodation, tours, cultural areas, road access), and to provide information about tourist places over the internet. Map-based information for tourists, which can be found on computer information kiosks or websites, is a popular application of GIS. Destinations are promoted over the Internet using this technology. Depending on the application, these maps can be interactive and allow real-time transactions to be conducted online, although limited (Farsari & Prastacos, 2004).

Creating a tourism resource inventory of a destination also helps to create a tourism information system. A tourism resources information system can be created using GIS in order to record, update and share the tourism attractions of a destination with other institutions and individuals. For example, Terzi (2020) lists the tourism attractions in Eskişehir (Turkey) on the basis of settlement and categories in the information system he prepared. It is possible to search within these places or categories. In the system, where information regarding tourism attractions is supported by photos and video content, maps for different types of tourism can be created and directions can be obtained. Users are informed by way of e-mail about the activities to be held regarding tourism attractions in the categories they choose, provided they subscribe to the system. In addition, this system allows queries regarding tourism planning with the province, district, settlement, road, water, stream, and elevation maps offered to users.

The geo-ecological uniqueness of each geo-ecotourism region in West Bengal was made by Acharya et al. (2022) with GIS to reveal the major tourist spots, as well as a detailed map of the potential points of each region. Filocamo et al. (2022) create an inventory of geosites and an information system about these geosites in the Matese National Park (Southern Italy), which is characterized by a rich geo-heritage with GIS. With the created geosite GIS database, it has become possible to create a geographical route passing the Matese Mountains. This inventory and information system created with GIS represents an important resource to support natural heritage and especially geo-heritage, local economy, and sustainable development related to geotourism initiatives.

Do: Determination of Sustainable Tourism Development Areas and Visitor Management

Changing the existing points in a destination by gaining attractiveness, improving accessibility, reducing randomness, intensifying the necessary infrastructural development, raising awareness, and accordingly preparing possible and potential tourist point maps that can be developed with tourism management are possible with GIS. Creating a database for morphometric features (vertical or horizontal articulation of relief, morphometric features of the terrain, slope and elevation of the land, exposure to impacts, and others), hydrological, soil, and geomorphological features and their cartographic representation is the basis for all future activities in terms of tourism planning. GIS makes it possible to determine the most suitable location for the creation of new tourist sites and infrastructure or to renovate existing ones, to plan new zones for the implementation of various tourism activities, and to calculate the maximum number of tourists allowed in a given area for a sustainable purpose (Pobrić & Sivac, 2022).

Acharya et al. (2022) emphasize that with the application of mathematical methods and geospatial techniques, and efficient results obtained from such analyzes, regions of conformity and their ranking can be made. It is stated that it is possible to encourage the development of geo-ecotourism and revive the tourism sector by identifying suitable areas in the context of sustainability. Geo-ecotourism is a mixture of geotourism that encourages the population to take an interest in the sustainable conservation of places by enabling them to appreciate geological landscapes or historical heritage sites, and ecotourism that aims to preserve the cultural and natural resources of the place.

The authors used GIS in their research to plan the sustainable development of geo-ecotourism in West Bengal (India), where there are many geomorphologically, geologically, and ecologically important tourist attractions. A geo-ecotourism map was created with different parameters in West Bengal. The results of the study contributed to the formation of location-specific planning for the development of geo-ecotourism in the state and the sustainable management of geo-ecotourism (Acharya et al., 2022).

Brundu et al. (2021) benefited from GIS in the case of Sardinia, an island known for its sea tourism, but whose rural and interior parts are not yet used as tourist attractions. In the study, rural tourism routes were created that can improve the characteristics of the region by combining different landscape assets in the context of the sustainability of rural tourism. The research of Gürbüz (2021) hoped to reduce the possible negative effects of activities based on intense coastal use on the northern shores of Gemlik Bay in Bursa Province (Turkey). It aimed to determine the potential of the area for diversifying tourism-recreational activities by considering the protection-use balance of the cultural and natural assets of the area. Accordingly, for the area to participate in sustainable tourism, the data of the area was examined using GIS and, as a result, five different recreational activities were determined in the area (Gürbüz, 2021).

Location suitability analysis is a well-known and widely developed application of GIS. In this way, it is ensured that suitable locations are determined indirectly or directly in the development of tourism. The main variables used to determine the capacity and potential of an area, or to be developed as a tourist destination, are geographical variables. GIS is used for ecological research areas, conservation areas, and recreational and development areas, as well as hotel layout planning. Tourist time-space analysis aims to understand the behavior of visitors or tourists. GIS can be a powerful tool in this type of analysis, providing a better understanding of tourist flows in a particular area or region. A better understanding of tourist behavior in travel management can lead to better infrastructure and operational management, environmental protection, and diffusion of benefits, such as economic gains (Farsari & Prastacos, 2004).

Many tourists can easily contribute to the deterioration of primary attractions. Therefore, it is necessary to properly manage the number of tourists visiting the attractions and to determine the maximum carrying capacity (Pobrić & Sivac, 2022). It is also possible to use different mathematical methods, in addition to the use of GIS alone, in the identification of sustainable tourism development areas and visitor management. A good example of this is the combined use of GIS and a mathematical selection method, OWA (Ordered Weighted Averaging).

Rezvani et al. (2022) emphasizes that integrating GIS with OWA contributes to appropriate decision-making. Decision-makers and managers can identify suitable areas by listing various alternatives. The application of the OWA model provides several strategies for managers and planners to consider risk parameters in their decision-making processes to intelligent resource management and to enhance sustainable tourism development in natural areas.

Watch: Monitoring the Impact of Tourism and Improving Resource Utilization

GIS includes layers of spatial information associated with different types of data. It is therefore a suitable tool for the analysis and assessment of the impact of tourism in a place (Boers & Cottrell, 2007). Measuring and monitoring tourism impact involves recording the changes that tourism development brings to destinations. This monitoring provides an assessment of the disadvantages and advantages of tourism, and also provides a good basis for all future activities (Pobrić & Sivac, 2022). Utilizing the analytical and modeling capabilities offered by GIS facilitates the monitoring of sustainable tourism. It is possible to monitor the effects caused by the number of tourists and to develop a GIS-based multimedia cultural archive. This can be used to predict possible effects by tracking requested parameters over time. GIS technology provides data integrity and management in sustainable tourism development that requires environmental, economic, and social knowledge (Farsari & Prastacos, 2004).

As an example of monitoring the effects of tourism and improving resource use, GIS was used to determine the spatial distribution of ethnic villages in Guizhou (China), and to analyze influencing factors and the structural characteristics of their spatial settlements. The formation mechanism of the spatial differentiation model of traditional villages in Guizhou is revealed from the perspective of the people and the physical geography. Most of the ethnic minority characteristic villages in Guizhou Province are

Plan, Do, Watch

located in areas with insufficient transportation, relatively underdeveloped economic development, and complex terrain.

Based on the research results, it has become possible to identify effective development strategies for the future development of ethnic minority villages in Guizhou (Zheng et al., 2022). The inventory and information system research on geosites of Filokamo et al. (2022) is also related to its contribution to the improvement of the geographical heritage of the Matese Mountains. This mountain area also contributes to greatly ameliorating other mountainous regions and, in general, the difficulties and constraints commonly characterized as land abandonment, depopulation, marginality, limits on mobility, and inaccessibility.

Today, climate change cause environmental hazards, such as wildlife stress, soil erosion, and degradation of nature. Together with GIS, remote sensing systems can identify vegetation or soil under stressful conditions. Therefore, it can help put forward preventive actions along with the guiding principles of sustainable tourism (Ramaano, 2022).

SOLUTIONS AND RECOMMENDATIONS

- The use of digital tools in the tourism industry has been becoming more common. These tools contribute to achieving goals related to social, economic, and environmental sustainability in tourism.
- An effective tourism strategy includes planning, making, and monitoring. It can be used in all the expressed stages of tourism activities of GIS.
- As in all industries, tourism is becoming knowledge intensive. Tourism inventories and information systems to be created through GIS can increase the efficiency of activities. Therefore, tourism can be made socio-economically sustainable.
- Tourism activities are becoming more important in national economies. GIS enables the identification of new tourism areas and the planning of existing destinations. As a result, it makes the continuity of tourism activities possible.
- Tourism is one of the industries criticized for its environmental effects. GIS ensures that the impact of tourism activities on the environment is determined, the results are eliminated and any negative effects are prevented before they occur. Accordingly, it harmonizes tourism with environmental sustainability.
- Smart movements are becoming more common. GIS is a part of smart tourism applications and contributes to its development.
- Mobility issues should be addressed through planning carried out to ensure the development of tourism that includes wider social, economic, and environmental objectives in the sustainable development of destinations.

FUTURE RESEARCH DIRECTIONS

Sustainability and smart movements are among the most remarkable topics in tourism research. In this sense, there is a need to empirically evaluate the contribution of GIS to social, economic, and environmental sustainability in tourism. In addition, it can show the value of GIS in research that measures or analyzes the contribution of GIS use to sustainable tourism in destinations where smart tourism infrastructure is developed.

CONCLUSION

In the UN Agenda of 2030, tourism occupies a prominent position as a critical sector that indirectly or directly affects several Sustainable Development Goals. The pursuit of sustainable tourism is built on the respectful use of the industry's core 'raw material', namely the vulnerable and precious link of cultural and natural resources, and the collaborative effort of everyone involved in tourism. Creating a sustainable tourism industry requires adequate political, social, and cultural infrastructure, as well as a broad participation of local communities in development projects. Therefore, it is necessary to pay attention to quality criteria and social goals in tourism industry development plans. This is because inappropriate, uncoordinated, and uncalculated development can produce many negative consequences. For example, it may have harmful effects on nature and the environment (Faghihi, 2021).

Sustainable tourism planning is associated with tourism infrastructure, which includes elements such as includes attractions (natural, cultural, man-made), service (accommodation, restaurants, shops, visitor information, tour and travel operations, money exchange, medical facilities, postal services, etc.), and transport facilities (both material infrastructure and transport services). Sustainable tourism planning requires spatial data collection and processing because all places and their interrelationships must be defined and analyzed within a spatial context. For this purpose, GIS can define tourism infrastructure elements as geometric, thematic, and topological (Jovanović & Njeguš, 2016: 262).

Tourism planning requires the availability of knowledge regarding natural resources and their attributes, cultural/heritage attractions, how resources are used by visitors, and social and economic impact. Ineffective tourism planning, feedback information on the impact of monitoring mechanisms, and planning decisions on the tourism resource are also needed (Bahaire & Elliott-White, 1999: 159). Tourist time-space analysis requires specific data on places visited, visitor's time spent, information used, routes chosen, motivation and perception. To date, most researchers have analyzed spatial tourism data with statistics. This approach requires data for every possible location in every period and region. These enormous amounts of data and tables make it difficult to see spatial relationships. GIS spatial data management is used effectively to see spatial relationships and to provide feedback for sustainable tourism development.

The increase in tourism indicates that the traditionally dispersed and overloaded tourism resource support is deteriorating (Zerihun, 2017). GIS can be usefully used in sustainable tourism practices. Approving a sustainable tourism plan integrated with GIS concerns perception, privileges, and attitudes among stakeholders. Therefore, it is also important how local people observe sustainable tourism. An approach endorsed by the local community can overcome poverty, promote local economic development, and reduce environmental degradation (Ramaano, 2022).

ACKNOWLEDGMENT

This research received no specific grant from any funding agency in the public, commercial, or not-for-profit sectors.

REFERENCES

Acharya, A., Mondal, B. K., Bhadra, T., Abdelrahman, K., Mishra, P. K., Tiwari, A., & Das, R. (2022). Geospatial analysis of geo-ecotourism site suitability using AHP and GIS for sustainable and resilient tourism planning in West Bengal, India. *Sustainability*, *14*(4), 2422. doi:10.3390u14042422

Akgiş İlhan, Ö. (2021). The rise of digitalization in the tourism industry during COVID-19: Cyber space, destinations, and tourist experiences. In *Handbook of Research on the Impacts and Implications of COVID-19 on the Tourism Industry* (pp. 843–862). IGI Global. doi:10.4018/978-1-7998-8231-2.ch041

Albuquerque, H., Costa, C., & Martins, F. (2018). The use of geographical information systems for tourism marketing purposes in Aveiro region (Portugal). *Tourism Management Perspectives*, *26*, 172–178. doi:10.1016/j.tmp.2017.10.009

Bahaire, T., & Elliott-White, M. (1999). The application of geographical information systems (GIS) in sustainable tourism planning: A review. *Journal of Sustainable Tourism*, *7*(2), 159–174. doi:10.1080/09669589908667333

Balasaraswathi, M., Srinivasan, K., Udayakumar, L., Sivasakthiselvan, S., & Sumithra, M. (2020). Big data analytic of contexts and cascading tourism for smart city. *Materials Today: Proceedings*. Advance online publication. doi:10.1016/j.matpr.2020.10.132

Beedasy, J., & Whyatt, D. (1999). Diverting the tourists: A spatial decision-support system for tourism planning on a developing island. *International Journal of Applied Earth Observation and Geoinformation*, *1*(3-4), 163–174. doi:10.1016/S0303-2434(99)85009-0

Bíl, M., Bílová, M., & Kubeček, J. (2012). Unified GIS database on cycle tourism infrastructure. *Tourism Management*, *33*(6), 1554–1561. doi:10.1016/j.tourman.2012.03.002

Boers, B., & Cottrell, S. (2007). Sustainable tourism infrastructure planning: A GIS-supported approach. *Tourism Geographies: An International Journal of Tourism Space. Place and Environment*, *9*(1), 1–21.

Brundu, B., Battino, S., & Manca, I. (2021, December). The sustainable tourism organization of rural spaces. The island of Sardinia in the era of" staycation. In *Proceedings of ICC2021-30th International Cartographic Conference, Florence (Italy)* (pp. 14-18). Academic Press.

Bulchand-Gidumal, J. (2022). Post-COVID-19 recovery of island tourism using a smart tourism destination framework. *Journal of Destination Marketing & Management*, *23*, 100689. doi:10.1016/j.jdmm.2022.100689

Campagna, M. (2005). GIS for sustainable development. In M. Campagna (Ed.), *GIS for sustainable development* (pp. 23–40). CRC Press. doi:10.1201/9781420037845-6

Chen, R. J. (2007). Geographic information systems (GIS) applications in retail tourism and teaching curriculum. *Journal of Retailing and Consumer Services*, *14*(4), 289–295. doi:10.1016/j.jretconser.2006.07.004

Cohen, B. (2014). *Smart City*. Retrieved on July 8, 2022, from: https://www.smart-circle.org/category/smart-city/

Eichelberger, S., Peters, M., Pikkemaat, B., & Chan, C. (2020). Entrepreneurial ecosystems in smart cities for tourism development: From stakeholder perceptions to regional tourism policy implications. *Journal of Hospitality and Tourism Management, 45*, 319–329. doi:10.1016/j.jhtm.2020.06.011

Faghihi, F. (2021). Tourism Model Based on Geospatial Information System (Case Study: Kurdistan Province). *EFFLATOUNIA-Multidisciplinary Journal, 5*(2).

Farsari, Y., & Prastacos, P. (2004). GIS applications in the planning and management of tourism. In A. A. Lew, C. M. Hall, & A. M. Williams (Eds.), *A companion to tourism: Blackwell companions to geography* (pp. 596–607). Blackwell Publishing. doi:10.1002/9780470752272.ch47

Filocamo, F., Rosskopf, C. M., Amato, V., & Cesarano, M. (2022). A Step towards a Sustainable Tourism in Apennine Mountain Areas: A Proposal of Geoitinerary across the Matese Mountains (Central-Southern Italy). *Geosciences, 12*(2), 100. doi:10.3390/geosciences12020100

Fonseca, A., & Gouveia, C. (2005). GIS for sustainable development. In M. Campagna (Ed.), *GIS for sustainable development* (pp. 23–40). CRC Press.

García-Milon, A., Juaneda-Ayensa, E., Olarte-Pascual, C., & Pelegrín-Borondo, J. (2020). Towards the smart tourism destination: Key factors in information source use on the tourist shopping journey. *Tourism Management Perspectives, 36*, 100730. doi:10.1016/j.tmp.2020.100730 PMID:32834961

González-Reverté, F. (2019). Building sustainable smart destinations: An approach based on the development of Spanish smart tourism plans. *Sustainability, 11*(23), 6874. doi:10.3390u11236874

Gretzel, U., Reino, S., Kopera, S., & Koo, C. (2015). Smart tourism challenges. *Journal of Tourism, 16*(1), 41–47.

Gretzel, U., Sigala, M., Xiang, Z., & Koo, C. (2015). Smart tourism: Foundations and developments. *Electronic Markets, 25*(3), 179–188. doi:10.100712525-015-0196-8

Guizzardi, A., Pons, F. M., Angelini, G., & Ranieri, E. (2021). Big data from dynamic pricing: A smart approach to tourism demand forecasting. *International Journal of Forecasting, 37*(3), 1049–1060. doi:10.1016/j.ijforecast.2020.11.006

Gürbüz, E. (2021). *Gemlik Körfezi kuzey kıyılarının sürdürülebilir turizm ve rekreasyon planlama kapsamında değerlendirilmesi* [Unpublished Master's thesis]. Bursa Uludağ University, Bursa, Turkey.

Hilty, L. M., & Aebischer, B. (2015). *ICT innovations for sustainability, advances in intelligent systems and computing*. Springer. doi:10.1007/978-3-319-09228-7

Hunter, W. C., Chung, N., Gretzel, U., & Koo, C. (2015). Constructivist research in smart tourism. *Asia Pacific Journal of Information Systems, 25*(1), 103–118. doi:10.14329/apjis.2015.25.1.105

Jovanović, V., & Njeguš, A. (2016). The application of GIS and its components in tourism. *Yugoslav Journal of Operations Research, 18*(2), 261–272. doi:10.2298/YJOR0802261J

Kim, H., Koo, C., & Chung, N. (2021). The role of mobility apps in memorable tourism experiences of Korean tourists: Stress-coping theory perspective. *Journal of Hospitality and Tourism Management, 49*, 548–557. doi:10.1016/j.jhtm.2021.11.003

Landres, P., Spildie, D. R., & Queen, L. P. (2001). *GIS Applications to wilderness management: Potential uses and limitations*. Fort Collins, CO: US Department of Agriculture, Forest Service, Rocky Mountain Research Station. General Technical Report RMRS-GTR-80.

Lampropoulos, V., Panagiotopoulou, M., & Stratigea, A. (2021). Assessing the performance of current strategic policy directions towards unfolding the potential of the culture–tourism nexus in the Greek Territory. *Heritage*, *4*(4), 3157–3185. doi:10.3390/heritage4040177

Lechner, A. M., Verbrugge, L. N., Chelliah, A., Ang, M. L. E., & Raymond, C. M. (2020). Rethinking tourism conflict potential within and between groups using participatory mapping. *Landscape and Urban Planning*, *203*, 103902. doi:10.1016/j.landurbplan.2020.103902

Lopez de Avila, A. (2015). Smart Destinations: XXI Century Tourism. Presented at the *ENTER2015 Conference on Information and Communication Technologies in Tourism*, Lugano, Switzerland.

Lu, C., Huang, J., Chen, C., Shu, M., Hsu, C., & Tapas Bapu, B. (2021). An energy-efficient smart city for sustainable green tourism industry. *Sustainable Energy Technologies and Assessments*, *47*, 101494. doi:10.1016/j.seta.2021.101494

Ma, D., Hu, J., & Yao, F. (2021). Big data empowering low-carbon smart tourism study on low-carbon tourism O2O supply chain considering consumer behaviors and corporate altruistic preferences. *Computers & Industrial Engineering*, *153*, 107061. doi:10.1016/j.cie.2020.107061

MacDonald, M. (2002). *Agendas for sustainability: Environment and development into the 21st century*. Routledge. doi:10.4324/9780203021057

Mango, J., Çolak, E., & Li, X. (2021). Web-based GIS for managing and promoting tourism in sub-Saharan Africa. *Current Issues in Tourism*, *24*(2), 211–227. doi:10.1080/13683500.2019.1711028

Neuhofer, B., Buhalis, D., & Ladkin, A. (2012). Conceptualising technology enhanced destination experiences. *Journal of Destination Marketing & Management*, *1*(1-2), 36–46. doi:10.1016/j.jdmm.2012.08.001

Pobrić, A., & Sivac, A. (2022). The application of GIS in tourism planning and sustainable tourism development. In *Proceedings of 8th International Tourism and Hospitality Management Congress* (pp. 456-462). Academic Press.

Rahayuningsih, T., Muntasib, E. H., & Prasetyo, L. B. (2016). Nature based tourism resources assessment using geographic information system (GIS): Case study in Bogor. *Procedia Environmental Sciences*, *33*, 365–375. doi:10.1016/j.proenv.2016.03.087

Rezvani, M., Nickravesh, F., Astaneh, A. D., & Kazemi, N. (2022). A risk-based decision-making approach for identifying natural-based tourism potential areas. *Journal of Outdoor Recreation and Tourism*, *37*, 100485. doi:10.1016/j.jort.2021.100485

Rolando, A., & Scandiffio, A. (2021). Historical agricultural landscapes: Mapping seasonal conditions for sustainable tourism. In *Proceedings of 28th CIPA Symposium "Great Learning & Digital Emotion"* (pp. 641-646). Academic Press.

Ramaano, A. I. (2022). Geographical information systems in sustainable rural tourism and local community empowerment: A natural resources management appraisal for Musina Municipality'Society. *Local Development & Society*, 1-32.

Scoones, I. (2007). Sustainability. *Development in Practice, 17*(4-5), 589–596. doi:10.1080/09614520701469609

Shafiee, S., Rajabzadeh Ghatari, A., Hasanzadeh, A., & Jahanyan, S. (2019). Developing a model for sustainable smart tourism destinations: A systematic review. *Tourism Management Perspectives, 31*, 287–300. doi:10.1016/j.tmp.2019.06.002

Tavitiyaman, P., Qu, H., Tsang, W. L., & Lam, C. R. (2021). The influence of smart tourism applications on perceived destination image and behavioral intention: The moderating role of information search behavior. *Journal of Hospitality and Tourism Management, 46*, 476–487. doi:10.1016/j.jhtm.2021.02.003

Terzi, S. (2020). *CBS destekli web tabanlı Eskişehir turizm kaynakları bilgi sistemi* [Unpublished Master's thesis]. Eskişehir Teknik University, Eskişehir, Turkey.

Vargas-Sánchez, A. (2016). Exploring the concept of smart tourist destination. *Enlightening Tourism. A Pathmaking Journal, 6*(2), 178-196.

Waleghwa, B., Heldt, T., Kati, V., & Niemelä, T. (2021). Public participation GIS in sustainable tourism planning; experiences from Sweden and Finland. In *Proceedings of 29th Nordic Symposium on Tourism and Hospitality Research (Akureyri)* (pp. 107-111). Academic Press.

Wang, X., Li, X., Zhen, F., & Zhang, J. (2016). How smart is your tourist attraction?: Measuring tourist preferences of smart tourism attractions via a FCEM-AHP and IPA approach. *Tourism Management, 54*, 309–320. doi:10.1016/j.tourman.2015.12.003

Wei, W. (2012). Research on the application of geographic information system in tourism management. *Procedia Environmental Sciences, 12*, 1104–1109. doi:10.1016/j.proenv.2012.01.394

World Commission on Environment and Development. (1987). *The Brundtland report, our common future*. Oxford University Press.

Xiang, Z. (2018). From digitization to the age of acceleration: On information technology and tourism. *Tourism Management Perspectives, 25*, 147–150. doi:10.1016/j.tmp.2017.11.023

Yang, B. (2016). GIS based 3-D landscape visualization for promoting citizen's awareness of coastal hazard scenarios in flood prone tourism towns. *Applied Geography (Sevenoaks, England), 76*, 85–97. doi:10.1016/j.apgeog.2016.09.006

Zerihun, M. E. (2017). Web based GIS for tourism development using effective free and open source software case study: Gondor town and its surrounding area, Ethiopia. *Journal of Geographic Information System, 9*(1), 47–58. doi:10.4236/jgis.2017.91004

Zheng, G. H., Jiang, D. F., Luan, Y. F., & Yao, Y. (2022). GIS-based spatial differentiation of ethnic minority villages in Guizhou Province, China. *Journal of Mountain Science, 19*(4), 1–14. doi:10.100711629-020-6627-9

ADDITIONAL READING

Arampatzis, G., Kiranoudis, C. T., Scaloubacas, P., & Assimacopoulos, D. (2004). A GIS-based decision support system for planning urban transportation policies. *European Journal of Operational Research*, *152*(2), 465–475. doi:10.1016/S0377-2217(03)00037-7

Bunruamkaew, K., & Murayama, Y. (2012). Land use and natural resources planning for sustainable ecotourism using GIS in Surat Thani, Thailand. *Sustainability*, *4*(3), 412–429. doi:10.3390u4030412

Gavilanes Montoya, A. V., Esparza Parra, J. F., Chávez Velásquez, C. R., Tito Guanuche, P. E., Parra Vintimilla, G. M., Mestanza-Ramón, C., & Vizuete, D. D. C. (2021). A nature tourism route through gis to improve the visibility of the natural resources of the Altar Volcano, Sangay National Park, Ecuador. *Land (Basel)*, *10*(8), 884. doi:10.3390/land10080884

Geertman, S., Pettit, C., Goodspeed, R., & Staffans, A. (2021). *Urban informatics and future cities*. Springer. doi:10.1007/978-3-030-76059-5

Jurkus, E., Taminskas, J., Povilanskas, R., Kontautienė, V., Baltranaitė, E., Dailidė, R., & Urbis, A. (2021). Delivering tourism sustainability and competitiveness in seaside and marine resorts with GIS. *Journal of Marine Science and Engineering*, *9*(3), 312. doi:10.3390/jmse9030312

Kaymaz, Ç. K., Çakır, Ç., Birinci, S., & Kızılkan, Y. (2021). GIS-Fuzzy DEMATEL MCDA model in the evaluation of the areas for ecotourism development: A case study of "Uzundere", Erzurum-Turkey. *Applied Geography (Sevenoaks, England)*, *136*, 102577. doi:10.1016/j.apgeog.2021.102577

Malczewski, J. (1999). *GIS and multicriteria decision analysis*. Wiley & Sons.

Omarzadeh, D., Pourmoradian, S., Feizizadeh, B., Khallaghi, H., Sharifi, A., & Kamran, K. V. (2022). A GIS-based multiple ecotourism sustainability assessment of West Azerbaijan province, Iran. *Journal of Environmental Planning and Management*, *65*(3), 490–513. doi:10.1080/09640568.2021.1887827

Sharma, P. (2021). *Geospatial technology and smart cities: ICT, geoscience modeling, GIS and remote sensing*. Springer. doi:10.1007/978-3-030-71945-6

Van Maarseveen, M., Martinez, J., & Flacke, J. (2019). *GIS in sustainable urban planning and management: A global perspective*. Taylor & Francis Group.

Wassler, P., & Fan, D. X. (2021). A tale of four futures: Tourism academia and COVID-19. *Tourism Management Perspectives*, *38*, 100818. doi:10.1016/j.tmp.2021.100818 PMID:34868836

KEY TERMS AND DEFINITIONS

Geographic Information System (GIS): this is the hardware, software, personnel, geographic data, and method that perform the functions of collecting, storing, processing, managing, spatial analysis, querying and presenting large volumes of geographic data to help solve complex social, economic and environmental problems.

Remote Sensing: this is the technique of recording and examining the earth and ground resources without establishing a physical connection with them. it is the task of determining the various features of the ground without any actual contact with the ground.

Smart Destination: a smart tourism destination is defined as an innovative tourism center built on a state-of-the-art infrastructure that is accessible to all, facilitates the interaction of visitors and ensures the sustainable development of tourist areas.

Smart Tourism: smart tourism is defined as tourism supported by physical infrastructure, social connections, public resources, and efforts in a destination to collect data from the human mind.

Sustainable Development: this is the principle of organizing to achieve human development goals while maintaining the ability of natural systems to provide the ecosystem services and natural resources on which the society and economy depend.

Sustainable Tourism: this is a concept encompassing the complete tourism experience, including economic, environmental, and social issues, as well as an interest in improving the tourist experience and meeting the needs of host communities.

Tourism Carrying Capacity: tourism carrying capacity is defined as the maximum number of tourists that any tourism destination can carry, without causing dissatisfaction for both the locals and the tourists, during the time it hosts the tourists.

Chapter 9
Sustainability as a Consequence of Memory and Memorable Experience

Selin Kama
https://orcid.org/0000-0002-2707-091X
Bitlis Eren University, Turkey

ABSTRACT

The degree of remembrance of an experience can affect an individual's contribution to social, cultural, economic, and environmental sustainability by transforming their behavior. In other words, memory and memorability are important predictors of sustainable behavior. Therefore, the focus of this study is to evaluate the memory and memorable experiences from the macro-sustainability perspective. Within this study, the impact of visitors' memorable experiences on sustainability and how sustainability shapes memorable experiences are evaluated conceptually. The results show that emotional and cognitive essence that makes tourism experiences memorable provides a competitive advantage for destinations by influencing the sustainability behaviors of visitors. In line with this study, the relationship between memory and sustainability behaviors of visitors must be evaluated via qualitative and quantitative methods.

INTRODUCTION

Tourism and recreation, which have an important capacity to create growth in destinations, have environmental, social, cultural, and economic effects arising from human behavior (Saarinen, 2006). In this respect, sustainability, which is one of the most affected areas by human behavior, is a leading concept in developmental practices and research (Thal, 2016). Most research related to the subject examine the effects of the environmental (Thal, 2016; Han, 2021), economic (Qiu et al., 2019), social and cultural (or socio-cultural) (Helgadóttir et al., 2019) dimensions of sustainability in destinations separately. The contribution of these studies can be viewed two-fold.

DOI: 10.4018/978-1-6684-4645-4.ch009

First, especially in the economic and socio-cultural dimension, the concerns of the local community or benefits from tourism and recreation mobility are addressed in the research. Second, it is investigated how the sustainability of a destination affects memorable experiences of tourists (Moliner-Tena et al., 2021). Although there is a necessity of subjecting sustainability to wider theoretical and practical order to ensure a safer future (Cohen, 2010) studies on holistic and cumulative effects of the macro-sustainability and the motivations of visitors' behavior are limited (Wan & Li, 2013).

This study discusses the sustainability from a macro perspective with the focus of memory and memorable experiences. In other words, in this study, rather than defining sustainability and the dimensions of sustainability or describing the known impact of people on sustainability, the impact of visitors' memorable experiences on sustainability, and how sustainability shapes memorable experiences are evaluated conceptually. Therefore, within the macro-sustainability perspective, the focus of this study is memory and memorable experiences.

Tourism and recreation businesses aim to offer visitors a new, intense and pleasurable feeling that stimulates the five senses to experience satisfying, unique and enriching experiences (Moliner-Tena et al., 2021). The fact that these experiences are unique enough to make an impact in the lives of visitors' (Jorgenson et al., 2019), and creating strong memories define the essence of memorable experience. Businesses use the ongoing perception of who and what we are, based on experiences of daily events, to activate memories, to create continuities, and to adapt the present to the trajectories of experience (Brown & Reavey, 2015). Many activities experienced by visitors during the travel process form a tourism memory and form a guideline for understanding visitor behaviors and trends (Kim et al., 2021). Therefore, although studies on memory are insufficient in terms of content and scope, have gained importance in tourism and recreation research to determine and measure the essence that makes experiences memorable (de Freitas Coelho & Gosling, 2020; Kim, 2012; Tung et al., 2017).

Additionally, it has been proven that experiences which are strong enough to stay in the minds of visitors motivate behavioral tendencies (Kim et al., 2010; Coudounaris & Sthapit, 2017; Kim et al., 2022) which in turn motivate sustainable behaviors. Memory studies bring sustainability into the context of memorable experiences in line with the meanings that visitors attribute to the place and the image created (Chandralal & Valenzuela, 2013; Kim et al. 2017). The main reason for this is that tourism and recreation, as a resource-intensive industry involving human activities, causes significant economic, social, and environmental impacts on local communities (Lu & Nepal, 2009).

Within the scope of this study, it is accepted that sustainability has an impact on memorable experiences, as well as memorable experiences have an impact on sustainability. In this context, the aim of this study is to examine the idea that the experiences that take place in the memory of the visitors' form the basis of the sustainable behavior through shaping emotions and thoughts. In this respect, the study seeks answers to the questions of how memory shapes memorable experiences and what effects memorable experiences have on sustainability behavior.

MEMORY

The ability of human being to remember past events causes the arrow of time to be twisted in a loop, returning to the reality of the mind, thus violating the law of the irreversibility of the flow of time (Tulving, 2002). This violation of time flow takes place in memory. Memory is a personal human ability that gains a place in one's imagination by influencing the mind as a result of the constant repetition of a past experience that defines the person and is meaningful for him/her (Gedi & Elam, 1996; Singer & Salovey, 2010). Memory is examined with its altered, transformed, and distorted structure in the mental life studies of psychologists and defined as the treasure and protector of everything in Cicero's De Oratore (Loftus, 1988).

On the other hand, based on the myths that have occurred in Greek mythology, Farmaki (2021) examines the concept of memory in the context of memory (Mnemosyne) and forgetfulness (Lethe), referring to two parallel rivers in the underworld, which represent the personification of goddesses. According to this legend, a group of deceased people are asked to drink from the waters of Lethe to forget their earthly life before their souls are reincarnated, while others drink the water of mnemosyne to remember and know everything. This legend shows that the mnemosyne, the river of memory, keeps memories of past lives alive. Adapted to today's conditions, as expressed in the legend, even if the memory is not related to previous lives, researchers explain memory by referring to the memorable aspects of an individuals' past experiences.

According to Gillis (1994), the first records about memory date back to the 19th century. Although it was not considered as a very important concept in terms of societies, archives were created for elite classes such as aristocrats, the church and the monarchical state in order to preserve past memories with genealogies, family portraits and biographies. Ordinary people, on the other hand, did not feel the need to record, objectify and preserve the past, as they felt it as a part of the present. Today, however, memory carries a much deeper meaning. Within this deep meaning, there is a uniqueness of each individual with a structure that evokes strong emotions with representative images that define who the person is, take important parts from lived experiences and crystallize the characteristic interest, motives or concerns for a short time (Singer & Salovey, 2010). Therefore, memory is the most basic way for an individual to exist as a human being and to make life sustainable. Therefore, it has gone beyond the records kept in the past, and has become an important concept for organizing people's lives through giving meaning to objects and places (Johnson, 1998).

Compared to ordinary events, extraordinary events that contain meaningful stimuli at a deep level, such as tourism and travel experiences, are remembered better and more vividly, as they are distinctive in terms of affective and cognitive evaluations (Kim, 2010). Keeping in mind, remembering and familiarity with the impressions of the visitors or the elements they perceive with their senses depending on the type and intensity of the existing associations in a particular destination seem to be effective in making the memory fully functional and perfect (Kirkpatrick, 1894). This association and intensity can be evaluated in terms of the accuracy of remembering a situation or phenomenon, the way the past is represented in the brain, the amount of accumulated information and the time that memories remain accessible (Klein, 2015).

In cognitive psychology, the importance of the event's similarity to the previous event, the credibility of the source (the credibility of the information and its integration into the memory), the probability of its realization and the degree of exposure to the experience is important for the memories of an event to be permanent in the memory (Braun-Latour et al., 2006). However, it should not be forgotten that recent events, events that are constantly repeated and constantly recalled, are more memorable, and new events that prevent repeating or recalling previous events may lead to the deletion of lived experiences from the mind (Waugh & Norman, 1965). In other words, visitors remember the lived experiences by associating them with previous similar experiences depending on the type and intensity of the associations, and these experiences, which are remembered over time, can be forgotten as a result of new experiences that replace them.

How and to what extent visitors remember the destinations, people and cultures visited (Ahmad & Hertzog, 2016) depends on the meaning and value of the experience. In studies referring to the value of experience, it is stated that memory is a dynamic process that is learned before the experience and affected by the interactions created after the journey (Braun-Latour et al., 2006). In this process, it is possible to reach a wide array of related memories by focusing on a single representative memory (Singer & Salovey, 2010).

For instance, as a result of the visual reflections of the touristic or recreational place or the visualization of an image in the mind of the individual, memory becomes active and effective (Kirkpatrick, 1894). Imagine being at an airport. The visual reflections at the airport can enable one person to remember the places seen in a loved destination, the food eaten and even the feelings felt, as well as the previous travels by plane. Research has been conducted on different aspects of memory to determine how these memories come to life in mind and to make them understandable.

Memory Classifications

There are various memory classes that have been widely studied to evaluate the visitor behavior and experiences in tourism and recreation research. In general, classifications are shaped under implicit and explicit memory (Farmaki, 2021; Droffelaar, 2021). In Explicit memory, sensory information is perceived, processed and recorded for conscious recall, and it has the ability to show long-term changes in behavior (Fariborz et al., 1996). Explicit memory, which contains facts and information about personal life, includes episodic and semantic memory (Jorgenson et al., 2019).

On the other hand, Implicit memory does not exist for conscious recall or awareness but refers to observable permanent changes associated with known past experiences (Fariborz et al., 1996). Depending on the importance in tourism and recreation research, long-term and short-term memory (Farmaki, 2021), episodic and semantic memory (Tulving, 2002), collective memory (Gedi & Elam, 1996; Wood, 2020; Johnson, 1998) and autobiographical memory (Jorgenson et al., 2019) are among the classes that need to be examined.

Short-term memory is used to refer to memory that occurred in the recent past, with a very short interval between presentation of material and recall (Gathercole, 1999). Short-term storage separates the memory system from the external environment, therefore, frees the individual from the responsibility of instant attention to environmental changes (Shiffrin & Atkinson, 1969: 180). It can temporarily keep a limited amount of information in an accessible state because of unconscious awareness and cannot be controlled (Cowan, 2008). Instant information that can be used to make decisions or evaluate situations (Jorgenson et al., 2019) is processed in the mind for 30 seconds or less and first transferred to the short-term storage of the mind, and then desired knowledge is transferred to the long-term memory, containing the permanent information (Shiffrin & Atkinson, 1969). Transferring certain events in one's life to *long-term memory* (Jorgenson, 2019) takes place in a three-stage process: encoding, consolidation and retrieval. According to Tung et al. (2017), in the first stage, the individual acquires event-specific information that includes extremely precise details such as the time and place of the experience, consisting of specific information and vivid moments, as well as authenticities acquired through the senses (i.e. olfactory and auditory cues). The second stage, consolidation, serves as a storage function during the transition to long-term memory. In the last stage, there is recalling and remembering the events in memory. Individuals retain places and faces longer when physical appearance or layout includes meaningful interactions (Mandler & Ritchey, 1977).

Episodic memory, which means knowing something (Droffelaar, 2021), emphasizes the conscious awareness of remembering a certain time and a certain situation in a mental time travel (Xu et al., 2021). Subjective sense of time, autonoetic awareness and self-refer are three central components of a neurocognitive (mind/brain) system that enables episodic memory (Tulving, 2002). In other words, it defines the information about what, where and when of the experience with the awareness of the self that has experienced the event in the past, which includes mental time travel. Since episodic memory is autobiographical in nature, it refers to personal experiences that carry information about time and location (Roediger & McDermott, 2013). Depending on the narrative structure (Xu et al., 2021), it defines the events in a sequence (Eichenbaum, 2013). For example, episodic memory occurs when a person remembers a playful employee and the fun times they had together from the time of the summer vacation, when he/she went to Antalya with family after successfully completing the school term. As can be understood from this example, episodic memory affects the transformation of experiences into narratives by storing various landscapes in the minds of tourists, re-experiencing them in memory, and routinely producing memories by drawing attention to the context of time and space (Xu et al., 2021). Therefore, it guides current and future behaviors in the process of remembering and familiarity (Fivush, 2011). Here, remembering requires recalling specific details about the event, while familiarity represents the feeling of having encountered with the item before but not being able to get more details (Cardona et al., 2020).

Semantic memory, which means remembering something (Droffelaar, 2021), hides facts about the world and uses them to know (Xu et al., 2021). Semantic memory is effective in accessing a wide array of related memories from a single sample, which has been described earlier in this chapter. Braun–Latour et al., (2006) states that when a tourist sees an advertisement of Disneyland, concepts related to the brand become active in the mind along with the past experiences at the resort. According to the researchers, while the mental model or semantic map of Disneyland evolves with the tourist's exposure to the media and other materials, it also creates reconstruction by harmonization with personal memories (autobiographical memories) of the overall experience felt at the facility.

Collective memory is a metaphoric concept, that defines a feature attached to a generalized entity such as society in subjective memories, contain representations of reality (Gedi & Elam, 1996; Gillis, 1994). For this reason, it changes the way of thinking about ones' selves, the past and place, and how we develop narratives, both in its special and universal form, by referring to the inseparable connection with the social and private lives of societies (Ahmad & Hertzog, 2016). In other words, it can be said that the collective memory shapes and even dictates the meaning that people with a common memory attribute to objects or events (Johnson, 1998). Social identities are defined in collective memory and maintained by remembering a sense of sameness over time and place, and what is remembered is defined by the assumed identity (Gillis, 1994). To help better understand the relationships between people and the environment within a socio-psychological structure, identity mediates between demographic variables such as race, gender, income, attitudes and ultimate behavior (Johnson, 1998). In tourism and recreation fields, collective memory provides a context for the design and consumption of experienced memories, emotional sharing of memories arising from experiences, sense of belonging, deep motivations and collective experiences (Wood, 2020). Applying to the physical memory of the place by using elements such as narratives, sound, light, decor, smell, size and location of the stage in places, affects the formation of emotional bonds with the present time by reinforcing the memories in the collective memory among former visitors (Bennett & Rogers, 2016).

Autobiographical memory, which is examined through its similarity with episodic memory, serves as social and emotional functions including self-advocacy and self-regulation in relation with the experiencer's ability to represent her/himself, referring to a meaningful sequence of events that defines the person or life (Fivush, 2011). It includes memories that are defined in everyday conversations about life and placed in a person's life story within a broad frame of reference (Jorgenson et al., 2019). Autobiographical memory, in addition to evaluating the present as framed by the past and the future, defines why remembering and thinking about the past takes place in daily life, self, psychodynamic integrity, social bonding, present and future behaviors within the scope of planning (Bluck, 2003). Visitor participation in hedonic activities and local culture encourages the formation and stimulation of autobiographical memories through enabling memories to be consciously or unconsciously recalled (Zhang et al., 2021). Similarly, an individual's memories of taking the first vacation as a family after meeting their spouse represent this form of memory, as they constitute self-biography (Jorgenson et al., 2019).

The memory classes described here detail how experiences from tourism and recreation become perceptible and memorable in the minds of visitors. On the other hand, Marscall (2012) defines the reflections of memory in the individual through two different concepts: return to memory and memory explosion. According to the researcher, the 'return to memory' is characterized by a broad societal interest in collective or social memory, manifested in the proliferation of monuments, museums, commemorative events and historical feature films. The return to memory can be explained, for example, in the context of cultural and heritage tourism.

According to Bajc (2006), visiting the cultural memory areas in order to experience life as it is, encourages sociality and identification with that social life, resulting in the formation of collective memories. The form of identity formed in these spaces ensures the continuity of the recording, preservation, and reconstruction of a common past and a common narrative that we define ourselves as members of such collective structures. The 'memory explosion', on the other hand, refers to the extraordinary international growth of the tourism industry and the simultaneous democratization of travel across all strata of society (Marschall, 2012).

MEMORABLE EXPERIENCES

In tourism and recreation services, when the focus shifted to staged experiences (Pine and Gilmore, 1998), businesses have sought new pleasant experiences, creative ideas that can satisfy visitors' wishes and innovative products/services in order to preserve the place in the memories of visitors (Azevedo, 2010). The main reason for this situation is the effort to make the experiences remarkable and memorable by ascribing meaning to them in a way that creates personal values, since not every tourism experience is strong enough to take a place in the memory (de Freitas Coelho & Gosling, 2020). In this context, it has been tried to establish a focal point in tourism and recreation research to understand exactly what is special, magnificent and the essence that makes the experience memorable (Tung & Ritchie, 2011). According to research, experiences that occur in memory depending on history or past experience act as a symbiosis between real travel and mental time travel, offering both a way to relax the past and a new experience to be remembered (Marschall, 2015).

Tourism and recreational businesses create environments suitable for consuming various meanings and images in the destination beyond just products and services (Caru & Cova, 2007) to influence the choices of visitors within various facilities and services (Angelkova et al., 2012). Experience emerges as a mixture of communication measured by the prediction of visitor expectations, physical performance of the business, evoked senses and evoked emotions in the interaction process between the business and the customer, which creates these images and meanings (Shaw, 2005).

Visitors evaluate experiences subjectively during the planning and preparation stages before the events, during the visit and in the recall process after the visit and gain emotional, cognitive and behavioral results (Tung & Ritchie, 2011). If these experiences include individual feelings, reflections, affect, expectations, consequentiality, and recollection, it is stated that the experience is memorable (Tung & Ritchie, 2011; de Freitas Coelho et al., 2018).

Memory and knowledge can be expressed as key concepts in the definition of memorable experiences. Memorable Tourism Experience (VTE) has been defined as a tourism experience that is positively remembered and recalled after the event (Kim et al., 2012). Here, the key concept of a memorable tourism experience is memory. According to Brown & Reavey (2015), memory should be associated with experience on a bipolar axis. Accordingly, one axis extends to the past and forward to a predicted future, while the other axis activates memory to inform current actions in relation to the changing world around. In other words, memory directs current and future behaviors by evaluating the current situation through past experiences. Therefore, according to Shafiee et al. (2021), memorable experiences should also be related to the perception and knowledge of the visitors about the place and the event. Destination-related information, such as the destination's images and attributes, are stored in semantic memory (Kim, 2014), and has an impact on decision-making behavior (Chandralal & Valenzuela, 2013).

In the memory literature, researchers have identified various factors that increase the memorization of an event, such as emotional effects, cognitive appraisals, and new events (Kim et al., 2010; Kim et al., 2012), and these factors constitute important components of the tourism experience that effect visitors' memory. These components are examined under seven headings: hedonism, innovation, local culture, knowledge, meaningfulness, refreshment, involvement. According to Rodrigues et al. (2022), each dimension creates an emotional, cognitive, or stimulating effect on visitors. Authors states that, while hedonism and refreshment are related to emotionality, knowledge and involvement should be handled in a cognitive structure.

On the other hand, meaningfulness, local culture and novelty create a stimulating effect on visitors. The seven elements must be considered in relation to each other in creating memorable and meaningful experiences. Breiby et al. (2020) suggest that when visitors enjoy any activity where they gain knowledge through active participation, they will attach meaning to the activities and want to be more involved in. This will probably encourage transformative, new and deeper understandings, leading to active interaction with the environment of people affected by products in social, cultural and physical contexts.

Hedonism

Hedonia, which is examined depending on the fact that pleasure is good and pain is bad, is based on pleasurable emotions such as joy, entertainment and fun (Lee & Jeong, 2020). The dominant component in the consumption of tourism and leisure activities is the pursuit of pleasure or hedonism (Hanna et al., 2018; Yu et al., 2019). In other words, a significant part of the value perceived by the visitors depends on the level of pleasure obtained, and the most important benefit obtained from the fun and enjoyable experiences defined as the hedonic value (Coudounaris & Sthapit, 2017). Hedonic value can be reflected in episodic memory as a narrative characterized by a happy existence (Xu et al., 2021; Lee & Jeong, 2020). For example, encoding the context in a musical, that causes hedonic feelings in the individual to experience more recall and less familiarity, creates positive effects on episodic memory (Cardona et al., 2020).

Novelty

Memory is to produce a meaningful explanation of a new event experienced in a cognitive perspective with a focus on reasoning and perceptual processes (Skavronskaya et al., 2019). For a visitor, the perception of novelty is related to the perceived novelty level of various objects such as historical places, the environment, and other people (Lee & Crompton, 1992). Therefore, even ordinary activities that an individual performs in a new place outside of their living space have the potential to occupy a strong place in memory as they increase the diversity and interest offered by the environment. The experience of eating lobster for the first time by the individual during the travel process may contribute to memory as a memorable dining experience (Stone et al., 2021).

It is possible that this situation arises from an attention, interest and desire to explore to meet the novelty quest. In addition, new experiences initiate different interaction and communication patterns, leading to the strengthening of the bonds established between the individual and other individuals or between the individual and the environment (Lee & Lee, 2021). As a result, it increases the willingness to take physical, psychological and social risks for the sake of various, new and complex emotions (Coudounaris & Sthapit, 2017).

Local Culture

Tourists' experiences are guided by social interactions between visitors and the host community, and the interaction between locals and tourists is defined as the most memorable aspect of the visit (Coudounaris & Sthapit, 2017). Therefore, researchers have tried to analyze the changes in traditional topics and behaviors, the role of local culture in visitors' holiday experience and the need to interact with the local population in order to understand the impact of tourism on local cultures and local cultures on tourism (Artal-Tur et al., 2018). Morgan and Xu (2009) state that the social motivations of the visitors are not to experience solely the 'high culture' of artistic and historical places, but to experience the behavior and lifestyle of the local people. Therefore, visitors interact with the local people to understand the local culture, and experiencing the local culture is considered an important motivation factor for travel (Yu et al., 2019). In this context, a cultural exchange, whether in artistic and historical places or in interactions with local people, can be seen as more likely to be remembered, as it includes novelty and surprise for the individual (de Freitas Coelho & Gosling, 2020).

Refreshment

As one of the push factors in tourism, refreshment is considered within the scope of inner peace and renewal which is associated with spiritual refreshment, getting away from daily life, escaping from the city, entertainment and comfort (Chen & Chen, 2015). Since it is defined as a state of renewal and relaxation in travel experiences, it is valued within the scope of psychological benefit (Coudounaris & Sthapit, 2017). Refreshment provides opportunities to participate in travel activities with invigorating experiences that offers refreshment of the mood positively and provides comfortable conditions for individuals to have affective or affectional communication and interaction (Lee & Lee, 2021).

Meaningfulness

Meaningfulness encourages a new way of looking at daily life by doing something important and valuable that can act as a catalyst for a visitor's personal growth and change (Sthapit et al., 2019; Wilson & Harris, 2006). The meaningfulness of travel experiences includes the effort to recognize the deep emotional and spiritual aspects and effects of visitors with a sense of self-confidence and empowerment in an area where they can explore, think, and analyze by considering their choices and perspectives on life (Wilson & Harris, 2006). Traveling to a meaningful touristic destination creates a context that enables individuals to have more accurate information about themselves, to face personal growth and to experience self-development (Kim et al., 2012; Lee & Lee, 2021). These subjective evaluations also include inquiries about how people can convey the meaning and benefits of travel experiences in their daily, changing lives when they return home (Sthapit et al., 2019).

Involvement

Studies on consumption behavior draw attention to three different aspects of participation in decision-making and communication behaviors. Michaelidou & Dibb (2008) define enduring involvement as an individual's commitment to a product or advertisement while situational involvement represents the focus of an individual's interest in purchasing a product. On the other hand, response involvement, refers to a behavioral orientation that includes information acquisition and decision processes. In tourism and leisure, involvement is accepted as an important feature of experiences in missed places and with desired activities (Coudounaris & Sthapit, 2017) that can be remembered by visitors in an intense and active experience process. When visitors find themselves involved in a leisure activity (Yu et al., 2019), they are more likely to have a memorable experience, as it increases the interest, enthusiasm, and sense of integrity in the activities (Lee & Lee, 2021).

Knowledge

The amount of knowledge that an individual keep in memory, functions as a determinant of behavioral attitudes (Abdullahi, 2017) by affecting the way of evaluation, interpretation and reaction to the stimuli in an environment (Blackwell et al., 2001). Knowledge gained from childhood through first-hand or socially transmitted experiences forms the basis of decision-making and has a vital influence on future actions (Selby, 2004). However, the ability of the information kept in mind to affect attitudes depends on the level of obtaining remarkable, accessible and compatible pieces of information from the person's memory (Lidman & Renström, 2011). To make a decision or provide a reliable basis for action, a person needs to manage the knowledge with personal skills and experience (Cooper, 2015).

Emphasis on sustainability in tourist destinations and events has a positive impact on visitor experiences, loyalty, word-of-mouth (WOM) intentions, and sustainability behaviors (Sisson & Alcorn, 2021). According to Angelkova et al. (2012), creating an attractive destination requires natural resources as well as universal natural and cultural heritage, delicious food and entertainment customized to the interests of modern tourists. For this reason, destinations should focus on destination features such as iconic touristic places and reach memorable experience factors such as perceived results of the trip, perceived opportunities for social interactions, feelings of pleasure and arousal (Chandralal & Valenzuela, 2013).

Memorable experiences begin with managers identifying and emphasizing the most important aspects of the destination's culture, history and the local lifestyle that distinguishes it from the rest of the tourism world, and a manageable number of activities/experiences/memories must be created for each of these aspects (Kim, 2014). In other words, these experiences should meet the desire to learn something new or learn how to do new things, as well as the opportunity to choose among classical activities based on a single attraction (Angelkova et al., 2012). Depending on the variety of the services, individuals grow mentally. For example, Kim et al. (2022) claim that recalling tourism experiences has a pleasant effect on the trip, leading to improved mental health and shaping various behavioral intentions. Additionally, developing inward (reward, freedom) or outward (joy, happiness, enthusiasm, vitality) positive emotions in the minds of visitors (de Freitas Coelho et al., 2018) will create the idea of staying longer, re-visiting or participating in more activities (Angelkova et al., 2012).

MEMORABLE EXPERIENCES AND SUSTAINABILITY

The sustainability movement, which was revived in the 1970s in line with the ideals of the environmental movement, was broadened by associating it with activities that promote long-term resilience in the society, culture and economy with individuals' cognitions, evaluations and beliefs (Pereira et al., 2012). When examined from a detailed point of view, Moliner-Tena et al. (2021) suggest the quality of life, the manners of behavior towards personnel, the use of local products and services, the degree of development of infrastructure and basic services are among the economic and social contexts. According to researchers, respect and care for the environment, energy and water saving, recycling, and the use of ecological products are seen among the subjects of tourism and recreation research with their environmental context. On the other hand, cultural sustainability is examined to define the bonds between local people and visitors.

While the natural, cultural, social, and economic resources of nations have little effect on attracting visitors, the superstructure is specially placed to attract and satisfy them (Ritchie & Crouch, 2010). Therefore, tourism businesses try to add value to visitor experiences by using the development of economic and environmental protection as marketing strategies (Wang et al., 2019). It is this value that turns sustainable resources into an attraction. Although the effect of social, cultural, environmental, and economic sustainability on creating memorable experiences in tourism and recreation research has been examined (Moliner-Tena et al., 2021), studies on how and in what way memorable experiences affect sustainability have been very scarce.

However, it is provable that there is a bidirectional relationship between sustainability and memorable experiences. This relationship, as can be understood from the narratives in this chapter, deals with the impact of sustainability on experience, and the impact of experience on sustainability. In terms of these contexts, it can be said that the emotional and cognitive essence that makes tourism experiences memorable provides a competitive advantage for destinations by influencing the sustainability behaviors of visitors.

Cognitive Component and Sustainability

Cognitive component, which refers to the awareness and interpretation of the stimulus, is organized around one's own reality in accordance with beliefs, knowledge and opinions about a place, experience, or another person (Moutinho, 1987). Cognitive maps created in the minds of individuals lead to the development of a cognitive understanding of the benefits and contradictions of sustainability in information processing and product perception of consumers by definition, classification and generalizations (Van Dam & Van Trijp, 2011). For example; An individual who is interested in outdoor recreation defines and classifies recreational environments suitable for different activities, and generalizes activities that can be performed in similar areas in his/her mind.

With this generalization, the identification of the benefits and contradictions of the sustainability of the subjected fields develops a cognitive understanding. The reason behind the behavior of individual is this understanding. Skavronskaya et al., (2017) explain this cognitive structure based on a theater scene. According to the researchers, the brain processes external perceptual stimuli, internal memories and the scenarios that represents the outside world as a play on the stage by combining it in a harmonious show, and the audience evaluates the stage show interactively. By producing neurotransmitters that stimulate bodily emotions with new input stimuli in the process of this show, individuals are motivated by commenting, and can influence the direction of the game. When evaluated in the context of sustainability, it is possible to say that various stimuli and unforgettable memories that affect the individual's awareness from the outside affect the interpretations of the place and this will affect the direction of sustainable behavior.

When sustainability is defined within the metaphors of innovation, memory, and instability rather than growth, balance, and stability, it becomes meaningful in memory, which has both ecological and social components in order to create excitement, determine alternative visions for the future, and build hope (Berkes et al., 2008). From the cognitive point of view, since the meanings formed in the memory are kept in the position of determinant of personal behaviors both directly and indirectly, it can be evaluated as a predictor of the sustainability behaviors of the person. In the simplest sense, this can be explained by the fact that the knowledge of how often the experience is remembered and shared with others transforms behaviors and interactions as it makes destinations manageable and marketable and permeates daily life (Jorgenson et al., 2019). According to Barber and Deale (2014), when individuals are relatively more aware of their environment and other people or encounter with businesses that help them become aware of sustainability practices, they become more concerned about others and society as a whole, and contribute to sustainability and interested in sustainable products and services. However, not every individual has cognitive skills that function in a superior quality. Therefore, it is necessary to open a separate parenthesis for neurodiversity in the relationship between memory and sustainability.

It is necessary to evaluate the memorable tourism experiences and sustainable tourism behaviors of neurodiverse individuals who tend to show unique travel-related motivations, perceptions and experiences while visiting a destination (Akyıldız, 2021). For example, individuals with autism spectrum disorder may prefer to follow the same route or eat the same food every day because they have difficulty in orientation and relaxation when there are changes in their routines (Raulston et al., 2019). The concept that is effective here is the level of recognition or familiarity that activates the cognitive aspect as a source of information. This can be best explained with the example of Mandler's (1980) butcher-in-the-bus.

According to Mandler, when an individual sees a familiar face on the bus, even if being not sure of recognizing the person or does not remember who he/she is, an interrogation begins in the memory, and with the additional information, it can be remembered that he is the butcher at the local supermarket. Therefore, it is inevitable for neurodiverse individuals to question the recognition level of the places they visit, despite of their limited cognitive skills. This level of recognition of the place can shape behavioral tendencies and revisit intention by encouraging memorable experiences and can motivate sustainable behaviors.

From another point of view, inclusive theater experiences have proven to have the potential to increase confidence levels, self-esteem, empathic abilities and being comfortable with others as well as improving communication and socialization skills (Kim et al., 2015). Therefore, neurodiverse individuals can gain the potential to perform sustainable behaviors through such recreational experiences, along with communication and socialization skills. Finally, it is necessary to restructure or reorganize transportation, accommodation, excursions, recreation, and other touristic activities in order to meet the needs and requests, and the plans made to provide the support, assistance and security that neurodiverse individuals need during their travels, and the execution of the trips by travel agencies (Hamed, 2013). This situation is effective for destination managers and operators in supporting environmental, social, and economic sustainability.

Emotional Component and Sustainability

Memories of the past create positive nostalgic feelings in the minds of individuals, trigger involuntary comparisons and are effective in decision-making processes (Marschall, 2012). This means focusing on memorable tourism experiences not only enables brands to grow over time, but also encourages the tendency to act more responsibly and sustainably when experiences develop emotional relationships and bonds in the minds of visitors (Dettori, 2019). Emotions directly influence behavioral intentions in leisure, marketing, and tourism settings such as festivals and events, providing a way of understanding the interaction between the environment and human in involved, refreshing and hedonic moments (Rodrigues et al., 2022; Santos et al., 2021).

Novelty, on the other hand, can increase tourists' sustainable experience and the desire and satisfaction for sustainable tourism by triggering emotional excitement and positive evaluations of perceived value (Liu et al., 2016). Sameer et al., (2021) argue that hedonism, which is among the dimensions of a memorable tourism experience, is positively related with overall consumption and sustainable or responsible consumption. According to researchers, those who value increasing pleasure, joy, and comfort as a source of happiness, have stronger sustainability-oriented behaviors. However, to provide the hedonic experience, the preservation of natural environments that offer space for visitors, depends on the fulfillment of sustainability in destination development and supporting infrastructures (Hanna et al., 2018).

Interaction with the local culture and history offers new and meaningful experiences, broadens visitors' horizons and changes their perspectives of memorable experiences and memorable experiences will lead to increased sustainability behavior (Han et al., 2020). In cultural tourism, depending on the average spending level of the visitors, it becomes possible to increase the level of economic sustainability and to create a more sustainable tourism model that improves the quality of life of local residents (Artal-Tur et al., 2018). For example, historical urban landscapes contribute to the maintenance of memory features related to local culture by representing the importance of remembering memories, as well as contributing to social sustainability with their effect on the formation of a sense of place, place identity, pride and quality of life (Hussein et al., 2020).

Therefore, the promotion of cultural and ethnic diversity by the destination and business managers will be remembered by the visitors, and is also effective in creating a sustainable destination (Artal-Tur et al., 2018). Also, it has been stated that museums, which are one of the important areas of promoting local cultures, provide sustainability in material collective memory forms by providing an objective record of the identities of certain communities, whether global, national, regional, or local (Merriman, 2008).

Breiby et al., (2020) sought to describe the impact of memorable experiences created by interactions between visitors and local community and manager and visitors on behavioral intentions and sustainability. According to researchers, the behavior of visitors who do not interact with host communities or natural environments can pose numerous associated sustainability issues for destinations. On the other hand, if visitors collaborate with producers or managers to create the value of the experience, they create a context for understanding how to improve destination sustainability and experience value. In this process, constantly updating the experiences and ensuring the permanence in memory (Glenberg, 1997: 7) affects the future travel plans, behaviors and emotions of tourists (Xu et al., 2021).

Memorable experiences are valuable for the sustainable development of tourist destinations (Wei et al., 2019), as they are designed to strengthen and reinforce the recall of pleasant memories (Chen et al., 2020). As a matter of fact, many psychological states such as believing, dreaming, desiring, intending, thinking, recognizing, searching, wandering, hope and fear transform the processes of planning, judging, categorizing, and decision making with memories of past experiences (Klein, 2015).

SOLUTIONS AND RECOMENDATIONS

The context of the sustainability structure, which expresses the ability of businesses to keep themselves in time (Kim et al., 2010), is carried to a much deeper and wider scope when searched within the context of macro sustainability of destinations. The rapid growth in tourism and recreation can sometimes be seen as worrying in terms of economic, cultural, and social sustainability. However, tourism and recreation, which have positive effects on community resilience and quality of life, can provide sustainability with practices of businesses as part of the management strategies to build more trust and comfort among the public (Helgadóttir et al., 2019).

Moreover, spatial planning, the laws and regulations related to cultural heritage, and the permissions and privileges to be granted for various activities will enhance the memorability of the local lifestyle, regional traditions, and abilities, and help determine the tendencies and behaviors of individuals towards economic, social, cultural and ecological sustainability (Murzyn-Kupisz, 2012). Additionally, spectacular scenery, attractions, friendly people, a unique culture and heritage serve the goal of reducing substitutability by providing experiences that are strong enough to be remembered (Hudson & Ritchie, 2009).

In a constantly changing and evolving macro environment, destination and business managers regularly monitor the environment to understand the "big picture" and see the transformations that are changing the tourism landscape (Ritchie & Crouch, 2010). By allocating resources effectively to the seven dimensions of the experience (Yu et al., 2019) while developing a program, managers encourage positive reactions that will be remembered by tourists with hedonism, novelty, meaningfulness, and social interactions, therefore, increasing recommendation and revisit intentions (Chen et al., 2020). In this manner, it is expected that the perceived memorable experiences will increase the positive memories accumulated in the mind and the sustainability behaviors in meaningful spaces. In other words, memorable tourism experiences raise awareness of visitors, and support the development of economically, culturally, socially, and environmentally efficient management systems.

FUTURE RESEARCH DIRECTIONS

The effects of memory and memorable tourism experiences on sustainability examined in this study has not been sufficiently covered in the literature. Therefore, there is a need for more in-depth research to enrich the findings obtained in the study. In this direction, it is possible to benefit from qualitative research in order to observe the sustainability behaviors of the visitors in the destinations or activity areas where they have memorable experiences and to learn their views on this subject. With another structure, it is possible to determine how much the visitors' views match with their actual practices. Although individuals verbally express that they exhibit sustainable behaviors, what is done and what is thought may not always be in a relationship with each other. In this direction, conducting surveys could provide a broad perspective for the objective evaluation of behaviors.

RESULT

In this empirical study, the dominant effect of sustainability on memorable tourism experiences, which is frequently encountered in the literature, is examined from a reverse perspective. More specifically, it has been examined how memorable tourism experiences shape behavioral tendencies towards the sustainability of the destination or place, depending on the place in the mind or memory of the visitors.

Memory can provide an emotional and cognitive attachment to places in the minds of individuals, by providing the opportunity to remember the places seen, meals eaten and even emotions felt. This type of attachment increases visitors' sensitivity to the place and maximizes sustainability behavior. If it is considered in more detail, for instance, the fact that episodic memory includes mindfulness will guide future behaviors and encourage the person to exhibit more positive attitudes. Visitors' experiences are also seen as a predictor of sustainability, since emotional, cognitive and stimulus structures (hedonism, innovation, local culture, knowledge, meaningfulness, refreshment, involvement) are revealed in different classes of memory.

Visitors who decide to visit a place with motives such as entertainment, relaxation and novelty seeking (Lee & Crompton, 1992) are promised to have memorable experiences in tourism and recreation areas where memories are produced (Coudounaris & Sthapit, 2017). Emotionality and cognition, which are at the core of memorable experiences, encourage the individual's sense of excitement and open the door to visions for the future. For this reason, it is seen that each dimension of memorable experiences, especially the local culture dimension, affects the social, economic, cultural, and environmental sustainability behavior both individually and holistically. Therefore, businesses and destinations develop an integrative and balanced approach in all dimensions of sustainability by using experiential marketing strategies and strengthening emotional connections with experiences that are strong enough to be in the minds of visitors (Dettori, 2019).

Since memory, as both a political and social structure, cannot exist outside of politics, social relations and self-history, it represents not what the person thinks about, but what the person thinks with (Gillis, 1994). Therefore, thoughts are involved in the representation of human behavior. However, the commodification of nostalgic feelings in the memory of individuals can mean exploitation by various actors in the market (Bartoletti, 2010). Considering the cultural structures in memory as eco-systems or habitats that sometimes need to be enlarged and sometimes cut off (Merriman, 2008), memory can have an impact on increasing sustainability by eliminating possible negative experiences in the minds of individuals. In the contemporary world, the intensive use of cultural heritage and its dictation to people for a full remembering process may hinder sustainability by causing the heritage to be rendered ineffective and worthless (Harrison, 2013).

REFERENCES

Abdullahi, B. B. (2017). Examining the influence of knowledge and attitude on the intention to adopt environmentally sustainable behaviour. *International Journal of Engineering Technology and Scientific Innovation*, *2*(6), 763–771.

Ahmad, R., & Hertzog, A. (2016). Tourism, memory and place in a globalizing world. *Tourism and Hospitality Research*, *16*(3), 201–205. doi:10.1177/1467358416641254

Akyildiz, A. (2021). Tourist Behavior of People with Autism Spectrum Disorder. *Travel and Tourism Research Association: Advancing Tourism Research Globally*, *2*.

Angelkova, T., Koteski, C., Jakovlev, Z., & Mitrevska, E. (2012). Sustainability and competitiveness of tourism. *Procedia: Social and Behavioral Sciences*, *44*, 221–227. doi:10.1016/j.sbspro.2012.05.023

Artal-Tur, A., Villena-Navarro, M., & Alamá-Sabater, L. (2018). The relationship between cultural tourist behaviour and destination sustainability. *Anatolia*, *29*(2), 237–251. doi:10.1080/13032917.2017.1414444

Azevedo, A. (2010). Designing unique and memorable experiences: Co-creation and the surprise factor. *International Journal of Hospitality and Tourism Systems*, *3*(1).

Bajc, V. (2006). Collective memory and tourism: Globalizing transmission through localized experience. *Journeys*, *7*(2), 1–14. doi:10.3167/jys.2006.070201

Barber, N. A., & Deale, C. (2014). Tapping mindfulness to shape hotel guests' sustainable behavior. *Cornell Hospitality Quarterly*, *55*(1), 100–114. doi:10.1177/1938965513496315

Bartoletti, R. (2010). 'Memory tourism' and commodification of nostalgia. *Tourism and Visual Culture*, *1*, 23–42.

Bennett, A., & Rogers, I. (2016). In the scattered fields of memory: Unofficial live music venues, intangible heritage, and the recreation of the musical past. *Space and Culture*, *19*(4), 490–501. doi:10.1177/1206331215623217

Berkes, F., Colding, J., & Folke, C. (Eds.). (2008). *Navigating social-ecological systems: building resilience for complexity and change*. Cambridge University Press.

Bluck, S. (2003). Autobiographical memory: Exploring its functions in everyday life. *Memory (Hove, England)*, *11*(2), 113–123. doi:10.1080/741938206 PMID:12820825

Braun-Latour, K. A., Grınley, M. J., & Loftus, E. F. (2006). Tourist memory distortion. *Journal of Travel Research*, *44*(4), 360–367. doi:10.1177/0047287506286721

Breiby, M. A., Duedahl, E., Øian, H., & Ericsson, B. (2020). Exploring sustainable experiences in tourism. *Scandinavian Journal of Hospitality and Tourism*, *20*(4), 335–351. doi:10.1080/15022250.2020.1748706

Brown, S. D., & Reavey, P. (2015). Turning around on experience: The 'expanded view'of memory within psychology. *Memory Studies*, *8*(2), 131–150. doi:10.1177/1750698014558660

Cardona, G., Rodriguez-Fornells, A., Nye, H., Rifà-Ros, X., & Ferreri, L. (2020). The impact of musical pleasure and musical hedonia on verbal episodic memory. *Scientific Reports*, *10*(1), 1–13. doi:10.103841598-020-72772-3 PMID:32999309

Caru, A., & Cova, B. (2007). *Consuming Experiences: An Introduction. Consuming Experience*. Routledge.

Chandralal, L., & Valenzuela, F. R. (2013). Exploring memorable tourism experiences: Antecedents and behavioural outcomes. *Journal of Economics. Business and Management*, *1*(2), 177–181.

Chen, L. J., & Chen, W. P. (2015). Push–pull factors in international birders' travel. *Tourism Management*, *48*, 416–425. doi:10.1016/j.tourman.2014.12.011

Chen, X., Cheng, Z. F., & Kim, G. B. (2020). Make it memorable: Tourism experience, fun, recommendation and revisit intentions of Chinese outbound tourists. *Sustainability*, *12*(5), 1904. doi:10.3390u12051904

Cohen, E. (2002). Authenticity, equity and sustainability in tourism. *Journal of Sustainable Tourism*, *10*(4), 267–276. doi:10.1080/09669580208667167

Cooper, C. (2015). Managing tourism knowledge. *Tourism Recreation Research*, *40*(1), 107–119. doi:10.1080/02508281.2015.1006418

Coudounaris, D. N., & Sthapit, E. (2017). Antecedents of memorable tourism experience related to behavioral intentions. *Psychology and Marketing*, *34*(12), 1084–1093.

Cowan, N. (2008). *What are the differences between long-term, short-term, and working memory?* (Vol. 169). Progress in Brain Research. doi:10.1016/S0079-6123(07)00020-9

de Freitas Coelho, M., & de Gosling, M. S. (2020). The essence of memorable experience. In S. K. Dixit (Ed.), *The Routledge Handbook of Tourism Experience Management and Marketing* (pp. 88–98). doi:10.4324/9780429203916-7

de Freitas Coelho, M., de Sevilha Gosling, M., & de Almeida, A. S. A. (2018). Tourism experiences: Core processes of memorable trips. *Journal of Hospitality and Tourism Management*, *37*, 11–22. doi:10.1016/j.jhtm.2018.08.004

Dettori, A. (2019). Sustainability as a matrix of experiential marketing. *International Journal of Marketing Studies*, *11*(2), 29–37. doi:10.5539/ijms.v11n2p29

Droffelaar, B. V. (2021). Episodic memories of wilderness experiences foster sustainable leadership style transformation. *Journal of Management Development*, *40*(6), 486–502. doi:10.1108/JMD-12-2020-0393

Eichenbaum, H. (2013). Memory on time. *Trends in Cognitive Sciences, 17*(2), 81–88. doi:10.1016/j.tics.2012.12.007 PMID:23318095

Fariborz, A., Thomas, L., Richard, L., Alan, L., Gordon, B., Teresa, M., & Schiff, E. Z. (1996). Affect, attachment, memory: Contributions toward psychobiologic integration. *Psychiatry, 59*(3), 213–239. doi:10.1080/00332747.1996.11024764 PMID:27702391

Farmaki, A. (2021). Memory and forgetfulness in tourism crisis research. *Tourism Management, 83*, 104210. doi:10.1016/j.tourman.2020.104210 PMID:32904475

Fivush, R. (2011). The development of autobiographical memory. *Annual Review of Psychology, 62*(1), 559–582. doi:10.1146/annurev.psych.121208.131702 PMID:20636128

Gathercole, S. E. (1999). Cognitive approaches to the development of short-term memory. *Trends in Cognitive Sciences, 3*(11), 410–419. doi:10.1016/S1364-6613(99)01388-1 PMID:10529796

Gedi, N., & Elam, Y. (1996). Collective memory—What is it? *History & Memory, 8*(1), 30–50.

Gillis, J. R. (1994). Introduction. Memory and identity: The history of a relationship. *Commemorations*, 1–24.

Glenberg, A. M. (1997). What memory is for. *Behavioral and Brain Sciences, 20*(1), 1–55. doi:10.1017/S0140525X97000010 PMID:10096994

Hamed, H. M. (2013). Tourism and autism: An initiative study for how travel companies can plan tourism trips for autistic people. *American Journal of Tourism Management, 2*(1), 1–14.

Han, H., Lee, S., & Hyun, S. S. (2020). Tourism and altruistic intention: Volunteer tourism development and self-interested value. *Sustainability, 12*(5), 2152. doi:10.3390u12052152

Hanna, P., Font, X., Scarles, C., Weeden, C., & Harrison, C. (2018). Tourist destination marketing: From sustainability myopia to memorable experiences. *Journal of Destination Marketing & Management, 9*, 36–43. doi:10.1016/j.jdmm.2017.10.002

Harrison, R. (2013). Forgetting to remember, remembering to forget: Late modern heritage practices, sustainability and the 'crisis' of accumulation of the past. *International Journal of Heritage Studies, 19*(6), 579–595. doi:10.1080/13527258.2012.678371

Helgadóttir, G., Einarsdóttir, A. V., Burns, G. L., Gunnarsdóttir, G. Þ., & Matthíasdóttir, J. M. E. (2019). Social sustainability of tourism in Iceland: A qualitative inquiry. *Scandinavian Journal of Hospitality and Tourism, 19*(4-5), 404–421. doi:10.1080/15022250.2019.1696699

Hudson, S., & Ritchie, J. B. (2009). Branding a memorable destination experience. The case of 'Brand Canada'. *International Journal of Tourism Research, 11*(2), 217–228. doi:10.1002/jtr.720

Hussein, F., Stephens, J., & Tiwari, R. (2020). Memory for social sustainability: Recalling cultural memories in Zanqit Alsitat historical street market, Alexandria, Egypt. *Sustainability, 12*(19), 8141. doi:10.3390u12198141

Johnson, C. Y. (1998). A consideration of collective memory in African American attachment to wildland recreation places. *Human Ecology Review*, 5–15.

Jorgenson, J., Nickerson, N., Dalenberg, D., Angle, J., Metcalf, E., & Freimund, W. (2019). Measuring visitor experiences: Creating and testing the tourism autobiographical memory scale. *Journal of Travel Research*, *58*(4), 566–578. doi:10.1177/0047287518764344

Kim, A. J., Stembridge, S., Lawrence, C., Torres, V., Miodrag, N., Lee, J., & Boynes, D. (2015). Neurodiversity on the stage: The effects of inclusive theatre on youth with autism. *International Journal of Education and Social Science*, *2*(9), 27–39.

Kim, J. H. (2010). Determining the factors affecting the memorable nature of travel experiences. *Journal of Travel & Tourism Marketing*, *27*(8), 780–796. doi:10.1080/10548408.2010.526897

Kim, J. H. (2014). The antecedents of memorable tourism experiences: The development of a scale to measure the destination attributes associated with memorable experiences. *Tourism Management*, *44*, 34–45. doi:10.1016/j.tourman.2014.02.007

Kim, J. H., Ritchie, J. B., & McCormick, B. (2012). Development of a scale to measure memorable tourism experiences. *Journal of Travel Research*, *51*(1), 12–25. doi:10.1177/0047287510385467

Kim, J. H., Ritchie, J. R., & Tung, V. W. S. (2010). The effect of memorable experience on behavioral intentions in tourism: A structural equation modeling approach. *Tourism Analysis*, *15*(6), 637–648. doi:10.3727/108354210X12904412049776

Kim, Y., Ribeiro, M. A., & Li, G. (2021). Tourism memory characteristics scale: Development and validation. *Journal of Travel Research*, 1–19.

Kim, Y., Ribeiro, M. A., & Li, G. (2022). Tourism memory, mood repair and behavioral intention. *Annals of Tourism Research*, *93*, 103369. doi:10.1016/j.annals.2022.103369

Kirkpatrick, E. A. (1894). An experimental study of memory. *Psychological Review*, *1*(6), 602–609. doi:10.1037/h0068244

Klein, S. B. (2015). What memory is. *Wiley Interdisciplinary Reviews: Cognitive Science*, *6*(1), 1–38. doi:10.1002/wcs.1333 PMID:26262926

Lee, K. J., & Lee, S. Y. (2021). Cognitive appraisal theory, memorable tourism experiences, and family cohesion in rural travel. *Journal of Travel & Tourism Marketing*, *38*(4), 399–412. doi:10.1080/10548408.2021.1921094

Lee, T. H., & Crompton, J. (1992). Measuring novelty seeking in tourism. *Annals of Tourism Research*, *19*(4), 732–751. doi:10.1016/0160-7383(92)90064-V

Lee, W., & Jeong, C. (2020). Beyond the correlation between tourist eudaimonic and hedonic experiences: Necessary condition analysis. *Current Issues in Tourism*, *23*(17), 2182–2194. doi:10.1080/13683500.2019.1611747

Lidman, K., & Renström, S. (2011). *How to design for sustainable behaviour? A review of design strategies and an empirical study of four product concepts* [Unpublished Master Thesis]. Chalmers University of Technology, Sweden.

Liu, C. H., Horng, J. S., Chou, S. F., Chen, Y. C., Lin, Y. C., & Zhu, Y. Q. (2016). An empirical examination of the form of relationship between sustainable tourism experiences and satisfaction. *Asia Pacific Journal of Tourism Research*, *21*(7), 717–740. doi:10.1080/10941665.2015.1068196

Loftus, E. F. (1988). *Memory*. Rowman & Littlefield Publishers.

Lu, J., & Nepal, S. K. (2009). Sustainable tourism research: An analysis of papers published in the Journal of Sustainable Tourism. *Journal of Sustainable Tourism*, *17*(1), 5–16. doi:10.1080/09669580802582480

Mandler, G. (1980). Recognizing: The judgment of previous occurrence. *Psychological Review*, *87*(3), 252–271. doi:10.1037/0033-295X.87.3.252

Mandler, J. M., & Ritchey, G. H. (1977). Long-term memory for pictures. *Journal of Experimental Psychology. Human Learning and Memory*, *3*(4), 386–396. doi:10.1037/0278-7393.3.4.386

Marschall, S. (2012). Tourism and memory. *Annals of Tourism Research*, *39*(4), 2216–2219. doi:10.1016/j.annals.2012.07.001

Marschall, S. (2015). 'Travelling down memory lane': Personal memory as a generator of tourism. *Tourism Geographies*, *17*(1), 36–53. doi:10.1080/14616688.2014.925963

Merriman, N. (2008). Museum collections and sustainability. *Cultural Trends*, *17*(1), 3–21. doi:10.1080/09548960801920278

Michaelidou, N., & Dibb, S. (2008). Consumer involvement: A new perspective. *The Marketing Review*, *8*(1), 83–99. doi:10.1362/146934708X290403

Moliner-Tena, M. Á., Monferrer-Tirado, D., Ferreres-Bonfill, J. B., & Rodríguez-Artola, R. M. (2021). Destination sustainability and memorable tourism experiences. *Sustainability*, *13*(21), 11996. doi:10.3390u132111996

Morgan, M., & Xu, F. (2009). Student travel experiences: Memories and dreams. *Journal of Hospitality Marketing & Management*, *18*(2-3), 216–236. doi:10.1080/19368620802591967

Murzyn-Kupisz, M. (2012). Cultural, economic and social sustainability of heritage tourism: issues and challenges. *Economic and Environmental Studies (E&ES)*, *12*(2), 113-133.

Pereira, E. M., Mykletun, R. J., & Hippolyte, C. (2012). Sustainability, daily practices and vacation purchasing: Are they related? *Tourism Review*, *67*(4), 40–54. doi:10.1108/16605371211277812

Pine, B. J., & Gilmore, J. H. (1998). Welcome to the experience economy. *Harvard Business Review*, *76*(4), 97–105. PMID:10181589

Qiu, H., Fan, D. X., Lyu, J., Lin, P. M., & Jenkins, C. L. (2019). Analyzing the economic sustainability of tourism development: Evidence from Hong Kong. *Journal of Hospitality & Tourism Research (Washington, D.C.)*, *43*(2), 226–248. doi:10.1177/1096348018777046

Raulston, T. J., Hansen, S. G., Machalicek, W., McIntyre, L. L., & Carnett, A. (2019). Interventions for repetitive behavior in young children with autism: A survey of behavioral practices. *Journal of Autism and Developmental Disorders*, *49*(8), 3047–3059. doi:10.100710803-019-04023-y PMID:31030312

Ritchie, J. R., & Crouch, G. I. (2010). A model of destination competitiveness/sustainability: Brazilian perspectives. *Revista de Administração Pública, 44*(5), 1049–1066. doi:10.1590/S0034-76122010000500003

Rodrigues, Á., Loureiro, S. M. C., Lins de Moraes, M., & Pereira, R. G. (2022). Memorable tourism experience in the context of astrotourism. *Anatolia*, 1-13.

Roediger, H. L. III, & McDermott, K. B. (2013). Two types of event memory. *Proceedings of the National Academy of Sciences of the United States of America, 110*(52), 20856–20857. doi:10.1073/pnas.1321373110 PMID:24319091

Saarinen, J. (2006). Traditions of sustainability in tourism studies. *Annals of Tourism Research, 33*(4), 1121–1140. doi:10.1016/j.annals.2006.06.007

Sameer, Y. M., Elmassah, S., Mertzanis, C., & El-Maghraby, L. (2021). Are happier nations more responsible? Examining the link between happiness and sustainability. *Social Indicators Research, 158*(1), 267–295. doi:10.100711205-021-02698-4

Santos, V., Sousa, B., Ramos, P., & Valeri, M. (2021). Emotions and involvement in tourism settings. *Current Issues in Tourism*, 1–6.

Selby, M. (2004). Consuming the city: Conceptualizing and researching urban tourist knowledge. *Tourism Geographies, 6*(2), 186–207. doi:10.1080/1461668042000208426

Shafiee, M. M., Foroudi, P., & Tabaeeian, R. A. (2021). Memorable experience, tourist-destination identification and destination love. *International Journal of Tourism Cities, 7*(3), 799–817. doi:10.1108/IJTC-09-2020-0176

Shaw, C. (Ed.). (2005). *Revolutionize your customer experience*. Palgrave Macmillan. doi:10.1057/9780230513457

Shiffrin, R. M., & Atkinson, R. C. (1969). Storage and retrieval processes in long-term memory. *Psychological Review, 76*(2), 179–193. doi:10.1037/h0027277

Singer, J. A., & Salovey, P. (2010). *Remembered self: emotion and memory in personality*. Simon and Schuster.

Sisson, A. D., & Alcorn, M. R. (2021). How was your music festival experience? Impacts on loyalty, word-of-mouth, and sustainability behaviors. *Event Management*.

Skavronskaya, L., Scott, N., Moyle, B., & Kralj, A. (2019). Novelty and the tourism experience. *Current Issues in Tourism*.

Skavronskaya, L., Scott, N., Moyle, B., Le, D., Hadinejad, A., Zhang, R., Gardiner, S., Coghlan, A., & Shakeela, A. (2017). Cognitive psychology and tourism research: State of the art. *Tourism Review, 72*(2), 221–237. doi:10.1108/TR-03-2017-0041

Solís-Radilla, M. M., Hernández-Lobato, L., Callarisa-Fiol, L. J., & Pastor-Durán, H. T. (2019). The importance of sustainability in the loyalty to a tourist destination through the management of expectations and experiences. *Sustainability, 11*(15), 4132. doi:10.3390u11154132

Sthapit, E., Del Chiappa, G., Coudounaris, D. N., & Björk, P. (2019). Tourism experiences, memorability and behavioural intentions: A study of tourists in Sardinia, Italy. *Tourism Review*, *75*(3), 533–558. doi:10.1108/TR-03-2019-0102

Stone, M. J., Migacz, S., & Sthapit, E. (2021). Connections between culinary tourism experiences and memory. *Journal of Hospitality & Tourism Research (Washington, D.C.)*, *46*(4), 797–807. doi:10.1177/1096348021994171

Thal, K. I. (2016). Macro Scale Assessment of Sustainability in Tourism. *Travel and Tourism Research Association: Advancing Tourism Research Globally*, *18*.

Tulving, E. (2002). Episodic memory: From mind to brain. *Annual Review of Psychology*, *53*(1), 1–25. doi:10.1146/annurev.psych.53.100901.135114 PMID:11752477

Tung, V. W. S., Lin, P., Qiu Zhang, H., & Zhao, A. (2017). A framework of memory management and tourism experiences. *Journal of Travel & Tourism Marketing*, *34*(7), 853–866. doi:10.1080/10548408.2016.1260521

Tung, V. W. S., & Ritchie, J. B. (2011). Exploring the essence of memorable tourism experiences. *Annals of Tourism Research*, *38*(4), 1367–1386. doi:10.1016/j.annals.2011.03.009

van Dam, Y. K., & van Trijp, H. C. (2011). Cognitive and motivational structure of sustainability. *Journal of Economic Psychology*, *32*(5), 726–741. doi:10.1016/j.joep.2011.06.002

Wan, Y. K. P., & Li, X. (2013). Sustainability of tourism development in Macao, China. *International Journal of Tourism Research*, *15*(1), 52–65. doi:10.1002/jtr.873

Wang, T. C., Cheng, J. S., Shih, H. Y., Tsai, C. L., Tang, T. W., Tseng, M. L., & Yao, Y. S. (2019). Environmental sustainability on tourist hotels' image development. *Sustainability*, *11*(8), 2378. doi:10.3390u11082378

Waugh, N. C., & Norman, D. A. (1965). Primary memory. *Psychological Review*, *72*(2), 89–104. doi:10.1037/h0021797 PMID:14282677

Wei, C., Zhao, W., Zhang, C., & Huang, K. (2019). Psychological factors affecting memorable tourism experiences. *Asia Pacific Journal of Tourism Research*, *24*(7), 619–632. doi:10.1080/10941665.2019.1611611

Wilson, E., & Harris, C. (2006). Meaningful travel: Women, independent travel and the search for self and meaning. *Tourism: An International Interdisciplinary Journal*, *54*(2), 161–172.

Wood, E. H. (2020). I remember how we all felt: Perceived emotional synchrony through tourist memory sharing. *Journal of Travel Research*, *59*(8), 1339–1352. doi:10.1177/0047287519888290

Xu, C., Zhong, S., Li, P., & Xiao, X. (2021). Tourist memory and childhood landscape. *Journal of Tourism and Cultural Change*, 1–21. doi:10.1080/14766825.2021.2015358

Yu, C. P., Chang, W. C., & Ramanpong, J. (2019). Assessing visitors' memorable tourism experiences (MTEs) in forest recreation destination: A case study in Xitou nature education area. *Forests*, *10*(8), 636. doi:10.3390/f10080636

Zhang, X., Chen, Z., & Jin, H. (2021). The effect of tourists' autobiographical memory on revisit intention: Does nostalgia promote revisiting? *Asia Pacific Journal of Tourism Research*, *26*(2), 147–166. doi:10.1080/10941665.2020.1718171

ADDITIONAL READING

Ahmad, R., & Hertzog, A. (2016). Tourism, memory and place in a globalizing world. *Tourism and Hospitality Research*, *16*(3), 201–205. doi:10.1177/1467358416641254

Berkes, F., Colding, J., & Folke, C. (Eds.). (2008). *Navigating social-ecological systems: building resilience for complexity and change*. Cambridge University Press.

Farmaki, A. (2021). Memory and forgetfulness in tourism crisis research. *Tourism Management*, *83*, 104210. doi:10.1016/j.tourman.2020.104210 PMID:32904475

Marschall, S. (2015). 'Travelling down memory lane': Personal memory as a generator of tourism. *Tourism Geographies*, *17*(1), 36–53. doi:10.1080/14616688.2014.925963

Winter, P. L., Selin, S., Cerveny, L., & Bricker, K. (2019). Outdoor recreation, nature-based tourism, and sustainability. *Sustainability*, *12*(1), 81. doi:10.3390u12010081

KEY TERMS AND DEFINITIONS

Hedonism: The emotional or well-being state that ensures a high level of satisfaction, pleasure, fun and happiness experienced during the visit.

Local Culture: Local features of cultural, historical or lifestyle specific to the destination visited.

Memorable Tourism Experience: Experiences that are powerful, meaningful, and unique enough to remember for a long time.

Memory: Mental activity that facilitates human life and directs behavior by mediating the recollection of events and facts.

Novelty: It refers to the curiosity awaking and surprising content in which the level of familiarity and knowledge of individuals is low in the process of visiting certain destinations or activity areas.

Sustainability: Macro environmental factors that need to be developed and sustained in social, cultural, economic, and environmental dimensions in order to facilitate and improve the living conditions of future generations.

Chapter 10
Tourism and Women

Ayse Deliormanli
https://orcid.org/0000-0001-9577-484X
Beykent University, Turkey

ABSTRACT

Gender-related issues have not lost their importance from the past to the present and are being carefully emphasized. As one of the important subjects of sociology, gender and gender discrimination continues to exist in the tourism sector as well. There are basic predispositions for both employment in tourism and the participation of women as consumers in tourism activities. The roles socially determined for women can create an obstacle for women to participate in working life. The same attitude is observed at the stage of women's participation in tourism activities. In particular, the risks and concerns faced by women traveling as a group or alone indicate the perspective on women has not changed. Based on this point of view, this study aims to present the relationship between gender and tourism, the experiences of women both in working life and in tourism activities as a tourist in a theoretical framework.

INTRODUCTİON

Regarding gender relations, the roles and responsibilities assigned to women or men by society are taken into consideration (Beavouir, 2010). Gender has always been regarded as a critical boundary issue in the sociological study of tourism (Cohen & Cohen, 2019). According to Kinnaird and Hall (1996), tourism encompasses processes consisting of complex and diverse realities along with often hierarchical and unequal relationships. Studies have illustrated that women, compared to men, are generally less capable of gaining access and benefiting from tourism jobs and the pertaining business world (Swain, 1995). The differences between men and women can be mitigated applying certain changes in the development of gender perception, and for this, sectors need to display a non-sexist approach.

Tourism is one of the leading and significant employment fields within the service sector. Concurrently, being among the sectors generating the most income, tourism plays a helpful role in reducing gender discrimination and the differences between men and women (Karaçar, 2018). The development of tourism has an impact on the change of women's position with respect to men and in the society itself, as well as

DOI: 10.4018/978-1-6684-4645-4.ch010

their different roles outside the home. It is clear that women work outside the household, participate in travels and even travel alone. Through the inclusion of women in working life, the economic power they have gained enables women to make purchases for the house and for themselves (Sürücü & Ak, 2018).

Positive developments in the economic sense initiated with the participation of women in business life, then they continued to participate in tourism activities in their spare time (Khan, 2011). In this part of the study, it has been tried to give a detailed theoretical framework and information on the women's participation in the tourism sector focusing on gender and women, women in the tourism sector, and women as tourists.

SOCIAL GENDER AND WOMEN

The basic values attributed to women are considered to be caring for family members. Sentences beginning with "What you call a woman…" lead to the limitations imposed on them (Beavouir, 2010). Regarding the use of their spare time, within the framework of the responsibilities associated with the roles set by society, women are prevented from being given a voice to express themselves. Not being outside for late times, not laughing loudly in public, not being intimate with the opposite sex and other predispositions supporting these stereotypes are the patterns of being a woman that is not difficult but is made difficult by the society. Such stereotypes, been in existence since ancient societies, restrict women's freedom of movement (Doğru, 2010).

The most important reason for this is the gender-oriented predispositions formed by social and cultural value judgments separating men and women (Kargiglioğlu & Özer, 2018). Gender can be expressed as all of the generalizations and expectations attributed to women and men by society (Ökten, 2009). Apart from the biological difference pertaining to the gender of the individuals, gender expresses the superiority and advantage of one sex over the other and constitutes the polarity of femininity and masculinity created by the patriarchal system. This view, in which women are most oppressed, has been criticized by various thinkers. In his work titled, *The Subjection of Women* on gender, J. S. Mill (1869) expressed the oppression of women as: "The dominance of one gender over the other is the greatest obstacle to the development of humanity, along with being wrong per se" (Donovan, 1997: 62).

In his book *State*, in which he expresses the ideal state, Plato elaborates on the thoughts of the sophists, he maintains that their idea of considering the people inherently good and equal, in fact, is a social order that corrupts people. In parallel with the thought proposed by the sophists, Plato emphasized that women and men have equal rights (Yücel, 2020).

The themes in gender and women's psychology actually reflect the social structuring of these concepts. Feminist theories see gender not as biological differences but as a socially constructed reality. According to the social configuration, as a result of not having the chance to experience the truth directly, the periphery is evaluated in light of the information obtained from previous experiences and the events.

In other words, it is a theoretical perspective describing the situation to make assumptions based on experience and beliefs rather than discovering the truth (Else-Quest & Hyde, 2021). As well as being a personal feature, gender is an important stimulus. For instance, when a baby is born as a boy or a girl, behaviors such as the reactions given by a woman or a man show the importance of the stimulus.

Social gender stereotypes can be defined as cultural beliefs interpreted concerning the behavior, interests, and personalities of men and women. Studies have revealed that the differences between men and women are felt even in modern communities (Else-Quest & Hyde, 2021). In their study, Ghavami and Peplau (2013) asked participants to describe men and women and elaborate on the data obtained. The themes obtained by the researchers are listed in order of frequency (from the most to the least):

Table 1. Top 15 Characteristics Listed for Women and Men. Source: Ghawami and Peplau, 2013

Women	Men
Duygusal (Emotional)	Uzun boylu (Tall)
Şefkatli (Caring)	Fiziksel olarak güçlü (Physically strong)
Yumuşak başlı (Soft)	Saygı duyulan (Respected)
Dış görünüşüne önem veren (Care about appearance)	Zeki (Intelligent)
Konuşkan (Talkative)	Yüksek statüye sahip (Have high status)
Minyon (Small build)	Lider (Leaders)
Uysal (Submissive)	Cinsiyetçi (Sexist)
Bağımlı (Dependent)	Sporsever (Like sports)
Anaç (Motherly)	Geçim sağlayan (Providers)
Kadınsı (Feminine) Manipülatif (Manipulative)	Agrasif (Aggressive) Sadakatsiz (Unfaithfu)
Çekici (Attractive) Seks objesi (Sexual objects) Maddiyatçı (Materialistic)	Hırslı (Ambitious) Kibirli (Arrogant) Dağınık (Messy)

The table shows that the stereotypes attributed to women and men have not changed over the years. For instance, the attitude of considering women as emotional, compassionate, and talkative has always been a characteristic of women in societies since past times. In the same way, the characteristics of being intelligent, strong, and a leader for men are among the social stereotypes (Else-Quest & Hyde, 2021). Despite the fact that there are critical predispositions to women's being outside the home, there are expectations for women's work (Duffy et al, 2015), and women at home are subject to complaints by their husbands in certain times and cases.

Presenting interview data contrary to this idea, Duffy et al. (2015), taken from an opinion put forth by one of the participants claiming that "a man works, a woman takes care of a house", underlined that there are both expectations for women and social predispositions continue to exist. Until recently, the economic roles of men and women differed. While men were responsible for bringing income to the household by working outside, women stayed at home and were in charge of household chores management. Cooking, bearing and raising children, and cleaning the house were the duties set for women (Sarmiento, 1998).

In the 20th century, through women starting to work outside the home in America, women began to have different roles. As a consequence of the increase in women's participation in the workforce, the division of labor between men and women in the market became more equal in a speedy fashion. While this situation progressed rapidly in the working environment, the responsibility sharing matters within the household took time. The time men spend on housework tends to increase as women's education, employment and earnings increase (Sarmiento, 1998). In addition to women's economic empowerment being a right, any sort of economic power gained will enable them to show the magnitude of their benefits for their families, and communities, resulting in national development (Ferguson, 2010). Initiating economic opportunities for women will pave the ground for a faster way of reducing poverty.

THE IMPACTS OF TOURISM ON SOCIAL GENDER

While existing gender definitions create an 'independent' effect on the formation of tourism workforce patterns in different fields, with the growth of tourism, it is also thought to contribute to changing the attitudes on gender definitions (Swain, 1995). Besides transforming cultures, customs and traditions into sold commodities, tourism also provides an understanding of the ideological structure of culture (Richards, 1996). The interactions among the tourists and local communities act as a means of reflecting these ideologies. The values and cultural structure of the local community will be shaped by the attitude towards the tourists. As Trucker (2007) maintains that tourism development continues to interact with other aspects of social change, as well as gender-based socio-spatial relationships in certain regions, studying these interactions will provide a better understanding of the ways in which gender-based identities are negotiated and reconstructed through tourism.

Emphasizing the necessity of considering gender norms as a negotiation, Meethan (2001) believes that gender norms are "continuities that include the global movement of people and tourists on the one hand, and locality dynamics on the other. The author states that the relationships on which tourism is based are dynamic, heterogeneous and mutually constructive among the visitor-host, client-tour guide, as well as the multinational and local organizations.

Safa (2018) maintains that tourism reduces women's dependence on their male partners and that expanding women's social activities outside the home is central to reducing gender inequality. In spite of the fact that the tourism sector provides employment opportunities for women, long working hours in the active season, shift system (night shift) and seasonal demands in the structure of the sector can create obstacles for women in their working fields. Accordingly, employing men instead of women is considered appropriate (Santero-Sanchez et al., 2015).

Therefore, despite the obstacles in tourism, in developed countries, women are employed in high-level jobs in glamorous hotels and restaurants (Goh & Lee, 2018). This opinion is on par with the ILO view that socially constructed gender roles are crucial for promoting sustainable tourism to which both men and women contribute, regardless of their biological differences (Mitra et al, 2022).

Another issue in which the gender phenomenon makes itself felt is the choice of profession. The definition of some jobs being as men's and some as women's jobs draws attention to the discrimination in choosing a profession. Therefore, the personnel to be selected are evaluated based on the employer's perception of gender (Parlaktuna, 2010). Kinnaird and Hall (1996) state that the careers in the tourism sector are separated by gender, and women are employed in most of the unqualified professions. Based on these statements, it can be said that gender differences differ within the framework of stereotypes expected from men and women (Nalbant & Korkmaz, 2019).

Along with offering significant opportunities for gender inequality, tourism creates difficulties as well (Rinaldi & Salerno, 2020). Concerning the development of women in the tourism sector within the gender equality development, Su et al. (2020) expressed their views on the fact that participation in cultural heritage exhibitions and tourism practices in rural areas will be effective in their development. Irrespective of the fact that women's status has improved with the development of tourism, there are also studies indicating that the barriers to achieving gender equality in the tourism sector continue to exist. Duffy et al. (2015) drew attention to the necessity of limiting women's participation in the tourism sector, maintaining that women's becoming economically and socially independent brings about new gender roles and status changes besides conflicts in family relations. It has also been stated that women entrepreneurs encounter ongoing discrimination regarding their education level and gender (Nomnga, 2017).

Gender inequality is a common and complex phenomenon rooted in the socio-economic culture of many countries (Mitra et al, 2022). In certain societies, women and tourism affairs can be approached more harshly. For example, in Islamic societies, women face discrimination in tourism participation due to social and cultural factors (Alrwajfah et al., 2020). The restrictions on women's participation in the tourism sector are related to religious and traditional constraints, political obstacles, women's role in decision-making, women's domestic roles and gender characteristics (Sönmez, 2001; Tucker, 2007; Trupp & Sunanta, 2017).

Stating that tourism contributes to the psychological, social, political and economic empowerment of women, Gil Arroyo et al. (2019), concluded that despite all these effects, traditional social cultures prevent women from fully enjoying the benefits of tourism. Due to these restrictions, gender inequalities in the tourism industry still make their presence felt today. In some studies, it has been indicated that the tourism perception develops more in men than in women and that the interest in tourism shows more positive developments in men. In a study on rural areas of New Zealand (Mason and Cheyne, 2000), it was found that men participate more in tourism development than women and perceive more positive effects.

Several scholars (Kinnard & Hall, 1996; Truker, 2007; Swain, 1995; Zhang & Zhang, 2020) have emphasized on the importance of gaining an understanding of how gender has shaped tourism processes over time and how gender has been shaped as a result of these processes. Due to culturally defined gender identity, roles and relationships, in many contexts, women miss out on employment opportunities and the associated benefits of tourism development (Trucker, 2007). Therefore, some tourism development projects focusing on the law income class have deliberately targeted the "economic empowerment" of women through encouraging and supporting women's participation in small and micro businesses (Ferguson, 2010).

The aim of such projects is an approach that deals with rural development within the scope of minimizing poverty in tourism (Doğan & Bilici, 2020). Another approach being effective in the development of local people is community-based tourism. With community-based tourism, while the cultural exchange between local people and tourists will be experienced, environmental and cultural values will be preserved as well (Yordam & Dusmezkalender, 2019).

TOURISM AND GENDER EQUALITY

The employment of women and the relative increase in their incomes and the change in their education levels confirm the rising status of women in the society. Changes in women's status in society are also reflected in the development of tourism. In addition, employment of women in the tourism industry results in changes in the society (Zhang & Zhang, 2020). Studies indicating that tourism theoretically contributes to gender equality and empowerment of women (Font et al, 2016: 1444; Cole, 2018) support this result. Cole (2018) advocates the existence of a relationship between tourism and women, believing that women experience positive changes in their status through the mentioned industry and that they can and should use tourism judiciously to improve their status. Zhang and Zhang (2020) determined that tourism enjoys a significant level of (1%) on gender equality in East and Southeast Asian countries and that tourism is a proper sector regarding improving gender equality.

The researchers concluded that in Muslim countries in Western Asia, women's workplaces were constrained by cultural traditions to "women's" workplaces as unique to women, and women were not socially welcomed to work in so-called "male" areas. In addition, the researchers maintain that the evaluation of the tourism field as a more "women's" field in Asian countries ensures more women employment in the tourism sectors in conservative societies. Additionally, the UNWTO (2019) report suggests information concerning the fact that most of the hosts in the Airbnb industry in Asia are women, showing that women are not only employed in a career, but also have the entrepreneurship opportunity. Enabling women to be economically free, this sector paves the ground for the emergence and development of education, skills and abilities along with financial support. Scientific studies, researches and reports prove that tourism is a sector that can be improved in terms of gender equality.

On account of development of the rural aspect of tourism and the emergence of rural tourism, there has been a change in the status of women living in rural areas. In particular, through supporting the necessary training of women in their work in tourism, public and non-governmental organizations have contributed to reducing the gender gap in Asia. For instance, there are women ministers in charge of tourism in the Philippines, Cambodia and Georgia in Asia (Zhang & Zhang, 2020). In certain regions of Asia, the impact of tourism can be seen in different areas.

Nonetheless, the effect of tourism on women's empowerment and gender equality is undeniable. The fact that women are employed in tourism in the face of gender inequality, as well as being able to travel as a tourist, sometimes with family, sometimes with groups, and sometimes alone, helps to break the gender perception. The place of women in tourism has started to rise not only as an employee but also as a consumer. Especially recently, studies on individual travel attract the attention of women, and enable women to develop their courage and self-confidence.

TOURISM AND WOMEN

Gender is part of the "basic" identity emerging early in life and continuing throughout life. While the "social gender" concept refers to the social, cultural and psychological aspects of men's and women's life, the term "gender" refers to the biological aspects of being a man or a woman (Jucan & Jucan, 2013). Considering gender in the tourism context, it can be said that tourism plays a mediating role in eliminating gender inequality. When tourism is considered as for a female in particular, negative reactions can be given to the participation in tourism activities. The notion that adventure, pleasure, excitement, and equivalent activities are unique to men is seen as the reason for negative reactions in women's participation in tourism. Beside tourism activities, women encounter many stereotypes that are suppressed by society in daily life (Korkmaz et al., 2019).

The tourism sector is also of great importance in promoting gender equality and increasing women's income and employment (Zhang & Zhang, 2020). With women starting to work and earn in tourism, cultural values dominated by patriarchal cultures gradually began to be questioned. Furthermore, especially in developing communities, families have opened their homes to tourism and entered the accommodation industry, resulting in increasing the earnings made by women and the rate of their work as a boss (Farmaki, 2019). As a rapidly growing and developing sector in the world, tourism brings important transformations for many countries (Çiçek et al., 2017).

In particular, its economic contributions are reflected in the sub-areas affecting the service sector directly or indirectly. Each service or product put into operation as necessary for the development of tourism reveals the demands for employment. Besides being hectic in terms of physical capital, the tourism sector requires a variety of skilled labor and, hence, investment in human capital (Sinclair, 1998).

The traditionally set gender roles affect women's participation in small-scale tourism businesses to a great extent (Garcia-Ramon et al., 1995). Mentioned more and more in the production field, women are in the position of important users in consumption areas as a result of developments in social change. Especially, in the travel context, the travel groups formed by women coming together gain momentum. Headings like women traveling alone, traveling on her own, and traveling women are popular tourism movements both in literature and in daily life. On social media platforms such as Facebook and Instagram, membership for groups formed as "women traveling group", women travelers, and women traveling the world with caravans are on the rise.

In addition, the same groups create pages on Instagram, share their experiences and motivate other female users. It is planned to write a chapter focusing on the changing roles of women in tourism and the changes that tourism itself creates in women. In this respect, we believe that this study trying to convey the knowledge of being a woman in tourism through channels such as blogs, vlogs, columns, and posts on social media will contribute to the literature (Sinclair, 1997).

WOMEN WORKING IN THE TOURISM SECTOR

In both developing and industrialized countries, tourism employment is gender-structured since most of the top jobs are held by men, whereas low-paid, part-time and seasonal jobs are predominantly performed by women (Zencirkıtan, 2017). It is known that women have been working since primitive societies (Karaçar, 2018). Women, who have been working since primitive societies, still take their place in working life today. However, women are exposed to some discrimination in their roles at every stage of their lives. Despite many developments in almost every field throughout history, women have always remained backstage (Akoğlan, 1996). In some societies, the value given to women was so meager that they were not even given the chance to survive. Starting with the industrial revolution, women began to be evaluated and recognized for the first time, and as of the 19th century, women's adaptation to business life was fully fulfilled. Women's initiation to participate in the service sector took place after the 1950s (Karaçar, 2018).

Equality and discrimination in gender-related issues are the circumstances faced by women. Equality, defined as "the state of being equal of two or more things" by the Turkish Language Institution, is also on par with the concepts like "equivalence (TLI, 2022). Discrimination concept expressing the state of being discriminated (TLI, 2022), refers to the processes of exclusion, exposure and separation of people (Doğrul, 2007). Women encounter many difficulties due to the gender roles directed at them. They work in many professions under unequal conditions, unequal wages and unequal employment standards (Zencirkıran, 2017).

Considered as the forefront of discrimination against women, Gender discrimination is felt in the form of the power imbalance between men and women, inequality in enjoying resources and opportunities, inability to benefit from basic services at equal rates, and constraints in business life (Demirbilek, 2007).

Taking into account the types of discrimination against women, it is known that gender discrimination in business life, discrimination between departments, discrimination based on power, inequality in wages and discrimination based on age come to the fore (Karaçar, 2018).

Although gender equality is recognized by law in many countries, inequalities between men and women persist, especially in employment. Many jobs performed by women, including cooking, cleaning, arranging the beds and welcoming, etc. directly and indirectly contribute to employment (Karaçar, 2018). Changes in social life have also been reflected in the production and consumption areas where women are involved, and some professions and jobs have begun to be regarded as women-oriented. It is observed that women have penetrated in the service sector, encompassing hostess and nursing jobs and in the education sector in particular. The tourism sector is one of these areas. Especially, the reception, housekeeping and kitchen areas (Tekin, 2017) are named as labor-intensive as well as feminine dominated areas (Akoğlan, 1996).

Men and women tend to concentrate on gender-based jobs considered appropriate for their gender (Costa et al, 2011). Despite mentioning the differences in terms of both genders (male and female), women remain backstage. In a way that, observably, in occupational hierarchies, men are represented in higher ranks and women are in lower ranks (vertical separation) (Gustafson, 2006). Stating that there are horizontal and vertical distinctions in gender discrimination in the tourism sector, as in other sectors, Karaçar (2018) argued that the horizontal gender distinction is formed by the classification of jobs as feminine and masculine, and the vertical gender distinction is formed by the existence of a gender pyramid. In the tourism sector, if men are in the top managerial positions, it becomes difficult for women to be promoted. The most outstanding premise of such circumstance is that although the number of female employees is higher than that of male employees, women are mostly employed at lower levels and/or women are paid less than men (Cave & Kılıç, 2010).

Çiçek et al. (2017) noted that the differences between men and women are also observed in terms of wages, and in the tourism industry women generally earn 10% to 15% less than men. Grasmuck and Espinal (2000) argued that developments in gender were effective in a woman's development of social roles outside the home through employment and the decrease in her economic independence from men. Tucker and Boonabaana (2012) maintain that women gain autonomy becoming independent through working, as well as they gain prestige as a result of their earnings and offer financial support to their families. According to Ferguson (2010), male-dominated household income will move away from male dominance thanks to the earnings and returns obtained by women, it can create a change in the balance of power within the household, and as a result, women can demand more rights and independence due to their increasing economic contribution.

So as to increase the economic power of women, many gender-sensitive regulations in the macroeconomic level are implemented every day. With such reform in regulations, the number of women entrepreneurs in the tourism sector has increased significantly. Taking advantage of the sharing economy and especially online platforms, women have made progress towards making a living not only for themselves but also for their families (Mitra et al, 2022). Women constitute a remarkable portion of the tourism workforce on a global scale. 55% of the online platform Airbnb's worldwide accommodation is allocated to them, (Farmaki & Kladou, 2020). Although women make up 60-70% of the workforce, there is a marked disparity in women's empowerment (ILO, 2010).

Tourism and Women

Empowering and educating girls and women and making full use of their talents and leadership in the global economy, politics and society are essential elements of success and development in the modern competitive world (Jucan & Jucan, 2013). The 2030 Agenda for Sustainable Development is among the works to be done to empower women. The women-oriented affairs engulfing the center of the agenda will be an important tool in realizing the commitments attributed to women (UNWTO, 2019). Women are recognized as key participants in the tourism labor market (Jafari & Scott, 2014). Religion, culture and society are key determinants of women's employment in tourism (Shakeela & Cooper, 2009). The observations made by the authors of this article indicate that in many hotel and tourism schools around the world, approximately 70% of students - the future workforce of tourism - are women and the percentage is increasing (Jafari & Scott, 2014). Various studies have also been conducted to analyze gender bias in the tourism sector focusing on general empowerment and community participation (Boley et al, 2017; Morgan & Winkler, 2020; Ferguson, 2011).

WOMEN LABOR FORCE IN THE TOURISM SECTOR

An increase in women's employment is highly effective in reducing poverty, sustaining economic growth and promoting women's empowerment and independence. Increasing female labor force participation and hours worked by women are proven to be the primary factors of growing Gross Domestic Product (GDP) for the G7 economies. Having more female employees at different levels in organizations contributes to diversity and innovation and can result in improved corporate governance. Women's elated presence in corporate leadership positions improves company performance in all areas of operation, including innovation, working environment and the associated values, leadership, accountability and external orientation.

Companies in the top quartile for female representation on executive committees enjoy an average of 47% higher return on equity than companies having no women on their boards of directors. In many countries, Travel and Tourism employs more women than most other industries, thence, the role of the industry in providing opportunities for women, especially in developing and emerging countries, cannot be underestimated. Despite the fact that many countries have taken important measures towards gender equality in education, health, economic and political dimensions, much remains to be done to achieve full equality. Irrespective of the progress made so far, women's workspace is far from equal to that of men. Indeed, in most countries, women receive on average only 60 to 75 percent of men's wages. According to the World Economic Forum, women hold only 34% of management positions, and on average only 18% of government ministers are women. For instance, according to the World Bank, only 5% of Travel and Tourism companies have a female general manager and only 4% have a female majority stake.

Travel and Tourism, particularly in developing countries, can provide women with more opportunities than many other sectors concerning the workforce participation, leadership, entrepreneurship and empowerment and can therefore have a tremendous impact on poverty reduction in rural communities. Worldwide, Travel and Tourism has almost twice as many female employers as any other industry, proving significant opportunities for women to run their own businesses in the industry. In this respect, Latin America is the leader, with more than half of tourism businesses run by women, the values which is more than twice the other sectors. Notably, compared to 20% in other sectors, more than 70% of tourism business owners in Panama and Nicaragua are women.

Indonesia, Malaysia, the Philippines and Thailand are among the prominent countries across Asia where more than half of the tourism businesses are run by women (WTTC Travel and Tourism, 2019). Looking at the change in the share of women in Travel and Tourism and the employment rate in the total economy between 2007 and 2017, it has been observed that the share of women's employment in the sector has also seen a significant improvement. Table 1 below shows the employment data of women in tourism by countries and countries.

Table 2. Changes in the share of women in Travel and Tourism and total economy employment (2007-2017)

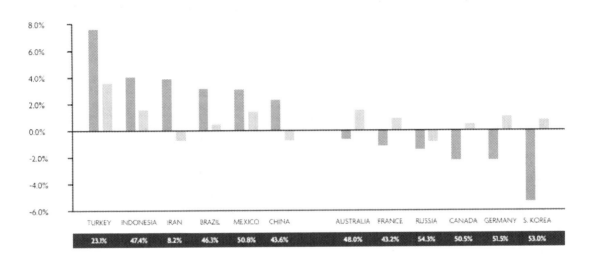

An increase in the travel activities of women has been witnessed in Muslim societies in recent years, and similarly, there has been an increase in opportunities for women in tourism in the patriarchal society structure such as the Middle East. It is supported by studies that almost 1 in 10 people working in tourism in the Middle East are women and this ratio is to increase. Published by the World Tourism Organization (UNWTO) and the Ministry of Tourism of the Kingdom of Saudi Arabia, the Regional Report on Women in Tourism in the Middle East maintains that besides this progress, improvements have been made in the field of gender in the tourism sector.

In addition, in the second edition of the Global Report on Women in Tourism, it was stated that 8% of the people employed in tourism in the region and 54% of the people employed in tourism at the global level are women (UNWTO, 2021). Based on the data published by The World Bank Group report in 2017, taken from interviews conducted with women in Costa Rica, Belize and Honduras, women have expressed their willingness to work in tourism and the sector provided them with a much better life than other paid jobs such as in the dairy or citrus industry. Younger women also said it was a great way to make a living and an opportunity to meet a wide variety of people and gain more confidence through these interactions (The World Bank Group, 2017).

WOMEN AS TOURISTS

Physical, social, and cultural needs of the individual are endless, but the resources to meet them are limited. Economic plan and movements are required to meet these needs. The ability of an individual to continue his life is achieved by consuming products and services. Consumptions are sometimes based on necessity and sometimes based on desires. Which product and service to be consumed depends entirely on the decision made by the consumer (Sürücü and Ak, 2018).

Evaluating the consumer concept in the tourism context (İçöz, 2001), tourists are considered as potential consumers as they consume goods and services. Consumption also differs in the context of gender differences. For instance, female consumers shop more emotionally than male consumers. In online shopping, women are more hesitant to buy compared to men. The reason for this is the high tendency to buy the product through touching and examining (Özdemir & Tokol, 2008).

Consequently, it is possible to separate the consumers as men and women and to produce and prepare services and products for these two groups as the consumption behavior of both groups differs. Historically, traveling has been more regarded as a male activity, though women have traveled as well. The spaces attributed to women have generally been private or domestic spaces such as home and family. Gender-oriented spaces or places have been considered and evaluated as a mechanism function by which a more powerful group maintains and consolidates its advantage over another less powerful group (Spain, 1992). Accordingly, through traveling or being away from home, women develop insight, power, and identities crossing the boundaries of the gendered space (Fan et al, 2021).

The values, beliefs, and preferred social life of a society affect the behavior toward men and women. The concepts attributed to gender may affect the decisions regarding travel at some point. In the early 1970s, the issues pertaining to women and gender were not included in the magazines. Men's experiences were considered universal (Myers, 2010). Traveling was attributed mainly to men depending on gender roles, and more importantly, there might be concerns about the safety of women during travel.

Especially in contemporary Western societies, there are more leisure options for women to access tourism and they have the required resources and opportunities. However, these options for women to access travel experiences may be restricted due to their social and gender-based position as women. Studies focusing on leisure time illustrate that leisure activities outside the home tend to be heavily restricted (Wilson & Litte, 2005).

Nonetheless, the desire of women to make their own decisions and travel alone or as a group reached an important point by the passage of time. Historical records reveal that women have traveled for centuries, and they still travel. It is stated that 35 million people travel alone in the USA as of 2005, a total of 47% of whom are women (Chiang & Jogaratnam, 2005). The change in the traditional family ideologies and the changing expectations about marriage and childcare has also enabled women to act more freely. It is to say that an increasing number of women around the world are realizing their independence, they are more motivated to travel than ever before and are starting to travel more.

By moving away from the identities like "wife", "mother", "girlfriend", and "housewife", women get the opportunity to travel alone for their own satisfaction and pleasure. Women of all ages now travel with groups of close friends, as two or as a single person (Myers, 2010). However, recently, traveling alone and exploring new places seems attractive to many travelers. When considered in this context, it can be stated that women traveling alone constitute a significant market (Chiang & Jogaratnam, 2005).

Due to the change in the image attributed to women during the period 1970-1980, women started to dominate in all types of travel, including business travel and even they started to make up a very high proportion of business travelers. Of course, this situation is also linked to the employment of women on a global scale (Wilson & Litte, 2005). Although the number of female tourists is increasing, compared to me, it may be riskier and more insecure due to many possible circumstances they may encounter during travel. However, risk-taking provides women with a crucial advantage in building their social identities and resisting social expectations (Yang & Khoo-Lattimore, 2017).

CONCLUSION

In the tourism industry, empowering all members of the population is essential to foster sustainable growth (Alarcón & Cole, 2019). As women generally work in jobs with low wages and flexible working hours, gender bias is important. Therefore, the main causes of gender inequality lie in gender inequalities in income and employment, as well as important social and cultural factors (Mitra et al., 2022). In this respect, tourism needs strengthening in social, political and cultural to reduce gender inequalities. In their study, Mitra et al. (2022) concluded that not all low-income countries promote general gender inequality through tourism.

The merits of a higher tourism income will begin to become evident when the income increases from tourism exceed expectations. As tourism develops, there will be an increase in employment and the created demand will not just be met by men, it will bring about opportunities for women as well. Therefore, low-income countries can develop themselves adopting balanced approaches to tourism resources and other economic activities. As a result of accrued income obtained from tourism, low-income countries adopting tourism activities will have economic and social benefits. Consequently, gender inequality will be reduced.

In their study, Sürücü and Ak (2018) stated that gender differences are not limited to travel preferences and that tourism businesses now offer services according to these gender differences. In recent years, arising from the transformation of women's travel activities into a more dynamic structure, tourism enterprises have started to organize their products according to the tastes of women. In this regard, hotel businesses try to appeal to women by placing lotions and scented soaps in rooms, and the beauty salons in the hotels also offer services to draw the attention of women.

At this point, there is an element to be considered is the security service offered to women. As for tourism, there are a number of problems faced by female consumers, and their solution is important. When traveling alone or with women's groups, women face uncomfortable situations such as sexual harassment (Khan, 2011).

Practices to be conducted by tourism businesses to address women's security concerns will increase the preference of businesses by women. This will increase the competition between businesses serving women consumers. The obstacles faced by women are not limited only during their travels, they actually start with the predispositions of the society even before the trip. Apostolopoulos and Sonmez (2001) argue that although women's travel behaviors reflect their own societal norms and values, cultural or religious restrictions on their social roles and socio-economic constraints are likely to determine their travel abilities and styles.

When the literature is examined, it is seen that there are differences in consumption behaviors between men and women. In particular, due to their nature, the gender-driven characteristics of women enabled them to have unique values. Therefore, men's consumption values and behaviors are different from those of women. Women adopt a more rigorous consumption approach than men. Tourism businesses should consider the gender discrimination exposed to women and the differences between men and women. Considering the importance of tourism in eliminating gender differences, the roles that it should assume become available.

REFERENCES

Alarcón, D. M., & Cole, S. (2019). No sustainability for tourism without gender equality. *Journal of Sustainable Tourism, 27*(7), 903–919. doi:10.1080/09669582.2019.1588283

Alrwajfah, M. M., Almeida-García, F., & Cortés-Macías, R. (2020). Females' perspectives on tourism's impact and their employment in the sector: The case of Petra, Jordan. *Tourism Management, 78*, 104069. doi:10.1016/j.tourman.2019.104069

Apostolopoulos, Y., & Sönmez, S. (2001). Working producers, leisured consumers: Women's experiences in developing regions. *Women as producers and consumers of tourism in developing regions*, 3-18.

Beauvoir, S. (2010). *Female second sex: Marriage age (Kadın ikinci cins: Evlilik çağı) (8.Basım)*. Payel Yayınları.

Boley, B. B., Ayscue, E., Maruyama, N., & Woosnam, K. M. (2017). Gender and Empowerment: Assessing Discrepancies Using the Resident Empowerment Through Tourism Scale. *Journal of Sustainable Tourism, 25*(1), 113–129. doi:10.1080/09669582.2016.1177065

Cave, P., & Kilic, S. (2010). The role of women in tourism employment with special reference to Antalya, Turkey. *Journal of Hospitality Marketing & Management, 19*(3), 280–292. doi:10.1080/19368621003591400

Chiang, C., & Jogaratnam, G. (2005). Why do women travel solo for purposes of leisure? *Journal of Vacation Marketing, 12*(1), 59–70. doi:10.1177/1356766706059041

Çiçek, D., Zencir, E., & Kozak, N. (2017). Women in Turkish tourism. *Journal of Hospitality and Tourism Management, 31*, 228–234. doi:10.1016/j.jhtm.2017.03.006

Cohen, S. A., & Cohen, E. (2019). New directions in the sociology of tourism. *Current Issues in Tourism, 22*(2), 153–172. doi:10.1080/13683500.2017.1347151

Costa, C., Carvalho, I., & Breda, Z. (2011). Gender inequalities in tourism employment: The Portuguese case. *Revista Turismo & Desenvolvimento*, (15), 39–54.

Demirbilek, S. (2007). A sociological study of gender discrimination. *Finance Political & Economic Comments, 44*(511).

Doğan, H., & Bilici, N. S. (2020). A Different Perspective to Rural Development Approach: Pro-Poor Tourism and Elazıg Case [Kırsal Kalkınma Yaklaşımına Farklı Bir Bakış: Yoksul Yanlısı Turizm ve Elazığ İli Örneği]. *Bartin Orman Fakültesi Dergisi, 22*(2), 332–340.

Doğru, A. (2010). *Glass ceiling barriers for woman employees and its effect on the job satisfaction: An example from Afyon Kocatepe University Faculty of meicine Master Thesis* [Kadın çalışanların cam tavan engelleri ve iş tatminine etkisi: Afyon Kocatepe Üniversitesi tıp fakültesi örneği)]. Yüksek lisans tezi, Dumlupınar Üniversitesi, Sosyal Bilimler Enstitüsü, İşletme Anabilim Dalı, Kütahya.

Doğrul, H. G. (2007). *Determinants of female labour supply in the urban labour markets and the effects of female labour supply on the wage structure: An application to Turkey [Kentsel alanlarda kadın işgücü arzının belirleyicileri ve kadın işgücü arzının ücret yapısı üzerindeki etkisi: Türkiye üzerine bir uygulama].* Yayınlanmamış Doktora Tezi, Dumlupınar Üniversitesi Sosyal Bilimler Enstitüsü.

Duffy, L. N., Kline, C. S., Mowatt, R. A., & Chancellor, H. C. (2015). Women in tourism: Shifting gender ideology in the DR. *Annals of Tourism Research, 52,* 72–86. doi:10.1016/j.annals.2015.02.017

Farmaki, A., & Kladou, S. (2020). Why do Airbnb hosts discriminate? Examining the sources and manifestations of discrimination in host practice. *Journal of Hospitality and Tourism Management, 42,* 181–189. doi:10.1016/j.jhtm.2020.01.005

Ferguson, L. (2010a). Tourism development and the restructuring of social reproduction in Central America. *Review of International Political Economy, 17*(5), 860–888. doi:10.1080/09692290903507219

Ferguson, L. (2010b). Interrogating 'gender' in development policy and practice: The World Bank, tourism and microenterprise in Honduras. *International Feminist Journal of Politics, 12*(1), 3–24. doi:10.1080/14616740903429080

Ferguson, L. (2011). Promoting gender equality and empowering women? Tourism and the third Millennium Development Goal. *Current Issues in Tourism, 14*(3), 235–249. doi:10.1080/13683500.2011.555522

Garcia-Ramon, M. D., Canoves, G., & Valdovinos, N. (1995). Farm tourism, gender and the environment in Spain. *Annals of Tourism Research, 22*(2), 267–282. doi:10.1016/0160-7383(94)00096-4

Ghavami, N., & Peplau, L. A. (2013). An intersectional analysis of gender and ethnic stereotypes: Testing three hypotheses. *Psychology of Women Quarterly, 37*(1), 113–127. doi:10.1177/0361684312464203

Gil Arroyo, C., Barbieri, C., Sotomayor, S., & Knollenberg, W. (2019). Cultivating women's empowerment through agritourism: Evidence from Andean communities. *Sustainability, 11*(11), 3058. doi:10.3390u11113058

Goh, E., & Lee, C. (2018). A workforce to be reckoned with: The emerging pivotal Generation Z hospitality workforce. *International Journal of Hospitality Management, 73,* 20–28. doi:10.1016/j.ijhm.2018.01.016

Grasmuck, S., & Espinal, R. (2000). Market success or female autonomy? Income, ideology, and empowerment among microentrepreneurs in the Dominican Republic. *Gender & Society, 14*(2), 231–255. doi:10.1177/089124300014002002

Gustafson, P. (2006). Work-related travel, gender and family obligations. *Work, Employment and Society, 20*(3), 513–530. doi:10.1177/0950017006066999

Harvey, M. J., Hunt, J., & Harris, C. C. Jr. (1995). Gender and community tourism dependence level. *Annals of Tourism Research, 22*(2), 349–366. doi:10.1016/0160-7383(94)00081-6

ILO. (2010). Developments and challenges in the hospitality and tourism sector. In *Issues paper for discussion at the Global Dialogue Forum for the Hotels, Catering, Tourism Sector*. Geneva: International Labour Organization.

Jafari, J., & Scott, N. (2014). Muslim world and its tourisms. *Annals of Tourism Research, 44*, 1–19. doi:10.1016/j.annals.2013.08.011

Karaçar, E. (2018). *Women and equality/discrimination in the tourism sector [Turizm sektöründe kadın ve eşitlik/ayrımcılık]*. İç. Turizm ve Kadın, Detay Yayıncılık.

Khan, S. (2011). Gendered leisure: Are women more constrained in travel for leisure? Tourismos. *An International Multidisciplinary Journal Of Tourism, 6*(1), 105–121.

Kinnaird, V., & Hall, D. (1996). Understanding tourism processes: A gender-aware framework. *Tourism Management, 17*(2), 95–102. doi:10.1016/0261-5177(95)00112-3

Korkmaz, M., Özkök, F., & Uluocak, Ş. (2019). Investigating the perspective of local people towards Women tourists in the context of gender roles Equality and life values: Gokceada case [Yerel halkın kadın turistlere yönelik bakış açısının toplumsal cinsiyet rolleri eşitliği ve yaşam değerleri bağlamında incelenmesi: Gökçeada örneği]. *Journal Of Life Economics, 6*(1), 35–60. doi:10.15637/jlecon.6.004

Kozak, M. A. (1996). Positions women hold in the accommodations industry, (Konaklama endüstrisinde kadının konumu). Anatolia. *Turizm Araştırmaları Dergisi, 7*(2), 16–23.

Mason, P., & Cheyne, J. (2000). Residents' attitudes to proposed tourism development. *Annals of Tourism Research, 27*(2), 391–411. doi:10.1016/S0160-7383(99)00084-5

Meethan, K. (2001). Tourism in Global Society: Place, Culture, Consumption. Basingstoke: Palgrave. *American Journal of Sociology*.

Mitra, S. K., Chattopadhyay, M., & Chatterjee, T. K. (2022). Can Tourism Development Reduce Gender Inequality? *Journal of Travel Research*.

Morgan, M. S., & Winkler, R. L. (2020). The third shift? Gender and empowerment in a women's ecotourism cooperative. *Rural Sociology, 85*(1), 137–164. doi:10.1111/ruso.12275

Myers, L. M. (2010). *Women's Independent Travel Experiences in New Zealand* [Doctoral thesis]. University of Sunderland.

Nalbant, F., & Korkmaz, T. (2019). Evaluation of Social Gender Equality on the Basis of Feminist Theory within the Context of Turkey [Feminist teori temelinde toplumsal cinsiyet eşitliğinin Türkiye bağlamında değerlendirilmesi]. *Artvin Çoruh Üniversitesi Uluslararası Sosyal Bilimler Dergisi, 5*(2), 165–186. doi:10.22466/acusbd.633806

Nomnga, V. J. (2017). Unlocking the potential of women entrepreneurs in the tourism and hospitality industry in the eastern Cape Province, South Africa. *Journal of Economics and Behavioral Studies, 9*(4(J)), 6–13. doi:10.22610/jebs.v9i4(J).1817

Nyaruwata, S., & Nyaruwata, L. T. (2013). Gender equity and executive management in tourism: Challenges in the Southern African Development Community (SADC) region. *African Journal of Business Management, 7*(21), 2059–2070.

Ökten, S. (2009). Gender and power: the system of gender in southeastern anatolia [Toplumsal cinsiyet ve iktidar: Güneydoğu Anadolu Bölgesi'nin toplumsal cinsiyet düzeni]. *Journal of International Social Research, 2*(8).

Özdemir, E., & Tokol, T. (2008). Marketing strategies for female consumers [Kadın tüketicilere yönelik pazarlama stratejileri]. *Anadolu University Journal of Social Sciences, 8*(2).

Parlaktuna, İ. (2010). Analysis of Gender-Based Occupational Discrimination in Turkey [Türkiye'de cinsiyete dayalı mesleki ayrımcılığın analizi]. *Ege Akademik Bakış, 10*(4), 1217–1230. doi:10.21121/eab.2010419607

Richards, G. (1996). Production and consumption of European cultural tourism. *Annals of Tourism Research, 23*(2), 261–283. doi:10.1016/0160-7383(95)00063-1

Rinaldi, A., & Salerno, I. (2020). The tourism gender gap and its potential impact on the development of the emerging countries. *Quality & Quantity, 54*(5), 1465–1477. doi:10.100711135-019-00881-x

Sabina, J. M., & Nicolae, J. C. (2013). Gender trends in tourism destination. *Procedia: Social and Behavioral Sciences, 92*, 437–444. doi:10.1016/j.sbspro.2013.08.698

Safa, H. I. (2018). *The myth of the male breadwinner: Women and industrialization in the Caribbean*. Routledge. doi:10.4324/9780429492754

Santero-Sanchez, R., Segovia-Pérez, M., Castro-Nuñez, B., Figueroa-Domecq, C., & Talón-Ballestero, P. (2015). Gender differences in the hospitality industry: A job quality index. *Tourism Management, 51*, 234–246. doi:10.1016/j.tourman.2015.05.025

Sarmiento, S. (1998). Household, gender, and travel. In Women's Travel Issues Second National Conference. Drachman Institute of the University of Arizona, Morgan State University,; Federal Highway Administration.

Sinclair, M. T. (1998). Tourism and economic development: A survey. *The Journal of Development Studies, 34*(5), 1–51. doi:10.1080/00220389808422535

Sönmez, S. (2001). Tourism behind the veil of Islam: Women and development in the Middle East. *Women as producers and consumers of tourism in developing regions*, 113-142.

Su, M. M., Wall, G., Ma, J., Notarianni, M., & Wang, S. (2020). Empowerment of women through cultural tourism: Perspectives of Hui minority embroiderers in Ningxia, China. *Journal of Sustainable Tourism*, 1–22. doi:10.1080/09669582.2020.1841217

Sürücü, Ö. A., & Ak, S. (2018). *Women as consumers in the tourism industry [Turizm sektöründe tüketici olarak kadın]*. İç. Turizm ve Kadın, Detay Yayıncılık.

Swain, M. B. (1995). Gender in tourism. *Annals of Tourism Research, 22*(2), 247–266. doi:10.1016/0160-7383(94)00095-6

Tekin, Ö. A. (2017). Gender perception in tourism industry: a study on five star hotel employees [Turizm sektöründe toplumsal cinsiyet algısı: beş yıldızlı otel çalışanları üzerine bir araştırma]. *Avrasya Sosyal ve Ekonomi Araştırmaları Dergisi*, *4*(12), 669–684.

Trupp, A., & Sunanta, S. (2017). Gendered practices in urban ethnic tourism in Thailand. *Annals of Tourism Research*, *64*, 76–86. doi:10.1016/j.annals.2017.02.004

Tucker, H. (2007). Undoing shame: Tourism and women's work in Turkey. *Journal of Tourism and Cultural Change*, *5*(2), 87–105. doi:10.2167/jtcc089.0

Tucker, H., & Boonabaana, B. (2012). A critical analysis of tourism, gender and poverty reduction. *Journal of Sustainable Tourism*, *20*(3), 437–455. doi:10.1080/09669582.2011.622769

Wilson, E., & Little, D. E. (2005). A "relative escape"? The impact of constraints on women who travel solo. *Tourism Review International*, *9*(2), 155–175. doi:10.3727/154427205774791672

Yang, E. C. L., & Khoo-Lattimore, C. (2017). Constructing Space and Self through Risk Taking: A Case of Asian Solo Female Travelers. *Journal of Travel Research*, *57*(4), 1–43.

Yücel, H. A. (2020). *Platon State [Devlet]*. Türkiye İş Bankası Kültür Yayınları.

Zencirkıran, M. (2017). *Sociology [Sosyoloji]*. Dora Yayıncılık, 6.

Zhang, J., & Zhang, Y. (2020). Tourism and gender equality: An Asian perspective. *Annals of Tourism Research*, *85*, 103067. doi:10.1016/j.annals.2020.103067

Chapter 11
Use of Blockchain in the Context of Sustainable Gastronomy

Mustafa Çağatay Kiziltaş
Sivas Cumhuriyet University, Turkey

Duran Cankül
Eskişehir Osmangazi University, Turkey

ABSTRACT

Global food systems, from agricultural production to processing, distribution, retail sale, food processing, and the resulting waste in the entire process in the supply chain, create greenhouse gas emissions that cause climate change. At the same time, some negative environmental effects such as misuse of spring water, environmental pollution, and loss of biodiversity may occur during the production of food. While access to food is a major problem in underdeveloped countries, food waste is a concern in developed countries. In addition, people want to trust the food they consume, and they want to know under what conditions the food they consume is produced and whether it comes to their table as promised. Especially in the field of gastronomy, many people are curious about the adventure of food. Issues such as traceability, transparency, reliability, and efficiency offered by blockchain technology ensure that waste can be prevented; on the other hand, it also provides the opportunity for consumers to monitor their food from field to table and provides a more sustainable food system.

INTRODUCTION

The concept of sustainability can be defined in general terms as efforts to leave a livable world to future generations. In other words, sustainability; conservation, development and improvement of environmental, social and economic resources to meet the needs of current and future generations. As concerns about climate change, loss of biodiversity and pollution on our planet become more common, investments in sustainable business practices and green technology have gained importance and businesses have begun to be encouraged in this area. Sustainability aims to protect the natural environment, human health and ecological balance without compromising people's lifestyles while promoting innovative practices.

As in all business areas, sustainability issues have started to gain importance in the field of gastronomy. Especially considering the food and beverage area, on the one hand, there are significant wastes in food, while on the other hand, people cannot access food items. Similarly, food wastage is experienced because the safety of foodstuffs is not assured. When these situations are examined, it is seen that there is a great obstacle in front of sustainability. It is thought that blockchain technology, which is a new technological development, can overcome many inefficiencies, especially in the food system.

By providing a new environment of trust and transparency in the food system, it reveals sustainability opportunities at every step of the food chain. Blockchain technology is thought to provide many advantages in gastronomy, such as traceability, transparency, reliability and efficiency. In this context, this study reveals the advantages of using blockchain technology in the field of gastronomy in terms of sustainability.

Sustainability and Gastronomy

Everything in the world has the potential to be exhausted, and due to the limited resources, it is necessary to be careful about the use of these resources and to transfer them to future generations. The term sustainability, which was introduced in this context, was first used by the German forester, Hans Carl von Carlowitz, in the text *Sylvicultura O economica* in 1712 to describe how forests should be managed in the long-term. After this process, the term sustainability did not gain validity until the 1980s (Scoones, 2007). The general acceptance of the concept of sustainability as a policy concept is based on the 1987 Brundtland Report.

This document is about the relationship between humanity's longing for a better life on the one hand and the limitations imposed by nature on the other (Kuhlman & Farrington, 2010). Sustainability actually refers to the endurance capacity of a resource. It is the ability to maintain continuity by emphasizing it. Sustainability which is compatible with the existence of the universe and the ability to maintain a certain stable outcome (Liu, 2017), is a goal of critical importance for human activity and development (Rosen, 2012). Over time, the concept of sustainability has managed to become a focus and an important goal for many people interested in environmental issues (Jickling, 2000).

Sustainability, which is a concept that aims to meet the needs of today without compromising the needs of future generations, can be perceived in different ways by different segments. When environmentalists talk about the concept of sustainability, they usually mean ecological sustainability. But when business people talk about sustainability, they mean the economic sustainability of their organizations (Rankin, 2014). The concept of sustainability is accepted by all stakeholders as a guiding principle for both public policy making and corporate strategies. A protected and undisturbed environment refers to a development that can meet the needs of the present without limiting the ability of future generations to meet their needs for social justice and economic prosperity (Finkbeiner, Schau, Lehmann, & Traverso, 2010). Sustainability aims to protect the natural environment, human health and ecological balance without compromising people's lifestyles while promoting innovative practices (Mason, 2020).

Sustainable development is one of the most difficult challenges facing humanity. Achieving the principle of sustainability requires addressing many fundamental issues at local, regional and global levels, and achieving the goals and objectives of sustainability poses great challenges for all segments of society. The basic principle of sustainable development is to improve human well-being and sustain these improvements over time, but the consequences of climate change and the increasing demand for energy and resources make this goal more difficult (Gavrilescu, 2011).

While the basic needs that people need to survive are met, natural resources are tried to be met by polluting them and even by producing at the expense of destruction (Lester, 2021). Sustainability policies examine how natural systems function, vary, and produce everything that ecology needs to stay in balance, while also recognizing that humans need these resources to sustain their modern lifestyle (Mason, 2020).

Sustainability has three main goals: environmental management, social responsibility, and economic well-being for both the organization and its stakeholders (Placet et al., 2005; Carter & Rogers, 2008; Finkbeiner et al., 2010; Rankin, 2014; Lester, 2021).

Preservation of the natural environment (conservation of natural resources) is a prerequisite for a well-functioning economy (economic growth that ensures economic vitality and human well-being) and social justice (improving the living conditions of the world's poor and promoting equal opportunities for all) (Finkbeiner et al., 2010; Hanss & Böhm, 2011). Therefore, it is very important to bring together the three pillars of sustainability, namely the environment, economy and social welfare, in national and international harmony in all areas of life (Finkbeiner et al., 2010).

The goals of sustainability are a plan to build a better and more sustainable future for all. It addresses global challenges faced such as poverty, inequality, climate change, environmental degradation, peace and justice (UN, 2021). It is thought that it can be widely used in the fight against global problems such as environmental pollution, climate change or poverty by developing sustainable lifestyles (Hanss & Böhm, 2011).

Sustainability has many benefits, both in the short- and long-term. The ecosystem of the world we live in cannot be preserved unless more sustainable choices are made. If processes detrimental to sustainability continue without change, it is likely that fossil fuels will run out, many animal species will become extinct, and the atmosphere will be irreparably damaged.

Within the scope of sustainability, especially the protection of the environment is the most emphasized element. It deals with the process of reducing carbon footprints, water use, non-degradable packaging and waste as part of the supply chain. Social sustainability is concerned with treating employees fairly and providing responsible, ethical and sustainable treatment to employees, stakeholders and the community in which a business operates.

For example, the business should operate using a sustainable workforce that includes fairly-paid, adult employees who can operate in a safe environment. Economically, sustainability is also seen as the simplest form of sustainability. To be economically viable, a business must be profitable and generate enough revenue to continue into the future. The challenge with this form of sustainability is finding the balance. Instead of focusing on making money at all costs, companies should try to make a profit by acting in accordance with other elements of sustainability (Twi-global, 2022).

As in all areas, the problems related to sustainability have become a very important issue in the world of gastronomy. Chefs, gastronomes, restaurant owners, managers, food journalists and many other professionals in the tourism industry are directly involved with themes such as food supply, income and living justice, energy use, water conservation and waste reduction. These issues have moved to a much more central stage in the tourism industry. (Zanella, 2020). In the context of sustainable gastronomy, it is thought that with the optimal use of environmental resources, basic ecological processes and biodiversity can be protected.

At the same time, cultural tolerance is built to ensure respect for the socio-cultural authenticity and values of the host communities. It is possible to provide stable employment opportunities for local people by building a viable economy that provides socio-economic benefits. It is thought that the creation of social services that increase the quality of life of the society and the problems related to food safety will contribute to the sustainability of gastronomy. (Fons et al., 2011).

Food is very important for the growth, reproduction and survival of all living organisms. Any substance or material that can be used as a food source such as carbohydrates, proteins, fats, vitamins and minerals can be called food (Premanandh, 2011). Nutrition is one of the most important elements for people to stay healthy. It is very important for individuals to consume the foods they need, taking into account their gender, age, physiological status, and daily work for a healthy diet (Saygın, et al., 2011). It is the characteristics specific to a particular region and nation defined by elements such as culture, language, religion, cuisine, social habits, music and art (Soeroso & Susilo, 2014).

A society's culture manifests itself in various ways in its art, language and literature, music and all kinds of religious and secular rituals. The same is true for foods. There are marked differences in the way different societies prepare similar foodstuffs. In primitive cultures, people who produce grains or collect seeds grind them into powder with simple methods and then convert these nutrients into edible form. Similarly, meat and fish products are often cut into pieces and brought into edible form by air, sun or fire drying. It is seen that different and more complex cooking and preparation techniques are used in developed societies (Hegarty & O'Mahony, 2001).

As a part of culture, cuisine and gastronomy are related to tourism in a very important way. Culinary culture has always been an important part of tourism experiences. Because tourists not only eat to avoid hunger or get sick, they also want to understand a region or country, their culture, and they can get information about a region and civilization from food (Soeroso & Susilo, 2014). Gastronomy is concerned not only with how food is prepared and eaten, but also with how food is grown, traded and valued. While being sensitive to environmental, social, physiological and economic well-being, it takes seriously the question of how to understand and influence food culture (Maberly & Reid, 2014).

Culinary culture has been a neglected area until recently. However, culinary culture is always the longest standing part of a culture and tradition. In other words, kitchens, where many different identities of a society come together and national feelings are felt most, are a mirror of daily life styles, religious beliefs, habits, customs and traditions. The change in eating habits in societies and the increase in the value of eating socially have been one of the reasons for the movements in tourism activities (Sormaz, et al., 2016). Many destinations and countries use food and food tourism for destination marketing by associating it with product development and regional identity issues (Muangasame & Park, 2019).

The availability of a local cuisine and local beverages provides consumers with unforgettable experiences and appears to support the satisfaction they will gain from the tourism movement in general (Alonso & Liu, 2011). Gastronomy has become an important factor in the competitiveness of touristic destinations (López-Guzmán & Sánchez-Cañizares, 2012), and has become an important attribute in the development of niche travel and niche destinations (Kivela & Crotts, 2006). Gastronomy has become a rapidly growing component of cultural tourism all over the world.

In addition to intercultural communication, it makes significant contributions to both social and economic development (Buluk & Eşitti, 2018). In parallel with the increase in competition among tourism destinations, it is seen that local culture has become an increasingly important source of new products and activities, which are put forward to attract tourists and have fun. In this regard, gastronomy has a very important role, because gastronomy is not only at the center of the tourist experience, but has also become an important source of identity formation in postmodern societies (Richards, 2002).

For centuries, one of the most important problems of humanity has been to meet the need for food (Koçak, 2016). With industrialization, globalization, increase in income level, campaigns and discounts, increase in leisure time and prolongation of retirement periods, changes have occurred in the field of food and beverage, as in many other areas. People started to eat not only to fill their stomachs but also to taste different pleasures (Hall, 2003). Food has now become a basic motivation for some human activities such as meetings, weddings, celebrations (Corigliano & Baggio, 2002). Today, the production of foods that are called edible, bringing them to a state that can be consumed, processing and cooking have reached the present day by passing through many stages over the years (Koçak, 2016).

For this reason, gastronomy is seen as an important source of cultural identity in post-modern societies (Buluk & Eşitti, 2018) and tourism is the most important consumer of this cultural identity (Fons et al., 2011). Tourism has become a key industry for the economic growth of many countries. Therefore, there is an increasing competitiveness between different destinations to attract as many tourists as possible. As a result, disciplines such as marketing have developed tools to differentiate some destinations from others, and concepts such as place branding and country brand have emerged. One of the most important factors that make up the country brand is gastronomy, because gastronomic tourism is a way to reduce the growing sustainability problem in tourism, as it affects the image of the country and its environment in different ways (Vázquez-Martinez, et al., 2019).

While gastronomy potentially represents the factors that increase the attractiveness and competitiveness of destinations, it contributes to the economic, social and environmental sustainability of destinations (Rinaldi, 2017). The contribution of the commercial foodservice industry to sustainability is highlighted by eight themes: food waste management, food safety and hygiene, food allergy management, provision of healthy meals, local food use, employment of disadvantaged people, staff well-being and noise level management (Bui & Filimonau, 2021). As a niche part of the tourism industry, gastronomy tourism is considered as one of the necessary elements for tourists to assimilate the culture and lifestyle of a destination that contains different traditional values related to the country they visit. The role played by gastronomic tourism has contributed significantly to the growth of gastronomic experiences among tourists, especially on the quality and sustainability of local food products and the landscape of traditions, culture and lifestyle (Sanip & Mustapha, 2020).

It is known that a significant part of the food produced all over the world is wasted and this leads to negative consequences for sustainability. Reducing food waste is seen as a very important problem for the food service industry (Martin-Rios et al. 2018). Although sufficient amount of food is produced for humans globally, access to food and safe food issues are a major problem in developing countries (Aiking & de Boer, 2004). Global food system, from agricultural production to processing, distribution, retail sale, food processing and the resulting waste in the entire process in the supply chain, greenhouse gas emissions that cause climate change occur. At the same time, some negative environmental effects such as misuse of spring water, environmental pollution and loss of biodiversity may occur during the production of food (Premanandh, 2011; Garnett, 2013).

Policy makers have begun to address these concerns, but issues related to food security and adequate nutrition are still major issues (Garnett, 2013). Nearly half of the world's population is affected by food insecurity, obesity/overweight or micronutrient deficiencies, indicating the need to reform the current food system (El Bilali et al., 2018). While hunger and malnutrition problems continue in developing countries, it is seen that unsafe food-borne diseases increase. Malnutrition and micronutrient deficiencies negatively affect the health of children and women and have led to the emergence of chronic diseases such as diabetes, hypertension, stroke and cancer (Belahsen, 2014).

Agriculture plays an important role in ensuring food security and sustainability for people in any country (Anshari et al., 2019). There has been an increased interest in sustainable food practices, food welfare, lower food carbon footprint, increase in popularity of organic foods, gourmet foods, gastronomic, authentic foods. The eight priorities of the sustainable food supply chains of the widely accepted UK Commission for Sustainable Development are summarized as follows (Smith, 2007):

1. to produce safe, healthy products, nutrition and access to information;
2. to support rural and urban economies and communities;
3. promoting sustainable livelihoods from sustainable land management;
4. to operate within the biological limits of natural resources;
5. reduce energy consumption, minimize inputs and use renewable energy;
6. to ensure worker welfare, training, safety and hygiene;
7. achieve high animal health and welfare standards;
8. to grow food and maintain resources for the public good

Adequate food nutrition security, which is the main problem of sustainable agri-food systems, has recently become a hotly debated issue (El Bilali, 2019). According to the World Health Organization (WHO) data, an average of 420,000 people die annually due to food poisoning. In the USA alone, the total cost caused by food safety concerns ranges from US$55.5 billion to US$93.2 billion annually. In addition, it has been observed that epidemic diseases caused by some imported fruits and vegetables in some parts of the world (Gutierrez, 2017). The main problem with sustainable food is how to make food production more environmentally sustainable and more resilient while more people are fed more effectively (Garnett, 2013).

Consumers around the world demand more information about the food they consume, where it comes from, the impact of production methods on our planet, and how workers and animals are treated in the process. Nearly 50% of consumers consider it important that the food they buy is produced in an environmentally sustainable way. Sustainability has ceased to be a choice and has become a necessity both for demanding consumers and for future business models.

Today, some of the consumers have realized the importance of sustainability awareness. According to studies, it is seen that approximately 78% of consumers are willing to change their consumption habits in order to reduce the environmental impact of their consumption by acting with sustainability awareness (IBM, 2021). According to researches, approximately one third of the food produced is wasted and more than one billion tons of food is wasted every year (IBM, Food waste, 2021). Thanks to Blockchain technology, which is thought to be able to overcome these problems, it is thought that sustainability and improvement opportunities will emerge at every step of the food chain by providing new levels of trust and transparency in the food ecosystem with a digital food supply chain (IBM, 2021).

BLOCKCHAIN

Blockchain was designed as a decentralized, insecure and anonymous general ledger in 2008, as a stability-oriented system that is constantly growing and confirms and records transactions (Jiang et al.,

2021). The blockchain technology underlying Bitcoin and other cryptocurrencies serves as a distributed ledger technology that keeps historical records of all transactions that occur in the peer-to-peer network (Crosby et al., 2016; Underwood, 2016; Iansiti & Lakhani, 2017; Ikeda, 2018; He et al., 2018; Boireau, 2018; Efanov & Roschin, 2018; Dinh, et al., 2018; Kim, 2018; Swan, 2018; Atlam & Wills, 2018; Muzammal et al., 2019; Lee, 2019; Bodkhe et al., 2020; Upadhyay et al., 2021).

Blockchain is a special data structure that stores transactions that have been made in the past. It is the case that users agree that all transactions taking place in the system are sequential (Dinh et al., 2018). With the rapid development in cryptocurrencies, blockchain has become a fundamental technology that has received a lot of attention (Ertz & Boily, 2019). A revolutionary new ecosystem has been built by providing the opportunity to transact and communicate over the Internet.

Blockchain aims to improve information security and transparency by sharing encrypted data between peer-to-peer networks. Due to the importance it attaches to security and trust, the demand for blockchain application is increasing in various business sectors, reducing costs by enabling direct peer-to-peer transactions between participants without intermediaries. It has great potential in areas where transaction reliability is important and transaction efficiency can be increased by reducing brokerage costs (Lee, 2019). Blockchain technology promises to change all existing business models and make financial services cheaper, thus contributing to better financial inclusion and even better economic wealth distribution (Schinckus, 2020).

The primary user of blockchain technology is the financial sector because it can solve significant process inefficiencies and a large cost base problem in this industry (Nofer et al., 2017). However, with the spread of Blockchain technology in recent years, it has been used exponentially in the use of various smart applications such as smart agriculture, smart health, supply chain and logistics, tourism and accommodation, energy management (Bodkhe et al., 2020). In addition, many applications such as smart contracts, smart properties, crowdfunding and digital assets are made possible by blockchain technology (Temizkan & Kızıltaş, 2021).

Blockchain 1.0 is the first generation of this technology and was launched in 2009 with the bitcoin network. It is in this generation that the first cryptocurrencies are created. With this idea came the issues of payment and cryptocurrency creation. With Blockchain 2.0, the implementation of smart contracts for various applications and financial services was introduced in 2010. In this generation, it is proposed to develop Blockchain technology with the Ethereum and Hyperledger frameworks.

Decentralized applications have been introduced with Blockchain 3.0. Various research areas such as healthcare, governance, IoT, supply chain, business and smart city have been considered to create decentralized applications. Blockchain 4.0 is mainly focused on services such as public ledger and distributed databases in real time. This level enables seamless integration of Industry 4.0 based applications. Smart contracts are used, which eliminates the need for paper-based contracts (Bodkhe, et al., 2020).

Blockchain and Sustainable Gastronomy

Food is an important part of the lives of people and human cultures around the world. The agriculture and food sector is recognized as a major global employment. Agricultural supply chain management is becoming one of the most complex and challenging processes due to its large number and heterogeneity of relevant stakeholders such as farmers, distributors and retailers as well as customers (Sajja et al., 2021). There are many components, such as supply chain management, crop insurance, and transportation of goods, that require the involvement of multiple parties, such as farmers, retailers, customers, wholesalers and assessors.

The existence of an intermediary (i.e., people or human-operated institutions) raises critical issues such as accessibility, relevance, security, and immutability (Kassanuk & Phasinam, 2021). In recent years, the greenhouse industry has come to an important position from the agricultural community due to its production capability. However, labor and energy consumption costs increase the production cost of the greenhouse by approximately 40-50%.

In addition, the security and accuracy of agricultural data, particularly for yield monitoring and analysis, has also become a challenging issue in existing greenhouse systems. The greenhouse requires a controlled environment and optimum parameter settings to increase food production. Therefore, even a small improvement in this area can bring significant improvements in total cost (Jamil et al., 2022). Important factors in developing more sustainable supply chains are identified as the type of supply chain involved and the individual business attitude towards extending responsibility for product quality to social and environmental performance within their supply chain. Interpersonal trust and working in accordance with standards are important to create more sustainable local and many preserved food supply chains, but classical methods are insufficient in this regard (Smith, 2007).

The combination of technology in e-farming can yield many benefits, such as shared benefits, enhanced coordination among value chain actors, and real-time decision-making for optimal resource allocation and their sustainable use in e-farming (Dey & Shekhawat, 2021). In this sense, Blockchain plays a very important role in replacing the traditional methods of storing, sorting and sharing agricultural data in a more reliable, immutable, transparent and decentralized way (Torky & Hassanein, 2020).

The transition to a low-carbon future requires visionary restructuring, from the interaction of infrastructure systems and services with consumers to planning, purchasing, financing, construction and operations. Adopting new technologies that deliver drastic reductions in greenhouse gas emissions is crucial to a successful transition. Blockchain technology has the potential to improve existing processes and systems by acting as a digital enabler in the infrastructure value chain (OECD, 2021). Blockchain technology, a disruptive technology that changes business and supply chain models, can change the way information is exchanged between actors in the chain using distributed software architecture and advanced computing.

Blockchain technology provides a platform to solve the problem of tracking product information in supply chain management (Ronaghi, 2021). Blockchain technology has started to be used in the agricultural industry. Blockchain can provide an efficient and robust mechanism to increase food traceability in the agrifood industry and a transparent and reliable way to verify the quality, safety and sustainability of agrifood (Xu et al., 2020), it is a fundamental technology creating a change in the improvement of supply chain sustainability (Abderahman & Karim, 2020).

Blockchain technology can trace the origin of food and thus help build reliable food supply chains and increase customer confidence. It makes it easy to use data-driven technology to make agriculture smarter as a covert way to store data. It also allows timely payments between stakeholders, used in conjunction with smart contracts that can be triggered by changes in data on the blockchain. The main applications of blockchain are agricultural insurance, smart agriculture, traceability, land registry, food supply chain, safety and security farms, e-commerce of agricultural products.

Agriculture is an important part of the economy of every country as it helps to feed the entire population. It enables connection and communication with all connected industries of the country (Sajja et al., 2021). Blockchain technology can trace the origin of food, help build reliable food supply chains and increase customer confidence. As a secure way to store data, it facilitates the use of data-driven technologies to make agriculture smarter. (Xu et al., 2020; Sajja et al., 2021). All information starts to be recorded in the system from the beginning of the first growing of the product. Where, when, and by whom the product is grown, for how long was it grown, under what conditions was it stored, under what conditions were the transfers made (if there is a cold chain, is there any breakage?) have easy access.

It is possible to access information such as paying attention to the use of resources during the growing process of the product, obtaining information about the people employed in the production process of the product, paying attention to the carbon footprints during the transfer stages.

The use of blockchain technology can prevent food fraud, food-borne diseases, illegal production and recalling food due to some negative reasons that can occur in the classical food supply chain system (Takyar, 2022). System users can see the source of the product and gain a clearer view of where inefficiencies and lack of sustainability exist in the entire supply chain. Farmers, producers and other food actors can automatically digitize and easily share audits, certifications and other records, demonstrating that they use and support sustainable and ethical practices.

By tracking every step of the food supply chain and sharing data in an immutable ledger, participants can ensure that the quality of promised goods is unquestionable (IBM, 2021). The use of blockchain technology is considered to be very beneficial when considering factors such as increasing data transparency, realizing data traceability, improving food safety and quality monitoring, and reducing the cost of financial transactions (Xu et al., 2020).

Blockchain technology offers the opportunity to certify the origin of the product, to ensure its quality and to certify the freshness of the product. It is also possible to record soil temperature and moisture levels, fertilizers, seeds used and weather conditions in the system. They can also use the data to predict weather conditions and take measures to protect crops, improve pricing tactics and promote sustainable farming practices. It helps to assess whether foods are kept in ideal storage conditions and whether the facility is certified to have such items on its premises. It helps determine if and when a facility inspection is done and what the rating is.

It also helps to monitor the storage environment when the cause of food spoilage is checked in the event of a recall, and the same data can be used for future use to prevent spoilage (Farmtoplate, 2022). Especially tourists want to trust the food they consume and they want to know under what conditions the food they consume is produced and whether it comes to their table as promised. Again, many people in the field of gastronomy and gastronomic tourism can wonder about the adventure of food. Issues such as traceability, transparency, reliability and efficiency offered by blockchain technology ensure that waste can be prevented, on the other hand, it also provides the opportunity for consumers to monitor their food from field to table and provides a more sustainable food system.

CONCLUSION

Food insecurity and hunger are the harbingers of health and economic development problems of people deprived of basic vital needs. Economic growth has pushed the boundaries of sustainability in agriculture, ecology and economy, raising deep concerns about food security at the global level. Therefore, food insecurity, reducing poverty and hunger are top priorities on the global agenda (Premanandh, 2011). Consumers around the world demand more information about their food, about where it comes from, the impact of production methods on our planet, and how workers and animals are treated in the process.

According to research, a total of 54% of consumers believe it is important to produce the food they buy in an environmentally sustainable way and a total of 78% of consumers are willing to change their food consumption habits to reduce their environmental impact (IBM, 2021). In addition, with one-third of all food produced is wasted, efforts to reduce food waste have become a global necessity.

Globally, it is thought that more than one billion tons of food goes to landfills for different reasons each year. Due to some doubts, a third of fresh food is wasted each year by consumers who are unsure of the quality of their food (IBM, Food waste, 2021). All these problems are seen as threats to sustainability. A digital food supply chain powered by blockchain provides new levels of trust and transparency in the food ecosystem, unlocking sustainability opportunities at every step of the food chain. Blockchain technology offers advantages such as traceability and transparency, reliability and efficiency in food and beverage. (Cankul & Kiziltas, 2020).

When the applications related to the subject are examined, Walmart company has spent millions of dollars to find the source of the epidemic that has arisen from the previously experienced diseased vegetables. Walmart now requires all vegetable suppliers to upload data to a blockchain that tracks the product back to the farm it came from. In the case of batch contamination, Walmart can monitor contaminated food in seconds compared to a manual process that takes weeks. This provides invaluable convenience, especially in product recalls. Nestlé uses a blockchain to trace the origins of the coffee produced by a coffee brand called Zoégas.

To increase product trust and transparency, The Rainforest Alliance provides its own certification information that guarantees the origins and sustainability practices of coffee cultivation. By scanning the QR code on the packaging, customers are able to view the processing certificate information for farmers, harvest time, roasting time and even the special shipment of their coffee. Brand Bumble Bee Foods records yellowfin tuna operations on a blockchain to increase traceability and eliminate fraud. The system can follow the movement of the fish in the supply chain from the moment it is caught to the moment it is sold in stores. Just like with the Nestle brand, customers can view information about where the tuna came from, the fishing community that caught it, and the size of the catch. Fair trade data is also displayed, providing customers with evidence that their money is not being used to finance unethical practices such as slavery and child labor.

The benefits of the use of blockchain technology in the field of food and beverage can be listed as follows; (Cankul & Kiziltas, 2020):

- It can provide traceability of food from farm to fork
- It can keep information about the history of food and beverages (food items)
- It provides the opportunity to control the supply chain in real time
- The process becomes more efficient by increasing the traceability of the supply chain
- It increases the overall performance of the supply chain by overcoming the problems of cooperation and trust in the supply chain
- It can provide a powerful solution by adding digital identity to document the authenticity of foods that can be imitated and cheated, to see the origin
- It can simplify supply chains by reducing the need for multiple intermediaries, thus eliminating some transaction costs
- It provides the opportunity to make directions via GPS in order to transport rapidly perishable products to close places, and products with long shelf life to farther places, and thus wastes can be prevented

- Thanks to the traceability it provides, it provides the opportunity to see whether the cold chain is broken by using parameters such as temperature, humidity and pressure in the transportation of perishable foods such as meat products, dairy products and fish
- It can increase the value of products by providing superior customer experience

When the advantages of using blockchain in the context of sustainable gastronomy are examined, the principle of healthy and quality life, which is also among the objectives of sustainable development, decent work and economic growth, industry innovation and infrastructure, reduction of inequalities, sustainable cities and communities, responsible production and consumption, climate action, water purposes such as life, terrestrial life are shaped directly in a positive way.

In this context, it is thought that encouraging the use of blockchain at every stage of the food and beverage field will help to build a more sustainable future. Necessary incentives and practical assistance should be provided for the use of blockchain to be more accessible and widely used. It is seen that the studies on the subject in the academic field are quite limited. For this reason, there is a need for more academic studies on the use of blockchain in the food and beverage industry.

REFERENCES

Abderahman, R., & Karim, R. (2020). Blockchain and supply chain sustainability. *Scientific Journal of Logistics, 16*(3), 363–372.

Alonso, A., & Liu, Y. (2011). The potential for marrying local gastronomy and wine: The case of the 'fortunate islands'. *International Journal of Hospitality Management, 30*(4), 974–981. doi:10.1016/j.ijhm.2011.02.005

Anshari, M., Almunawar, M., Masri, M., & Hamdan, M. (2019). Digital Marketplace and FinTech to Support Agriculture Sustainability. *Energy Procedia, 156*, 234–238. doi:10.1016/j.egypro.2018.11.134

Atlam, H., & Wills, G. (2018). Technical aspects of blockchain and IoT. *Advances in Computers*, 115.

Bodkhe, U., Tanwar, S., Parekh, K., Khanpara, P., Tyagi, S., Kumar, N., & Alazab, M. (2020). Blockchain for Industry 4.0: A Comprehensive Review. In *Deep Learning Algorithms for Internet of Medical Things* (pp. 79764-79800). IEEE Access.

Boireau, O. (2018). Securing the blockchain against hackers. *Network Security, 2018*(1), 8–11. doi:10.1016/S1353-4858(18)30006-0

Bui, H., & Filimonau, V. (2021). A recipe for sustainable development: Assessing transition of commercial foodservices towards the goal of the triple bottom line sustainability. *International Journal of Contemporary Hospitality Management, 33*(10), 3535–3563. doi:10.1108/IJCHM-03-2021-0330

Cankül, D., & Kızıltaş, M. (2020). Yiyecek İçecek İşletmelerinde Tedarik Zinciri ve Blokzincir Teknolojisi. *Journal of Gastronomy, Hospitality, and Travel, 3*(2), 244–259.

Carter, C., & Rogers, D. (2008). A Framework of Sustainable Supply Chain Management: Moving Toward New Theory. *International Journal of Physical Distribution & Logistics Management, 38*(5), 360–387. doi:10.1108/09600030810882816

Crosby, M., Nachiappan, Pattanayak, P., Verma, S., & Kalyanaraman, V. (2016). BlockChain Technology: Beyond Bitcoin. *Applied Innovation Review*, *2*, 6–19.

Dey, K., & Shekhawat, U. (2021). Blockchain for sustainable e-agriculture: Literature review, architecture for data management, and implications. *Journal of Cleaner Production*, *316*, 1–17. doi:10.1016/j.jclepro.2021.128254

Dinh, T., Liu, R., Zhang, M., Chen, G., Ooi, B., & Wang, J. (2018). *Untangling Blockchain: A Data Processing View of Blockchain Systems*. IEEE Transactions on Knowledge and Data Engineering.

Efanov, D., & Roschin, P. (2018). The All-Pervasiveness of the Blockchain Technology. *Procedia Computer Science*, *123*, 116–121. doi:10.1016/j.procs.2018.01.019

El Bilali, H., Callenius, C., Strassner, C., & Probst, L. (2018). Food and nutrition security and sustainability transitions in food systems. *Food and Energy Security*, *8*(2), 1–20.

Ertz, M., & Boily, É. (2019). The rise of the digital economy: Thoughts on blockchain technology and cryptocurrencies for the collaborative economy. *International Journal of Innovation Studies*, *3*(4), 84–93. doi:10.1016/j.ijis.2019.12.002

Farmtoplate. (2022). *Blockchain for Food Tracking and Tracing*. https://www.farmtoplate.io/how-it-works/

Finkbeiner, M., Schau, E., Lehmann, A., & Traverso, M. (2010). Towards Life Cycle Sustainability Assessment. *Sustainability*, *2*(10), 3309–3322. doi:10.3390u2103309

Gavrilescu, M. (2011). *Sustainability. In Comprehensive Biotechnology*. Pergamon.

Hanss, D., & Böhm, G. (2011). Sustainability seen from the perspective of consumers. *International Journal of Consumer Studies*, *36*(6), 678–687. doi:10.1111/j.1470-6431.2011.01045.x

He, Q., Xu, Y., Liu, Z., He, J., Sun, Y., & Zhang, R. (2018). rivacy-preserving Internet of Things device management scheme based on blockchain. *International Journal of Distributed Sensor Networks*, *14*(11), 1–12. doi:10.1177/1550147718808750

Hegarty, J., & O'Mahony, G. (2001). Gastronomy: A phenomenon of cultural expressionism and an aesthetic for living. *International Journal of Hospitality Management*, *20*(1), 3–13. doi:10.1016/S0278-4319(00)00028-1

Iansati, M., & Lakhani, K. (2017). The Truth About Blockchain. Harvard Business Review. *Harvard Business Review*, *95*(1), 4–11.

IBM. (2021). *Food waste*. Benefits of IBM Food Trust: https://www.ibm.com/blockchain/resources/7-benefits-ibm-food-trust/#food-waste

IBM. (2021). *Sustainability*. Benefits of IBM Food Trust: https://www.ibm.com/blockchain/resources/7-benefits-ibm-food-trust/#sustainability

Ikeda, K. (2018). Security and Privacy of Blockchain and Quantum Computation. *Advances in Computers*, *111*, 199–228. doi:10.1016/bs.adcom.2018.03.003

Jamil, F., Ibrahim, M., Ullah, I., Kim, S., Kahng, H., & Kim, D.-H. (2022). Optimal smart contract for autonomous greenhouse environment based on IoT blockchain network in agriculture. *Computers and Electronics in Agriculture*, *192*, 1–18. doi:10.1016/j.compag.2021.106573

Jickling, B. (2000). A Future for Sustainability? *Water, Air, and Soil Pollution*, *123*(1/4), 467–476. doi:10.1023/A:1005211410123

Kassanuk, T., & Phasinam, K. (2021). Design of blockchain based smart agriculture framework to ensure safety and security. *Materials Today: Proceedings*, 1–4.

Kim, S. (2018). Blockchain for a Trust Network Among Intelligent Vehicles. *Advances in Computers*, *111*, 43–68. doi:10.1016/bs.adcom.2018.03.010

Kivela, J., & Crotts, J. (2006). Tourism and Gastronomy: Gastronomy's Influence on How Tourists Experience a Destination. *Journal of Hospitality & Tourism Research (Washington, D.C.)*, *30*(3), 354–377. doi:10.1177/1096348006286797

Kuhlman, T., & Farrington, J. (2010). What is Sustainability? *Sustainability*, *2*(11), 3436–3448. doi:10.3390u2113436

Lee, J. (2019). A decentralized token economy: How blockchain and cryptocurrency can revolutionize business. *Business Horizons*, *62*(6), 773–784. doi:10.1016/j.bushor.2019.08.003

Lester, A. (2021). *Sustainability. In Project Management, Planning and Control*. Butterworth-Heinemann.

Liu, S. (2017). *What is Sustainability? In Bioprocess Engineering Kinetics, Sustainability, and Reactor Design*. Elsevier. doi:10.1016/C2015-0-04891-2

López-Guzmán, T., & Sánchez-Cañizares, S. (2012). Gastronomy, Tourism and Destination Differentiation: A Case Study in Spain. *Revue d'Economie Financiere*, *1*, 63–72.

Maberly, C., & Reid, D. (2014). Gastronomy: An approach to studying food. *Nutrition & Food Science*, *44*(4), 272–278. doi:10.1108/NFS-02-2014-0013

Mason, M. (2020). *What Is Sustainability and Why Is It Important?* Environmental Science: https://www.environmentalscience.org/sustainability

Muangasame, K., & Park, E. (2019). *Food Tourism, Policy and Sustainability: Behind the Popularity of Thai Food. In Food Tourism in Asia*. Springer. doi:10.1007/978-981-13-3624-9_9

Muzammal, M., Qu, Q., & Nasrulin, B. (2019). Renovating Blockchain With Distributed Databases: An open source system. *Future Generation Computer Systems*, *90*, 105–117. doi:10.1016/j.future.2018.07.042

Nofer, M., Gomber, P., Hinz, O., & Schiereck, D. (2017). Blockchain – A Disruptive Technology. *Business & Information Systems Engineering*, *59*(3), 183–187. doi:10.100712599-017-0467-3

OECD. (2021). *Blockchain Technologies as a Digital Enabler for Sustainable*. https://www.oecd.org/finance/Blockchain-technologies-as-a-digital-enabler-for-sustainable-infrastructure-key-findings.pdf

Placet, M., Anderson, R., & Fowler, K. (2005). Strategies for Sustainability. *Research Technology Management*, *48*(5), 32–41. doi:10.1080/08956308.2005.11657336

Premanandh, J. (2011). Factors affecting food security and contribution of modern technologies in food sustainability. *Journal of the Science of Food and Agriculture, 91*(15), 2707–2714. doi:10.1002/jsfa.4666 PMID:22002569

Rankin, W. (2014). *Sustainability. In Treatise on Process Metallurgy*. Elsevier.

Richards, G. (2002). *Gastronomy: an essential ingredient in tourism production and consumption? In Tourism and Gastronomy*. Routledge.

Rinaldi, C. (2017). Food and Gastronomy for Sustainable Place Development: A Multidisciplinary Analysis of Different Theoretical Approaches. *Sustainability, 9*(10), 1–25. doi:10.3390u9101748

Ronaghi, M. (2021). A blockchain maturity model in agricultural supply chain. *Information Processing in Agriculture, 8*(3), 398–408. doi:10.1016/j.inpa.2020.10.004

Rosen, M. (2012). Engineering Sustainability: A Technical Approach to Sustainability. *Sustainability, 4*(9), 2270–2292. doi:10.3390u4092270

Sajja, G., Rane, K., Phasinam, K., Kassanuk, T., Okoronkwo, E., & Prabhu, P. (2021). Towards applicability of blockchain in agriculture sector. *Materials Today: Proceedings*, 1–4. doi:10.1016/j.matpr.2021.07.366

Sanip, M., & Mustapha, R. (2020). Sustainability of Gastronomic Tourism in Malaysia: Theoretical Context. *International Journal of Asian Social Science, 10*(8), 417–425. doi:10.18488/journal.1.2020.108.417.425

Schinckus, C. (2020). The good, the bad and the ugly: An overview of the sustainability of blockchain technology. *Energy Research & Social Science, 69*, 1–10. doi:10.1016/j.erss.2020.101614

Scoones, I. (2007). Sustainability. *Development in Practice, 17*(4-5), 589–596. doi:10.1080/09614520701469609

Smith, B. (2007). Developing sustainable food supply chains. *Philosophical Transactions of the Royal Society of London. Series B, Biological Sciences, 363*(1492), 849–861. doi:10.1098/rstb.2007.2187 PMID:17766237

Soeroso, A., & Susilo, Y. (2014). Traditional Indonesian Gastronomy as a Cultural Tourism Attraction. *Journal of Applied Economics in Developing Countries, 1*(1), 45–59.

Sormaz, U., Akmese, H., Gunes, E., & Aras, S. (2016). Gastronomy in Tourism. *Procedia Economics and Finance, 39*, 725–730. doi:10.1016/S2212-5671(16)30286-6

Swan, M. (2018). Blockchain for Business: Next-Generation Enterprise Artificial Intelligence Systems. *Advances in Computers, 111*, 121–162. doi:10.1016/bs.adcom.2018.03.013

Take Action for the Sustainable Development Goals. (2021). https://www.un.org/sustainabledevelopment/sustainable-development-goals/

Takyar, A. (2022). *Food Supply Chain Blockchain- Solving Food Supply Problems*. https://www.leewayhertz.com/supply-chain-blockchain-reinventing-food-supply/

Temizkan, R., & Kızıltaş, M. (2021). Turizm Bağlamında Kültürel ve Doğal Kaynakların Korunmasında Fon Sağlama AracıOlarak NFT. *Journal of Tourism and Gastronomy Studies*, *9*(4), 3079–3091. doi:10.21325/jotags.2021.935

Torky, M., & Hassanein, A. (2020). Integrating blockchain and the internet of things in precision agriculture: Analysis, opportunities, and challenges. *Computers and Electronics in Agriculture*, *178*, 1–23. doi:10.1016/j.compag.2020.105476

Underwood, S. (2016). Blockchain beyond bitcoin. *Communications of the ACM*, *59*(11), 15–17. doi:10.1145/2994581

Upadhyay, A., Mukhuty, S., Kumar, V., & Kazancoglu, Y. (2021). Blockchain technology and the circular economy: Implications for sustainability and social responsibility. *Journal of Cleaner Production*, *293*, 1–7. doi:10.1016/j.jclepro.2021.126130

Vázquez-Martinez, U., Sanchís-Pedregosa, C., & Leal-Rodríguez, A. (2019). IsGastronomy A Relevant Factor for Sustainable Tourism? An Empirical Analysis of Spain Country Brand. *Sustainability*, *11*(9), 1–13. doi:10.3390u11092696

What Is Sustainability and Why Is It So Important? (2022). https://www.twi-global.com/technical-knowledge/faqs/faq-what-is-sustainability

Xu, J., Guo, S., Xie, D., & Yan, Y. (2020). Blockchain: A new safeguard for agri-foods. *Artificial Intelligence in Agriculture*, *4*, 153–161. doi:10.1016/j.aiia.2020.08.002

Zanella, M. (2020). On the challenges of making a sustainable kitchen: Experimenting with sustainable food principles for restaurants. *Research in Hospitality Management*, *10*(1), 29–41. doi:10.1080/22243534.2020.1790207

Chapter 12
Visitors' Perceptions of Homestay Management in Nepal:
Evidence From Structural Equation Modelling

Niranjan Devkota
https://orcid.org/0000-0001-9989-0397
Quest International College, Pokhara University, Nepal

Shreedhar Khamcha
Quest International College, Pokhara University, Nepal

Sahadeb Upretee
Central Washington University, USA

Udaya Raj Paudel
Quest International College, Pokhara University, Nepal

Surendra Mahato
Nepal Commerce Campus, Tribhuvan University, Nepal

ABSTRACT

Tourists' visits to rural areas are increasingly experiencing growth; however, there is no literature available to reveal how the Nepalese community has taken advantage of tourism as an opportunity to increase income. The study assesses the visitors' perception of homestay management in one of the indigenous homestay areas: Gabhar Valley, Nepal. Based on an explanatory research design, primary data was collected from 285 tourist guests using the structural equation modelling (SEM) technique which was applied to find the visitors perceptions about homestay management. This study found there is positive and significant influence on visitors' intension to visit using homestay. Variables such as environmental concerns indeed exert a positive influence on their subjective norms and perceived moral obligation, which in turn influence their intention to visit homestay as expected. This study concludes that as homestay programs contribute significantly towards environmental concern and rural livelihood, it is an effective tourism tool for economic sustainability.

DOI: 10.4018/978-1-6684-4645-4.ch012

INTRODUCTION

Nepal, a small country on the southern slopes of the Himalayas, borders China in the North and India in the East, West and South. This small Himalayan Democratic Republic shares an open border with India, the southern neighbor. Nepal is less industrialized but rich in natural beauty (Thapa, 2016). With its mild climates, Nepal enjoys one of the richest biodiversity and multiethnic communities to lure tourists from different geographical areas around the globe. To cash this rich biodiversity and multiethnicity of rural Nepal, rural entrepreneurs developed homestays as one of the viable tourism industries recently. However, the management of these homestays needs professional improvements. The homestay program enables tourists to experience the unique culture and lifestyle of the local people (Subedi, 2016). Homestays intend to attract tourists with a particular demographic profile who desire authentic experiences. Homestay tourism is popular in many destinations; it adds indigenous sociocultural richness to the tourist experience. Homestays strengthen local people's social and economic capacities (Budhathoki, 2013).

Homestay started as a community-based initiative in the 1970s and has seen a significant rise in local community engagement. Muslim et al. (2018) state that varied ecological areas, abundant biodiversity and distinct cultural identity of different ethnic groups make Nepal one of the most interesting tourist destinations in the world. The mountainous landscapes of Nepal enable it to make a low-cost, eco-friendly tourist destination for socioeconomic development and poverty reduction. The purpose of homestays depends on the sociocultural context of a county. Homestay management not only helps local people to play their part in conserving the natural habitat but also serves to safeguard indigenous culture and livelihoods and raise wealth for community members as a change in sustainable growth (Zhang & Tang, 2021). Homestay management concept is ecotourism, promoting local resources, well management leadership, the discipline of every host family and quality services and facilities available to the tourists (Basak et al., 2021). Homestays must consider basic facilities like toilets and bathrooms with standard sanitation practices. Despite the emerging concept of homestays as an industry, the regulatory authority has not yet developed a monitoring and assessment system to maintain the quality standard. An authentic monitoring and assessment system would help visitors, stakeholders, and local governments (Walter et al., 2018). The development of the homestay industry involves comprehensive planning, infrastructure construction, and aggressive promotion. In the meantime, the homestay industry also significantly contributes to generating income for local people and preserving the cultural legacy of indigenous people.

The concept of rural tourism is popular these days. Visiting the pristine natural beauty of rural Nepal creates opportunities for recreation and rural economic growth. Homestays promote rural tourism. Homestays in different countries have different quality measurements. Standard quality management attracts local and foreign tourists, enabling local entrepreneurs to earn more. Generating income in the local area contributes to sociocultural development and higher living standards by reducing local people's poverty and exploring the local culture, food, art and handicraft, and natural beauty (Biswakarma, 2015; Pasanchay & Schott, 2021). Tourism can affect community development; it may impact local population structure, transform the forms and types of occupation, change values, influence traditional lifestyles, and modify consumption patterns (KC, 2021).

Rural tourism has the goals of helping tourists schedule a journey, choose a tour and minimise its effect on the environment. It is a key economic growth strategy which leads rural economies through income generation, job creation and entrepreneurship. Village tourism is undoubtedly instrumental in alleviating poverty. Adequate and appropriate policies and interventions encourage homestay entrepreneurs with appropriate services to improve the economic status of vulnerable and disadvantaged local residents (Pasa, 2020). Subedi (2016) argued development of the tourism sector contributed to an increase in employment and income, as well as an improvement in the country's balance of payments. The homestay industry could be a thriving option for foreign exchange, providing opportunities for various sectors like hotels, motels, restaurants, catering services, etc.

In recent years, the community-based homestay has been a fast-growing rural tourism enterprise (Jamaludin et al., 2012). It fosters ecotourism around the globe by uplifting the local community and other enterprises such as fruit production and processing, etc. Nepal, where the export potential of manufactured goods is limited, cannot ignore the role of tourism, as its multifaceted impact on the balance of payments diversifies the economy, increases income and creates jobs. The homestay industry has emerged as sustainable tourism in rural Nepal. Tourists who desire to be a part of local traditions and interact with the local community to understand the local culture, cuisine, and natural attraction prefer homestay.

In homestay management, there are some research issues in the Nepalese context. To thrive, operators have to cope with crucial problems, such as seeking ways to improve the experience of travelers to customers and building a meaning for the brand that holds an intrinsic and special image or brand equity (Shen & Liu, 2015). The problems of cultural geography have arisen since the beginning of the 20th century and over the last three decades internationally. In advance, after the Industrial Revolution, the West still reveals that biology is contrary to tradition (Fatimah, 2015). The last issue we need to address is the atmosphere and intent of the measurement (Moutinho, 1987). Today homestay has focused on local tourists and generating income in rural areas.

I took theoretical insights from the theory of planned behavior for this study. This theory understands and predicts compotation, which implies the immediate determination of behavioral intentions and the perception of behavioral control in certain circumstances. Compartmental intentions are determined by three factors: behavioral attitudes, subjective standards and perceived behavioral control (Ajzen, 1985; Quintal et al., 2010; Rizzo & Columna, 2020). This theory has been successfully applied in my research to assess the model of tourists' perceived value, place attachment, re-visit intentions, the conceptual model of travel behavior, TPB of the tourist motivation model, and the conceptual framework of consumers' visit intention of green hotels. My previous experience indicates the theory would address the issues of homestay management. The planned behavior theory and model consider my research visitors' perceptions, i.e., behavioral attitudes, subjective standards and perceived behavioral control in homestay management.

Homestay is part of the tourism industry. It includes homestay quality and service performance for local tourism benefit. Homestay promotes rural tourism; contributes to rural development. In the south Asian context, people perceive homestays to attract people from different cultures contributing to cultural exchange and integrity. It has a positive impact on economic, sociocultural development and environmental protection. Similarly, the east Asian concept of homestay management has to community base participation and sustainable development modifications: adding, continuing, customizing, transforming and repairing.

Murphy highlights the cultural characteristics of a homestay destination, such as its heritage, structures, rituals, architectural features, food, tradition, artworks, music, handwork and dance, which provide visitors with simple and strong attractions (as cited in Biswakarma, 2015). In many destinations, home tourism is very popular; it gives the tourists authentic sociocultural wealth. In China, aesthetic and escapist experiences are significant predictors of visitors' perceived functional, emotional and social value (Zhao et al., 2022). Similarly, in Indonesia, expectation and perceived value had a greater impact on re-visit intention than satisfaction and visitor management (Damanik & Yusuf, 2021). At the same time, houses are an enticing alternative tourism product for a nation that does not emphasize extensive investment in infrastructure but has a wealth of tourism in rural communities (Acharya & Halpenny, 2013).

The environment of the building and its amenities, service quality and house operation and management is more critical for homestays and their customer classes (Hu et al., 2012). The basic equipment to be changed is street lighting to ensure visitors are comfortable and protected. The Tourism Board should oversee the regularly scheduled homestay. The regulatory bodies should routinely collect feedback from hosts and visitors; places to be improved should be addressed as quickly as possible (Jamaludin et al., 2012).

In the homestay, issues need to be addressed urgently for effective functioning. Local governments have to formulate policies addressing homestays' problems as an industry, and regulatory authorities should implement these policies effectively. The central government has to make the visa system hassle-free to attract foreign tourists. The government should create a favorable environment, infrastructure development, internet facilities, advertisement of the local areas, and indigenous foods in the international media. The local entrepreneurs should improve their services, maintaining the socio- tourist relationship. The entrepreneur has to give high-quality services and the taste of local food, traditional culture, homestay quality infrastructure and other facilities.

This research assesses the visitor's perception of homestay management at Gabhar Valley in Nepal. More particularly, this study seeks to answer the questions; What is the visitor's opinion on homestay? How do the visitors perceive their stay in the homestays of Gabhar Valley? What is the managerial solution for homestay management at Gabhar Valley?

The paper is structured as follows: Section 2 discusses the methods used in the study. Likewise, Section 3 presents the results of the study and data analysis; Section 4 discusses the results of this study. Section 5 concludes with recommendations.

RESEARCH METHODS

The approach used for the current study is presented in this section. It includes the framework (theoretical and conceptual), functional interpretation of independent and dependent variables used, research hypothesis, study area, population and sample, and data collection techniques and procedures.

Theoretical Framework

The theoretical framework is the study plan (Dickson et al., 2018). Theoretically, the demand for various individuals in terms of tourism perception, attitudes, norms, beliefs, behavioral purposes etc., has been discussed.

The theory of planned behavior has been applied to study beliefs, attitudes, behavioral intentions and behaviors in different fields (Ajzen, 1985; Alzubaidi et al., 2021). Similarly, the reaction action theory predicts how individuals act subject to their past perspectives and social expectations. Hofstede's Cultural Dimensions Theory (2007) says that four cultural dimensions related to work, including power distance, avoidance of ambiguity, individualism and male entity, were established to examine labor-related cultural values in various countries. Community development theory says that social capital and community capacity are closely linked. Social capital is also seen as a social cohesion factor (Hofstede, 2007). Another theory of travel behavior explains the important links between travel and satisfaction with travel. Several important elements of travel behavior, such as travel frequency, mode and distance, are also calculated as factors that affect travel satisfaction (Arroyo et al., 2020; Han et al., 2020). Community participation theory explains the basic concept required to acquire insight and skills to exchange ideas amongst themselves. This can also impact tourism planning to improve their awareness of problems and potentially enhance innovative policies and practices (Chakraborty, 2019). Chakraborty (2019) said that attitudes could positively and negatively affect a person.

Thus, how indigenous people can enhance homestay management issues are the major apprehension in order to find a balance between socioeconomic transformation, rural tourism and rural infrastructure, preserving biodiversity and flavoring localness. The homestay management provides vital support for uplifting the social standards of indigenous people. Thus, homestay management and its performance influence a large number of variables. To conclude, the Gabhar Valley homestay has taken from TPB theory. This theory explains visitors' behavior, subjective norms, perceived moral behavior, the attitude of intention to visit, intention to visit homestay and perceived behavior control, etc., so this theory and model fit my research design.

Conceptual Framework

A conceptual framework, as a manuscript, is designed to develop and systematize concepts, empirical studies and theories of ideas or issues (Rocco & Plakhotnik, 2009). The conceptual structure describes the condition of knowledge through a literature review. In general, it identifies and summarizes the state of knowledge and the methodological basis of the research project to identify gaps in our understanding of a phenomenon or problem (Varpio et al., 2020). This structure enables the researcher to describe the term, map the field or study concept, systematic relationships and identify literature gaps (Leshem & Trafford, 2007).

Homestay has been a growing industry in Nepal (Subedi, 2016). There are several models, i.e., tourist perceived value, travel behavior, tourist motivation, and extended theory of planned behavior model, describing the homestay management for providing a sound conceptual framework. The researcher has used five models based on the theory of planned behavior. The first model is the tourist perceived value model. The independent variables are tourism resource and service value, cultural value, social value, and cost value. On the other hand, the dependent variables are the intentions of re-visit, place dependency place identity. Similarly, another model used is the travel behavior model. The Independent variables of this model are built environment, socioeconomic attitude, individual attitude, and lifestyle. And dependent variable is travel behavior. Another model used is the tourist motivation model. The independent variables are the motivation of visiting the destination, attitude toward visiting the destination, subjective norm toward visiting the destination, and perceived behavior control toward visiting the destination. The dependent variable is the intention to the destination and actual behavior of visiting the destination. The fourth model used for the study is the extended theory of planned behavior. The finding revealed that tourism, personality, subjective standards, perceived behaviors, and moral components help define and understand homestay and tourism management. Lastly, TBP of rural tourism social media model is used for homestay management. This model has explained three key aspects: intentions, conditions and origins for systematic and sustainable homestay management.

Figure 1. Conceptual Framework

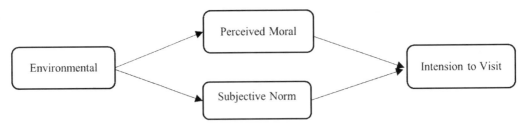

Environmental Concern and Positive Subjective Norms: Subjective norms for the degree of social pressure a person experiences concerning his behavior (Alzubaidi et al., 2021). In other words, subjective norms are perceived opinions of significant others who are close/important to the individual and which influence his/her decision-making. It also means that the individual is under social pressure from other people or groups. Most previous studies have confirmed that subjective norms positively affect behavioral intentions by examining the relationship between people's subjective norms and behavioral intentions (Han et al., 2010; Taylor & Todd, 1995). In the homestay, visitors have a positive relationship between environmental concerns and subjective norms.

H_{01}: Environmental Concern has no significant relation with Subjective Norms.

Environmental Concern and Positive Perceived Moral Obligation: A perceived moral obligation implies that a person feels responsible for performing a particular moral behavior when faced with a moral situation (Alzubaidi et al., 2021; Beck & Ajzen, 1991). Moral obligation is a personal criterion by which a person is willing to perform a certain behavior based on his responsibility or duty. Previous research has shown that a person's moral considerations play an important role in predicting intentions when a person's self-interest is linked to others (Kaiser & Scheuthle, 2003). The perceived moral obligation measures six items regarding safety and protection (Chen, 2016). Similarly, behavior, discomfort, difficulty, and reduction were adopted (Alsaad et al., 2020). Environmental concerns have to play major roles in the homestay management for the visitor. And a perceived moral obligation has human behavior: visitors visit clean. Environmental concerns have a positive relationship with perceived moral obligation.

H_{02}: Environmental Concern has no significant relation with Perceived Moral Obligation.

Positive Subjective Norm and Intension to Visit Homestays: Homestays are products originating from the concept of protecting the environment and visiting them is a special treat to protect the environment. Previous research has shown that environmentally conscious consumers would favor environment-friendly products or services, including visits to family homestays (Han & Kim, 2010). Consumer attitudes, subjective norms, perceived control over behavior and perceived moral obligations to move households into the family influence concerns for the environment (Kaiser & Scheuthle, 2003). This hypothesis shows the relationship between positive subjective norms and the intention to visit the homestay.

H_{03}: Subjective has no significant relation with Intention to Visit Homestays.

Perceives Moral Obligation and Intension to Visit Homestay: Moral obligation is a personal standard by which an individual is ready to act on his/her personal responsibilities or duties. Past research has shown that the moral considerations of a person play a significant role in the prediction of purpose when the self-interest of the individual contradicts others (Chen & Tung, 2014; Kurland, 1995). People who are important to consumers think they should stay with families; then, they will have more intentions to move to families due to higher levels of social pressure. If a consumer has a high level of perceived moral obligation, he or she is more likely to visit the homestay and vice versa (Han & Kim, 2010). This hypothesis has a positive relationship between perceived moral obligation and intention to visit the homestay.

H_{04}: Perceived moral obligation has no significant relation with the intention to visit Homestays.

Environmental concerns and positive attitude toward visiting homestay: Taking care of the environment is a general approach to protecting the environment. It is an essential factor determining the change in people's behavior towards more incredible environmental friendliness (Dunlap & Van Liere, 2014; Weigel & Weigel, 1978). Attitude is a psychological feeling and a positive or negative evaluation that occurs when a person exhibits a specific behavior (Chen & Tung, 2014). The more positive people's attitudes are, the more positive their behavioral intentions will be, and vice versa (Taylor & Todd, 1995). In homestay management, visitors have a positive relationship with environmental concerns leading to a positive attitude to visiting homestay.

H_{05}: Environmental concerns have no significant relation with an intention to visit the homestay.

Variables and Construct

This study is based on prior literature, both conceptually and empirically. Indeed, the factors employed in this study are commonly found in homestay and tourism management literature. The current study looks at four elements of visitors' perceptions of homestay management. As shown in Table 1, four latent constructs of the study consisted of 15 observed items; four items for environmental concerns, three for subjective norms, three for perceived moral obligation and four for intention to visit the homestay. We measured the variables using a five-point Likert scale, where one indicates 'strongly disagree' and five 'strongly agree'.

Study Area and Population

The survey was conducted to collect empirical data through face-to-face interaction with guests who stayed at the homestays in the Gabhar valley. Similarly, a survey questionnaire was used to collect data for hypothesis testing from various locations in the Gabhar valley. The study area is located in Banke National Park (Subedi et al., 2020). Likewise, the geographical coordinates of Gabhar valley of Banke District consist of 28°27" N latitude and 81°68" E longitude (Chaulagain, 2021). The study area consists of 28 homestays in the Gabhar valley divided into two locations (i.e., Main Gabhar and Mini Gabhar Valley). We used a quantitative method with convenience sampling to obtain the sample data to accomplish the study's research aims. We used a 280 sample size. Our respondents were the visitors who visited the Gabhar valley homestay. We used the formula n = z^2pq/l^2 (Adam, 2020) to determine the sample size.

Table 1. Variable Construct

Construct	Observed Variables	Variable Notation	Description
Environmental Concern	Awareness	EC1	Worried about the world's environment
	Human interference	EC2	Human interference produces disastrous consequences
	Balance	EC3	The balance of nature is delicate and easily upset
	Care	EC4	Environmental problems should be care
Subjective Norms	Staying	SN1	Staying in a homestay when travelling
	Align local culture	SN2	Mitigate with local culture
	Important people	SN3	Motivate important people to stay in homestay
Perceived Moral Obligation	Obligation	PMO1	Natural resource protection is obligated
	behavior	PMO2	Behave in an environmentally friendly way
	Pondering	PMO3	Pondering ethical issues
	Moral aspects	PMO4	The moral aspects of my decisions
Intention to Visit Homestay	Effort	IVH1	An effort to stay at a homestay
	Intent	IVH2	Intent to visit homestay in near future
	Want	IVH3	I want to visit a homestay in future
	Circumstances	IVH4	If circumstances allow, I will visit a homestay

Instrument and Procedure for Data Collection

To ensure consistency, we used a mixed-method study for analysis. We used three processes to combine these two forms of analysis. In the beginning, a series of preliminary interviews generated the data and confirmed the appropriate matrix for the second stage, which was a quantitative investigation. The fundamental topics that composed the different aspects were reviewed informally with the homestay and hospitality specialists. We drew each construct's characterization from various definitions available in the literature. In the third stage, we asked experts a series of questions to lay a solid foundation for validating our structured questionnaire. We used a five-point Likert scale to assess each latent construct (Strongly agree= 5; Strongly disagree= 1). We informed all participants that participating in the study was completely optional and that any information they provided would be confidential. To achieve maximum accuracy, we conducted data cleaning before processing the raw data in the statistical software. Because we screened the surveys immediately when respondents submitted questionnaires, they had no anomalous results. We used a structured questionnaire to collect primary data. The questionnaire used for the study was divided into three groups (i.e. demographic profiles, visitors' perception of homestay and managerial solution). All dimensions are assessed using a structured, customized questionnaire developed from previous research, with some adjustments made to account for the study's objectives and setting. We inserted the data in the kobo toolbox when the questionnaire was finalized. Similarly, a Pre-test of 20 responders was also undertaken to ensure that the information was clear and easy to understand. Based on responses of 280 respondents, EFA was conducted using SPSS and inferential was conducted using AMOS.

Data Analysis

We analyzed the collected data to achieve the objective of the study. We used both descriptive and inferential analysis methods. We used descriptive data to describe the socio-demographic characteristics, the general opinion of homestay management and managerial solution. Likewise, we conducted an inferential analysis to analyze the statistical relationship of hypothesized models. We used SPSS and SEM techniques to analyze the data and draw conclusions. To begin, we conducted an exploratory factor analysis using SPSS version 22.0 through Principal Component Analysis. Second, using AMOS version 22.0, a two-stage technique was applied to test the research model. This study used EFA to determine a measure's factor structure, a measurement model to verify data validity, and a structural model to determine each structural parameter's significance, direction, and magnitude.

RESULT AND ANALYSIS

Socio-Demographic Analysis

A total of 280 respondents provided information to the survey in this study. Regarding gender, (51%) were male, whereas females were (49%). Regarding marital status, the majority (66%) of respondents were married, indicating that married visitors were more attracted to the homestay. Most respondents (42.11%) were in the age group 31-40, followed by 40% of respondents in the age group 21-30, indicating that youths are more attracted to visiting homestays of different ethnic groups. We divided the respondents into four groups based on their educational levels. With 67.46%, bachelor's degree and +2 was the highest level of education. Meanwhile, 18.25% of respondents had a master's degree or more. The rest completed secondary education (SLC) or those below primary education (19.12%). Regarding employment, most respondents worked in both the public and private sectors (43.87%). There were 13.33% businessmen, 12.63% students and others respectively. According to our findings, most respondents (40.70%) who visited the Gabhar valley homestay earned a median salary (20,000-30,000).

General Opinion of Homestay Management

We found that 92.63% of the respondents visited and stayed in homestays, and only 7.37% did not visit any homestay and stayed at night. The data indicated that most people have visited and stayed in new homestays. Among them, 28.77% of visitors have visited the Gabhar Valley. Similarly, 14.04% visited Dalla Gaun homestay, 13.33% visited Sauraha homestay, 12.98% visited Bandipur homestay, 10.53% visited Ghale Gaun homestay, 7.37% visited Tanahusur homestay, 4.21% has visited Sirubari homestay and 1.4% has visited other. Our study revealed that 44.21% of tourists stayed for one day, 31.23% of tourists spent two days, 18.95% of respondents spent three days, and 5.61% of the tourists spent more than three days.

There are seven different activities, i.e., livelihood, culture and tradition, people hospitality, surrounding greenery and conserved wildlife, national park/ protected area, local food and taste, local place and environment and agro-experience. Regarding the taste of food, 27.37% of the respondents gave 1st rank to local foods and taste. Likewise, 20.35% gave 2nd rank to surrounding greenery and conserved wildlife. The livelihood culture and tradition, people hospitality got the third rank, i.e., 17.54%. People hospitality ranked fourth, i.e., 10.88% of respondents. The fifth rank is Argo-experience, i.e., 9.12%. The sixth rank was national park/ protected area, i.e., 8.77%. Local place and environment received seventh rank, i.e., 5.96%.

Figure 2. Homestay Promotional

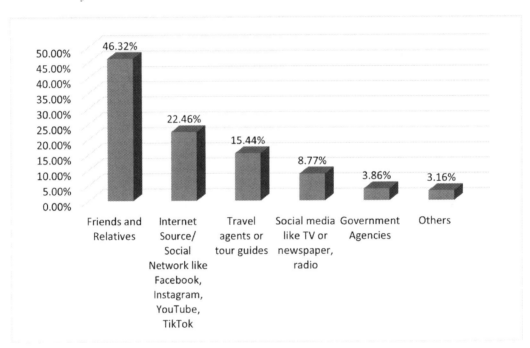

Managerial Solution

Our 90.18% of respondents believed the homestays are manageable, whereas only 9.82% of tourists believe they are not. They can manage by making it tourist friendly, improving rooms facility, the attractiveness of homes decoration, cleanness of homes, facility for tourist guild, Tharu foods, cultural dance and tradition etc. has manageable. Our study reveals that most respondents find homestay owners and homestays family members responsible for homestay management by homestay owners and homestays family members. 84.91%, 82.46%, 29.47%, 28.42% and 9.82% believe homestay owners, homestay family members, homestay management committee, government and others are responsible for homestay management, respectively.

Our study has revealed that 47.02% of guests had very good feedback and only 5.26% had extremely bad feedback for homestay at Gabhar Valley. It indicates that guests liked their homestay foods, homestay hospitality for guests, natural environment and, Tharu culture, livelihood.

Table 2. Improvement and Suggestions at Gabhar Valley Homestay. Source: Filed Study

SN	Suggestions for Gabhar Valley	No of Visitors	Percentage
1	Improvement of local food, culture and tradition	75	26.32%
2	Improvement in linguistic and communication	20	7.02%
3	Policy implementation by local government	60	21.05%
4	More advertisements throughout social media	40	14.04%
5	Development infrastructure, i.e., blacktop road, internet facility, etc.	50	17.54%
6	Establish a museum, cultural ornament	30	10.53%
7	Improvement of tourist's information desk	10	3.51%

Inferential Analysis

Summary Statistics

The summary statistics are presented, including the mean, median, standard deviation, skewness, and kurtosis of the reported manifest variables. The mean ranges from 3.764 to 4.586, and the standard deviation ranges from 0.902 to 1.217, indicating that the data are consistent. The skewness value lies from -2.815 to -0.751 in our study, which lies above -3 and below 0, which shows that it has a negative skewness, i.e., the tail of the left side of the distribution is longer (Kallner 2018). Likewise, in kurtosis, the values lie above -0.028 to 7.682, representing the high peak kurtosis distribution. The calculation of fit for distribution is kurtosis. It means that data is usually distributed. Hence, it allows further analysis.

Exploratory Factor Analysis

To determine the underlying dimensions of the perceived value scale, researchers used exploratory factor analysis (EFA) using varimax rotation. The study revealed that the KMO value is 0.735, and the value of Bartlett's test is 0.000, which is less than 5%, suggesting that the data used by the researcher is suitable for a structural reduction. The commonalities of all the items retained for the study were more than 0.5, suggesting that extracted factors explained more of the variance of an individual item. Similarly, the Cronbach alpha score of 4 latent constructs ranged from 0.807 to 0.843, exceeding the minimum threshold value (i.e., 0.70), implying good internal consistency. Furthermore, the total variance for a single factor is 19.84%, less than 50%, showing that common method bias (CMB) does not affect our data and indicates that these latent constructs are suitable for further process. As a result of the low factor loading (i.e., less than 0.50), some observed items were removed, leaving only 15 items from four latent constructs for further analysis.

Measurement Model

Before analyzing the structural model, the measurement models were estimated using Anderson and Gerbing two-step technique (1988). We performed confirmatory factor analysis on the 15 observed items corresponding to four constructs. We used CMIN/df, RMR, GFI, CFI, TLI, IFI, RMSEA, and CMIN/df to test the model's goodness of fit. The result of CFA showed that all latent variables fulfill the criteria and indicate a good model is fit for the study purpose.

On the other hand, we assessed the validity of data collected by considering convergent and discriminant validity. The convergent validity shows the degree to which indicators of selected latent constructs coverage or share of a significant proportion of variance in general. Standardized factor loadings were used to determine the validity of the observed items, which showed that they were significant and indicative of their latent construct. For convergent validity, they must assure certain conditions: i.e. CR>0.7, CR>AVE and AVE>0.5. All latent constructs composite reliability (CR) readings were higher than the benchmark value of 0.70, and all Average Variance Extracted (AVE) values were higher than the recommended value of 0.50 (See Table 3). The results showed that our study's entire data set met all the validity criteria.

Discriminant validity shows the degree to which a construct is actually distinctive from other latent constructs and is calculated using AVE and Maximum Shared Variance (MSV). The two prerequisites for assuring discriminant validity are AVE > MSV and AVE > r (i.e. correlation). Because both MSV and the correlation of four latent components were found to be lower than their respective AVE values, the overall discriminant validity component was significant (See Table 3). The square roots of the AVE values and respective loadings were all higher than their corresponding inner-construct correlations and cross-loadings, demonstrating satisfactory discriminant validity, as shown in Table 4.

Table 3. Validity and Reliability

Construct	Indicator	Factor Loading	CRONBACH'S ALPHA	CR	AVE	MSV
Environmental Concern	EC1	0.809	0.843	0.844	0.577	0.003
	EC2	0.792				
	EC3	0.841				
	EC4	0.852				
Perceived Moral Obligation	PMO1	0.759	0.810	0.815	0.528	0.020
	PMO2	0.822				
	PMO3	0.854				
	PMO4	0.752				
Intention to Visit Homestay	IVH1	0.803	0.807	0.808	0.513	0.020
	IVH2	0.787				
	IVH3	0.792				
	IVH4	0.794				
Subjective Norms	SN1	0.875	0.840	0.815	0.528	0.020
	SN2	0.836				
	SN3	0.891				

Figure 3. Path Analysis

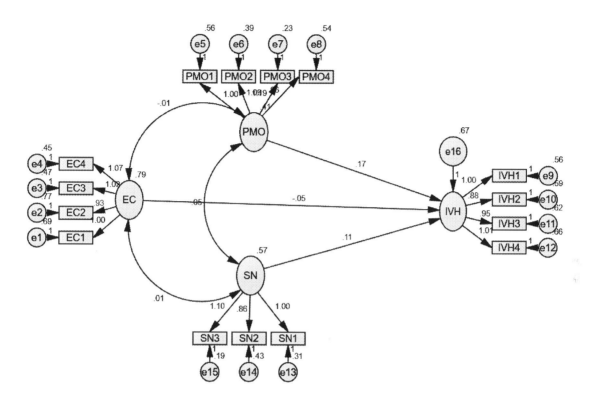

Table 4. Latent Construct Correlation

	IVH	EC	PMO	SN
IVH	**0.716**			
EC	-0.056	**0.760**		
PMO	0.141	-0.025	**0.727**	
SN	0.115	0.017	0.094	**0.802**

Test of Hypothesis

An empirical structural equation model was created and tested to examine if the hypothesized theoretical model was consistent with the acquired data. Three exogenous constructs (i.e., *Environmental Concern, Perceived Moral Obligation, and Subjective Norms*) and one endogenous construct (i.e. *Intention to Visit homestay*) were used to test the theoretical model. The proposed model's path coefficients, R-squared values, and structural relationship between research variables are shown in Figure 2. The R-squared values show the variations explained by individual constructs, while the path coefficients represent the strength of the association between dependent and independent latent constructs. Table 6 displays the standardized regression weights for the direct paths associated with the hypothesized model generated from the model's outcomes. All the hypotheses with P-value less than 0.05 are accepted, which means there are significant relationships between dependent and independent variables. H_{01}, H_{02} and H_{05} hypotheses are accepted as p<0.05 (see Table 5), and the remaining hypotheses are rejected. This indicates that environmental concern has a significant relationship with subjective norms, perceived moral obligation and intention to visit the homestay. Whereas perceived moral obligation and subjective norms had an insignificant relationship between intention to visit homestays.

The theory of mediation examines the interaction between variables of the study (i.e., dependent variable and independent variable). While looking at the relationship between variables, it needs to be determined whether mediators are present or not (Lee et al., 2015). For our analysis, SOBEL test is used. For the relation to be supported, the required criteria is P<0.05. In our, the p-value of both the relationship EC→PMO→IVH and EC→SN→IVH with a=-0.020 & b=0.121 and a= 0.031 & b=0.084 respectively is greater than 0.05. So, we concluded that there is no mediating effect of the mediating variable in the relationship between environmental concern and intension to visit the homestay.

Table 5. Hypothesis Testing Results

Hypothesis	Significant/ Insignificant	Conclusion
H_{01}: Environmental Concern →Subjective Norms	Significant	Reject
H_{02}: Environmental Concern →Perceived Moral Obligation	Significant	Reject
H_{03}: Subjective Norms →Intention to Visit Homestays	Insignificant	Hypothesis Fail to Reject
H_{04}: Perceived Moral Obligation →Intention to Visit Homestays	Insignificant	Hypothesis Fail to Reject
H_{05}: Environmental Concern → Intention to Visit Homestays	Significant	Reject

DISCUSSION

This study investigated the tourists' intention to visit Gabhar Valley homestay in Banke, Nepal. The findings showed that subjective norms perceived moral obligation and environmental concerns, as hypothesized, had a significant impact on tourist intention to visit a homestay. These findings are comparable to those of earlier studies (Chen & Tung, 2014; Kim & Han, 2010). However, in line with the observations report of Bamberg's (2003) study, the findings of this empirical study indicate that tourists' environmental concern is positively connected to their subjective norms and perceived moral obligation, as measured by their intention to acquire knowledge about green homestay goods. Similarly, guests perceived moral obligation influences their intentions to visit a homestay. Furthermore, the mediation analysis results show that tourists' environmental concerns might indirectly influence their intentions to visit a homestay through subjective norms and perceived moral obligation (Chen & Tung, 2014).

In summary, our research findings provide some theoretical contributions to the literature and provide insight into visitors' intentions to visit homestays. Our results support the argument that if visitors' subjective norms toward visiting homestay are favorable, and visitors' subjective norms and moral obligation to support homestay are good, visitors are more likely to visit homestay. The findings also support the TPB model as a research framework for explaining visitors' intentions to visit a homestay. Furthermore, our data show that environmental concerns significantly impacted visitors' subjective norms. This indicates that if Nepalese tourists are concerned about the environment, they will establish favorable subjective standards (Chen & Tung, 2014).

The study's results have many implications for homestay policy formulation and program implementation. When visitors are worried about the environment, the data suggest that they will have a more favorable subjective norm and perceived moral obligation. Therefore, to increase public awareness about the environment, the authorities must focus on raising the idea of environmental protection. In doing so, the government might concentrate on public education or school-based environmental education. For example, the environmental protection administration can create documentary films to persuade consumers of the importance of the environment and confront them with practical problems related to the environment, and give some appropriate ideas and recommendations for them to follow. Visitors will take a more favorable subjective norm, perceived model obligation, and conduct appropriately as long as they sense a higher degree of environmental concern (Chen & Tung, 2014).

A variety of communication strategies, such as media ads and sponsorship schemes, can stimulate tourists' ecological concerns while raising their knowledge of the benefits of visiting a homestay. Our findings indicate that tourists are more interested in staying at rural and community homestays when they have more favorable subjective norms and a perceived moral obligation. As long as guests realize that visiting a community homestay is good for the environment, their subjective norms and perceived moral obligation to visit such a homestay may improve. Moreover, to increase visitors' perceived moral obligation, the government and education should educate everyone that they have a moral obligation to protect our only living environment. They should not only start some eco-friendly programs on their own but also urge others to join them. After all, maintaining the quality of the human living environment is everyone's responsibility worldwide (Chen & Tung, 2014; Kim & Han, 2010).

There is one more item to address. Our empirical study indicates that visitors' impression of the ease with which they may visit a community homestay is a significant factor in their intention to visit a homestay. If tourists believe that community homestays are conveniently accessible, they will be more likely to choose them. Therefore, whether there are enough homestay options for tourists to select from has become a major issue. However, there have been few homestays in Nepal thus far. When homestay owners are urged to go green and apply for the Green Mark, the government's communications and incentive initiatives are critical. Of course, the authorities involved should instill in homestay owners and family members the environmental need for the financial incentive to go green. At the same time, they should educate customers on distinguishing the Green Mark and choosing mark-bearers when the opportunity arises (Chen & Tung, 2014; Kunjuraman & Hussin, 2017).

Different factors cause inactivity among natural-level visitors. The most prominent one is a lack of knowledge. The homestay accommodation industry should effectively communicate messages that explain the goals of their environmental protection policies to make visitors understand the concepts behind operating green homestays to build up the simple use of local resources and the durability of established homestays. The management committee of homestays can remind guests of their social responsibility to conserve the environment besides their personal needs and desires (Goldstein et al., 2007). However, recognizing community homestays among Nepalese and international tourists is still in its early stages. The homestays accommodation industry applies discounts for not asking for fresh towels every day or for not using homestays offered hygiene and sanitation items (Tsai & Tsai, 2008). Hopefully, the various methods of information distribution and education dedicated by the government and the homestay lodging sector, as described above, will inspire travelers with environmental concerns to visit rural homestays.

CONCLUSION

The primary goal of this study was to understand visitors' perceptions of homestay management. Likewise, the study's specific objectives were to identify visitors' opinions on homestay and to analyze their perceptions of homestay management at Gabhar Valley. This research concludes that visitors were interested in visiting homestays and preferred to stay for a short time, i.e., 1/2 days. Majority visit there for local foods and taste, surrounding greenery & conserved and livelihood cultural & tradition. This research concludes that the majority of guests know about the Gabhar Valley homestay through their friends and relations and from social media like Internet sources/ social networks like Facebook, Instagram, YouTube, TikTok etc. This study found that homestay management should improve service quality. To improve the service quality, the owners should create a tourist-friendly environment and improve room facilities. They need to make homes attractive with adequate decoration, hygiene, and sanitation. They should train tourist guides with the knowledge of Tharu foods, cultural dance and tradition etc. Owners and homestays family members should be responsible for homestay management. The study found that tourists had serious concerns about the environment. It impacts subjective norms, perceived moral obligations and intention to re-visit homestays, whereas subjective norms and perceived moral obligations did not influence intention to visit homestays. Therefore, while managing the homestays, the owners must mainly focus on environmental concerns. And the result also revealed that subjective norms and perceived moral obligation do not play the mediating variable as there is no significant relationship with dependent variables.

REFERENCES

Acharya, B. P., & Halpenny, E. A. (2013). Homestays as an alternative tourism product for sustainable community development: A case study of women-managed tourism product in rural Nepal. *Tourism Planning & Development*, *10*(4), 367–387. doi:10.1080/21568316.2013.779313

Adam, A. M. (2020). Sample size determination in survey research. *Journal of Scientific Research and Reports*, *26*(5), 90–97. doi:10.9734/jsrr/2020/v26i530263

Adhikari, S. (2021). *Role of gender diversity on banking performance in Kathmandu valley* [Unpublish MBA Thesis]. Pokhara University, Pokhara, Kastki, Nepal.

Ajzen, I. (1985). From intentions to actions: A theory of planned behavior. *Action Control*, 11–39. doi:10.1007/978-3-642-69746-3_2

Ajzen, I. (1991). The theory of planned behavior. Academic Press. *Inc*, *50*(11), 179–211. doi:10.1080/10410236.2018.1493416

Allua, S., & Thompson, C. B. (2009). Inferential statistics. *Air Medical Journal*, *28*(4), 168–171. doi:10.1016/j.amj.2009.04.013 PMID:19573763

Alzubaidi, H., Slade, E. L., & Dwivedi, Y. K. (2021). Examining antecedents of consumers' pro-environmental behaviors: TPB extended with materialism and innovativeness. *Journal of Business Research*, *122*(1), 685–699. doi:10.1016/j.jbusres.2020.01.017

Arroyo, R., Ruiz, T., Mars, L., Rasouli, S., & Timmermans, H. (2020). Influence of values, attitudes towards transport modes and companions on travel behavior. *Transportation Research Part F: Traffic Psychology and Behaviour, 71*, 8–22. doi:10.1016/j.trf.2020.04.002

Bamberg, S. (2003). How does environmental concern influence specific environmentally related behaviors? A new answer to an old question. *Journal of Environmental Psychology, 23*(1), 21–32. doi:10.1016/S0272-4944(02)00078-6

Basak, D., Bose, A., Roy, S., Chowdhury, I. R., & Sarkar, B. C. (2021). Understanding sustainable homestay tourism as a driving factor of tourist's satisfaction through structural equation modelling: A case of Darjeeling Himalayan region, India. *Current Research in Environmental Sustainability, 3*, 100098. doi:10.1016/j.crsust.2021.100098

Biswakarma, G. (2015). On the dimensionality of measuring tourist satisfaction towards homestay. *International Journal of Hospitality and Tourism Systems, 8*(2), 1–13. doi:10.21863/ijhts/2015.8.2.014

Budhathoki, B. (2013). *Impact of homestay tourism on livelihood: A case study of Ghale Gaun, Lamjung, Nepal* [Unpublish Master Thesis]. Norwegian University, Oslo, Norway.

Chakraborty, B. (2019). Homestay and women empowerment: A case study of women managed tourism product in Kasar Devi, Uttarakhand, India. *Tourism International Scientific Conference, 4*(1), 202–216. http://www.tisc.rs/proceedings/index.php/hitmc/article/view/252

Chaulagain, T. R. (2021). *Population and households characteristics*. In Central Bureau of Statistics.

Chen, M. F., & Tung, P. J. (2014). Developing an extended theory of planned behavior model to predict consumers' intention to visit green hotels. *International Journal of Hospitality Management, 36*(4), 221–230. doi:10.1016/j.ijhm.2013.09.006

Damanik, J., & Yusuf, M. (2022). Effects of perceived value, expectation, visitor management, and visitor satisfaction on re-visit intention to Borobudur Temple, Indonesia. *Journal of Heritage Tourism, 17*(2), 174–189. doi:10.1080/1743873X.2021.1950164

Dickson, A., Adu-Agyem, J., & Emad Kamil, H. (2018). Theoretical and conceptual framework: Mandatory ingredients of quality research. *International Journal of Scientific Research, 7*(1), 438–441.

Dunlap, R. E., & Van Liere, K. D. (2014). The "new environmental paradigm.". *The Journal of Environmental Education, 9*(4), 10–19. doi:10.1080/00958964.1978.10801875

Fatimah, T. (2015). The impacts of rural tourism initiatives on cultural landscape sustainability in borobudur area. *Procedia Environmental Sciences, 28*(2), 567–577. doi:10.1016/j.proenv.2015.07.067

Gerbing, R., Matthay, K. K., Perez, C., Seeger, R. C., Brodeur, G. M., Shimada, H., Atkinson, J. B., Black, C. T., Haase, G. M., Stram, D. O., Swift, P., & Lukens, J. N. (1998). Successful treatment of stage III neuroblastoma based on prospective biologic staging: A children's cancer group study. *Journal of Clinical Oncology, 16*(4), 1256–1264. doi:10.1200/JCO.1998.16.4.1256 PMID:9552023

Goldstein, N. J., Griskevicius, V., & Cialdini, R. B. (2007). Invoking social norms: A social psychology perspective on improving hotels' linen-reuse programs. *The Cornell Hotel and Restaurant Administration Quarterly, 48*(2), 145–150. doi:10.1177/0010880407299542

Han, H., Hsu, L. T., & Sheu, C. (2010). Application of the Theory of Planned Behavior to green hotel choice: Testing the effect of environmentally friendly activities. *Tourism Management, 31*(3), 325–334. doi:10.1016/j.tourman.2009.03.013

Han, H., & Kim, Y. (2010). An investigation of green hotel customers' decision formation: Developing an extended model of the theory of planned behavior. *International Journal of Hospitality Management, 29*(4), 659–668. doi:10.1016/j.ijhm.2010.01.001

Han, Y., Zhang, T., & Wang, M. (2020). Holiday travel behavior analysis and empirical study with integrated travel reservation information usage. *Transportation Research Part A, Policy and Practice, 134*, 130–151. doi:10.1016/j.tra.2020.02.005

Hofstede, G. (2007). Cultural dimensions explained. *Itim International*, 1–3. http://www.geert-hofstede.com/hofstede_mexico.shtml

Hu, Y. C., Wang, J. H., & Wang, R. Y. (2012). Evaluating the performance of Taiwan homestay using analytic network Process. *Hindawi Publishing Corporation Mathematical Problems in Engineering, 2012*(2), 1–25. doi:10.1155/2012/827193

Jamaludin, M., Othman, N., & Awang, A. R. (2012). Community based homestay programme: A personal experience. *Procedia: Social and Behavioral Sciences, 42*(7), 451–459. doi:10.1016/j.sbspro.2012.04.210

Kaiser, F. G., & Scheuthle, H. (2003). Two challenges to a moral extension of the theory of planned behavior: Moral norms and just world beliefs in conservationism. *Personality and Individual Differences, 35*(5), 1033–1048. doi:10.1016/S0191-8869(02)00316-1

Kallner, A. (2018). Logarithms and exponents formulas. *Laboratory Statistics, 5*(3), 1–140. doi:10.1016/B978-0-12-814348-3.00001-0

Kc, B. (2021). Ecotourism for wildlife conservation and sustainable livelihood via community-based homestay: A formula to success or a quagmire? *Current Issues in Tourism, 24*(9), 1227–1243. doi:10.1080/13683500.2020.1772206

Kim, Y., & Han, H. (2010). Intention to pay conventional-hotel prices at a green hotel - a modification of the theory of planned behavior. *Journal of Sustainable Tourism, 18*(8), 997–1014. doi:10.1080/09669582.2010.490300

Kunjuraman, V., & Hussin, R. (2017). Challenges of community-based homestay programme in Sabah, Malaysia: Hopeful or hopeless? *Tourism Management Perspectives, 21*, 1–9. doi:10.1016/j.tmp.2016.10.007

Kurland, N. B. (1995). Ethical intentions and the theories of reasoned action and planned behavior. *Journal of Applied Social Psychology, 25*(4), 297–313. doi:10.1111/j.1559-1816.1995.tb02393.x

Lee, H., Herbert, R. D., & McAuley, J. H. (2015). Mediation analysis. *Journal of the American Medical Association, 314*(15), 1637–1638. doi:10.1001/jama.2015.13480 PMID:26501539

Leshem, S., & Trafford, V. (2007). Overlooking the conceptual framework. *Innovations in Education and Teaching International, 44*(1), 93–105. doi:10.1080/14703290601081407

Madden, T. J., Ellen, S. P., & Ajzen, I. (2018). A comparison of the theory of planned behavior and the theory of reasoned action. *Society for Personality and Social Psychology Inc., 18*(1), 3–9. doi:10.1177/0146167292181001

Moutinho, L. (1987). Consumer behavior in tourism. *European Journal of Marketing, 21*(10), 5–44. doi:10.1108/EUM0000000004718

Muslim, H. F. M., Numata, S., & Yahya, N. A. (2018). Development of Malaysian homestay tourism: A review. *The International Journal of Tourism Science, 12*(3), 65–74.

Pasa, R. B. (2020). Performance evaluation of Amaltari bufferzone community homestay of Kawasoti municipality, Nawalpur. *Journal of the Humanities and Social Sciences, 25*(7), 1–10. doi:10.9790/0837-2507040110

Pasanchay, K., & Schott, C. (2021). Community-based tourism homestays' capacity to advance the Sustainable Development Goals: A holistic sustainable livelihood perspective. *Tourism Management Perspectives, 37,* 100784. doi:10.1016/j.tmp.2020.100784

Pett, M. A., Lackey, N. R., Sullivan, J., & Robinson, S. (Eds.). (2003). Making sense of Factor Analysis (1st ed.). SAGE Publication International Education and Professional Publisher. doi:10.4135/9781412984898

Quintal, V. A., Lee, J. A., & Soutar, G. N. (2010). Risk, uncertainty and the theory of planned behavior: A tourism example. *Tourism Management, 31*(6), 797–805. doi:10.1016/j.tourman.2009.08.006

Rizzo, T. L., & Columna, L. (2020). Theory of planned behavior. Routledge Handbook of Adapted Physical Education, 326–346. doi:10.4324/9780429052675-25

Rocco, S. T., & Plakhotnik, S. M. (2009). Literature reviews, conceptual frameworks, and theoretical frameworks: Terms, functions, and distinctions. *Human Resource Development Review, 8*(1), 120–130. doi:10.1177/1534484309332617

Shen, C. C., & Liu, D. J. (2015). Correlation between the homestay experience and brand equity using the yuehetang rural residence as a case study. *Journal of Hospitality and Tourism Technology, 6*(1), 59–72. doi:10.1108/JHTT-01-2015-0008

Subedi, P., Joshi, R., Poudel, B., & Lamichhane, S. (2020). Status of human-wildlife conflict and assessment of crop damage by wild animals in buffer zone area of Banke national park, Nepal. *Asian Journal of Conservation Biology, 9*(2), 196–206.

Subedi, S. (2016). *Effects of homestay in rural tourism* [Unpublish Master Thesis]. Tribhuvan University, Kirtipur, Kathmandu, Nepal.

Taylor, S., & Todd, P. (1995). Understanding household garbage reduction behavior: A test of an integrated model. *Journal of Public Policy & Marketing, 14*(2), 192–204. doi:10.1177/074391569501400202

Tenzin, K., Mee-Udon, F., & Prampesit, R. (2019). Community opinion towards a village homestay program in Soe, a small nomadic community in the North-West of Bhutan. *African Journal of Hospitality, Tourism and Leisure, 8*(3), 1–10.

Thapa, S. (2016). *Rural tourism in Nepal: Case study of Tanahusur homestay of Tanahu* [Unpublish Master Thesis]. Tribhuvan University, Kirtipur, Kathmandu, Nepal.

Tsai, C. W., & Tsai, C. P. (2008). Impacts of consumer environmental ethics on consumer behaviors in green hotels. *Journal of Hospitality & Leisure Marketing, 17*(3–4), 284–313. doi:10.1080/10507050801984974

Varpio, L., Paradis, E., Uijtdehaage, S., & Young, M. (2020). The distinctions between theory, theoretical framework, and conceptual framework. *Academic Medicine, 95*(7), 989–994. doi:10.1097/ACM.0000000000003075 PMID:31725464

Walter, P., Regmi, K. D., & Khanal, P. R. (2018). Host learning in community-based ecotourism in Nepal: The case of Sirubari and Ghalegaun homestays. *Tourism Management Perspectives, 26*(February), 49–58. doi:10.1016/j.tmp.2018.02.002

Weigel, R., & Weigel, J. (1978). Environmental concern: The development of a measure. *Environment and Behavior, 10*(1), 3–15. doi:10.1177/0013916578101001

White-Davis, T., Edgoose, J., Brown Speights, J. S., Fraser, K., Ring, J. M., Guh, J., & Saba, G. W. (2018). Addressing racism in medical education: An interactive training module. *Family Medicine, 50*(5), 364–368. doi:10.22454/FamMed.2018.875510 PMID:29762795

Wong, A., & Sohal, A. (2002). An examination of the relationship between trust, commitment and relationship quality. *International Journal of Retail & Distribution Management, 30*(1), 34–50. doi:10.1108/09590550210415248

Zhang, X., & Tang, J. (2021). A Study of Emotional Solidarity in the Homestay Industry between Hosts and Tourists in the Post-Pandemic Era. *Sustainability, 13*(13), 7458. doi:10.3390u13137458

Zhang, Y., Washington, W. M., Weatherly, J. W., Meehl, G. A., Semtner, A. J., Bettge, T. W., Craig, A. P., Strand, W. G., Arblaster, J., Wayland, V. B., & James, R. (2000). Parallel climate model (PCM) control and transient simulations. *Climate Dynamics, 16*(10–11), 755–774. doi:10.100700382000007

Zhao, Y., Chau, K. Y., Shen, H., & Duan, X. (2022). Relationship between perceived value, satisfaction and behavioral intention of homestays in the experience economy of mainland China. *Anatolia*, 1-12.

Chapter 13
Sustainable Inventory Management in Hotels

Tipparat Laohavichien
Department of Technology and Operations Management, Kasetsart University, Thailand

Lawrence D. Fredendall
Department of Management, Clemson University, USA

ABSTRACT

The objectives of this chapter are to present inventory planning and control systems in the hotel industry and to examine how to use the existing inventory management practices in the hotel industry to promote sustainability based on the concept of a triple bottom line (i.e., economic, social, and environmental sustainability). Yield or revenue management is the method most hotels use to manage their perishable inventory (rooms). The basic principle of yield management is that hotels achieve maximum revenue by matching customer needs with the right room rate and the right time of sale. Yield management directly promotes economic and social sustainability but indirectly fosters environmental sustainability. In addition, techniques and models for managing nonperishable hotel inventory are discussed, including the EOQ model, JIT and Lean systems, and the ABC classification. Moreover, radio-frequency identification (RFID), the technology used to support the effectiveness of a sustainable inventory management system, is discussed, and finally, further research is provided.

INTRODUCTION

Business organizations across the world now face increasing pressure from the government, customers, and stakeholders to demonstrate corporate sustainability. Sustainability is based on the concept that the consequences of people's activity and organization's operations that meet the needs of this generation today should not negatively impact the next generation's future needs (United Nations, 1987, p. 24). However, the term "sustainability" has been interpreted in many different ways. A survey of more than 1,500 executives and managers worldwide revealed a wide variety of sustainability definitions. Some

DOI: 10.4018/978-1-6684-4645-4.ch013

focused only on environmental impact, while others integrated many aspects such as economic, societal, cultural, and personal implications (Bern et al., 2009). By integrating sustainability within their operations, corporations not only demonstrate their responsibility to the world and the next generations, but they can also improve financial performance (Klassen & McLaughlin, 1996), gain customer loyalty (Lee et al., 2017), establish corporate reputation (Kim et al., 2015), and increase competitiveness (Ruiz Molina et al., 2022).

Sustainability management includes formulating, implementing, and evaluating the decisions and actions related to sustainable practices for both the environment and socioeconomic system. These decisions and actions are made at the individual, organizational and societal levels (Starik & Kanashiro, 2013). Many businesses achieve a sustainability orientation by focusing on long-term goals related to the well-being of the environment, society, and economy. Using institution theory, sustainability is defined within an institution's environment, including a degree of environmental regulation, societal expectations on organization responsibility, and national business systems that vary across countries (Song, 2020).

John Elkington coined the term "Triple Bottom Line (TBL)" in 1994 (Elkington, 2004). TBL, also known as "People, Planet, Profit (PPP)," uses three indexes---social (people), environmental (planet), and economic (profit) to measure a firm's sustainability (Goel, 2010). Well-known organizations such as Shell, AT&T, Clorox, Toyota, Timberland, and Dow Chemical have used the term TBL in their annual report and other press releases (Norman & MacDonald, 2004; Dhiman, 2008). Therefore, the TBL concept is regarded in operations management as to how sustainability is implemented (Kleindorfer et al., 2005). Sustainable operations management incorporates social, environmental, and economic responsibilities into the company's culture, strategy, and operations with the purpose of sustainable performance achievement.

In operations management, social sustainability means that an organization's business practices should both be fair to stakeholders and engage in activities that give back to society. For example, ensuring employees and people in the surrounding community have a good quality of life, encouraging diversity in the workplace, engaging in corporate social responsibility (CSR) programs, and so forth. Environmental sustainability is related to the efficient use of energy recourses, reduction of waste and pollution, and minimizing consumption of harmful materials, and so forth. Economic sustainability refers to the business practices that concern long-term financial performance and cost-efficiency. Typically, costs in this context are operationalized as production and service costs, such as the costs of outsourced goods and services, recycling, inventory holding, etc.

Business organizations exert effort to achieve economic sustainability because it is at the core of their business operations. Businesses need to have financial performance that satisfies stakeholders to survive in their industry. Therefore, some organizations are reluctant to pursue environmental and social sustainability because environmental and social sustainability activities may increase their costs (Hutchins & Sutherland, 2008) and may not directly affect their business performance. Consequently, customers, government, community, and society are the main drivers that pressure the company to consider environmental and social sustainability in their operations. Kleindorfer et al. (2005) proposed a dynamic framework for companies to use to achieve sustainable operations. The framework offers four types of business strategies involved in sustainable operations management as follows:

1. Improve current internal operations using continuous processes that lead to sustainability, such as waste reduction, natural resources consumption reduction, etc. This strategy is called "current internal strategies."
2. Improve the impact of business suppliers' and customers' processes on the society, the environment, and the economy by analyzing the current supply chains and finding a better choice of materials and methods. This strategy is called "current external strategies."
3. Investigate capabilities to improve organizational operations in the future, such as developing substitutes for non-recycled inputs, redesigning product or service processes to reduce energy consumption and pollution emission, etc. This strategy is called "internal strategies for the future."
4. Develop capabilities in the whole supply chain for long-term sustainability. This strategy is called "external strategies for the future."

This dynamic framework for sustainable operations management means that businesses could adopt different sustainable practices at both the inter-organizational and intraorganizational levels. But a critical business practice area consists of inventory management practices; these are crucial sustainable practices at the inter-organizational level (Pattnaik et al., 2021). Inventory management is an essential issue in operations management. Traditional inventory management focuses on the organization's tangible assets. The basic classical inventory management model is the Economic Order Quantity (EOQ) model. This was developed by Ford Harris in 1915 to examine the two major inventory decisions: how much to order and when to order. The EOQ model is one of the oldest, most commonly known, and easy-to-use techniques. The assumptions of the EOQ model are the following (Heizer & Render, 2011, p. 507):

1. Demand is known, constant, and independent
2. Lead time is known and constant
3. Inventory receipt is one batch at one time
4. Quantity discounts are not allowed
5. Only setup cost, holding cost, and item cost are considered

While these assumptions make it an easy model to use, the EOQ model ignores environmental costs such as warehouse emission costs, transport pollution costs, and social factors. So as formulated, the EOQ model does not support corporate sustainability in terms of TBL. In addition, the EOQ model applies to goods manufacturing firms more than services. This is because services as a process are perishable and time dependent.

For example, if a person missed a doctor's appointment yesterday, s/he cannot go back to yesterday to obtain the treatment. Another implicit assumption of the EOQ model was that stocked items have infinite shelf lives---nonperishable (Bakker et al., 2012). Consequently, the EOQ model is not appropriate for a service organization where everything is perishable, and it does not align with the concept of sustainability. This chapter examines inventory planning and control systems in the hotel industry to identify whether current hotel inventory management practices promote sustainability in terms of TBL. In addition, techniques and models for managing hotel inventory will be discussed and further research will be provided.

BACKGROUND

Operations management views the operations systems as consisting of three components: inputs, conversion process or transformation, and outputs. There are two forms of outputs: goods and services. Many key differences exist between goods and services. The most notable difference is that goods are tangible, while services are intangible. Activities involved in creating goods and/or services occur in all kinds of organizations, but the activities differ between goods and services organizations. For example, service processes require a much higher degree of interaction with customers than manufacturing processes require. The service facility needs to be designed for customers to be present for a face-to-face service, while a manufacturing plant does not require an area for customers to be present. Goods can be made in a plant distant from the customer, with no direct interaction between the producer and customer, which is not the case with service.

There are two types of service organizations: 1) pure services, and 2) core services (Sharma & Patterson, 1999). Examples of pure services are legal, consulting, and teaching. These services focus on giving clients an action that is intangible. On the other hand, core service providers are the service organizations that must also manage tangible goods. For example, hospitals provide healthcare services as a core service but also need many tangible goods to provide services. These goods include protective masks, medicines, needles, etc. A hotel is another example of a core service organization. The hotel's main core service is the provision of sleeping accommodations, but the hotel's services also include providing tangibles, such as meals, beverages, newspapers, and so forth.

Therefore, the hotel industry uses an inventory planning and control system for both their: 1) core service's inventory management and 2) inventory management of the tangibles necessary for the hotel operations. Inventory management can affect the hotel's service perceived quality and customer satisfaction. For example, customers will be unhappy with the hotel accommodation service if a hotel stocks out of beverages.

MANAGING CORE-SERVICE INVENTORY IN HOTELS

A hotel is a service organization whose core service is the number of available rooms for customers. So, inventory management in the form of capacity planning is a crucial hotel function. The room must be available when the customer wants to stay. A room night cannot be stored for use later. Therefore, demand management is essential to hotel capacity management. Customer demand constantly fluctuates and, as stated earlier, a room night cannot be stored.

The hotel's inability to use a buffer to smooth customer demand, which is similar to inventory buffers in goods industries, creates a challenge in designing an economic, social, and environmentally responsible inventory system in a competitive environment. Yield management is a technique to incorporate capacity and demand management to generate the maximum revenue.

Yield Management

Yield management, which is also referred to as revenue management, was first developed in the airline industry by American Airlines (Viglia & Abrate, 2019). American Airlines started research on managing revenue from its reservations inventory in the early 1960s. In 1987, American Airlines used the term "yield management" in its annual report, referring to "selling the right seats to the right customers at the right price." As a result, yield management improved American Airlines' financial performance (Smith et al., 1992). Since then, yield management has been employed in other service organizations to manage their perishable inventory.

Yield management" is a method to maximize the profit or revenue of service organizations with high fixed costs and low variable costs, such as hotels, car rentals, and cruises. The firm incorporates customer demand and the organization's capacity to create a pricing policy that maximizes revenue (Davis, Aquilano, & Chase, 2003). The concept of yield management is to sell the right inventory unit to the right type of customer at the right time and at the right price (Kimes, 1989). Therefore, service organizations can achieve maximum income (yield per available inventory unit) by deciding how much of each type of inventory to allocate to different customer demands with different prices.

In the hotel industry, it is difficult to fill rooms with full-price customers. Therefore, hotels fill rooms by offering discounted price incentives and using yield management systems to balance the high utilization of rooms achieved with lower room rates versus lower room utilization at a higher room rate. While an unoccupied room represents an opportunity cost, the hotels must decide the rooms-night to sell at a discount rate while ensuring room-night are available to sell to later-booking full rate customers. Therefore, revenue per available room is a measure of the hotel's yield. Yield management is most effective under the following conditions (Kimes, 1989), which hotels meet:

1. Demand is highly fluctuating and can be segmented by customer.
2. Service or product can be reserved or sold in advance of consumption.
3. The capacity is relatively fixed.
4. Inventory is perishable.
5. Variable costs are low.
6. Fixed costs are high.

Operating Yield Management in Hotel

Yield management has been used in the hotel industry since the 1990s, and it improves revenue (Lockyer, 2007). For example, Marriott international hotels using yield management improved revenue by US$25-35 million in 1991. However, not all hotels successfully implement yield management (Baker & Collier, 1999). Successful yield management depends on internal agreement about the variable room rate policy. To achieve this goal, the hotels must provide: (1) different prices to different customer segments or (2) different prices for a different service time. For example, the hotels need to charge a cheaper rate for customers who made a reservation in advance than for a walk-in customer for the same type of room.

Likewise, the hotels may charge a cheaper rate for the same customers to stay on weekdays than on weekends in the same kind of room. This allows the hotel to control customer demand by pricing management. Hotels use a mechanism called a fence to prevent customers from changing their decision from a high rate to a low rate (Zhang & Bell, 2010). Many types of fences, such as the pattern of purchase (e.g., reservation before a certain date, a different method of distribution channel), customer characteristics (e.g., minimum number grouped, minimum purchase times), and product/service characteristics (e.g., refund penalty, changing penalty) are used.

The hotels also need to control the customer's duration of stay, which refers to how long customers use a particular service. Duration is measured by the number of nights staying at the hotel, and it can be classified as predictable or unpredictable (Kimes & Chase, 1998). A predictable stay duration helps the hotels maximize profit or revenue better than an erratic customer stay. Therefore, length of stay control is crucial in yield management and helps hotels manage their capacity by requiring customers to stay for a minimum number of nights (Choi & Kimes, 2002).

Yield management incorporates many inputs to determine the most profitable matching of demand for the hotel's capacity. For example, variable cost per room, average daily, occupancy rate, and overbooking policy are some inputs. There are four different approaches to obtaining the best solution. These include mathematical programming, marginal revenue, threshold curve, and expert systems analyses (Kimes, 1989). The marginal revenue and threshold curve are the two most popular methods, while mathematical programming and expert systems may give a more accurate result, but they require more time to solve the problem. This is a problem in the hotel's context where the decision-making needs to be fast.

Marginal Revenue Analysis

Marginal revenue refers to the incremental revenue organization earns from selling an extra one unit of product or service. In hotels, when the sale of rooms reaches a certain level, the probability of selling one more room is about zero, and the revenue from the rooms is zero. Marginal revenue analysis is that hotels should protect a certain number of rooms with a high room rate for potential customers until the expected revenue from that additional protected high room rate is equal to the actual level of the lower room rate. The optimal room allocation occurs when the marginal revenue for the last room sold at the higher room rate is the same as the one with the lower rate. For instance, in the case that the hotel guests are only divided into backpack and business groups. Business guests are willing to pay higher room rates than backpackers. Then the hotels want to keep the room with a high rate for the business guests first to receive the maximum revenue. This type of room would not sell to the backpackers until the last room was sold to the business guest at a rate equal to or less than the rate selling to the backpackers in a different kind of room.

Threshold Approach

The mechanism of the threshold approach is to compare the threshold value, which refers to actual past booking demand over time (generally between 60 to 90 days), with the current hotel's actual booking. The differences between the threshold and the actual current level are considered to be the need to adjust the room rate to generate the maximum revenue. A typical booking record of a hotel on a particular day can be demonstrated in Figure 1.

Figure 1 shows the threshold curve of a given day. It can be seen that the reservations booked are negatively related to the number of days before arrival. However, the pattern of the threshold curve may not be the same from day to day of a week. For instance, the bookings for Saturday usually are higher than Tuesday due to the nature of the hotel business. Figure 2 shows the threshold band formed from the threshold curves of each day (Monday to Sunday) for 60 days before the guest's arrival.

Figure 1.

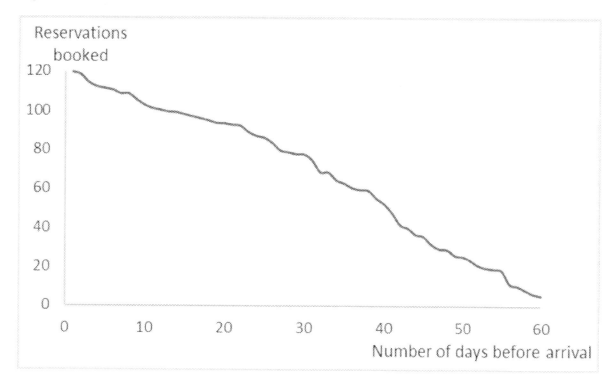

Figure 2.

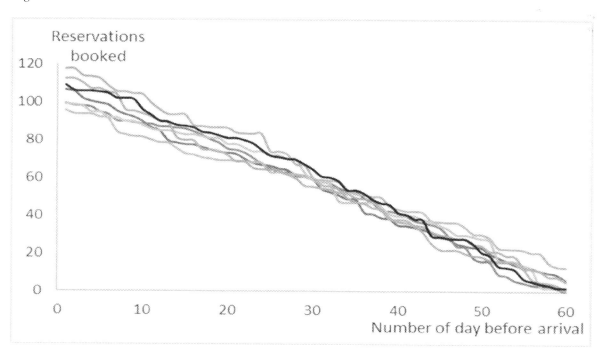

In practice, room rates should be adjusted to gain the highest revenue when the actual reservation on a particular day is outside the threshold band. Figure 3 shows that five days before the arrival day, the actual reservations fall below the threshold band; the hotel manager should open discount rates to motivate more reservations. On the other hand, ten days before the arrival day, the actual reservations exceed the upper level of the threshold band; the hotel manager should increase the room rates and still reserve rooms for emergency guests who are willing to pay.

Figure 3.

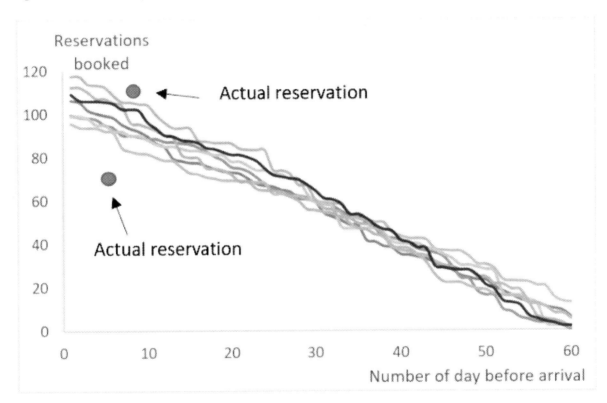

The threshold approach shows many practical advantages. It is simple to install, provides good daily recommendations, and can detect the booking process (Relihan, 1989).

A hotel's yield management program affects sustainability through the way it manages the relevant ethical issues. Yield management has proven high profitability and shows good hotel financial performance; however, increasing yield through the practice of "overbooking" to compensate for customers' cancellations and no-shows creates problems for the overbooked customer, and overbooking is considered illegal in some places (Jones & Hamilton, 1992).

Overbooking is also associated with increased costs. When more customers show up than available rooms, the hotel needs to compensate the customer. This includes transportation expenses, new hotel transfer costs, discount rates for the next stay, and so forth. Another yield management ethical issue is the length of stay control. Many customers view the length of stay control as an unfair practice, which then affects the hotel's reputation, and, eventually, its revenue (Lee et al., 2021). Length of stay control

Sustainable Inventory Management in Hotels

creates the situation that the customer pays different prices for different days during the same booking (the start date and leaving date of stay, type of room, purchase channel, amenities provided), and this variable room rate is criticized by customers (Ivanov & Zhechav, 2012).

Hotels need a culture to support yield management for it to be successful. (Jones & Hamilton, 1992; Viglia & Abraye, 2020). This culture starts with disseminating the yield management concept to all levels of employees. Every level of an employee must understand the yield management concept and understand how to effectively manage the customer who was overbooked. In addition to culture, it is important that information technology and computer software be needed to support yield management. These can help analyze demand with speed and precision.

It is known that the accuracy of demand forecast is a big part that contributes to the success of yield management. However, the technology is only as good as those dealing with it know how to analyze the data correctly and make the right decision. Nowadays, information and communication technology advances have changed the hotel reservation system. Tradition hotel booking systems have three distribution channels, including property management, central reservation, and travel agencies. Currently, online travel agencies have become an additional popular distribution channel for hotels (Choi & Kimes, 2002; Viglia & Abraye, 2020). This channel enables customers to easily compare prices and adjust their pricing based on the inventory (number of rooms) level and remaining time in the selling season (Pang et al., 2015).

Consequently, the ability to manage the system to provide real-time information to ensure no gap in connectivity has been critical to effectively managing yield. In addition, each distribution channel has a different cost to hotels. Therefore, the best managerial practice for hotels is to use the reservation system that incurs the least cost if there is sufficient customer demand in that channel (Choi & Kimes, 2002).

Does Yield Management Promote Sustainability?

It is clear yield management promotes economic sustainability for hotels. Yield management focuses on maximizing revenue and reducing costs. In addition, hotels can generate revenue from guests who purchase food, beverages, and souvenirs during their stay.

Yield management also positively contributes to society. Social sustainability focuses on the effect of the business on stakeholders---both inside the company (e.g., shareholders, employees, suppliers, and customers) and external, including the local community and society. Successful yield management keeps the hotels in operation, which maintains the quality of life in terms of infrastructure and utilities, public transportation, wifi service, etc., for the surrounding community. In addition, yield management promotes social sustainability by influencing a broader supply chain by creating partnerships and facilitating cooperation with travel agency companies and other organizations to offer group discounts.

The relationship between yield management and environmental sustainability should not be seen in isolation (Northcote & Macbeth, 2006). There are no negative and positive direct effects of yield management on environmental sustainability in hotels. However, the indirect impact could incur in the form of tourism. Successful implementation of yield management in hotels can persuade more tourists to stay. Increased tourist numbers may cause a decline in environmental quality, for instance, through increased traffic congestion. On the other hand, increased visitor numbers may stimulate heritage conservation (Hall & Page, 1999). However, the physical effects of tourism on the environment are not fully understood (Hall & Lew 1998).

MANAGING NONPERISHABLE INVENTORY IN THE HOTEL

Tangible Inventory

As mentioned earlier, the hotel is not a pure service organization. Therefore, hotels have to deal with intangibles inventory planning and control. The major tangibles inventory in the hotel are as follows: liquor, food, soft beverages, bedding supplier, stationery items, and hotel amenities such as towels, toothpaste, hairdryer, shampoo, soap, and so forth. The following sections present the techniques to manage a hotel's nonperishable inventory, including the sustainable EOQ model, Just-in-Time and Lean Systems, and the ABC classification.

Sustainable EOQ Model

The most famous hotel nonperishable inventory management method is based on the EOQ model. EOQ is one of the oldest and most commonly used techniques to control inventory. It is purely an economic model in classical inventory control theory (Arslan & Turkay, 2013). The model is designed to find the optimum order quantity to minimize total cost under a deterministic setting. The inventory costs associated with the EOQ are holding (carrying) cost and set up (ordering) cost. However, the original EOQ did not incorporate and evaluate sustainability measurement in terms of environmental and social in the model.

Traditionally, inventory management aims to maintain the service level by improving the efficiency of activities in the supply chain with the goal of reducing the total cost. However, the increasing attention to sustainability issues urges businesses to review their strategies and operations to be more realistic with the current business environment. As a result, many scholars and practitioners have increased their focus on sustainability in inventory management.

Therefore, newer versions of the EOQ model incorporating environment and social sustainability measures are shown in Table 1. Most of the studies in Table 1 developed a mathematical or simulation model under different conditions by providing numerical examples, graphical presentation, and sensitivity analysis.

Based on Table 1, the sustainable inventory planning and control systems modify the original EOQ model that considers only economic criteria by incorporating environmental and social basis. It is clear most studies measure environmental sustainability by carbon emission. The carbon emission involved in the inventory system is generated from three sources: (1) warehousing or storage of items, (2) transportation or vehicle of items, and (3) disposal of obsolete items.

Hotel managers need to be aware of the following issues regarding a sustainable inventory control system for managerial practices. First, waste is generated from poor inventory management systems in the form of carbon emissions. For example, damaged inventory items due to inefficient transportation mode and packaging design. The second is the lot size of the items ordered. The small batches mean more ordering costs and more shipment numbers but less holding costs. Therefore, in terms of environmental sustainability, a small lot size seems worse than a large lot size---the more shipment numbers, the more carbon dioxide emission generated from the transportation. Third, the location of the supplier is also essential because it affects transportation costs---the farther the supplier, the more negative effect on the environment.

Table 1. Selected Sustainable EOQ models

Sustainable measures	Managerial Major Findings	Sources
(1) Carbon footprint (2) Working hours required to perform the operation. It is considered a social measure of sustainability.	The optimal cost of the sustainable EOQ model that incorporates the carbon tax is greater than the traditional EOQ model when the policy remains the same.	Arslan and Turkay (2013)
Carbon emission	The cost difference between the traditional EOQ and sustainable EOQ is low when considering the same single mode of transportation. However, when considering multimode (road-rail) transportation, the sustainable EOQ cost is lower than the traditional EOQ.	Battini et al. (2014)
Carbon emission	The sustainable EOQ model can help reduce transportation costs and carbon emissions by ordering items in larger quantities and less frequently than the traditional EOQ.	Bonney and Jaber (2011)
(1) Carbon footprint (2) The injury rate caused by ordering and warehousing operations is assessed as a social measure of sustainability.	Formulated a multiobjective model by including carbon footprint and the injury rate into the original EOQ model. The conclusion is that the carbon footprint from storing goods that require refrigeration can outweigh the benefits of full truckload shipment.	Bouchery et al. (2012)
Carbon emission	Incorporate carbon emissions into the original EOQ model to ensure that carbon emissions can be reduced without significantly increasing costs via operational adjustment.	Chen et al. (2013)
Carbon emission	Order quantity and backorder quantity increase when organizations consider the environmental cost. Therefore, fewer delivery orders will reduce carbon emissions.	Daryanto et al. (2021)
(1) air pollution emission (2) noise (3) congestion (4) accidents	Propose a sustainable order quantity inventory model modified from the EOQ model by considering the stochastic variability of the supplier's lead time. As a result, the total cost is minimized when the order quantity and the transportation speed increase.	Digiesi et al. (2013)
Carbon emission	The optimal order size of the sustainable EOQ model under the carbon emission trading mechanism is between the optimal order size of traditional EOQ and the optimal order size that minimizes carbon emissions. Carbon emission levels depend on the carbon price.	Hua et al. (2011)
Carbon emission	An environmental strategy is more significant for cheaper and green-labeled products. A public mechanism such as a carbon tax will decrease total and marginal emissions.	Hovelaque & Bironneau (2015)
Carbon emission cost	The inclusion of the carbon emissions costs and imperfect quality items provides helpful information on setting the appropriate lot sizes to achieve minimum costs.	Kazemi (2016)
(1) Gas emission (2) Water waste	The costs and environmental pollution can be reduced by providing a sustainable inventory model that adds environmental ergonomics.	Zadjafar & Gholamian (2018)

Just-in-Time and Lean Systems in Hotels

To support sustainability, carrying a lower inventory level will require a smaller warehouse and less energy consumed in cooling or heating the warehouse. The concept of keeping the inventory at the minimum level is called Just-in-Time (JIT). Taiichi Ohno developed JIT at the Toyota Motor Company in Japan. JIT gained worldwide notability in the 1970s. Many well-known organizations have implemented JIT as a part of their operations, such as Honda, Ford, Boeing, and IBM. The central idea of JIT is to eliminate all waste. Therefore, excess inventory is considered a waste in JIT (Reid & Sanders, 2005).

Although JIT originated in the manufacturing industry, JIT can be applied to service organizations like hotels in which inventory involves purchasing activities that aim to minimize the stock of tangible inventory from suppliers to zero or as near to zero as possible. Based on the basic principles of a JIT inventory system, JIT purchasing requires items are shipped in small quantities at frequent intervals. JIT purchasing benefits organizations in the following: reducing inventory level, reducing space needed, and reducing energy consumption, which in turn reduce cost (Barow, 2002). Al-Aomar & Hussain (2019) empirically studied 54 experts from 5-star hotels in the United Arab Emirates and found that JIT was the first top priority of the technique to control hotel inventory.

JIT purchasing, as stated earlier, definitely supports the TBL in terms of economic sustainability---reducing cost. It also advocates social sustainability. To fulfill JIT purchasing by ordering a small lot size at frequent times can be smoothly possible with reliable local suppliers. By supporting local suppliers, it is evidence that JIT promotes social sustainability. Nevertheless, JIT purchasing does not fully address environmental sustainability characteristics. On the one hand, it supports environmental sustainability by reducing energy consumption from the small warehouse size. On the other hand, it can be said that JIT purchasing is not promoted environmental sustainability due to the frequent delivery of a small lot. The more shipping times, the more carbon emission.

While there is not much extant literature on JIT in hotels, some researchers use the term "Lean System" to refer to JIT. Although JIT and lean systems are often used interchangeably, there is little difference. JIT emphasizes problem-solving that focuses on reducing inventory, while lean operations emphasize eliminating waste and understanding the customer wants (Heizer & Render, 2008, p. 642). Any activities that use resources but do not add value to customers are a waste in the lean system. Ohno identified seven wastes in the operations system: overproduction, waiting time, transportation, inventory, motion, overprocessing, and defective. Obviously, inventory is one type of waste. Therefore, the literature showed that some studies incorporate the lean technique to manage inventory items in hotels, including Al-Aomar and Hussain (2018), Rauch et al. (2020), and Hussain et al. (2019).

Al-Aomar and Hussain (2018) studied 30 hotels with 3, 4, and 5-star rates in Abu Dhabi of the United Arab Emirates (UAE). The results identified a lean-based categorization of waste in hotels' inventory as follows: (1) keeping too much amount of food and drinks, (2) improper storage and excessive storage of equipment, tools, and so forth. The benefit of the lean technique is cost-effective as less waste (i.e., less excessive inventory) means lower cost. Rauch et al. (2020) performed a case study of one of the biggest and noblest 4-star hotels in Italy and found that by using lean in purchasing and warehouse management, this hotel saves 25,000 Euro per year.

Hussain et al. (2019) empirically assess the effect of integrated lean and green practices on the sustainable performance of the hotel supply chain in the United Arab Emirates. The result showed that lean and green practices substantially impact sustainable performance in all three aspects: economic, social, and environmental performances.

Based on the literature, it can be concluded that the lean system of minimizing waste is well compliant with sustainability. In addition, the concept of lean thinking itself is also amenable to sustainability. This is because one of the lean thinking goals is the long-term benefits for the organization. To realize the dominant result of lean takes time. It requires changes in the mindset of people, and systems, which cannot occur in a few days (Rauch, 2016).

ABC Inventory Classification in Hotels

ABC inventory classification is a method of categorizing on-hand inventory items according to the annual value volume to determine the control level and frequency of inventory items checkup. It assumes that a small percentage of causes have a huge effect, so if the organization focuses on a few vital inventory items (i.e., Class A items), it can reduce costs.

The inventory items in the hotel that are suitable for the ABC classification system include liquor, soft beverage, and tobacco (Kumar & Soni, 2017).

However, the literature showed that the usage rate of the ABC inventory system is only moderate level (Kiboko, 2017). The ABC inventory system supports economic sustainability by allowing managers to control class A-items to avoid a frequent backlog (Teunter et al., 2010). However, the practice of ABC inventory classification itself does not directly affect social and environmental sustainability.

RADIO FREQUENCY IDENTIFICATION (RFID)

Apart from the appropriate practices used to control a hotel's inventory, the technology supporting inventory management, such as Radio Frequency Identification (RFID), can provide an effective solution for sustainable inventory management systems, especially in the hotel chain and hotel group. RFID is a real-time information technology that uses electronic tags to store, send and receive data over wireless radio waves. The RFID tag has a chip and an antenna that transmits an item's unique identification (ID) number to a reader containing details associated with that ID number (Alwadi, 2017).

Many well-known organizations confirm that RFID is one factor that reinforces the success of their inventory management system, such as Wal-Mart, Procter & Gamble, Kraft, Gillette, and Metro AG (a German retailer) (Finch, 2006, p. 399). With RFID, hotels can eliminate the need for manual counting of items. This would help hotels keep accurate and up-to-date records of inventory status.

Öztayşi et al. (2009) categorized RFID applications in the tourism industry into four groups: (1) human tracking and control systems such as E-passport and tracking customers with special needs. (2) assets and valuables tracking systems. For example, hotel RFID-tagged valuable paints can be grouped into this category: (3) contactless payment systems (i.e., payment in the hotel, keyless room entry), and (4) RFID-based information devices. The device that is designed to inform the customers by giving information about nearby objects is categorized into this group, such as mobile phone integrated systems used in museums to educate investors regarding the exhibited objects.

The case study of RFID in a branch of a five-star hotel chain located on the Mediterranean Sea was investigated by Öztayşi et al. (2009). The results show that the hotel employed the RFID applications in the access control system, payment systems, tracking systems, kiosk and information management, and preference capturing, such as a system developed to learn the customer preferences in temperature and light of the room, etc. The benefits of RFID are illustrated by Chen (2013), who performed a case study of a hotel in Taipei, Taiwan. The findings revealed that RFID benefits include: (1) improved speed, flexibility, accuracy, and security of information, (2) improved service quality and customer satisfaction, (3) saved costs, and (4) enhanced object visibility and customer experiences.

Aluri and Palakurthi (2009) compare the customer attitudes and intentions to use RFID in the U.S.A. and European hotels. The results show that there is no significant difference between the attitudes and intentions of customers in the USA and European hotels to use RFID. Overall, RFID is a technology that supports a successful inventory management system. RFID technology can bring development in hotel sustainability management and operations to improve performance.

FURTHER RESEARCH DIRECTIONS

The ultimate goal of business in inventory planning and control systems is to generate the highest profit by reducing costs. However, it is likely that to create a sustainable inventory management system, only cost minimization may not be the best solution. Further research in inventory planning and control systems must consider additional performance measures that reflect environmental and social concerns.

The extant literature shows that most studies in hotel inventory management fall into two groups: (1) presenting concepts, benefits, and cautions of each inventory management method and (2) proposing mathematical models with the simulation technique and sensitivity analysis. Most of the mathematical model studies were interpreted from the engineering perspective. Sometimes, they are too technical for the business management context. More future research that focuses on inventory control from the viewpoint of managers and business practices is needed and needs to be "practically significant" (Tracy, 2010).

Good research comprehends how practitioners deal with specific problems and provide implications on how to act. Additional case studies would provide more insight information into sustainability inventory management. With the case study, the researchers can share and talk with participants. This would help enhance the credibility of the research result. Further research in sustainable inventory management may incorporate marketing aspects in yield management to investigate if the different distribution channels: hotel direct (hotel website and hotel front desk), central reservation offices, travel agents, and online agents affect the efficiency of yield management differently.

Moreover, the COVID-19 pandemic has decreased the number of tourists staying at the hotels, especially foreign tourists. Hence, the yield or revenue generated from other functions of the hotels, such as fitness centers, spas, and restaurants, are important contributions and promote hotel sustainability. The effect of COVID-19 should urge the hotel to reconsider the policy of cancellation fees. Some tourists may cancel the booking due to COVID-19 illness or the travel restriction. Indeed, further research may empirically study the effect of yield management on environmental and social sustainability.

Most of the studies in the sustainability EOQ inventory model's settings are in the countries where the carbon emission trading systems and markets exist. However, this mechanism is not applicable in many countries. Hence, further research on the sustainability inventory model in those countries with no carbon emission trading system is interesting to investigate. Additionally, studies examining and comparing sustainability practices in different types of a hotel, such as casino hotels versus convention hotels, may provide more views for managers.

There are limited studies on sustainability in terms of JIT, ABC inventory classification, and lean techniques in the hotel industry, and all these techniques are not equally potential for hotels. Therefore, further studies may design exploratory approaches to study the particular requirements of the hotel industry.

CONCLUSION

Sustainability in the hotel industry is an emerging requirement for better business practices. This chapter proposes a literature review on hotel inventory management in response to sustainability perspectives. In achieving sustainability, hotel executives should adopt environmental and social considerations as well as the traditional economic goal based on the triple bottom line concept. Unfortunately, the extant literature showed that few organizations could achieve the three objectives simultaneously. By the nature of business, profits are the evidence of economic sustainability. Therefore, business organizations cannot stay in the business industry if they are not achieving economic sustainability in accordance with "the going concern" assumption in accounting. For an organization to be a going concern, it must be able to continue operating long enough to carry out its commitments, goals, objectives, and so on. Clearly, achieving economic sustainability is the first priority for most business organizations.

Based on the literature review of the hotel industry, all the inventory management systems practices in the hotel industry support sustainability in terms of economics. However, the methods used to manage the nonperishable inventory in hotels are more concise with a sustainability concept than those used to manage the hotel's perishable inventory. Literature showed that inventory analysis in perishable is more challenging and complicated than it is for nonperishable. This is due to the nature of the perishable inventory, which is different from nonperishable inventory. These differences in the hotels are: (1) capacity is an inventory for the core service of hotels. The hotels cannot be sure that their perishable capacity reserved by a customer will be used; (2) customers are present in the process of perishable inventory management, but no customers are present in the hotel's nonperishable inventory management. Therefore, errors or any mistakes that happen in front of customers need to be promptly solved with appropriate actions

In terms of perishable inventory in the hotel industry, yield management has been the most outstanding technique for inventory planning and control systems. The two most common approaches to obtaining the best solution in yield management are marginal revenue and the threshold value. Yield management responded to economic sustainability in the first place by its concept and followed by social sustainability. However, environmental sustainability is not directly affected by yield management. For nonperishable inventory management, the EOQ model is the most dominant technique.

Since the traditional EOQ model does not consider the issue of sustainability in terms of environment and social, researchers and academics have been adding more measurements into it in order to reflect the concern of sustainability. Many studies integrated carbon emissions into the traditional EOQ model, which measures the emissions generated from vehicles transporting inventory items, the warehouse keeping the items, and the disposal of obsolete items. Hence, most alternative EOQ models are compliant with economic and environmental sustainability. On the other hand, few studies incorporate social sustainability into the traditional EOQ model. More tools and techniques have been used in hotels' nonperishable inventory management in the last decade besides the EOQ model, including JIT, Lean, and ABC classification. JIT and lean seem to support sustainability more than the ABC classification.

In addition, information technology and computer software are required for a successful sustainable inventory management system in this era. A real-time hotel reservation software that passes the information from guests to the hotel's backend is necessary for effective yield management. The essential of having real-time reservation software is also to serve the customer behavior that has been changed. It is expected that by 2023 more than 700 million travelers will be booking hotels primarily online (Lacalle, 2021).

Additionally, information technology such as RFID is essential for updating and tracking information in hotels' inventory control processes and customer behaviors. RFID offers time-saving and security of information to customers while offering cost-saving to hotels. Finally, future research is still needed in the area of sustainable hotel inventory management and control. Certainly, future research may include case study analysis and actual data collection instead of using a simulation technique or deriving a mathematical model. The case study will obtain more insight and information on the significant managerial practice contribution. Overall, management scholars must contribute valuable knowledge to real-world sustainable practices.

REFERENCES

Al-Aomar, R., & Hussain, M. (2018). An assessment of adopting lean techniques in the construct of hotel supply chain. *Tourism Management*, *69*, 553–565. doi:10.1016/j.tourman.2018.06.030

Al-Aomar, R., & Hussain, M. (2019). Exploration and prioritization of lean techniques in a hotel supply chain. *International Journal of Lean Six Sigma*, *10*(1), 375–396. doi:10.1108/IJLSS-10-2017-0119

Aluri, A. K., & Palakurthi, R. R. (2009). A comparative study of consumer attitudes and intentions to use RFID technologies in the U.S. and European hotel industry. In *Proceedings of 27th EuroCHRIE Annual Conference* (pp. 500-511). HAAGA-HELIA University of Applied Science.

Alwadi, A., Gawanmeh, A., Parvin, S., & Al-karaki, J. N. (2017). Smart solutions for RFID based inventory management systems: A survey. *Scalable Computing: Practice and Experience*, *18*(4), 347–360. doi:10.12694cpe.v18i4.1333

Arslan, M. C., & Turkay, M. (2013). EOQ revisited with sustainability considerations. *Foundations of Computing and Decision Sciences*, *38*(4), 223–249. doi:10.2478/fcds-2013-0011

Baker, T. M., & Collier, D. A. (1999). A comparative revenue analysis of hotel yield management heuristics. *Decision Sciences*, *30*(1), 239–263. doi:10.1111/j.1540-5915.1999.tb01608.x

Bakker, M., Riezebos, J., & Teunter, R. H. (2012). Review of inventory systems with deterioration since 2001. *European Journal of Operational Research*, *221*(2), 275–284. doi:10.1016/j.ejor.2012.03.004

Barlow, G. L. (2002). Just-in-time: Implementation within the hotel industry—a case study. *International Journal of Production Economics*, *80*(2), 155–167. doi:10.1016/S0925-5273(02)00315-8

Berns, M., Townend, A., Khayat, Z., Balagopal, B., Reeves, M., Hopkins, M. S., & Kruschwitz, N. (2009). Sustainability and Competitive Advantage. *MIT Sloan Management Review*, *51*(1), 19–26.

Bonney, M., & Jaber, M. Y. (2011). Environmentally responsible inventory model: Non-classical models for a non-classical era. *International Journal of Production Economics*, *133*(1), 43–53. doi:10.1016/j.ijpe.2009.10.033

Bouchery, Y., Ghaffari, A., Jemai, Z., & Dallery, Y. (2012). Including sustainability criteria into inventory models. *European Journal of Operational Research*, *222*(2), 229–240. doi:10.1016/j.ejor.2012.05.004

Chen, T. F. (2013). Applying FEID technology in tourism industry: The case study of hotel in Taipei. *Advanced Materials Research*, *630*, 439–445. doi:10.4028/www.scientific.net/AMR.630.439

Chen, X., Benjaafar, S., & Elomri, A. (2013). The carbon-constrained EOQ. *Operations Research Letters*, *41*(2), 172–179. doi:10.1016/j.orl.2012.12.003

Choi, S., & Kimes, S. E. (2002). Electronic distribution channels' effect on hotel revenue management. *The Cornell Hotel and Restaurant Administration Quarterly*, *43*(3), 23–31. doi:10.1177/0010880402433002

Daryanto, Y., Wee, H., & Wu, K. (2021). Revisiting sustainable EOQ model considering carbon emission. *International Journal of Manufacturing Technology and Management*, *35*(1), 1–11. doi:10.1504/IJMTM.2021.114697

Davis, M. M., Aquilano, N., & Chase, R. (2003). *Fundamentals of Operations Management*. McGraw-Hill Irwin.

Dhiman, S. (2008). Products, People, and Planet: The Triple Bottom-Line Sustainability Imperative. *Journal of Global Business Issues*, *2*(2), 51–57.

Digiesi, S., Mossa, G., & Mummolo, G. (2013). Supply lead time uncertainty in a Sustainable Order Quantity inventory model. *Management and Production Engineering Review*, *4*(4), 15–27. doi:10.2478/mper-2013-0034

Elkington, J. (2004). Enter the triple bottom line. In A. Henriques & J. Richardson (Eds.), *The triple bottom line: Does it all add up* (pp. 1–16). Taylor & Francis.

Finch, B. J. (2006). *Operations Now: Profitability, Processes, Performance*. McGraw-Hill.

Geraghty, M. K., & Johnson, E. (1997). Revenue Management Saves National Car Rental. *INFORMS Journal on Applied Analytics*, *27*(1), 107–127. doi:10.1287/inte.27.1.107

Goel, P. (2010). Triple Bottom Line Reporting: An Analytical Approach for Corporate Sustainability. *Journal of Finance. Accounting and Management*, *1*(1), 27–42.

Hall, M., & Lew, A. (Eds.). (1998). *Sustainable Tourism Development: Geographical Perspectives*. Addison Wesley Longman.

Hall, M., & Page, S. (1999). *The Geography of Tourism and Recreation: Environment, Place and Space*. Routledge.

Heizer, J., & Render, B. (2008). *Operations Management*. Pearson.

Heizer, J., & Render, B. (2011). *Operations Management*. Pearson.

Hovelaque, V., & Bironneau, L. (2015). The carbon-constrained EOQ model with carbon emission dependent demand. *International Journal of Production Economics*, *164*, 285–291. doi:10.1016/j.ijpe.2014.11.022

Hua, G., Cheng, T. C. E., & Wang, S. (2011). Managing carbon footprints in inventory management. *International Journal of Production Economics*, *132*(2), 178–185. doi:10.1016/j.ijpe.2011.03.024

Hussain, M., Al-Aomar, R., & Melhem, H. (2019). Assessment of Lean-green practices on the sustainable performance of hotel supply chain. *International Journal of Contemporary Hospitality Management, 31*(6), 2448–2467. doi:10.1108/IJCHM-05-2018-0380

Hutchins, M. J., & Sutherland, J. W. (2008). An exploration of measures of social sustainability and their application to supply chain decisions. *Journal of Cleaner Production, 16*(15), 1688–1698. doi:10.1016/j.jclepro.2008.06.001

Ivanov, S., & Zhechev, V. (2012). Hotel revenue management – a critical literature review. *Tourism: An International Interdisciplinary Journal, 60*(2), 175–197.

John, E. (1998). Accounting for the triple bottom line. *Measuring Business Excellence, 2*(3), 18–22. doi:10.1108/eb025539

Jones, P., & Hamilton, D. (1992). Yield management: Putting people in the big picture. *The Cornell Hotel and Restaurant Administration Quarterly, 33*(1), 89–95. doi:10.1177/001088049203300126

Kazemi, N., Abdul-Rashid, S. H., Ghazilla, R. A. R., Shekarian, E., & Zanoni, S. (2016). Economic order quantity models for items with imperfect quality and emission considerations. *International Journal of Systems Science: Operations & Logistics, 5*(2), 99–115.

Kiboko, A. B. (2017). *Inventory management practices and operational performance of hotels in Mombasa, Kenya* [Unpublished master project]. The University of Nairobi.

Kim, H., Hur, W., & Yeo, J. (2015). Corporate brand trust as mediator in the relationship between customer perception of CSR, corporate hypocrisy and corporate reputation. *Sustainability, 7*(4), 3683–3694. doi:10.3390u7043683

Kimes, S. E. (1989). Yield management: A tool for capacity-constrained service firms. *Journal of Operations Management, 8*(4), 348–363. doi:10.1016/0272-6963(89)90035-1

Kimes, S. E., & Chase, R. B. (1998). The Strategic Levers of Yield Management. *Journal of Service Research, 1*(2), 156–166. doi:10.1177/109467059800100205

Klassen, R. D., & McLaughlin, C. P. (1996). The Impact of Environmental Management on Firm Performance. *Management Science, 42*(8), 1199–1214. doi:10.1287/mnsc.42.8.1199

Kleindorfer, P. R., Singhal, K., & Wassenhove, L. N. V. (2005). Sustainable Operations Management. *Production and Operations Management, 14*(4), 482–492. doi:10.1111/j.1937-5956.2005.tb00235.x

Kumar, N., & Soni, R. (2017). ABC Analysis in the hospitality sector: A case study. *Operations & Supply Chain Management*, (Special Issue), 1–3.

Lacalle, E. (2021, April 2). *How does an online hotel reservation system work?* [Web blog message]. Retrieved on September 2, 2021, from: https://www.mews.com/en/blog/hotel-reservation-system

Lee, C. Y., Chang, W. C., & Lee, H. C. (2017). An investigation of the effects of corporate social responsibility on corporate reputation and customer loyalty – evidence from the Taiwan non-life insurance industry. *Social Responsibility Journal, 13*(2), 355–369. doi:10.1108/SRJ-01-2016-0006

Lee, M., Jeong, M., & Shea, L. J. (2021). Length of stay control: Is it a fair inventory management strategy in hotel market? *Tourism Economics, 27*(2), 307–327. doi:10.1177/1354816619901207

Lockyer, T. (2007). Yield management: The case of the accommodation industry in New Zealand. *International Journal of Revenue Management, 1*(4), 315–326. doi:10.1504/IJRM.2007.015536

Norman, W., & MacDonald, C. (2004). Getting to the bottom of "triple bottom line. *Business Ethics Quarterly, 14*(2), 243–262. doi:10.5840/beq200414211

Northcote, J., & Macbrth, J. (2006). Conceptualizing yield sustainable tourism management. *Annals of Tourism Research, 33*(1), 199–220. doi:10.1016/j.annals.2005.10.012

Öztayşi, B., Baysan, S., & Akpinar, F. (2009). Radio frequency identification (RFID) in hospitality. *Technovation, 29*(9), 618–624. doi:10.1016/j.technovation.2009.05.014

Pang, Z., Berman, O., & Hu, M. (2015). Up Then Down: Bid-Price Trends in Revenue Management. *Production and Operations Management, 24*(7), 1135–1147. doi:10.1111/poms.12324

Pattnaik, S., Nayak, M. M., Abbate, S., & Centobelli, P. (2021). *Recent trends in sustainable inventory model: A literature review*. doi:10.3390/su132111756

Rauch, E., Damian, A., Holzner, P., & Matt, D. T. (2016). Lean hospitality-application of lean management methods in the hotel sector. *Procedia CIRP, 41*, 614–619. doi:10.1016/j.procir.2016.01.019

Rauch, E., Matt, D. T., & Linder, C. (2020). Lean management in hospitality: Methods, applications and future directions. *International Journal of Services and Operations Management, 36*(3), 303–326. doi:10.1504/IJSOM.2020.108115

Reid, R. D., & Sanders, N. R. (2005). *Operations Management: An Integrated Approach*. Wiley.

Relihan, W. J. III. (1989). The yield-management approach to hotel-room pricing. *The Cornell Hotel and Restaurant Administration Quarterly, 30*(May), 40–45. doi:10.1177/001088048903000113

Rivera, J. (2001). Does it pay to be green in the developing world? Participation in a Costa Rican voluntary environmental program and its impact on hotels' competitive advantage. In Academy of Management Proceedings (vol. 2001, pp. C1-C6). Academic of Management.

Ruiz Molina, M. E., Belda-Miquel, S., Hytti, A., & Gil-Saura, I. (2022). Addressing sustainable food management in hotels: Proposing a framework and examining hotel groups. *British Food Journal, 124*(2), 462–492. doi:10.1108/BFJ-12-2020-1171

Sharma, N., & Patterson, P. G. (1999). The impact of communication effectiveness and service quality on relationship commitment in consumer, professional services. *Journal of Services Marketing, 13*(2), 151–170. doi:10.1108/08876049910266059

Slaper, T. F., & Hall, T. J. (2011). The triple bottom line: What is it and how does it work. *Indiana Business Review, 86*(1), 4–8.

Song, H.-C. (2020). Sufficiency economy philosophy: Buddhism-based sustainability framework in Thailand. *Business Strategy and the Environment, 29*(8), 2995–3005. doi:10.1002/bse.2553

Starik, M., & Kanashiro, P. (2013). Toward a theory of sustainability management: Uncovering and integrating the nearly obvious. *Organization & Environment*, *26*(1), 7–30. doi:10.1177/1086026612474958

Teunter, R. H., Babai, M. Z., & Syntetos, A. A. (2009). ABC Classification: Service Levels and Inventory Costs. *Production and Operations Management*, *19*(3), 343–352. doi:10.1111/j.1937-5956.2009.01098.x

Tracy, S. J. (2010, December). (20100. Qualitative Quality: Eight "Big-Tent" Criteria for Excellent Qualitative Research. *Qualitative Inquiry*, *16*(10), 837–851. doi:10.1177/1077800410383121

United Nations. (1987). *Report of the World Commission on Environment and Development*. Retrieved on June 2, 2021, from: https://tind-customer-undl.s3.amazonaws.com/6a11aad7-f822-40e6-9717-04ceb0726149?response-content-disposition=attachment%3B%20filename%2A%3DUTF-8%27%27A_42_427-EN.pdf&response-content-type=application%2Fpdf&X-Amz-Algorithm=AWS4-HMAC-SHA256&X-Amz-Expires=86400&X-Amz-Credential=AKIAXL7W7Q3XFWDGQKBB%2F20220417%2Feu-west-1%2Fs3%2Faws4_request&X-Amz-SignedHeaders=host&X-Amz-Date=20220417T070036Z&X-Amz-Signature=809ae6fa2c686138676265d0a5783d35a2232ddb671f0e3a0d6da5dc35e99087

Viglia, G., & Abrate, G. (2020). Revenue and yield management: A perspective article. *Tourism Review*, *75*(1), 294–298. doi:10.1108/TR-04-2019-0117

Zadjafar, M. A., & Gholamian, M. R. (2018). A sustainable inventory model by considering environmental ergonomics and environmental pollution, case study: Pulp and paper mills. *Journal of Cleaner Production*, *199*, 444–458. Advance online publication. doi:10.1016/j.jclepro.2018.07.175

Zhang, M., & Bell, P. (2010). Price fencing in the practice of revenue management: An overview and taxonomy. *Journal of Revenue and Pricing Management*, *11*(2), 146–159. doi:10.1057/rpm.2009.25

ADDITIONAL READING

Becken, S., & Simmons, D. (2008). Using the concept of yield to assess the sustainability of different tourist types. *Ecological Economics*, *67*(3), 420–429. doi:10.1016/j.ecolecon.2007.12.025

Faber, N., Jorna, R., & Engelen, J. V. (2005). The sustainability of "sustainability" – a study into the conceptual foundations of the notion of "sustainability.". *Journal of Environmental Assessment Policy and Management*, *7*(1), 1–33. doi:10.1142/S1464333205001955

Gimenez, C., Sierra, V., & Rodon, J. (2012). Sustainable operation: Their impact on the triple bottom line. *International Journal of Production Economics*, *140*(1), 149–159. doi:10.1016/j.ijpe.2012.01.035

Hampl, N., & Loock, M. (2013). Sustainable development in retailing: What is the impact on store choice? *Business Strategy and the Environment*, *22*(3), 202–216. doi:10.1002/bse.1748

Kumar, A., Luthra, S., Mangla, S. K., & Kazançoğlu, Y. (2020). COVID-19 impact on sustainable production and operations management. *Sustainable Operations and Computers*, *1*, 1–7. doi:10.1016/j.susoc.2020.06.001

Rahman, I. (2018). The interplay of product involvement and sustainable consumption: An empirical analysis of behavioral intentions related to green hotels, organic wines and green cars. *Sustainable Development*, *26*(4), 399–414. doi:10.1002d.1713

Raynolds, P. C., & Braithwaite, R. W. (1997). Whose yield is it anyway? Compromise options for sustainable boat tour ventures. *International Journal of Contemporary Hospitality Management*, *9*(2), 70–74. doi:10.1108/09596119710164803

Sarkis, J., Helms, M. M., & Hervani, A. A. (2010). Reverse logistics and social sustainability. *Corporate Social Responsibility and Environmental Management*, *17*(6), 337–354. doi:10.1002/csr.220

Schrettle, S., Hinz, A., Scherrer-Rathje, M., & Friedli, T. (2014). Turning sustainability into action: Explaining firms' sustainability efforts and their impact on firm performance. *International Journal of Production Economics*, *147*, 73–84. doi:10.1016/j.ijpe.2013.02.030

Stevenson, W. J. (2007). *Operations management international student edition with global readings*. McGraw-Hill.

KEY TERMS AND DEFINITIONS

ABC Inventory System: A method to manage nonperishable inventory by classifying inventory items into three groups: Class A, B, and C based on annual consumption value. Class A represents the highest money usage, accounting for a small number of items in inventory. Class C, on the hand, describes the lowest money usage, which accounts for a large number of items in inventory, while class B is in the middle.

Economic Sustainability: Refers to the organization's aim to carry out its business in a way that can continue for an everlasting time and is also concerned with long-term financial performance.

Environmental Sustainability: Refers to the organization's purpose to continue its business for a never-ending time and is also concerned with its impact on environmental issues, such as pollution, emission into the air, water, and soil, waste, toxic materials, and energy and water consumptions, etc.

EOQ (Economic Order Quantity) Model: The mathematics model designed to calculate the appropriate order size of nonperishable inventory items by incorporating demand, ordering, or set up cost, and holding or carrying cost. The objective of this model is to minimize the total cost (carry cost and ordering cost) incurred.

Inventory: One type of the organization asset. It refers to the stock of any resource used in an organization for current or future operations and can be perishable or nonperishable.

JIT: Stand for Just-in-Time. It is a technique to manage inventory. It originated in Japan's Toyota company. The goal of JIT is to keep the inventory at the minimum level.

Social Sustainability: Refers to the ability of the organization to perform its business for an endless time and contribute to the well-being of the community, society, and country where they locate.

Sustainability: Refers to the intention of the organization to continue its operation for an undefined time. At the same time, the organization needs to perform in a way that does not negatively affect the next generation's well-being while still achieving the organization's current goals.

Triple Bottom Line (TBL): The three organizational performances in response to sustainability. It consists of economic, social, and environmental performances.

Yield Management: A method used to manage perishable inventory in a service organization to maximize the revenue by incorporating customer demand, firm capacity, and pricing policy.

Chapter 14
Revitalization of Creative Tourism in Post-Pandemic Environment in Thailand

Duangthida Pattano
Universiti Sains Malaysia, Malaysia

Shankar Chelliah
Universiti Sains Malaysia, Malaysia

ABSTRACT

The spread of the COVID-19 pandemic has had a significant negative impact on many tourist destinations around the world, including Thailand. A shift in typical vacation behavior has emerged as a major issue in the global tourism industry as a result of travel restriction and social distancing issues. In the new normal scenario of COVID-19 pandemic, creative tourism, which focuses on participating in onsite activities and interacting with people, is facing challenges. It is important to pay attention to what tourists consider when making decisions about future travel plans, especially in creative tourism. This chapter focuses on tourist motivation, travel decisions, and travel practices for service providers, all of which are discussed in terms of how Thailand's creative tourism potential can be revitalized. Furthermore, an integrated model of creative tourism is proposed in predicting future travel behavior related to health risk concerns. Several potential implications and concerns for managerial decision-making in service and marketing contexts are discussed.

INTRODUCTION

The tourism industry is one of the largest and fastest growing industries with leading contribution in term of economic, social, and cultural sectors. According to The Travel and Tourism Competitiveness Report 2019 (World Economic Forum, 2019), the World Tourism Organization (UNWTO) predicts that global international tourist arrivals will reach 1.8 billion by 2030. By 2030, emerging economy destinations are expected to have the highest growth in international tourist arrivals, accounting for a total of 57% of global international tourist arrivals. With the great deal of benefits on travel and tourism sectors, many countries have developed and promoted destinations to expand their market share. Moreover, the Asia Pacific region is expected to enjoy higher-than-global arrivals growth at 4.9% through 2030 (Ministry of Tourism and Sports Thailand, 2017).

Simultaneously, several critical global issues and challenges (such as sustainability, technological and innovation advancement, human connection, health and safety protocols, experience travel with mental wellness, protecting workforce and communities, social responsibility, and woman empowerment) have been widely discussed in order to implement strategies for shifting industry toward a more sustainable future (WTTC, 2021). Nevertheless, tourism is one of many industries affected by disasters, whether natural or pandemic/epidemic, which has a significant impact on tourist intentions to visit a destination (Pahrudin et al., 2021).

In the era of the COVID-19 pandemic, many restrictions and regulations on human mobility affect into travel decision in term of health and safety issue. According to the Global Summit Report (WTTC, 2021), it is important time for turning the crisis to the opportunity to notions of recovery, reshape, rethink, reboot and rebuilding the travelers confidence. As a result, future travel intention and behavior must be considered strongly and seriously as a shift change of a new normal practice. Several researchers investigated factors underlying travel risk perception and travel intention during and after a pandemic to predict tourist behavior (Chien et al., 2017; Godovykh et al., 2020; Li et al., 2021; Samdin et al., 2021; Tseng et al., 2021).

Additionally, the influence of other travel decision determinants on travel intention are significant into tourism researches such as social media (Li et al., 2021; Yu et al., 2021), and destination trust (Shin et al., 2022). Sine tourist behavior is a major issue in the tourism industry, a new scenario in the tourism industry must be revised and proposed based on the new normal environment. For more than a decade, the concept of creative tourism has been debated and proposed as a unique experience for such destinations. In principle, creative tourism is defined as a niche kind of cultural tourism with a unique, authentic, and meaningful tourist experience.

Creative tourism has been recognized as a new category of experience tourism that offer tourists to develop their creative potential as active tourist in learning and experience in such destination (Ali et al., 2016a; Zhang & Xie, 2019). Tourists have transformed into active seekers of new and engaging experiences (Zatori et al., 2018). Stakeholders (such as tourists, locals, trainers, entrepreneurs, and so on) must interact with one another in various forms of learning in order to achieve the core value of creative tourism experience. Creative attractions are not like commodities that are bought routinely (Dean & Suhartanto, 2019).

Many studies have discovered various variables and factors contributing to creative tourism experience when it comes to consumption. In line with Zhang and Xie (2019), the researchers explore tourists' perception through an empirical study of participation, motivation and authenticity and point out sightseeing, social contact, self-improvement and escape as primary motivations for participating in creative activities. Pull motivation factors impacts visitor behavioral intention to re-experience while push motivation to re-experience is strengthen by experience quality and perceived value (Dean & Suhartanto, 2019). Therefore, not only experience quality, perceived value, and satisfaction but also the motivation factors should be considered in the model of behavioral intention.

Many dimensions of experience quality in creative tourism have been investigated, including escape, recognition, peace of mind, unique involvement, interactivity, and learning. (Ali et al., 2016; Dean et al., 2019; Suhartanto et al., 2018, 2020; Wang et al., 2020). On the other hand, the construct of experience namely education, aesthetics, entertainment, and escapism are claimed in the studies of Chang et al. (2014) and Singh & Nazki (2019). For cultural experiences across the contexts of attractions, events and tours, in Hong Kong, Richards et al. (2020) identifies four dimensions of experience (cognitive, conative, affective and novelty) through structural equation modelling to track the relationship between visitor experiences and behavioural outcomes.

The importance of tourist experience on psychological perspective is extended in research. How tourists and visitor experience places, and how the perception of places is shaped by deep psychological constructs (Ram et al., 2016). The exploration of this study focusing on creative leisure travel using a positive psychology perspective confirms that the satisfaction of creative tourists' psychological need and the experience of positive emotions directly impacts subjective well-being. Additionally, psychological needs satisfaction acts as an important antecedent of behavioral intention to revisit creative tourist attractions (Huang et al., 2020). In addition, Chen and Chou (2019) defines the "perceived coolness" term adopted in creative tourism experience model of Generation Y, the antecedences are investigated; namely, uniqueness, identification, and attractiveness.

Many scholars emphasize the role of culture and creativity in integrating approaches geared toward sustainable development (Henche et al., 2020; Henriques & Moreira, 2019; Pulido-Fernández et al., 2021). To achieve sustainable creative tourism, creative tourism experiences must be managed in collaboration with the local community, and created social, environmental, and economic benefits for all stakeholders (Baixinho et al., 2021). Combining creativity in a unique location is important in terms of creating quality vacations for tourists (Eirini & Kostas, 2017).

However, it can vary depending on the context (Carvalho et al., 2019), such as the geographic scale of place for designing sustainable creative tourism (Baixinho et al., 2021). Other perceptions are proposed, such as cultural events and festivals in the setting environment (Guerreiro et al., 2019; Rachão et al., 2021; Zhang et al., 2019). More tourists spending money boosts economic growth (Buonincontri et al., 2017; Pulido-Fernández et al., 2021). These contribute to a tourist destination's success.

Moreover, co-creative behaviour among stakeholders like locals, tourists, including service providers are highlighted (Pera, 2017; Richards, 2018; Slak Valek, 2020). Carvalho et al. (2019) cites the co-creation being a key factor for tourist creative experience in term of tourists' involvement, engagement, participation and interactivity on their consumption process toward satisfaction and future behavioral intentions, that influence to destination image (Slak Valek, 2020).

On the festival providers, co-creation experience can enhance attendees' satisfaction through both the performers and other festival goers (Zhang et al., 2019). Co-creation is recognized as a trend for creative tourism development, in which tourists become co-producers and co-consumers of experiences (Richards, 2020). Participation in activity and involvement in networking with relevant stakeholders are primarily dominated by the creative experience and co-creation concept.

The growth of cultural and creative tourism is part of a broader trend toward creating appealing places for people to live, work, and visit (OECD, 2014) while creative tourism is considered as new opportunities for adding value of goods and services through creativities (UNCTAD, 2021). Many academics have discovered the important role of creativity in tourist destinations. Creativity has become a strategy in placemaking, with cities and regions attempting to increase their attractiveness to the creative class, support the creative industries, or become "creative cities" (Richards, 2020). Underpinning tourism based on the idea of creative industry, creative tourism is emerging as a new product for destinations to add value of social and economic aspects (Huang et al., 2019).

On the other hand, cultural and creative tourism have been claimed as significant tourism types in new normal travel environment. Corresponding, a new model of creative initiatives are debated how to respond to and recover from the crisis (OECD, 2020). Both domestic and international travelers are drawn to the culture and creative industries, new visitor regulations on social distancing and facility modification, for example, these must be implemented (UNWTO, 2021).

Domestic travelers, for example, can engage and reengage with their own culture, heritage, and local communities for new experiences. International visitors may be inspired to rediscover local culture and creative industries. While this type of tourism necessitates closer participation, pandemic prevention has declared the importance of COVID-19 controls. Creative tourism appears to have limited growth potential with new normal travel practices and restrictions on social distancing and health-protection regulations. The core value of creative tourism may not be recognized. As a result, it remains unclear how to encourage and persuade tourists to engage in creative tourism experiences.

Creative tourism allows tourists to deeply experience by learning and doing for knowledge and skills development. With this specific tourism, it is not limited with only one actor, that involves the co-creation of participations, interaction and sharing with locals and creative professionals for first-hand experience. While people and place are recognized and applied in pandemic practices and prevention regulations, a shift of tourist behavior may change and need to redesign. Regarding unpredictable travel intentions in unprecedent crisis, it is important to understand what tourists are motivated for future travel, how tourists design their travel experience, and how much tourists concern on engaging the creative activities. Meanwhile, this will pursue to understand main concerns on tourists' perception through the creative tourism destinations, including in Thailand.

Creative Tourism in Thailand

Travel and tourism are widely recognized as significant activities in Thailand, and they play a significant role in a strategic pillar of the economy. Thailand's tourism industry was ranked among the top ten destinations and top ten tourism earners in the world (UNWTO, 2020). Thailand scored among the top 35 economies due to a combination of natural and cultural resources as well as strong price competitiveness (World Economic Forum, 2019). From the report, Thailand (31st) has South- East Asia's largest T&T GDP, which is reinforced by some of Asia-Pacific's most attractive natural resources (10th) and most efficient tourist services infrastructure (14th) (World Economic Forum, 2019).

Thailand's weaknesses, on the other hand, were in the environment, safety, and cleanliness. According to the Ministry of Tourism and Sports (2020), the number of international visitors to Thailand increased from more than 35 million in 2017 to 38.28 million in 2018, with a total expenditure of more than 1,800 billion Thai baht. While tourists continued to outnumber 39.8 million in 2019, revenue totaled 1,933 billion Thai baht. Domestic visitors, on the other hand, increased steadily from 158 to nearly 167 million in 2018, before falling slightly to 166.84 million in 2019. Domestic tourist spending in Thailand increased from 990 billion Thai Baht in 2017 to 1,084 billion Thai Baht in 2019.

Surprisingly, it is clear the domestic tourist is another critical segment in shifting the economic growth of Thailand's tourism industry. As a result, the country has benefited from a large number of tourists, both international and domestic, resulting in significant revenue, despite the fact that some severe and unpleasant situations have occurred, causing tourism to take a short break. While the number of tourist arrivals was nearly 40 million in 2019, with the outbreak of the COVID-19 pandemic crisis, it plummeted dramatically in the first quarter of 2020, then fell to zero, and then to a very limited number of tourists by the end of the year 2020.

Recognizing the potential contribution of tourism growth, cultural and creative tourism has been highlighted in Thailand's 20-year National strategy (2018-2037), the 12th National Economic and Social Development Plan (2018-2021) and the second National Tourism Development Plan (2017-2021). According to the 20-year National Strategy (2018-2037), with creating diversity tourism of the tourism sector is addresses as part of the Master Plan under the National Strategy for Competitiveness Advancement. Thailand's Tourism Vision for 2036 has been presented in The Second Thailand National Tourism Development Plan (2017 - 2021), as *"Thailand will be a World's leading quality destination, through balanced development while leveraging Thainess to contribute significantly to the country's socio-economic development and wealth distribution inclusively and sustainably"* (Ministry of Tourism and Sports Thailand, 2017).

Therefore, to become a world-class high-quality destination, the primary strategic objectives and targets focus on improving Thailand's tourism industry's overall quality and capabilities, as well as supporting sustainable growth that capitalizes on the great value of "Thainess". Reasonably, creative and cultural tourism is one of quality tourism experience to support for achieving the country's growth.

Through marketing strategies, the concept of creative tourism has also been introduced to other parties in the travel and tourism sector by Tourism Authority of Thailand. Many tourism campaigns have been broadly publicized by Tourism Authority of Thailand (TAT) through several themes such as in 2012 "Discover the Other you", in 2015-2016 in "Hidden Gem", in 2016 "Unique Thai Local Experience", and in 2018 "Amazing Thailand Go Local". Particularly, TAT released its market plan 2017, in line with the Thailand 4.0 strategy which aim to transform the country into a value-based economy through innovation, knowledge, technology, and creativity.

Since 2017, the strategies have been continuously promoted in collaboration with other 55 (provincial) secondary tourist destinations, in accordance with policies such as the tax break for tourism spending. Furthermore, concepts like "Village of the World," "Creative Thailand," and "The Link" were obviously launched to add value in the context of creative tourism experience activities for local communities. Destinations or local communities, on the other hand, face new challenges in developing new products and services to serve newcomers.

Significantly, the UNESCO Creative Cities Network (UCCN) has designated four dominant cities in Thailand, including Phuket as a 'Creative City of Gastronomy' in 2015, Chiang Mai as a 'Creative City of Crafts and Folk Art' in 2017, and Bangkok as a 'Creative City of Design' and Sukhothai as a 'Creative City of Crafts and Folk Art' in 2019. These are significantly increasing Thailand's profile in terms of cultural and creative tourism cities.

Significantly, the concept of creative tourism in Thailand was first implemented as community-based tourism, as it was anticipated as an active tool for adding value to cultures and improving the quality of life in the local community (Wisansing, 2019). Since 2003 Designated Areas for Sustainable Tourism Administration (DASTA) has shared the concept of creative tourism and run pilot projects for emerging creative community-based tourism.

DASTA, which is in charge of Thailand's tourism development program geared toward sustainability, facilitates creative programming for communities, with nine designated areas for more than 80 communities that are currently being planned and developed. A wide range of creative activities in which visitors can learn and participate through first-hand experience, marketing plans and strategies have been revised and launched to motivate tourists from around the world. One of the DASTA handbooks published in 2020, titled, "Be a Local Artist for a Day," contains a collection of 21 creative tourism experiences launched in 11 provinces to promote creative communities, such as Tin-Chok Textile weaving in Sukhothai province, mask art in Loie province, Lanna Egg Cuisine in Nan province, and White clay ceramic in Ranong province, to name a few examples. From these, it is clear that Thailand offers a diverse range of creative tourism destinations for visitors to enjoy.

While Thailand is proclaimed in the uniqueness and charming cultural and historical destination, the concept of creativity has been practiced in tourism industry to reshape or reinvent existing local values and assets. Being more competitive advantage is highlighted on destinations with a high value of cultural assets and resources (Bednárová et al., 2018; Salinas Fernández et al., 2020; World Economic Forum, 2019), while Thailand always addresses the country with a diverse range of culture, tradition, local wisdom, and distinctive living styles. Creative tourism is widely regarded as an essential component for increasing the value of Thailand's tourism industry (Richards et al., 2018), which can boost the country's competitive advantage. Therefore, to draw demands and meet new tourist expectation and behavior trend, creative tourist destinations should be more investigate and rebuild some practical to regions.

Tourism Industry Challenges in a Pandemic

While many countries attempt to take preventative and health measures against this pandemic, several tourism researchers have focused on understanding travel behavior with a focus on the effects of the COVID-19 pandemic. Tourism is defined as a very vulnerable sector in uncertain and unprecedented situations, particularly health situations, where tourist perceptions of health-risk and safety measures vary greatly (Bhati et al., 2020; Rather, 2021; Sánchez-Cañizares et al., 2021). Even so, in a pandemic environment, it is unclear and unpredictable behavioral intention of choosing a travel destination and participating in tourist activities.

Rasoolimanesh et al. (2021) noted that perceptions of a health risk at a destination have a negative impact on tourist perceptions, destination image, and travel intentions, while travel attitude is important factor for travel decision (Sánchez-Cañizares et al., 2021). The issue of building trust is highlight in the study of Shin et al. (2022). The study confirmed that the political and interactional trust levels are required for domestic tourism travel decisions, along with strong ensuring safety via social distancing measures. Furthermore, building destination trust is critical for countries that rely heavily on international visitors, because international visitors are less likely to visit a destination they do not trust.

Notably, tourist perspectives during and after the pandemic may reveal a variety of insights influencing future travel decisions and behavior. While the study of the COVID-19 tourism impacts include all participants in travel stakeholders, it may not be consistent (Abbas et al., 2021). These are affected by many variables such as the tourism industry's size, venue, management, and governance types. They also emphasize that leisure and business travel, as well as local and individual tourists, have very different travel needs, so the consequences of COVID-19 impacts are critical for discussion in specific markets. As a result, how tourists' behaviors and preferences change after the end of lockdown, as well as the factors influencing the changes, merit further investigation (Li et al., 2021).

Despite the fact that tourists perceive a severe spread of COVID-19 risk, existing tourism and hospitality literature fails to answer the question of how it affects tourism decisions (Zaman et al., 2022). In particular, the uniqueness of the creative tourism experiences are sought a high level of involvement, participation, and interaction to achieve a creative tourism experience (Richards et al., 2018). This means that tourists and travel stakeholders such as service providers and local residents must actively participate in the creative process; however, social distancing and other health measures for health risk protection and prevention tend to influence the decision-making process and behavioral intention for travel.

In a sense of safety for Chinese, five experienced safety dimensions were classified; safety information were scored at highest level among safety concerns, tourism environment, facilities and services, and regional culture (Zou & Meng, 2020). On the other hand, visitor relationships to the cultures they visit need rethinking following the pandemic COVID-19 (Einarsson & Sorin, 2020). It is reasonable to believe that risk perception can influence tourists' decisions not only about traveling to such destination but also about avoiding or participating in creative tourism activities. How to encourage tourists to visit and participate in creative tourism activities during and post pandemic is still ambiguous. Hence, understanding influencing factors is critical particularly for Thailand to position itself as a creative tourism destination.

Developing physical features or objects at destinations would be beneficial and increase destination attraction; however, in a pandemic environment, these are less of a concern. Destination managers must understand future tourist behavior. People are fearful and nervous, they do not want to travel during the coronavirus outbreak (Vos, 2020). Although reasons for traveling are various physical and psychological needs, making decisions on travelling is less common during the covid-19 era. Based on reviews, tourist's perception, awareness and attitudes on health and risk concerns are needed more understanding on their travel intention and behavior.

Likewise, Abbas et al. (2021) stated that understanding direct COVID-19 tourism impacts, attitudes, and practices in gaining the leisure industry's boom and recovery is beneficial to government officials, scholars, and tourism firms in reinvesting in the tourism industry following the pandemic. In doing so, this chapter could be expected to make significant contributions to the short- and long-term planning and development strategies of such creative destinations, particularly in Thailand. Travel operators and local service providers could make clear and raise awareness of the potential practices and well-operation to sustainably and effectively boost either the value of the tourist experience or the growth of creative tourism.

With keeping in mind, the principles of creative tourism associated with travel behavior intention have been investigated in several previous studies (Ali et al., 2016; Dean & Suhartanto, 2019; Wang et al., 2020; Zhang & Xie, 2019). More investigation, however, is required to clarify in the new normal environment. Regarding unpredictable travel intentions in unprecedent crisis, travel restrictions and travel anxiety stop people from traveling in order to avoid risk (Bratić et al., 2021), as evidenced by the decrease in tourist numbers shown in current travel statistics. Making decisions on travelling is less common during the covid-19 era, therefore, tourist's perception, awareness and attitudes on health and risk concerns are needed more understanding on their travel intention and behavior. Given that the preliminary study, the study was conducted to gain insight into Thailand's creative tourism context and significant factors influencing tourists' travel intentions in light of the current pandemic environment.

As a result of the preliminary study's findings, there is a significant demand for travel to Thailand when the pandemic is over or at a low risk. Most tourists are willing to travel after the pandemic account for more than 80% of respondents, while only 16.7% of them are willing to stay at home for a while. According to preliminary research, Thailand tourism still has a great deal of potential to encourage tourists in terms of leisure and recreational activities, as well as cultural tourism. With little attention, creative tourism is less appealing to tourists, regardless of the fact that a wide range of creative tourism products have been promoted and are available throughout the country as main attractions in both first and secondary tier city destinations. Furthermore, escapism or relaxation were identified as primary motivations for an upcoming trip to Thailand based on the findings. Other factors, such as self-development and social contact, as well as a focus on hands-on activities for learning and participation, can influence them to travel in the future.

Based upon the preliminary findings, there appears to be uncertainty on the demand side, particularly in tourist travel decisions to travel and experience, especially in the context of creative tourism. Besides, current issues concern the creative tourism experience, such as location and accessibility, security and safety, the environment at the location, and cleanliness and sanitary conditions. These are critical issues for local service providers to consider for supporting creative tourism.

As can be seen, it is important to understand what tourists are motivated for future travel, how tourists design their travel experience, and how much tourists concern on engaging the creative activities. The values of creative tourism experience may be limited in new normal travel practices and restrictions on social distancing and health-protection regulations. There have been numerous studies on travel intention to Thailand; however, the majority of the studies appear to confirm this relationship in normal circumstances. As a result, understanding the determinant factors influencing tourists' intentions and behaviors in the new normal travel situation is pivotal for the government sector, private sectors (such as tourist service providers and other related-tourism businesses), and local communities to effectively manage creative tourism destinations and achieve tourist experience goals.

A Way Forward for Creative Tourism

Meanwhile, several perspectives on future travel intention to Thailand and experience in creative tourism are reviewed and explored into a preliminary study. To connect this knowledge gap and develop the value of creative tourism experiences, three main areas are focused on: tourists' motivation, travel decisions, and travel practices for service providers, all of which are discussed how Thailand's creative tourism potential could be revitalized in the next new situation.

To begin, the motivation of tourists is crucial in determining travel intention and influencing specific behavior in creative tourism. Since motivation is viewed as a psychological structure that accounts for an individual's need as a human trait, understanding why people travel and what they require while traveling is critical. People are away from home for a variety of reasons and travel to various destinations. In general, sun, sand, and sea tourist destinations have been claimed as the most popular leisure and recreational activities for international tourists visiting Thailand, as well as cultural tourism.

Interestingly, the respondents from the preliminary study revealed that escapism or recreation associated with self-development and social contact could be as major tourist motivation for participating in creative activities. They are generally willing to travel around Thailand after the pandemic for recreation, and they are open-minded to learning something new from new people in order to improve their abilities and skills. They may be encouraged to visit and participate in a variety of creative tourism activities available in Thailand's cities and local communities as a result.

Motivation factors, whether push or pull, are significant issues for developing marketing and destination management across various types of tourist attractions (Dean & Suhartanto, 2019). With the constructs of creativity, potential tourists can be motivated for intended participation through interaction and contact with stakeholders. Zhang and Xie (2019) explained that participatory experience incorporating authentic experiences into tourism products can increase the popularity of creative tourism. Other recent studies have revealed various motivators in the construction of cultural and creative tourism destinations, such as cultural contact (Lai et al., 2021), social interaction (Remoaldo et al., 2020), co-creation in specific food-related activities (Rachão et al., 2021) and uniqueness in a heritage context (Karagöz & Uysal, 2020), all of which reflect tourists' learning and understanding of different cultures.

If people have a powerful motivation to perform a behavior, the likelihood of that behavior being carried out is high (Sujood et al., 2021; Ulker-Demirel & Ciftci, 2020). As a result, incorporating motivational constructs may greatly assist in understanding more specific tourists 'needs in creative tourism, for example, a combination of sightseeing, self-improvement, escape, and relaxation (Zhang & Xie, 2019). Thailand can evidently consider utilizing unique aspects of creative products and services, as well as employing specific tourist desires such as co-creation, cultural contact, or interaction, which can encourage potential tourists to visit creative destinations in the aftermath of a pandemic.

The level of interest in participating in activities, on the other hand, can vary. Rachão et al. (2021) discovered a difference through interest in participating in specific food-related activities across generational cohorts and gender. Baby boomers and male tourists, on the other hand, were less eager to participate in cooking classes with locals than Generations X, Y, Z, and female tourists (Rachão et al., 2021). In terms of the effects of the COVID-19 pandemic situation, destination managers should pay closer attention to what motivational determinants demonstrate the essential of tourism product suppliers or tourists. According to some recent studies, some shifting influences on travel motivation and behavior, such as increasing social non-interaction with the destination space in Chinese tourists (Zhang et al., 2021), decreasing potential tourists' motivation toward all local food consumption Dedeoğlu et al. (2022), and preferring intact tourism in the new normal (Bae & Chang, 2021).

It is evident that people are likely to avoid traveling to crowded destinations and prefer destinations with fewer people. It seems that service providers are struggling to provide unique and authentic experiences through interacting and participating under COVID-19 risk perception. Consequently, creative tourism marketing and planning strategies must reflect current tourist demand in new normal situation, which is linked to multi-construct motivation with acknowledging a relationship with visitors, the local community, and among creative tourism participants themselves. As a result, a better understanding of specific tourist motivations is a critical issue for both tourists and service providers.

Next, travel planning and decision-making involve a number of concerns. In terms of choosing tourist destinations, destination characteristics are the most important consideration when planning the trip. This finding supports a previous tourism study (Bratić et al., 2021), which acknowledged the significance of destination attributes when making travel-related decisions in leisure travel. Furthermore, several studies perceived destination attributes as major components of destination image in various aspects such as destination attractiveness and accommodation service in Vietnam (Viet et al., 2020), and 'celebrations' (festivals, feats and fairs) in the Algarve region (Guerreiro et al., 2019).

Similarly, in the findings of Ahmad et al. (2020), the results indicate that physical factors are the main factors that influence tourists' visit intention. This means that tourists perceive the image of destination strongly in the process of decision making. Evidently, destination image plays a significant role in influencing tourists' decision making process to travel and to choose destination (Chaulagain et al., 2019; Desfiandi & Singagerda, 2019; Kanwel et al., 2019; Karl et al., 2021; Tan & Wu, 2016). Nevertheless, the destination's image can be perceived as positive or negative (Perpiña et al., 2019). These factors can influence which destinations should be visited and which should be avoided.

Especially in light of the current COVID-19 pandemic, health risk perception at such destination is commonly debated in terms of predicting potential for travel behavioral intention (Ahmad et al., 2020; Godovykh et al., 2020; Nazir et al., 2021; Rasoolimanesh et al., 2021; Su et al., 2021). Because of the current COVID outbreak, the preliminary findings suggest that major concerns for travelers to consider when planning their next trip to Thailand: clear entry requirements, convenient facilities and infrastructure, and a higher percentage of vaccination rate at the destination.

Furthermore, other factors that may influence potential tourists to visit the country have been identified; cleaner and safer environments, and clear standard operating procedures, lists of dark-red zones or red zones under strict enforcement of maximum COVID-19 controls, and awards on safety and health certificates. This study, on the other hand, shows that perception of COVID-19 as a travel-related risk leads to a planned shift in a number of related travel behaviors, as previous study mentioned (Bratić et al., 2021).

According to some studies on behavioral intention change as health risk perception, Pahrudin et al. (2021) concluded that important determinants such as finding a vaccine, adhering to health protocols, and physical distance influence the decision to visit post-pandemic Indonesia. Though, some decision-making factors that influence travel intention after a pandemic differ between domestic and international travel intention (Shin et al., 2022). It can be said that the travel decision making to travel destination is no single process. Destination attributes and other concerns either individual or social concerns are leading to predict behavioral intention. Therefore, understanding these concerns can help to reduce the negative perception of a destination and make Thailand a preferred destination for tourists.

In the context of creative tourism, the number of participants and size become more important factors to consider when arranging a creative tourist experience in a pandemic environment. In comparison, respondents are more likely to participate in creative tourism experiences individually rather than in groups. More importantly, the findings of (Remoaldo et al., 2020) support the potential of creative tourism, which is well positioned to significantly contribute to post-pandemic tourism, whereas creative tourism is, by definition, intended for small groups (e.g., families and social bubbles).

From the survey, those who are prefer group activities toward creative tourism experience, they express on fascination, creativity, fun and sharing social life. On the other hand, some respondents are more willing to participate in activities in a small group with similar interests, with family and friends, than in a large group, which is less personal. Nonetheless, many tourists prefer on individual with regards to several aspects such as independent, convenient, exclusive, creative, flexible, and timing. Furthermore, location and accessibility, as well as security and safety, are regarded as critical factors in attracting tourists to participate in and experience creative tourism. Others are environment at place and cleanliness and sanitary at, affordability, information availability (about activities, price, services), and health concerns and number of participations shown the possible concerns.

Previous research (Tseng et al., 2021) supports the findings, and as a result, people are more influenced by factors such as their perception of current physical and mental health impact in traveling when planning a future trip. To extend the study, the theory of planned behavior factors on post-pandemic travel intention can be used to explain greater intention to visit destinations (Pahrudin et al., 2021), despite the fact that the effects vary depending on the type of travel (Shin et al., 2022). As a result, it can be summed that a lack of knowledge about health and risk measures, precautions, and a flexible pattern of creative activities may result in fewer tourists coming.

Numerous significant implications and impacts are addressed based on literature reviews and preliminary study results for destination managers and service providers to understand how the perception of health risk will affect tourism and tourist-related decisions and behaviour in the coming years. As a result, travel practices for service providers require an attention focused on changes in consumer behavior and travel demand (Gössling et al., 2020). A recent review of travel literature indicates that the effects of the COVID-19 pandemic cause to new tourism trends and new emerging and potential travel markets, for example short-distance and local trip (Li et al., 2021), domestic tourism and longer stays in one place (Remoaldo et al., 2020), the solo travel and senior tourist markets for domestic and international travel (Shin et al., 2022), niche travel and prefer smaller groups and being free independent travelers (FITs) (Surawattananon et al., 2021).

Moreover, destination management organizations need to put more promotion effort to motivate tourist behavior intention. For example, primary motivations such cultural experience, novelty and sensory appeal factors can increase the intention of local food consumption (Dedeoğlu et al., 2022). Continuing to support the growth of creative tourism, motivational factors such as pursuing personal interests and curiosities; and developing new skills that can be major driven factors influencing creative tourism participation, with associated diversity of destination characteristics can enhance domestic tourism and longer stays at destinations (Remoaldo et al., 2020).

A more recent COVID-19 impacts in traveling concern on physical health protection and prevention. Therefore, travel practices for tourist consumption involve on traveler and trip related aspects. (Dedeoğlu et al., 2022) proposed factors such as vaccinations, masks, and social distancing measures, they may influence people's willingness to travel and participate in tourism activities, whereas less crowded attractions are expected (Surawattananon et al., 2021). Regarding social interactivity with other tourists, mainstream and big scale tasting rooms should be downsized and probably be more restricted and exclusive (Rachão et al., 2021). Similar to the previous study, Lai et al. (2021) confirmed that providing personalized cultural products and services can provide tourists with a sense of exclusivity and novelty, enhancing their cultural memories. Health and safety information is critical issues for communication to the broader public, this can reduce intrapersonal and social distancing constraints (Shin et al., 2022).

Given this, the culinary motivation of potential tourists can reduce negative effects of COVID-19 risk perception (Dedeolu et al., 2022). Therefore, increasing availability of and channels offering destination information in today's digital and mobile era would be respond high tourist demand for more convenient, accurate and reliable destination safety information (Zou & Meng, 2020). Furthermore, travel intention may be influenced by health and safety information preferences, media, perceived government effectiveness, and local safety practices (Samdin et al., 2021). Related research on travel planning determinants emphasis developing an engagement strategy, Backhaus et al. (2022) suggested that developing a relationship with a potential customer would eventually lead to a purchase, for example a community of travelers or personalized inspirational itineraries could be effective.

Besides, recognition in terms of better, more comfortable travel, personalized service, and maintaining affordable prices is a significant issue for future enhancements in tourist experience (Abbas et al., 2021). More specifically, in terms of flexibility and distinctiveness, creative tourism experiences can be customized to tourists. Therefore, tourism service providers may need to consider new strategies as a new paradigm that facilitates individuals' need to drive their desire to travel and experience, minimize perceived risks, and develop the connection between tourists and destinations.

Tourists' behavioral intentions are determined by a multitude of important factors related to destination selection, whereas the value and roles of tourists in creative tourism are represented in terms of first-hand experience consumption based on sociocultural capital. Furthermore, existing research studies on COVID-19 tourism impacts and related research revealed a shift in tourist behavior when the health risk was perceived. As a result, the growing popularity of creative tourism experiences in a stressful environment requires raising awareness in order to revitalize the industry. From this point of view, this study developed an integrated creative destination tourism model that is applicable in predicting future travel behavior related to health risk concerns during the pandemic situation, hence understanding tourist behavior that may impact intention to visit.

As illustrated in Figure 1, the overall model is based on a theoretical review that underpins creative tourism development (Carvalho et al., 2019; Richards, 2011). This input-process-output model provides a framework for understanding the factors that influence tourist travel intention to participate in creative tourism experiences. Travel decision determinants are divided into two categories: traveler-related determinants, which include travel motives related to tourists' need and desire for creative experiences, and destination-related determinants, which are based on creativity (activity, background, environment, people, and product) that are available at destinations.

These two major determinants are based on tourists' preferences for cultural contact, cultural learning, and co-creation for adding value and achieving the value of creative tourism. As a distinct effect of overall destination image component influence on travel behavior, embedding for creative cities/communities (such as events, festivals, creative spaces, and creative networks) and travel practices based on health risk concerns could be a major driving force in the process of destination image building.

In addition to these factors, behavioral intentions may change after the pandemic is over. As a result, attitude has been widely adopted as one of the constructs in the theory of planned behavior to explain travel behavior, which then influences travel decisions during the pandemic (whether to travel or not to travel). Thus, this study proposes the integrated framework for further research could include adding and/or removing items, as well as modifying the model into various disciplines (such as psychology, business, entrepreneurships, community-based tourism and so on).

Figure 1. An Integrated Creative Tourism Destination Framework

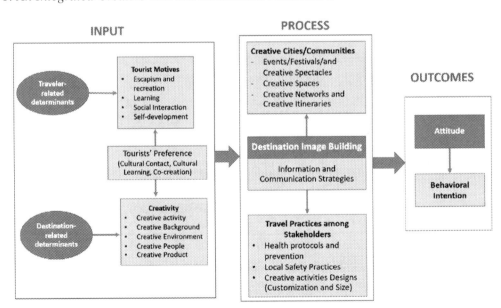

CONCLUSION

Creative tourism, with a focus on interaction with people and place, appears to be blurred in terms of further possibilities and limitations. Uncertainty in the pandemic environment, as well as health risk concerns, cause tourists to think more carefully about when and where they should go, as well as what they should do at destinations. It is critical to consider how the future of creative tourism should look in order to continue moving forward in the next new situations. If they extremely concern on health risk at destination or tourism activities, they might have negative perception. They may prefer other types of tourism that do not require them to interact with people and maintain social distance, such as leisure tourism, rather than travel for the sake of experiencing creative tourism.

Moreover, tourists' perceptions of risk have a significant impact on their interests (Zaman et al., 2022). Hence, understanding behavior intention among tourists in the context of creative tourism is advantage considering the pandemic crisis. This study will pursue to understand tourist intention on visit the creative tourism destinations in Thailand. While creative tourism has been widely promoted and spotted in tourism marketing strategies for tourists' experiences on uniqueness and authenticity, it is still lacking in strength.

With the restriction and regulation related to hygiene and social distancing, all tourism products and services in creative tourism have been affected in unprecedented ways. Therefore, this will be negative or positive impacts for judgement in decision making on future travel intention at creative tourism destination. Through participatory activities on learning, interactivity, and co-creation, these have an impact on the value of creative tourism activities, then local tourism providers need to understand individual's mindset, whether they have experience with parties or individuals.

How destination developers and marketers in Thailand establish proper strategies for attracting tourists' future travel intention are still new challenges in the context of creative tourism during and post pandemic. A number of noticeable travel practices for service providers can be recognized, such as knowledge of health standards, protocols, and guidelines including update and reliable health and safety information. Further, well-designed activities and modified facilities, such as downsized, flexible, exclusive, and personalized patterns, can most likely ensure all health safety and increase the quality of creative experience.

On the other hand, new tourism trends and potential travel market segmentation can be considered to predict the critical factors for potential tourists and to promote creative tourism destinations with different marketing strategies. Tourism marketers/managers must devise unique marketing tactics/strategies in the COVID-19 pandemic environment, emphasizing the role of fear and perceived risk (Rather, 2021). To move forward, all stakeholders, particularly service providers in Thailand's creative tourism, must concentrate on the aforementioned elements, which must improve customer-service related touchpoints and products.

As a result, in the aftermath of a pandemic, creativity can help to differentiate marketing positioning and redesigning approach of creative tourist experience with more confidence to ensure risk-free traveler. The challenge now is to collectively learn from this global tragedy to optimize the development of sustainable tourism (Gössling et al., 2020). Given that there are many different types of crises and disasters, and each event is likely to be unique, it is important to document as much information as possible so that one can be better prepared for future possibilities in countering and recovery strategies (Yeh, 2021).

Although it is unlikely when the pandemic crisis will end, the tourism proposition must focus on ensuring future growth and sustainability, as well as responding to travel demand and preference. As a result, more research on creative tourism in Thailand is required to better understand who creative tourists are and why they seek to engage in creative activities. This study could serve as a reference for academics and destination marketing organization to improve knowledge and understanding on travel intention and behavior in the time of the spread of the COVID-19.

To extend what tourists look seriously on their decision making for future travel intention should be paid attention for adding value of creative tourism. In addition, the key points related to the influence of behavioral travel intention are also proposed; which can encompass as the integrated framework for future research. The future study can be projected how the opportunity can be used to think beyond recovery and address several aspects that help pave the way for a better future, particularly in the context of creative tourism.

LIMITATIONS AND FUTURE RESEARCH DIRECTIONS

This study should be discussed in providing the foundation for future studies in the travel intention of creative tourism context during a pandemic situation. Since this current study's sample size is small, the study's findings may not be generalizable. A larger sample size could be advantageous in future studies to provide more accurate data. Second, the creative tourism participant profiles and motivations data in relation to the different types of creative tourism activities in which the tourists were engaged, it would be valuable to conduct further analysis in the context of creative tourism (Remoaldo et al., 2020).

Third, different types of tourism and tourist stages can have various effects on tourist behavior (Lai et al., 2021); therefore, additional research could help to clarify the path of tourist behavior in pre-, during-, and post-trip. Finally, the researchers believe that during and after a crisis, tourist behavior and consumption in creative tourism could be extended. For example, escapism and less crowded attractions, as well as technology or digitalization, may become more visible. As a result, future research may consider how these variables influence tourist loyalty and interconnect among stakeholders.

REFERENCES

Abbas, J., Mubeen, R., Iorember, P. T., Raza, S., & Mamirkulova, G. (2021). Exploring the impact of COVID-19 on tourism: Transformational potential and implications for a sustainable recovery of the travel and leisure industry. *Current Research in Behavioral Sciences*, *2*(March), 100033. doi:10.1016/j.crbeha.2021.100033

Ahmad, A., Jamaludin, A., Zuraimi, N. S. M., & Valeri, M. (2020). Visit intention and destination image in post-Covid-19 crisis recovery. *Current Issues in Tourism*, *0*(0), 1–6. doi:10.1080/13683500.2020.1842342

Ali, F., Ryu, K., & Hussain, K. (2016). Influence of Experiences on Memories, Satisfaction and Behavioral Intentions: A Study of Creative Tourism. *Journal of Travel & Tourism Marketing*, *33*(1), 85–100. doi:10.1080/10548408.2015.1038418

Backhaus, C., Heussler, T., & Croce, V. (2022). Planning Horizon in International Travel Decision-Making: The Role of Individual and Cultural Determinants. *Journal of Travel Research*. Advance online publication. doi:10.1177/00472875211066112

Bae, S. Y., & Chang, P. J. (2021). The effect of coronavirus disease-19 (COVID-19) risk perception on behavioural intention towards 'untact' tourism in South Korea during the first wave of the pandemic (March 2020). *Current Issues in Tourism*, 24(7), 1017–1035. doi:10.1080/13683500.2020.1798895

Baixinho, A., Santos, C., Couto, G., de Albergaria, I. S., da Silva, L. S., Medeiros, P. D., & Simas, R. M. N. (2021). Islandscapes and sustainable creative tourism: A conceptual framework and guidelines for best practices. *Land (Basel)*, 10(12), 1–17. doi:10.3390/land10121302

Bednárová, Ľ., Kiseľáková, D., & Onuferová, E. (2018). Competitiveness analysis of tourism in the European Union and in the Slovakia. *Geo Journal of Tourism and Geosites*, 23(3), 759–771. doi:10.30892/gtg.23312-326

Bhati, A. S., Mohammadi, Z., Agarwal, M., Kamble, Z., & Donough-Tan, G. (2020). Motivating or manipulating: The influence of health-protective behaviour and media engagement on post-COVID-19 travel. *Current Issues in Tourism*, 24(15), 2088–2092. doi:10.1080/13683500.2020.1819970

Bratić, M., Radivojević, A., Stojiljković, N., Simović, O., Juvan, E., Lesjak, M., & Podovšovnik, E. (2021). Should i stay or should i go? Tourists' covid-19 risk perception and vacation behavior shift. *Sustainability (Switzerland)*, 13(6), 3573. Advance online publication. doi:10.3390u13063573

Buonincontri, P., Morvillo, A., Okumus, F., & van Niekerk, M. (2017). Managing the experience co-creation process in tourism destinations: Empirical findings from Naples. *Tourism Management*, 62, 264–277. doi:10.1016/j.tourman.2017.04.014

Carvalho, R. M. F., Costa, C. M. M. da, & Ferreira, A. M. A. P. (2019). Review of the theoretical underpinnings in the creative tourism research field. *Tourism & Management Studies*, 15(SI), 11–22. doi:10.18089/tms.2019.15SI02

Chang, L.-L., Backman, K. F., & Huang, Y. C. (2014). Creative tourism: A preliminary examination of creative tourists' motivation, experience, perceived value and revisit intention. *International Journal of Culture, Tourism and Hospitality Research*, 8(4), 401–419. doi:10.1108/IJCTHR-04-2014-0032

Chaulagain, S., Wiitala, J., & Fu, X. (2019). The impact of country image and destination image on US tourists' travel intention. *Journal of Destination Marketing & Management*, 12(January), 1–11. doi:10.1016/j.jdmm.2019.01.005

Chen, C. F., & Chou, S. H. (2019). Antecedents and consequences of perceived coolness for Generation Y in the context of creative tourism - A case study of the Pier 2 Art Center in Taiwan. *Tourism Management*, 72(February), 121–129. doi:10.1016/j.tourman.2018.11.016

Chien, P. M., Sharifpour, M., Ritchie, B. W., & Watson, B. (2017). Travelers' Health Risk Perceptions and Protective Behavior: A Psychological Approach. *Journal of Travel Research*, 56(6), 744–759. doi:10.1177/0047287516665479

Dean, D., & Suhartanto, D. (2019). The formation of visitor behavioral intention to creative tourism: The role of push–Pull motivation. *Asia Pacific Journal of Tourism Research*, *24*(5), 393–403. doi:10.1 080/10941665.2019.1572631

Dean, D., Suhartanto, D., & Kusdibyo, L. (2019). Predicting Destination Image in Creative Tourism: A Comparative between Tourists and Residents. *International Journal of Applied Business Research*, *1*(01), 1–15. doi:10.35313/ijabr.v1i01.36

Dedeoğlu, B. B., Mariani, M., Shi, F., & Okumus, B. (2022). The impact of COVID-19 on destination visit intention and local food consumption. *British Food Journal*, *124*(2), 634–653. doi:10.1108/BFJ-04-2021-0421

Desfiandi, A., & Singagerda, F. S. (2019). Destination Choices in Travel Decisions. *Scholars Bulletin*, *05*(10), 593–603. doi:10.36348b.2019.v05i10.008

Einarsson, S., & Sorin, F. (2020). Circular Economy in travel and tourism: A conceptual framework for a sustainable, resilient and future proof industry transition. CE360 Alliance. doi:10.1002/col.10105

Eirini, T., & Kostas, K. (2017). The evolution of alternative forms of Tourism: A theoretical background. *Business & Entrepreneurship Journal*, *6*(1), 1–4.

Godovykh, M., Pizam, A., & Bahja, F. (2020). Antecedents and outcomes of health risk perceptions in tourism, following the COVID-19 pandemic. *Tourism Review*, *76*(4), 737–748. doi:10.1108/TR-06-2020-0257

Gössling, S., Scott, D., & Hall, C. M. (2020). Pandemics, tourism and global change: A rapid assessment of COVID-19. *Journal of Sustainable Tourism*, *29*(1), 1–20. doi:10.1080/09669582.2020.1758708

Guerreiro, M. M., Henriques, C., & Mendes, J. (2019). Cultural and Creative Tourism: The Case of 'Celebrations' in the Algarve Region. *Journal of Spatial and Organizational Dynamics*, *VII*(4), 320–338.

Henche, B. G., Salvaj, E., & Cuesta-Valiño, P. (2020). A sustainable management model for cultural creative tourism ecosystems. *Sustainability (Switzerland)*, *12*(22), 1–21. doi:10.3390u12229554

Henriques, C., & Moreira, M. (2019). Turismo Criativo e Sustentabilidade Urbana: Os Casos de Lisboa e Porto. *Revista Portuguesa de Estudos Regionais*, *51*, 93–114.

Huang, Y. C., Chang, L. L., & Backman, K. F. (2019). Detecting common method bias in predicting creative tourists behavioural intention with an illustration of theory of planned behaviour. *Current Issues in Tourism*, *22*(3), 307–329. doi:10.1080/13683500.2018.1424809

Huang, Y. C., Cheng, J. S., & Chang, L. L. (2020). Understanding Leisure Trip Experience and Subjective Well-Being: An Illustration of Creative Travel Experience. *Applied Research in Quality of Life*, *15*(4), 1161–1182. doi:10.100711482-019-09727-y

Kanwel, S., Lingqiang, Z., Asif, M., Hwang, J., Hussain, A., & Jameel, A. (2019). The influence of destination image on tourist loyalty and intention to visit: Testing a multiple mediation approach. *Sustainability (Switzerland)*, *11*(22), 6401. Advance online publication. doi:10.3390u11226401

Karagöz, D., & Uysal, M. (2020). Tourists' Need for Uniqueness as a Representation of Differentiated Identity. *Journal of Travel Research*. Advance online publication. doi:10.1177/0047287520972804

Karl, M., Kock, F., Ritchie, B. W., & Gauss, J. (2021). Affective forecasting and travel decision-making: An investigation in times of a pandemic. *Annals of Tourism Research*, *87*, 103139. doi:10.1016/j.annals.2021.103139

Lai, S., Zhang, S., Zhang, L., Tseng, H. W., & Shiau, Y. C. (2021). Study on the influence of cultural contact and tourism memory on the intention to revisit: A case study of cultural and creative districts. *Sustainability (Switzerland)*, *13*(4), 1–18. doi:10.3390u13042416

Li, X., Gong, J., Gao, B., & Yuan, P. (2021). Impacts of COVID-19 on tourists' destination preferences: Evidence from China. *Annals of Tourism Research*, *90*, 103258. doi:10.1016/j.annals.2021.103258 PMID:34924648

Ministry of Tourism and Sports Thailand. (2017). *The Second National Tourism Development Plan (2017-2021)*. Author.

Nazir, M. U., Yasin, I., & Tat, H. H. (2021). Destination image's mediating role between perceived risks, perceived constraints, and behavioral intention. *Heliyon*, *7*(7), e07613. doi:10.1016/j.heliyon.2021.e07613 PMID:34368481

OECD. (2020). *Culture Shock: COVID-19 and the Cultural and Creative Sectors*. OECD. https://read.oecd-ilibrary.org/view/?ref=135_135961-nenh9f2w7a&title=Culture-shock-COVID-19-and-the-cultural-and-creative-sectors

Pahrudin, P., Chen, C.-T., & Liu, L.-W. (2021). A modified theory of planned behavioral: A case of tourist intention to visit a destination post pandemic Covid-19 in Indonesia. *Heliyon*, *7*(10), e08230. doi:10.1016/j.heliyon.2021.e08230 PMID:34708160

Pera, R. (2017). Empowering the new traveller: Storytelling as a co-creative behaviour in tourism. *Current Issues in Tourism*, *20*(4), 331–338. doi:10.1080/13683500.2014.982520

Perpiña, L., Camprubí, R., & Prats, L. (2019). Destination Image Versus Risk Perception. *Journal of Hospitality & Tourism Research (Washington, D.C.)*, *43*(1), 3–19. doi:10.1177/1096348017704497

Pulido-Fernández, J. I., García-Suárez, J. A., & Rodríguez-Díaz, B. (2021). Proposal for an index to measure creativity in urban-cultural destinations. *International Journal of Tourism Research*, *23*(1), 89–105. doi:10.1002/jtr.2396

Rachão, S. A. S., de Jesus Breda, Z., de Oliveira Fernandes, C., & Joukes, V. N. P. M. (2021). Drivers of experience co-creation in food-and-wine tourism: An exploratory quantitative analysis. *Tourism Management Perspectives*, *37*(May). doi:10.1016/j.tmp.2020.100783

Ram, Y., Björk, P., & Weidenfeld, A. (2016). Authenticity and place attachment of major visitor attractions. *Tourism Management*, *52*, 110–122. doi:10.1016/j.tourman.2015.06.010

Rasoolimanesh, S. M., Seyfi, S., Rastegar, R., & Hall, C. M. (2021). Destination image during the COVID-19 pandemic and future travel behavior: The moderating role of past experience. *Journal of Destination Marketing & Management*, *21*(February), 100620. doi:10.1016/j.jdmm.2021.100620

Rather, R. A. (2021). Monitoring the impacts of tourism-based social media, risk perception and fear on tourist's attitude and revisiting behaviour in the wake of COVID-19 pandemic. *Current Issues in Tourism, 0*(0), 1–9. doi:10.1080/13683500.2021.1884666

Remoaldo, P., Serra, J., Marujo, N., Alves, J., Gonçalves, A., Cabeça, S., & Duxbury, N. (2020). Profiling the participants in creative tourism activities: Case studies from small and medium sized cities and rural areas from Continental Portugal. *Tourism Management Perspectives, 36*(May), 100746. doi:10.1016/j.tmp.2020.100746 PMID:32953432

Richards, G. (2011). Creativity and tourism. The state of the art. *Annals of Tourism Research, 38*(4), 1225–1253. doi:10.1016/j.annals.2011.07.008

Richards, G. (2018). Cultural tourism: A review of recent research and trends. *Journal of Hospitality and Tourism Management, 36*, 12–21. doi:10.1016/j.jhtm.2018.03.005

Richards, G. (2020). Designing creative places: The role of creative tourism. *Annals of Tourism Research, 85*(March), 102922. doi:10.1016/j.annals.2020.102922

Richards, G., & Jutamas Jan Wisansing, E. P. (2018). Creating creative tourism toolkit. *Designated Areas for Sustainable Tourism Administration (Public Organization)-DASTA*. https://www.researchgate.net/profile/Greg-Richards-2/publication/330425066_Creating_Creative_Tourism_Toolkit/links/5c4046e0458515a4c72beeba/Creating-Creative-Tourism-Toolkit.pdf

Richards, G., King, B., & Yeung, E. (2020). Experiencing culture in attractions, events and tour settings. *Tourism Management, 79*(February), 104104. doi:10.1016/j.tourman.2020.104104

Salinas Fernández, J. A., Serdeira Azevedo, P., Martín Martín, J. M., & Rodríguez Martín, J. A. (2020). Determinants of tourism destination competitiveness in the countries most visited by international tourists: Proposal of a synthetic index. *Tourism Management Perspectives, 33*(September), 100582. doi:10.1016/j.tmp.2019.100582

Samdin, Z., Abdullah, S. I. N. W., Khaw, A., & Subramaniam, T. (2021). Travel risk in the ecotourism industry amid COVID-19 pandemic: Ecotourists' perceptions. *Journal of Ecotourism, 0*(0), 1–29. doi:10.1080/14724049.2021.1938089

Sánchez-Cañizares, S. M., Cabeza-Ramírez, L. J., Muñoz-Fernández, G., & Fuentes-García, F. J. (2021). Impact of the perceived risk from Covid-19 on intention to travel. *Current Issues in Tourism, 24*(7), 970–984. doi:10.1080/13683500.2020.1829571

Shin, H., Nicolau, J. L., Kang, J., Sharma, A., & Lee, H. (2022). Travel decision determinants during and after COVID-19: The role of tourist trust, travel constraints, and attitudinal factors. *Tourism Management, 88*(December), 104428. doi:10.1016/j.tourman.2021.104428

Singh, R., & Nazki, A. (2019). Investigating the influencing factors of Tourist Behavior towards Creative Tourism and its Relationship with Revisit Intention. *African Journal of Hospitality, Tourism and Leisure, 8*(1), 1–28.

Slak Valek, N. (2020). Word-of-art: Contribution of artists-in-residence to a creative tourism destination. *Journal of Tourism and Cultural Change, 18*(2), 81–95. doi:10.1080/14766825.2018.1467920

Su, D. N., Tran, K. P. T., Nguyen, L. N. T., Thai, T. H. T., Doan, T. H. T., & Tran, V. T. (2021). Modeling behavioral intention toward traveling in times of a health-related crisis. *Journal of Vacation Marketing*. Advance online publication. doi:10.1177/13567667211024703

Suhartanto, D., Agustina, R., Wibisono, N., & Leo, G. (2018). The Application of Structural Equation Modelling for Predicting the Link between Motivation and Experience Quality in Creative Tourism. *MATEC Web of Conferences, 218*, 4–9. 10.1051/matecconf/201821804001

Suhartanto, D., Brien, A., Primiana, I., Wibisono, N., & Triyuni, N. N. (2020). Tourist loyalty in creative tourism: The role of experience quality, value, satisfaction, and motivation. *Current Issues in Tourism, 23*(7), 867–879. doi:10.1080/13683500.2019.1568400

Sujood, Hamid, S., & Bano, N. (2021). Behavioral Intention of Traveling in the period of COVID-19: An application of the Theory of Planned Behavior (TPB) and Perceived Risk. *International Journal of Tourism Cities*, (July). Advance online publication. doi:10.1108/IJTC-09-2020-0183

Surawattananon, N., Reancharoen, T., Prajongkarn, W., Chunanantatham, S., Simakorn, Y., & Gultawatvichai, P. (2021). *Revitalising Thailand's tourism sector*. https://www.bot.or.th/Thai/MonetaryPolicy/EconomicConditions/AAA/250624_WhitepaperVISA.pdf

Tan, W. K., & Wu, C. E. (2016). An investigation of the relationships among destination familiarity, destination image and future visit intention. *Journal of Destination Marketing & Management, 5*(3), 214–226. doi:10.1016/j.jdmm.2015.12.008

Tseng, K. C., Lin, H. H., Lin, J. W., Chen, I. S., & Hsu, C. H. (2021). Under the covid-19 environment, will tourism decision making, environmental risks, and epidemic prevention attitudes affect the people's firm belief in participating in leisure tourism activities? *International Journal of Environmental Research and Public Health, 18*(14), 1–20. doi:10.3390/ijerph18147539 PMID:34300013

Ulker-Demirel, E., & Ciftci, G. (2020). A systematic literature review of the theory of planned behavior in tourism, leisure and hospitality management research. *Journal of Hospitality and Tourism Management, 43*(September), 209–219. doi:10.1016/j.jhtm.2020.04.003

Viet, B. N., Dang, H. P., & Nguyen, H. H. (2020). Revisit intention and satisfaction: The role of destination image, perceived risk, and cultural contact. *Cogent Business and Management, 7*(1), 1796249. Advance online publication. doi:10.1080/23311975.2020.1796249

Vos, J. De. (2020). *Since January 2020 Elsevier has created a COVID-19 resource centre with free information in English and Mandarin on the novel coronavirus COVID- 19*. Elsevier.

Wang, C., Liu, J., Wei, L., & Zhang, T. (2020). Impact of tourist experience on memorability and authenticity: A study of creative tourism. *Journal of Travel & Tourism Marketing, 37*(1), 48–63. doi:10.1080/10548408.2020.1711846

Wisansing, J. (2019). *Creative Tourism Initiatives in Thailand : DASTA Model*. https://www.academia.edu/39983241/Title_Creative_Tourism_Initiatives_in_Thailand_DASTA_Model

World Economic Forum. (2019). *The Travel and Tourism Competitiveness Report 2019* [El Informe de Competitividad de Viajes y Turismo 2019]. https://www3.weforum.org/docs/WEF_TTCR_2019.pdf

World Tourism Organization (UNWTO). (2021). *UNWTO Inclusive Recovery Guide – Sociocultural Impacts of Covid-19, Issue 2: Cultural Tourism (Issue 2)*. doi:10.18111/9789284422579

WTTC. (2021). *WTTC global summit: Uniting the world for recovery*. WTTC.

Yeh, S. S. (2021). Tourism recovery strategy against COVID-19 pandemic. *Tourism Recreation Research*, *46*(2), 188–194. doi:10.1080/02508281.2020.1805933

Yu, M., Li, Z., Yu, Z., He, J., & Zhou, J. (2021). Communication related health crisis on social media: A case of COVID-19 outbreak. *Current Issues in Tourism*, *24*(19), 2699–2705. doi:10.1080/13683500.2020.1752632

Zaman, K., Bashir, S., Afaq, Z., & Khan, N. (2022). Covid-19 Risk Perception of Travel Destination Development and Validation of a Scale. *SAGE Open*, *12*(1). doi:10.1177/21582440221079622

Zatori, A., Smith, M. K., & Puczko, L. (2018). Experience-involvement, memorability and authenticity: The service provider's effect on tourist experience. *Tourism Management*, *67*, 111–126. doi:10.1016/j.tourman.2017.12.013

Zhang, C. X., Fong, L. H. N., & Li, S. N. (2019). Co-creation experience and place attachment: Festival evaluation. *International Journal of Hospitality Management*, *81*(May), 193–204. doi:10.1016/j.ijhm.2019.04.013

Zhang, C. X., Wang, L., & Rickly, J. M. (2021). Non-interaction and identity change in Covid-19 tourism. *Annals of Tourism Research*, *89*, 103211. doi:10.1016/j.annals.2021.103211

Zhang, Y., & Xie, P. F. (2019). Motivational determinates of creative tourism: A case study of Albergue art space in Macau. *Current Issues in Tourism*, *22*(20), 2538–2549. doi:10.1080/13683500.2018.1517733

Zou, Y., & Meng, F. (2020). Chinese tourists' sense of safety: Perceptions of expected and experienced destination safety. *Current Issues in Tourism*, *23*(15), 1886–1899. doi:10.1080/13683500.2019.1681382

KEY TERMS AND DEFINITIONS

Creative Tourism: This is a type of niche tourism that transforms mass cultural tourism by enhancing the value of creativity and cultural capitals through participation, interaction, and learning.

Health Risk Perception: Risk perception on health is one of the factors that influence an individual's decision to travel or participate in activities, as evidenced by various forms of communication. When tourists encounter a risky related health crisis, they may experience some negative consequences such as mental effects (such as fear, worry, and unsafety), uncertainty for travel plans with restrictions, and additional expenditures.

Pandemic Situation/Environment: This study focuses on the COVID-19 outbreak, which refers to human disease conditions that have significantly affected into the global recession in the hospitality and tourism industry and have resulted in significant changes in travel behavior.

Service Providers: This means to all local and business entrepreneurs, and other work sectors related to tourists who provide services and products to satisfy tourists' needs at destinations.

Tourist Behavior Intention: This study is to examine how people's decision intentions to travel or not travel as a result of the pandemic situation have changed. This includes the future behavior to participate or avoid in the tourist activities based on health and safety concerns.

Travel Motivation: This study looks into reasons or purposes which encourage tourists to travel and why tourists travel and involve in creative tourism experience.

Travel Practices: This can be claimed as important guidelines for destination managers, marketers, and service providers including local entrepreneurs to aware and prepare well for providing future tourists.

Chapter 15
Does Brand Equity Matter?
How Chinese Tourists View Wine Brand Equity When Making Wine Tourism Decisions – A Case Study of European Wine Tourism From the Perspective of the Chinese Market

Poshan Yu

https://orcid.org/0000-0003-1069-3675

Soochow University, China & Australian Studies Centre, Shanghai University, China

YuHan Wang

Independent Researcher, China

Emanuela Hanes

Independent Researcher, Austria

ABSTRACT

This chapter examines how tourism in the hypercompetitive world can create a flexible mean to generate advantages and maintain advantages to achieve sustainable development. This chapter reflects the international wine business and global wine tourism by studying the wine tourism in the tourism industry, and studies the driving forces and factors of the sustainable development of tourism economy with wine tourism as the core. This work also reflects the demands and preferences of Chinese consumers on global wine business and wine tourism from the perspective of consumers through a Chinese case study and a questionnaire survey. After nearly 2 years of COVID-19 lockdown, the authors investigate which international wine tourism region(s) Chinese tourists most want to go after the COVID-19 lockdown and why. This study attempts to measure the wine brand equity (WBE) on travel intention based upon surveying Chinese travelers' data.

DOI: 10.4018/978-1-6684-4645-4.ch015

INTRODUCTION

Tourism is one of the world's largest employment industries and a vital strategic sector. Tourism is even the pillar of many countries' national economy. Tourism can be said to be a resource formed by the local unique cultural environment, natural scenery, and regional characteristics. It is the basic resources for tourism destination development. Whether a region's resources can truly become a tourism resource is influenced by a variety of factors such as time, space, human demand preferences, and social development. After the relevant resources are discovered and developed in a specific area, they will become part of the tourism infrastructure and thus competition of a region. With the expansion of travel networks around the world, tourists are focusing on core destinations (Gao et al., 2022).

How a scenic spot stands out among many scenic spots becomes the winning condition for tourism development. In modern tourism, transportation plays an increasingly important role in providing tourism services (Nave et al., 2021). Although the COVID-19 pandemic has closed borders to many countries, reducing the flow of people, the transportation of tourists and the demand of tourists are still very relevant factors to plan for the post-Covid-19 revival (Henseler et al., 2022). The tourism market continues to rise steadily, promoting the level of economic development in regions enjoying tourism resources and restoring and improving the quality of life of local people.

Tourism has developed rapidly on both the supply and demand sides. In terms of travel demand, although the spread of COVID-19 has hindered travels, with the easing of the epidemic, people have more disposable income accumulated in recent years and an increased demand and desire for travelling. In terms of supply, all countries and regions are deeply aware of the limitation of tourism resources and have invested substantial money and manpower to develop tourism, build tourist destinations and develop tourist products. In such a tourism development environment, the competition between the international tourism industries is also more intense. How to obtain competitive advantages in the context of global tourism hypercompetition and keep the advantages in the process of development has become the focus of research.

To maintain competitive advantages and remove obstacles in development under the background of global super competition, the developers of tourism projects are more inclined to develop industries and tourism projects with sustainable development power (Nave et al., 2021). Product updates in tourism industry are relatively rare, and product updates in the tourism industry are relatively infrequent, and the speed from decision-making to implementation is slow. Most tourism consumers are foreign tourists, and there is a gap between their payment and experience.

With the low probability of tourists returning to the same area, the characteristics of the tourism products make brand building very difficult and brand loyalty hard to maintain. To improve the intention of customers to return, tourism project developers must develop a sustainable tourism economy and provide good customer service (Byrd et al., 2016). In the development of tourism, we can observe a continuous refinement of the tourism sector. From the 1990s, there is a rise of special interest tourism in the tourism industry (McKercher et al., 2005). Wine tourism belongs to special interest tourism, and designs tourism products around specific wine products with the goal to attract tourists from all over the world. Visitors visit wineries and wine regions to experience wine-related production and lifestyle, including tasting wine and food, as well as experiencing wine culture and other recreational activities.

Wine tourism has become a new driving force for the sustainable development of tourism, so the potential for wine-related special interest tourism and food tourism in the context of global hypercompetition is high. Wine has a focus on quality-of-life consumption and enjoys a high reputation globally.

Wine tourism is an investment focusing on quality, and wine tourism must be emotionally immersive (Martins et al., 2017). Compared with other types of tourism, wine tourism spends more on corresponding products sales, tasting experience, dining consumption and accommodation in wine tourism destinations.

Tourists also prefer tours that offer a wide range of cultural and outdoor attractions (Getz & Brown, 2006). This enables wine tourism to gain advantages in international competition. It has become the focus of wine tourism project developers how to leverage and maintain these advantages in the context of global competition. While cooperation is generally considered to be conducive to sustainable tourism development, the complexity of tourism systems is based on interaction and interdependence (Vodeb, 2012).

Therefore, tourism systems rarely appear as single cooperation, but more in the form of cooperative competition - a process in which cooperation and competition or conflict coexist (Nguyen et al., 2022). The best strategy is to choose moderate cooperation in the case of existing competition and to choose small-scale competition in the case of long-term cooperation, to stabilize and improve the original advantage.

Competition and uncertainty of demand are significant drivers of innovation. Different stakeholders of wine tourism should take advantage of international super competition to innovate tourism models and realize sustainable development of wine tourism (Nguyen et al., 2021). In the planning of wine tourism projects, traditional wine brands and wineries have become the main force to build the reputation of wine tourism. Studies have shown that the strength of wine brands equity (WBE) is conducive to the successful development of wine tourism industry. By identifying the main advantages and disadvantages of wine tourism industry, wine brands can easily form a full-service wine tourism industry chain and form a tourism hot spot (Gómez et al., 2015b). Wine brands use effective strategies of telling good brand stories to attract consumers (Frost et al., 2020).

However, there remains an obvious knowledge gap in identifying whether wine brand equity can predict tourists' intention to visit. There is also literature showing that managers overestimate the influence of wine brand equity, and thus fail to meet consumer needs in strategy formulation (Gómez et al., 2015a). From the perspective of consumers, this chapter will measure which factors in wine brands influence consumers' (tourists) intentions and choices of wine tourism destinations.

China's rapid economic development has given Chinese consumers strong purchasing power, while consumers are eager to incorporate Western trends and lifestyles into their lives, thus increasing their willingness to consume for example wine. China is the world's sixth largest consumer of wine. The value of consumer wine increased for three consecutive years from 2016 to 2019. At the same time, the number of Chinese consumers traveling abroad has increased (Figure 1). Wine tourism economy and wine production show a positive growth trend.

In 2019, the Novel Coronavirus pandemic took the world by storm, dealing a severe blow to the global tourism industry (Kudo et al., 2021). With effective control in individual countries and the development of novel coronavirus vaccines, many countries are gradually bringing the spread of COVID-19 under control. With the normalization of epidemic prevention and control, Chinese consumers' demand for outbound tourism is increasing day by day. This chapter focuses on consumers' demand for wine tourism. The influence of wine brand equity on consumers' wine travel intentions was explored through questionnaires. This work advances the theoretical research on sustainable development of tourism and contributes to improving the competitiveness of wine brands in the global competition. Through the case study, it provides meaningful practical insights for wine tourism stakeholders for attracting Chinese consumers (tourists) more effectively.

Figure 1. Wine consumption worldwide in 2020. Data source: International Organisation of Vine and Wine; Various sources (Trade Press); Food and Agriculture Organization of the United Nations

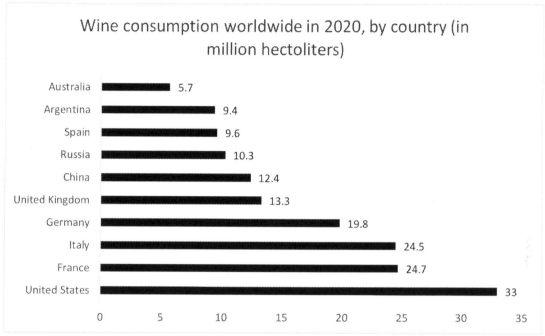

Data source: International Organisation of Vine and Wine; Various sources (Trade Press); Food and Agriculture Organization of the United Nations

METHODOLOGY

The purpose of this chapter is to examine whether wine brand equity matters when consumers make travel decisions. This chapter uses bibliometric analysis to examine hotspots of prior research in wine tourism. Previously unknown patterns are revealed by collecting a large amount of relevant information over a certain range. By collecting a large amount of relevant information on a field or a topic, it helps researchers to understand the full picture of a research area and to construct links between publications in different subfields. Bibliometric research methods provide quantitative statistical analysis of the number of publications, the number of core networks, and other aspects (Yue et al., 2021).

This chapter uses CiteSpace 5.8.R3 software to analyze keyword co-occurrence and co-citation networks in the field of wine tourism research and to construct a model of wine tourism development. The keywords of a chapter reflect the key content of the chapter. Scholars often use keywords when searching the field. The connections between keywords represent recognition among authors, and when enough authors accept these connections and use similar keywords in their chapters, these connections form hot spots and themes in the research field (Chen et al., 2018). The analysis of co-cited chapters was also conducted for the main research content of the chapter in the field of wine brand equity-related areas, and the hot spots and frontiers of research in the field of wine brand equity were discussed to capture the impact of wine brand equity on the travel decisions made by consumers.

The literature search was conducted using the subject terms in the Web of Science database, and the chapters were searched by the keywords "wine tourism" and "wine brand equity". Among the filtered records, chapters with full-text content were selected and duplicate content was removed to obtain the data records of the literature, which were analyzed using CiteSpace software. Using a questionnaire research method, a total of 302 responses from Chinese consumers were collected additionally. The set of questions and the data collected from the questionnaire were used to study the extent to which Chinese consumers know about wine brand equity and the extent to which wine brand equity influences consumers' decision making in wine tourism. The sample data collected through the questionnaire provides a more intuitive picture of the overall Chinese consumers' consumption tendencies.

Finally, to reflect the embodiment of wine brand equity in wine tourism practices, a case study approach was utilized. Case studies are usually selected on a small scale to be more representative and pragmatic. Using small-scale studies to find potential interest or usefulness that can be referenced within a common context simplifies complex overall research and helps to address very complex issues (Tight, 2017).

The case study approach is often used as a general discussion and is a qualitative approach to research, where different cases are selected so that the breadth and variation of the research area can be discussed in subsequent case studies. It also allows for a more precise analysis of a specific field or subfield of the field, a systematic evaluation, and a review of successful or unsuccessful cases. In the process of review, the strategies used in the cases related to the topic of the chapter are discovered and the strategies are replicated with more examples (Tight, 2017).

The purpose of this chapter is to examine the role of wine brand equity in wine tourism, and therefore to select developed and emerging wine countries and examine how wine brands in each of these countries have improved their wine brand equity to attract consumers. The study examines how wine countries at different stages of wine tourism can enhance their wine brand equity to attract consumers. To summarize consumers' perceptions of wine brand equity and their willingness to spend for wine tourism, and to provide common and individual strategies for wine brands to enhance wine brand equity.

LITERATURE REVIEW

To review the previous chapters on international trade and global tourism, keywords in the database of "Web of Science Core Collection" are used in the literature retrieval process in this paragraph. In order to study global business and international tourism, we searched chapters with key words "global business" and "global tourism" and limited the literature type to book chapters and chapters. The time span of retrieval is from the year of keyword occurrence to 2022. CiteSpace was then used to remove chapters without full text and duplicate records. The CiteSpace time slice was set to one year to analyze the keyword co-occurrence and co-citation networks as well as the cluster analysis formed between chapters. A total of 855 literature records from 1998 to 2022 were selected as literature samples for this study.

CiteSpace 5.8.R3 was used to analyze and screen out the top 25 keywords with the highest occurrence of keywords in 855 literature records (Figure 2). It can be found that since 2012, from the perspective of consumers, travel choice has gradually become the research direction and hotspot of scholars. Corresponding to this is the consumption level of hot consumers studied from 2016 to 2017. It is impossible to achieve a balance to study global commerce and global tourism only from the demand side. The collaborative working system on the supply side has become a hot keyword of research after 2014 after the consumer demand is clearly defined.

Figure 2. Top 25 Keywords of "global business" and "global tourism"

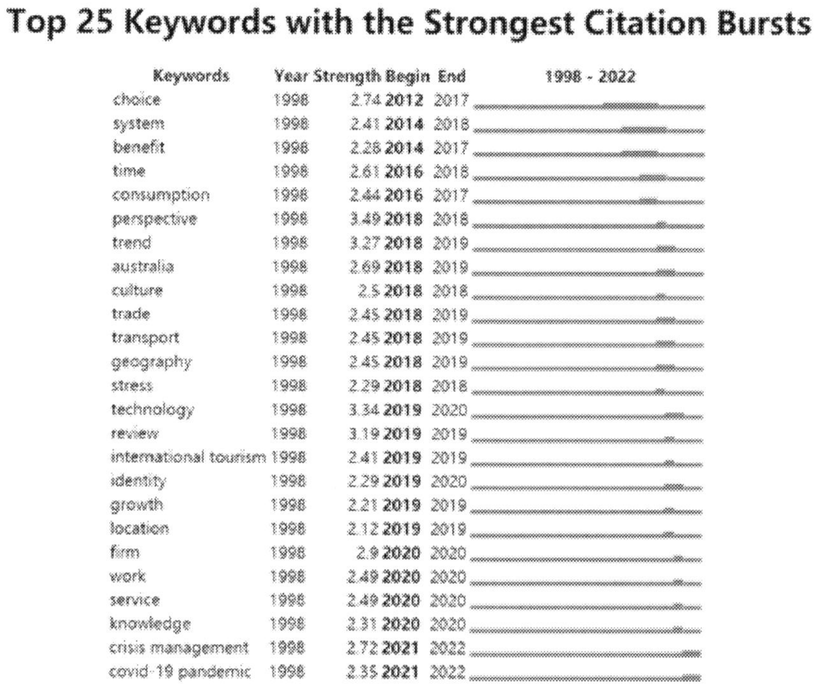

Top 25 Keywords with the Strongest Citation Bursts

Keywords	Year	Strength	Begin	End	1998 - 2022
choice	1998	2.74	2012	2017	
system	1998	2.41	2014	2018	
benefit	1998	2.28	2014	2017	
time	1998	2.61	2016	2018	
consumption	1998	2.44	2016	2017	
perspective	1998	3.49	2018	2018	
trend	1998	3.27	2018	2019	
australia	1998	2.69	2018	2019	
culture	1998	2.5	2018	2018	
trade	1998	2.45	2018	2019	
transport	1998	2.45	2018	2019	
geography	1998	2.45	2018	2019	
stress	1998	2.29	2018	2018	
technology	1998	3.34	2019	2020	
review	1998	3.19	2019	2019	
international tourism	1998	2.41	2019	2019	
identity	1998	2.29	2019	2020	
growth	1998	2.21	2019	2019	
location	1998	2.12	2019	2019	
firm	1998	2.9	2020	2020	
work	1998	2.49	2020	2020	
service	1998	2.49	2020	2020	
knowledge	1998	2.31	2020	2020	
crisis management	1998	2.72	2021	2022	
covid-19 pandemic	1998	2.35	2021	2022	

From the end of 2019 to the beginning of 2020 when COVID-19 swept the world, crisis management of tourism and the recovery of tourism after COVID-19 became a new research direction. Understanding the relationship between disaster events and tourism can help destination managers make joint decisions regarding recovery, reconstruction and marketing (Rossello et al., 2020). The hotel and tourism industry is vulnerable to crises of various sources and ranges, and it has been an academic attempt in recent years to conceptualize crisis management (Berbekova et al., 2021). In tourism, micro and small enterprises account for the majority of the global tourism and hospitality industry and contribute to the economic livelihood of many regions. They have the characteristics of small scale and high diversity. But because of these characteristics, it has become one of the sectors vulnerable to crisis and external impact (Pham et al., 2021).

To intuitively display the correlation of previous research directions, CiteSpace visual view is used to present key nodes (Figure 3). The centrality of tourism companies is linked to the dramatic impact on the landscapes they operate in (Rosato et al., 2021). The management direction and mode of tourism enterprises have become a key node. From 2020 to 2022, the global tourism industry suffered huge losses due to COVID-19. Crisis management, including disaster management and risk management, has become a hot topic for hotel and tourism organizations (Wut et al., 2021).

The service mode and performance of tourism areas determine consumers' satisfaction degree and subsequent consumption tendency. The decision of consumer travel destination influences the management planning of tourism area. There is a lack of research on whether wine brand equity can be a factor in attracting consumers to wine tourism.

Figure 3. "Global business" and "Global tourism"

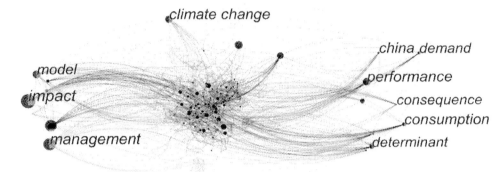

Figure 4. "global business" and "global tourism" Clusters visualization

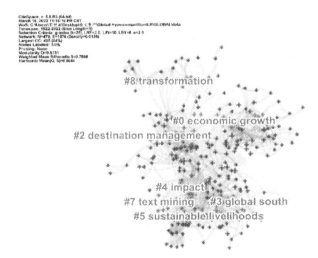

Table 1. Clusters of "global business" and "global tourism"

Cluster ID	Cluster Labels	Mean Year	Size	Top term
0	economic growth	2017	63	economic growth; autoregressive distributed lag approach;
2	destination management	2015	54	destination management; google places;
3	global south	2018	44	sharing economy; destination management organizations;
4	impact	2016	38	climate change; adaptive capacity;
5	sustainable livelihoods	2015	36	sustainable livelihoods; blue economy;
7	text mining	2012	28	sentiment analysis; text mining;
8	transformation	2014	22	climate change; multivariate adaptive regression spline;

From 1998 to 2022, a total of 855 literature records form seven clusters, (Figure 4 & Table 1) which include the following: economic growth, destination management, global south, impact, sustainable livelihoods, text mining and transformation (Filter clusters with a cluster size greater than 10 for visual view, so the cluster ID lacks the numbers 1 and 6). Tourism drives economic growth and has become the mainstay of many countries' economies (Zhang & Dong, 2021) as well as strengthens the degree of economic dependence between regions (Chen et al., 2021).

Tourism also plays an important role in establishing friendly relations between people and thus promotes the socio-economic growth of the country, being also an important part of the country's foreign exchange reserves and providing direct and indirect employment to the population (Thommandru et al., 2021). Tourism is inseparable from the development and management of tourism destinations by tourism enterprises and tourism organizations. Tourism enterprises and organizations need to establish the connection between consumers and travel destinations through storytelling strategies (Hartman et al., 2019). With the continuous development of the tourism industry, the sustainable development of a region's tourism has become a key indicator to judge the quality of tourism destination management (Lozano-Oyola et al., 2019). Successful development of sustainable purposes is considered as a function and result of effective governance (Roxas et al., 2020). Sustainable tourism has become a requirement for suppliers, and sustainable tourism shows the competitiveness of this tourist destination in the super competition.

However, the needs of tourists for sustainable tourism products are often ignored (Mach & Ponting, 2021). Sustainable development of tourism cannot be realized only by adjusting the sustainable strategy from the supply side, as there has not been a critical number of tourists willing to pay more for sustainable features of tourism products yet (Liu et al., 2022). We can see that tourists with different incomes and different needs are divided into different tourist markets, and tourists who are willing to pay more for tourism also regard sustainability as part of the competitiveness of tourism products. The same holds true for the planning of the wine tourism.

In the tourism industry, competition is mainly manifested as competition within and between destinations (Nguyen et al., 2022). Tourism destinations are affected by four main factors: 1. Core resources and attraction factors (such as geographical, cultural and historical activities), 2. Supporting factors and resources (accessibility and infrastructure construction, etc.), 3. Destination management (e.g., resource management, marketing, messaging), 4. Qualification determinants (e.g., location, dependency, security, cost) (Crouch & Ritchie, 1999). Of course, tourism destination competitiveness is also affected by the global macro- and micro- environments.

Tourism competitiveness refers to the ability of a region to optimize its attractiveness to residents and non-residents, to provide quality, innovative and attractive travel services to consumers (tourists), and to gain market share in domestic and global markets, while ensuring sustainable use of tourism resources. A major goal of tourism competitiveness is how to shape the image of tourist destination. The image of a tourist destination refers to the synthesis of people's perception, impression, and viewpoint of a tourist destination, as well as the cognition and concept of society, politics, economy, life, and culture (Zhang & Dong, 2021). Destination competition refers to the competition among competitive destinations that have similar tourism resources and attract similar tourist groups within the region (Pan & Lee, 2011).

The higher the similarity of tourist destinations, the greater the intensity of competition will be. To gain an edge over the competition, wine tourism was explored as a strategy to develop food tourism and special interest tourism. Wine tourism can effectively differentiate consumers' consumption levels. As mentioned above, classifying consumers with different needs can effectively improve the sustainability of travel products. To study the relationship between wine tourism and sustainable tourism, as well as the hot spots and frontiers of previous research. In the process of literature retrieval, keywords in the database of "Web of Science Core Collection" are used to retrieve chapters. The key words are "wine tourism" and "sustainable tourism". CiteSpace was used to remove chapters without full text, and 326 records were obtained from 1995 to 2022.

Figure 5. Clusters of "wine tourism" and "sustainable tourism"

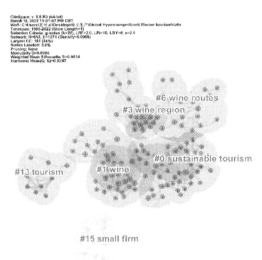

Applying cluster analysis, we can show that wine and sustainable tourism form two large clusters (Figure 5). Research topics in wine tourism literature and sustainable tourism research are inseparable. The food tourism research boom emerged in 2001 and again in 2013 because of sustainable development trends in the industry (Figure 6). Wine tourism can be defined as the combination between tourism and wine production, that is, it consists of a series of wine production-related visits and experience-related activities (Gu et al., 2021).

Wine tourism can also be understood as the activity of conducting tourism dedicated to discovering wine, wine regions and wine production processes (Nave et al., 2021). Wine tourism is not only created by tourism organizations and departments. Wine tourism is a form of tourism formed by interaction between tourists, wine production team, management system and other attributes of winery. Wine tourism influences the sustainable development of tourism areas from three dimensions: environment, society and economy (Sun & Drakeman, 2020).

Tourism research tends to focus on policy makers' management strategies but ignores the impact of tourism enterprises' brand equity on consumers' choice of destination. Wine brand equity is divided into three levels of brand analysis, namely destination brand, outbound brand and wine tourism destination brand (Gómez et al., 2015b). Wine brand equity can be used as a destination for wine tourism, as well as a powerful tool to distinguish wine regions or wine tourism destinations from their competitors. Wine brand equity develops and strengthens the emotional connection between the destination and the consumer. Wine brands also increase the added value of wine tourism and maintain the strong competi-

Does Brand Equity Matter?

tiveness of wine tourism in the tourism sector. This chapter will fill the gap in how wine brand equity affects travel decisions.

Figure 6. Clusters and keywords occurrence timeline

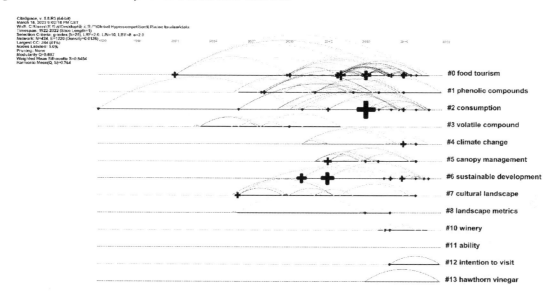

DEVELOPMENT AND POTENTIAL OF WINE TOURISM AND INTERNATIONAL WINE BUSINESS IN GLOBAL HYPERCOMPETION

Wine has always been an integral part of Western culture, and as a key element in tourism, wine is closely related to the service industry and tourism (Nicolosi et al., 2016). Wine tourism is a form of tourism that combines tourists' motivation to travel with the experience of wine producing areas. It is a visit to vineyards, wineries, wine culture festivals and wine exhibitions (Hall, 2005). Because wine tourism takes tasting wine and experiencing the characteristics of wine producing areas as the main purpose of tourism, the atmosphere of wine festivals has a significant impact on tourist satisfaction (Mason & Paggiaro, 2012). Wine tourism is also summarized as a special interest tourism, which has become a strong growth area of tourism in many countries (Bruwer, 2003).

Wine tourism is different from natural scenery tourism and historical and cultural city tourism as tourists who choose wine tourism are more inclined to a lifestyle experience. Visitors are interested not only in tasting wine, but also in the wider wine-related experience (Priilaid et al., 2020). The suppliers of wine tourism have changed from traditional tour operators to wineries and tour operators cooperating together. Wine merchants, wine brands and travel agencies form a network relationship of wine tourism (Musso & Francioni, 2015).

Wine brand equity is a business card of the wine region. The demand side of wine tourism is divided more carefully. The consumers of wine tourism are divided into wine lovers, those who are interested in wine and curious tourists according to their consumption ability and habits. The classification is based on the amount of wine consumed during wine tourism. Wine lovers are the most likely to make wine purchases, while in wine tourism, curious travelers are the least likely to make wine and related purchases. It is found that the original intention of the design of wine tourism routes is to better distribute wine and wine-related products.

The starting point of wine tourism route development is to cooperate with the supply side to distribute wine products, from traditional wine making to wine product promotion, this series of promotions and developments cannot be done without the support of wine brand equity. Wine tourism is an economic activity and an emerging form of tourism that increases the sales of wineries and expands knowledge about wine and vintages in the regions where it occurs (Gómez et al., 2015a). Managers of wine tourism tend to overestimate the brand equity of wine in this region (Gómez et al., 2015b). With the tremendous growth of wine tourism in recent years, the starting point of route design of wine tourism has gradually shifted from the supply end to the demand end. Food and wine-related tourism for the local development will not only increase the sales of wine products, but also provide a new way to build sustainable tourism and create jobs in the local area.

Wine is a more quality-oriented investment than traditional tourism, with visitors spending more on products, tasting experiences, meals and accommodation. This also requires wine tourism to consider the satisfaction of tourists and consumers. Wineries and wine products are the attraction of wine tourism but only a part of the many tourist attractions in a region, if all the tourism resources of the region can be integrated to play the advantages of wine tourism. Tour operators and services are key drivers of the increase in the number of wine visitors, but the appeal of the product has a greater long-term impact (Torres et al., 2021).

When conducting wine tourism experience, tourists pay more attention to the immersive experience. Wine brands that have built up enough wine brand equity should be able to offer consumers a better wine tourism experience. The experience of wine tourism, whether active or passive, needs to be enhanced by an immersive experience (Thanh and Kirova, 2018). The co-creation of tourist experience and the interaction between tourists and local residents influence the level of wine tourism participation (Rachão et al., 2021). Wine tourism is a sensory experience. Customers pay more attention to the service quality during the tourism and increase wine knowledge during the travel (Getz & Brown, 2006). Because of this, the development of wine tourism projects is now measured by the satisfaction degree of consumers and tourists. Tourists' satisfaction depends primarily on their understanding and trust of wine regions. Tourism is a difficult product given that improving the loyalty of tourists and consumers to wine brands is an urgent problem to be solved (Santeramo et al., 2017).

Tourist experience is closely related to the corresponding supporting facilities. Wine tourism is closely related to catering, accommodation, tourism crafts and environmental safety. The degree of tourist satisfaction is also affected by spatial proximity, agglomeration and the availability of transportation hubs (Gu et al., 2021). Wine tourism has changed from a simple added value of product sales to a unique means of improving the domestic and international tourism image of wine producing areas.

The wine industry has a long history and traditional distribution models have carved up much of the global market. Due to the globalization of the wine industry and the intensification of competition, the presence of multinational enterprises and small- and medium-sized enterprises in the global market is increasing (Jiménez-Asenjo & Filipescu, 2019). The emergence of wine tourism provides advantages for wine enterprises that take the lead in developing wine tourism projects. Wine brands provide consumers with an opportunity to understand and experience new wine products, and thus improve brand awareness and increase profits. Developing wine tourism provides additional sales channels for wine distribution in close interaction with visitors and consumers, while giving direct feedback on the wine market information.

Wine tourism is a relatively new industry sector (Byrd et al., 2016). Wine tourism is the product of the innovative development of the wine industry, which expands development on the basis of the original vineyards and wine chateaux. Wine producers engage in a variety of co-value creating activities, and the hospitality and tourism of wine tourism creates previously untapped value (Crick et al., 2020). Wine tourism adjusts the objectives, distribution channels, prices and communication methods of wine brands, and also indirectly adjusts the product range, brand name and brand positioning within the wine industry (Jiménez-Asenjo & Filipescu, 2019). Wine tourism is a way for the wine industry to enhance its industrial competitiveness.

Different tourist destinations have different tourism attributes, and they attach different importance to specific attributes of wine brands to achieve successful marketing (Getz & Brown, 2006). Attracting tourists by telling good stories about wine regions is also a means to maintain competitive advantages (Frost et al., 2020). Resources and capabilities as well as strategy jointly determine competitive advantages (Lorenzo et al., 2018).

Institutional, regulatory, and professional aspects of wine tourism should not prevent wine regions from realizing their potential as wine tourism destinations. Wine tourism policy makers should fully consider the challenges posed by international competition and seize the opportunities in the new challenges (Festa et al., 2020). The formation of wine brand equity is conducive to the successful development of wine tourism, identifying strengths and weaknesses in the industry, providing relevant information and formulating strategies in line with the development of wine brand equity (Gómez et al., 2015a).

On the basis of limited tourism resources, wine tourism industry is facing cooperation and competition (Crick & Crick, 2021). Wine tourism will need to intrinsically carry out sustainable development strategies in order to maintain the competitiveness of wine tourism compared with other traditional tourism (Nave et al., 2021). How to carry out uncommon wine tourism activities has become a requirement for the design of wine tourism routes (Priilaid et al., 2020). When developing wine tourism routes, we should firmly grasp the advantages of the origin of wine, so as to maintain the advantages in international competition (Rodrigues et al., 2020).

CHARACTERISTICS OF EUROPEAN TOP WINE TOURISM AND THE STRATEGY OF WINE TOURISM: WINE BRAND EQUITY FORMATION

Europe is the world's most famous wine-producing continent and has the longest wine-making history. Several European countries are leading the way in wine production and export (Correia et al., 2019). Wines in Europe form amazing diversity due to differences between regions, landforms, grape varieties, and climates. Loyal supporters usually frequent a certain country, region, or brand of wine. Areas with large vineyard areas are one of the most important factors in the formation of a quality wine region. With a long history of wine development, European vineyards have a worldwide influence. Europe had the largest share of the world's vineyards in 2020.

Among European countries, Spain accounts for 13.1 percent of the world's vineyard area, with the advantages of primitive natural conditions. France and Italy are not far behind, with 10.9% and 9.8% of the world's vineyard area, respectively (Figure 7).

Figure 7. Share of world vineyard surface area in European countries in 2020. Data source: OIV; FAO

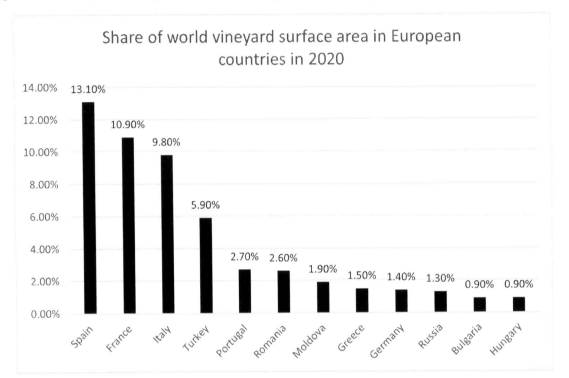

Because of the advantages of natural conditions, Spain, France, and Italy have a long tradition of wine production, of continuous wine industry development and in forming world-renowned brands. In wine production Italy, France, Spain also far ahead of other wine - making European countries. Proximity to the target market is considered ideal for a tourist destination, and wine tourism is no exception (Soontiens et al., 2018). Leading wine production and more convenient international trade provide the possibility of developing wine tourism for traditional wine producing countries. Wine tourism is a growing activity that contributes to the economic development of wine regions (Thanh & Kirova, 2018).

Wine creates a driver for travel (Rachão et al., 2021). Wine brand equity guarantees the quality of wine tourism. In the field of wine tourism, the development of wine tourism in each country and region is divided into five life cycles: the construction of wineries at the beginning, the recognition of wine brands, the outstanding performance of wine producing areas, the construction of wine tourism and the maturity of wine tourism, and the decline of wine tourism (Boatto et al., 2013). In the initial stage of the development of wine tourism, there were few reception facilities in wine producing areas, and wineries were not well-known and wine production was small.

The countries of Italy, France and Spain have accumulated a certain level of popularity of wine brands, wine production and they also ensure the global supply. Their wine brands build wine brand equity through product quality. These countries have passed the initial stage of wine tourism development while developing their wine industry. In the stage of wine tourism being recognized by more tourists, wine tourism needs to pay more attention to quality, perfect reception facilities, increase levels of wine production, and implement a stable cooperation between public institutions and private companies with good network relations improving the popularity of wine tourism. In the mature stage of wine tourism, wine tourism areas will form special festivals about wine, and the region will become active with wine (Velikova & Dodd, 2016). Italy, Spain, and France are the most important destinations for wine tourism. This is in line with having Europe's largest vineyard share and a long wine-making history.

Figure 8. Leading countries for wine tourism worldwide as of 2021 (index score). Data source: Bounce

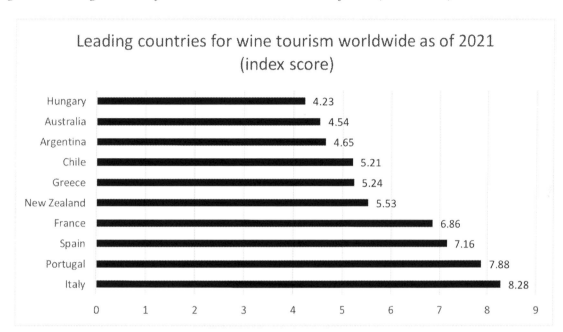

Data source: Bounce

As the world's largest wine producer, Italy has gained a leading position in wine tourism (Figure 8) amongst the traditional wine countries and actively seeks new opportunities in the wine market. Wine tourism is becoming more and more important in the tourism industry and a successful phenomenon (Festa et al., 2020). As one of the most excellent tourism countries in the world, wine tourism has occupied an important position in the total output value of Italy, with a large and rapid growth. The supply of Italian wine tours is ample and the quality of service is emphasized (Boatto et al., 2013).

Italian wine equity is reflected in the global share of Italian wines. For foreign tourists to Italy, the unique variety of food and wine in Italy is the second biggest attraction after Italian art and fashion. And wine tourism, a special interest tourism, is often the part of the trip that brings the most memorable and unique experience for tourists and consumers. Tuscany is one of Italy's most attractive regions for wine tourism, due to its natural beauty and rich cultural history. According to the data, the most important factors for tourists to choose Italian wine tourism are beautiful natural scenery, local traditional culture and wine quality. Italian wine brands emphasize that the natural beauty of the wine region is also part of the wine brand equity (Figure 9).

Piedmont and Veneto also show strong attraction. They have a competitive advantage especially in the field of wine cellar and wine museum visits. Visits to museums and monuments are also important factors in Italian wine tourism (Figure 10).

Figure 9. Most important factors when choosing a food and wine destination in Italy in 2021. Data source: Roberta Garibaldi

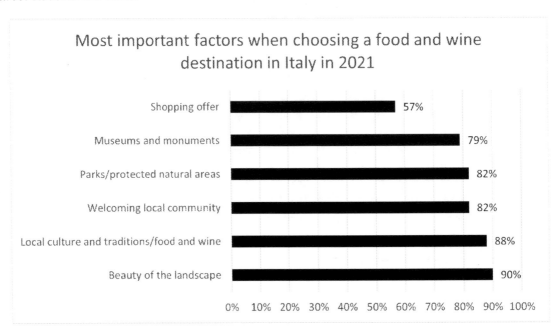

In terms of Italian wine brands, they have realized the economic benefits brought by wine tourism and paid more attention to the planning of wine tourism. In addition to the new Italian wine cellars, there are plans to cater to wine tourists by incorporating architectural planning as an effective way to build wine brand equity, such as the construction of tasting rooms and wine sales stores. In the strategy of wine brand equity, wine tourism has been an important part of the commercial development blueprint. Wine brands and government policies work together to promote the excellent development of the wine industry (Santeramo et al., 2017).

As one of the "Old World" wine producing countries, Spain has the most extensive vineyard coverage, but also has a very long wine-producing history (Figure 7). Grape planting and winemaking in the territory are colorful and leads to excellent quality due to different climate, soil and grape varieties. The diversity of wine brings with it the diversity of local traditions and culture, coupled with the profound history of wine making, Spain is also a leading country in wine tourism (Figure 8).

Spanish wine tourism connects Spain's regional culture, nature and rural wine regions, increasing the commercial value of rural areas and thereby increasing employment opportunities. Spanish wine brands enhance wine brand equity through regional culture to further attract tourists. Wine tourism is an opportunity to develop the traditional Spanish wine industry and plays a decisive role in attracting tourists and consumers to regions associated with wine.

In 2020, the Autonomous community of Castile and Leon in Spain has developed eight wine tours, which are matched by eight museums related to wine culture in the autonomous community (Figures 11 & 12). This facilitates the link between culture and tourism in Spain's wine regions to create a higher value for visitors.

Figure 10. Opinions on most attractive Italian enotourism regions 2021, by tourism type. Data source: Associazione Nazionale Città del Vino (Osservatorio Nazionale sul Turismo del Vino)

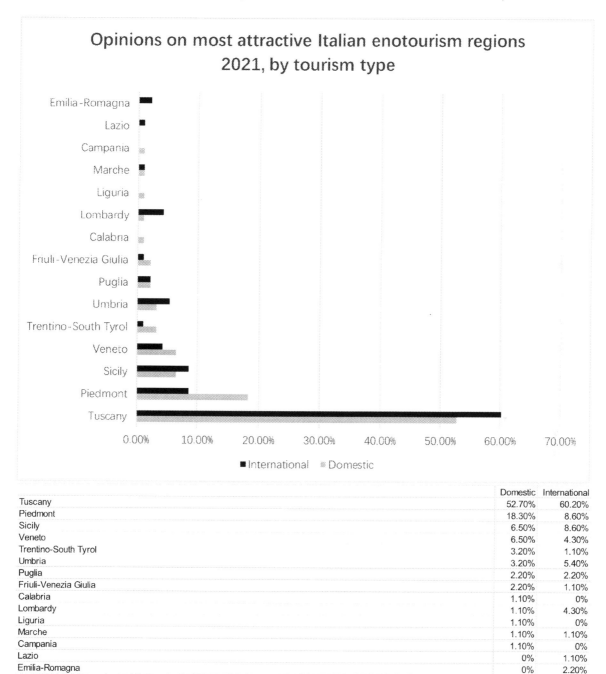

	Domestic	International
Tuscany	52.70%	60.20%
Piedmont	18.30%	8.60%
Sicily	6.50%	8.60%
Veneto	6.50%	4.30%
Trentino-South Tyrol	3.20%	1.10%
Umbria	3.20%	5.40%
Puglia	2.20%	2.20%
Friuli-Venezia Giulia	2.20%	1.10%
Calabria	1.10%	0%
Lombardy	1.10%	4.30%
Liguria	1.10%	0%
Marche	1.10%	1.10%
Campania	1.10%	0%
Lazio	0%	1.10%
Emilia-Romagna	0%	2.20%

Data source: Associazione Nazionale Città del Vino (Osservatorio Nazionale sul Turismo del Vino)

Figure 11. Number of wine routes in Spain in 2020, by autonomous community. Data source: Asociación Española de Ciudades del Vino

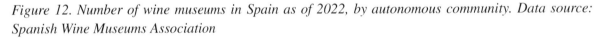

Data source: Asociación Española de Ciudades del Vino

Figure 12. Number of wine museums in Spain as of 2022, by autonomous community. Data source: Spanish Wine Museums Association

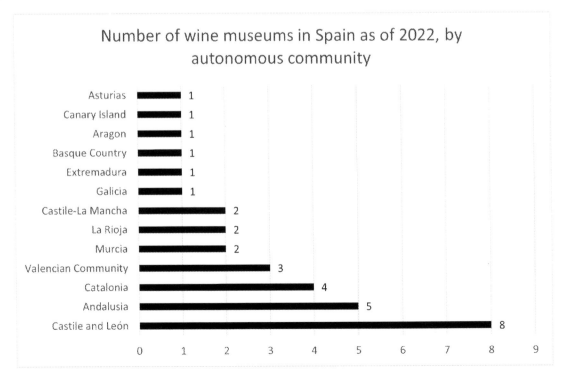

Wineries in Spain are named after the wine regions. This tendency is also applied by the wine industry. Naming wine products and tourist destinations after the areas of origin is a guarantee of quality with the reference to outstanding or famous wine regions (Gómez et al., 2015a). Spanish wine brands play a role in protecting the brand value system. It also provides a means of value for tourists and consumers to choose suitable destinations. Spanish wine brands improve the long-term utility of wine brand equity through customer relationship management and understanding the needs of tourists (Gómez et al., 2015b).

Wine industry is an important industry of France. With various rules and regulations, standardized wine production process, France formed a complete set of wine production and development model to promote the development of French wine quickly. They comprise the world-famous Chateau Lafite Rothschild, Chateau Latour, Chateau Margaux wine brands, amongst others.

Wine tourism is also a huge industry in France, one of the world's leading wine tourism destinations. Visitors can experience numerous famous French vineyards and explore a variety of smaller vineyards (Song et al., 2019). In the face of the impact of new world wine producing countries on the French wine industry and to cope with the high intensity of international competition, the proportion of wine tourism establishment in France is increasing. Since 1934, wine tourism routes have been launched in Burgundy and Champagne. France is also the number one tourist destination country, thus making French wine and tourism a perfect combination. French wine brands use regional culture to enhance wine brand equity.

Different regional cultural systems are reflected in different cultural landscapes (Mitchell et al., 2012). Compared with other countries, French wine estates exudes solemn and elegant atmosphere, seemingly low-key but rich in historical deposits. French wine tourism includes the local characteristics of the garden scenery and leisure and entertainment, tourists can appreciate the beautiful address of the wine estate, feel the art of French life. This is the number one reason people visit Bordeaux in France (Figure 13). On the other hand, tourists and consumers can have a deeper understanding of wine culture and participate in the production and appreciation of wine. This is the second biggest attraction for tourists and consumers. Wine tourism in France offers a unique experience for visitors.

French wine brand brings French wine not only fame, but also the guarantee of quality behind the brand. French wine brands have a good positioning, giving play to the elegant and high-end characteristics of French wine brands (Gómez et al., 2015b). Each major French wine brand clearly defines the audience and designs novel and unique wine tourism routes without losing style, which conforms to consumers' immersive travel experience. French wine brands also improve the industry chain related to wine tourism, improve transportation, accommodation and catering conditions, to provide tourists with the best sightseeing experience.

As a traditional wine country, Portugal has a profound influence on wine tourism. When it comes to the characteristics of Portuguese wine, we find minority brands, fine and diversified selections. Every drop of Portuguese wine is hailed as Portugal's prized treasure. Portuguese wine brands capture the unique flavor of Portuguese wine to enhance wine brand equity and competitiveness.

Although Portugal does not have extensive vineyard coverage area, but Portugal's unique indigenous grape varieties bring Portuguese wine unique flavor. Although the geographical area of the vineyard is small, the microclimatic conditions of each region are very different, forming a unique geomorphic characteristic. The different climate also brings the rich diversity of Portuguese wine, and Portuguese wine brands can offer a variety of wines for different occasions.

Figure 13. Main reasons for visiting wine tourist sites in Bordeaux, France in 2019. Data source: Gironde Tourisme; Various sources (Le Conseil Interprofessionnel du Vin de Bordeaux, Comité Régional du Tourisme de Nouvelle-Aquitaine)

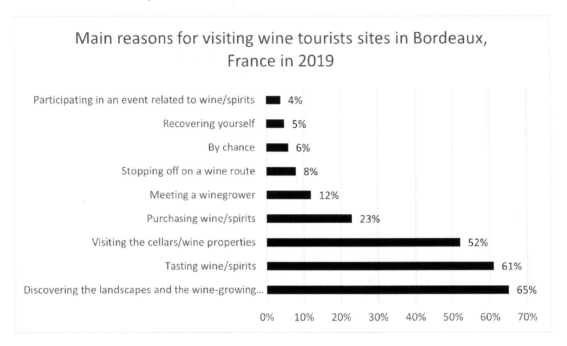

Figure 14. Number of wine museums and wine routes in Portugal 2022. Data source: Statista; Instituto da Vinha e do Vinho

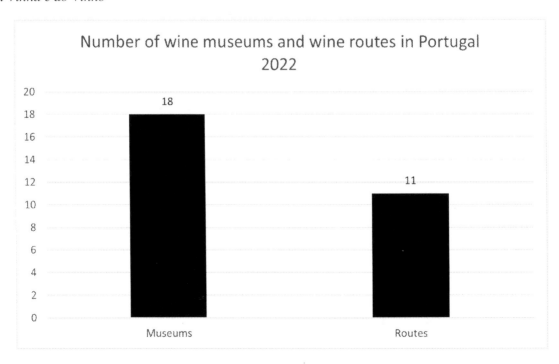

To better adapt to the increasingly competitive wine market, Portuguese wine brands have launched a global tour of Portuguese wine to tell the story of their wine and attract more consumers (Frost et al., 2020) by giving consumers the opportunity to taste Portuguese wine. At the same time, Portuguese wine brands and the Portuguese tourism industry welcome visitors from all over the world to visit the wine producing regions with rich wine culture. As of February 2022, Portugal has launched 11 official wine tours and established 18 wine tourism museums (Figure 14). Wine tourism facilities in Portugal offer full packages, so tourists can not only taste the wine, but also experience the cultural heritage of Portuguese wine.

GLOBAL "WINE PRODUCTS + TRAVELLING EXPERIENCES" FROM CHINESE PERCEPTION

As the second largest economy in the world, China's domestic economy is developing rapidly and its wine consumption demand is constantly rising. This also promotes the continuous upgrading and innovation of the wine industry. Chinese wine consumption market has experienced four distinct development phases. During the second phase from 1990 to 1999, more and more foreign capital entered the food and beverage market. China's wine retail industry has implemented fixed-point experiments on imported wine, and the share of imported wine in the Chinese market has further increased.

Many domestic retailers in China have set off a wave of learning from foreign distributors. Domestic wine companies and international wine companies have begun to establish relationships and conduct governance of relationships (Ellegaard & Medlin, 2018). In the second stage of the wine consumption market development, large, medium and small distributors implemented the format of specialty stores. Chain stores and supermarkets also appeared and gradually became a trend. On different occasions, wine began to become synonymous with fashion and health, and wine gradually appeared on the table of Chinese families.

During the third stage, from 2000 to 2010, wine products began to appear in the form of winery wines and well-known wine brand wines, and more internationally renowned wine brands were introduced into the Chinese market, the cross-border investment and acquisition of wine brands have become more frequent. In the wine distribution market, due to the saturation of the market, the retail industry has gradually begun to merge and integrate wine brands with more market shares and wide influence have emerged. There are significant differences in dietary consumption patterns, preferences and purchasing choices among people from different cultures or geographical regions (Rodrigues & Parr, 2019).

Although wine has gradually increased its influence in the Chinese market since 1949, the traditional Chinese liquor "baijiu" is still the mainstream liquor in the context of Chinese traditional culture, and the economic indicators of baijiu have been leading for a long time. The proportion of grape wine in the total number of beverages in the country is still very low. Since 2011, in the fourth developmental stage of the Chinese wine consumption market, the development of technology has become a major change in the organization of wine and wine tourism industry (Martins et al., 2017).

Traditional advertising sales gradually decline, emerging e-commerce platforms become the main front for wine brand publicity, and new digital sales models emerge. Small- and medium-sized wine enterprises play an important role in the dissemination of innovation (Menna & Walsh, 2019). The Chinese market has an unprecedented strong demand for overseas tourism, medical care, entertainment, and education. After the development stages described above, the wine industry is now a driving force for general development in China.

To understand wine products and travel experiences in the Chinese market, a total of 302 valid questionnaires on wine brands, wine tourism and consumer decisions were completed by Chinese consumers and analyzed. According to the collected data, more than 60% of people have been in contact with wine brands, which also proves that wine can be widely accepted by consumers in China (Figure 15). Wine origin and wine brands are closely linked. Among those who have been in contact with wine, traditional offline physical store purchase is still the main buying mode of many consumers (Figure 16).

Chinese traditional consumption concepts pursue the word of mouth of the product. In the way of contacting the wine brand, the word-of-mouth recommendation of friends and relatives is the most important influencing factor. A total of 64.02% mentioned the recommendation of friends and relatives for a certain wine brand. The establishment of reputation of this wine brand can be spread by clustering in the Chinese market and form a point-to-point propaganda mode.

In the fourth stage of the wine market development, due to the popularity of smart phones and mobile terminals, many new media have become the main front of wine brand promotion, and the communication environment is more interactive, digital, and online as before. After contacting wine brands through the above channels, most consumers have a new understanding of the wine brands behind the wine products. This gradually improves the interest of Chinese consumers in imported wine brands. Among them, a total of 84.66% respondents who have been in contact with wine said that traditional advertising and new media publicity can help deepen their understanding of wine brands (Figure 17).

Figure 15. Proportion of consumers who have been exposed to wine brands in China

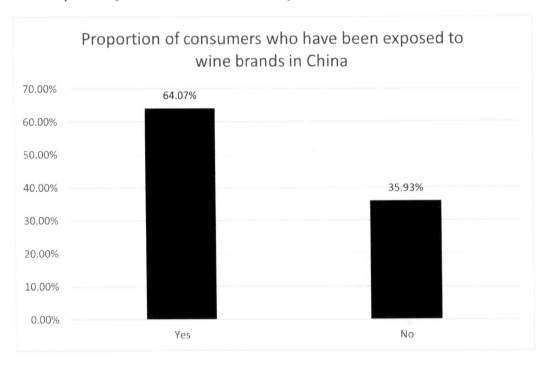

Does Brand Equity Matter?

Figure 16. The way Chinese consumers approach wine brands

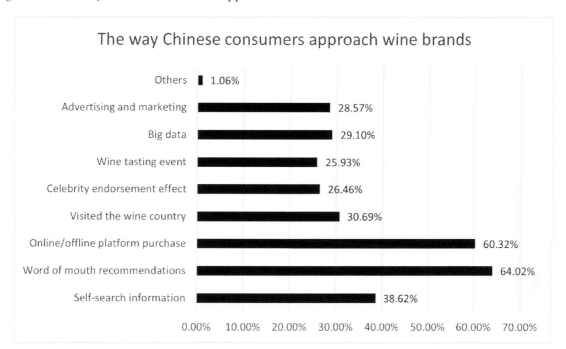

In the measurement of wine brand equity, we aim to study which wine brand equity components will affect consumers' purchasing decisions. The questionnaire deals with the value and assets of wine brands from the perspective of Chinese consumers, aiming to make a successful wine brand an important asset to create added value for the company and consumers from the perspective of consumers. Good wine brand equity adds value to the product as well as the wine service (Figure 18).

Based on the questionnaire collection of Chinese wine consumers, wine brand equity can be divided into five aspects: brand awareness of wine (reflected by the long history of a wine brand), product quality of wine brand, public reputation of wine brand, service quality of wine brand and cost performance of wine product. In marketing literature, brand assets are divided into brand awareness, perceived quality, brand association, brand loyalty, and other proprietary brand assets (Gómez et al., 2015b). The division of wine brand equity basically conforms to the division of original marketing literature.

Wine brand awareness, wine brand product quality and wine brand service are all perceptual recognition of wine brand equity, while wine brand loyalty is a behavioral component (Kim et al., 2009). From the perspective of Chinese consumers, more attention was paid to the quality of wine brand products, as well as the long history and popularity of wine brands. Such recognition of wine brand equity is inseparable from the consumption habits of Chinese consumers. The main purpose of Chinese consumers to buy imported wine is to give it to their friends and relatives as a gift, followed by consumers' personal appreciation and drinking (Figure 19). From this we can support the thesis that standardization of international unified packaging and publicity, cross-cultural marketing communication and localization of packaging and publicity are still needed (Celhay et al., 2020).

Figure 17. Chinese consumers' interest in learning about wine brands

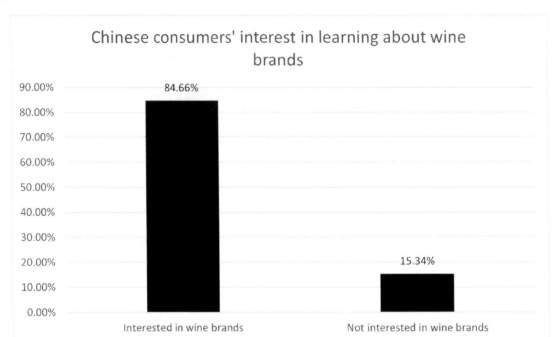

Figure 18. The embodiment of wine brand equity from the perspective of Chinese consumers

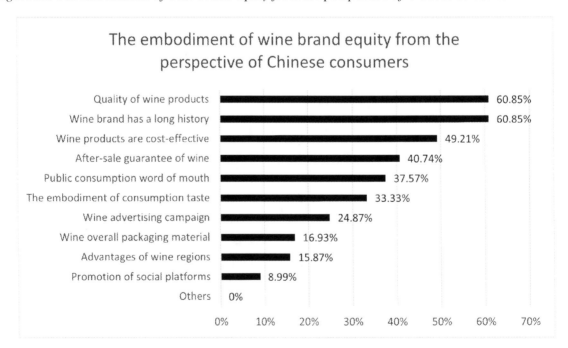

Figure 19. Reasons why Chinese consumers buy wine

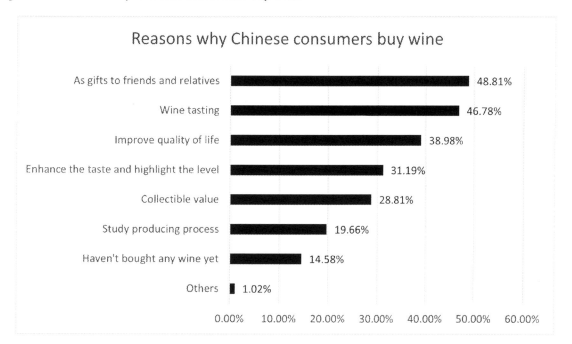

Trust attributes play an important role in consumer's product evaluation and purchase behavior, but are often underestimated (Lerro et al., 2021). This leads to related problems in the wine brand loyalty, as Chinese consumers are not opting for a single brand but must be combined with their own needs and in-depth knowledge of the market positioning of the wine products. Wine is typically bought after comparing many types of wine brands. Chinese consumers are surprisingly consistent on this point. Among 295 questionnaires effectively answered in this question, a total of 80% of consumers need to compare several wines according to their own needs before buying (Figure 20). Consumers pursue consumption experience when buying wine products, and the dimensions of feeling, emotion and cognition affect wine consumption experience at different levels (Oyinseye et al., 2022).

As a new special interest tourism, wine tourism plays an important role in increasing the added value of wine industry (Thanh & Kirova, 2018). It is also a sustainable development strategy for many wine brands, and consumers have positive feedback on sustainable wine tourism (Lerro et al., 2021). Consumers can understand the wine producing areas of the wine brand through the wine brand to better plan wine tourism. In the survey of Chinese consumers, it is found that only 11.86% of consumers will know the wine region of the brand after learning about it. Most consumers said they do not know much about the wine region of the wine brand they are familiar with, and do not pay attention to the wine region. This implies obstacles for wine brands to promote wine tourism (Figure 21).

After in-depth understanding of wine brands, Chinese consumers remain conservative in choosing their favorite wine brands for wine tourism, and 50.85% of them choose not to carry out wine tourism projects of a wine brand because they trust it (Figure 22). Although wine brand equity acts as a security for the quality of the brand development of wine tourism projects, Chinese consumers still are influenced more by the elements of experience and co-creation, possibilities for visitors to interact with local residents and with tourism employees, as well as dining satisfaction and travel immersion (Rachão et al., 2021).

Figure 20. The influence of wine brands on Chinese consumers

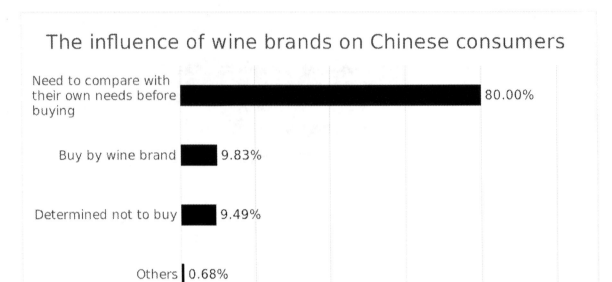

Figure 21. Chinese consumers' perception of wine regions

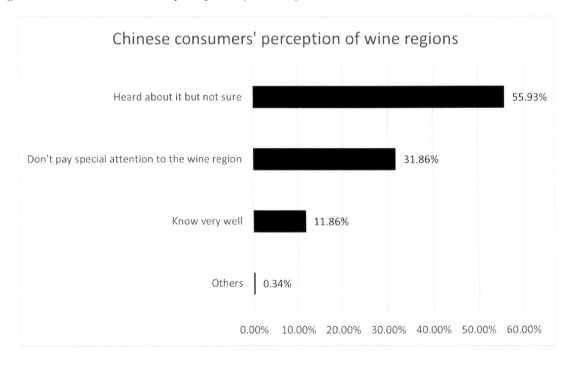

Figure 22. The willingness of Chinese consumers to choose wine tourism because of the wine brand equity

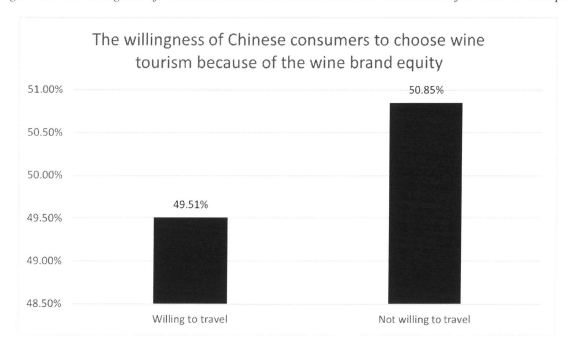

Word-of-mouth recommendation, product attraction, tourism services, network information and recommendation of tourism operators also influence consumers' decision-making on tourism routes (Torres et al., 2021). Wine brands not only need to create good product quality, but also need to create a strong tourism image in the wine tourism industry (Güzel et al., 2021).

CHINESE MARKET DEMAND FOR INTERNATIONAL WINE TOURISM

As the world's second largest economy, China's growth and the increase in disposable income of residents as well as the increased leisure time has led to a strong demand for tourism. Since 2020 the development of Chinese tourism has been severely hampered by the impact of COVID-19. What will be the trend of tourism demand in China under the impact of the COVID-19? What are the long-term and short-term impacts of the COVID-19 on tourist destinations, accommodation, and tourism?

The results of the survey are presented and analyzed below. In Table 2, we show the basic information of the participants. The sample age of this survey is concentrated between 18 and 50 years old. It is not difficult to understand that the group interested in wine brands and wine tourism is getting younger. This is closely related to the transformation of the consumption concept of the young generation in the Chinese market. As a traditional liquor-producing country, China began to introduce wine in 1950.

After four stages of market development, the wines with good quality and unique taste are highly sought after by the younger generation. It can be seen from the questionnaire that young people are most interested in wine tourism. Young people are curious, willing to accept new things and willing to improve the quality of life within their ability, which perfectly fits the characteristics of the crowd for wine tourism. Wine brand equity is an important factor in attracting young consumers.

Table 2. Basic information of respondents

Basic information of respondents		Number	Percentage
Gender	male	135	44.70%
	female	167	55.30%
Age	Under the age of 18	7	2.32%
	18-30	165	54.64%
	31-40	75	24.83%
	41-50	40	13.25%
	51-60	8	2.65%
	60 years old and above	7	2.32%
Annual disposable income (RMB)	Less than 100,000 yuan	135	45.76%
	100,000-300,000 yuan	101	34.24%
	More than 300,000 - 500,000 yuan	42	14.24%
	More than 500,000 yuan - 1 million yuan	14	4.75%
	More than 1 million yuan	3	1.02%

However, due to the impact of the COVID-19, the global economy has slowed. With uncertain income and living security, the income of Chinese residents has also fluctuated, which is bound to affect consumers' demand and plans for travel. According to the different gradients of consumers' annual disposable income (RMB) designed in the questionnaire, it is found that even under the background of different incomes, the choice of two or three trips in one year is the choice with the largest proportion in corresponding income gradient (Figure 23).

This shows that China's tourism market still has strong resilience under the conditions of the COVID-19. This also indirectly indicates that the novel coronavirus disease has suppressed a strong consumer travel demand, and Chinese residents' desire to travel has greatly increased, thus increasing the possibility of Chinese consumers choosing wine tourism and increasing their travel budget.

Affected by the COVID-19 epidemic, 58.64% of consumers choose to travel within China, and 20.34% choose to travel outside China (Figure 24). Even if the epidemic is effectively controlled, it will still take a longer time for Chinese consumers to build up their psychological attitude towards tourism safety. However, the traditional European outbound tourism projects are still warmly reflected in the questionnaire, and the hot tourist areas in Europe still accumulate a large tourism demand in the Chinese market.

The unique natural scenery of Europe attracted 71.19% of the potential consumers in the survey sample, and the unrepeatable natural scenery became the number one driving force to attract Chinese tourists and consumers. European food tasting is the second most popular consumption trend of Chinese tourists and tasting activities of European historical wine products are indispensable in the food tasting (Figure 25), as can be seen by a strong response for the project of travel experience in European wine regions.

The enhancement of wine brand equity can be achieved by upgrading wine amenities to meet the stated goals. Taking wine tourism as the main part of tourism activities, not only as an additional item of European tourism, 39.32% respondents are still willing to visit wineries, learn winemaking, participate in wine tasting and other wine tourism-related activities. Chinese consumers have shown an open attitude towards wine tourism in Europe. The impact of the epidemic on the Chinese market has depressed consumers' demand for overseas tourism, but after the epidemic is lifted, the demand for Wine tourism in Europe will jump-start with considerable numbers.

Figure 23. The relationship between income and tourism frequency (per year)

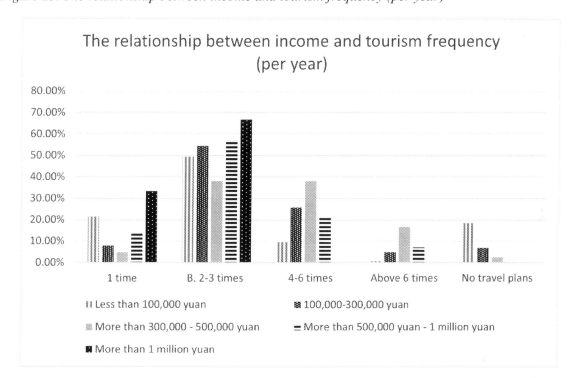

To further study the demand for European wine tourism in the Chinese market, 302 respondents were surveyed on their perceptions of wine brands. Among them, a total of 64.07% respondents said they had contact with wine brands. The degree of wine brand customer perception is also an important indicator of wine brand equity. European wine brands have a wide recognition in the Chinese market, which lays a foundation for wine brands to carry out wine tourism, but also for European wine brands to promote wine tourism in the Chinese market has played a good role (Figure 15).

Consumers' perception of wine origin helps consumers make decisions about wine tourism. The survey found that 31.86% of Chinese consumers do not pay special attention to wine regions, and 55.93% of consumers have heard about wine regions but do not pursue precise regions (Figure 21). Before making travel decisions, consumers will refer to the travel experience on social platforms to have a general understanding of the destination and make travel planning before choosing the region to travel.

To study consumers' understanding of wine producing regions, it is found that Chinese consumers are relatively familiar with the wine producing regions of traditional big wine producing countries such as France, Italy and Spain (Figure 26). This is consistent with the previous survey on the influence of wine producing countries in the Chinese market. These "Old World" wine countries with a long wine making history and high-quality wine brand assets, they accumulated a good reputation and see a good response on the Chinese market.

Figure 24. The willingness of Chinese consumers to choose tourist routes

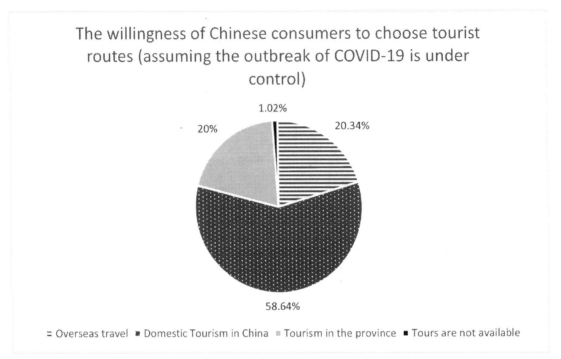

Figure 25. Reasons to travel to Europe

The survey data also show that the influence of emerging wine countries in China is still unable to compete with traditional wine countries, the promotion of wine producing areas of emerging wine countries has not been fully developed in the Chinese market, and the promotion strategies of emerging wine countries need to be adjusted and strengthened. Emerging wine countries remain unable to enhance that wine brand equity through visibility.

Figure 26. Wine countries that Chinese consumers know

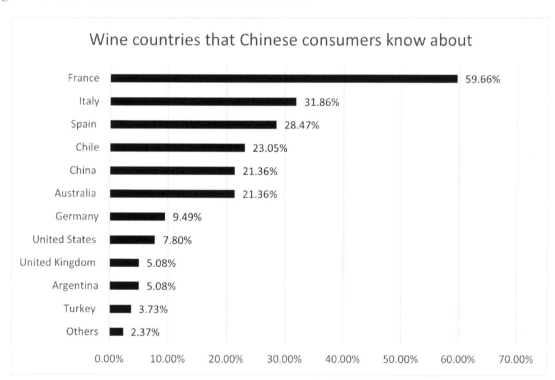

Traditional European wine products have been distributed in China, Chinese consumers have a preliminary understanding of wine brands, and Chinese consumers have a preliminary understanding of the existing wine tourism routes, which also affects the demand for wine tourism in the Chinese market. The survey shows that consumers in the Chinese market are not very interested in participating in tourism fairs or other forums that can promote tourism routes. It can be seen from the data that nearly half of the respondents have not actively participated in the forums for introducing tourism routes (Figure 22).

Inadequate campaigns may hinder consumers from making wine tourism decisions. Among the consumers who participated in the forum, the promotion of wine tourism was relatively positive, with only 9.21% of respondents saying that they had neither heard of wine tourism nor knew much about it. However, the consumers who have a comprehensive understanding of wine tourism only account for 37.5% of the surveyed population, and more consumers stay at the stage of hearing about wine tourism but not knowing deeply. In this case, more in-depth promotion of wine tourism routes by wine brands can effectively improve this situation, wine tourism in the Development of the Chinese market there is a large space for development (Figure 27).

When Chinese consumers make wine tourism decisions, wine brand equity will become a factor affecting consumers' decisions. However, according to the data the vast majority of consumers will not only consider wine brand equity and the influence of wine brand. In choosing wine tourism, the basic travel budget, transportation convenience and food and beverage service conditions are all considered by consumers (Figure 28). The density of scenic spots on wine tourism routes can maximize the advantages of wine tourism routes. Wine brand developers should maximize the diversity and richness of tourism routes in developing wine tourism routes, so that tourists and consumers can have novel travel experience.

To summarize the results of the questionnaire, there are few examples of wine tourism in China's tourism industry. The country's wine tourism market is broad, and Chinese consumers have high expectations for wine tourism. Most tourists are open to wine tourism and willing to try wine tourism routes. Our findings will help researchers and practitioners to better understand the perception of Chinese wine tourism brands by deepening Chinese consumers' understanding of wine tourism routes.

Figure 27. The promotion effect of wine tourism in the Chinese market

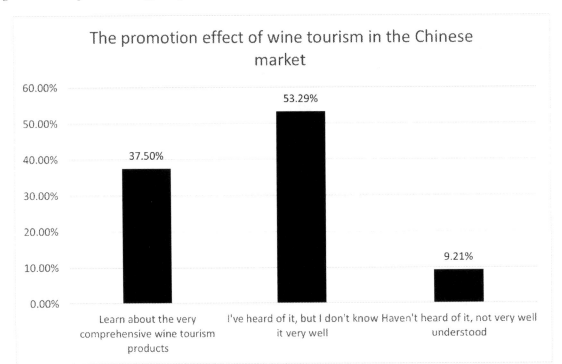

Figure 28. Factors influencing tourism decisions

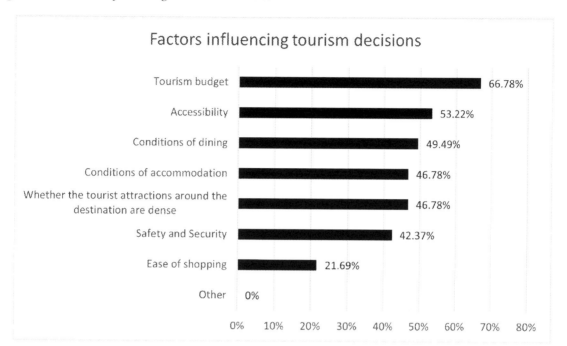

CASE STUDIES

European Developed Countries and Emerging Countries Wine Tourism Flexible Strategy for the Chinese Market

As a country with the most outstanding wine industry development, France has laid a foundation for the development of wine tourism. The emergence of new world wines has made France's traditional wine industry feel the pressure of global competition. Wine industry is one of the pillar industries in France. As an industry that can increase the added value of wine industry, wine tourism has the vitality of a new industry. Wine tourism has become an integral part of French tourism.

The development of French wine brand equity cannot be separated from the long history of French winemaking, and the French wine tourism industry has a history of more than 70 years. From a global perspective, wine tourism is an emerging special interest tourism industry with broad prospects for development. Based on the popular demand of tourism, French wine tourism enables consumers and tourists to experience the rich and interesting local wine producing areas and provides individual service and perfect reception places.

French wine brands improve the impact of their wine brands by improving their winemaking techniques, thus increasing their wine brand equity. French wine is close to the needs of consumers from the aspects of wine making technology, but also from the level of history, architecture, culture, food, and friends. They are well equipped to provide consumers with immersive tour experiences so that tourists experience the charm of wine culture, and the art of life. The cross-fertilization of cultures is also an important way to enhance the equity of wine brands.

Take wine tourism in Bordeaux, France for example. Bordeaux is the largest wine region in the world, with the largest vineyard coverage in France. The unique natural conditions provide natural advantages for Bordeaux to develop wine tourism. Bordeaux adopts the Winery Route Mode (WRM) to develop wine tourism. The WRM is a mode that attracts and receives tourists by gathering many winemakers in the region. This enables the advantage of a scaling effect (Boivin & Tanguay, 2019) of the Bordeaux wine brand cluster development. As one of the most important wine producing regions in France, Bordeaux has many wine chateaux, such as Lafite, Chateau Latour, Petrus, and Chateau Mouton Rothschild.

The establishment of wine chateaux and brands has provided Bordeaux with global popularity. The influence of French wine brands in The Chinese market is inseparable from the active marketing of Bordeaux wine brands. Each Bordeaux wine estate has its own history. Wine brands take advantage of the benefits of cluster development to improve wine brand equity. These wineries are developed in clusters in Bordeaux, and the culture of wine tourism is built on the cultural diversity of many wineries. The cultural diversity also enriches the local wine brand equity and lays the foundation for the development of wine tourism.

The development of wine tourism routes integrates the resources of wineries in the Bordeaux region. As the wineries are connected with each other, they conduct unified planning to provide tourists with rich tourism resources and diverse wine-making cultures. The development of winery clusters in the Bordeaux region has greatly reduced the time and cost consumers spend on transportation, effectively solving the problem of limited travel budgets in the survey. Bordeaux wine tourism combines the primary, secondary and tertiary industries, and wine tourism provides impetus for the development of the wine industry (Cusin & Passebois-Ducros, 2015).

Bordeaux became the best tourist region in Europe in 2015 due to the hospitality of the people of Bordeaux. Bordeaux wine tourism focuses on the construction of reception facilities. Well-established wine tourism facilities reflect the equity of the wine brand. Perfect tourist reception facilities guarantee the satisfaction of wine tourists. Among the famous Bordeaux chateaux, there are tasting rooms, reception centers, exhibition rooms and picnic areas with natural scenery. Tourists can experience the local customs and customs of Bordeaux through contact with local people, which improves the satisfaction of consumers (Ponsignon & Derbaix, 2020).

Wine brand equity provides a guarantee for wine tourism development. France Bordeaux also has rich wine tourism products and Bordeaux wine brands jointly carry out the French Bordeaux Wine Festival where tourists can taste the wine of many chateaux. During the Bordeaux Wine Festival, local folk performances are held, and fireworks are provided by fireworks companies to bring consumers a multi-sensory experience. Walking along the Garonne river to the cruise ship, and travel options abound. Abundant tourism products provide tourists with abundant choices and enrich the personalized needs of tourists. At the same time, the festival of wine culture is carried out to create a high-quality image of Bordeaux wine brand tourism.

The effective use of the natural beauty of wine tourism is a reflection of what wine brands have to offer. Tuscany is Italy's best-known wine region and the most attractive wine destination for both Italy and the world. Tuscany has become the center of Italian wine tourism due to its long human history and beautiful natural scenery. Tuscany is characterized by its varied landscape, unique romantic characteristics, ancient towns and rural tourism, which provide wine brands and profound cultural heritage for local wineries (Randelli et al., 2014).

Wine brand equity is reflected in the mastery of and reaction to consumer consumption habits. The development of tourism in Tuscany is in line with the travel habits of consumers. After the COVID-19 outbreak, consumers no longer pursue luxurious metropolitan tourism, but prefer to travel routes with beautiful natural environment and unique landscapes. Tuscan wine brands take advantage of the natural landscape of their wineries, promote the combination of wine tourism and natural scenery, and emphasize the harmony between ecological environment and wine production (Domi & Belletti, 2022).

Castello Banfi, one of the most beautiful wineries in Brunello di Montalcino, is a well-known winery in Italy. It enjoys the title of "Art Winery". In the short period of 30 years, this winery has won the reputation of "the best winery in Italy" many times. Winery tourism facilities are complete, numerous wine tourism activities, standard wine tasting, characteristic wine tasting, wine cellar visit and winery visit, equipped with travel gift shop to better meet the needs of consumers.

Wine brand equity also needs to focus on the ability to integrate resources. As an art city of world civilization, Italian wine brands also integrate wine tourism resources and culture and art tourism resources. Through the architectural style and urban layout of the old winery, wine products are brought to every tourist's journey. Wine brands open wine tasting related tourism products, consumers can have a good perception of wine tasting art, experience the Love of Italian people for wine.

With the largest vineyard coverage in the world, Wine tourism in Spain is also very mature. Tradition, craftsmanship and innovation have pushed Spanish wines to the top of the world. Spanish grape farmers apply the perfect combination of ancestral planting techniques and modern planting technology, and their wines' taste is famous internationally. In addition, the soil and climate of the Iberian Peninsula are suitable for the growth of various special types of grapes, and the taste of various wines is unique and distinct. Follow the wine Trail to discover Spain's different landscapes and cultural heritage, sample authentic wines and immerse yourself in its rich culture.

Wine brand equity reflects the culture of the wine brand, while wine culture contributes to the growth of wine brand equity. A quick way to learn about Spanish culture is to taste the wines while visiting a wine estate. Rioja is a popular destination for Wine tourism in Spain. Wine tours in Spain include tours of related wine museums and thus attract more visitors. Spanish wine brand La Rioja Alta has taken advantage of the spectacular landscape of the grapevine fields of the Rioja Mountains to develop wine Tours, visiting various museums and explanation centers, and bringing wine to travel tables for consumers to taste. Spanish baroque churches, castles, monasteries and wine estates complement each other, adding to the historical and artistic heritage displayed in Spanish wine tourism.

Wine brand equity demonstrates strong product competitiveness and attracts consumers to wine tourism. As a tiny landlocked country, Switzerland is surrounded by big wine-producing countries such as France and Italy, and the reputation of Swiss wine is not widely spread. However, the quality of Swiss wine is still recognized by the majority of consumers. Although the export volume is less than 1% of the global wine market, Swiss domestic and international consumers through the high-quality wine products attracted to Switzerland for wine tour.

The first-hand experience of consumers is often a value that can be overlooked, while a good ecological perspective builds up a reputation for wine brands. The Pfyn-Finges Nature Park in Switzerland focuses on wine tourism, attracting visitors through traditional wine-picking techniques. The Swiss wine tourism industry has created a number of natural parks, covering more than 80 vineyards. By telling the story of the development of Swiss wine, Swiss wine brands add the story of the transformation from the agricultural name of the region to the story of grape planting and wine-making village into the wine tourism routes. In the promotion, they convey the concept of sustainable development to consumers and let them experience the unique experience of close contact with nature.

The history of wine development in the emerging wine world is much less ancient than that of the "Old World" wine producers. Wine brand equity also differs from that of "Old World" wine producing countries. Although Napa Valley, as an excellent wine tourism demonstration case in the United States, does not belong to Europe, it can make Bordeaux in France change its wine marketing strategy, which is worth learning from the emerging developing countries (Hira & Swartz, 2014).

Emerging wine brand equity differs from old world wine brands in that it is more about having novel product development. Napa Valley wineries cluster together to facilitate unified planning and management. In terms of product design, many Napa Valley wine brands have developed many tourism products such as wine train, grape sampling, winery tour, wine tasting, vineyard ecological tour and so on. The diversity of products gives consumers more choices, and consumers can choose their own personalized tourism programs.

Wine brand equity makes a natural distinction for consumers. Napa Valley Wine brands offer Tours for all income levels. It is divided into high, middle and low-end tourist routes, based on refined metrics of market demands. Their mottos are: Be proactive in marketing and promote yourself through well-known wine events. Make full use of celebrity effect, maintain good cooperative relations with entertainment, media, and art circles, hold exhibitions to improve the influence of wineries and drive wine tourism industry. Napa Valley is a typical wine tourism-centered industry model, which drives the development of wine industry through good tourism benefits and is worth learning from and referencing for emerging wine countries.

CONCLUSION AND RECOMMENDATION

The purpose of this chapter is to explore whether wine brand equity has an impact on consumers' wine travel decisions. This chapter first reviews the literature of international commerce and tourism, summarizes the development trend of international commerce and tourism, and provides research direction and ideas for the development trend of wine industry and wine tourism. As a new tourism mode, wine contributes to the sustainable development of wine industry. Wine tourism combines the first, second and third industries to inject vitality into more industries.

This chapter summarizes the characteristics of top European wine tourism from the development of wine tourism itineraries in the top European wine countries, combined with specific wine brand assets. Then from the perspective of Chinese consumers, through a questionnaire survey, we studied the Chinese consumers' perception of imported wine brands. We analyzed whether wine brands play a decisive role in consumers' wine travel decisions. Research shows that the wine brand is an effective guarantee of the quality of wine tourism products, and Chinese consumers are more willing to choose the brand with which they are familiar for wine tourism.

However, wine brand equity does not play a decisive role in the decision-making of wine tourism, and consumers are also affected by multiple factors such as travel budget, travel safety and transportation convenience. Chinese consumers are showing keen interest in European wine Tours and remain open to buying European wine after the COVID-19 pandemic ends. Finally, through case studies, we showcased mature wine tourism development strategies and the wine tourism strategy of new world wine countries as valuable advice for countries currently developing their wine tourism.

Developing countries and new world wine countries need to build their own wine brands through the quality of wine products as soon as possible. The quality of wine products is the premise and foundation of wine tourism. Only through the guarantee of wine brand equity can the wine market attract more consumers convincingly and establish a good reputation for its own wine brand.

Companies that already have mature wine brands should actively market in China. The Chinese market's perception of wine brands is still stuck in the "Old World" wine brands, emerging wine countries should seize this market gap. More wine brand promotion, through star endorsement, star effect, advertising, offline wine tasting activities, etc., can attract more consumers and form a good reputation among consumers, thus increasing the influence of wine brand equity in the Chinese market.

We already have wine brands recognized by consumers. When developing wine tourism routes, we should fully consider the consumption level of the Chinese market and design diversified products to meet the needs of consumers with different income levels to choose wine tourism routes. Through hierarchical positioning, market segmentation, design of high-end wine tourism and public wine tourism routes, stakeholders can meet the needs of consumers with personalized wine tourism routes.

The understanding of wine tourism in the Chinese market is still in its infancy, and more consumers have never had an in-depth understanding of wine tourism routes. Wine brands should push their wine tourism products into more tourism forums and make wine tourism an emerging tourism model in China. This could be facilitated by building special publicity websites to provide consumers with convenient consulting services and preview services and provide experience services at the appropriate time (Dai et al., 2022) as well as by taking the initiative in marketing, formulating, and implementing promotion strategies of wine tourism, and constantly adjusting in practice to adapt to the Chinese market. Stakeholders can use brand marketing, experience marketing, network marketing, film marketing and sustainable marketing and other ways to expand the popularity of wine tourism in the market and improve consumers' recognition of wine tourism.

European wine tourism in China has lost the advantage of geographical proximity of consumption, which emphasizes the cooperation between wineries and wine brands in the same region, unified planning, and the formation of a unique wine tourism system. Can consumers experience the culture of different wineries in one trip, solving the geographical disadvantage of being far away from the target consumer group?

Wine tourism is a tourism focusing on quality, wine brands should pay more attention to the construction of reception facilities, improve the reception facilities of tourists, to ensure the quality of service is the guarantee of wine tourism satisfaction. Visitors immerse themselves in the wine estate tourism experience. Cooperate with more service industries to provide a complete tourism service supply chain.

This chapter provides suggestions for developing wine tourism routes and management strategies for wine brands to maintain their advantages in international competition. Wine as a special interest tourism in the future development is bound to have broad prospects.

ACKNOWLEDGMENT

The authors extend sincere gratitude to:
- Our colleagues from Soochow University, The Australian Studies Centre of Shanghai University, The European Business University of Luxembourg and Krirk University as well as the indepen-

dent research colleagues who provided insight and expertise that greatly assisted the research, although they may not agree with all of the interpretations/conclusions of this chapter.
- China Knowledge for supporting our research.
- The Editor and the International Editorial Advisory Board (IEAB) of this book who initially desk reviewed, arranged a rigorous double/triple blind review process and conducted a thorough, minute and critical final review before accepting the chapter for publication.
- All anonymous reviewers who provided very constructive feedbacks for thorough revision, improvement and fine tuning of the chapter.

REFERENCES

Berbekova, A., Uysal, M., & Assaf, A. G. (2021). A thematic analysis of crisis management in tourism: A theoretical perspective. *Tourism Management, 86*, 86. doi:10.1016/j.tourman.2021.104342

Boatto, V., Galletto, L., Barisan, L., & Bianchin, F. (2013). The development of wine tourism in the Conegliano Valdobbiadene area. *Wine Economics and Policy, 2*(2), 93–101. doi:10.1016/j.wep.2013.11.003

Boivin, M., & Tanguay, G. A. (2019). Analysis of the determinants of urban tourism attractiveness: The case of Québec City and Bordeaux. *Journal of Destination Marketing & Management, 11*, 67–79. doi:10.1016/j.jdmm.2018.11.002

Bruwer, J. (2003). South African wine routes: Some perspectives on the wine tourism industry's structural dimensions and wine tourism product. *Tourism Management, 24*(4), 423–435. doi:10.1016/S0261-5177(02)00105-X

Byrd, E. T., Canziani, B., Hsieh, Y.-C., Debbage, K., & Sonmez, S. (2016). Wine tourism: Motivating visitors through core and supplementary services. *Tourism Management, 52*, 19–29. doi:10.1016/j.tourman.2015.06.009

Celhay, F., Cheng, P., Masson, J., & Li, W. (2020). Package graphic design and communication across cultures: An investigation of Chinese consumers' interpretation of imported wine labels. *International Journal of Research in Marketing, 37*(1), 108–128. doi:10.1016/j.ijresmar.2019.07.004

Chen, C., Song, M., & Heo, G. E. (2018). A scalable and adaptive method for finding semantically equivalent cue words of uncertainty. *Journal of Informetrics, 12*(1), 158–180. doi:10.1016/j.joi.2017.12.004

Chen, J., Cui, F., Balezentis, T., Streimikiene, D., & Jin, H. (2021). What drives international tourism development in the Belt and Road Initiative? *Journal of Destination Marketing & Management, 19*, 19. doi:10.1016/j.jdmm.2020.100544

Correia, L., Gouveia, S., & Martins, P. (2019). The European wine export cycle. *Wine Economics and Policy, 8*(1), 91–101. doi:10.1016/j.wep.2019.04.001

Crick, J. M., & Crick, D. (2021). Coopetition and family-owned wine producers. *Journal of Business Research, 135*, 319–336. doi:10.1016/j.jbusres.2021.06.046

Crick, J. M., Crick, D., & Tebbett, N. (2020). Competitor orientation and value co-creation in sustaining rural New Zealand wine producers. *Journal of Rural Studies, 73*, 122–134. doi:10.1016/j.jrurstud.2019.10.019

Cusin, J., & Passebois-Ducros, J. (2015). Appropriate persistence in a project: The case of the Wine Culture and Tourism Centre in Bordeaux. *European Management Journal*, *33*(5), 341–353. doi:10.1016/j.emj.2015.04.001

Dai, F., Wang, D., & Kirillova, K. (2022). Travel inspiration in tourist decision making. *Tourism Management*, 90.

Domi, S., & Belletti, G. (2022). The role of origin products and networking on agritourism performance: The case of Tuscany. *Journal of Rural Studies*, *90*, 113–123. doi:10.1016/j.jrurstud.2022.01.013

Ellegaard, C., & Medlin, C. J. (2018). Finding good relationships – intended and realized relational governance of international fine wine exchanges. *Journal of World Business*, *53*(6), 794–805. doi:10.1016/j.jwb.2018.06.003

Festa, G., Shams, S. M. R., Metallo, G., & Cuomo, M. T. (2020). Opportunities and challenges in the contribution of wine routes to wine tourism in Italy – A stakeholders' perspective of development. *Tourism Management Perspectives*, *33*, 33. doi:10.1016/j.tmp.2019.100585

Frost, W., Frost, J., Strickland, P., & Smith Maguire, J. (2020). Seeking a competitive advantage in wine tourism: Heritage and storytelling at the cellar-door. *International Journal of Hospitality Management*, *87*, 87. doi:10.1016/j.ijhm.2020.102460

Gao, J., Peng, P., Lu, F., & Claramunt, C. (2022). A multi-scale comparison of tourism attraction networks across China. *Tourism Management*, *90*, 90. doi:10.1016/j.tourman.2022.104489

Getz, D., & Brown, G. (2006). Critical success factors for wine tourism regions: A demand analysis. *Tourism Management*, *27*(1), 146–158. doi:10.1016/j.tourman.2004.08.002

Gómez, M., González-Díaz, B., & Molina, A. (2015a). Priority maps at wine tourism destinations: An empirical approach in five Spanish wine regions. *Journal of Destination Marketing & Management*, *4*(4), 258–267. doi:10.1016/j.jdmm.2015.09.003

Gómez, M., Lopez, C., & Molina, A. (2015b). A model of tourism destination brand equity: The case of wine tourism destinations in Spain. *Tourism Management*, *51*, 210–222. doi:10.1016/j.tourman.2015.05.019

Gu, Q., Zhang, H., Huang, S., Zheng, F., & Chen, C. (2021). Tourists' spatiotemporal behaviors in an emerging wine region: A time-geography perspective. *Journal of Destination Marketing & Management*, *19*, 19. doi:10.1016/j.jdmm.2020.100513

Güzel, Ö., Ehtiyar, R., & Ryan, C. (2021). The Success Factors of wine tourism entrepreneurship for rural area: A thematic biographical narrative analysis in Turkey. *Journal of Rural Studies*, *84*, 230–239. doi:10.1016/j.jrurstud.2021.04.021

Hall, C. M. (2005). Biosecurity and wine tourism. *Tourism Management*, *26*(6), 931–938. doi:10.1016/j.tourman.2004.06.011

Hartman, S., Parra, C., & De Roo, G. (2019). Framing strategic storytelling in the context of transition management to stimulate tourism destination development. *Tourism Management*, *75*, 90–98. doi:10.1016/j.tourman.2019.04.014

Henseler, M., Maisonnave, H., & Maskaeva, A. (2022). Economic impacts of COVID-19 on the tourism sector in Tanzania. *Annals of Tourism Research Empirical Insights, 3*.

Hira, A., & Swartz, T. (2014). What makes Napa Napa? The roots of success in the wine industry. *Wine Economics and Policy, 3*(1), 37–53. doi:10.1016/j.wep.2014.02.001

Jiménez-Asenjo, N., & Filipescu, D. A. (2019). Cheers in China! International marketing strategies of Spanish wine exporters. *International Business Review, 28*(4), 647–659. doi:10.1016/j.ibusrev.2019.01.001

Kim, S. H., Abbasi, F., Lamendola, C., & Reaven, G. M. (2009). Effect of moderate alcoholic beverage consumption on insulin sensitivity in insulin-resistant, nondiabetic individuals. *Metabolism: Clinical and Experimental, 58*(3), 387–392. doi:10.1016/j.metabol.2008.10.013 PMID:19217456

Kudo, T., Lahey, R., Hirschfeld, C. B., Williams, M. C., Lu, B., Alasnag, M., Bhatia, M., Henry Bom, H.-S., Dautov, T., Fazel, R., Karthikeyan, G., Keng, F. Y. J., Rubinshtein, R., Better, N., Cerci, R. J., Dorbala, S., Raggi, P., Shaw, L. J., Villines, T. C., & ... . (2021). Impact of COVID-19 Pandemic on Cardiovascular Testing in Asia. *Journal of the American College of Cardiology: Asia, 1*, 187–199.

Lerro, M., Yeh, C.-H., Klink-Lehmann, J., Vecchio, R., Hartmann, M., & Cembalo, L. (2021). The effect of moderating variables on consumer preferences for sustainable wines. *Food Quality and Preference, 94*, 94. doi:10.1016/j.foodqual.2021.104336

Liu, Z., Wang, A., Weber, K., Chan, E. H. W., & Shi, W. (2022). Categorisation of cultural tourism attractions by tourist preference using location-based social network data: The case of Central, Hong Kong. *Tourism Management, 90*, 90. doi:10.1016/j.tourman.2022.104488

Lorenzo, J. R. F., Rubio, M. T. M., & Garcés, S. A. (2018). The competitive advantage in business, capabilities and strategy. What general performance factors are found in the Spanish wine industry? *Wine Economics and Policy, 7*(2), 94–108. doi:10.1016/j.wep.2018.04.001

Lozano-Oyola, M., Blancas, F. J., Gonzalez, M., & Caballero, R. (2019). Sustainable tourism tags to reward destination management. *Journal of Environmental Management, 250*, 109458. doi:10.1016/j.jenvman.2019.109458 PMID:31472380

Mach, L., & Ponting, J. (2021). Establishing a pre-COVID-19 baseline for surf tourism: Trip expenditure and attitudes, behaviors and willingness to pay for sustainability. *Annals of Tourism Research Empirical Insights, 2*.

Martins, J., Gonçalves, R., Branco, F., Barbosa, L., Melo, M., & Bessa, M. (2017). A multisensory virtual experience model for thematic tourism: A Port wine tourism application proposal. *Journal of Destination Marketing & Management, 6*(2), 103–109. doi:10.1016/j.jdmm.2017.02.002

Mason, M. C., & Paggiaro, A. (2012). Investigating the role of festivalscape in culinary tourism: The case of food and wine events. *Tourism Management, 33*(6), 1329–1336. doi:10.1016/j.tourman.2011.12.016

Mckercher, B., Ho, P. S. Y., & Du Cros, H. (2005). Relationship between tourism and cultural heritage management: Evidence from Hong Kong. *Tourism Management, 26*(4), 539–548. doi:10.1016/j.tourman.2004.02.018

Menna, A., & Walsh, P. R. (2019). Assessing environments of commercialization of innovation for SMEs in the global wine industry: A market dynamics approach. *Wine Economics and Policy, 8*(2), 191–202. doi:10.1016/j.wep.2019.10.001

Mitchell, R., Charters, S., & Albrecht, J. N. (2012). Cultural systems and the wine tourism product. *Annals of Tourism Research, 39*(1), 311–335. doi:10.1016/j.annals.2011.05.002

Musso, F., & Francioni, B. (2015). Agri-Food Clusters, Wine Tourism and Foreign Markets. The Role of Local Networks for SME's Internationalization. *Procedia Economics and Finance, 27*, 334–343. doi:10.1016/S2212-5671(15)01004-7

Nave, A., Laurett, R., & Do Paço, A. (2021). Relation between antecedents, barriers and consequences of sustainable practices in the wine tourism sector. *Journal of Destination Marketing & Management, 20*, 20. doi:10.1016/j.jdmm.2021.100584

Nguyen, T. Q. T., Johnson, P., & Young, T. (2022). Networking, coopetition and sustainability of tourism destinations. *Journal of Hospitality and Tourism Management, 50*, 400–411. doi:10.1016/j.jhtm.2022.01.003

Nguyen, V. K., Natoli, R., & Divisekera, S. (2021). Innovation and productivity in tourism small and medium enterprises: A longitudinal study. *Tourism Management Perspectives, 38*, 38. doi:10.1016/j.tmp.2021.100804

Nicolosi, A., Cortese, L., Nesci, F. S., & Privitera, D. (2016). Combining Wine Production and Tourism. The Aeolian Islands. *Procedia: Social and Behavioral Sciences, 223*, 662–667. doi:10.1016/j.sbspro.2016.05.381

Oyinseye, P., Suárez, A., Saldaña, E., Fernández-Zurbano, P., Valentin, D., & Sáenz-Navajas, M.-P. (2022). Multidimensional representation of wine drinking experience: Effects of the level of consumers' expertise and involvement. *Food Quality and Preference, 98*, 98. doi:10.1016/j.foodqual.2022.104536

Pan, Y.-J., & Lee, L.-S. (2011). Academic Performance and Perceived Employability of Graduate Students in Business and Management – An Analysis of Nationwide Graduate Destination Survey. *Procedia: Social and Behavioral Sciences, 25*, 91–103. doi:10.1016/j.sbspro.2011.10.531

Pham, L. D. Q., Coles, T., Ritchie, B. W., & Wang, J. (2021). Building business resilience to external shocks: Conceptualising the role of social networks to small tourism & hospitality businesses. *Journal of Hospitality and Tourism Management, 48*, 210–219. doi:10.1016/j.jhtm.2021.06.012

Ponsignon, F., & Derbaix, M. (2020). The impact of interactive technologies on the social experience: An empirical study in a cultural tourism context. *Tourism Management Perspectives, 35*, 35. doi:10.1016/j.tmp.2020.100723

Priilaid, D., Ballantyne, R., & Packer, J. (2020). A "blue ocean" strategy for developing visitor wine experiences: Unlocking value in the Cape region tourism market. *Journal of Hospitality and Tourism Management, 43*, 91–99. doi:10.1016/j.jhtm.2020.01.009

Rachão, S. A. S., De Jesus Breda, Z., De Oliveira Fernandes, C., & Joukes, V. N. P. M. (2021). Drivers of experience co-creation in food-and-wine tourism: An exploratory quantitative analysis. *Tourism Management Perspectives, 37*, 37. doi:10.1016/j.tmp.2020.100783

Randelli, F., Romei, P., & Tortora, M. (2014). An evolutionary approach to the study of rural tourism: The case of Tuscany. *Land Use Policy, 38*, 276–281. doi:10.1016/j.landusepol.2013.11.009

Rodrigues, H., & Parr, W. V. (2019). Contribution of cross-cultural studies to understanding wine appreciation: A review. *Food Research International (Ottawa, Ont.), 115*, 251–258. doi:10.1016/j.foodres.2018.09.008 PMID:30599939

Rodrigues, H., Rolaz, J., Franco-Luesma, E., Saenz-Navajas, M. P., Behrens, J., Valentin, D., & Depetris-Chauvin, N. (2020). How the country-of-origin impacts wine traders' mental representation about wines: A study in a world wine trade fair. *Food Research International (Ottawa, Ont.), 137*, 109480. doi:10.1016/j.foodres.2020.109480 PMID:33233142

Rosato, P. F., Caputo, A., Valente, D., & Pizzi, S. (2021). 2030 Agenda and sustainable business models in tourism: A bibliometric analysis. *Ecological Indicators, 121*, 121. doi:10.1016/j.ecolind.2020.106978

Rossello, J., Becken, S., & Santana-Gallego, M. (2020). The effects of natural disasters on international tourism: A global analysis. *Tourism Management, 79*, 104080. doi:10.1016/j.tourman.2020.104080 PMID:32287755

Roxas, F. M. Y., Rivera, J. P. R., & Gutierrez, E. L. M. (2020). Mapping stakeholders' roles in governing sustainable tourism destinations. *Journal of Hospitality and Tourism Management, 45*, 387–398. doi:10.1016/j.jhtm.2020.09.005

Santeramo, F. G., Seccia, A., & Nardone, G. (2017). The synergies of the Italian wine and tourism sectors. *Wine Economics and Policy, 6*(1), 71–74. doi:10.1016/j.wep.2016.11.004

Song, H., Livat, F., & Ye, S. (2019). Effects of terrorist attacks on tourist flows to France: Is wine tourism a substitute for urban tourism? *Journal of Destination Marketing & Management, 14*, 14. doi:10.1016/j.jdmm.2019.100385

Soontiens, W., Dayaram, K., Burgess, J., & Grimstad, S. (2018). Bittersweet? Urban proximity and wine tourism in the Swan Valley Region. *Tourism Management Perspectives, 28*, 105–112. doi:10.1016/j.tmp.2018.08.008

Sun, Y.-Y., & Drakeman, D. (2020). Measuring the carbon footprint of wine tourism and cellar door sales. *Journal of Cleaner Production, 266*, 266. doi:10.1016/j.jclepro.2020.121937

Thanh, T. V., & Kirova, V. (2018). Wine tourism experience: A netnography study. *Journal of Business Research, 83*, 30–37. doi:10.1016/j.jbusres.2017.10.008

Thommandru, A., Espinoza-Maguiña, M., Ramirez-Asis, E., Ray, S., Naved, M., & Guzman-Avalos, M. (2021). Role of tourism and hospitality business in economic development. *Materials Today: Proceedings*. Advance online publication. doi:10.1016/j.matpr.2021.07.059

Tight, M. (2017). *Understanding Case Study Research: Small-scale Research with Meaning*. Academic Press.

Torres, J. P., Barrera, J. I., Kunc, M., & Charters, S. (2021). The dynamics of wine tourism adoption in Chile. *Journal of Business Research, 127*, 474–485. doi:10.1016/j.jbusres.2020.06.043

Velikova, N., & Dodd, T. (2016). Sustainability of the Wine Market though Emerging Consumer Segments: The Case of U.S. Hispanic Consumers. *Agriculture and Agricultural Science Procedia, 8*, 81–87. doi:10.1016/j.aaspro.2016.02.011

Vodeb, K. (2012). Competition In Tourism In Terms of Changing Environment. *Procedia: Social and Behavioral Sciences, 44*, 273–278. doi:10.1016/j.sbspro.2012.05.030

Wut, T. M., Xu, J., & Wong, S.-M. (2021). Crisis management research (1985–2020) in the hospitality and tourism industry: A review and research agenda. *Tourism Management, 85*, 85. doi:10.1016/j.tourman.2021.104307

Yue, Y., Li, X., Zhang, D., & Wang, S. (2021). How cryptocurrency affects economy? A network analysis using bibliometric methods. *International Review of Financial Analysis, 77*, 77. doi:10.1016/j.irfa.2021.101869

Zhang, J., & Dong, L. (2021). Image Monitoring and Management of Hot Tourism Destination Based on Data Mining Technology in Big Data Environment. *Microprocessors and Microsystems, 80*, 80. doi:10.1016/j.micpro.2020.103515

APPENDIX

About wine brands, wine tourism and consumer decisions

Questionnaires

Dear Consumers,

Hello! In order to better understand consumers' cognition of wine brands, the understanding and planning of wine tourism. We need your help completing this questionnaire. The results of the questionnaire are not used for any purpose other than relevant academic research. Please read each question below carefully and choose the option that you think best suits you. There is no right or wrong in your answer, please answer each question, thank you for your cooperation.

Basic information investigation

1. Your gender is:
    A. Male
    B. Female
2. Your age group:
    A. under 18 years of age (questionnaire closed).
    B. 18-30
    C. 31-40
    D. 41-50
    E. 51-60
    F. 60 years of age or older
3. Your current occupation:
4. Your disposable annual income (equivalent to nominal currency).
    A. 100,000 yuan or less
    B. 100,000-300,000 yuan
    C. More than 300,000 yuan - 500,000 yuan
    D. 500,000 yuan or more - 1 million yuan
    E. 1 million yuan or more

The issue of wine brand equity

5. Have you ever been exposed to a wine brand?
    A. Yes
    B. No (skip to question 9).
6. How have you ever been exposed to wine brands? (Multiple choice)
    A. Access information on your own
    B. Testimonials from friends and family
    C. Make purchases in physical stores
    D. Have been to wine regions to make purchases

      E.   Celebrity endorsements
      F.   Take part in some wine tastings
      G.   Big data
      H.   Others

7. Contact the wine brand through the above channels
    A. Helps deepen your interest in learning about wine/wine brands
    B. Doesn't increase your interest in learning about wine/wine brands

8. What do you think is the value of the wine brand? Multiple choice questions
    A. Wine product quality
    B. Wine after-sales guarantee
    C. Wine products are cost-effective
    D. Wine brands have a long history
    E. Wine advertising campaigns
    F. The embodiment of consumer taste
    G. Popular consumer reputation
    H. The overall packaging material of the wine
    I. Promotion of social platforms
    J. Wine region advantage
    K. Others

9. If conditions permit, would you buy wine because of the wide influence of the wine brand?
    A. Anyone with this brand will buy it
    B. You need to compare multiple things according to your own needs before purchasing
    C. Resolutely do not buy
    D. Others

10. The reason why you buy wine [multiple choice question].
    A. Taste fine wines
    B. Collectible value
    C. Elevate the level of taste and highlighting
    D. As a gift for friends and family
    E. Research on brewing processes
    F. Improve the quality of life
    G. I have not purchased wine at the moment
    H. Others

Wine tourism related issues

11. How many trips per year do you plan?
    A. 1 time
    B. 2-3 times
    C. 4-6 times
    D. 6 times or more
    E. No travel plans

12. If the COVID-19 epidemic is effectively controlled, which tour route will you choose?
    A. Overseas travel
    B. Domestic travel
    C. Intra-provincial travel
    D. Others
13. If you choose Europe as your travel destination, what do you think attracts you? Multiple choice questions
    A. Cultural history (art galleries, museums, etc.).
    B. Nature (beaches, mountains, etc.).
    C. Medical facilities (travel activities while treating abroad).
    D. Food tasting (national specialties).
    E. Wine region experience (visit to a winery, learn to make, participate in a wine tasting, etc.).
    F. Bustling metropolis (shopping, modern city excursions, etc.).
    G. Extreme sports (skydiving, cross-country skiing, etc.).
    H. Others
14. Have you ever participated in a travel expo or other forum for introducing tourism projects?
    A. Participated (skip to 15 questions).
    B. Did not participate (skip to 16 questions).
15. Did you learn about wine tourism in the above forum? (Wine tourism: visit famous wineries and appellations, experience picking and making wine, tasting wine, learning about wine, making wine purchases, etc.).
    A. Learn about the very comprehensive wine tourism products
    B. I've heard of it, but I don't know it very well
    C. Haven't heard of it, not very well understood
16. As a consumer, when it comes to wine culture tourism, which countries come to mind first? (Wine tourism: visit famous wineries and appellations, experience picking and making wine, taste wine, learn about wine, buy wine, etc.)
    A. Spain
    B. France
    C. Italy
    D. Chile
    E. Australia
    F. China
    G. Germany
    H. United States
    I. Argentina
    J. United Kingdom
    K. Turkey
    L. Others
17. Among the wine brands you buy, do you know the wine regions of that brand? Multiple Choice Questions
    A. Very knowledgeable
    B. Slightly heard but not sure

C. Do not pay special attention to the production area
D. Others
18. Will you choose wine travel because you prefer a certain wine brand [Judgment Question].
    A. Yes
    B. No
19. After choosing a wine tourism destination based on the wine brand, what factors will affect your travel? Multiple choice questions
    A. Convenience of transportation
    B. Travel budget
    C. Catering conditions
    D. Whether the tourist attractions around the destination are dense
    E. Accommodation conditions
    F. Safety and security
    G. Ease of shopping
    H. Others
20. If you can travel to Europe after the pandemic is over, will you add wine tourism to your itinerary?
    A. Yes
    B. Possibly
    C. No

Thank you for taking the time to participate in this survey, I wish you a happy life, thank you.

Chapter 16
Culture as a Critical Enabler for Tourism Destination Development

Manuela Presutti
University of Bologna, Italy

Francesco Barbini
Campus of Rimini, Italy

Massimo Ferdinandi
Campus of Rimini, Italy

Jessica Cattabiani
Campus of Rimini, Italy

ABSTRACT

The relationship between cultural heritage and tourism has stimulated the theoretical debate for many years. While it is evident that cultural attractions have the potential to be critical assets for tourism policymakers and destinations, tourist behaviors are often seen as potential harm to both the preservation of cultural heritage and the development of a profound cultural experience. Nevertheless, a growing number of experiences show that a sound management of cultural tourism can generate substantial social, economic, and even environmental benefits. This chapter aims to investigate the trajectories and strategies tourism destinations can adopt to leverage their (material and immaterial) cultural assets, improve their brand, and eventually, enhance their competitive position in the tourism markets, with particular reference to the case of Parma Italian Capital of Culture 2020.

Culture as a Critical Enabler for Tourism Destination Development

INTRODUCTION

Culture is increasingly becoming a constant demand in the hypercompetitive world of tourism as a growing number of tourists choose to travel driven by cultural reasons, in a quest for a place's cultural expressions in their broadest sense, from history and heritage to arts, festivals, music, or even gastronomy. Therefore, an increasing number of tourists are not just willing to visit a territory, but also to participate in its heritage and anything a destination may offer in terms of culture. These trends are highlighted by most recent reports issued by UNWTO and UNESCO, which show how rapidly the impact of culture for sustainability issue on global markets has increased.

The aim of this chapter is to understand how a tourism destination can leverage its (material and immaterial) sustainable cultural assets improve its brand and, eventually, to enhance its competitive position on the international hypercompetitive tourism markets. This contribution particularly focuses on the concept of sustainable culture and its different constitutive elements like history, heritage, arts, and music, without overlooking other important elements like industrial heritage and food and wine. Strongly connected to cultural tourism will be analyzed in this research also creative tourism.

Finally, the role of the Destination Management Organization in the planning and development of the destination will also be investigated, considering both sustainable goals and the Covid-19 pandemic impact. No study has applied the themes of culture and sustainability at the tourist destination level. In this direction, this is the first empirical contribution aimed at investigating the trajectories and strategies tourism destinations can adopt to leverage their (material and immaterial) sustainable cultural assets, improve their brand and, eventually, enhance their competitive position in the actual hypercompetitive tourism markets.

We explore this interesting and original issue by focusing on the Parma Italian Capital of Culture case study. The case study analyzes the tourism-related consequences from the designation of Parma as 2020 Italian Capital of Culture. The Candidacy Project - interpreted from the outset as a real sustainable territorial program - has allowed us to grasp how innovative and sustainable cultural policies are the foundations for transformative development, not only economic, but above all society in a city context.

THEORETICAL FRAMEWORK: CULTURAL TOURISM, SUSTAINABILITY, AND HYPERCOMPETITION

Tourism and culture are the two cornerstones of the concept of cultural tourism. At the same time, cultural aspects play a pivotal role in the overall 2030 Agenda's success, including in areas where connections may only be implicit. In practice, as evidence collected over the years has amply demonstrated, cultural aspects, including active participation in cultural life, the development of individual and collective cultural liberties, the safeguarding of tangible and intangible cultural heritage, and the protection and promotion of diverse cultural expressions, are core components of sustainable social development. They can also have positive effects in other areas of sustainable development.

For cultural organizations, the Sustainable Development Goals create both challenges and opportunities. The main aim is to ensure culture's effective contribution to the global policy agenda. The most critical opportunities lie in demonstrating culture's importance to society and supporting advocacy. The role of culture in building a more sustainable world is now widely recognized and reflected in the international agenda. The case and discussion presented in this chapter describe the role of culture as a sector of activity and its transversal contribution across different SDGs and policy areas.

This research refers to the term culture as to the prerogative of the broadest attractiveness of a tourism destination according to a sustainable perspective. This kind of definition made its first appearance in relation of cultural productions, more specifically both in terms of process of culture and products resulting from that process (Richards, 1996).

Therefore, within the context of this chapter, notwithstanding both definitions are strictly interrelated, the term culture should not be misunderstood with "the derivatives of experience, more or less organized, learned or created by the individuals of a population, including those images and their interpretations (meanings) transmitted from past generations, from contemporaries, or formed by individuals themselves" (Avruch, 1998).

Furthermore, sustainable development, or "development that meets the needs of the present without compromising the ability of future generations to meet their own needs" (World Commission on Environment, 1987, p. 43), is a crucial issue to be deeply studied. Consequently, most organizations increasingly started demonstrating their contributions to social, economic, and environmentally sustainable development goals. Although initially considered a component of social sustainability, culture is now of equal importance to economic, environmental, and social concerns in enabling sustainable development (Hawkes, 2001).

Consequently, sustainable tourism can be considered a kind of tourism with more benefits than negative impacts, especially relating to the environment, the economy, and communities. Sustainable and responsible tourism should make destinations better for people to live in and visit. These aspects are very relevant in the actual strategic dimension, where the times have changed and have ushered in a new era of competition known as *hypercompetition*, which can be defined as organizations' use of tactics to disrupt the competitive advantage held by industry leaders.

The interrelation between those two definitions can be found in the broader definition of cultural tourism proposed by ATLAS Cultural Tourism Research Project which refers to the latter as to "the movement of persons to cultural attractions away from their normal place of residence, with the intention to gather new information and experiences to satisfy their cultural needs" (Richards, 1996, p. 24). Therefore, it is reasonable to refer to cultural tourism as a definable niche within the broad range of tourism activities, but encompasses all experiences absorbed by the visitor to a place that is beyond their own living environment" (ICOMOS, 1999, p. 22).

The Coherently with the ATLAS' definition, the World Tourism Organization (UNWTO, 2019) defines cultural tourism as "a type of tourism activity in which the visitor's essential motivation is to learn, discover, experience, and consume the tangible and intangible cultural attractions/products in a tourism destination". Continuing in the search to propose a more complete and articulated definition of cultural tourism, several typologies of cultural tourism have been identified:

- heritage tourism (tourism products and activities concerning the fostering of natural and cultural heritage)
- cultural thematic routes (tourism products and activities classified according to different cultural themes such as spiritual, industrial, artistic, gastronomic, etc.)
- cultural city tourism (products and activities are developed and promoted in Capitals of Culture)
- traditions and ethnic tourism (products and activities concern the involvement in tourism of local culture and ethnic traditions)

- event and festival tourism (products and activities are elaborated according to the organization of cultural festivals and events)
- religious tourism and pilgrimage routes (tourism products and activities are organized basing on the visit of religious sites and the experience of pilgrimage routes)
- creative culture and creative tourism (tourism products and activities concern the experience of traditional cultural and artistic activities as well as of cultural industries such as cinema and multimedia)

In addition, it is noteworthy mentioning the development of tourism products and activities in the field of rural tourism (according to local traditions and lifestyle) and in the creation of products and activities related to gastronomy tourism (wine and food) (Csapó, 2012). As stated by Richards (2013, p. 297), "culture and tourism were two of the major growth industries of the 20th century, and towards the end of the century the combination of these two sectors into cultural tourism had become one of the most desirable development options for countries and regions around the world".

In this framework, creative tourism represents a supplementary element to cultural tourism. Indeed, creative tourism refers to the "creation of experiences, and the active involvement of the consumer in the production of those experiences" (Richards, 2001, p.2) and it is defined as the "tourism which offers visitors the opportunity to develop their creative potential through active participation in courses and learning experiences which are characteristic of the holiday destination where they are undertaken" (Richards & Raymond, 2000, p.19). Creative tourism can be conceived as an innovative approach to cultural tourism in which tourists shift from a passive consumption of experiences to an active involvement in the development of their own experiences.

While the concept of creative tourism is not new (e.g., Richards, 2001), it paves the way to new trends and innovations where creativity becomes the core element of the cultural experience: it adds value to the experience, broadens the concept of culture, allows greater sustainability (Richards, 2009). Overall, creative tourism is based on the correlation between creativity and experience where creativity triggers the experience and experience is triggered by creativity. In the tourism domain, creativity can be leveraged in two different ways: as a background for tourism or as a tourist activity.

According to UNESCO, creative tourism stimulates the development of a new generation of tourism which involves higher interactions between the various actors who interact within the tourism destination; in particular, tourists communicate with the destination in an informative, social and inclusive way by involving in the interaction local people and their culture (UNESCO, 2006).

If cultural tourism is mostly concerned with the simultaneous promotion and protection of cultural heritage, creative tourism concerns the development of a tourist experience based on the involvement of people in creative activities (Bastenegar & Hassani, 2019). Moreover, from a cultural tourism perspective, creative tourism leads some benefits in terms of culture, namely (Bastenegar & Hassani, 2019):

- the creation of satisfying and authentic experiences
- an active participation between tourists and local people to create networks
- learning and development of creative capacities and skills
- the development of self-esteem and self-awareness
- the development of new products and processes which reflects the values of a culture
- the development of new creative spaces

As a matter of fact, creative tourism is widely recognized as a growing sector since it impacts economy, society, culture, and environment (Pimenta et al., 2021) and supports the destinations willing to attract investors and tourists (Stipanović & Rudan, 2015). The improvement of creative tourism can only be achieved through the active engagement of local people and the involvement of stakeholders who, through various initiatives, promote the destination and stimulate its economy (Stipanović & Rudan, 2015).

Alternatively, Lindroth et al. (2007) argue that creative tourism may foster the propagation of culture from local people to visitors and it may encourage the establishment of relationship between tourists and residents or even endorse tourists' need for self-development. Finally, creativity stimulates destinations to identify tourists' needs, improving satisfaction and destination brand loyalty, as tourism products and experiences reflect emotions and memories of the tourism destination (Kim et al., 2018).

THE MANAGEMENT AND GOVERNANCE OF A CULTURAL TOURISM DESTINATION

According to the UNWTO Tourism Guidelines (2019, p. 14) a tourism destination is "a physical space with or without administrative and/or analytical boundaries in which a visitor can spend an overnight. It is the cluster (co-location) of products and services, and of activities and experiences along the tourism value chain and a basic unit of analysis of tourism. A destination incorporates various stakeholders and can network to form larger destinations. It is also intangible with its image and identity which may influence its market competitiveness", while, from the tourists' point of view, a tourism destination is a place "outside of their normal place of residence" (Bornhorst et al., 2009: 2). A tourism destination bases its role and its success on the enhancement of social and economic well-being of local people who live in the destination, and on its capability to provide tourists with a wide range of activities and experiences (Bornhorst et al., 2009).

Usually, the complex interdependences between the subjects operating in the destination are coordinated by an ad-hoc organization: the Destination Management Organization (DMO). Specifically, a DMO is "the leading organizational entity which may encompass the various authorities, stakeholders and professionals and facilitates partnerships towards a collective destination vision" (UNWTO, 2019: 12). Regarding the several functions that a DMO should perform, the UNWTO Guidelines for Institutional Strengthening of DMOs (UNWTO, 2019) summarized he most relevant: strategic planning, implementation of tourism policy, monitoring, crisis management, promotion, marketing and branding, coordination, competitiveness, sustainability, innovation, governance, tourism culture and brand identity.

The overall efficiency of a DMO depends on its capability to combine three critical tasks (UNWTO, 2019): a) strategic leadership; b) correct execution, and c) efficient governance. The first task concerns the strategic leadership, it "means harnessing of stakeholders' efforts and energy towards a collective vision, mapping a strategy for achieving the vision, communicating and advocating the advantages and principles of effective tourism management, promoting public-private partnerships, etc." (UNWTO, 2019, p. 17). Leadership is aimed at achieving a sound management of the destination through the establishment common values and vision, and it also embraces coordination, responsibility, short and long-term policies.

The second task regards the effective execution of destination management functions. The execution clarifies the DMO's roles in relation to other tourism organizations. A correct execution requires an appropriate organizational structure and a coherent budget (UNWTO, 2019, p. 18). Through a strategic plan it is possible to define the roadmap with programs regarding financial and human resources, potential stakeholders, key performance indicators and other measurements which allow the destination to behave towards its goals. The strategic plan is one of the fundamental tools for the development of the destination brand and awareness; while in the past the strategic plan was usually formulated on five-year period, now the tendency is to decrease the term to two or three years while considering a longer-term plan that can even involve a period of 10 years.

The last key task of a successful DMO is the presence of an efficient governance system, which means "providing awareness and guidance for the industry on quality and excellence, promoting sustainable and responsible tourism and efficient and transparent corporate governance (e.g., financial, administrative and HR practices, speedy/flexible execution, performance monitoring, evaluation, management and others)" (UNWTO, 2019, p. 20). "Destination governance relates to the development and implementation of a cohesive tourism destination policy, an appropriate institutional framework to ensure the effective implementation of this policy and a consistent operational system" (UNWTO, 2019: 20).

It is necessary for the destination to adopt a comprehensive approach ranging from strategic policies to consistent governance, where governance is composed of two main dimensions:

1. Directive capacity of government, in terms of coordination and collaboration with stakeholders
2. Directive effectiveness, in terms of skills and resources available

Hence, a DMO may achieve its aims by creating a brand, in this case a destination brand, that embodies the values and culture of the destination in question while also attracting tourists' attention. Keller (1993) proposed a "Customer-Based Brand Equity Model" which considers the brand not as a monolithic dimension but as a sum of various components (the identities of a brand). The first point is to create the brand equity which can be defined, according to Keller (1993, p.8), as "the differential effect of brand knowledge on consumer response to the marketing of the brand", "a brand is said to have positive […] brand equity if consumers react more favorably to the product, price, promotion, or distribution of the brand […]". Customers are more interested in the brand identity, thus both brand equity and brand identity produce multiple benefits, mostly in terms of revenues and production, cost limitation and protection from other competitors (Keller, 1993; Ritchie & Ritchie, 1998).

Actually, brand knowledge (or brand equity) is dependent on brand awareness and brand image, which are related to the brand's strength in the minds of customers (Keller, 1993). Reference is made to brand awareness as "the strength of the brand node or trace in memory, as reflected by consumers' ability to identify the brand under different conditions" (Keller, 1993, p. 3). In turn, brand awareness is divided into brand recognition and brand recall where recognition means how easy it is recognized the brand and brand recall refers to the ability of the consumer to recall the brand from the mind (Keller, 1993).

The second necessary condition that together with brand awareness create a brand is brand image (Keller, 1993). Brand image is defined "as perceptions about a brand as reflected by the brand associations held in consumer memory" (Keller, 1993: 3) or as "the set of feelings, ideas and attitudes that consumers have about a brand" (Pereira et al., 2012, p. 82). To brand image, it specifically comprises two further different dimensions: the cognitive and the affective dimensions. The first one refers to beliefs and knowledge about physical features while the second one is about the feelings towards the features and its environment (Baloglu & McCleary, 1999; Pereira et al., 2012).

Besides, "brand image is made up of three types of interconnected associations that consumers hold perceptions on: product attributes, benefits, and attitudes. Attributes are the descriptive characteristics that a consumer believes the product has. Attributes include physical characteristics of a product, price [...]. 'Benefits are the personal value consumers attach to the product attributes' [...], attitudes are how the consumers evaluate a brand (favorably or unfavorably) and often are the basis for consumer behavior. Attitudes are a function of the first two associations: attributes and benefits" (Keller 1993; Schaar, 2013, p. 3).

Nonetheless, the brand image of a brand depends on the processes of interpretation that consumers have about the brand concerned (Pereira et al., 2012. Besides Keller (1993), another "Customer-Based Brand Equity Model" was proposed by Aaker (1991). Aaker (1991), different to Keller, defines brand equity as the "set of brand assets and liabilities linked to a brand, its name and symbol, that add to or subtract from the value provided by a product or service to a firm and/or to that firm's customers" (Aaker, 1991, p. 27). In addition, he divides those assets and liabilities into five categories (Fig. 8) on which brand equity is built: brand loyalty, name recognition, perceived quality, brand connections in addition to perceived quality, and additional proprietary brand assets (patents, trademarks, etc.) (Aaker, 1991; Ritchie & Ritchie, 1998).

Focusing on brand and tourism, we suggest that a tourism destination is not only the "place towards which people travel and where they choose to stay for a while [...]" (Leiper, 1995, p. 87; Pereira et al., 2012, p. 81), it is also a cognitive and subjective concept that is interpreted according to the type of tourist and on the basis of its travel experience, background and features (Pereira et al., 2012). To resume, a destination brand should undertake different roles in the pre-experience phase which regards the identification, the differentiation, the anticipation, the expectation, and the reassurance of the destination and its experience while in the post-experience phase, a destination brand plays the role of consolidation and reinforcement of the memories in the destination.

As Ritchie and Ritchie (1998) say a destination brand is only the initial step of a larger process of destination management, which involves not only theories and concepts about branding applied to a destination, but rather the application of theoretical models as regards to the phase of branding and marketing of a destination brand.

Starting with the model presented by Cai (2002), it is possible to observe that destination branding is considered a process that turns around the vertical axis composed of brand element, brand identity and brand image building. This process starts with the identification and selection of the already existing destination brand elements in view of building "brand associations that reflect the attributes, affective, and attitudes components" of a destination image (Cai, 2002, p. 725). Basing on this model, the designing of the destination brand image is built according to the tourists' perceptions and to what the DMO desires to create depending on the three components that characterize the brand image association (Cai, 2002).

In doing so, the gap between what is perceived by tourists and what is projected by the DMO may be evaluated. The evaluation allows to create the desired image which is coherent with brand identity and the application of marketing programs, marketing communications and managing secondary associations (Cai, 2002). Are considered marketing programs the improvement of tourist experience, the development of attractions, the selection of channel of distribution and so on; while marketing communications concern the selection of the optimal media communication which support the marketing program in the fostering of brand identity; and finally, managing secondary associations derive completely from the relationship that the place has with the tourist and not from the marketing strategy applied by the DMO (Cai, 2002).

A further model has been developed by Ekinci (2003), who states that an effective destination able to attract tourists depends on a real destination positioning strategy, and what is necessary to do is the creation and management of a unique destination image. The image can be considered an evaluation of the destination and it can vary from one person to another (Ekinci, 2003). Moreover, Ekinci (2003) argues that this destination branding process starts when it is included the emotional attachment in the evaluation of the destination image, and according to this author "destination branding represents the emotional component of the destination image. [...] Only branded destinations would establish an instant emotional link with their customers" (Ekinci, 2003, p. 22).

The second step of this process regards exactly to destination branding which involves more precisely the establishment of relationships between the destination and tourists. Furthermore, this branding process is aimed at establishing a connection with destination image and tourist self-image; in fact, one of the key points of destination branding is the presence of brand personality, since it emphasizes the human part of the destination image (Ekinci, 2003). Basically, the destination image is described by using brand personality traits. What Ekinci (2003) wants to highlight is that clearer is the identity of the destination in tourist's mind, easier is the destination to be branded.

In addition, the relationship between destination image and tourist self-image implicates the inclusion of tourist basic and emotive needs, which incorporate his lifestyle and value system (Pereira et al., 2012). So, the DMO, in order to create an effective destination positioning strategy and destination image, needs to reflect not only on the emotional link and personal human traits connected with the destination but also on the designing of those destination experiences or products which emphasizes the brand values highlighted in Ekinci's model (Pereira et al., 2012).

THE CASE OF PARMA ITALIAN CAPITAL OF CULTURE 2020

The close relationships existing between tourism and the promotion of cultural heritage are effectively shown in the case of the candidacy of the city of Parma as the Italian Capital of Culture 2020. Indeed, the designation of the city of Parma as the Italian Capital of Culture for the year 2020 results from a careful and cohesive planning process aimed at integrating the different cultural assets available to achieve long-term cultural development and attract national and international visitors. This process has eventually become an occasion to build up local pride and establish stronger ties between the local actors involved in culture and tourism.

This case represents a flagship of how culture and tourism, when properly coordinated, may boost the attractiveness of a tourism destination while preserving its material and immaterial cultural heritage. It is a situation in which social and economic sustainability become aligned and reinforce each other. The facts and data presented in the following have been gathered through a desk survey on documents and official reports issued by the Municipality and the organizing committee and through interviews with the most relevant local policy makers and destination managers.

We had a privileged point of view in data collection since one of the authors has worked there for about six months. Interviews were conducted during this period for a total of over 300 minutes. One of the authors also did an internship in the structure, thus observing all the various mechanisms directly.

Parma 2020: Destination Branding, Governance, and Strategies

With more than 190,000 residents, Parma is the second largest city of Emilia-Romagna region. Founded by Etruscans, it flourished under the Romans and became an important road hub on the Via Aemilia and Via Claudia. Its rich history is expressed by the tangible cultural heritage still existing. Furthermore, Parma has been home to important poets, musicians, film makers. Finally, Parma is one of the most important hus of the so-called Food Valley, the work-known district of food and gastronomy. Indeed, Emilia-Romagna has the greatest number in Italy and in Europe of agri-food products classified under the categories of PDO and PGI.

In 2015, Parma has been designated as UNESCO Creative City of Gastronomy: "Parma and its territory are universally known for their incomparable gastronomic heritage that offers products to the whole world, such as Parmigiano Reggiano (Parmesan cheese) and Prosciutto di Parma (Parma ham). Parma's agri-food sector is represented throughout the food production chain, from the cultivation of raw materials to the promotion of cuisine through events, gastronomy schools, and food museums".

This designation is the result of a unique mix of tradition, talent, and innovation (Malcevschi, 2016) and of a "unique combination of anthropological expressions that constitute the identity, the history and the know-how of the community, a culture linked to a material and immaterial heritage" (Parma Municipality, p. 2). After the designation as UNESCO Creative City of Gastronomy, Parma run for the title of Italian Capital of Culture, in the belief that "culture is well-being for the community and furthermore a vehicle for the economic and social development, culture is a place of freedom and democracy, space and time of inclusion and individual and community growth" (2020 Parma Committee, 2018, p. 4).

The "Italian Capital of Culture" is an initiative aimed at supporting, encouraging, and enhancing the autonomous planning and implementation capabilities of Italian cities in the field of culture. It aims at leveraging the value of culture for social cohesion, the conflict-free integration, identity preservation, creativity, innovation, growth and economic development and individual and collective well-being.

The specific outcomes pursued by Parma included the following:

- Stimulate a culture of integrated design and strategic planning
- Urge cities and territories to consider cultural development as the paradigm for their economic progress and social cohesion
- Enhance the cultural and natural heritage
- Improve services for tourists
- Develop cultural and creative industries
- Promote processes of urban regeneration and development

The 2020 Parma Committee was soon established to draft the candidacy dossier and to engage the local stakeholders. The founders of the Committee were the Municipality of Parma, the Association "Parma, io ci sto!", and Unione Parmense degli Industriali (local Manufacturers' Association). The Committee had to plan and implement all the activities related to Parma as Italian Capital of Culture and the achievement of goals.

A new brand able to reflect the values and vision of Parma - "Parma 2020 - La cultura batte il tempo" - was created to reflect the characteristics of "a city which is alive, breathes and develops along different time frames. The brand "Parma 2020 - La cultura batte il tempo" refers to culture as a decisive factor in the connection among diverse temporal and social dimensions, as a place of "timing inclusion" which means working to hold together memories, working on places and inside places, working on social groups and with social groups; but it also means preparing expositions, museums and laboratories, theatre performances, cinema, libraries, meeting places and so forth to express culture on a broad spectrum" (2020 Parma Committee, 2018).

The Parma 2020 Project

The candidature dossier defined the goals that "Parma 2020" intended to achieve. The city was divided into seven Districts, which correspond to the different areas of the city. In addition, the project of "Parma 2020" also involved a Pilot Project and the organization of Officine Contemporanee. Districts have been defined in order to emphasize the genius faber of the city and to optimize the forms of coexistence and cultural sharing whereas Officine has taken its name from officina parmigiana, which Pasolini described with regard to the culture of the territory of Parma constituted of heritage, culture, and creativity (2020 Parma Committee, 2018).

The districts corresponded to significant areas of the city, and they represented the means through which social conflicts are reduced and competitiveness increased, they are the Parma's personalities and "express points of excellence of the local cultural proposition" (2020 Parma Committee, 2018, p. 23):

- I Chiostri del Correggio – District of culture of agri-food excellence: this District is the heart of Parma 2020, it is the place of the venue aimed at developing Parma tourist policies which regard to the promotion of tourist offer and tourist welcoming; it will be host the Destination Management Organization (DMO) of Parma, the unified ticket office for all museums and the thematic laboratories for agri-food excellences, culture, and innovation
- Aemilia 187 B.C. – University socio-cultural District: it is the student hub, the meeting place for Erasmus students and the venue for those associations that the University of Parma wants to valorize
- Ospedale Vecchio – Social, Civil and Popular Memory District: with the project "The Future of Memory" this District promotes the dialogue between history, identity and innovation
- Workout Pasubio – Creative enterprise and urban regeneration District: this District is a testing place, after a process of renovation, this area will become a space for all people who want to be creative; it will host a coworking and fablab space, and a workshop space open to everyone who want to confront about policies and regeneration practices
- Il Parco della Musica – District of music production and congress activities: this area situated within the park ex-Eridania will host spaces for production, listening and music learning additionally to all activities connected to the events organized in collaboration with Auditorium Niccolò Paganini
- La Cittadella dei Ragazzi – District of educational culture: the area of Cittadella is a tangible heritage of military architecture, today is an urban park attended by all residents; the ex-hostel located inside the park will be renovated to become a recreative and cultural space for intergenerational and inclusive purposes
- La Cittadella del Cinema – District of Cinema: this District is becoming a pole for Advance Education, experiment, and production in film and audiovisual

Districts were considered the point of reference for worksites and productions always related to the project of "Parma 2020". I Chiostri del Correggio – District of culture of agri-food excellence- was conceived as the pulsing heart of "Parma 2020", the place where to summon and welcome tourists, the venue for the Destination Management Organization (DMO) of Parma, the unified ticket office for all museums and the thematic laboratories for agri-food excellences, culture, and innovation.

In parallel, the Pilot Project was organized into several actions: exhibitions, a special event and four Open Calls. One of the exhibitions programmed for the Pilot Project was "The Future of Memory" which has the aim of regenerating the Oltretorrente area through the creation of a multimedia itinerary based on the interconnections between past, present, and future.

The Pilot Project was also composed of four Open Calls, these Calls aimed to consolidate the relationship between public and private systems, with particular attention on the development of cultural and creative enterprises and on the inclusion of all the socio-economic sectors of Districts. The first Call, "Cultura per tutti, cultura di tutti", had the goal to expand culture to young people, families, elders, and people with disabilities through the development of customized cultural products and experiences. The second Call, "Industrie Creativity-Driven", aimed at bringing culture and creativity in enterprises as an opportunity to innovate the brand, products and services offered, but also to improve the worktime and workspaces.

"Temporary Signs – Bando per artisti under 35" was the third project promoted as Open Call and it was open to all young artists under 35 who wanted to propose a particular project with the goal to requalify the urban area. The last Open Call, "Creating Sustainability, con il coinvolgimento delle Città Creative UNESCO" was dedicated to the network of the UNESCO "Creative Cities". This Call wanted to identifiy and award the strategies that have been able to valorize tangible and intangible cultural heritage in terms of inclusion, innovation, and sustainability.

The final element that characterized "Parma 2020 – La cultura batte il tempo" was the Officine Contemporanee, which has been aimed at expressing the value of culture through different strategies and media. Considering that in the period 2012-2016 Parma experienced a +25% in number of tourist arrivals, reaching 700,000 tourists (2020 Parma Committee, 2018), the municipality set the goal of achieving, thanks the interventions and the actions to be activated in 2020, 1,000,000 tourist arrivals in 2022. Parma has actually invested on the combination of culture and tourism, supported by sustainability, innovation and accessibility.

Immediately after its designation as the Italian Capital of Culture for 2020, Parma acted to establish of a Destination Management Organization (DMO). The DMO had to be responsible for the development and management of tourism-related activities in the territory of Parma. Another goal of the DMO was to integrate the plan of "Parma 2020" with the tools that are already used for tourism promotion, with a further improvement in digital and social media marketing strategies. The DMO had also to manage the city's new official tourist and cultural online platform, which included a calendar of events, the tourist cards, and an online and offline database.

The online platform was intended to facilitate the tourists' access to information, services and bookings. On different social media, a competent staff had to properly promote the Parmesan territory; in parallel, another team had to develop of a multimedia tourist guide named "App Percorsi Parma" inspired by principles of accessibility and multiculturalism. In addition to the app, an integrated system of itineraries had to be planned to orientate properly manage the flow of tourists in the city: the different itineraries, which covered different themes (historical, cultural, spiritual) have finally been published online to implement the level and the quality of the service.

An important section of the dossier of candidature dealt with the definition of measures for assessing the results and the outcomes achieved by the "Parma 2020" project. The assessment system was based on four dimensions, with specific measures for each of them:

1. Social impact (Number of applications to open calls; Number of associations involved; Number of enterprises involved; Number of young people involved)
2. Economic impact (Arrivals of Italian tourists; Arrivals of foreign tourists; Average stay in the city; Involvement of enterprises in the cultural and creative production system)
3. Participation in events (Number of participants in specific initiatives; Number of visits in museums, theatres, and cultural events; Results from customer satisfaction analysis)
4. Visibility, image and reputation (Reputation from social networks and campaigns; Number of users of online platforms and itinerary system; Number of international press releases and press coverage)

As described in Cai's model (2002), the process starts with the identification and selection of the existing brand elements which compose the brand image. By applying this to the case of Parma, it can be said that the already existing brand elements may be identified in the distinction of the city into seven Districts since, even though Districts were not specified before the candidacy, cultural attractions and heritage were already present in the territory. Basing on this and on the already existing perceptions of tourists, the 2020 Parma Committee has worked on the creation of the destination brand image.

Another model that may be applied to the case of "Parma 2020" is the model analyzed by Cai and Hsu (2009). This framework considers extremely important starting from the decision-making process of the tourist which consists of brand knowledge, brand trust and brand loyalty. On the basis of this process of decision-making, it is possible to develop a model of branding for the destination. The model (Cai & Hsu, 2009) starts from the point of brand knowledge composed of awareness and image; then, with the next step is built brand trust in the minds of tourists, what tourists may expect from the destination; and with the last phase it is developed all the possible behavioral intentions, which corresponds to the construction of brand loyalty.

The other model that may be applied to this case study is the one developed by Tasci and Gartner (2009). This model is distinctive from the others since it starts the process of destination branding by doing a qualitative and quantitative research and it is divided in two-side perspectives, the supply side and the demand side; the research is asked to all individuals who fall into these two categories. Only after the research, done through questionnaires and interviews, it is possible to know which are the elements that characterize the destination image and identity according to the persons questioned.

With a confrontation on both the supply-side, who gives a projected image and identity of the destination, and the demand-side, who gives a different perception of the image and identity of the destination, it is achievable a fit between the two parts. This fit regards the definition of the name of the destination brand, its logo, the slogan, and so on and so forth. The creation of the destination brand as consequence leads to the definition and creation of the elements that compose the destination brand equity, thus awareness, image, quality, value, loyalty, associations and so on.

The Results of Parma 2020 and the Impact of COVID-19

The designation as Italian Capital of Culture should have been only for the year 2020. Unfortunately, due to the COVID-19 pandemic situation, the Ministry of Cultural Heritage decided to extend the Parma designation as Italian Capital of Culture also to the year 2021.

Hence, the 2020 Parma Committee organized an online meeting "Parma 2020+21: la forza di un'idea" (the strength of an idea) to expose the new actions planned designed to extend the project "Parma 2020 – La cultura batte il tempo" (culture beats time). The meeting wanted not only to remark the strengths of the original project and the evolution of the program, but also to set new objectives, actions, and measures to deal with the situation caused by the pandemic.

Moreover, the meeting stated that the project of "Parma 2020" is based on four intangible and transversal assets which take as reference the high relevance of the relationship between the public and private sectors. This relationship allows to finance the 59% of the entire program and project, where 32% is financed by the private system, 44% by public institutions and 24% by bank foundations. Hence, the project uses a public-private territorial model.

The plan for year 2021 has implied a digitalization of the programme by organizing the events also on online platforms. The planning of events introduced also two further appointments connected to the new asset "culture as a cure" dealing with the topics of culture and health and the tax exemption of the costs of culture. These two appointments reached 12,100 interactions.

Globally, considering that the program of "Parma 2020" started in 2019, a total of 664 events have been realized in 20 months, and most of them were organized online. With reference to the asset "culture and enterprise", the Open Call "Imprese Creativity-Driven" reached in numbers over 500 enterprises with 15 participants to the call; a total of 150 were the meetings organized, 20 were conventions and talks arranged both offline and online and 16 were the speakers and testimonials involved; finally, a total of 50 were the candidate projects and 80 were the creators who participated in this Open Call. "Culture and sustainability" through the application of UNESCO Thematic Indicators for Culture in 2030 Agenda easily achieved its goals.

The initiative called "#miimpegnoaparma" aimed to involve citizens with the purpose of promoting an active participation in city life and enhancing of cultural experiences: 945 volunteers collaborated in more than 200 events. Because of COVID-19, the digital strategy of "Parma 2020+21" has been reinforced: Parma has launched an online cultural platform where it was possible to visit all exhibitions, expositions, and museums directly from a computer or smartphone; these online immersive visits were accompanied by exceptional tourist guides such as Vittorio Sgarbi, Arturo Carlo Quintavalle and Barnaba Fornasetti. For the occasion, two short movies inspired by Bernardo Bertolucci, "Parma, una storia d'amore – Atto I" and "Parma, una storia d'amore – Atto II" were produced to narrate the city and its territory through the eyes of a boy and a girl.

Furthermore, through a transmedia strategy, the Committee of "Parma 2020+21" has been able to implement effective social media campaigns, which allowed to diversify the message on different social networks on the basis of the target audience, thus reaching the widest possible target.

A dedicated page has been published on SkyArte, with docufilms and broadcasting services, a page related to the project "Parma 2020+21" on Google Art & Culture, and some filters, GIFs, and Instagram Reels have been made available on Instagram; alternatively, on Spotify, it has been created a playlist with the music created by the great masters of this territory, Verdi and Toscanini. On magazines, "Parma 2020+21" narrated and described its territory and heritage; collections of tailor-made editorial contents were published by Corriere della Sera, DoveViaggi and Gazzetta di Parma. Overall, "Parma 2020+21" was reported on 1,373 newschapters and on 4,000 online newschapters, it was mentioned on 269 weekly magazines and 346 magazines; 437 were the TV, and 88 were the radio services.

Furthermore, the Committee "Parma 2020" decided to present an initiative called "La seconda notte è nostra!" (the second night is ours) aimed at attracting higher number of tourists in form at least two nights, with the second night subsided by the Municipality of Parma. Finally, some new cultural events events have been organized during the summer period: "I Like Parma 2021" organized in the month of May, "Parma 360 Festival della creatività contemporanea" from May to August, "Parma Estate 2021" with numerous cultural events, and the "Settembre Gastronomico".

CONCLUSION

The importance given by the designation as Italian Capital of Culture highlights the relevance of sustainable culture in the improvement and development of the tourism destination; in fact, in this research, it has been reported, about this matter, the case study of the city of Parma nominated Italian Capital of Culture for the years 2020 and 2021. Furthermore, to the case have been applied several models to identify which kind of process the city of Parma has applied for the development of the city, its destination brand and image on the occasion of the designation; to give further relevance to the work projected and developed by the city a comparative analysis has been done.

However, being designated as Capital of Culture is an important recognition, the city nominated has been chosen to be the showcase and representation of the value of culture, nationally and internationally. Here, culture expresses in its broaden sense what composes the territory, which is its history, its heritage and so on; museums, expositions and installations attract visitors from every corner of the world, whereas complementary elements such as gastronomy, creativity and community give further relevance to the concept of culture.

By embracing a broad and systemic vision, cultural investments were aimed both to increase tourist attractiveness and to form a stable and lasting relational capital, in the awareness that the combination of "Culture and Social" is an essential lever to establish a renewed future for the territories, through integration, inclusion, and promotion of well-being and higher quality of life. What emerges from the variegated cultural offer of Parma are the substantial opportunities of this city in proposing itself as a tourist destination of interest for visitors belonging to different cultures, therefore visitors who give priority, for example, to visiting a museum instead of visiting an exhibition or to participate in an event related to local culinary traditions or vice versa.

Therefore, it is reasonable to consider Parma as a tourist destination, potentially attractive, for example, both for visitors who recognize and appreciate cultural traditions as a distinctive element of civilization (for example, Chinese culture) and for visitors more oriented towards the discovery of innovation in the field of creative tourism. Under a cultural profiling perspective, since Parma is not a particularly well-known destination in the world, if compared, for example, to Rome or Venice, its promotion abroad could have as its main objective those cultures more inclined to explore lesser-known tourist destinations. To better explain how different cultures relate to the popularity of a tourist destination, we can refer to the cultural dimension of Geert Hofstede (1980) named **uncertainty avoidance**.

The Dutch sociologist refers to uncertainty avoidance as to "the extent to which a society feels threatened by uncertain and ambiguous situations and tries to avoid these situations by providing greater career stability, establishing more formal rules, not tolerating deviant ideas and behaviors, and believing in absolute truths and the attainment of expertise". The connection between this definition and the different cultural mental processes of choosing a tourist destination is quite intuitive.

There are cultures in the world more inclined to explore little-known tourist destinations and others that feel more comfortable visiting universally recognized places and cities. For example, Indonesian tourists, who have a fair propensity to deal with unfamiliar situations, may be more inclined to visit Parma than Japanese tourists, who might prefer the "safer" Rome.

The designation is an important opportunity for the city whose programming is extended for the whole year of candidacy; for the occasion, the city should be prepared to receive visitors; a process of urban regeneration based on sustainable assets is always an optimal choice to give a new look to the city, furthermore infrastructures, transport facilities, tourist facilities and so on should be appropriate to host tourists. In the case of "Parma 2020+21 – La cultura batte il tempo", the city has proposed a program which involve culture through its history and heritage, fine arts, music, gastronomy, but the program has also presented events and exhibitions related to the concepts of innovation, sustainability and creativity, giving priority to the relationship between the private and public sector and community.

The city of Parma has taken the opportunity of the candidacy as Italian Capital of Culture for the years 2020 and 2021 to create and develop a new destination image and brand with the aim to increase the number of visitors by facilitating the recognition of the city in the minds of tourists. However, the city's efforts to adjust to changes have been hampered by the COVID-19 pandemic, nevertheless, Parma has tried to adapt to changes. development. Next year, this city must work a lot on the essence of its destination branding defines as "a complex process of identification, organization and coordination of all the variables that have an impact on the destination's image" (Ruiz-Real et al., 2020, p. 3).

Consequently, the role of DMO will be more and more important for the creation and development of the destination branding and the management of the Parma sustainable destination not only at local but especially international level. However, with a view to sustainability, in particular in the Covid and post-Covid periods, the effective role of the DMO in this context requires measuring the contribution of Culture to sustainable development. It is not possible to translate the concept of Culture back to a universally accepted definition, and it is not easy, compared to other areas of evaluation, to find relevant and significant data.

Furthermore, quantitative indicators are not sufficient for Culture. The indicators - in all domains, and particularly in the cultural domain, which has significant qualitative and intangible effects - should be considered as necessary premises, useful for providing support and basis for policy decisions, which always have a more complex character and not only call for multiple shreds of evidence and sources, but also value positions that require mediation between different interests and objectives.

In terms of the implications for governance, we can consider the following aspects to leverage:

- Systematization of the experience from a knowledge-transfer perspective, given the upcoming initiatives of the Italian Capital of Culture. The Parma experience can represent an essential wealth of learning regarding constraints and opportunities for cities that will present their candidacy in the coming years

- Strengthening of the data collection infrastructure to guide policy design. The evaluation experiences increase the attention towards strategic accountability on the client's part. It would be worth investing in building a solid data collection infrastructure to steer the public decision maker's point of view concerning policy design. At the same time, a greater level of accountability would help settle a trusting relationship between the citizen and the Public Administration
- Strengthening the sustainability of the collaborative processes of the local cultural actors. The experience of Parma should emphasize the importance of interventions based on public-private partnerships. Collaboration processes require a substantial investment, not only in financial terms: the most strategic action for the partnership's success is linked to the management of network dynamics. At the same time, to encourage an integrated and collaborative approach, the Public Administration should invest in efficient resource allocation methods, favoring collaboration over competition.

REFERENCES

Aaker, D. A. (1991). *Managing brand equity: Capitalizing on the value of a brand name*. The Free Press.

Atilgan, E., Akinci, S., Aksoy, S., & Kaynak, E. (2009). Customer-based brand equity for global brands: A multinational approach. *Journal of Euromarketing*, *18*(2), 155–132.

Avruch, K. (1998). *Culture & conflict resolution*. US Institute of Peace Press.

Baloglu, S., & McCleary, K. W. (1999). A model of destination image formation. *Annals of Tourism Research*, *26*(4), 868–897.

Bastenegar, M., & Hassani, A. (2019). Spiritual understanding and experience in the creative tourism of gastronomy. *International Journal of Tourism and Spirituality*, *3*(2), 43–67.

Bornhorst, T., Ritchie, J. B., & Sheehan, L. (2010). Determinants of tourism success for DMOs & destinations: An empirical examination of stakeholders' perspectives. *Tourism Management*, *31*(5), 572–589.

Cai, L. A. (2002). Cooperative branding for rural destinations. *Annals of Tourism Research*, *29*(3), 720–742.

Cai, L. A., & Hsu, C. H. C. (2009). Brand knowledge, trust and loyalty - A conceptual model of destination branding. In *Proceedings of the International CHRIE Conference*. University of Massachusetts Amherst.

Crompton, J. L. (1979). An Assessment of the image of Mexico as a vacation destination and the influence of geographical location upon that image. *Journal of Travel Research*, *17*(4), 18–23.

Csapó, J. (2012). The role and importance of cultural tourism in modern tourism industry. In M. Kasimoglu (Ed.), *Strategies for Tourism Industry - Micro and Macro Perspectives* (pp. 201–232). IntechOpen.

Ekinci, Y. (2003). From destination image to destination branding: An emerging area of research. *e-Review of Tourism Research*, *1*(2), 21-24.

Hawkes, J. (2001). *The Fourth pillar of sustainability: Culture's essential role in public planning*. Common Ground Publishing.

Hofstede, G. (1980). Motivation, leadership, and organization: Do American theories apply abroad? *Organizational Dynamics*, 9(1), 42–63.

ICOMOS. (1999). *International cultural tourism charter*. Retrieved on August 4, 2020, from: http://www.whitr-ap.org/themes/69/userfiles/download/2013/2/28/vqev6ibfgtbbewh.pdf

Keller, K. L. (1993). Conceptualizing, measuring, and managing customer-based brand equity. *Journal of Marketing*, 57(1), 1–22.

Kim, H., Stepchenkova, S., & Babalou, V. (2018). Branding destination co-creatively: A case study of tourists' involvement in the naming of a local attraction. *Tourism Management Perspectives*, 28, 189–200.

Leiper, N. (1995). *Tourism management*. RMIT Press.

Lew, A. A., & Wong, A. (2004). Sojourners, guanxi and clan associations. Social capital and overseas Chinese tourism to China. In T. Coles & D. J. Timothy (Eds.), *Tourism, Diasporas and Space, Contemporary Geographies of Leisure, Tourism and Mobility* (pp. 202–214). Taylor and Francis.

Lindroth, K., Ritalahti, J., & Soisalon-Soininen, T. (2007). Creative tourism in destination development. *Tourism Review*, 62(3/4), 53–58.

Malcevschi, A. (2016). The Parma University strategy for managing UNESCO designated sites. *Sustainable Mediterranean*, 72, 40–42.

Parma Committee. (2018). *Dossier di candidatura di Parma a Capitale Italiana della Cultura 2020* [Parma Candidacy Dossier as Italian Capitsl of Culture 2020]. Retrieved on June 2, 2021, from: https://parma2020.it/it/verso-parma2020/

Pereira, R. L. G., Correia, A. L., & Schutz, R. L. A. (2012). Destination branding: A critical overview. *Journal of Quality Assurance in Hospitality & Tourism*, 13(2), 81–102.

Pimenta, C. A. M., Cadima Ribeiro, J., & Remoaldo, P. (2021). The relationship between creative tourism and local development: A bibliometric approach for the period 2009-2019. *Tourism & Management Studies*, 17(1), 5–18.

Richards, G. (1996). *Cultural tourism in Europe*. CAB International.

Richards, G. (2001). The experience industry and the creation of attractions. In G. Richards (Ed.), *Cultural attractions and European tourism* (pp. 55–71). Tilburg University.

Richards, G. (2009). Creative tourism and local development. In R. Wurzburger, A. Pattakos, & S. Pratt (Eds.), *Creative tourism: A global conversation* (pp. 78–90). Sunstone Press.

Richards, G. (2013). Tourism development trajectories. From culture to creativity? In M. Smith & G. Richards (Eds.), *The Routledge handbook of cultural tourism* (pp. 297–303). Routledge.

Richards, G., & Raymond, C. (2000). Creative tourism. *ATLAS News*, 23, 16–20.

Ritchie, B. J. R., & Ritchie, R. J. B. (1998). The branding of tourism destination: Past achievements and future trends in destination marketing – scope and limitations. *Proceedings of the 48th Congress of the Annual Congress of the International Association of Scientific Experts in Tourism*.

Ruiz-Real, J. L., Uribe-Toril, J., & Gázquez-Abad, J. C. (2020). Destination branding: Opportunities and new challenges. *Journal of Destination Marketing & Management, 17*, 100453.

Schaar, R. (2013). Destination branding: A snapshot. *UW-L Journal of Undergraduate Research, 16*, 1–10.

Stipanović, C., & Rudan, E. (2015). Creative tourism in destination brand identity. *International Journal – Vallis Aurea, 1*(1), 75-83. DOI: doi:10.2507/IJVA.1.1.7.7

Tasci, A. D. A., & Gartner, W. C. (2009). A practical framework for destination branding. In L. A. Cai, W. C. Gartner, & A. M. Munar (Eds.), *Tourism branding: Communities in action* (pp. 149–158). Emerald Group Publishing.

UNESCO. (2006). *Towards sustainable strategies for creative tourism.* In Discussion Report of the Planning Meeting for 2008 International Conference on Creative Tourism, Santa Fe, NM.

UNWTO. (2019a). *UNWTO Tourism definitions.* World Tourism Organization.

UNWTO. (2019b). *UNWTO Guidelines for institutional strengthening of destination management organizations (DMOs) - Preparing DMOs for new challenges.* World Tourism Organization.

Although senior tourism is a significant segment for thermal hotels, this segment will not provide satisfying profitability. Hotel managers must diversify targeted markets with other social groups to decrease the potential risks of the one-segment operation. Within this context, disabled people could be an excellent segment to enable diversity in market segmentation. Hence, contrary to general belief, numerous people live in communities with disability status, whether natal or ensuing. Although they have some special needs in a social environment, disabled people need to be integrated into all aspects of social life. Based on this reality, all social facilities and atmospheres should be accessible for disabled people.

Hence, they should also have a right to access touristic attractions and facilities without boundaries. In sum, seniors and disabled people should be considered a target segment for thermal hotel operations. Thermal hotels offer those people a rich and diversified context based on their curative treatments, such as thermal pools, SPA units, physiotherapy, hydrotherapy, and clinical treatments. At this point, thermal hotel management needs to answer this critical question: "Is our hotel accessible for these groups?"

Accessibility refers to "how easy something is to reach ... for somebody with a disability" (Oxford Dictionary, 2021) in terms of disability seen in communities. In the tourism industry, accessibility is evaluated in two primary dimensions: physical accessibility and accessibility to information. Physical accessibility refers to meeting the specific needs of individuals with various limitations or disabilities in accommodation, transportation, travel, communication infrastructure, etc. Accessibility to information, on the other hand, is the total satisfaction of more comprehensive information that individuals with disabilities need within the tourism system.

Both physical accessibility and accessibility to information start before the travel decision, extend during the vacation experience and continues after the experience (Buhalis et al., 2005). With increasing awareness of accessibility, tour operators have begun to offer accessible tourism activities and destinations in the form of package tours, taking into account the demands of disabled or senior individuals (Gandin, 2018). Today, thermal hotels struggle to get a share of this market segment, and accessibility is becoming more critical every day for thermal hotels.

Based on the relevant acknowledged above, this study focuses on searching for accessibility of thermal and SPA units for seniors and disabled people. As a conceptual framework, the terms of accessibility and its importance, accessibility in tourism, senior tourism, and accessibility, accessibility for disabled people in tourism, and accessibility in thermal hotels subjects will be explained based on existing literature. Then a case study is performed in relevance to the research subject. Thermal hotels operated in Afyonkarahisar were chosen for the case study since Afyonkarahisar is one of the most famous thermal tourism destinations in Türkiye. The research process consists of qualitative research methods and starts with observation. In the observation period, researchers visited thermal hotels with an observation form indicating a checklist for accessibility to thermal hotels.

Semi-structured interviews were performed with managers of thermal hotels after completing observations. There are seven five-star thermal hotels in Afyonkarahisar; thus, semi-structured interviews were conducted with the general managers of those hotels. At this stage, on the one hand, it is planning to check the reliability of the observation results; on the other hand, it is planning to gather more detailed data about the accessibility of seniors and disabled people to relevant services. Then, both the results of observation and semi-structured interviews were analyzed. Data decoding, theme determining, the conceptualization of the themes, and data encoding processes were performed for interview forms. Eventually, all gathered findings were discussed; and some theoretical and managerial evaluations were made.

CONCEPTUAL FRAMEWORK

Accessibility in Tourism and Accessible Tourism

In a broad sense, the term accessibility could conceptualize as *having an opportunity to access, use or own something (desire, opportunity, product, service, etc.)*. It is generally accepted that the term accessibility derived from the Late Latin word accessibilitas to French as accessibilité or a native formation of *accessible + ity*. As a native formation, the word accessible dates back to two Latin words accedere and accessus. The Latin phrase accedere refers to "approach, go to, come near, enter upon," while accessus means "a coming near, an approach; an entrance." Then, the word accessus has begun to be used in French and English, and it is the root of the word accessibility.

In daily talks, accessibility could be used to indicate a technological, technical, social, or psychological context (Etmyonline, 2022). The American Psychological Association (APA), by adopting a psychological approach, defines the adjective accessibility as "*....of a building or other site and its facilities and fixtures: easy to approach, enter, or use, particularly by people with disabilities*" (APA, 2022).

The concept of accessibility is a phenomenon with its continuously increasing importance and validity both in tourism and other industries. Further, the relevant matter and truth of the concept continually become essential based on the diversifying tourism services and the observed variety of customer demands. Leiper (1990) states that the tourism system consists of five basic elements that are interdependent. Within this context, a tourism system should involve at least a tourist, an origin, a transportation zone, a touristic destination, and a travel and tourism industry facilitating mobility in the tourism system. In this system, as a sine qua non part of the touristic activities, indispensably, are affected by other people they have communicated with and other environmental factors such as socio-cultural, economic, technologic, physical, political, and political-legal environments (Darcy & Buhalis, 2011).

Hence, the success of the tourism system mainly depends on enabling the tourists' satisfaction by delivering high-quality tourism services. Based on this fact, in tourism, all touristic infrastructure and superstructure elements must rightly be served to tourists with safe, comfortable, and economical means of transport. The destinations that do not meet the demands of the tourists' consisting of infants, elders, and handicapped people who want to experience touristic services, will be isolated from the tourism system in the process of time (UNWTO, 2013). Again, the destinations and the touristic enterprises that are accessible but isolated from the system will not contribute to the travel and tourism system. Thus, in each phase of the travel experience, accessibility should be provided throughout the system meanwhile supporting tourists to access demanded services (Buhalis et al., 2005).

Based on all these facts, accessibility in tourism should be enabled for each part presented in the tourism system. In touristic destinations, accessibility is generally composed of physical accessibility and the accessibility to information. Physical accessibility refers to meeting visitors' special needs and requirements without excepting people with disabilities in the process of tourism experience consisting of accommodation, transportation, food and beverage facilities, sightseeing, communication, and other aspects.

Accessibility to information, on the other hand, completely meets of more comprehensive/detailed needs and requirements of the people with disabilities in the tourism system (Buhalis et al., 2005). Both physical accessibility and accessibility to information facts start before the transportation phase, come into their own during travel experience with a large spectrum, and continue even after the travel experience. Accordingly, both governmental and private tourism establishments should make an effort to provide accessibility to the destination or, in other words, an on-site destination (Buhalis, 2005), and should consider the relevant tourism services given in Table 1.

In tourism services, physical accessibility varies based on individuals' impairments or disabilities, while access to information is equally essential for each individual. Within this context, all destination amenities, attractions, services, and activities should be pre-designed for the needs and requirements of people with disabilities. Additionally, and more importantly, all information barriers decreasing or delimiting travel amenities for people with disability should be actively pre-eliminated. However, it should not be forgotten that accessibility to information is vital for people with disabilities and for everyone who participates or will participate in the tourism experience.

Because having all acknowledged accessibility in a destination will considerably affect potential visitors' holiday decisions and reservations. Thus, designing and applying creative multi-dimensional knowledge strategies throughout the destination is essential. Moreover, those innovative strategies should focus on standard criteria that are important for all and should be developed by considering the crucial knowledge-searching characteristics of market segments.

Table 1. Destination Services Evaluated within the Scope of Accessibility in Tourism. **Source:** *Adapted and summarized from Buhalis et al. (2005)*

Amenities	*Accommodation services*	Hotels Holiday resorts	Apart-hotels Farmhouses	Camping/caravans Cottages/bungalows	Pensions
	Retailing	Shopping centres	Markets	Department stores	Gift shops
	Entertainment	Cinemas and Theatres	Clubs	Pubs	Casinos
	Catering services	Restaurants	Cafes	Fast food enterprises	Terraces and taverns
Attractions	*Heritage*	Monuments	Archaeological sites	Historical buildings	Stately homes
	Events	Festivals Artistic activities	Sportive activities	Religious activities	The conference, congress, etc.
	Artificial structures	Architectural elements Muses	Archaeological elements	Artistic galleries	Spa etc.
	Natural attractions	Beaches Waterfalls	Rivers	Woodland	Landscapes Parks / gardens
	Artificial	- Disneyland, Waxwork museum, etc.			
	Purpose-built	Activity centers	Theme parks	Wild life parks	Observatories
Ancillary services	*Public services*	Health organizations Real-time operating systems	National tourism organizations Local tourism organizations		Security services Embassies
	Private services	Health organizations Communication bureaus	Travel insurance org. Tour(ist) guides Banks		Exchange offices Tour programs Timetables
Touristic activities		(Sportive) fishing Artistic painting	Sailing Cycling Golf	Nature exploration Trekking	Swimming Diving

It is well-known that the success of destination marketing depends on delivering the knowledge of accessibility amenities in the destination to potential tourists (Buhalis, 2005). This is also closely related to the holiday decision process since the primary aim of potential visitors is to get enjoyed from touristic attractiveness.

Hence, a potential visitor searches a variety of travel options and selects one among them that serves the best their travel aims. Meanwhile, deciding among travel options requires comprehensive searches that consist of price-quality comparisons or determination of advantages and disadvantages of the tourism product. Accessibility to information constitutes one of the essential elements in this phase. Moreover, this is much more important for people with disabilities. For instance, the lack of information about available parks for disabled people or the lack of information about the presence of wheelchair-using infrastructure directly affects the decision process of people with disabilities (Israeli, 2002).

Given these realities, accessibility in tourism services should embody the whole tourism chain consisting of destination management, marketing, and promotion activities, urban and architectural environments, transportation services, lodging, food and beverage services, meeting and events management, cultural activities, and others relevant tourism services. Within this context, it should be possible to get tourism services in equal conditions for people with limited participation in tourism services, particularly those with disabilities. In other words, people with disabilities and others with barriers to getting tourism services should receive all physical environments, transportation services, touristic information and communication amenities, and all other public services and amenities in urban, rural, and coastal areas (UNWTO, 2013).

According to World Health Organisation forecasts, approximately one billion people who make up 15% of the world's population are disabled, and the world population is rapidly getting older. The growing proportion of disabled people in communities of the world population's rapid aging trend causes essential changes in individuals' lives, behaviors and environments, and economical products and services. The tourism and travel industry is also inevitably facing those changes (Tomej, 2019). Hence, the World Tourism Organisation estimates that the travel of people with disabilities will increase in the long view.

Accessibility is integral to responsible and sustainable tourism activities within this context. Facilitating travel and tourism experiences of people with disabilities is a human responsibility and a good job opportunity with economic returns. At this point, enhancing accessibility conditions of tourists with accessible tourism becomes more important in terms of both the financial expectations of tourism suppliers and locals and providing new job opportunities in tourism (UNWTO, 2016b). Within this construct, accessible tourism could be characterized by some features listing below (Babu, Dixit, & Yadav, 2010):

- Accessible tourism involves a series of practices aimed to provide facilitators to individuals with barriers in terms of relational ability as a tourist
- Those individuals have some special needs at different phases of staying and traveling. To facilitate their tourism experience, their unique needs should be met
- Accessible tourism encompasses all individuals with some accessibility barriers at differing levels regarding participation in tourism, leisure, and recreation activities. People with disabilities (visual, hearing, mobility, and mental development), people who need special care due to their health problems, older people, and those who need care services temporarily constitute the overall community participating in accessible tourism.

- In accessible tourism, non-accessibility to tourism opportunities is not often the fundamental issue. However, it comes to the forefront to provide opportunities to eliminate restrictions on accessibility by working with common sense.

Although accessible tourism is a widespread phenomenon, especially in recent decades, an internationally accepted definition is still not developed (UNWTO, 2016a). On the other hand, numerous studies have already been conducted in a popular research area. Basically, two main factors making challenging to make a common definition of accessible tourism. First, various terms have been synonymous in different studies subjecting accessible tourism and its growth over time. For example, Inclusive Tourism, Adapted Tourism, Tourism for All, Barrier-Free Tourism, Easy Access Tourism, and Universal Tourism terms have been used to define the content of accessible tourism. Nonetheless, all these terms contain significant differences in extent and scope. On the other hand, in correlating the term accessibility to tourism, researchers have intended to make comprehensive definitions that involve concrete factors. Still, they could not agree on a common definition.

Although today the term accessible tourism has become more precise and more distinct due to its growing period, there is still not an internationally common definition that satisfies everyone (UNWTO, 2016a). Buhalis and Darcy (2011), who states that the majority of accessible tourism definitions focus on the accessibility of functional elements of tourism, reconsider Darcy and Dickson's (2009) accessible tourism definition, and they define it as follows;

Accessible tourism is a form of tourism that involves collaborative processes between stakeholders that enables people with access requirements, including mobility, vision, hearing, and cognitive dimensions of access, to function independently and with equity and dignity through the delivery of universally designed tourism products, services, and environments. This definition adopts a whole of life approach where people through their lifespan benefit from accessible tourism provision. These include people with permanent and temporary disabilities, seniors, obese, families with young children and those working in safer and more socially sustainably designed environments.

Based on this comprehensive definition, we could make a short version of accessible tourism: "Accessible tourism means accessibility of particularly people with disabilities to physical environments, transportation services, communication channels, and other public services delivering in terms of the tourism system in equal conditions as everyone." By the way, definitions of accessible tourism are mainly commentaries on the relationships between the needs of a particular community, such as people with disabilities, and their accessibility to those needs (Babu, Dixit, & Yadav, 2010). Additionally, accessible tourism consists of five primary dimensions knowledge, transportation, everyday essentials, multi-purpose designs, and accessibility. The knowledge dimension refers to the strategies about which information should be gathered, how to retrieve needed information, and how to deliver that information. It also refers to presenting information to make it accessible for everyone.

As a second dimension, transportation refers to the availability of vehicles for everyone in terms of transport and mobility from one point to another at the destination. In accessible tourism, common needs are providing car park areas that facilitate mobility, consideration of all parties in communication, especially with the sign language and Braille, adequate announcements and directions in each phase of the tourism experience, enabling signs for all parties, and founding a well-designed infrastructure that enables people with disabilities could independently float around. Multi-purpose designs as another dimension of accessible tourism design touristic products, environments, event programs, and other services without requiring any adaptation or unique design. Finally, the accessibility dimension serves all information about facilitators in the destination, such as visiting hours of the areas, distances of touristic attractiveness, transportation amenities, guidance services, and so forth. (Wiastuti, Adiati, & Lestari, 2018).

Accessibility of Disabled Tourists

Due to the everchanging features of touristic demand in the tourism industry, tourism suppliers must follow new demographic challenges and transformations in society to develop their tourism products and market segmentations (Nikitina & Vorontsova, 2015). Studying the changes in society provides good insights into determining future tourism demand trends (Alén, Domínguez, & Lasada, 2012). At this point, considering the aging of the population is one of the most critical indicators to develop new tourism products and set out sustainable tourism policies. The World Health Organization (WHO) states that the number and proportion of people aged 60 and over is steadily increasing. WHO also reveals that the number of people aged 60 and over was more than 1 billion in 2019 and will increase to 1.4 billion by 2030, projected to 2.1 billion by 2050 (WHO, 2021).

This transformation originates from aging and has some significant outcomes, such as reducing the workforce worldwide and developing new segments of the tourism industry called senior tourism (Patiar, 2015). Although there are different conceptualizations for this tourism segment, such as mature tourism, third age tourism, geriatric tourism, grey tourism or elderly tourism, these all denotations focus on the traveling of elderly people. This type of tourism is a growing segment because elderly people are healthier than past, travel much more, prefer longer staying at greater distances, and are prone to spend money on vacations (Patiar, 2015). Śniadek (2006) aligns some characteristics of the senior/elderly market as below;

- Due to the rapid aging (Every six seconds someone in the world becomes an elder/senior) of the world population, senior tourism has unusual growth dynamics
- Senior people devote 40% more than younger people to tourism and recreation activities
- Elderly people tend to spend much more on holidays (they spend 74% more on typical holidays)
- Elderly people attend touristic or recreational activities since they want to maintain their good health and physical condition as long as possible
- Today, elderly people, particularly bay bloomers, spend their free time on self-education, fun, and entertainment rather than staying with their family. Thus, they perceive tourism activities as a prize, especially in their retirement period
- They tend to participate in tourism activities during in low or off-season rather than during the high season
- In senior tourism, social reasons should also consider, such as gaining health with fewer expenses

In senior tourism, accessibility is the crucial link of touristic experiences since elderly people are the primary beneficiaries of accessibility (Alén, Domínguez, & Lasada, 2012). The importance of accessibility increases much more, especially when elderly people have difficulties or barriers to receiving touristic activities. Thus, both tourism companies and travel agencies should provide complete and truthful information to elderly people (Lindqvist & Björk, 2000). Meanwhile, it is necessary to fulfill their accessibility requirements to develop the senior tourism market (Wang, 2011). In other words, suppliers need to consider that, in the tourism experience, elderly people demand special conditions or services based on their age and state of health (Patiar, 2015).

Although all elderly people demand special services during their trip in terms of accessibility, these requirements differ due to their health status. Even some elderly people are directly considered in the group of people with disabilities since they have some impairments or disabilities. If an elderly person is aging actively, they expect universal service standards. In contrast, many elderly people living with some health problems or disabilities insistently require additional services to enjoy their vacation fully.

Wang (2011) asserts three major accessibility issues in the senior tourism market following as accessibility to facilities, availability and accessibility of information resources, and affordability of travel activities. In terms of accessibility, elderly people generally demand special meals, including dietary, want to use a shower instead of the bathtub in hotel rooms, prefer healthcare services in the hotel and close by, and require well-designed transportation that meets each movement's needs (UNWTO, 2016a).

Having personal assistance in using new technologies, getting language support in new destinations, making trips with tourist guides aware of elderly people's needs, and contacting local people without any barriers could also be added to elderly people's other accessibility requirements. At this point, destination management and tourism enterprises in the destination should focus on delivering tourism services appropriately to elderly people with full access.

In the tourism industry, enabling accessibility of disabled tourists to complete services and amenities is a central concern within accessible tourism efforts.

Within this point of view, people with disabilities in tourism, namely disabled tourists, are those whose *effective participation in society on an equal basis with others in travel, accommodation, and other tourism services is hindered by the barriers in the environment they are in, as well as by attitudinal barriers* (UNWTO, 2016b). UNWTO (2013) enunciates that accessibility should be presented throughout the tourism chain for disabled tourists and make some valuable suggestions for accommodation/hotel enterprises as below;

- There should be fully accessible hotel rooms for disabled tourists that are located close to the emergency exit and hotel entrance
- In these rooms, including bathrooms and terraces, disabled tourists should be able to move around independently and comfortably and use all devices and equipment without assistance
- All devices and actuators in the rooms should be designed according to Universal Design principles
- There should be alarm systems suitable for deaf people and other guests in guest rooms and throughout the hotel
- Hotel enterprises should accept guide dogs when visually impaired persons accommodate the hotel

Although the UNWTO continually endeavors to create awareness about accessibility tourism and active participation of disabled people in tourism activities with similar conditions, many tourism enterprises tend to ignore this segment due to its market share. Artar and Karabacakoğlu (2003) state that disabled people face many problems with receiving adequate service delivery for their special needs, emphasize do's, and make numerous recommendations to provide high satisfaction for disabled tourists.

Among all precious recommendations, the authors also make suggestions for hotel enterprises presented in table 2. As seen in the table, hotels need to deliver a comprehensive service for disabled tourists, from the parking area to all other using areas with suitable arrangements in line with the unique needs.

Table 2. Accessibility Issues in hotels. Source: Adapted and summarized from Artar & Karabacakoğlu (2003)

Entrance	- A separated and sufficient parking area with appropriate signings - A barrier-free movement area and closeness to the entrance gate - Tactile walking paths and effective color contrast for visually impaired people - Handicap ramps enable easy access to the reception area - Availability of bell-button/help-button with easy access, next to stairs - A second entrance door that designed for disabled tourists without stairs or a revolving system
Reception	- A special check/in desk designed lower than the normal one - Proper lightning that especially enables lip-reading - Availability of a convenient sitting area in the lobby - Anti-allergic mats in the lobby -Telephones with Braille and/or inductive coupler
Common areas	- Corridors with barrier-free decorations and convenient width (at least allowing two wheelchairs) - Grab bars in the corridor, lift, and other areas - Lift buttons with Braille and audio guided lifts - Banistered stairs specially designed for convenient usage and - Availability of toilette for handicapped people
Restaurants, cafes	- Entrance hall with tactile walking path or mats allowing easy movement with wheelchair - Availability of portable dining tables and chairs for disabled tourists, or a separated area - Rounded corner dining tables and convenient width (more than 91,5 cm) between tables - Accessible buffet station and bar desk (lower design for disabled tourists) - Audio guidance or visual signs
Guest rooms	- Rooms locating at ground floor or accessible with lifts - Room doors with at least 75 cm width that allows wheelchair - Switches and remote controllers and other devices with Braille and easy access - Make-up table and wardrobe that is convenient for use with a wheelchair - High-contrasted or marked steps with anti-slip tape - High-contrasted info brochures and menus with enlarged letters or with Braille - General instructions and fire instructions with Braille - Availability of help buttons both in bedroom and bathroom - Room doors with automatic unlocking in case of emergency - Telephones with Braille or inductive coupler - Audio assistance for room service - Well-designed room plan for easy movement in the room
Bathrooms	- High-contrasted walls and equipment - Grab bars for usage - Help button with easy access - Banistered toilette and bathtub - High-contrasted or embossed towels - Hotel guest amenities designed for the people with disabilities - Nonslip floor design or mats

Accessibility Issues in Thermal Hotels

Thermal tourism is a bidirectional tourism activity formed based on tourism supply and demand to take advantage of thermal springs consisting of curative and mineralized waters (Özbek & Özbek, 2008). Thermal tourism, in one direction, is a curative movement with its' medical and control centers. On the other hand, it is a social movement that facilitates communication among people and provides relaxation (Monti, 2003). Meanwhile, the bidirectional characteristic of thermal tourism makes it difficult to position it as a distinct tourism type.

In literature, thermal tourism is generally categorized as a sub-branch of health tourism with Spa-wellness and medical tourism activities. In particular, thermal tourism is closely related to Spa-wellness activities. Because it also embodies very similar activities to Spa-wellness and beauty treatments (Boekstein, 2014), it is also used to maintain health and medical treatments (Temizkan & Çiçek, 2015). Thermal tourism, similar to therapeutic applications based on natural sources (sea, sun, climate, etc.), uses thermal water, peloids, and gases to maintain health and medical treatments (Charlier & Chaineux, 2009).

In thermal tourism, thermal hotels or hot springs are the touristic establishments that meet individuals' basic needs and thermal treatment requirements when traveling from their residence to thermal tourism destinations. In this context, a thermal hotel can be defined as a year-round establishment convenient for meeting 14–21 days long treatment needs, accommodation, and all kinds of requirements with its structure and features (Özbek & Özbek, 2008). On the other hand, in Türkiye, The Ministry of Culture and Tourism defines thermal establishments as "… the establishments consisting of a variety of units such as hot springs and thalassotherapy where natural therapeutic elements are used for health purposes", according to the Regulation on the Qualifications of Tourism Establishments.

In the Regulation, these establishments are categorized into two groups: the thermal facilities with accommodation and the thermal facilities without accommodation service. Thermal facilities with accommodation services are the establishments operating and licensed with accommodation establishments and named by specifying the type and class of the accommodation facilities they are located in (Turizm Tesislerinin Niteliklerine İlişkin Yönetmelik, 2019). Additionally, in Türkiye, Ministry-certified facilities for thermal tourism are mostly hotel types.

Hotel establishments for thermal tourism are more comprehensive and distinct than regular hotels in their organizational structure and physical constructions. These establishments serve both healthy people and people with health problems. Thus, they both need to be designed as multi-purposed and have an extensive organizational structure to meet all tourists' requirements. A thermal hotel generally consists of three main parts: accommodation facility, recreation areas, and thermal cure center. The accommodation facility of thermal hotels is similar to other hotel enterprises in their organizational structure. By the way, a dietary kitchen is the most distinct feature of the accommodation facility.

Thermal hotels are establishments that require long-term accommodation ranging up to 3 weeks, especially for curative treatments. Thus, they also need to have recreational areas that allow tourists to enjoy their time. In this context, recreational areas can contain a variety of amenities such as walking areas, sports areas, game saloons, libraries, cinemas, shopping centers, TV halls, concert halls, animation shows, cycling horse-riding routes, and regions. The cure center is crucial in differentiating thermal hotels from other hotel businesses.

Although differentiating according to the qualifications of thermal water and the features of other conditions, the main amenities of a cure center are balneotherapy, physiotherapy, and other additional services. Within the context of balneotherapy services, there can be regular swimming pools, treatment pools, special treatment baths, showers, massages, mud baths, steam baths, and gas baths. Additionally, there can be a thermal drinking unit, inhalation unit, subcutaneous injection unit, mixed-applications, sauna, Turkish bath, and ozone bath based on the establishment's scale. Physiotherapy units generally involve electro physiotherapy and radiotherapy. In addition, a cure center can have other services such as epilation, skincare, post-operative care and treatment, dental treatment, dietary services, climate-therapy and heliotherapy.

In Türkiye, thermal hotels must primarily have the Regulation on the Qualifications of Tourism Establishments standards and hospitality enterprises' qualifications (Aslan, 2015). However, the physical design of a thermal hotel should be created to meet the demands and needs of old and disabled tourists as well as normal tourists. In this direction, ENAT (European Network for Accessible Tourism) criteria and practices are the reference sources for the practices in hotel businesses in Türkiye. Physical Accessibility Control List of ENAT is geared towards ensuring accessibility of facilities for people with disabilities (Olcay, Giritlioğlu & Parlak, 2014).

Table 3. Some issues about accessibility (Article 21 of the Communiqué on the Implementation of the Regulation on the Qualifications of Tourism Establishments)

Headings	Regulations
Entrance	1) Entrance places at different levels are arranged following the movement of the physically disabled. If there is a threshold, the arrangement is made at a suitable height and chamfered to ensure the passage. 2) The entrance door of the facility is arranged so that its width is at least 100 cm.
Common areas and toilets	1) Door width is arranged to be at least 90 cm. If there is a threshold, the arrangement is made at a suitable height and chamfered to ensure the passage. 2) Equipment such as closets, washbasins, siphons, and faucets are arranged so that physically disabled people can use them. A grab bar is placed at the height of 85-95 cm from the floor covering, suitable for the use of the physically disabled, on the sides of the toilet bowl. 3) Mirrors are arranged at eye level or tilted forward 10-15 degrees, with the lower edge at a maximum height of 90 cm from the finished floor. 4) Enough space allows the wheelchair to make a complete turn, and the floor is covered with non-slippery material. 5) Accessories such as soap dispensers, towel holders, and paper holders are mounted at 50-120 cm from the finished floor. 6) There is an alarm system or telephone connected to the reception.
Bedrooms	1) Rooms are furnished and decorated with items of appropriate size and location so that the people with physical disabilities can move freely and use the room; Unbalanced, sharp-edged items are not kept. An emergency warning system is provided in at least one client's bedroom for the hearing impaired. 2) The width of the room entrance door is arranged to be at least 90 cm, and information boards showing the room number are set for the visually impaired use. 3) The floor covering is arranged for wheelchair use. 4) Wardrobe doors are arranged as sliding or without doors, with a maximum hanger height of 140 cm. 5) Electrical switches and sockets and all control and control panels in the room are arranged at the height of a maximum of 120 cm and at least 40 cm from the floor. 6) There is a central lighting button at the bedside. 7) In addition to the arrangements made in the public toilets in the room bathrooms, shower arrangements are made following the use of the people with physical disabilities. In these sections, seating and grab bars are provided in appropriate places. The bathroom door opening is arranged in a way that allows for easy movement. 8) For room arrangements, fractions are not taken into account in the evaluation of the one percent rate stipulated in the Regulation.
Lifts	1) The door is arranged with a photocell so that the closing interval is not shorter than five seconds. 2) The control buttons are arranged at the height of 90 cm-120 cm from the floor covering and are suitable for the use of the visually impaired. 3) Grab bars are provided in the cabin 85-95 cm from the floor. 4) Cabin floor covering is arranged for wheelchair use. 5) There is voice information in the cabin.
Dining tables	1) A table arrangement with a minimum of 70 cm height and at least 50 cm width with knee space is made. 2) The distance between tables is regulated to accommodate wheelchair access.

In Türkiye, the most up-to-date resource regarding accessibility in tourism establishments is in subparagraph (b) of the first paragraph of Article 18 of the Regulation on the Qualifications of Tourism Establishments. In subparagraph (b), accessibility is referred to as "In establishments with a total capacity of eighty rooms or more, and at least one room in four and five-star hotels, in one percent of the total room capacity, as well as in the facility entrance, elevators, public toilets, and at least one catering unit, daily facilities, break and in entertainment centres, accessibility arrangements are made as specified in the minimum qualifications of their types. These regulations are indicated by special signs."

According to subparagraph (b) of Article 18 of the Regulation, Article 21 of the Communiqué on the Implementation of the Regulation on the Qualifications of Tourism Establishments (Communiqué No: 2019/1) defines the principles regarding accessibility regulations. In Communiqué, accessibility regulations are defined in main headings as entrance, common areas and toilets, bedrooms, barrier-free accessibility, and food & beverage units. Some essential points of this Regulation can be summarized in Table 3.

In Türkiye, Regulations regarding the accessibility of Ministry-certificated hotels are also valid for thermal hotel enterprises. However, when the relevant regulations are examined, it is seen that there are not enough regulations for visually impaired people. In addition, although the service areas differ according to the types of hotels, it is noteworthy that these issues are not adequately addressed in the relevant principles.

For instance, in the cure center, one of the most critical sections in thermal hotel businesses, the regulations regarding how elderly and disabled individuals benefit from the services are not included in the communiqué. Scientific researches on thermal hotel businesses and general accommodation businesses (Baydeniz & Türkoğlu, 2021; Yılmazer, Kalpaklıoğlu, & Yılmaz, 2020; Olcay, Giritlioğlu, & Parlak, 2014) are also indicates that hotel businesses are at a low level in terms of physical accessibility, especially for disabled individuals.

A CASE STUDY ABOUT ACCESSIBILITY OF THERMAL HOTELS

Sample, Procedure, and Data Analysis

With the aim of presenting the accessibility of thermal hotels, this study explores which facilities and adjustments are being considered by thermal hotels for disabled tourists during service production. For this purpose, observations were made in selected thermal hotels in Afyonkarahisar, a city in western Türkiye, and semi-structured interviews were held with the top managers of these hotels (Table 4).

Table 4. Participants and Interviewing Summary

Participants	Position of Participant	Duration of Interview	Date of Interview
Participant-A	General Manager	45 min.	April 4th, 2022
Participant-B	Sales & Marketing Manager	35 min.	April 4th, 2022
Participant-C	Assistant General Manager	25 min.	April 5th, 2022
Participant-D	Sales Executive	40 min.	April 5th, 2022

Accessibility of Thermal Hotels for Disabled and Elderly Tourists

Although there are seven 5-star thermal hotels in Afyonkarahisar, researchers interviewed with four hotel managers based on the acceptance of appointment demands. Thermal hotels were chosen as a research area because they include services mainly for the elderly and disabled guests. These guests have some physical needs and may demand services such as physiotherapy. For this reason, thermal hotels were chosen as the population, with the thought that there may be more arrangements in this direction. The judgment sampling method, one of the non-probability sampling methods, was used to determine the participants. The main reason for choosing the Judgement sampling method is the desire to benefit from the participants' views at the maximum level in line with the purpose of the study.

In qualitative research, data about individuals and places are collected in their natural environment, and the inductive method is used in data analysis (Creswell, 2007, p. 37). Considering the inductive method, this study adopts an interpretative approach as it tries to understand the phenomena, uses qualitative data, and considers the environment in which the phenomenon takes place. The interpretative paradigm is adopted because a subjective interpretation is made to reveal the similarities and differences of the data obtained through observation and interview and to reach a common conclusion because of the evaluations made regarding these differences. In this context, by shuttling between deduction and induction and constantly making evaluations, the researchers are sought insights, general rules, patterns, and the saturation of the research question.

Figure 1 shows our analytical approach from data collection to data visualization. In the data collection phase, we both made observations and conducted interviews with senior managers of thermal hotels. At this point, we reached the relevant hotels approximately an hour earlier than appointment time and controlled accessibility facilities in general areas through our checklist chart, which is adopted from Tutuncu and Lieberman's (2016) study about the accessibility of hotels for people with visual impairments.

We also asked some questions to hotel staff to learn whether they were informed and are aware of accessibility issues. Within the data pre-processing phase, transcribing the data and text classification were made, and the text document was uploaded to the software. The following phases were coding and collating the data, subsuming codes under potential themes, mapping codes & themes, and portraying the relations between codes.

Figure 1. Phases from data collection to data visualization

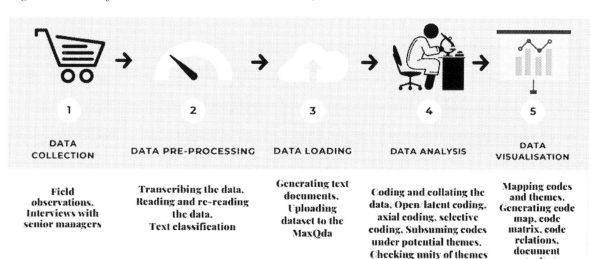

As a powerful method of analysing qualitative data, a thematic analysis is conducted to understand experiences, thoughts, or behaviors across the data set (Kiger & Varpio, 2020). The six-step process framework (Table 5) for conducting thematic analysis is adopted (Braun & Clarke, 2006).

In the first step of the thematic analysis, the researchers read the texts in detail at different times by first converting the information obtained from interviews into question-by-question texts. The first ideas were noted during the readings, and the foundation of data analysis was laid. In the second stage, firstly, the interview texts were uploaded to the MaxQda2020 software. Afterwards, the data related to each code was collated by systematically coding throughout the entire data set. Coding was conducted with open/latent, axial, and selective coding. Open coding is used to reveal the visible meanings in the text, while latent coding is used to indicate the invisible but implied meanings in the text.

Axial coding was used to determine the relationships between code categories, and selective coding was used to determine basic categories. After data coding, potential themes were created, and codes were defined under themes. Code Frequencies were determined in order to detect the most frequently repeated codes after the coding processes were completed. Code Map (conflicting codes) and Code matrix browser tools were used to determine the relationships between codes.

Table 5. Phases of thematic analysis. Source: Adapted from Braun and Clarke (2006)

Phase	Description of the process	Our way/path of analysis
Familiarizing yourself with your data:	Transcribing data (if necessary), reading and re-reading the data, and noting initial ideas.	• Transcribing and revisiting the data • Reading and re-reading the data in detail • Text classification
Generating initial codes:	Coding interesting features of the data in a systematic fashion across the entire data set, collating data relevant to each code.	• Defining and applying specific rules to segment each text • Separating the assumptions, factors, possibilities, and limits unit by unit • Coding and collating the data • Open/latent coding, axial coding, selective coding
Searching for themes:	Collating codes into potential themes, gathering all data relevant to each potential theme.	• Subsuming codes under potential themes • Assigning potential themes and sub-themes • Identifying codes with themes and sub-themes
Reviewing themes:	Checking if the themes work with the coded extracts (Level 1) and the entire data set (Level 2), generating a thematic 'map' of the analysis.	• Checking unity of themes with coded extracts • Mapping thematic approach
Defining and naming themes:	Ongoing analysis to refine the specifics of each theme and the overall story the analysis tells, generating clear definitions and names for each theme.	• Refining each theme and sub-themes • Defining and naming themes
Producing the report:	The final opportunity for analysis. Selection of vivid, compelling extract examples, the final analysis of selected extracts, relating back of the analysis to the research question and literature, producing a scholarly report of the analysis.	• Selecting extract comments • Identifying with research question and literature • Reporting • Mapping codes and themes, generating code map, code matrix, code relations, document portrait, etc.

RESULTS

Observation Results

During the observation period, we checked which of the applications related to accessibility were carried out in hotels with the help of an accessibility chart. The chart is adopted from Tutuncu and Lieberman's (2016) study about the accessibility of hotels for people with visual impairments (Table 6).

Table 6. Hotel Accessibility Checklist for Hotel Managers

Area	Recommendations (all places where applicable)	Hotel A	Hotel B	Hotel C	Hotel D
Entrance	**Signage**				
	Tactile maps and signs	X	X	X	
	Braille information about services and equipment		X	X	
	Large print with adequate contrast			X	
	The standard placement for the signage		X	X	
	Audio information in elevators	X	X	X	X
	Large signs in elevators	X	X	X	X
	Lighting, color, and contrast				
	Contrasts of walls and surfaces				
	Colors are not conflicting (for instance, the sofa is a different color than rug)				
	Brightness sufficient for guests with visual impairments		X		
	Mark glass doors and thresholds for outside areas		X	X	X
	Reception desk				
	A tactile map of the hotel		X	X	
	Orientation to hotel and room, including electric devices	X	X	X	X
	Braille information about shuttle services (how far, where, timing)		X	X	
	Auditory information		X	X	X
	Training of front office staff	X	X	X	X
	Special needs of guests with visual impairments		X	X	X
	Communication	X	X	X	X
	Hotel services for guests with visual impairments		X		X
Guest rooms	**Electronics**				
	Position of outlet accessible	X	X		X
	Consistent placement of light switches	X	X	X	X
	Telephone with tactile markings		X		X
	Directions and tactile markings with Braille in the room				
	TV remote control with directions and tactile markings and Braille				
	Heating and cooling systems with tactile markings and Braille		X		
	Sockets not blocked by furniture	X	X	X	X
	The standard height for the sockets	X	X	X	X

continues on following page

Table 6. Continued

Area	Recommendations (all places where applicable)	Hotel A	Hotel B	Hotel C	Hotel D
Guest rooms	**Bathroom**				
	Marking for shower or bath (hot and cold water taps identification)				
	Marking for shampoo, conditioner, lotion				
	Sign for the towel bar				
	Sign for electricity				
	Sign for hairdryer				
	Other room settings				
	Key cards marked for easy access	X	X	X	X
	Mini-bar, menu (large print or sign for prices)				
	Sign for beverages (regular coffee packet or decaf)				
	Terrace or balcony with warning tape or markers				
	Windows accessible to guest	X	X	X	X
	Braille information and tactile map about the layout of the room		X		
	Emergency instructions and other policies		X		
	Auditory information (via a phone extension or digitally downloadable)				
	Training of housekeeping staff	X	X	X	
	Special needs of guests with visual impairments (position of personal items)		X		
	Communication			X	X
	Room services for guests with visual impairments		X		X
Other hotel areas	**Restaurants and menus**				
	Position of the food on the plate			X	X
	Tactile or large print menu				
	Prices clearly displayed		X		
	Chair position related to lighting		X		
	Bar position related to lighting		X		
	Auditory information or closed captioning				
	Staff training		X	X	
	Interactive vending machines				

continues on following page

According to our observations before the interviews, it is observed that necessary directions such as tactile maps and signs, audio information and large signs in elevators, glass door marks, and thresholds for outside areas are available. We also observed that the light switches have consistent placement, the standard height for the sockets is appropriate and not blocked by furniture, and windows are accessible to disabled guests. However, we noted the lack of some arrangements such as contrasts of walls and surfaces, a tactile map of the room, directions and tactile markings with Braille in the room, auditory information, and so forth. (Table 6).

Table 6. Continued

Area	Recommendations (all places where applicable)	Hotel A	Hotel B	Hotel C	Hotel D
Recreation amenities	**Gym**				
	Tactile markings on fitness machines				
	A tactile map of the room				
	Floor markings for directions from one form of equipment to another				
	Free weights do not block fitness machines				X
	Pool				
	Deepness must be clearly marked	X	X		
	Stairs clearly marked		X		
	Elevators clearly marked	X	X		
	Tactile markings in the environment				
	Tactile markings or a rug around the perimeter		X		
	Mat for accessibility			X	
	Guide bar for accessibility		X		
	Railing from the locker room entrance				
Recreation amenities	**Entertainment**				
	Accessible list of local attractions		X		
	Described movies				
	A tactile map of recreation areas				
	Conference rooms and hallways				
	Tactile ground surface indicators crossing areas		X		
	Rug one color with no decorations for safety				
	The contrast of walls, steps, thresholds				
	Tactile maps and signage				

Interview Results

As a result of the data analysis in the research, a total of 20 codes with four different themes and a total of 167 frequencies were determined. Since codes such as Accessibility adjustments and accessibility are also included under different themes, the number of frequencies has increased to 190 (Table 7). The first of the themes was determined as *Theme 1: Observations about Accessibility*, which reflects the general thoughts and approaches of the managers determined as the participants. Under this theme, two codes were identified: observation and niche market.

The observation code was created for statements thought to include the managers' comments other than estimation, which are not based on statistical data. The codes determined under the theme of *Theme 2: Accessibility adjustments* regarding the arrangements made by thermal hotels for disabled guests are accessible, adjustments, directional signs, informing, and education. *Theme 3: Accessibility in Service Encounter* contains codes such as accessible, accompaniment, and functionality, which are determined by the managers' comments regarding their approach towards such guests during the service encounter. The last theme is "Theme 4: Cost-benefit", which is related to the policy understood due to the coding of hidden content and includes codes such as alternative cost, exceptional customer services, utilitarianism, and service cost.

The Code Map (Figure-2), which is prepared after coding the visible or hidden content in the text, visually reveals the frequency of the relevant codes and shows the relationships between codes. The colored circles on the map show the frequency of the codes according to their sizes. The lines between the codes represent the relationship between them. Code Map shows which codes are associated with other code groups.

Table 7. Code overview

Color	Theme	Code	f
●	Observations about Accessibility	Observation	14
●		Niche market	3
●	Accessibility adjustments	Accessibility adjustments	18
●		Accessible	13
●		Education	13
●		Legal obligation	12
●		Directional signs	4
●		Informing	2
●	Cost-benefit	Cost-benefit	16
●		Face-to-face contact	13
●		Alternative cost	10
●		Lack of demand	9
●		Utilitarianism	6
●		Exceptional customer service	4
●		Caring	3
●		Service cost	3
●	Accessibility in Service Encounter	Accessibility adjustments	18
●		Accessible	13
●		Functionality	11
●		Accompaniment	5

To view the color image, please see the electronic version of the chapter

The data analysis shows a similarity for many subjects; therefore, athough the codes are under different themes, they are related to each other. One of the salient among these relations is the relations between Alternative cost-Service cost-Cost benefit-Accessibility adjustments codes. These relationships result from managers' cost-benefit approaches to guests with disabilities. In particular, the fact that visually impaired guests represent a low part of the total demand, the risk of physical arrangements disrupting the normal functioning of the hotel, and the thought that it would be more appropriate to design areas for all guests, confirmed the close relationship between these codes.

Figure 2. Code map

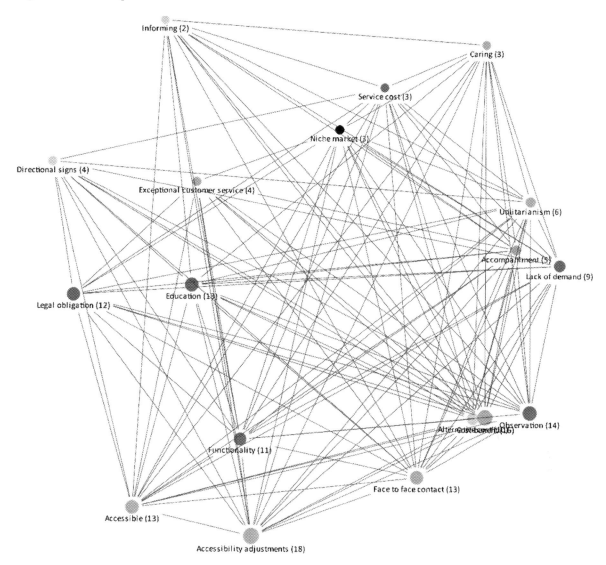

Other remarkable relationships are utilitarianism-lack of demand, legal obligation-functionality, exceptional customer service face-to-face contact, and education-informing codes. It has been understood that the arrangements for the disabled guests are not profitable due to the lack of demand, the arrangements for the disabled guests are carried out in connection with the legal obligations, unexpected services are provided to eliminate the negative perception that may occur due to the inadequate regulations, and a face-to-face service approach is developed by training certain employees such as guest relations. Figure 3 shows the relationships between codes obtained with the code matrix browser tool visually.

Figure 3. Code matrix browser

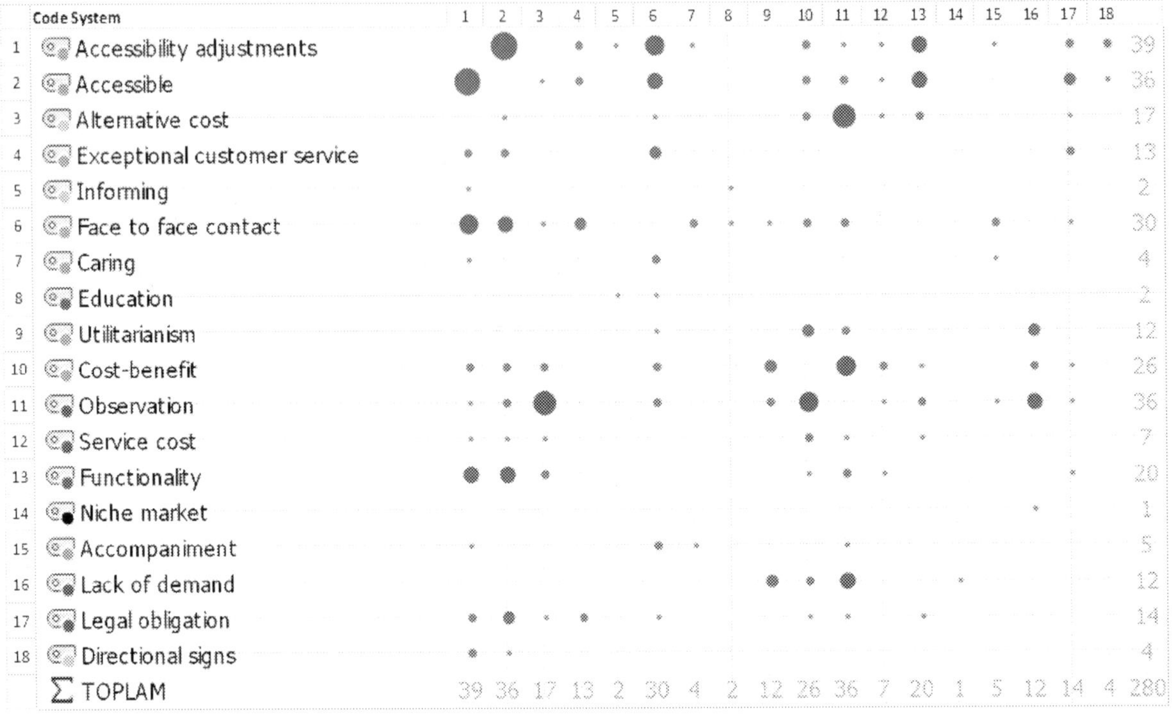

Code System	1	2	3	4	5	6	7	8	9	10	11	12	13	14	15	16	17	18	Total
1 Accessibility adjustments		●		•		●				•		•	●		•		•	•	39
2 Accessible	●			•		●				•		•	●				•	•	36
3 Alternative cost			•			•				•	●		•				•		17
4 Exceptional customer service	•	•				●											•		13
5 Informing	•								•										2
6 Face to face contact	●	●	•	•			•		•	•	•	•	•		•		•		30
7 Caring	•					•									•				4
8 Education									•	•									2
9 Utilitarianism									•	●	•				●				12
10 Cost-benefit		•	•	•		•				●	●	•	•			•	•		26
11 Observation	•	•	●			•			•	●		•	•			•	●	•	36
12 Service cost		•	•							•	•		•						7
13 Functionality	●	●	•							•	•	•					•		20
14 Niche market																•			1
15 Accompaniment	•				•	•				•									5
16 Lack of demand										●	•	●			•				12
17 Legal obligation	•	●	•	•	•					•	•		•						14
18 Directional signs	•	•																	4
∑ TOPLAM	39	36	17	13	2	30	4	2	12	26	36	7	20	1	5	12	14	4	280

Theme 1: Observations about Accessibility

Participants think that physical regulations regarding accessibility may adversely affect the functionality of the service delivery process. They state that there is routine traffic during service encounters in hotels, especially in busy times, and that service cars and cleaning machines in general areas such as lobbies and restaurants cause noise due to materials that may physically interfere with the operation, such as ground surface indicators.

"Adjustments for disabled guests can often make the hotel disabled for other guests."

"Once we make the facility accessible to the disabled, the facility becomes disabled for those who work for other guests."

Although efforts related to accessibility in thermal hotels are mainly handled through physical elements, it is among the most critical findings obtained in the interviews that any specific arrangement was made for the visually impaired guests. It has been observed that the main reason for this is insufficient demand. They also implied that they looked at the impaired guests market as a niche market and emphasized that they rarely have guests from this market.

"If the demand is high, more investment will be made, but in this case, it makes more sense to give one-on-one care staff."

"Since the demand is not so high, following such a strategy does not seem profitable. It seems more advantageous to solve the problem with personnel."

"There is no such demand in the market."

"We are not conducting a separate marketing effort for the visually impaired guests market."

Managers believe visually impaired guests always come to their establishments with a companion, so there is no need for such arrangements. However, they stated that they assigned a staff member for the visually impaired guests. In the interviews, the participants constantly expressed their observations about this.

"We have about five disabled guests a year. They always have their companions with them."

"The best solution seems to be to serve such guests with accompanying staff."

Theme 2: Accessibility Adjustments

In the thermal hotels included in the research, regulations for disabled individuals are carried out with a particular focus on legal requirements. It has been understood that the number of rooms for the disabled is determined by considering the limit specified in the law. It has been observed that the physical regulations are similarly based on legal requirements, and there are opinions that the audits are effective in this. Managers also emphasized that it would be more appropriate to consider all guests' expectations in regulations regarding accessibility. Associated with it; participants have made comments such as the following:

"The hotel is designed to be accessible to everyone."

"The physically handicapped people can easily move around the hotel."

"Standard layout is essential in the area, but equipment and devices are placed based on the accessibility."

"Informing" and "education" are among the codes determined under the theme of accessibility adjustments. In this context, managers are stated that the relevant personnel is informed when necessary, the tactile map prepared in Braille alphabet is kept at the entrance of the hotel, the ground surface indicators start from the outside of the hotel to the reception, but these indicators are not elsewhere as it physically affects the routine traffic; personnel is given periodic training about disabled people, and the training is mainly on body language. Comments on this are as follows:

"Information to the guests is made starting from the reception."

"We have a tactile map and ground surface indicators in the lobby."

"We provide body language training to our guest relations personnel and inform them in this way."

"We provide periodic training to the personnel by the department managers on the service for the disabled."

"The staff was trained for the hearing-impaired alphabet."

"Although it is not mandatory, we care about training our personnel on this subject."

Another code determined within the scope of accessibility adjustments was "directional signs." With this code, the managers stated that there are directional signs in Braille alphabet prepared especially for the physically disabled guests at specific points of the hotel, that arrangements are made for the visually impaired guests in the elevators, and the menus are prepared for the visually impaired guests are not available in the relevant rooms and restaurants:

"Only elevators and telephones have markings for the visually impaired."

"The elevators have directives with Braille alphabet."

"There is no embossed menu etc., prepared for visually impaired guests in our rooms and our restaurant. Our staff helps in such cases."

Theme 3: Accessibility in Service Encounter

During the interviews, one of the practical issues was the approach developed regarding accessibility during the service encounter. The managers expressed the issues they find objectionable regarding the regulations for accessibility. They stated that it is a more advantageous method to provide one-on-one service with their personnel in this regard. In this direction, it has been understood that they are trying to prevent the problem by assigning trained personnel, especially for their visually impaired guests.

"We reserve a special table for them in the restaurant."

"The restaurant staff prepares the guest's food and brings it to the guest. One-on-one service is available at the restaurant."

"They fulfill all kinds of demands during service delivery."

"General usage principles have been taken into account in our regulations."

Functionality was one of the codes determined under the "Accessibility in Service Encounter" theme. Managers stated that plans regarding the settlement were made to enable the disabled guests to move freely even without personnel during the service encounter. Some arrangements had already been made in the rooms for the disabled and other areas as per legal obligations. They also stated that they prioritize functionality in all areas. However, there are no special adjustments; they can make arrangements in accordance with the guests' expectations upon request and that the layout plans are made in line with the legal criteria and for the use of all guests.

"The hotel is designed to be accessible to everyone."

"The physically handicapped people can easily move around the hotel."

"These rooms are designed following legal criteria."

"Standard layout is essential in the area, but the equipment is placed based on the accessibility."

Another code determined under this theme was the "companion." They stated that visually impaired guests usually come with a companion and have never encountered a contrary situation. They also stated that they are personally interested in visually impaired guests. It is not appropriate to make arrangements for them in the entire hotel; instead, it would be a more satisfying approach to be accompanied by the staff. The participants' opinions about this code are as follows:

"We deal with our guests in this situation individually."

"We have never had a visually impaired guest come by himself before."

Theme 4: Cost-benefit

The striking thing about the latent coding in the research was that the hotels acted according to the cost-benefit approach in the regulations regarding disabled individuals. Since the demand for this market is not sufficient, it has been understood that the prevailing opinion is that the return of making the said regulations will not be at a satisfactory level. It has been determined that the managers act by considering issues such as alternative cost of services, utilitarianism, and service cost while making decisions about such regulations. From this point of view, codes such as alternative cost, lack of demand, utilitarianism, and service cost were determined under the theme of cost-benefit. Comments on these codes are as follows:

"The use of service trolleys, bellboy trolleys, etc., is challenging and generates excessive noise."

"There are good facilities for the disabled, but many are costly."

"There are two electric chairs for disabled guests in our hotel, which were purchased for 5000 Euros. However, this price is too exaggerated; it does not yield the same amount."

The approach to providing one-to-one service to disabled individuals stood out as the common understanding of all interviewed managers. Along with the one-to-one service, it has been observed that the unexpected customer services approach is mainly applied to prevent the deficiencies in the regulations for disabled people from causing negativity. The participants commented that they could gain the appreciation of other guests by serving with an approach that emphasizes service diversification for such guests.

"We offer special services for people with disabilities….. …..Other guests appreciate such situations."

"We offer in-room catering for the disabled."

"A guest requested special arrangements for his room. We redesigned his room in a short time as he requested"

CONCLUSION

It is the shared responsibility of all tourism stakeholders to create conditions that will enable everyone to enjoy the right to participate in tourism. In this context, hotels are also required to make arrangements in the organizational and physical structure for disabled guests. The legal basis of the practices for the disabled guests in hotels in Türkiye is the principles regarding the practices for the disabled people in the communiqué on the implementation of the Regulation on the qualifications of tourism establishments. The relevant principles are that the regulations for the physically disabled people are predominant; however, it shows that visually impaired tourists, considered the most disadvantaged group, are insufficient.

Studies on the practices for the disabled in hotels (Baydeniz & Türkoğlu, 2021; Yılmazer, Kalpaklıoğlu, & Yılmaz, 2020; Olcay, Giritlioğlu & Parlak, 2014) indicated that there is no effort or target for disabled individuals as a managerial strategy and the regulations for disabled people are focused on legal coercion. Thermal hotels are hotels where healthy and sick individuals use the same environment. These aspects constitute the hotels that should have the most regulations for disabled individuals.

In line with this basic information, this study aims to portray the accessibility of thermal hotels for disabled guests using observation and a semi-structured interviewing form. For this purpose, observation was made in relevant hotels, and interviews were conducted with thermal hotel managers. The main findings obtained as a result of the observation and interviews are as follows:

- According to our observations before interviews, it is observed that necessary directions such as tactile maps and signs, audio information and large signs in elevators, glass door marks, and thresholds for outside areas are available. We also observed that the light switches have consistent placement, the standard height for the sockets are appropriate and not blocked by furniture, and the windows are accessible to disabled guests. Our observations have similarities with interview results
- Arrangements are made for only physical disabilities within the scope of accessibility in thermal hotels
- Arrangements for the disabled are focused on legal requirements
- Thermal hotels organize rooms for the disabled only as specified in the law
- In the hotel's thermal-SPA units, there are no special efforts related to accessibility, and routine arrangements are made
- Especially visually impaired people come to the hotel with an accompanying person
- They think that allocating special personnel to these guests instead of making arrangements for the guests with visual impairments will create more satisfaction
- It is believed that the arrangements for the disabled in the hotels can often create obstacles for the guests who are not disabled
- Practices for the disabled in hotels create difficulties and obstacles in executing service activities

Another finding that was reached in the study is whether any specific arrangement was made for the visually impaired guests. According to the observations of managers, these guests constitute a small demand, so arrangements for them are not mandatory for the hotels. In addition, participants think that physical regulations regarding accessibility may adversely affect the functionality of the service delivery process.

This idea is the product of the concern that the regulations for disabled people hinder the operability during the service delivery process, where the traffic is primarily heavy. A wider guest group may be disturbed by this. This study also shows that regulations for disabled individuals are carried out with a particular focus on legal requirements. Legal obligations oblige thermal hotels to act within legal limits. For this reason, it was understood that they only designed rooms for the disabled as much as the limited in the law. Hotels acted according to the cost-benefit approach in the regulations regarding disabled individuals. Thermal hotel managers do not consider disabled people as a market segment.

However, when disabled people come to their hotels, they ironically offer personalized (significantly visually impaired) services and do not hesitate to allocate staff for this. They stated that providing one-on-one service with their personnel is more advantageous. Along with the one-on-one service, it has been observed that the unexpected customer services approach is mainly applied to prevent the deficiencies in the regulations for disabled people from causing negativity.

SOLUTIONS, RECOMMENDATIONS AND FUTURE RESEARCH DIRECTIONS

This study aimed to reveal the accessibility of thermal hotels, conducted in a limited sample. However, it hits the high spots of accessibility issues for thermal tourism services. It is revealed that, contrary to general expectation, thermal hotel managers handle the accessibility facilities in terms of cost-benefit approach and demand generation capacity of disabled people rather than UNWTO's tourism for all approach. Thus, services delivered to disabled tourists mostly have one-on-one service characteristics. Furthermore, some accessibility adjustments are disregarded due to functionality and to provide an efficient service to hotel guests. At this point, hotel managers should reconsider the accessibility of the hotel and the thermal services within the context of ethics, human rights and UNWTO's tourism for all approach.

Additionally, they should reconsider the demand generation potential of disabled tourists. It is because delivering high-quality services to disabled tourists will highly contribute to the company's image, and hotels have a chance to meet higher demands beyond their expectations. Moreover, they could use accessibility as a promotional strategy to attract the niche market of people with special needs. To bring this strategy into action, hotel managers should comprehensively explain the potential benefits of this strategy to entrepreneurs of thermal hotels and try to convince them to make more investments in accessibility. On the other hand, much more academic research focusing on daily service procedures should be conducted to create awareness about the needs of disabled or elderly tourists.

Within this context, more comprehensive academic research involving both tourists' and managers' opinions, the demand size of disabled tourism, the satisfaction and expectations of the disabled tourists for the services provided in thermal hotels, or using qualitative and quantitative research methods must be carried out. Moreover, the accessibility projects should be run with the association among hotels, academicians and governmental establishments such as the UN, EU, or national foundations. This study's findings are valid for Afyonkarahisar. In addition, the interviewed managers mostly host Turkish tourists, so the results may vary with tourists with different cultures and socioeconomic structures.

REFERENCES

APA. (2022). *APA dictionary*. Accessible at https://dictionary.apa.org/accessible

Arasıl, T. (1991). Using of the thermal waters in the field of health [Termal Suların Sağlık Alanında Kullanımı]. *Anatolia Dergisi. Mayıs-Haziran, 17-18*, 45–48.

Artar, Y., & Karabacakoğlu, Ç. (2003). *Accessible Tourism Report: Investigation of infrastructure opportunities in accommodation facilities for the development of disabled tourism in Turkey* [Engelsiz Turizm Raporu: Türkiye'de engelliler turizminin geliştirilmesine yönelik konaklama tesislerindeki altyapı imkanlarının araştırılması]. Retrieved on July 4, 2020, from: https://www.devturkiye.org/Projeler/Engelsiz-Tatil-Koyu/Engelsiz-Turizm-Raporu/

Aslan, Z. (2015). Service standards in thermal tourism enterprises [Termal Turizm İşletmelerinde Hizmet Standartları]. Turizm Sağlık ve Hukuk Sempozyumu, 23-42.

Babu, S. S., Dixit, S., & Yadav, C. (2010). *A report on problems and prospects of accessible tourism in India*. Indian Institute of Tourism and Travel Management.

Baydeniz, E., & Türkoğlu, T. (2021). Evaluation of applications for guests with disabled at thermal hotel enterprises: An application in Afyonkarahisar [Termal Otel İşletmelerinde Engelli Misafirlere Yönelik Uygulamaların Değerlendirilmesi: Afyonkarahisar İlinde Bir Uygulama]. *Journal of Tourism and Gastronomy Studies, 5*(Special Issue), 442–452. doi:10.21325/jotags.2021.966

Boekstein, M. (2014). Tourism, Health and Changing Role of Thermal-Springs Should South Africa Reposition Its Thermal Spring Tourism Product. *African Journal of Hospitality, Tourism and Leisure, 3*(2), 1–8.

Buhalis, D., Eichhorn, V., Michopoulou, E., & Miller, G. (2005). Accessibility market and stakeholder analysis. University of Surrey One-Stop Shop for Accessible Tourism in Europe (OSSATE).

Charlier, R. H., & Chaineux, M.-C. P. (2009). The Healing Sea: A Sustainable Coastal Ocean Resource: Thalassotherapy. *Journal of Coastal Research, 25*(4), 838–856. doi:10.2112/08A-0008.1

Communiqué on the Implementation of the Regulation on the Qualifications of Tourism Facilities [Turizm Tesislerinin Niteliklerine İlişkin Yönetmeliğin Uygulanmasına Dair Tebliğ (Tebliğ No: 2019/1)]. (n.d.). Retrieved on October 19, 2020, from: https://www.resmigazete.gov.tr/eskiler/2019/11/20191127-6.htm

Darcy, S., & Buhalis, D. (2011). Introduction: From disabled tourists to accessible tourism. In S. Buhalis & S. Darcy (Eds.), *Accessible Tourism: Concepts and Issues* (pp. 1–20). Channel View Publications Ltd.

Etmyonline. (2022). Accessible at: https://www.etymonline.com/search?q=accessibility&ref=searchbar_searchhint

Gandin, S. (2018). Tourism promotion and disability: still a (linguistic) taboo? A preliminary study. In M. Bielenia-Grajewska & E. Cortes De Los Rios (Eds.), *Innovative perspectives on tourism discourse* (pp. 55–73). IGI Global. doi:10.4018/978-1-5225-2930-9.ch004

Israeli, A. A. (2002). A preliminary investigation of the importance of site accessibility factors for disabled tourists. *Journal of Travel Research, 41*(1), 101–104. doi:10.1177/004728750204100114

Lindqvist, L. J., & Björk, P. (2000). Perceived safety as an important quality dimension among senior tourists. *Tourism Economics*, *6*(2), 151–158. doi:10.5367/000000000101297541

Monti, S. (2003). Thermalism Between Past and Future. *Proceedings of the Conference the Cultural Turn in Geography.*

Olcay, A., Giritlioğlu, İ., & Parlak, Ö. (2014). Comparison of hotel business arrangements for accessible tourism between ENAT(European Network For Accessible Tourism) and Turkey [ENAT (European Network For Accessible Tourism-Avrupa Erişilebilir Turizm Ağı) ile Türkiye'nin Erişilebilir Turizme Yönelik Otel İşletmelerini Kapsayan Düzenlemeleri ve Bu Düzenlemelerin Karşılaştırılması]. *Gazi Üniversitesi Turizm Fakültesi Dergisi*, *2*, 127–144.

Oxford Dictionary. (2021). Accessible at: https://www.oxfordlearnersdictionaries.com/definition/english/accessibility?q=accessibility

Özbek, D., & Özbek, T. (2008). Integration of Geothermal Resources into Health and Thermal Tourism [Jeotermal Kaynakların Sağlık ve Termal Turizme Entegrasyonu]. *Jeoloji Mühendisleri Odası Haber Bülteni*, *2-3*, 99–113.

Özbek, T. (1991). Thermal tourism in the World and Turkey and its importance [Dünya'da ve Türkiye'de Termal Turizmin Önemi]. *Anatolia Dergisi*, *17-18*, 15–29.

Patiar, S. (2015). *Handbook senior tourism*. Grŵp Llandrillo Menai.

Regulation on the Qualifications of Tourism Facilities [Turizm Tesislerinin Niteliklerine İlişkin Yönetmelik]. (n.d.). Retrieved on September 22, 2021, from: https://www.mevzuat.gov.tr/MevzuatMetin/21.5.1134.pdf

Śniadek, J. (2006). Age of Seniors–A Challenge for tourism and leisure industry. *Studies in the Physical Culture and Tourism*, *13*(1), 103–105.

Temizkan, S. P., & Çiçek, D. (2015). The concept of health tourism and its characteristics. [Sağlık Turizmi Kavramı ve Özellikleri]. In S. P. Temizkan (Ed.), *Health Tourism* [Sağlık Turizmi] (pp. 11–36). Detay Yayıncılık.

Tomej, K. (2019). Accessible and equitable tourism services for travellers with disabilities: From a charitable to a commercial footing. In S. O. Idowu & R. Schmidpeter (Eds.), *Corporate sustainability and responsibility in tourism* (pp. 65–78). Springer. doi:10.1007/978-3-030-15624-4_4

Tutuncu, O., & Lieberman, L. (2016, May-June). Accessibility of Hotels for People with Visual Impairments: From Research to Practice. *Journal of Visual Impairment & Blindness*, 163–175.

UNWTO. (2013). Recommendations on accessible tourism. Madrid, Spain: World Tourism Organization (UNWTO) Publications.

UNWTO. (2016a). Manual on accessible tourism for all: Principles, tools and best practices - Module I: Accessible tourism - definition and context. Madrid, Spain: World Tourism Organization (UNWTO) Publications.

UNWTO. (2016b). *Highlights of the 1st UNWTO conference on accessible tourism in Europe (San Marino, 19-20 November 2014),* Madrid, Spain: World Tourism Organization (UNWTO) Publications.

WHO. (2021). *Ageing*. Retrieved on January 13, 2022, from: https://www.who.int/health-topics/ageing#tab=tab_1

Wiastuti, R. D., Adiati, M. P., & Lestari, N. S. (2018). Implementation of accessible tourism concept at museums in Jakarta. *IOP Conference Series: Earth and Environmental Science, 126*(1), 1-9.

Wnag, Y. (2011). Ageing travel market and accessibility requirements. In S. Buhalis & S. Darcy (Eds.), *Accessible Tourism: Concepts and Issues* (pp. 1–20). Channel View Publications Ltd.

Yılmazer, A., Kalpaklıoğlu, N. Ü., & Yılmaz, S. (2020). A research on the expectations of disabled individuals from hospitality enterprises for tourism participation and current situation determination [Engelli Bireylerin Turizme Katılımına Yönelik Konaklama İşletmelerinden Beklentileri ve Mevcut Durum Tespitine İlişkin Bir Araştırma]. *Türk Turizm Araştırmaları Dergisi, 4*(3), 2821–2839.

Chapter 18
Current Trends in Sustainable Tourism in the Indian Context

Sunita Jatav
School of Management (PG), Dr.Vishwanath Karad, MIT World Peace University, Pune, India

ABSTRACT

Indian tourism is rich with culture, heritage, ecology, and natural beauty across the country. The tourism sector plays a vital role for foreign exchange earnings and gross domestic product (GDP) in India. India's travel and tourism business ranks 7th internationally, contributing almost 9.6% to GDP, and is expected to rise 6.9% annually over the next decade to rank 4th. This will have a multiplier effect on India's socio-economic progress via improved infrastructure, job creation, and skill development. India was ranked 10th among 185 countries in 2019. India is a globally and digitally advanced nation in term of planning, booking, and positive experience for travel and tour. Indian middle class people's disposable income is increasing, which creates a positive impact on outbound tourism. The Indian travel market is projected to grow to US$125 billion by 2027. This study identifies best practices and the need for sustainable tourism in India's growth.

TOURISM IN INDIA

The tourist industry has a significant impact on the global economy in terms of both the amount of money it brings in and the amount of money it costs. One of the primary drivers of the service industry in India is tourism and hospitality. All around India, visitors may experience a wide range of cultural, historical, and natural attractions. India's tourism industry plays a critical part in the country's economy and foreign currency revenues. From 2016 to 2019, foreign currency profits climbed at a Compound Annual Growth Rate (CAGR) of 7% but fell in 2020 because of the COVID-19 pandemic.

The tourist industry is anticipated to provide 53 million jobs by the year 2029 (IBEF, Indian Tourism Hospitality Report October 2021). According to the rules (World Travel & Tourism Council [WTTC] 2007), in 2019 India was placed 10th out of 185 nations in terms of digital advancement in the planning, booking, and good travel and tourism experience. Tourists from India are benefiting from a rise in disposable money among the country's middle class. Travel in India is expected to expand by US$125

DOI: 10.4018/978-1-6684-4645-4.ch018

billion in the next decade. By 2027, India's airline sector is expected to quadruple in size because of the country's high-quality airport infrastructure and increased passport access. Use of air travel has resulted in an increase in demand for hotels in both local and foreign markets.

In 2019, India received more than 10 million FTAs, and in April 2021, India's share of FTAs will surpass that of the United States, Germany, Canada, the Maldives, France, and Australia combined. A total of 29 airports in India have been able to increase their share of FTA from -84 percent after COVID-19. More than US$59 billion in income is estimated to be generated by the FTA by 2028. Post-pandemic development is projected for both foreign and domestic tourism in India; hence, most international hotels are expanding their presence in the country. According to the Federation of Hotel and Restaurant Associations of India (FHRAI), the Indian hotel industry lost US$17.8 billion in revenue due to the COVID-19 pandemic (IBEF, 2021). Unsurprisingly, the pandemic has become a catalyst for serious consideration regarding sustainability and safety.

SUSTAINABLE TOURISM

According to the World Tourism Organization (WTO), sustainable tourism principles include environmental, economic, and socio-cultural components of tourism development, and an appropriate balance must be maintained between these three dimensions to ensure its long-term sustainability. UNEP and the World Trade Organization (2005). To ensure a destination's long-term viability, sustainable tourism evaluates the needs of visitors, the tourism industry, environmental conditions, as well as the host communities. Sustainable tourism research has grown from the study of tourism, economics, and environmental management, as per Buckley (2012).

Sustainable tourism is no longer a reactive reaction to (bad) tourist challenges state Bramwell and Lane (1993), but a solution that creates positive change. Green Step is the lifeline for sustainable tourism, which provides assessments and enhancement in the hospitality industry. The concept of sustainability has received huge attention and attraction in the tourism industry. The main intention of sustainable was for growth of society, economic development, environmental safety, and cultural knowledge (Sancho et al., 2002; Perez et al, 2013).

Several businesses in the service industry have taken an important step towards sustainability by establishing a target for their organization's sustainability. Environmentally friendly items were in high demand from customers of services. Environmental deterioration was gradually recognized by both small and large service sector organizations which use environmentally friendly goods and services to avoid it. The tourism industry is one of the most significant and fastest growing in the world, making it an ideal candidate for the application of environmental protection principles based on sustainability (World Travel & Tourism Council [WTTC] 2007).

The United Nations (UN) has established 12 primary goals for sustainable tourism, which would limit the degradation of tourism in all nations, for development and economic prosperity (UNWTO, 2013). In India and throughout the globe, there are several efforts made by both private and public organizations. Initiatives focused on trash management, transportation management, the most effective use of electronic resources for promotion, green marketing, and environmentally friendly activities. Sustainable techniques have been developed by different hotels and tourist-based businesses, such as eco label, prizes for implementing green projects, and educational campaigns on responsible tourism.

Current Trends in Sustainable Tourism in the Indian Context

For many nations, tourism is an important source of money and jobs including India. In India, all 28 states benefit from tourism in some manner. Himachal Pradesh, Jammu, Kashmir, the eastern seven sister states, Kerala, Uttaranchal/Uttarakhand, and a slew of other states in India are known for their natural beauty and rely heavily on tourism for their primary source of income. Degradation of natural resources, brought on by increased tourism, has resulted in disasters such as the Uttarakhand floods of 2013. Disasters occur when natural resources are heavily mined. The hotel business is one of the primary tourist industries that poses a significant danger to the environment because of its high use of energy, water, and less durable items.

Although the hotel industry is a critical component of the tourist industry, its development and use of global and natural resources contribute to environmental damage. To ensure client satisfaction, hotels provide services such as warm water, lights, water, pools, food and beverages as well as linens and towels that are non-recyclable. This has an indirect impact on the environment. Tourists can handle the challenges hotels provide, while safeguarding and developing the future of their destinations and their requirements.

Due to the negative impact of the pandemic and many natural hazards, many organizations were highly affected, so governments and public policy maker like India are working to overcome the challenges. Some innovative and environment-friendly steps have taken by organization, states and countries which are giving guideline to other for sustainable tourism.

Green for Sustainable Tourism

Environmental damage is rising globally, thus everyone must use eco-friendly goods and services. People's changing lifestyles require them to use eco-friendly items. Therefore, advertising green goods and services to tourists is crucial. Ottman (2010) detailed green marketing concepts in *The New Rules of Green Marketing*. Sixteen of the 17 green marketing guidelines apply to environmentally friendly travel as provided below:

1. Green goods perform as well as or better than conventional items and are often worth a premium price.
2. Green encourages the development of creative goods and services that may result in increased customer value, improved branding, and a stronger business.
3. Values Guide Consumer Purchasing: Historically, people made purchasing decisions primarily based on price, performance, and convenience.
4. A Life-Cycle Approach is Necessary: Individual characteristics such as recyclable, organic, or energy efficient are critical.
5. Manufacturer and Retailer Reputation Count Now More Than Ever: Buyers are turning over packages and asking, "Who makes this brand?" "Were environmental and social criteria met throughout production?"
6. Save me! Today's consumers buy greener brands to help protect their health, save money, or because they simply work better.
7. Sustainability is a critical consumer desire that has evolved into an inherent part of product quality.
8. The most environmentally friendly goods feature novel ideas with much less impactful business approaches.

9. Consumers do not have to possess items; services may suit their requirements just as well, if not better.
10. Green customers are heavily affected by the recommendations of friends and family, as well as third-party sources of information.
11. Consumers that are environmentally conscious trust companies that are transparent.
12. Green Consumers Don't Expect Perfection: Continue to improve and report on your progress.
13. Environmentalists are no longer seen as adversaries.
14. Nearly Everyone is a Corporate Stakeholder: No longer limited to consumers, workers, and investors, corporate stakeholders today include environmentalists, educators, and children even the unborn.
15. Authenticity: It is not sufficient to put on a recycling emblem or make a claim about biodegradability. Genuine brands include important environmental advantages into their goods.
16. Keep it Simple: Plato was an advocate for the environment, stating that "simplicity is beauty." Consumers nowadays are avoiding pointless purchases and getting rid of gadgets and gizmos that offer no value to their lives.

Pillar of Sustainable Tourism

Non-profits, businesses, and governments encourage sustainable tourism (OECD, 2002; UNEP, 2005; European Environmental Agency, 2006). Diverse governmental and private projects show tourism may enhance resource usage, waste management, and transportation. Despite visitors' declining interest in green policies, business and government have launched green initiatives. Institutions utilise eco-labels, certification systems, communication, and awareness efforts. UN organisations like UNWTO encourage three-pillar sustainable tourism (environmental, sociocultural, and economic).

Sustainable tourism is now a trend in academic tourism and programming, as well as various tourist regulations and legislation. Tourism can promote economic, cultural, and environmental sustainability

Figure 1.

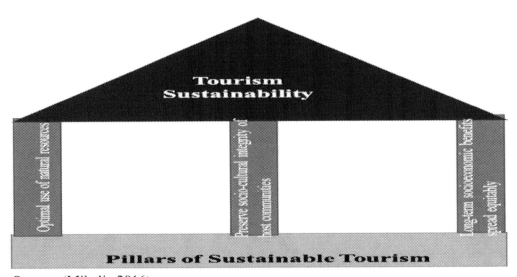

Source: (Mihalic 2016).

and transformation. Clean environments, diversified cultures, and pleasant communities are important for tourism. Tourism's influence extends beyond monetary and currency benefits. People's thinking, acting, communicating, and living in communities are changing. Cultural preservation, resource management, trash management, business and social ethics, sustainable development, and inclusive growth affect many industries (Mihalic 2016).

Aim of Sustainable Tourism

- Economic Viability
- Local Prosperity
- Employment Quality
- Social Equity
- Visitor Fulfilment
- Local Management
- Community Wellbeing
- Cultural Richness
- Physical Integrity
- Biological Diversity
- Resource Efficiency
- Environmental Integrity

The UN has 12 sustainable tourism goals (UNWTO 2013): 1) Destinations should be long-lasting and profitable; 2) Reduce tourist spending leaks; 3) Improve job number, quality, pay, and circumstances; 4) Fair economic and social advantages for the host community; 5) Safe, enriching visit without discrimination; 6) Destination planning and decision-making by local communities; 7) Protect communal structures and activities against degradation; 8) Preserve culture, heritage, and architecture; 9) Maintain landscape quality; 10) Contribute to habitat, forum, and wildlife conservation 11) Minimize non-renewable tourist infrastructures and operations; 12) Reduce waste and pollution.

New paradigms also emphasise the demand side, pushing visitors to pick sustainable items despite a price premium and resource austerity. It preserves local citizens' well-being and promotes global sustainability, including Sustainable Development Goals (SDGs). Accordingly, sustainable tourism development must suit current visitor requirements while safeguarding and developing future areas and needs. Sustainable tourism development must meet present tourist requirements while protecting and growing future opportunities in the same region.

Dimension of Sustainable Tourism

- **Responsible Tourism:** Reduces harmful social, economic, and environmental consequences to greatest extent possible. Industry has adopted this approach since sustainability might suggest wider aspects that are beyond its purview
- **Ecotourism:** Traveling to unspoiled natural locations in an environmentally conscious manner. All types of tourism have the potential to be sustainable, but not all forms of tourism have the potential to be ecotourism

- **Geotourism:** Preservation and enhancement initiatives should be on preserving and strengthening an area's "feeling of place," rather than on the efforts of the industry
- **Voluntourism:** Emphasize the importance of "giving back to the community" via volunteer activity

Benefits of Sustainable Tourism Practices

Regulating and managing tourism's negative repercussions will not establish a viable economic paradigm. Tourism may help towns economically, socially, and environmentally. Tourism sector values may and should be mutually reinforcing, and policies that encourage them may benefit both the company and the community (Singh, 2013).

Benefits of Adopting Sustainable Tourism:

- Tourism enterprises- long term profitability and corporate image
- Local communities- Increased prosperity but without exploitation or damage to their quality of life
- Tourists- High quality experience in safe and attractive environments; Low impacts of travelling
- Environmentalists- Valuable source of income for conservation
- It assures long-term development as well as predictability in the future
- However, the long-term savings outweigh any initial costs
- It is easier for corporations to promote their goods and services if they consider environmental concerns
- It facilitates entry into new markets and gives businesses an edge in the marketplace

PROMOTION OF NEW DESTINATION TOURISM VIA SUSTAINABILITY

Cruise tourism: Cruise tourism is one of the world's fastest-growing leisure industries. According to official forecasts, India's cruise tourism sector would handle 1.2 million passengers by 2020. India is also using its 7,500 kilometers of coastline to expand its cruise tourism business. The Dream Hotel Group said in April, 2021 that it will spend US$300 million in India's cruise business over the following three to five years. Cordelia Cruises will start operating cruises in India in May, 2021 in conjunction with Waterways Leisure Tourism Private Limited.

Rural Tourism: Considering the majority of India's population lives in rural regions, the country has a significant amount of untapped potential for the growth of rural tourism. This may be of economic and social value to the local community, as well as enable contact between visitors and residents, which can result in an experience that is rewarding for both parties.

Eco Tourism: The country of India is often referred to be a hotspot for bio-diversity and the country's vast natural history is unrivalled in many respects. By the end of 2020, the country will have a total of 566 sanctuaries in addition to its 104 national parks. Such a significant foundation of useful resources provides the incentive for the practise of a range of alternative types of tourism, many of which are currently in operation. The Indian Council of Agricultural Research-Central Coastal Agricultural Research

Institute (ICAR-CCARI), which has its headquarters in Old Goa, inaugurated the agro-eco tourism (AET) module in January, 2021 as a possible alternative to traditional tourism (IBEF 2022).

Sustainable Tourism Industry: A Global and Indian Overview

Travel and tourism contribute to economic growth and job creation. Travel and tourism employed 109 million people in 2016. The sector supported 292 million jobs globally in 2016, generating US$7.6 trillion (including indirect and induced impacts). In 2010, this industry accounted for 10.2% of global GDP and one-tenth of total employment. Recent natural catastrophes have impacted several businesses, including travel and tourism, generating sustainability concerns. Sustainability is a concern in some of the world's fastest-growing tourist destinations, such as developing countries with big populations. International visitor proportion relative to local population is an indicator of tourism effect.

In 2016, foreign visitors outnumbered Icelanders 5.1 to 1. Europe's highest rates are in Croatia (3.3) and Montenegro (1.1). (2.6 to 1). This ratio shows where large-scale growth may strain infrastructure and produce environmental and social difficulties. Sustainability will grow more essential as more consumers and corporations travel responsibly, yet consumer commitment to responsible tourism remains low.

Only 20% of travel companies have been asked about a trip's sustainability, according to ABTA, and the typical tourist doesn't believe they can make a difference. These numbers are minor, but analysts believe they signal sustained tourism growth. The graph below compares a Green Scenario against business as usual in the tourism industry from 2010 to 2050.

Figure 2.

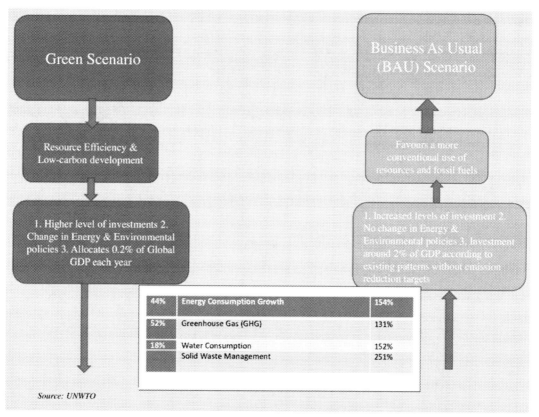

India's diverse landscape and microcosms of culture, art, architecture, and heritage provide a wide range of tourist attractions. In 2016, FTAs rose 10.7%. 2016 FTAs were 88.9 lakh compared. 80.3 lakh in 2015. India received 84.5% of FTAs through air, 14.8% by land, and 0.7% by water. Delhi and Mumbai airports led India's FTAs. Foreign visitors are predicted to climb 7.1% year from 2005 through 2025. Domestic tourist visits rose 15.5% in 2016 over 2015 and 13.8% over the previous decade. In 2016, had 1653 million domestic tourist visits which was up from 1,432 million in 2015. Indian tourism creates foreign currency and jobs. India can harness its unrivalled tourist potential by guiding investments with legislation.

Key Statistics for Indian Tourism

- *Higher Investments:* As a percentage of overall investments in 2016, tourism contributed 5.7 percent to capital investment, with annual growth predicted to reach 5.7 percent per year from 2017 to 2027, much higher than the world average of 4.5 percent.
- *Visitor Exports:* The contribution of visitor exports to overall exports is expected to grow at a rate of 6.1 percent per year between 2017–27, compared to a global average growth rate of 4.3 percent per annum.
- *Foreign Tourist Arrivals:* FTAs were 7.68 million in 2014, a total of 8.03 million in 2015, and 8.89 million in 2016. In 2014, FTAs totalled 7.68 million. FTA's CAGR is 8.45%, compared to 4-5% globally. The World Tourism Organization predicts 15.3 million international tourists in India by 2025.
- *Foreign Exchange Earnings:* In January-April 2017, there were 35.85 lakh FTAs, a 15.4% increase over previous year. 5.82 lakh tourists arrived on e-Tourist Visas, up 48.8% from the previous year. During January-April 2017, FEEs were INR 61,605 crore, up 18.9% from the previous year. This is a 15% rise over the same time last year.
- *Contribution to GDP:* In 2016, India was rated third out of 184 nations in terms of the overall contribution of travel and tourism to the country's GDP. In 2016, the tourism and hospitality industry made a direct contribution to GDP of USD 71.53 billion, according to the World Bank. A compound annual growth rate of 14.05 percent in direct contribution of tourism and hospitality to GDP is predicted to be achieved between 2006 and 2017.
- *Employment Generation:* The Indian tourist industry is expected to sustain 41 million employments by 2017, with the number of jobs expected to rise to around 49.8 million by 2027, according to estimates.
- *Domestic Tourism*: Expenditures on domestic travel generated 82.5 percent of 2015's direct Travel and Tourism GDP in contrast to 17.5% of that year's total visitor exports. Visitor spending on domestic travel will rise 7.8% annually to INR 13,305.5 billion in 2026, while visitor exports will rise 7.2% annually to INR 2,625.6 billion in 2026.

Source: Ministry of Tourism, Govt. of India

CURRENT AND FUTURE TOURISM BUSINESS IN INDIA

The World Travel and Tourism Council (2018) estimates the direct contribution of travel and tourism to GDP in 2017 was INR 943.3 billion (US$91.3 billion), or 3.7% of overall GDP. It is anticipated to increase by 7.1% each year from 2018 to 2028, reaching INR 12, 777.9 billion (US$194.7 billion), or 3.9% of total GDP in 2028. In 2017 tourism provided 26,148,000 jobs, representing five percent of all employment. By 2028, this will rise by 2.1% per year to 33,195,000 employment (5.3 percent of the total workforce). Tourism investment will rise. In 2017, investments were INR 2,706.1 billion (US$41.6 billion), or 6.3% of total investment. It's expected to grow by 6.7% per annum during the next 10 years, reaching INR 5,546.3 billion (US$85.2 billion) in 2028, or 6.1% of the total. Travel and tourism are major economic drivers.

India came in third place in the World Travel and Tourism Council's (WTTC) Economic Impact 2019 report for travel and tourism GDP growth, behind only China and the Philippines. The travel and tourism business in India brought in a total of US$121.9 billion in income in 2013, which is equivalent to 4.7 percent of the country's overall GDP. In the year 2020, it is responsible for the employment of 31,785,200 persons, which is 7.3 percent of the entire workforce. Despite the pandemic, domestic travellers spent INR 7201.4 billion on travel in 2020, while international travellers spent INR 890.7 billion (WTTC Economic Impact Report, 2020).

As per the WTTC, the travel and tourism business are accountable for around 10 percentage points of the global gross domestic product. It is estimated that by the year 2025, it will be able to contribute a total of 12 trillion dollars to the growth of the global economy. (Report Published by the McKinsey Global Institute in 2020) It has become one of the industries that is increasing at the pace that is the most rapid all over the globe.

The tourism sector contributed with US$121.9 billion to the GDP in 2020; by 2028, it is anticipated to have increased to US$512 billion. A compound annual growth rate (CAGR) of 21.1% is anticipated for the medical tourism industry between 2020 and 2027. After reaching an estimated value of US$75 billion in Fiscal Year 2020, the travel industry in India is expected to more than double to US$125 billion by Fiscal Year 2027. It is anticipated that by the year 2028, the number of visitors from other countries would reach 30.5 million.

India offers a wide variety of specialised tourist options, including cruises, medical, wellness, sports, MICE, ecotourism, film, rural, and religious tourism, among others. After the pandemic issue is resolved, the government intends to take use of the region's tourism potential by throwing up the doors to visitors from South Asian countries. Free loans are being made available by the government to micro, small, and medium-sized businesses (MSMEs) to assist them in coping with the crisis and reviving the economy overall, particularly the tourist industry (IBEF, 2022).

Key Initiatives in Sustainable tourism by Indian Government

As part of India's federal structure, tourism falls under the State list of the Indian constitution, which means that state governments and union territory administrations are in charge of issues such as land, transportation, hotels, industry, law and order, and the development of tourism infrastructure. The Indian Ministry of Tourism develops and promotes national tourism policies and programmes. The Ministry also coordinates and supplements the efforts of the State Governments/Union Territory Administrations, promotes private investment, strengthens promotional and marketing efforts, and provides skilled labour resources.

State tourism ministries promote India as a tourist destination, while 14 abroad offices promote India as a tourist destination. The India Tourism Development Corporation (ITDC) is a government-owned corporation. It helps build tourist infrastructure. Other tourism-related services offered by ITDC include transportation, duty-free shopping, entertainment, promotional material development, and professional advice.

Government Initiatives

Tourism is one of the only industries that operates in rural regions and vulnerable ecosystems, where cultural heritage protection is as vital as natural heritage. Recognizing the problem of balancing tourist numbers with historical preservation, the Ministry of Tourism is developing regulatory tools to lead the sector towards resource conservation and reducing negative environmental and social consequences.

With the establishment of the Global Sustainable Tourism Council in 2010, the Ministry took on the task of adapting the GSTC criteria for sustainable tourism to the Indian context, while also considering additional criteria, including GSTC. In this global context, the 12th Five Year Plan aggressively integrated sustainable tourism and its different aspects focusing on:

- Under the 'Atithi Devo Bhavah' programme, a major social awareness campaign is being conducted
- Schools, non-governmental organizations, industrial groups, and other organizations are being enlisted to participate in long-term cleaning campaigns in popular tourist sites. All companies and people that participate in this project will be given with appropriate incentives and recognition
- The provision of Central Financial Assistance for the construction of roadside facilities, such as biodegradable toilets, is given the highest priority

A non-profit organization created in 2008 to promote and enforce ecologically responsible and sustainable tourism practices, Ecotourism Society of India (ESOI) and the Ministry of Tourism released the Sustainable Tourism Criteria for India (STCI) in 2016. The criteria were established for Tour Operators, Accommodation and Beaches, and Backwaters, Lakes and Rivers. The Ministry has also developed rules for approving hotel projects and for categorizing and re-categorizing existing hotels.

Hotels must integrate eco-friendly methods such as sewage treatment plants, rainwater harvesting systems, waste management systems, pollution control, non-chlorofluorocarbon (CFC) refrigeration and air conditioning equipment, energy, and water conservation measures from the start of the project. Additionally, tour companies certified by the Ministry of Tourism must sign a vow to fully follow Sustainable Tourism practices, keeping with the finest environmental and heritage preservation requirements. As numerous players in sustainable tourism, such as airlines, lie beyond the Ministry of Tourism's control, the Sustainable Tourism Criteria for India now only encompass tour operators and the hotel industry.

Current Trends in Sustainable Tourism in the Indian Context

Table 1. State Level Key initiatives to promote sustainable tourism

State Name	Policy and Promotional Related Initiatives	Institutional Initiatives	Infrastructure and Capacity Building, New Products
Andhra Pradesh	Partnered with UNWTO to promote sustainable tourism		Coastal Tourism Circuit in Sri Potti Sriramalu, Nellore under Swadesh Darshan Scheme Community based eco-tourism development has been taken up at a cost of INR 2.5 cr at Bairutla and Pacharla in Nallamala forest
Assam			Majuli Sustainable Tourism Development Project' to encourage a carbon free tourism experience in the island
Chhattisgarh	Provisions to promote Eco tourism, rural tourism, adventure tourism and tourism promotion through Special Tourism Areas/Zones		Tribal tourism circuit has been identified for development under Swadesh Darshan Scheme
Gujarat	Homestay policy		Ambardi Lion Safari Park
Himachal Pradesh	HP Eco Tourism Policy 2017		Infrastructure Development Investment Program for Tourism (IDIPT)
Karnataka	Declared "2017 – Year of the Wild" Adventure Tourism Policy and Homestay Policy under preparation	Jungle Lodges & Resorts - Joint Venture of Department of Tourism and Department of Forest Karnataka Eco-Tourism Development Board (KEDB)	
Kerala	Re-branding Kerala as 'Land of Adventure		Introduction of Coracle Ride as part of the Seethathode - Gavi Popular Tourism (SGPT) project 10 forest-centered ecotourism circuit projects
Madhya Pradesh	Madhya Pradesh Forest (Entertainment and Wildlife experience) Rule 2015	Madhya Pradesh Ecotourism Development Board	
Maharashtra	Mahabhraman Scheme		Signed MoU with AirBnB to promote unique experiences Pustakanche Gaon (village of books) Concept
Odisha	Odisha Ecotourism Policy 2013		42 eco-tourism facilities across 23 forest divisions
Sikkim	Sikkim Ecotourism Policy 2011	Sikkim Ecotourism Council	Sikkim Himalayan Home Stay Program
Tamil Nadu		Vehicle Safari at Sathyamangalam Tiger Reserve (STR) Tree-Top Rest Houses Mangrove Ecotourism at Karankadu	
Telangana		Telangana Samskruthika Sarathi	Integrated Development of Eco Tourism Circuit in Mahabubnagar District with an outlay of INR 91.62 cr Tribal Tourism Circuit in Warangal District
Uttarakhand	Draft Uttarakhand Tourism Policy 2017	Uttarakhand Tourism Development Board (UTDB)	

Best Practices with Cases of Global and Indian (Developing and Underdeveloped Nations)

Country Case Studies, Indian State Case Studies, Indian Institute Case Studies

1. **Slovenia**: Slovenia is one of the pioneering countries advancing the cause of sustainable tourism and overall sustainable development with a strategic objective of becoming a green boutique destination for demanding visitors looking for a diversified and active experience, tranquilly and personal well-being. Nearly 13% of Slovenia's GDP comes from tourism, which accounts for 8% of all exports and 37% of all service exports, according to the country's official statistics. To boost the competitiveness of Slovenian attractions, the Slovenian Tourism Board is undertaking the ambitious Slovenia Green programme Tourism officials have been adopting Europe's Travel Indicators (ETIS) and the Global Sustainable Tourism Council (GSTC) standards since 2015 to create a comprehensive certification programme that takes into consideration Slovenia's national features at both the destination and provider levels.

   Slow Tourism is a network that Gorenjska and Gorika, two Slovenian areas, have formed with neighbouring regions in Italy. Eco-accommodations, restaurants, and other small enterprises are included in this category. Meeting locals, learning about traditions like cheese-making and folk music, and engaging in low-impact, "slow" activities like hiking, biking, and rafting are all part of the experience. The Slovenian government has approved the Sustainable Development Strategy for Slovenian Tourism 2017-2021 to create competitive advantages and promote systemic solutions in this field.

2. **Bhutan**: One of the few nations in the world where sustainability is woven into the fabric of society and public policy is Bhutan. According to its Gross National Happiness Index (GNH), the only carbon-negative nation on Earth, sustainable development, environmental protection, cultural preservation, and good governance all play a role. The Bhutanese economy relies heavily on tourism, which accounts for more than 9% of GDP, generates the hardest currency reserves, and provides the most job opportunities in a landlocked mountainous nation. The government has made a strategic decision to focus on "high value, low impact" tourism as a strategy for attracting visitors. Travelers visiting Bhutan must be accompanied by a licenced tour operator who will handle all their travel arrangements while in the country and arrive by Druk Air, which flies from just a few Asian cities. All guests are required to pay a daily tariff, which in low season starts at US$200 and goes up to US$250 in high season. To support the free health care and education system, as well as the construction of tourist infrastructure, this daily tariff includes US$65 in 'sustainable tourism' royalty. Visitors from neighbouring countries, known as "regional tourists," are exempt from this provision (residents of India, Bangladesh, and the Maldives do not need a visa). The fact that Bhutanese tourism continues to flourish despite the high barrier of high costs is evidence of the model's effectiveness. Tourists from the top 20 overseas markets continue to stay in the country for an average of seven nights. It is noteworthy to state the nation is able to generate significant income from a relatively small number of tourists owing to the greater average expenditure per tourist facilitated by policy processes. Faster economic development and greater self-sufficiency are the two main goals of the present government's RISE programme (Rapid Investment in Selected Enterprise). In the tourism industry, the goal is to increase yield per visitor while also doubling the

number of visitors. However, this growth must be evenly distributed across the nation and year-round. (Source: National Council of Bhutan)

3. **Barcelona**: Barcelona's tourist history is rather short. Catalonia's seashore became a popular tourist destination in the 1960s. During the 1992 Olympics in Barcelona, the city's striking and picturesque architecture was brought to the attention of the rest of the globe. Through an extensive urban rehabilitation effort and a redevelopment of the city's waterfront, the city was converted into a cosmopolitan Mediterranean beachside metropolis. As a result of the Olympic Games, Barcelona became a significant European tourist destination. However, the unexpected surge in tourism also drew in the bad aspects, such as drugs, gambling, and prostitution, which resulted in a very hostile local population. Aside from enhancing the quality of tourist experiences by attracting more return visitors and increasing spending, the systemic changes have also fostered a climate of trust and cooperation between the city's residents and the city's government, cementing Barcelona's status as an undisputed icon of modern urban tourism. An annual tourist profile and a citizen impression survey have been in place in Barcelona for many years, and recently upgraded to provide more information on tourist-heavy neighbourhoods. As part of an effort to improve tourism management, the Barcelona Provincial Council and the Barcelona Tourism Consortium are working together to establish a Tourist Activity Observatory86 that uses sensors and cell phone data. Through face-to-face meetings, talks, and debates, as well as proposal collecting trolleys, the city has established a wide variety of tools for people to participate in the city's decision-making process. Rather than creating its own institutions, Barcelona prefers to involve its inhabitants in decision making via open government rather than rely on tourism (Goodwin, 2016).

4. **Kerala**: Kerala is a national leader in community-based tourism strategies that have been implemented effectively. Nature, wellness (ayurvedic), tradition, culture, and food are just a few of the numerous offerings that India has to offer visitors, thanks to its lush coastline and backwaters. As a result of the reduction in agriculture, tourism has played a vital role in counterbalancing it. The state has established an organisation to promote and manage responsible tourism. Since its inception in the 1980s, the Alleppey Tourism Development Cooperative (ATDC) Society has been one of the country's first community-based tourism models that has been functioning effectively for almost three decades. It is worth noting that the Alleppey Tourism Development Cooperative (ATDC) Society is one of the country's first community-based tourism models, having been in operation for over three decades and exhibiting a model of commercial sustainability for local communities. The organisation was established in 1987 under the provisions of the State Cooperatives Act with the primary goal of securing sustainable livelihoods for local populations who were increasingly finding agriculture to be unprofitable at the time. After seeing the success that cooperative models had brought to the state in areas such as agricultural loans and marketing, cotton weaving, and beedi production, the local communities were persuaded to establish India's first tourism cooperative focused on houseboats. This was despite the fact that there had been no precedent for cooperative models in the tourism sector. As a result, the individual boat owners were responsible for the operational elements of their boats, with the ATDC acting as the centralised marketing face for all houseboat owners, allowing for greater scalability. Boat owners were urged to make the necessary modifications to their rice boats to meet the demands of tourists, and finance for these modifications was made available via an agreement with a banking cooperative. Nevertheless, no governmental subsidies were provided in this case, which in part encouraged the locals to guarantee that their business model was a success (George, 2007).

5. **Karnataka**: Karnataka has firmly established itself as India's prime destination for wildlife tourism as a result of its constant conservation efforts over the years. This vast expanse of natural land contains the Nilgiri Biosphere Reserve, which has five national parks and twenty-five wildlife sanctuaries (of which seven are bird sanctuaries), and this vast expanse of natural land offers a wide range of chances for nature-based tourist activities. Jungle Lodges and Resorts (JLR), one of the earliest examples of public-private partnership (PPP) in tourism, was established as a joint venture between the Government of Karnataka and Tiger Tops Jungle Lodges in 1980 with the goal of promoting eco-tourism, wildlife tourism, adventure tourism, and various outdoor activities such as trekking, camping, white water rafting, joy fishing, and other activities that are non-consumptive components of eco-tourism and aid in environmental conservation. Although Tiger Tops withdrew from the partnership in 1987 and sold its stake to the government, the brand continued to flourish and is now considered to be one of the greatest instances of a government-led organisation operating at the efficiency levels of the private sector today. Today, the resort attracts a diverse range of international and domestic visitors, the vast majority of whom are well educated and have a great love for the natural world. Having grown from a single resort in Karnataka to a network of 18 resorts and two heritage hotels, each with its own distinctive characteristics, it has achieved a remarkable level of consistency in positive consumer feedback as well as adherence to policies of local employment and procurement, which contribute to the overall sustainability model. (Economic Survey of Karnataka, 2016-17).
6. **Sikkim**: Because of the natural beauty and distinct indigenous culture of Sikkim, it has been striving to develop tourism with a conservative approach in line with the neighbouring country of Bhutan. This includes keeping an eye on carrying capacity violations and devising mechanisms to diversify tourism in the hinterland while avoiding undue pressure on the fragile mountain ecosystem. Because of Sikkim's advantage of having an enormously diverse landscape combined with a distinct culture, the state government implemented two progressive policy mechanisms that distinguished it from all other states in India as well as its other Himalayan counterparts: first, it became the first state to be declared completely organic, thereby automatically incentivizing the state's agriculture sector; and second, it became the first state to implement an ecotourism policy, which made it stand out among all other states in India as well as its other. The Sikkim Himalayan Home Stay Program promotes ecotourism in rural parts of Sikkim by providing accommodation in Himalayan homes. It is backed by the United Nations Educational, Scientific, and Cultural Organization (UNESCO), the Norwegian Government, and the Principality of Andorra, and is executed by the Ecotourism and Conservation Society of Sikkim (ECOSS), a nongovernmental organisation. It is possible to participate in the Sikkim Himalayan Homestays Program at Dzongu (North Sikkim), Pastanga (East Sikkim), Yuksam (West Sikkim), and Kewzing (South Sikkim) (South Sikkim). A number of new rural ecotourism sites are being developed by ECOSS in East Sikkim, South Sikkim, Ray Mindu, and Lingee Payong, among other locations (East Sikkim).
7. **ITC Hotels**: ITC Hotels, one of the world's greenest hotel groups, has carved out a unique position for itself via its relentless pursuit of new standards in energy efficiency, water efficiency, solid waste recycling, and carbon reduction, among other areas. ITC Hotels, which embodies the ethos of 'Responsible Luxury,' began its journey in establishing green buildings with the ITC Green Centre in 2004. Today, 13 of ITC's hotels are certified LEED Platinum, the highest level of certification awarded by the United States Green Building Council, and the company has received numerous awards and accolades for its environmental efforts and commitment.

Current Trends in Sustainable Tourism in the Indian Context

8. **CGH Earth**: CGH Earth, which is synonymous with experiencing holidays that have a strong emphasis on sustainability, history, wellness, and environment, provides luxury travel experiences across 17 hotels in three Indian states, including Kerala, Rajasthan, and Rajasthan. It has followed the core philosophy of 'experience over ostentation' since 1988, when the company was awarded the management contract for the property on Bangaram Island in Lakshadweep. CGH earth has carved out an exclusive niche for itself in the luxury hotel segment by adopting a highly sensitised value system that requires every property to adhere strictly to the local environment and culture.

For example, the Spice Hamlet in Thekkady, in the southern Indian state of Kerala, is constructed in the style of an ancient mountain village, with thatched roofs made of elephant grass and cottages constructed using traditional methods. The Coconut Lagoon was constructed using materials salvaged from 150-year-old, demolished buildings, while the Marari Beach Resort is comprised of 16 cottages with coconut palm thatched-roofs, which are organised in the style of an ancient fishing hamlet on the island of Bali. Instead of being a plain vanilla hotel firm, the organisation has turned itself into one of the leading responsible tourist operators, as seen by the change in its name from the Casino Group of Hotels (CGH) to the Clean, Green and Healthy Organization (CGO) (CGH). A holistic tourist ecosystem that extends 'beyond the property' is being established at CGH Earth, which is one of the greatest instances of this. Because of the success of its yoga and Ayurveda-based health products throughout the world, the firm is hoping to grow into other areas of India as well as other parts of the world.

Best Practices for Sustainable Tourism and Need

- According to the Green Hotel Association (2008), green hotels, also called environmentally friendly hotels, save water and energy, use environmentally friendly products, and reduce emissions and waste disposals to protect the natural environment while reducing operational costs. Green hotels are eco-friendly. Green hotel operations help safeguard the environment, but consumers don't want to forgo service quality or comfort.
- Sustainable tourism considers tourists, industry, environment, and host communities. We want sustainable tourism. Sustainable tourism should optimize natural resource utilization while sustaining ecological processes and protecting biodiversity. Promote intercultural understanding and tolerance by preserving the host community's cultural and traditional values. Ensure long-term economic sustainability, give socioeconomic advantages to all stakeholders, and provide sustainable employment, income, and social services to host communities (WTO & UNEP, 2005). Promoting ecotourism usually involves highlighting its contribution to sustainable tourism. Sustainability is "filling current visitor and host community needs while protecting and expanding future prospects." Meeting economic, social, and aesthetic needs while protecting cultural integrity, ecological processes, biological diversity, and life support systems will be challenging. Best Practices for sustainability include the following:
    1. Nila Foundation started as a non-profit in 2004. TBY promotes "responsible tourism" in Kerala, India. TBY pioneered sustainable tourist excursions along Nila in Kerala, India. The river that fed Kerala's ancient civilisation is now restoring its lost wonders. TBY's South African market grew rapidly in 2011. TBY has promoted Sri Lanka since 2012. TBY uses tourism to solve development challenges because of its local roots. TBY helps the community's people, culture, heritage, lifestyle, livelihood, and future.

2. It is important to note that the Global Sustainable Tourism Council's Criteria are the minimal requirements for achieving social, environmental, cultural and economic sustainability. The Criteria are meant to be tailored to local circumstances and reinforced by additional criteria for the particular place and activity.
3. Economic viability: To secure the long-term success and advantages of tourist locations and businesses.
4. Maximize the contribution of tourism to the host destination's economic development, particularly the amount of tourist expenditure kept locally.
5. Employment quality and social equity: Workforce development, wages, benefits, and accessibility for everyone without regard to gender, handicap, or other factors.
6. Visitor fulfilment: Providing a safe, comfortable, and gratifying experience for all guests, regardless of gender, handicap, or other factors.
7. Community wellbeing: The quality of life in local communities is to be maintained and strengthened by ensuring access to resources, facilities, and life support systems while preventing social deterioration and exploitation.
8. Cultural richness, integration and mutual understanding: Respect and strengthen the historic history, unique culture, customs, and originality of host communities. Respect for and understanding of cultural diversity is a cornerstone of sustainable development.
9. Physical integrity: To preserve and improve the quality of IHR, both rural and distant, and to prevent environmental damage.
10. Mountain biological diversity: In terms of aesthetic effects, much research has focused on rural landscapes and how they influence and are influenced by tourism. The integrity and aesthetic quality of constructed and natural landscapes in rural and urban regions should be equally valued.
11. Resource efficiency: Resources are finite and non-renewable in tourist development and operation.
12. Environmental purity: Minimize contamination of air, water, and land by tourist businesses and guests.

Status of Sustainable Tourism for Developing and Developing Countries

The world and local economies rely heavily on the ever-expanding business of tourism. It is vital to the country's economic, social, and cultural well-being, and it offers real prospects for long-term progress. Urban and rural areas alike are seeing an increase in demand for environmentally friendly vacations, but many nations have struggled to publicise this trend. Locals and tourists' perceptions of tourism destinations in cities and rural regions alike have been altered significantly by digital communication platforms such as social media and others (Langemeyer et al., 2018; Magno & Cassia, 2018). The globalisation of rural vitality is being fuelled by the urbanisation of rural areas (Long et al., 2019).

There are a variety of facets to rural tourism, including the economy, the community, and the natural environment. It has an impact on the environment and the economy because of its ties to people, space, and things (Nepal, 2007; Wang et al., 2016; Xia et al., 2011). It is possible that village tourism may help the local economy, provide jobs, and improve people's lives. Overburdening infrastructure and diminishing local resources are some of the drawbacks (Gao & Zhang, 2019; Liu et al., 2020; Torres & Momsen, 2005). Understanding the impact of tourism on village sustainability is critical.

In many nations, rural areas serve as a storehouse of natural and historical significance, and this serves as a special selling feature for countryside holidays (Lane, 1994) Research in rural tourism focuses on the role and justification of the joint management department in the tourism sector. Some rural tourism studies focus on the impact of over tourism on the local environment and the level of local dissatisfaction (Diaz-Parra & Jover, 2020; Fletcher, 2019; Liu et al., 2019). Researchers are increasingly concentrating on how tourism earnings help relieve poverty and generate employment in rural areas of the country (Carius & Job, 2019; Higgins-Desbiolles et al., 2019).

Development is gradual in rural areas of developing countries, according to the author's discussion of World Heritage Sites in impoverished nations. Communities and the environment are impacted by tourism. In many developing nations, large-scale tourism-related ventures are either operated by foreign investors or a hegemonic alliance between international firms and corrupt local governments (Franceschini, 2020; Jeyacheya & Hampton, 2020).

Factors Affecting Sustainability for Indian Tourists

Tourism literature focuses on foreign guests, not domestic. US tourists drive business optimism. Knowing how domestic tourists buy is key. It helps identify feasible market categories and establish tourism segmentation strategies. With this knowledge, local governments and tourism marketing groups may make better decisions. According to India Tourism Statistics, Government of India (2018), domestic tourist visits in India grew by 13.1% annually from 1991 to 2017 compared to 8.6% for foreign visitors. Microstudies are used to research tourism in the US, AU, EA, and EU. First research to examine Indian domestic tourism expenditure in South Asia.

Ahmad et al. (2020) found "no publications by experts located exclusively in India," indicating a dearth of tourism study in India. Indian Monthly per-capita consumer spending, a proxy for family income, boosts Indian visitor spending. Families use their growing riches for status, partner recruiting and retention, and parenting.

Tourist spending rises with affluence. Per-capita monthly consumption may be endogenous. Female-headed households in India spend less, altering resource ownership policies. India should boost woman-owned resources. Tourism and women's groups benefit. Developing countries should encourage female property ownership to empower women. Due to poorer tourist packages, regular wage employees spend less on tourism in India than self-employed farmers.

Indian tourism should not affect the environment. India's tourism might grow with a greener atmosphere. If India's tourism sector emphasises green natural areas, it may attract more income earners. Most families vacation in hotels near nature. This form of dwelling gives them a natural view from the balcony and connects them to nature. Nature can revive travellers. Nature improves travellers' physical, mental, and spiritual wellness (Louv, 2008).

Key Issues and Challenges

Although sustainable tourism promotes itself as a cure for reducing the negative consequences of tourist activities without sacrificing on the economic benefits, its mainstream acceptance has faced certain difficulties, particularly in a developing tourism economy such as India.

1. **Change in Consumer Outlines:** Inbound tourism comes from a more mature market that favours sustainable tourism products, whereas the domestic tourist industry is relatively young and dominated by mass tourism activities and attractions. Changing the domestic visitor's mindset towards sustainable tourism items is a major challenge for sustainable tourism in India.
2. **Low Adoption of Sustainable Practices**: The tourism industry may benefit from standards and certification systems that assist it embrace sustainable practises, especially when it comes to water, electricity, and waste management. The Ministry of Tourism created Sustainability Tourism Criteria for India (STCI), which adapts GSTC to the Indian context. Acceptance of these ideas remains minimal, partly due to expensive certification costs in certain cases.
3. **Price Barriers:** Many sustainable tourism goods are priced pricier than their conventional equivalents because of the greater input and localization expenses required. The upshot is that a large number of visitors, particularly those from the United States, are forced to settle with mass tourism-based lifestyles, even if they have a preference for sustainable tourism goods.
4. **Capacity Creation in Rural Areas:** One aspect is providing the necessary tourist infrastructure; the other is motivating people, especially in rural areas, to participate in tourism by developing skills in hospitality and commercial operations. Energizing a rural population with poor literacy and limited access to basic essentials may be tough.
5. **Informed Policy Frameworks:** Policies must be based on evidence if they are to be readily accepted and executed by the industry, hence data collection, analysis, and monitoring are essential. Data collecting efforts must be maintained and collaborative, with the use of existing statistical frameworks and indicators depending on requirements. The acquired data must also be utilised to guide actual tourist management in practise, which calls for further efforts.

Sustainable Tourism Issues in India

In India, tourism is built on biodiversity, forests, rivers, and culture and legacy. The problems in this sector include keeping them in their original form, making them accessible to domestic and international tourists, and protecting local communities' economic interests and history.

- India's tourism hotspots need talent development and community participation. Sustainable tourism requires all-levels community engagement
- The Sustainable Tourism Criteria for India calls for metrics to standardise hotels and other service providers' environmental responsibility. It places a low priority on developing skills in subsectors and the host community
- Without executive processes to implement policies, skill acquisition suffers. Lower-level stakeholders lack incentives to use sustainable practises. Sustainable practises need strong policy instruments and regulatory mechanisms, which India lacks (Sustainable Tourism Index, 2018)
- Terrorism and brutality against women also deter visitors from visiting India. When crimes occur in tourist locations, foreign visitors decrease. It affects India's worldwide security rating.
- Women, Peace and Security Index ranked India 131st out of 153 nations in 2017 and 137th out of 162 in 2018 (Institute for Economics and Peace, 2018). Therefore, India's host community and tourist sector require a sustainable policy framework (Sustainable Tourism Index, 2018).
- New tourism goods like education tourism (art, theatre, archaeology, history PhD students) and rural tourism provide potential.

SOLUTIONS AND RECOMMENDATIONS

The foregoing debate on sustainability concerns in the hotel business shows that customers are still not ready to adopt green goods and services. This challenge may be overcome by increasing consumer knowledge of green goods and services, making green products and services more widely available, and providing value for money. These technologies may help firms and hotels keep clients for longer. Consumer lifestyles are changing which demand creative items. They are aware that the environment is deteriorating, therefore corporations and hotels are developing green goods and services, but consumers are not ready to embrace them. Before moving further, it is critical to establish the consumer's wants and desires. It is advised that hoteliers offer green services without compromising consumer satisfaction; they should know their customers' preferences when booking hotels and deliver the finest green services for their money.

India's Sustainable Tourism Policies and its Implication

- The National Tourist Policy 2021 is a comprehensive plan for expanding the tourist business responsibly and sustainably. The policy is structured on ten guiding principles, five national missions, and five institutional missions, all supported by a governance and institutional framework
- The policy aims to strengthen the conditions for tourism development in the country, support tourism-related businesses, and expand tourism subsectors
- The national tourism plan focuses on sustainable and green tourism and making the sector more user-friendly for operators and tourists
- Sustainable tourism should encourage environmental, biodiversity, economic, socio-cultural, certification, IEC, capacity building, and governance
- After COVID-19, the government has moved its focus to the tourist sector's resilience, sustainability, and interconnection
- Shrestha Ek Bharat is a key policy to connect and comprehend people from various States/UT. It strives to develop a continuous and organized cultural connection in tourism, traditions and music, food, sports, best practices, and so forth
- The Policy aims to mainstream sustainability into the tourism sector, making it more energy-efficient and climate-sound, consuming less water, reducing waste, conserving biodiversity, cultural heritage, and traditional values, supporting intercultural understanding and tolerance, generating local income, and integrating local communities to improve livelihoods and reduce poverty. Ecotourism benefits locals and the environment (National Tourism Policy, 2021)
- Private and public bodies involved in tourism in India ought to center their attention on the reasons why domestic and international tourists visit India in the related travel subfields of ecotourism, nature-based tourism, protected area tourism, backpacker tourism, volunteer tourism, cultural tourism, and rural tourism (Mody, 2015)

FUTURE RESEARCH

Numerous new destinations have developed, battling fiercely for more footfalls, and many companies inside destinations are also competing. Congestion, environmental quality, and socio-cultural fabric are all factors that might negatively impact a destination's competitive edge. The goal is to coordinate investments and innovations such that they enhance rather than detract from competitive advantage. For long-term destination success and, consequently, a steady flow of resources, the competitive advantage must be maintained or increased over time.

Sustainable tourism needs collaboration between host communities, visitors, and the corporate and governmental sectors. The public sector must establish planning, regulation, and monitoring procedures that meet the demands of the specialized market and the tourist development strategy. The business sector is especially concerned in enhancing the destination's competitiveness and ensuring that the rules of the game are appropriately defined and applied.

REFERENCES

Ahmad, N., Menegaki, A. N., & Al-Muharrami, S. (2020). Systematic literature review of tourism growth nexus: An overview of the literature and a content analysis of 100 most influential papers. *Journal of Economic Surveys, 34*(5), 1068–1110. doi:10.1111/joes.12386

Bramwell, B., & Lane, B. (1993). Sustainable tourism: An evolving global approach. *Journal of Sustainable Tourism, 1*(1), 1–5. doi:10.1080/09669589309450696

Buckley, R. (2012). Sustainable tourism: Research and reality. *Annals of Tourism Research, 39*(2), 528–546. doi:10.1016/j.annals.2012.02.003

Carius, F., & Job, H. (2019). Community involvement and tourism revenue sharing as contributing factors to the UN sustainable development goals in jozani-chwaka bay national park and biosphere reserve, zanzibar. *Journal of Sustainable Tourism, 27*(6), 826–846. doi:10.1080/09669582.2018.1560457

Diaz-Parra, I., & Jover, J. (2020). Overtourism, place alienation and the right to the city: Insights from the historic centre of seville, Spain. *Journal of Sustainable Tourism, 29*(2–3), 158–175.

Fletcher, R. (2019). Ecotourism after nature: Anthropocene tourism as a new capitalist "fix". *Journal of Sustainable Tourism, 27*(4), 522–535. doi:10.1080/09669582.2018.1471084

Franceschini, I. (2020). As far apart as earth and sky: A survey of Chinese and Cambodian construction workers in sihanoukville. *Critical Asian Studies, 52*(4), 1–18. doi:10.1080/14672715.2020.1804961

Gao, J., & Zhang, L. (2019). Exploring the dynamic linkages between tourism growth and environmental pollution: New evidence from the Mediterranean countries. *Current Issues in Tourism, 24*(1), 49–65. doi:10.1080/13683500.2019.1688767

George, B. P. (2007). Alleppey Tourism Development Cooperative: The Case of Network Advantage. *The Innovation Journal.*

Goodwin, H. (2016). Managing Tourism in Barcelona. *Progress in Responsible Tourism*, 28-48.

Götz, K., Loose, W., Schmied, M., & Schubert, S. (2002). *Mobility Styles in Leisure Time: Reducing the environmental impacts of leisure and tourism travel.* Freiburg, Germany: Oko-Institut eV.

Higgins-Desbiolles, F., Carnicelli, S., Krolikowski, C., Wijesinghe, G., & Boluk, K. (2019). Degrowing tourism: Rethinking tourism. *Journal of Sustainable Tourism, 27*(12), 1926–1944. doi:10.1080/09669 582.2019.1601732

Initiative, T. O. (2003). *Sustainable Tourism: The Tour Operators' Contribution.* TOI.

Jeyacheya, J., & Hampton, M. P. (2020). Wishful thinking or wise policy? Theorising tourism-led inclusive growth: Supply chains and host communities. *World Development, 131,* 104960. doi:10.1016/j.worlddev.2020.104960

Lane, B. (1994). Sustainable rural tourism strategies: A tool for development and conservation. *Journal of Sustainable Tourism, 2*(1–2), 102–111. doi:10.1080/09669589409510687

Langemeyer, J., Calcagni, F., & Baró, F. (2018). Mapping the intangible: Using geolocated social media data to examine landscape aesthetics. *Land Use Policy, 77,* 542–552. doi:10.1016/j.landusepol.2018.05.049

Long, H., Zhang, Y., & Tu, S. (2019). Rural vitalization in China: A perspective of land consolidation. *Journal of Geographical Sciences, 29*(4), 517–530. doi:10.100711442-019-1599-9

Louv, R. (2008). *Last child in the woods: Saving our children from nature-deficit disorder.* Algonquin Books.

Magno, F., & Cassia, F. (2018). The impact of social media influencers in tourism. *Anatolia, 29*(2), 288–290. doi:10.1080/13032917.2018.1476981

Mihalic, T. (2016, January 16). Sustainable-responsible tourism discourse e Towards 'responsustable' tourism. *Journal of Cleaner Production, 111*(Part B), 461-470. doi:10.1016/j.jclepro.2014.12.062

Mody, Day, J., Sydnor, S., Jaffe, W., & Lehto, X. (2014). The different shades of responsibility: Examining domestic and international travelers' motivations for responsible tourism in India. *Tourism Management Perspectives, 12,* 113–124. doi:10.1016/j.tmp.2014.09.008

Nepal, S. K. (2007). Tourism and rural settlements Nepal's Annapurna region. *Annals of Tourism Research, 34*(4), 855–875. doi:10.1016/j.annals.2007.03.012

OECD. (2002). *Household Tourism Travel: Trends, Environmental Impacts and Policy Response.* Retrieved on April 22, 2022, from: https://www.oecd.org/

Ottman, J. A. (2011). *The New Rules of Green marketing: Strategies, Tools, and Inspiration for Sustainable Branding* (1st ed.). Routledge., doi:10.4324/9781351278683

Pérez, V., Guerrero, F., González, M., Pérez, F., & Caballero, R.Pérez at al. (2013). Composite indicator for the assessment of sustainability: The case of Cuban nature-based tourism destinations. *Ecological Indicators, 29,* 316–324. doi:10.1016/j.ecolind.2012.12.027

Sancho, A., García, G., Pedro, A., & Yagüe, R. M. (2002). *Sustainability audit in tourist destinations.*

Singh, G. (2013). A study of evolution and practice of green marketing by various companies in India. *International Journal of Management and Social Sciences Research, 2*, 49–56.

Torres, R., & Momsen, J. (2005). Planned tourism development in Quintana Roo, Mexico: Engine for regional development or prescription for inequitable growth? *Current Issues in Tourism, 8*(4), 259–285. doi:10.1080/13683500508668218

UNEP. (2005). Making tourism more sustainable. In *A guide for policy makers*. UNEP and WTO.

UNWTO. (2013). Sustainable Tourism for Development. Madrid: World Tourism Organization.

Upham, P. (2001). A comparison of sustainability theory with UK and European airports policy and practice. *Journal of Environmental Management, 63*(3), 237–248. doi:10.1006/jema.2001.0469 PMID:11775497

Visit. (2005). *The Tourism Market: Potential Demand for Products*. Retrieved on September 22, 2021, from: http://www.your-visit.info/brochure/en/070.htm#nachfrage

Wang, L., & Yotsumoto, Y. (2019). Conflict in tourism development in rural China. *Tourism Management, 70*, 188–200. doi:10.1016/j.tourman.2018.08.012

World Tourism Organization. (2020b). *International tourism growth continues to outpace the global economy*. UNWTO. Retrieved on July 6, 2022, from: https://www.unwto.org/international-tourism-growth-continues-to-outpace-the-economy

World Travel and Tourism Council. (2007). *United States: The 2007 travel & tourism economic research*. Retrieved on May 19, 2021, from: http://www.wttc.travel/bin/pdf/original_pdf_file/1unitedstates.pdf

Xia, J. C., Zeephongsekul, P., & Packer, D. (2011). Spatial and temporal modelling of tourist movements using Semi-Markov processes. *Tourism Management, 32*(4), 844–851. doi:10.1016/j.tourman.2010.07.009

Chapter 19
Evaluation of the Disaster Tourism Potential of Countries

Zekiye Göktekin
https://orcid.org/0000-0003-1666-6109
Faculty of Health Sciences, Gümüşhane University, Turkey

Ahmet Bahadır Şimşek
https://orcid.org/0000-0002-7276-2376
Faculty of Health Sciences, Gümüşhane University, Turkey

ABSTRACT

Disasters are tragic events that cause losses. The curiosity of people to feel sadness and pain motivates disaster tourism. Each disaster region has the potential for disaster tourism, which offers various benefits. This chapter covers the evaluation of the disaster tourism potential of countries with the fuzzy-TOPSIS method. The criteria affecting the disaster tourism potential as the number of dead, injured, affected, and homeless people were weighted according to the evaluations of the decision-makers. Disasters that occurred worldwide between 1980-2022 were analyzed with the criteria weights based on the countries where they occurred. Decision-makers mostly evaluated the number of deaths and homeless as more effective in affecting the desire to visit a disaster area and the attractiveness of the region. Among 90 countries, it has been determined that Sri Lanka and the Russian Federation are the two countries with the highest disaster tourism potential as to the number of losses/disasters, while Ethiopia is the country with the lowest disaster tourism potential.

INTRODUCTION

Disasters are tragic events that cause the loss of life and property. Landmarks such as monuments, museums, and disaster heritage sites symbolizing tragedies attract tourists (Lin et al., 2021). Chernobyl, Hiroshima, and Pompeii are the most popular disaster destinations. Places like these pave the way for visitors to empathize with the victims and feel what has happened. The curiosity of people to feel sadness and pain motivates disaster tourism. In addition, the fact that the media gives a global character by

DOI: 10.4018/978-1-6684-4645-4.ch019

announcing disasters to large masses triggers the growth of disaster tourism (Sharpley & Wright, 2018). Thus, many ordinary places have become attractive destinations after the disaster (Shondell Miller, 2008). In this context, each disaster region has the potential for disaster tourism, which offers various benefits.

This chapter examines the benefits that prompt countries to consider the tourism potential of disasters in two dimensions: i) Economic, ii) Risk reduction. Disasters occur as undesirable events, but the tourism activity after it creates a positive effect. This situation is considered the "blessing in disguise" effect and attracts the attention of many researchers (Biran et al., 2014; Zhang et al., 2009). Although disaster tourism is the subject of ethical debates since it is fed with pain (Rucinska & Lechowicz, 2014), it is seen that it has become a tourism sector with a serious economic size under "Dark Tourism" (Caisarina et al., 2021; Lin et al., 2018). On the other hand, disaster tourism makes significant contributions to the objectives of disaster management, such as increasing resilience and reducing risk (Fountain & Cradock-Henry, 2020; Lin et al., 2021).

The people living in a disaster region organize their entire lives to increase their resilience against the negative effects of disasters. By adopting this living environment in which they were born, new generations grow up with higher disaster resistance compared to their peers in different geographies. Additionally, disaster tourism can be implemented as a strategy to improve local livelihoods and build community resilience (Liu-Lastres et al., 2020). Additionally, disaster destinations play the role of "Disaster Storytelling" to visitors (Nagamatsu et al., 2021). It encompasses the activities of drawing, painting, singing, drama, or photography as well as verbal or written narratives as a means of conveying lessons learned from a disaster, sharing emotions, and developing empathy for others (Tanaka et al., 2021).

All kinds of touristic actions associated with the disaster, such as tours, entertainment, dramas, and museums, tell visitors about the disaster. In this context, visitors are informed about the causes, negligence, and consequences of the disaster and become more conscious individuals than before the visit. If the issue is handled in terms of tourism organizers, another stakeholder, it should be emphasized that the disaster tourism potential of a region can change with its exposure to disaster (Huang et al., 2022).

Ide (2009) categorizes disaster areas in terms of tourism into four types. Type A: The region was a tourist destination before the disaster and continues after. Type B: The region became a tourist destination after the disaster. Type C: The region was a tourist destination before the disaster and could not continue after. Type D: The region was not a tourist destination before the disaster. It became a touristic center after the disaster but could not maintain its status. This classification reminds the variability of disaster tourism destinations, that new destinations can be created at any time and existing destinations may disappear.

It is home truth that a tourist's interest in a disaster destination is proportional to the magnitude of the losses caused by the disaster. This can be attributed to the 3-factor theory.

The 3-factor theory is an effective evaluation method for tourist satisfaction (Deng, 2007; Lin et al., 2021). The three factors of the theory can be explained as follows. Basic factor attributes will lead to dissatisfaction when they fail to meet tourist needs, but these attributes will not cause tourist satisfaction even if they fully meet their needs. Performance factor attributes will lead to satisfaction when they meet tourist needs, but dissatisfaction when they fail to meet those needs. Excitement factor attributes will lead to satisfaction when they meet tourist needs, but these attributes will not cause tourist dissatisfaction even if they do not fully meet tourist needs.

While there is an opportunity to improve by intervening in the basic and performance factor attributes within the framework of disaster tourism, it is not possible to interfere with the excitement factor attributes. The excitement factor attributes are all about the losses caused by the disaster. At this point, the size of the losses plays an important role in the satisfaction of the tourists. If the disaster tourism potential of countries is to be evaluated effectively, the only thing that cannot be intervened, disaster losses, should be focused on.

Evaluation of countries in terms of disaster tourism potential is the aim of this chapter.

The main motivation of the study can be explained as follows. Just as countries can benefit from familiar tourism activities such as sun-sand tourism, ski tourism, and surfing tourism, as much as possible, they also have the right to benefit from tourism activities that are emergent after disasters, as much as possible. If it is assumed that the desire of a tourist who is interested in disaster tourism to visit a disaster destination is directly proportional to the number of injuries and loss of life caused by the disaster, the attractiveness of countries in terms of disaster tourism increases in proportion to disaster-related losses.

Just as Mediterranean countries are centers of sun-sand tourism, countries that have suffered great losses in disasters are centers of disaster tourism. With this understanding, the authors evaluated the disaster tourism potential of countries by focusing on disaster-related losses. This chapter specifically evaluates countries in terms of pure disaster tourism potential, the contribution of the findings to disaster tourism stakeholders (policymakers, tourism organizers, and tourists) can be highlighted as follows. i) It promotes policymakers to discover the disaster tourism potential of the country and to question how they can benefit from this potential. It also motivates the development of policies and regulations to increase the level of benefit from disaster tourism. ii) It boosts tourism organizers to inspect their destination portfolios and to determine the countries they will focus on for the new destination that they have not included in their operations before. iii) Lists the attractive countries for tourists in terms of disaster tourism.

In this manner, it allows them to organize their visit plans and routes in detail in a way that will increase their satisfaction. In addition to its contributions to disaster tourism stakeholders, as far as the authors' knowledge, it is the first study to evaluate the disaster tourism potential of countries based on disaster losses. In this respect, it can be claimed that it contributed to the limited disaster tourism literature in terms of its approach to the subject and broadened the vision of the relevant researchers.

The remainder of the study is organized as follows. Research on the assessment of disaster potential is discussed in Section 2. The methodology of the research is presented in Section 3. The implementation and findings are presented in Section 4. Section 5 contains conclusions and future directions.

BACKGROUND

This section examines studies on disaster tourism and the evaluation of tourism potential. Existing research is divided into the evaluation of region-specific tourism potential and comparison of tourism potential of many regions. Some of the studies in the first group can be summarized as follows. Ebrahim and Ganguli (2017) investigated Bahrain's medical tourism potential to determine its contribution to the economy and roadmap for public and private sector players. In the study, which makes use of quantitative analysis techniques, it is emphasized that Bahrain has the potential to gain competitiveness in the medical tourism sector and what can be done to make the most of this potential.

Mileva (2018) made a preliminary assessment of the dark tourism potential in Bulgaria. In the research, first, the inventory and classification of the main touristic places for dark tourism were made, and then the applicability of dark tourism was discussed with the stakeholders. It has been revealed that dark tourism in Bulgaria is a type of tourism that is relatively unknown, unexplored, difficult to distinguish, and intertwined with other types of tourism. Mikaeili and Aytuğ (2019) researched the cultural tourism potential of the Jolfa Region on the northern border of Iran. He emphasized that to develop cultural tourism in Iran, cultural activities specific to Iran such as sea, religious tourism, and traditional music festivals should be developed.

The tourism potential comparison-oriented studies in the second group are as follows. Puška et al. (2021) aimed to determine the areas to be supported by evaluating the rural areas in Bosnia-Herzegovina's Brčko Region in terms of tourism potential. A total of six rural areas were analyzed using multi-criteria decision-making techniques with the help of 3 experts. While the criterion weights were determined by the Full Consistency Method (FUCOM), the analysis was carried out with the fuzzy Measurement Alternatives and Ranking according to the COmpromise Solution (MARCOS) method.

It has been determined that the Bijela settlement has the highest rural tourism potential. Thus, suggestions were made to policymakers to direct the limited economic resource to the right region. Hoang et al. (2018) evaluated the tourism potential of Vietnam's Central Highlands with a multi-criteria approach. In the study, geographic information systems were used to measure the distances between the fields. Criterion weights were determined by Analytical Hierarchy Process (AHP) and criteria were determined by Principal Component Analysis (PCA). In the study, a total of 99 areas with environmental tourism and 45 cultural tourism potential were determined. In addition, it was emphasized that improving the tourism infrastructure, service quality, connections with other touristic places, and diversifying tourism products are necessary to increase the attractiveness of regional destinations.

Nouri et al. (2008) compared the strategic and ecological areas located on the northern coastline of the Persian Gulf in the south of Iran in terms of tourism potential. Regions were evaluated by a simple scoring method with three main and four sub-criteria. It has been determined that the Kangan region has potential for the tourism sector. The Naiband Gulf took first place with 20 points, Asalouyeh with 18 points, and the Taheri and Kangan Ports took last place with 16 and 15 points, respectively. The necessity of ecotourism quality improvement and environmental management planning for the northern coastline of the Persian Gulf was emphasized.

Ranjan (2016) evaluated the tourism potential of the states for the effective use of limited resources within the framework of India's economy plans. An integrated visual decision aid model of preference ranking organization method for enrichment evaluation (PROMETHEE) and geometrical analysis for interactive aid (GAIA), which are multi-criteria decision-making techniques, were used in the analysis. A total of 29 states were evaluated with 11 criteria. Jammu and Kashmir, and Jharkhand were determined as the states with the best and worst tourism potential, respectively.

In the studies examined in general, it is aimed either to reveal the tourism potential of a region or to evaluate the tourism potential of more than one region for the effective use of limited economic resources. Apart from case studies, various methodological approaches are presented in the literature for the evaluation of tourism potential (Ramírez-Guerrero et al., 2021; Yan et al., 2017; Zhang et al., 2021). Existing studies on disaster tourism have mostly focused on the effects of disasters on tourism, tourists' intention to visit the disaster site, and tourism disaster management. Many studies are emphasizing that disasters have a significant negative impact on tourism in the region and that despite large expenditures, tourism has a very difficult time recovering (Faulkner, 2001; Wang, 2009; Huan, Beaman, & Shelby, 2004; Huang & Min, 2002; Mao, Ding, & Lee, 2010).

Regarding this issue, which the tourism sector suffers from, some researchers have stated that sector stakeholders can cope with the negative effects of disasters by preparing for disasters, by constantly assessing tourism disaster risks and offered various suggestions for this (Orchiston, 2012; Huang, Tseng, & Petrick, 2008; Becken & Hughey, 2013; Mair, Ritchie, & Walters, 2016; Xu & Grunewald, 2009). Tsai & Chen (2010, 2011) focused on the disaster risk assessment of Taiwan's tourism industry for possible devastating earthquakes and developed an earthquake disaster assessment model.

Faulkner and Vikulov (2001), and Faulkner (2001) focused on tourism disaster management plans of tourism destinations and stated that if good planning is done, the difficulties that disasters will bring can be overcome and developed a model for tourism disaster management. Ritchie (2008, 2004) focused on the importance of understanding crises and disasters for the tourism industry, and called for a more comprehensive, integrative, strategic, and proactive approach to tourism disaster management, emphasizing the need for cooperation with internal and external stakeholders in this direction.

Hystad and Keller (2008) conducted a follow-up study to investigate what a local tourism industry experienced in the long term after a major forest fire disaster, what recovery strategies were initiated, the effects that remained, and how tourism disaster management changed. and proposed a framework to increase tourism disaster management at the destination level. In addition, authors encounter studies to determine the target audience and to reach them, to examine the tourists' intention to visit disaster-related regions and the factors affecting these intentions (Li, Wen, & ng, 2018; Huan, Beaman & Shelby, 2004; Wright & Sharpley, 2018; Chew & Jahari, 2014; Rittichainuwat & Chakraborty, 2009). There are different findings regarding tourists' intentions to visit destinations they deem risky. It can be mentioned both positive and negative findings.

Huan, Beaman, and Shelby (2004) found that disasters negatively affect the image of tourism destinations as they increased risk perception. Similarly, Çetinsöz and Ege (2013) stated in their study that perceived risk is a critical antecedent of the intention to revisit a destination. Chew and Jahari (2014) examined the relationship between the perceived risk of destination and the intention to revisit there after the 2011 Japan Fukushima Disaster and found that the perceived physical risk directly negatively affects the intention to revisit.

However, despite being affected by the disaster, it was concluded that the intention to revisit the destination is relatively high when high risk is not perceived for the destination. Wright and Sharpley (2018) investigated the perceptions and reactions of the residents towards the emerge of disaster tourism after the earthquake that occurred in L'Aquila, Italy in 2009, and revealed that the public's perceptions of disaster tourism changed from negative to positive over time.

METHODOLOGY

The approach adopted to evaluate countries in terms of disaster potential consists of three main stages (see Figure 1).

In the first stage, data on disaster losses of countries were obtained from the Emergency Events Database (EM-DAT). EM-DAT allows users to data on disaster losses by filtering based on time, disaster class, and region. However, there is no filtering option for disaster losses. In the second stage, disasters with data in each criterion are filtered and decision-makers who will evaluate the attractiveness of disasters in terms of the losses they cause are determined. Since it would not be feasible and economical for each decision-maker to evaluate the attractiveness of hundreds of disaster records individually, an evaluation template is taken from each decision-maker for each criterion.

Figure 1. Stages of methodology

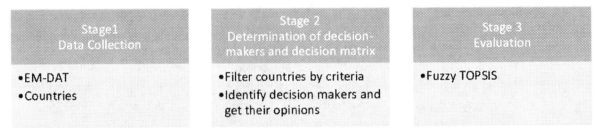

(Alt Text is not required, screen readers can read this figure.)

In the third stage, disaster losses of countries are converted into linguistic expressions using templates taken from decision-makers. Thus, it is determined how interesting each disaster is for each decision-maker in each criterion. Each country is represented by a single record by averaging the records of the same country. Multi-criteria decision-making techniques are used to make the final evaluation of the countries.

Multi-criteria decision-making (MCDM) literature offers effective solutions to different decision environments where many alternatives should be evaluated by considering many criteria. In an MCDM problem, in the presence of m alternatives ($A_1, A_2, ..., A_m | i=1,2,...,m$) and n criteria ($C_1, C_2, ..., C_n | j=1,2,...,n$), the performance of the A_i in the C_j is shown as x_{ij}. $w_j \in W = \{w_1,...,w_n\}$ is the importance of criteria C_j. By default, MCDM techniques assume that the decision matrix and weights are known exactly and that there is a single decision-maker. There are also extensions of the techniques that are compatible with different decision environments such as uncertain data, and group decision-making.

MCDM techniques attempt to simulate the decision maker's evaluation environment.

In some conditions, the decision-maker may have difficulty expressing x_{ij} and C_j with numbers. In such cases, the decision-maker may refer to linguistic expressions to express himself more easily. In some cases, alternatives may need to be evaluated by multiple decision-makers with different expertise or perspectives. In such cases, the opinions of the decision-makers should be taken into consideration. Linguistic expressions and group decision-making are widely used in research on tourism destinations (Dadashpour Moghaddam et al., 2022; Genç & Filipe, 2016; Ghasemi et al., 2021; Huang & Peng, 2012; Luštický & Bína, 2014).

In this study, the extension of the technique for order performance by similarity to ideal solution (TOPSIS), which is a well-known MCDM technique, which can handle group decision-making and linguistic expressions proposed by Chen (2000), is adopted. Developed by Hwang and Yoon (1981), TOPSIS is based on obtaining positive and negative ideal solutions from the decision matrix and calculating the relative distance of each alternative from the ideal solution. It ranks the alternatives in descending order of their relative closeness to the ideal solution. The TOPSIS is frequently preferred because it does not contain complex mathematical operations and its results are easily explained and interpreted.

Fuzzy-TOPSIS Technique with Group Decision Making

The inadequacy of crisp data to model the decision environment, and the often-ambiguous nature of human judgments which is difficult to quantify, motivates Fuzzy-TOPSIS Technique with Group Decision Making, an extension of TOPSIS. Chen (2000) proposed a model that includes the following steps to solve multi-person, multi-criteria decision-making problems in a fuzzy environment.

Step 1. Identify the decision-maker group and evaluation criteria and alternatives.

The decision-making group should include people who are familiar with the alternatives and have a good grasp of the evaluation criteria. To avoid decision-maker bias, the contrast between decision-maker profiles is preferred.

Step 2. Identify linguistic expressions for evaluation of criteria and alternatives.

Chen (2000) suggests the linguistic expressions and corresponding fuzzy numbers in Table 1.

Table 1. Linguistic expressions and their corresponding fuzzy numbers

Triangular FNs for the importance of criteria		Triangular FNs for the evaluation of alternatives	
Linguistic Expression	**Fuzzy Numbers**	**Linguistic Expression**	**Fuzzy Numbers**
Very High (VH)	(0.9,1.0,1.0)	Very Good (VG)	(9,10,10)
High (H)	(0.7,0.9,1.0)	Good (G)	(7,9,10)
Medium (MH)	(0.5,0.7,0.9)	Medium Good (MG)	(5,7,9)
Medium (M)	(0.3,0.5,0.7)	Fair (F)	(3,5,7)
Medium Low (ML)	(0.1,0.3,0.5)	Medium Poor (MP)	(1,3,5)
Low (L)	(0.0,0.1,0.3)	Poor (P)	(0,1,3)
Very Low (VL)	(0.0,0.0,0.1)	Very Poor (VP)	(0,0,1)

Step 3. Convert criterion weights and alternative performances from linguistic expressions to fuzzy numbers.

With the translation in Table 1, linguistic expressions can be easily converted to fuzzy numbers. In the case of K decision-makers, the fuzzy numbers obtained from each decision-maker can be aggregated as follows.

$$\tilde{x}_{ij} = \frac{1}{K}\left[\tilde{x}_{ij}^1 + \tilde{x}_{ij}^2 + \ldots + \tilde{x}_{ij}^K\right]$$

$$\tilde{w}_j = \frac{1}{K}\left[\tilde{w}_j^1 + \tilde{w}_j^2 + \ldots + \tilde{w}_j^K\right]$$

where $\tilde{x}_{ij}^{K}$ and $\tilde{w}_{ij}^{K}$ are the fuzzy number equivalent of the *k*th decision maker's linguistic expression for alternative and criterion, respectively.

Step 4. Calculate the fuzzy decision matrix and the normalized fuzzy decision matrix.

The fuzzy decision matrix and the weight set are shown as:

$$\tilde{D} = \begin{bmatrix} \tilde{x}_{11} & \cdots & \tilde{x}_{1n} \\ \vdots & \ddots & \vdots \\ \tilde{x}_{m1} & \cdots & \tilde{x}_{mn} \end{bmatrix}, \quad \tilde{W} = \begin{bmatrix} \tilde{w}_1, \tilde{w}_2, \ldots, \tilde{w}_n \end{bmatrix}$$

Where $\tilde{x}_{ij}$ and $\tilde{w}_j$ are triangular fuzzy numbers that are described as $\tilde{x}_{ij} = (a_{ij}, b_{ij}, c_{ij})$ and $\tilde{w}_j = (w_{j1}, w_{j2}, w_{j3})$.

$\tilde{R}$ denotes normalized fuzzy decision matrix.

$$\tilde{r}_{ij} = \left(\frac{a_{ij}}{c_j^*}, \frac{b_{ij}}{c_j^*}, \frac{c_{ij}}{c_j^*} \right), \quad j \in B$$

$$\tilde{r}_{ij} = \left(\frac{a_j^-}{c_{ij}}, \frac{a_j^-}{b_{ij}}, \frac{a_j^-}{a_{ij}} \right), \quad j \in C$$

$$c_j^* = \max_i c_{ij} \mid j \in B$$

$$a_j^- = \min_i a_{ij} \mid j \in C$$

Where sets *B* and *C* cover the benefit and cost criteria, respectively.

Step 5. Calculate the weighted normalized fuzzy decision matrix.

$\tilde{V}$ denotes weighted normalized fuzzy decision matrix.

$$\tilde{V} = \tilde{r}_{ij} * \tilde{w}_j$$

Step 6. Specify fuzzy positive ideal solution (FPIS) and fuzzy negative ideal solution (FNIS).

A^* and A^- denote fuzzy positive ideal solution (FPIS) and fuzzy negative ideal solution (FNIS), respectively.

Evaluation of the Disaster Tourism Potential of Countries

$$A^* = \left(\tilde{v}_1^*, \tilde{v}_2^*, \ldots, \tilde{v}_n^*\right)$$

$$A^- = \left(\tilde{v}_1^-, \tilde{v}_2^-, \ldots, \tilde{v}_n^-\right)$$

where $\tilde{v}_j^* = (1,1,1)$ and $\tilde{v}_j^- = (0,0,0)$.

Step 7. Calculate the distance of each alternative from FPIS and FNIS, respectively.

d_i^* and d_i^- denote the distance of each alternative from A^* and A^-, respectively.

$$d_i^* = \sum_{j=1}^{n} d\left(\tilde{v}_{ij}, \tilde{v}_j^*\right)$$

$$d_i^- = \sum_{j=1}^{n} d\left(\tilde{v}_{ij}, \tilde{v}_j^-\right)$$

where

$$d(\tilde{x}, \tilde{y}) = \sqrt{\frac{1}{3}\left[(\tilde{x}_1 - \tilde{y}_1)^2 + (\tilde{x}_2 - \tilde{y}_2)^2 + (\tilde{x}_3 - \tilde{y}_3)^2\right]}$$

is distance measurement function between two fuzzy numbers.

Step 8. Calculate the closeness coefficient of each alternative.

CC_i denotes the closeness coefficient of each alternative.

$$CC_i = \frac{d_i^-}{d_i^* + d_i^-}$$

Step 9. Rank all alternatives in descending order of the closeness coefficient.

If the CC equation is considered, it is seen that the alternative close to FPIS and far from FNIS will get a score converging to 1. The final ranking is obtained by sorting in descending order of CC.

IMPLEMENTATION AND FINDINGS

In this section, the implementation of evaluating the disaster tourism potential of countries with the Fuzzy-TOPSIS method is included. The implementation steps are shown in Figure 2:

Figure 2. The implementation steps

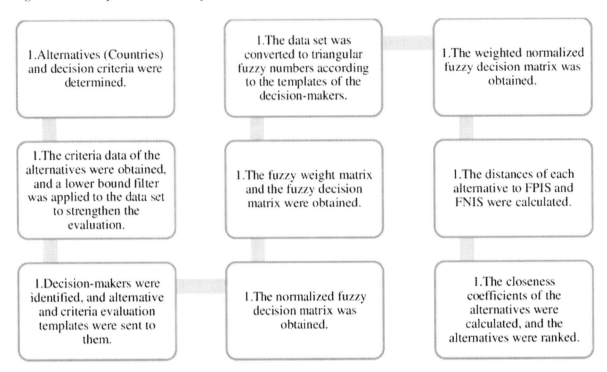

EM-DAT is a global database that stores, categorizes, and freely offers essential core data about disasters worldwide. It was developed in 1988 to rationalize decision-making in disaster preparedness, to provide an objective basis for efforts to assess vulnerability and set priorities (The Centre for Research on the Epidemiology of Disasters (CRED), 2016).

To evaluate the disaster tourism potential of the countries, the authors considered the number of deaths, injured, affected, and homeless people because of disasters as evaluation criteria. According to the database, deaths (C1) comprise "dead and missing people"; injured people (C2) mean "people suffering from physical injuries, trauma, or an illness requiring immediate medical assistance as a direct result of a disaster"; affected people (C3) represent "people requiring immediate assistance during an emergency"; homeless people (C4) involve "number of people whose house is destroyed or heavily damaged and therefore need shelter after an event" (EM-DAT, n.d.).

For the evaluation, data on all the above-mentioned four criteria of all disasters (22.362) that occurred worldwide between 1980 and 2022 was accessed. The list was filtered so that each criterion value for each disaster was "at least 1", thus a data set containing a total of 434 disasters was obtained. The decision-makers whose descriptive characteristics are given in Table 2 were asked to evaluate the criteria in terms of significance and to assign an evaluation template to evaluate the disaster tourism potential of the countries exposed to these disasters. A sample evaluation template (the evaluation template of the decision-maker with DM1 code) is given in Table 3. The disasters and criteria in the list were labeled according to the subjective evaluations of these 8 decision-makers who visited many countries, and tourist destinations.

Each country was represented by a single record by averaging the records of the same country (Thus, a total of 90 countries were obtained.), and finally, the Fuzzy Decision Matrix and the Fuzzy Importance Weights of Criteria data set are formed (Table 4, Table 5, Table 6).

Table 4 presents the decision makers' evaluations of the criteria. Accordingly, DM3 coded decision-maker evaluated C1 (Number of deaths) as "Effective" and C4 (Number of homeless people) as "Very effective" in evaluating the disaster tourism potential. According to DM3, the order of the criteria's importance is C4>C1>C2>C3.

Table 2. Profiles of decision-makers

Code	Descriptive characteristics of decision-makers
DM1	Female, 28 years old, Ph.D. (Disaster Management)
DM2	Male, 29 years old, Ph.D. (Physics)
DM3	Female, 30 years old, Ph.D. (Physics)
DM4	Male, 28 years old, Ph.D. (Law)
DM5	Female, 30 years old, Ph.D. (Psychiatric Nursing)
DM6	Male, 27 years old, M.Sc. (Civil Engineering)
DM7	Female, 25 years old, M.Sc. (Disaster Management)
DM8	Male, 28 years old, M.Sc. (Law, Education)

Table 3. DM1's evaluation template

Lower Bound	C_1: Number of *deaths* in the event	Upper Bound
100.001	Very effective	+
20.001	Effective	100.000
5.001	Medium Good Effective	20.000
1.001	Medium Effective	5.000
501	Medium Poor Effective	1.000
101	Poor Effective	500
-	Very Poor Effective	100

Lower Bound	C_2: Number of *injured* in the event	Upper Bound
50.001	Very effective	+
25.001	Effective	50.000
10.001	Medium Good Effective	25.000
5.001	Medium Effective	10.000
2.001	Medium Poor Effective	5.000
1.001	Poor Effective	2.000
-	Very Poor Effective	1.000

Lower Bound	C_3: Number of *affected* by the event	Upper Bound
1.000.001	Very effective	+
500.001	Effective	1.000.000
100.001	Medium Good Effective	500.000
30.001	Medium Effective	100.000
10.001	Medium Poor Effective	30.000
1.001	Poor Effective	10.000
-	Very Poor Effective	1.000

Lower Bound	C_4: Number of *homeless* due to the event	Upper Bound
50.001	Very effective	+
20.001	Effective	50.000
10.001	Medium Good Effective	20.000
5.001	Medium Effective	10.000
2.001	Medium Poor Effective	5.000
1.001	Poor Effective	2.000
-	Very Poor Effective	1.000

Table 4. DMs' linguistic expressions for the criteria importance weights

Code	C_1	C_2	C_3	C_4
DM1	Very effective	Medium effective	Medium poor effective	Medium effective
DM2	Very effective	Medium poor effective	Poor Effective	Effective
DM3	Effective	Medium-high effective	Poor Effective	Very effective
DM4	Very effective	Medium effective	Medium poor effective	Very effective
DM5	Very effective	Medium-high effective	Medium poor effective	Effective
DM6	Very effective	Effective	Poor Effective	Poor Effective
DM7	Very effective	Medium effective	Medium-high effective	Very effective
DM8	Very effective	Very effective	Medium effective	Very effective

Table 5. Fuzzy importance weights of criteria

Code	C_1			C_2			C_3			C_4		
DM1	0,8	1,0	1,0	0,3	0,5	0,7	0,1	0,3	0,5	0,3	0,5	0,7
DM2	0,8	1,0	1,0	0,1	0,3	0,5	0,0	0,1	0,3	0,7	0,9	1,0
DM3	0,7	0,9	1,0	0,5	0,7	0,9	0,0	0,1	0,3	0,8	1,0	1,0
DM4	0,8	1,0	1,0	0,3	0,5	0,7	0,1	0,3	0,5	0,8	1,0	1,0
DM5	0,8	1,0	1,0	0,5	0,7	0,9	0,1	0,3	0,5	0,7	0,9	1,0
DM6	0,8	1,0	1,0	0,7	0,9	1,0	0,0	0,1	0,3	0,0	0,1	0,3
DM7	0,8	1,0	1,0	0,3	0,5	0,7	0,5	0,7	0,9	0,8	1,0	1,0
DM8	0,8	1,0	1,0	0,8	1,0	1,0	0,3	0,5	0,7	0,8	1,0	1,0
Weights	0,8	1,0	1,0	0,4	0,6	0,8	0,1	0,3	0,5	0,6	0,8	0,9

The evaluations of the decision-makers by using linguistic expressions about the criteria are converted into triangular fuzzy numbers by giving the membership function. For example, (0.9, 1.0, 1.0) membership functions are assigned to a criterion rated as "Very Effective". The same process is applied for the evaluation of each decision-maker and as a result, Table 5 is obtained and the countries are evaluated according to these criteria weights.

Table 6 contains the disaster data of the countries classified according to the rating scales of the decision-makers in Table 3. This table is the decision matrix used in the evaluation.

Table 6. Fuzzy decision matrix

Country	C_1			C_2			C_3			C_4		
Afghanistan	0,2	0,4	0,5	0,2	0,3	0,4	0,5	0,7	0,8	0,6	0,7	0,8
Algeria	0,3	0,4	0,5	0,3	0,4	0,5	0,4	0,5	0,6	0,5	0,6	0,7
Antigua and Barbuda	0,0	0,0	0,1	0,0	0,0	0,2	0,3	0,5	0,7	0,3	0,5	0,7
⋮	⋮	⋮	⋮	⋮	⋮	⋮	⋮	⋮	⋮	⋮	⋮	⋮
Zimbabwe	0,3	0,5	0,7	0,2	0,3	0,4	0,7	0,9	0,9	0,7	0,9	1,0

As a result, the disaster tourism potential of 90 countries was evaluated with the Fuzzy-TOPSIS technique according to the criteria above, the criteria importance weights and the scales of the decision-makers, and the ranking in Table 7 was obtained.

Table 7. Ranking of countries

Rank	Country
1	Sri Lanka
2	Russian Federation (the)
3	Dominican Republic (the)
4	Maldives
5	Turkey
6	Bangladesh
7	Nepal
8	Zimbabwe
10	Benin
9	India
11	Iran (the Islamic Republic of)
12	Bolivia (Plurinational State of)
13	Korea (the Democratic People's Republic)
14	Sudan (the)
15	China
16	Greece
17	Madagascar
18	Chad
19	Algeria
20	Chile
⋮	⋮
88	Denmark
89	Egypt
90	Ethiopia

CONCLUSION AND FUTURE RESEARCH DIRECTIONS

People's curiosity about tragic events such as disasters has enabled disaster areas to become tourist attractions. Although ethical concerns and criticisms about disaster tourism continue, it is possible to observe a positive paradigm shift. It is thought that disaster tourism can create a positive value in terms of its attractiveness such as reviving the regions affected by disasters, providing tourists with various emotional experiences such as empathizing with disaster victims, and adapting to the disaster environment (Rucińska & Lechowicz 2014; Genç, 2018).

Thanks to disaster tourism, the local livelihoods of the disaster area can be improved and the resilience of local people and tourists to disasters can increase. Disaster tourism sites are classified according to the variability of pre-disaster and post-disaster tourism potential. This classification shows the variability of disaster tourism destinations, and that they can disappear and new destinations can come into existence at any time. According to the three-factor theory, which is an effective evaluation method, tourist satisfaction is evaluated according to the basic factor, the performance factor, and the excitement factor (Deng, 2007; D. Lin et al., 2021). While the basic factor and the performance factor can be developed and changed, the excitement factor is completely specific to the nature of the destination.

In disaster tourism, this factor emerges as the destruction caused by the disaster. In this respect, disaster losses should be focused on to effectively evaluate the disaster tourism potential. The desire of visiting the disaster destination of a tourist who is interested in disaster tourism increases according to the size of the loss of life and property caused by the disaster. When viewed from this aspect, just as Mediterranean countries are the attraction centers of sun-sand tourism, countries that have suffered great losses due to disasters can also be the attraction center of disaster tourism, and they can benefit as much as possible from tourism activities that occur after disasters.

This study, in which the authors evaluate countries according to their disaster tourism potential, contributes to tourism stakeholders such as policymakers, tourism suppliers, and tourists in the following ways: i) discovering disaster tourism potentials of countries for policymakers and developing appropriate policies, ii) adding new disaster destinations to their activities for tourism suppliers, iii) providing tourists with disaster destinations where they can create their visit plans and routes, iv) affording ground for a raising disaster awareness by increasing the public's disaster risk perception. In addition, it can be said that this study, which is the first known to evaluate the disaster tourism potential according to disaster losses, expands the vision of the researchers.

In other words, it can be said that the thing that most affects people's curiosity about a disaster area is the loss of life caused by the disaster. According to the research results, decision-makers mostly evaluated the number of dead and homeless criteria as more effective in terms of affecting the desire to visit a disaster area and the attractiveness of the region in terms of tourism. Among the criteria, the criterion that was evaluated as "with the relatively least impact "was the "number of affected". Contrary to death, homelessness, and injury, it is relatively difficult to envision the phenomenon of "being affected by disasters".

In addition, losses, and national and international migrations due to disasters, have been a hot button in the world in recent years. For these reasons, it was thought that people might have approached the phenomenon of "being homeless" more sensitively. Considering the findings on countries' rankings, according to the number of losses/the number of disasters, it has been determined that Sri Lanka and the Russian Federation are the two countries with the highest disaster tourism potential among 90 countries, while Ethiopia is the country with the lowest disaster tourism potential. Looking at the dataset, it was seen that Ethiopia has suffered from only a disaster (which caused both loss of life and other negative effects) since 1980, which resulted in 28 deaths and 1.000 people becoming homeless.

However, there are also countries such as China and Indonesia, which rank lower due to the high frequency of exposure to disasters and relatively low losses. It may also be useful to consider the disaster tourism potential of such countries that have a low loss/disaster rate but are frequently heard their names with disasters.

As can be seen from the data, no country seems safe from disaster. Disasters are increasing their effects day by day. Disaster risk reduction has become a global issue (Wang, Peng, Huang, & Deng, 2022). To effectively manage the disaster phenomenon, international collaborations have been developed, currently the Sendai framework, one of the basic principles of which is "to understand disaster risk", is in effect (United Nations Office for Disaster Risk Reduction, n.d.). Countries have been making changes in their management systems, organizing various campaigns, education and training, deepening their disaster research, and focusing on projects (Disaster and Emergency Management Presidency of Türkiye, n.d.; Republic of Turkey Ministry of National Education, 2021).

In essence, societies are trying to increase the perception of disaster risk to survive. Therewithal, for the tourism sector, which is trying to keep up with the pace of the developing world, disaster tourism seems to be a unique field. The unique nature of each disaster and the multifaceted emotions it evokes make this field attractive. Not every country is aware of this situation. However, it is also possible to talk about countries that open disaster areas to tourism and thus both keep tourism alive, create a godsend for healing the wounds of the locals and thuswise increase the disaster risk perception. With such aspects, the determination of countries with disaster tourism potential can be a guide to the stakeholders.

The authors believe this study that was conducted for this purpose will also catch the fancy-of-field researchers. For future research, it can suggest expanding the criteria pool (such as the economic effects of disasters, the situation, and potential in pre-disaster of the region), to get opinions from more decision-makers, and repeating the analyzes by including the tourism-related factors of the countries (such as infrastructure, accommodation, human resources). Apart from these, disaster tourism and related factors can be studied by using different methods.

The authors believe disaster tourism is timeless due to the uniqueness of disasters. It would not be wrong to say that it is getting popular day by day in the current situation. With the increase in the frequency, destructiveness, and diversity of disasters, countries have focused on disaster management. In the future, interest in disaster tourism will increase to increase disaster risk perception, disaster awareness, and resilience to disasters, with studies, focused on disaster risk reduction. At this point, cooperation between the two field authorities is of great importance. Considering the long-term, unique, and sustainable search of the tourism industry for a new tourism area, disaster tourism emerges as a unique field.

In this paradigm shift, the authors consider that even a small effort by the actors of the tourism industry can bring great positive values. In this respect, the authors can suggest that tourism industry actors should evaluate their businesses in terms of disaster risk, be prepared for potential hazards, and not ignore the role of the media at this point. It may be good to inform the tourists visiting the destination about the danger and risk situation of the region, introduce the disaster management systems of the region, provide basic training for emergencies, and convince them that they can do "disaster tourism in a safe area" by including these studies in the advertising and marketing processes.

Again, apart from tourism actors, disaster tourism is a unique disaster education material for disaster managers too. It is known that the disaster preparedness behavior of societies that are frequently exposed to disasters is better than other societies. This situation is mostly associated with a high perception of disaster risk in the disaster management literature. Factors such as real disaster areas, drills, and interaction with disaster victims play a major role in increasing the perception of disaster risk. For these reasons, as mentioned in previous studies, if this reciprocal relationship between disaster and tourism fields can be well understood and managed, both fields will provide significant benefits.

REFERENCES

Disaster and Emergency Management Presidency of Türkiye. (2022). *81 İlde Eş Zamanlı Deprem Tatbikatı Gerçekleştirildi*. Retrieved on May 2, 2022, from: https://www.afad.gov.tr/81-ilde-es-zamanli-deprem-tatbikati-gerceklestirildii-merkezicerik

Disaster and Emergency Management Presidency of Türkiye [AFAD]. (n.d.a). *Projelerimiz*. Retrieved on September 22, 2021, from: https://www.afad.gov.tr/projelerimiz

Disaster and Emergency Management Presidency of Türkiye [AFAD]. (n.d.b). *Afete Hazır Türkiye*. Retrieved on September 22, 2021, from: https://www.afad.gov.tr/afete-hazir-turkiye

Asia-Pacific Network for Global Change Research. (n.d.). *Projects under "Risk and resilience"*. Retrieved on October 30, 2021, from: https://www.apn-gcr.org/themes/risk-and-resilience/projects-under-risk-and-resilience/

Asian Development Bank. (n.d.). *Projects &Tenders*. Retrieved on September 22, 2021, from: https://www.adb.org/projects?terms=disaster

Association of Caribbean States. (n.d.). *Projects in Disaster Risk Reduction*. Retrieved on December 3, 2021, from: http://www.acs-aec.org/index.php?q=disaster-risk-reduction/projects

Becken, S., & Hughey, K. F. D. (2013). Linking tourism into emergency management structures to enhance disaster risk reduction. *Tourism Management, 36*, 77–95. doi:10.1016/j.tourman.2012.11.006

Biran, A., Liu, W., Li, G., & Eichhorn, V. (2014). Consuming post-disaster destinations: The case of Sichuan, China. *Annals of Tourism Research, 47*, 1–17. doi:10.1016/j.annals.2014.03.004

Caisarina, I., Omar, S. I., Rafie, M., & Afandi, N. A. A. (2021). The provision of travel advice to tourists visiting disaster area: The case of Banda Aceh. *IOP Conference Series. Earth and Environmental Science, 630*(1), 012030. doi:10.1088/1755-1315/630/1/012030

Centre for Research on the Epidemiology of Disasters. (2016). *Ongoing projects: Emergency events database (EM-DAT)*. Retrieved on March 1, 2022, from: https://www.cred.be/projects/EM-DAT

Centre for Research on the Epidemiology of Disasters. (n.d.). *EM-DAT The international disaster database: Guidelines*. Retrieved on March 1, 2022, from: https://www.emdat.be/guidelines

Çetinsöz, B. C., & Ege, Z. (2013). Impacts of perceived risks on tourists' revisit intentions. *An International Journal of Tourism and Hospitality Research, 24*(2), 173–187. doi:10.1080/13032917.2012.743921

Chen, C. T. (2000). Extensions of the TOPSIS for group decision-making under fuzzy environment. *Fuzzy Sets and Systems, 114*(1), 1–9. doi:10.1016/S0165-0114(97)00377-1

Chew, Y. E. T., & Jahari, S. A. (2014). Destination image as a mediator between perceived risks and revisit intention: A case of post-disaster Japan. *Tourism Management, 40*, 382–393. doi:10.1016/j.tourman.2013.07.008

Dadashpour Moghaddam, M., Ahmadzadeh, H., & Valizadeh, R. (2022). A GIS-Based Assessment of Urban Tourism Potential with a Branding Approach Utilizing Hybrid Modeling. *Spatial Information Research*, *2022*(3), 1–18. doi:10.100741324-022-00439-4

Deng, W. (2007). Using a revised importance-performance analysis approach: The case of Taiwanese hot springs tourism. *Tourism Management*, *28*(5), 1274–1284. doi:10.1016/j.tourman.2006.07.010

Ebrahim, A. H., & Ganguli, S. (2017). Strategic priorities for exploiting Bahrain's medical tourism potential. *Journal of Place Management and Development*, *10*(1), 45–60. doi:10.1108/JPMD-03-2016-0011

Faulkner, B. (2001). Towards a framework for tourism disaster management. *Tourism Management*, *22*(2), 135–147. doi:10.1016/S0261-5177(00)00048-0

Faulkner, B., & Vikulov, S. (2001). Katherine, washed out one day, back on track the next: A post-mortem of a tourism disaster. *Tourism Management*, *22*(4), 331–344. doi:10.1016/S0261-5177(00)00069-8

Fountain, J., & Cradock-Henry, N. (2020). Recovery, risk and resilience: Post-disaster tourism experiences in Kaikōura, New Zealand. *Tourism Management Perspectives*, *35*, 100695. doi:10.1016/j.tmp.2020.100695

Genç, R. (2018). Catastrophe of Environment: The Impact of Natural Disasters on Tourism Industry. *Journal of Tourism & Adventure*, *1*(1), 86–94. doi:10.3126/jota.v1i1.22753

Genç, T., & Filipe, J. A. (2016). A fuzzy MCDM approach for choosing a tourism destination in Portugal. *International Journal of Business and Systems Research*, *10*(1), 23–44. doi:10.1504/IJBSR.2016.073688

Ghasemi, P., Mehdiabadi, A., Spulbar, C., & Birau, R. (2021). Ranking of Sustainable Medical Tourism Destinations in Iran: An Integrated Approach Using Fuzzy SWARA-PROMETHEE. *Sustainability*, *13*(2), 683. doi:10.3390u13020683

Hoang, H. T. T., Truong, Q. H., Nguyen, A. T., & Hens, L. (2018). Multicriteria Evaluation of Tourism Potential in the Central Highlands of Vietnam: Combining Geographic Information System (GIS), Analytic Hierarchy Process (AHP) and Principal Component Analysis (PCA). *Sustainability*, *10*(9), 3097. doi:10.3390u10093097

Huan, T. C., Beaman, J., & Shelby, L. (2004). No-escape natural disaster mitigating impacts on tourism. *Annals of Tourism Research*, *31*(2), 255–273. doi:10.1016/j.annals.2003.10.003

Huang, J., & Min, J. (2002). Earthquake devastation and recovery in tourism: The Taiwan case. *Tourism Management*, *23*(2), 145–154. doi:10.1016/S0261-5177(01)00051-6

Huang, J. H., & Peng, K. H. (2012). Fuzzy Rasch model in TOPSIS: A new approach for generating fuzzy numbers to assess the competitiveness of the tourism industries in Asian countries. *Tourism Management*, *33*(2), 456–465. doi:10.1016/j.tourman.2011.05.006

Huang, L., Zheng, Q., Yin, X., Luo, M., & Yang, Y. (2022). "Double-edged sword": The effect of cultural distance on post-disaster tourism destination recovery. *Tourism Review*, *77*(1), 146–162. doi:10.1108/TR-03-2021-0113

Huang, Y. C., Tseng, Y. P., & Petrick, J. F. (2008). Crisis Management Planning to Restore Tourism After Disasters. *Journal of Travel & Tourism Marketing*, *23*(2-4), 203–221. doi:10.1300/J073v23n02_16

Hwang, C.-L., & Yoon, K. (1981). Methods for Multiple Attribute Decision Making. In *Multiple Attribute Decision Making*. Springer. doi:10.1007/978-3-642-48318-9_3

Hystad, P. W., & Keller, P. C. (2008). Towards a destination tourism disaster management framework: Long-term lessons from a forest fire disaster. *Tourism Management*, 29(1), 151–162. doi:10.1016/j.tourman.2007.02.017

Ide, A. (2009). Categorization and future direction of recoveries by tourism. *The International Journal of Tourism Science*, 2, 31–38. https://ci.nii.ac.jp/naid/110008606971

Li, F., Wen, J., & Ying, T. (2018). The influence of crisis on tourists' perceived destination image and revisit intention: An exploratory study of Chinese tourists to North Korea. *Journal of Destination Marketing & Management*, 9, 104–111. doi:10.1016/j.jdmm.2017.11.006

Lin, D., Jiang, Z., & Qu, H. (2021). Asymmetric Effects of Quality of Life on Residents' Satisfaction: Exploring a Newborn Natural Disaster Tourism Destination. *International Journal of Environmental Research and Public Health*, 18(21), 11577. doi:10.3390/ijerph182111577 PMID:34770091

Lin, Y., Kelemen, M., & Tresidder, R. (2018). Post-disaster tourism: Building resilience through community-led approaches in the aftermath of the 2011 disasters in Japan. *Journal of Sustainable Tourism*, 26(10), 1766–1783. doi:10.1080/09669582.2018.1511720

Liu-Lastres, B., Mariska, D., Tan, X., & Ying, T. (2020). Can post-disaster tourism development improve destination livelihoods? A case study of Aceh, Indonesia. *Journal of Destination Marketing & Management*, 18, 100510. doi:10.1016/j.jdmm.2020.100510

Luštický, M., & Bína, V. (2014). Application of Fuzzy Benchmarking Approach for Strategic Planning of Tourism Destination. *Journal of Quality Assurance in Hospitality & Tourism*, 15(4), 327–355. doi:10.1080/1528008X.2014.921779

Mair, J., Ritchie, B. W., & Walters, G. (2016). Towards a research agenda for post-disaster and post-crisis recovery strategies for tourist destinations: A narrative review. *Current Issues in Tourism*, 19(1), 1–26. doi:10.1080/13683500.2014.932758

Mao, C. K., Ding, C. G., & Lee, H. Y. (2010). Post-SARS tourist arrival recovery patterns: An analysis based on a catastrophe theory. *Tourism Management*, 31(6), 855–861. doi:10.1016/j.tourman.2009.09.003 PMID:32287733

Mikaeili, M., & Aytuğ, H. K. (2019). Evaluation of Iran's Cultural Tourism Potential from the European Union Perspective: Jolfa Region. *Advances in Science. Technology and Innovation*, 115–130. doi:10.1007/978-3-030-10804-5_12

Mileva, S. V. (2018). Potential of development of dark tourism in Bulgaria. *International Journal of Tourism Cities*, 4(1), 22–39. doi:10.1108/IJTC-05-2017-0029

Republic of Turkey Ministry of National Education. (2021). *Okullarda Afet Risk Yönetimi Projesi*. Retrieved from https://iegm.meb.gov.tr/www/okullarda-afet-risk-yonetimi-projesi/icerik/454

Nagamatsu, S., Fukasawa, Y., & Kobayashi, I. (2021). Why Does Disaster Storytelling Matter for a Resilient Society? *Journal of Disaster Research*, 16(2), 127–134. doi:10.20965/jdr.2021.p0127

Nouri, J., Danehkar, A., & Sharifipour, R. (2008). Evaluation of ecotourism potential in the northern coastline of the Persian Gulf. *Environmental Geology*, *55*(3), 681–686. doi:10.100700254-007-1018-x

Orchiston, C. (2012). Seismic risk scenario planning and sustainable tourism management: Christchurch and the Alpine Fault zone, South Island, New Zealand. *Journal of Sustainable Tourism*, *20*(1), 59–79. doi:10.1080/09669582.2011.617827

Puška, A., Pamucar, D., Stojanović, I., Cavallaro, F., Kaklauskas, A., & Mardani, A. (2021). Examination of the Sustainable Rural Tourism Potential of the Brčko District of Bosnia and Herzegovina Using a Fuzzy Approach Based on Group Decision Making. *Sustainability*, *13*(2), 583. doi:10.3390/su13020583

Ramírez-Guerrero, G., García-Onetti, J., Arcila-Garrido, M., & Chica-Ruiz, J. A. (2021). A Tourism Potential Index for Cultural Heritage Management through the Ecosystem Services Approach. *Sustainability*, *13*(11), 6415. doi:10.3390u13116415

Ritchie, B. (2008). Tourism Disaster Planning and Management: From Response and Recovery to Reduction and Readiness. *Current Issues in Tourism*, *11*(4), 315–348. doi:10.1080/13683500802140372

Ritchie, B. W. (2004). Chaos, crises and disasters: A strategic approach to crisis management in the tourism industry. *Tourism Management*, *25*(6), 669–683. doi:10.1016/j.tourman.2003.09.004

Rittichainuwat, B. N., & Chakraborty, G. (2009). Perceived travel risks regarding terrorism and disease: The case of Thailand. *Tourism Management*, *30*(3), 410–418. doi:10.1016/j.tourman.2008.08.001

Rucinska, D., & Lechowicz, M. (2014). Natural hazard and disaster tourism. *Miscellanea Geographica*, *18*(1), 17–25. doi:10.2478/mgrsd-2014-0002

Sharpley, R., & Wright, D. (2018). Disasters and Disaster Tourism: The Role of the Media. In The Palgrave Handbook of Dark Tourism Studies (pp. 335-354). London: Palgrave Macmillan. doi:10.1057/978-1-137-47566-4_14

Shondell Miller, D. (2008). Disaster tourism and disaster landscape attractions after Hurricane Katrina: An auto-ethnographic journey. *International Journal of Culture, Tourism and Hospitality Research*, *2*(2), 115–131. doi:10.1108/17506180810880692

Tanaka, N., Ikaptra, Kusano, S., Yamazaki, M., & Matsumoto, K. (2021). Disaster Tourism as a Tool for Disaster Story Telling. *Journal of Disaster Research*, *16*(2), 157–162. doi:10.20965/jdr.2021.p0157

The World Bank. (n.d.). *Natural Disaster Risk Management Project*. Retrieved from https://projects.worldbank.org/en/projects-operations/project-detail/P073361

Tsai, C. H., & Chen, C. W. (2010). An earthquake disaster management mechanism based on risk assessment information for the tourism industry-a case study from the island of Taiwan. *Tourism Management*, *31*(4), 470–481. doi:10.1016/j.tourman.2009.05.008

Tsai, C. H., & Chen, C. W. (2011). The establishment of a rapid natural disaster risk assessment model for the tourism industry. *Tourism Management*, *32*(1), 158–171. doi:10.1016/j.tourman.2010.05.015

United Nations Office for Disaster Risk Reduction. (n.d.). *What is the Sendai Framework for Disaster Risk Reduction?* Retrieved from https://www.undrr.org/implementing-sendai-framework/what-sendai-framework

Wang, X., Peng, L., Huang, K., & Deng, W. (2022). Identifying the influence of disaster education on the risk perception of rural residents in geohazard-prone areas: A propensity score-matched study. *International Journal of Disaster Risk Reduction, 71*, 102795. doi:10.1016/j.ijdrr.2022.102795

Wang, Y. S. (2009). The impact of crisis events and macroeconomic activity on Taiwan's international inbound tourism demand. *Tourism Management, 30*(1), 75–82. doi:10.1016/j.tourman.2008.04.010 PMID:32287727

Wright, D., & Sharpley, R. (2018). Local community perceptions of disaster tourism: The case of L'Aquila, Italy. *Current Issues in Tourism, 21*(14), 1569–1585. doi:10.1080/13683500.2016.1157141

Xu, J., & Grunewald, A. (2009). What Have We Learned? A Critical Review of Tourism Disaster Management. *Journal of China Tourism Research, 5*(1), 102–130. doi:10.1080/19388160802711444

Yan, L., Gao, B. W., & Zhang, M. (2017). A mathematical model for tourism potential assessment. *Tourism Management, 63*, 355–365. doi:10.1016/j.tourman.2017.07.003

Zhang, S., Wu, Z., Ma, Z., Liu, X., & Wu, J. (2021). Wasserstein distance-based probabilistic linguistic TODIM method with application to the evaluation of sustainable rural tourism potential. *Economic Research-Ekonomska Istraživanja, 35*(1), 409–437. doi:10.1080/1331677X.2021.1894198

Zhang, Y., Qu, H., & Tavitiyaman, P. (2009). The determinants of the travel demand on international tourist arrivals to Thailand. *Asia Pacific Journal of Tourism Research, 14*(1), 77–92. doi:10.1080/10941660902728080

KEY TERMS AND DEFINITIONS

Dark Tourism: The act of visiting destinations linked with tragedy, death, suffering, and destruction.

Dark Tourist: A person who is interested in dark tourism and visits dark tourism destinations.

Disaster: The situation in which the existing capacity and resources are insufficient in the face of the destructive effects caused by human actions or nature.

Disaster Risk Reduction: All efforts to reduce disaster potential/probability.

Disaster Tourism: The act of visiting disaster-affected or disaster-related places.

Disaster Tourist: A person who is interested in disaster tourism and visits disaster tourism destinations.

Fuzzy-TOPSIS: A method that examines decision-making problems in a fuzzy environment where the performance of alternatives and the importance of criteria are defined imprecisely.

Multi-Criteria Decision-Making: Approaches and methods that try to reach the best/appropriate solution in decision-making processes where more than one criterion must be considered.

Tourism Destination: Geographic area or zone visited by tourists for touristic purposes.

Tourism Disaster Management: The process of integrating the actors and factors affecting tourism into disaster management (Tourism management in which the disaster phenomenon is considered.).

Chapter 20
Eco-Gastronomy, Sustainability, and Art:
A Design Study With the Chefs of the Future

Gonca Babadağ
Anadolu University, Turkey

Sema Ekincek
https://orcid.org/0000-0001-9186-9323
Anadolu University, Turkey

ABSTRACT

Sustainability refers to the careful use of natural resources by considering future generations. Especially in the food sector, the sustainability of resources and the reduction of environmental impacts are very important. The relationship between gastronomy and sustainability might be described using the term "eco-gastronomy." As practitioners of gastronomy, it is very important that chefs recognize the ecosystem, protect natural resources, and respect the natural environment. In this context, the aim of the study is to provide potential chef candidates with the opportunity to express their emotions via creative design by incorporating sustainability, eco-gastronomy, and art. A total of 21 students were included in the study. With these students, designs related to both sustainability and gastronomy were realized, and they were enabled to design and present sustainable green restaurant logos and slogans in accordance with the concept they determined. Consequently, it was seen that the design stages and creativity stages of the students were exactly the same.

DOI: 10.4018/978-1-6684-4645-4.ch020

INTRODUCTION

Sustainability is focusing on meeting the needs of present generations without neglecting future generations. While the concept of sustainability is associated with the economic and social elements that are expected to be developed by the elements that are expected to be sustainable, such as nature, ecosystem, and social structure, it also focuses on goals, determinants, values, and practices. The food industry, which grows on a global scale with the increasing need for food, causes environmental damage such as environmental pollution, infertility of soils, ecological problems brought about by transportation conditions to distant regions, and excessive water consumption. Especially in the food sector, the sustainability of resources and the reduction of environmental impacts are very important.

Gastronomy is defined as a reflection of the preparation, cooking, presentation, and consumption of food, as well as a field that explores the art of eating (Scarpato, 2002a; Kivela & Crotts, 2006).

Quality and healthy nutrition have been distinguishing elements of sustainable development. In this vein, gastronomy is seen as an essential part of sustainable development. This stems from gastronomy's effect on sustainable regional development. The relationship between gastronomy and sustainability might be described using the term "eco-gastronomy". Eco-gastronomy comprises cooking and eating styles that also consider environmental concerns in determining, preparing, and marketing the content of gastronomy that reflects cooking and specialty dishes (Nillson, 2013). This field is not only about nutrition but also about consuming qualified, delicious, and healthy food. As curiosity in gastronomy and environmental consciousness expand, there is a growing focus on eco-gastronomy today.

Today, it is important for chefs to recognize the ecosystem and respect the natural environment (Ekincek, 2020). The duty of a chef who is an expert in the field of gastronomy and culinary arts is not only cooking but also respecting the environment and food beyond cooking. Chefs must be familiar with natural raw materials, educated about the environment, and respectful of the earth, all of which should be expressed in their products. It is of great importance to raise the chef candidates' attention to create this necessity and awareness.

Creativity, which is at the forefront in culinary work as in other areas, guides the chefs in keeping up with innovations and introducing new products (Horng & Hu, 2008).

Similarly, Uçuk and Özkanlı (2017) evaluated the relationship between art, design, and gastronomy, particularly in terms of creativity and presentation. Chefs who are experts in the realm of gastronomy and culinary arts are expected to do more than just cooking; they must also demonstrate creativity during presentation while respecting the setting and the food. Ekincek (2020) underlines the necessity of chefs today recognizing the ecosystem and respecting the natural environment, stating that artistic productions and kitchen designs are similar in terms of creativity. Hence, individuals who will be trained in the field of gastronomy and culinary arts must develop their art and design knowledge (Çağlayan, 2019), aesthetic perspectives, creativity, and awareness of sustainability.

Examining the literature, it has been seen that there is a gap in working together on sustainability, gastronomy and art. In this context, the aim of the study is to provide potential chef candidates with the opportunity to express their emotions via creative design by incorporating sustainability, eco gastronomy, and art. In addition, it is aimed to raise awareness of environmental concerns in prospective chefs who are an important part of gastronomy and sustainable tourism.

In the first part of the study, students who are future chef candidates were informed about sustainability, art, and gastronomy. Then, the students were taught what this relationship was by the question-and-answer method. In this context, the place of soil, water, and plastic in human life and their effect on food were discussed. In addition, the artworks created by contemporary artists on these concepts were examined. Sustainability and eco gastronomy-themed presentations by the chefs were also investigated. In this way, the study was help students to understand the connections between gastronomy, art, and sustainability.

In the second part of the study, the design phase was conducted. It was ensured that 21 students will be formed in groups of three. These student groups were asked to reflect on contemporary works of art and plate presentations and determine a concept with their groupmates. Further, they were asked to make a design by associating this concept with both sustainability and gastronomy. They were provided to design their sustainable green restaurants logo and slogan for the concept they determined in groups in these designs. At the end of the activity, they were asked to present what they wanted to tell in design briefly.

LITERATURE

Sustainability

Following the Industrial Revolution, industrial developments and their socio-cultural ramifications have resulted in a slew of environmental problems, including global warming, air pollution, water pollution, soil pollution, forest destruction, biological diversity. While the rise in population puts strain on resources, the unconscious use of resources accelerates the rate of resource consumption. This leads to a disregard for future generations' needs. Sustainability refers to the careful use of natural resources, the reduction of waste that pollutes the environment, the shift to renewable energy sources, and the prevention of the future by acting fairly and in accordance with needs while serving the demands of the present generation (Commission of the European Communities [COM], 2001).

Thus, in its most basic form, sustainability refers to as "ensuring that current situations are maintained in the future" (Kök & Güngör, 2021). The foundation of sustainability is *"the ongoing and protective appraisal of resources, particularly the use of renewable resources without surpassing the limitations of renewal, and the notion of equality between today's people and future generations"* (Yaylı, 2012). It also necessitates a shift toward renewable energy sources and waste minimization.

While the concept of sustainability is associated with the economic and social elements that are expected to be developed by the elements that are expected to be sustainable, such as nature, ecosystem, and social structure, it also focuses on goals, determinants, values, and practices. Food is undoubtedly one of the dimensions of sustainability that has a multi-layered structure in terms of its biological, economic, historical, sociological, aesthetic, and political dimensions.

Indeed, while rapid population growth causes the global food sector to expand, it also creates a paradoxical area that is difficult to resolve, such as rapid resource consumption, environmental pollution, soil infertility, ecological problems caused by transportation modes to distant regions, and excessive water consumption. Therefore, the sustainable and efficient use of natural resources, especially in the food and beverage sector, is important in terms of limiting the negative environmental effects of the sector (Axelos et. al., 2018).

Sustainable Food and Eco-Gastronomy

Sustainable food incorporates different dimensions such as before, during and after service. In fact, during and after sustainable food production, it is vital to avoid harming the environment, to respect living things, to protect living and non-living nature, to avoid polluting resources and to use them responsibly, to establish appropriate working conditions for employees, and to provide consumers with natural and healthy products. When it comes to sustainable food, the aim is to avoid polluting the air, water, and soil, to safeguard all living and non-living elements of the environment, to use energy and resources at an optimum level and to obtain healthy products (Dzene & Eglīte, 2012; Ötleş & Cagindı, 2004).

Sustainable food is directly correlated to the field of gastronomy. Gastronomy is described as *"a food culture or culinary art in which food and beverages are prepared in a methodical sequence within the confines of hygiene and sanitation standards and presented in a pleasing manner to the eye and palate"* (Dilsiz, 2010, p. 3). Scarpato (2002a, p. 4) defines gastronomy in the scientific context with all its dimensions related to food as *"the production of food and the means by which it is produced; political economy; processing, storage, transportation and processing of food; preparation and cooking; food and style; chemistry of food, digestion and physiological effects of food; food choices, customs, and traditions"*. Gastronomy is also expressed as *"healthful, well-arranged, pleasant and delicious cuisine"* (Hatipoğlu, 2014, p. 10).

Altınel (2009) explained the differences between gastronomy and eating/drinking with the difference between wrapping any fabric around and dressing, because gastronomy includes the presentation phase as well as the preparation and cooking of the food. In the literature, sustainable gastronomy is also expressed with the concept of eco-gastronomy (Scarpato, 2002b).

Eco-gastronomy, which prioritizes public health, requires social justice and welfare to be observed at all stages, including production, sale, and consumption of food (Scarpato, 2002b; Güneş, 2019). Eco-gastronomy supports the knowledge of the growing conditions of food, consuming food in season, preserving traditional taste, transferring traditional cooking techniques to future generations, preserving food diversity and authenticity (Akdağ & Üzülmez, 2017; Öztopçu & Akar, 2019; Scarpato, 2002b). Eco-gastronomy, which promotes the reuse of food leftovers for a variety of purposes, helps to conserve resources and minimize waste.

Based on healthy and organic nutrition, eco-gastronomy supports local production within the framework of sustainability. As improving the living conditions of people living in the world, considering the needs of future generations is the basic philosophy of sustainability (Öztopçu and Akar, 2019), it is necessary to create quality and healthy nutritional conditions in the most efficient and fair way with sufficient resources. It is thought that it takes up to 1500 miles for a food to come from field to plate.

This situation reveals that energy and resource consumption continues not only in the production of food products, but also in a variety of other areas such as transportation, packaging, and preservation under appropriate conditions, as well as the environmental damage it causes until it reaches the point of consumption. As sustainable food also includes processing, packaging, labeling, storage and marketing of products (Ötleş & Çağındı, 2004), eco-gastronomy supports local agriculture and food production.

Besides, local products are always fresher and tastier (GRA, 2012). Figure 1 shows the primary benefits (Güneş, 2019; Öztopçu & Akar, 2019; Scarpato, 2002b) of eco-gastronomy, which combines the realm of gastronomy with environmental concerns. Sustainability allows individuals to change their way of thinking without having to lower their living standards. Hence, a sustainable life requires individuals to consider the environment in their decisions, to try to carry out their actions without harming the environment, to protect the environment and to use resources carefully.

Today, the increasing awareness of the necessity of sustainable life has led consumers to turn to environmentally friendly foods. This situation necessitated restaurants reviewing the food habits of the producers, paving the path for the establishment of sustainable restaurants (Güneş, 2019). Indeed, choosing local, healthful, and organic meals, as well as including vegetarian and diet items on menus, can be viewed as crucial steps toward sustainability. (Jang et al., 2011; Legrand et al., 2010). However, the conditions of being a sustainable restaurant are not limited to this. Considering the production process, working hours and open days of restaurants, they are the businesses that use the most energy compared to other businesses in the service sector. For this reason, it is important for restaurants to use green practices in terms of sustainability (Namkung & Jang, 2013).

Designations like "Green Restaurant" or "Sustainable Restaurant" assigned to the restaurants with the greatest level of environmental responsibility are highly essential in terms of promoting and outlining what a restaurant should focus on when it comes to sustainability. Some of the criteria for being a green restaurant include efficient water usage, decreasing waste and prioritizing recycling, utilizing sustainable durable items and construction materials, sustainable food use, energy use, transparency and education, and lowering pollution and chemical use (Green Restaurant Association, 2019): The sustainable restaurant award is given to restaurants that use locally, organically, seasonally, and ethically sourced products, provide suitable working conditions for their employees, encourage healthy eating, use an environmentally friendly approach in food supply, do not harm the environment in waste disposal, and use resources effectively.

Figure 1. Primary benefits of Eco-Gastronomy

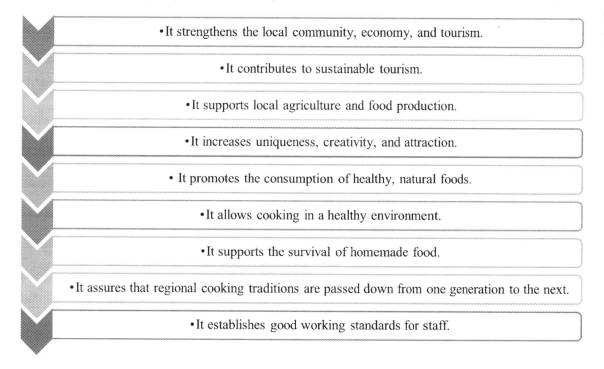

Narisawa, one of the outstanding restaurants worldwide to receive this award, is a Japanese restaurant. Japanese ingredients are combined with French cooking skills in this two-Michelin-starred restaurant, which claims to create a sustainable environment for both the soul and the body. Le Manoir aux Quat'Saisons, one of the sustainable restaurants, is situated in a luxury boutique hotel in Oxfordshire, England. In 2012, Raymond Blanc, the restaurant's

chef and owner, was elected President of the Sustainable Restaurant Association. The ingredients of this two-Michelin-star restaurant are produced in a two-acre vegetable garden. This restaurant delivers modern French cuisine made with fresh and seasonal ingredients.

Brae, an Australian restaurant built on a 30-acre organic farm near Birregurra, can be viewed as a sustainable restaurant that follows nature's production-consumption cycle. The restaurant utilizes no artificial additives or processes and serves contemporary cuisine that are visually appealing and made with seasonal, nutritious, and organic ingredients. Land renewal initiatives are visible in the area where the farm is located, and biodiversity is boosted by planting over 1000 native trees and plants.

Solar energy is employed in the area with olive groves, fruit trees, bees, and free-range hens, and waste is recycled back into the environment through composting. Recycling is given great importance in this restaurant, which produces very little waste and prevents waste. This restaurant, which collaborates with sustainable producers and supports local farmers, is said to treat both suppliers and employees fairly and respectfully. In this context, it is seen that it has all the qualifications that a sustainable restaurant should have.

Figure 2 Narisawa (Tokyo, Japan)

Figure 3. Le Manoir aux Quat'Saisons (Oxfordshire, England)

Figure 4. Brae (Birregurra, Australia)

The Relationship Between Eco-Gastronomy and Ecological Art

Having an interdisciplinary structure, gastronomy is directly or indirectly related to many fields such as anthropology, history, sociology, economy, chemistry, agriculture, ecology, medicine, and modern technologies (Altınel, 2009; Brillat-Savarin, 1994; Scarpato, 2002b). Culinary arts and food science are disciplines that cover food preparation, nutrition, cooking techniques, aesthetics, and cultural knowledge. Furthermore, creativity is one of the most important components of culinary art and the advancement of the culinary industry (Jeou-Shyan & Lee, 2007).

This is important for revealing the relationship between gastronomy and art because the connection between the need for nourishment and flavor and visuality, rather than the act of eating and drinking, has given rise to an artistic perspective in the realm of gastronomy and brought art and gastronomy closer together (Çağlayan, 2019; Ekincek, 2020; Sipahi, Ekincek & Yılmaz, 2017). Consequently, food is consumed not simply to satisfy physiological requirements, but also to provide aesthetic pleasure in accordance with other pursuits and expectations now (Ekincek, 2020).

Art, which is intertwined with aesthetics and includes order and harmony (Akdoğan, 2001; Turani, 2019), can be defined as *"the reflection and transmission of emotions and thoughts, perceptions and images (your dreams, your images, your plans), desires and wishes to the senses through various means in a beautiful, creative and original way"* (Özsoy and Mamur, 2019, p. 26). Considering that behind every traditional food that is healthy, delicious, pleasing to the eye and based on sustainability, there is a centuries-old knowledge, skill, intelligence, and creativity (Kurnaz, 2017), the common points of art and gastronomy emerge. From this perspective, knowledge, aesthetics, acquiring a product using proper procedures and techniques with specific tools, eliciting various feelings and pleasures in the customer, uniqueness, and creativity can all be seen as common aspects of gastronomy and art.

Cooking is the art of adapting dishes and making them taste good (This, 2005).

Craftsmen practicing the profession of cooking are now defined as artists. The most obvious example of introducing chefs as artists is Ferran Adrià, who made a name for himself with his innovative and creative cuisine. There is an important gastronomy and creativity literature examining Ferran Adria and restaurant elBulli (Planellas & Svejenova, 2007; de Solier, 2010; Opazo, 2012; Domene, 2013; Capdevila et al., 2015, 2018; Jimenez-Mavillard & Suarez, 2022). One of the most influential chefs, especially known for his "techno-cuisine", Adrià was the only chef invited to Documenta, a contemporary art exhibition held every five years in Kassel. As a result of the transformation from chef to "artist", Adrià joined Documenta 12 and transformed El Bulli into another venue for artistic activity (Domene, 2013).

Even if Ferran Adria does not work directly on eco-gastronomy, he promotes local and traditional food culture and attaches importance to gastronomy education. In addition, most of the published studies on culinary creativity have focused on the kitchens of Michelin-starred chefs or innovative leaders such as Ferran Adrià (Albors-Garrigos et al., 2013).

As art presents situations that were not perceived, felt, or were ignored by others before, within the framework of an aesthetic expression, with an intensity of emotion, it allows people to take action on issues such as environmental problems and sustainability. Given the quickly growing and unavoidable environmental challenges, art has never been more important in affecting people and utilizing both mind and emotions. The understanding of art, which focuses on environmental and nature problems, is explained with the term 'ecological art' in the literature.

Ecological art is an interdisciplinary art movement founded on the harmonious coexistence of human being and nature (Bianco, 2000). Ecological art is defined as *"artistic approaches with ethical responsibilities to both human and nonhuman living communities"* (Gablik, 1991, p. 22). Ecological artists question stereotyped notions and practices that no longer serve the world's future, propose adjustments, and demonstrate the effectiveness of these changes (Carruthers, 2006). Ecological artists, rather than unveiling artistic masterpieces, urge individuals to take responsible acts toward the environment by directing them to question or by making direct attempts for improvement themselves.

Ecological artists such as David Buckland, who brought together scientists, artists, and educators on an expedition to confront global climate change and raise awareness, Jalila Essaidi, who combined her biology-based artistic productions with creative and critical thinking mechanisms with the new materials she developed, Alexis Rockman, who describes the division between human being and the natural world in his paintings depicting the effects of global warming and genetic engineering, and Nele Avezado, who uses ice sculptures to draw attention to global warming and major environmental disasters all use art as a tool to raise awareness against environmental threats (Carruthers, 2006; Graham, 2007; Susamoğlu, 2018, Mamur, 2017).

Agnes Denes, an eco-artist, used wheat as a metaphor of food, energy, trade, and economy in her artwork "Wheatfield: A Confrontation" on the human-nature interaction. In the study, a two-acre wheat field in Manhattan near Wall Street and the World Trade Center opposite of the Statue of Liberty was turned into a wheat field, referring to waste, hunger, and ecological concerns, and highlighting our misplaced priorities.

Eco-Gastronomy, Sustainability, and Art

Figure 5. Agnes Denes, Wheatfield, 1982

Figure 6. Jackie Brookner's artworks

Jackie Brookner, an eco-artist who questions whether humans are smarter than other animals and underlines the dependence of all living things' life on the breathing phenomena, frequently collaborates with ecologists. It is seen that large-scale water treatment projects and biosculptures are generally built on wetlands and rivers and have an ecosystem feature. The artist emphasizes that there is no waste in natural ecosystems. The artwork, "The Gift of Water," in which two big hands reach for water in a public pool, depicts algae acting as a filter without the need of chemicals (Uysal, 2009).

METHODOLOGY

Although creativity is a crucial element in art, technical and scientific studies, the kitchen; includes all three elements. Creativity, which is at the forefront in culinary work as in other areas, guides the chefs in keeping up with innovations and introducing new products (Horng & Hu, 2008). In this context, it is intended to give future chef candidates the opportunity to create designs in which they may convey their sentiments and opinions about sustainability. In this study basic qualitative research method was used.

Basic qualitative research is a type of qualitative research that specifies general, basic, and explanatory studies. The researcher is interested in the meaning of the phenomenon in the people concerned (Merriam, 2009). It is expected that questioning the relationship between eco-gastronomy and ecological art will play a significant role in raising the awareness of students studying gastronomy for a sustainable life. From this start point, the research was conducted in three steps.

Figure 7. Initial stage of the activity

In the initial stage of the research, inquiries were conducted into the relationship between eco-gastronomy and ecological art to raise awareness about worldwide environmental problems. At this stage, an interactive presentation was prepared and information on environmental problems was made, restaurants based on sustainability, chef presentations, and artistic productions of ecological artists were reviewed.

It was thus intended to stimulate students' mental processes such as distinguishing, questioning, associating, analyzing, and evaluating.

In the second stage of the study, the students were provided with a suitable setting to work in groups. It was ensured that 21 students will be formed in groups of three. These student groups were asked to reflect on contemporary works of art and plate presentations and determine a concept with their groupmates. At this stage, students in the gastronomy department, as future chefs, were instructed to envisage themselves running a restaurant that is environmentally conscious and respects sustainability. Encouraging students to brainstorm within the group, it was ensured that they questioned the relationship between gastronomy and sustainability and recognized the importance of individual effort in solving environmental concerns. The groups were then asked to investigate the sustainability-art-gastronomy relationship and create designs, such as logos, slogans, or images, that reflect this relationship. They were ensured to reflect these designs on the materials provided to them, such as cups, plates, and cloth bags, by thinking they might be utilized in sustainable restaurants (Figure 9 and 10). It was assumed that the mental activity performed throughout the initial stage of the study would result in creative and aesthetic products.

Figure 8. Second stage of the activity

Figure 9. Examples of students' cloth bag designs

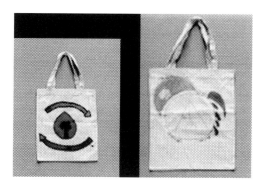

Figure 10. Examples of students' plate and cup designs

In the third stage of the study, the students were given the opportunity to present what they wanted to convey in their designs. Through the products they created, the students were able to demonstrate their efforts toward environmental concerns as well as their inquiries about sustainability-art-gastronomy relationship.

FINDINGS

The results of the content analysis of student products, observations made by the researchers during the process, and student presentations show that four stages of the creativity process are employed. It is a well-known fact that creativity is an inherent skill that can be developed and be reawakened when the right conditions are formed and preventing factors are eliminated, even if it has been suppressed (Türkcan & Babadağ, 2021). Herrmann argues that creativity has four stages: preparation, incubation, illumination, and verification (San, 2008).

In the preparation stage of the creativity process, the problem situation is identified and information on the solution of the problem is gathered. At this stage, examples of sustainable restaurants and ecological art were reviewed in the interactive presentation on environmental problems to trigger creativity. In the incubation stage, where the problem situation was examined in more detail, the students were given the opportunity to brainstorm by forming groups and to question the relationship between eco-gastronomy and ecological art. At this stage, it was intended to stimulate mental processes such as distinguishing, questioning, associating, analyzing, and evaluating. It was observed that this stage was completed in different times in each group.

During the illumination stage, students learned that they could play an active part in resolving environmental problems in the context of the sustainable restaurant they envisaged. They created very creative designs with the concept of sustainability at this stage. In the verification stage, where students evaluate whether the situation that emerged during the illumination stage meet the need for the problem identified in the preparation stage, the students were given the opportunity to exhibit their designs and share their evaluations.

Figure 11.

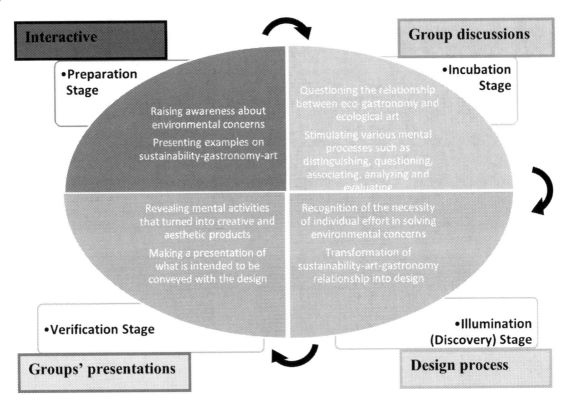

DISCUSSION

In this study, the authors aimed to offer potential chef candidates the opportunity to express their feelings through creative design by bringing together sustainability, eco gastronomy and art. In this context, future chef candidates are provided with the opportunity to produce designs in which they can use their creativity and to express their feelings and thoughts on sustainability. In the literature, it is seen that the subject of creativity is frequently mentioned in the studies on chefs (Horng & Hu, 2009; Peng, Lin & Baum, 2013; Roque et al., 2018; Lee et al., 2019; 2020; Stierand, 2020; Lee, 2021). However, in this study, unlike the literature, sustainability and eco gastronomy are discussed together with creativity and art.

In addition, it was ensured that the chef candidates use the creative process to create artistic products and express themselves through art. Slavich, Cappetta, and Salvemini (2014) stated that chefs write texts and sketch with colored pencils to create creative products. In this regard, they stated that creative teamwork is of special importance in the formation of future outstanding chefs because it represents a unique opportunity to involve them in creative practice. In this study, the subject of eco-gastronomy was discussed and the chef candidates were given the opportunity to express themselves through teamwork.

In the initial stage of the study, which consists of three stages, the relationship between the concepts of sustainability, sustainable food, eco-gastronomy and ecological art was examined, and students, as future chef candidates, made inquiries about what they can do individually on the basis of sustainability before, during, and after the service. In the second stage of the study, students were given the opportunity to turn their mental activities into creative and concrete designs. In the third stage of the study, students were allowed to present what they wanted to convey in the designs they created. During the process in which creative processes take place, the information at hand was questioned, analyzed, evaluated, and embodied with the goal of contributing to permanent learning.

The results of the study are similar to the stages of the kitchen creativity process model adapted by Horng and Hu (2008). In addition, Horng and Hu (2009) stated that the results of the tests conducted after the implementation of the creative cuisine curriculum showed an improvement in the creativity process of the students. Similar to the results of their study, Bouty and Gomez (2013) state that creativity in the kitchen has three different aspects: "creative teamwork", "idea development", and "naming", respectively.

Study findings also include stages such as teamwork, idea development and naming in eco gastronomy and art activity. In addition, this study shows that education and awareness-raising experiences have an impact on creativity. Creative chefs, as practitioners of gastronomy, are of great importance in eco gastronomy and gastronomy tourism. Because chefs are also defined as a value chain in gastronomic tourism (UNWTO, 2018). It has been revealed that the chef candidates offer creative products for eco gastronomy with the aim of making people think, emphasizing some problems, making analogies to works of art and drawing attention to the issue of sustainability.

At this point, it has been seen that the stages in the creative process (San, 2008) are the same as the chef candidates' process of designing products for eco gastronomy. In this study, an environment was created for the chefs to learn about sustainability and eco gastronomy within the ecological art practice. In this context, the fact that chef candidates receive eco-gastronomy education and increase their environmental awareness will also contribute to the support of sustainable tourism in the region (Scarpato, 2002b), because it is of great importance that the chefs are conscious as the practitioners of gastronomy to successfully realize eco-gastronomy and sustainable tourism in a region.

CONCLUSION

The multidimensional and complex character of environmental problems necessitates an interdisciplinary approach. In this regard, the effect of eco-gastronomy and ecological art was employed in this study to raise awareness of environmental concerns among students studying in the gastronomy department and to make them understand the significance of individual actions. The study aims to increase the awareness of the students, who are the chefs of the future, about the environment and ecosystem, and to enable them to express their thoughts on sustainability and eco gastronomy through art. Besides, it was aimed that the students, as future chef candidates, will recognize their abilities to actively participate in sustainability and solving environmental problems.

Providing education on eco gastronomy to chef candidates is important in terms of sustainable tourism. Conducting art activities for this will strengthen the creativity and artistic direction of the chefs. As a result of the study, it was determined that the education of chefs in eco gastronomy contributed positively to the creative product creation processes. Raising creative chefs with environmental awareness in the field of gastronomy will make great contributions to the region in terms of eco gastronomy and sustainable tourism. In addition to this, it is a unique study subject to increase the creativity of the chef candidates and to express their awareness of the environment with artistic products. This study is expected to form a basis for further research on eco gastronomy and art.

In the application phase of the research, the students created very creative designs using the concept of sustainability. In the research, it was seen that the application stages of the students and the stages of creativity were exactly the same. As a result of the study, the students who are future chef candidates were provided to internalize the subject of eco-gastronomy and express it with art. It is thought that these chefs will be more sensitive to the environment, region, country, and the world. In addition, these chef candidates, who are practitioners of eco-gastronomy, will also contribute to sustainable tourism.

REFERENCES

Akdağ, G., & Üzülmez, M. (2017). Sürdürülebilir gastronomi turizmi kapsamında otantik yiyeceklere yönelik bir inceleme [A review of authentic food within the scope of sustainable gastronomic tourism]. *Journal of Tourism and Gastronomy Studies, 5*(2), 301-309.

Akdoğan, B. (2001). Sanat, Sanatçı, Sanat Eseri ve Ahlak [Art, Artist, Artwork and Ethics]. *Ankara Üniversitesi İlahiyat Fakültesi Dergisi, 42*(1), 213–245.

Albors-Garrigos, J., Barreto, V., García-Segovia, P., Martínez-Monzó, J., & Hervás-Oliver, J. L. (2013). Creativity and innovation patterns of haute cuisine chefs. *Journal of Culinary Science & Technology, 11*(1), 19–35. doi:10.1080/15428052.2012.728978

Altınel, H. (2009). *Gastronomide menü yönetimi* [Menu management in gastronomy] [Yüksek Lisans Tezi, İstanbul Üniversitesi Sosyal Bilimler Enstitüsü]. Erişim adresi: http://nek.istanbul.edu.tr:4444/ekos/TEZ/44835.pdf

Axelos, M., Basinskiene, L., Darcy-Vrillon, B., Ruyck, H. D., Pou, A. M., Salaseviciene, A., & Bianco, A. (2000). *Ecological Art and Ethics*. Retrieved on March 11, 2020, from: http://ecologicalart.org/ecartandet.html

Bouty, I., & Gomez, M. L. (2013). Creativity in Haute Cuisine: Strategic Knowledge and Practice in Gourmet Kitchens. *Journal of Culinary Science & Technology, 11*(1), 80–95. doi:10.1080/15428052.2012.728979

Brillat-Savarin, J. A. (1994). The physiology of taste. New York: Penguin.

Brookner, J. (2004). *Materials, Ecological Aesthetics Art in Environmental Design: Theory and Practice* (H. Strelow, Ed.). Birkhauser.

Çağlayan, E. (2019). Temel sanat eğitimi dersinin gastronomi ve mutfak sanatları eğitimindeki yeri ve önemi [The place and importance of basic art education course in gastronomy and culinary arts education]. *İnsan ve Toplum Bilimleri Araştırmaları Dergisi, 8*(4), 3084-3095.

Capdevila, I., Cohendet, P., & Simon, L. (2015). Establishing New Codes for Creativity through Haute Cuisine. The Case of Ferran Adrià and elBulli. Academic Press.

Capdevila, I., Cohendet, P., & Simon, L. (2018). From a local community to a global influence. How elBulli restaurant created a new epistemic movement in the world of haute cuisine. *Industry and Innovation, 25*(5), 526–549. doi:10.1080/13662716.2017.1327844

Carruthers, B. (2006). Art, Sweet Art. *Alternatives Journal, 32*(4/5), 24–27.

Commission of the European Communities. (2001). *A sustainable Europe for a better World: A European Union strategy for sustainable development.* Communication From The Commission. Retrieved on September 22, 2021, from: https://eur-lex.europa.eu/legal-content/EN/TXT/PDF/?uri=CELEX:52001DC0264&from=EN

De Solier, I. (2010). Liquid nitrogen pistachios: Molecular gastronomy, elBulli and foodies. *European Journal of Cultural Studies, 13*(2), 155–170. doi:10.1177/1367549409352275

Dilsiz, B. (2010). *Türkiye'de Gastronomi ve Turizm (İstanbul Örneği)* [Gastronomy and Tourism in Turkey (Istanbul Example)]. Yüksek Lisans Tezi. İstanbul Üniversitesi Sosyal Bilimler Enstitüsü.

Domene, M. (2013). El Bulli: Contemporary intersections between food, science, art and late capitalism. *Barcelona Investigación Arte Creación, 1*(1), 100–126. doi:10.17583/brac.2013.v1i1.a611.100-126

Dzene, S., & Eglīte, A. (2012). Perspective of sustainable food consumpiton in Latvia. *Annual 18th International Scientific Conference Proceedings, 2*, 210-215.

Ekincek, S. (2020). *Yenilebilir Sanat: Gastronomide Yemeğin Sanatsal Boyutunun İncelenmesi* [Edible Art: Examining the Artistic Dimension of Food in Gastronomy] [Yayımlanmamış Doktora Tezi]. Eskişehir: Anadolu Üniversitesi. GRA (Green Restaurant Association). Retrieved on December 14, 2021, from: www.dinegreen.weebly.com

Graham, M. A. (2007). Art, Ecology and Art Education: Locating. *Studies in Art Education, 48*(4), 375–391. doi:10.1080/00393541.2007.11650115

Güneş, S. G. (2019). Eco-gastronomy, Tourism and Sustainability: The Rise of Sustainable Restaurants in the World. *Erasmus International Academic Research Symposium on Educational and Social Sciences*, 67-84.

Horng, J. S., & Hu, M. L. (2008). The mystery in the kitchen: Culinary creativity. *Creativity Research Journal, 20*(2), 221–230. doi:10.1080/10400410802060166

Horng, J. S., & Hu, M. L. (2009). The creative culinary process: Constructing and extending a four-component model. *Creativity Research Journal, 21*(4), 376–383. doi:10.1080/10400410903297956

Huttunen, M. (2018). *Assessment of Research and Innovation on Food Systems by European Member States.* Standing Committee on Agricultural Research (SCAR) Strategic Working Group on Food Systems.

Jang, J. Y., Kim, G. W., & Bonn, M. A. (2011). Generation Y Consumers' Selection Attributes and Behavioral İntentions Concerning Green Restaurants. *International Journal of Hospitality Management*, *30*(4), 803–811. doi:10.1016/j.ijhm.2010.12.012

Jeou-Shyan, & Lee, H. Y.-C. (2007). What does it take to be a creative culinary artist? *Journal of Culinary Science & Technology*, *5*(2-3), 5–22. doi:10.1300/J385v05n02_02

Jimenez-Mavillard, A., & Suarez, J. L. (2022). A computational approach for creativity assessment of culinary products: The case of elBulli. *AI & Society*, *37*(1), 331–353. doi:10.100700146-021-01183-3

Kivela, J. & Crotts, C., J. (2006). Tourism and Gastronomy: Gastronomy's Influence on How Tourists Experience a Destinations. *Journal of Hospitality & Tourism Research*, *30*(3), 354-377.

Kurnaz, A. (2017). *Sürdürülebilir gastronomi kapsamında yeşil restoranların hizmet kalite algısının GRSERV ile ölçümü: İstanbul örneği* [Measurement of service quality perception of green restaurants within the scope of sustainable gastronomy with GRSERV: The example of Istanbul]. [Doktora tezi]. Adnan Menderes Üniversitesi Sosyal Bilimler Enstitüsü.

Lee, K. S. (2021). Expressionist view of culinary creativity: A culinary theory exercised with specialty coffee. *International Journal of Gastronomy and Food Science*, *23*, 100311. doi:10.1016/j.ijgfs.2021.100311

Lee, K. S., Blum, D., Miao, L., & Tomas, S. R. (2019). The duality of a pastry chef's creative process. *Events and Tourism Review*, *2*(1), 21–29. doi:10.18060/22958

Lee, K. S., Blum, D., Miao, L., & Tomas, S. R. (2020). The creative minds of extraordinary pastry chefs: An integrated theory of aesthetic expressions - a portraiture study. *International Journal of Contemporary Hospitality Management*, *32*(9), 3015–3034. doi:10.1108/IJCHM-04-2020-0329

Legrand, W., Sloan, P., Simons-Kaufmann, C., & Fleisher, S. (2010). A Review of Restaurant Sustainable Indicators. In Advances in Hospitality and Leisure (vol. 6). Emerald Group Publishing Limited.

Mamur, N. (2017). Ekolojik Sanat: Çevre Eğitimi ile Sanatın Kesişme Noktası [Ecological Art: The Intersection Point of Environmental Education and Art]. *Mersin Üniversitesi Eğitim Fakültesi Dergisi*, *13*(3), 1000–1016. doi:10.17860/mersinefd.316297

Merriam, S. B. (2009). *Qualitative research: A guide to design and implementation*. John Willey & Sons.

Namkung, Y., & Jang, S. (2013). Effects of Restaurant Green Practices on Brand Equity Formation: Do Green Practices Really Matter? *International Journal of Hospitality Management*, *33*, 85–95. doi:10.1016/j.ijhm.2012.06.006

Nilsson, J. H. (2013). *Nordic Eco-gastronomy. Sustainable Culinary Systems: Local Foods, Innovation, Tourism and Hospitality* (C. M. Hall & S. Gössling, Eds.). Routledge.

Opazo, M. P. (2012). Discourse as driver of innovation in contemporary haute cuisine: The case of elBulli restaurant. *International Journal of Gastronomy and Food Science*, *1*(2), 82–89. doi:10.1016/j.ijgfs.2013.06.001

Ötleş, S., & Çağındı, Ö. (2004). Ekolojik Gıdaların Önemi ve Ekolojik Üzüm Üretimi [Importance of Ecological Foods and Ecological Grape Production]. *Akademik Gida Dergisi*, *2*(2), 36–38.

Özsoy, V., & Mamur, N. (2019). Görsel Sanatlar Öğrenme ve Öğretim Yaklaşımları [Visual Arts Learning and Teaching Approaches]. Ankara: Pegem Akademi.

Öztopçu, A. (2019). Eko-gastronomi ve sürdürülebilir bölgesel kalkınma [Eco-gastronomy and sustainable regional development]. *International Social Mentality and Researcher Thinkers Journal, 5*(24), 1432–1443. doi:10.31576mryj.354

Peng, K. L., Lin, M. C., & Baum, T. (2013). The constructing model of culinary creativity: An approach of mixed methods. *Quality & Quantity, 47*(5), 2687–2707. doi:10.100711135-012-9680-9

Planellas, M., & Svejenova, S. (2007). *Creativity: Ferran Adria*. Presented at the annual meeting ExpoManagement, Madrid, Spain. Retrieved from http://www. elBulli. com/esade/CasoFerranAd ria_and _elBulli-ESADE_en. pdf

Roque, J., Guastavino, C., Lafraire, J., & Fernandez, P. (2018). Plating influences diner perception of culinary creativity. *International Journal of Gastronomy and Food Science, 11*, 55–62. doi:10.1016/j.ijgfs.2017.11.006

San, İ. (2008). Sanat ve Eğitim [Arts and Education] [Dördüncü Baskı]. Ankara: Ütopya Yayınevi.

Scarpato, R. (2002a). Gastronomy as a tourist product: the perspective of gastronomy studies. In A.-M. Hjalager & G. Richards (Eds.), *Sustainable gastronomy as a tourist product* (pp. 51–70). Routledge.

Scarpato, R. (2002b). Tourism Gastronomy. In A.-M. Hjalager & G. Richards (Eds.), *Sustainable gastronomy as a tourist product* (pp. 132–152). Routledge.

Sipahi, S., Ekincek, S., & Yılmaz, H. (2017). Gastronominin sanatsal kimliğinin estetik üzerinden incelenmesi [Examining the artistic identity of gastronomy through aesthetics]. *Journal of Tourism and Gastronomy Studies, 5*(3), 381–396. doi:10.21325/jotags.2017.100

Slavich, B., Cappetta, R., & Salvemini, S. (2014). Creativity and the Reproduction of cultural products: The experience of Italian Haute Cuisine chefs. *International Journal of Arts Management, 16*, 29–71.

Stierand, M. (2020). Culinary Creativity. In M. Runco & S. Pritzker (Eds.), *Encyclopedia of Creativity* (pp. 296–300). Elsevier. doi:10.1016/B978-0-12-809324-5.23684-5

Stierand, M., & Dörfler, V. (2016). The role of intuition in the creative process of expert chefs. *The Journal of Creative Behavior, 50*(3), 178–185. doi:10.1002/jocb.100

Susamoğlu, F. (2018). Güncel Sanatta Ekolojik Yaklaşımlar ve Ekozofi Kavramı [Ecological Approaches in Contemporary Art and the Concept of Ecosophy]. *Atatürk Üniversitesi Güzel Sanatlar Enstitüsü Dergisi, 41*, 96–103. doi:10.32547/ataunigsed.453183

This, H. (2005). *Molecular Gastronomy - Exploring the Science of Flavor* (M. B. Debevoise, Trans.). Columbia University Press.

Turani, A. (2019). Dünya Sanat Tarihi [World Art History] [Genişletilmiş Basım]. İstanbul: Remzi Kitabevi.

Türkcan, B., & Babadağ, G. (2021). İlkokulda görsel sanatlar öğretimi [Visual arts teaching in primary school]. In İ. Korkmaz (Ed.), İlkokulda öğretim öğretmen el kitabı içinde (pp. 333-364). Pegem Akademi.

Uçuk, C., & Özkanlı, O. (2017). Gastronomi turizmi: Tabak prezentasyonunun gastronomi turizmindeki yeri [Gastronomy tourism: The place of plate presentation in gastronomy tourism]. *Uluslararası Kırsal Turizm ve Kalkınma Dergisi*, *1*(1), 51–54.

UNWTO. (2018). *Report on Gastronomy Tourism: The Case of Japan*. Affiliate Members Report: Volume Seventeen. Retrieved on March 30, 2022, from:www.e-unwto.org

Uysal, H. F. (2009). *Çağdaş Sanat ve Ekosistem* [Contemporary Art and Ecosystem]. Yüksek Lisans Tezi. Marmara Üniversitesi Güzel Sanatlar Enstitüsü.

Yaylı, H. (2012). Çevre Etiği Bağlamında Kalkınma, Çevre ve Nüfus [Development, Environment and Population in the Context of Environmental Ethics]. *Süleyman Demirel Üniversitesi Sosyal Bilimler Enstitüsü Dergisi*, *1*(15), 151–169.

Chapter 21
Food and Beverage Operations and Safety:
The Global Scenario

Birsen Bulut Solak
https://orcid.org/0000-0003-1583-1504
Selcuk University, Turkey

Feridun Aydınlı
https://orcid.org/0000-0002-0230-5129
Selcuk University, Turkey

Sakib Bin Amin
https://orcid.org/0000-0003-2363-9045
North South University, Bangladesh

ABSTRACT

For the past three years the COVID-19 pandemic has received much global attention due to the high risk of fatality and human-to-human transmission. This pandemic has forced changes in every sector as well as in different aspects of everyone's daily lives. Travelling has had a critical role in contributing to its transmission by negatively influencing the majority of public health. The hospitality and tourism industry is subject to being immediately influenced by the external environment. This chapter explains how COVID-19 has affected food and beverage operations and safety in the sector and the global economy. New rules and regulations are described in detail. The future of food and beverage operations has changed by integrating technology, touchless contact, social distancing, and hygiene precautions, focusing on domestic travel, virtual tourism, and luxury travel.

INTRODUCTION

The COVID-19 pandemic seems to be a warning course to the public community to start preparing for an open, transparent, and coordinated action by all relevant stakeholders (Bin Salem & Jagadeesan, 2020). Moreover, the pandemic has completely changed most of things enormously in global, and substantially influenced the global economy, particularly the tourism sector. The pandemic outcomes have also been effectively visible on the country's outbound, inbound, and domestic tourism, business and adventure travels, food and beverage operations and cruise holidays (Kaushal & Srivastava, 2021).

In addition to these effects, each country has also been facing negative effects on their economies due to the COVID-19 pandemic, with marketing problems throughout goods transport chains especially food supplement being one of the worst-hit areas. Without a medical solution to the pandemic, tourists were reluctant to travel, despite the protective measures taken by transport and hospitality companies. Travelling has also had a critical character in contributing to the transmission of these diseases by negatively affecting the majority of public health. Aside from initial lockdowns and gradual unlocking of economic activities, public has been encouraged to ensure social distancing, practice appropriate hygiene, face mask wearing and avoiding gatherings unless critically needed (Sharma, 2020). Activities to recover the sector, governments at various levels have initiated check-ins with relevant COVID-19 negative reports, encouragement on minimum days stay at hospitality establishments (Cond´e Nast Traveller, 2020).

In the extant literature, researchers have also widely used perceived severity (PS) and perceived vulnerability (PV) to foresee customer behaviors that might be influenced by an event or disease such as foodborne illness (Ali, Harris, & Ryu, 2019). Accordingly, it was assumed that customers who had high PS and PV may use online takeaway services to minimize the possibility of risk to the COVID-19 from dining out at restaurants. One study also uncovered situation-appropriate resulted under the COVID-19 pandemic situation precisely, showing that younger customers (Generation Y/Z) were more willing to utilize online food order than older customers (Generation X/Baby Boomers) (Hong et al, 2021). This could be because of customers's awares about the low risk of getting sick with COVID-19 from food reported at the Center for Disease Control and Prevention (CDC) (Centers for Disease Control and Prevention [CDC], 2020).

According to another study published by Yacoub and ElHajjar (2021), it was found that hotel operations in Lebanon had witnessed a new normal characterised by more in-room dining rather than buffet dining due to COVID-19 pandemic, and the wearing of face masks becoming the norm as well. It was also found that, many hotels had attempted to minimize expenditure by ensuring that staff took their annual holidays, while room and food costs were adjusted according to market demands (Yacoub & ElHajjar 2021).

This chapter is aimed to reveal the effects of the COVID-19 pandemic on food and beverage operations and the changes in food and beverage service processes during and after the pandemic. Accordingly, the chapter examined the global impacts of COVID-19 and gathered information about the ongoing pandemic for readers. Then, the effects of this pandemic on the tourism and accommodation sector on a global scale and its impact on the food and beverage departments were continued to be summarized.

The recent pandemic has threatened the food supply, security and supply system, and changes in food and beverage operations are discussed in order to prevent this situation in this study as well. Moreover, the literature review in this section is based on selected articles concerning accommodation and tourism in light of the health and food crises affecting the tourism industry to varying degrees. For these purposes, most of the relevant studies accessed through databases were used. After the articles were scanned and

Food and Beverage Operations and Safety

duplicates were removed, a total of 55 full-text studies were entitled to be read in full by the authors, and at the end of this process, material related to the chapter was excluded.

BACKGROUND

Global Effects of COVID-19 Across Two-Time Frames

In the last decade, there have been some significant viruses: H1N1 (Hemagglutinin type 1 and neuraminidase type 1), AIDS (Acquired Immunodeficiency Syndrome), NDM1 (New Delhi Metallo-β-lactamase 1), and COVID-19 which occurred in epidemics/pandemics worldwide. COVID-19, one of these important viruses, has a 2% case fatality rate. Simultaneously, International Committee on Taxonomy of Viruses (ICTV) also named this novel coronavirus as SARS-CoV-2 (Gorbalenya et al., 2020). COVID-19, similar to the severe acute respiratory syndrome (SARS) which occurred in 2003, is an airborne disease, and surpasses its counterparts in morbidity and mortality (Yang et al., 2020).

However, epidemiological evidence points at the COVID-19 outbreak to have association with a seafood market in Wuhan city in Hubei province in China (Xu et al., 2020). The first case was also reported on December 12, 2019 in China, but by the month end in January 2020, the virus had infected around two thousand people in the country (Wu et al., 2020). From the feasible place of origin, the zoonotic transmission began and spread in countries across the world and turned into a global outbreak.

This became possible due to the virus's highly transmissible among humans' population (Gautam & Rivedi, 2020; Liu et al., 2020). Moreover, recent studies have found the potential transmission of the SARS-CoV-2 virus from environmental surfaces, including water, food and other commonly touched fomites (Kampf, Todt, Pfaender, & Steinmann, 2020). In addition, the COVID-19 pandemic has been observed to be a uniquely effective incident as well as a major public health crisis in world history (Fong et al., 2020). Thereby, the COVID-19 has been acrossing the planet since March 11, 2020 (WHO, 2020).

It also resulted in the announcement of a pandemic by the World Health Organization (WHO) on March 11, 2020 (WHO, 2020). COVID-19 continues to spread with approximately 512 million confirmed cases in more than 227 countries, resulting in over 6.3 million deaths by July 09, 2022 (CoronaBoard, 2022).

With the declaration of the pandemic as a Formidable Epidemic Disease on March 27, 2020, the most countries governments announced a set of restrictions and social-distancing protocols including: (a) suspension of international flights except cargo and evacuation air planes with an imposition of a 14-day quarantine for returning residents, (b) suspension of domestic flight and passenger railway train, (c) reduction of public transportation capacity to below 60%, (d) closure of educational institutions, (e) movement restrictions from cities to the counties, (f) recommendation for public to stay and work from home and the banning of public gatherings including places of worship, hotels, restaurants and bars, (g) requirement for all people to wear face masks while in public places (Nechifor et al., 2021).

Practicing implementing partial and social distancing or complete lockdown were the familiar measures taken at local and international levels to decrease the transmission of COVID-19. Restriction on almost all activities involving human gathering was a difficult outcome of the measures taken to stop rapid spreading of COVID-19, and planet has gradually got used to the new ways of industrial functioning which has involved more virtual and less physical interactions (Jawed et al., 2020). Employers did not only keep their facilities clean and employees' safe, but they also had to assure that they did not create additional exposures for their customers or suppliers, and this created a dangerous incident of overlapping nature (Jawed et al., 2020).

Under this quarantine, household revenue was influenced directly through a contraction of economic activity from partial or full business closure leading to lower earnings from employment and other rents. At its turn, the lower household revenue may have translated into lower require across the consumption basket with further negative feedback influences on economic activity. The evolution of the pandemic outside the country also affected the economy negatively in multi-ways. The reduction in commodity and service require in other countries found out a contraction of exports and tourism with severe implications over the activity of export-oriented sectors such as horticulture (Nechifor et al., 2021). Thereby, the COVID-19 pandemic has influenced all national economies through a multitude of impact channels.

Effects of COVID-19 on the Tourism and Hotel sectors

Tourism, which enables a country to obtain economic, social, and cultural gains, is seen as one of the most important global industries. For this reason, developed and developing countries with tourism potential are trying to intensify their tourism activities to increase their welfare levels. In this direction, countries have accelerated their economic development by increasing their incomes (Çetintaş & Bektaş, 2008). However, natural disasters, political instability, internal conflicts, wars between countries, and pandemics such as COVID-19 not only affect the regions where the crisis is experienced, but also the whole world (Ritchie, 2004).

Natural crises are caused by earthquakes and hurricanes or are human-made which are caused by terrorist events or industrial accidents. These periods of crises are also often characterized by uncertainty, unpredictability, and an inability to regulate the functioning of a system (Koehl, 2011; Beirman & Van Walbeek, 2011). As mentioned above, one of the sectors most affected by these crisis periods is the tourism sector. Crises, which are marginal events that greatly affect the tourism industry, often jeopardize the market potential and attractiveness of a region or tourism destination (Beirman & Van Walbeek, 2011). The COVID-19 pandemic crisis has greatly threatened the tourism industry. As with the recent COVID-19 pandemic, any pandemic can immediately reduce the flow of inbound and outbound tourism due to tourists' decision not to visit certain geographic areas or destinations and/or government restrictions to stop the spread of the disease (Zhang et al., 2020).

The global impact of COVID-19 on tourism has been devastating as it has led to a decline in tourism activity due to suspension of air travel, social distancing protocols and quarantines in many countries around the world (Rogerson & Baum, 2020). Travelers who wanted to have an outdoor experience due to nature, rural tourism, and road travel preferred because of travel restrictions were the tourists most affected by the pandemic. Health and safety measures and cancellation policies are among the main concerns of consumers, while last-minute bookings have increased due to the volatility of developments regarding the pandemic and travel restrictions (UNWTO, 2021).

However, the current global pandemic has significantly affected the normal functioning of the tourism industry, resulting in job loss in the sector, reduced revenues for businesses in the tourism and hospitality sectors, and loss of tax revenues for governments. In addition, the desire of people to travel to closer destinations was cited as a positive development in the domestic tourism market. As a result of these effects, Ateljevic mentioned that life will not be the same as before due to the COVID-19 pandemic (2020), but Nepal also emphasized that the COVID-19 pandemic allows the tourism industry to reset itself (2020).

In addition, Brouder stated that tourism sector managers should examine new supplies and demands after the COVID-19 pandemic, and that new investment routes can be opened for the tourism sector if mandatory conditions are met (2020). The impacts of COVID-19 as word cloud expressing in simple way were seen in Figure 1.

Figure 1. Word cloud expressing the key socio-economic and ecological effects of the pandemic on the tourism (Soluki et al., 2021)

The pandemic has led to significant changes in the world. To mitigate the impact, governments have taken radical measures by closing an entire country or the most affected cities, as well as banning entry to their borders, quarantine measures and restriction of human movements etc., resulting in a major blow to the global tourism industry. Reporting a cost from US$910 billion to US$1.2 trillion in export revenues from tourism due to bans can be given as an example of significant changes. (Hassan, Knio, & Bellos 2022). The COVID-19 pandemic has emerged as an unprecedented situation in the tourism industry, and the impact of this pandemic has resulted in a 22% double-digit drop in international tourist arrivals in the first quarter of 2020 compared to the same period in 2019.

While tourism in the world decreased significantly (Niewiadomsky, 2020), tourist arrivals decreased by 57% in March, a total of 67 million international tourists and a loss of export revenue of approximately US$80 billion were observed. The Asia/Pacific region fell by 35% and Europe fell by 19%, followed by the Americas (% -15), Africa (-12%) and the Middle East (-11%). Europe hosted 221 million tourists with a loss of 70%. In 2017, it regressed to 30 years earlier with a 74% loss. As mentioned above, the negative effects of pandemics such as COVID-19 have greatly affected the tourism sector.

Accordingly, Gössling et al. (2020) examined the impact of previous pandemics and the impact of the COVID-19 pandemic on the global tourism industry, the airline and hospitality industries following travel restrictions and the massive shutdown. The study figured out how a pandemic could change society, national economies and the tourism industry. In this direction, many tourism destinations had to cease operations due to canceled reservations, limited logistics, job losses, reduced sales, quarantine measures and travel bans. This situation dealt a heavy blow to the accommodation sector in the tourism sector. F Furthermore, social distancing has put pressure on the hospitality industry, where many accommodation establishments have had to immediately cease their operations and/or significantly minimize those (Fotidatis et al., 2021). Accordingly, hotel occupancy rates decreased in all regions. In China, where the virus emerged, guest entries to accommodation businesses decreased by 89%. Hotels belonging to the world-famous MGM chain ceased activities due to the quarantine in Las Vegas, Nevada

USA (Hospitalitynet, 2020a). Hotel occupancy rates in Germany fell by more than 36% compared to 2019, making Cologne the most affected city in Germany. More than two-thirds of revenues were lost compared to March 2019 due to postponed and canceled business trips. The tourism industry in Rome, Italy collapsed after a 94% decrease in hotel occupancy rates (Hospitalitynet, 2020b).

The situation was the same in Turkey's two most important tourism cities, Istanbul and Antalya. Hotel occupancy rate in Istanbul decreased from 72.1% in March 2019 to 29% in March 2020. Hotel occupancy rates in Antalya, which was 78.4% in March 2019, decreased to 29% in March 2020 (TUROB, 2020). Interestingly, European hotels, which had occupancy rate of 11% in April 2020, entered a partial recovery period and experienced relief by increasing their occupancy rate to 26.5% in July of the same year.

Despite the partial recovery, these rates were still hopeless. Average cost per room in hotels was - 20.9% and - 73.4% of revenue per usable room, respectively, in July 2019 (STR, 2020a). Unfortunately, Africa could not experience such a rapid economic recovery. The African hospitality sector saw an occupancy rate of 16.9% through July 2020, down 72.9% from the same period of 2019. Average cost per room for African hotels was 10.8% and 75.8% of revenue per available room in July 2019, respectively (STR, 2020b).

The North American hotel occupancy rate, which reached 42.1% in August 2020, showed a strong recovery at the end of the summer. Of course, this rate shows a 45.2% decrease compared to 2019. North American hotels experienced a 59.4% decrease in average revenue per room (STR, 2020c). As can be understood from these data, the accommodation industry all over the world has deeply felt the negative effects of the COVID-19 pandemic. To mitigate these effects, governments around the world have provided incentive and severance packages to individuals and small and medium-sized enterprises (SMEs) who lost their jobs in the hospitality industry and the tourism sector as a whole (Dube, Nhamo, & Chikodzi, 2021).

The choice of traveling and visiting a destination depends on tourists' perceptions of safety and security (Taylor & Toohey, 2007). Hotels and restaurants are also facilities that host intense human use. Visitor concerns about the pandemic are growing, as interaction between guests and staffs is high at these properties. Accordingly, the official of one of the accommodation facilities outlines some of the restructuring that has already taken place during the pandemic (Soliku et al., 2021). Face mask wearing was made mandatory during the restructuring process until a sustainable solution is available (COVID-19 vaccine) (Kaushal & Srivastava, 2021). This restructuring is necessary to ensure the safety of both customers and employees, and to increase customers' confidence in protecting their services (Gössling et al., 2020).

Hotels still operating during the COVID-19 pandemic have been asked to adopt and maintain high-level security service norms and security operation standards. The hospitality industry needs to restructure its operations, particularly with seating arrangements in restaurants, accommodation arrangements in dorms, and other common areas such as swimming pools, sports facilities, and reception areas, among others. Such restructuring issues may include the temporary cancellation of services such as use of swimming pools, dormitory accommodation, and buffet meals.

Instead, the use of contactless menu boards, routine disinfection of tables, contactless payment systems, the promotion of takeaways in restaurants and screening of dinners should be encouraged. In addition, regardless of the type of operations, managers should consider creating specific task forces to address hygiene issues and related training and awareness rising among employees (Kaushal & Srivastava, 2021).

EFFECTS OF COVID-19 ON THE FOOD AND BEVERAGE SECTOR

The COVID-19 response among all stakeholders, including governments, regulators, the agri-food industry, and consumers, has the potential to change food security, and promoting such needs depends in part on future research into food safety costs, performance assessments and risk communication. (Roy, 2020). The impact of tourism activity in the rapid spread of the COVID-19 pandemic to the world is quite high (Nicola et al., 2020).

Some measures had to be taken to reduce this effect. Catering operations have been shut down, limited, or forced to only offer take-out services. New operational models and restrictions during the pandemic process were applied in the sector (Bucak & Yiğit, 2021). These measures resulted in significant employment and income loss in the food and beverage industry (Cho, Lee, & Winters, 2020). Therefore, the food and beverage industry has a direct connection with these effects and measures (Bucak & Yiğit, 2021), because when the historical process is followed, the crises that emerged in the world have affected the food and beverage industry together with other sectors operating in the tourism sector (Okat, Bahçeci, & Ocak, 2020). Like other global crises, the COVID-19 pandemic has deeply affected the food and beverage industry.

The impacts of COVID-19 are summarized in Figure 2. For example, in China where the COVID-19 pandemic started, a total of 94% of catering establishments have been adversely affected since the start of the pandemic, and the number of customers has decreased by more than 69% (Yılmaz & Şahin, 2021). Food and beverage businesses operating in countries on the European continent have been adversely affected by the COVID-19 pandemic. For example, takeaway sales in the United Kingdom decreased by 56.4% and bar sales by 60% in March, 2020 (Luty, 2020a). Similarly, the year 2020 in Germany was analyzed compared to the previous year.

Within the scope of the measures taken to prevent the spread of the disease, a 90% decrease was observed in the sales of the restaurants serving the table in March, with the reduction of the working hours of the restaurants. Afterwards, only take-out service was provided (Luty, 2020b). Similarly, it was the same in the United States. As a result of the general measures taken to slow down the effect of the pandemic and attention to social distance, as of May 6, 2020, the sales of restaurants serving table decreased by 100% compared to the previous year (Lock, 2020). It was clear that the COVID-19 pandemic was causing an unprecedented socio-economic impact (Dolnicar & Zare, 2020).

Williams and Kayaoğlu pointed out that the accommodation and food and beverage sectors in the European Union (EU) contribute 19.7% and 58.7%, respectively, to the overall employment in the tourism industry (2020). The restriction and closure of businesses therefore had disastrous effects on businesses and workers in the tourism sector. For example, it was determined that more than eight million people working in the restaurant industry in the United States lost their jobs at the end of April, 2020 due to the impact of the COVID-19 pandemic, and the restaurant industry lost approximately $80 billion in revenue simultaneously (NRA, 2020).

On the other hand, in Turkey it was seen that the food and beverage sector that ended its activities the most with the effect of the pandemic (TEPAV, 2020). Accordingly, the loss of employment in the tourism and food and beverage sector in a year was determined as 205,000 Turkish Lira (Bucak & Yiğit, 2021). Due to these negativities, central governments have taken some measures to reduce income loss. Central government or local public institutions have offered financial packages to food and beverage companies to cover various expenses to maintain their activities and ensure their sustainability for food security outcomes as seen in the Figure 2. Considering the restrictions applied in some countries, it has been observed that some support and incentives such as grants, tax reductions, and debt reductions are provided to the food and beverage industry (Dube et al., 2021).

Figure 2. Interactions between COVID-19 quarantine effects and government recovery measures leading to food security outcomes

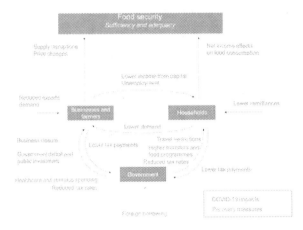

Effects of the COVID-19 Pandemic Crisis on the Restaurant Industry

COVID-19 measures and customer reluctance to eat in restaurants has led to a rapid decline in restaurant sales because consumers were afraid of service encounters with restaurant staff and other customers. Therefore, this has greatly affected the restaurant industry (Kim, Bonn, & Cho, 2021) and caused unprecedented damage to the global restaurant industry (Lock, 2020). As previously mentioned, more than eight million employees working in the restaurant industry were on leave until April, 2020, and in April, 2020 consumption in restaurants/bars fell to the lowest level since October, 1984 (NRA, 2020). The pandemic has also negatively affected human behavior (Hong et al., 2021).

Individuals use the information they collect to assess the risk they face and ultimately decide to take advantage of preventive behaviors to deal with the upcoming risks (Ali, Harris, & Ryu, 2019; Cahyanto et al., 2016). Food safety risk perception (FSRP) plays an extremely important role in the decision-making process of customers who buy food (Frewer et al., 2009). Accordingly, the coronavirus changed customer behavior to prefer online takeaway (Hong et al., 2021). In this direction, restaurants sought ways to survive in this process (NPD, 2020). For this reason, they have turned to online food delivery services due to the advantages of contactless ordering and contactless delivery. This service has gained high demands by bringing food and beverages to customers' doorsteps on a global scale (Maida, 2020).

Indeed, the growing demand for food and beverages online has been increasing daily due to the COVID-19 pandemic (FAO, 2020a). While the rate of those who brought and ate food from home was 13% before COVID-19, this rate is predicted to reach 49% after COVID-19 (Ekonomist, 2020, p. 9). The total revenue of the global online food delivery service market was estimated at approximately US$107.4 billion in 2019, while it is expected to exceed US$182.3 billion by 2024 (Statista, 2020).

Therefore, more customers around the world can use online food delivery services to avoid human contact with restaurant staff and other customers in the wake of the pandemic. There is also limited research examining the impact of customer perceptions of health risk on customer intention to use online meal delivery during the COVID-19 pandemic (Hong et al., 2021).

Effects of COVID-19 on Food Safety

Since food is the basic requirement for life, food safety is the discipline that describes how food is handled and stored in such a way as to prevent food diseases. Essential protocols of food safety for health risks are a critical issue for commercial applications of business applications (Han et al., 2021; Tuncer & Akoğlu, 2020). For all food safety systems, effective control systems of vehicles are necessary for public health and protection. New food packaging has also been created so loaders can be loaded from both exporting and importing companies to develop food safety systems and to adopt and market risk-based food safety policies (M&M Technologies, 2012).

Once food has emerged with COVID 19 again, food safety measures are extremely important. Developments in the pandemic process have made it mandatory to establish food safety systems based on COVID 19 as well (Farias & Santos Gomesdos, 2020). The pandemic has also ushered in a new era in the food industry. Evaluating the potential impact of the virus on food safety has become an entirely important issue for governments, the food industry, and consumers around the world. At the point where nutrition is important for human life, the definition of food and beverage safety culture has also expanded, but the main purpose of food and beverage safety has remained the same. Besides these, droplets from the mouths of individuals by coughing, sneezing and speaking loudly stand out as the primary mode of transmission of COVID-19, which effect food and beverage safety.

Close social distances of people also increase the risk of transmission of the virus (Borouiba, 2020). Furthermore, contact with surfaces or objects contaminated with COVID-19 are indicated as a secondary transmission route (Chan et al., 2015; WHO, 2020c; Çiftçi & Çoksuer, 2020; Güngör & Yıldız, 2020). Infected hands, especially of staffs and shop customers, can be the cause of COVID 19 transmission because while shopping, people carefully select ripe fruits and intact vegetables, especially when purchasing food; they check the contents of the product on the box. Therefore, contamination can be a cause because these foods have been touched, bought, or re-shelfed by others (Duda-Chodak et al., 2020). Figure 3 summarizes the proposed safety measures for the food sector during the pandemic at each stage of the food chain from farms to consumer.

In some studies regarding the life span of COVID-19 on surfaces, it has been determined that COVID-19 can survive for three hours in the air, four hours on copper material, 24 hours in cardboard packaging, and up to 72 hours on stainless steel and plastic surfaces (van Doremalen et al., 2020). In another study, it was also observed that COVID-19 can survive up to nine days on inanimate surfaces such as metal, glass or plastic (Kampf, Todt, Pfaender, & Steinman, 2020). According to the US Food and Drug Administration (FDA), WHO, European Food Safety Authority (EFSA), CDC, USDA Animal and Plant Health Supervision Service (APHIS), and the Institute of Food Technologists, COVID-19 is not transmitted through food and water.

However, the possibility of spreading the virus by consuming food served on contaminated surfaces, during packaging in a contaminated room, or by transmission during the handling or sharing of food with an infected person cannot be ignored. For the longevity of COVID-19, there is no alternative to developing an accurate and rapid detection method for food can on food surfaces and the planner SARS-CoV-2.

The COVID-19 virus is first transmitted by saliva from themes and words, just like humans. One research also shows that the COVID-19 virus is transmitted through water (Galanakis, 2020). The SARS-CoV and MERS-CoV viruses, which are close to the COVID-19 virus, can also survive for two years in a frozen state (Hatipoğlu, 2021). Some solutions were also prepared safety practices for the possibility of contracting this COVID-19 virus, 0.5% sodium peroxide, 0.1% hypochlorite (i.e. broth)-71% ethanol or disinfectant ready to use to generate the in-use CoV contamination within 1 minute after exposure (Pressman, Naidu, & Clemens, 2020).

Duan et al. suggested that ultraviolet light irradiation for 60 minutes on several coronaviruses in culture resulted in undetectable viral infectivity as well (2003). Some researchers are also observed at 56°C after the duration and temperatures of several coronaviruses: 90 minutes at 67°C for 60 minutes and 30 minutes at 75°C in 2003 (Mullis et al., 2012). Coronaviruses can also survive longer in low-temperature environments. It has been found that the survival time of coronaviruses is reduced in high-temperature environments (Casanova et al., 2010).

Accordingly, in general cooking SARS-CoV disappears in the region of 70°C. This ascending, COVID-19 can also be rendered susceptible by ultraviolet light, thermal exposure at 65°C, alkaline pH >12 or acidic pH <3. Several viruses were affected by heating experiments to 56°C, such as routine tissue wound samples (Henwood, 2020). The COVID-19 virus has been cited as the top food safety issue for food processing and preparation in the United States according to the International Food Information Council (IFIC) 2020 Food and Health Survey (IFIC, 2020). Regarding food safety after the pandemic, many restaurants, cafes, and health authorities in Central Europe at the start of the pandemic crisis stopped serving rare steak and meat as a general precaution against viruses and pathogens, although foodborne transmission of SARS-CoV-2 is not supported by scientific evidence (Euractiv, 2020).

Moreover, some companies in the USA (such as those carrying out meat processing) have entirely ceased production during the pandemic (Reiley, 2020). Transportation for cooking or processing food has minimized SARS-CoV-2 transmission on travel through a potentially contaminated food. On the tissue surface, including the skin, it can be easily elevated by washing with soap and alcohol hand sanitizers can be excluded (Darnell et al., 2004). In this direction, it is explained with the applied food technique, starting from the steps of personal food input acceptance, preparation, processing, and service-delivery process.

All staff in the food and beverage sectors have been trained on pandemic and hygiene. In the sector, it was also given personal equipment, clothes were put on, and weight was given. All wore personal masks, gave importance to personal hygiene, and paid attention to social distance. In addition, food samples for food safety were taken and examined during the day. Moreover, food service at home is considered to be handled with clean hands due to pandemic concerns. Figure 3 also shows all measures step by step for the food sector.

Changes Occured in the Food and Beverage Sector after COVID-19

The COVID-19 pandemic has brought some changes in food and beverage businesses, as in many sectors. As mentioned earlier, many countries had to take various measures to prevent the spread of the pandemic. Accordingly, as part of the pandemic measures, many restaurants were also closed, forced to provide limited service or forced to provide takeaway service (Dedeoğlu & Boğan, 2021). These measures created recession in food and beverage businesses (Teachout & Zipfel, 2020). The stagnation experienced also led to significant changes in the dimension of supply and demand.

Figure 3. Summarizes the proposed safety measures for the food sector during the pandemic at each stage of the food chain from farms to consumer

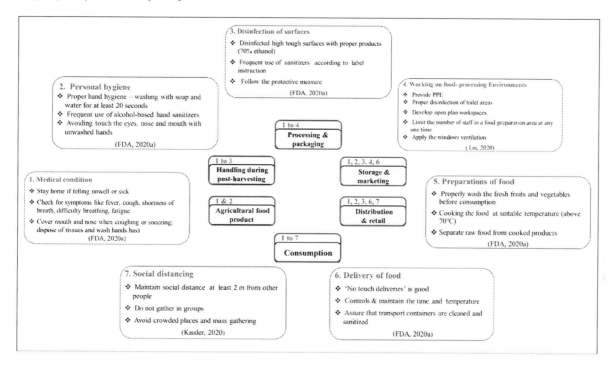

For example, when the recent pandemic is analyzed in terms of supply, it has threatened the sustainability of businesses (Okat et al., 2020). The fact that COVID-19 is a contagious disease, concerns about the act of eating (Kim, Kim, Lee, & Tang, 2020), measures such as quarantine and social/physical distance implemented limit the movement of people by determining where they can go, with whom they can meet and where they can eat, in food and beverage establishments. This has gradually reduced the consumption rate (İflazoğlu & Aksoy, 2020). Individuals who prefer to consume their meals at home (Cömert & Yeşilyurt, 2021) differ significantly in the amounts and types of foods they need to prepare meals (Goddard, 2020).

Thus, consumer consumption of food at home has affected the entire food and beverage industry, especially restaurants, economically, socially, and psychologically. Simultaneously, the recommendations of the central and local governments to stay at home within the scope of COVID-19 measures (Kim & Lee, 2020), the fact that the pandemic causes a decrease in consumer incomes, and the fact that the prices of food products are unnecessary and expensive cause consumers to decrease their demands and not to buy happened (Cranfield, 2020). In this situation, the differentiation of consumer perception and some changes in consumption behaviors along with the pandemic were among the effects of the pandemic on the demand dimension.

Food and beverage businesses, which had to cease during COVID-19, resumed their activities with the decrease in cases and the spread of vaccine applications. However, in this normalization period, some changes have occurred as stated before. In particular, food and beverage businesses have turned to more innovation studies and paid extra attention to hygiene and sanitation (Demirdelen, Alrawadieh, & Çiftçi, 2021). Intermittent ventilation of the environment in food and beverage businesses, not taking customer clothes, choosing disposable materials, measuring the temperature of guests and staff, using disinfectants at the tables, using masks by customers and staff, and providing services by staff in open buffet presentations (Karamustafa, Ülker, & Akçay, 2021).

It is seen as important changes to keep a distance of at least 1.5 meters and 60 centimeters between tables, and to clean dining tables and furniture, tabletop equipment with disinfectants after each use (Ministry of Culture and Tourism, 2020). In addition, the pandemic has increased the use of takeway services, contactless payment, package service, QR codes, and digital menus, thus resuting in a large increase in automation. In fact, this rapid change in terms of food and beverage businesses is expected to be more common in the future (Demirdelen, Alrawadieh, & Çiftçi, 2021).

Effects of the Pandemic Crisis on Food Insecurity

Food security is the constant availability, accessibility, and usability of food necessary for a healthy life. Disruption in availability, accessibility, usability, and continuity creates food insecurity (Demir & Esen, 2021). Food insecurity is a multifaceted issue affected by a variety of environmental and personal determinants that require a comprehensive solution (USDA, 2021). The concept of Moderate Food Insecurity refers to the uncertainty of the possibility of accessing food in sufficient quantity and/or quality. The concept of severe food insecurity refers to situations where food is depleted, no food is eaten for days, and human health and well-being are at great risk (FAO, 2020; Çalışır, 2021).

The 2019 United Nations Report states that 26.4% of the world's population, 52.5% of the African population, 30.9% of the Latin American population, 22.8% of the Asian population, and 8% of the population of North America and Europe experienced moderate or severe food insecurity during 2018. There are significant disparities between Europe and North America, which is defined as the "global north", and sub-Saharan Africa, South America, and Asia, which is referred to as the "global south".

The common features of these regions with moderate and severe food insecurity are in and around the tropical zone, rich natural resources, and including very rich forests and wildlife. These regions are also very rich in terms of natural resources and correspond to regions where ecological diversity is under threat. Regions of food insecurity are also the origins of major pandemics for the past two decades (FAO, 2020; Holst, 2020; Çalışır, 2021).

Disaster situations, including pandemics, hurricanes, wildfires, and earthquakes disproportionately affect those most at risk of experiencing food insecurity. The COVID-19 pandemic has also led to widespread reductions in global food security, affecting vulnerable households in almost every country in the world (Rudin-Rush et al., 2022). For example, food insecurity is rampant in the United States and has increased sharply as a result of social distancing policies and the economic disruption brought on by the coronavirus disease 2019 (COVID-19) pandemic.

Prior to COVID-19, a total of one in nine households in the United States were food insecure (Coleman-Jensen, 2019; Leddy et al., 2020). However, in the first four months of the pandemic, food insecurity in the United States increased by 26%. Massachusetts had the largest increase in food insecurity across the USA (47%) at the start of the pandemic. In 2019, 1 in 12 Massachusetts, 1 in 8 in 2020, and 1 in 10 in 2021 experienced food insecurity (Ohri-Vachaspati et al., 2021; The Greater Boston Food Bank, 2021; Nelson et al., 2022).

In addition, food insecurity was more common in rural and poor areas. For example, it was stated that in 2020, a total of 8.18 million people were in crisis in South Africa and 1.16 million people were in an emergency in terms of food insecurity, and it was stated that this number would increase to 9.60 million and 2.20 million, respectively, by March, 2021 (IPC, 2021; Ngarava, 2022). It is believed the effect of COVID-19 in the emergence of this situation is quite high. The increase in food insecurity has brought along household stress, various chronic diseases, and health problems (Leddy et al., 2020).

Additionally, the COVID-19 pandemic has had the greatest impact on human behavior changes (Laato, Islam, Farooq, & Dhir, 2020). At the beginning of the pandemic, when it comes to the possibility of the transmission of the coronavirus to food, people looked more cautiously at the food and the places they consume. People's food insecurity has increased and this has caused great damage to the restaurant industry (Kim, Bonn, & Cho, 2021).

Effects of the COVID-19 Pandemic Crisis on the Food Supply System

The food supply chain can be thought of as a chain of five segments, which are agricultural production, preprocessing, processing, distribution, retail, service, and consumption, as seen in Figure 3 above. It is a complex network of interconnected actors working to obtain the food, rather than a singular chain of specific actors. This chain starts with the agricultural producer and the food supplied at this stage moves through various manufacturing methods (Soğancılar, Dereli, & Arı, 2022). The uninterrupted flow in the food supply chain is of great importance as it provides well-being and security for customers and is a source of income and profit for individuals and businesses that are part of the chain (Gholami-Zanjani et al., 2021).

Food supply and security have faced negative impacts from the impact of the COVID-19 pandemic. Strict quarantine measures in China at the beginning of 2020, followed by further restrictions in Europe and the USA, have damaged the international movement of goods and people, with significant effects on international trade and tourism (Nichifor et al., 2021). However, the COVID-19 measures to close food markets implemented in many countries have changed the demand for food products and disrupted the continuity of the flow in the global food system (Stephens et al., 2020). These disruptions also significantly affected the international and national mobility of many basic necessities, especially foodstuffs.

Under such strict quarantine conditions, where most logistics activities stopped, shortages of foodstuffs became inevitable. For example, it was determined that the availability of vegetables, fruits and edible oils in India dropped to 10%. On the other hand, when the production in the farms is considered, a 20% decrease was determined in the production of vegetables and fruits. However, farms were found to have minimal impact on their prices (Mahajan & Tomar, 2021). At the same time, buyers sometimes experienced empty shelves in shops at the beginning of the epidemic, as food supply accelerated due to the sudden surge in demand (OECD, 2020; Bartender, Das, & Kanti De, 2021).

Moreover, it was observed that long-life milk and other foods with a long storage period were rapidly depleted in supermarkets in France and Germany in the first months of the pandemic due to social panic as seen in Table 1 (Hatipoğlu, 2021). In addition, countries had to make new regulations on their exports and imports during this period. For example, although Russia is a wheat exporter country, it stopped exporting during the pandemic and aimed to meet the possible food needs of its own citizens due to the uncertainty of how long the pandemic will last. The situation was similar in this process in Turkey. Onions, potatoes, and lemons (due to the increase in consumption and high demand against COVID-19 because of containing vitamin C) have tied their exports to special permits (Torun Kayabaşı, 2020).

The COVID-19 pandemic has caused labor shortages in certain labor-intensive areas such as animal care, agriculture, planting, gathering, and harvesting (Stephens et al., 2020). In Italy, for example, over 25% of food production is dependent on 370,000 regular seasonal workers brought from abroad. The closure of borders and the consequent cessation of human movement have revealed the fact that crops can be left to rot in the fields. This is also true for the UK and Germany. That is because in the UK the horticultural sector employs around 80,000 seasonal workers a year. On the other hand, Germany needs 300,000 workers to harvest fruits such as asparagus. In this process, the UK and Germany had difficulties in finding workers due to travel restrictions between countries (Defra, 2020; Petetin, 2020, pp. 327-328; Hatipoğlu, 2021).

Due to COVID-19, cherry and grape tomato shipments in the USA decreased by 50% and 47%, respectively, compared to 2019 levels. Businesses closed between April and June when more than 3,000 workers at 30 meat processing plants in the US tested positive for COVID-19 and a total of 44 workers died. Approximately 45,000 workers were affected by these closures. This directly affected meat processing volumes and fell 40% below 2019 levels (Luckstead et al., 2020, pp. 384-388; Walters et al., 2020, p. 2).

COVID-19 has been shown to affect the entire cycle from farm to customer (Bartender, Das, & Kanti De, 2021).

Security measures are extremely important to ensure the continuity of the food supply in this cycle. The most important of these measures are health problems of food sector personnel, personal hygiene, use of necessary personal protective equipment such as gloves and masks, cleaning of surfaces and working environments, safe preparation, transportation, and delivery of products, and maintaining food and physical distance. However, the potential risk is greater due to the high human interaction in the final stages of the food supply chain. Therefore, the measures taken at these stages are extremely important (Aday & Aday, 2020; Hatipoglu, 2021), because coronaviruses cannot reproduce in food and need an animal or human host to reproduce (Shariatifar & Molaee-aghaee, 2019).

Therefore, all stakeholders, including staff and consumers working in the food industry, must comply with food handlers' adequate sanitation and hygienic practice rules and at least the maximum requirements of food handlers to protect themselves from transmission of the COVID-19 virus (Olaimat et al., 2020). In addition, the food industry during the COVID-19 pandemic and the upcoming post-quarantine period must strictly follow Food Safety Management Systems (FSMS) based on Hazard Analysis Critical Control Point (HACCP) principles to prevent food contamination at all stages of food processing, production, packaging, and food processing.

Table 1. Food Production in France and Germany in March 2020. Source: (Liu, 2020; Hatipoğlu, 2021)

Country	Manufacturing Sub-Industry	Industrial Production Index (2015=100)	Compare to Previous Month	Compare to Same Month Last Year
France	Food Products Manufacturing	97	-% 2.3	-% 0.3
	Beverage Manufacturing	86.6	-% 12.7	-% 15.8
	Motor Vehicles, Trailers and Semi-Trailers	52.1	-% 49.1	-% 54.4
	Total Manufacturing	85	-% 18.3	-% 19.3
Germany	Food Products Manufacturing	99.8	-% 1.1	-% 4.1
	Beverage Manufacturing	101.2	-% 6.6	% 0.9
	Motor Vehicles, Trailers and Semi-Trailers	60.7	-% 31.1	-% 37.7
	Total Manufacturing	89.5	-% 11.5	-% 14.5

Food and Beverage Operations and Safety

All businesses operating in the food industry must strictly comply with the Food Safety Management Systems (FSMS) principles given for HACCP principles and stay up to date with new data on viruses when necessary. Food businesses and industries, including accommodation, where HACCP protocols do not apply, should be assigned a specialist who will stay in contact with public health authorities to seek advice in the event of an outbreak. Staff working in food and beverage businesses should be provided with soap, warm water, hand disinfectant for regular use, and hand washing stations with posters to inform effective use (Yılmaz & Beyter, 2021).

CONCLUSION

The tourism industry and government have an important role to play in the recovery efforts as the tourism industry differently post-pandemic. Consequently, it has been expected that the consequences of COVID-19 would result in a significant decline in value industries hotels, airlines, cruise lines, and car rentals. The decline has been significant enough in each industry to show concerns over the long-term outlook for each of these industries. The recent food and beverage safety trends during pandemic within two frames have still been discussed globally in this book's chapter which is based on different scientific materials, reports, and statistics from various scientific sources (i.e., the World Travel and Tourism Council [WTTC], the United Nations World Tourism Organization [UNWTO] and so forth).

However, the future of food and beverage operations in hotels has changed by integrating technology, touchless contact, social distancing, and hygiene precautions, focusing on domestic travel, virtual tourism, and luxury travel. With the recent pandemic events, robots also present an extra opportunity for financial benefits and expansion. Robots of the technology industry have been evolving in many restaurants and cafes that employ robots to prepare food and serve their customers. Using of kitchen technologies as robots is increasing after the COVID-19 pandemic in kitchens.

However, integrating technology especially robotization may further increase unemployment and turn enterprises into fabricated manufacturing enterprises. Food and beverage safety trends are also being changed. There will also be more organic and healthy foods menu planning processes and in the markets to strengthen immunity in as well. It is also suggested that kitchens will change to produce personally instead of these systems. However, the potential risk is greater due to the high human interaction in the final stages of the food supply chain.

Another issue is that there will be change in the menu planning process in the food and beverage sector post-pandemic. Menu planning processes of the chefs will be based on local and healthy products after the post-pandemic. It is found that employees who do not have a certificate after COVID-19 will not work in the food and beverage sector. Absolutely, the COVID pandemic is still reshaping existing patterns of tourism industry demand in a globalized inter-dependent world. In light of the COVID-19 pandemic, there will be more research conducted for the future of world. It is also concluded that the negative impacts of pandemic outbreaks such as the differentiation of consumer perception and some changes in consumption behaviors will be enormous on the tourism sector and supporting sectors in the world's poorest economies.

REFERENCES

Aday, S., & Aday, M. S. (2020). Impact of COVID-19 on the food supply chain. *Food Quality and Safety*, *4*(4), 167–180. doi:10.1093/fqsafe/fyaa024

Ali, F., Harris, K. J., & Ryu, K. (2019). Consumers' return intentions towards a restaurant with foodborne illness outbreaks: Differences across restaurant type and consumers' dining frequency. *Food Control*, *98*, 424–430. doi:10.1016/j.foodcont.2018.12.001

Ateljevic, I. (2020). Transforming the (tourism) world for good and re(generating) the potential 'new normal'. *Tourism Geographies*, *22*(3), 467–475. Advance online publication. doi:10.1080/14616688.2020.1759134

Barman, A., Das, R., & Kanti De, P. (2021). Impact of COVID-19 in food supply chain: Disruptions and recovery strategy. *Current Research in Behavioral Sciences*, *2*, 100017. doi:10.1016/j.crbeha.2021.100017

Beirman, D., & Van Walbeek, B. (2011). *Bounce back: Tourism risk, crisis and recovery management guide*. The Pacific Asia Travel Association.

Bin Salem, S., & Jagadeesan, P. (2020). COVID-19 from food safety and biosecurity perspective. *The Open Food Science Journal*, *12*(1-2).

Bourouiba, L. (2020). Turbulent gas clouds and respiratory pathogen emissions: Potential implications for reducing transmission of COVID-19. *Journal of the American Medical Association*, *323*(18), 1837–1838. doi:10.1001/jama.2020.4756 PMID:32215590

Brouder, P. (2020). Reset redux: Possible evolutionary pathways towards the transformation of tourism in a COVID-19 world. *Tourism Geographies*, *22*(3), 484–490. Advance online publication. doi:10.1080/14616688.2020.1760928

Bucak, T., & Yigit, S. (2021). The future of the chef occupation and the food and beverage sector after the COVID-19 outbreak: Opinions of Turkish chefs. *International Journal of Hospitality Management*, *92*, 102682. doi:10.1016/j.ijhm.2020.102682 PMID:33071426

Cahyanto, I., Pennington-Gray, L., Thapa, B., Srinivasan, S., Villegas, J., Matyas, C., & Kiousis, S. (2016). Predicting information seeking regarding hurricane evacuation in the destination. *Tourism Management*, *52*, 264–275. doi:10.1016/j.tourman.2015.06.014

Casanova, L. M., Jeon, S., Rutala, W. A., Weber, D. J., & Sobsey, M. D. (2010). Effects of air temperature and relative humidity on coronavirus survival on surfaces. *Applied and Environmental Microbiology*, *76*(9), 2712–2717. doi:10.1128/AEM.02291-09 PMID:20228108

Centers for Disease Control and Prevention. (2020). *COVID-19 surveillance and data analytics*. Retrieved on April 10, 2020, from: https://www.cdc.gov/coronavirus/2019-ncov/php/open-america/surveillance-data-analytics.html

Chan, J. F.-W., Yuan, S., Kok, K. H., Wang, K. K.-W., Chu, H., & Yang, J. (2015). A familial cluster of pneumonia associated with the 2019 novel coronavirus indicating person-to-person transmission: A study of a family cluster. *Lancet*, *395*(10223), 514–523. doi:10.1016/S0140-6736(20)30154-9 PMID:31986261

Cho, S. J., Lee, J. Y., & Winters, J. V. (2020). *COVID-19 Employment status impacts on food sector workers. 13334: 1.* ZA Discussion.

Coleman-Jensen, A., Rabbitt, M. P., Gregory, C. A., & Singh, A. (2019). Household Food Security in the United States in 2018. United States Department of Agriculture (USDA).

Cond'e Nast Traveller. (2020). *Himachal pradesh reopens for tourists, but many kullu- manali hotels to stay closed.* Retrieved on September 05, 2020, from: https://www.cntraveller.in/story/himachal-pradesh-covid-19-negative-test-minimum-5-day-booking-travel-new-rules-2020/

CoronaBoard. (2022). Retrieved on July 7, 2022, from: https://coronaboard.com/global/

Cömert, M., & Yeşilyurt, B. (2021). The impact of the changes caused by the Covid-19 pandemic on consumer behaviors on food and beverage businesses. *Journal of Tourism and Gastronomy Studies, 9*(3), 1622–1638. doi:10.21325/jotags.2021.859

Cranfield, J. A. (2020). Framing Consumer Food Demand Responses In A Viral Pandemic. *Canadian Journal of Agricultural Economics/Revue canadienne d'agroeconomie, 68*(2), 151-156.

Çalışır, H. (2021). *Anthropocene to the Covid-19 Epidemic.* Academic Press.

Çetintaş, H., & Bektaş, Ç. (2008). Türkiye'de turizm ve ekonomik büyüme arasındaki kısa ve uzun dönemli ilişkiler. *Anatolia: Turizm Araştırmaları Dergisi, 19*(1), 37–44.

Çiftçi, E., & Çoksuer, F. (2020). Novel Coronavirus Infection: COVID-19. *Flora Journal of Infectious Diseases and Clinical Microbiology, 25*(1), 9–18.

Darnell, M., Subbrao, K., Feinstone, S., & Taylor, D. (2004). Inactivation of the coronavirus that induces severe acute respiratory syndrome, SARS-CoV. *Journal of Virological Methods, 121*(1), 85–91. doi:10.1016/j.jviromet.2004.06.006 PMID:15350737

Dedeoğlu, B. B., & Boğan, E. (2021). The motivations of visiting upscale restaurants during the covid-19 pandemic: The role of risk perception and trust in government. *International Journal of Hospitality Management, 95*, 102905. doi:10.1016/j.ijhm.2021.102905

DEFRA. (2018). *Horticulture Statistics 2018.* Retrieved on September 11, 2021, from: https://assets.publishing.service.gov.uk/government/uploads/system/uploads/attachment_data/file/1003952/hort-report-01aug19.pdf

Demir, O., & Esen, A. (2021). Destructive Economic Effects of Covid 19 and Transformation Need in Turkish Economy. *Journal of Emerging Economies and Policy, 6*(1), 88–105.

Dolnicar, S., & Zare, S. (2020). COVID19 and airbnb-disrupting the disruptor. *Annals of Tourism Research, 102961.* Advance online publication. doi:10.1016/j.annals.2020.102961 PMID:32834218

Duan, S. M., Zhao, X. S., & Wen, R. F. (2003). Stability of SARS coronavirus in human specimens and environment and its sensitivity to heating and UV irradiation. *Biomedical and Environmental Sciences, 16*(3), 246–255. PMID:14631830

Dube, K., Nhamo, G., & Chikodzi, D. (2021). COVID-19 cripples global restaurant and hospitality industry. *Current Issues in Tourism, 24*(11), 1487–1490. doi:10.1080/13683500.2020.1773416

Duda-Chodak, A., Lukasiewicz, M., Ziec, G., Florkiewicx, A., & Filipiak-Florkiewicz, A. (2020). Covid-19 pandemic and food: Present knowledge, risks, consumers fears and safety. *Trends in Food Science & Technology, 105*, 145–160. doi:10.1016/j.tifs.2020.08.020 PMID:32921922

Ekonomist E-Dönüşüm Dergisi. (2020). *Dijitalleşmeyle yeni normale dönülüyor*. Retrieved on February 14, 2021, from: https://www.qnbefinans.com/uploads/20200925115031437.pdf

Euractiv. (2020). *No evidence of COVID-19 transmission through food, says EFSA*. Retrieved on August 14, 2021, from: https://www.euractiv.com/section/coronavirus/news/no-evidence-of-covid-19-transmission-through food-says-efsa/

Farias, D. P., & Santos Gomesdos, M. G. (2020). COVID-19 outbreak: What should be done to avoid food shortages? *Trends in Food Science & Technology, 102*, 291–292. doi:10.1016/j.tifs.2020.06.007 PMID:32834501

FAO. (2020). *Hunger and food insecurity*. Retrieved on September 22, 2021, from: https://www.fao.org/hunger/en/

Food and Agriculture Organization. (2020). *Q&A: COVID-19 pandemic–impact on food and agriculture*. Retrieved on September 11, 2020, from: http://www.fao.org/2019-ncov/q-and-a/impact-on-food-and-agriculture/en/

Fong, L. H. N., Law, R., & Ye, B. H. (2020). Outlook of tourism recovery amid an epidemic: Importance of outbreak control by the government. *Annals of Tourism Research*, 102951. PMID:32836566

Fotiadis, A., Polyzos, S., & Tzung-Cheng, T. C. H. (2021). The good, the bad and ugly on Covid-19 tourism recovery. *Annals of Tourism Research, 87*, 103117. doi:10.1016/j.annals.2020.103117 PMID:33518847

Frewer, L., de Jonge, J., & van Kleef, E. (2009). Consumer perceptions of food safety. *Medical Science, 2*, 243.

Galanakis, C. M. (2020). The food systems in the era of the coronavirus (COVID-19) pandemic crisis. *Foods, 9*(4), 523. doi:10.3390/foods9040523 PMID:32331259

Gautam, S., & Trivedi, U. (2020). Global implications of bio-aerosol in pandemic. *Environment, Development and Sustainability, 22*(5), 3861–3865. doi:10.100710668-020-00704-2 PMID:34172977

Gholami-Zanjani, S. M., Klibi, W., Jabalemeli, M. S., & Pishvaee, M. S. (2021). The design of resilient food supply chain networks prone to epidemic disruptions. *International Journal of Production Economics, 233*, 108001. doi:10.1016/j.ijpe.2020.108001

Goddard, E. (2020). The impact of covid-19 on food retail and food service in Canada: preliminary assessment. *Canadian Journal of Agricultural Economics/Revue Canadienne D'agroeconomie*, 1-5.

Gorbalenya, A. E., Baker, S. C., Baric, R. S., de Groot, R. J., Drosten, C., & Gulyaeva, A. A. (2020) Severe acute respiratory syndrome-related coronavirus: The species and its viruses – a statement of the Coronavirus Study Group. BioRxiv. doi:10.1101/2020.02.07.937862

Gössling, S., Scott, D., & Hall, C. M. (2020). Pandemics, tourism and global change: A rapid assessment of COVID-19. *Journal of Sustainable Tourism*, 1–20.

Güngör, E. Ö., & Yaldız, N. (2020). *Sars-Cov-2 (Covid – 19) And Food Safety. In Tam Metin Bildiriler Kitabı–Sağlık Bilimleri.* Concovid.

Han, S., Roy, P. K., Hossain, M. I., Byun, K. H., Choi, C., & Sang-Do, H. (2021). COVID-19 pandemic crisis and food safety: Implications and inactivation strategies. *Trends in Food Science & Technology, 109*, 25–36. doi:10.1016/j.tifs.2021.01.004 PMID:33456205

Hassan, V., Knio, M., & Bellos, G. (2022). Chapter 13 - How COVID-19 will change the future of tourism industry. In COVID-19: Tackling Global Pandemics through Scientific and Social Tools. Academic Press.

Hatipoğlu, A., (2021). *Covid-19 Pandemisinin küresel gıda tedarik zincirine etkileri.* Academic Press.

Henwood, F. A. (2020). Coronavirus disinfection in histopathology. *Journal of Histotechnology, 43*(2), 102–104. doi:10.1080/01478885.2020.1734718 PMID:32116147

Holst, J. (2020). Global Health – emergence, hegemonic trends and biomedical reductionism. *Globalization and Health, 16*(1), 1–11. doi:10.118612992-020-00573-4 PMID:32375801

Hong, C., Choi, H., Choi, C., & Joung, D. (2021). Factors affecting customer intention to use online food delivery services before and during the COVID-19 pandemic. *Journal of Hospitality and Tourism Management, 48*, 509–518. doi:10.1016/j.jhtm.2021.08.012

Hospitalitynet. (2020a). *MGM resorts international statement on temporary closure of Las Vegas properties.* Retrieved on March 16, 2022, from: https://www.hospitalitynet.org/news/4097568.html

Hospitalitynet. (2020b). *Coronavirus hits German hotel industry hard: more than every-3-guests stay away.* Retrieved on March 16, 2022, from: https://www.hospitalitynet.org/performance/4097569.html

IPC. (2021). *South Africa: IPC Acute Food Insecurity Analysis.* IPC.

İflazoğlu, N., & Aksoy, M. (2020). A study on the quality of the service consumers expect from food and beverage enterprises during the Covid-19 outbreak. *Journal of Tourism and Gastronomy Studies, 8*(4), 3362–3377. doi:10.21325/jotags.2020.766

Jawed, I., Tareen, F.R., Cauhan, K., & Nayeem, M. (2020). Food safety and COVID-19: Limitations of HACCP and the way forward. *The Pharma Innovation Journal, 9*(5), 1-4.

Kaushal, V., & Srivastava, S. (2021, January). Hospitality and tourism industry amid COVID-19 pandemic: Perspectives on challenges and learnings from India. *International Journal of Hospitality Management, 92*, 102707. doi:10.1016/j.ijhm.2020.102707 PMID:33024348

Kampf, G., Todt, D., Pfaender, S., & Steinmann, E. (2020). Persistence of coronaviruses on inanimate surfaces and their inactivation with biocidal agents. *The Journal of Hospital Infection, 104*(3), 246–251. doi:10.1016/j.jhin.2020.01.022 PMID:32035997

Karamustafa, K., Ülker, M., & Akçay, S. (2021). A Qualitative Study On Changes In Food And Beverage Service Processes Based On The Covid-19 Pandemic. *Journal of Consumer and Consumption Research, 13*(1), 33–69.

Kim, J., Kim, J., Lee, S. K., & Tang, L. R. (2020). Effects Of Epidemic Disease Outbreaks On Financial Performance Of Restaurants: Event Study Method Approach. *Journal of Hospitality and Tourism Management, 43*, 32–41. doi:10.1016/j.jhtm.2020.01.015

Kim, J., & Lee, J. C. (2020). Effects of COVID-19 on preferences for private dining facilities in restaurants. *Journal of Hospitality and Tourism Management, 45*, 67–70. doi:10.1016/j.jhtm.2020.07.008

Kim, K., Bonnb, M. A., & Choc, M. (2021). Clean safety message framing as survival strategies for small independent restaurants during the COVID-19 pandemic. *Journal of Hospitality and Tourism Management, 46*, 423–431. doi:10.1016/j.jhtm.2021.01.016

Koehl, D. (2011). *Toolbox for crisis communications in tourism: Checklists and best practices*. Univerza v Ljubljani, Ekonomska fakulteta, Madrid.

IFIC. (2020). *COVID-19 pandemic transforms the way we shop, eat and think about food, according to IFIC's 2020 Food & Health Survey*. Retrieved on April 24, 2022, from: https://foodinsight.org/wp-content/uploads/2020/06/2020-Food-and-Health-Survey-.pdf

Laato, S., Islam, A. N., Farooq, A., & Dhir, A. (2020). Unusual purchasing behavior during the early stages of the COVID-19 pandemic: The stimulus-organism-response approach. *Journal of Retailing and Consumer Services, 57*, 102224. doi:10.1016/j.jretconser.2020.102224

Leddy, A. M., Whittle, H. J., Shieh, J., Ramirez, C., Ofotokun, I., & Weiser, S. D. (2020). Exploring the role of social capital in managing food insecurity among older women in the United States. *Social Science & Medicine, 265*, 113492. doi:10.1016/j.socscimed.2020.113492 PMID:33162195

Lock, S. (2020). Daily year-on-year impact of COVID-19 on global restaurant dining. *Statista*. https://www.statista.com/statistics/1103928/coronavirus-restaurant-visitation-impact/

Liu, S. (2020). Food supply pressure in France and Germany during COVID-19: Causes from manufacturing. *Journal of Agriculture, Food Systems, and Community Development, 9*(4), 139–142. doi:10.5304/jafscd.2020.094.007

Luckstead, J., Nayga, R. M. Jr, & Snell, H. A. (2020). Labor Issues in the Food Supply Chain Amid the COVID-19 Pandemic. *Applied Economic Perspectives and Policy, 43*(1), 382–400. doi:10.1002/aepp.13090 PMID:33173571

Luty, J. (2020a). *Decline in pub, bar and restaurant sales due to covid-19 In The UK 2020*. Retrieved on March 23, 2022, from: https://www.statista.com/statistics/1105174/uk-pub-and-restaurant-sales-fall-due-to-covid-19/

Luty, J. (2020b). *Year-over-year daily change in seated restaurant diners due to the coronavirus (Covid-19) pandemic in Germany from February 24, 2020 to February 20, 2022*. Retreived on March 23, 2022, from: https://www.statista.com/statistics/1105090/coronavirus-restaurant-visitation-impact-german/

Mahajan, K., & Tomar, S. (2021). COVID-19 and supply chain disruption: Evidence from food markets in India. *American Journal of Agricultural Economics, 103*(1), 35–52. doi:10.1111/ajae.12158 PMID:33230345

Maida, J. (2020). Analysis on impact of Covid-19- online on-demand food delivery services market 2019-2023. *Businesswire*. Retrieved on November 11, 2021, from: https://www.businesswire.com/news/home/20200430005160/en/Analysis-Impact-Covid-19–Online-On-Demand-Food-Delivery

Ministry of Culture and Tourism. (2020). *Safe tourism certification program*. Retrieved on July 4, 2021, from: https://www.ktb.gov.tr/?_dil=1

Mullis, L., Saif, L. J., Zhang, Y., Zhang, X., & Azevedo, M. S. (2012). Stability of bovine coronavirus on lettuce surfaces under household refrigeration conditions. *Food Microbiology, 30*(1), 180–186. doi:10.1016/j.fm.2011.12.009 PMID:22265299

M&M Technologies. (2012). *M&M Technologies Food Safety and Food Security*. Retrieved on June 1, 2020, from: https://www.foodsafetymagazine.com/signature-series/food-safety-and-food-security/

National Restaurant Association (NRA). (2020). *Restaurant sales fell to their lowest real level in over 35 years*. Retrieved on September 19, 2021, from: https://restaurant.org/articles/news/restaurant-sales-fell-to-lowest-level-in-35-years.

Nechifor, V., Ramos, M. P., Ferrari, E., Laichena, J., Kihiu, E., Omanyo, D., Musamali, R., & Kiriga, B. (2021). Food security and welfare changes under COVID-19 in Sub-Saharan Africa: Impacts and responses in Kenya. *Global Food Security, 28*.

Nelson, E., Bangham, C., Modi, S., Liu, X., Codner, A., Hicks, J. M., & Greece, J. (2022). Understanding the impacts of COVID-19 on the determinants of food insecurity: A state-specific examination. *Preventive Medicine Reports, 28*, 101871.

Nepal, S. K. (2020). Travel and tourism after COVID-19 – business as usual or opportunity to reset? *Tour. Geogr.* doi:10.1080/14616688.2020.1760926

Ngarava, S. (2022). Empirical analysis on the impact of the COVID-19 pandemic on food insecurity in South Africa. *Physics and Chemistry of the Earth Parts A/B/C, 103180*.

Nichifor, E., Lixandroiu, R. C., Sumedrea, S., Chițu, I. B., & Bratucu, G. (2021). How can SMEs become more sustainable? Modelling the M-commerce consumer behaviour with contingent free shipping and customer journey's touchpoints optimisation. *Sustainability, 13*, 6845. https://doi.org/10.3390/su13126845

Nicola, M., Alsafi, Z., Sohrabi, C., Kerwan, A., Al-Jabir, A., Iosifidis, C., Agha, M., & Agha, R. (2020). The socio-economic implications of the coronavirus and COVID-19 pandemic: a review. *Int. J. Surg.* doi:10.1016/j.ijsu.2020.04.018

Niewiadomsky, P. (2020). COVID-19: From temporary de-globalisation to a rediscovery of tourism? *Tourism Geographies, 22*(3), 651–656.

NPD. (2020). *Online food orders, delivery surge amid COVID-19 lockdown*. Retrieved on May 24, 2021, from: https://www.npd.com/wps/portal/npd/us/news/press-releases/2020/while-total-us-re staurant-traffic-declines-by-22-in-march-digital-and-delivery-orders-jump-by-over- 60/

OECD. (2020). *Supporting livelihoods during the Covid-19 crisis: closing the gaps in safety nets*. Retrieved on January 23, 2022, from: https://www.oecd.org/coronavirus/en

Ohri-Vachaspati, P., Acciai, F., & DeWeese, R. S. (2021). SNAP participation among low-income US households stays stagnant while food insecurity escalates in the months following the COVID-19 pandemic. *Preventive Medicine Reports, 24*, 101555.

Okat, Ç., Bahçeci, V. & Ocak, E. (2020). Evaluating İmpacts Of COVID-19 (New Coronavirus) Pandemic Crisis On Food & Beverage Entreprises. *International Journal of Contemporary Tourism Research*, 201-218.

Olaimat, A. N., Shahbaz, H. M., Fatima, N., Munir, S., & Holley, R. A. (2020). Food safety during and after the era of COVID-19 pandemic. *Frontiers in Microbiology*, 1854.

Pressman, P., Naidu, A. S., & Clemens, R. (2020). COVID-19 and food safety: Risk management and future considerations. *Nutrition Today, 55*(3), 125-128.

Reiley, L. (2020). Stress-baking and hoarding have led to a retail egg shortage. There are eggs in the pipeline, but maybe not enough. *The Washington Post*. Retrieved on July 24, 2020, from: https://www.washingtonpost.com/business/2020/03/26/shortages-eggs-stress-baking/

Ritchie, B. W. (2004). Chaos, crises and disasters: A strategic approach to crisis management in the tourism industry. *Tourism Management, 25*(6), 669–683.

Rogerson, C. M., & Baum, T. (2020). COVID-19 and African tourism research agendas. *Development Southern Africa, 37*(5), 727–741.

Roy, D. (2020). *World food safety day 2020: COVID-19 offers an opportunity for India's food systems to deliver on safety and health*. Retrieved on June 16, 2020, from: https://www.ifpri.org/blog/world-food-safety-day-2020-covid-19-offers-opportunity-indias-food-systems-deliver-safety-and/

Rudin-Rush, L., Michler, J. D., Josephson, A., & Bloem, J. R. (2022). Food insecurity during the first year of the COVID-19 pandemic in four African countries. *Food Policy, 111*, 102306.

Shariatifar, N., & Molaee-aghaee, E. (2019). Novel Coronavirus 2019 (COVID-19): Important tips on food safety. *Journal of Food Safety and Hygiene, 5*(1), 58–59.

Sharma, S. (2020). *Distancing, masks key to stopping covid-19 spread: study*. https://www.hindustantimes.com/india-news/social-distancing-masks-eye-wear-and-hand-washing-work-best-in-combination-study/story-yROOhsGvHO0Zp7eAZpJmjJ.htm

Statista. (2020). *eServices Report 2020*. Retrieved on July 22, 2021, from: https://www.statista.com/study/42306/eservices-report/

Soğancılar, N., Dereli, Z., & Arı, G. S. (2022). Food Security in the COVID 19 Pandemic: Impacts Related to Food Supply. *Alanya Academic Review Journal, 6*(2), 2333–2349.

Soliku, O., Kyiire, B., Mahama, A., & Kubio, C. (2021). Tourism amid COVID-19 pandemic: Impacts and implications for building resilience in the eco-tourism sector in Ghana's Savannah region. *Heliyon, 7*, 07892.

Stephens, E. C., Martin, G., van Wijk, M., Timsina, J., & Snow, V. (2020). Editorial: Impacts of COVID-19 on agricultural and food systems worldwide and on progress to the sustainable development goals. *Agricultural Systems, 183*, 102873.

STR. (2020a). *STR: Europe hotel performance for July 2020*. Retrieved on March 17, 2022, from: https://str.com/press-release/str-europe-hotel-performance-july-2020

STR. (2020b). *STR: Middle East and Africa hotel performance for July 2020*. Retrieved on March 17, 2022, from: https://str.com/press-release/str-middle-east-and-africa-hotel-performance-july-2020

STR. (2020c). *STR: Canada hotel results for week ending 29 August*. Retrieved on March 17, 2022, from: https://str.com/press-release/str-canada-hotel-results-week-ending-29-august

Taylor, T., & Toohey, K. (2007). Perceptions of terrorism threats at the 2004 Olympic games: Implications for sport events. *Journal of Sport & Tourism, 12*(2), 99–114. https://doi.org/10.1080/14775080701654754

Teachout, M., & Zipfel, C. (2020). *The economic impact of Covid-19 lockdowns in sub-Saharan Africa*. International Growth Centre.

The Greater Boston Food Bank. (2021). *Food Insecurity Remains Well Above Pre-Pandemic Levels*. Retrieved on February 20, 2022, from: https://www.gbfb.org/2021/04/01/food-insecurity-remains-well-above-pre-pandemic-levels/

Torun Kayabaşı, E. (2020). The Effect of COVID-19 on Agricultural Production. *Eurasian Journal of Research in Social and Economics, 7*(5), 38–45.

Tuncer, T., & Akoğlu, A. (2020). Food safety knowledge of food handlers working in hotel kitchens in Turkey. *Food Health, 6*(2), 77–89. doi:10.3153/FH20009

TEPAV. (2020). Retrieved on August 9, 2020, from: https://www.tepav.org.tr/upload/files./15967816977.TEPAV_Istihdam_Izleme_Bulteni_SGK_Mayis_2020.pdf

TUROB. (2020). *Big bill to world tourism; STR March 2020 report*. Retrieved on March 15, 2022, from: https://www.turob.com/tr/bilgi-merkezi/basin-bultenleri/2020/show/32/dunya-turizmine-buyuk-fatura-str-mart-2020-

UNWTO. (2020). *Tourism highlights 2019 Edition*. Retrieved on March 13, 2022, from: https://www.unwto.org/taxonomy/term/347?page=1

UNWTO. (2021). *Covıd-19 and tourism: tourism in pre-pandemic times*. Retrieved on March 13, 2022, from: https://www.unwto.org/covid-19-and-tourism-2020

USDA. (2021). *Food Insecurity Measurement*. Retrieved on March 24, 2022, from: https://www.ers.usda.gov/topics/food-nutrition-assistance/food-security-in-the-u-s/measurement/#measurement

Walters, L., Wade, T., & Suttles, S. (2020). Food and agricultural transportation challenges amid the COVID-19 Pandemic. *Choices Magazine, 35*(3), 1–8.

Williams, C. C., & Kayaoğlu, A. (2020). COVID-19 and undeclared work: Impacts and policy responses in Europe. *The Service Industries Journal*, 1–18. .1080/02642069.2020.1757073. doi:https://doi.org/10

WHO. (2020). *COVID-19 and food safety: Guidance for food businesses: interim guidance*. Retrieved on April 24, 2022, from: https://www.who.int/publications/i/item/COVID-19-and-food-safety-guidance-for-food-businesses

Xu, Z., Elomri, A., Kerbache, L., & El Omri, A. (2020). Impacts of COVID-19 on global supply chains: Facts and perspectives. *IEEE Engineering Management Review*, *48*(3), 153–166.

van Doremalen, N., Bushmaker, T., Morris, D. H., Holbrook, M. G., Gamble, A., Williamson, B. N., & Munster, V. J. (2020). Aerosol and surface stability of SARS-CoV-2 as compared with SARS-CoV-1. *The New England Journal of Medicine*, *382*(16), 1564–1567.

Yacoub, L., & ElHajjar, S. (2021). How do hotels in developing countries manage the impact of COVID-19? The case of Lebanese hotels. *Int. J. Contemp. Hospit. Manag.*

Yang, Y., Zhang, H., & Chen, X. (2020). Coronavirus pandemic and tourism: Dynamic stochastic general equilibrium modeling of infectious disease outbreak. *Annals of Tourism Research*. https://www.ncbi.nlm.nih.gov/pmc/articles/PMC7147856/

Yılmaz, İ., & Beyter, N. (2021). Changes in the measures taken in food and beverage units for food safety after covid-19. *Journal of Tourism and Gastronomy Studies*, *5*(Special Issue), 321–346.

Yılmaz, M., & Şahin, M. K. (2021). Parents' willingness and attitudes concerning the COVID-19 vaccine: A cross-sectional study. *International Journal of Clinical Practice*, *75*, e14364.

Zhang, K., Hou, Y., & Li, G. (2020). Threat of infectious disease during an outbreak: Influence on tourists' emotional responses to disadvantaged price inequality. *Annals of Tourism Research*, *84*, 102993.

Chapter 22
Sustainable Practices in Indian Aviation

Mallika Sankar
https://orcid.org/0000-0002-9296-8478
Christ University, India

Priyanka Michael
Christ University, India

Suja John
Christ University, India

ABSTRACT

Air travel produces about three percent of carbon dioxide emissions worldwide. The air travel industry requires an enduring vision that focuses on sustainable practices in the entire aviation sector, which will be a significant aspect of the future of civil aviation. The study adopts a systematic review to portray significant challenges, issues, and best practices in the worldwide aviation industry, highlighting the Indian scenario to establish future exploration in India. The chapter extensively investigates the latest sustainable developments in the airline business, the logical agreement on its ecological effects, and steps taken for sustainability.

INTRODUCTION

Aviation must be an important travel segment of our society, driving economic, social, and cultural development worldwide. In India, the aviation industry contributes approximately 1.5% of the country's Gross Domestic Product (GDP) and supports eight million jobs. India is one of the fastest-growing aviation markets globally and is on track to hold the world's third-biggest position in the civil aviation market by 2030 (Business Standard, 2021). Air India is the national carrier and plays a significant role in associating India with the world. Indigo, Spice Jet, Go First, Vistara, and Air Asia are other players sharing their space in the Indian civil aviation industry.

DOI: 10.4018/978-1-6684-4645-4.ch022

Indian civil aviation at present stands at around $900 Mn and is anticipated to grow to US$4.33 billion by 2025, increasing at a Compound Annual Growth Rate (CAGR) of about 14-15%. The air-traffic recorded 131 million travellers in 2016, of which 100 million were homegrown. The most prominent aircraft by worldwide traveller traffic was Jet Airways which moved more than 10 million travellers throughout India in 2016, trailed by Air India and AI Express (8.8 million). Emirates (5.46 million) was the most prominent international airline working in India in the third spot. (Sinha, 2017). Though this is a million-dollar business, air travel has serious ecological effects concerning land acquisition issues and greenhouse gas emissions.

SUSTAINABILITY IN AVIATION INDUSTRY

Sustainable development did not gain any recognition until a German tax accountant and mining administrator Hans Carl von Carlowitz, laid its groundwork in his book *Sylvicultura Oeconomica* in 1713. He poignantly argued the philosophy of short-term financial gains in managing primary resources about wood. This concept gained importance in the late 20th century when the depletion of natural resources became alarming due to rapid economic growth. The first report on environmental concerns came into being by the International Union for Conservation of Nature (IUCN) in 1951. It aimed at bridging the gap between economy and ecology for a sustainable future.

Another significant report on the foundation of policies for sustainable development was *The Limits of Growth* evolved in the think tank of the Club of Rome in 1972. It highlighted the finiteness of natural resources, which is exhausting rapidly with population growth. Owing to the need of the hour, the United Nations Environment Programme (UNEP) was formed at the 1972 Stockholm Conference. The most well-known definition of sustainability comes from the 1987 Brundtland Commission report by the World Commission on Environment and Development (WCED) called *Our Common Future* as "meeting the needs of the present without compromising the ability of future generations to meet their own needs" (Jarvie, 2016).

Sustainability works on our lives' nature, secure our environment, and conserves regular assets of people for the future. Sustainable aviation is a system that sets out the aggregate methodology to handle the test of guaranteeing a cleaner, calmer, and brighter future by establishing comprehensive practices from assembling to operations to client care. Becoming environmentally viable and feasible is not just easy for the aviation sector. Improving a sustainable flying mode is essential for airlines, passengers, and the planet. Multiple tactics are followed by airlines of all sizes to reduce fuel consumption to carbon emissions. Most airlines are currently working with their regular operational flights by utilizing alternative fuel options. Nonetheless, the accessibility of biofuel feedstock stays a significant hindrance to inevitable use.

There are three types of sustainability pillars: the environmental, social, and economic pillars (Purvis et al., 2019). In the environmental aspect of sustainability, organizations focus on decreasing their carbon impressions, bundling waste, water utilization, and their general impact on the climate. They helpfully affect the planet and can likewise have a favorable monetary effect. Social paradigms reflect that a reasonable share of the business needs to be kept aside for helping and endorsement of its workers, partners, and the local area it works in. The ways to deal with getting and keeping up with this help are different.

However, it comes down to treating representatives decently and being a decent neighbour and local area, both locally and internationally. Economically a business should be productive to sustain itself in the market. Things that fit under the financial support point should also incorporate consistency and appropriate administration (Bettie, 2021). Furthermore, Sustainability in the aeronautics business can be accomplished by creating frameworks that respect the climate, cultivate financial worth, and upgrade public activity quality (Elhmoud & Kutty, 2020). The three vast parts of aeronautics supportability incorporate the following:

a) Ecological sustainability comprises the standard asset framework reliance
b) Monetary support, which expounds the financial ability, economic improvement, and monetary sensibility
c) Social reasonableness clarifies social honesty, security, individual well-being, and the predominance of life

The regulation by the International Civil Aviation Organisation (ICAO) regarding environmental concerns of the Aviation industry paved the way for the formation of the Carbon Offsetting and Reduction Scheme for International Aviation (CORSIA) on October 6, 2016. ICAO signed an agreement to curb and manage the enormous 100 million tonnes of CO_2 emissions by flights annually. Airports produce a minor portion of aviation emissions, but they are critical infrastructure governing passenger mobility and essential for long-term growth.

Airports impact climate, energy, air quality, water, biodiversity, and noise, among other environmental factors. The primary source of direct airport emissions is energy consumption. Airport operators can reduce their carbon footprint by improving insulation, energy efficiency and using renewable energy sources for electricity, heating, and conditioning. (Chokhani, 2021).

Some of the significant airport environmental issues include:

- Emission and environmental capacity: Aircraft emissions, both at ground level and altitude can have various detrimental consequences for air quality, temperature, and the ozone layer. From the ground to higher altitudes, the gases and particles released by aircraft engines can cause harm at various stages of flight. One of the adverse effects of airplane emissions at ground level, when airports are involved, is the degradation of air quality, which can directly influence human health (André, 2004).
- Noise issues: Aircraft noise has been one of the most significant sources of excessive noise caused by human activities since the beginning of the aviation industry. The engines, which comprise two essential types of jet and piston engines, and the aircraft frame are two sources of aircraft noise. Airports are regarded as critical contributors to the problem of excessive noise since airplanes make more noise during take-off and landing, and noise pollution is one of the most apparent environmental hazards of airport activities from a community's perspective (Sameh & Scavuzzi, 2016).
- Land Utilisation: When it comes to deciding whether to build or expand an airport, airport operators must strike a balance between maximizing capacity and future growth potential on the one hand and minimizing the associated environmental impacts on the other. Airport operators can achieve the best possible results by having appropriate and effective environmental management that develops and implements approaches and a mechanism to integrate airports and their activi-

ties into sustainable development plans. This means striking the best possible balance between the airport's growth, maximizing its social and economic benefits, and satisfying communities and regulators (Sameh, 2018).

Trends and Practices in the Aviation Industry

Newer planes, such as the Airbus A350 and Boeing 737 MAX, use less fuel per passenger (Aviation Benefits Beyond Borders, 2019). Airlines save money on fuel by using more efficient methods and reducing weight.

- On the ground: A small generator called an auxiliary power unit (APU) is installed in the aircraft's tail. Many airports are now installing fixed electrical ground power and pre-conditioned air at their gates, letting pilots turn off the APU and save fuel and noise when on the ground (Aviation Benefits Beyond Borders, 2019).
- Departure: There are mechanisms in operation, such as single-engine taxiing or in progress, such as self-driving devices, that allow aircraft to taxi from the gate to the runway without utilizing full engine power.
- Cruise: Airlines are devising new techniques to minimize the weight of a wide range of objects transported, including food service trolleys, seats, carpets, and loading only the right amount of water for each flight rather than filling the tanks every time. As a result, tremendous savings are realized.
- Arrival: New technology enables far more precise observation of each aircraft's location, resulting in a complete picture of the traffic environment. This has led to the development of a new technology known as continuous descent operations, which allows planes to nearly 'glide' into the airport with their engines turned off. This saves fuel and minimizes the amount of noise generated in the surrounding area.

Residents who live near airports may be disturbed by aircraft noise (Aviation Benefits Beyond Borders, 2019). The industry has been attempting to reduce noise for decades, and it has made significant progress. The noise levels have been cut in half in the last ten years. According to the International Civil Aviation Organization (ICAO), the number of individuals exposed to airplane noise worldwide decreased by 35% between 1998 and 2004. The Boeing 787 and Airbus A380, two of the most recent colossal aircraft, have minimal noise 'footprints.' Airlines and pilots can apply noise reduction methods such as lower thrust take-off, displacement landing thresholds, and continuous descent operations with the help of air navigation service providers and airport operators.

Aircraft and engine manufacturers worldwide are setting the standard for greener manufacturing. Some companies even require such measures throughout their whole manufacturing supply chain. Pratt and Whitney aspires to achieve zero waste in its factories by 2025, with all waste being recycled. Energy consumption will be optimized, and greenhouse gas emissions will be decreased by 80%. The corporation wants to eliminate water waste and reduce water use by 80% (Aviation Benefits Beyond Borders, 2018). Despite hiring 13,000 additional people and constructing a large production site, Boeing and Kaiser reduced hazardous waste by 18%, CO_2 levels by 9%, energy use by 3%, and water intake by 2%, according to a five-year environmental audit.

Boeing diverted 79 percent of its solid waste from landfills in 2012, improving 36% from 2007. Airbus became the first aerospace business to acquire ISO environmental certification in January 2007, covering all its manufacturing locations, products, and services throughout its entire lifecycle. The program had already produced the following results in 2012 by 30% lower energy use, 43% lower water consumption, and 46% lower non-recycled waste generation CO_2 emissions were reduced by 34%.

Challenges in the Aviation Industry

Airlines are confronted with several new sustainability issues such as sustainability reporting, sustainable procurement and supply chain management, cabin waste recycling, and the substitution of single-use plastics.

- **Sustainability reporting:** Although the number of aviation firms providing separate sustainability reports has expanded dramatically over the years, over half of those companies no longer do so. As a result, if the aviation industry believes in the benefits of engaging in sustainability issues and sincerely wants to improve its sustainability reporting practices, then boards of directors may encourage companies to integrate sustainability issues into their operations by allocating the necessary financial and human resources. The panels may also create a special sustainability committee or department to address sustainability issues and reporting methods (Karaman et al., 2018).
- **Sustainable procurement and supply chain management:** In today's environment, Supply Chain Management enables firms to remain competitive and expand their benefits, as the market's rapid development, more incredible rivalry, and the need to improve customer service quality offer new challenges for businesses. Supply Chain Management enables optimizing all value chain operations, from raw material supply to end-user service. (Makarova & Pavlov, 2017).
- **Cabin waste recycling:** To lower the environmental footprint, airlines realize the necessity of minimizing, reusing, and recycling cabin waste from their flight operations. Cabin garbage levels might increase in the next 10 years if wiser control is not implemented. IATA wants to see cabin trash laws simplified and harmonized and technical solutions that cut industry costs and contribute to the circular economy. (IATA, n.d.).
- **Substitution of single-use plastics:** According to the International Air Transport Association (IATA), airlines generate around 6.7 million tons of cabin garbage. Plastic is a significant component of this waste stream and a global problem. There is also the issue of food waste. According to IATA, unopened food and drink account for 20 to 30% of overall waste. Many airlines have replaced single-use plastics with more sustainable alternatives like bamboo, paper, cardboard cutlery, and other biodegradable options (Paddison, 2020).

Initiatives and Successful Strategies in Global Aviation Industry

Air New Zealand: Air New Zealand has implemented several programs to reduce single-use plastic on its flights to remove roughly 55 million plastic items from its fleet. Individual plastic water bottles have been eliminated from the airline's Business Premier and Premium Economy cabins and its Works Deluxe offering on Tasman and Pacific Island trips. Individual plastic sauce packets are withdrawn from Business Premier cabins on mainland North America and Hong Kong routes. Instead, customers will be served sauce in recyclable dishes, saving an estimated 200,000 plastic packets from being thrown away each year (Asaf, 2019).

Scandinavian Airlines: Scandinavian Airlines (SAS) is the latest airline to announce plans to phase out in-flight duty-free shopping as part of a 25% reduction in emissions by 2030. While the change aligns with a movement toward in-flight e-commerce, it will assist in reducing the aircraft's total weight, which will save fuel and reduce emissions. Tax-free sales are a popular feature onboard SAS flights, but the airline has noticed a shift in passenger purchase behavior, with sustainability becoming a key consideration (Caswell, 2019).

Etihad Airways: To raise awareness about plastic pollution, Etihad Airways claimed to be the first airline in the United Arab Emirates to run a flight without any single-use plastics on board. According to the airline, over 95% of single-use plastic products used in Etihad's aircraft cabins have removed from the Earth Day flight, Etihad saved nearly 50 kilograms of plastic from being dumped (Etihad Airways, 2019).

Qantas Airlines: Qantas has stated that it has completed the first-ever commercial flight with no landfill waste, starting with a goal to eliminate 75% of the airline's garbage by the end of 2021 and cut 100 million single-use plastics by the end of 2020. Approximately 1,000 single-use plastic goods, such as individually packaged milk and vegemite, were replaced with sustainable alternatives or removed entirely from the trip. Meal containers made from sugar cane and cutlery manufactured from corn starch were among the alternative goods used on the aircraft, both of which are compostable. Customers were also encouraged to use digital boarding passes and electronic bag tags whenever feasible. Employees were on hand to ensure that any paper passes or tags were disposed of in an environmentally friendly manner (Qantas Newsroom, 2019).

Singapore Airlines: Singapore Airlines (SIA) is also expanding the use of sustainable ingredients in inflight meals, minimizing food waste on board, and reducing the usage of plastics for inflight products. SIA presently uses customer surveys, data analytics, and employee feedback, and it collaborates with its caterers to prevent food waste after flights. The airline has also indicated that it intends to automate data collecting and expand its use of artificial intelligence and machine learning to predict consumer consumption habits better and reduce cabin food waste (Singapore Airlines, 2019).

Emirates Airlines: Emirates provides facilities for sustainability in the United Arab Emirates (UAE) with the installation of solar power systems through the Emirates Engine Maintenance Centre and Emirates Flight Catering to provide renewable electricity. The airline is dedicated to responsible consumption by making thoughtful decisions about what they buy, where they get them, how they dispose of garbage, and how they use water and electricity (Otley, 2021).

Qatar Airways: The Qatar Airways Group is reaffirming its commitment to environmental sustainability by showcasing its significant environmental efforts. The airline is the first in the Middle East to get the highest level of accreditation from the IATA Environmental Assessment Programme. Qatar Airways has pledged to achieve net-zero carbon emissions by 2050, joining the first global alliance to commit to a common goal of carbon neutrality (Doyle, 2021).

Initiatives and Successful Strategies in India Aviation Industry

The Ministry of Civil Aviation in India plans to accomplish a reasonable and comprehensive development of the aviation industry in the nation and cure the ecological concerns presented by the industry. The Indian Government has proposed a Green Aviation Policy to make an administrative structure to heal the environmental issues created by the aviation industry by distinguishing key approach regions that require core values and guidelines. The Green Aviation Policy intends to figure out arrangements regarding environmental concerns relating to the natural administration framework.

Airport expert preparation, green foundation program, clamor for the executives, ozone-depleting substance discharges and ecological change, local air quality, energy and resource protection, solar-based and other renewable power (Singhania et al., 2019) were a few initiatives proposed through Green Aviation Policy. India satisfied its deliberate characteristic of diminishing the outflow power of its GDP by 21% as of 2005 levels (Jain, 2022). Before 2030, it is adjusted to procure a 35% markdown. India has also appeared the most recent environment and energy targets, creating 450 gigawatts (GW) of environmentally friendly power utilization by 2030.

Approximately 40 percent of the Indian airspace was under the Indian defence authorities, and most of the routes were restricted for civil aircraft movement. Due to this, most civil aircraft navigational routes had to circumvent these restricted areas by adding carbon emissions and losing fuel and time. Airport Authority of India (AAI) has executed technical fixes for route enhancement like shortening and fixing significant air routes, Reduced Horizontal Separation (RHS), Performance-based Navigation (PBN), and Flexible Use of Airspace (FUA) drive (ICAO, 2016). The Airport Carbon Accreditation program freely evaluates the activities of air terminals through six levels of certification and is an ideal intercession to battle environmental change. Implementation of onsite renewable energy is another indicator of sustainability. Since 2014, India has introduced solar technology at 44 airports, accomplishing a decrease of roughly 57,600 tons of CO_2 each annum at AAI Airports. Infrastructure building, which is one more fundamental part of extending the country's common avionics industry, has been brought under a green and manageability centre. Delhi, Mumbai, and Bengaluru International Airports have effectively gotten a 'Gold rating' by the International Green Building Organisation. While Jammu, Chandigarh, and Tirupati air terminals have earned a "4-star rating" by Green Rating for Integrated Habitat Assessment (GRIHA), India's own particular green structure rating framework (Puri, 2021).

ICAO has cautioned that the flight business needs to plan for severe interruptions due to environmental change. It needs to utilize clean innovation and mechanisms to lessen its carbon impression alongside other ecological effects. Investigating the utilization of bio-jet fuels, energy-productive foundations, electric vehicles, green maneuvering vehicles, legitimate administrative systems, and favorable economic situations are a few options helping reduce greenhouse gas in the aviation industry. Airplane noise close to the airport presents significant well-being and natural risk raising public concerns. It will probably affect future tasks and the extension and advancement of air terminals. The aeronautics partners are reliably cooperating to diminish noise through innovation, process improvement, and land use arranging. Be that as it may, the commotion around air terminals might be reduced by appropriate land use arranging, which should be tended to with government partners (Ministry of Civil Aviation, 2019).

Aviation emission discharge levels should be consistently observed and controlled through proper framework and transformation measures. Green Aviation improvement is a persistent stream of cycles, and the achievements can be accomplished by aggregating activities from different circles of exercise. Few initiatives may include better-streamlined airplane plan and assembling, greener fuel sources like power modules and biofuels, effective motors, course enhancement and organization advancement, productive executives' air traffic, coercive regulative arrangements, and positive financial measures (Sarkar, 2012).

Though the Indian aviation sector merely accounts for approximately 2 percent of global anthropogenic CO_2 emissions, including international and domestic aviation, India needs to take action to develop a better way to decarbonize the aviation sector.

Acknowledging the environmental impact of air travel, the "International Air Transport Association" (IATA) has designed three goals, viz., 1.5% per annum fuel efficiency improvement, neutral carbon growth, and net-zero emissions, to mitigate the climate impact from the aviation sector and to reduce its carbon footprint.

To lessen the impact on the environment, the Indian government has adopted many new initiatives to mitigate the climate change and environmental challenges and implemented many best practices to mobilize the situation. Cochin International Airport Ltd. is the world's first air terminal entirely fuelled by sun-based energy (CIAL, 2017). Chandigarh and Vadodara airports in India have embraced new green building activities. Indira Gandhi International Airport in Delhi is a "carbon neutral" air terminal (Ministry of Civil Aviation, 2020).

Carbon neutrality is a condition of net-zero carbon dioxide emissions and balancing emitting carbon and absorbing carbon from the atmosphere in carbon sinks. It might get completed by adjusting outflows of carbon dioxide with expulsion or killing discharges from society. As of October 2016, the Carbon Offsetting and Reduction Scheme for International Aviation (CORSIA) has been initiated, and sixty-six nations offering over 85% of the worldwide aeronautics movement have chosen to participate in this instrument from the early stage willingly (ICAO, 2016).

India is becoming more mindful of this worldwide concern and has made significant aviation and environmental change strides. The Airport Authority of India (AAI) has attempted different feasible advancement projects across various airports in the country. The key initiatives and successful strategies of various airlines in India include fleet renewal, technology adaptation, SAF, and various operational and infrastructure improvements.

Fleet renewal is one of the innovative models that most airlines in India have adopted. This is a new initiative to switch the existing aircraft with additional fuel-efficient models. In addition to this, new airplanes have enlisted into aviation service in the last decade, and every new generation of aircraft is 15-20 percent more fuel-efficient than the previous. Nearly 50 percent of the in-service fleet in India is A320neo and airlines have an order book for over 850 A320neo and 737MAX aircraft.

Along with this, research and development for new technology aircraft with electric, hydrogen, or hybrid engines are advancing in India that can substantially reduce CO_2 emissions. Airbus is expected to launch a hydrogen-powered airliner in 2035 under the ZEROe project. India enjoys practical, sustainable aviation fuel (SAF) benefits, including a colossal market scope. Being one of the world's least expensive environment-friendly power makers, it has more than adequate and economical feedstocks.

Despite severe supportability guidelines, India's SAF feedstock has a promising future. India can lead and construct its guide for introducing SAF by utilizing global cross-practical aptitude to support the neighbourhood partners. The objective of using sustainable aviation fuels, or SAFs, is to decrease the quantity of ozone-depleting substances transmitted during the lifetime of the energies, from creation to burning, contrasted to current petrol-based jet powers. The size of that decrease relies upon the cycle used to make the fuel and the carbon source. And surprisingly, however, some SAFs boasts critical outflow decreases, and few are made at a vast scale (Boerner, 2021).

SAF can reduce CO_2 emissions, and the aviation industry has made a lot of progress in proving its operational safety and reliability, with over 350,000 flights operated using SAF since 2011. However, only a handful of flights have been completed in India. India is well placed to develop a SAF industry given the wide availability of feedstocks and low cost of renewable energy.

The airlines and airports can put a broad range of operational and infrastructure improvements to reduce CO2 emissions. These may include optimizing the use of airstrips and airspace, adopting biofuel and weight-saving measures, constructing greener airports, and optimum air traffic management. Delhi Airport has installed Fixed Electric Ground Power (FEGP) at all its stands to reduce airline emissions by up to 40% and reduce noise on the apron. The aviation sector also relies on carbon offsetting to fill the emission gaps as an interim resolution.

Sustainable Aviation and Corporate Social Responsibility (CSR) in the Aviation Industry

Corporate Social Responsibility (CSR) is one source of competitive advantage in today's aviation business, which operates in a highly competitive environment. This industry has several negative consequences, including noise, carbon dioxide emissions, pollution, and working conditions. CSR is a strategic corporate activity that can help ensure the aviation industry's long-term viability (Serhan et al., 2018). Airlines value corporate social responsibility and sustainability for a variety of reasons. Social power, public image, money and wealth, and conformity are all factors that influence corporate social responsibility. CSR is a means for certain airlines to obtain social influence.

The "green movement" is a well-known social and environmental movement, and consumers are drawn to companies that follow ethical business methods (Dunbar, 2018). People are susceptible to environmental issues in every business as pollution concerns increase. According to Kim et al. (2020), one of the most critical CSR initiatives in the airline business is environmental protection and safety concerns from customers' perspectives. Consumers regard environmental responsibility as just as necessary as safety issues that could mean the difference between life and death. CSR initiatives have made many organized sectors more accountable to local communities in lowering the environmental impact. It has also been used in the aviation sector to encourage positive behavior.

Regulators are preparing to set emissions reduction targets for the aviation industry in a world increasingly concerned about climate change and seeing the aviation industry's release of greenhouse gas (GHG) emissions at high altitudes as problematic. From educators' perspectives, industry players, and the society in which they operate, CSR in the aviation business is an essential topic. The aviation sector is one of the most critical linkages in the tourism industry. It has a variety of consequences on society in terms of job creation, environmental impact, and community involvement. Various airlines participate in CSR in some form or another on a national and worldwide level. These practices include everything from community work to giving passengers "free miles" to starting environmental research (Singh, 2015).

All airlines in Indian Aviation Industry also follow many CSR initiatives. Indigo is the leading airline in the Indian aviation market, follows many CSR initiatives for children education, women empowerment, environmental support, preservation of heritage sites, and hunger relief initiatives (IndigoReach, n.d.). SpiceJet follows CSR practices such as hunger, poverty, malnutrition, preventive healthcare, water and sanitation, education, employability and livelihoods enhancement, gender equality and women empowerment, senior citizens care, rural development, slum area development. Vistara's CSR practices aiming at Children and Education encourages the underprivileged children to pursue secondary education and a healthy lifestyle to assist them in realizing their goals.

To enhance the employability skills, they provide poor children and young women with practical occupational skills and encouraging them to pursue careers in aviation or similar fields. For ensuring environmental sustainability and ecological balance they also promote natural resource conservation.

Along with this, the organization also follow the most common forms of community outreach through donations and grants volunteering by employees and payroll donations, providing air travel and cargo space access (Air Vistara, n.d.).

Air India Express also follows the CSR practices such as providing education, skill development, women empowerment, environment and community development, drinking water, sanitation, rural development/ slum development, childcare, conservation of natural resources, promoting and developing of art and culture, public libraries, promotion and development of traditional arts and handicrafts, sports, health care (Air India Express, n.d.).

GoFirst Airlines is one of the group companies in the Wadia Group, and this group uses the word philanthropy for its CSR activities. Between 1908 and 1956, the Wadia group's philanthropy included the creation of five gardens in Mumbai. In addition, Mumbai has hospitals, and Pune has a college. Sir Ness Wadia Foundation, a non-profit trust founded in 1969, has worked to assist earthquake victims in Latur and provide scholarships to underprivileged groups in drought relief (GoFirst Airline, n.d.).

India's commercial carriers keep developing new and productive airplanes aiming at reduction in CO_2 discharges over numerous years. Both government and industry's flow envisioned that Indian market will have more modest hydrogen-energized and electrically-fuelled airplanes take to the skies during the 2030s. All airline companies targeting at productive planes ultimately to make them reasonable and sustainable (Sethi, 2021). Cultivating a SAF industry wouldn't just diminish carbon emissions in aviation. However, it would likewise battle air contamination from crop burning, do various green jobs, work on farmers' income, and settle waste management issues (Wolff et al., 2021).

The aviation industry has entered the era of industry 5.0, including robots, the Internet of Things (IoT), Artificial Intelligence (AI), and many other remote sensing machines. The future innovations in AI and IoT will be incorporated into the aviation industry, enhancing passenger experience in airlines and boarding process in airport ground handling (Chakraborty et al., 2021). Some of the sustainable innovations that already exist are Radio Frequency Identification (RFID)which smoothens the method of baggage handling further. Real-time data dissemination with an on-ground team has enhanced the security measure of airline services.

A passenger can track the airplane on the ground with real-time tracking enabled systems. Human touch is reduced in airports, with self-check-in kiosks being installed in major airports in India. The recent installation of mobile kiosks by SITA can be observed in Mumbai's Chhatrapati Shivaji Maharaj International Airport (SITA, 2020). Printable baggage barcodes and RFID tags are directly sent to passengers via email to stick to their baggage.

CONCLUSION

Sustainability brings efficacy and generates return on investment in the aviation sector over a period of time. Despite the pandemic, the Indian airline industry continued to drive its sustainability initiatives to establish innovative methods for ecological sustainability. Sustainability is the need of the hour, and India's aviation sector is embracing it with open arms. The airlines in India have realised that "sustainable operations are not only good for the environment, but they also enable higher efficiency, including cost and time savings".

The sustainability measures adopted in Indian aviation are ranging from energy neutrality ways, use of renewable power sources, conservation of more water than consumption, zero emission philosophy, waste and waste-water management, automation of ground support equipment, battery-operated baggage freight loader, portable baggage transfer belt and implementation of vehicle-mounted transfer rollers. These initiatives not only reduced man-hours per flight, but also bring in cost savings.

REFERENCES

Agarwal, R. K. (2012). *Review of Technologies to Achieve Sustainable (Green) Aviation*. Recent Advances in Aircraft Technology.

Air India Express. (n.d.). *CSR Policies*. Retrieved on March 22, 2022, from: https://www.airindiaexpress.in/en/about-us/csr

Air Vistara. (n.d.). *CSR and Sustainability*. Retrieved on December 13, 2021, from: https://www.airvistara.com/in/en/csr-and-sustainability#:~:text=Corporate%20Social%20Responsibility%20(CSR)%20is,to%20help%20achieve%20their%20dreams

André, R. (2004). *Take Back the Sky: Protecting Communities in the Path of Aviation Expansion*. Retrieved on March 21, 2022, from: https://www.raeandre.com/take_back_the_sky__protecting_communities_in_the_path_of_aviation_expansion_17444.htm

Asaf, S. (2019, July 8). Air New Zealand rolls out measures to reduce single-use plastic waste on flights. *Business Traveller*. Retrieved on January 22, 2022, from: https://www.businesstraveller.com/business-travel/2019/07/08/air-new-zealand-rolls-out-measures-to-reduce-single-use-plastic-waste-on-flights/

Aviation Benefits Beyond Borders. (2018). *Greener manufacturing*. Retrieved on October 7, 2021, from: https://aviationbenefits.org/environmental-efficiency/greener-manufacturing/

Aviation Benefits Beyond Borders. (2019a). *Efficient technology*. Retrieved on October 7, 2021, from: https://aviationbenefits.org/environmental-efficiency/climate-action/efficient-technology/

Aviation Benefits Beyond Borders. (2019b). *Operational improvements*. Retrieved on October 7, 2021, from: https://aviationbenefits.org/environmental-efficiency/climate-action/operational-improvements/

Aviation Benefits Beyond Borders. (2019c). *Reducing noise*. Retrieved on October 7, 2021, from: https://aviationbenefits.org/environmental-efficiency/reducing-noise/

Bettie, A. (2021, June). The 3 Pillars of Corporate Sustainability. *Investopedia*. Retrieved on October 19, 2021, from: https://www.investopedia.com/articles/investing/100515/three-pillars-corporate-sustainability.asp

Caswell, M. (2019, June 5). SAS to stop inflight duty-free sales. *Business Traveller*.

Chakraborty, S., Chakravorty, T., & Bhatt, V. (2021, March). IoT and AI driven sustainable practices in airlines as enabler of passenger confidence, satisfaction and positive. In *Conference Proceedings, International Conference on Artificial Intelligence and Smart Systems (ICAIS)* (pp. 1421-1425). IEEE. 10.1109/ICAIS50930.2021.9395850

Chokhani, S. (2021, November 30). *How airports in India contribute to aviation's sustainability goals.* ICF. Retrieved on March 4, 2022, from: https://www.icf.com/insights/transportation/airports-contribute-india-sustainability-goals

CIAL. (2017). *CIAL will double solar power plant capacity by February: Chief Minister.* https://cial.aero/Pressroom/newsdetails.aspx?news_id=381&news_status=A

CSRBox. (2020). *SpiceJet.* Retrieved on November 11, 2021, from: https://csrbox.org/India_Company_Haryana-SpiceJet-Limited_6243

Doyle, C. (2021, June 1). Qatar Airways highlights environmental sustainability initiatives. *Aviation Business News.* Retrieved on November 8, 2021, from: https://www.aviationbusinessnews.com/cabin/airlines/qatar-airways-group-highlights-environmental-sustainability-initiatives/

Dunbar, E. (2018). Corporate Social Responsibility and Sustainability. *Learning to Give.* Retrieved on June 2, 2021, from: https://www.learningtogive.org/resources/corporate-social-responsibility-and-sustainability

Elhmoud, E. R., & Kutty, A. A. (2020). Sustainability Assessment in Aviation Industry: A MiniReview on the Tools, Models, and Methods of Assessment. *IEOM Society International*, 1–11. http://ieomsociety.org/harare2020/papers/324.pdf

Etihad Airways. (2019, April 17). *Etihad Airways to Operate Single-Use Plastic Free Flight on Earth Day as Part of Its Commitment to Sustainability.* Retrieved on August 21, 2021, from: https://www.etihad.com/en/news/etihad-airways-to-operate-single-use-plastic-free-flight-on-earth-day-as-part-of-its-commitment-to-sustainability#:~:text=Abu%20Dhabi%2C%20United%20Arab%20Emirates,the%20effects%20of%20plastic%20pollution

Fitzgerald, P. P., & David-Cooper, R. (2018). Corporate Social Responsibility in the Aviation Industry. Cambridge University Press. doi:10.1017/9781316594216.016

Harijono, H. D. (2013). Aircraft trailing vortices - Cirrus cloud interaction and green aircraft technology: An overview. *Proceeding of the 2013 IEEE International Conference on Space Science and Communication*, 318-323. https://www.businesstraveller.com/business-travel/2019/06/05/sas-to-stop-inflight-duty-free-sales/

IANS. (2021, November 18). *India is now the world's third-largest domestic aviation market: Scindia.* Retrieved on January 13, 2022, from: https://www.business-standard.com/article/economy-policy/india-now-world-s-third-largest-domestic-aviation-market-scindia-121111900056_1.html

IAT. (n.d.). *Aviation environment and sustainability.* Retrieved on March 15, 2022, from: https://www.iata.org/contentassets/a33c39219430432fb241f7b9ac5a145c/environment.pdf

IATA. (n.d.). *Cabin waste.* Retrieved on March 15, 2022, from: https://www.iata.org/en/programs/environment/cabin-waste/

ICAO. (2016). *Performance-Based Navigation (PBN) Implementation Road Map.* Retrieved on July 22, 2021, from: https://www.icao.int/safety/pbn/PBNStatePlans/India%20PBN%20implementation%20plan.pdf

ICAO. (2016, October). *A historic agreement was reached to mitigate international aviation emissions*. Retrieved on July 22, 2021, from: https://www.icao.int/Newsroom/Pages/Historic-agreement-reached-to-mitigate-international-aviation-emissions.aspx

IndigoReach. (n.d.) *Social changes that reach everywhere, everyone.* Indigo Airlines. Retrieved on August 14, 2021, from: https://www.goindigo.in/csr.html

Jain, B. (2022, January). *The Green Aviation Opportunity*. Invest India. https://www.investindia.gov.in/team-india-blogs/green-aviation-opportunity

Jarvie, M. E. (2016, May). Brundtland Report. In *Encyclopedia Britannica*. Retrieved on September 11, 2021, from: https://www.britannica.com/topic/Brundtland-Report

Karaman, A. S., Kilic, M., & Uyar, A. (2018). Sustainability reporting in the aviation industry: Worldwide evidence. *Emerald Insight, 9*(4), 362–391. doi:10.1108/SAMPJ-12-2017-0150

Kim, Y., Lee, S. S., & Roh, T. (2020). Taking Another Look at Airline CSR: How Required CSR and Desired CSR Affect Customer Loyalty in the Airline Industry. *Sustainability, 12*(10), 1–19. doi:10.3390u12104281

Krietsch Boerner, L. (2021, September). *Airlines want to make flights more sustainable. How will they do it?* Retrieved on December 19, 2021, from: https://cen.acs.org/environment/sustainability/Airlines-want-make-flight-sustainable/99/i32

Lin, Z. M. (2013). Making aviation green. *Advances in Manufacturing, 1*(1), 42–49. doi:10.100740436-013-0008-3

Makarova, E. L., & Pavlov, P. V. (2017). Supplier Management Improvement in Aviation Industry: A Case Study of Beriev Aircraft Company. *International Journal of Supply Chain Management, 6*(1), 41–54.

Maurya, A. (2013). Environmental Impact of the Flying Scenario: An Approach Towards Sustainable Air Transportation: A Case Study of India. *OIDA International Journal of Sustainable Development, 5*(12), 107–118.

Ministry of Civil Aviation. (2020, November). *GMR's Delhi Airport to become Net Zero Carbon Emission Airport*. Retrieved on October 29, 2021, from: https://www.newdelhiairport.in/blog/gmr-delhi-airport-to-become-net-zero-carbon-emission-airport

Ministry of Civil Aviation Government of India. (2019, March). *White Paper on National Green Aviation Policy*. Retrieved on October 14, 2021, from: https://www.civilaviation.gov.in/sites/default/files/Whitepaper%20on%20National%20Green%20Aviation%20Policy.pdf

Otley, T. (2021, June 18). Emirates promotes its sustainable operations. *Business Traveller*. https://www.businesstraveller.com/features/emirates-promotes-its-sustainable-operations/

Paddison, L. (2020, January 16). Airline Cabin Waste Is Aviation's Other Environmental Crisis. *Huffpost*. Retrieved on December 8, 2021, from: https://www.huffpost.com/entry/plane-waste-cabin-plastic-food_n_5e1c5868c5b650c621e1cc89

Puri, H. S. (2021, June 11). Indian Aviation: Sustainable Development is in the air. *The Daily Guardian*. Retrieved on July 22, 2021, from: https://thedailyguardian.com/indian-aviation-sustainable-development-is-in-the-air/

Purvis, B., Mao, Y., & Robinson, D. (2019). Three pillars of sustainability: In search of conceptual origins. *Sustainability Science*, *14*(3), 681–695. doi:10.100711625-018-0627-5

Qantas Newsroom. (2019, May 8). *Qantas Operates World's First Zero Waste Flight*. Retrieved on August 4, 2021, from: https://www.qantasnewsroom.com.au/media-releases/qantas-operates-worlds-first-zero-waste-flight/

Rathore, H., Nandi, S., & Jakhar, S. K. (2020, November 27). The future of Indian aviation from the perspective of environment-centric regulations and policies. *IIMB Management Review*, *13*(4), 434–447. doi:10.1016/j.iimb.2020.11.003

Sameh, M. M., & Scavuzzi, J. (2016). *Environmental Sustainability Measures for Airports*. McGill, Centre for Research in Air and Space Law. Retrieved on October 7, 2021, from: https://www.mcgill.ca/iasl/files/iasl/vii_sustainability_and_environmental_protection_measures_for_airports_final.pdf

Sarkar, A. N. (2012, August). *Evolving Green Aviation Transport System: A Holistic Approach to Sustainable Green Market Development*. Retrieved on November 2, 2021, from: https://www.scirp.org/html/5-2360021_22479.htm?pagespeed=noscript

Serhan, C., Abboud, P., & Shahoud, R. (2018). Corporate Social Responsibility Practices in the Aviation Industry. *International Journal of Research in Business Studies and Management*, *5*(9), 1–14.

Singapore Airlines. (2019, May 21). *SIA Significantly Stepping Up In-Flight Sustainability Initiatives*. Retrieved on May 11, 2021, from: https://www.singaporeair.com/en_UK/es/media-centre/press-release/article/?q=en_UK/2019/January-March/ne0819-190321

Singh, V. K. (2015, June 1). Corporate Social Responsibility within the Dynamics of Aviation Industry – with Special Reference to India. *Indian Journal of Air and Space Law*, *1*(57). Advance online publication. doi:10.2139srn.2973713

Singhania, K., Pandey, S., & Makuny, A. (2019, September). *National Green Aviation Policy: India's Step Towards Emission Cuts*. Retrieved on February 14, 2021, from https://www.mondaq.com/india/aviation/847444/national-green-aviation-policy-india39s-step-towards-emission-cuts

Sinha, S. (2017, February 22). Notebandi fails to impact international travel. *The Times of India*. Retrieved on August 23, 2020, from: https://timesofindia.indiatimes.com/business/india-business/notebandi-fails-to-impact-international-travel/articleshow/57283096.cms

SITA. (2020, September 11). *Mumbai Airport introduces mobile-enabled kiosks to meet new COVID-19 requirements*. Retrieved on October 17, 2021, from: https://www.sita.aero/pressroom/news-releases/mumbai-airport-introduces-mobile-enabled-kiosks-to-meet-new-covid-19-requirements/

Srivastava, T. (2015, June). India attempts flexible use of airspace to cut time and costs. *Hindustan Times*. Retrieved on December 4, 2020, from: https://www.hindustantimes.com/business/india-attempts-flexible-use-of-airspace-to-cut-time-costs/story-GadQM0aQXoLGONWTO4lIFJ.html

Vahora, S. I., & Mishra, P. C. B. (2017). Benchmarking: Green Aviation Transport System. *Kalpa Publications in Civil Engineering, 1*, 259–264. https://easychair.org/publications/open/h5Q

Wolff, C., Uppink, L., & Malhotra, S. G. (2021, June 10). How India can become a leader in sustainable aviation fuel. *World Economic Forum*. Retrieved on August 19, 2021, from: https://www.weforum.org/agenda/2021/06/how-india-can-become-a-leader-in-sustainable-aviation-fuel-saf-carbon-emissions-transportation-air-quality-pollution-covid/

Chapter 23
Transformation or Retaining the Status Quo:
Multinational Hospitality Companies and SME Collaboration on Sustainability in Emerging Countries

Sibel Yamak
University of Wolverhampton, UK

Mine Karatas-Ozkan
University of Southampton, UK

Eun Sun Godwin
University of Wolverhampton, UK

Samia Mahmood
https://orcid.org/0000-0002-6103-1578
University of Wolverhampton, UK

Roya Rahimi
University of Wolverhampton, UK

ABSTRACT

This chapter focuses on the dynamics of MHC-SME collaboration on sustainability in an emerging country context. The findings show that MHC sustainability policy is generally driven from headquarters and that economic sustainability has priority over environmental and social sustainability. By contrast, SMEs appear to be able to initiate fully sustainable strategies based on the culture, tradition, family history, industry, and ethical standing of the owners. The interaction of MHCs and SMEs in relation to sustainability involves varying factors at the macro, meso, and micro levels. However, the micro level factor (i.e., human agency) seems to be the determining factor of the relationship. The authors provide rich contextual data by adopting a qualitative research method (case study) based on primary data, which is rare in international business literature.

DOI: 10.4018/978-1-6684-4645-4.ch023

INTRODUCTION

A small hotel in Sri Lanka, the Kip, is fully decorated with ethnic furniture. No plastic is used, and the hotel offers cleaning products and engages in composting and donating food. This hotel is no exception among such sustainable small and medium-size enterprises (SMEs), which develop novel products and experiences influencing the awareness of customers, suppliers, and other organizations such as multinational hospitality companies (MHCs). Just a decade ago the term green hotels or green practices in the hospitality industry used to bring visions of fringe environmentalism and a high cost for minimal benefit however, nowadays hotel businesses realized that a strategy good for the world can also be good for the bottom line (Chan et al., 2014).

The hospitality industry is always associated with its negative impacts on the environment. Although it is not among the great polluters such as the metallurgical or chemical industry, however, its size, rapid growth, and reliance on natural resources make it clear that environmentally sustainable actions are necessary. Many sustainability challenges generate boundaryless settings and entail systemic transformations beyond the capacity of individual businesses and, therefore, collaboration is key at the intersection of local, national, and international organizations. The role of multinational enterprises in general, and multinational hospitality companies (MHCs) in particular, is critical in all these sustainability-related developments, anchored mostly in the United Nations (UN) Sustainable Development Goals (SDGs) (e.g., Biermann et al., 2017; Fukuda-Parr, 2016; Kolk et al., 2020; UNCTAD, 2015).

Sustainability has gained popularity in the tourism and hospitality industry recently (Iyer and Jarvis, 2019; Ertuna et al., 2019; Hatipoglu et al., 2019)However, the drivers for, and nature of, the collaboration between MHCs and SMEs is not fully investigated by the previous studies and academic research has not yet picked up this trend (Ertuna et al., 2019; Hatipoglu et al., 2019), particularly in relation to the MHC and SME relationship in an emerging country. Multinational enterprises, including MHCs, face increasing pressures to be sustainable and/or responsible from several stakeholders, such as customers, home and host governments, public authorities, and investors (European Commission, 2018; Schoenmaker, 2017, 2018; Schramade, 2016; 2017). Their role as 'good corporate citizens' has received growing attention (Kolk & Lenfant 2010).

This good citizenship is often associated with their ascribed role of changing and positively influencing the business environment in the host country, including their relationship with SMEs. More specifically, in the tourism and hospitality industry, MHCs' role is particularly significant considering the industry's complex stakeholder profile encompassing those at both international and national (home and host country) levels, and the industry's additional sensitivity to local contexts (e.g., culture, tradition and nature) (Hatipoglu et al., 2019; Iyer & Jarvis, 2019; MacKenzie & Gannon, 2019) including SMEs. As mentioned earlier, taking a critical approach to problematize the collaboration between MHCs and SMEs, this work aims to understand the drivers for, and nature of, their collaboration in the domain of sustainability, and whether – and if so, how – this collaboration generates value for both parties.

Scholars have identified the need to widen the geographical scope of sustainability research (Pisani et al., 2017). This contextual and geographical expansion of knowledge pertains to leveraging the importance of sustainable development agendas for emerging countries in particular. The authors believe that discussion of this issue in the tourism and hospitality industry from a developing country context will bring divergent perspectives on sustainability issues and practices (Ertuna et al., 2019). It is crucial to understand the operationalization of key pillars of sustainability in the sector, as well as to assess the relationship between sustainable practices and profits (Iyer & Jarvis, 2019).

Equally, it is important to learn about how to harmonize traditional cultures with contemporary frameworks of sustainability (*ibid*). Sustainable development is about rethinking human-nature relationships, re-examining current doctrines of progress and modernity, and proposing alternative visions of the world (Banerjee, 2007, p. 92). Similarly, sustainability can be defined as an engaged state of critical social and moral consciousness and awareness since businesses and individuals exist as part of an intergenerational and interconnected enduring ecosystem (Koe Hwee Nga, & Shamuganathan, 2010). Hence, collaboration forms the key mechanism to achieve sustainability in its broadest sense.

Given our emphasis on a broader notion of sustainability, its three pillars – economic, environmental, and social (Lozano et al., 2015; Svensson et al., 2010) should be mentioned. Originally, economic and environmental imperatives of sustainability attracted more attention from academics and business practitioners, despite the increasing importance of social sustainability reflected in recent events and cases across the globe. The authors take a view that there should be a more holistic and contextually integrated approach to sustainability. However, sustainability agendas and associated academic literature are often dominated by industrialized countries and transnational organizations reflecting the interests of large corporations with economic growth orientations, all of which are embedded in Western-based capitalist perspectives (Banerjee, 2007).

Considering the importance of local culture and tradition in the tourism and hospitality industry, context sensitivity is critical (Ertuna et al., 2019). With the emphasis on *context*, the interaction between key actors and their collaboration is crucial for sustainability. Nevertheless, there have not been enough attempts to link MHCs and SMEs in collaborating for sustainability, despite their substantial interaction and business relationships in emerging countries. Such interaction is often treated as a 'black box' (Contreras et al., 2012; Narula & Dunning, 2010). This study focuses on achieving a better understanding of this 'black box' by unpacking the nature of the collaboration on sustainability between MHCs and local SMEs in the tourism sector.

Arguably, the tourism and hospitality industry, with its complex multinational spaces and multiple layers of stakeholders, presents an excellent opportunity to address this topic beyond the traditional approach to sustainability underpinned by measurement (see Iyer & Jarvis, 2019, for measurement dimension). Furthermore, small businesses in the tourism and hospitality sector have attracted less attention (Khatter et al., 2019). The overall research question of the current study is as follows: what is the nature of collaboration on sustainability between MHCs and local SMEs in the hospitality sector?

This triggers two following inter-related sub-research questions:

- What are the drivers and dynamics of MHC-SME collaboration in sustainability?
- What constitutes its transformative value for both parties, if any?

The findings of the study have both theoretical and empirical contributions. They will be discussed in detail in the next sections.

LITERATURE REVIEW

Mhcs and Sustainability

Hotel businesses operate 24/7 with frequent consumption of water, energy, and non-durable products by the customers and employees (Deng & Burnett, 2002). As a result, hotel companies face increasing pressure to pay more attention to environmental issues (Olya et al., 2021; Khatter et al., 2019). A different number of studies have explored sustainability management practices in hotels (Oriade et al.,2021). It has been used with different labels such as environmental management practices, green practices, sustainable practices, sustainable development practices, environmentally friendly practices, sustainability man-agreement tools, and sustainability initiatives.

Despite all these labels, the core is a routine practice by organizations to reduce damaging the environment (Mensah, 2014). One of the main challenges hotel business faces is the balance between environmental performance, limited resources, public legitimacy, burdensome litigation, and profitability issues (Mathur & Khanna, 2017; Chan et al., 2013; Hsieh, 2012; Chan et al.,2014). Hence to maintain corporate competitiveness and save costs, implementing environmental programs such as managing energy and water consumption and reducing waste is increasing steadily in the hotel industry (Sourvinou & Filimonau, 2018; Han et al., 2018).

More recently, multinational hotel business face a higher level of pressures and demands from various groups of stakeholders, including global consumers, international governance organizations, home and host country regulatory bodies, and local communities for implementing sustainable practices (Raub et al., 2019; Ng & Tavitiyaman, 2020).In the tourism and hospitality industry context, the view on the role of MHCs in the host country development is mixed. Some studies argue that such multinational tourism corporations can fill institutional voids often observed in many developing countries (Hatipoglu et al., 2019) such as "loose regulations, weak protection of private property rights, gaps in social policy by the state" (Ertuna et al., 2019, p. 2568). In so doing they can gain legitimacy in these host countries (*ibid*). Other studies raise concerns over the negative impact of "unfettered tourism" (Mackenzie & Gannon, 2019, p. 2411), particularly on the environment, by many MHCs, which can often be neglected by developing host country governments whose economies rely heavily on this sector (Khatter et al., 2019; ibid).

At the same time, research has paid unbalanced attention to large firms, leaving sustainable practice in SMEs relatively neglected (Darcy et al., 2014; Hörisch, Johnson, & Schaltegger, 2015; Langwell & Heaton, 2016; Shields & Shelleman, 2015). The tourism section is not an exception (Khatter et al., 2019; Kornilaki, Thomas, & Font, 2019). This can limit our understanding of sustainable business, particularly in emerging countries, as SMEs play important roles in such countries.

While there are several challenges that SMEs in emerging economies face relating to sustainability such as lack of stakeholder pressure, time and financial resource constraints, weaker government regulation, and culture (Yadav et al., 2018), the OECD report (2017, p.7) claims that the key challenge is for SMEs to find "appropriate knowledge partners and networks" and to integrate this knowledge into their firms by developing their management practices. Similar challenges are observed in tourism and hospitality as small businesses face lesser pressure from stakeholders, which affects their motivations to address sustainability issues further (Khatter et al., 2019).

Considering the significance of SMEs' role in emerging economies and the constraints they face when implementing sustainable business, our study looks at the dynamics and potential value of the collaboration between MHCs and SMEs in terms of sustainability. There is a dearth of research investigating such links between these two in emerging countries. The United Nations World Tourism Organisation (UNWTO) asserts the potential contribution from tourism to all the UN Sustainable Development Goals (SDGs) (Raub et al., 2019; UNWTO, 2015).

Collaboration Between MHCs and SMEs in Emerging Countries

Due to growing pressure around sustainable practices from global stakeholders, multinational corporations employ 'universal sustainability strategies' throughout their international business, including their supply chains or other similar business networks in host countries (Nishii & Özbilgin, 2007).This is usually through their own codes of conduct (Locke & Romis, 2007), as internal tools are often seen to be more influential than external ones such as globally certified rating systems (Kolk et al., 2020). In this way, local SMEs might be influenced by these sustainable practices if they are involved in the multinational's supply chain or interact with them through different business networks. SMEs in emerging economies are often slow to adopt sustainable practices for several reasons, such as lack of stakeholder pressure, time and financial resource constraints, weaker government regulation and culture, and the context of SME operations (Yadav et al., 2018).

In multinationals' usual standardized social and environmental sustainability programs, social issues appear to have attracted limited attention compared with environmental issues (Banerjee, 2007; Halme et al., 2020; Taticchi et al., 2013; Wahga, Blundel, & Schaefer, 2018). Similarly, in the tourism and hospitality industry there is a narrow scope (such as environmental rather than socio-cultural) as a result of which the expectations of the multiplicity of their stakeholders are ignored (Font & Lynes, 2018).

Understanding local context is critical for unpacking the complexity of the collaboration between MHCs and SMEs – thus, the 'black-box' as stated in the introduction. In addition, there is significant ambiguity in defining what sustainable tourism is at the global level of sustainability goals, such as SDGs or UN-designated Sustainable Tourism for Development (MacKenzie & Gannon, 2019); hence, these goals tend to neglect specificity and context in sustainability issues faced by hospitality firms (Raub et al., 2019). This lack of context in sustainable strategies can limit effective collaboration between MHCs and local SMEs. In numerous examples of ethical 'blunders', which have tarnished several well-known global multinational brands (see Banerjee, 2007; Lane & Maznevski, 2019 for example), it often turns out that these unethical issues were caused by local contractors rather than by multinationals.

It is often the case that multinationals take rather passive and reactive attitudes toward such matters and avoid full responsibility to maintain corporate reputation (Camilleri, 2017; Xu et al., 2019). Multinationals' usual 'paternalistic practices' without considering local issues and their lack of sensitivity context sensitivity have significant implications for their collaboration with SMEs, particularly in emerging countries. In their efforts to prioritize global demands from their parent organization and other stakeholders, multinational subsidiaries tend to dominate this collaborative relationship. They often regulate SMEs "beyond any legal regulation and against the interests of the SMEs" in local economies in terms of sustainability agenda (Morsing & Perrini, 2009, p.3).

Given that large firms are characterized by their risk-averse behavior and that large and small firms have different timescales and resources that they can deploy, any risks involved can disproportionately be put on to the side of SMEs (Young, 2013) in the process of their collaboration. For example, if SMEs do not put enough information in their reports or into the public domain due to resource constraints, they might receive low ratings in the relevant areas (Schoenmaker, 2018), which might have a knock-on effect on their interaction with MHCs.

Departing from this literature base, the current study focusses on explaining the dynamics of the collaboration between MHCs and local SMEs in their sustainability practice and exploring the drivers and the value of this collaboration in the context of a developing nation. This response to the research gap as identified by different scholars (Ertuna et al., 2019; Jia et al., 2018; Wahga et al., 2018). The collaboration between multinationals and SMEs remains a 'black box' (Contreras et al., 2012). Unpacking this black box, the present study has posed two inter-related research questions:

- What are the drivers and dynamics of MHC-SME collaboration in sustainability?
- What constitutes its transformative value for both parties, if any?

In addressing these questions and exploring the drivers and what is happening in this 'black box', this study not only contributes to addressing this gap but also generates policy and practice implications on sustainable development in the context of emerging countries.

METHOD

Research Setting: Turkey

The hospitality industry is one of the main pillars of the Turkish economy due to its massive contribution to economic and social development. In the last few decades, there has been much encouragement from the government for mass tourism in Turkey along with foreign investments. While the focus on mass tourism has been crucial for the economic development of Turkey, it has also attracted a lot of criticism about its negative environmental, social, cultural, and economic impacts (Egresi 2016). This encouraged a lot of businesses to take initiative for more sustainable practices toward giving more attention to minimizing their possible negative impacts on the environment and at the same time, benefit local communities with the positive aspects of increased tourist traffic (Tousan, 2001; Kisi, 2019; Ekinci, 2014).

Despite all efforts, these initiative remains underdeveloped in the Turkish hospitality industry, particularly in the SMEs. In general hotel managers mostly lack the necessary environmental knowledge and interest to meet the basic objectives of social and environmental responsibility. It is thus necessary to develop an integrated system of policy and practice that involves not only the hotel management and staff, but also all parties concerned with environmental protection and sustainability, and to re-evaluate and reconsider national, local, and hotel policies and training activities (Erdogan et al., 2007).

The specific geographical context for this study is the city of Bodrum, which is located in the South Aegean coast of Turkey and is a highly attractive tourist destination with many domestic and international airlines operating in the summer period in particular. There is fierce competition between international hotel and restaurant chains and local companies in making investments in the hospitality sector in Bodrum as the further potential of the town is acknowledged in international fora (Hurriyet, 2022). The attractiveness of the town is associated with price, accessibility, promotion and marketing and quality of service, alongside safety and security (Gunaydin, Ozer, & Ataman, 2021).

Research Approach, Design and Sample

A qualitative approach employing a case study design was adopted to address the research questions. Qualitative research designs are more tuned with exploring the MHC-SME interaction in relation to sustainability, as qualitative methods are well-matched for this type of exploratory research with inductive reasoning and theory building. As suggested by De Urioste-Stone, McLaughlin, Daigle and Fefer (2018) for tourism research, current study have utilized exploratory case study design, which allows for the discovery of relevant constructs and components of complex relationships leading to development of a model. The sample included 10 cases: five MHCs (hotel chains) and five SMEs in Bodrum, a well-developed tourist destination in Turkey.

This study used purposive snowballing sampling (Patton, 2014). The authors contacted one of the largest congress tourism companies in Turkey to identify sustainable multinational hotels among those that do business in Bodrum. The company provided us with the names of five hotels. Four of them were subsidiaries of multinationals that originated from developed countries, and one from a developing country background. The authors wrote letters to these hotels' management and explained the purpose of the study and sent them the preliminary areas/questions for exploration. It was ensured that company names or any identifying information would be kept strictly confidential throughout the study. Once the hotels approved the objectives/study, the authors asked for an appointment with the responsible person in charge of (or most knowledgeable about) sustainability activities/strategies and general management of the hotel.

The interviews with the designated managers took place in the respective hotels. During the interviews each respondent was asked for the names of SMEs with which they collaborated. This gave us the second part of our sample, which is composed of SMEs. The authors were given the names of nine SMEs in total, and five agreed to take part in the study. The SMEs were all located in Bodrum, mostly in the food and agricultural sector, apart from one in arts and crafts.

Production of Empirical Material

The authors conducted in-depth interviews lasting from 45 to 90 minutes with a total of 13 managers/owners of these 10 companies in October 2019. Most of the interviews were recorded except one (during which detailed notes were taken). The interview questions ranged from the history of the company; sustainability approach, strategies, and practices; key drivers and motivation for sustainability; and collaboration with MHCs or SMEs in terms of the source, development, and end of this collaboration.

The data sources were triangulated by conducting searches on the companies in social media accounts (Instagram and Twitter), as well as by checking the news on Google and their website. The authors also checked the headquarters' sustainability policies/activities in the case of MHCs. The authors conducted company visits, which enabled them to observe the production and service facilities on site.

The authors used thematic analysis and followed a structured approach as described by Boyatzis (1998) and Leitch et al. (2013). The analysis started with the careful examination of the data obtained from the related Google pages, social media, and company websites (of both the headquarter and the subsidiary in the case of MHCs). This enabled us to familiarize ourselves with each case. In the next stage, the broad themes were differentiated by identifying major activities and motivations, followed by the identification of intra-case themes. The authors identified the similarities and differences in creating patterns. In the coding stage, generated labels were generated. Two different researchers independently coded the data for reliability purposes and identified the major emerging themes. In the event of disagreement between the two researchers, the theme was dropped from analysis or reconstructed until full agreement was reached.

The authors also cross-checked the brief summaries of interview data with the archival data they had collected. At the final stage of explanation and abstraction, the authors underlined our contribution to the extant literature by checking the differences and similarities between our findings and existing theories. In so doing, and aligned with the case study design, the authors went through iterative stages of description, analysis, and interpretation (based on Wolcott, 1991). This allowed the researchers to generate rich accounts of cases studied as well as to move beyond such descriptive accounts to offer insightful findings and build a model of the transformative capacity of collaboration between MHC and SME actors. Our cases are presented in this section leading to the analysis of key themes in the findings section of our chapter.

FINDINGS

Our findings reveal the importance of a multiplicity of factors shaping the MHC-SME collaboration on sustainability in emerging countries. In line with our research questions, the authors present the cases first and then explain the drivers and dynamics of MHC-SME collaboration in sustainability below, along with the implications for the transformative value of such collaboration.

Descriptive Account of Cases

Case 1: MHC1 (Based on the Interview With the Hotel Manager)

Business Activity:

This hotel is a subsidiary of a developed country MHC collaborating with a Turkish partner on a management contract basis for their operation in Bodrum. The hotel has 66 rooms and is targeting a higher end market.

Sustainability and Collaboration:

It is ranked second in the internal sustainability certification of its headquarters and awarded with the green star label by the Turkish Ministry of Culture and Tourism (MCT) for environmental sustainability. Its environmental sustainability includes the use of organic food and implementing waste management and recycling processes. It has water- and energy-saving policies such as using reverse osmosis for sustainable water usage in irrigation. They produce olive from olive trees in the compound and organize an environment week each year. They plant trees abroad (Brazil) and in Turkey, aim to reduce single-use plastics, and give excess food to animal shelters.

Their social sustainability practices include buying from local suppliers, financial contribution to the foundation for disabled people, and helping village schools and the poor. There is a wish tree where the hotel guests and employees can contribute to the needs of the surrounding communities. They also have a policy against human trafficking which is designed by the headquarter. However, on the hotel website or on its social media accounts, there is no mention of sustainability. The management claims that around 10% of its business is with SMEs. They think it is easier to manage small businesses which do not want to lose the opportunity to collaborate with an MHC.

Case 2: MHC2 (Based on the Interview With Assistant General Manager and Technical Manager)

Business Activity:

This hotel belongs to a developed country MHC collaborating with a Turkish partner on a management contract basis for their operation in Bodrum. It is a high-end hotel with 108 rooms which operates six months a year.

Sustainability and Collaboration:

It is awarded with a green star label by the MCT for environmental sustainability which is an extension of the headquarter policy. They annually organize a week where environmental and social sustainability is promoted through projects (helping the poor and different associations, cleaning the beaches, and so forth). They eliminate single-use plastics and recycle some waste (e.g., chemical waste is sent to related companies for recycling). However, there is neither water recycling nor recycling of the food waste. They tried to preserve the maximum number of trees during the construction phase. Energy consumption is controlled and reduced by high technological infrastructure of the hotel (high efficiency in air conditioning) to reduce cost. They prioritize customer satisfaction at the expense of sustainability.

The hotel's social sustainability policy involves local sourcing of the needs of the hotel (food, furniture, technical services, and so forth). They prefer to buy food from local family businesses because the quality of the food is rated higher when it is not industrialized. There is no mention of sustainability on the company webpage. The management claimed that around 10% of its business is with SMEs where guarantee in price, continuous supply or consistent quality can become a problem. They use word of mouth and personal visits to select SMEs.

Case 3: MHC3 (Based on the Interview With Hotel Operations Manager and Sales Manager)

Business Activity:

This hotel is wholly owned by a developed country MHC. It has 285 rooms and 352 houses with an all-inclusive business model.

Sustainability and Collaboration:

It has a green star award from the MCT and green key award from the Turkish Foundation for Environmental Education (TFEE). They cultivate pesticide-free olives, vegetables, and mandarins for their own use in the hotel. Chickens are raised against the scorpions. It also has a zero-waste policy. Compost is generated from the organic waste which is used as fertilizer. Water recycling and reverse osmosis are used for sustainable water usage. They reduce the plastic usage. Recycling is encouraged in the guest rooms as well. There is a voluntary green team to clean the environment within and outside the premises. Services such as environmental sensitivity training for the employees and for the children of the hotel guests are also available. The kids' program includes activities such as cow milking, and vegetable growing. The headquarter designs the general policy but the subsidiary management team decided to become a green hotel with different vegetable and fruit production facilities. Electric vehicles are used in the hotel. They expect their suppliers to be environmentally conscious. Animal welfare protection is a priority in selecting water sports equipment.

Its social sustainability policy includes treating the employees like internal guests to lead to lower turnover and higher satisfaction among the workforce. Each winter they collaborate with the universities and provide training to tourism students. They support local suppliers and local cultural heritage by providing space to Bodrum slippers, ice cream, and other local crafts and brands in their premise. Sustainability is the major marketing tool for the hotel.

The supplies from SMEs are reported by the management to constitute 40% of the total. Personal acquaintances and experiences are important in the selection of SMEs. There is a long-term relationship and exchange of knowledge between the hotel (on food safety and training) and SMEs (on geographical products).

Case 4: MHC4 (Based on the Interview With General Manager)

Business Activity:

This hotel is a subsidiary of a developing country multinational enterprise. It was established by a female entrepreneur who sold it recently to the multinational. It is a high-end hotel with 74 rooms and operates six months a year.

Sustainability and Collaboration:

There is no central sustainability policy imposed by the headquarters, but the environment and the trees are kept as a result of the environmental affinity and personal choice of the founder. They do not have waste management or energy-saving activities and customer satisfaction is prioritized at the expense of sustainability. For example, only glass and paper are recycled and solar panels are not used because of the cost and adverse effect on the panorama. In terms of its social sustainability, the hotel sources some food and textiles locally, hire legally required number of disabled people on a yearly basis, and support traditional handcrafts by providing a sale space in the hotel. SMEs are said to constitute 30% of their collaborations. They prefer companies with consistent quality and appropriate prices.

Case 5: MHC5 (Based on the Interview With Quality Manager)

Business Activity:

This hotel is a franchise of a developed country MHC. A Turkish partner is in charge of the operation in Bodrum. The hotel has 487 rooms and is open for six months a year with an all-inclusive business model.

Sustainability and Collaboration:

It is awarded with green star label by the MCT and green key label by the TFEE. The headquarters provide the sustainability policy which incorporates SDGs. Due to a short-time period of business and being a franchise there is a large flexibility in its implementation. Their approach is that they do not have sufficient time to conduct more than 10 sustainability projects during their very busy 6-month period of business.

In terms of environmental sustainability policy, they started to switch to LED lighting to avoid harmful effects of fluorescent lamps and to electric vehicles with charging facilities as well. They grow some of their vegetables and herbs without using harmful chemicals. Activities such as water recycling and biological purification of the waste-water are also conducted. They have a sophisticated recycling system, but they do not have a composting facility. Voluntary teams of employees clean different areas. For social sustainability they have clear policies and training to fight human trafficking. They support the activities of the Bodrum Municipality in relation to disabled people, mothers, and children. They hire disabled people to fulfil their legal responsibility.

The management has reported that supplies from SMEs (mainly food and beverages) constitute 5% of the total, the main reason being the difficulties SMEs are experiencing in competing with the large companies in terms of costs. The purchasing department of the hotel deals with the selection of the SMEs. The purchasing managers have their networks where they exchange ideas about potential suppliers. Taste of the product and the price are important factors. Suppliers' capacity and compatibility with the food safety standards are indispensable. Geographical proximity of the supplier is important to reduce costs. They are not able to impose sustainability rules on the suppliers.

Case 6: SME1 (Based on the Interview With Owner)

Business Activity:

This is a family business which produces mainly olive oil, vegetables, and herbs.

Sustainability and Collaboration:

Sustainability is their major investment and survival tool. They are very ambitious about environmental sustainability, aiming for zero waste. They try to recycle their waste coming from both the business and family although the Municipality does not serve that area. Organic waste is used as animal food or fertilizer. They do not use artificial fertilizers. They promote and preserve the local seeds. They also demonstrated their ethical consideration about health and fair treatment of customers, and high sensitivity to natural resource depletion.

For social sustainability, the co-owner (a lady with a high school degree) involves the neighbors in the production process of certain food. She trains the students at nearby schools about olive oil production, recycling, and environmental sustainability. She hires women to provide them with an opportunity to work. She also pushes local authorities and schools to pay more attention to the preservation of geographical products. She advocates the employment of the local workforce in local crafts and industries and points to the problem of the workforce being absorbed by MHCs to tourism and limiting the chances of local industries.

The manager's view is that the relationship with MHCs can be difficult. There is an unbalanced power structure. Some do not pay their purchases appropriately, or intermediaries ask for commissions over the purchase. When conflict happens SME1 tends not to overreact and just avoids the specific MHC for future interaction. However, there have also been fruitful collaborations where they learn how to treat customers and how to improve their products. They also transfer their knowledge to MHCs. For example, they taught MHC3 how to trim the olive trees and how to preserve the olive oil. Through their relationship and network with their neighbors, colleagues, and tourists they have opportunities to interact with MHCs.

Case 7: SME2 (Based on the Interview With Owner)

Business Activity:
This is a well-known family-run handicraft company in Bodrum.

Sustainability and Collaboration:
They do not have an environmental sustainability policy even though they were once victims of an environmental disaster (flooding) and lost their shop. In social sustainability terms, they collaborate with the arts and crafts foundations to preserve and develop cultural heritage. SME2 values social inclusion and hires women for the business.

They have established collaborations with MHCs to sell their crafts (through their personal relations and reputation). However, one collaboration with a multinational hotel was not successful as SME2 was not able to interact with the customers due to the architectural structure of the space. This resulted in financial issues and poor economic sustainability. At that stage, MHC4 offered a space in its hotel with a feasible agreement. According to the owner, this successful interaction is also due to the 'compatibility of mentality'.

Case 8: SME3 (Based on the Interview With Owner)

Business Activity:
This is a company established by a female entrepreneur who has a degree in environmental engineering. The company produces wine, olive oil, and other food products.

Sustainability and Collaboration:
They have a high level of expertise in environmental sustainability. She is the first entrepreneur to invest in this area which has swiftly become populated by other sustainable producers. SME3 adopts zero waste policy. They do not use pesticides and artificial fertilizers by using chicken against the scorpions and cats against the rats and snakes. The ducks in the pool provide natural fertilizer. They respect the ecological balance in all their production. They also offer restaurant services with their products. They have attracted customers via social media. Hotels which need natural and local products for their customers have been attracted to their high-quality products. Its sustainability strategy has been its uniqueness.

It trains the personnel of the MHCs on how to offer wine and promotes its sustainability policy to adopt in their hotels. She is a role model for businesses and MHC3. She uses her network in her interactions with the hotels.

Case 9: SME4 (Based on the Interview With Manager of the Retail Unit)

Business Activity:
This is a family business specializing in dairy products.

Sustainability and Collaboration:
They emphasize traditional production with the milk from the breeds of Bodrum. They do not use artificial ingredients and their recipes are the same for more than two decades. However, their interpre-

tation of sustainability focuses on traditional production. They have no recycling activities. For social sustainability, they organize female workforces in different villages and buy different products from them.

They supply dairy products and olives to several MHCs in Bodrum. They mainly collaborate with the high-end hotels. However, the cyclical nature of the business (e.g., some hotels are closed during the winter) is a challenge.

Case 10: SME5 (Based on the Interview With Owner)

Business Activity:

This is a family business specialized on mandarins. They have developed patented products and also have geographical identification for their products.

Sustainability and Collaboration:

Their environmental sustainability comes from their natural product with no additives, artificial ingredients, or sugar. For that reason, their products need to be sold quickly. They do not use pesticides in their production. The wife of the owner innovates new value-added products and adds them to the existing product range to deplete the mandarin stock as quickly as possible. They do not do much about recycling; only organic food waste is recycled. The majority of the workforce is female. They have limited trading capacity with the MHCs which seek low-cost products. The company has high production costs which impede them from competing with other companies. The relationship with the MHCs is on and off. They have tried to have a stall in the premises of MHCs to market their products. However, they stopped the collaboration with MHCs not taking care of their stall.

Sustainability as Perceived and Practised by MHCs and SMEs

State-of-art in sustainability should be defined clearly for both parties. In all MHCs interviewed, sustainability policies are centrally defined and orchestrated by the headquarters (with varying levels of imposition). SDGs are incorporated in those policies, which in turn are followed and shared by employees via internal digital platforms. Preventing human trafficking as a part of social sustainability is an example of this. However, the extent to which sustainability is implemented depends largely on (i) the host country, (ii) specific geographical area within the country, (iii) the hotels' business models, and (iv) their interaction with the key stakeholders. Host country characteristics include regulatory frameworks and strength of public authorities.

For example, in relation to waste management (environmental sustainability), there are neither compulsory policies/regulations locally imposed nor infrastructure for it organized by public authorities:

"We don't do compost; we asked the Municipality how to do it but they were not aware of it; they don't have the know-how" (MHC1).

"As to segregation of waste, we have done it ourselves; and when we asked public authorities for further stages, they said that they cannot serve that geographical area and they don't have a system as such" (SME1).

This leaves sustainable practices to voluntary action by businesses. The voluntary nature of sustainability practice is highly evident in our data. Spatial dimension – in other words, specific geographical location – is equally important to understand sustainability approaches. Such aspects of the local context include climate, agriculture-based local economy and its impact on tourism, and flow of international tourists. For instance, local supply of food and beverage and protecting local products and nature form the kind of environmental sustainability observed, while preservation of cultural heritage constitutes social sustainability. These local dynamics characterize MHC-SME interaction in our study:

"We buy food and beverages from local companies since the area is rich agriculturally... We even produce olive oil from the trees in our land. We consult local manufacturers on how to trim our trees and produce oil" (MHC3).

Business models of the hotels seem to influence sustainability approaches to a large extent, particularly for MHCs. All-inclusive and high-end hotels differ in their sustainability practice. The luxury hotel concept does not necessarily align with sustainability and customer satisfaction is a priority in high-end hotels. The trade-off between minimum possible and minimum acceptable is often observed:

"We cannot place solar panels on the roofs because this may deteriorate the view of some rooms. Customer satisfaction is our priority" (MHC4).

In all-inclusive models, the cost is the first consideration. They minimize the energy cost when facing performance targets as it has economic implications. This demonstrates the prevalence of economic sustainability over other types.

"We cannot switch to glass bottles to reduce plastic use. This may significantly increase our costs since this is an all-inclusive model". (MHC5)

This business model-driven dimension implies that the sustainability practices of MHCs and SMEs are largely driven and constrained by economic sustainability. The authors observed the interwoven and dual nature of economic and social sustainability; in other words, economic sustainability often reinforces and constrains social sustainability. This applies to environmental sustainability as well, all of which in turn shapes the interaction between MHCs and SMEs. For instance, in MHC5, an all-inclusive hotel, protection of small enterprises is considered as an important part of their value chain, which demonstrates a notion of social sustainability. However, economic sustainability, manifested in profit-driven understanding and cost minimization dominates their interaction:

"The small businesses cannot afford lower prices we seek" (MHC5).

The seasonal nature of the businesses is another component of the business model affecting MHC-SME collaboration in sustainability. Lack of continuity in employment of the workforce deters MHCs from adopting regular training on, and systematic implementation of, sustainability. However, MHC4 presents a compelling case of turning this situation into an opportunity to address social sustainability by employing disabled employees on a full-time basis beyond the six-month operations.

"Most of our workforce is hired for six months since the premise operates only six months. However, we hire disabled people for a year-long contract" (MHC4).

The authors observe that SME understanding and practice of sustainability in the majority of our cases prioritizes environmental sustainability. Environmental sustainability is practised in these SMEs in a unique and informed way despite the unregulated macro-environment whereby the government office (Ministry of Environment and Urbanism) often has a counter argument towards the sustainability practice. Environmental sustainability seems to determine the survival of the business for most SMEs (three out of five cases) due to the nature of their business (mainly in the food industry) and the methods that they use:

"We are using chicken to get rid of scorpions and in our pool where we store water for irrigation we raise ducks so that the water is rich in fertilizer...Despite the common knowledge to dispose of olive pomace, we transfer it back to the soil as it nourishes and acts a fertilizer. This is what we have learned in our visits in Italy" (SME3).

Environmental sustainability is followed by some examples of social sustainability practices, as in the case of MHC4 employing people with disability, and gender and age-based recruitment of staff. These initiatives demonstrate commitment to social inclusion in most of our case SMEs, whereby women play an active role in innovation and management of the enterprise:

"I prefer to employ women as part of our social inclusion policy; instead of having 50-kilo bags of olives, I use 30 kilo-bags for women to carry" (SME1).

"We rely so much on the female workforce... we collect milk from over 100 local producers" (SME4).

Dynamics of MHC and SME Collaboration

As part of MHC and SME collaboration MHCs' selection and retention processes of local suppliers and business partners are integral steps towards inclusive and sustainable economic growth. However, a formal selection process does not exist between the MHCs and SMEs in our study. Instead, human agency plays a crucial role in MHCs' selection and maintaining the collaboration with the SMEs. By human agency, the authors refer to managerial agency, partner and owner-manager influence, employees and even customers. SMEs seem to be usually shy or less powerful in initiating the collaboration with the MHCs whilst the MHCs consider mainly economic sustainability and then other sustainability dimensions in choosing supplier SMEs. Geographical proximity is one important criterion (i.e. MHCs' preference to collaborate with local SMEs) for cost minimization reasons (economic sustainability), reducing pollution (environmental sustainability) and protection of local enterprises in order to create jobs (social sustainability):

"Locally sourcing our needs is a company policy. We even buy from the greengrocer down the street" (MHC1).

"The employee of the hotel used to live in our village. He taught us how to improve our product and services and introduced us to the hotel" (SME1).

SMEs' capacity as suppliers and their compatibility to collaborate with the MHC are two other criteria across all the cases. All MHCs in our sample apply regular audits and checks to SMEs on food safety that affect the quality of their service and customer satisfaction directly. MHCs usually do not check other sustainability dimensions in SMEs.

"Before we decide to buy food from local companies, we conduct regular checks on their production to make sure that they are compliant with food safety procedures – namely HACCP. We supervise them and inform them on how to be compliant" (MHC2).

"It is impossible to impose on all the suppliers to be fully sustainable. For this the hotels need to act together. A single hotel cannot influence all the suppliers" (MHC1).

In unpacking the 'black box in the collaboration between MHCs and SMEs, there exist opportunities and challenges for both parties (MHCs and SMEs). Here, MHCs' continuous engagement with SMEs plays an important role for MHC-SME collaboration on sustainability while this engagement is largely determined by the business seasonality of MHCs as well as the competitive power of SMEs. In most cases, MHCs' breaking up with SMEs occurs due to the SMEs' incapability in lowering their costs or to provide consistent, continuous, and high-quality supply in their competition with larger supplier firms (economic sustainability).

The collaboration between our case MHCs and SMEs is highly characterized by human agency. For instance, the power of purchasing managers and other employees, such as a sustainability-driven chef of the hotel, in influencing decisions to work with SMEs also has an impact on financial or other business-related challenges. In more detail, payment delays caused by MHCs or requests for commissions claimed by different intermediaries deteriorate the relationship between MHCs and SMEs. Power dynamics between MHCs and SMEs are often unbalanced while the relative importance placed on sustainability issues differs between them accordingly. SMEs perceive themselves as relatively powerless in their relationship with MHCs, which can lead to SMEs' lack of willingness to collaborate:

"Large suppliers can get their payments from large hotels but we cannot. One hotel has not paid our delivery. We stopped working with them without making noise. We need to be careful not to hurt anyone" (SME1).

"I am producing agricultural products which are free from pesticides and artificial fertilizers. This is a demanding process. I do not have time to spend in managing the relationship with the large hotels" (SME5).

Another important finding is that sustainability is a *product* as well as a *process* for MHCs collaborating with SMEs in an emerging country context. Their customers often request sustainability in the form of, for instance, protection of local produce, increasing interest in cultural heritage (social sustainability), and/or green activities for children (environmental sustainability). Such customer-driven awareness has a mediating force in collaborating with SMEs. This is also coupled by digital transformation, particularly use of social media, which enhances accessibility and outreach to SMEs by a multitude of actors including customers and other suppliers. Such actors and intermediaries also become agents for MHC-SME collaboration in endorsing sustainability:

"The customers of the hotels find us through Tripadvisor and they request local wine from their hotels" (SME3).

"We have improved on sustainability since Germans request sustainability" (SME1).

The authors also find that knowledge exchange occurs between MHCs and SMEs in developing sustainable practices. Transfer of sustainability practice is usually observed in the form of providing advice, setting standards, as well as role-modelling. However, an interesting finding is that the exchange occurs in a two-way street whereby SMEs also train MHCs particularly in localized sustainability such as preservation of olive trees (environmental sustainability) or maintaining the architectural integrity of hotels for cultural heritage (social sustainability).

This kind of transformative practice, as an outcome of the sustainability-related collaboration, entails learning and unlearning to embed sustainability in organizational practice. However, at the same time, sustainability appears to be an add-on practice in MHCs as it is not fully embedded in their overall strategic outlook and subsequent practice. Economic growth overrides sustainable development in their business approach.

DISCUSSION AND CONTRIBUTIONS

A Multi-Layered Model of MHC-SME Collaboration on Sustainability

Overall, our findings on sustainability and MHCs confirm their usual market-oriented approach to sustainability, whereby greater emphasis is put on the end-customer and interests of multiple stakeholders, as referred to in the extended literature (Li, Zhou and Wu, 2017; Mori et al., 2015).In this approach, neoliberal understanding of sustainability is legitimized in such a way that all sustainability activities have to be related to economic sustainability. In other words, environmental and social sustainability can co-exist if they serve the purpose of economic sustainability. Protection of environment and addressing social issues, such as poverty, equality and respecting diversity of employees, can go hand in hand if they meet the economic objectives. This underpins the collaboration between MHCs and SMEs in our cases.

This utilitarian approach adopted by MHCs bears a resemblance to reactionary behavior, as opposed to the proactive behaviour put forward in the extant literature (Ike et al., 2019). However, most of the participant SMEs, as represented by their owners, in our study are highly proactive in adopting sustainability practices as part of their survival strategies. For them, sustainability is the right action not through judgment of its consequences, but by a series of considerations of the underpinning values and ethics pertaining to sustainability.

This deontological view on sustainability of SMEs contrasts with the pragmatic stance and adoption of sustainable practice by MHCs, which often results in a tick-box exercise. This aligns with the recent debate in the literature pertaining to differences in corporate social responsibility (CSR) understandings between owner-managers and professional managers (Yamak, Ergur, Karatas-Ozkan, & Tatli, 2019) as the SMEs in our sample were managed by their owners and MHCs by professional managers.

The findings of the study lend themselves to development of a multi-layered framework for MHC-SME collaboration on sustainability, as shown in Figure 1. At the macro-institutional level, SDGs have significant weight, being implicitly embedded in the MHC policy frameworks whereas, for SMEs, sustainable development is explicitly reflected in their discourse and practice, without them necessarily being cognizant of SDGs as such. Growing concerns about the future of local context and business survival characterize SMEs' approach to sustainability, which demonstrates a high level of consciousness about sustainable development and a collective approach to addressing SDG-related challenges.

This is part of their transformation process investigating how to change and evolve their understanding and practices in the light of useful experiences for future (York, 2009). The prevailing cultural idiosyncratic conditions of host countries and the local environment impact highly on this process (Gallego-Alvarez & Ortas, 2017). SMEs, particularly those owned and/or managed by women, tend to show sensitivity towards the historical, archaeological, and cultural heritage and integrity of the location. In that sense, they have a more holistic perspective to sustainability than MHCs have with their centralized sustainability codes and policies. This concurs with the findings of García-Sánchez et al. (2019), who highlighted the positive impact of female representation in senior management for sustainability.

Figure 1.

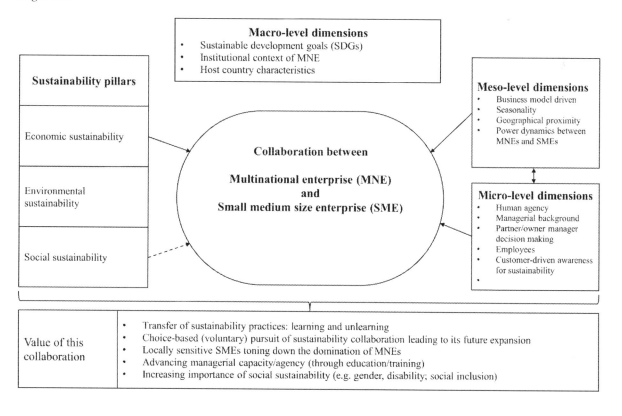

At the meso-relational level, organizational dimensions such as business models, seasonality of businesses and customer-driven sustainability motivation prevail in the MHC-SME collaboration on sustainability. From a business model perspective, competing forces that prioritize different sustainability pillars in different circumstances determine the relationship. Basic service provider hotels, as opposed to all-inclusive hotels, are more inclined to collaborate with SMEs, because their profit margin allows room for such collaboration, and they have a customer-base which is increasingly conscious of the issue. However, the limited capacity of the SMEs regarding the consistent and high-quality supply of the goods acts as a main barrier in the collaboration with the MHCs (Hennart, 2020).

At the interplay of meso- and micro-layers, tension is observed in unpacking the black box of the relationship from a perspective of three pillars of sustainability. MHCs, which empower women by integrating them into the labor market, also attract the workforce to tourism industry. This social sustainability initiative of MHCs has an adverse impact on SMEs and the rest of the local economy. SMEs fight against this by initiating training in agriculture, arts, and crafts to sustain cultural practices and local production. Clearly, this is linked to social sustainability from a stakeholder theory perspective whereby the input versus output aspects of stakeholders should be critically assessed (Hussain, Ajmal, Gunasekaran, & Khan, 2018). Socially, sustainable practices require more transformation and assimilation within organizations, due to the high involvement of human interaction (Riikkinen et al., 2017).

The micro-level dimension is particularly important in addressing the research questions set for this study. Human agency, in its most inclusive sense, is the determining factor shaping sustainability orientations. It also affects the emergence and continuity of MHC-SME collaboration. Despite the structural imposition of sustainability frameworks by MHC headquarters, implementation of such frameworks at a subsidiary level is decided by managers, who actively use their knowledge and decision-making capacity to choose who to interact with, when, and how. Managerial autonomy through exercise of agency is particularly evident in the process of initiating collaboration with SMEs on sustainability. The extent of agency varies according to circumstances, encapsulating individual as well as collective action (Buhr, 2002).

Kolk and Tulder (2010, p.119) argue that managers of MHCs particularly enjoy the 'moral free space' (Donaldson, 1996, p.56), in which the absence of tightly prescriptive frameworks for sustainability provides them with the autonomy to chart their own course of action. Contextual backdrop (i.e. emerging country context) is also instrumental in exercising this liberal approach in forming their collaboration with SMEs. For instance, on the SME side, MacKenzie and Gannon (2019) argue for the role of individual entrepreneurs and leaders, who understand the importance of sustainable tourism and that of effective collaboration with the host country government and local networks, using Costa Rica's ecotourism case. The role of such a business approach in sustainable development is critical in the tourism and hospitality industry of emerging countries (Hatipoglu et al., 2019).

This multi-layered framework of MHC-SME collaboration on sustainability can be concluded with inherent outcomes. The concurrent transformation of MHCs and SMEs lies at the heart of this. This transformative experience is multi-dimensional, due to the voluntary nature of sustainable practice evolving in organizations, the intersectionality of sustainability pillars applied in different circumstances, and a variety of trade-offs that subsequently come to the fore, with transfer of sustainable practices between two parties, which also brings about domination and exploitation of one against the other in some cases.

However, SMEs that have managed to retain the local, cultural, and environmental integrity of their touristic businesses show resistance to domination through innovation and a highly sensitized and culturally embedded approach to sustainability. They take initiatives to start collaboration with local authorities and other SMEs. The outcomes of such collaboration in this study demonstrate that SMEs and MHCs are subject to sustainability discourse from multiple sources and stakeholders. They develop agentic capacity to internalize these discourses and put them into action, the extent and nature of which vary according to the business requirements. This process also acts as a mechanism for increasing the trust of stakeholders in the sustainability commitment (García-Sánchez & Martinez-Ferrero, 2017) exercised through MHC-SME collaboration.

Contributions to Scholarship on Sustainability in Tourism

This study sheds light on the MHC-SME relationship in the area of sustainability in the tourism and hospitality industry in an emerging country. Our findings extend the understanding of the 'black box' and delineate the role of human agency in the interaction between MHCs and SMEs. They also show the exchange of knowledge between MHCs and SMEs in the domain of sustainable practices in tourism. The previous literature mainly focused on the transfer of knowledge from MHCs to SMEs, but the findings of the current study show that SMEs also contribute to the knowledge base of MHCs with regards to sustainability. The relationship between MHCs and SMEs regarding sustainability depends on the context, resources of the geographical area, business model and seasonality, among others.

In addition to our contribution to scholarship on sustainability in tourism and hospitality research, our findings on local SMEs' proactiveness in sustainable practice in emerging countries could provide a new perspective to address other neglected issues in academic knowledge, such as sustainability and SMEs.

Contributions to Practice and Policy

As there is high enthusiasm for sustainability at both policy and practice levels, the authors make contributions in three domains: businesses, political and legal, and society. First, for *businesses*, MHC-SME collaboration can bring visibility to SMEs and the local context in relation to sustainability, which is highly important for further development of sustainability practices in the latter, particularly in the developing/emerging market context.

However, SME owner-managers should be mindful of the dual nature of this strategic exchange (i.e., both positive and negative aspects and outcomes of this transformation) when collaborating with MHCs. Our findings suggest that MHCs can also benefit from the dynamic capacity and agility of SMEs, as well as their in-depth localized knowledge of the area. In addition, discussion on MHC-SME collaboration will encourage supporting intermediary organizations, such as co-operatives, which can empower and enable collective and co-ordinated action of SMEs in order to resist domination by MHCs.

Second, for the practitioners in the *political and legal* domain, understanding of MHC-SME collaboration and its different configurations might help investors and public authorities to identify areas of deficiency and potential improvement in relation to sustainability practices in tourism and hospitality businesses. Sustainability transparency – through the introduction of new requirements, compelling changes, and proactive behavior in MHC-SME collaboration – is essential for public authorities to take on board.

Last, at the *societal* level, social sustainability, as manifested in the social inclusion of disadvantaged groups (e.g., gender, disability) into the labour market and engagement with the community, as discussed in this study, has obvious benefits for society. Critical assessment of the outcomes of MHC-SME collaboration should also be undertaken by societal members in order to understand both the mutual benefits and drawbacks of such collaboration in terms of their impact on social sustainability.

CONCLUSION AND OPPORTUNITIES FOR FUTURE RESEARCH

The authors have conducted multiple-case study-based research on sustainability in an emerging market, which addresses the nature and dynamics of collaboration on sustainability (i.e. economic, environmental, and social sustainability) between MHCs and SMEs. The sustainability practice of MHCs and their approach to collaboration with SMEs is characterized by a neo-liberal/market-oriented approach, with top-down/centralized sustainability policies reflecting important stakeholders' pressure, such as SDGs or customer demand. Our SME cases show their own unique way of implementing sustainability practices, which are highly localized, encompassing a wider community. Their view on sustainability differs with a deontological approach, rather than having an explicitly targeted agenda such as SDGs. This outcome is a novel finding compared with the extant literature.

Our model encapsulates these dynamics from a multi-layered perspective: The collaboration between MHCs and SMEs is determined by the interaction of macro-meso-micro factors. First, macro-level factors, such as the SDG-based sustainability codes and policies of MHCs (e.g., criteria used for choosing SME partners; choice of interaction with local SMEs), are prevalent. Second, meso-level factors such as business models (all-inclusive versus premium service), affect the nature and continuity of collaboration as economic sustainability is often prioritized over others. Third, micro-level factors, such as human agency, determine the fundamental view on sustainability and subsequent practices and decisions on the collaboration between MHCs and SMEs. Our findings suggest that influence and knowledge transfer do not only occur from MHCs to SMEs, but also in the reverse direction as well. Therefore, transformative value of this collaboration is observed for both parties.

This study provides several new opportunities for future research. First, future studies might explore how MHCs' own sustainability policies can be effectively developed and implemented by reflecting differing host country tourism contexts, including their relationship with local SMEs. Second, future studies need to address missing policy gaps in many emerging countries for holistic development in sustainable tourism by shifting the focus from the agenda of, and guidance from, MHCs to supporting local SMEs and equipping them with relevant tools for MHC-SME collaboration. Last, future studies on SMEs and sustainable tourism might also view the issues with an altered stance from the conventional idea that SMEs lack interest and willingness in sustainable business to a new understanding of how they are already employing innovative sustainability practices in their own unique way and contributing to sustainable development agenda in the context of emerging countries.

REFERENCES

Banerjee, S. B. (2007). *Corporate Social Responsibility: The Good, the Bad and the Ugly*. Edward Elgar. doi:10.4337/9781847208552

Barkemeyer, R. (2009). Beyond compliance—Below expectations? CSR in the context of international development. *Business Ethics (Oxford, England), 18*(3), 273–288. doi:10.1111/j.1467-8608.2009.01563.x

Biermann, F., Kanie, N., & Kim, R. E. (2017). Global governance by goal-setting: The novel approach of the UN Sustainable Development Goals. *Current Opinion in Environmental Sustainability, 26-27,* 26–31. doi:10.1016/j.cosust.2017.01.010

Boyatzis, R. E. (1998). *Transforming qualitative information: Thematic analysis and code.* Sage.

Buhr, N. (2002). A structuration view on the initiation of environmental reports. *Critical Perspectives on Accounting, 13*(1), 17–38. doi:10.1016/S1045-2354(00)90441-6

Camilleri Mark, A. (2017). The rationale for responsible supply chain management and stakeholder engagement. *Journal of Global Responsibility, 8*(1), 111–126. doi:10.1108/JGR-02-2017-0007

Chan, E. S., Hon, A. H., Chan, W., & Okumus, F. (2014). What drives employees' intentions to implement green practices in hotels? The role of knowledge, awareness, concern and ecological behaviour. *International Journal of Hospitality Management, 40,* 20–28. doi:10.1016/j.ijhm.2014.03.001

Chan, W. W., Yeung, S., Chan, E. S. W., & Li, D. (2013). Hotel heat pump hot water sys-tems: Impact assessment and analytic hierarchy process. *International Journal of Contemporary Hospitality Management, 25*(3), 428–446. doi:10.1108/09596111311311053

Contreras, O. F., Carrillo, J., & Alonso, J. (2012). Local Entrepreneurship within Global Value Chains: A Case Study in the Mexican Automotive Industry. *World Development, 40*(5), 1013–1023. doi:10.1016/j.worlddev.2011.11.012

Darcy, C., Hill, J., McCabe, T. J., & McGovern, P. (2014). A consideration of organisational sustainability in the SME context: A resource-based view and composite model. *European Journal of Training and Development, 38*(5), 398–414. doi:10.1108/EJTD-10-2013-0108

De Urioste-Stone, S., McLaughlin, W. J., Daigle, J. J., & Fefer, J. P. (2018). Applying case study methodology to tourism research. In *Handbook of research methods for tourism and hospitality management.* Edward Elgar Publishing. doi:10.4337/9781785366284.00042

Deng, S. M., & Burnett, J. (2002). Energy use and management in hotels in Hong Kong. *IJHM, 21*(4), 371–380.

Donaldson, T. (1996). Values in tension: Ethics away from home. *Harvard Business Review, 74,* 48–62.

Egresi, I. (2016). Tourism and sustainability in Turkey: Negative impact of mass tourism development. In *Alternative tourism in Turkey* (pp. 35–53). Springer. doi:10.1007/978-3-319-47537-0_3

Ekinci, M. B. (2014). The Cittaslow philosophy in the context of sustainable tourism development; the case of Turkey. *Tourism Management, 41,* 178–189. doi:10.1016/j.tourman.2013.08.013

Erdogan, N., & Baris, E. (2007). Environmental protection programs and conservation practices of hotels in Ankara, Turkey. *Tourism Management, 28*(2), 604–614. doi:10.1016/j.tourman.2006.07.003

Ertuna, B., Karatas-Ozkan, M., & Yamak, S. (2019). Diffusion of sustainability and CSR discourse in the hospitality industry: Dynamics of local context. *International Journal of Contemporary Hospitality Management*, *31*(6), 2564–2581. doi:10.1108/IJCHM-06-2018-0464

European Commission. (2018). *Proposal for a Regulation of the European Parliament and of the Council on the establishment of a framework to facilitate sustainable investment*. European Commission.

Font, X., & Lynes, J. (2018). Corporate social responsibility in tourism and hospitality. *Journal of Sustainable Tourism*, *26*(7), 1027–1042. doi:10.1080/09669582.2018.1488856

Fukuda-Parr, S. (2016). From the Millennium Development Goals to the Sustainable Development Goals: Shifts in purpose, concept, and politics of global goal setting for development. *Gender and Development*, *24*(1), 43–52. doi:10.1080/13552074.2016.1145895

Gallego-Álvarez, P. I., & Ortas, P. E. (2017). Corporate environmental sustainability reporting in the context of national cultures: A quantile regression approach. *International Business Review*, *26*(2), 337–353. doi:10.1016/j.ibusrev.2016.09.003

Gunaydin, Y., Özgür, Ö., & Ataman, D. (2021). Influence of pull factors on the travel motivation of foreign tourists towards Bodrum-Turkey destination. *Journal of Tourism Theory and Research*, *7*(1), 11–21. doi:10.24288/jttr.823952

Halme, M., Rintamäki, J., Knudsen, J. S., Lankoski, L., & Kuisma, M. (2020). When Is There a Sustainability Case for CSR? Pathways to Environmental and Social Performance Improvements. *Business & Society*, *59*(6), 1181–1227. doi:10.1177/0007650318755648

Han, H., Lee, J. S., Trang, H. L. T., & Kim, W. (2018). Water conservation and waste reduction management for increasing guest loyalty and green hotel practices. *International Journal of Hospitality Management*, *75*, 58–66. doi:10.1016/j.ijhm.2018.03.012

Hatipoglu, B., Ertuna, B., & Duygu, S. (2019). Corporate social responsibility in tourism as a tool for sustainable development. *International Journal of Contemporary Hospitality Management*, *31*(6), 2358–2375. doi:10.1108/IJCHM-05-2018-0448

Hennart, J. F. (2020). More than intent: A bundling model of MNE–SME interactions. *Journal of International Business Studies*, *51*(7), 1176–1194. doi:10.105741267-020-00352-8

Hörisch, J., Johnson, M. P., & Schaltegger, S. (2015). Implementation of Sustainability Management and Company Size: A Knowledge-Based View. *Business Strategy and the Environment*, *24*(8), 765–779. doi:10.1002/bse.1844

Hsieh, Y. C. (2012). Hotel companies' environmental policies and practices: A content analysis of their web pages. *International Journal of Contemporary Hospitality Management*, *24*(1), 97–121. doi:10.1108/095961112

Hurriyet (2022, June 19). *Yatirimcinin gozu Bodrum'da*. hurriyet.com

Hussain, M., Ajmal, M. M., Gunasekaran, A., & Khan, M. (2018). Exploration of social sustainability in healthcare supply chain. *Journal of Cleaner Production*, *203*, 977–989. doi:10.1016/j.jclepro.2018.08.157

Ike, M., Donovan, J. D., Topple, C., & Masli, E. K. (2019). A holistic perspective on corporate sustainability from a management viewpoint: Evidence from Japanese manufacturing multinational enterprises. *Journal of Cleaner Production, 216*, 139–151. doi:10.1016/j.jclepro.2019.01.151

Iyer, G., & Jarvis, L. (2019). CSR adoption in the multinational hospitality context. *International Journal of Contemporary Hospitality Management, 31*(6), 2376–2393. doi:10.1108/IJCHM-06-2018-0451

Jia, F., Zuluaga-Cardona, L., Bailey, A., & Rueda, X. (2018). Sustainable supply chain management in devel,oping countries: An analysis of the literature. *Journal of Cleaner Production, 189*, 63–278. doi:10.1016/j.jclepro.2018.03.248

Khatter, A., McGrath, M., Pyke, J., White, L., & Lockstone-Binney, L. (2019). Analysis of hotels' environmentally sustainable policies and practices. *International Journal of Contemporary Hospitality Management, 31*(6), 2394–2410. doi:10.1108/IJCHM-08-2018-0670

Kişi, N. (2019). A strategic approach to sustainable tourism development using the A'WOT hybrid method: A case study of Zonguldak, Turkey. *Sustainability, 11*(4), 964. doi:10.3390u11040964

Koe Hwee Nga, J., & Shamuganathan, G. (2010). The Influence of Personality Traits and Demographic Factors on Social Entrepreneurship Start Up Intentions. *Journal of Business Ethics, 95*(2), 259–282. doi:10.100710551-009-0358-8

Kolk, A., Kourula, A., Pisani, N., & Westermann-Behaylo, M. (2020). The state of international business, corporate social responsibility and development: key insights and an application to practice. In P. Lund-Thomsen, M. W. Hansen, & A. Lindgreen (Eds.), *Business and Development Studies: Issues and perspective*. Routledge.

Kolk, A., & Lenfant, F. (2010). MNC Reporting on CSR and Conflict in Central Africa. *Journal of Business Ethics, 93*(S2), 241–255. doi:10.100710551-009-0271-1

Kolk, A., & van Tulder, R. (2010). International business, corporate social responsibility and sustainable development. *International Business Review, 19*(2), 119–125. doi:10.1016/j.ibusrev.2009.12.003

Kornilaki, M., Thomas, R., & Font, X. (2019). The sustainability behaviour of small firms in tourism: The role of self-efficacy and contextual constraints. *Journal of Sustainable Tourism, 27*(1), 97–117. doi:10.1080/09669582.2018.1561706

Lane, H. W., & Maznevski, M. L. (2019). *International Management Behavior: Global and Sustainable Leadership* (8th ed.). Cambridge University Press. doi:10.1017/9781108637152

Langwell, C., & Heaton, D. (2016). Using human resource activities to implement sustainability in SMEs. *Journal of Small Business and Enterprise Development, 23*(3), 652–670. doi:10.1108/JSBED-07-2015-0096

Leitch, C. M., McMullan, C., & Harrison, R. T. (2013). The development of entrepreneurial leadership: The role of human, social and institutional capital. *British Journal of Management, 24*(3), 347–366. doi:10.1111/j.1467-8551.2011.00808.x

Li, E. L., Zhou, L., & Wu, A. (2017). The supply-side of environmental sustainability and export performance: The role of knowledge integration and international buyer involvement. *International Business Review*, *26*(4), 724–735. doi:10.1016/j.ibusrev.2017.01.002

Locke, R., & Romis, M. (2007). Improving Work Conditions in a Global Supply Chain. *MIT Sloan Management Review*, *48*, 54.

Lozano, R., Carpenter, A., & Huisingh, D. (2015). A review of 'theories of the firm' and their contributions to Corporate Sustainability. *Journal of Cleaner Production*, *106*, 430–442. doi:10.1016/j.jclepro.2014.05.007

MacKenzie, N., & Gannon, M. J. (2019). Exploring the antecedents of sustainable tourism development. *International Journal of Contemporary Hospitality Management*, *31*(6), 2411–2427. doi:10.1108/IJCHM-05-2018-0384

Mathur, S., & Khanna, K. (2017). Sustainability practices as a competitive edge in five star hotels of Delhi: A study on manager's perception. *International Research Journal of Management. IT and Social Sciences*, *4*(6), 1–9.

Mori, K., Fujii, T., Yamashita, T., Mimura, Y., Uchiyama, Y., & Hayashi, K. (2015). Visualization of a City Sustainability Index (CSI): Towards transdisciplinary approaches involving multiple stakeholders. *Sustainability*, *7*(9), 12402–12424. doi:10.3390u70912402

Morsing, M., & Perrini, F. (2009). CSR in SMEs: Do SMEs matter for the CSR agenda? *Business Ethics (Oxford, England)*, *18*(1), 1–6. doi:10.1111/j.1467-8608.2009.01544.x

Narula, R., & Dunning, J. H. (2010). Multinational Enterprises, Development and Globalization: Some Clarifications and a Research Agenda. *Oxford Development Studies*, *38*(3), 263–287. doi:10.1080/13600818.2010.505684

Ng, A. W., & Tavitiyaman, P. (2020). Corporate social responsibility and sustainability initiatives of multinational hotel corporations. In *International business, Trade and Institutional Sustainability* (pp. 3–15). Springer. doi:10.1007/978-3-030-26759-9_1

Nishii, L. H., & Özbilgin, M. F. (2007). Global diversity management: Towards a conceptual framework. *International Journal of Human Resource Management*, *18*(11), 1883–1894. doi:10.1080/09585190701638077

OECD. (2017). *Enhancing the Contributions of SMEs in a Global and Digitalised Economy*. Retrieved on June 27, 2019, from: https://www.oecd.org/mcm/documents/C-MIN-2017-8-EN.pdf)

Olya, H., Altinay, L., Farmaki, A., Kenebayeva, A., & Gursoy, D. (2021). Hotels' sustainability practices and guests' familiarity, attitudes and behaviours. *Journal of Sustainable Tourism*, *29*(7), 1063–1081. doi:10.1080/09669582.2020.1775622

Oriade, A., Osinaike, A., Aduhene, K., & Wang, Y. (2021). Sustainability awareness, management practices and organisational culture in hotels: Evidence from developing countries. *International Journal of Hospitality Management*, *92*, 92. doi:10.1016/j.ijhm.2020.102699

Patton, M. Q. (2014). *Qualitative Research & Evaluation Methods Integrating Theory and Practice* (4th ed.). Sage Publications.

Pisani, N., Kourula, A., Kolk, A., & Meijer, R. (2017). How global is international CSR research? Insights and recommendations from a systematic review. *Journal of World Business, 52*(5), 591–614. doi:10.1016/j.jwb.2017.05.003

Raub, S. P., & Martin-Rios, C. (2019). "Think sustainable, act local" – a stakeholder-filter-model for translating SDGs into sustainability initiatives with local impact. *International Journal of Contemporary Hospitality Management, 31*(6), 2428–2447. doi:10.1108/IJCHM-06-2018-0453

Riikkinen, R., Kauppi, K., & Salmi, A. (2017). Learning Sustainability? Absorptive capacities as drivers of sustainability in MNCs' purchasing. *International Business Review, 26*(6), 1075–1087. doi:10.1016/j.ibusrev.2017.04.001

Rodgers, P., Stokes, P., Tarba, S., & Khan, Z. (2019). The Role of Non-market Strategies in Establishing Legitimacy: The Case of Service MHCs in Emerging Economies. *Management International Review, 59*(4), 515–540. doi:10.100711575-019-00385-8

Schoenmaker, D. (2017). Investing for the common good: a sustainable finance framework. In *Essay and Lectures Series*. Bruegel.

Schoenmaker, D. (2018). *Sustainable investing: How to do it. Policy Contribution, 23*. Bruegel.

Schramade, W. (2016). Bridging Sustainability and Finance: The Value Driver Adjustment Approach. *Journal of Applied Corporate Finance, 28*(2), 17–28. doi:10.1111/jacf.12170

Schramade, W. (2017). Investing in the UN Sustainable Development Goals: Opportunities for Companies and Investors. *Journal of Applied Corporate Finance, 29*(2), 87–99. doi:10.1111/jacf.12236

Shields, J., & Shelleman, J. M. (2015). Integrating Sustainability into SME Strategy. *Journal of Small Business Strategy, 25*, 59–78.

Sourvinou, A., & Filimonau, V. (2018). Planning for an environmental management programme in a luxury hotel and its perceived impact on staff: An exploratory case study. *Journal of Sustainable Tourism, 26*(4), 649–667. doi:10.1080/09669582.2017.1377721

Svensson, G., Wood, G., & Callaghan, M. (2010). A corporate model of sustainable business practices: An ethical perspective. *Journal of World Business, 45*(4), 336–345. doi:10.1016/j.jwb.2009.08.005

Taticchi, P., Tonelli, F., & Pasqualino, R. (2013). Performance measurement of sustainable supply chains: A literature review and a research agenda. *International Journal of Productivity and Performance Management, 62*(8), 782–804. doi:10.1108/IJPPM-03-2013-0037

Tosun, C. (2001). Challenges of sustainable tourism development in the developing world: The case of Turkey. *Tourism Management, 22*(3), 289–303. doi:10.1016/S0261-5177(00)00060-1

UNCTAD. (2015). *World Investment Report - Reforming international investment governance*. UNCTAD.

UNWTO. (2015). *Tourism in the 2030 agenda*. Retrieved on March 29, 2021, from: https://www.unwto.org/tourism-in-2030-agenda

Wahga, A. I., Blundel, R., & Schaefer, A. (2018). Understanding the drivers of sustainable entrepreneurial practices in Pakistan's leather industry. *International Journal of Entrepreneurial Behaviour & Research, 24*(2), 382–407. doi:10.1108/IJEBR-11-2015-0263

Wolcott, H. F. (1994). *Transforming qualitative data: Description, analysis, and interpretation.* Sage Publications.

Xu, M., Cui, Y., Hu, M., Xu, X., Zhang, Z., Liang, S., & Qu, S. (2019). Supply chain sustainability risk and assessment. *Journal of Cleaner Production, 225*, 857–867. doi:10.1016/j.jclepro.2019.03.307

Yadav, N., Gupta, K., Rani, L., & Rawat, D. (2018). Drivers of Sustainability Practices and SMEs: A Systematic Literature Review. *European Journal of Sustainable Development, 7*(4), 531–544. doi:10.14207/ejsd.2018.v7n4p531

Yamak, S., Ergur, A., Karatas-Ozkan, M., & Tatli, A. (2019). CSR and Leadership Approaches and Practices: A Comparative Inquiry of Owners and Professional Executives. *European Management Review, 16*(4), 1097–1114. doi:10.1111/emre.12318

York, J. G. (2009). Pragmatic Sustainability: Translating Environmental Ethics into Competitive Advantage. *Journal of Business Ethics, 85*(S1), 97–109. doi:10.100710551-008-9950-6

Young, L. (2013). *Growing your business - A report on growing micro businesses.* Retrieved on June 11, 2019, from: https://assets.publishing.service.gov.uk/government/uploads/system/uploads/attachment_data/file/198165/growing-your-business-lord-young.pdf

Chapter 24
Using the Technology Acceptance Model in Tourism Businesses

Mahmut Barakazi
Harran University, Turkey

ABSTRACT

It is seen that technological elements are frequently used to provide a better quality tourism experience and to expand the comfort zone. It is understood that many tourism businesses, especially in the fields of accommodation, travel, and gastronomy, have gained a more competitive structure by developing their technological infrastructure. In this direction, the suitability of the technology acceptance model (TAM), which was first developed by Davis and based on two basic elements, in terms of tourism enterprises is associated with examples. It is understood that the perceived convenience and usefulness within the scope of the research is met positively in terms of tourism services. In addition, it is thought the quality-of-service perception will be increased by better using the opportunities brought by technology in tourism. The goal is to contribute to the relevant literature by evaluating the effect of the TAM model on the tourism sectors from a general perspective.

INTRODUCTION

Tourism activities are gaining more and more importance day by day in terms of obtaining travel experience and cultural units. However, as a result of the economic development of touristic destinations and the improvement of infrastructure activities, tourism movements have started to create awareness. This situation has created an intensely competitive environment in the field of tourism and has led to developments in marketing and promotion. Tourism businesses (e.g., accommodation, travel, recreation, and others) that want to engage in a better promotion activity compared to their competitors are trying to improve their infrastructure with technological tools in parallel with technological developments.

DOI: 10.4018/978-1-6684-4645-4.ch024

At this point, innovative and digital services are offered that consider the technological service demands of people. People who start to use mass media more frequently, especially social media, can realize their touristic purchases or their intention to choose destinations in these areas. Technological tools such as internet-based reservation systems, online payment, smart menus and artificial intelligence-supported robotic systems are becoming very necessary for tourism businesses. In addition, tourism businesses need to have qualified personnel and technology-sensitive consumers who can use technological elements.

Because the technological requirement at the point of supply and demand must show similar characteristics for tourism businesses to be sustainable. However, it is understood that technology be fully achieved in cases where the technological infrastructure is insufficient, and the level of technological acceptability is not at the desired level. Therefore, tourism businesses must focus on the concept of technology acceptability as well as strengthen their technological infrastructure.

The technology acceptance model, which is one of the most frequently studied models on the level of technological use, was put forward for the first time by Davis (1989). Developing the theory of reasoned action is presented in the form of a model that determines the behavior of people towards the use or acceptance of new technologies. In the technology acceptance model (TAM), the user's intention is understood by determining the ease of use and perceived usefulness of technological tools (Sadiq & Adil, 2021).

To better understand the development of TAM, it is necessary to understand its emergence process and theories. The ever-increasing need for technology in the daily life of users was being examined psychologically in terms of acceptance or rejection. However, with the inclusion of behaviors and intentions in the process over time, TAM has begun to be expressed in a wide area. In this direction, elements such as traditional lifestyle, character and personal factors find their place in the technology acceptability model. Normative beliefs and motivation to comply are also expressed as behaviors that directly affect individuals' perceived technology acceptability.

In its simplest form, TAM is explained as perceived usefulness and attitude towards technology, as well as behavior and reason for technology use (Marangunić & Granić, 2015: 82). In terms of the tourism sector, uses such as the technology acceptability model, online reservation, internet-based ticket purchase and rating of the tourism experience in virtual environments are evaluated within this scope (McCloskey, 2004: 50). There are the following studies in the literature on the technology acceptability model in the relationship between tourism and technology; It is discussed and implemented how users accept artificial intelligence (AI) robots in hotels (Go et al., 2020).

The factors affecting the use of the technology acceptance model in social media marketing by tour operators are investigated (Matikiti et al., 2018). Patients are uses using the technology acceptance model to explain the e-purchase intention in health tourism (Phatthana & Mat, 2011). The technology acceptability of the intention to make an online reservation in the context of e-tourism is high (Sahli & Legohérel, 2016). Mobile-based tourism shopping is adopted by users, technology acceptability model studies in the relationship between tourism and technology are available in the related literature, as it affects tourist intentions and the perception of technology compatibility affects acceptance intentions (Gu et al., 2019).

Technological tools, which are an important strategic target for hotel organizations to improve their operational performance and strategic competitive power, are being used in all departments. In this context, businesses that develop hotel front office systems with the TAM system, which is an expanded technology acceptance model, examine the relationship between perceived value and consumer acceptance. In addition, the attitudes and real behaviors of consumers who buy touristic services that offer technological tools in the hotel are revealed (Kim et al., 2008). In addition to the accommodation sector, travel businesses that offer package tours, especially transportation, focus on digital service providers to benefit more from technological opportunities and minimize physical infrastructure expenses.

In this context, various technological service tools are offered to people who want to purchase travel services. However, it is necessary to determine the effect of the technological possibilities offered in terms of perceived ease of use and benefits. It is revealed that individuals who purchase online travel services provide positive feedback on perceived ease of use and their usage intentions can be explained by associating them with the TAM model (Setiawan & Widanta, 2021).

In terms of businesses providing recreation and entertainment services, the technology acceptance model reveals similar results. It is important to what extent individuals who visit museums and historical cultural heritage sites perceive the smart tourism content they use during their travels. There are significant positive effects in the study, in which the relationship between the use of technological tools in museums or other touristic areas and their perceived usefulness during the touristic experience (Jeong et al., 2021). In addition, it is emphasized that both the perceived ease of use and the level of perceived usefulness have a significant impact on the intention to use technology.

In the light of all this information, it is seen that technological use and perceived use are positive in all activities that provide tourism services, especially accommodation, travel businesses and recreation services. For this reason, it is thought that the evaluation of tourism activities and their relationship status should be the subject of further studies, especially in the technology acceptance model. In this way, it can be determined whether the rate of technology use is in line with the perceived need. In other words, it is necessary to reveal whether the technological services offered by tourism enterprises work for the users.

The theoretical background first gives an idea about the conceptual framework of the TAM model. In the second part, the relationship of the TAM model is explained in terms of tourism enterprises. Finally, the importance of the relationship was tried to be explained with an example event.

BACKGROUND

Technology Acceptance Model (TAM)

The origin of the technology acceptance model (TAM) is based on the theory of reasoned action, which is the determinant of consciously intended behaviors (Lu et al., 2003). The technology acceptance model (TAM) is one of the most popular theories used to explain the reasons for the use of information systems. With this model, the acceptable behaviors and reactions of individuals towards technology were examined and confirmed by various studies (Surendran, 2012). TAM can be explained by building on two basic factors. One of these factors is perceived usefulness, while the other is perceived usefulness in the short and long term.

Davis two factors in terms of perceived usefulness and perceived ease of use; He summarized it as "the degree to which a person believes that using a particular system will improve job performance" and "the degree to which a person believes that using a particular system will not require effort" (Chau, 1996). However, it is revealed that these two factors are affected by external variables and gain different dimensions. In this context, the main external factors affecting the model; It has been determined that there are social factors, cultural factors and political factors.

Social factors are classified as foreign languages known other than mother tongue, physical and mental skills, social personality and communication disposition, as well as other facilitating conditions. Cultural factors are called social factors, especially traditional lifestyle, teachings, normative beliefs, and ethical and moral values. Political factors, on the other hand, are expressed as the differences between technological tools and political perspectives. In other words, it is about the extent to which the attitude toward technology is accepted or allowed by the political circles.

The main purpose of TAM is to be able to interpret by examining the effect of external variables on internal beliefs, attitudes and intentions. It is suggested that perceived ease of use and perceived usefulness are the two most important factors in explaining system usage (Legris et al., 2003). Based on TAM's main components and external factors, Davis gave the final version of this model in Figure 1 (Surendran, 2012);

Figure 1. Technology Acceptance Model (Davis, 1989)

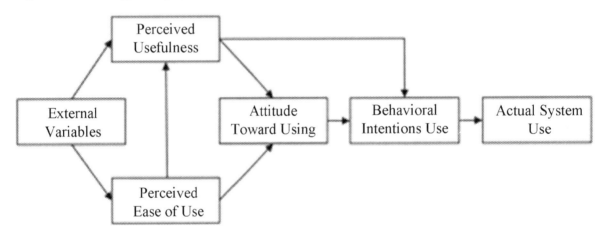

TAM has developed by applying different tests to examine how different technological tools, which have increased rapidly in recent years, are perceived. The role of digital collaboration, which is one of the most important practitioners of technology in human life, in the adoption of technology has begun to be considered. In this context, digital cooperation is defined as providing coordination between people with similar tasks based on electronic technologies. With the emergence of the World Wide Web at the end of the 20th century, the impact of the technology acceptance model began to increase gradually as a result of the introduction of e-mail, file sharing and communicative processes (Dasgupta et al., 2002).

However, it is stated that this model has shortcomings, and it is revealed that TAM relationships are not confirmed in all studies. In various studies with different users and systems, many different results have been obtained then the predicted effects. For this reason, it is thought that the model should be developed (King & He, 2006). From this point of view, Lucas and Spitler (1999) expanded TAM by including new variables such as the perceived system quality level and valid norms in the model. The new model was tested considering the two control variables workload and previous performance output, and different results were obtained in terms of technology adoption.

Geffen and Straub (2000), on the other hand, argue that most of the studies based on Davis's TAM model fail to examine the importance of perceived ease of use in the adoption of information technology.

They reveal that perceived ease of use affects the perceived usefulness of the system, and usefulness affects the user's intention to use information technology. They also thought that perceived ease of use heavily influenced the experience of actual use. When they looked at the relationship between perceived ease of use and internal and external features of information technologies, they found that there was an effect at various levels.

According to Davis (1989), the basis of the TAM model, perceived ease of use of a system affects its perceived usefulness, while perceived ease of use and perceived usefulness affect the use of the system. These three approaches explain the relationships outlined in TAM. Lucas and Spitler (1999) used another hypothesis in addition to TAM and tested the results of using information systems in their work on intermediary workstations. The aim here is to reveal the impact of information technology adoption on performance. They also draw attention to the relationship between technology and user experience by addressing the effect of system usage on individual performance.

Venkatesh and Davis (2000) reconsidered the structure of the original TAM, using empirical findings to assess the importance of the traditional structures of the models. In their revised model, known as TAM2, they excluded attitudes but retained perceived usefulness and ease of use. In addition, the TAM2 approach added measures of subjective norms in various dimensions to capture social influences. Factors such as subjective norms, indicators of social influences, and personality traits (e.g., colleagues, friends, supervisors) were contemplated.

However, in the new model, they put forward the idea that people's target technological perceptions can explain behaviors about the applicability of individuals to their work or daily routines at work. Compared to the first TAM approach, it was concluded that TAM2 significantly expands the range of indirect effects of remote estimators (e.g., social norms, relevance, and so forth) on intentions to use, while emphasizing the central role of perceived usefulness and ease of use. Shown as follows (TAM2), which has many similarities with the original TAM approach, but differs in content and number, which is the basis of the legacy of the technology acceptance literature (Venkatesh & Davis, 2000).

Figure 2. Technology Acceptance Model 2 (Venkatesh ve Davis, 2000)

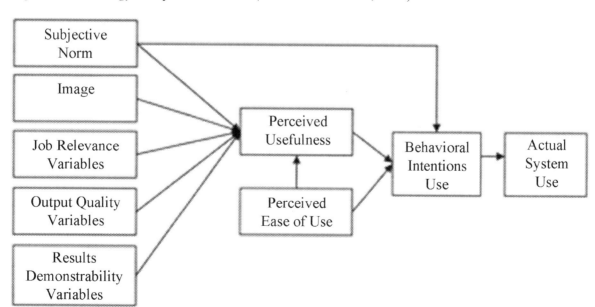

THE RELATIONSHIP BETWEEN TAM AND TOURISM

Understanding the reactions of people to the emergence of innovative technologies is very important for tourism businesses that provide people-oriented services. Businesses operating in all areas of the tourism sector closely follow current developments and update their service providers accordingly (Jacob et al., 2003). On the other hand, due to the intense use of technological tools by individuals participating in tourism activities, the infrastructure must be at a level that can respond to this. With the beginning of the internet age in technological developments, digital fields have started to be included in human life (Gretzel et al., 2015).

This process, which started with Web 2.0, has reached today in the form of smartphones, mobile applications, and artificial intelligence-supported information services. People who have the intention to travel more, especially in the light of positive developments in leisure and income, have started to find the destination they want to go to, the hotel they want to stay and the recreational activities they want to participate in, using technology tools. Today, tourism movements are no longer expected to take place without technological opportunities.

At this point, it is a necessity in terms of sustainable tourism understanding to determine how the differences brought by technology are perceived or accepted by touristic consumers.

Research on the acceptance of various informatics applications such as smartphone applications and different types of software in the service sector, especially in tourism, has determined the psychological variable that predicts usage intentions. With TAM, it is stated that perceived usefulness and perceived ease of use affect attitudes towards technology applications and usage intentions are supported by high-level motivation tools. These variables, which are well summarized in the technology acceptance model (TAM) first developed by Davis, have helped to specifically explain technological perceptions in the last 20 years (Ketididis et al., 2012).

In addition, approaches such as the original TAM and other alternative technological acceptance models are among the areas that should be applied carefully for a sector such as tourism with a complex structure and multidimensional differences. In this context, researchers have examined shopping intentions and technological usage levels over digital platforms by applying TAM to different areas of technology such as tourism and shopping. They reveal that digital purchasing behaviors consist of a theoretical framework information system (Technology Acceptance Model), marketing (Consumer Behavior) and psychology (Flow and Environmental Psychology). The emotional and cognitive reactions of people who visit a web page marketing digital-based tourism products for the first time were examined and their acceptance and approval intentions were evaluated.

Within the scope of the research, it was concluded that the perceived usefulness of the digital website strongly supported the purchase intention, while the emotional and cognitive responses revealed positive outcomes (Jan & Contreras, 2011). From this point of view, the ideas about how the technology acceptance model is put forward in the fields such as accommodation, travel, and recreation, which are the main branches of the tourism sector, are given in detail by evaluating the relevant literature and observation.

TAM in Terms of Accommodation Businesses

Accommodation businesses are one of the most important service providers in the tourism industry. For the realization of tourism activities, it is necessary to stay at the destination. In this context, the physical accommodation capacities of the destination are evaluated first while making travel plans. The intense competition environment brought by globalization and chain establishments has led to an increase in comfort and special needs in accommodation businesses.

Accommodation businesses, which can respond to the demands of consumers and produce the services they need, come to the fore. Accommodation businesses are divided into many departments, including front desk, housekeeping, catering and other support services. In each of these departments, technological tools are used and digital developments are closely followed. In the front office department, guests are welcomed and checked in. Various services are also offered for them to make reservations and communicate. In this context, the front office, which provides services from the first moment the guests start to receive accommodation service until the last time, frequently uses technological tools to increase the service quality.

For example, traditional room keys have been in the background by using smart cards recently. On the other hand, with smart wristbands and descriptive mobile services, guests can meet their needs with these technological tools. With the introduction of reservation systems in digital areas, time and cost savings were achieved by eliminating the intermediaries between accommodation establishments and guests (Morosan & Jeong, 2008).

At this point, it has become possible to say that a two-way interaction has occurred by establishing a direct connection. In addition, a wide range of services that can be obtained in the front office department can be reached with web-based digital information. Considering the intention of the employees in the front office department to show a rapid tendency towards innovations, it is predicted that the use of technology will be similarly accepted.

In the study conducted on front-office employees through the TAM framework, it is stated that the employees' perspective on technology is very positive and they have positive implications for the relationship between information system quality and perceived value (Kim et al., 2008). In addition, in a study on the acceptance of WBT by employees in the front office department using an extension of the TAM model, it was determined that the dimensions of entertainment, organizational support and information quality were significantly affected, and perceived ease was found to be high (Hasanien et al., 2014).

Housekeeping services, which carry out laundry, dry cleaning, and general square cleaning activities, especially room services in accommodation establishments, try to take advantage of technological opportunities to the fullest. Because hygiene and sanitation processes should be done meticulously with technological tools and control processes should be created via computer. It is extremely important to transfer the room status to digital media after it is prepared with the relevant forms between the front desk and housekeeping services. In this way, transactions can be carried out quickly and practically in the hotel workflow process. Considering all this process, it is necessary to understand whether the employees accept technology and whether they have it at a sufficient level due to the intense use of technology in housekeeping (Venkatesh & Davis, 2000).

In a study in which advanced TAM models were tested in the context of smart housekeeping applications, it was determined that perceived usefulness and perceived ease of use had a positive and significant effect on attitude (Hamid et al., 2020). On the other hand, it is important for the hotel circulation that the housekeeping staff communicate about the room status by communicating via radio or mobile phone. At this point, the technological acceptability and perceptions of the employees support the business process.

Food and beverage services are one of the focal points in tourism businesses in terms of meeting the nutritional needs of the guests and making them feel good. In recent years, the interest in healthy nutrition and conscious consumption as well as innovative cuisine can be met by food and beverage services. Technological tools such as the use of smart robots during the service, beverage machines, e-menu and robotic kitchen tools with artificial intelligence are frequently used in this department. However, competent employees who are equipped to use these technological tools need to plan the workflow process correctly. However, technological tools, which are being used intensively, can cause employment problems by reducing the need for human labor.

This situation can be perceived negatively by people and feelings of dissatisfaction with technology can develop. Due to the progress of science and the rapid impact of discoveries on food and beverage businesses, a structure independent of technological tools is not expected to be sustainable. At this point, the important thing is to design the technology and human relationship correctly and develop it based on mutual benefit.

In a study on the payment systems used in food and beverage businesses, it was understood that the factors affecting the acceptance of technology create the perception of appropriate usage areas for the growth and development of the business. It is seen that the perception of technological acceptance is realized by determining various positive relations between the TAM and food and beverage payment systems. It has been concluded that the perceived usefulness of payment systems benefits the information quality of the employees and entertains them while learning. Therefore, the implementation of the technology adoption strategy is important in terms of both better learning for the employees and providing efficiency to the business (Ramos & Castro, 2017).

In another study, how Artificial Intelligence (AI) tools can help restaurants improve service quality and create a better customer experience has been discussed and examined with TAM. It is stated that robots, chatbots, face recognition systems and voice-activated technological tools used in food and beverage businesses have positive effects in terms of perceived usefulness. It is said that restaurants using artificial intelligence technology are seen as advantageous in terms of convenience perceived by employees and consumers (Cheong et al., 2021). In another study, he tried to examine the perception of restaurant robots using a trust, interaction and output quality and the technology acceptance model (TAM) and found that attitude positively affects perceived usefulness and acceptance. It was also concluded that perceived ease of use affects attitude positively.

Considering that perceived ease of use significantly increases perceived usefulness, the TAM relationship in restaurants can be better understood. It was concluded that perceived ease of use significantly determines perceived usefulness in terms of trust and output quality as well as interaction (Lee et al., 2018). In a study based on TAM integration, the effect of e-commerce adoption in food and beverage businesses on perceived usefulness and perceived ease of use was examined and the hypotheses put forward were supported. At the point of adoption of e-commerce, it is observed that sensory perceived ease of use and usefulness perceptions have improved from the TAM model, while individual skills have also increased in this direction (Nguyen et al., 2022).

In a study conducted to investigate the external factors that affect the acceptance of technology used by employees in tourism enterprises, they were asked to evaluate their technology experiences within the scope of the TAM. It was concluded that two mediating factors will affect the relationship between external variables and technological acceptance for system use, and the relationship has been confirmed. It has been determined that there is an external variable that will affect the acceptance of technology by users with food and beverage experience, and task fit leads to the perceived usefulness of technology (Stamam et al., 2012).

It is possible to talk about the existence of this connection, based on the studies in which payment systems and smart technological device usage in food and beverage businesses are associated with the technology acceptance model. In addition, testing this relationship in other areas will reveal information that will provide serious benefits in terms of service quality

In other support departments offered in accommodation establishments, there are service providers such as entertainment, spa, technical services and sales for guests. These elements play the role of complementing the main service products and meeting other needed needs. Technological use is intense in these departments, as in the main service products. For this reason, determining the perception of technological acceptability and usefulness becomes very important.

Concerts, performing arts, daytime activities and dance shows in the entertainment area gain a different dimension thanks to the technological infrastructure. There is a need for employees who use technological equipment well, especially in sound systems and light management. In spa services, the ambiance and space visuals are provided with technological tools. To ensure that accommodation businesses are provided with electricity, communication, and device controls sustainably, technical services employees who are constantly operating should be selected from people who are prone to technology use. As a matter of fact, with the rapid change and updating of innovative technologies, it is a necessity for employees who manage digital devices to keep up with this situation.

Finally, it is seen that sales offices are used to meet personal needs in accommodation businesses. These stores can offer services such as markets, souvenirs and hairdressers to their customers. They use especially relaxing music and wi-fi facilities and their technological infrastructure to ensure customer satisfaction.

A study of stimuli influencing behavioral intentions to use mobile entertainment in the FULL framework in Malaysia revealed that perceived usefulness and perceived ease of use had a positive effect on perceived enjoyment. In other words, it is understood that entertainment-based technological tools support the model in TAM (Leong et al., 2013). Similarly, it is seen that third age groups point to perceived usefulness as the reason for using and accepting entertaining technology. It is stated that perceived ease of use is perceived as a prerequisite for entertaining and interactive digital communication (Dogruel et al., 2015). Relationships with the concept of TAM were examined in a study on a business providing spa services.

While it has been determined that spa services technologies have a positive and significant effect on perceived usefulness and perceived ease of use, it is understood that personalized digital options increase service quality (Devi & Suartana, 2014). Technology is always a big help for businesses looking to sell and all digital tools that can grab the attention of builders are often used. In this context, a study examining the effects of sales employees' beliefs and attitudes on technology use, it is tried to explain the relations with the TAM model. It provides evidence that support services and personal innovation influence perceived ease of use of technology by field salespeople, while TAM has been found to play an important role in the sales force context. This scope is increasing day by day through e-sales and mobile applications, and the competitive aspect of accommodation businesses comes to the fore (Huang et al., 2021).

Figure 3. TAM and Hospitality Businesses Relationship (By Author)

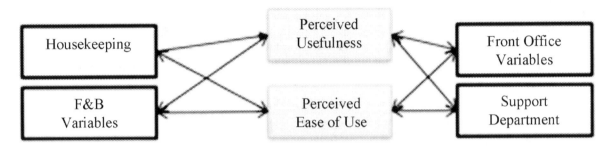

TAM in Terms of Travel Businesses

Developments in the field of transportation have directly affected people's intention to travel and have created an important source of motivation. With the decrease in costs and transportation time, travel movements have reached a different dimension and made it possible for tourism activities where people from all walks of life can meet. People who can make intercontinental travels, especially thanks to the airplane and high-speed train transportation, are more interested in innovations brought by technology. People who get the chance to watch movies, have wi-fi facilities and use their transactions through digital mobile applications while traveling are closely related to technology.

In this context, it is important to determine the perceptions of acceptance and usefulness by evaluating travel businesses within the framework of TAM. Travel businesses generally provide services in four areas: airlines, railways, seaways, and highways. Today, airlines, which provide the fastest and safest means of transportation, are growing day by day and becoming a mode of transportation preferred by more and more people. Businesses that offer airline services can offer high-tech infrastructure as a business need and carry out almost all their transactions in digital environments.

For example, in the process of purchasing flight tickets, seat selection, extra baggage allowance, food selection and special preferences (large packages, specially packaged products, instruments, pets, etc.), the preference of web environments show the tendency toward technology. On the other hand, the comparison of service quality and prices is also carried out in these digital environments and information about the subject is obtained. In particular, airline companies that want to provide luxury services such as first-class equip their aircraft with technological opportunities and various entertainment-themed activities are put forward.

With the use of technology-based virtual reality (VR) in tourism, interest in this subject has started to increase. In a study on the attitudes and experiences of airline customers of 360-degree VR videos, it was concluded that the TAM model was rated positively against the participants' VR experience dimensions. It is said that using VR contributes to perceived usefulness and acceptance, as well as contributing to target marketing and promotion (Gibson & O'Rawe, 2018). In another study on travel businesses, tourist behavior is analyzed in the FULL coverage of Web 2.0-based and Travel 2.0 websites. Concretely, there is an attempt to explain by generalizing the behavioral information about TAM's intentions to use the relevant sites. It reveals that TAM has an impact on individuals using blogs, social networks, and virtual communities and that it develops a mutually beneficial relationship (Muñoz-Leiva et al., 2012).

It is stated that users who prefer high-tech high-speed trains have technological awareness and, in this context, they behave following the technology acceptability model (Givoni, 2006). In addition, it is thought that these vehicles, which provide comfort and time savings, will appeal to the perceived ease of use and usefulness by attracting the attention of technology-related individuals in the future. Within the framework of the full model, there is no scientific study about tourism activities carried out by the sea. However, while it is stated that technology has a significant leverage effect in cruise tourism, it is said that technology plays an active role in defining and communicating tourist experiences.

In this respect, it is understood that the technological effects, indirectly, not directly, affect the crisis tourism and positively reflect on the perceived usefulness and technology acceptance (Tiago et al., 2018). As a result of the improvements made in the field of highways, wide highways, ring roads and web-based toll payment systems have been used frequently. This situation has led to an increase in road trips, as well as paving the way for a comfortable journey.

In addition, transportation has gained a different dimension with the equipping of road vehicles with the latest technological possibilities. Traveling has become a pleasant experience as vehicles, especially electric vehicles, have autonomous driving, lane tracking system, navigation, sensory equipment, and other services. At this point, manufacturers trying to use all the possibilities offered by technology are aware of the perception and acceptance level of technology (Ward et al., 2017). A study that determined how people use digital tools with the help of an extended technology acceptance model revealed that perceived ease of use (PEOU) and perceived usefulness level had a positive effect on behavioral intention.

It supports perceived usefulness by offering many technological possibilities such as unified payment interface-based transactions with digital tools, toll collection on highways, car identification and quick balance arrangements (Sarmah et al., 2021). Considering the general approaches, the idea that all vehicles used in travel services will provide a better touristic experience with technological equipment is getting stronger.

Figure 4. TAM and Transportation (Travel Businesses) (By Author)

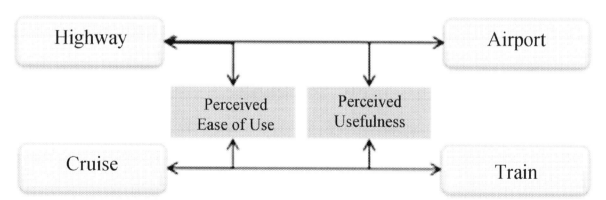

TAM in Terms of Gastronomy and other Tourism Businesses

People who want to transform their nutritional needs into a delicious experience during their touristic travels are interested in local products and innovative gastronomic trends. To this end, gastronomy businesses also update their service elements depending on demand and use intense technological elements (Baltescu, 2016). In particular, businesses that have started to use smart robots to improve the standard recipes and to have a certain quality in the service outputs see technology as a strategic target in every area from the service area to the kitchen (Rodgers, 2007). In addition, in terms of hygiene and sanitation, digital tools such as cleaning robots, contactless cooking devices and smart beverage machines are shown as examples of technological developments in the field of gastronomy (Nayik et al., 2015).

On the other hand, it is stated that it is more willing to purchase services from technological tools so that consumers feel more comfortable, do not experience emotional problems and do not stress in terms of time. The frequent use of technological equipment, which is constantly needed in gastronomy activities, also explains its relationship with technology in terms of process management. In this respect, the importance of perceived usefulness and convenience in gastronomy services emerges.

Molecular gastronomy, one of the gastronomy types, is a culinary approach that requires technology knowledge applications. In this respect, molecular gastronomy, which requires a technological infrastructure, is closely followed by technology-savvy people. In a study on the explanation of perceptions and behavioral intentions about molecular gastronomy within the framework of the technology acceptance model, it is stated that perceived usefulness is more important than perceived ease of use in terms of molecular gastronomy. It is seen that a positive perspective toward molecular cuisine is revealed between the perception of ease of use and behavioral intention (Chi, 2011).

Apart from accommodation, travel and gastronomy services, many tourism businesses such as recreational activities and tourist guiding also maintain their existence in close relation to technology. The microphones and digital wireless headphones used by the guides during the tour make the experience even better. On the other hand, it facilitates travel with technological tools with its smart mobile applications and destination information with QR codes.

It is stated that the technology used in the travel experience supports the perceived usefulness (PU) and perceived ease of use (PEU) in the research, which investigates the applicability of touristic travels within the framework of TAM. In addition, it is revealed that there is a noticeable increase in the service perception quality of travelers with technological tools (Singh & Srivastava, 2019). The necessity of technological infrastructure is needed in recreational activities such as event management, congress organizations and animation activities. There is a high level of sensitivity to technology, especially in terms of stage shows, light shows, and simultaneous translation processes.

In this context, it is necessary not to be deprived of technology for the realization of recreational activities and a better perception of the service provided. In a study examining recreation and leisure information sharing within the scope of the technology acceptance model, it was found that self-efficacy and subjective norm variables significantly and positively affect perceived ease of use and attitude towards perceived usefulness. In addition, considering that subjective norms and attitude values significantly affect behavioral intention to share information, the importance of technological perception is emphasized in sharing recreation and leisure information (Huang et al., 2015).

Looking at the two basic elements of the technology acceptance model, it is seen that it is related to all services in the tourism sector. There is mutual benefit in terms of both the perception of quality of touristic services and the benefit of consumers. In this context, the bidirectional relationship between tourism enterprises and the technology acceptance model is shown in Figure 5.

Figure 5. Relationship between TAM and tourism businesses (By Author)

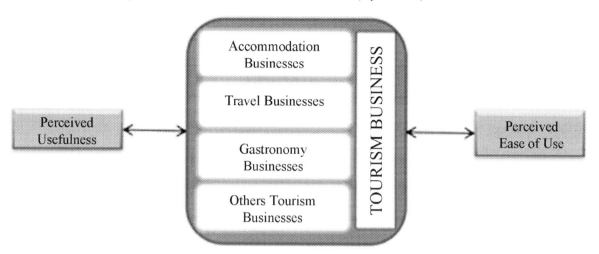

CONCLUSION

It is a well-known fact that all businesses in the tourism industry need to constantly improve their service quality and infrastructure opportunities, as they are in an intensely competitive environment (Buhalis, 1998). In particular, with the change in consumer demands and the increasing sensitivity to technology, the tendency towards innovative approaches of all tourism services continues to increase. At this point, it has been concluded that there are interconnected relations in this research, in which the perceptions of the acceptability and usefulness of technology are evaluated in terms of tourism businesses.

In addition, it is observed that tourism organizations that cannot integrate technological approaches into their business at a sufficient level are at a disadvantage in the competitive environment. Although the COVID-19 epidemic, which emerged in 2020, has hurt the development of tourism movements, it supports the TAM model in terms of the use of contactless payment and remote digital ordering methods (Gretzel et al., 2020). In this respect, it is possible to say that crisis periods can create positive and negative opportunities for the relationship between tourism and technology.

Thanks to the increasing use of digital media, virtually supported tourism festivals (Hossain et al., 2022), eco-friendly ecotourism activities (Guan, 2022) and smart tourism mobile applications to improve the quality of the destination experience (Um & Chung, 2021) are frequently tourism movements is used. In this context, considering the recent studies on the relationship between tourism and technology, it is seen that these two relationships are getting stronger.

A CASE STUDY: THE MARSHMALLOW HOTEL

The Marshmallow Hotel was established in 1927 in a small town to provide accommodation services with its authentic architecture. Until the 21st century, it welcomed visitors to its destination in a nice way and provided interesting experiences. However, he cared too much about traditional lifestyle and service elements and had prejudices against innovative developments. Although this situation was not a problem in the first years, it was reflected in the hotel in the form of negative feedback with the development of technology and the change in demands. The hotel management, who did not want to use smart kitchen tools, stayed away from the loss of time in service times and mass production opportunities.

For this reason, he could not serve his customers within the required time. In addition, due to the lack of technological tools in the rooms, the quality of service in the areas of cleanliness and comfort began to decrease gradually. Marshmallow Hotel, which lost customers rapidly after all these events, started to investigate why it was left behind by other competitors. Developing its service tools with technological tools as a result of research, the hotel also informed its staff in this direction and became one of the pioneers of the approach that integrates technology and authenticity by offering innovative services. The hotel, which managed to return to its old successful days, realized that technology and innovations are not things to worry about, and beyond that when done correctly, they will make the business more successful. In line with this case study, it is understood that technology is not an element of choice, and it is seen that it should be accepted as a necessity at the point of meeting the needs of the age.

REFERENCES

Baltescu, C. A. (2016). Culinary experiences as a key tourism attraction. Case Study: Brasov County. *Bulletin of the Transilvania University of Brasov. Economic Sciences. Series V*, *9*(2), 107.

Buhalis, D. (1998). Strategic use of information technologies in the tourism industry. *Tourism Management*, *19*(5), 409–421. doi:10.1016/S0261-5177(98)00038-7

Chau, P. Y. (1996). An empirical assessment of a modified technology acceptance model. *Journal of Management Information Systems*, *13*(2), 185–204. doi:10.1080/07421222.1996.11518128

Cheong, Y. S., Seah, C. S., Loh, Y. X., & Loh, L. H. (2021, September). Artificial Intelligence (Ai) In The Food And Beverage Industry: Improves The Customer Experience. In *2021 2nd International Conference on Artificial Intelligence and Data Sciences (AiDAS)* (pp. 1-6). IEEE.

Chi, H-K. (2011). The application of the technology acceptance model and theory of reasoned action on the molecular gastronomy message. *Journal of Global Business Management*.

Dasgupta, S., Granger, M., & McGarry, N. (2002). User acceptance of e-collaboration technology: An extension of the technology acceptance model. *Group Decision and Negotiation*, *11*(2), 87–100. doi:10.1023/A:1015221710638

Davis, F. D. (1989). Perceived usefulness, perceived ease of use, and user acceptance of information technology. *Management Information Systems Quarterly*, *13*(3), 319–340. doi:10.2307/249008

Devi, N. L. N. S., & Suartana, I. W. (2014). Analisis technology acceptance model (TAM) terhadap penggunaan sistem informasi di Nusa Dua Beach Hotel & SPA. *E-Journal Akuntansi*, *6*(1), 167–184.

Dogruel, L., Joeckel, S., & Bowman, N. D. (2015). The use and acceptance of new media entertainment technology by elderly users: Development of an expanded technology acceptance model. *Behaviour & Information Technology*, *34*(11), 1052–1063. doi:10.1080/0144929X.2015.1077890

Gibson, A., & O'Rawe, M. (2018). Virtual reality as a travel promotional tool: Insights from a consumer travel fair. In *Augmented reality and virtual reality* (pp. 93–107). Springer. doi:10.1007/978-3-319-64027-3_7

Givoni, M. (2006). Development and impact of the modern high-speed train: A review. *Transport Reviews*, *26*(5), 593–611. doi:10.1080/01441640600589319

Go, H., Kang, M., & Suh, S. C. (2020). Machine learning of robots in tourism and hospitality: Interactive technology acceptance model (iTAM)–cutting edge. *Tourism Review*, *75*(4), 625–636. Advance online publication. doi:10.1108/TR-02-2019-0062

Gretzel, U., Fuchs, M., Baggio, R., Hoepken, W., Law, R., Neidhardt, J., Pesonen, J., Zanker, M., & Xiang, Z. (2020). e-Tourism beyond COVID-19: A call for transformative research. *Information Technology & Tourism*, *22*(2), 187–203. doi:10.100740558-020-00181-3

Gretzel, U., Sigala, M., Xiang, Z., & Koo, C. (2015). Smart tourism: Foundations and developments. *Electronic Markets*, *25*(3), 179–188. doi:10.100712525-015-0196-8

Gu, D., Khan, S., Khan, I. U., & Khan, S. U. (2019). *Understanding mobile tourism shopping in Pakistan: An integrating framework of innovation diffusion theory and technology acceptance model*. Mobile Information Systems. doi:10.1155/2019/1490617

Guan, C., Rani, T., Yueqiang, Z., Ajaz, T., & Haseki, M. I. (2022). Impact of tourism industry, globalization, and technology innovation on ecological footprints in G-10 countries. *Economic Research-Ekonomska Istraživanja*, 1-17.

Hamid, R., Ong, M. H. A., Razak, I. R. A., Ismail, T. A. T., Ramli, N., & Nawawi, Z. M. W. N. W. (2020). User acceptance of smart housekeeping: A study of TAM model prototype in hotel industry. *International Journal of Supply Chain Management*, *9*(3), 308–314.

Hasanien, A., Essawy, M., & Moussa, M. (2014). The Impact of Web-based Training Characteristics on Transfer of Training: An Application on Hotel Front Office Department. *Egyptian Journal of Tourism Studies*, *13*(2).

Hossain, S. F. A., Ahsan, F. T., Nadi, A. H., Ahmed, M., & Neyamah, H. (2022). Exploring the Role of Technology Application in Tourism Events, Festivals and Fairs in the United Arab Emirates: Strategies in the Post Pandemic Period. In *Technology Application in Tourism Fairs, Festivals and Events in Asia* (pp. 313–330). Springer. doi:10.1007/978-981-16-8070-0_19

Huang, H. C., Chang, S. S., & Lou, S. J. (2015). Preliminary investigation on recreation and leisure knowledge sharing by LINE. *Procedia: Social and Behavioral Sciences*, *174*, 3072–3080. doi:10.1016/j.sbspro.2015.01.1100

Huang, X., Sun, S., & Law, R. (2021). A Reflection of Core Marketing Subjects in E-Hospitality Programmes: The IPO Model. *Journal of Quality Assurance in Hospitality & Tourism*, *22*(3), 336–344. doi:10.1080/1528008X.2020.1774033

Jacob, M., Tintoré, J., Aguiló, E., Bravo, A., & Mulet, J. (2003). Innovation in the tourism sector: Results from a pilot study in the Balearic Islands. *Tourism Economics*, *9*(3), 279–295. doi:10.1177/135481660300900303

Jan, A. U., & Contreras, V. (2011). Technology acceptance model for the use of information technology in universities. *Computers in Human Behavior, 27*(2), 845–851. doi:10.1016/j.chb.2010.11.009

Jeong, E. S., Choi, S. R., & Son, M. Y. (2021). A Study on Intention to Use of Smart Tourism Contents through Extended Technology Acceptance Model: Case of Visitors to the National Museum of Korea. *Journal of Digital Convergence, 19*(9), 115–123. doi:10.14400/JDC.2021.19.9.115

Ketikidis, P., Dimitrovski, T., Lazuras, L., & Bath, P. A. (2012). Acceptance of health information technology in health professionals: An application of the revised technology acceptance model. *Health Informatics Journal, 18*(2), 124–134. doi:10.1177/1460458211435425 PMID:22733680

Kim, T. G., Lee, J. H., & Law, R. (2008). An empirical examination of the acceptance behaviour of hotel front office systems: An extended technology acceptance model. *Tourism Management, 29*(3), 500–513. doi:10.1016/j.tourman.2007.05.016

King, W. R., & He, J. (2006). A meta-analysis of the technology acceptance model. *Information & Management, 43*(6), 740–755. doi:10.1016/j.im.2006.05.003

Lee, W. H., Lin, C. W., & Shih, K. H. (2018). A technology acceptance model for the perception of restaurant service robots for trust, interactivity, and output quality. *International Journal of Mobile Communications, 16*(4), 361–376. doi:10.1504/IJMC.2018.092666

Legris, P., Ingham, J., & Collerette, P. (2003). Why do people use information technology? A critical review of the technology acceptance model. *Information & Management, 40*(3), 191–204. doi:10.1016/S0378-7206(01)00143-4

Leong, L. Y., Ooi, K. B., Chong, A. Y. L., & Lin, B. (2013). Modeling the stimulators of the behavioral intention to use mobile entertainment: Does gender really matter? *Computers in Human Behavior, 29*(5), 2109–2121. doi:10.1016/j.chb.2013.04.004

Lu, J., Yu, C., Liu, C., & Yao, J. E. (2003). Technology acceptance model for wireless Internet. *Internet Research, 13*(3), 206–222. doi:10.1108/10662240310478222

Marangunic, N., & Granic, A. (2015). Technology acceptance model: A literature review from 1986 to 2013. *Universal Access in the Information Society, 14*(1), 81–95. doi:10.100710209-014-0348-1

Matikiti, R., Mpinganjira, M., & Roberts-Lombard, M. (2018). Application of the Technology Acceptance Model and the Technology–Organization–Environment Model to examine social media marketing use in the South African tourism industry. *South African Journal of Information Management, 20*(1), 1–12. doi:10.4102ajim.v20i1.790

McCloskey, D. (2004). Evaluating electronic commerce acceptance with the technology acceptance model. *Journal of Computer Information Systems, 44*(2), 49–57. doi:10.1080/08874417.2004.11647566

Morosan, C., & Jeong, M. (2008). Users' perceptions of two types of hotel reservation Web sites. *International Journal of Hospitality Management, 27*(2), 284–292. doi:10.1016/j.ijhm.2007.07.023

Muñoz-Leiva, F., Hernández-Méndez, J., & Sánchez-Fernández, J. (2012). Generalising user behaviour in online travel sites through the Travel 2.0 website acceptance model. *Online Information Review, 36*(6), 879–902. Advance online publication. doi:10.1108/14684521211287945

Nayik, G. A., Muzaffar, K., & Gull, A. (2015). Robotics and food technology: A mini review. *Journal of Nutrition & Food Sciences*, *5*(4), 1–11. doi:10.4172/2155-9600.1000384

Nguyen, X. T., Nguyen, T. H., Dang, H. P., Pham, T. L. P., Bui, T. T., Tran, N. M., ... Nguyen, N. P. (2022). E-commerce Adoption in Distribution: An Empirical Study on Household Businesses in Food and Beverage Industry. *Journal of Distribution Science*, *20*(2), 65–77. doi:10.15722/jds.20.02.202202.65

Phatthana, W., & Mat, N. K. N. (2011). The Application of Technology Acceptance Model (TAM) on health tourism e-purchase intention predictors in Thailand. In *2010 International conference on business and economics research* (Vol. 1, pp. 196-199). Academic Press.

Ramos, Y., & Castro, A. O. (2017). Point-Of-Sales Systems in Food and Beverage Industry: Efficient Technology and Its User Acceptance. *Journal of Information Sciences and Computing Technologies*, *6*(1), 582–591.

Rodgers, S. (2007). Innovation in food service technology and its strategic role. *International Journal of Hospitality Management*, *26*(4), 899–912. doi:10.1016/j.ijhm.2006.10.001

Sadiq, M., & Adil, M. (2021). Ecotourism related search for information over the internet: A technology acceptance model perspective. *Journal of Ecotourism*, *20*(1), 70–88. doi:10.1080/14724049.2020.1785480

Sahli, A. B., & Legohérel, P. (2016). The tourism web acceptance model: A study of intention to book tourism products online. *Journal of Vacation Marketing*, *22*(2), 179–194. doi:10.1177/1356766715607589

Sarmah, R., Dhiman, N., & Kanojia, H. (2021). Understanding intentions and actual use of mobile wallets by millennial: An extended TAM model perspective. *Journal of Indian Business Research*, *13*(3), 361–381. Advance online publication. doi:10.1108/JIBR-06-2020-0214

Setiawan, P., & Widanta, A. (2021). The effect of trust on travel agent online use: Application of the technology acceptance model. *International Journal of Data and Network Science*, *5*(3), 173–182. doi:10.5267/j.ijdns.2021.6.015

Singh, S., & Srivastava, P. (2019). Social media for outbound leisure travel: a framework based on technology acceptance model (TAM). *Journal of Tourism Futures*. doi:10.1108/JTF-10-2018-0058

Stamam, M. S. M., Nenin, M., Hashim, R., & Radzi, S. M. (2012). Food and beverage technology and employees' acceptance in 4 and 5 star hotels in Kuala Lumpur, Malaysia. *Current Issues In Hospitality And Tourism Research And Innovations*, 237.

Surendran, P. (2012). Technology acceptance model: A survey of literature. *International Journal of Business and Social Research*, *2*(4), 175–178. doi:10.18533/ijbsr.v2i4.161

Tiago, F., Couto, J., Faria, S., & Borges-Tiago, T. (2018). Cruise tourism: Social media content and network structures. *Tourism Review*, *73*(4), 433–447. Advance online publication. doi:10.1108/TR-10-2017-0155

Um, T., & Chung, N. (2021). Does smart tourism technology matter? Lessons from three smart tourism cities in South Korea. *Asia Pacific Journal of Tourism Research*, *26*(4), 396–414. doi:10.1080/1094166 5.2019.1595691

Venkatesh, V., & Davis, F. D. (2000). A theoretical extension of the technology acceptance model: Four longitudinal field studies. *Management Science*, *46*(2), 186–204. doi:10.1287/mnsc.46.2.186.11926

Ward, C., Raue, M., Lee, C., D'Ambrosio, L., & Coughlin, J. F. (2017, July). Acceptance of automated driving across generations: The role of risk and benefit perception, knowledge, and trust. In *International Conference on Human-Computer Interaction* (pp. 254-266). Cham, Switzerland: Springer. 10.1007/978-3-319-58071-5_20

Chapter 25
Sustainable Tourism and an Analysis of Opportunities for and Challenges to Researchers and Professionals

Fatima L. Carvalho
https://orcid.org/0000-0002-1189-8843
Cinturs, University of Algarve, Portugal

Silvia C. Fernandes
https://orcid.org/0000-0002-1699-5415
Faculty of Economics, Cinturs, University of Algarve, Portugal

ABSTRACT

This work analyzes academic work from 2004 to 2020 with an influence on the blueprint for sustainable tourism innovation strategies. Criteria used include verifying which are the main concerns, the contribution of sustainability indices, and implications to practitioners and high educational institutions in the area. This is increasingly important due to present and future challenges undermining the existence of a sustainable tourism industry. Accurate metrics can empower destinations, and higher education and its inner research must have a key role in the development of effective instruments. The challenge comprises selecting and monitoring them for sustainable tourism policy. Educational and research institutes with tourism studies should include in their syllabuses real cases and tools for developing key sustainability models and metrics to integrate and respond more promptly to critical challenges and trends.

DOI: 10.4018/978-1-6684-4645-4.ch025

INTRODUCTION

Sustainable tourism is defined as the creation and promotion of a tourism industry that preserves or enhances a country's social, cultural, or environmental capital. Data reveals that the environmental strength of a country is directly related to tourism revenue. Although there is no evidence of direct causality, the more pristine the natural environment of a local the more tourists are willing to access it. Consequently, as the natural capital deteriorates, destinations lose revenue. It is important to recognize that processes and activities associated with tourism also damage the environment.

Given the close relationship between natural resources and a very large segment of the tourism industry, a lack of progress on fostering sustainability will reduce tourism development opportunities. Besides environment, also cultural and socio-economic issues become involved in this equation of tourism sustainability (Simão & Partidário, 2012). Many works and reports discuss this subject, revealing its increasing importance for today's global and local decisions about tourism development. This chapter aims to establish what proportion of academic works, listed in the scientific repository of open access in Portugal (RCAAP), have proposed innovative governance strategies for sustainable tourism. And among these, which portion has used approaches grounded on international/national sustainability indices.

Thus, the main objective is to investigate in what ways academic research (e.g., doctoral theses, papers, reports) has reacted to the projections on the growing pressure that tourism is placing on the environment and society today. The related research questions are the following:

1) Is the application of sustainability indices an important concern of academic works?
2) Do they give practical recommendations from their appliance?

The academic production object of study was produced in Portuguese and Brazilian higher education institutions. The first period considered was 2004-2017, due to a first project for the University of Algarve in Portugal. Then, especially due to the current pandemic impact on tourism, an increased number of works was considered in the period 2018-2020.

To accomplish this aim, next sections are structured as follows: section 2 approaches the trends in sustainable tourism research; section 3 presents the research framework used in the present study; and section 4 develops a content analysis on the collected documents using *Nvivo* software. Section 5 discusses the results obtained and section 6 further use. Finally, the last section concludes the study referring implications for tourism planners and education/research in the area.

The Portuguese Context

Portuguese higher education is organized in a *binary* system, integrating university education and polytechnic education. In the years 2015/16, the number of master and PhD students increased slightly. Regarding graduation in the tourism area, master's degrees accounted for 21.3% of their total number, while doctoral programs represented 3.2%. The areas of engineering, business, law, and health exhibited the uppermost expression.

The Bologna process then inspired considerable curricular changes in tourism degrees in a way that this area was fully integrated in the European space for higher education to enhance its employability/mobility. During the first period under review (2004-2017), a total of 80 PhD dissertations were concluded in Portugal. The themes focused on tourism management and planning; heritage, and development; and cultural tourism.

The University of Aveiro had the largest number of doctoral theses in tourism, followed by the Faculty of Economics at Algarve's University. This last was followed by the Institute of Geography at Lisbon's University. The themes developed at the University of Aveiro were more related with rural tourism, destination competitiveness, tourist behaviour, and investment factors. And those developed at the Faculty of Economics at Algarve's University were mainly related to destination's image, welfare, and economic evaluation. Finally, those developed at the Institute of Geography were mostly related to tourism management and cultural tourism.

The Brazilian Context

Brazilian education experimented great changes in the first decade of 21st century. Educational policies in Brazil provided conditions for new initiatives to emerge and allow a considerable diversity of educational projects in higher education (Mota & Almeida, 2016), to meet the diversified demand of different regions in the country. It was necessary to create federal institutes, linked to the education system, to promote a rapid expansion of higher education offer. This became more relevant in tourism studies since the National Tourism Plan was established and the policies of qualification in tourism have intensified (Mota & Anjos, 2012).

The OASISBr Portal

This Brazilian portal of open access publications is a multi-disciplinary search engine, allowing free access to the scientific production of authors linked to Brazilian universities and research institutes. In the first timespan (2004-2017), a total of 24 works directly approach the theme of sustainability in tourism among which eight consider sustainability indices (see Table 1).

There is a growing trend in addressing these metrics. The other works focused on other areas such as: environmental concerns, local communities, rural tourism, creative cities, and behaviors. Santos (2013) argues that tourism sustainability indicator systems are important tools, because they can provide essential information that contributes to understand the activity and drive better the efforts. Thus, the author used the system of indicators SISDTur as one of the most complete methodologies.

The applicability of indices should include four important steps: map and identify the network of social actors involved with the activity (to study their relations); improve the system of indicators according to the specificities involved; define a set of analytical criteria for the metrics of each system's dimension and propose actions for developing an activity aligned with sustainability principles.

Cordeiro (2008) also studied sustainability indicators and compared six approaches: UNWTO's system of indicators; the system of tourism indicators of Macaronesia; the Eurostat for sustainable tourism Core Set Indicator (CSI); the National Geographic's Destination Scorecard; the barometer of tourism sustainability; and the Tourism Ecological footprint. The author found that, among these methodologies, the most apt include the Ecological footprint, Destination Scorecard, and Sustainability barometer.

Table 1. *List of publications with references to sustainability indices. Source: Own elaboration*

	Reference
1	IBGE Brazilian Institute of Geography and Statistics. Sustainable development indicators: Brazil (2015) Coordination of Natural Resources and Environmental Studies [and] Coordination of Geography. – Rio de Janeiro: IBGE, 2015. 352p. ISSN 1517-1450, 10
2	Brandão, C.N. (2012) Indigenous tourism as a factor for local and sustainable development: A multi-case study in indigenous communities in Roraima. (Brazil) (Master Dissertation). Fundação Getulio Vargas School of Business Administration in São Paulo, Brazil
3	Oliveira_Huascar (2009) Evaluation of the indicators of the tourist potential of the municipality of Itapipoca (Ceará): Subsidies for the sustainable development of tourism (Master Dissertation). Federal University of Ceará, Regional Postgraduate Program in Development and Environment, Brazil
4	Andrade, Beatriz Bittencourt (2006) Tourism and sustainability in the city of Florianópolis: An application of the Ecological Footprint method. Florianópolis, (Master Dissertation). Federal University of Santa Catarina, Postgraduate Program in Administration, Santa Catarina, Brazil
5	Silva_Francisca de Paula (2005) Sustainable higher education: an analysis of tourism courses. PhD thesis. Federal University of Bahia, Faculty of Education, Brazil
6	Amazonas_Iuri (2014) Environmental management in hotels: Technologies and sustainable practices applied in hotels in João Pessoa-PB (Master Dissertation). Federal University of Paraíba. Regional Postgraduate Program in Development and Environment, Paraíba, Brazil
7	Silva, Michel Robinson (2014) Environmental perception and sustainable tourism: Analysis of the impacts of tourism in coastal areas of the greater João Pessoa (Master Dissertation). Federal University of Paraíba. Center for Natural and Exact Sciences Regional graduate program in development and the environment, Paraiba, Brazil
8	Freitas, N.R.; Souza, P.A.R.; Zambra, E.M.; Romeiro, M.C.; Pereira, R.S. (2014) Management and sustainability in tourism activity: An analysis of discussions in the last decade in Brazil. Brazilian Journal of Ecotourism, São Paulo, 7(2), 394-411

TRENDS IN SUSTAINABLE TOURISM RESEARCH

The present study inspected the academic production of Portuguese and Brazilian higher education, using the keywords: sustainable tourism, sustainability index, and governance. Regarding the work developed in Portuguese institutions, one could observe a growing trend to address sustainability and governance (mainly in more recent works, from 2015 to 2017). And this production relates these areas especially to stakeholders and environment.

In previous years, it was more related to growth, local development, and economic evaluation (Stilwell, 2011). This author debated on indicators applied to the development of Portuguese tourism. Although indicator systems are uncertain and imperfect models of the reality, this author's work adapted a system to the Portuguese reality, which proposed the GIST (Group of Tourism Sustainability Indicators) to assess the state of Portuguese tourism. It is based on the three pillars of sustainability (social, environmental, and economic) and on the strategic lines for development, as outlined by Portuguese Strategic Plan for Tourism (PENT, 2015).

Further academic works aimed to identify tourism impact in various dimensions of sustainable development. Carvalho (2012) approached sustainable tourism and ecotourism in the Portuguese reality analysing the importance of ecotourism certification as a tool to determine standards of quality via indices/criteria. This work used a set of indicators to evaluate Zmar - Eco Camping Resort.

It proposed an ecotourism certification program founded on the selection and analysis of indices based on international references such as: the Mohonk Agreement (2000), the STSC Final Report (2003), the Québec Declaration (2002), the European Ecotourism Labelling Standard (Eco-Destinet, 2009), and the Global Sustainable Tourism Criteria (GSTC, 2009).

The criteria for a system of certification for sustainable tourism resulted in four main categories:

(A) Structural criteria: (a.1) the certification target and which sectors it touches; (a.2) the certification label; (a.3) levels of classification; (a.4) methodologies applied; (a.5) auditing; (a.6) planning and environmental management and evaluation mechanisms; (a.7) legal conformity; (a.8) staff training; (a.9) client satisfaction; (a.10) rigorous marketing; (a.11) design and the construction of buildings and infrastructures; (a.12) interpretation and the offer of educational materials;

(B) Socio-economic criteria: (b.1) community development; (b.2) local employment; (b.3) acquisition of local services and goods; (b.4) support for small and local entrepreneurs as well as the strengthening of competences in the local community; (b.5) local communities and their involvement in the elaboration and application of codes of conduct; (b.6) human rights; (b.7) equal contracts for men and women; (b.8) legal protection of national and international employees; (b.9) guarantee of basic services such as water, energy and sanitation;

(C) Cultural patrimony criteria: (c.1) code of conduct during local visits, provision of information on local culture and community; (c.2) negotiation of exhibition of historical or archaeological artefacts; (c.3) protection of places and preservation of properties with cultural relevance as well as access to residents; (c.4) incorporation of culture using local art elements in architecture and other forms of cultural patrimony;

(D) Environmental criteria: (d.1) conservation of resources in acquisition policies; (d.2) attention to consumer goods with a reduction of disposable materials and a programme to minimize packaging.

Considering the context of higher education in the two countries, and the trends in sustainable tourism research, next section introduces the research framework with focus on the research questions proposed to discern lessons and implications.

RESEARCH FRAMEWORK

As previously referred, the research questions are: 1) is the application of sustainability indices an important concern of academic works?; ad 2) do they give practical recommendations from their appliance? Then, related key aspects include the following: what contents stand out; what differences exist between the academic production in Portugal and Brazil; and how topics such as sustainability, environment, governance, planning, and regulation relate to sustainable tourism.

The main database used in this work is RCAAP (Portuguese scientific Open Access Repository). Documents as theses, reports and academic chapters were collected. The aim is to identify what kind of innovative strategies for sustainable tourism have been discussed within the research developed in higher education institutions. These works can be authored by Portuguese or Brazilian students. Another source used was the Brazilian portal of scientific publications (OASISBr), a multi-disciplinary search engine that allows free access to the scientific production from Brazilian universities and research institutes.

A first sample (from 2004-2017) has 70 'stable'[1] works, which include master dissertations, PhD dissertations, scientific papers, and reports. The method used to analyze these multiple documents was a content analysis, assisted by *Nvivo*, a software designed for qualitative analysis. First, Figure 1 illustrates the underlying areas that emerged from the content analysis developed (*nodes*).

These nodes, or six thematic areas (tourism, governance, planning, sustainability, regulation, environment), that emerged from a first qualitative approach to the sample collected, are now used as keyworks for queries and comparison with the next time span. There is here a central node called *sustainability indexes*. These are central tools for policy makers, governments, and non-governmental organizations to discern and monitor new and effective policies for sustainable tourism.

Figure 1. Guiding framework for the qualitative analysis

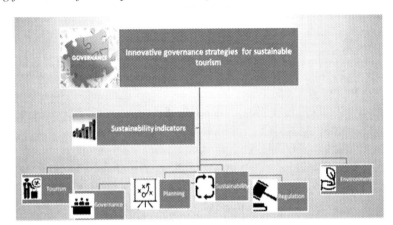

DETAILED CONTENT ANALYSIS

This work's objectives can benefit from a qualitative approach. A qualitative research intends to evaluate or explain social, cultural, and economic phenomena. Related works have analyzed data from interviews, surveys, web pages, audio-visual material, theses, and journal chapters. The *Nvivo* tool for qualitative analysis can help to explore and find patterns in these data. It was used to organize the documents of the first timespan on sustainable tourism. Having in mind the research questions proposed, queries were applied to answer them. Thus, next section presents the results obtained through queries that involved the cases (documents) and the nodes (themes).

Results from Coding Cases

Coding is one of the several techniques tailored to make sense from data. The way coding is handled depends on the methodology and research design. In this research, the cases correspond to the types of works collected from the databases used. These types are PhD and master dissertations, journal chapters, reports, and bachelor dissertations. These works make up the sample collected in the first timespan (2004-2017). Then, the cases are gathered into nodes which are the topics/themes that emerge, which perform the guiding framework for applying the queries (see Figure 1).

Results from Coding Nodes

Coding a sample's content to topics/themes will produce the main nodes. This is fundamental in most qualitative projects as it organizes the material collected into broad areas. It tends to be a cumulative rather than a one-stage process, as a node can be submitted to more detailed coding. Once we open a node in *Nvivo*, it shows all its content which can be text, audio, video, pictures, webpage, etc. (coded in the node). It also can be linked to a memo to describe its analytical insights or its coding into other topic(s).

Exploring the content from the works collected, a first query was the *word frequency* (word cloud). This exploratory technique shows that, when entailing all data, the central term is "tourism". The word cloud obtained illustrates a closer connection of tourism to the term 'development' than to terms as 'sustainable' or 'sustainability'. In addition, there is a low relevance of the term 'indicators' (low frequency in the cloud).

This corroborates the fewer number of empirical works that explore sustainability indexes. Handling qualitative data tends to be an iterative process to explore, code, memo, code more, query, and so forth. Then, according to another output - project map (Figure 2) - that involves both cases and nodes, the topics tourism, regulation, and environment appear at the center of it.

Figure 2. Project map of the academic production collected

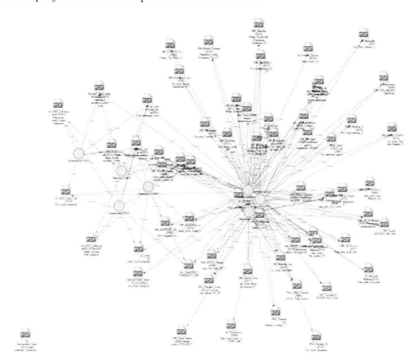

For example, among international reports, the one from World Economic Forum (2017) highlights the topic 'sustainability indices' 311 times and has the highest mentions of tourism (1741), environment (359), governance (197) and regulation (154). Analysing the journal chapters, Dias (2016) has a work related with environmental sustainability measurement, mentioning 'sustainability indicators' 22 times and 'sustainability index' 16 times. Wimmler, Hejazi, Fernandes, Moreira and Connors (2015), whose work has a multi-criteria method applied to renewable energy, also highlighted the topic 'sustainability index'. Ferreira, Silva, Seixas, Lopes, Fortes, Reis, Poseiro, Capitão, Malvarez, and Tenedório (2014) whose chapter is about resource evaluation, is the one that most highlights the topic governance.

DISCUSSION AND LESSONS

The process of coding brings us closer to the data gathered to ask questions such as: 'how do data help answer this research question?'. Coding facilitates the use of queries and visualizations, allowing look for connections among topics and enhance understanding. Queries and maps nurture the iterative nature of qualitative research and help investigate hunches as we progress in a project. They can help us focus on the questions we want to ask and prompt us to code accordingly.

They also help determine whether we need to gather additional files or re-frame the questions asked before. The techniques of querying and re-coding contribute to integrate results for better comparison and discussion. Thus, from a query based on clustering the nodes obtained, figure 3 illustrates two main trends: 1) one that reflects the use of sustainability indicators for regulation/governance matters; and 2) another where sustainability issues relate to planning.

Figure 3. Hierarchy chart of clustering nodes

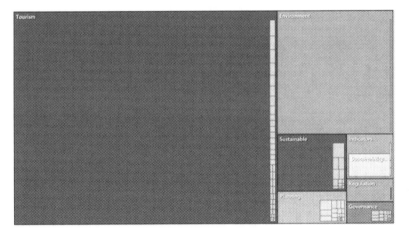

This scenario, combined with the previous outputs, suggests an increasing concern with regulation and governance, and a consequent use of sustainability indices. This reminds the need of effective and lasting policy measures. However, quantitative indexes for governance and planning continue to be weakly approached. The majority of works collected mention these issues on a more theoretical/descriptive way.

Comparing the Two Countries

Comparing the works from Portugal and Brazil, the former focus more on topics related to territorial planning, stakeholders involved, natural destinations, governance, rural tourism, and resources. The latter focus more on topics related to environmental education, local power (re)definition, participation, ecological footprint, and ethical issues. Thus, Portuguese research on sustainable tourism has given emphasis to resources/ stakeholders and Brazilian research emphasizes local power/community.

This is in line with a focus of Brazilian academy on local policies, in regions where the universities are placed. This is related with the Brazilian context that expects public power, local community, and companies join forces to define a tourism development plan. Also, the Brazilian case reveals a higher diversity of themes, due to its educational policies that have provided conditions for initiatives, such as educational projects, in higher education to meet the demands of the diverse regions of this country.

NEW CHALLENGES FOR TOURISM

The rationale of sustainable tourism approach in the timespan 2004-2017 relates more to a conceptual evolution of sustainability, seen as an abstraction that incorporates trans-disciplinarity, participation, social learning, and adaptation (Gibson & Hasan, 2005; Norton, 2005). In the subsequent time range of 2018-2020 (a period included in this research due to the pandemic impacts on tourism and resulting challenges), the literature continued to discuss high-level international documents, such as the resolution adopted by the General Assembly on the promotion of sustainable tourism for poverty eradication and environment protection.

The main difference between the two timespans considered is that in the first, the authors are under the impact of foundational documents defending sustainable development as a philosophy that should be directed as a tourism policy. In the second phase, the basic concern is on the implementation of projects and instruments for regulation and management of sustainable tourism. This trend in the most recent research reflects the inclusion of the keyword *implementation* in the related literature (Carvalho, 2021).

Figure 4. Recent research interests on tourism

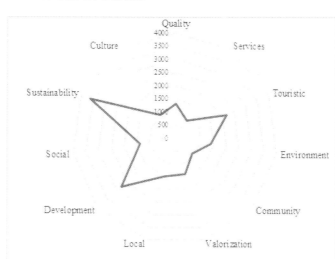

After analyzing the first dataset (2004-2017), the second one (2018-2020) is composed by documents from RCAAP and from the Web of Science (using the same criteria and keywords previously applied). We acknowledge that, perhaps due to the pandemic impacts, the literature has been focusing more on sustainability instruments and indices. Additionally, the interest on topics related with environment and community aspects is increasing (Figure 4).

In this second analytical phase, sustainable development concept was permeated by topics such as tourism experience, management, and governance (Huang, Chang, Chung, Yin, & Yen, 2019). These authors defined sustainable tourism as "market-oriented" whereas traditional tourism is "sales oriented". New research, especially in Portugal and Spain, has privileged policies and strategies for planning and developing local tourism. Connections between tourism, cultural activities, and sustainability have been explored.

This change is consistent with the United Nations Resolution (General Assembly) which recognized that "sustainable tourism, including ecotourism, represented, in many countries, an important driver of sustainable economic growth and decent job creation for all" (UN Resolution, 2018, p. 4). This new 'type' of tourism can contribute to achieve internationally agreed development goals.

Sustainability Implementation

For an in-depth analysis, a recent literature review based on Prisma Statement for systematic literature reviews, used the Web of Science core collection and other repositories. From a total of 430 records screened, 106 stable documents were selected and submitted to a content analysis again in the software *Nvivo*. This review revealed that sustainable tourism *implementation* already permeated the literature pre-2018, encompassing eight categories of interest: 1) Adaptive resource management; 2) Carbon mitigation approach; 3) Community-based conservation areas and community-based ecotourism; 4) Community-based natural resource management; 5) Multi-objective optimization model; 6) Social re-investment strategy; 7) Tourism sustainability certification, and 8) Transition management.

The broad literature on sustainable tourism also suggests that. Larson and Poudyal (2012) already approached the notion of adaptive resource management. Gössling, Ring, Dwyer, Andersson, and Hall (2016) referred the carbon mitigation approach, which targets managerial aspects through optimizing a tourism demand mix. Jamal and Stronza (2009) clarified that community-based conservation areas refer to areas owned by the community with two important characteristics: 1) ensuring long-term sustainability of tourism and natural resources, and 2) local ownership and management of tourism enterprises and activities.

Working on poverty alleviation and environmental sustainability, Mbaiwa (2011) already incorporated the notion of community-based natural resource management. Blackman and Rivera (2011) referred certification initiatives in which producers adhere to environmental and social-welfare production standards. Certification drives producers to improve their environmental, social, and economic performance. And the transition management strategy offers a theoretical framework for stakeholders involved in policy implementation processes of sustainable tourism (Gössling, Hall, Ekström, Engeset, & Aall, 2012).

Most recent research continues to emphasize sustainability implementation issues. Arbolino, Boffardi, De, and Lopollo (2021) referred the multi-objective optimization model which analyzes environmental, social, and economic impacts of tourism activities to select those that maximize stakeholder utility. The multi-criteria dimension methods allow practitioners to simultaneously address a multiplicity of issues related to tourism policymaking, facilitating an effective appraisal of the effects of tourism policies.

Kudratova, Huang, and Zhou (2018) suggest an integrated optimization approach in which sustainability cost is quantified and reinvestment strategy is adopted.

In conclusion, the present study acknowledges that implementation strategies such as the 'community-based natural resource management' and the 'tourism certification approach' covered 60% of all mentions on methods of sustainability implementation in the selected literature. Thus, they should be treated as leading drivers of sustainable tourism today. Yet more work is needed to explain how a certain destination or tourism business meet set standards over time, and across several national contexts.

CONCLUSION

In general, this work highlights that sustainable tourism development requires integrated approaches to management, supported by the right indicators. As WTO (2013) already suggested, metrics are tools that provide accurate information for decision-making, leading to better planning and solutions. They can signal important trends and contribute to discuss risks and impacts to destinations. And are mostly useful when measured repeatedly and consistently through monitoring programs. When information is available over time on a regular basis, more effective use of indicators can occur what provides context for a better understanding of changes and of their relevance as policy priorities.

Regarding the research questions, about if the application of sustainability indices is an important concern of academic works and if they give practical recommendations from their appliance, the present study showed that quantitative indexes for sustainability governance are still weakly approached. Some works approached their application to support innovative governance in tourism, but on a theoretical/descriptive way. Then, related key aspects were analyzed through a content analysis (themes that stand out; differences between the academic production in Portugal and Brazil; and how sustainability, environment, governance, planning, and regulation relate to tourism).

A guiding framework and queries were derived which highlighted that literature pre-2018 emphasized development and regulation in relation to tourism. Sustainability and environment came later in this timespan. Additionally, Portuguese research on sustainable tourism has given emphasis to resources and stakeholders, while Brazilian research emphasized local power and community. This is related with the Brazilian context that expects from public power, local community, and companies a joint definition of a tourism development plan. Brazil also reveals a higher diversity of themes, due to the demanding projects of its various regions.

Then another time range was considered, due to recent developments. Comparing both timespans, changes in the literature concerning sustainable tourism seem to reflect the conceptual evolution of sustainability, a multi-layered notion affected by current challenges. Specially in the second time-span (post-2018), conceptual development of sustainable tourism gained more pragmatism due to the need to test and compare tourism sustainability implementation models and governance across several contexts (Huang et al., 2019).

The need to introduce new tools to measure tourism sustainability can be found in international reports and projects developed worldwide (Guilarte & Quintáns, 2019). The aim of measures development and monitoring is not only for measurement purpose, but for better research and decision-making. The information generated by governments, private and public organizations, or through research, can be important for building the right sustainability indicators. Then, turning them accessible and sharable is the route to informed decision-making and involvement of all stakeholders. This can empower destinations, providing the necessary data to negotiate development standards, future investments, joint ventures, and sharing benefits.

However, academic studies often have been one-time initiatives (i.e., there is the initial study of a problem and the establishment of baseline information, but without follow-up through continuous monitoring). Then, a challenge to the academy is obtaining sufficient resources to support its ongoing role in implementing key instruments and measures, as well as their validation. Another challenge is to transform the new information generated into forms that can be easily understood and used by practitioners and policy makers. Additionally, by tourism professionals to be familiar with the indexes and their monitoring practices. Thus, education/training institutions should include, in their tourism studies curricula, real cases and methodologies for developing and testing sustainability models and metrics.

REFERENCES

Arbolino, R., Boffardi, R., De Simone, L., & Lopollo, G. (2021). Multi-objective optimization technique: A novel approach in tourism sustainability planning. *Journal of Environmental Management*, 285(1), 112016. doi:10.1016/j.jenvman.2021.112016 PMID:33561732

Blackman, A., & Rivera, J. (2011). Producer-Level Benefits of Sustainability Certification. *Conservation Biology*, 25(6), 1176–1185. doi:10.1111/j.1523-1739.2011.01774.x PMID:22070273

Carvalho, F. (2021). The status of resource management and certification in tourism sustainability implementation literature. *Journal of Spatial and Organizational Dynamics*, 9(2), 91–114.

Carvalho, N. (2012). Ecoturismo - Estudo de caso: Zmar-Eco Camping Resort. Projeto final de licenciatura, Universidade Atlântica, Portugal.

Cordeiro, I. (2008). *Instrumentos de avaliação da sustentabilidade do turismo: Uma análise crítica* [Master's Thesis]. Universidade Nova de Lisboa, Portugal.

Dias, J. (2016). Environmental sustainability measurement in the Travel & Tourism Competitiveness Index: An empirical analysis of its reliability. *Ecological Indicators*, 73, 589–596. doi:10.1016/j.ecolind.2016.10.008

Eco-Destinet. (2009). *Eco-Destinet (2007-2009)*. Retrieved on September 8, 2018, from: https://destinet.eu/who-who/civil-society-ngos/ecotrans/ecotrans-projects-activities/2006-2010/EETLS_Blueprint_Draft_Final_web.pdf

Ferreira, J., Silva, S., Seixas, L., Lopes, A., Fortes, C., Reis, M., Poseiro, P., Capitão, R., Malvarez, G., & Tenedório, J. (2014). *The resource valuation and the challenge of coastal ecosystem-based management implementation*. Retrieved on August 8, 2018, from: http://repositorio.lnec.pt:8080/handle/123456789/1007022

Final Report, S. T. S. C. (2003). *Sustainable Tourism Stewardship Council raising the standards and benefits of sustainable tourism and ecotourism certification*. Retrieved on August 16, 2018, from: http://usir.salford.ac.uk/44065/1/STSC%202002%20-final-report.pdf

Gibson, R., & Hassan, S. (2005). *Sustainability assessment: Criteria and processes*. Routledge.

Gössling, S., Hall, C. M., Ekström, F., Engeset, A., & Aall, C. (2012). Transition management: A tool for implementing sustainable tourism scenarios? *Journal of Sustainable Tourism, 20*(6), 899–916. doi:10.1080/09669582.2012.699062

Gössling, S., Ring, A., Dwyer, L., Andersson, A., & Hall, C. M. (2016). Optimizing or maximizing growth? A challenge for sustainable tourism. *Journal of Sustainable Tourism, 24*(4), 527–548. doi:10.1080/09669582.2015.1085869

GSTC - Global Sustainable Tourism Council. (2009). *GSTC mission and impacts*. Retrieved on November 9, 2018, from: https://www.gstcouncil.org/about/about-us/

Guilarte, Y., & Quintáns, D. (2019). Using big data to measure tourist sustainability: Myth or reality? *Sustainability, 11*(20), 5641. doi:10.3390u11205641

Huang, R.-Y., Chang, W.-J., Chung, Y.-C., Yin, Y.-S., & Yen, J. C. (2019). A literature review of sustainable tourism (1990-2016): Development trajectory and framework. *International Journal of Tourism & Hospitality Reviews, 6*(1), 20–49. doi:10.18510/ijthr.2019.613

Jamal, T., & Stronza, A. (2009). Collaboration theory and tourism practice in protected areas: Stakeholders, structuring and sustainability. *Journal of Sustainable Tourism, 17*(2), 169–189. doi:10.1080/09669580802495741

Kudratova, S., Huang, X., & Zhou, X. (2018). Sustainable project selection: Optimal project selection considering sustainability under reinvestment strategy. *Journal of Cleaner Production, 203,* 469–481. doi:10.1016/j.jclepro.2018.08.259

Larson, L., & Poudyal, N. (2012). Developing sustainable tourism through adaptive resource management: A case study of Machu Picchu, Peru. *Journal of Sustainable Tourism, 20*(7), 917–938. doi:10.1080/09669582.2012.667217

Mbaiwa, J. (2011). The effects of tourism development on the sustainable utilisation of natural resources in the Okavango Delta, Botswana. *Current Issues in Tourism, 14*(3), 251–273. doi:10.1080/13683500.2011.555525

Mohonk Agreement. (2000). *Proposal for an International Certification Program for Sustainable Tourism and Ecotourism*. Retrieved on November 9, 2018, from: https://earthcheck.org/media/23533/mohonk.pdf

Mota, K., & Almeida, J. (2016). Educação superior em turismo, hospitalidade e lazer no Brasil: Análise do panorama de cursos ofertados frente ao contexto contemporâneo. *Revista Turismo & Desenvolvimento, 26,* 65–77.

Mota, K., & Anjos, F. (2012). Educação superior em turismo no Brasil: Análise da oferta de cursos superiores no Nordeste brasileiro pelos institutos federais. *Revista Brasileira de Pesquisa em Turismo, 6*(1), 48–63. doi:10.7784/rbtur.v6i1.461

Norton, B. (2005). Sustainability: A philosophy of adaptive ecosystem management. *Ecoscience, 13*(4), 565–566. doi:10.2980/1195-6860(2006)13[565:SAPOAE]2.0.CO;2

PENT - Plano Estratégico Nacional do Turismo. (2015). *Ministério da Economia e do Emprego*. Retrieved on May 14, 2020, from: https://www.portugal.gov.pt/media/820185/20130111%20consulta%20publica%20pent.pdf

Québec Declaration. (2002). *Québec Declaration on Ecotourism*. Retrieved on September 22, 2021, from: https://www.gdrc.org/uem/eco-tour/quebec-declaration.pdf

Santos, J. (2013). *Sistema de indicadores de sustentabilidade para o turismo: aplicação de uma abordagem participativa em Porto de Galinhas, PE* [Master's Dissertation]. Universidade Federal de Pernambuco.

Simão, J., & Partidário, M. (2012). How does tourism planning contribute to sustainable development? *Sustainable Development*, *20*(6), 372–385. doi:10.1002d.495

Stilwell, D. (2011). *Indicadores de sustentabilidade aplicados ao contexto do desenvolvimento turístico português* [Dissertação de Mestrado]. Faculty of Sciences, University of Lisbon.

United Nations Resolution (2018). *The Report of the Second Committee* (A/73/542).

Wimmler, C., Hejazi, G., Fernandes, E., Moreira, C., & Connors, S. (2015). Multi-criteria decision support methods for renewable energy systems on islands. *Journal of Clean Energy Technologies*, *3*(3), 185–195. doi:10.7763/JOCET.2015.V3.193

World Economic Forum. (2017). *Travel and Tourism Competitiveness Report*. Retrieved on August 20, 2018, from: https://reports.weforum.org/travel-and-tourism-competitiveness-report-2017/

World Tourism Organisation (WTO). (2013). *Sustainable Tourism for Development, European Commission*. Retrieved on August 16, 2018, from: https://www.e-unwto.org/doi/pdf/10.18111/9789284415496

ENDNOTE

[1] 'Stable' in the sense of being the downloadable documents that better fitted the keywords and criteria used.

Chapter 26
Adoption of the Sharing Economy in the Tourism and Hospitality Industry in Developing Countries

Kiril Kjiroski
Faculty of Computer Science and Engineering, University "Ss. Cyril and Methodius" in Skopje, Macedonia

Smilka Janeska Sarkanjac
https://orcid.org/0000-0001-6480-6722
Faculty of Computer Science and Engineering, University "Ss. Cyril and Methodius" in Skopje, Macedonia

Sasho Josimovski
Faculty of Economics, University "Ss. Cyril and Methodius" in Skopje, Macedonia

Ljubomir Drakulevski
Faculty of Economics, University "Ss. Cyril and Methodius" in Skopje, Macedonia

Branislav Sarkanjac
Faculty of Philosophy, University "Ss. Cyril and Methodius" in Skopje, Macedonia

ABSTRACT

The tourism and hospitality industry has been affected by sharing economy platforms and eco-systems, which constitute disruptive innovations (i.e., innovations that create new markets and value networks while disrupting existing ones and displacing industry incumbents). As the third-largest socioeconomic activity within the European Union (EU), tourism can be considered an engine for economic development, accounting for about 8% between 2007 and 2016, while it has been close to 10% worldwide. This chapter examines the potential of the sharing economy in the tourism and hospitality sectors to disrupt the incumbent tourist regions and proposes sharing economy platforms for the introduction of new destinations in developing countries such as the Republic of Macedonia. It is crucial to examine the issue of the sharing economy from a governance perspective. The authors contend that sharing economy should be a part of a comprehensive national tourism policy based on contemporary governance principles and on experiences of other countries.

DOI: 10.4018/978-1-6684-4645-4.ch026

INTRODUCTION

The sharing economy concept involves direct exchange of goods and services over the internet using online marketplaces. Also known as "collaborative consumption", "on-demand economy", "gig economy", "access economy", or "peer-to-peer (P2P) economy", it is a hybrid market model of P2P exchange that has experienced rapid growth in the last few years.

Currently, the sharing economy is present in nearly every aspect of our daily lives, and it continues to create new niches traditionally occupied by businesses, not individuals (Hawksworth et al., 2014). Hawksworth also makes predictions of future growth in the sharing economy, which should increase by multiple times more than traditional economies in similar economic fields.

The sharing economy began to grow exponentially following the world's greatest economic and financial crisis in 2008. This is not an accident. During his re-election campaign in 2004, US President Bush proclaimed an 'ownership society': "The greater the ownership in America, the greater the vitality of the nation." However, the ownership society, pushed by major banks and their subprime mortgages as well as credit default swaps, collapsed in 2008. 'Ownership hadn't made the U.S. vital; it had just about ruined the country' (Walsh 2011). The sharing economy has been historically rooted in bartering from ancient times and in more recent forms of organizations and activities such as cooperatives, mutual societies, associations, foundations, and tontines. Working class, poor, and minority communities have perpetuated these practices since very early times. The sharing economy concept was preceded by companies such as eBay (1995), Wikipedia (2001), PayPal (1998), Facebook (2004), YouTube (2005), Couchsurfing and Freecycle (both 2003), and so forth.

The sharing economy of the 21st century does not innovate the types of services and goods that are exchanged, but rather the way and the scope of doing the exchange. The innovation of the P2P economy lies in its process of connecting consumers and providers-and in the social benefits that the transactions bring. Shared resources were initially intended to be shared between individuals, but later evolved into consumer-to-consumer and supplier-to-consumer collaborations. Common threads of the sharing economy are disintermediation, the sharing of excess capacity, and increased productivity (Schor 2016).

PricewaterhouseCoopers (2015) conducted a large-scale survey on sharing economies, concluding it was here to stay. They estimate that the online sharing economy will be worth US$335 billion by 2025; if one factors in offline or physical sharing economies, it amounts to over US$1 trillion. P2P companies are getting close to or surpassing the largest incumbent competitors in traditional segments of their markets. According to Cusumano (2015), Airbnb, one of the most prominent representatives of the sharing economy, was worth approximately US$31 billion in 2017, surpassing Hilton (US$25 billion) and Marriott (US$20 billion) as well as Intercontinental Hotel Group, owner of the Holyday Inn chain (US$9 billion). It is estimated that Uber is worth between $28 and $66 billion, surpassing its incumbent competitors: Avis - US$6.34 billion and Hertz - US$12.4 billion. Sharing economy models are also developing at a rapid pace. It took the Hilton hotel group 93 years to build an inventory of more than 610,000 rooms in over 88 countries. In contrast, it took Airbnb only four years to compile 650,000 rooms in 192 countries, none of which they own, as Lauren Capelin, Chief Knowledge Officer of the Collaborative Lab, pointed out at the 13th International Luxury Travel Market Conference in 2014. The sharing economy now accounts for approximately 40% of the overall world outbound accommodation market (ITB Berlin, 2014).

Nonetheless, there is little agreement among scholars and practitioners regarding this economic model, as it has provoked fierce controversy. A prominent group of proponents of the sharing economy are stating that it is an economic model of the future, an innovative, transformative, choice-enhancing, as well as altruistic, communal, and environmentally sound one. Conversely, its opponents claim that it is a likable way for greedy capitalists to monetize the desperation of people in the post-crisis economy while sounding generous; others file lawsuits pertaining to labor law violations or zoning regulations, confront P2P companies in large demonstrations around the globe, and press governments to take direct regulation action. Governing bodies have responded in a variety of ways, from non-intervention to creating new regulatory regimes to sporadically enforcing compliance with regulations on some of these services to complete bans (Aloni, 2016).

In balancing the two types of potential of the sharing economy, governments around the world are trying to protect the traditional, incumbent businesses in their markets from the P2P companies, while at the same time creating the regulatory environment that will allow the sharing economy to succeed (European Parliament 2016). To that end, the European Commission, in an effort to examine the sector's overall contribution to the European economy as well as the current social and legal environment regarding the sharing economy, has launched a formal assessment of this sector with the self-explanatory title of "The Cost of Non-Europe in the Sharing Economy". Their findings are as follows:

The assessment of existing EU and national legislation confirms that there are still significant implementation gaps and areas of poor economic performance. The subsequent examination of areas where it was believed that an economic potential exists highlighted that substantial barriers remain, hindering the achievement of the goals set out in the existing legislation. Moreover, some issues are not or are insufficiently addressed (e.g. status of workers employed by sharing economy service providers). Consequently, more European action would be necessary to achieve the full economic potential of the sharing economy. In doing so, policy-makers should seek to ensure an adequate balance between creative freedom for business and the necessary regulatory protection (European Parliament 2016).

The reasons for participating in the sharing economy vary, which is not surprising given that the concept offers a variety of platforms and activities. Web sites for conducting e-business and applying the sharing concept offer generally lower prices than other market alternatives. It is easy to distribute the goods and services offered through the supply chain to producers or consumers and away from so-called "mediators", so the costs of this type of trade are lower. Through these platforms, visitors and hosts can establish genuine relationships that are not possible within traditional tourism systems. The main enablers of the sharing economy are mostly internet-related and include cloud databases, online data analysis, social media, and mobile technologies (Schor, 2016).

The sharing economy is not monolithic, it is driven by different market needs and can take a centralized, decentralized, or combined approach (PwC, 2017). Basic characteristics of the sharing economy in tourism include the following:

- It tends to be decentralized, consumer-to-consumer in nature
- The consumer owns the assets while the business only maintains the platform
- Revenue is primarily generated by consumers while businesses charge small fees for usage of their platforms

- Direct investments are relatively small, since much of the supply is created and consumed by consumers
- Scalability and viability depend on the number of customers that increase

As the third largest socioeconomic activity within the European Union, tourism can be considered an engine for economic development, generating revenues from accommodation, food consumption, shopping, local transportation, and local services for host countries. According to 'Global Travel Statistics for 2016', report by global travel wholesaler HotelsPro, a total of 58% of international tourists visit Europe, making the continent the number one tourist destination worldwide. The contribution of tourism to the gross domestic product of Europe has been about 8% between 2007 and 2016, while it has been close to 10% worldwide.

In general, tourism and hospitality are regarded as complementary, overlapping industries, and they will be discussed as a whole in this chapter.

The main difference between the two industries is that tourism is concerned with attractions, activities, and events while hospitality is concerned with providing accommodation, travel, food, wellness, and so forth. The hospitality industry is in fact a major supplier of tourism services. When one develops, the other usually follows. Social media is another very important actor in this analysis. In today's economy, social media and sharing economy can be seen as two aspects of a paradigm shift. It is a positive feedback loop that feeds off each other's penetration into our daily lives.

Furthermore, there is a distinction between a tourist and a traveler. Mass tourism in the 21st century has resulted in tourists becoming a metaphor for shallowness, contamination, and inauthenticity. The term "traveler" refers to different behaviors adopted by individuals to combat the problems they associate with tourism, with better ways to interact cross-culturally, and with differentiated, esoteric, and individualized activities (Week 2012). Generally, travelers utilize sharing economy platforms and design their own tours, as opposed to tourists who travel with tours organized by a travel agency.

This chapter examines the potential of the sharing economy in the tourism and hospitality sectors to disrupt the incumbent tourist regions and proposes sharing economy platforms for the introduction of new destinations in developing countries such as the Republic of Macedonia. This chapter should answer the question that was posed in the Dredge & Gyimóthy's (2015) paper: 'Is the collaborative economy (partially or entirely) good and/or desirable?', applying the question on the tourism and hospitality sector in developing countries. Also, the chapter should propose governance models for successful adoption of sharing economy in the tourism and hospitality sector in developing countries.

THE SHARING ECONOMY AND TOURISM AND HOSPITALITY INDUSTRY

The sharing economy is considered a disruptive innovation, one that creates new markets and value networks while disrupting existing industry incumbents. Tourism and hospitality are two industries that have been affected by the sharing economy. Travelers are replacing tourists in increasing numbers. Traditional travel agencies are rapidly disappearing, replaced by platforms such as Booking.com; airline tickets are increasingly purchased online. Empirical studies have revealed that Airbnb's offerings compete directly with that of one and two-star hotels (Guttentag, 2015).

Tourism and ride sharing represent the two largest segments of the sharing economy market. In the tourism and hospitality sectors, accommodation is the most common form of sharing economy model. By taking advantage of the sharing economy, the tourism industry can increase available accommodation resources during peak periods, eliminating the need to construct new accommodation facilities. Individual homeowners can rent their rooms, apartments, or houses efficiently through an electronic platform. This gives them increased credibility and authenticity, while also helping potential customers decide on a possible rental offer based on another individual's experience. Accommodation sharing is motivated by economics and the willingness of the supplier to reduce his own comfort to increase his own budget. Alternatively, users may have access to superior accommodations which are too expensive to own, or they may rent accommodations, which are priced much less than those offered by most commercial organizations (PwC, 2017).

PwC's research (2016) focuses on five key sectors of the sharing economy that facilitate transactions between individuals and organizations using online platforms. Four of them (all but the last) have direct relevance to the tourism and hospitality industry:

- Peer-to-peer accommodation: the sharing of unused space in homes or renting out holiday homes to travelers
- Peer-to-peer transportation: sharing a ride, a car, or a parking space with another individual
- On-demand household services: platforms which enable households to find freelancers to assist them with household tasks, such as the delivery of food and DIY projects on demand
- On demand professional services: freelance marketplaces that offer businesses on-demand access to administrative, consulting, and accounting services
- Collaborative finance: financial transactions are conducted directly between individuals without the involvement of traditional financial institutions

Figure 1 below illustrates the top areas in the tourism and hospitality industry occupied by sharing economy models, along with the corresponding online platforms.

Another aspect of disruption of this economic model is decentralization of accommodation (i.e., the displacement of traditional tourist destinations by new ones).

According to the OECD, sharing companies may bring tourists to destinations that were previously less popular. For example, a 2016 study by the Observatoire Valaisin du Tourisme looking at the impact of Airbnb on tourism in Switzerland found that Airbnb has expanded the city-break niche market in some Swiss cities where the high cost of hotel stays had previously hindered some tourists from staying there (European Parliament 2017).

However, tourism has the potential to contribute to employment, economic growth, and development in developing countries (Vujovic et al. 2016). Most developing countries fail to attract capital investments for the development of their traditional tourism systems. Botsman (2014) claims: "Airbnb's model (and other similar sharing economy models) is 'asset light'; it does not need to build or own inventory, but instead facilities access to existing assets, such as spare rooms, holiday houses, entire islands, or treehouses". In this way, developing countries may overcome the lack of heavy investments to develop their tourism industry.

Figure 1. Sharing economy and tourism. Source: Dredge, D., and Gyimóthy, S. (2015). The collaborative economy and tourism: Critical perspectives, questionable claims and silenced voices. Tourism Recreation Research, 40(3), 286-302

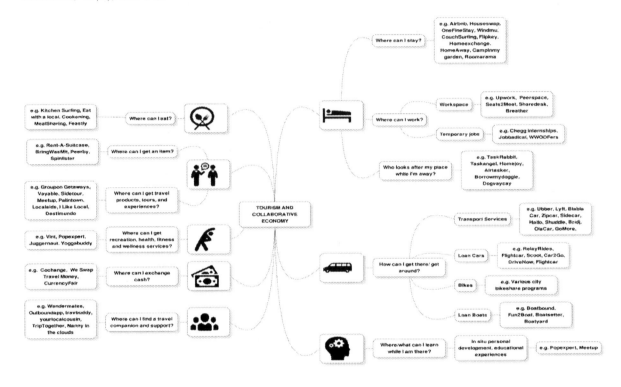

Many researchers are skeptical of the redistribution of power and information offered by new platforms. They argue that there is an illusion of participation, crowd power and customer sovereignty (Munar & Gyimóthy 2013). Social technologies are neither transparent nor emancipatory; rather, they produce and demonstrate new types of power asymmetries, social hierarchies and influential positions (Labrecque, Esche, Mathwick, Nowak, & Hofacker, 2013).

The quantitative studies that measure sharing economy showed that the people engaged in it are mostly urban, employed in managerial, professional, and administrative jobs, rather than rural, ethnic, unemployed or pensioned ones (Stokes et al., 2014; Tussyadiah, 2015). In Dredge and Gyimóthy's (2015) paper, they claim that the sharing economy phenomenon, or sharing economy fad, may be driven and influenced by people with high cultural, digital, and networking capital. This thesis is accompanied by the claim that much attention has been paid to shareable cities rather than shareable countryside.

TOURISM AND HOSPITALITY INDUSTRY IN THE REPUBLIC OF MACEDONIA

There are 12 main types of tourism that generate substantial demand worldwide, including several niche types (Ministry of Economy of the Republic of Macedonia, 2016):

- Sun and Beach Tourism
- City Tourism
- Culture Tourism
- Cruise Tourism
- Business/MICE Tourism
- Health and Spa Tourism
- Mountain / Winter Tourism
- Lake Tourism
- Adventure Tourism
- Nature/Eco Tourism
- Pilgrimage Tourism
- Visiting Family / Friends

In the Republic of Macedonia, the official statistics of the State Statistics Office indicate that accommodations and food service activities, since there are no data on tourism, accounted for less than 1.3% of GDP in 2013, 2014, and 2015. Figure 2 shows the number of tourist arrivals and the number of tourist nights spent in the Republic of Macedonia between 1960 and 2015. The tourist arrivals and tourist nights spent at the peak in the late 1980s have not yet been replicated. According to the Ministry of Economy of the Republic of Macedonia (2016), tourism in Macedonia contributed 5.2% to the national Gross Domestic Product (GDP) in 2014, and was US$288 per inhabitant, which is much higher than the average value for Europe and the world.

Tourism in Macedonia was responsible for 33.100 jobs or 4,7% of total employment. It is also important to note that Macedonia's government spends only 1,3% of its total budget on tourism, a modest percentage when compared with Greece (8%), Slovenia (4,3%) and Seychelles (22.4%). Ohrid and Struga, the two towns on the Ohrid Lake, traditional tourist destinations, generated 46% of annual overnight stays in Macedonia, and over 94% in popular lake destinations was generated in July and August. Consequently, the vast majority of tourism activities in Macedonia are traditional in nature. A

As can be seen in Figure 3, Macedonia is a landlocked country with three large lakes in the southeast and southwest of the country. However, there are a number of areas that can be used to develop a rich and interesting tourist offer. In its 2016 Strategic document (Ministry of Economy of the Republic of Macedonia, 2016), the Macedonian Ministry of Economy analyzed these locations.

Analyzing the main categories of tourism that generate substantial demand worldwide, in the case of Republic of Macedonia, since it is a landlocked country, cannot focus on Sun and Beach Tourism or Cruise Tourism. In view of its size (about two million inhabitants) and economic power, Business/MICE Tourism and Visiting Family/Friends might not be considered significant tourist types. The strategy should be focused on the following types of tourism: City Tourism, Culture Tourism, Health & Spa Tourism, Mountain/Winter Tourism, Lake Tourism, Adventure Tourism or Nature/Eco Tourism. They may all be affected by the technological disruption brought about by sharing economy platforms.

The Ministry of Economy of the Republic of Macedonia has developed a Strategy for the Development of Tourism in the Republic of Macedonia in 2009, which was reviewed and updated in January 2016, for the period 2016-2020. The sharing economy or the platforms that enable it are not mentioned in this strategy. However, one of the trends that is noted is the use of information technology:

It is expected that the use of the internet for purchasing and comparing tourism products and services will continue to grow. As a consequence, the consumer will assume more and more control. E-purses, secure credit cards, and other electronic payment systems will be developed. etc. The new developments will simplify the transfer of money as well as eliminate concerns about excessive transfer charges, exchange rates, and the security of moving money online.

Figure 2. Number of tourist arrivals and the number of tourist nights spent in the Republic of Macedonia in the period 1960-2015. Data source: Dimitrov, N., Koteski, C., & Jakovlev, Z. (2018). Analysis tourist trends of the Republic of Bulgaria in the Republic of Macedonia. SocioBrains, Issue 41, January 2018, 130-137

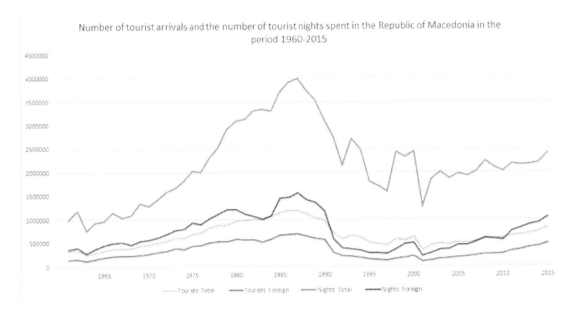

The Strategy notes the following global trends in tourism:

- Health
- Less leisure time
- Increasing travel experience
- Information technology
- Demographics
- Climate change
- Macroeconomic trends
- Political factors
- Safety and security
- Lifestyle
- Trends in marketing
- Transport

Figure 3. Topographical map of Republic of Macedonia

The main tourist attractions in Macedonia include the three Macedonian lakes, the city of Skopje as a city tourism destination, several smaller mountain resorts, located primarily in the western part of the country, and wine tourism in the main wine-growing region of the Vardar Valley (still in its early stages). The hot water springs of Macedonia are also popular (currently used primarily for healing purposes). Despite its significance, the strategy is a mainstream document that treats tourists, not travelers, and overlooks important trends. In particular, the use of sharing economy platforms in tourism has been overlooked. Essentially, the strategy does not consider new platforms and the sharing economy as vehicles for industry growth.

EXAMPLES OF PROMOTING TOURIST DESTINATIONS

Many nations have taken advantage of Internet technologies, social media, and the sharing economy, which have led to the development of new tourist offers, increasing tourism numbers and revenues, as well as restructuring their tourism industry. Traditional tourist destinations such as Italy are considering the new trends (In Italia sharing economy nel turismo frenata da scarsa digitalizzazione, 2017).

Not-so-traditional ones are deliberating this as well: "The volumes of the five leading areas of sharing economy are forecast to grow 25-fold globally in 10 years. We must deal with regulations favoring sharing economy in European countries already today, because people's preferences and habits are changing, and this holds big economic potential" (Estonia supports expansion of sharing economy 2016).

A review of some of the sharing economy in tourism initiatives will be presented as part of this study, selecting those that can be applied to the Republic of Macedonia. Examples are taken from tourism campaigns in Catalonia, Michigan and Aruba. There is also the case of Kamaishi City in Japan. In addition, a brief analysis of the platforms that can help attract tourists will be presented, such as TripAdvisor and Foursquare. At the end of this section the Macedonian online tourist platform in the field sharing economy, WhenInX, will be analyzed.

Catalunya Experience

The Catalan Tourist Board (CTB) was established by the government of Catalonia to promote tourism in the region. As CTB's public face on social networks, The Catalunya Experience developed with the intent of sharing knowledge and becoming opinion leaders regarding the attractive tourist destination. The company has a strong presence on several social media platforms such as Facebook with over 1,222,489 followers, Twitter with over 67,500 followers and over 19,100 tweets, over 264,000 Instagram followers with over 2,249,000 posts with the hashtag #catalunyaexperience, and over 7.000 subscribers to their YouTube channel with over 2,1550,00 views.

It has been an extremely successful campaign, with a steady increase in followers and viewers. They also take part in European tourism initiatives, such as family tourism in 2014, inland and mountain tourism in 2015, gastronomy and wine tourism in 2016, and this year's initiative for cultural tourism, trying to position themselves as "a key, differentiating factor for the destination, with tourism playing an essential role" (Agència Catalana de Turisme, 2018).

Figure 4 illustrates the increase in individual tourists over the past few years. Authors have used data from the National Institute of Statistics which is available at https://www.ine.es. Data is taken from October, 2015 through February, 2020. Each new year starts with January data, which are aggregated on a yearly basis.

Pure Michigan

Pure Michigan began as an advertising campaign by Travel Michigan for the US state of Michigan in 2006. They began by focusing on their own region, but soon began to attract tourists from neighboring states and Canada. Initially, they focused on social media presences such as YouTube, Facebook, Twitter, and Instagram, featuring actor Tim Allen's voice. Tourism reports (Tourism Economics, 2015; Longwoods International, 2016; Longwoods International, 2017) indicate the Pure Michigan campaign has been successful as measured by generated trips, visitor spending, and generated taxes.

The number of reported ROI numbers is constantly rising, starting from a regional Return on Investment (ROI) of US$2.11 on every US$1 spent on campaign, to a combined ROI of US$12.96 on a regional and national level in 2011, and reaching a combined ROI of US$18.62 in 2016. In terms of absolute numbers, the success of this campaign can also be seen in the increase of 250% in the number of generated trips (from 700,000 to over 2.5 million), an increase of 700% in their spending (US$188

Figure 4. Tourism movement on borders for Catalonia. Source: Instituto Nacional de Estadística. Source: https://www.ine.es/jaxiT3/Datos.htm?t=10823#!tabs-grafico

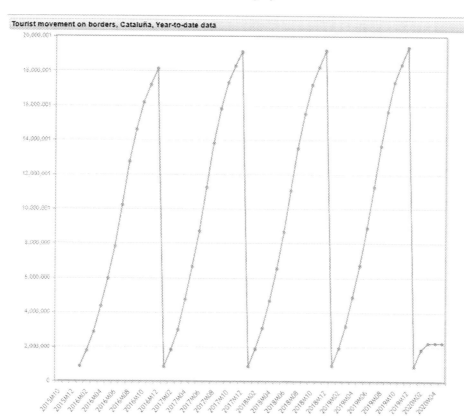

million to US$1.532 billion), and an increase of 360% in the amount of state taxes generated (US$13.1 million compared to US$60.9 million).

Pure Michigan has become a recognizable trademark due to the use of this brand by groups and individuals for sponsorship events, promotion, and other initiatives. In addition to advertising some of Michigan's most spectacular destinations, Pure Michigan's logo has now found application in different areas, such as connecting businesses (Pure Michigan Business Connect, 2018), promoting fitness programs (Pure Michigan Fitness, 2015), uniting Michigan's regions through sports (Pure Michigan Sports, 2017), and many other commercial and cultural endeavors.

Aruba

Aruba is a small island country in the southern Caribbean, located near the coast of South America and north of Venezuela. The country is a former Netherlands colony with Dutch as the official language and approximately 100,000 inhabitants living over an area of 193 square kilometers. The popularity of Aruba as a tourist destination in the Caribbean in recent years, along with its beautiful weather, beaches, and variety of entertainment, has led to Aruba having some of the most expensive accommodations and hotels in the world. Official Aruba tourism sites, such as https://www.aruba.com and https://www.

visitaruba.com, feature larger resorts, hotels, and vacation rentals. Smaller home and room owners are being left out, which allows entrepreneurs to use an avant-garde approach, such as the agreement between the Aruba Tourism Authority and Airbnb.

The Government of Aruba and the Aruba Tourism Authority initiated investigations and discussions which resulted in modifications in their tourist offerings, such as imposing a cap on the growth of all-inclusive resorts (Government of Aruba Argues in Favor of Limiting Growth of All-Inclusive Resorts, 2016). According to their reasoning, almost 80 percent of travel expenditures go to airlines, hotels, and other international companies, rather than to local businesses or workers (Archer, 2016).

As tourism accounts for 91% of Aruba's GDP and 93% of its employment, the island has had to turn to other forms of tourism and limit all-inclusive hotel packages. Airbnb, the world's leading community-driven hospitality company, and Aruba Tourism Authority signed an agreement in 2016 (Feliciano, 2016), that will position Aruba as a regional leader in the sharing economy and promote tourism on the island. A framework would be created to assist the Aruba Tourism Authority (ATA) and Airbnb to address the issue of taxes, host accommodation standards, and regulations and ensure that they are in accordance with Aruba's tourism policy.

Currently, there are more than 1,400 Aruba vacation rentals listed on Airbnb, serving more than 14,000 annual visitors and averaging 4.8 out of 5 stars. Aruba's positive experience with Airbnb was closely followed by other Caribbean countries, resulting in Airbnb signing a series of innovative and promising partnerships in the Caribbean, including with Curaçao, Jamaica, Bermuda, Anguilla, and the Caribbean Tourism Organization (CTO).

Kamaishi City

Kamaishi City in Japan was one of the host cities for the Rugby World Cup and as such, was expected to experience large increases in accommodation and transportation demand. Therefore, the city government partners with sharing enterprises to provide additional resources:

- Partnership with Airbnb for the use of farmhouse accommodation and community sites, as well as English guidebooks
- Partnership with TABICA, a platform bringing closer local daily life and customs through guides and workshops, and promoting tourism in the area
- Partnership with COGICOGI for bicycle rental service
- Partnership with ShareNori for visitor transport through their car-sharing program

PLATFORMS AND APPLICATIONS

There are many platforms and applications on the internet that facilitate and facilitate sharing economy and tourism as shown in Figure 1. Increasingly, the use of computers and the Internet enables people to share rides, hire accommodations, share workspace, storage, delivery, and logistics, share fashion, establish, and maintain B2B relationships, and many more services. The following section provides an overview of a few platforms that can assist in developing alternative tourist destinations, such as Republic of Macedonia.

TripAdvisor

Founded in 2000 by Stephen Kaufer and Nick Shanny, TripAdvisor is an online travel research company dedicated to assisting travelers and tourists around the world in planning and booking their perfect journey. According to TripAdvisor, it is the world's largest travel site, listing over 7.5 million accommodations (hotels, bed and breakfasts, specialty lodging, vacation rentals) as well as attractions, restaurants, and destinations. They have expanded into 49 markets in under 20 years, receiving over 450 million unique visitors each month. They have 20 websites in their portfolio, such as Airfarewatchdog, BookingBuddy, Citymaps, Cruise Critic, Family Vacation Critic, FlipKey, GateGuru etc. They are located in more than 40 countries around the world and have posted over 600 million reviews and opinions.

TripAdvisor has added new features in recent years, such as Road Trips - an online tool that helps travelers plan driving routes in the United States, including maps, hotels, attractions, and restaurants, as well as the best of – according to TripAdvisor, an extensive collection of award-winning hotels, destinations, beaches, airlines, and vacation rentals. These new inclusions are helping them keep up the pace set by market newcomers and their new ideas. Looking for means to increase their members and reviewers, since 2012 they have included connections to social networks, allowing their Facebook- and Google-connected users to select reviews from their social-network circles.

Even today they have one of the largest and most devoted customer group, still proudly presenting their "owl" logo, with one green (places to go) and one red eye (places to avoid).

Foursquare

Foursquare is a technology company focused on improving consumer experiences and business solutions via location intelligence. For that purpose, Foursquare has developed two applications; namely, Foursquare City Guide, which assists users in discovering new places based on Foursquare community recommendations, and Foursquare Swarm, an application similar to a lifelog that logs places visited. Their technology assists companies in locating, measuring, and communicating with their clients. Apple, Uber, Twitter, Microsoft, Samsung, and many other companies use Foursquare.

Foursquare has a large community and their platforms such as City Guide and Foursquare Swarm attract more than 50 million users each month. In Foursquare, check-ins are used to keep track of visited places, and they already have more than 12 billion Swarm check-ins with 9 million unique check-ins recorded in just one day. Using this technology, they have mapped more than 105 locations around the globe. Foursquare currently employs 250 individuals in the United States, London, and Singapore.

An interesting aspect of Foursquare is that businesses do not need to submit formal applications to appear on their map. Users are responsible for building business coverage on Foursquare. With the Swarm application, people can register their current location, along with places and businesses on the map, and share their comments, experiences, and evaluations.

Regarding their business model (Carpenter, 2016; Miller, 2017), it is noteworthy that they have begun to monetize their large customer base developed since 2009. Foursquare location intelligence data is used primarily by:

- Data licensing: Foursquare licenses their gathered data to companies such as Microsoft, Twitter, Apple, and so forth. They claim that more than 40% of their revenue stems from this activity

- Location-based digital targeting: Foursquare's Pinpoint application is using client location data for targeted communication based on their preferences, demographics and visit history
- Foot traffic analytics: Foursquare possess a database of more than 105 million places, and precisely determines user location in real time using machine learning, while also identifies hidden trends and predicts future customer behavior. Companies such as Apple are using it to accurately predict their sales figures, or sales drop, such as in the case of Chipotle.

Foursquare has proven to be most valuable to tourist attractions, since the location data gathered with the help of Swarm allows them to gather information about places their customers visit, as well as their impressions and feedback. As a demonstration of the power of their location technology, the company has provided their Location Based Travel and Tourism Insights (2017), in which they provide comprehensive information about the travel industry in the US, including the following:

- Days with most traffic, divided by the type of transit (automobile, airplane, or train)
- Analysis of hotel versus alternative accommodation
- Top travel destinations and their occupation, provided with the help of foot traffic pattern analysis
- Marketing and measurement help and other helpful content, including audience segmentation, real-time targeting, measure impact, understanding regional preferences, and customized recommendations

WhenInX

WhenInX (Do as the locals do) is an online marketplace for visitors to explore and book outdoor activities, cultural experiences, and events hosted by locals. Unlike traditional travel agencies, which directly sell to customers, they try to match travelers with local "experts", or hosts, who act as the service providers. Its approach is similar to other sharing economy online marketplaces (such as Airbnb, Couchsurfing, etc.) with the exception of connecting visitors with local "experts" and helping them discover hidden beauty.

Launched in September, 2017, the platform has over 1,100 registered users and achieves more than 25,000 page views per day. This project was funded by Macedonian Fund for Innovations and Technology Development. After providing software services to international clients for many years, the Macedonian company Webgliders decided to finally develop a product that will become a recognized brand. WhenInX authors have been working on their unique idea since 2015, when there were no other similar platforms on the global stage. Although there are now multiple platforms addressing this unique tourism niche, the absence of such offerings in the region gives them the opportunity to succeed. On the WhenInX portal, they provide means for safe online purchasing, while still seeking ways to engage users by providing unique experiences that can only be obtained from this platform.

Currently, the platform offers over 100 tours, primarily in Macedonia and Portugal (Island of Madeira), but they expect to expand to neighboring countries (such as Slovenia, Croatia, Serbia, Bulgaria, and Turkey). In addition to opening new tours, WhenInX plans to launch a marketing campaign that will promote their platform, enhance their credibility and make them more attractive to consumers, both tourists and operators of alternative tourism. Their efforts include organizing the second annual festival When In Krushevo (June 29-30, 2018), which will offer online reservations for mountain climbing, mountain biking, canoeing, tandem paragliding, and museum tours. They admit that the main cause of their losing market share is the lack of the resources required for a more intensive marketing campaign rather than a lack of promotional ideas.

DISCUSSION

Below we discuss the adoption of sharing economy in tourism and hospitality, and its potential positive impact on the tourism industry in Macedonia. Any developing country that is interested in developing its tourism economy can easily replicate the conclusions and recommendations of this analysis. To evaluate Macedonia's growth potential as a viable tourist destination by using new technologies and platforms, the possibilities of implementing them in the Macedonian context should be explored. The first step is to conduct a comparative analysis of their use in the campaigns cited in this paper. Data on social networks and platforms were collected in August, 2018.

Similar to the campaigns such as #CatalunyaExperience and #PureMichigan, #MacedoniaTimeless has been undertaken by the Agency for Promotion and Support of Tourism in Macedonia. Table 1 makes it apparent that all three campaigns have been using social media to distribute their messages, but Macedonia's campaign is far behind Catalonia's (the results in favor of Catalonia are approximately 25 times higher on Facebook, 67 times higher on Twitter, and 5 times higher on Youtube), and even behind Michigan's campaign results (approximately 22 times higher on Facebook, 477 times higher on Twitter, and eight times higher on Youtube).

According to an analysis of Youtube data, Catalonia's campaign has created twice as much creative (video spots) as Michigan's campaign has. From this, it can be concluded that Macedonia's participation in social networks and reaching 50,000 potential tourists via Facebook is far from satisfactory. The factors of insufficient commitment on the part of the organizers, or insufficient founding, or possibly both, inhibit the achievement of more significant results.

Table 1. Comparation of #MacedoniaTimeless, #CatalunyaExperience and #PureMichigan campaigns

	#MacedoniaTimeless	#CatalunyaExperience	#PureMichigan
Facebook	50,742 liked 50,394 followed	1,274,749 liked 1,270,758 followed	1,170,910 liked 1,119,809 followed
Instagram	5,226 followers	282,000 followers	573,000 followers
Twitter	427 Tweets 997 Followers	20,400 Tweets 67.300 Followers 25.000 Likes	26,900 Tweets 476,000 Followers 18,500 Likes
Youtube	1,422 subscribers 83 videos 103,000 views max	7,241 subscribers 159 videos 265,000 views max	11,802 subscribers 738 videos 295,000 views max

In Table 2, data provided by AirBnB and booking.com are compared regarding accommodation facilities offered in Macedonia and Aruba on these platforms. Figures are comparable, and one of the destinations offers more facilities on one of the platforms, while the other country is more present on the competitor's platform.

Table 2. Comparation of Macedonia and Aruba on AirBnB and Booking.com

	Macedonia	Aruba
# rentals offered on AirBnB	430	1,400
# rentals offered on Booking.com	1,817	367

It would be possible to draw parallels between platforms offered by Kamaishi City in Japan (TABICA, COGICOGI and SjareNori) and WhenInX. TABICA offers very special local experiences to travelers, such as traveling with a nun, experiencing a harvest day on a farm, fishing experience, and so on. This is similar to the concept of WhenInX. The COGICOGI bike sharing platform represents a trend that is not very popular in the Republic of Macedonia, although there have been attempts to popularize bike sharing in Skopje, the capital of the country (Lokalno 2018). The ShareNori system is a tool for car sharing, where a person with a vehicle can, for a monetary compensation, lend out their car or even take full advantage of the vehicle for a limited time.

There are some examples of this type of service being offered in Macedonia, although in an extremely informal and unregulated manner, through Facebook groups, where communication is conducted exclusively in Macedonian, which makes it unusable for foreign tourists and travelers, and there is currently no broader platform for use. To evaluate their use of this platform for promotion, the destinations included in our analysis on TripAdvisor are compared below.

Table 3. Comparison of destinations included in TripAdvisor analysis

TripAdvisor	R. Macedonia	Aruba	Catalonia	Michigan	Kamaishi City
Total # of reviews and opinions	54,156	438,791	4,752,556	1,335,817	439
# Hotels	/	37	1,848	1,483	/
# B&B & Inns	/	/	1,370	755	/
# Vacation Rentals	/	719	15,092	1,509	20
# Restaurants	/	427	30,147	23,344	202
# Things to do	/	/	7,827	5,733	/
Total	54,156	439,974	4,808,840	1,368,641	661
Popularity compared to R. Macedonia (factor)		8,12	88,79	25,27	0,012

From Table 3, which represents data from TripAdvisor about researched destinations, we can discern relatively developed tourist destinations, such as Catalonia and Michigan, from the other, obviously undeveloped destinations. In the case of Kamaishi City, the case can be entirely separated because the city uses local platforms and does not use TripAdvisor or similar Western platforms, so their numbers do not have relevance to the evaluation of this tourist destination. Upon comparing Aruba and Macedonia, it can be concluded there are at least 10 times more people commenting and rating content on Aruba than on Macedonia. In the case of Macedonia, TripAdvisor does not even provide data about accommodation facilities, restaurants, or fun activities, which is enough to discourage tourists from considering Macedonia as a viable option and give up on the idea of visiting the country.

The situation with Foursquare is similar, despite the fact that they, due to their local geolocation nature, do not provide detailed statistical analyses of countries, regions, or cities. The WhenInX platform represents an excellent starting point, thanks to the large number of included tours (more than 100 Things to Do), 1.100 registered users, and 25.000 site visits. By providing this platform with a powerful boost, it can function as the engine of tourism development in Macedonia through regionalization and perhaps globalization.

As previously mentioned, there is some uncertainty regarding how much new platforms can contribute to developing tourist destinations. However, Catalonia, Michigan, and Aruba demonstrate that new approaches in tourism work for them. These initiatives have all set out to achieve different goals with similar means, and simultaneously, they have demonstrated that modern social technologies can assist in improving image (in the case of Pure Michigan), that they can help balance the economic gains more in favor of the local economy compared with international travel agencies (in the case of Aruba), or that they help in promoting new tourism initiatives and creating personal relationships with potential tourists (in the case of the Catalonia Experience).

One more example of comparison between a developed and a developing country, in terms of tourist volume and revenue derived from them, although neither country is well known for its traditional tourism. Compare, for example, Mecklenburg-Vorpommern, a state in Germany, to the Republic of Macedonia. Mecklenburg-Vorpommern (23,174 km^2) is about the size of Macedonia (25,713km^2). Mecklenburg-Vorpommern has a population of about 1.600.000, which is close to Republic of Macedonia (about 2,000,000) and both countries had similar starting points in 1989 following the fall of the Berlin Wall (Mecklenburg-Vorpommern until 1989 was part of the German Democratic Republic (East Germany), Macedonia until 1991 was part of Yugoslavia).

Mecklenburg-Vorpommern saw 7.57 million arrivals in 2016 and 30.3 million overnight stays, according to the statistical office (Statistisches Amt) in the state. In 2016, Mecklenburg-Western Pomerania tourists spent approximately 7.74 billion Euros, among other things, for overnight stays, restaurant visits, groceries, and shopping. The tourist added value is estimated at nearly 4.1 billion Euros. Macedonia is lagging significantly behind. In 2015, the State Statistical Office of the Republic of Macedonia reported 816,000 tourist arrivals, and 2,394,000 overnight stays. The total revenue was US$270 million dollars. Though it might seem impossible to ever reach the numbers of Mecklenburg-Vorpommern, but without a vision and long-term goals any development in Macedonia is severely limited by the fuzzy politics of the country.

GOVERNANCE IMPLICATIONS AND SIGNIFICANCE OF THE STUDY

A good or effective sharing economy should involve activities such as supervision, coordination, and regulation of small businesses within the tourism industry. As a result, it is important to examine the sharing economy from the perspective of governance. In the authors' opinion, sharing economy should be a part of a comprehensive national tourism policy, which incorporates contemporary governance principles and a comparison of governance practices from different countries.

There are many definitions of the concept of governance. Different authors refer to different forms of governance. For example, Kooiman (1993) refers to the sociopolitical governance which includes as many political actors and normative debates as possible.

Social-political governance must be regarded as a continuous process of interaction between public or private actors. They act in conjunction in co-arrangements. Contemporary political governance unfolds from a plurality of governing actors. Social-political governance would cover all those interactive settings in which both public and private actors participate to create opportunities for development of tourism, and which are related to the institutions responsible for development of tourism in which the governing activities occur.

In socio-political governance traditional hierarchical governance and social self-organization are complementary and there is sufficient autonomy at the micro level. We believe that this autonomy is very important for sharing economy in tourism and hospitality.

Creating more concrete governing models such as co-management, co-steering, and co-guidance is the goal. The role of research centers, forward-looking visions, and ICT-based social innovations can be added to this definition of governance. Research centers for the development of tourism should be interconnected with research centers at national and local levels, research centers at universities and research centers at economic chambers in Macedonia. It is essential that the major political parties as well as independent Non-Governmental Organizations (NGOs) and so-called "Think Tanks" participate in this complex process of governance in tourism. Presently, such centers are largely inactive or nonexistent.

Private initiatives, such as WhenInX, can facilitate the government's interest in playing a more active role in governing the sharing economy, especially with regards to empowering citizens to improve their potential and to attract more travelers, which in turn contributes to economic growth. This chapter is also intended to encourage other private initiatives and demonstrate that, with the involvement of private sector entities, developing countries such as Republic of Macedonia can be included on the global map of travelers, and develop their overall tourism and hospitality industries.

It is emphasized throughout the chapter that social media is closely intertwined with sharing economy platforms to have a positive impact on the tourism and hospitality sectors. It is the authors' strong belief that platforms such as WhenInX, with proper support from Macedonia's ministry, can represent a rewarding opportunity to attract tourists. These visitors will also require travel, accommodation, and other hospitality services, which will have a positive impact on locals beyond those offering the attraction in question.

The government should support such initiatives and help promote them through social media channels to provide a more detailed, up-to-date, and better presented view of what the country has to offer. In turn, that will attract travelers to visit these sites, as well as establish a connection between travelers and locals.

The following limitations apply to this analysis. All platforms and social media analyzed in this chapter represent some of the most contemporary trends in global relations. It is understandable that they are, in any case, not the only means to stimulate interest in places and events. It has previously been possible to tickle people's imaginations with advertisements in newspapers, radio, television, and billboards, and there is no doubt that there will be new forms of communication in the future. This economic area is so dynamic that it needs to be constantly monitored to analyze and determine the best methods to promote development of the tourism and hospitality industries.

CONCLUSION

In this chapter the authors have tried to answer the modification of the question that was posed in the Dredge and Gyimóthy (2015) paper: 'Is the collaborative economy (partially or entirely) good and/or desirable?', modifying it into 'Is the collaborative economy (partially or entirely) good and/or desirable for us? Do sharing economy potentials in the tourism and hospitality sector offer the possibility of disrupting incumbent tourism and hospitality markets at the same time as allowing new destinations to be introduced, such as the Republic of Macedonia? How can this be achieved? Should Catalunya Experience, Pure Michigan, and Aruba be considered role models? Are AirBnb, TripAdvisor, FourSquare, and WhenInX the main online platforms that could contribute to Macedonia's development as a popular tourist destination? Are these opinion makers overestimated, and have they lived up to the trust placed in them? Finally, how will these investments in new technologies contribute to the improvement of the economy of the country?

The Internet and social media have become indispensable in our connected world for building and maintaining the image of a country, a company, or even an individual. It would therefore be worthwhile for Macedonia to become involved with the above-mentioned social media and sharing economy models. In absolute terms, Macedonia lags behind more current and popular tourist destinations, such as Catalonia and Aruba, and on the other hand, underrepresents itself, as compared to destinations which reinvent and improve their own image, such as Michigan. It is, of course, of utmost importance for the country to reap economic benefits, to find its own voice and message when communicating with prospective tourists. In developing countries, without their own underdeveloped private sector, the government themselves should take responsibility and support such initiatives and campaigns.

With comparative analysis conducted from different research centers throughout the country and benchmarking the potential of the sharing economy, a long-term vision and realistic goals can be set. Despite the lack of academic research on sharing economy and tourism in low-income countries, the authors believe that sharing economy in tourism offers a good opportunity to use so-called idle assets in Macedonia. The controversial concept of capitalization of poverty (De Sotto, 1989) may prove to be viable. According to the European Commission, the cost of including non-Macedonia in the sharing economy would be too high. There is the potential for the Republic of Macedonia to utilize the sharing economy to develop its tourism and hospitality sectors. A roadmap to this goal is provided in this chapter.

REFERENCES

Agència Catalana de Turisme. (2018). *2018 Year of Cultural Tourism*. Retrieved on January 16, 2018, from: http://act.gencat.cat/2018-year-of-cultural-tourism/?lang=en

Aloni, E. (2016). Pluralizing the Sharing Economy. *Washington Law Review (Seattle, Wash.), 91*, 1397.

Archer, D. (2016). *Keeping its destination profitable and its people happy: Aruba's cap on all-inclusive resorts*. Retrieved on November 16, 2016, from: https://destinationthink.com/keeping-destination-profitable-people-happy-aruba-cap-on-all-inclusive-resorts/

Berlin, I. T. B. (2014). *ITB world travel trends report 2014/2015*. Messe Berlin GmbH.

Botsman, R. (2014). *Collaborative economy services: Changing the way we travel*. Retrieved on July 2, 2018, from: http://www.collaborativeconsumption.com/2014/06/25/collaborative-economy-services-changing-the-way-we-travel/

Britannica, tourism topic. (n.d.). Retrieved on July 2, 2018, from: https://www.britannica.com/topic/tourism

Carpenter, W. (2016). *An Inside Look at Foursquare's Business Model.* Retrieved on February 15, 2016, from: https://www.investopedia.com/articles/markets/021516/inside-look-foursquares-business-model.asp

Cusumano, M. A. (2015). How traditional firms must compete in the sharing economy. *Communications of the ACM, 58*(1), 32–34. doi:10.1145/2688487

Dimitrov, N., Koteski, C., & Jakovlev, Z. (2018, January). Analysis tourist trends of the Republic of Bulgaria in the Republic of Macedonia. *SocioBrains,* (41), 130–137.

Discover Hospitality. (2015). *What is Hospitality?* Retrieved on July 2, 2018, from: https://web.archive.org/web/20150814071021/http://discoverhospitality.com.au/what-is-hospitality

Dredge, D., & Gyimóthy, S. (2015). The collaborative economy and tourism: Critical perspectives, questionable claims and silenced voices. *Tourism Recreation Research, 40*(3), 286–302. doi:10.1080/02508281.2015.1086076

European Parliament. (2016). *The Cost of Non-Europe in the Sharing Economy.* January 2016 - PE 558.777. European Added Value Unit.

European Parliament. (2017). Tourism and the sharing economy. January 2017 — PE 595.897. Juul, M., Members' Research Service.

Feliciano, S. (2016). *Airbnb and Aruba Tourism Authority Sign Historic, Tourism Agreement.* Retrieved on November 1, 2018, from: https://www.prnewswire.com/news-releases/airbnb-and-aruba-tourism-authority-sign-historic-tourism-agreement-300358342.html

Foursquare Location Based Travel and Tourism Insights. (2018). Retrieved on July 15, 2018, from: https://www2.foursquare.com/l/310041/are-Traveler-Insights-2017-pdf/2frvtp

Guttentag, D. (2015). Airbnb: Disruptive innovation and the rise of an informal tourism accommodation sector. *Current Issues in Tourism, 18*(12), 1192–1217. doi:10.1080/13683500.2013.827159

Hawksworth, J., & Vaughan, R. (2014). *The sharing economy–sizing the revenue opportunity.* Retrieved on July 20, 2018, from: https://www.pwc.co.uk/issues/megatrends/collisions/sharingeconomy/the-sharing-economysizing-therevenue-opportunity.html

Kooiman, J. (Ed.). (1993). *Modern governance: New government-society interactions.* Sage.

Labrecque, L. I., vor dem Esche, J., Mathwick, C., Novak, T. P., & Hofacker, C. F. (2013). Consumer power: Evolution in the digital age. *Journal of Interactive Marketing, 27*(4), 257–269.

Lokalno. (2018). *In Europe it is a trend, in Skopje it did not take.* Retrieved on August 15, 2018, from: https://lokalno.mk/vo-evropa-e-trend-a-vo-skopje-ne-zazhivea-iznajmuvaneto-velosipedi/

Longwoods International. (2016). *Michigan 2015 Tourism Advertising Evaluation and Image Study.* Retrieved on July 20, 2018, from: https://www.michiganbusiness.org/cm/Files/Reports/MI%202015%20National%20Regional%20Ad%20Evaluation%20Image%20Study_Final%20Report.pdf

Longwoods International. (2017). *Michigan 2016 Tourism Advertising Evaluation and Image Study.* Retrieved on July 20, from: https://www.michiganbusiness.org/cm/Files/Reports/MI%202016%20National%20%20Regional%20Ad%20Evaluation%20%20Image%20Study%20Final%20Report%20(003).pdf

Map of Republic of Macedonia. (n.d.). Retrieved on February 10, 2019, from https://www.novamakedonija.com.mk/prilozi/izbor/%D1%81%D0%BB%D1%83%D1%87%D0%B0%D1%98%D0%BE%D1%82-%D0%BC%D0%B0%D0%BA%D0%B5%D0%B4%D0%BE%D0%BD%D0%B8%D1%98%D0%B0-%D0%B8%D0%BB%D0%B8-%D0%BA%D0%B0%D0%BA%D0%BE-%D0%B4%D0%B0-%D1%98%D0%B0/

Miller, N. (2017). *After Years of Challenges, Foursquare Has Found its Purpose -- and Profits.* Retrieved on September 15, 2018, from https://www.entrepreneur.com/article/290543

Ministry of Economy of the Republic of Macedonia. (2016). *National Tourism Strategy Republic of Macedonia.* Kohl, C.H., & Partner.

Munar, A. M., & Gyimóthy, S. (2013). Critical digital tourism studies. In *Tourism social media: Transformations in identity, community and culture* (pp. 245–262). Emerald Group Publishing Limited.

PricewaterhouseCoopers, L. L. P. (2015). *The sharing economy.* Report, Consumer Intelligence Series.

Pure Michigan Business Connect. (2018). Retrieved on April 8, 2018, from: https://www.michiganbusiness.org/pmbc/

Pure Michigan Fitness. (2015). Retrieved on April 8, 2018, from: https://michiganfitness.org/pure-michigan-fitness

Pure Michigan Sports. (2017). Retrieved on April 8, 2018, from: http://www.puremichigansports.org

Schor, J. (2016). Debating The Sharing Economy. *Journal of Self-Governance & Management Economics, 4*(3).

Stokes, K., Clarence, E., Anderson, L., & Rinne, A. (2014). *Making sense of the UK collaborative economy.* Nesta.

Tavel Agent Central. (2016). *Government of Aruba Argues in Favor of Limiting Growth of All-inclusives.* Retrieved on July 15, 2018, from: https://www.travelagentcentral.com/government-aruba-argues-favor-limiting-growth-all-inclusives

Telles, R., Jr. (2016). Digital Matching Firms: A New Definition in the "Sharing Economy" Space. ESA Issue Brief, 01-16.

The Baltic Course. (2016). *Estonia supports expansion of sharing economy.* Retrieved on July 2, 2018, from: http://www.baltic-course.com/eng/analytics/?doc=115999

Tourism Economics, an Oxford Economics Company. (2015). *The Economic Impact of Travel in Michigan Tourism Satellite Account Calendar Year 2014.* Retrieved on May 22, 2018, from: https://www.michiganbusiness.org/cm/Files/Reports/Michigan-2014-Tourism-Economic-Impact.pdf

Travelnostop. (2017). *In Italia sharing economy nel turismo frenata da scarsa digitalizzazione*. Retrieved on January 26, 2017, from: https://www.travelnostop.com/news/dati-e-statistiche/in-italia-sharing-economy-nel-turismo-frenata-da-scarsa-digitalizzazione_140073

Tussyadiah, I. P. (2015). An exploratory study on drivers and deterrents of collaborative consumption in travel. In *Information and communication technologies in tourism 2015* (pp. 817–830). Springer.

Vujovic, S. M., Ćurčić, N. V., & Miletić, V. S. (2016). The influence of tourism on the circular flow of an economic process. *Economics of Agriculture*, *1*, 323–337.

Walsh, B. (2011). Today's smart choice: Don't own. Share. *Times International*, *1*(3), 49.

Week, L. (2012). I am not a tourist: Aims and implications of "traveling". *Tourist Studies*, *12*(2), 186–203.

KEY TERMS AND DEFINITIONS

Developing Country: This refers to low- and middle-income generating countries (LMIC), that are relatively less developed, or in some cases underdeveloped countries with a less developed industrial base and a low Human Development Index (HDI) relative to developed countries.

Disruptive Innovation: Product that displaces (disrupts) established order in certain eco-system. It doesn't necessarily implies emerging of a new product, but it involves great increase in product adoption by wider public.

Hospitality: The hospitality industry is a broad category of fields within the service industry that includes lodging, food and drink service, event planning, theme parks, travel, and tourism. It includes hotels, tourism agencies, restaurants, and bars.

On Demand: Goods or services that are available when customers need them.

Peer-to-Peer: Term mostly used in computer networks, to describe connections between independent and equal computers. Here it refers to a direct exchange of goods, services and currency, enabled by Internet, Web applications and social networks.

Republic of Macedonia: Landlocked country in the Balkans region, north of Greece, south of Serbia, East of Bulgaria and West of Albania, with area of approximately 25.700 square kilometers, defined by the central valley of river Vardar, with mostly rugged terrain. It has three large lakes – Lake Ohrid and Lake Prespa in the south-west and Lake Dojran in the south-east.

Sharing Economy: Model of economy, where goods are provided and purchased by individuals rather than companies, most often involving some Internet application or social network.

Social Platform: A web-based technology that enables the development, deployment and management of social media solutions and services. It provides the ability to create social media websites and services with complete social media network functionality.

Tourism: Traveling to and staying in places outside their usual environment for leisure or business. Tourism industry consists of businesses that sell products or services to these travelers, also known as "tourists".

Tourist: A person which goes to a different place with the purpose of enjoying and experiencing most famous events and locations offered by certain place or country.

Traveler: A person which goes to a different place with the purpose of experiencing authentic people, food, etc. Travelers tend to blend in with their hosts and adopt their hosts' way of living while visiting.

Compilation of References

Parma Committee. (2018). *Dossier di candidatura di Parma a Capitale Italiana della Cultura 2020* [Parma Candidacy Dossier as Italian Capitsl of Culture 2020]. Retrieved on June 2, 2021, from: https://parma2020.it/it/verso-parma2020/

Aaker, D. A. (1991). *Managing brand equity: Capitalizing on the value of a brand name.* The Free Press.

Abbas, J., Mubeen, R., Iorember, P. T., Raza, S., & Mamirkulova, G. (2021). Exploring the impact of COVID-19 on tourism: Transformational potential and implications for a sustainable recovery of the travel and leisure industry. *Current Research in Behavioral Sciences*, *2*(March), 100033. doi:10.1016/j.crbeha.2021.100033

Abderahman, R., & Karim, R. (2020). Blockchain and supply chain sustainability. *Scientific Journal of Logistics*, *16*(3), 363–372.

Abdullahi, B. B. (2017). Examining the influence of knowledge and attitude on the intention to adopt environmentally sustainable behaviour. *International Journal of Engineering Technology and Scientific Innovation*, *2*(6), 763–771.

Abram, N. J., Henley, B. J., Sen Gupta, A., Lippmann, T. J., Clarke, H., Dowdy, A. J., Sharples, J. J., Nolan, R. H., Zhang, T., Wooster, M. J., Wurtzel, J. B., Meissner, K. J., Pitman, A. J., Ukkola, A. M., Murphy, B. P., Tapper, N. J., & Boer, M. M. (2021). Connections of climate change and variability to large and extreme forest fires in Southeast Australia. *Communications Earth & Environment*, *2*(1), 8. Advance online publication. doi:10.103843247-020-00065-8

Acharya, A., Mondal, B. K., Bhadra, T., Abdelrahman, K., Mishra, P. K., Tiwari, A., & Das, R. (2022). Geospatial analysis of geo-ecotourism site suitability using AHP and GIS for sustainable and resilient tourism planning in West Bengal, India. *Sustainability*, *14*(4), 2422. doi:10.3390u14042422

Acharya, B. P., & Halpenny, E. A. (2013). Homestays as an alternative tourism product for sustainable community development: A case study of women-managed tourism product in rural Nepal. *Tourism Planning & Development*, *10*(4), 367–387. doi:10.1080/21568316.2013.779313

Adam, A. M. (2020). Sample size determination in survey research. *Journal of Scientific Research and Reports*, *26*(5), 90–97. doi:10.9734/jsrr/2020/v26i530263

Adamson, M., Hamilton, R., Hutchison, K., Kazmierowski, K., Lau, J., Madejski, D., & Macdonald, N. (2005). *Environmental impact of computer information technology in an institutional setting: A case study at The University Of Guelph.* Retrieved on April 22, 2021, from: https://www.uoguelph.ca/isc/documents/050602environcs_000.pdf

Aday, S., & Aday, M. S. (2020). Impact of COVID-19 on the food supply chain. *Food Quality and Safety*, *4*(4), 167–180. doi:10.1093/fqsafe/fyaa024

Adhikari, S. (2021). *Role of gender diversity on banking performance in Kathmandu valley* [Unpublish MBA Thesis]. Pokhara University, Pokhara, Kastki, Nepal.

Compilation of References

Adner, R., & Kapoor, R. (2016). Innovation ecosystems and the pace of substitution: Re-examining technology S-curves. *Strategic Management Journal*, *37*(4), 625–648. doi:10.1002mj.2363

Agarwal, R. K. (2012). *Review of Technologies to Achieve Sustainable (Green) Aviation*. Recent Advances in Aircraft Technology.

Agència Catalana de Turisme. (2018). *2018 Year of Cultural Tourism*. Retrieved on January 16, 2018, from: http://act.gencat.cat/2018-year-of-cultural-tourism/?lang=en

Ahmad, A., Jamaludin, A., Zuraimi, N. S. M., & Valeri, M. (2020). Visit intention and destination image in post-Covid-19 crisis recovery. *Current Issues in Tourism*, *0*(0), 1–6. doi:10.1080/13683500.2020.1842342

Ahmad, N., Menegaki, A. N., & Al-Muharrami, S. (2020). Systematic literature review of tourism growth nexus: An overview of the literature and a content analysis of 100 most influential papers. *Journal of Economic Surveys*, *34*(5), 1068–1110. doi:10.1111/joes.12386

Ahmad, R., & Hertzog, A. (2016). Tourism, memory and place in a globalizing world. *Tourism and Hospitality Research*, *16*(3), 201–205. doi:10.1177/1467358416641254

Air India Express. (n.d.). *CSR Policies*. Retrieved on March 22, 2022, from: https://www.airindiaexpress.in/en/about-us/csr

Air Vistara. (n.d.). *CSR and Sustainability*. Retrieved on December 13, 2021, from: https://www.airvistara.com/in/en/csr-and-sustainability#:~:text=Corporate%20Social%20Responsibility%20(CSR)%20is,to%20help%20achieve%20their%20dreams

Ajzen, I. (1985). From intentions to actions: A theory of planned behavior. *Action Control*, 11–39. doi:10.1007/978-3-642-69746-3_2

Ajzen, I. (1991). The theory of planned behavior. Academic Press. *Inc*, *50*(11), 179–211. doi:10.1080/10410236.2018.1493416

Akat, Ö. (2000). *Pazarlama ağırlıklı turizm işletmeciliği*. Ekin Kitabevi.

Akdağ, G., & Üzülmez, M. (2017). Sürdürülebilir gastronomi turizmi kapsamında otantik yiyeceklere yönelik bir inceleme [A review of authentic food within the scope of sustainable gastronomic tourism]. *Journal of Tourism and Gastronomy Studies*, *5*(2), 301-309.

Akdoğan, B. (2001). Sanat, Sanatçı, Sanat Eseri ve Ahlak [Art, Artist, Artwork and Ethics]. *Ankara Üniversitesi İlahiyat Fakültesi Dergisi*, *42*(1), 213–245.

Akgiş İlhan, Ö. (2021). The rise of digitalization in the tourism industry during COVID-19: Cyber space, destinations, and tourist experiences. In *Handbook of Research on the Impacts and Implications of COVID-19 on the Tourism Industry* (pp. 843–862). IGI Global. doi:10.4018/978-1-7998-8231-2.ch041

Akın, M. H. (2021). Yeşil bilişim uygulamalarının turizm sektörü açısından değerlendirilmesi: Kavramsal bir inceleme [Evaluation of green computing practices in terms of tourism: A conceptual evaluation]. In *2021 III. International Sustainable Tourism Congress* (pp. 319-325). ISTC.

Akyildiz, A. (2021). Tourist Behavior of People with Autism Spectrum Disorder. *Travel and Tourism Research Association: Advancing Tourism Research Globally*, *2*.

Al-Aomar, R., & Hussain, M. (2018). An assessment of adopting lean techniques in the construct of hotel supply chain. *Tourism Management*, *69*, 553–565. doi:10.1016/j.tourman.2018.06.030

Al-Aomar, R., & Hussain, M. (2019). Exploration and prioritization of lean techniques in a hotel supply chain. *International Journal of Lean Six Sigma, 10*(1), 375–396. doi:10.1108/IJLSS-10-2017-0119

Alarcón, D. M., & Cole, S. (2019). No sustainability for tourism without gender equality. *Journal of Sustainable Tourism, 27*(7), 903–919. doi:10.1080/09669582.2019.1588283

Albareda, L., & Hajikhani, A. (2019). Innovation for Sustainability: Literature Review and Bibliometric Analysis. In N. Bocken, P. Ritala, L. Albareda, & R. Verburg (Eds.), *Innovation for Sustainability: Business Transformations Towards a Better World* (pp. 35–58). Palgrave Macmillan. doi:10.1007/978-3-319-97385-2_3

Albors-Garrigos, J., Barreto, V., García-Segovia, P., Martínez-Monzó, J., & Hervás-Oliver, J. L. (2013). Creativity and innovation patterns of haute cuisine chefs. *Journal of Culinary Science & Technology, 11*(1), 19–35. doi:10.1080/15428052.2012.728978

Albuquerque, H., Costa, C., & Martins, F. (2018). The use of geographical information systems for tourism marketing purposes in Aveiro region (Portugal). *Tourism Management Perspectives, 26*, 172–178. doi:10.1016/j.tmp.2017.10.009

Alcalde-Giraudo, A., Fernández-Hernández, R., Paradinas-Márquez, C., Sánchez-González, P., & García-Muiña, F. E. (2021). Marketing approach to Nordic tourism. *Technological Forecasting and Social Change, 163*, 120441. doi:10.1016/j.techfore.2020.120441

AlFarraj, O., Alalwan, A. A., Obeidat, Z. M., Baabdullah, A., Aldmour, R., & Al-Haddad, S. (2021). Examining the impact of influencers' credibility dimensions: attractiveness, trustworthiness and expertise on the purchase intention in the aesthetic dermatology industry. *Review of International Business and Strategy*. doi:10.1108/RIBS-07-2020-0089

Ali, F., Harris, K. J., & Ryu, K. (2019). Consumers' return intentions towards a restaurant with foodborne illness outbreaks: Differences across restaurant type and consumers' dining frequency. *Food Control, 98*, 424–430. doi:10.1016/j.foodcont.2018.12.001

Ali, F., Ryu, K., & Hussain, K. (2016). Influence of Experiences on Memories, Satisfaction and Behavioral Intentions: A Study of Creative Tourism. *Journal of Travel & Tourism Marketing, 33*(1), 85–100. doi:10.1080/10548408.2015.1038418

Alkhowaiter, W. (2016). The Power of Instagram in Building Small Businesses. *Social Media: The Good, the Bad, and the Ugly, 9844*, 59-64. doi:10.1007/978-3-319-45234-0_6

Allua, S., & Thompson, C. B. (2009). Inferential statistics. *Air Medical Journal, 28*(4), 168–171. doi:10.1016/j.amj.2009.04.013 PMID:19573763

Aloni, E. (2016). Pluralizing the Sharing Economy. *Washington Law Review (Seattle, Wash.), 91*, 1397.

Alonso, A., & Liu, Y. (2011). The potential for marrying local gastronomy and wine: The case of the 'fortunate islands'. *International Journal of Hospitality Management, 30*(4), 974–981. doi:10.1016/j.ijhm.2011.02.005

Alrwajfah, M. M., Almeida-García, F., & Cortés-Macías, R. (2020). Females' perspectives on tourism's impact and their employment in the sector: The case of Petra, Jordan. *Tourism Management, 78*, 104069. doi:10.1016/j.tourman.2019.104069

Altınel, H. (2009). *Gastronomide menü yönetimi* [Menu management in gastronomy] [Yüksek Lisans Tezi, İstanbul Üniversitesi Sosyal Bilimler Enstitüsü]. Erişim adresi: http://nek.istanbul.edu.tr:4444/ekos/TEZ/44835.pdf

Aluri, A. K., & Palakurthi, R. R. (2009). A comparative study of consumer attitudes and intentions to use RFID technologies in the U.S. and European hotel industry. In *Proceedings of 27th EuroCHRIE Annual Conference* (pp. 500-511). HAAGA-HELIA University of Applied Science.

Compilation of References

Alves, C. J., Lok, T. C., Luo, Y. B., & Hao, W. (2021). *Crisis management for small business during the COVID-19 outbreak: Survival, resilience and renewal strategies of firms in Macau.* www.researchsquare.com/article/rs-34541/v1

Alvesson, M., & Sköldberg, K. (2009). *Reflexive methodology: New vistas for qualitative research* (2nd ed.). Sage.

Alwadi, A., Gawanmeh, A., Parvin, S., & Al-karaki, J. N. (2017). Smart solutions for RFID based inventory management systems: A survey. *Scalable Computing: Practice and Experience*, *18*(4), 347–360. doi:10.12694cpe.v18i4.1333

Alzubaidi, H., Slade, E. L., & Dwivedi, Y. K. (2021). Examining antecedents of consumers' pro-environmental behaviors: TPB extended with materialism and innovativeness. *Journal of Business Research*, *122*(1), 685–699. doi:10.1016/j.jbusres.2020.01.017

André, R. (2004). *Take Back the Sky: Protecting Communities in the Path of Aviation Expansion.* Retrieved on March 21, 2022, from: https://www.raeandre.com/take_back_the_sky__protecting_communities_in_the_path_of_aviation_expansion_17444.htm

Andreeva, T., & Kianto, A. (2011). Knowledge processes, knowledge-intensity and innovation: A moderated mediation analysis. *Journal of Knowledge Management*, *15*(6), 1016–1034. doi:10.1108/13673271111179343

Angelkova, T., Koteski, C., Jakovlev, Z., & Mitrevska, E. (2012). Sustainability and competitiveness of tourism. *Procedia: Social and Behavioral Sciences*, *44*, 221–227. doi:10.1016/j.sbspro.2012.05.023

Anshari, M., Almunawar, M., Masri, M., & Hamdan, M. (2019). Digital Marketplace and FinTech to Support Agriculture Sustainability. *Energy Procedia*, *156*, 234–238. doi:10.1016/j.egypro.2018.11.134

APA. (2022). *APA dictionary.* Accessible at https://dictionary.apa.org/accessible

Apostolopoulos, Y., & Sönmez, S. (2001). Working producers, leisured consumers: Women's experiences in developing regions. *Women as producers and consumers of tourism in developing regions*, 3-18.

Arasıl, T. (1991). Using of the thermal waters in the field of health [Termal Suların Sağlık Alanında Kullanımı]. *Anatolia Dergisi. Mayıs-Haziran*, *17-18*, 45–48.

Arbeláez-Campillo, D., Rojas-Bahamón, M. J., & Arbeláez-Encarnación, T. (2018). Apuntes para el debate de las categorías ciudadanía universal, derechos humanos y globalización. Notes for the debate of the categories universal citizenship, human rights and globalization. *Cuestiones Políticas*, *34*(61), 139–160.

Arbolino, R., Boffardi, R., De Simone, L., & Lopollo, G. (2021). Multi-objective optimization technique: A novel approach in tourism sustainability planning. *Journal of Environmental Management*, *285*(1), 112016. doi:10.1016/j.jenvman.2021.112016 PMID:33561732

Arbulú, I., Razumova, M., Rey-Maquieira, J., & Sastre, F. (2021). Can domestic tourism relieve the COVID-19 tourist industry crisis? The case of Spain. *Journal of Destination Marketing & Management*, *20*, 100568. doi:10.1016/j.jdmm.2021.100568

Archer, D. (2016). *Keeping its destination profitable and its people happy: Aruba's cap on all-inclusive resorts.* Retrieved on November 16, 2016, from: https://destinationthink.com/keeping-destination-profitable-people-happy-aruba-cap-on-all-inclusive-resorts/

Arıkan, R. (2011). *Research Methods and Techniques* [Araştırma Yöntem ve Teknikleri]. Nobel Akademi Publishing.

Arjona, M. F. (2020). *Sustainability in hospitality and tourism sector.* Society Publishing.

Arroyo, R., Ruiz, T., Mars, L., Rasouli, S., & Timmermans, H. (2020). Influence of values, attitudes towards transport modes and companions on travel behavior. *Transportation Research Part F: Traffic Psychology and Behaviour*, *71*, 8–22. doi:10.1016/j.trf.2020.04.002

Arslan, M. C., & Turkay, M. (2013). EOQ revisited with sustainability considerations. *Foundations of Computing and Decision Sciences*, *38*(4), 223–249. doi:10.2478/fcds-2013-0011

Artal-Tur, A., Villena-Navarro, M., & Alamá-Sabater, L. (2018). The relationship between cultural tourist behaviour and destination sustainability. *Anatolia*, *29*(2), 237–251. doi:10.1080/13032917.2017.1414444

Artar, Y., & Karabacakoğlu, Ç. (2003). *Accessible Tourism Report: Investigation of infrastructure opportunities in accommodation facilities for the development of disabled tourism in Turkey* [Engelsiz Turizm Raporu: Türkiye'de engelliler turizminin geliştirilmesine yönelik konaklama tesislerindeki altyapı imkanlarının araştırılması]. Retrieved on July 4, 2020, from: https://www.devturkiye.org/Projeler/Engelsiz-Tatil-Koyu/Engelsiz-Turizm-Raporu/

Arunanondchai, J., & Fink, C. (2006). Trade in health services in the ASEAN region. *Health Promotion International*, *21*(suppl_1), 59–66. doi:10.1093/heapro/dal052 PMID:17307958

Asaf, S. (2019, July 8). Air New Zealand rolls out measures to reduce single-use plastic waste on flights. *Business Traveller*. Retrieved on January 22, 2022, from: https://www.businesstraveller.com/business-travel/2019/07/08/air-new-zealand-rolls-out-measures-to-reduce-single-use-plastic-waste-on-flights/

Asan, K. (2022). Measuring the impacts of travel influencers on bicycle travellers. *Current Issues in Tourism*, *25*(6), 978–994. doi:10.1080/13683500.2021.1914004

Asian Development Bank. (n.d.). *Projects &Tenders*. Retrieved on September 22, 2021, from: https://www.adb.org/projects?terms=disaster

Asia-Pacific Network for Global Change Research. (n.d.). *Projects under "Risk and resilience"*. Retrieved on October 30, 2021, from: https://www.apn-gcr.org/themes/risk-and-resilience/projects-under-risk-and-resilience/

Aslan, Z. (2015). Service standards in thermal tourism enterprises [Termal Turizm İşletmelerinde Hizmet Standartları]. Turizm Sağlık ve Hukuk Sempozyumu, 23-42.

Association of Caribbean States. (n.d.). *Projects in Disaster Risk Reduction*. Retrieved on December 3, 2021, from: http://www.acs-aec.org/index.php?q=disaster-risk-reduction/projects

Ateljevic, I. (2020). Transforming the (tourism) world for good and re(generating) the potential 'new normal'. *Tourism Geographies*, *22*(3), 467–475. Advance online publication. doi:10.1080/14616688.2020.1759134

Atilgan, E., Akinci, S., Aksoy, S., & Kaynak, E. (2009). Customer-based brand equity for global brands: A multinational approach. *Journal of Euromarketing*, *18*(2), 155–132.

Atkeson, A. (2020). What will be the economic impact of COVID-19 in the US? Rough estimates of disease scenarios. *National Bureau of Economic Research*, *26*, 21–25. doi:10.3386/w26867

Atlam, H., & Wills, G. (2018). Technical aspects of blockchain and IoT. *Advances in Computers*, 115.

ATTA. (2018). *2018 Trends Report: Continued Growth, Innovative Marketing Technology*. Retrieved on May 9, 2020, from: https://www.adventuretravelnews.com/2018-trends-report-continued-growth-innovative-marketing-technology

Autio, E., Sapienza, H. J., & Almeida, J. G. (2000). Effects of age at entry, knowledge intensity, and imitability on international growth. *Academy of Management Journal*, *43*(5), 909–924.

Compilation of References

Aviation Benefits Beyond Borders. (2018). *Greener manufacturing*. Retrieved on October 7, 2021, from: https://aviationbenefits.org/environmental-efficiency/greener-manufacturing/

Aviation Benefits Beyond Borders. (2019a). *Efficient technology*. Retrieved on October 7, 2021, from: https://aviationbenefits.org/environmental-efficiency/climate-action/efficient-technology/

Aviation Benefits Beyond Borders. (2019b). *Operational improvements*. Retrieved on October 7, 2021, from: https://aviationbenefits.org/environmental-efficiency/climate-action/operational-improvements/

Aviation Benefits Beyond Borders. (2019c). *Reducing noise*. Retrieved on October 7, 2021, from: https://aviationbenefits.org/environmental-efficiency/reducing-noise/

Avruch, K. (1998). *Culture & conflict resolution*. US Institute of Peace Press.

Axelos, M., Basinskiene, L., Darcy-Vrillon, B., Ruyck, H. D., Pou, A. M., Salaseviciene, A., & Bianco, A. (2000). *Ecological Art and Ethics*. Retrieved on March 11, 2020, from: http://ecologicalart.org/ecartandet.html

Azevedo, A. (2010). Designing unique and memorable experiences: Co-creation and the surprise factor. *International Journal of Hospitality and Tourism Systems*, *3*(1).

Babu, S. S., Dixit, S., & Yadav, C. (2010). *A report on problems and prospects of accessible tourism in India*. Indian Institute of Tourism and Travel Management.

Backhaus, C., Heussler, T., & Croce, V. (2022). Planning Horizon in International Travel Decision-Making: The Role of Individual and Cultural Determinants. *Journal of Travel Research*. Advance online publication. doi:10.1177/00472875211066112

Bae, S. Y., & Chang, P. J. (2021). The effect of coronavirus disease-19 (COVID-19) risk perception on behavioural intention towards 'untact' tourism in South Korea during the first wave of the pandemic (March 2020). *Current Issues in Tourism*, *24*(7), 1017–1035. doi:10.1080/13683500.2020.1798895

Bahaire, T., & Elliott-White, M. (1999). The application of geographical information systems (GIS) in sustainable tourism planning: A review. *Journal of Sustainable Tourism*, *7*(2), 159–174. doi:10.1080/09669589908667333

Baiomy, M. A. E. A., Jones, E., Elias, A. N. E., & Dinana, T. R. (2013). Menus as Marketing Tools: Developing a Resort Hotel Restaurant Menu Typology. *Journal of Tourism Research & Hospitality*, *2*(2), 1–10. doi:10.4172/2324-8807.1000116

Baixinho, A., Santos, C., Couto, G., de Albergaria, I. S., da Silva, L. S., Medeiros, P. D., & Simas, R. M. N. (2021). Islandscapes and sustainable creative tourism: A conceptual framework and guidelines for best practices. *Land (Basel)*, *10*(12), 1–17. doi:10.3390/land10121302

Bajc, V. (2006). Collective memory and tourism: Globalizing transmission through localized experience. *Journeys*, *7*(2), 1–14. doi:10.3167/jys.2006.070201

Baker, S. R., Farrokhnia, R. A., Meyer, S., Pagel, M., & Yannelis, C. (2020). How does household spending respond to an epidemic? Consumption during the 2020 COVID-19 pandemic. *Review of Asset Pricing Studies*, *10*(4), 834–862. doi:10.1093/rapstu/raaa009

Baker, T. M., & Collier, D. A. (1999). A comparative revenue analysis of hotel yield management heuristics. *Decision Sciences*, *30*(1), 239–263. doi:10.1111/j.1540-5915.1999.tb01608.x

Bakhshi, H., McVittie, E., & Simmie, J. (2008). *Creating Innovation: Do the creative industries support innovation in the wider economy?* Nesta.

Bakker, M., Riezebos, J., & Teunter, R. H. (2012). Review of inventory systems with deterioration since 2001. *European Journal of Operational Research*, *221*(2), 275–284. doi:10.1016/j.ejor.2012.03.004

Balaban, V., & Marano, C. (2010). Medical tourism research: A systematic review. *International Journal of Infectious Diseases*, *14*, e135. doi:10.1016/j.ijid.2010.02.1784

Balasaraswathi, M., Srinivasan, K., Udayakumar, L., Sivasakthiselvan, S., & Sumithra, M. (2020). Big data analytic of contexts and cascading tourism for smart city. *Materials Today: Proceedings*. Advance online publication. doi:10.1016/j.matpr.2020.10.132

Baloglu, S., & McCleary, K. W. (1999). A model of destination image formation. *Annals of Tourism Research*, *26*(4), 868–897.

Baltacı, A. (2017). Miles-Huberman Model in Qualitative Data Analysis [Nitel veri analizinde Miles-Huberman modeli]. *A Journal of Ahi Evran University Institute of Social Sciences*, *3*(1), 1-15.

Baltacı, A. (2018). A Conceptual Review of Sampling Methods and Sample Size Problems in Qualitative Research [Nitel araştırmalarda örnekleme yöntemleri ve örnek hacmi sorunsalı üzerine kavramsal bir inceleme]. *Journal of Bitlis Eren University Institute of Social Sciences.*, *7*(1), 231–274.

Baltescu, C. A. (2016). Culinary experiences as a key tourism attraction. Case Study: Brasov County. *Bulletin of the Transilvania University of Brasov. Economic Sciences. Series V*, *9*(2), 107.

Băltescu, C. A., Neacșu, N. A., Madar, A., Boșcor, D., & Zamfirache, A. (2022). Sustainable Development Practices of Restaurants in Romania and Changes during the COVID-19 Pandemic. *Sustainability*, *14*(7), 3798. doi:10.3390u14073798

Bamberg, S. (2003). How does environmental concern influence specific environmentally related behaviors? A new answer to an old question. *Journal of Environmental Psychology*, *23*(1), 21–32. doi:10.1016/S0272-4944(02)00078-6

Bamberry, G., & Wickramasekara, R. (2012). Domestic and international strategies in the Queensland Wine Industry. *International Journal of Wine Business Research*, *24*(4), 302–318. doi:10.1108/17511061211280347

Banerjee, S. B. (2007). *Corporate Social Responsibility: The Good, the Bad and the Ugly*. Edward Elgar. doi:10.4337/9781847208552

Bansal, R., & Saini, S. (2022). Leveraging Role of Social Media Influences in Corporate World—An Overview. *Journal of Global Marketing*, *5*(1), 1–5.

Baral, M. M., & Verma, A. (2021). Analysing factors impacting the adoption of green computing in Indian universities. In S. Kumar, R. Raja, A. K. S. Kuswaha, S. Kumar, & R. K. Patra (Eds.), *Green computing and its applications* (pp. 109–130). Nova Science Publishers.

Barber, N. A., & Deale, C. (2014). Tapping mindfulness to shape hotel guests' sustainable behavior. *Cornell Hospitality Quarterly*, *55*(1), 100–114. doi:10.1177/1938965513496315

Barbier, E. B., Burgess, J., & Folke, C. (1994). *Paradise Lost? The Ecological Economics of Biodiversity*. Earthscan Publication Limited.

Barbier, E. B., Burgess, J., & Folke, C. (2019). *Paradise Lost? The ecological economics of biodiversity* (Vol. 2). Routledge. doi:10.4324/9780429342219

Barefoot, D., & Szabo, J. (2010). *Friends with benefits: A social media-marketing handbook*. William Pollock.

Barkemeyer, R. (2009). Beyond compliance—Below expectations? CSR in the context of international development. *Business Ethics (Oxford, England)*, *18*(3), 273–288. doi:10.1111/j.1467-8608.2009.01563.x

Barlow, G. L. (2002). Just-in-time: Implementation within the hotel industry—a case study. *International Journal of Production Economics*, *80*(2), 155–167. doi:10.1016/S0925-5273(02)00315-8

Compilation of References

Barman, A., Das, R., & Kanti De, P. (2021). Impact of COVID-19 in food supply chain: Disruptions and recovery strategy. *Current Research in Behavioral Sciences*, *2*, 100017. doi:10.1016/j.crbeha.2021.100017

Barrows, C. W., & Powers, T. (2008). *Introduction to in the hospitality industry*. John Wiley & Sons.

Bartoletti, R. (2010). 'Memory tourism' and commodification of nostalgia. *Tourism and Visual Culture*, *1*, 23–42.

Basak, D., Bose, A., Roy, S., Chowdhury, I. R., & Sarkar, B. C. (2021). Understanding sustainable homestay tourism as a driving factor of tourist's satisfaction through structural equation modelling: A case of Darjeeling Himalayan region, India. *Current Research in Environmental Sustainability*, *3*, 100098. doi:10.1016/j.crsust.2021.100098

Bastenegar, M., & Hassani, A. (2019). Spiritual understanding and experience in the creative tourism of gastronomy. *International Journal of Tourism and Spirituality*, *3*(2), 43–67.

Bathelt, H., Cohendet, P., Henn, S., & Simon, L. (Eds.). (2017). *The Elgar companion to innovation and knowledge creation*. Edward Elgar Publishing. doi:10.4337/9781782548522

Baydeniz, E., & Türkoğlu, T. (2021). Evaluation of applications for guests with disabled at thermal hotel enterprises: An application in Afyonkarahisar [Termal Otel İşletmelerinde Engelli Misafirlere Yönelik Uygulamaların Değerlendirilmesi: Afyonkarahisar İlinde Bir Uygulama]. *Journal of Tourism and Gastronomy Studies*, *5*(Special Issue), 442–452. doi:10.21325/jotags.2021.966

Baysal, A., & Küçükaslan, N. (2007). *Beslenme ilkeleri ve menü planlaması*. Ekin Yayınları.

Beauvoir, S. (2010). *Female second sex: Marriage age (Kadın ikinci cins: Evlilik çağı) (8.Basım)*. Payel Yayınları.

Bechky, B. A. (2003). Sharing meaning across occupational communities: The transformation of understanding on a production floor. *Organization Science*, *14*(3), 312–330. doi:10.1287/orsc.14.3.312.15162

Becken, S., & Hughey, K. F. D. (2013). Linking tourism into emergency management structures to enhance disaster risk reduction. *Tourism Management*, *36*, 77–95. doi:10.1016/j.tourman.2012.11.006

Bednárová, Ľ., Kiseľáková, D., & Onuferová, E. (2018). Competitiveness analysis of tourism in the European Union and in the Slovakia. *Geo Journal of Tourism and Geosites*, *23*(3), 759–771. doi:10.30892/gtg.23312-326

Beedasy, J., & Whyatt, D. (1999). Diverting the tourists: A spatial decision-support system for tourism planning on a developing island. *International Journal of Applied Earth Observation and Geoinformation*, *1*(3-4), 163–174. doi:10.1016/S0303-2434(99)85009-0

Beirman, D., & Van Walbeek, B. (2011). *Bounce back: Tourism risk, crisis and recovery management guide*. The Pacific Asia Travel Association.

Beladi, H., Chao, C. C., Ee, M. S., & Hollas, D. (2019). Does medical tourism promote economic growth? A cross-country analysis. *Journal of Travel Research*, *58*(1), 121–135. doi:10.1177/0047287517735909

Belias, D., Velissariou, E., Kyriakou, D., Vasiliadis, L., Mantas, C., Sdrolias, L., Aspridis, G., & Kakkos, N. (2017). The importance of Customer Relationship Management and social media in the Greek wine tourism industry. *Innovative Approaches to Tourism and Leisure*, 249–259. doi:10.1007/978-3-319-67603-6_19

Bennett, A., & Rogers, I. (2016). In the scattered fields of memory: Unofficial live music venues, intangible heritage, and the recreation of the musical past. *Space and Culture*, *19*(4), 490–501. doi:10.1177/1206331215623217

Berbekova, A., Uysal, M., & Assaf, A. G. (2021). A thematic analysis of crisis management in tourism: A theoretical perspective. *Tourism Management*, *86*, 86. doi:10.1016/j.tourman.2021.104342

Berkes, F., Colding, J., & Folke, C. (Eds.). (2008). *Navigating social-ecological systems: building resilience for complexity and change*. Cambridge University Press.

Berlin, I. T. B. (2014). *ITB world travel trends report 2014/2015*. Messe Berlin GmbH.

Berne-Manero, C., & Marzo-Navarro, M. (2020). Exploring how influencer and relationship marketing serve corporate sustainability. *Sustainability*, *12*(11), 4392. doi:10.3390u12114392

Berns, M., Townend, A., Khayat, Z., Balagopal, B., Reeves, M., Hopkins, M. S., & Kruschwitz, N. (2009). Sustainability and Competitive Advantage. *MIT Sloan Management Review*, *51*(1), 19–26.

Bettie, A. (2021, June). The 3 Pillars of Corporate Sustainability. *Investopedia*. Retrieved on October 19, 2021, from: https://www.investopedia.com/articles/investing/100515/three-pillars-corporate-sustainability.asp

Bhati, A. S., Mohammadi, Z., Agarwal, M., Kamble, Z., & Donough-Tan, G. (2020). Motivating or manipulating: The influence of health-protective behaviour and media engagement on post-COVID-19 travel. *Current Issues in Tourism*, *24*(15), 2088–2092. doi:10.1080/13683500.2020.1819970

Bhatti, Y., Taylor, A., Harris, M., Wadge, H., Escobar, E., Prime, M., Patel, H., Carter, A. W., Parston, G., Darzi, A. W., & Udayakumar, K. (2017). Global lessons in Frugal innovation to improve health care delivery in the United States. *Health Affairs*, *36*(11), 1912–1919. doi:10.1377/hlthaff.2017.0480 PMID:29137503

Biermann, F., Kanie, N., & Kim, R. E. (2017). Global governance by goal-setting: The novel approach of the UN Sustainable Development Goals. *Current Opinion in Environmental Sustainability*, *26-27*, 26–31. doi:10.1016/j.cosust.2017.01.010

Bilgin, A. (2003). Turkish Religious Foundation Encyclopedia of Islam [Türkiye Diyanet Vakfı İslam Ansiklopedisi]. Academic Press.

Bíl, M., Bílová, M., & Kubeček, J. (2012). Unified GIS database on cycle tourism infrastructure. *Tourism Management*, *33*(6), 1554–1561. doi:10.1016/j.tourman.2012.03.002

Bin Salem, S., & Jagadeesan, P. (2020). COVID-19 from food safety and biosecurity perspective. *The Open Food Science Journal*, *12*(1-2).

Biran, A., Liu, W., Li, G., & Eichhorn, V. (2014). Consuming post-disaster destinations: The case of Sichuan, China. *Annals of Tourism Research*, *47*, 1–17. doi:10.1016/j.annals.2014.03.004

Biswakarma, G. (2015). On the dimensionality of measuring tourist satisfaction towards homestay. *International Journal of Hospitality and Tourism Systems*, *8*(2), 1–13. doi:10.21863/ijhts/2015.8.2.014

Blackman, A., & Rivera, J. (2011). Producer-Level Benefits of Sustainability Certification. *Conservation Biology*, *25*(6), 1176–1185. doi:10.1111/j.1523-1739.2011.01774.x PMID:22070273

Bluck, S. (2003). Autobiographical memory: Exploring its functions in everyday life. *Memory (Hove, England)*, *11*(2), 113–123. doi:10.1080/741938206 PMID:12820825

Boatto, V., Galletto, L., Barisan, L., & Bianchin, F. (2013). The development of wine tourism in the Conegliano Valdobbiadene area. *Wine Economics and Policy*, *2*(2), 93–101. doi:10.1016/j.wep.2013.11.003

Bocken, N., Ritala, P., Albareda, L., & Verburg, R. (2019). Introduction: Innovaion for Sustainability. In N. Bocken, P. Ritala, L. Albareda, & R. Verburg (Eds.), *Innovation for Sustainability: Business Transformations Towards a Better World* (pp. 1–20). Palgrave Macmillan. doi:10.1007/978-3-319-97385-2_1

Bodkhe, U., Tanwar, S., Parekh, K., Khanpara, P., Tyagi, S., Kumar, N., & Alazab, M. (2020). Blockchain for Industry 4.0: A Comprehensive Review. In *Deep Learning Algorithms for Internet of Medical Things* (pp. 79764-79800). IEEE Access.

Boekstein, M. (2014). Tourism, Health and Changing Role of Thermal-Springs Should South Africa Reposition Its Thermal Spring Tourism Product. *African Journal of Hospitality, Tourism and Leisure*, *3*(2), 1–8.

Boers, B., & Cottrell, S. (2007). Sustainable tourism infrastructure planning: A GIS-supported approach. *Tourism Geographies: An International Journal of Tourism Space. Place and Environment*, *9*(1), 1–21.

Boireau, O. (2018). Securing the blockchain against hackers. *Network Security*, *2018*(1), 8–11. doi:10.1016/S1353-4858(18)30006-0

Boivin, M., & Tanguay, G. A. (2019). Analysis of the determinants of urban tourism attractiveness: The case of Québec City and Bordeaux. *Journal of Destination Marketing & Management*, *11*, 67–79. doi:10.1016/j.jdmm.2018.11.002

Boley, B. B., Ayscue, E., Maruyama, N., & Woosnam, K. M. (2017). Gender and Empowerment: Assessing Discrepancies Using the Resident Empowerment Through Tourism Scale. *Journal of Sustainable Tourism*, *25*(1), 113–129. doi:10.1080/09669582.2016.1177065

Bonney, M., & Jaber, M. Y. (2011). Environmentally responsible inventory model: Non-classical models for a non-classical era. *International Journal of Production Economics*, *133*(1), 43–53. doi:10.1016/j.ijpe.2009.10.033

Boons, F., & Lüdeke-Freund, F. (2013). Business models for sustainable innovation: State-of-the-art and steps towards a research agenda. *Journal of Cleaner Production*, *45*, 9–19. doi:10.1016/j.jclepro.2012.07.007

Booth, N., & Matic, J. A. (2011). Mapping and leveraging influencers in social media to shape corporate brand perceptions. *Corporate Communications*, *16*(3), 184–191. doi:10.1108/13563281111156853

Bornhorst, T., Ritchie, J. B., & Sheehan, L. (2010). Determinants of tourism success for DMOs & destinations: An empirical examination of stakeholders' perspectives. *Tourism Management*, *31*(5), 572–589.

Boroujeni, M., Saberian, M., & Li, J. (2021). Environmental impacts of COVID-19 on Victoria, Australia, witnessed two waves of coronavirus. *Environmental Science and Pollution Research International*, *28*(11), 14182–14191. doi:10.100711356-021-12556-y PMID:33506421

Botsman, R. (2014). *Collaborative economy services: Changing the way we travel*. Retrieved on July 2, 2018, from: http://www.collaborativeconsumption.com/2014/06/25/collaborative-economy-services-changing-the-way-we-travel/

Bouchery, Y., Ghaffari, A., Jemai, Z., & Dallery, Y. (2012). Including sustainability criteria into inventory models. *European Journal of Operational Research*, *222*(2), 229–240. doi:10.1016/j.ejor.2012.05.004

Bourouiba, L. (2020). Turbulent gas clouds and respiratory pathogen emissions: Potential implications for reducing transmission of COVID-19. *Journal of the American Medical Association*, *323*(18), 1837–1838. doi:10.1001/jama.2020.4756 PMID:32215590

Bouty, I., & Gomez, M. L. (2013). Creativity in Haute Cuisine: Strategic Knowledge and Practice in Gourmet Kitchens. *Journal of Culinary Science & Technology*, *11*(1), 80–95. doi:10.1080/15428052.2012.728979

Boyatzis, R. E. (1998). *Transforming qualitative information: Thematic analysis and code*. Sage.

Boyd, D. M., & Ellison, N. B. (2008). Social Network Sites: Definition, History, and Scholarship. *Journal of Computer-Mediated Communication*, *13*(1), 210–230. doi:10.1111/j.1083-6101.2007.00393.x

Brabazon, T., Winter, M., & Gandy, B. (2014). Mark(ET)ing the bottle: Using QR codes to build new wine regions. *SpringerBriefs in Business*, 87–96. doi:10.1007/978-981-287-059-9_8

Braczyk, H. J., Cooke, P., & Heidenreich, M. (Eds.). (2003). *Regional innovation systems: the role of governances in a globalized world*. Routledge. doi:10.4324/9780203330234

Bramwell, B., & Lane, B. (1993). Sustainable tourism: An evolving global approach. *Journal of Sustainable Tourism, 1*(1), 1–5. doi:10.1080/09669589309450696

Bratić, M., Radivojević, A., Stojiljković, N., Simović, O., Juvan, E., Lesjak, M., & Podovšovnik, E. (2021). Should i stay or should i go? Tourists' covid-19 risk perception and vacation behavior shift. *Sustainability (Switzerland), 13*(6), 3573. Advance online publication. doi:10.3390u13063573

Braun-Latour, K. A., Grınley, M. J., & Loftus, E. F. (2006). Tourist memory distortion. *Journal of Travel Research, 44*(4), 360–367. doi:10.1177/0047287506286721

Breiby, M. A., Duedahl, E., Øian, H., & Ericsson, B. (2020). Exploring sustainable experiences in tourism. *Scandinavian Journal of Hospitality and Tourism, 20*(4), 335–351. doi:10.1080/15022250.2020.1748706

Breier, M., Kallmuenzer, A., Clauss, T., Gast, J., Kraus, S., & Tiberius, V. (2021). The role of business model innovation in the hospitality industry during the COVID-19 crisis. *International Journal of Hospitality Management, 92*, 102723. doi:10.1016/j.ijhm.2020.102723

Brewer, P., & Sebby, G. A. (2021). The effect of online restaurant menus on consumers' purchase intentions during the COVID-19 pandemic. *Int J Hosp Manag., 94*. . doi:10.1016/j.ijhm.2020.102777

Brillat-Savarin, J. A. (1994). The physiology of taste. New York: Penguin.

Britannica, tourism topic. (n.d.). Retrieved on July 2, 2018, from: https://www.britannica.com/topic/tourism

Brix, J. (2017). Exploring knowledge creation processes as a source of organizational learning: A longitudinal case study of a public innovation project. *Scandinavian Journal of Management, 33*(2), 113–127. doi:10.1016/j.scaman.2017.05.001

Brookner, J. (2004). *Materials, Ecological Aesthetics Art in Environmental Design: Theory and Practice* (H. Strelow, Ed.). Birkhauser.

Brotherton, B. (1999). Towards a definitive view of the nature of hospitality and hospitality management. *International Journal of Contemporary Hospitality Management, 11*(4), 165–173. doi:10.1108/09596119910263568

Brouder, P. (2020). Reset redux: Possible evolutionary pathways towards the transformation of tourism in a COVID-19 world. *Tourism Geographies, 22*(3), 484–490. Advance online publication. doi:10.1080/14616688.2020.1760928

Brown, S. D., & Reavey, P. (2015). Turning around on experience: The 'expanded view' of memory within psychology. *Memory Studies, 8*(2), 131–150. doi:10.1177/1750698014558660

Brundtland, G. (1987). *Report of the World Commission on Environment and Development: Our Common Future*. Academic Press.

Brundu, B., Battino, S., & Manca, I. (2021, December). The sustainable tourism organization of rural spaces. The island of Sardinia in the era of" staycation. In *Proceedings of ICC2021-30th International Cartographic Conference, Florence (Italy)* (pp. 14-18). Academic Press.

Bruwer, J. (2003). South African wine routes: Some perspectives on the wine tourism industry's structural dimensions and wine tourism product. *Tourism Management, 24*(4), 423–435. doi:10.1016/S0261-5177(02)00105-X

Bruwer, J., & Rueger-Muck, E. (2018). Wine tourism and hedonic experience: A motivation-based experiential view. *Tourism and Hospitality Research, 19*(4), 488–502. doi:10.1177/1467358418781444

Bucak, T., & Yigit, S. (2021). The future of the chef occupation and the food and beverage sector after the COVID-19 outbreak: Opinions of Turkish chefs. *International Journal of Hospitality Management, 92*, 102682. doi:10.1016/j.ijhm.2020.102682 PMID:33071426

Buckley, R. (2012). Sustainable tourism: Research and reality. *Annals of Tourism Research*, *39*(2), 528–546. doi:10.1016/j.annals.2012.02.003

Budhathoki, B. (2013). *Impact of homestay tourism on livelihood: A case study of Ghale Gaun, Lamjung, Nepal* [Unpublish Master Thesis]. Norwegian University, Oslo, Norway.

Buhalis, D., & Law, R. (2008). Progress in information technology and tourism management: 20 years on and 10 years after the Internet—The state of eTourism research. *Tourism Management*, *29*(4), 609-623. doi:10.1016/j.tourman.2008.01.005

Buhalis, D., Eichhorn, V., Michopoulou, E., & Miller, G. (2005). Accessibility market and stakeholder analysis. University of Surrey One-Stop Shop for Accessible Tourism in Europe (OSSATE).

Buhalis, D. (1998). Strategic use of information technologies in the tourism industry. *Tourism Management*, *19*(5), 409–421. doi:10.1016/S0261-5177(98)00038-7

Buhr, N. (2002). A structuration view on the initiation of environmental reports. *Critical Perspectives on Accounting*, *13*(1), 17–38. doi:10.1016/S1045-2354(00)90441-6

Bui, H., & Filimonau, V. (2021). A recipe for sustainable development: Assessing transition of commercial foodservices towards the goal of the triple bottom line sustainability. *International Journal of Contemporary Hospitality Management*, *33*(10), 3535–3563. doi:10.1108/IJCHM-03-2021-0330

Bulchand-Gidumal, J. (2022). Post-COVID-19 recovery of island tourism using a smart tourism destination framework. *Journal of Destination Marketing & Management*, *23*, 100689. doi:10.1016/j.jdmm.2022.100689

Buonincontri, P., Morvillo, A., Okumus, F., & van Niekerk, M. (2017). Managing the experience co-creation process in tourism destinations: Empirical findings from Naples. *Tourism Management*, *62*, 264–277. doi:10.1016/j.tourman.2017.04.014

Burgess, J. (1982). Perspectives on gift exchange and hospitable behavior. *International Journal of Hospitality Management*, *1*(1), 49–57. doi:10.1016/0278-4319(82)90023-8

Bu, Y., Parkinson, J., & Thaichon, P. (2020). Digital Content Marketing as a catalyst for e-WOM in food tourism. *Australasian Marketing Journal*, *29*(2), 142–154. doi:10.1016/j.ausmj.2020.01.001

Byrd, E. T., Canziani, B., Hsieh, Y.-C., Debbage, K., & Sonmez, S. (2016). Wine tourism: Motivating visitors through core and supplementary services. *Tourism Management*, *52*, 19–29. doi:10.1016/j.tourman.2015.06.009

Caballero-Danell, S., & Mugomba, C. (2007). Medical Tourism and its Entrepreneurial Opportunities-A conceptual framework for entry into the industry. *rapport nr.: Master Thesis 2006: 91*.

Çağlayan, E. (2019). Temel sanat eğitimi dersinin gastronomi ve mutfak sanatları eğitimindeki yeri ve önemi [The place and importance of basic art education course in gastronomy and culinary arts education]. *İnsan ve Toplum Bilimleri Araştırmaları Dergisi*, *8*(4), 3084-3095.

Cahyanto, I., Pennington-Gray, L., Thapa, B., Srinivasan, S., Villegas, J., Matyas, C., & Kiousis, S. (2016). Predicting information seeking regarding hurricane evacuation in the destination. *Tourism Management*, *52*, 264–275. doi:10.1016/j.tourman.2015.06.014

Cai, L. A., & Hsu, C. H. C. (2009). Brand knowledge, trust and loyalty - A conceptual model of destination branding. In *Proceedings of the International CHRIE Conference*. University of Massachusetts Amherst.

Cai, L. A. (2002). Cooperative branding for rural destinations. *Annals of Tourism Research*, *29*(3), 720–742.

Caisarina, I., Omar, S. I., Rafie, M., & Afandi, N. A. A. (2021). The provision of travel advice to tourists visiting disaster area: The case of Banda Aceh. *IOP Conference Series. Earth and Environmental Science*, *630*(1), 012030. doi:10.1088/1755-1315/630/1/012030

Çalışır, H. (2021). *Anthropocene to the Covid-19 Epidemic*. Academic Press.

Çallı, D. S. (2015). Uluslararası seyahatlerin tarihi gelişimi ve son seyahat trendleri doğrultusunda Türkiye'nin konumu. *Turar Turizm ve Araştırma Dergisi*, *4*(1), 4–28.

Caloghirou, Y., Kastelli, I., & Tsakanikas, A. (2004). Internal capabilities and external knowledge sources: Complements or substitutes for innovative performance? *Technovation*, *24*(1), 29–39. doi:10.1016/S0166-4972(02)00051-2

Caloghirou, Y., & Protogerou, A. (2015). Knowledge-intensive entrepreneurship: Exploring a taxonomy based on the AEGIS survey. In *Dynamics of Knowledge Intensive Entrepreneurship* (pp. 119–144). Routledge.

Camilleri Mark, A. (2017). The rationale for responsible supply chain management and stakeholder engagement. *Journal of Global Responsibility*, *8*(1), 111–126. doi:10.1108/JGR-02-2017-0007

Campagna, M. (2005). GIS for sustainable development. In M. Campagna (Ed.), *GIS for sustainable development* (pp. 23–40). CRC Press. doi:10.1201/9781420037845-6

Campbell, C., & Farrell, J. R. (2020). More than meets the eye: The functional components underlying influencer marketing. *Business Horizons*, *63*(4), 469–479. doi:10.1016/j.bushor.2020.03.003

Campbell, C., & Grimm, P. E. (2019). The Challenges Native Advertising Poses: Exploring Potential Federal Trade Commission Responses and Identifying Research Needs. *Journal of Public Policy & Marketing*, *38*(1), 110–123. doi:10.1177/0743915618818576

Campos, A. C., Mendes, J., Valle, P. O. D., & Scott, N. (2018). Co-creation of tourist experiences: A literature review. *Current Issues in Tourism*, *21*(4), 369–400. doi:10.1080/13683500.2015.1081158

Cankül, D., & Kızıltaş, M. (2020). Yiyecek İçecek İşletmelerinde Tedarik Zinciri ve Blokzincir Teknolojisi. *Journal of Gastronomy, Hospitality, and Travel*, *3*(2), 244–259.

Capdevila, I., Cohendet, P., & Simon, L. (2015). Establishing New Codes for Creativity through Haute Cuisine. The Case of Ferran Adrià and elBulli. Academic Press.

Capdevila, I., Cohendet, P., & Simon, L. (2018). From a local community to a global influence. How elBulli restaurant created a new epistemic movement in the world of haute cuisine. *Industry and Innovation*, *25*(5), 526–549. doi:10.1080/13662716.2017.1327844

Cardona, G., Rodriguez-Fornells, A., Nye, H., Rifà-Ros, X., & Ferreri, L. (2020). The impact of musical pleasure and musical hedonia on verbal episodic memory. *Scientific Reports*, *10*(1), 1–13. doi:10.103841598-020-72772-3 PMID:32999309

Carius, F., & Job, H. (2019). Community involvement and tourism revenue sharing as contributing factors to the UN sustainable development goals in jozani-chwaka bay national park and biosphere reserve, zanzibar. *Journal of Sustainable Tourism*, *27*(6), 826–846. doi:10.1080/09669582.2018.1560457

Carpenter, W. (2016). *An Inside Look at Foursquare's Business Model*. Retrieved on February 15, 2016, from: https://www.investopedia.com/articles/markets/021516/inside-look-foursquares-business-model.asp

Carrera, P. M., & Bridges, J. F. (2006). Globalization and healthcare: Understanding health and medical tourism. *Expert Review of Pharmacoeconomics & Outcomes Research*, *6*(4), 447–454. doi:10.1586/14737167.6.4.447 PMID:20528514

Carruthers, B. (2006). Art, Sweet Art. *Alternatives Journal*, *32*(4/5), 24–27.

Carson, D. B., & Carson, D. A. (2019). *Disasters, market changes and 'the big smoke': Understanding the decline of remote tourism in Katherine*. Perspectives on Rural Tourism Geographies. doi:10.1007/978-3-030-11950-8_6

Carter, C., & Rogers, D. (2008). A Framework of Sustainable Supply Chain Management: Moving Toward New Theory. *International Journal of Physical Distribution & Logistics Management, 38*(5), 360–387. doi:10.1108/09600030810882816

Caru, A., & Cova, B. (2007). *Consuming Experiences: An Introduction. Consuming Experience*. Routledge.

Carvalho, N. (2012). Ecoturismo - Estudo de caso: Zmar-Eco Camping Resort. Projeto final de licenciatura, Universidade Atlântica, Portugal.

Carvalho, R. M. F., Costa, C. M. M. da, & Ferreira, A. M. A. P. (2019). Review of the theoretical underpinnings in the creative tourism research field. *Tourism & Management Studies, 15*(SI), 11–22. doi:10.18089/tms.2019.15SI02

Carvalho, F. (2021). The status of resource management and certification in tourism sustainability implementation literature. *Journal of Spatial and Organizational Dynamics, 9*(2), 91–114.

Casanova, L. M., Jeon, S., Rutala, W. A., Weber, D. J., & Sobsey, M. D. (2010). Effects of air temperature and relative humidity on coronavirus survival on surfaces. *Applied and Environmental Microbiology, 76*(9), 2712–2717. doi:10.1128/AEM.02291-09 PMID:20228108

Caswell, M. (2019, June 5). SAS to stop inflight duty-free sales. *Business Traveller*.

Cave, P., & Kilic, S. (2010). The role of women in tourism employment with special reference to Antalya, Turkey. *Journal of Hospitality Marketing & Management, 19*(3), 280–292. doi:10.1080/19368621003591400

Celhay, F., Cheng, P., Masson, J., & Li, W. (2020). Package graphic design and communication across cultures: An investigation of Chinese consumers' interpretation of imported wine labels. *International Journal of Research in Marketing, 37*(1), 108–128. doi:10.1016/j.ijresmar.2019.07.004

Centers for Disease Control and Prevention. (2020). *COVID-19 surveillance and data analytics*. Retrieved on April 10, 2020, from: https://www.cdc.gov/coronavirus/2019-ncov/php/open-america/surveillance-data-analytics.html

Centre for Research on the Epidemiology of Disasters. (2016). *Ongoing projects: Emergency events database (EM-DAT)*. Retrieved on March 1, 2022, from: https://www.cred.be/projects/EM-DAT

Centre for Research on the Epidemiology of Disasters. (n.d.). *EM-DAT The international disaster database: Guidelines*. Retrieved on March 1, 2022, from: https://www.emdat.be/guidelines

Çetinsöz, B. C., & Ege, Z. (2013). Impacts of perceived risks on tourists' revisit intentions. *An International Journal of Tourism and Hospitality Research, 24*(2), 173–187. doi:10.1080/13032917.2012.743921

Çetintaş, H., & Bektaş, Ç. (2008). Türkiye'de turizm ve ekonomik büyüme arasındaki kısa ve uzun dönemli ilişkiler. *Anatolia: Turizm Araştırmaları Dergisi, 19*(1), 37–44.

ÇevreOnline. (2015). *Elektromanyetik kirlilik*. https://cevreonline.com/elektromanyetik-kirlilik/

Chakraborty, B. (2019). Homestay and women empowerment: A case study of women managed tourism product in Kasar Devi, Uttarakhand, India. *Tourism International Scientific Conference, 4*(1), 202–216. http://www.tisc.rs/proceedings/index.php/hitmc/article/view/252

Chakraborty, S., Chakravorty, T., & Bhatt, V. (2021, March). IoT and AI driven sustainable practices in airlines as enabler of passenger confidence, satisfaction and positive. In *Conference Proceedings, International Conference on Artificial Intelligence and Smart Systems (ICAIS)* (pp. 1421-1425). IEEE. 10.1109/ICAIS50930.2021.9395850

Chandralal, L., & Valenzuela, F. R. (2013). Exploring memorable tourism experiences: Antecedents and behavioural outcomes. *Journal of Economics. Business and Management*, *1*(2), 177–181.

Chan, E. S., Hon, A. H., Chan, W., & Okumus, F. (2014). What drives employees' intentions to implement green practices in hotels? The role of knowledge, awareness, concern and ecological behaviour. *International Journal of Hospitality Management*, *40*, 20–28. doi:10.1016/j.ijhm.2014.03.001

Chang, L.-L., Backman, K. F., & Huang, Y. C. (2014). Creative tourism: A preliminary examination of creative tourists' motivation, experience, perceived value and revisit intention. *International Journal of Culture, Tourism and Hospitality Research*, *8*(4), 401–419. doi:10.1108/IJCTHR-04-2014-0032

Chan, J. F.-W., Yuan, S., Kok, K. H., Wang, K. K.-W., Chu, H., & Yang, J. (2015). A familial cluster of pneumonia associated with the 2019 novel coronavirus indicating person-to-person transmission: A study of a family cluster. *Lancet*, *395*(10223), 514–523. doi:10.1016/S0140-6736(20)30154-9 PMID:31986261

Chan, W. W., Yeung, S., Chan, E. S. W., & Li, D. (2013). Hotel heat pump hot water sys-tems: Impact assessment and analytic hierarchy process. *International Journal of Contemporary Hospitality Management*, *25*(3), 428–446. doi:10.1108/09596111311311053

Charlier, R. H., & Chaineux, M.-C. P. (2009). The Healing Sea: A Sustainable Coastal Ocean Resource: Thalassotherapy. *Journal of Coastal Research*, *25*(4), 838–856. doi:10.2112/08A-0008.1

Chatti, W. (2021). Moving towards environmental sustainability: Information and communication technology (ICT), freight transport, and CO2 emissions. *Heliyon*, *7*(10), e08190. doi:10.1016/j.heliyon.2021.e08190 PMID:34729432

Chatzigeorgiou, C. (2017). Modelling the impact of social media influencers on behavioural intentions of millennials: The case of tourism in rural areas in Greece. *Journal of Tourism, Heritage & Services Marketing*, *3*(2), 25-29. doi:10.5281/zenodo.1209125

Chaulagain, S., Wiitala, J., & Fu, X. (2019). The impact of country image and destination image on US tourists' travel intention. *Journal of Destination Marketing & Management*, *12*(January), 1–11. doi:10.1016/j.jdmm.2019.01.005

Chaulagain, T. R. (2021). *Population and households characteristics*. In Central Bureau of Statistics.

Chau, P. Y. (1996). An empirical assessment of a modified technology acceptance model. *Journal of Management Information Systems*, *13*(2), 185–204. doi:10.1080/07421222.1996.11518128

Chen, C. F., & Chou, S. H. (2019). Antecedents and consequences of perceived coolness for Generation Y in the context of creative tourism - A case study of the Pier 2 Art Center in Taiwan. *Tourism Management*, *72*(February), 121–129. doi:10.1016/j.tourman.2018.11.016

Chen, C. T., Cheng, C. C., & Hsu, F. S. (2015). GRSERV scale: An effective tool for measuring consumer perceptions of service quality in green restaurants. *Total Quality Management and Business Excellence*, *26*(3-4), 355-367.

Chen, C. T. (2000). Extensions of the TOPSIS for group decision-making under fuzzy environment. *Fuzzy Sets and Systems*, *114*(1), 1–9. doi:10.1016/S0165-0114(97)00377-1

Chen, C., Song, M., & Heo, G. E. (2018). A scalable and adaptive method for finding semantically equivalent cue words of uncertainty. *Journal of Informetrics*, *12*(1), 158–180. doi:10.1016/j.joi.2017.12.004

Chen, J., Cui, F., Balezentis, T., Streimikiene, D., & Jin, H. (2021). What drives international tourism development in the Belt and Road Initiative? *Journal of Destination Marketing & Management*, *19*, 19. doi:10.1016/j.jdmm.2020.100544

Chen, L. J., & Chen, W. P. (2015). Push–pull factors in international birders' travel. *Tourism Management*, *48*, 416–425. doi:10.1016/j.tourman.2014.12.011

Chen, M. F., & Tung, P. J. (2014). Developing an extended theory of planned behavior model to predict consumers' intention to visit green hotels. *International Journal of Hospitality Management*, *36*(4), 221–230. doi:10.1016/j.ijhm.2013.09.006

Chen, R. J. (2007). Geographic information systems (GIS) applications in retail tourism and teaching curriculum. *Journal of Retailing and Consumer Services*, *14*(4), 289–295. doi:10.1016/j.jretconser.2006.07.004

Chen, T. F. (2013). Applying FEID technology in tourism industry: The case study of hotel in Taipei. *Advanced Materials Research*, *630*, 439–445. doi:10.4028/www.scientific.net/AMR.630.439

Chen, X., Benjaafar, S., & Elomri, A. (2013). The carbon-constrained EOQ. *Operations Research Letters*, *41*(2), 172–179. doi:10.1016/j.orl.2012.12.003

Chen, X., Cheng, Z. F., & Kim, G. B. (2020). Make it memorable: Tourism experience, fun, recommendation and revisit intentions of Chinese outbound tourists. *Sustainability*, *12*(5), 1904. doi:10.3390u12051904

Cheong, Y. S., Seah, C. S., Loh, Y. X., & Loh, L. H. (2021, September). Artificial Intelligence (Ai) In The Food And Beverage Industry: Improves The Customer Experience. In *2021 2nd International Conference on Artificial Intelligence and Data Sciences (AiDAS)* (pp. 1-6). IEEE.

Chesbrough, H. (2006). Open innovation: a new paradigm for understanding industrial innovation. *Open innovation: Researching a new paradigm*, *400*, 0-19.

Chew, Y. E. T., & Jahari, S. A. (2014). Destination image as a mediator between perceived risks and revisit intention: A case of post-disaster Japan. *Tourism Management*, *40*, 382–393. doi:10.1016/j.tourman.2013.07.008

Chhabra, A., Munjal, M., Mishra, P. C., Singh, K., Das, D., Kuhar, N., & Vats, M. (2021). Medical tourism in the Covid-19 era: Opportunities, challenges and the way ahead. *Worldwide Hospitality and Tourism Themes*, *13*(5), 660–665. doi:10.1108/WHATT-05-2021-0078

Chi, H-K. (2011). The application of the technology acceptance model and theory of reasoned action on the molecular gastronomy message. *Journal of Global Business Management*.

Chiang, C., & Jogaratnam, G. (2005). Why do women travel solo for purposes of leisure? *Journal of Vacation Marketing*, *12*(1), 59–70. doi:10.1177/1356766706059041

Chien, P. M., Sharifpour, M., Ritchie, B. W., & Watson, B. (2017). Travelers' Health Risk Perceptions and Protective Behavior: A Psychological Approach. *Journal of Travel Research*, *56*(6), 744–759. doi:10.1177/0047287516665479

Choi, S., & Kimes, S. E. (2002). Electronic distribution channels' effect on hotel revenue management. *The Cornell Hotel and Restaurant Administration Quarterly*, *43*(3), 23–31. doi:10.1177/0010880402433002

Chokhani, S. (2021, November 30). *How airports in India contribute to aviation's sustainability goals*. ICF. Retrieved on March 4, 2022, from: https://www.icf.com/insights/transportation/airports-contribute-india-sustainability-goals

Chopra, A., Avhad, V., & Jaju, A. S. (2021). Influencer marketing: An exploratory study to identify antecedents of consumer behavior of millennial. *Business Perspectives and Research*, *9*(1), 77–91. doi:10.1177/2278533720923486

Cho, S. J., Lee, J. Y., & Winters, J. V. (2020). *COVID-19 Employment status impacts on food sector workers. 13334: 1*. ZA Discussion.

CIAL. (2017). *CIAL will double solar power plant capacity by February: Chief Minister*. https://cial.aero/Pressroom/newsdetails.aspx?news_id=381&news_status=A

Çiçek, D., Zencir, E., & Kozak, N. (2017). Women in Turkish tourism. *Journal of Hospitality and Tourism Management*, *31*, 228–234. doi:10.1016/j.jhtm.2017.03.006

Çiftçi, E., & Çoksuer, F. (2020). Novel Coronavirus Infection: COVID-19. *Flora Journal of Infectious Diseases and Clinical Microbiology*, *25*(1), 9–18.

Clarke, A., & Chen, W. (2009). *International Hospitality Management*. Routledge. doi:10.4324/9780080547312

Cockburn, I. M., & Henderson, R. M. (1998). Absorptive capacity, coauthoring behavior, and the organization of research in drug discovery. *The Journal of Industrial Economics*, *46*(2), 157–182. doi:10.1111/1467-6451.00067

Cohen, B. (2014). *Smart City*. Retrieved on July 8, 2022, from: https://www.smart-circle.org/category/smart-city/

Cohen, E. (2002). Authenticity, equity and sustainability in tourism. *Journal of Sustainable Tourism*, *10*(4), 267–276. doi:10.1080/09669580208667167

Cohen, S. A., & Cohen, E. (2019). New directions in the sociology of tourism. *Current Issues in Tourism*, *22*(2), 153–172. doi:10.1080/13683500.2017.1347151

Coleman-Jensen, A., Rabbitt, M. P., Gregory, C. A., & Singh, A. (2019). Household Food Security in the United States in 2018. United States Department of Agriculture (USDA).

Collins, C. (2020). 08, 07). Productivity in a pandemic. *Science*, *369*(6504), 603. doi:10.1126cience.abe1163 PMID:32764040

Cömert, M., & Yeşilyurt, B. (2021). The impact of the changes caused by the Covid-19 pandemic on consumer behaviors on food and beverage businesses. *Journal of Tourism and Gastronomy Studies*, *9*(3), 1622–1638. doi:10.21325/jotags.2021.859

Commission of the European Communities. (2001). *A sustainable Europe for a better World: A European Union strategy for sustainable development*. Communication From The Commission. Retrieved on September 22, 2021, from: https://eur-lex.europa.eu/legal-content/EN/TXT/PDF/?uri=CELEX:52001DC0264&from=EN

Communiqué on the Implementation of the Regulation on the Qualifications of Tourism Facilities [Turizm Tesislerinin Niteliklerine İlişkin Yönetmeliğin Uygulanmasina Dair Tebliğ (Tebliğ No: 2019/1)]. (n.d.). Retrieved on October 19, 2020, from: https://www.resmigazete.gov.tr/eskiler/2019/11/20191127-6.htm

Cond'e Nast Traveller. (2020). *Himachal pradesh reopens for tourists, but many kullu- manali hotels to stay closed*. Retrieved on September 05, 2020, from: https://www.cntrav eller.in/story/himachal-pradesh-covid-19-negative-test-minimum-5-day-booking-travel-new-rules-2020/

Connell, J. (2013). Medical tourism in the Caribbean islands: A cure for economies in crisis? *Island Studies Journal*, *8*(1), 115–130. doi:10.24043/isj.280

Constantinides, E. (2014). Foundations of Social Media Marketing. *Procedia: Social and Behavioral Sciences*, *148*(1), 40–57. doi:10.1016/j.sbspro.2014.07.016

Contreras, O. F., Carrillo, J., & Alonso, J. (2012). Local Entrepreneurship within Global Value Chains: A Case Study in the Mexican Automotive Industry. *World Development*, *40*(5), 1013–1023. doi:10.1016/j.worlddev.2011.11.012

Cooke, P., & Schwartz, D. (2007). Key drivers of contemporary innovation and creativity. *European Planning Studies*, *15*(9), 1139–1141. doi:10.1080/09654310701528997

Cooper, C. (2015). Managing tourism knowledge. *Tourism Recreation Research*, *40*(1), 107–119. doi:10.1080/02508281.2015.1006418

Cordeiro, I. (2008). *Instrumentos de avaliação da sustentabilidade do turismo: Uma análise crítica* [Master's Thesis]. Universidade Nova de Lisboa, Portugal.

CoronaBoard. (2022). Retrieved on July 7, 2022, from: https://coronaboard.com/global/

Correia, L., Gouveia, S., & Martins, P. (2019). The European wine export cycle. *Wine Economics and Policy*, 8(1), 91–101. doi:10.1016/j.wep.2019.04.001

Costa, C., Carvalho, I., & Breda, Z. (2011). Gender inequalities in tourism employment: The Portuguese case. *Revista Turismo & Desenvolvimento*, (15), 39–54.

Costa, G., Glinia, E., Goudas, M., & Antoniou, P. (2004). Recreational services in resort hotels: Customer satisfaction aspects. *Journal of Sport & Tourism*, 9(2), 117–126. doi:10.1080/14775080410001732541

Cotterell, D., Hales, R., Arcodia, C., & Ferreira, J.-A. (2019). Overcommitted to tourism and under committed to sustainability: The urgency of teaching "strong sustainability" in tourism courses. *Journal of Sustainable Tourism*, 27(7), 882–902. doi:10.1080/09669582.2018.1545777

Coudounaris, D. N., & Sthapit, E. (2017). Antecedents of memorable tourism experience related to behavioral intentions. *Psychology and Marketing*, 34(12), 1084–1093.

Cowan, N. (2008). *What are the differences between long-term, short-term, and working memory?* (Vol. 169). Progress in Brain Research. doi:10.1016/S0079-6123(07)00020-9

Cranfield, J. A. (2020). Framing Consumer Food Demand Responses In A Viral Pandemic. *Canadian Journal of Agricultural Economics/Revue canadienne d'agroeconomie*, 68(2), 151-156.

Crick, J. M., & Crick, D. (2021). Coopetition and family-owned wine producers. *Journal of Business Research*, 135, 319–336. doi:10.1016/j.jbusres.2021.06.046

Crick, J. M., Crick, D., & Tebbett, N. (2020). Competitor orientation and value co-creation in sustaining rural New Zealand wine producers. *Journal of Rural Studies*, 73, 122–134. doi:10.1016/j.jrurstud.2019.10.019

Crompton, J. L. (1979). An Assessment of the image of Mexico as a vacation destination and the influence of geographical location upon that image. *Journal of Travel Research*, 17(4), 18–23.

Crosby, M., Nachiappan, Pattanayak, P., Verma, S., & Kalyanaraman, V. (2016). BlockChain Technology: Beyond Bitcoin. *Applied Innovation Review*, 2, 6–19.

Csapó, J. (2012). The role and importance of cultural tourism in modern tourism industry. In M. Kasimoglu (Ed.), *Strategies for Tourism Industry - Micro and Macro Perspectives* (pp. 201–232). IntechOpen.

CSRBox. (2020). *SpiceJet*. Retrieved on November 11, 2021, from: https://csrbox.org/India_Company_Haryana-SpiceJet-Limited_6243

Cusin, J., & Passebois-Ducros, J. (2015). Appropriate persistence in a project: The case of the Wine Culture and Tourism Centre in Bordeaux. *European Management Journal*, 33(5), 341–353. doi:10.1016/j.emj.2015.04.001

Cusumano, M. A. (2015). How traditional firms must compete in the sharing economy. *Communications of the ACM*, 58(1), 32–34. doi:10.1145/2688487

Dadashpour Moghaddam, M., Ahmadzadeh, H., & Valizadeh, R. (2022). A GIS-Based Assessment of Urban Tourism Potential with a Branding Approach Utilizing Hybrid Modeling. *Spatial Information Research*, 2022(3), 1–18. doi:10.100741324-022-00439-4

Dahlstrom, M. F. (2014). Using narratives and storytelling to communicate science with nonexpert audiences. *Proceedings of the National Academy of Sciences of the United States of America*, *111*(supplement_4), 13614–13620. doi:10.1073/pnas.1320645111 PMID:25225368

Dai, F., Wang, D., & Kirillova, K. (2022). Travel inspiration in tourist decision making. *Tourism Management*, 90.

Damanik, J., & Yusuf, M. (2022). Effects of perceived value, expectation, visitor management, and visitor satisfaction on re-visit intention to Borobudur Temple, Indonesia. *Journal of Heritage Tourism*, *17*(2), 174–189. doi:10.1080/1743873X.2021.1950164

Damar, M., & Gökşen, Y. (2018). Yeşil bilişim yaklaşımıyla kullanıcı ve kurum odaklı enerji yönetim sistemi. *Dokuz Eylül Üniversitesi Mühendislik Fakültesi Fen ve Mühendislik Dergisi*, *20*(58), 259–274. doi:10.21205/deufmd.2018205821

Darcy, C., Hill, J., McCabe, T. J., & McGovern, P. (2014). A consideration of organisational sustainability in the SME context: A resource-based view and composite model. *European Journal of Training and Development*, *38*(5), 398–414. doi:10.1108/EJTD-10-2013-0108

Darcy, S., & Buhalis, D. (2011). Introduction: From disabled tourists to accessible tourism. In S. Buhalis & S. Darcy (Eds.), *Accessible Tourism: Concepts and Issues* (pp. 1–20). Channel View Publications Ltd.

Darnell, M., Subbrao, K., Feinstone, S., & Taylor, D. (2004). Inactivation of the coronavirus that induces severe acute respiratory syndrome, SARS-CoV. *Journal of Virological Methods*, *121*(1), 85–91. doi:10.1016/j.jviromet.2004.06.006 PMID:15350737

Darwazeh, D., Clarke, A., & Wilson, J. (2021). Framework for Establishing a Sustainable Medical Facility: A Case Study of Medical Tourism in Jordan. *WORLD (Oakland, Calif.)*, *2*(3), 351–373. doi:10.3390/world2030022

Daryanto, Y., Wee, H., & Wu, K. (2021). Revisiting sustainable EOQ model considering carbon emission. *International Journal of Manufacturing Technology and Management*, *35*(1), 1–11. doi:10.1504/IJMTM.2021.114697

Dasgupta, S., Granger, M., & McGarry, N. (2002). User acceptance of e-collaboration technology: An extension of the technology acceptance model. *Group Decision and Negotiation*, *11*(2), 87–100. doi:10.1023/A:1015221710638

Davis, F. D. (1989). Perceived usefulness, perceived ease of use, and user acceptance of information technology. *Management Information Systems Quarterly*, *13*(3), 319–340. doi:10.2307/249008

Davis, M. M., Aquilano, N., & Chase, R. (2003). *Fundamentals of Operations Management*. McGraw-Hill Irwin.

De Bruin, A., & Jelinčić, D. A. (2016). Toward extending creative tourism: Participatory experience tourism. *Tourism Review*, *71*(1), 57–66. doi:10.1108/TR-05-2015-0018

de Freitas Coelho, M., & de Gosling, M. S. (2020). The essence of memorable experience. In S. K. Dixit (Ed.), *The Routledge Handbook of Tourism Experience Management and Marketing* (pp. 88–98). doi:10.4324/9780429203916-7

de Freitas Coelho, M., de Sevilha Gosling, M., & de Almeida, A. S. A. (2018). Tourism experiences: Core processes of memorable trips. *Journal of Hospitality and Tourism Management*, *37*, 11–22. doi:10.1016/j.jhtm.2018.08.004

De Solier, I. (2010). Liquid nitrogen pistachios: Molecular gastronomy, elBulli and foodies. *European Journal of Cultural Studies*, *13*(2), 155–170. doi:10.1177/1367549409352275

De Urioste-Stone, S., McLaughlin, W. J., Daigle, J. J., & Fefer, J. P. (2018). Applying case study methodology to tourism research. In *Handbook of research methods for tourism and hospitality management*. Edward Elgar Publishing. doi:10.4337/9781785366284.00042

De Veirman, M., Cauberghe, V., & Hudders, L. (2017). Marketing through Instagram influencers: The impact of number of followers and product divergence on brand attitude. *International Journal of Advertising, 36*(5), 798–828. doi:10.1080/02650487.2017.1348035

Dean, D., & Suhartanto, D. (2019). The formation of visitor behavioral intention to creative tourism: The role of push–Pull motivation. *Asia Pacific Journal of Tourism Research, 24*(5), 393–403. doi:10.1080/10941665.2019.1572631

Dean, D., Suhartanto, D., & Kusdibyo, L. (2019). Predicting Destination Image in Creative Tourism: A Comparative between Tourists and Residents. *International Journal of Applied Business Research, 1*(01), 1–15. doi:10.35313/ijabr.v1i01.36

Dedeoğlu, B. B., & Boğan, E. (2021). The motivations of visiting upscale restaurants during the covid-19 pandemic: The role of risk perception and trust in government. *International Journal of Hospitality Management, 95*, 102905. doi:10.1016/j.ijhm.2021.102905

Dedeoğlu, B. B., Mariani, M., Shi, F., & Okumus, B. (2022). The impact of COVID-19 on destination visit intention and local food consumption. *British Food Journal, 124*(2), 634–653. doi:10.1108/BFJ-04-2021-0421

DEFRA. (2018). *Horticulture Statistics 2018*. Retrieved on September 11, 2021, from: https://assets.publishing.service.gov.uk/government/uploads/system/uploads/attachment_data/file/1003952/hort-report-01aug19.pdf

Delgado, M. (2020). The co-location of innovation and production in clusters. *Industry and Innovation, 27*(8), 842–870. doi:10.1080/13662716.2019.1709419

DeLorenzo, J., & Techera, E. J. (2018). Ensuring good governance of marine wildlife tourism: A case study of ray-based tourism at Hamelin Bay, Western Australia. *Asia Pacific Journal of Tourism Research, 24*(2), 121–135. doi:10.1080/10941665.2018.1541186

Demirbilek, S. (2007). A sociological study of gender discrimination. *Finance Political & Economic Comments, 44*(511).

Demir, O., & Esen, A. (2021). Destructive Economic Effects of Covid 19 and Transformation Need in Turkish Economy. *Journal of Emerging Economies and Policy, 6*(1), 88–105.

Deng, S. M., & Burnett, J. (2002). Energy use and management in hotels in Hong Kong. *IJHM, 21*(4), 371–380.

Deng, W. (2007). Using a revised importance-performance analysis approach: The case of Taiwanese hot springs tourism. *Tourism Management, 28*(5), 1274–1284. doi:10.1016/j.tourman.2006.07.010

Denizer, D. (2005). *Food and Beverage Management in Hospitality Businesses* [Konaklama İşletmelerinde Yiyecek ve İçecek Yönetimi]. Detay Publishing.

Desfiandi, A., & Singagerda, F. S. (2019). Destination Choices in Travel Decisions. *Scholars Bulletin, 05*(10), 593–603. doi:10.36348b.2019.v05i10.008

Dettori, A. (2019). Sustainability as a matrix of experiential marketing. *International Journal of Marketing Studies, 11*(2), 29–37. doi:10.5539/ijms.v11n2p29

Devi, N. L. N. S., & Suartana, I. W. (2014). Analisis technology acceptance model (TAM) terhadap penggunaan sistem informasi di Nusa Dua Beach Hotel & SPA. *E-Journal Akuntansi, 6*(1), 167–184.

Dewald, B., Bruin, B. J., & Jang, Y. J. (2014). US consumer attitudes towards "green" restaurants. *Anatolia, 25*(2), 171–180. doi:10.1080/13032917.2013.839457

Dey, K., & Shekhawat, U. (2021). Blockchain for sustainable e-agriculture: Literature review, architecture for data management, and implications. *Journal of Cleaner Production, 316*, 1–17. doi:10.1016/j.jclepro.2021.128254

Dhiman, S. (2008). Products, People, and Planet: The Triple Bottom-Line Sustainability Imperative. *Journal of Global Business Issues*, *2*(2), 51–57.

Dhirasasna, N. N., Becken, S., & Sahin, O. (2020). A systems approach to examining the drivers and barriers of renewable energy technology adoption in the hotel sector in Queensland, Australia. *Journal of Hospitality and Tourism Management*, *42*, 153–172. doi:10.1016/j.jhtm.2020.01.001

Dias, J. (2016). Environmental sustainability measurement in the Travel & Tourism Competitiveness Index: An empirical analysis of its reliability. *Ecological Indicators*, *73*, 589–596. doi:10.1016/j.ecolind.2016.10.008

Diaz-Parra, I., & Jover, J. (2020). Overtourism, place alienation and the right to the city: Insights from the historic centre of seville, Spain. *Journal of Sustainable Tourism*, *29*(2–3), 158–175.

Dickson, A., Adu-Agyem, J., & Emad Kamil, H. (2018). Theoretical and conceptual framework: Mandatory ingredients of quality research. *International Journal of Scientific Research*, *7*(1), 438–441.

Dietz, S., & Neumayer, E. (2007). Weak and strong sustainability in the SEEA: Concepts and measurement. *Ecological Economics*, *61*(4), 617–626. doi:10.1016/j.ecolecon.2006.09.007

Digiesi, S., Mossa, G., & Mummolo, G. (2013). Supply lead time uncertainty in a Sustainable Order Quantity inventory model. *Management and Production Engineering Review*, *4*(4), 15–27. doi:10.2478/mper-2013-0034

Dilsiz, B. (2010). *Türkiye'de Gastronomi ve Turizm (İstanbul Örneği)* [Gastronomy and Tourism in Turkey (Istanbul Example)]. Yüksek Lisans Tezi. İstanbul Üniversitesi Sosyal Bilimler Enstitüsü.

Dimitrov, N., Koteski, C., & Jakovlev, Z. (2018, January). Analysis tourist trends of the Republic of Bulgaria in the Republic of Macedonia. *SocioBrains*, (41), 130–137.

Dinh, T., Liu, R., Zhang, M., Chen, G., Ooi, B., & Wang, J. (2018). *Untangling Blockchain: A Data Processing View of Blockchain Systems. IEEE Transactions on Knowledge and Data Engineering*.

DiPietro, B., R., C. Y., & Partlow, C. (2013). Green practices in upscale foodservice operations: Customer perceptions and purchase intentions. *International Journal of Contemporary Hospitality Management*, *25*(5), 779–796. doi:10.1108/IJCHM-May-2012-0082

Disaster and Emergency Management Presidency of Türkiye [AFAD]. (n.d.a). *Projelerimiz*. Retrieved on September 22, 2021, from: https://www.afad.gov.tr/projelerimiz

Disaster and Emergency Management Presidency of Türkiye [AFAD]. (n.d.b). *Afete Hazır Türkiye*. Retrieved on September 22, 2021, from: https://www.afad.gov.tr/afete-hazir-turkiye

Disaster and Emergency Management Presidency of Türkiye. (2022). *81 İlde Eş Zamanlı Deprem Tatbikatı Gerçekleştirildi*. Retrieved on May 2, 2022, from: https://www.afad.gov.tr/81-ilde-es-zamanli-deprem-tatbikati-gerceklestirildii-merkezic-erik

Discover Hospitality. (2015). *What is Hospitality?* Retrieved on July 2, 2018, from: https://web.archive.org/web/20150814071021/http://discoverhospitality.com.au/what-is-hospitality

Dixon, S. (2022a, June 15). *Social network penetration worldwide from 2018 to 2027*. https://www.statista.com/statistics/260811/social-network-penetration-worldwide/#:~:text=In%202021%2C%20approximately%2056%20percent,amounted%20to%204.59%20billion%20users

Dixon, S. (2022b, July 26). *Most popular social networks worldwide as of January 2022, ranked by number of monthly active users*. https://www.statista.com/statistics/272014/global-social-networks-ranked-by-number-of-users/

Compilation of References

Dixon, S. (2022c, September 16). *Number of social media users worldwide from 2018 to 2027*. https://www.statista.com/statistics/278414/number-of-worldwide-social-network-users/

Doğan, H., & Bilici, N. S. (2020). A Different Perspective to Rural Development Approach: Pro-Poor Tourism and Elazig Case [Kırsal Kalkınma Yaklaşımına Farklı Bir Bakış: Yoksul Yanlısı Turizm ve Elazığ İli Örneği]. *Bartin Orman Fakültesi Dergisi*, 22(2), 332–340.

Doğdubay, M., & Saatçi, G. (2014). *Menu Engineering* [Menü Mühendisliği]. Detay Publishing.

Doğru, A. (2010). *Glass ceiling barriers for woman employees and its effect on the job satisfaction: An example from Afyon Kocatepe University Faculty of meicine Master Thesis* [Kadın çalışanların cam tavan engelleri ve iş tatminine etkisi: Afyon Kocatepe Üniversitesi tıp fakültesi örneği)]. Yüksek lisans tezi, Dumlupınar Üniversitesi, Sosyal Bilimler Enstitüsü, İşletme Anabilim Dalı, Kütahya.

Dogruel, L., Joeckel, S., & Bowman, N. D. (2015). The use and acceptance of new media entertainment technology by elderly users: Development of an expanded technology acceptance model. *Behaviour & Information Technology*, 34(11), 1052–1063. doi:10.1080/0144929X.2015.1077890

Doğrul, H. G. (2007). *Determinants of female labour supply in the urban labour markets and the effects of female labour supply on the wage structure: An application to Turkey [Kentsel alanlarda kadın işgücü arzının belirleyicileri ve kadın işgücü arzının ücret yapısı üzerindeki etkisi: Türkiye üzerine bir uygulama]*. Yayınlanmamış Doktora Tezi, Dumlupınar Üniversitesi Sosyal Bilimler Enstitüsü.

Dolnicar, S., & Zare, S. (2020). COVID19 and airbnb-disrupting the disruptor. *Annals of Tourism Research*, 102961. Advance online publication. doi:10.1016/j.annals.2020.102961 PMID:32834218

Domene, M. (2013). El Bulli: Contemporary intersections between food, science, art and late capitalism. *Barcelona Investigación Arte Creación*, 1(1), 100–126. doi:10.17583/brac.2013.v1i1.a611.100-126

Domi, S., & Belletti, G. (2022). The role of origin products and networking on agritourism performance: The case of Tuscany. *Journal of Rural Studies*, 90, 113–123. doi:10.1016/j.jrurstud.2022.01.013

Donaldson, T. (1996). Values in tension: Ethics away from home. *Harvard Business Review*, 74, 48–62.

Doyle, C. (2021, June 1). Qatar Airways highlights environmental sustainability initiatives. *Aviation Business News*. Retrieved on November 8, 2021, from: https://www.aviationbusinessnews.com/cabin/airlines/qatar-airways-group-highlights-environmental-sustainability-initiatives/

Drăghici, C. C., Diaconu, D., Teodorescu, C., Pintilii, R. D., & Ciobotaru, A. M. (2016). Health tourism contribution to the structural dynamics of the territorial systems with tourism functionality. *Procedia Environmental Sciences*, 32, 386–393. doi:10.1016/j.proenv.2016.03.044

Dredge, D., & Gyimóthy, S. (2015). The collaborative economy and tourism: Critical perspectives, questionable claims and silenced voices. *Tourism Recreation Research*, 40(3), 286–302. doi:10.1080/02508281.2015.1086076

Droffelaar, B. V. (2021). Episodic memories of wilderness experiences foster sustainable leadership style transformation. *Journal of Management Development*, 40(6), 486–502. doi:10.1108/JMD-12-2020-0393

Duan, S. M., Zhao, X. S., & Wen, R. F. (2003). Stability of SARS coronavirus in human specimens and environment and its sensitivity to heating and UV irradiation. *Biomedical and Environmental Sciences*, 16(3), 246–255. PMID:14631830

Dube, K., Nhamo, G., & Chikodzi, D. (2021). COVID-19 cripples global restaurant and hospitality industry. *Current Issues in Tourism*, 24(11), 1487–1490. doi:10.1080/13683500.2020.1773416

Duda-Chodak, A., Lukasiewicz, M., Ziec, G., Florkiewicx, A., & Filipiak-Florkiewicz, A. (2020). Covid-19 pandemic and food: Present knowledge, risks, consumers fears and safety. *Trends in Food Science & Technology, 105*, 145–160. doi:10.1016/j.tifs.2020.08.020 PMID:32921922

Duffy, L. N., Kline, C. S., Mowatt, R. A., & Chancellor, H. C. (2015). Women in tourism: Shifting gender ideology in the DR. *Annals of Tourism Research, 52*, 72–86. doi:10.1016/j.annals.2015.02.017

Dunbar, E. (2018). Corporate Social Responsibility and Sustainability. *Learning to Give*. Retrieved on June 2, 2021, from: https://www.learningtogive.org/resources/corporate-social-responsibility-and-sustainability

Dunlap, R. E., & Van Liere, K. D. (2014). The "new environmental paradigm.". *The Journal of Environmental Education, 9*(4), 10–19. doi:10.1080/00958964.1978.10801875

Dwityas, N. A., & Briandana, R. (2017). Social media in travel decision making process. *International Journal of Humanities and Social Science, 7*(7), 193–201.

Dwyer, L. (2018). Saluting while the ship sinks: The necessity for tourism paradigm change. *Journal of Sustainable Tourism, 26*(1), 29–48. doi:10.1080/09669582.2017.1308372

Dyllick, T., & Muff, K. (2016). Clarifying the meaning of sustainable business: Introducing a typology from business-as-usual to true business sustainability. *Organization & Environment, 29*(2), 156–174. doi:10.1177/1086026615575176

Dzene, S., & Eglīte, A. (2012). Perspective of sustainable food consumpiton in Latvia. *Annual 18th International Scientific Conference Proceedings, 2*, 210-215.

Dziallas, M., & Blind, K. (2019). Innovation indicators throughout the innovation process: An extensive literature analysis. *Technovation, 80*, 3–29. doi:10.1016/j.technovation.2018.05.005

Ebrahim, A. H., & Ganguli, S. (2017). Strategic priorities for exploiting Bahrain's medical tourism potential. *Journal of Place Management and Development, 10*(1), 45–60. doi:10.1108/JPMD-03-2016-0011

Ebrahim, A. H., & Ganguli, S. (2019). A comparative analysis of medical tourism competitiveness of India, Thailand and Singapore. *Tourism: An International Interdisciplinary Journal, 67*(2), 102–115.

Eco-Destinet. (2009). *Eco-Destinet (2007-2009)*. Retrieved on September 8, 2018, from: https://destinet.eu/who-who/civil-society-ngos/ecotrans/ecotrans-projects-activities/2006-2010/EETLS_Blueprint_Draft_Final_web.pdf

Efanov, D., & Roschin, P. (2018). The All-Pervasiveness of the Blockchain Technology. *Procedia Computer Science, 123*, 116–121. doi:10.1016/j.procs.2018.01.019

Egresi, I. (2016). Tourism and sustainability in Turkey: Negative impact of mass tourism development. In *Alternative tourism in Turkey* (pp. 35–53). Springer. doi:10.1007/978-3-319-47537-0_3

Eichelberger, S., Peters, M., Pikkemaat, B., & Chan, C. (2020). Entrepreneurial ecosystems in smart cities for tourism development: From stakeholder perceptions to regional tourism policy implications. *Journal of Hospitality and Tourism Management, 45*, 319–329. doi:10.1016/j.jhtm.2020.06.011

Eichenbaum, H. (2013). Memory on time. *Trends in Cognitive Sciences, 17*(2), 81–88. doi:10.1016/j.tics.2012.12.007 PMID:23318095

Eide, D., & Hoarau-Heemstra, H. (2022). Innovation for sustainable destinations: The role of certification and partnership. In I. Booyens & O. Brouder (Eds.), *Handbook of Innovation for Sustainable Tourism* (pp. 112–139). Edward Elgar Publishing.

Compilation of References

Einarsson, S., & Sorin, F. (2020). Circular Economy in travel and tourism: A conceptual framework for a sustainable, resilient and future proof industry transition. CE360 Alliance. doi:10.1002/col.10105

Eirini, T., & Kostas, K. (2017). The evolution of alternative forms of Tourism: A theoretical background. *Business & Entrepreneurship Journal*, *6*(1), 1–4.

Ekincek, S. (2020). *Yenilebilir Sanat: Gastronomide Yemeğin Sanatsal Boyutunun İncelenmesi* [Edible Art: Examining the Artistic Dimension of Food in Gastronomy] [Yayımlanmamış Doktora Tezi]. Eskişehir: Anadolu Üniversitesi. GRA (Green Restaurant Association). Retrieved on December 14, 2021, from: www.dinegreen.weebly.com

Ekinci, Y. (2003). From destination image to destination branding: An emerging area of research. *e-Review of Tourism Research*, *1*(2), 21-24.

Ekinci, M. B. (2014). The Cittaslow philosophy in the context of sustainable tourism development; the case of Turkey. *Tourism Management*, *41*, 178–189. doi:10.1016/j.tourman.2013.08.013

Ekonomist E-Dönüşüm Dergisi. (2020). *Dijitalleşmeyle yeni normale dönülüyor*. Retrieved on February 14, 2021, from: https://www.qnbefinans.com/uploads/20200925115031437.pdf

El Bilali, H., Callenius, C., Strassner, C., & Probst, L. (2018). Food and nutrition security and sustainability transitions in food systems. *Food and Energy Security*, *8*(2), 1–20.

El Yaagoubi, W. L., & Machrafi, M. (2021). Social Media Influencers, Digital Marketing, and Tourism in Morocco. *Economic and Social Development: Book of Proceedings*, 145-152.

Elektronik Atıkların Geri Dönüşümü (EAGD). (2016). *Türkiye'de ve Dünya'da e-atık*. https://www.eagd.org.tr/turkiyede-ve-dunyada-e-atik/

Elhmoud, E. R., & Kutty, A. A. (2020). Sustainability Assessment in Aviation Industry: A MiniReview on the Tools, Models, and Methods of Assessment. *IEOM Society International*, 1–11. http://ieomsociety.org/harare2020/papers/324.pdf

Elkington, J. (1994). Towards the Sustainable Corporation: Win-Win-Win Business Strategies for Sustainable Development. *California Management Review*, *36*(2), 90–100. doi:10.2307/41165746

Elkington, J. (1998). *Cannibals with Forks: The Triple Bottom Line of 21st Century Business*. New Society Publishers.

Elkington, J. (2004). Enter the triple bottom line. In A. Henriques & J. Richardson (Eds.), *The triple bottom line: Does it all add up* (pp. 1–16). Taylor & Francis.

Ellegaard, C., & Medlin, C. J. (2018). Finding good relationships – intended and realized relational governance of international fine wine exchanges. *Journal of World Business*, *53*(6), 794–805. doi:10.1016/j.jwb.2018.06.003

Epler Wood, M., Milstein, M., & Ahamed-Broadhurst, K. (2019). *Destinations at Risk: The Invisible Burden of Tourism*. Retrieved on September 22, 2020, from: www.thetravelfoundation.org.uk

Erdogan, B. Z. (1999). Celebrity endorsement: A literature review. *Journal of Marketing Management*, *15*(4), 291–314. doi:10.1362/026725799784870379

Erdogan, N., & Baris, E. (2007). Environmental protection programs and conservation practices of hotels in Ankara, Turkey. *Tourism Management*, *28*(2), 604–614. doi:10.1016/j.tourman.2006.07.003

Erkol Bayram, G., & Bayram, A. T. (2017). Uluslararası seyahat işletmelerinin türleri, görev, yetki ve sorumlulukları. In B. Zengin, M. Sarıışık, & C. Avcıkurt (Eds.), *Uluslararası seyahat işletmeciliği* (pp. 41–66). Detay Yayıncılık.

Ertuna, B., Karatas-Ozkan, M., & Yamak, S. (2019). Diffusion of sustainability and CSR discourse in the hospitality industry: Dynamics of local context. *International Journal of Contemporary Hospitality Management*, *31*(6), 2564–2581. doi:10.1108/IJCHM-06-2018-0464

Ertz, M., & Boily, É. (2019). The rise of the digital economy: Thoughts on blockchain technology and cryptocurrencies for the collaborative economy. *International Journal of Innovation Studies*, *3*(4), 84–93. doi:10.1016/j.ijis.2019.12.002

Etihad Airways. (2019, April 17). *Etihad Airways to Operate Single-Use Plastic Free Flight on Earth Day as Part of Its Commitment to Sustainability*. Retrieved on August 21, 2021, from: https://www.etihad.com/en/news/etihad-airways-to-operate-single-use-plastic-free-flight-on-earth-day-as-part-of-its-commitment-to-sustainability#:~:text=Abu%20Dhabi%2C%20United%20Arab%20Emirates,the%20effects%20of%20plastic%20pollution

Etmyonline. (2022). Accessible at: https://www.etymonline.com/search?q=accessibility&ref= searchbar_searchhint

Euractiv. (2020). *No evidence of COVID-19 transmission through food, says EFSA*. Retrieved on August 14, 2021, from: https://www.euractiv.com/section/coronavirus/news/no-evidence-of-covid-19-transmission-through food-says-efsa/

European Commission. (2018). *Proposal for a Regulation of the European Parliament and of the Council on the establishment of a framework to facilitate sustainable investment*. European Commission.

European Commission. (n.d.). *Corporate Sustainability Reporting*. Retrieved on June 2, 2020, from: https://ec.europa.eu/info/business-economy-euro/company-reporting-and-auditing/company-reporting/corporate-sustainability-reporting_en

European Parliament. (2016). *The Cost of Non-Europe in the Sharing Economy*. January 2016 - PE 558.777. European Added Value Unit.

European Parliament. (2017). Tourism and the sharing economy. January 2017 — PE 595.897. Juul, M., Members' Research Service.

Evans, G. (2009). *From cultural quarters to creative clusters–creative spaces in the new city economy*. Institute of Urban History.

Evans, S., Vladimirova, D., Holgado, M., Van Fossen, K., Yang, M., Silva, E. A., & Barlow, C. Y. (2017). Business model innovation for sustainability: Towards a unified perspective for creation of sustainable business models. *Business Strategy and the Environment*, *26*(5), 597–608. doi:10.1002/bse.1939

Factor, A., Ulhøi, J. P., & Romm, N. (2021). Research on small and medium-sized enterprises and Sustainability. *Sustainability and Small and Medium-Sized Enterprises*, 26–47. doi:10.4324/9780429426377-2-2

Faghihi, F. (2021). Tourism Model Based on Geospatial Information System (Case Study: Kurdistan Province). *EFFLATOUNIA-Multidisciplinary Journal*, *5*(2).

FAO. (2020). *Hunger and food insecurity*. Retrieved on September 22, 2021, from: https://www.fao.org/hunger/en/

Farias, D. P., & Santos Gomesdos, M. G. (2020). COVID-19 outbreak: What should be done to avoid food shortages? *Trends in Food Science & Technology*, *102*, 291–292. doi:10.1016/j.tifs.2020.06.007 PMID:32834501

Fariborz, A., Thomas, L., Richard, L., Alan, L., Gordon, B., Teresa, M., & Schiff, E. Z. (1996). Affect, attachment, memory: Contributions toward psychobiologic integration. *Psychiatry*, *59*(3), 213–239. doi:10.1080/00332747.1996.11024764 PMID:27702391

Farmaki, A. (2021). Memory and forgetfulness in tourism crisis research. *Tourism Management*, *83*, 104210. doi:10.1016/j.tourman.2020.104210 PMID:32904475

Farmaki, A., & Kladou, S. (2020). Why do Airbnb hosts discriminate? Examining the sources and manifestations of discrimination in host practice. *Journal of Hospitality and Tourism Management*, *42*, 181–189. doi:10.1016/j.jhtm.2020.01.005

Farmtoplate. (2022). *Blockchain for Food Tracking and Tracing*. https://www.farmtoplate.io/how-it-works/

Farsari, Y., & Prastacos, P. (2004). GIS applications in the planning and management of tourism. In A. A. Lew, C. M. Hall, & A. M. Williams (Eds.), *A companion to tourism: Blackwell companions to geography* (pp. 596–607). Blackwell Publishing. doi:10.1002/9780470752272.ch47

Fatimah, T. (2015). The impacts of rural tourism initiatives on cultural landscape sustainability in borobudur area. *Procedia Environmental Sciences*, *28*(2), 567–577. doi:10.1016/j.proenv.2015.07.067

Faulkner, B. (2001). Towards a framework for tourism disaster management. *Tourism Management*, *22*(2), 135–147. doi:10.1016/S0261-5177(00)00048-0

Faulkner, B., & Vikulov, S. (2001). Katherine, washed out one day, back on track the next: A post-mortem of a tourism disaster. *Tourism Management*, *22*(4), 331–344. doi:10.1016/S0261-5177(00)00069-8

Feliciano, S. (2016). *Airbnb and Aruba Tourism Authority Sign Historic, Tourism Agreement*. Retrieved on November 1, 2018, from: https://www.prnewswire.com/news-releases/airbnb-and-aruba-tourism-authority-sign-historic-tourism-agreement-300358342.html

Felix, R., Rauschnabel, P. A., & Hinsch, C. (2017). Elements of strategic social media marketing: A holistic framework. *Journal of Business Research*, *70*(1), 118–126. doi:10.1016/j.jbusres.2016.05.001

Femenia-Serra, F., & Gretzel, U. (2020). Influencer Marketing for Tourism Destinations: Lessons from a Mature Destination. *Information and Communication Technologies in Tourism*, 65-78.

Femenia-Serra, F., Gretzel, U., & Alzua-Sorzabal, A. (2022). Instagram travel influencers in #quarantine: Communicative practices and roles during COVID-19. *Tourism Management*, *89*, 104454. Advance online publication. doi:10.1016/j.tourman.2021.104454

Ferguson, L. (2010a). Tourism development and the restructuring of social reproduction in Central America. *Review of International Political Economy*, *17*(5), 860–888. doi:10.1080/09692290903507219

Ferguson, L. (2010b). Interrogating 'gender' in development policy and practice: The World Bank, tourism and microenterprise in Honduras. *International Feminist Journal of Politics*, *12*(1), 3–24. doi:10.1080/14616740903429080

Ferguson, L. (2011). Promoting gender equality and empowering women? Tourism and the third Millennium Development Goal. *Current Issues in Tourism*, *14*(3), 235–249. doi:10.1080/13683500.2011.555522

Ferreira, J., Silva, S., Seixas, L., Lopes, A., Fortes, C., Reis, M., Poseiro, P., Capitão, R., Malvarez, G., & Tenedório, J. (2014). *The resource valuation and the challenge of coastal ecosystem-based management implementation*. Retrieved on August 8, 2018, from: http://repositorio.lnec.pt:8080/handle/123456789/1007022

Festa, G., Shams, S. M. R., Metallo, G., & Cuomo, M. T. (2020). Opportunities and challenges in the contribution of wine routes to wine tourism in Italy – A stakeholders' perspective of development. *Tourism Management Perspectives*, *33*, 33. doi:10.1016/j.tmp.2019.100585

Filocamo, F., Rosskopf, C. M., Amato, V., & Cesarano, M. (2022). A Step towards a Sustainable Tourism in Apennine Mountain Areas: A Proposal of Geoitinerary across the Matese Mountains (Central-Southern Italy). *Geosciences*, *12*(2), 100. doi:10.3390/geosciences12020100

Final Report, S. T. S. C. (2003). *Sustainable Tourism Stewardship Council raising the standards and benefits of sustainable tourism and ecotourism certification*. Retrieved on August 16, 2018, from: http://usir.salford.ac.uk/44065/1/STSC%202002%20-final-report.pdf

Finch, B. J. (2006). *Operations Now: Profitability, Processes, Performance*. McGraw-Hill.

Finkbeiner, M., Schau, E., Lehmann, A., & Traverso, M. (2010). Towards Life Cycle Sustainability Assessment. *Sustainability*, *2*(10), 3309–3322. doi:10.3390u2103309

Firth, R., Kala, J., Lyons, T. J., & Andrys, J. (2017). An analysis of regional climate simulations for Western Australia's wine regions—Model evaluation and future climate projections. *Journal of Applied Meteorology and Climatology*, *56*(7), 2113–2138. doi:10.1175/JAMC-D-16-0333.1

Fisher, C., & Sood, K. (2014). What is driving the growth in medical tourism? *Health Marketing Quarterly*, *31*(3), 246–262. doi:10.1080/07359683.2014.936293 PMID:25120045

Fitzgerald, P. P., & David-Cooper, R. (2018). Corporate Social Responsibility in the Aviation Industry. Cambridge University Press. doi:10.1017/9781316594216.016

Fivush, R. (2011). The development of autobiographical memory. *Annual Review of Psychology*, *62*(1), 559–582. doi:10.1146/annurev.psych.121208.131702 PMID:20636128

Fletcher, R. (2019). Ecotourism after nature: Anthropocene tourism as a new capitalist "fix". *Journal of Sustainable Tourism*, *27*(4), 522–535. doi:10.1080/09669582.2018.1471084

Flew, T., & Kirkwood, K. (2020). The impact of COVID-19 on cultural tourism: Art, culture and communication in four regional sites of Queensland, Australia. *Media International Australia*, *178*(1), 16–20. doi:10.1177/1329878X20952529

Fong, L. H. N., Law, R., & Ye, B. H. (2020). Outlook of tourism recovery amid an epidemic: Importance of outbreak control by the government. *Annals of Tourism Research*, 102951. PMID:32836566

Font, X., & Lynes, J. (2018). Corporate social responsibility in tourism and hospitality. *Journal of Sustainable Tourism*, *26*(7), 1027–1042. doi:10.1080/09669582.2018.1488856

Food and Agriculture Organization. (2020). *Q&A: COVID-19 pandemic–impact on food and agriculture*. Retrieved on September 11, 2020, from: http://www.fao.org/2019-ncov/q-and-a/impact-on-food-and-a griculture/en/

Fotiadis, A., Polyzos, S., & Tzung-Cheng, T. C. H. (2021). The good, the bad and ugly on Covid-19 tourism recovery. *Annals of Tourism Research*, *87*, 103117. doi:10.1016/j.annals.2020.103117 PMID:33518847

Fountain, J., & Cradock-Henry, N. (2020). Recovery, risk and resilience: Post-disaster tourism experiences in Kaikōura, New Zealand. *Tourism Management Perspectives*, *35*, 100695. doi:10.1016/j.tmp.2020.100695

Foursquare Location Based Travel and Tourism Insights. (2018). Retrieved on July 15, 2018, from: https://www2.foursquare.com/l/310041/are-Traveler-Insights-2017-pdf/2frvtp

Franca, R. P., Iano, Y., Monteiro, A. C. B., & Arthur, R. (2020). Better transmission of information focused on green computing through data transmission channels in cloud environments with rayleigh fading. In B. Balusamy, N. Chilamkurti, & S. Kadry (Eds.), *Green Computing in Smart Cities: Simulation and Techniques* (pp. 71–94). Springer Nature.

Franceschini, I. (2020). As far apart as earth and sky: A survey of Chinese and Cambodian construction workers in sihanoukville. *Critical Asian Studies*, *52*(4), 1–18. doi:10.1080/14672715.2020.1804961

Freberg, K., Graham, K., McGaughey, K., & Freberg, L. A. (2011). Who are the social media influencers? A study of public perceptions of personality. *Public Relations Review*, *37*(1), 90–92. doi:10.1016/j.pubrev.2010.11.001

Compilation of References

Frewer, L., de Jonge, J., & van Kleef, E. (2009). Consumer perceptions of food safety. *Medical Science*, 2, 243.

Frost, W., Frost, J., Strickland, P., & Smith Maguire, J. (2020). Seeking a competitive advantage in wine tourism: Heritage and storytelling at the cellar-door. *International Journal of Hospitality Management*, 87, 87. doi:10.1016/j.ijhm.2020.102460

Fukuda-Parr, S. (2016). From the Millennium Development Goals to the Sustainable Development Goals: Shifts in purpose, concept, and politics of global goal setting for development. *Gender and Development*, 24(1), 43–52. doi:10.1080/13552074.2016.1145895

Fullerton, J. A., & Kendrick, A. (2011). Australia tourism advertising: A test of the bleed-over effect among us travelers. *Place Branding and Public Diplomacy*, 7(4), 244–256. doi:10.1057/pb.2011.17

Furlong, Y., & Finnie, T. (2020). Culture counts: The diverse effects of culture and society on mental health amidst COVID-19 outbreak in Australia. *Irish Journal of Psychological Medicine*, 37(3), 237–242. doi:10.1017/ipm.2020.37 PMID:32406358

Galanakis, C. M. (2020). The food systems in the era of the coronavirus (COVID-19) pandemic crisis. *Foods*, 9(4), 523. doi:10.3390/foods9040523 PMID:32331259

Galati, A., Crescimanno, M., Tinervia, S., & Fagnani, F. (2017). Social media as a strategic marketing tool in the Sicilian wine industry: Evidence from Facebook. *Wine Economics and Policy*, 6(1), 40–47. doi:10.1016/j.wep.2017.03.003

Gallego-Álvarez, P. I., & Ortas, P. E. (2017). Corporate environmental sustainability reporting in the context of national cultures: A quantile regression approach. *International Business Review*, 26(2), 337–353. doi:10.1016/j.ibusrev.2016.09.003

Gandin, S. (2018). Tourism promotion and disability: still a (linguistic) taboo? A preliminary study. In M. Bielenia-Grajewska & E. Cortes De Los Rios (Eds.), *Innovative perspectives on tourism discourse* (pp. 55–73). IGI Global. doi:10.4018/978-1-5225-2930-9.ch004

Ganguli, S., & Ebrahim, A. H. (2017). A qualitative analysis of Singapore's medical tourism competitiveness. *Tourism Management Perspectives*, 21, 74–84. doi:10.1016/j.tmp.2016.12.002

Gao, J., Peng, P., Lu, F., & Claramunt, C. (2022). A multi-scale comparison of tourism attraction networks across China. *Tourism Management*, 90, 90. doi:10.1016/j.tourman.2022.104489

Gao, J., & Zhang, L. (2019). Exploring the dynamic linkages between tourism growth and environmental pollution: New evidence from the Mediterranean countries. *Current Issues in Tourism*, 24(1), 49–65. doi:10.1080/13683500.2019.1688767

García-Milon, A., Juaneda-Ayensa, E., Olarte-Pascual, C., & Pelegrín-Borondo, J. (2020). Towards the smart tourism destination: Key factors in information source use on the tourist shopping journey. *Tourism Management Perspectives*, 36, 100730. doi:10.1016/j.tmp.2020.100730 PMID:32834961

Garcia-Ramon, M. D., Canoves, G., & Valdovinos, N. (1995). Farm tourism, gender and the environment in Spain. *Annals of Tourism Research*, 22(2), 267–282. doi:10.1016/0160-7383(94)00096-4

Gardner, C. A., Acharya, T., & Yach, D. (2007). Technological and social innovation: A unifying new paradigm for global health. *Health Affairs*, 26(4), 1052–1061. doi:10.1377/hlthaff.26.4.1052 PMID:17630448

Gathercole, S. E. (1999). Cognitive approaches to the development of short-term memory. *Trends in Cognitive Sciences*, 3(11), 410–419. doi:10.1016/S1364-6613(99)01388-1 PMID:10529796

Gatti, M., Pirez, F. J., Frioni, T., Squeri, C., & Poni, S. (2018). Calibrated, delayed-cane winter pruning controls yield and significantly postpones berry ripening parameters in *vitis vinifera* L. cv. Pinot Noir. *Australian Journal of Grape and Wine Research*, 24(3), 305–316. doi:10.1111/ajgw.12330

Gautam, S., & Trivedi, U. (2020). Global implications of bio-aerosol in pandemic. *Environment, Development and Sustainability*, *22*(5), 3861–3865. doi:10.100710668-020-00704-2 PMID:34172977

Gavrilescu, M. (2011). *Sustainability. In Comprehensive Biotechnology*. Pergamon.

Gavrilović, Z., & Maksimović, M. (2018). Green innovations in the tourism sector. *Strategic Management*, *23*(1), 36–42. doi:10.5937/StraMan1801036G

Gedi, N., & Elam, Y. (1996). Collective memory—What is it? *History & Memory*, *8*(1), 30–50.

Gegez, A. E. (2007). *Marketing Research* [Pazarlama Araştırmaları]. Beta Publishing.

Genç, R. (2018). Catastrophe of environment: The impact of natural disasters on tourism industry. *Journal of Tourism & Adventure*, *1*(1), 86–94. doi:10.3126/jota.v1i1.22753

Genç, T., & Filipe, J. A. (2016). A fuzzy MCDM approach for choosing a tourism destination in Portugal. *International Journal of Business and Systems Research*, *10*(1), 23–44. doi:10.1504/IJBSR.2016.073688

Georgea, R., Stainton, H., & Adu-Ampong, E. (2021). Word-of-Mouth Redefined: A Profile of Influencers in the Travel and Tourism Industry. *Journal of Smart Tourism*, *1*(3), 31–44. doi:10.52255marttourism.2021.1.3.6

George, B. P. (2007). Alleppey Tourism Development Cooperative: The Case of Network Advantage. *The Innovation Journal*.

Geraghty, M. K., & Johnson, E. (1997). Revenue Management Saves National Car Rental. *INFORMS Journal on Applied Analytics*, *27*(1), 107–127. doi:10.1287/inte.27.1.107

Gerbing, R., Matthay, K. K., Perez, C., Seeger, R. C., Brodeur, G. M., Shimada, H., Atkinson, J. B., Black, C. T., Haase, G. M., Stram, D. O., Swift, P., & Lukens, J. N. (1998). Successful treatment of stage III neuroblastoma based on prospective biologic staging: A children's cancer group study. *Journal of Clinical Oncology*, *16*(4), 1256–1264. doi:10.1200/JCO.1998.16.4.1256 PMID:9552023

Getz, D., & Brown, G. (2006). Critical success factors for wine tourism regions: A demand analysis. *Tourism Management*, *27*(1), 146–158. doi:10.1016/j.tourman.2004.08.002

Geyser, W. (2022, February 8). *The State of Influencer Marketing 2020: Benchmark Report*. https://influencermarketinghub.com/influencer-marketing-benchmark-report-2020/

Ghasemi, B., Khalijian, S., Daim, T. U., & Mohammadipirlar, E. (2021). Knowledge management performance measurement based on World-Class Competitive Advantages to develop strategic-oriented projects: Case of Iranian oil industry. *Technology in Society*, *67*, 101691. doi:10.1016/j.techsoc.2021.101691

Ghasemi, P., Mehdiabadi, A., Spulbar, C., & Birau, R. (2021). Ranking of Sustainable Medical Tourism Destinations in Iran: An Integrated Approach Using Fuzzy SWARA-PROMETHEE. *Sustainability*, *13*(2), 683. doi:10.3390u13020683

Ghavami, N., & Peplau, L. A. (2013). An intersectional analysis of gender and ethnic stereotypes: Testing three hypotheses. *Psychology of Women Quarterly*, *37*(1), 113–127. doi:10.1177/0361684312464203

Ghazinoory, S., Sarkissian, A., Farhanchi, M., & Saghafi, F. (2020). Renewing a dysfunctional innovation ecosystem: The case of the Lalejin ceramics and pottery. *Technovation*, *96*, 102122. doi:10.1016/j.technovation.2020.102122

Gholami-Zanjani, S. M., Klibi, W., Jabalemeli, M. S., & Pishvaee, M. S. (2021). The design of resilient food supply chain networks prone to epidemic disruptions. *International Journal of Production Economics*, *233*, 108001. doi:10.1016/j.ijpe.2020.108001

Compilation of References

Gibson, A., & O'Rawe, M. (2018). Virtual reality as a travel promotional tool: Insights from a consumer travel fair. In *Augmented reality and virtual reality* (pp. 93–107). Springer. doi:10.1007/978-3-319-64027-3_7

Gibson, R., & Hassan, S. (2005). *Sustainability assessment: Criteria and processes*. Routledge.

Gifford, E., & McKelvey, M. (2019). Knowledge-intensive entrepreneurship and S3: Conceptualizing strategies for sustainability. *Sustainability*, *11*(18), 4824. doi:10.3390u11184824

Gil Arroyo, C., Barbieri, C., Sotomayor, S., & Knollenberg, W. (2019). Cultivating women's empowerment through agritourism: Evidence from Andean communities. *Sustainability*, *11*(11), 3058. doi:10.3390u11113058

Gilg, A., Barr, S., & Ford, N. (2005). Green consumption or sustainable lifestyles? Identifying the sustainable consumer. *Futures*, *37*(6), 481–504. doi:10.1016/j.futures.2004.10.016

Gillis, J. R. (1994). Introduction. Memory and identity: The history of a relationship. *Commemorations*, 1–24.

Givoni, M. (2006). Development and impact of the modern high-speed train: A review. *Transport Reviews*, *26*(5), 593–611. doi:10.1080/01441640600589319

Glenberg, A. M. (1997). What memory is for. *Behavioral and Brain Sciences*, *20*(1), 1–55. doi:10.1017/S0140525X97000010 PMID:10096994

Glucksman, M. (2017). The rise of social media influencer marketing on lifestyle branding: A case study of Lucie Fink. *Elon Journal of Undergraduate Research in Communications*, *8*(2), 77-87.

Goddard, E. (2020). The impact of covid-19 on food retail and food service in Canada: preliminary assessment. *Canadian Journal of Agricultural Economics/Revue Canadienne D'agroeconomie*, 1-5.

Godovykh, M., Pizam, A., & Bahja, F. (2020). Antecedents and outcomes of health risk perceptions in tourism, following the COVID-19 pandemic. *Tourism Review*, *76*(4), 737–748. doi:10.1108/TR-06-2020-0257

Goel, P. (2010). Triple Bottom Line Reporting: An Analytical Approach for Corporate Sustainability. *Journal of Finance. Accounting and Management*, *1*(1), 27–42.

Goffi, G., Cucculelli, M., & Masiero, L. (2019). Fostering tourism destination competitiveness in developing countries: The role of sustainability. *Journal of Cleaner Production*, *209*, 101–115. doi:10.1016/j.jclepro.2018.10.208

Go, H., Kang, M., & Suh, S. C. (2020). Machine learning of robots in tourism and hospitality: Interactive technology acceptance model (iTAM)–cutting edge. *Tourism Review*, *75*(4), 625–636. Advance online publication. doi:10.1108/TR-02-2019-0062

Goh, E., & Lee, C. (2018). A workforce to be reckoned with: The emerging pivotal Generation Z hospitality workforce. *International Journal of Hospitality Management*, *73*, 20–28. doi:10.1016/j.ijhm.2018.01.016

Gökşen, Y., Damar, M., & Doğan, O. (2016). Yeşil bilişim: Bir kamu kurumu örneği ve politika önerileri. *Ege Academic Review*, *16*(4).

Goldstein, N. J., Griskevicius, V., & Cialdini, R. B. (2007). Invoking social norms: A social psychology perspective on improving hotels' linen-reuse programs. *The Cornell Hotel and Restaurant Administration Quarterly*, *48*(2), 145–150. doi:10.1177/0010880407299542

Gómez, M., González-Díaz, B., & Molina, A. (2015a). Priority maps at wine tourism destinations: An empirical approach in five Spanish wine regions. *Journal of Destination Marketing & Management*, *4*(4), 258–267. doi:10.1016/j.jdmm.2015.09.003

Gómez, M., Lopez, C., & Molina, A. (2015b). A model of tourism destination brand equity: The case of wine tourism destinations in Spain. *Tourism Management*, *51*, 210–222. doi:10.1016/j.tourman.2015.05.019

González-Reverté, F. (2019). Building sustainable smart destinations: An approach based on the development of Spanish smart tourism plans. *Sustainability*, *11*(23), 6874. doi:10.3390u11236874

Goodwin, H. (2016). Managing Tourism in Barcelona. *Progress in Responsible Tourism*, 28-48.

Gorbalenya, A. E., Baker, S. C., Baric, R. S., de Groot, R. J., Drosten, C., & Gulyaeva, A. A. (2020) Severe acute respiratory syndrome-related coronavirus: The species and its viruses – a statement of the Coronavirus Study Group. BioRxiv. doi:10.1101/2020.02.07.937862

Gössling, S., Hall, C. M., Ekström, F., Engeset, A., & Aall, C. (2012). Transition management: A tool for implementing sustainable tourism scenarios? *Journal of Sustainable Tourism*, *20*(6), 899–916. doi:10.1080/09669582.2012.699062

Gössling, S., Ring, A., Dwyer, L., Andersson, A., & Hall, C. M. (2016). Optimizing or maximizing growth? A challenge for sustainable tourism. *Journal of Sustainable Tourism*, *24*(4), 527–548. doi:10.1080/09669582.2015.1085869

Gössling, S., Scott, D., & Hall, C. M. (2020). Pandemics, tourism and global change: A rapid assessment of COVID-19. *Journal of Sustainable Tourism*, *29*(1), 1–20. doi:10.1080/09669582.2020.1758708

Götz, K., Loose, W., Schmied, M., & Schubert, S. (2002). *Mobility Styles in Leisure Time: Reducing the environmental impacts of leisure and tourism travel*. Freiburg, Germany: Oko-Institut eV.

Graham, M. A. (2007). Art, Ecology and Art Education: Locating. *Studies in Art Education*, *48*(4), 375–391. doi:10.1080/00393541.2007.11650115

Granstrand, O., & Holgersson, M. (2020). Innovation ecosystems: A conceptual review and a new definition. *Technovation*, *90*, 102098. doi:10.1016/j.technovation.2019.102098

Grasmuck, S., & Espinal, R. (2000). Market success or female autonomy? Income, ideology, and empowerment among microentrepreneurs in the Dominican Republic. *Gender & Society*, *14*(2), 231–255. doi:10.1177/089124300014002002

Gretzel, U. (2018). Influencer Marketing in Travel and Tourism. *Advances in Social Media for Travel, Tourism and Hospitality: New Perspectives, Practice and Cases*, 147-156.

Gretzel, U., Fuchs, M., Baggio, R., Hoepken, W., Law, R., Neidhardt, J., Pesonen, J., Zanker, M., & Xiang, Z. (2020). e-Tourism beyond COVID-19: A call for transformative research. *Information Technology & Tourism*, *22*(2), 187–203. doi:10.100740558-020-00181-3

Gretzel, U., Reino, S., Kopera, S., & Koo, C. (2015). Smart tourism challenges. *Journal of Tourism*, *16*(1), 41–47.

Gretzel, U., Sigala, M., Xiang, Z., & Koo, C. (2015). Smart tourism: Foundations and developments. *Electronic Markets*, *25*(3), 179–188. doi:10.100712525-015-0196-8

Grönroos, C. (1999). Internationalization strategies for services. *Journal of Services Marketing*, *13*(4/5), 290–297. doi:10.1108/08876049910282547

Grosseck, G. (2009). To use or not to use web 2.0 in higher education? *Procedia: Social and Behavioral Sciences*, *1*(1), 478–482. doi:10.1016/j.sbspro.2009.01.087

GSTC - Global Sustainable Tourism Council. (2009). *GSTC mission and impacts*. Retrieved on November 9, 2018, from: https://www.gstcouncil.org/about/about-us/

Compilation of References

Guan, C., Rani, T., Yueqiang, Z., Ajaz, T., & Haseki, M. I. (2022). Impact of tourism industry, globalization, and technology innovation on ecological footprints in G-10 countries. *Economic Research-Ekonomska Istraživanja*, 1-17.

Gu, D., Khan, S., Khan, I. U., & Khan, S. U. (2019). *Understanding mobile tourism shopping in Pakistan: An integrating framework of innovation diffusion theory and technology acceptance model*. Mobile Information Systems. doi:10.1155/2019/1490617

Guerreiro, M. M., Henriques, C., & Mendes, J. (2019). Cultural and Creative Tourism: The Case of 'Celebrations' in the Algarve Region. *Journal of Spatial and Organizational Dynamics*, *VII*(4), 320–338.

Guilarte, Y., & Quintáns, D. (2019). Using big data to measure tourist sustainability: Myth or reality? *Sustainability*, *11*(20), 5641. doi:10.3390u11205641

Guizzardi, A., Pons, F. M., Angelini, G., & Ranieri, E. (2021). Big data from dynamic pricing: A smart approach to tourism demand forecasting. *International Journal of Forecasting*, *37*(3), 1049–1060. doi:10.1016/j.ijforecast.2020.11.006

Gunaydin, Y., Özgür, Ö., & Ataman, D. (2021). Influence of pull factors on the travel motivation of foreign tourists towards Bodrum-Turkey destination. *Journal of Tourism Theory and Research*, *7*(1), 11–21. doi:10.24288/jttr.823952

Güneş, S. G. (2019). Eco-gastronomy, Tourism and Sustainability: The Rise of Sustainable Restaurants in the World. *Erasmus International Academic Research Symposium on Educational and Social Sciences*, 67-84.

Güngör, E. Ö., & Yaldız, N. (2020). *Sars-Cov-2 (Covid – 19) And Food Safety. In Tam Metin Bildiriler Kitabı–Sağlık Bilimleri*. Concovid.

Gupta, M. K., Rajachar, V., & Prabha, C. (2015). Medical tourism: A new growth factor for Indian healthcare industry. *International Journal of Research in Medical Sciences*, *3*(9), 2161–2163. doi:10.18203/2320-6012.ijrms20150597

Gu, Q., & Huang, S. (2018). Profiling Chinese wine tourists by wine tourism constraints: A comparison of Chinese Australians and long-haul Chinese tourists in Australia. *International Journal of Tourism Research*, *21*(2), 206–220. doi:10.1002/jtr.2255

Gu, Q., Qiu, H., King, B. E. M., & Huang, S. (2019). Understanding the wine tourism experience: The roles of facilitators, constraints, and involvement. *Journal of Vacation Marketing*, *26*(2), 211–229. doi:10.1177/1356766719880253

Gu, Q., Zhang, H., Huang, S., Zheng, F., & Chen, C. (2021). Tourists' spatiotemporal behaviors in an emerging wine region: A time-geography perspective. *Journal of Destination Marketing & Management*, *19*, 19. doi:10.1016/j.jdmm.2020.100513

Gürbüz, E. (2021). *Gemlik Körfezi kuzey kıyılarının sürdürülebilir turizm ve rekreasyon planlama kapsamında değerlendirilmesi* [Unpublished Master's thesis]. Bursa Uludağ University, Bursa, Turkey.

Gürdal, M. (2015). *Turizm ulaştırması – Paket tur organizasyonu ve yönetimi*. Nobel Yayıncılık.

Gustafson, P. (2006). Work-related travel, gender and family obligations. *Work, Employment and Society*, *20*(3), 513–530. doi:10.1177/0950017006066999

Guttentag, D. (2015). Airbnb: Disruptive innovation and the rise of an informal tourism accommodation sector. *Current Issues in Tourism*, *18*(12), 1192–1217. doi:10.1080/13683500.2013.827159

Güzel, Ö., Ehtiyar, R., & Ryan, C. (2021). The Success Factors of wine tourism entrepreneurship for rural area: A thematic biographical narrative analysis in Turkey. *Journal of Rural Studies*, *84*, 230–239. doi:10.1016/j.jrurstud.2021.04.021

Hall, C. M. (2005). Biosecurity and wine tourism. *Tourism Management*, *26*(6), 931–938. doi:10.1016/j.tourman.2004.06.011

Hall, C. M. (2011). Health and medical tourism: A kill or cure for global public health? *Tourism Review*, *66*(1/2), 4–15. doi:10.1108/16605371111127198

Hall, C. M. (2018). Resilience theory and tourism. In J. Saarinen & A. M. Gill (Eds.), *Resilient Destinations and Tourism* (pp. 34–47). Routledge. doi:10.4324/9781315162157-3

Hall, C. M., & Seyfi, S. (2020). COVID-19 pandemic, tourism and degrowth. In C. M. Hall, L. Lundmark, & J. J. Zhang (Eds.), *Degrowth and Tourism* (pp. 220–238). Routledge. doi:10.4324/9780429320590-17

Hall, M., & Lew, A. (Eds.). (1998). *Sustainable Tourism Development: Geographical Perspectives*. Addison Wesley Longman.

Hall, M., & Page, S. (1999). *The Geography of Tourism and Recreation: Environment, Place and Space*. Routledge.

Halme, M., Rintamäki, J., Knudsen, J. S., Lankoski, L., & Kuisma, M. (2020). When Is There a Sustainability Case for CSR? Pathways to Environmental and Social Performance Improvements. *Business & Society*, *59*(6), 1181–1227. doi:10.1177/0007650318755648

Hamed, H. M. (2013). Tourism and autism: An initiative study for how travel companies can plan tourism trips for autistic people. *American Journal of Tourism Management*, *2*(1), 1–14.

Hamid, R., Ong, M. H. A., Razak, I. R. A., Ismail, T. A. T., Ramli, N., & Nawawi, Z. M. W. N. W. (2020). User acceptance of smart housekeeping: A study of TAM model prototype in hotel industry. *International Journal of Supply Chain Management*, *9*(3), 308–314.

Han, H., Hsu, L. T., & Sheu, C. (2010). Application of the Theory of Planned Behavior to green hotel choice: Testing the effect of environmentally friendly activities. *Tourism Management*, *31*(3), 325–334. doi:10.1016/j.tourman.2009.03.013

Han, H., & Kim, Y. (2010). An investigation of green hotel customers' decision formation: Developing an extended model of the theory of planned behavior. *International Journal of Hospitality Management*, *29*(4), 659–668. doi:10.1016/j.ijhm.2010.01.001

Han, H., Lee, J. S., Trang, H. L. T., & Kim, W. (2018). Water conservation and waste reduction management for increasing guest loyalty and green hotel practices. *International Journal of Hospitality Management*, *75*, 58–66. doi:10.1016/j.ijhm.2018.03.012

Han, H., Lee, S., & Hyun, S. S. (2020). Tourism and altruistic intention: Volunteer tourism development and self-interested value. *Sustainability*, *12*(5), 2152. doi:10.3390u12052152

Han, J., & Chen, H. (2021). *Millennial social media users' intention to travel: the moderating role of social media influencer following behavior*. International Hospitality Review.

Hanna, P., Font, X., Scarles, C., Weeden, C., & Harrison, C. (2018). Tourist destination marketing: From sustainability myopia to memorable experiences. *Journal of Destination Marketing & Management*, *9*, 36–43. doi:10.1016/j.jdmm.2017.10.002

Han, S., Roy, P. K., Hossain, M. I., Byun, K. H., Choi, C., & Sang-Do, H. (2021). COVID-19 pandemic crisis and food safety: Implications and inactivation strategies. *Trends in Food Science & Technology*, *109*, 25–36. doi:10.1016/j.tifs.2021.01.004 PMID:33456205

Hanss, D., & Böhm, G. (2011). Sustainability seen from the perspective of consumers. *International Journal of Consumer Studies*, *36*(6), 678–687. doi:10.1111/j.1470-6431.2011.01045.x

Han, Y., Zhang, T., & Wang, M. (2020). Holiday travel behavior analysis and empirical study with integrated travel reservation information usage. *Transportation Research Part A, Policy and Practice*, *134*, 130–151. doi:10.1016/j.tra.2020.02.005

Harford, T. (2017). *Fifty Inventions That Shaped the Modern Economy* [Modern Ekonomiyi Şekillendiren Elli İcat]. Pegasus Publishing.

Harijono, H. D. (2013). Aircraft trailing vortices - Cirrus cloud interaction and green aircraft technology: An overview. *Proceeding of the 2013 IEEE International Conference on Space Science and Communication*, 318-323. https://www.businesstraveller.com/business-travel/2019/06/05/sas-to-stop-inflight-duty-free-sales/

Harmon, R. R., & Auseklis, N. (2009). Sustainable IT services: Assessing the impact of green computing practices. In *PICMET'09-2009 Portland International Conference on Management of Engineering & Technology* (pp. 1707-1717). IEEE.

Harrison, R. (2013). Forgetting to remember, remembering to forget: Late modern heritage practices, sustainability and the 'crisis' of accumulation of the past. *International Journal of Heritage Studies*, *19*(6), 579–595. doi:10.1080/13527258.2012.678371

Hartman, S., Parra, C., & De Roo, G. (2019). Framing strategic storytelling in the context of transition management to stimulate tourism destination development. *Tourism Management*, *75*, 90–98. doi:10.1016/j.tourman.2019.04.014

Harvey, M. J., Hunt, J., & Harris, C. C. Jr. (1995). Gender and community tourism dependence level. *Annals of Tourism Research*, *22*(2), 349–366. doi:10.1016/0160-7383(94)00081-6

Hasanien, A., Essawy, M., & Moussa, M. (2014). The Impact of Web-based Training Characteristics on Transfer of Training: An Application on Hotel Front Office Department. *Egyptian Journal of Tourism Studies*, *13*(2).

Hassan, V., Knio, M., & Bellos, G. (2022). Chapter 13 - How COVID-19 will change the future of tourism industry. In COVID-19: Tackling Global Pandemics through Scientific and Social Tools. Academic Press.

Hassen, T.B., Bilali, E. H., & Allahyari, M. (2020). Impact of COVID-19 on food behavior and consumption in Qatar. *Sustainability*, *12*(17), 6973.

Hatipoğlu, A., (2021). *Covid-19 Pandemisinin küresel gıda tedarik zincirine etkileri*. Academic Press.

Hatipoglu, B., Ertuna, B., & Duygu, S. (2019). Corporate social responsibility in tourism as a tool for sustainable development. *International Journal of Contemporary Hospitality Management*, *31*(6), 2358–2375. doi:10.1108/IJCHM-05-2018-0448

Hausmann, R., Hidalgo, C. A., Bustos, S., Coscia, M., & Simoes, A. (2014). *The atlas of economic complexity: Mapping paths to prosperity*. MIT Press. doi:10.7551/mitpress/9647.001.0001

Hawkes, J. (2001). *The Fourth pillar of sustainability: Culture's essential role in public planning*. Common Ground Publishing.

Hawksworth, J., & Vaughan, R. (2014). *The sharing economy–sizing the revenue opportunity*. Retrieved on July 20, 2018, from: https://www.pwc.co.uk/issues/megatrends/collisions/sharingeconomy/the-sharing-economysizing-therevenue-opportunity.html

Hegarty, J., & O'Mahony, G. (2001). Gastronomy: A phenomenon of cultural expressionism and an aesthetic for living. *International Journal of Hospitality Management*, *20*(1), 3–13. doi:10.1016/S0278-4319(00)00028-1

He, H., & Zhu, L. (2020). Online shopping green product quality supervision strategy with consumer feedback and collusion behavior. *PLoS One*, *15*(3), e0229471. Advance online publication. doi:10.1371/journal.pone.0229471 PMID:32126092

Heiskanen, E., & Jalas, M. (2000). *Dematerialization through services-A review and evaluation of the debate*. The Ministry of the Environment.

Heizer, J., & Render, B. (2008). *Operations Management*. Pearson.

Helgadóttir, G., Einarsdóttir, A. V., Burns, G. L., Gunnarsdóttir, G. Þ., & Matthíasdóttir, J. M. E. (2019). Social sustainability of tourism in Iceland: A qualitative inquiry. *Scandinavian Journal of Hospitality and Tourism*, *19*(4-5), 404–421. doi:10.1080/15022250.2019.1696699

Henche, B. G., Salvaj, E., & Cuesta-Valiño, P. (2020). A sustainable management model for cultural creative tourism ecosystems. *Sustainability (Switzerland)*, *12*(22), 1–21. doi:10.3390u12229554

Hennart, J. F. (2020). More than intent: A bundling model of MNE–SME interactions. *Journal of International Business Studies*, *51*(7), 1176–1194. doi:10.105741267-020-00352-8

Henriques, C., & Moreira, M. (2019). Turismo Criativo e Sustentabilidade Urbana: Os Casos de Lisboa e Porto. *Revista Portuguesa de Estudos Regionais*, *51*, 93–114.

Henseler, M., Maisonnave, H., & Maskaeva, A. (2022). Economic impacts of COVID-19 on the tourism sector in Tanzania. *Annals of Tourism Research Empirical Insights*, 3.

Henwood, F. A. (2020). Coronavirus disinfection in histopathology. *Journal of Histotechnology*, *43*(2), 102–104. doi:10.1080/01478885.2020.1734718 PMID:32116147

He, Q., Xu, Y., Liu, Z., He, J., Sun, Y., & Zhang, R. (2018). rivacy-preserving Internet of Things device management scheme based on blockchain. *International Journal of Distributed Sensor Networks*, *14*(11), 1–12. doi:10.1177/1550147718808750

Hernández-Espallardo, M., Sánchez-Pérez, M., & Segovia-López, C. (2011). Exploitation-and exploration-based innovations: The role of knowledge in inter-firm relationships with distributors. *Technovation*, *31*(5-6), 203–215. doi:10.1016/j.technovation.2011.01.007

Herrera, M. R. G., Sasidharan, V., Hernández, J. A. Á., & Herrera, L. D. A. (2018). Quality and sustainability of tourism development in Copper Canyon, Mexico: Perceptions of community stakeholders and visitors. *Tourism Management Perspectives*, *27*, 91–103. doi:10.1016/j.tmp.2018.05.003

Heslinga, J., Groote, P., & Vanclay, F. (2019). Strengthening governance processes to improve benefit-sharing from tourism in protected areas by using stakeholder analysis. *Journal of Sustainable Tourism*, *27*(6), 773–787.

Hiatt, J. (2006). *ADKAR: a model for change in business, government, and our community*. Prosci.

Hidalgo, C. A., Klinger, B., Barabási, A. L., & Hausmann, R. (2007). The product space conditions the development of nations. *Science*, *317*(5837), 482–487. doi:10.1126cience.1144581 PMID:17656717

Higgins-Desbiolles, F. (2020). Socialising tourism for social and ecological justice after COVID-19. *Tourism Geographies*, *22*(3), 610–623. doi:10.1080/14616688.2020.1757748

Higgins-Desbiolles, F., Carnicelli, S., Krolikowski, C., Wijesinghe, G., & Boluk, K. (2019). Degrowing tourism: Rethinking tourism. *Journal of Sustainable Tourism*, *27*(12), 1926–1944. doi:10.1080/09669582.2019.1601732

Hilty, L. M., & Aebischer, B. (2015). *ICT innovations for sustainability, advances in intelligent systems and computing*. Springer. doi:10.1007/978-3-319-09228-7

Hira, A., & Swartz, T. (2014). What makes Napa Napa? The roots of success in the wine industry. *Wine Economics and Policy*, *3*(1), 37–53. doi:10.1016/j.wep.2014.02.001

Hjalager, A. M. (2002). Repairing innovation defectiveness in tourism. *Tourism Management*, *23*(5), 465–474. doi:10.1016/S0261-5177(02)00013-4

Hjalager, A. M. (2009). Innovations in travel medicine and the progress of tourism—Selected narratives. *Technovation*, 29(9), 596–601. doi:10.1016/j.technovation.2009.05.012

Hoang, H. T. T., Truong, Q. H., Nguyen, A. T., & Hens, L. (2018). Multicriteria Evaluation of Tourism Potential in the Central Highlands of Vietnam: Combining Geographic Information System (GIS), Analytic Hierarchy Process (AHP) and Principal Component Analysis (PCA). *Sustainability*, 10(9), 3097. doi:10.3390u10093097

Hoarau-Heemstra, H., & Eide, D. (2016). Values and concern: Drivers of innovation in experience-based tourism. *Tourism and Hospitality Research*, 19(1), 15–26. doi:10.1177/1467358416683768

Høegh-Guldberg, O., Maziliauske, E., Eide, D., & Ryan, A. W. (2022). Innovation for Sustainability in World Heritage Destinations: Opportunities and Challenges of the Idealistic Paradigm. In C. Ribeiro de Almeida, J. C. Martins, A. R. Gonçalves, S. Quinteiro, & M. L. Gasparini (Eds.), *Handbook of Research on Cultural Tourism and Sustainability* (pp. 56–83). IGI Global. doi:10.4018/978-1-7998-9217-5.ch004

Høegh-Guldberg, O., Seeler, S., & Eide, D. (2021). Sustainable Visitor Management to Mitigate Overtourism – What, Who, and How. In A. Sharma & H. Azizul (Eds.), *Over-tourism as Destination Risk: Impacts and Solutions* (pp. 167–186). Emerald Publishing Limited. doi:10.1108/978-1-83909-706-520211012

Hofstede, G. (2007). Cultural dimensions explained. *Itim International*, 1–3. http://www.geert-hofstede.com/hofstede_mexico.shtml

Hofstede, G. (1980). Motivation, leadership, and organization: Do American theories apply abroad? *Organizational Dynamics*, 9(1), 42–63.

Holst, J. (2020). Global Health – emergence, hegemonic trends and biomedical reductionism. *Globalization and Health*, 16(1), 1–11. doi:10.118612992-020-00573-4 PMID:32375801

Hong, C., Choi, H., Choi, C., & Joung, D. (2021). Factors affecting customer intention to use online food delivery services before and during the COVID-19 pandemic. *Journal of Hospitality and Tourism Management*, 48, 509–518. doi:10.1016/j.jhtm.2021.08.012

Hopkins, L., Labonté, R., Runnels, V., & Packer, C. (2010). Medical tourism today: What is the state of existing knowledge? *Journal of Public Health Policy*, 31(2), 185–198. doi:10.1057/jphp.2010.10 PMID:20535101

Hörisch, J., Johnson, M. P., & Schaltegger, S. (2015). Implementation of Sustainability Management and Company Size: A Knowledge-Based View. *Business Strategy and the Environment*, 24(8), 765–779. doi:10.1002/bse.1844

Horng, J. S., & Hu, M. L. (2008). The mystery in the kitchen: Culinary creativity. *Creativity Research Journal*, 20(2), 221–230. doi:10.1080/10400410802060166

Horng, J. S., & Hu, M. L. (2009). The creative culinary process: Constructing and extending a four-component model. *Creativity Research Journal*, 21(4), 376–383. doi:10.1080/10400410903297956

Horowitz, M. D. (2007). Medical tourism-health care in the global economy. *Physician Executive*, 33(6), 24. PMID:18092615

Hospitalitynet. (2020a). *MGM resorts international statement on temporary closure of Las Vegas properties*. Retrieved on March 16, 2022, from: https://www.hospitalitynet.org/news/4097568.html

Hospitalitynet. (2020b). *Coronavirus hits German hotel industry hard: more than every-3-guests stay away*. Retrieved on March 16, 2022, from: https://www.hospitalitynet.org/performance/4097569.html

Hossain, S. F. A., Ahsan, F. T., Nadi, A. H., Ahmed, M., & Neyamah, H. (2022). Exploring the Role of Technology Application in Tourism Events, Festivals and Fairs in the United Arab Emirates: Strategies in the Post Pandemic Period. In *Technology Application in Tourism Fairs, Festivals and Events in Asia* (pp. 313–330). Springer. doi:10.1007/978-981-16-8070-0_19

Hovelaque, V., & Bironneau, L. (2015). The carbon-constrained EOQ model with carbon emission dependent demand. *International Journal of Production Economics*, *164*, 285–291. doi:10.1016/j.ijpe.2014.11.022

Hsieh, Y. C. (2012). Hotel companies' environmental policies and practices: A content analysis of their web pages. *International Journal of Contemporary Hospitality Management*, *24*(1), 97–121. doi:10.1108/095961112

Hsu, C. H., & Powers, T. (2008). *Marketing Hospitality*. John Wiley and Sons.

Hua, G., Cheng, T. C. E., & Wang, S. (2011). Managing carbon footprints in inventory management. *International Journal of Production Economics*, *132*(2), 178–185. doi:10.1016/j.ijpe.2011.03.024

Huang, C. Y., Shen, Y. Z., Lin, H. X., & Chang, S. S. (2007). Bloggers' motivations and behaviors: A model. *Journal of Advertising Research*, *47*(4), 472–484. doi:10.2501/S0021849907070493

Huang, H. C., Chang, S. S., & Lou, S. J. (2015). Preliminary investigation on recreation and leisure knowledge sharing by LINE. *Procedia: Social and Behavioral Sciences*, *174*, 3072–3080. doi:10.1016/j.sbspro.2015.01.1100

Huang, J. H., & Peng, K. H. (2012). Fuzzy Rasch model in TOPSIS: A new approach for generating fuzzy numbers to assess the competitiveness of the tourism industries in Asian countries. *Tourism Management*, *33*(2), 456–465. doi:10.1016/j.tourman.2011.05.006

Huang, J., & Min, J. (2002). Earthquake devastation and recovery in tourism: The Taiwan case. *Tourism Management*, *23*(2), 145–154. doi:10.1016/S0261-5177(01)00051-6

Huang, L., Zheng, Q., Yin, X., Luo, M., & Yang, Y. (2022). "Double-edged sword": The effect of cultural distance on post-disaster tourism destination recovery. *Tourism Review*, *77*(1), 146–162. doi:10.1108/TR-03-2021-0113

Huang, O., & Copeland, L. (2020). GEN Z, Instagram Influences, and Hashtags' Influence on Purchase Intention of Apparel. *Academy of Marketing Studies Journal*, *24*(3), 1–14.

Huang, R.-Y., Chang, W.-J., Chung, Y.-C., Yin, Y.-S., & Yen, J. C. (2019). A literature review of sustainable tourism (1990-2016): Development trajectory and framework. *International Journal of Tourism & Hospitality Reviews*, *6*(1), 20–49. doi:10.18510/ijthr.2019.613

Huang, X., Sun, S., & Law, R. (2021). A Reflection of Core Marketing Subjects in E-Hospitality Programmes: The IPO Model. *Journal of Quality Assurance in Hospitality & Tourism*, *22*(3), 336–344. doi:10.1080/1528008X.2020.1774033

Huang, Y. C., Chang, L. L., & Backman, K. F. (2019). Detecting common method bias in predicting creative tourists behavioural intention with an illustration of theory of planned behaviour. *Current Issues in Tourism*, *22*(3), 307–329. doi:10.1080/13683500.2018.1424809

Huang, Y. C., Cheng, J. S., & Chang, L. L. (2020). Understanding Leisure Trip Experience and Subjective Well-Being: An Illustration of Creative Travel Experience. *Applied Research in Quality of Life*, *15*(4), 1161–1182. doi:10.100711482-019-09727-y

Huang, Y. C., Tseng, Y. P., & Petrick, J. F. (2008). Crisis Management Planning to Restore Tourism After Disasters. *Journal of Travel & Tourism Marketing*, *23*(2-4), 203–221. doi:10.1300/J073v23n02_16

Compilation of References

Huan, T. C., Beaman, J., & Shelby, L. (2004). No-escape natural disaster mitigating impacts on tourism. *Annals of Tourism Research*, *31*(2), 255–273. doi:10.1016/j.annals.2003.10.003

Hudson, S. (2008). *Tourism and Hospitality Marketing: a global perspective.* Sage. doi:10.4135/9781446280140

Hudson, S., & Ritchie, J. B. (2009). Branding a memorable destination experience. The case of 'Brand Canada'. *International Journal of Tourism Research*, *11*(2), 217–228. doi:10.1002/jtr.720

Hu, H. H., Parsa, H. G., & Self, J. (2010). The dynamics of green restaurant patronage. *Cornell Hospitality Quarterly*, *51*(3), 344–362. doi:10.1177/1938965510370564

Hunter, W. C., Chung, N., Gretzel, U., & Koo, C. (2015). Constructivist research in smart tourism. *Asia Pacific Journal of Information Systems*, *25*(1), 103–118. doi:10.14329/apjis.2015.25.1.105

Hurriyet (2022, June 19). *Yatirimcinin gozu Bodrum'da.* hurriyet.com

Hussain, M., Ajmal, M. M., Gunasekaran, A., & Khan, M. (2018). Exploration of social sustainability in healthcare supply chain. *Journal of Cleaner Production*, *203*, 977–989. doi:10.1016/j.jclepro.2018.08.157

Hussain, M., Al-Aomar, R., & Melhem, H. (2019). Assessment of Lean-green practices on the sustainable performance of hotel supply chain. *International Journal of Contemporary Hospitality Management*, *31*(6), 2448–2467. doi:10.1108/IJCHM-05-2018-0380

Hussein, F., Stephens, J., & Tiwari, R. (2020). Memory for social sustainability: Recalling cultural memories in Zanqit Alsitat historical street market, Alexandria, Egypt. *Sustainability*, *12*(19), 8141. doi:10.3390u12198141

Hutchins, M. J., & Sutherland, J. W. (2008). An exploration of measures of social sustainability and their application to supply chain decisions. *Journal of Cleaner Production*, *16*(15), 1688–1698. doi:10.1016/j.jclepro.2008.06.001

Huttunen, M. (2018). *Assessment of Research and Innovation on Food Systems by European Member States.* Standing Committee on Agricultural Research (SCAR) Strategic Working Group on Food Systems.

Hu, Y. C., Wang, J. H., & Wang, R. Y. (2012). Evaluating the performance of Taiwan homestay using analytic network Process. *Hindawi Publishing Corporation Mathematical Problems in Engineering*, *2012*(2), 1–25. doi:10.1155/2012/827193

Hwang, C.-L., & Yoon, K. (1981). Methods for Multiple Attribute Decision Making. In *Multiple Attribute Decision Making.* Springer. doi:10.1007/978-3-642-48318-9_3

Hysa, B., Karasek, A., & Zdonek, I. (2021). Social media usage by different generations as a tool for sustainable tourism marketing in society 5.0 idea. *Sustainability*, *13*(3), 1018. doi:10.3390/su13031018

Hystad, P. W., & Keller, P. C. (2008). Towards a destination tourism disaster management framework: Long-term lessons from a forest fire disaster. *Tourism Management*, *29*(1), 151–162. doi:10.1016/j.tourman.2007.02.017

IANS. (2021, November 18). *India is now the world's third-largest domestic aviation market: Scindia.* Retrieved on January 13, 2022, from: https://www.business-standard.com/article/economy-policy/india-now-world-s-third-largest-domestic-aviation-market-scindia-121111900056_1.html

Iansati, M., & Lakhani, K. (2017). The Truth About Blockchain. Harvard Business Review. *Harvard Business Review*, *95*(1), 4–11.

IAT. (n.d.). *Aviation environment and sustainability.* Retrieved on March 15, 2022, from: https://www.iata.org/contentassets/a33c39219430432fb241f7b9ac5a145c/environment.pdf

IATA. (n.d.). *Cabin waste.* Retrieved on March 15, 2022, from: https://www.iata.org/en/programs/environment/cabin-waste/

IBM. (2021). *Food waste*. Benefits of IBM Food Trust: https://www.ibm.com/blockchain/resources/7-benefits-ibm-food-trust/#food-waste

IBM. (2021). *Sustainability*. Benefits of IBM Food Trust: https://www.ibm.com/blockchain/resources/7-benefits-ibm-food-trust/#sustainability

ICAO. (2016). *Performance-Based Navigation (PBN) Implementation Road Map*. Retrieved on July 22, 2021, from: https://www.icao.int/safety/pbn/PBNStatePlans/India%20PBN%20implementation%20plan.pdf

ICAO. (2016, October). *A historic agreement was reached to mitigate international aviation emissions*. Retrieved on July 22, 2021, from: https://www.icao.int/Newsroom/Pages/Historic-agreement-reached-to-mitigate-international-aviation-emissions.aspx

ICOMOS. (1999). *International cultural tourism charter*. Retrieved on August 4, 2020, from: http://www.whitr-ap.org/themes/69/userfiles/download/2013/2/28/vqev6ibfgtbbewh.pdf

Ide, A. (2009). Categorization and future direction of recoveries by tourism. *The International Journal of Tourism Science*, *2*, 31–38. https://ci.nii.ac.jp/naid/110008606971

IFIC. (2020). *COVID-19 pandemic transforms the way we shop, eat and think about food, according to IFIC's 2020 Food & Health Survey*. Retrieved on April 24, 2022, from: https://foodinsight.org/wp-content/uploads/2020/06/2020-Food-and-Health-Survey-.pdf

İflazoğlu, N., & Aksoy, M. (2020). A study on the quality of the service consumers expect from food and beverage enterprises during the Covid-19 outbreak. *Journal of Tourism and Gastronomy Studies*, *8*(4), 3362–3377. doi:10.21325/jotags.2020.766

Ikeda, K. (2018). Security and Privacy of Blockchain and Quantum Computation. *Advances in Computers*, *111*, 199–228. doi:10.1016/bs.adcom.2018.03.003

Ike, M., Donovan, J. D., Topple, C., & Masli, E. K. (2019). A holistic perspective on corporate sustainability from a management viewpoint: Evidence from Japanese manufacturing multinational enterprises. *Journal of Cleaner Production*, *216*, 139–151. doi:10.1016/j.jclepro.2019.01.151

ILO. (2010). Developments and challenges in the hospitality and tourism sector. In *Issues paper for discussion at the Global Dialogue Forum for the Hotels, Catering, Tourism Sector*. Geneva: International Labour Organization.

IndigoReach. (n.d.) *Social changes that reach everywhere, everyone*. Indigo Airlines. Retrieved on August 14, 2021, from: https://www.goindigo.in/csr.html

Ingrassia, M., Bellia, C., Giurdanella, C., Columba, P., & Chironi, S. (2022). Digital Influencers, Food and Tourism—A New Model of Open Innovation for Businesses in the Ho. Re. Ca. Sector. *Journal of Open Innovation: Technology, Market, and Complexity*, *8*(1), 50. doi:10.3390/joitmc8010050

Initiative, T. O. (2003). *Sustainable Tourism: The Tour Operators' Contribution*. TOI.

InnovasjonNorge. (2021). *Nasjonal reiselivsstrategi 2030 – Sterke inntrykk med små avtrykk*. Retrieved on July 4, 2021, from: https://www.regjeringen.no/no/tema/naringsliv/reiseliv/nasjonal-reiselivsstrategi-2030-sterke-inntrykk-med-sma-avtrykk/id2893884/

Instagram Business Team. (2021, January 25). *Introducing Professional Dashboard*. https://business.instagram.com/blog/announcing-instagram-professional-dashboard?locale=en_GB

Ionel, M. (2016). Hospitality industry. *Ovidius University Annals: Economic Sciences Series*, *1*(1), 187–191.

Iordache, C., Ciochină, I., & Roxana, P. (2013). Medical tourism–between the content and socio-economic development goals. Development strategies. *Romanian Journal of Marketing*, (1).

IPC. (2021). *South Africa: IPC Acute Food Insecurity Analysis*. IPC.

Ismail, A., Kassim, A., & Zahari, M. S. (2010). Responsiveness of restaurateurs towards the implementation of environmentally-friendly practices. *South Asian Journal of Tourism and Heritage*, *3*(2), 1–10.

Israeli, A. A. (2002). A preliminary investigation of the importance of site accessibility factors for disabled tourists. *Journal of Travel Research*, *41*(1), 101–104. doi:10.1177/004728750204100114

Isyanto, P., Sapitri, R. G., & Sinaga, O. (2020). Micro Influencers Marketing and Brand Image to Purchase Intention of Cosmetic Products Focallure. *Systematic Review Pharmacy*, *11*(1), 601–605.

ITU. (2008). *ITU and climate change, international telecommunication union*. https://www.itu.int/dms_pub/itu-t/oth/23/01/T23010000030002PDFE.pdf

Ivanov, S., & Zhechev, V. (2012). Hotel revenue management – a critical literature review. *Tourism: An International Interdisciplinary Journal*, *60*(2), 175–197.

Iyer, G., & Jarvis, L. (2019). CSR adoption in the multinational hospitality context. *International Journal of Contemporary Hospitality Management*, *31*(6), 2376–2393. doi:10.1108/IJCHM-06-2018-0451

Iyer, V. R., Chakraborty, S., & Dey, N. (2015). Advent of information technology in the world of tourism. In N. Ray (Ed.), *Emerging Innovative Marketing Strategies in the Tourism Industry* (pp. 44–53). IGI Global. doi:10.4018/978-1-4666-8699-1.ch003

Jacob, M., Tintoré, J., Aguiló, E., Bravo, A., & Mulet, J. (2003). Innovation in the tourism sector: Results from a pilot study in the Balearic Islands. *Tourism Economics*, *9*(3), 279–295. doi:10.1177/135481660300900303

Jafari, J. (1983). Anatomy of the travel industry. *The Cornell Hotel and Restaurant Administration Quarterly*, *24*(1), 71–81. doi:10.1177/001088048302400112

Jafari, J., & Scott, N. (2014). Muslim world and its tourisms. *Annals of Tourism Research*, *44*, 1–19. doi:10.1016/j.annals.2013.08.011

Jain, B. (2022, January). *The Green Aviation Opportunity*. Invest India. https://www.investindia.gov.in/team-india-blogs/green-aviation-opportunity

Jamal, T., & Stronza, A. (2009). Collaboration theory and tourism practice in protected areas: Stakeholders, structuring and sustainability. *Journal of Sustainable Tourism*, *17*(2), 169–189. doi:10.1080/09669580802495741

Jamaludin, M., Othman, N., & Awang, A. R. (2012). Community based homestay programme: A personal experience. *Procedia: Social and Behavioral Sciences*, *42*(7), 451–459. doi:10.1016/j.sbspro.2012.04.210

Jamil, F., Ibrahim, M., Ullah, I., Kim, S., Kahng, H., & Kim, D.-H. (2022). Optimal smart contract for autonomous greenhouse environment based on IoT blockchain network in agriculture. *Computers and Electronics in Agriculture*, *192*, 1–18. doi:10.1016/j.compag.2021.106573

Jan, A. U., & Contreras, V. (2011). Technology acceptance model for the use of information technology in universities. *Computers in Human Behavior*, *27*(2), 845–851. doi:10.1016/j.chb.2010.11.009

Jang, J. Y., Kim, G. W., & Bonn, M. A. (2011). Generation Y Consumers' Selection Attributes and Behavioral Intentions Concerning Green Restaurants. *International Journal of Hospitality Management*, *30*(4), 803–811. doi:10.1016/j.ijhm.2010.12.012

Jang, W., Kim, J., Kim, S., & Chun, J. W. (2020). The role of engagement in travel influencer marketing: The perspectives of dual process theory and the source credibility model. *Current Issues in Tourism*. Advance online publication. doi:10.1080/13683500.2020.1845126

Jarvie, M. E. (2016, May). Brundtland Report. In *Encyclopedia Britannica*. Retrieved on September 11, 2021, from: https://www.britannica.com/topic/Brundtland-Report

Jashi, C. (2013). Significance of Social Media Marketing in Tourism. *8th Silk Road International Conference "Development of Tourism in Black and Caspian Seas Regions*, 37-40.

Jawed, I., Tareen, F.R., Cauhan, K., & Nayeem, M. (2020). Food safety and COVID-19: Limitations of HACCP and the way forward. *The Pharma Innovation Journal, 9*(5), 1-4.

Jeong, E. S., Choi, S. R., & Son, M. Y. (2021). A Study on Intention to Use of Smart Tourism Contents through Extended Technology Acceptance Model: Case of Visitors to the National Museum of Korea. *Journal of Digital Convergence, 19*(9), 115–123. doi:10.14400/JDC.2021.19.9.115

Jeou-Shyan, & Lee, H. Y.-C. (2007). What does it take to be a creative culinary artist? *Journal of Culinary Science & Technology, 5*(2-3), 5–22. doi:10.1300/J385v05n02_02

Jeyacheya, J., & Hampton, M. P. (2020). Wishful thinking or wise policy? Theorising tourism-led inclusive growth: Supply chains and host communities. *World Development, 131*, 104960. doi:10.1016/j.worlddev.2020.104960

Jia, F., Zuluaga-Cardona, L., Bailey, A., & Rueda, X. (2018). Sustainable supply chain management in devel,oping countries: An analysis of the literature. *Journal of Cleaner Production, 189*, 63–278. doi:10.1016/j.jclepro.2018.03.248

Jiao, Y., Gao, J., & Yang, J. (2015, December). Social Value and Content Value in Social Media: Two Ways to Flow. *Journal of Advanced Management Science, 3*(4), 299–306. doi:10.12720/joams.3.4.299-306

Jickling, B. (2000). A Future for Sustainability? *Water, Air, and Soil Pollution, 123*(1/4), 467–476. doi:10.1023/A:1005211410123

Jiménez-Asenjo, N., & Filipescu, D. A. (2019). Cheers in China! International marketing strategies of Spanish wine exporters. *International Business Review, 28*(4), 647–659. doi:10.1016/j.ibusrev.2019.01.001

Jimenez-Mavillard, A., & Suarez, J. L. (2022). A computational approach for creativity assessment of culinary products: The case of elBulli. *AI & Society, 37*(1), 331–353. doi:10.100700146-021-01183-3

Jindal, G., & Gupta, M. (2012). Green computing "future of computers". *International Journal of Emerging Research in Management &Technology*, 14-18.

John, E. (1998). Accounting for the triple bottom line. *Measuring Business Excellence, 2*(3), 18–22. doi:10.1108/eb025539

Johnson, B., & Christensen, L. (2012). *Educational Research, Quantitative, Qualitative, and Mixed Approaches*. SAGE Pub. Inc.

Johnson, C. Y. (1998). A consideration of collective memory in African American attachment to wildland recreation places. *Human Ecology Review*, 5–15.

Jolly, D., & Dimanche, F. (2009). Investing in technology for tourism activities: Perspectives and challenges. *Technovation, 9*(29), 576–579. doi:10.1016/j.technovation.2009.05.004

Jones, P. J. S. (2021). A governance analysis of Ningaloo and Shark Bay Marine Parks, Western Australia: Putting the 'eco' in tourism to build resilience but threatened in long-term by climate change? *Marine Policy, 127*, 103636. doi:10.1016/j.marpol.2019.103636

Compilation of References

Jones, P., & Hamilton, D. (1992). Yield management: Putting people in the big picture. *The Cornell Hotel and Restaurant Administration Quarterly, 33*(1), 89–95. doi:10.1177/001088049203300126

Jørgensen, M. T., Hansen, A. V., Sørensen, F., Fuglsang, L., Sundbo, J., & Jensen, J. F. (2021). Collective tourism social entrepreneurship: A means for community mobilization and social transformation. *Annals of Tourism Research, 88*, 103171. doi:10.1016/j.annals.2021.103171

Jorgenson, J., Nickerson, N., Dalenberg, D., Angle, J., Metcalf, E., & Freimund, W. (2019). Measuring visitor experiences: Creating and testing the tourism autobiographical memory scale. *Journal of Travel Research, 58*(4), 566–578. doi:10.1177/0047287518764344

Jovanović, V., & Njeguš, A. (2016). The application of GIS and its components in tourism. *Yugoslav Journal of Operations Research, 18*(2), 261–272. doi:10.2298/YJOR0802261J

Kaiser, F. G., & Scheuthle, H. (2003). Two challenges to a moral extension of the theory of planned behavior: Moral norms and just world beliefs in conservationism. *Personality and Individual Differences, 35*(5), 1033–1048. doi:10.1016/S0191-8869(02)00316-1

Kallner, A. (2018). Logarithms and exponents formulas. *Laboratory Statistics, 5*(3), 1–140. doi:10.1016/B978-0-12-814348-3.00001-0

Kampf, G., Todt, D., Pfaender, S., & Steinmann, E. (2020). Persistence of coronaviruses on inanimate surfaces and their inactivation with biocidal agents. *The Journal of Hospital Infection, 104*(3), 246–251. doi:10.1016/j.jhin.2020.01.022 PMID:32035997

Kanagal, N. B. (2015). Innovation and product innovation in marketing strategy. *Journal of Management and Marketing Research, 18*(4).

Kang, M., & Schuett, M. A. (2013). Determinants of sharing travel experiences in social media. *Journal of Travel & Tourism Marketing, 30*(1-2), 93–107. doi:10.1080/10548408.2013.751237

Kanwel, S., Lingqiang, Z., Asif, M., Hwang, J., Hussain, A., & Jameel, A. (2019). The influence of destination image on tourist loyalty and intention to visit: Testing a multiple mediation approach. *Sustainability (Switzerland), 11*(22), 6401. Advance online publication. doi:10.3390u11226401

Kaplan, A. M., & Haenlein, M. (2010). Users of the world, unite! The challenges and opportunities of Social Media. *Business Horizons, 53*(1), 59–68. doi:10.1016/j.bushor.2009.09.003

Käpylä, J., Laihonen, H., Lönnqvist, A., & Carlucci, D. (2011). Knowledge-intensity as an organisational characteristic. *Knowledge Management Research and Practice, 9*(4), 315–326. doi:10.1057/kmrp.2011.23

Kara, A. (2010). Swine flu [Domuz gribi]. *Journal of Child Health and Diseases, 53*, 21–25. PMID:21140890

Karaca, E., & Nergiz Güçlü, H. (2021). Examination of Menu Designs of Restaurants During COVID 19 Pandemic: Examples of Restaurant A (Bulgaria) and Restaurant B (Turkey) [COVID-19 Salgın Sürecinde Restoranların Menü Tasarımlarının İncelenmesi: Restoran A (Bulgaristan) ve Restoran B (Türkiye) Örneği]. *Journal of Social Sciences of Mus Alparslan University, 9*(3), 703-713.

Karaçar, E. (2018). *Women and equality/discrimination in the tourism sector [Turizm sektöründe kadın ve eşitlik/ayrımcılık]*. İç. Turizm ve Kadın, Detay Yayıncılık.

Karaca, Ş. (2021). Sağlık turizminde pazarlama. In Ş. Karaca (Ed.), *Multidisipliner yaklaşımla sağlık turizmi* (pp. 215–238). Nobel Yayıncılık.

Karagiannis, D., & Andrinos, M. (2021). The role of sustainable restaurant practices in city branding: The case of Athens. *Sustainability*, *13*(4), 2271. doi:10.3390u13042271

Karagöz, D., & Uysal, M. (2020). Tourists' Need for Uniqueness as a Representation of Differentiated Identity. *Journal of Travel Research*. Advance online publication. doi:10.1177/0047287520972804

Karaküçük, S., & Gürbüz, B. (2007). *Rekreasyon ve kent(li)leşme*. Gazi Kitapevi.

Karaman, A. S., Kilic, M., & Uyar, A. (2018). Sustainability reporting in the aviation industry: Worldwide evidence. *Emerald Insight*, *9*(4), 362–391. doi:10.1108/SAMPJ-12-2017-0150

Karamustafa, K., Ülker, M., & Akçay, S. (2021). A Qualitative Study On Changes In Food And Beverage Service Processes Based On The Covid-19 Pandemic. *Journal of Consumer and Consumption Research*, *13*(1), 33–69.

Karl, M., Kock, F., Ritchie, B. W., & Gauss, J. (2021). Affective forecasting and travel decision-making: An investigation in times of a pandemic. *Annals of Tourism Research*, *87*, 103139. doi:10.1016/j.annals.2021.103139

Kassanuk, T., & Phasinam, K. (2021). Design of blockchain based smart agriculture framework to ensure safety and security. *Materials Today: Proceedings*, 1–4.

Kaur, K., & Kumar, P. (2020). Social media usage in Indian beauty and wellness industry: A qualitative study. *The TQM Journal*, *33*(1), 17–32. doi:10.1108/TQM-09-2019-0216

Kaushal, V., & Srivastava, S. (2021, January). Hospitality and tourism industry amid COVID-19 pandemic: Perspectives on challenges and learnings from India. *International Journal of Hospitality Management*, *92*, 102707. doi:10.1016/j.ijhm.2020.102707 PMID:33024348

Kazemi, N., Abdul-Rashid, S. H., Ghazilla, R. A. R., Shekarian, E., & Zanoni, S. (2016). Economic order quantity models for items with imperfect quality and emission considerations. *International Journal of Systems Science: Operations & Logistics*, *5*(2), 99–115.

Kc, B. (2021). Ecotourism for wildlife conservation and sustainable livelihood via community-based homestay: A formula to success or a quagmire? *Current Issues in Tourism*, *24*(9), 1227–1243. doi:10.1080/13683500.2020.1772206

Keller, K. L. (1993). Conceptualizing, measuring, and managing customer-based brand equity. *Journal of Marketing*, *57*(1), 1–22.

Ketikidis, P., Dimitrovski, T., Lazuras, L., & Bath, P. A. (2012). Acceptance of health information technology in health professionals: An application of the revised technology acceptance model. *Health Informatics Journal*, *18*(2), 124–134. doi:10.1177/1460458211435425 PMID:22733680

Khan, H. (2021). Buying behavior of online consumers during COVID-19 – buying behavior, payment mode, and critical factors affecting consumers buying behavior during the pandemic. *Journal of Management and Training for Industries*, *8*(2), 1–23. doi:10.12792/JMTI.8.2.1

Khan, S. (2011). Gendered leisure: Are women more constrained in travel for leisure? Tourismos. *An International Multidisciplinary Journal Of Tourism*, *6*(1), 105–121.

Khatter, A., McGrath, M., Pyke, J., White, L., & Lockstone-Binney, L. (2019). Analysis of hotels' environmentally sustainable policies and practices. *International Journal of Contemporary Hospitality Management*, *31*(6), 2394–2410. doi:10.1108/IJCHM-08-2018-0670

Kiatkawsin, K., & Sutherland, I. (2020). Examining luxury restaurant dining experience towards sustainable reputation of the Michelin restaurant guide. *Sustainability*, *12*(5), 2134. doi:10.3390u12052134

Compilation of References

Kiboko, A. B. (2017). *Inventory management practices and operational performance of hotels in Mombasa, Kenya* [Unpublished master project]. The University of Nairobi.

Kılıç, Y., & Babat, B. V. (2000). *Quality Function Deployment: A Hypothetical Approach on Food and Beverage Establishment* [Kalite Fonksiyon Göçerimi: Yiyecek-İçecek İşletmelerine Yönelik Kuramsal Bir Yaklaşım]. Karamanoğlu Mehmetbey University Journal of Social and Economic Research.

Kim, A. J., Stembridge, S., Lawrence, C., Torres, V., Miodrag, N., Lee, J., & Boynes, D. (2015). Neurodiversity on the stage: The effects of inclusive theatre on youth with autism. *International Journal of Education and Social Science*, *2*(9), 27–39.

Kimes, S. E. (1989). Yield management: A tool for capacity-constrained service firms. *Journal of Operations Management*, *8*(4), 348–363. doi:10.1016/0272-6963(89)90035-1

Kimes, S. E., & Chase, R. B. (1998). The Strategic Levers of Yield Management. *Journal of Service Research*, *1*(2), 156–166. doi:10.1177/109467059800100205

Kim, H., Hur, W., & Yeo, J. (2015). Corporate brand trust as mediator in the relationship between customer perception of CSR, corporate hypocrisy and corporate reputation. *Sustainability*, *7*(4), 3683–3694. doi:10.3390u7043683

Kim, H., Koo, C., & Chung, N. (2021). The role of mobility apps in memorable tourism experiences of Korean tourists: Stress-coping theory perspective. *Journal of Hospitality and Tourism Management*, *49*, 548–557. doi:10.1016/j.jhtm.2021.11.003

Kim, H., Stepchenkova, S., & Babalou, V. (2018). Branding destination co-creatively: A case study of tourists' involvement in the naming of a local attraction. *Tourism Management Perspectives*, *28*, 189–200.

Kim, J. H. (2010). Determining the factors affecting the memorable nature of travel experiences. *Journal of Travel & Tourism Marketing*, *27*(8), 780–796. doi:10.1080/10548408.2010.526897

Kim, J. H. (2014). The antecedents of memorable tourism experiences: The development of a scale to measure the destination attributes associated with memorable experiences. *Tourism Management*, *44*, 34–45. doi:10.1016/j.tourman.2014.02.007

Kim, J. H., Ritchie, J. B., & McCormick, B. (2012). Development of a scale to measure memorable tourism experiences. *Journal of Travel Research*, *51*(1), 12–25. doi:10.1177/0047287510385467

Kim, J. H., Ritchie, J. R., & Tung, V. W. S. (2010). The effect of memorable experience on behavioral intentions in tourism: A structural equation modeling approach. *Tourism Analysis*, *15*(6), 637–648. doi:10.3727/108354210X12904412049776

Kim, J., Kim, J., Lee, S. K., & Tang, L. R. (2020). Effects Of Epidemic Disease Outbreaks On Financial Performance Of Restaurants: Event Study Method Approach. *Journal of Hospitality and Tourism Management*, *43*, 32–41. doi:10.1016/j.jhtm.2020.01.015

Kim, J., & Lee, J. C. (2020). Effects of COVID-19 on preferences for private dining facilities in restaurants. *Journal of Hospitality and Tourism Management*, *45*, 67–70. doi:10.1016/j.jhtm.2020.07.008

Kim, K., Bonnb, M. A., & Choc, M. (2021). Clean safety message framing as survival strategies for small independent restaurants during the COVID-19 pandemic. *Journal of Hospitality and Tourism Management*, *46*, 423–431. doi:10.1016/j.jhtm.2021.01.016

Kim, S. (2018). Blockchain for a Trust Network Among Intelligent Vehicles. *Advances in Computers*, *111*, 43–68. doi:10.1016/bs.adcom.2018.03.010

Kim, S. H., Abbasi, F., Lamendola, C., & Reaven, G. M. (2009). Effect of moderate alcoholic beverage consumption on insulin sensitivity in insulin-resistant, nondiabetic individuals. *Metabolism: Clinical and Experimental*, *58*(3), 387–392. doi:10.1016/j.metabol.2008.10.013 PMID:19217456

Kim, T. G., Lee, J. H., & Law, R. (2008). An empirical examination of the acceptance behaviour of hotel front office systems: An extended technology acceptance model. *Tourism Management*, *29*(3), 500–513. doi:10.1016/j.tourman.2007.05.016

Kim, Y., & Han, H. (2010). Intention to pay conventional-hotel prices at a green hotel - a modification of the theory of planned behavior. *Journal of Sustainable Tourism*, *18*(8), 997–1014. doi:10.1080/09669582.2010.490300

Kim, Y., Lee, S. S., & Roh, T. (2020). Taking Another Look at Airline CSR: How Required CSR and Desired CSR Affect Customer Loyalty in the Airline Industry. *Sustainability*, *12*(10), 1–19. doi:10.3390u12104281

Kim, Y., Ribeiro, M. A., & Li, G. (2021). Tourism memory characteristics scale: Development and validation. *Journal of Travel Research*, 1–19.

Kim, Y., Ribeiro, M. A., & Li, G. (2022). Tourism memory, mood repair and behavioral intention. *Annals of Tourism Research*, *93*, 103369. doi:10.1016/j.annals.2022.103369

King, W. R., & He, J. (2006). A meta-analysis of the technology acceptance model. *Information & Management*, *43*(6), 740–755. doi:10.1016/j.im.2006.05.003

Kinnaird, V., & Hall, D. (1996). Understanding tourism processes: A gender-aware framework. *Tourism Management*, *17*(2), 95–102. doi:10.1016/0261-5177(95)00112-3

Kirkpatrick, E. A. (1894). An experimental study of memory. *Psychological Review*, *1*(6), 602–609. doi:10.1037/h0068244

Kişi, N. (2019). A strategic approach to sustainable tourism development using the A'WOT hybrid method: A case study of Zonguldak, Turkey. *Sustainability*, *11*(4), 964. doi:10.3390u11040964

Kivela, J. & Crotts, C., J. (2006). Tourism and Gastronomy: Gastronomy's Influence on How Tourists Experience a Destinations. *Journal of Hospitality & Tourism Research*, *30*(3), 354-377.

Kivela, J., & Crotts, J. (2006). Tourism and Gastronomy: Gastronomy's Influence on How Tourists Experience a Destination. *Journal of Hospitality & Tourism Research (Washington, D.C.)*, *30*(3), 354–377. doi:10.1177/1096348006286797

Klassen, R. D., & McLaughlin, C. P. (1996). The Impact of Environmental Management on Firm Performance. *Management Science*, *42*(8), 1199–1214. doi:10.1287/mnsc.42.8.1199

Kleindorfer, P. R., Singhal, K., & Wassenhove, L. N. V. (2005). Sustainable Operations Management. *Production and Operations Management*, *14*(4), 482–492. doi:10.1111/j.1937-5956.2005.tb00235.x

Klein, S. B. (2015). What memory is. *Wiley Interdisciplinary Reviews: Cognitive Science*, *6*(1), 1–38. doi:10.1002/wcs.1333 PMID:26262926

Kliewe, T., Davey, T., & Baaken, T. (2013). Creating a sustainable innovation environment within large enterprises: A case study on a professional services firm. *Journal of Innovation Management*, *1*(1), 55–84. doi:10.24840/2183-0606_001.001_0006

Knight, H., Megicks, P., Agarwal, S., & Leenders, M. A. A. M. (2018). Firm Resources and the development of environmental sustainability among small and medium-sized enterprises: Evidence from the Australian wine industry. *Business Strategy and the Environment*, *28*(1), 25–39. doi:10.1002/bse.2178

Koe Hwee Nga, J., & Shamuganathan, G. (2010). The Influence of Personality Traits and Demographic Factors on Social Entrepreneurship Start Up Intentions. *Journal of Business Ethics*, *95*(2), 259–282. doi:10.100710551-009-0358-8

Compilation of References

Koehl, D. (2011). *Toolbox for crisis communications in tourism: Checklists and best practices*. Univerza v Ljubljani, Ekonomska fakulteta, Madrid.

Kolk, A., Kourula, A., Pisani, N., & Westermann-Behaylo, M. (2020). The state of international business, corporate social responsibility and development: key insights and an application to practice. In P. Lund-Thomsen, M. W. Hansen, & A. Lindgreen (Eds.), *Business and Development Studies: Issues and perspective*. Routledge.

Kolk, A., & Lenfant, F. (2010). MNC Reporting on CSR and Conflict in Central Africa. *Journal of Business Ethics*, *93*(S2), 241–255. doi:10.100710551-009-0271-1

Kolk, A., & van Tulder, R. (2010). International business, corporate social responsibility and sustainable development. *International Business Review*, *19*(2), 119–125. doi:10.1016/j.ibusrev.2009.12.003

Kooiman, J. (Ed.). (1993). *Modern governance: New government-society interactions*. Sage.

Korkmaz, M., Özkök, F., & Uluocak, Ş. (2019). Investigating the perspective of local people towards Women tourists in the context of gender roles Equality and life values: Gokceada case [Yerel halkın kadın turistlere yönelik bakış açısının toplumsal cinsiyet rolleri eşitliği ve yaşam değerleri bağlamında incelenmesi: Gökçeada örneği]. *Journal Of Life Economics*, *6*(1), 35–60. doi:10.15637/jlecon.6.004

Kornilaki, M., Thomas, R., & Font, X. (2019). The sustainability behaviour of small firms in tourism: The role of self-efficacy and contextual constraints. *Journal of Sustainable Tourism*, *27*(1), 97–117. doi:10.1080/09669582.2018.1561706

Kortt, M. A., Sinnewe, E., & Pervan, S. J. (2018). The gender wage gap in the tourism industry: Evidence from Australia. *Tourism Analysis*, *23*(1), 137–149. doi:10.3727/108354217X15143857878697

Kostopoulos, K., Papalexandris, A., Papachroni, M., & Ioannou, G. (2011). Absorptive capacity, innovation, and financial performance. *Journal of Business Research*, *64*(12), 1335–1343. doi:10.1016/j.jbusres.2010.12.005

Kozak, M. A. (1996). Positions women hold in the accommodations industry, (Konaklama endüstrisinde kadının konumu). Anatolia. *Turizm Araştırmaları Dergisi*, *7*(2), 16–23.

Kozak, M., Keser, D., Büken, M. E., & Zaimoğlu, Z. (2019). İklim Değişikliği İle Mücadelede Soframızdaki Yiyeceklerin Karbon Ayak İzi [The Carbon Footprint of the Food on Our Table in Combating Climate Change]. *International Symposium on Advanced Engineering Technologies*, 920-925.

Kraus, S., Clauss, T., Breier, M., Gast, J., Zardini, A., & Tiberius, V. (2020). The economics of COVID-19: initial empirical evidence on how family firms in five European countries cope with the corona crisis. *International Journal of Entrepreneurial Behavior & Research*.

Krietsch Boerner, L. (2021, September). *Airlines want to make flights more sustainable. How will they do it?* Retrieved on December 19, 2021, from: https://cen.acs.org/environment/sustainability/Airlines-want-make-flight-sustainable/99/i32

Kruk, M. E., Pate, M., & Mullan, Z. (2017). Introducing the Lancet Global Health Commission on high-quality health systems in the SDG era. *The Lancet. Global Health*, *5*(5), 480–481. doi:10.1016/S2214-109X(17)30101-8 PMID:28302563

Kudo, T., Lahey, R., Hirschfeld, C. B., Williams, M. C., Lu, B., Alasnag, M., Bhatia, M., Henry Bom, H.-S., Dautov, T., Fazel, R., Karthikeyan, G., Keng, F. Y. J., Rubinshtein, R., Better, N., Cerci, R. J., Dorbala, S., Raggi, P., Shaw, L. J., Villines, T. C., & .... (2021). Impact of COVID-19 Pandemic on Cardiovascular Testing in Asia. *Journal of the American College of Cardiology: Asia*, *1*, 187–199.

Kudratova, S., Huang, X., & Zhou, X. (2018). Sustainable project selection: Optimal project selection considering sustainability under reinvestment strategy. *Journal of Cleaner Production*, *203*, 469–481. doi:10.1016/j.jclepro.2018.08.259

Kuhlman, T., & Farrington, J. (2010). What is Sustainability? *Sustainability*, *2*(11), 3436–3448. doi:10.3390u2113436

Kumar, N., & Soni, R. (2017). ABC Analysis in the hospitality sector: A case study. *Operations & Supply Chain Management*, (Special Issue), 1–3.

Kumar, S., Raja, R., Kuswaha, A. K. S., Kumar, S., & Patra, R. K. (2021). *Green computing and its applications*. Nova Science Publishers. doi:10.52305/ENYH6923

Kunjuraman, V., & Hussin, R. (2017). Challenges of community-based homestay programme in Sabah, Malaysia: Hopeful or hopeless? *Tourism Management Perspectives*, *21*, 1–9. doi:10.1016/j.tmp.2016.10.007

Kurland, N. B. (1995). Ethical intentions and the theories of reasoned action and planned behavior. *Journal of Applied Social Psychology*, *25*(4), 297–313. doi:10.1111/j.1559-1816.1995.tb02393.x

Kurnaz, A. (2017). *Sürdürülebilir gastronomi kapsamında yeşil restoranların hizmet kalite algısının GRSERV ile ölçümü: İstanbul örneği* [Measurement of service quality perception of green restaurants within the scope of sustainable gastronomy with GRSERV: The example of Istanbul]. [Doktora tezi]. Adnan Menderes Üniversitesi Sosyal Bilimler Enstitüsü.

Kusumadewi, N. M. W. (2021). Persuasion Mechanism of Social Media Influencers in Tourism. *IJISET - International Journal of Innovative Science, Engineering & Technology*, *8*(8), 76–79.

Kvale, S., & Brinkman, S. (2009). Interview quality. *Interviews: Learning the craft of qualitative research interviewing*, 161-175.

Laato, S., Islam, A. N., Farooq, A., & Dhir, A. (2020). Unusual purchasing behavior during the early stages of the COVID-19 pandemic: The stimulus-organism-response approach. *Journal of Retailing and Consumer Services*, *57*, 102224. doi:10.1016/j.jretconser.2020.102224

Labrecque, L. I., vor dem Esche, J., Mathwick, C., Novak, T. P., & Hofacker, C. F. (2013). Consumer power: Evolution in the digital age. *Journal of Interactive Marketing*, *27*(4), 257–269.

Lacalle, E. (2021, April 2). *How does an online hotel reservation system work?* [Web blog message]. Retrieved on September 2, 2021, from: https://www.mews.com/en/blog/hotel-reservation-system

Lacorde, M. (2019). Assessing the environmental characteristics of the Margaret River Wine Region, Australia. *International Journal of Applied Geospatial Research*, *10*(3), 1–24. doi:10.4018/IJAGR.2019070101

Lacroix, L., & Milliot, E. (2021). The Butterfly Effect of COVID-19: Toward an Adapted Model of Commodity Supply. In M. A. Marinov & S. T. Marinova (Eds.), *COVID-19 and International Business* (pp. 192–204). Routledge.

Lai, S., Zhang, S., Zhang, L., Tseng, H. W., & Shiau, Y. C. (2021). Study on the influence of cultural contact and tourism memory on the intention to revisit: A case study of cultural and creative districts. *Sustainability (Switzerland)*, *13*(4), 1–18. doi:10.3390u13042416

Lalangan, K. (2020). *Social Media in Tourism: The Impacts of Travel Content on YouTube and Instagram*. Academic Press.

Lampropoulos, V., Panagiotopoulou, M., & Stratigea, A. (2021). Assessing the performance of current strategic policy directions towards unfolding the potential of the culture–tourism nexus in the Greek Territory. *Heritage*, *4*(4), 3157–3185. doi:10.3390/heritage4040177

Landres, P., Spildie, D. R., & Queen, L. P. (2001). *GIS Applications to wilderness management: Potential uses and limitations*. Fort Collins, CO: US Department of Agriculture, Forest Service, Rocky Mountain Research Station. General Technical Report RMRS-GTR-80.

Lane, B. (1994). Sustainable rural tourism strategies: A tool for development and conservation. *Journal of Sustainable Tourism*, *2*(1–2), 102–111. doi:10.1080/09669589409510687

Lane, H. W., & Maznevski, M. L. (2019). *International Management Behavior: Global and Sustainable Leadership* (8th ed.). Cambridge University Press. doi:10.1017/9781108637152

Langemeyer, J., Calcagni, F., & Baró, F. (2018). Mapping the intangible: Using geolocated social media data to examine landscape aesthetics. *Land Use Policy*, *77*, 542–552. doi:10.1016/j.landusepol.2018.05.049

Langwell, C., & Heaton, D. (2016). Using human resource activities to implement sustainability in SMEs. *Journal of Small Business and Enterprise Development*, *23*(3), 652–670. doi:10.1108/JSBED-07-2015-0096

Larson, L., & Poudyal, N. (2012). Developing sustainable tourism through adaptive resource management: A case study of Machu Picchu, Peru. *Journal of Sustainable Tourism*, *20*(7), 917–938. doi:10.1080/09669582.2012.667217

Law, R., Buhalis, D., & Cobanoglu, C. (2014). Progress on information and communication technologies in hospitality and tourism. *International Journal of Contemporary Hospitality Management*, *26*(5), 727–750. doi:10.1108/IJCHM-08-2013-0367

Lechner, A. M., Verbrugge, L. N., Chelliah, A., Ang, M. L. E., & Raymond, C. M. (2020). Rethinking tourism conflict potential within and between groups using participatory mapping. *Landscape and Urban Planning*, *203*, 103902. doi:10.1016/j.landurbplan.2020.103902

Leddy, A. M., Whittle, H. J., Shieh, J., Ramirez, C., Ofotokun, I., & Weiser, S. D. (2020). Exploring the role of social capital in managing food insecurity among older women in the United States. *Social Science & Medicine*, *265*, 113492. doi:10.1016/j.socscimed.2020.113492 PMID:33162195

Lee, C. Y., Chang, W. C., & Lee, H. C. (2017). An investigation of the effects of corporate social responsibility on corporate reputation and customer loyalty – evidence from the Taiwan non-life insurance industry. *Social Responsibility Journal*, *13*(2), 355–369. doi:10.1108/SRJ-01-2016-0006

Lee, H., Herbert, R. D., & McAuley, J. H. (2015). Mediation analysis. *Journal of the American Medical Association*, *314*(15), 1637–1638. doi:10.1001/jama.2015.13480 PMID:26501539

Lee, J. (2019). A decentralized token economy: How blockchain and cryptocurrency can revolutionize business. *Business Horizons*, *62*(6), 773–784. doi:10.1016/j.bushor.2019.08.003

Lee, K. J., & Lee, S. Y. (2021). Cognitive appraisal theory, memorable tourism experiences, and family cohesion in rural travel. *Journal of Travel & Tourism Marketing*, *38*(4), 399–412. doi:10.1080/10548408.2021.1921094

Lee, K. S. (2021). Expressionist view of culinary creativity: A culinary theory exercised with specialty coffee. *International Journal of Gastronomy and Food Science*, *23*, 100311. doi:10.1016/j.ijgfs.2021.100311

Lee, K. S., Blum, D., Miao, L., & Tomas, S. R. (2019). The duality of a pastry chef's creative process. *Events and Tourism Review*, *2*(1), 21–29. doi:10.18060/22958

Lee, K. S., Blum, D., Miao, L., & Tomas, S. R. (2020). The creative minds of extraordinary pastry chefs: An integrated theory of aesthetic expressions - a portraiture study. *International Journal of Contemporary Hospitality Management*, *32*(9), 3015–3034. doi:10.1108/IJCHM-04-2020-0329

Lee, M., Han, H., & Lockyer, T. (2012). Medical tourism—Attracting Japanese tourists for medical tourism experience. *Journal of Travel & Tourism Marketing*, *29*(1), 69–86. doi:10.1080/10548408.2012.638564

Lee, M., Jeong, M., & Shea, L. J. (2021). Length of stay control: Is it a fair inventory management strategy in hotel market? *Tourism Economics*, *27*(2), 307–327. doi:10.1177/1354816619901207

Lee, T. H., & Crompton, J. (1992). Measuring novelty seeking in tourism. *Annals of Tourism Research*, *19*(4), 732–751. doi:10.1016/0160-7383(92)90064-V

Lee, W. H., Lin, C. W., & Shih, K. H. (2018). A technology acceptance model for the perception of restaurant service robots for trust, interactivity, and output quality. *International Journal of Mobile Communications*, *16*(4), 361–376. doi:10.1504/IJMC.2018.092666

Lee, W., & Jeong, C. (2020). Beyond the correlation between tourist eudaimonic and hedonic experiences: Necessary condition analysis. *Current Issues in Tourism*, *23*(17), 2182–2194. doi:10.1080/13683500.2019.1611747

Legrand, W., Sloan, P., Simons-Kaufmann, C., & Fleisher, S. (2010). A Review of Restaurant Sustainable Indicators. In Advances in Hospitality and Leisure (vol. 6). Emerald Group Publishing Limited.

Legris, P., Ingham, J., & Collerette, P. (2003). Why do people use information technology? A critical review of the technology acceptance model. *Information & Management*, *40*(3), 191–204. doi:10.1016/S0378-7206(01)00143-4

Leiper, N. (1995). *Tourism management*. RMIT Press.

Leitch, C. M., McMullan, C., & Harrison, R. T. (2013). The development of entrepreneurial leadership: The role of human, social and institutional capital. *British Journal of Management*, *24*(3), 347–366. doi:10.1111/j.1467-8551.2011.00808.x

Leitner, M. J., & Leitner, S. F. (2012). *Leisure enhancement*. Sagamore Publishing LLC.

Leonard, S., Parsons, M., Olawsky, K., & Kofod, F. (2013). The role of culture and traditional knowledge in climate change adaptation: Insights from East Kimberley, Australia. *Global Environmental Change*, *23*(3), 623–632. doi:10.1016/j.gloenvcha.2013.02.012

Leong, L. Y., Ooi, K. B., Chong, A. Y. L., & Lin, B. (2013). Modeling the stimulators of the behavioral intention to use mobile entertainment: Does gender really matter? *Computers in Human Behavior*, *29*(5), 2109–2121. doi:10.1016/j.chb.2013.04.004

Lerro, M., Yeh, C.-H., Klink-Lehmann, J., Vecchio, R., Hartmann, M., & Cembalo, L. (2021). The effect of moderating variables on consumer preferences for sustainable wines. *Food Quality and Preference*, *94*, 94. doi:10.1016/j.foodqual.2021.104336

Leshem, S., & Trafford, V. (2007). Overlooking the conceptual framework. *Innovations in Education and Teaching International*, *44*(1), 93–105. doi:10.1080/14703290601081407

Lester, A. (2021). *Sustainability. In Project Management, Planning and Control*. Butterworth-Heinemann.

Lew, A. A., & Wong, A. (2004). Sojourners, guanxi and clan associations. Social capital and overseas Chinese tourism to China. In T. Coles & D. J. Timothy (Eds.), *Tourism, Diasporas and Space, Contemporary Geographies of Leisure, Tourism and Mobility* (pp. 202–214). Taylor and Francis.

Lidman, K., & Renström, S. (2011). *How to design for sustainable behaviour? A review of design strategies and an empirical study of four product concepts* [Unpublished Master Thesis]. Chalmers University of Technology, Sweden.

Li, E. L., Zhou, L., & Wu, A. (2017). The supply-side of environmental sustainability and export performance: The role of knowledge integration and international buyer involvement. *International Business Review*, *26*(4), 724–735. doi:10.1016/j.ibusrev.2017.01.002

Li, F., Wen, J., & Ying, T. (2018). The influence of crisis on tourists' perceived destination image and revisit intention: An exploratory study of Chinese tourists to North Korea. *Journal of Destination Marketing & Management*, *9*, 104–111. doi:10.1016/j.jdmm.2017.11.006

Lin, D., Jiang, Z., & Qu, H. (2021). Asymmetric Effects of Quality of Life on Residents' Satisfaction: Exploring a Newborn Natural Disaster Tourism Destination. *International Journal of Environmental Research and Public Health*, *18*(21), 11577. doi:10.3390/ijerph182111577 PMID:34770091

Lindberg, F., Fitchett, J., & Martin, D. (2019). Investigating sustainable tourism heterogeneity: Competing orders of worth among stakeholders of a Nordic destination. *Journal of Sustainable Tourism*, *27*(8), 1277–1294. doi:10.1080/09669582.2019.1614188

Lindqvist, L. J., & Björk, P. (2000). Perceived safety as an important quality dimension among senior tourists. *Tourism Economics*, *6*(2), 151–158. doi:10.5367/000000000101297541

Lindroth, K., Ritalahti, J., & Soisalon-Soininen, T. (2007). Creative tourism in destination development. *Tourism Review*, *62*(3/4), 53–58.

Lindskov, A. (2021). Hypercompetition: a review and agenda for future research. *Competitiveness Review: An International Business Journal*. doi:10.1108/CR-06-2021-0097

Lin, Y., Kelemen, M., & Tresidder, R. (2018). Post-disaster tourism: Building resilience through community-led approaches in the aftermath of the 2011 disasters in Japan. *Journal of Sustainable Tourism*, *26*(10), 1766–1783. doi:10.1080/09669582.2018.1511720

Lin, Z. M. (2013). Making aviation green. *Advances in Manufacturing*, *1*(1), 42–49. doi:10.100740436-013-0008-3

Liu, C. H., Horng, J. S., Chou, S. F., Chen, Y. C., Lin, Y. C., & Zhu, Y. Q. (2016). An empirical examination of the form of relationship between sustainable tourism experiences and satisfaction. *Asia Pacific Journal of Tourism Research*, *21*(7), 717–740. doi:10.1080/10941665.2015.1068196

Liu, I. C., & Chen, C. C. (2013). Cultural issues in medical tourism. *American Journal of Tourism Research*, *2*(1), 78–83. doi:10.11634/216837861302318

Liu-Lastres, B., Mariska, D., Tan, X., & Ying, T. (2020). Can post-disaster tourism development improve destination livelihoods? A case study of Aceh, Indonesia. *Journal of Destination Marketing & Management*, *18*, 100510. doi:10.1016/j.jdmm.2020.100510

Liu, S. (2017). *What is Sustainability? In Bioprocess Engineering Kinetics, Sustainability, and Reactor Design*. Elsevier. doi:10.1016/C2015-0-04891-2

Liu, S. (2020). Food supply pressure in France and Germany during COVID-19: Causes from manufacturing. *Journal of Agriculture, Food Systems, and Community Development*, *9*(4), 139–142. doi:10.5304/jafscd.2020.094.007

Liu, Z., Wang, A., Weber, K., Chan, E. H. W., & Shi, W. (2022). Categorisation of cultural tourism attractions by tourist preference using location-based social network data: The case of Central, Hong Kong. *Tourism Management*, *90*, 90. doi:10.1016/j.tourman.2022.104488

Li, X., Gong, J., Gao, B., & Yuan, P. (2021). Impacts of COVID-19 on tourists' destination preferences: Evidence from China. *Annals of Tourism Research*, *90*, 103258. doi:10.1016/j.annals.2021.103258 PMID:34924648

Li, X., & Liu, Q. (2020). Social media use, eHealth Literacy, disease knowledge, and preventive behaviors in the COVID-19 pandemic: Cross-sectional study on Chinese netizens. *Journal of Medical Internet Research*, *22*(10), e19684. Advance online publication. doi:10.2196/19684 PMID:33006940

Li, Z., & Gao, X. (2021). Makers' relationship network, knowledge acquisition and innovation performance: An empirical analysis from china. *Technology in Society*, *66*, 101684. doi:10.1016/j.techsoc.2021.101684

Lock, S. (2020). Daily year-on-year impact of COVID-19 on global restaurant dining. *Statista.* https://www.statista.com/statistics/1103928/coronavirus-restaurant-visit ation-impact/

Lock, S. (2022a, January 7). *Forecasted change in revenue from the travel and tourism industry due to the coronavirus (COVID-19) pandemic worldwide from 2019 to 2020.* https://www.statista.com/forecasts/1103426/covid-19-revenue-travel-tourism-industry-forecast

Lock, S. (2022b, August 22). *Global tourism industry-statistics and facts.* https://www.statista.com/topics/962/global-tourism/#topicHeader__wrapper

Locke, R., & Romis, M. (2007). Improving Work Conditions in a Global Supply Chain. *MIT Sloan Management Review*, *48*, 54.

Lockyer, T. (2007). Yield management: The case of the accommodation industry in New Zealand. *International Journal of Revenue Management*, *1*(4), 315–326. doi:10.1504/IJRM.2007.015536

Loftus, E. F. (1988). *Memory*. Rowman & Littlefield Publishers.

Lokalno. (2018). *In Europe it is a trend, in Skopje it did not take*. Retrieved on August 15, 2018, from: https://lokalno.mk/vo-evropa-e-trend-a-vo-skopje-ne-zazhivea-iznajmuvaneto-velosipedi/

Long, H., Zhang, Y., & Tu, S. (2019). Rural vitalization in China: A perspective of land consolidation. *Journal of Geographical Sciences*, *29*(4), 517–530. doi:10.100711442-019-1599-9

Longwoods International. (2016). *Michigan 2015 Tourism Advertising Evaluation and Image Study*. Retrieved on July 20, 2018, from: https://www.michiganbusiness.org/cm/Files/Reports/MI%202015%20National%20Regional%20Ad%20Evaluation%20Image%20Study_Final%20Report.pdf

Longwoods International. (2017). *Michigan 2016 Tourism Advertising Evaluation and Image Study*. Retrieved on July 20, from: https://www.michiganbusiness.org/cm/Files/Reports/MI%202016%20National%20Regional%20Ad%20Evaluation%20%20Image%20Study%20Final%20Report%20(003).pdf

Lopez de Avila, A. (2015). Smart Destinations: XXI Century Tourism. Presented at the *ENTER2015 Conference on Information and Communication Technologies in Tourism*, Lugano, Switzerland.

López-Guzmán, T., & Sánchez-Cañizares, S. (2012). Gastronomy, Tourism and Destination Differentiation: A Case Study in Spain. *Revue d'Economie Financiere*, *1*, 63–72.

Lorenzini, B. (1994). The green restaurant, part II: Systems and service. *Restaurants & Institutions*, (104), 119–136.

Lorenzo, J. R. F., Rubio, M. T. M., & Garcés, S. A. (2018). The competitive advantage in business, capabilities and strategy. What general performance factors are found in the Spanish wine industry? *Wine Economics and Policy*, *7*(2), 94–108. doi:10.1016/j.wep.2018.04.001

Lou, C., & Yuan, S. (2019). Influencer marketing: How message value and credibility affect consumer trust of branded content on social media. *Journal of Interactive Advertising*, *19*(1), 58–73. doi:10.1080/15252019.2018.1533501

Louv, R. (2008). *Last child in the woods: Saving our children from nature-deficit disorder*. Algonquin Books.

Lozano-Oyola, M., Blancas, F. J., Gonzalez, M., & Caballero, R. (2019). Sustainable tourism tags to reward destination management. *Journal of Environmental Management*, *250*, 109458. doi:10.1016/j.jenvman.2019.109458 PMID:31472380

Lozano, R., Carpenter, A., & Huisingh, D. (2015). A review of 'theories of the firm' and their contributions to Corporate Sustainability. *Journal of Cleaner Production*, *106*, 430–442. doi:10.1016/j.jclepro.2014.05.007

Lu, C., Huang, J., Chen, C., Shu, M., Hsu, C., & Tapas Bapu, B. (2021). An energy-efficient smart city for sustainable green tourism industry. *Sustainable Energy Technologies and Assessments*, *47*, 101494. doi:10.1016/j.seta.2021.101494

Luckstead, J., Nayga, R. M. Jr, & Snell, H. A. (2020). Labor Issues in the Food Supply Chain Amid the COVID-19 Pandemic. *Applied Economic Perspectives and Policy*, *43*(1), 382–400. doi:10.1002/aepp.13090 PMID:33173571

Lu, J., & Nepal, S. K. (2009). Sustainable tourism research: An analysis of papers published in the Journal of Sustainable Tourism. *Journal of Sustainable Tourism*, *17*(1), 5–16. doi:10.1080/09669580802582480

Lu, J., Yu, C., Liu, C., & Yao, J. E. (2003). Technology acceptance model for wireless Internet. *Internet Research*, *13*(3), 206–222. doi:10.1108/10662240310478222

Lundberg, A. K., Granås Bardal, K., Vangelsten, B. V., Brynildsen, M., Bjørkan, R., Bjørkan, M., & Richardson, T. K. (2020). *Strekk i laget. En kartlegging av hvordan FNs bærekraftsmål implementeres i regional og kommunal planlegging*. Academic Press.

Luštický, M., & Bína, V. (2014). Application of Fuzzy Benchmarking Approach for Strategic Planning of Tourism Destination. *Journal of Quality Assurance in Hospitality & Tourism*, *15*(4), 327–355. doi:10.1080/1528008X.2014.921779

Luty, J. (2020a). *Decline in pub, bar and restaurant sales due to covid-19 In The UK 2020*. Retrieved on March 23, 2022, from: https://www.statista.com/statistics/1105174/uk-pub-and-restaurant-sales-fall-due-to-covid-19/

Luty, J. (2020b). *Year-over-year daily change in seated restaurant diners due to the coronavirus (Covid-19) pandemic in Germany from February 24, 2020 to February 20, 2022*. Retreived on March 23, 2022, from: https://www.statista.com/statistics/1105090/coronavirus-restaurant-visitation-impact-german/

M&M Technologies. (2012). *M&M Technologies Food Safety and Food Security*. Retrieved on June 1, 2020, from: https://www.foodsafetymagazine.com/signature-series/food-safety-and-food-security/

Maberly, C., & Reid, D. (2014). Gastronomy: An approach to studying food. *Nutrition & Food Science*, *44*(4), 272–278. doi:10.1108/NFS-02-2014-0013

MacDonald, M. (2002). *Agendas for sustainability: Environment and development into the 21st century*. Routledge. doi:10.4324/9780203021057

Mach, L., & Ponting, J. (2021). Establishing a pre-COVID-19 baseline for surf tourism: Trip expenditure and attitudes, behaviors and willingness to pay for sustainability. *Annals of Tourism Research Empirical Insights*, 2.

MacKenzie, N., & Gannon, M. J. (2019). Exploring the antecedents of sustainable tourism development. *International Journal of Contemporary Hospitality Management*, *31*(6), 2411–2427. doi:10.1108/IJCHM-05-2018-0384

Ma, D., Hu, J., & Yao, F. (2021). Big data empowering low-carbon smart tourism study on low-carbon tourism O2O supply chain considering consumer behaviors and corporate altruistic preferences. *Computers & Industrial Engineering*, *153*, 107061. doi:10.1016/j.cie.2020.107061

Madden, T. J., Ellen, S. P., & Ajzen, I. (2018). A comparison of the theory of planned behavior and the theory of reasoned action. *Society for Personality and Social Psychology Inc.*, *18*(1), 3–9. doi:10.1177/0146167292181001

Madhok, A. (2021). Globalization, de-globalization, and re-globalization: Some historical context and the impact of the COVID pandemic. *Business Research Quarterly*, *24*(3), 199–203. doi:10.1177/23409444211008904

Maghradze, D., Aslanishvili, A., Mdinaradze, I., Tkemaladze, D., Mekhuzla, L., Lordkipanidze, D., Jalabadze, M., Kvavadze, E., Rusishvili, N., McGovern, P., This, P., Bacilieri, R., Failla, O., Cola, G., Mariani, L., Toffolatti, S. L., Lorenzis, G. D., Bianco, P. A., Quaglino, F., ... Davitashvili, L. (2019). Progress for research of grape and wine culture in Georgia, the South Caucasus. *BIO Web of Conferences, 12*, 03003. 10.1051/bioconf/20191203003

Magno, F., & Cassia, F. (2018). The impact of social media influencers in tourism. *Anatolia, 29*(2), 288–290. doi:10.1080/13032917.2018.1476981

Mahajan, K., & Tomar, S. (2021). COVID-19 and supply chain disruption: Evidence from food markets in India. *American Journal of Agricultural Economics, 103*(1), 35–52. doi:10.1111/ajae.12158 PMID:33230345

Maida, J. (2020). Analysis on impact of Covid-19- online on-demand food delivery services market 2019-2023. *Businesswire*. Retrieved on November 11, 2021, from: https://www.businesswire.com/news/h ome/20200430005160/en/Analysis-Impact-Covid-19–Online-On-Demand-Food-Delivery

Mair, J., Ritchie, B. W., & Walters, G. (2016). Towards a research agenda for post-disaster and post-crisis recovery strategies for tourist destinations: A narrative review. *Current Issues in Tourism, 19*(1), 1–26. doi:10.1080/13683500.2014.932758

Makarova, E. L., & Pavlov, P. V. (2017). Supplier Management Improvement in Aviation Industry: A Case Study of Beriev Aircraft Company. *International Journal of Supply Chain Management, 6*(1), 41–54.

Makedon, V., Drobyazko, S., Shevtsova, H., Maslosh, O., & Kasatkina, M. (2019). Providing security for the development of high-technology organizations. *Journal of Security & Sustainability Issues, 8*(4), 757–772. doi:10.9770/jssi.2019.8.4(18)

Malcevschi, A. (2016). The Parma University strategy for managing UNESCO designated sites. *Sustainable Mediterranean, 72*, 40–42.

Malerba, F. (Ed.). (2004). *Sectoral systems of innovation: concepts, issues and analyses of six major sectors in Europe*. Cambridge University Press. doi:10.1017/CBO9780511493270

Mamur, N. (2017). Ekolojik Sanat: Çevre Eğitimi ile Sanatın Kesişme Noktası [Ecological Art: The Intersection Point of Environmental Education and Art]. *Mersin Üniversitesi Eğitim Fakültesi Dergisi, 13*(3), 1000–1016. doi:10.17860/mersinefd.316297

Mandler, G. (1980). Recognizing: The judgment of previous occurrence. *Psychological Review, 87*(3), 252–271. doi:10.1037/0033-295X.87.3.252

Mandler, J. M., & Ritchey, G. H. (1977). Long-term memory for pictures. *Journal of Experimental Psychology. Human Learning and Memory, 3*(4), 386–396. doi:10.1037/0278-7393.3.4.386

Mango, J., Çolak, E., & Li, X. (2021). Web-based GIS for managing and promoting tourism in sub-Saharan Africa. *Current Issues in Tourism, 24*(2), 211–227. doi:10.1080/13683500.2019.1711028

Mao, C. K., Ding, C. G., & Lee, H. Y. (2010). Post-SARS tourist arrival recovery patterns: An analysis based on a catastrophe theory. *Tourism Management, 31*(6), 855–861. doi:10.1016/j.tourman.2009.09.003 PMID:32287733

Map of Republic of Macedonia. (n.d.). Retrieved on February 10, 2019, from https://www.novamakedonija.com.mk/prilozi/izbor/%D1%81%D0%BB%D1%83%D1%87%D0%B0%D1%98%D0%BE%D1%82-%D0%BC%D0%B0%D0%BA%D0%B5%D0%B4%D0%BE%D0%BD%D0%B8%D1%98%D0%B0-%D0%B8%D0%BB%D0%B8-%D0%BA%D0%BA%D0%BE-%D0%B4%D0%B0-%D1%98%D0%B0/

Marangunic, N., & Granic, A. (2015). Technology acceptance model: A literature review from 1986 to 2013. *Universal Access in the Information Society, 14*(1), 81–95. doi:10.100710209-014-0348-1

Compilation of References

Marschall, S. (2012). Tourism and memory. *Annals of Tourism Research*, *39*(4), 2216–2219. doi:10.1016/j.annals.2012.07.001

Marschall, S. (2015). 'Travelling down memory lane': Personal memory as a generator of tourism. *Tourism Geographies*, *17*(1), 36–53. doi:10.1080/14616688.2014.925963

Martins, J., Gonçalves, R., Branco, F., Barbosa, L., Melo, M., & Bessa, M. (2017). A multisensory virtual experience model for thematic tourism: A Port wine tourism application proposal. *Journal of Destination Marketing & Management*, *6*(2), 103–109. doi:10.1016/j.jdmm.2017.02.002

Marwick, A. E. (2015). *You May Know Me from YouTube: (Micro-) Celebrity in Social Media*. https://en-gb.facebook.com/business

Mason, M. (2020). *What Is Sustainability and Why Is It Important?* Environmental Science: https://www.environmentalscience.org/sustainability

Mason, M. C., & Paggiaro, A. (2012). Investigating the role of festivalscape in culinary tourism: The case of food and wine events. *Tourism Management*, *33*(6), 1329–1336. doi:10.1016/j.tourman.2011.12.016

Mason, P., & Cheyne, J. (2000). Residents' attitudes to proposed tourism development. *Annals of Tourism Research*, *27*(2), 391–411. doi:10.1016/S0160-7383(99)00084-5

Mathur, S., & Khanna, K. (2017). Sustainability practices as a competitive edge in five star hotels of Delhi: A study on manager's perception. *International Research Journal of Management. IT and Social Sciences*, *4*(6), 1–9.

Matikiti, R., Mpinganjira, M., & Roberts-Lombard, M. (2018). Application of the Technology Acceptance Model and the Technology–Organization–Environment Model to examine social media marketing use in the South African tourism industry. *South African Journal of Information Management*, *20*(1), 1–12. doi:10.4102ajim.v20i1.790

Mattsson, J., Sundbo, J., & Fussing-Jensen, C. (2005). Innovation systems in tourism: The roles of attractors and scene-takers. *Industry and Innovation*, *12*(3), 357–381. doi:10.1080/13662710500195967

Maurya, A. (2013). Environmental Impact of the Flying Scenario: An Approach Towards Sustainable Air Transportation: A Case Study of India. *OIDA International Journal of Sustainable Development*, *5*(12), 107–118.

Mayakul, T., Kiattisin, S., & Prasad, R. (2018). A sustainable medical tourism framework based on the enterprise architecture design: The case in Thailand. *Journal of Green Engineering*, *8*(3), 359–388. doi:10.13052/jge1904-4720.838

Mbaiwa, J. (2011). The effects of tourism development on the sustainable utilisation of natural resources in the Okavango Delta, Botswana. *Current Issues in Tourism*, *14*(3), 251–273. doi:10.1080/13683500.2011.555525

McCloskey, D. (2004). Evaluating electronic commerce acceptance with the technology acceptance model. *Journal of Computer Information Systems*, *44*(2), 49–57. doi:10.1080/08874417.2004.11647566

McGarty, T. (2021). COVID-19: Mutations and Infectivity. Massachusetts Institute of Technology.

Mckercher, B., Ho, P. S. Y., & Du Cros, H. (2005). Relationship between tourism and cultural heritage management: Evidence from Hong Kong. *Tourism Management*, *26*(4), 539–548. doi:10.1016/j.tourman.2004.02.018

Meethan, K. (2001). Tourism in Global Society: Place, Culture, Consumption. Basingstoke: Palgrave. *American Journal of Sociology*.

Mell, P., & Grance, T. (2011). The NIST definition of cloud computing. *NIST SPECIAL Publication*, 800-145.

Memiş, H. (2017). *Yiyecek ve içecek işletmelerinde hizmet kalitesinin DINESERV modeli ile ölçümü: Çanakkale ili örneği* [Unpublished master's thesis]. University of Çanakkale Onsekiz Mart, Çanakkale, Turkey.

Menacer, R., & Becherair, A. (2019). The impact of the tourism sector on economic growth in Algeria: An analytical and econometric study (1990-2014). *Management & Economics Research Journal, 1*(1), 174–189. doi:10.48100/merj.v1i1.21

Mengü, C. (2018). *Seyahat işletmelerinde yönetim ve operasyon stratejileri*. Detay Yayıncılık.

Menna, A., & Walsh, P. R. (2019). Assessing environments of commercialization of innovation for SMEs in the global wine industry: A market dynamics approach. *Wine Economics and Policy, 8*(2), 191–202. doi:10.1016/j.wep.2019.10.001

Merriam, S. B. (2009). *Qualitative research: A guide to design and implementation*. John Willey & Sons.

Merriman, N. (2008). Museum collections and sustainability. *Cultural Trends, 17*(1), 3–21. doi:10.1080/09548960801920278

Michaelidou, N., & Dibb, S. (2008). Consumer involvement: A new perspective. *The Marketing Review, 8*(1), 83–99. doi:10.1362/146934708X290403

Mickoleit, A. (2010). *Greener and smarter: ICTs, the environment and climate change. OECD Green Growth Papers, No. 2010-01*. OECD Publishing. doi:10.1787/5k9h3635kdbt-

Mihalic, T. (2016, January 16). Sustainable-responsible tourism discourse e Towards 'responsustable' tourism. *Journal of Cleaner Production, 111*(Part B), 461-470. doi:10.1016/j.jclepro.2014.12.062

Mikaeili, M., & Aytuğ, H. K. (2019). Evaluation of Iran's Cultural Tourism Potential from the European Union Perspective: Jolfa Region. *Advances in Science. Technology and Innovation*, 115–130. doi:10.1007/978-3-030-10804-5_12

Mikalef, P., Boura, M., Lekakos, G., & Krogstie, J. (2019). Big data analytics capabilities and innovation: The mediating role of dynamic capabilities and moderating effect of the environment. *British Journal of Management, 30*(2), 272–298. doi:10.1111/1467-8551.12343

Mileham, A. (2022, February 3). *Chinese tariffs cost Australian exports AUS$1BN as overall exports plummet*. The Drinks Business. Retrieved July 20, 2022, from https://www.thedrinksbusiness.com/2022/02/chinese-tariffs-cost-australian-exports-1-billion-as-overall-value-of-exports-plummet-by-30/

Miles, M. B., & Huberman, A. M. (1984). *Qualitative data analysis*. SAGE Publications.

Mileva, S. V. (2018). Potential of development of dark tourism in Bulgaria. *International Journal of Tourism Cities, 4*(1), 22–39. doi:10.1108/IJTC-05-2017-0029

Miller, N. (2017). *After Years of Challenges, Foursquare Has Found its Purpose -- and Profits*. Retrieved on September 15, 2018, from https://www.entrepreneur.com/article/290543

Milör, V. (2021, 04, 0). *The "Ghost kitchen" application has been on the rise during the pandemic period* ["Ghost kitchen" uygulaması pandemi döneminde yükselişe geçti]. Gastro Table. https://www.gastromasa.com/ghost-kitchen-uygulamasi-pandemi-doneminde-yukselise-gecti/

Minazzi, R. (2014). Social media impacts on travel suppliers: Social media marketing. *Social Media Marketing in Tourism and Hospitality*, 77–126. doi:10.1007/978-3-319-05182-6_4

Ministries. (2016). *Norway's follow-up of Agenda 2030 and the Sustainable Development Goals*. Ministry of Foreign Affairs. Retrieved on February 14, 2020, from: https://www.regjeringen.no/en/dokumenter/follow-up-sdg2/id2507259/

Ministry of Civil Aviation Government of India. (2019, March). *White Paper on National Green Aviation Policy*. Retrieved on October 14, 2021, from: https://www.civilaviation.gov.in/sites/default/files/Whitepaper%20on%20National%20Green%20Aviation%20Policy.pdf

Ministry of Civil Aviation. (2020, November). *GMR's Delhi Airport to become Net Zero Carbon Emission Airport*. Retrieved on October 29, 2021, from: https://www.newdelhiairport.in/blog/gmr-delhi-airport-to-become-net-zero-carbon-emission-airport

Ministry of Culture and Tourism. (2020). *Safe tourism certification program*. Retrieved on July 4, 2021, from: https://www.ktb.gov.tr/?_dil=1

Ministry of Economy of the Republic of Macedonia. (2016). *National Tourism Strategy Republic of Macedonia*. Kohl, C.H., & Partner.

Ministry of Tourism and Sports Thailand. (2017). *The Second National Tourism Development Plan (2017-2021)*. Author.

Mitchell, R., Charters, S., & Albrecht, J. N. (2012). Cultural systems and the wine tourism product. *Annals of Tourism Research*, *39*(1), 311–335. doi:10.1016/j.annals.2011.05.002

Mitra, S. K., Chattopadhyay, M., & Chatterjee, T. K. (2022). Can Tourism Development Reduce Gender Inequality? *Journal of Travel Research*.

Moaniba, I. M., Lee, P. C., & Su, H. N. (2020). How does external knowledge sourcing enhance product development? Evidence from drug commercialization. *Technology in Society*, *63*, 101414. doi:10.1016/j.techsoc.2020.101414

Mody, Day, J., Sydnor, S., Jaffe, W., & Lehto, X. (2014). The different shades of responsibility: Examining domestic and international travelers' motivations for responsible tourism in India. *Tourism Management Perspectives*, *12*, 113–124. doi:10.1016/j.tmp.2014.09.008

Mohammed, M. A., Muhammed, D. A., & Abdullah, J. M. (2015). Green computing beyond the traditional ways. *Int. J. of Multidisciplinary and Current Research*, *3*.

Mohonk Agreement. (2000). *Proposal for an International Certification Program for Sustainable Tourism and Ecotourism*. Retrieved on November 9, 2018, from: https://earthcheck.org/media/23533/mohonk.pdf

Mokhare, K., Satpute, A., Pal, V., & Badwaik, P. (2021). Impact of influencer marketing on travel and tourism. *International Journal of Advance Research and Innovative Ideas in Education*, *7*(1), 1098–1105.

Moliner-Tena, M. Á., Monferrer-Tirado, D., Ferreres-Bonfill, J. B., & Rodríguez-Artola, R. M. (2021). Destination sustainability and memorable tourism experiences. *Sustainability*, *13*(21), 11996. doi:10.3390u132111996

Monti, S. (2003). Thermalism Between Past and Future. *Proceedings of the Conference the Cultural Turn in Geography*.

Morgan, M. S., & Winkler, R. L. (2020). The third shift? Gender and empowerment in a women's ecotourism cooperative. *Rural Sociology*, *85*(1), 137–164. doi:10.1111/ruso.12275

Morgan, M., & Xu, F. (2009). Student travel experiences: Memories and dreams. *Journal of Hospitality Marketing & Management*, *18*(2-3), 216–236. doi:10.1080/19368620802591967

Mori, K., Fujii, T., Yamashita, T., Mimura, Y., Uchiyama, Y., & Hayashi, K. (2015). Visualization of a City Sustainability Index (CSI): Towards transdisciplinary approaches involving multiple stakeholders. *Sustainability*, *7*(9), 12402–12424. doi:10.3390u70912402

Morosan, C., & Jeong, M. (2008). Users' perceptions of two types of hotel reservation Web sites. *International Journal of Hospitality Management*, *27*(2), 284–292. doi:10.1016/j.ijhm.2007.07.023

Morsing, M., & Perrini, F. (2009). CSR in SMEs: Do SMEs matter for the CSR agenda? *Business Ethics (Oxford, England)*, *18*(1), 1–6. doi:10.1111/j.1467-8608.2009.01544.x

Mostafa, M. (2007). A hierarchical analysis of the green consciousness of the Egyptian consumer. *Psychology and Marketing*, *24*(5), 445–473. doi:10.1002/mar.20168

Mota, K., & Almeida, J. (2016). Educação superior em turismo, hospitalidade e lazer no Brasil: Análise do panorama de cursos ofertados frente ao contexto contemporâneo. *Revista Turismo & Desenvolvimento*, *26*, 65–77.

Mota, K., & Anjos, F. (2012). Educação superior em turismo no Brasil: Análise da oferta de cursos superiores no Nordeste brasileiro pelos institutos federais. *Revista Brasileira de Pesquisa em Turismo*, *6*(1), 48–63. doi:10.7784/rbtur.v6i1.461

Moutinho, L. (1987). Consumer behavior in tourism. *European Journal of Marketing*, *21*(10), 5–44. doi:10.1108/EUM0000000004718

Mowery, D. C., & Oxley, J. E. (1995). Inward technology transfer and competitiveness: The role of national innovation systems. *Cambridge Journal of Economics*, *19*(1), 67–93.

Muangasame, K., & Park, E. (2019). *Food Tourism, Policy and Sustainability: Behind the Popularity of Thai Food. In Food Tourism in Asia*. Springer. doi:10.1007/978-981-13-3624-9_9

Mudambi, S. M., & Schuff, D. (2010). Research note: What makes a helpful online review? A study of customer reviews on Amazon. com. *MIS Quarterly*, 185-200.

Müller, H. (2001). Tourism and Hospitality in the 21st Century. In S. Medlik & A. Lockwood (Eds.), *Tourism and Hospitality in the 21st Century* (pp. 61–70). Routledge. doi:10.1016/B978-0-7506-5627-6.50008-0

Mullis, L., Saif, L. J., Zhang, Y., Zhang, X., & Azevedo, M. S. (2012). Stability of bovine coronavirus on lettuce surfaces under household refrigeration conditions. *Food Microbiology*, *30*(1), 180–186. doi:10.1016/j.fm.2011.12.009 PMID:22265299

Munar, A. M., & Gyimóthy, S. (2013). Critical digital tourism studies. In *Tourism social media: Transformations in identity, community and culture* (pp. 245–262). Emerald Group Publishing Limited.

Muñoz-Leiva, F., Hernández-Méndez, J., & Sánchez-Fernández, J. (2012). Generalising user behaviour in online travel sites through the Travel 2.0 website acceptance model. *Online Information Review*, *36*(6), 879–902. Advance online publication. doi:10.1108/14684521211287945

Murugesan, S. (2008). Harnessing Green IT: Principles and Practices. *IT Professional*, *10*(1), 24–33. doi:10.1109/MITP.2008.10

Murugesan, S., & Gangadharan, G. R. (2012). *Harnessing green IT: Principles and practices*. Wiley. doi:10.1002/9781118305393

Murzyn-Kupisz, M. (2012). Cultural, economic and social sustainability of heritage tourism: issues and challenges. *Economic and Environmental Studies (E&ES)*, *12*(2), 113-133.

Muslim, H. F. M., Numata, S., & Yahya, N. A. (2018). Development of Malaysian homestay tourism: A review. *The International Journal of Tourism Science*, *12*(3), 65–74.

Musso, F., & Francioni, B. (2015). Agri-Food Clusters, Wine Tourism and Foreign Markets. The Role of Local Networks for SME's Internationalization. *Procedia Economics and Finance*, *27*, 334–343. doi:10.1016/S2212-5671(15)01004-7

Muzammal, M., Qu, Q., & Nasrulin, B. (2019). Renovating Blockchain With Distributed Databases: An open source system. *Future Generation Computer Systems*, *90*, 105–117. doi:10.1016/j.future.2018.07.042

Compilation of References

Myers, L. M. (2010). *Women's Independent Travel Experiences in New Zealand* [Doctoral thesis]. University of Sunderland.

Nagamatsu, S., Fukasawa, Y., & Kobayashi, I. (2021). Why Does Disaster Storytelling Matter for a Resilient Society? *Journal of Disaster Research*, *16*(2), 127–134. doi:10.20965/jdr.2021.p0127

Nalbant, F., & Korkmaz, T. (2019). Evaluation of Social Gender Equality on the Basis of Feminist Theory within the Context of Turkey [Feminist teori temelinde toplumsal cinsiyet eşitliğinin Türkiye bağlamında değerlendirilmesi]. *Artvin Çoruh Üniversitesi Uluslararası Sosyal Bilimler Dergisi*, *5*(2), 165–186. doi:10.22466/acusbd.633806

Namkung, Y., & Jang, S. (2013). Effects of Restaurant Green Practices on Brand Equity Formation: Do Green Practices Really Matter? *International Journal of Hospitality Management*, *33*, 85–95. doi:10.1016/j.ijhm.2012.06.006

Narula, R., & Dunning, J. H. (2010). Multinational Enterprises, Development and Globalization: Some Clarifications and a Research Agenda. *Oxford Development Studies*, *38*(3), 263–287. doi:10.1080/13600818.2010.505684

National Restaurant Association (NRA). (2020). *Restaurant sales fell to their lowest real level in over 35 years*. Retrieved on September 19, 2021, from: https://restaurant.org/articles/news/restaurant-sales-fell-to-lowest-level-in-35-years.

Nave, A., Laurett, R., & Do Paço, A. (2021). Relation between antecedents, barriers and consequences of sustainable practices in the wine tourism sector. *Journal of Destination Marketing & Management*, *20*, 20. doi:10.1016/j.jdmm.2021.100584

Nayik, G. A., Muzaffar, K., & Gull, A. (2015). Robotics and food technology: A mini review. *Journal of Nutrition & Food Sciences*, *5*(4), 1–11. doi:10.4172/2155-9600.1000384

Nazir, M. U., Yasin, I., & Tat, H. H. (2021). Destination image's mediating role between perceived risks, perceived constraints, and behavioral intention. *Heliyon*, *7*(7), e07613. doi:10.1016/j.heliyon.2021.e07613 PMID:34368481

Nechifor, V., Ramos, M. P., Ferrari, E., Laichena, J., Kihiu, E., Omanyo, D., Musamali, R., & Kiriga, B. (2021). Food security and welfare changes under COVID-19 in Sub-Saharan Africa: Impacts and responses in Kenya. *Global Food Security*, *28*.

Nelson, E., Bangham, C., Modi, S., Liu, X., Codner, A., Hicks, J. M., & Greece, J. (2022). Understanding the impacts of COVID-19 on the determinants of food insecurity: A state-specific examination. *Preventive Medicine Reports*, *28*, 101871.

Nepal, S. K. (2020). Travel and tourism after COVID-19 – business as usual or opportunity to reset? *Tour. Geogr.* doi:10.1080/14616688.2020.1760926

Nepal, S. K. (2007). Tourism and rural settlements Nepal's Annapurna region. *Annals of Tourism Research*, *34*(4), 855–875. doi:10.1016/j.annals.2007.03.012

Neuhofer, B., Buhalis, D., & Ladkin, A. (2012). Conceptualising technology enhanced destination experiences. *Journal of Destination Marketing & Management*, *1*(1-2), 36–46. doi:10.1016/j.jdmm.2012.08.001

Neumayer, E. (2013). *Weak versus Strong Sustainability: Exploring the Limits of Two Opposing Paradigms* (4th ed.). Edward Elgar Publishing. doi:10.4337/9781781007082

Ng, A. W., & Tavitiyaman, P. (2020). Corporate social responsibility and sustainability initiatives of multinational hotel corporations. In *International business, Trade and Institutional Sustainability* (pp. 3–15). Springer. doi:10.1007/978-3-030-26759-9_1

Ngarava, S. (2022). Empirical analysis on the impact of the COVID-19 pandemic on food insecurity in South Africa. *Physics and Chemistry of the Earth Parts A/B/C*, 103180.

Nguyen, T. Q. T., Johnson, P., & Young, T. (2022). Networking, coopetition and sustainability of tourism destinations. *Journal of Hospitality and Tourism Management*, *50*, 400–411. doi:10.1016/j.jhtm.2022.01.003

Nguyen, V. K., Natoli, R., & Divisekera, S. (2021). Innovation and productivity in tourism small and medium enterprises: A longitudinal study. *Tourism Management Perspectives*, *38*, 38. doi:10.1016/j.tmp.2021.100804

Nguyen, X. T., Nguyen, T. H., Dang, H. P., Pham, T. L. P., Bui, T. T., Tran, N. M., ... Nguyen, N. P. (2022). E-commerce Adoption in Distribution: An Empirical Study on Household Businesses in Food and Beverage Industry. *Journal of Distribution Science*, *20*(2), 65–77. doi:10.15722/jds.20.02.202202.65

NHO Reiseliv/The Norwegian Hospitality Association. (2020). *Koronavirus*. https://www.nhoreiseliv.no/vi-mener/koronavirus/

Nichifor, E., Lixandroiu, R. C., Sumedrea, S., Chițu, I. B., & Bratucu, G. (2021). How can SMEs become more sustainable? Modelling the M-commerce consumer behaviour with contingent free shipping and customer journey's touchpoints optimisation. *Sustainability*, *13*, 6845. https://doi.org/10.3390/su13126845

Nicola, M., Alsafi, Z., Sohrabi, C., Kerwan, A., Al-Jabir, A., Iosifidis, C., Agha, M., & Agha, R. (2020). The socio-economic implications of the coronavirus and COVID-19 pandemic: a review. *Int. J. Surg*. doi:10.1016/j.ijsu.2020.04.018

Nicolosi, A., Cortese, L., Nesci, F. S., & Privitera, D. (2016). Combining Wine Production and Tourism. The Aeolian Islands. *Procedia: Social and Behavioral Sciences*, *223*, 662–667. doi:10.1016/j.sbspro.2016.05.381

Niewiadomsky, P. (2020). COVID-19: From temporary de-globalisation to a rediscovery of tourism? *Tourism Geographies*, *22*(3), 651–656.

Nikolova, M. S. (2020). *Behavioral Economics for Tourism: Perspectives on Business and Policy in the Travel Industry*. Academic Press.

Nilsen, H. R. (2010). The joint discourse 'reflexive sustainable development'—From weak towards strong sustainable development. *Ecological Economics*, *69*(3), 495–501. doi:10.1016/j.ecolecon.2009.11.011

Nilsson, J. H. (2013). *Nordic Eco-gastronomy. Sustainable Culinary Systems: Local Foods, Innovation, Tourism and Hospitality* (C. M. Hall & S. Gössling, Eds.). Routledge.

Nishii, L. H., & Özbilgin, M. F. (2007). Global diversity management: Towards a conceptual framework. *International Journal of Human Resource Management*, *18*(11), 1883–1894. doi:10.1080/09585190701638077

Nofer, M., Gomber, P., Hinz, O., & Schiereck, D. (2017). Blockchain – A Disruptive Technology. *Business & Information Systems Engineering*, *59*(3), 183–187. doi:10.100712599-017-0467-3

Nomnga, V. J. (2017). Unlocking the potential of women entrepreneurs in the tourism and hospitality industry in the eastern Cape Province, South Africa. *Journal of Economics and Behavioral Studies*, *9*(4 (J)), 6–13. doi:10.22610/jebs.v9i4(J).1817

Nonaka, I., & Takeuchi, H. (1995). *The Knowledge-creating Company: How Japanese companies create the dynamics of innovation*. Oxford University Press.

Nordregio. (n.d.). *Welcome to Agenda 2030 at the local level*. https://nordregioprojects.org/agenda2030local/

Norman, W., & MacDonald, C. (2004). Getting to the bottom of "triple bottom line. *Business Ethics Quarterly*, *14*(2), 243–262. doi:10.5840/beq200414211

Northcote, J., & Macbrth, J. (2006). Conceptualizing yield sustainable tourism management. *Annals of Tourism Research*, *33*(1), 199–220. doi:10.1016/j.annals.2005.10.012

Norton, B. (2005). Sustainability: A philosophy of adaptive ecosystem management. *Ecoscience*, *13*(4), 565–566. doi:10.2980/1195-6860(2006)13[565:SAPOAE]2.0.CO;2

Compilation of References

Nouri, J., Danehkar, A., & Sharifipour, R. (2008). Evaluation of ecotourism potential in the northern coastline of the Persian Gulf. *Environmental Geology, 55*(3), 681–686. doi:10.100700254-007-1018-x

NPD. (2020). *Online food orders, delivery surge amid COVID-19 lockdown*. Retrieved on May 24, 2021, from: https://www.npd.com/wps/portal/npd/us/news/press-releases/2020/while-total-us-re staurant-traffic-declines-by-22-in-march-digital-and-delivery-orders-jump-by-over- 60/

Nyamogosa, H. M., & Obonyo, G. O. (2022). Sustainable business strategies for fast-food restaurant growth: Fast-food restaurant managers' perspectives in lake region economic block, Kenya. *Journal of Hospitality and Tourism, 2*(1), 1–15. doi:10.47672/jht.958

Nyaruwata, S., & Nyaruwata, L. T. (2013). Gender equity and executive management in tourism: Challenges in the Southern African Development Community (SADC) region. *African Journal of Business Management, 7*(21), 2059–2070.

O'Connor, N., Cowhey, A., & O'Leary, S. (2016). Social media and the Irish tourism and hospitality industry: The customer experience. *Ereview of Tourism Research, 13*.

OECD. (2002). *Household Tourism Travel: Trends, Environmental Impacts and Policy Response*. Retrieved on April 22, 2022, from: https://www.oecd.org/

OECD. (2005). Oslo manual: guidelines for collecting and interpreting innovation data (3rd ed.). Paris: OECD.

OECD. (2017). *Enhancing the Contributions of SMEs in a Global and Digitalised Economy*. Retrieved on June 27, 2019, from: https://www.oecd.org/mcm/documents/C-MIN-2017-8-EN.pdf)

OECD. (2020). *Culture Shock: COVID-19 and the Cultural and Creative Sectors*. OECD. https://read.oecd-ilibrary.org/view/?ref=135_135961-nenh9f2w7a&title=Culture-shock-COVID-19-and-the-cultural-and-creative-sectors

OECD. (2020). *Supporting livelihoods during the Covid-19 crisis: closing the gaps in safety nets*. Retrieved on January 23, 2022, from: https://www.oecd.org/coronavirus/en

OECD. (2021). *Blockchain Technologies as a Digital Enabler for Sustainable*. https://www.oecd.org/finance/Blockchain-technologies-as-a-digital-enabler-for-sustainable-infrastructure-key-findings.pdf

Oğur, S., Hayta, Ş., & Bekmezci, D. H. (2021). Food safety risks and precautions during the COVID-19 pandemic. epidemic. In Epidemic, agriculture and food [COVID-19 pandemisi sürecinde gıda güvenliği riskleri ve önlemleri]. Tasav, 91-100.

Oğuz, M. (2021). *The Number of Restaurants in Istanbul Has Dropped to 20 Thousand* [İstanbul'da Restoran Sayısı 20 Binlere Düştü]. Tourism Diary, Tourism and Travel Newspaper. https://www.turizmgunlugu.com/2021/02/13/istanbulda-restoran-sayisi-20-binlere-dustu/

Ohri-Vachaspati, P., Acciai, F., & DeWeese, R. S. (2021). SNAP participation among low-income US households stays stagnant while food insecurity escalates in the months following the COVID-19 pandemic. *Preventive Medicine Reports, 24*, 101555.

Okat, Ç., Bahçeci, V. & Ocak, E. (2020). Evaluating İmpacts Of COVID-19 (New Coronavirus) Pandemic Crisis On Food & Beverage Entreprises. *International Journal of Contemporary Tourism Research*, 201-218.

Ökten, S. (2009). Gender and power: the system of gender in southeastern anatolia [Toplumsal cinsiyet ve iktidar: Güneydoğu Anadolu Bölgesi'nin toplumsal cinsiyet düzeni]. *Journal of International Social Research, 2*(8).

Okumus, B. (2020). Food Tourism Research: A perspective article. *Tourism Review, 76*(1), 38–42. doi:10.1108/TR-11-2019-0450

Olaimat, A. N., Shahbaz, H. M., Fatima, N., Munir, S., & Holley, R. A. (2020). Food safety during and after the era of COVID-19 pandemic. *Frontiers in Microbiology*, 1854.

Olcay, A., Giritlioğlu, İ., & Parlak, Ö. (2014). Comparison of hotel business arrangements for accessible tourism between ENAT(European Network For Accessible Tourism) and Turkey [ENAT (European Network For Accessible Tourism-Avrupa Erişilebilir Turizm Ağı) ile Türkiye'nin Erişilebilir Turizme Yönelik Otel İşletmelerini Kapsayan Düzenlemeleri ve Bu Düzenlemelerin Karşılaştırılması]. *Gazi Üniversitesi Turizm Fakültesi Dergisi, 2*, 127–144.

Olsen, S. J., Azziz-Baumgartner, E., Budd, A. P., Brammer, L., Sullivan, S., Pineda, R. F., Cohen, C., & Fry, A. M. (2020). Decreased influenza activity during the COVID-19 pandemic—United States, Australia, Chile, and South Africa, 2020. *American Journal of Transplantation, 20*(12), 3681–3685. doi:10.1111/ajt.16381 PMID:33264506

Olya, H., Altinay, L., Farmaki, A., Kenebayeva, A., & Gursoy, D. (2021). Hotels' sustainability practices and guests' familiarity, attitudes and behaviours. *Journal of Sustainable Tourism, 29*(7), 1063–1081. doi:10.1080/09669582.2020.1775622

Önaçan, M. B. K. (2019). Küresel ısınmaya karşı yeşil bilişim kapsamında alınabilecek bireysel önlemler. *Turkish Studies-Social Sciences, 14*(6), 3283–3302. doi:10.29228/TurkishStudies.39715

Ong, Y. X., Sun, T., & Ito, N. (2022). Beyond Influencer Credibility: The Power of Content and Parasocial Relationship on Processing Social Media Influencer Destination Marketing Campaigns. *Information and Communication Technologies in Tourism, 2022*, 110–122. doi:10.1007/978-3-030-94751-4_11

Opazo, M. P. (2012). Discourse as driver of innovation in contemporary haute cuisine: The case of elBulli restaurant. *International Journal of Gastronomy and Food Science, 1*(2), 82–89. doi:10.1016/j.ijgfs.2013.06.001

OpenTable. (2020). *The state of the restaurant industry*. https://www.opentable.com/state-of-industry#:~:text=In%20March%202020%2C%20OpenTable%20launched,%2C%20states%2C%20and%20countries%20reopen

Orchiston, C. (2012). Seismic risk scenario planning and sustainable tourism management: Christchurch and the Alpine Fault zone, South Island, New Zealand. *Journal of Sustainable Tourism, 20*(1), 59–79. doi:10.1080/09669582.2011.617827

Oriade, A., Osinaike, A., Aduhene, K., & Wang, Y. (2021). Sustainability awareness, management practices and organisational culture in hotels: Evidence from developing countries. *International Journal of Hospitality Management, 92*, 92. doi:10.1016/j.ijhm.2020.102699

Ormond, M., & Mainil, T. (2015). Government and governance strategies in medical tourism. In *Handbook on medical tourism and patient mobility* (pp. 154–163). Edward Elgar Publishing. doi:10.4337/9781783471195.00025

Otcenásková, T., Bures, V., & Mikulecká, J. (2012). Principal Starting Points of Organisational Knowledge Intensity Modelling. *Journal of Organizational Knowledge Management, 2012*, 1.

Ötleş, S., & Çağındı, Ö. (2004). Ekolojik Gıdaların Önemi ve Ekolojik Üzüm Üretimi [Importance of Ecological Foods and Ecological Grape Production]. *Akademik Gida Dergisi, 2*(2), 36–38.

Otley, T. (2021, June 18). Emirates promotes its sustainable operations. *Business Traveller*. https://www.businesstraveller.com/features/emirates-promotes-its-sustainable-operations/

Ott, K. (2003). The case for strong sustainability. *Greifswald's environmental ethics*, 59-64.

Ottenbacher, M., Harrington, R., & Parsa, H. G. (2009). Defining the hospitality discipline: A discussion of pedagogical and research implications. *Journal of Hospitality & Tourism Research (Washington, D.C.), 33*(3), 263–283. doi:10.1177/1096348009338675

Compilation of References

Ottman, J. A. (2011). *The New Rules of Green marketing: Strategies, Tools, and Inspiration for Sustainable Branding* (1st ed.). Routledge., doi:10.4324/9781351278683

Overton, J., Murray, W. E., & Howson, K. (2019). Doing good by drinking wine? Ethical value networks and upscaling of wine production in Australia, New Zealand and South Africa. *European Planning Studies*, *27*(12), 2431–2449. doi: 10.1080/09654313.2019.1628181

Oxford Dictionary. (2021). Accessible at: https://www.oxfordlearnersdictionaries.com/definition/ english/ accessibility?q=accessibility

Oyinseye, P., Suárez, A., Saldaña, E., Fernández-Zurbano, P., Valentin, D., & Sáenz-Navajas, M.-P. (2022). Multidimensional representation of wine drinking experience: Effects of the level of consumers' expertise and involvement. *Food Quality and Preference*, *98*, 98. doi:10.1016/j.foodqual.2022.104536

Özbek, D., & Özbek, T. (2008). Integration of Geothermal Resources into Health and Thermal Tourism [Jeotermal Kaynakların Sağlık ve Termal Turizme Entegrasyonu]. *Jeoloji Mühendisleri Odası Haber Bülteni*, *2-3*, 99–113.

Özbek, T. (1991). Thermal tourism in the World and Turkey and its importance [Dünya'da ve Türkiye'de Termal Turizmin Önemi]. *Anatolia Dergisi*, *17-18*, 15–29.

Özdemir, E., & Tokol, T. (2008). Marketing strategies for female consumers [Kadın tüketicilere yönelik pazarlama stratejileri]. *Anadolu University Journal of Social Sciences*, *8*(2).

Özel, Ç. H. (2012). Otelcilik endüstrisi. In M. Akoğlan Kozak (Ed.), *Otel işletmeciliği* (pp. 1–28). Detay Yayıncılık.

Özsoy, V., & Mamur, N. (2019). Görsel Sanatlar Öğrenme ve Öğretim Yaklaşımları [Visual Arts Learning and Teaching Approaches]. Ankara: Pegem Akademi.

Öztayşi, B., Baysan, S., & Akpinar, F. (2009). Radio frequency identification (RFID) in hospitality. *Technovation*, *29*(9), 618–624. doi:10.1016/j.technovation.2009.05.014

Öztopçu, A. (2019). Eko-gastronomi ve sürdürülebilir bölgesel kalkınma [Eco-gastronomy and sustainable regional development]. *International Social Mentality and Researcher Thinkers Journal*, *5*(24), 1432–1443. doi:10.31576mryj.354

Ozturk, A., Umit, K., Medeni, I. T., Ucuncu, B., Caylan, M., Akba, F., & Medeni, T. D. (2011). Green ICT (Information and communication technologies): A review of academic and practitioner perspectives. *International Journal of e-Business and eGovernment Studies*, *3*(1), 1-16.

Öztürk, F. (2020). *Thousands of Businesses Shut Down During the Pandemic Process* [Pandemi Sürecinde Binlerce İşletme Kepenk İndirdi]. BBC News/Türkçe. https://www.bbc.com/turkce/haberler-dunya-55258396

Paddison, L. (2020, January 16). Airline Cabin Waste Is Aviation's Other Environmental Crisis. *Huffpost*. Retrieved on December 8, 2021, from: https://www.huffpost.com/entry/plane-waste-cabin-plastic-food_n_5e1c5868c5b650c621e1cc89

Pahrudin, P., Chen, C.-T., & Liu, L.-W. (2021). A modified theory of planned behavioral: A case of tourist intention to visit a destination post pandemic Covid-19 in Indonesia. *Heliyon*, *7*(10), e08230. doi:10.1016/j.heliyon.2021.e08230 PMID:34708160

Pai, S., & Thomas, R. (2008). Immune deficiency or hyperactivity-Nfkappa b illuminates autoimmunity. *Journal of Autoimmunity*, *31*(3), 245–251. doi:10.1016/j.jaut.2008.04.012 PMID:18539434

Pang, Z., Berman, O., & Hu, M. (2015). Up Then Down: Bid-Price Trends in Revenue Management. *Production and Operations Management*, *24*(7), 1135–1147. doi:10.1111/poms.12324

Pan, Y.-J., & Lee, L.-S. (2011). Academic Performance and Perceived Employability of Graduate Students in Business and Management – An Analysis of Nationwide Graduate Destination Survey. *Procedia: Social and Behavioral Sciences*, *25*, 91–103. doi:10.1016/j.sbspro.2011.10.531

Parlaktuna, İ. (2010). Analysis of Gender-Based Occupational Discrimination in Turkey [Türkiye'de cinsiyete dayalı mesleki ayrımcılığın analizi]. *Ege Akademik Bakış*, *10*(4), 1217–1230. doi:10.21121/eab.2010419607

Pasanchay, K., & Schott, C. (2021). Community-based tourism homestays' capacity to advance the Sustainable Development Goals: A holistic sustainable livelihood perspective. *Tourism Management Perspectives*, *37*, 100784. doi:10.1016/j.tmp.2020.100784

Pasa, R. B. (2020). Performance evaluation of Amaltari bufferzone community homestay of Kawasoti municipality, Nawalpur. *Journal of the Humanities and Social Sciences*, *25*(7), 1–10. doi:10.9790/0837-2507040110

Patel, S. B., Umar, R., Patel, N., & Chugh, R. (2019). Likes, comments and shares on social media: Exploring user engagement with a state tourism facebook page. *International Journal of Web Based Communities*, *15*(2), 1. doi:10.1504/IJWBC.2019.10020618

Patiar, S. (2015). *Handbook senior tourism*. Grŵp Llandrillo Menai.

Patra, R. J., Rao, M. V., Balmuri, K., Konda, S., & Chande, M. K. (2021). High-performance computing and fault tolerance technique implementation in cloud computing. In S. Kumar, R. Raja, A. K. S. Kuswaha, S. Kumar, & R. K. Patra (Eds.), *Green computing and its applications* (pp. 255–310). Nova Science Publishers.

Pattnaik, S., Nayak, M. M., Abbate, S., & Centobelli, P. (2021). *Recent trends in sustainable inventory model: A literature review*. doi:10.3390/su132111756

Patton, M. Q. (2014). *Qualitative Research & Evaluation Methods Integrating Theory and Practice* (4th ed.). Sage Publications.

Pavithra, A. (2021). Towards developing a comprehensive conceptual understanding of positive hospital culture and approaches to healthcare organisational culture change in Australia. *Journal of Health Organization and Management*, *36*(1), 105–120. doi:10.1108/JHOM-10-2020-0385 PMID:33837683

Pazowski, P. (2015). Green computing: latest practices and technologies for ICT sustainability. In *Managing Intellectual Capital and Innovation for Sustainable and Inclusive Society, Joint International Conference* (pp. 1853-1860). Academic Press.

Peng, K. L., Lin, M. C., & Baum, T. (2013). The constructing model of culinary creativity: An approach of mixed methods. *Quality & Quantity*, *47*(5), 2687–2707. doi:10.100711135-012-9680-9

PENT - Plano Estratégico Nacional do Turismo. (2015). *Ministério da Economia e do Emprego*. Retrieved on May 14, 2020, from: https://www.portugal.gov.pt/media/820185/20130111%20consulta%20publica%20pent.pdf

Pera, R. (2017). Empowering the new traveller: Storytelling as a co-creative behaviour in tourism. *Current Issues in Tourism*, *20*(4), 331–338. doi:10.1080/13683500.2014.982520

Pereira, E. M., Mykletun, R. J., & Hippolyte, C. (2012). Sustainability, daily practices and vacation purchasing: Are they related? *Tourism Review*, *67*(4), 40–54. doi:10.1108/16605371211277812

Pereira, R. L. G., Correia, A. L., & Schutz, R. L. A. (2012). Destination branding: A critical overview. *Journal of Quality Assurance in Hospitality & Tourism*, *13*(2), 81–102.

Compilation of References

Pérez, V., Guerrero, F., González, M., Pérez, F., & Caballero, R.Pérez at al. (2013). Composite indicator for the assessment of sustainability: The case of Cuban nature-based tourism destinations. *Ecological Indicators*, *29*, 316–324. doi:10.1016/j.ecolind.2012.12.027

Perkumienė, D., Pranskūnienė, R., Vienažindienė, M., & Grigienė, J. (2020). The right to a clean environment: Considering Green Logistics and sustainable tourism. *International Journal of Environmental Research and Public Health*, *17*(9), 3254. doi:10.3390/ijerph17093254 PMID:32392737

Perkumienė, D., Vienažindienė, M., & Švagždienė, B. (2019). Cooperation perspectives in sustainable medical tourism: The case of Lithuania. *Sustainability*, *11*(13), 3584. doi:10.3390u11133584

Perpiña, L., Camprubí, R., & Prats, L. (2019). Destination Image Versus Risk Perception. *Journal of Hospitality & Tourism Research (Washington, D.C.)*, *43*(1), 3–19. doi:10.1177/1096348017704497

Pett, M. A., Lackey, N. R., Sullivan, J., & Robinson, S. (Eds.). (2003). Making sense of Factor Analysis (1st ed.). SAGE Publication International Education and Professional Publisher. doi:10.4135/9781412984898

Pham, L. D. Q., Coles, T., Ritchie, B. W., & Wang, J. (2021). Building business resilience to external shocks: Conceptualising the role of social networks to small tourism & hospitality businesses. *Journal of Hospitality and Tourism Management*, *48*, 210–219. doi:10.1016/j.jhtm.2021.06.012

Phatthana, W., & Mat, N. K. N. (2011). The Application of Technology Acceptance Model (TAM) on health tourism e-purchase intention predictors in Thailand. In *2010 International conference on business and economics research* (Vol. 1, pp. 196-199). Academic Press.

Pimenta, C. A. M., Cadima Ribeiro, J., & Remoaldo, P. (2021). The relationship between creative tourism and local development: A bibliometric approach for the period 2009-2019. *Tourism & Management Studies*, *17*(1), 5–18.

Pine, B. J., & Gilmore, J. H. (1998). Welcome to the experience economy. *Harvard Business Review*, *76*(4), 97–105. PMID:10181589

Pisani, N., Kourula, A., Kolk, A., & Meijer, R. (2017). How global is international CSR research? Insights and recommendations from a systematic review. *Journal of World Business*, *52*(5), 591–614. doi:10.1016/j.jwb.2017.05.003

Pisano, G. P., & Shih, W. C. (2009). Restoring american competitiveness. *Harvard Business Review*, *87*(7/8), 114–125.

Placet, M., Anderson, R., & Fowler, K. (2005). Strategies for Sustainability. *Research Technology Management*, *48*(5), 32–41. doi:10.1080/08956308.2005.11657336

Planellas, M., & Svejenova, S. (2007). *Creativity: Ferran Adria*. Presented at the annual meeting ExpoManagement, Madrid, Spain. Retrieved from http://www. elBulli. com/esade/CasoFerranAd ria_and _elBulli-ESADE_en. pdf

Pobrić, A., & Sivac, A. (2022). The application of GIS in tourism planning and sustainable tourism development. In *Proceedings of 8th International Tourism and Hospitality Management Congress* (pp. 456-462). Academic Press.

Pollock, A. (2019). *Regenerative Tourism: The Natural Maturation of Sustainability*. Retrieved on August 22, 2020, from: https://medium.com/activate-the-future/regenerative-tourism-the-natural-maturation-of-sustainability-26e6507d0fcb

Ponsignon, F., & Derbaix, M. (2020). The impact of interactive technologies on the social experience: An empirical study in a cultural tourism context. *Tourism Management Perspectives*, *35*, 35. doi:10.1016/j.tmp.2020.100723

Pop, R.-A., Săplăcan, Z., Dabija, D.-C., & Alt, M.-A. (2021). The impact of social media influencers on travel decisions: The role of trust in consumer decision journey. *Current Issues in Tourism*. Advance online publication. doi:10.1080/13683500.2021.1895729

Potts, J., Hartley, J., Banks, J., Burgess, J., Cobcroft, R., Cunningham, S., & Montgomery, L. (2008). Consumer co-creation and situated creativity. *Industry and Innovation*, *15*(5), 459–474. doi:10.1080/13662710802373783

Pourkhani, A., Abdipour, K., Baher, B., & Moslehpour, M. (2019). The impact of social media in business growth and performance: A scientometrics analysis. *International Journal of Data and Network Science*, *3*(3), 223–244. doi:10.5267/j.ijdns.2019.2.003

Powell, W. W., Koput, K. W., & Smith-Doerr, L. (1996). Interorganizational collaboration and the locus of innovation: Networks of learning in biotechnology. *Administrative Science Quarterly*, *41*(1), 116–145. doi:10.2307/2393988

Premanandh, J. (2011). Factors affecting food security and contribution of modern technologies in food sustainability. *Journal of the Science of Food and Agriculture*, *91*(15), 2707–2714. doi:10.1002/jsfa.4666 PMID:22002569

Pressman, P., Naidu, A. S., & Clemens, R. (2020). COVID-19 and food safety: Risk management and future considerations. *Nutrition Today*, *55*(3), 125-128.

PricewaterhouseCoopers, L. L. P. (2015). *The sharing economy*. Report, Consumer Intelligence Series.

Priilaid, D., Ballantyne, R., & Packer, J. (2020). A "blue ocean" strategy for developing visitor wine experiences: Unlocking value in the Cape region tourism market. *Journal of Hospitality and Tourism Management*, *43*, 91–99. doi:10.1016/j.jhtm.2020.01.009

Pueyo, T. (2020). *Coronavirus: Why You Must Act Now*. https://tomaspueyo.medium.com/coronavirus-act-today-or-people-will-die-f4d3d9cd99ca

Pulido-Fernández, J. I., García-Suárez, J. A., & Rodríguez-Díaz, B. (2021). Proposal for an index to measure creativity in urban-cultural destinations. *International Journal of Tourism Research*, *23*(1), 89–105. doi:10.1002/jtr.2396

Pure Michigan Business Connect. (2018). Retrieved on April 8, 2018, from: https://www.michiganbusiness.org/pmbc/

Pure Michigan Fitness. (2015). Retrieved on April 8, 2018, from: https://michiganfitness.org/pure-michigan-fitness

Pure Michigan Sports. (2017). Retrieved on April 8, 2018, from: http://www.puremichigansports.org

Puri, H. S. (2021, June 11). Indian Aviation: Sustainable Development is in the air. *The Daily Guardian*. Retrieved on July 22, 2021, from: https://thedailyguardian.com/indian-aviation-sustainable-development-is-in-the-air/

Purvis, B., Mao, Y., & Robinson, D. (2019). Three pillars of sustainability: In search of conceptual origins. *Sustainability Science*, *14*(3), 681–695. doi:10.100711625-018-0627-5

Puška, A., Pamucar, D., Stojanović, I., Cavallaro, F., Kaklauskas, A., & Mardani, A. (2021). Examination of the Sustainable Rural Tourism Potential of the Brčko District of Bosnia and Herzegovina Using a Fuzzy Approach Based on Group Decision Making. *Sustainability*, *13*(2), 583. doi:10.3390/su13020583

Qantas Newsroom. (2019, May 8). *Qantas Operates World's First Zero Waste Flight*. Retrieved on August 4, 2021, from: https://www.qantasnewsroom.com.au/media-releases/qantas-operates-worlds-first-zero-waste-flight/

Qiu, H., Fan, D. X., Lyu, J., Lin, P. M., & Jenkins, C. L. (2019). Analyzing the economic sustainability of tourism development: Evidence from Hong Kong. *Journal of Hospitality & Tourism Research (Washington, D.C.)*, *43*(2), 226–248. doi:10.1177/1096348018777046

Quadros, M. X. (2022, February 3). 12 tried-and-true ways to promote your blog posts. *HubSpot Blog*. Retrieved April 5, 2022, from https://blog.hubspot.com/marketing/blog-promotion-tactics

Québec Declaration. (2002). *Québec Declaration on Ecotourism*. Retrieved on September 22, 2021, from: https://www.gdrc.org/uem/eco-tour/quebec-declaration.pdf

Quintal, V. A., Lee, J. A., & Soutar, G. N. (2010). Risk, uncertainty and the theory of planned behavior: A tourism example. *Tourism Management*, *31*(6), 797–805. doi:10.1016/j.tourman.2009.08.006

Rachão, S. A. S., de Jesus Breda, Z., de Oliveira Fernandes, C., & Joukes, V. N. P. M. (2021). Drivers of experience co-creation in food-and-wine tourism: An exploratory quantitative analysis. *Tourism Management Perspectives*, *37*(May). doi:10.1016/j.tmp.2020.100783

Radu-Daniel, P., Cristian, B., Constantin, D. C., & Irina, S. (2014). Territorial imbalances in the distribution of creative industries in the North-Eastern Development Region. *Procedia: Social and Behavioral Sciences*, *122*, 179–183. doi:10.1016/j.sbspro.2014.01.1323

Raftery, D. (2017). Producing value from Australia's vineyards: An ethnographic approach to 'The quality turn' in the Australian Wine Industry. *Journal of Political Ecology*, *24*(1). Advance online publication. doi:10.2458/v24i1.20877

Rahayuningsih, T., Muntasib, E. H., & Prasetyo, L. B. (2016). Nature based tourism resources assessment using geographic information system (GIS): Case study in Bogor. *Procedia Environmental Sciences*, *33*, 365–375. doi:10.1016/j.proenv.2016.03.087

Raja, S. P. (2021). Green computing: A future perspective and the operational analysis of a data center. *IEEE Transactions on Computational Social Systems*.

Ramaano, A. I. (2022). Geographical information systems in sustainable rural tourism and local community empowerment: A natural resources management appraisal for Musina Municipality' Society. *Local Development & Society*, 1-32.

Ramírez-Guerrero, G., García-Onetti, J., Arcila-Garrido, M., & Chica-Ruiz, J. A. (2021). A Tourism Potential Index for Cultural Heritage Management through the Ecosystem Services Approach. *Sustainability*, *13*(11), 6415. doi:10.3390u13116415

Ramos, Y., & Castro, A. O. (2017). Point-Of-Sales Systems in Food and Beverage Industry: Efficient Technology and Its User Acceptance. *Journal of Information Sciences and Computing Technologies*, *6*(1), 582–591.

Ram, Y., Björk, P., & Weidenfeld, A. (2016). Authenticity and place attachment of major visitor attractions. *Tourism Management*, *52*, 110–122. doi:10.1016/j.tourman.2015.06.010

Randelli, F., Romei, P., & Tortora, M. (2014). An evolutionary approach to the study of rural tourism: The case of Tuscany. *Land Use Policy*, *38*, 276–281. doi:10.1016/j.landusepol.2013.11.009

Rankin, W. (2014). Sustainability. In *Treatise on Process Metallurgy*. Elsevier.

Rasoolimanesh, S. M., Seyfi, S., Rastegar, R., & Hall, C. M. (2021). Destination image during the COVID-19 pandemic and future travel behavior: The moderating role of past experience. *Journal of Destination Marketing & Management*, *21*(February), 100620. doi:10.1016/j.jdmm.2021.100620

Rather, R. A. (2021). Monitoring the impacts of tourism-based social media, risk perception and fear on tourist's attitude and revisiting behaviour in the wake of COVID-19 pandemic. *Current Issues in Tourism*, *0*(0), 1–9. doi:10.1080/13683500.2021.1884666

Rathore, H., Nandi, S., & Jakhar, S. K. (2020, November 27). The future of Indian aviation from the perspective of environment-centric regulations and policies. *IIMB Management Review*, *13*(4), 434–447. doi:10.1016/j.iimb.2020.11.003

Ratnasari, R. T., Gunawan, S., Pitchay, A. A., & Mohd Salleh, M. C. (2021). Sustainable medical tourism: Investigating health-care travel in Indonesia and Malaysia. *International Journal of Healthcare Management*, •••, 1–10.

Raub, S. P., & Martin-Rios, C. (2019). "Think sustainable, act local" – a stakeholder-filter-model for translating SDGs into sustainability initiatives with local impact. *International Journal of Contemporary Hospitality Management, 31*(6), 2428–2447. doi:10.1108/IJCHM-06-2018-0453

Rauch, E., Damian, A., Holzner, P., & Matt, D. T. (2016). Lean hospitality-application of lean management methods in the hotel sector. *Procedia CIRP, 41*, 614–619. doi:10.1016/j.procir.2016.01.019

Rauch, E., Matt, D. T., & Linder, C. (2020). Lean management in hospitality: Methods, applications and future directions. *International Journal of Services and Operations Management, 36*(3), 303–326. doi:10.1504/IJSOM.2020.108115

Raulston, T. J., Hansen, S. G., Machalicek, W., McIntyre, L. L., & Carnett, A. (2019). Interventions for repetitive behavior in young children with autism: A survey of behavioral practices. *Journal of Autism and Developmental Disorders, 49*(8), 3047–3059. doi:10.100710803-019-04023-y PMID:31030312

Regulation on the Qualifications of Tourism Facilities [Turizm Tesislerinin Niteliklerine İlişkin Yönetmelik]. (n.d.). Retrieved on September 22, 2021, from: https://www.mevzuat.gov.tr/MevzuatMetin/21.5.1134.pdf

Reid, R. D., & Bojanic, D. C. (2009). *Hospitality marketing management.* John Wiley and Sons.

Reid, R. D., & Sanders, N. R. (2005). *Operations Management: An Integrated Approach.* Wiley.

Reiley, L. (2020). Stress-baking and hoarding have led to a retail egg shortage. There are eggs in the pipeline, but maybe not enough. *The Washington Post.* Retrieved on July 24, 2020, from: https://www.washingtonpost.com/business/2020/03/26/shortages-eggs-stress-baking/

Relihan, W. J. III. (1989). The yield-management approach to hotel-room pricing. *The Cornell Hotel and Restaurant Administration Quarterly, 30*(May), 40–45. doi:10.1177/001088048903000113

Remoaldo, P., Serra, J., Marujo, N., Alves, J., Gonçalves, A., Cabeça, S., & Duxbury, N. (2020). Profiling the participants in creative tourism activities: Case studies from small and medium sized cities and rural areas from Continental Portugal. *Tourism Management Perspectives, 36*(May), 100746. doi:10.1016/j.tmp.2020.100746 PMID:32953432

Republic of Turkey Ministry of National Education. (2021). *Okullarda Afet Risk Yönetimi Projesi.* Retrieved from https://iegm.meb.gov.tr/www/okullarda-afet-risk-yonetimi-projesi/icerik/454

Rezvani, M., Nickravesh, F., Astaneh, A. D., & Kazemi, N. (2022). A risk-based decision-making approach for identifying natural-based tourism potential areas. *Journal of Outdoor Recreation and Tourism, 37*, 100485. doi:10.1016/j.jort.2021.100485

Richards, G., & Jutamas Jan Wisansing, E. P. (2018). Creating creative tourism toolkit. *Designated Areas for Sustainable Tourism Administration (Public Organization)-DASTA.* https://www.researchgate.net/profile/Greg-Richards-2/publication/330425066_Creating_Creative_Tourism_Toolkit/links/5c4046e0458515a4c72beeba/Creating-Creative-Tourism-Toolkit.pdf

Richards, G. (1996). *Cultural tourism in Europe.* CAB International.

Richards, G. (1996). Production and consumption of European cultural tourism. *Annals of Tourism Research, 23*(2), 261–283. doi:10.1016/0160-7383(95)00063-1

Richards, G. (2001). The experience industry and the creation of attractions. In G. Richards (Ed.), *Cultural attractions and European tourism* (pp. 55–71). Tilburg University.

Richards, G. (2002). *Gastronomy: an essential ingredient in tourism production and consumption? In Tourism and Gastronomy.* Routledge.

Compilation of References

Richards, G. (2009). Creative tourism and local development. In R. Wurzburger, A. Pattakos, & S. Pratt (Eds.), *Creative tourism: A global conversation* (pp. 78–90). Sunstone Press.

Richards, G. (2011). Creativity and tourism. The state of the art. *Annals of Tourism Research*, *38*(4), 1225–1253. doi:10.1016/j.annals.2011.07.008

Richards, G. (2013). Tourism development trajectories. From culture to creativity? In M. Smith & G. Richards (Eds.), *The Routledge handbook of cultural tourism* (pp. 297–303). Routledge.

Richards, G. (2016). The challenge of creative tourism. *Ethnologies (Québec)*, *38*(1-2), 31–45. doi:10.7202/1041585ar

Richards, G. (2018). Cultural tourism: A review of recent research and trends. *Journal of Hospitality and Tourism Management*, *36*, 12–21. doi:10.1016/j.jhtm.2018.03.005

Richards, G. (2018). Tourism, an underestimated driving force for the creative economy. *Revista Turismo em Análise*, *29*(3), 387–395. doi:10.11606/issn.1984-4867.v29i3p387-395

Richards, G. (2020). Designing creative places: The role of creative tourism. *Annals of Tourism Research*, *85*(March), 102922. doi:10.1016/j.annals.2020.102922

Richards, G., King, B., & Yeung, E. (2020). Experiencing culture in attractions, events and tour settings. *Tourism Management*, *79*(February), 104104. doi:10.1016/j.tourman.2020.104104

Richards, G., & Raymond, C. (2000). Creative tourism. *ATLAS News*, *23*, 16–20.

Richardson, S., March, R., Lewis, J., & Radel, K. (2015). Analysing the impact of the 2011 natural disasters on the Central Queensland tourism industry. *Tourism Crisis and Disaster Management in the Asia-Pacific*, 149–160. doi:10.1079/9781780643250.0149

Riikkinen, R., Kauppi, K., & Salmi, A. (2017). Learning Sustainability? Absorptive capacities as drivers of sustainability in MNCs' purchasing. *International Business Review*, *26*(6), 1075–1087. doi:10.1016/j.ibusrev.2017.04.001

Rinaldi, A., & Salerno, I. (2020). The tourism gender gap and its potential impact on the development of the emerging countries. *Quality & Quantity*, *54*(5), 1465–1477. doi:10.100711135-019-00881-x

Rinaldi, C. (2017). Food and Gastronomy for Sustainable Place Development: A Multidisciplinary Analysis of Different Theoretical Approaches. *Sustainability*, *9*(10), 1–25. doi:10.3390u9101748

Ristic, R., Danner, L., Johnson, T. E., Meiselman, H. L., Hoek, A. C., Jiranek, V., & Bastian, S. E. P. (2019). Wine-related aromas for different seasons and occasions: Hedonic and emotional responses of wine consumers from Australia, UK and USA. *Food Quality and Preference*, *71*, 250–260. doi:10.1016/j.foodqual.2018.07.011

Ritala, P. (2019). Innovation for Sustainability: Sceptical, Pragmatic, and Idealist Perspectives on the Role of Business as a Driver for Change. In N. Bocken, P. Ritala, L. Albareda, & R. Verburg (Eds.), *Innovation for Sustainability: Business Transformations Towards a Better World* (pp. 21–34). Palgrave Macmillan. doi:10.1007/978-3-319-97385-2_2

Ritchie, B. (2008). Tourism Disaster Planning and Management: From Response and Recovery to Reduction and Readiness. *Current Issues in Tourism*, *11*(4), 315–348. doi:10.1080/13683500802140372

Ritchie, B. J. R., & Ritchie, R. J. B. (1998). The branding of tourism destination: Past achievements and future trends in destination marketing – scope and limitations. *Proceedings of the 48th Congress of the Annual Congress of the International Association of Scientific Experts in Tourism*.

Ritchie, B. W. (2004). Chaos, crises and disasters: A strategic approach to crisis management in the tourism industry. *Tourism Management*, *25*(6), 669–683. doi:10.1016/j.tourman.2003.09.004

Ritchie, B. W., & Jiang, Y. (2019). A review of research on tourism risk, crisis and disaster management: Launching the annals of tourism research curated collection on tourism risk, crisis and disaster management. *Annals of Tourism Research*, *79*, 102812. doi:10.1016/j.annals.2019.102812

Ritchie, J. R., & Crouch, G. I. (2010). A model of destination competitiveness/sustainability: Brazilian perspectives. *Revista de Administração Pública*, *44*(5), 1049–1066. doi:10.1590/S0034-76122010000500003

Rittichainuwat, B. N., & Chakraborty, G. (2009). Perceived travel risks regarding terrorism and disease: The case of Thailand. *Tourism Management*, *30*(3), 410–418. doi:10.1016/j.tourman.2008.08.001

Rivera, J. (2001). Does it pay to be green in the developing world? Participation in a Costa Rican voluntary environmental program and its impact on hotels' competitive advantage. In Academy of Management Proceedings (vol. 2001, pp. C1-C6). Academic of Management.

Rizzo, T. L., & Columna, L. (2020). Theory of planned behavior. Routledge Handbook of Adapted Physical Education, 326–346. doi:10.4324/9780429052675-25

Robert, I. (1996). Alexandrie 1830-1930: Historie d'une communaute citadine. Institut Fran͵ais d'Archéologie Orientale.

Roberts, P. (1999). Product innovation, product-market competition and persistent profitability in the US pharmaceutical industry. *Strategic Management Journal*, *20*(7), 655–670. doi:10.1002/(SICI)1097-0266(199907)20:7<655::AID-SMJ44>3.0.CO;2-P

Robinson, R. (2020). *The 7 top social media sites you need to care about in 2020*. Preuzeto.

Rocco, S. T., & Plakhotnik, S. M. (2009). Literature reviews, conceptual frameworks, and theoretical frameworks: Terms, functions, and distinctions. *Human Resource Development Review*, *8*(1), 120–130. doi:10.1177/1534484309332617

Rodgers, P., Stokes, P., Tarba, S., & Khan, Z. (2019). The Role of Non-market Strategies in Establishing Legitimacy: The Case of Service MHCs in Emerging Economies. *Management International Review*, *59*(4), 515–540. doi:10.100711575-019-00385-8

Rodgers, S. (2007). Innovation in food service technology and its strategic role. *International Journal of Hospitality Management*, *26*(4), 899–912. doi:10.1016/j.ijhm.2006.10.001

Rodrigues, Á., Loureiro, S. M. C., Lins de Moraes, M., & Pereira, R. G. (2022). Memorable tourism experience in the context of astrotourism. *Anatolia*, 1-13.

Rodrigues, H., & Parr, W. V. (2019). Contribution of cross-cultural studies to understanding wine appreciation: A review. *Food Research International (Ottawa, Ont.)*, *115*, 251–258. doi:10.1016/j.foodres.2018.09.008 PMID:30599939

Rodrigues, H., Rolaz, J., Franco-Luesma, E., Saenz-Navajas, M. P., Behrens, J., Valentin, D., & Depetris-Chauvin, N. (2020). How the country-of-origin impacts wine traders' mental representation about wines: A study in a world wine trade fair. *Food Research International (Ottawa, Ont.)*, *137*, 109480. doi:10.1016/j.foodres.2020.109480 PMID:33233142

Rodriguez, M., Doloreux, D., & Shearmur, R. (2017). Variety in external knowledge sourcing and innovation novelty: Evidence from the KIBS sector in Spain. *Technovation*, *68*, 35–43. doi:10.1016/j.technovation.2017.06.003

Roediger, H. L. III, & McDermott, K. B. (2013). Two types of event memory. *Proceedings of the National Academy of Sciences of the United States of America*, *110*(52), 20856–20857. doi:10.1073/pnas.1321373110 PMID:24319091

Rogerson, C. M., & Baum, T. (2020). COVID-19 and African tourism research agendas. *Development Southern Africa*, *37*(5), 727–741.

Roggio, A. (2018, January 2). Live streaming can promote ecommerce products. *Practical Ecommerce*. Retrieved April 5, 2022, from https://www.practicalecommerce.com/live-streaming-can-promote-ecommerce-products

Rolando, A., & Scandiffio, A. (2021). Historical agricultural landscapes: Mapping seasonal conditions for sustainable tourism. In *Proceedings of 28th CIPA Symposium "Great Learning & Digital Emotion"* (pp. 641-646). Academic Press.

Romão, J., & Nijkamp, P. (2019). Impacts of innovation, productivity and specialization on tourism competitiveness–a spatial econometric analysis on European regions. *Current Issues in Tourism*, *22*(10), 1150–1169. doi:10.1080/13683500.2017.1366434

Ronaghi, M. (2021). A blockchain maturity model in agricultural supply chain. *Information Processing in Agriculture*, *8*(3), 398–408. doi:10.1016/j.inpa.2020.10.004

Roque, J., Guastavino, C., Lafraire, J., & Fernandez, P. (2018). Plating influences diner perception of culinary creativity. *International Journal of Gastronomy and Food Science*, *11*, 55–62. doi:10.1016/j.ijgfs.2017.11.006

Rosato, P. F., Caputo, A., Valente, D., & Pizzi, S. (2021). 2030 Agenda and sustainable business models in tourism: A bibliometric analysis. *Ecological Indicators*, *121*, 121. doi:10.1016/j.ecolind.2020.106978

Rosen, M. (2012). Engineering Sustainability: A Technical Approach to Sustainability. *Sustainability*, *4*(9), 2270–2292. doi:10.3390u4092270

Rossello, J., Becken, S., & Santana-Gallego, M. (2020). The effects of natural disasters on international tourism: A global analysis. *Tourism Management*, *79*, 104080. doi:10.1016/j.tourman.2020.104080 PMID:32287755

Roth, R. E. (2020). Cartographic design as visual storytelling: Synthesis and review of map-based narratives, genres, and tropes. *The Cartographic Journal*, *58*(1), 83–114. doi:10.1080/00087041.2019.1633103

Roxas, F. M. Y., Rivera, J. P. R., & Gutierrez, E. L. M. (2020). Mapping stakeholders' roles in governing sustainable tourism destinations. *Journal of Hospitality and Tourism Management*, *45*, 387–398. doi:10.1016/j.jhtm.2020.09.005

Roy, D. (2020). *World food safety day 2020: COVID-19 offers an opportunity for India's food systems to deliver on safety and health*. Retrieved on June 16, 2020, from: https://www.ifpri.org/blog/world-food-safety-day-2020-covid-19-offers-opportunity-indias-food-systems-deliver-safety-and/

Rucinska, D., & Lechowicz, M. (2014). Natural hazard and disaster tourism. *Miscellanea Geographica*, *18*(1), 17–25. doi:10.2478/mgrsd-2014-0002

Rudin-Rush, L., Michler, J. D., Josephson, A., & Bloem, J. R. (2022). Food insecurity during the first year of the COVID-19 pandemic in four African countries. *Food Policy*, *111*, 102306.

Ruiz Molina, M. E., Belda-Miquel, S., Hytti, A., & Gil-Saura, I. (2022). Addressing sustainable food management in hotels: Proposing a framework and examining hotel groups. *British Food Journal*, *124*(2), 462–492. doi:10.1108/BFJ-12-2020-1171

Ruiz-Real, J. L., Uribe-Toril, J., & Gázquez-Abad, J. C. (2020). Destination branding: Opportunities and new challenges. *Journal of Destination Marketing & Management*, *17*, 100453.

Saarinen, J. (2006). Traditions of sustainability in tourism studies. *Annals of Tourism Research*, *33*(4), 1121–1140. doi:10.1016/j.annals.2006.06.007

Saarinen, J. (2014). Critical Sustainability: Setting the Limits to Growth and Responsibility in Tourism. *Sustainability*, *6*(1), 1–17. doi:10.3390u6010001

Saarinen, J. (2019). Communities and sustainable tourism development: Community impacts and local benefit creation in tourism. In S. McCool & K. Bosak (Eds.), *A research agenda for sustainable tourism* (pp. 206–222). Edward Elgar Publishing. doi:10.4337/9781788117104.00020

Sabina, J. M., & Nicolae, J. C. (2013). Gender trends in tourism destination. *Procedia: Social and Behavioral Sciences*, *92*, 437–444. doi:10.1016/j.sbspro.2013.08.698

Sabri Ülker Foundation. (2021). *COVID-19 nutritional behavior research from the Sabri Ülker Foundation* [Sabri Ülker Vakfı'ndan COVID-19 dönemi beslenme davranışları araştırması]. www.sabriulkerfoundation.org/tr/sabri-ulker-vakfindan-covid-19-donemi-beslenme-davranislari-arastirmasi

Sadiq, M., & Adil, M. (2021). Ecotourism related search for information over the internet: A technology acceptance model perspective. *Journal of Ecotourism*, *20*(1), 70–88. doi:10.1080/14724049.2020.1785480

Safa, H. I. (2018). *The myth of the male breadwinner: Women and industrialization in the Caribbean*. Routledge. doi:10.4324/9780429492754

Sagar, S., & Pradhan, N. (2020). A review: Recent trends in green computing. In B. Balusamy, N. Chilamkurti, & S. Kadry (Eds.), *Green Computing in Smart Cities: Simulation and Techniques* (pp. 19–34). Springer Nature.

Saha, B. (2014). Green computing. *International Journal of Computer Trends and Technology*, *14*(2), 46–50. doi:10.14445/22312803/IJCTT-V14P112

Sahebalzamani, S., Jørgensen, E. J. B., Bertella, G., & Nilsen, E. R. (2022). A Dynamic Capabilities Approach to Business Model Innovation in Times of Crisis. *Tourism Planning & Development*, •••, 1–24. doi:10.1080/21568316.2022.2107560

Sahli, A. B., & Legohérel, P. (2016). The tourism web acceptance model: A study of intention to book tourism products online. *Journal of Vacation Marketing*, *22*(2), 179–194. doi:10.1177/1356766715607589

Sajja, G., Rane, K., Phasinam, K., Kassanuk, T., Okoronkwo, E., & Prabhu, P. (2021). Towards applicability of blockchain in agriculture sector. *Materials Today: Proceedings*, 1–4. doi:10.1016/j.matpr.2021.07.366

Salinas Fernández, J. A., Serdeira Azevedo, P., Martín Martín, J. M., & Rodríguez Martín, J. A. (2020). Determinants of tourism destination competitiveness in the countries most visited by international tourists: Proposal of a synthetic index. *Tourism Management Perspectives*, *33*(September), 100582. doi:10.1016/j.tmp.2019.100582

Samdin, Z., Abdullah, S. I. N. W., Khaw, A., & Subramaniam, T. (2021). Travel risk in the ecotourism industry amid COVID-19 pandemic: Ecotourists' perceptions. *Journal of Ecotourism*, *0*(0), 1–29. doi:10.1080/14724049.2021.1938089

Sameer, Y. M., Elmassah, S., Mertzanis, C., & El-Maghraby, L. (2021). Are happier nations more responsible? Examining the link between happiness and sustainability. *Social Indicators Research*, *158*(1), 267–295. doi:10.100711205-021-02698-4

Sameh, M. M., & Scavuzzi, J. (2016). *Environmental Sustainability Measures for Airports*. McGill, Centre for Research in Air and Space Law. Retrieved on October 7, 2021, from: https://www.mcgill.ca/iasl/files/iasl/vii_sustainability_and_environmental_protection_measures_for_airports_final.pdf

San, İ. (2008). Sanat ve Eğitim [Arts and Education] [Dördüncü Baskı]. Ankara: Ütopya Yayınevi.

Sánchez-Cañizares, S. M., Cabeza-Ramírez, L. J., Muñoz-Fernández, G., & Fuentes-García, F. J. (2021). Impact of the perceived risk from Covid-19 on intention to travel. *Current Issues in Tourism*, *24*(7), 970–984. doi:10.1080/13683500.2020.1829571

Sancho, A., García, G., Pedro, A., & Yagüe, R. M. (2002). *Sustainability audit in tourist destinations*.

Sandberg, D. S. (2017). Medical tourism: An emerging global healthcare industry. *International Journal of Healthcare Management*, *10*(4), 281–288. doi:10.1080/20479700.2017.1296213

Sanip, M., & Mustapha, R. (2020). Sustainability of Gastronomic Tourism in Malaysia: Theoretical Context. *International Journal of Asian Social Science*, *10*(8), 417–425. doi:10.18488/journal.1.2020.108.417.425

Santeramo, F. G., Seccia, A., & Nardone, G. (2017). The synergies of the Italian wine and tourism sectors. *Wine Economics and Policy*, *6*(1), 71–74. doi:10.1016/j.wep.2016.11.004

Santero-Sanchez, R., Segovia-Pérez, M., Castro-Nuñez, B., Figueroa-Domecq, C., & Talón-Ballestero, P. (2015). Gender differences in the hospitality industry: A job quality index. *Tourism Management*, *51*, 234–246. doi:10.1016/j.tourman.2015.05.025

Santos, J. (2013). *Sistema de indicadores de sustentabilidade para o turismo: aplicação de uma abordagem participativa em Porto de Galinhas, PE* [Master's Dissertation]. Universidade Federal de Pernambuco.

Santos, V., Sousa, B., Ramos, P., & Valeri, M. (2021). Emotions and involvement in tourism settings. *Current Issues in Tourism*, 1–6.

Saravanakumar, M., & SuganthaLakshmi, T. (2012). Social Media Marketing. *Life Science Journal*, *9*(4), 4444-4451. http://www.lifesciencesite.com/lsj/life0904/670_13061life0904_4444_4451.pdf

Sarıışık, M., Çavuş, Ş., & Karamustafa, K. (2010). *Profosyonel restoran yönetimi, ilkeler, uygulamalar ve örnek olaylar*. Detay Yayıncılık.

Sarkar, A. N. (2012, August). *Evolving Green Aviation Transport System: A Holistic Approach to Sustainable Green Market Development*. Retrieved on November 2, 2021, from: https://www.scirp.org/html/5-2360021_22479.htm?pagespeed=noscript

Sarkar, N. I., & Gul, S. (2020). Green Computing and internet of things for smart cities: Technologies, challenges, and implementation. In B. Balusamy, N. Chilamkurti, & S. Kadry (Eds.), *Green Computing in Smart Cities: Simulation and Techniques* (pp. 35–50). Springer Nature.

Sarmah, R., Dhiman, N., & Kanojia, H. (2021). Understanding intentions and actual use of mobile wallets by millennial: An extended TAM model perspective. *Journal of Indian Business Research*, *13*(3), 361–381. Advance online publication. doi:10.1108/JIBR-06-2020-0214

Sarmiento, S. (1998). Household, gender, and travel. In Women's Travel Issues Second National Conference. Drachman Institute of the University of Arizona, Morgan State University,; Federal Highway Administration.

Scarpato, R. (2002a). Gastronomy as a tourist product: the perspective of gastronomy studies. In A.-M. Hjalager & G. Richards (Eds.), *Sustainable gastronomy as a tourist product* (pp. 51–70). Routledge.

Scarpato, R. (2002b). Tourism Gastronomy. In A.-M. Hjalager & G. Richards (Eds.), *Sustainable gastronomy as a tourist product* (pp. 132–152). Routledge.

Schaar, R. (2013). Destination branding: A snapshot. *UW-L Journal of Undergraduate Research*, *16*, 1–10.

Schaffer, N. (2017, September 7). Social Media Promotion - 11 effective ways to boost your content. *11 Effective Ways to Use Social Media to Promote Your Content*. Retrieved April 5, 2022, from http://www.curata.com/blog/11-effective-ways-to-use-social-media-to-promote-your-content/

Schinckus, C. (2020). The good, the bad and the ugly: An overview of the sustainability of blockchain technology. *Energy Research & Social Science*, *69*, 1–10. doi:10.1016/j.erss.2020.101614

Schoenmaker, D. (2017). Investing for the common good: a sustainable finance framework. In *Essay and Lectures Series*. Bruegel.

Schoenmaker, D. (2018). *Sustainable investing: How to do it. Policy Contribution, 23*. Bruegel.

Schor, J. (2016). Debating The Sharing Economy. *Journal of Self-Governance & Management Economics*, *4*(3).

Schouten, A. P., Janssen, L., & Verspaget, M. (2020). Celebrity vs. Influencer endorsements in advertising: The role of identification, credibility, and Product-Endorser fit. *International Journal of Advertising*, *39*(2), 258–281. doi:10.1080/02650487.2019.1634898

Schramade, W. (2016). Bridging Sustainability and Finance: The Value Driver Adjustment Approach. *Journal of Applied Corporate Finance*, *28*(2), 17–28. doi:10.1111/jacf.12170

Schramade, W. (2017). Investing in the UN Sustainable Development Goals: Opportunities for Companies and Investors. *Journal of Applied Corporate Finance*, *29*(2), 87–99. doi:10.1111/jacf.12236

Schubert, F. (2008). *Exploring and predicting consumers' attitudes and behaviours towards green restaurants*. The Degree Master's of Science in the Graduate School of The Ohio State University.

Scoones, I. (2007). Sustainability. *Development in Practice*, *17*(4-5), 589–596. doi:10.1080/09614520701469609

Secilmis, C., Ozdemir, C., & Kılıç, İ. (2021). How travel influencers affect visit intention? The roles of cognitive response, trust, COVID-19 fear and confidence in vaccine. *Current Issues in Tourism*, 1–16.

Seeler, S., Høegh-Guldberg, O., & Eide, D. (2021). Impacts on and Responses of Tourism SMEs and MEs on the COVID-19 Pandemic–The Case of Norway. In S. K. Kulshreshtha (Ed.), *Virus Outbreaks and Tourism Mobility* (pp. 177–193). Emerald Publishing Limited. doi:10.1108/978-1-80071-334-520211016

Seidman, İ. E. (1991). *Interviewing as qualitative research: A guide for researchers in education and the social sciences*. Teachers College Press.

Selby, M. (2004). Consuming the city: Conceptualizing and researching urban tourist knowledge. *Tourism Geographies*, *6*(2), 186–207. doi:10.1080/1461668042000208426

Selwyn, T. (2013). Hospitality. In M. Smith & G. Richards (Eds.), *The Routledge Handbook of Cultural Tourism*. Routledge.

Sequira, T. (2021). *New COVID variant found in Finland may not shop up in test*. Helsinki Times. https://www.helsinkitimes.fi/finland/news-in-brief/18735-new-covid-variant-found-in-finland-may-not-show-up-in-tests.html

Serhan, C., Abboud, P., & Shahoud, R. (2018). Corporate Social Responsibility Practices in the Aviation Industry. *International Journal of Research in Business Studies and Management*, *5*(9), 1–14.

Sesar, V., Hunjet, A., & Kozina, G. (2021). Influencer marketing in travel and tourism: Literature review. *Economic and Social Development: Book of Proceedings*, 182-192.

Setiawan, P., & Widanta, A. (2021). The effect of trust on travel agent online use: Application of the technology acceptance model. *International Journal of Data and Network Science*, *5*(3), 173–182. doi:10.5267/j.ijdns.2021.6.015

Shafiee, M. M., Foroudi, P., & Tabaeeian, R. A. (2021). Memorable experience, tourist-destination identification and destination love. *International Journal of Tourism Cities*, *7*(3), 799–817. doi:10.1108/IJTC-09-2020-0176

Shafiee, S., Rajabzadeh Ghatari, A., Hasanzadeh, A., & Jahanyan, S. (2019). Developing a model for sustainable smart tourism destinations: A systematic review. *Tourism Management Perspectives*, *31*, 287–300. doi:10.1016/j.tmp.2019.06.002

Compilation of References

Shahbaznezhad, H., Dolan, R., & Rashidirad, M. (2021). The role of social media content format and platform in Users' engagement behavior. *Journal of Interactive Marketing, 53*, 47-65. doi:10.1016/j.intmar.2020.05.001

Shariatifar, N., & Molaee-aghaee, E. (2019). Novel Coronavirus 2019 (COVID-19): Important tips on food safety. *Journal of Food Safety and Hygiene, 5*(1), 58–59.

Sharma, S. (2020). *Distancing, masks key to stopping covid-19 spread: study.* https://www.hindustantimes.com/india-news/social-distancing-masks-eye-wear-and-hand-washing-work-best-in-co mbination-study/story-yROOhsGvHO0Z-p7eAZpJmjJ.htm

Sharma, N., & Patterson, P. G. (1999). The impact of communication effectiveness and service quality on relationship commitment in consumer, professional services. *Journal of Services Marketing, 13*(2), 151–170. doi:10.1108/08876049910266059

Sharma, S. K., Gayathri, N., Rakesh Kumar, S., Ramesh, C., Kumar, A., & Modanval, R. K. (2020). Green ICT, communication, networking, and data processing. In B. Balusamy, N. Chilamkurti, & S. Kadry (Eds.), *Green Computing in Smart Cities: Simulation and Techniques* (pp. 151–170). Springer Nature.

Sharma, S., & Verma, H. V. (2018). *Social Media Marketing: Evolution and Change.* Springer Nature. doi:10.1007/978-981-10-5323-8_2

Sharpley, R., & Wright, D. (2018). Disasters and Disaster Tourism: The Role of the Media. In The Palgrave Handbook of Dark Tourism Studies (pp. 335-354). London: Palgrave Macmillan. doi:10.1057/978-1-137-47566-4_14

Shaw, C. (Ed.). (2005). *Revolutionize your customer experience.* Palgrave Macmillan. doi:10.1057/9780230513457

Shen, C. C., & Liu, D. J. (2015). Correlation between the homestay experience and brand equity using the yuehetang rural residence as a case study. *Journal of Hospitality and Tourism Technology, 6*(1), 59–72. doi:10.1108/JHTT-01-2015-0008

Shields, J., & Shelleman, J. M. (2015). Integrating Sustainability into SME Strategy. *Journal of Small Business Strategy, 25*, 59–78.

Shiffrin, R. M., & Atkinson, R. C. (1969). Storage and retrieval processes in long-term memory. *Psychological Review, 76*(2), 179–193. doi:10.1037/h0027277

Shin, H., Nicolau, J. L., Kang, J., Sharma, A., & Lee, H. (2022). Travel decision determinants during and after COVID-19: The role of tourist trust, travel constraints, and attitudinal factors. *Tourism Management, 88*(December), 104428. doi:10.1016/j.tourman.2021.104428

Shondell Miller, D. (2008). Disaster tourism and disaster landscape attractions after Hurricane Katrina: An auto-ethnographic journey. *International Journal of Culture, Tourism and Hospitality Research, 2*(2), 115–131. doi:10.1108/17506180810880692

Shriedeh, F. (2019). The impact of medical tourist relationship management dimensions on innovation capabilities. *Business and Economic Review, 9*(3), 70–86. doi:10.5296/ber.v9i3.14955

Sigala, M. (2019). The transformational power of wine tourism experiences: The socio-cultural profile of Wine Tourism in South Australia. *Social Sustainability in the Global Wine Industry*, 57–73. doi:10.1007/978-3-030-30413-3_5

Sigala, M., & Haller, C. (2018). The impact of social media on the behavior of wine tourists: A typology of power sources. *Management and Marketing of Wine Tourism Business*, 139–154. doi:10.1007/978-3-319-75462-8_8

Simão, J., & Partidário, M. (2012). How does tourism planning contribute to sustainable development? *Sustainable Development, 20*(6), 372–385. doi:10.1002d.495

Simoes, A. J. G., & Hidalgo, C. A. (2011, August). The economic complexity observatory: An analytical tool for understanding the dynamics of economic development. *Workshops at the twenty-fifth AAAI conference on artificial intelligence.*

Sinclair, M. T. (1998). Tourism and economic development: A survey. *The Journal of Development Studies*, *34*(5), 1–51. doi:10.1080/00220389808422535

Singapore Airlines. (2019, May 21). *SIA Significantly Stepping Up In-Flight Sustainability Initiatives.* Retrieved on May 11, 2021, from: https://www.singaporeair.com/en_UK/es/media-centre/press-release/article/?q=en_UK/2019/January-March/ne0819-190321

Singer, J. A., & Salovey, P. (2010). *Remembered self: emotion and memory in personality.* Simon and Schuster.

Singh, S., & Srivastava, P. (2019). Social media for outbound leisure travel: a framework based on technology acceptance model (TAM). *Journal of Tourism Futures.* doi:10.1108/JTF-10-2018-0058

Singhania, K., Pandey, S., & Makuny, A. (2019, September). *National Green Aviation Policy: India's Step Towards Emission Cuts.* Retrieved on February 14, 2021, from https://www.mondaq.com/india/aviation/847444/national-green-aviation-policy-india39s-step-towards-emission-cuts

Singh, G. (2013). A study of evolution and practice of green marketing by various companies in India. *International Journal of Management and Social Sciences Research*, *2*, 49–56.

Singh, R., & Nazki, A. (2019). Investigating the influencing factors of Tourist Behavior towards Creative Tourism and its Relationship with Revisit Intention. *African Journal of Hospitality, Tourism and Leisure*, *8*(1), 1–28.

Singh, V. K. (2015, June 1). Corporate Social Responsibility within the Dynamics of Aviation Industry – with Special Reference to India. *Indian Journal of Air and Space Law*, *1*(57). Advance online publication. doi:10.2139srn.2973713

Sinha, S. (2017, February 22). Notebandi fails to impact international travel. *The Times of India.* Retrieved on August 23, 2020, from: https://timesofindia.indiatimes.com/business/india-business/notebandi-fails-to-impact-international-travel/articleshow/57283096.cms

Sipahi, S., Ekincek, S., & Yılmaz, H. (2017). Gastronominin sanatsal kimliğinin estetik üzerinden incelenmesi [Examining the artistic identity of gastronomy through aesthetics]. *Journal of Tourism and Gastronomy Studies*, *5*(3), 381–396. doi:10.21325/jotags.2017.100

Sisson, A. D., & Alcorn, M. R. (2021). How was your music festival experience? Impacts on loyalty, word-of-mouth, and sustainability behaviors. *Event Management.*

SITA. (2020, September 11). *Mumbai Airport introduces mobile-enabled kiosks to meet new COVID-19 requirements.* Retrieved on October 17, 2021, from: https://www.sita.aero/pressroom/news-releases/mumbai-airport-introduces-mobile-enabled-kiosks-to-meet-new-covid-19-requirements/

Skavronskaya, L., Scott, N., Moyle, B., & Kralj, A. (2019). Novelty and the tourism experience. *Current Issues in Tourism.*

Skavronskaya, L., Scott, N., Moyle, B., Le, D., Hadinejad, A., Zhang, R., Gardiner, S., Coghlan, A., & Shakeela, A. (2017). Cognitive psychology and tourism research: State of the art. *Tourism Review*, *72*(2), 221–237. doi:10.1108/TR-03-2017-0041

Slak Valek, N. (2020). Word-of-art: Contribution of artists-in-residence to a creative tourism destination. *Journal of Tourism and Cultural Change*, *18*(2), 81–95. doi:10.1080/14766825.2018.1467920

Slaper, T. F., & Hall, T. J. (2011). The triple bottom line: What is it and how does it work. *Indiana Business Review*, *86*(1), 4–8.

Compilation of References

Slavich, B., Cappetta, R., & Salvemini, S. (2014). Creativity and the Reproduction of cultural products: The experience of Italian Haute Cuisine chefs. *International Journal of Arts Management*, *16*, 29–71.

Sloan, P., Legrand, W., & Chen, J. S. (2013). Sustainability in the hospitality industry: Principles of sustainable operations (2nd ed.). New York: Routledge.

Smith, B. (2007). Developing sustainable food supply chains. *Philosophical Transactions of the Royal Society of London. Series B, Biological Sciences*, *363*(1492), 849–861. doi:10.1098/rstb.2007.2187 PMID:17766237

Smith, B. E. (2013). *Green computing: Tools and techniques for saving energy, money, and resources*. CRC Press. doi:10.1201/b15098

Smith, M., & Puczkó, L. (2014). *Health, tourism and hospitality: Spas, wellness and medical travel*. Routledge. doi:10.4324/9780203083772

Smith, P. C., & Forgione, D. A. (2007). Global outsourcing of healthcare: A medical tourism decision model. *Journal of Information Technology Case and Application Research*, *9*(3), 19–30. doi:10.1080/15228053.2007.10856117

Śniadek, J. (2006). Age of Seniors–A Challenge for tourism and leisure industry. *Studies in the Physical Culture and Tourism*, *13*(1), 103–105.

Soeroso, A., & Susilo, Y. (2014). Traditional Indonesian Gastronomy as a Cultural Tourism Attraction. *Journal of Applied Economics in Developing Countries*, *1*(1), 45–59.

Soğancılar, N., Dereli, Z., & Arı, G. S. (2022). Food Security in the COVID 19 Pandemic: Impacts Related to Food Supply. *Alanya Academic Review Journal*, *6*(2), 2333–2349.

Soliku, O., Kyiire, B., Mahama, A., & Kubio, C. (2021). Tourism amid COVID-19 pandemic: Impacts and implications for building resilience in the eco-tourism sector in Ghana's Savannah region. *Heliyon*, *7*, 07892.

Solís-Radilla, M. M., Hernández-Lobato, L., Callarisa-Fiol, L. J., & Pastor-Durán, H. T. (2019). The importance of sustainability in the loyalty to a tourist destination through the management of expectations and experiences. *Sustainability*, *11*(15), 4132. doi:10.3390u11154132

Song, H.-C. (2020). Sufficiency economy philosophy: Buddhism-based sustainability framework in Thailand. *Business Strategy and the Environment*, *29*(8), 2995–3005. doi:10.1002/bse.2553

Song, H., Livat, F., & Ye, S. (2019). Effects of terrorist attacks on tourist flows to France: Is wine tourism a substitute for urban tourism? *Journal of Destination Marketing & Management*, *14*, 14. doi:10.1016/j.jdmm.2019.100385

Son, I. S., Huang, S., & Padovan, D. (2021). Realising the goals of event leveraging: The tourism and hospitality SME Perspective. *Journal of Hospitality and Tourism Management*, *49*, 253–259. doi:10.1016/j.jhtm.2021.09.018

Sönmez, S. (2001). Tourism behind the veil of Islam: Women and development in the Middle East. *Women as producers and consumers of tourism in developing regions*, 113-142.

Soonthonsmai, V. (2007). Environmental or Green Marketing as Global Competitive Edge: Concept, Synthesis, and Implication. *EABR (Business) and ETLC (Teaching) Conference Proceeding*.

Soontiens, W., Dayaram, K., Burgess, J., & Grimstad, S. (2018). Bittersweet? Urban proximity and wine tourism in the Swan Valley Region. *Tourism Management Perspectives*, *28*, 105–112. doi:10.1016/j.tmp.2018.08.008

Sormaz, U., Akmese, H., Gunes, E., & Aras, S. (2016). Gastronomy in Tourism. *Procedia Economics and Finance*, *39*, 725–730. doi:10.1016/S2212-5671(16)30286-6

Sottini, V. A., Barbierato, E., Bernetti, I., & Capecchi, I. (2021). Impact of climate change on wine tourism: An approach through social media data. *Sustainability*, *13*(13), 7489. doi:10.3390u13137489

Sourvinou, A., & Filimonau, V. (2018). Planning for an environmental management programme in a luxury hotel and its perceived impact on staff: An exploratory case study. *Journal of Sustainable Tourism*, *26*(4), 649–667. doi:10.1080/09669582.2017.1377721

Spenceley, A., & Rylance, A. (2019). The contribution of tourism to achieving the United Nations Sustainable Development Goals. In S. F. McCool & K. Bosak (Eds.), *A research agenda for sustainable tourism* (pp. 107–125). Edward Elgar Publishing. doi:10.4337/9781788117104.00015

Srivastava, T. (2015, June). India attempts flexible use of airspace to cut time and costs. *Hindustan Times*. Retrieved on December 4, 2020, from: https://www.hindustantimes.com/business/india-attempts-flexible-use-of-airspace-to-cut-time-costs/story-GadQM0aQXoLGONWTO4lIFJ.html

Stamam, M. S. M., Nenin, M., Hashim, R., & Radzi, S. M. (2012). Food and beverage technology and employees' acceptance in 4 and 5 star hotels in Kuala Lumpur, Malaysia. *Current Issues In Hospitality And Tourism Research And Innovations*, 237.

Starik, M., & Kanashiro, P. (2013). Toward a theory of sustainability management: Uncovering and integrating the nearly obvious. *Organization & Environment*, *26*(1), 7–30. doi:10.1177/1086026612474958

Statista Research Department. (2022, August 19). *Influencer marketing market size worldwide from 2016 to 2022*. https://www.statista.com/statistics/1092819/global-influencer-market-size/

Statista. (2020). *eServices Report 2020*. Retrieved on July 22, 2021, from: https://www.statista.com/study/42306/eservices-report/

Stephens, E. C., Martin, G., van Wijk, M., Timsina, J., & Snow, V. (2020). Editorial: Impacts of COVID-19 on agricultural and food systems worldwide and on progress to the sustainable development goals. *Agricultural Systems*, *183*, 102873.

Sthapit, E., Del Chiappa, G., Coudounaris, D. N., & Björk, P. (2019). Tourism experiences, memorability and behavioural intentions: A study of tourists in Sardinia, Italy. *Tourism Review*, *75*(3), 533–558. doi:10.1108/TR-03-2019-0102

Stierand, M. (2020). Culinary Creativity. In M. Runco & S. Pritzker (Eds.), *Encyclopedia of Creativity* (pp. 296–300). Elsevier. doi:10.1016/B978-0-12-809324-5.23684-5

Stierand, M., & Dörfler, V. (2016). The role of intuition in the creative process of expert chefs. *The Journal of Creative Behavior*, *50*(3), 178–185. doi:10.1002/jocb.100

Stilwell, D. (2011). *Indicadores de sustentabilidade aplicados ao contexto do desenvolvimento turístico português* [Dissertação de Mestrado]. Faculty of Sciences, University of Lisbon.

Stipanović, C., & Rudan, E. (2015). Creative tourism in destination brand identity. *International Journal – Vallis Aurea*, *1*(1), 75-83. Doi:10.2507/IJVA.1.1.7.7

Stokes, K., Clarence, E., Anderson, L., & Rinne, A. (2014). *Making sense of the UK collaborative economy*. Nesta.

Stone, M. J., Migacz, S., & Sthapit, E. (2021). Connections between culinary tourism experiences and memory. *Journal of Hospitality & Tourism Research (Washington, D.C.)*, *46*(4), 797–807. doi:10.1177/1096348021994171

Storm, M. (2022, March 18). 5 types of social media for growing your business strategy. *WebFX*. Retrieved April 5, 2022, from https://www.webfx.com/blog/social-media/types-of-social-media/

Compilation of References

STR. (2020a). *STR: Europe hotel performance for July 2020*. Retrieved on March 17, 2022, from: https://str.com/press-release/str-europe-hotel-performance-july-2020

STR. (2020b). *STR: Middle East and Africa hotel performance for July 2020*. Retrieved on March 17, 2022, from: https://str.com/press-release/str-middle-east-and-africa-hotel-performance-july-2020

STR. (2020c). *STR: Canada hotel results for week ending 29 August*. Retrieved on March 17, 2022, from: https://str.com/press-release/str-canada-hotel-results-week-ending-29-august

Streimikiene, D., Svagzdiene, B., Jasinskas, E., & Simanavicius, A. (2021). Sustainable tourism development and competitiveness: The systematic literature review. *Sustainable Development*, *29*(1), 259–271. doi:10.1002d.2133

Strickland, P., Williams, K. M., Laing, J., & Frost, W. (2016). The use of social media in the wine event industry: A case study of the high country harvest in Australia. *Successful Social Media and Ecommerce Strategies in the Wine Industry*, 74–92. doi:10.1057/9781137602985_5

Subedi, S. (2016). *Effects of homestay in rural tourism* [Unpublish Master Thesis]. Tribhuvan University, Kirtipur, Kathmandu, Nepal.

Subedi, P., Joshi, R., Poudel, B., & Lamichhane, S. (2020). Status of human-wildlife conflict and assessment of crop damage by wild animals in buffer zone area of Banke national park, Nepal. *Asian Journal of Conservation Biology*, *9*(2), 196–206.

Su, D. N., Tran, K. P. T., Nguyen, L. N. T., Thai, T. H. T., Doan, T. H. T., & Tran, V. T. (2021). Modeling behavioral intention toward traveling in times of a health-related crisis. *Journal of Vacation Marketing*. Advance online publication. doi:10.1177/13567667211024703

Suhartanto, D., Agustina, R., Wibisono, N., & Leo, G. (2018). The Application of Structural Equation Modelling for Predicting the Link between Motivation and Experience Quality in Creative Tourism. *MATEC Web of Conferences, 218*, 4–9. 10.1051/matecconf/201821804001

Suhartanto, D., Brien, A., Primiana, I., Wibisono, N., & Triyuni, N. N. (2020). Tourist loyalty in creative tourism: The role of experience quality, value, satisfaction, and motivation. *Current Issues in Tourism*, *23*(7), 867–879. doi:10.1080/13683500.2019.1568400

Sujood, Hamid, S., & Bano, N. (2021). Behavioral Intention of Traveling in the period of COVID-19: An application of the Theory of Planned Behavior (TPB) and Perceived Risk. *International Journal of Tourism Cities*, (July). Advance online publication. doi:10.1108/IJTC-09-2020-0183

Sujová, E., Čierna, H., & Żabińska, I. (2019). Application of digitization procedures of production in practice. *Management Systems in Production Engineering*, *27*(1), 23–28. doi:10.1515/mspe-2019-0004

Su, M. M., Wall, G., Ma, J., Notarianni, M., & Wang, S. (2020). Empowerment of women through cultural tourism: Perspectives of Hui minority embroiderers in Ningxia, China. *Journal of Sustainable Tourism*, 1–22. doi:10.1080/09669582.2020.1841217

Sundbo, J., Orfila-Sintes, F., & Sørensen, F. (2007). The innovative behaviour of tourism firms—Comparative studies of Denmark and Spain. *Research Policy*, *36*(1), 88–106. doi:10.1016/j.respol.2006.08.004

Sun, J. W. (2000). Dematerialization and sustainable development. *Sustainable Development*, *8*(3), 142–145. doi:10.1002/1099-1719(200008)8:3<142::AID-SD139>3.0.CO;2-H

Sun, Y.-Y., & Drakeman, D. (2020). Measuring the carbon footprint of wine tourism and cellar door sales. *Journal of Cleaner Production*, *266*, 266. doi:10.1016/j.jclepro.2020.121937

Sun, Y.-Y., & Drakeman, D. (2021). The double-edged sword of wine tourism: The economic and environmental impacts of wine tourism in Australia. *Journal of Sustainable Tourism*, *30*(4), 932–949. doi:10.1080/09669582.2021.1903018

Surawattananon, N., Reancharoen, T., Prajongkarn, W., Chunanantatham, S., Simakorn, Y., & Gultawatvichai, P. (2021). *Revitalising Thailand's tourism sector*. https://www.bot.or.th/Thai/MonetaryPolicy/EconomicConditions/AAA/250624_WhitepaperVISA.pdf

Surendran, P. (2012). Technology acceptance model: A survey of literature. *International Journal of Business and Social Research*, *2*(4), 175–178. doi:10.18533/ijbsr.v2i4.161

Sürücü, Ö. A., & Ak, S. (2018). *Women as consumers in the tourism industry [Turizm sektöründe tüketici olarak kadın]*. İç. Turizm ve Kadın, Detay Yayıncılık.

Susamoğlu, F. (2018). Güncel Sanatta Ekolojik Yaklaşımlar ve Ekozofi Kavramı [Ecological Approaches in Contemporary Art and the Concept of Ecosophy]. *Atatürk Üniversitesi Güzel Sanatlar Enstitüsü Dergisi*, *41*, 96–103. doi:10.32547/ataunigsed.453183

Svensson, G., Wood, G., & Callaghan, M. (2010). A corporate model of sustainable business practices: An ethical perspective. *Journal of World Business*, *45*(4), 336–345. doi:10.1016/j.jwb.2009.08.005

Swain, M. B. (1995). Gender in tourism. *Annals of Tourism Research*, *22*(2), 247–266. doi:10.1016/0160-7383(94)00095-6

Swan, M. (2018). Blockchain for Business: Next-Generation Enterprise Artificial Intelligence Systems. *Advances in Computers*, *111*, 121–162. doi:10.1016/bs.adcom.2018.03.013

Szymańska, E. (2016). *Consumer participation in the health tourism innovation process. Ekonomia i Zarządzanie, 8(4)*.

Take Action for the Sustainable Development Goals. (2021). https://www.un.org/sustainabledevelopment/sustainable-development-goals/

Takyar, A. (2022). *Food Supply Chain Blockchain- Solving Food Supply Problems*. https://www.leewayhertz.com/supply-chain-blockchain-reinventing-food-supply/

Tanaka, N., Ikaptra, Kusano, S., Yamazaki, M., & Matsumoto, K. (2021). Disaster Tourism as a Tool for Disaster Story Telling. *Journal of Disaster Research*, *16*(2), 157–162. doi:10.20965/jdr.2021.p0157

Tan, B. C., & Yeap, P. F. (2012). What drives green restaurant patronage intention? *International Journal of Business and Management*, *7*(2), 215. doi:10.5539/ijbm.v7n2p215

Tan, W. K., & Wu, C. E. (2016). An investigation of the relationships among destination familiarity, destination image and future visit intention. *Journal of Destination Marketing & Management*, *5*(3), 214–226. doi:10.1016/j.jdmm.2015.12.008

Tasci, A. D. A., & Gartner, W. C. (2009). A practical framework for destination branding. In L. A. Cai, W. C. Gartner, & A. M. Munar (Eds.), *Tourism branding: Communities in action* (pp. 149–158). Emerald Group Publishing.

Taticchi, P., Tonelli, F., & Pasqualino, R. (2013). Performance measurement of sustainable supply chains: A literature review and a research agenda. *International Journal of Productivity and Performance Management*, *62*(8), 782–804. doi:10.1108/IJPPM-03-2013-0037

Tavel Agent Central. (2016). *Government of Aruba Argues in Favor of Limiting Growth of All-inclusives*. Retrieved on July 15, 2018, from: https://www.travelagentcentral.com/government-aruba-argues-favor-limiting-growth-all-inclusives

Tavitiyaman, P., Qu, H., Tsang, W. L., & Lam, C. R. (2021). The influence of smart tourism applications on perceived destination image and behavioral intention: The moderating role of information search behavior. *Journal of Hospitality and Tourism Management*, *46*, 476–487. doi:10.1016/j.jhtm.2021.02.003

Compilation of References

Taylor, N., Miller, P., Coomber, K., Livingston, M., Scott, D., Buykx, P., & Chikritzhs, T. (2021). The impact of a minimum unit price on wholesale alcohol supply trends in the Northern Territory, Australia. *Australian and New Zealand Journal of Public Health*, *45*(1), 26–33. doi:10.1111/1753-6405.13055 PMID:33559964

Taylor, S., & Todd, P. (1995). Understanding household garbage reduction behavior: A test of an integrated model. *Journal of Public Policy & Marketing*, *14*(2), 192–204. doi:10.1177/074391569501400202

Taylor, T., & Toohey, K. (2007). Perceptions of terrorism threats at the 2004 Olympic games: Implications for sport events. *Journal of Sport & Tourism*, *12*(2), 99–114. https://doi.org/10.1080/14775080701654754

Teachout, M., & Zipfel, C. (2020). *The economic impact of Covid-19 lockdowns in sub-Saharan Africa*. International Growth Centre.

Tekin Çevik, İ. (2020). Changing Consumer Behavior In The Pandemic Process [Pandemi Sürecinde Değişen Tüketici Davranışları]. *BMIIJ*, *8*(2), 2331–2347.

Tekin, Ö. A. (2017). Gender perception in tourism industry: a study on five star hotel employees [Turizm sektöründe toplumsal cinsiyet algısı: beş yıldızlı otel çalışanları üzerine bir araştırma]. *Avrasya Sosyal ve Ekonomi Araştırmaları Dergisi*, *4*(12), 669–684.

Telles, R., Jr. (2016). Digital Matching Firms: A New Definition in the "Sharing Economy" Space. ESA Issue Brief, 01-16.

Temesgen, A., Storsletten, V., & Jakobsen, O. (2019). Circular Economy – Reducing Symptoms or Radical Change? *Philosophy of Management*. Advance online publication. doi:10.100740926-019-00112-1

Temizkan, R., & Kızıltaş, M. (2021). Turizm Bağlamında Kültürel ve Doğal Kaynakların Korunmasında Fon Sağlama AracıOlarak NFT. *Journal of Tourism and Gastronomy Studies*, *9*(4), 3079–3091. doi:10.21325/jotags.2021.935

Temizkan, S. P., & Çiçek, D. (2015). The concept of health tourism and its characteristics. [Sağlık Turizmi Kavramı ve Özellikleri]. In S. P. Temizkan (Ed.), *Health Tourism* [Sağlık Turizmi] (pp. 11–36). Detay Yayıncılık.

Tenzin, K., Mee-Udon, F., & Prampesit, R. (2019). Community opinion towards a village homestay program in Soe, a small nomadic community in the North-West of Bhutan. *African Journal of Hospitality, Tourism and Leisure*, *8*(3), 1–10.

TEPAV. (2020). Retrieved on August 9, 2020, from: https://www.tepav.org.tr/upload/files. /15967816977.TEPAV_Istihdam_Izleme_Bulteni_SGK_Mayis_2020.pdf

Terzi, S. (2020). *CBS destekli web tabanlı Eskişehir turizm kaynakları bilgi sistemi* [Unpublished Master's thesis]. Eskişehir Teknik University, Eskişehir, Turkey.

Teunter, R. H., Babai, M. Z., & Syntetos, A. A. (2009). ABC Classification: Service Levels and Inventory Costs. *Production and Operations Management*, *19*(3), 343–352. doi:10.1111/j.1937-5956.2009.01098.x

Thal, K. I. (2016). Macro Scale Assessment of Sustainability in Tourism. *Travel and Tourism Research Association: Advancing Tourism Research Globally*, *18*.

Thanh, T. V., & Kirova, V. (2018). Wine tourism experience: A netnography study. *Journal of Business Research*, *83*, 30–37. doi:10.1016/j.jbusres.2017.10.008

Thapa, S. (2016). *Rural tourism in Nepal: Case study of Tanahusur homestay of Tanahu* [Unpublish Master Thesis]. Tribhuvan University, Kirtipur, Kathmandu, Nepal.

The Baltic Course. (2016). *Estonia supports expansion of sharing economy*. Retrieved on July 2, 2018, from: http://www.baltic-course.com/eng/analytics/?doc=115999

The Greater Boston Food Bank. (2021). *Food Insecurity Remains Well Above Pre-Pandemic Levels*. Retrieved on February 20, 2022, from: https://www.gbfb.org/2021/04/01/food-insecurity-remains-well-above-pre-pandemic-levels/

The World Bank. (n.d.). *Natural Disaster Risk Management Project*. Retrieved from https://projects.worldbank.org/en/projects-operations/project-detail/P073361

This, H. (2005). *Molecular Gastronomy - Exploring the Science of Flavor* (M. B. Debevoise, Trans.). Columbia University Press.

Thommandru, A., Espinoza-Maguiña, M., Ramirez-Asis, E., Ray, S., Naved, M., & Guzman-Avalos, M. (2021). Role of tourism and hospitality business in economic development. *Materials Today: Proceedings*. Advance online publication. doi:10.1016/j.matpr.2021.07.059

Thorat, S. B., Kishor, S. B., & Meghe, B. (2013). Social media marketing mix: Applicability review for marketing in education. *International Proceedings of Economics Development and Research, 59*(4), 16-20. DOI: .2013.V59.4 doi:10.7763/IPEDR

Tiago, F., Couto, J., Faria, S., & Borges-Tiago, T. (2018). Cruise tourism: Social media content and network structures. *Tourism Review, 73*(4), 433–447. Advance online publication. doi:10.1108/TR-10-2017-0155

Tight, M. (2017). *Understanding Case Study Research: Small-scale Research with Meaning*. Academic Press.

Tolay, İ., & Sinclair, L. (2020). *Instincts to help you understand consumer need in uncertain times* [Belirsiz zamanlarda tüketici ihtiyacını anlamanıza yardımcı olacak içgüdüler]. https://www.thinkwithgoogle.com/intl/tr-tr/icgoruler/t%C3%BCketici-trendleri/belirsiz-zamanlarda-tuketici-ihtiyacini-anlamaniza-yardimci-olacak-icgoruler-11-mayis-2020/

Tomej, K. (2019). Accessible and equitable tourism services for travellers with disabilities: From a charitable to a commercial footing. In S. O. Idowu & R. Schmidpeter (Eds.), *Corporate sustainability and responsibility in tourism* (pp. 65–78). Springer. doi:10.1007/978-3-030-15624-4_4

Torkington, K., Stanford, D., & Guiver, J. (2020). Discourse (s) of growth and sustainability in national tourism policy documents. *Journal of Sustainable Tourism, 28*(7), 1041–1062. doi:10.1080/09669582.2020.1720695

Torky, M., & Hassanein, A. (2020). Integrating blockchain and the internet of things in precision agriculture: Analysis, opportunities, and challenges. *Computers and Electronics in Agriculture, 178*, 1–23. doi:10.1016/j.compag.2020.105476

Torres, J. P., Barrera, J. I., Kunc, M., & Charters, S. (2021). The dynamics of wine tourism adoption in Chile. *Journal of Business Research, 127*, 474–485. doi:10.1016/j.jbusres.2020.06.043

Torres, R., & Momsen, J. (2005). Planned tourism development in Quintana Roo, Mexico: Engine for regional development or prescription for inequitable growth? *Current Issues in Tourism, 8*(4), 259–285. doi:10.1080/13683500508668218

Torun Kayabaşı, E. (2020). The Effect of COVID-19 on Agricultural Production. *Eurasian Journal of Research in Social and Economics, 7*(5), 38–45.

Tosun, C. (2001). Challenges of sustainable tourism development in the developing world: The case of Turkey. *Tourism Management, 22*(3), 289–303. doi:10.1016/S0261-5177(00)00060-1

Tourism Economics, an Oxford Economics Company. (2015). *The Economic Impact of Travel in Michigan Tourism Satellite Account Calendar Year 2014*. Retrieved on May 22, 2018, from: https://www.michiganbusiness.org/cm/Files/Reports/Michigan-2014-Tourism-Economic-Impact.pdf

Tracy, S. J. (2010, December). (20100. Qualitative Quality: Eight "Big-Tent" Criteria for Excellent Qualitative Research. *Qualitative Inquiry, 16*(10), 837–851. doi:10.1177/1077800410383121

Travel Guides. (2021, December 18). *7 most beautiful regions in Australia*. Touropia. Retrieved April 24, 2022, from https://www.touropia.com/regions-in-australia-map/

Travelnostop. (2017). *In Italia sharing economy nel turismo frenata da scarsa digitalizzazione*. Retrieved on January 26, 2017, from: https://www.travelnostop.com/news/dati-e-statistiche/in-italia-sharing-economy-nel-turismo-frenata-da-scarsa-digitalizzazione_140073

Trupp, A., & Sunanta, S. (2017). Gendered practices in urban ethnic tourism in Thailand. *Annals of Tourism Research*, *64*, 76–86. doi:10.1016/j.annals.2017.02.004

Tsai, C. H., & Chen, C. W. (2010). An earthquake disaster management mechanism based on risk assessment information for the tourism industry-a case study from the island of Taiwan. *Tourism Management*, *31*(4), 470–481. doi:10.1016/j.tourman.2009.05.008

Tsai, C. H., & Chen, C. W. (2011). The establishment of a rapid natural disaster risk assessment model for the tourism industry. *Tourism Management*, *32*(1), 158–171. doi:10.1016/j.tourman.2010.05.015

Tsai, C. W., & Tsai, C. P. (2008). Impacts of consumer environmental ethics on consumer behaviors in green hotels. *Journal of Hospitality & Leisure Marketing*, *17*(3–4), 284–313. doi:10.1080/10507050801984974

Tseng, K. C., Lin, H. H., Lin, J. W., Chen, I. S., & Hsu, C. H. (2021). Under the covid-19 environment, will tourism decision making, environmental risks, and epidemic prevention attitudes affect the people's firm belief in participating in leisure tourism activities? *International Journal of Environmental Research and Public Health*, *18*(14), 1–20. doi:10.3390/ijerph18147539 PMID:34300013

Tsen, W. S., & Cheng, B. K. L. (2021). Who to find to endorse? Evaluation of online influencers among young consumers and its implications for effective influencer marketing. *Young Consumers*, *22*(2), 237–253. doi:10.1108/YC-10-2020-1226

Tucker, H. (2007). Undoing shame: Tourism and women's work in Turkey. *Journal of Tourism and Cultural Change*, *5*(2), 87–105. doi:10.2167/jtcc089.0

Tucker, H., & Boonabaana, B. (2012). A critical analysis of tourism, gender and poverty reduction. *Journal of Sustainable Tourism*, *20*(3), 437–455. doi:10.1080/09669582.2011.622769

Tulving, E. (2002). Episodic memory: From mind to brain. *Annual Review of Psychology*, *53*(1), 1–25. doi:10.1146/annurev.psych.53.100901.135114 PMID:11752477

Tuncer, T., & Akoğlu, A. (2020). Food safety knowledge of food handlers working in hotel kitchens in Turkey. *Food Health*, *6*(2), 77–89. doi:10.3153/FH20009

Tung, V. W. S., Lin, P., Qiu Zhang, H., & Zhao, A. (2017). A framework of memory management and tourism experiences. *Journal of Travel & Tourism Marketing*, *34*(7), 853–866. doi:10.1080/10548408.2016.1260521

Tung, V. W. S., & Ritchie, J. B. (2011). Exploring the essence of memorable tourism experiences. *Annals of Tourism Research*, *38*(4), 1367–1386. doi:10.1016/j.annals.2011.03.009

Tura, N., Mortimer, G., & Kutvonen, A. (2019). Exploring the Pitfalls of Systemic Innovations for Sustainability. In N. Bocken, P. Ritala, L. Albareda, & R. Verburg (Eds.), *Innovation for Sustainability: Business Transformations Towards a Better World* (pp. 157–175). Palgrave Macmillan. doi:10.1007/978-3-319-97385-2_9

Turani, A. (2019). Dünya Sanat Tarihi [World Art History] [Genişletilmiş Basım]. İstanbul: Remzi Kitabevi.

Türkcan, B., & Babadağ, G. (2021). İlkokulda görsel sanatlar öğretimi [Visual arts teaching in primary school]. In İ. Korkmaz (Ed.), İlkokulda öğretim öğretmen el kitabı içinde (pp. 333-364). Pegem Akademi.

Turkina, E., Oreshkin, B., & Kali, R. (2019). Regional innovation clusters and firm innovation performance: An interactionist approach. *Regional Studies*, *53*(8), 1193–1206. doi:10.1080/00343404.2019.1566697

Türkiye Bilişim Derneği – TBD. (2010). *Belge Grubu Raporu – Çevreci Bilişim*. TBD/Kamu-BIB/2010-BG.

Turner, L. (2007). 'First world health care at third world prices': Globalization, bioethics and medical tourism. *Biosocieties*, *2*(3), 303–325. doi:10.1017/S1745855207005765

Turner, R. K., Turner, R. K., Pearce, D. W., & Bateman, I. (1993). *Environmental economics: an elementary introduction*. Johns Hopkins University Press.

Türnüklü, A. (2000). A Qualitative Research Technique That Can Be Used Effectively in Educational Research: Interview [Eğitimbilim Araştırmalarında Etkin Olarak Kullanılabilecek Nitel Bir Araştırma Tekniği: Görüşme]. *Educational Management in Theory and Practice*, *24*, 543–559.

TUROB. (2020). *Big bill to world tourism; STR March 2020 report*. Retrieved on March 15, 2022, from: https://www.turob.com/tr/bilgi-merkezi/basin-bultenleri/2020/show/32/dunya-turizmine-buyuk-fatura-str-mart-2020-

Tussyadiah, I. P. (2015). An exploratory study on drivers and deterrents of collaborative consumption in travel. In *Information and communication technologies in tourism 2015* (pp. 817–830). Springer.

Tutuncu, O., & Lieberman, L. (2016, May-June). Accessibility of Hotels for People with Visual Impairments: From Research to Practice. *Journal of Visual Impairment & Blindness*, 163–175.

Twitter Marketing Services. (n.d.). https://www.brafton.com/services/twitter-marketing-services/

Uçuk, C., & Özkanlı, O. (2017). Gastronomi turizmi: Tabak prezentasyonunun gastronomi turizmindeki yeri [Gastronomy tourism: The place of plate presentation in gastronomy tourism]. *Uluslararası Kırsal Turizm ve Kalkınma Dergisi*, *1*(1), 51–54.

Ulker-Demirel, E., & Ciftci, G. (2020). A systematic literature review of the theory of planned behavior in tourism, leisure and hospitality management research. *Journal of Hospitality and Tourism Management*, *43*(September), 209–219. doi:10.1016/j.jhtm.2020.04.003

Um, T., & Chung, N. (2021). Does smart tourism technology matter? Lessons from three smart tourism cities in South Korea. *Asia Pacific Journal of Tourism Research*, *26*(4), 396–414. doi:10.1080/10941665.2019.1595691

UNCTAD. (2015). *World Investment Report - Reforming international investment governance*. UNCTAD.

Underwood, S. (2016). Blockchain beyond bitcoin. *Communications of the ACM*, *59*(11), 15–17. doi:10.1145/2994581

UNEP. (2005). Making tourism more sustainable. In *A guide for policy makers*. UNEP and WTO.

UNEPIE. (1996). Eco-efficiency and cleaner production, charting the course to sustainability. UNEPIE.

UNESCO. (2006). *Towards sustainable strategies for creative tourism*. In Discussion Report of the Planning Meeting for 2008 International Conference on Creative Tourism, Santa Fe, NM.

United Nations Office for Disaster Risk Reduction. (n.d.). *What is the Sendai Framework for Disaster Risk Reduction?* Retrieved from https://www.undrr.org/implementing-sendai-framework/what-sendai-framework

United Nations Resolution (2018). *The Report of the Second Committee* (A/73/542).

Compilation of References

United Nations. (1987). *Report of the World Commission on Environment and Development.* Retrieved on June 2, 2021, from: https://tind-customer-undl.s3.amazonaws.com/6a11aad7-f822-40e6-9717-04ceb0726149?response-content-disposition=attachment%3B%20filename%2A%3DUTF-8%27%27A_42_427-EN.pdf&response-content-type=application%2Fpdf&X-Amz-Algorithm=AWS4-HMAC-SHA256&X-Amz-Expires=86400&X-Amz-Credential=AKIAXL7W7Q3XFWDGQKBB%2F20220417%2Feu-west-1%2Fs3%2Faws4_request&X-Amz-SignedHeaders=host&X-Amz-Date=20220417T070036Z&X-Amz-Signature=809ae6fa2c686138676265d0a5783d35a2232ddb671f0e3a0d-6da5dc35e99087

United Nations. (2021). *The global food crises.* www.un.org/esa/socdev/rwss/docs/2011/chapter4.pdf

UNWTO. (2013). Recommendations on accessible tourism. Madrid, Spain: World Tourism Organization (UNWTO) Publications.

UNWTO. (2013). Sustainable Tourism for Development. Madrid: World Tourism Organization.

UNWTO. (2015). *Tourism in the 2030 agenda.* Retrieved on March 29, 2021, from: https://www.unwto.org/tourism-in-2030-agenda

UNWTO. (2016a). Manual on accessible tourism for all: Principles, tools and best practices - Module I: Accessible tourism - definition and context. Madrid, Spain: World Tourism Organization (UNWTO) Publications.

UNWTO. (2016b). *Highlights of the 1st UNWTO conference on accessible tourism in Europe (San Marino, 19-20 November 2014),* Madrid, Spain: World Tourism Organization (UNWTO) Publications.

UNWTO. (2018). *Report on Gastronomy Tourism: The Case of Japan.* Affiliate Members Report: Volume Seventeen. Retrieved on March 30, 2022, from:www.e-unwto.org

UNWTO. (2019). *International Tourism Highlights, 2019 Edition.* UNWTO.

UNWTO. (2019a). *UNWTO Tourism definitions.* World Tourism Organization.

UNWTO. (2019b). *UNWTO Guidelines for institutional strengthening of destination management organizations (DMOs) - Preparing DMOs for new challenges.* World Tourism Organization.

UNWTO. (2020). *Tourism highlights 2019 Edition.* Retrieved on March 13, 2022, from: https://www.unwto.org/taxonomy/term/347?page=1

UNWTO. (2021). *Covıd-19 and tourism: tourism in pre-pandemic times.* Retrieved on March 13, 2022, from: https://www.unwto.org/covid-19-and-tourism-2020

Upadhyay, A., Mukhuty, S., Kumar, V., & Kazancoglu, Y. (2021). Blockchain technology and the circular economy: Implications for sustainability and social responsibility. *Journal of Cleaner Production, 293,* 1–7. doi:10.1016/j.jclepro.2021.126130

Upadhyay, P. (2011). Comparative and competitive advantages of globalised India as a medical tourism destination. *International Journal of Engineering and Management Sciences, 2*(1), 26–34.

Upham, P. (2001). A comparison of sustainability theory with UK and European airports policy and practice. *Journal of Environmental Management, 63*(3), 237–248. doi:10.1006/jema.2001.0469 PMID:11775497

USDA. (2021). *Food Insecurity Measurement.* Retrieved on March 24, 2022, from: https://www.ers.usda.gov/topics/food-nutrition-assistance/food-security-in-the-u-s/measurement/#measurement

Usta, Ö. (2014). *Turizm genel ve yapısal yaklaşım.* Detay Yayıncılık.

Utomo, S. B., Triyonowati, & Mildawati, T. (2022). *Virtual tour as an alternative for destination marketing during the pandemic of COVID-19*. International Conference on Government Education Management and Tourism.

Uysal, H. F. (2009). *Çağdaş Sanat ve Ekosistem* [Contemporary Art and Ecosystem]. Yüksek Lisans Tezi. Marmara Üniversitesi Güzel Sanatlar Enstitüsü.

Vahora, S. I., & Mishra, P. C. B. (2017). Benchmarking: Green Aviation Transport System. *Kalpa Publications in Civil Engineering, 1*, 259–264. https://easychair.org/publications/open/h5Q

van Dam, Y. K., & van Trijp, H. C. (2011). Cognitive and motivational structure of sustainability. *Journal of Economic Psychology, 32*(5), 726–741. doi:10.1016/j.joep.2011.06.002

Van der Waldt, D. L. R., Van Loggerenberg, M., & Wehmeyer, L. (2009). Celebrity endorsements versus created spokespersons in advertising: A survey among students. *Suid-Afrikaanse Tydskrif vir Ekonomiese en Bestuurswetenskappe, 12*(1), 100–114. doi:10.4102ajems.v12i1.263

van Doremalen, N., Bushmaker, T., Morris, D. H., Holbrook, M. G., Gamble, A., Williamson, B. N., & Munster, V. J. (2020). Aerosol and surface stability of SARS-CoV-2 as compared with SARS-CoV-1. *The New England Journal of Medicine, 382*(16), 1564–1567.

van Hoorik, P., Bomhof, F., & Meulenhoff, P. (2010). Assessing the positive and negative impacts of ICT on people, planet and profit. In *International Conference on Green Computing* (pp. 45-50), SCITEPRESS.

Vargas-Sánchez, A. (2016). Exploring the concept of smart tourist destination. *Enlightening Tourism. A Pathmaking Journal, 6*(2), 178-196.

Varpio, L., Paradis, E., Uijtdehaage, S., & Young, M. (2020). The distinctions between theory, theoretical framework, and conceptual framework. *Academic Medicine, 95*(7), 989–994. doi:10.1097/ACM.0000000000003075 PMID:31725464

Vassakis, K., Petrakis, E., Kopanakis, I., Makridis, J., & Mastorakis, G. (2019). Location-Based Social Network Data for Tourism Destinations. *Big Data and Innovation in Tourism, Travel, and Hospitality*, 105-114. doi:10.1007/978-981-13-6339-9_7

Vázquez Vicente, G., Martín Barroso, V., & Blanco Jiménez, F. J. (2021). Sustainable tourism, economic growth and employment—The case of the wine routes of Spain. *Sustainability, 13*(13), 7164. doi:10.3390u13137164

Vázquez-Martinez, U., Sanchís-Pedregosa, C., & Leal-Rodríguez, A. (2019). IsGastronomy A Relevant Factor for Sustainable Tourism? An Empirical Analysis of Spain Country Brand. *Sustainability, 11*(9), 1–13. doi:10.3390u11092696

Velikova, N., & Dodd, T. (2016). Sustainability of the Wine Market though Emerging Consumer Segments: The Case of U.S. Hispanic Consumers. *Agriculture and Agricultural Science Procedia, 8*, 81–87. doi:10.1016/j.aaspro.2016.02.011

Venkatesh, V., & Davis, F. D. (2000). A theoretical extension of the technology acceptance model: Four longitudinal field studies. *Management Science, 46*(2), 186–204. doi:10.1287/mnsc.46.2.186.11926

Viet, B. N., Dang, H. P., & Nguyen, H. H. (2020). Revisit intention and satisfaction: The role of destination image, perceived risk, and cultural contact. *Cogent Business and Management, 7*(1), 1796249. Advance online publication. doi:10.1080/23311975.2020.1796249

Viglia, G., & Abrate, G. (2020). Revenue and yield management: A perspective article. *Tourism Review, 75*(1), 294–298. doi:10.1108/TR-04-2019-0117

Visit. (2005). *The Tourism Market: Potential Demand for Products*. Retrieved on September 22, 2021, from: http://www.your-visit.info/brochure/en/070.htm#nachfrage

Compilation of References

Vodeb, K. (2012). Competition In Tourism In Terms of Changing Environment. *Procedia: Social and Behavioral Sciences*, *44*, 273–278. doi:10.1016/j.sbspro.2012.05.030

Volberda, H. W. (1996). Toward the flexible form: How to remain vital in hypercompetitive environments. *Organization Science*, *7*(4), 359–374. doi:10.1287/orsc.7.4.359

Volberda, H. W., Foss, N. J., & Lyles, M. A. (2010). Perspective—Absorbing the concept of absorptive capacity: How to realize its potential in the organization field. *Organization Science*, *21*(4), 931–951. doi:10.1287/orsc.1090.0503

Von Hippel, E. (2005). Democratizing innovation: The evolving phenomenon of user innovation. *Journal für Betriebswirtschaft*, *55*(1), 63–78. doi:10.100711301-004-0002-8

Vos, J. De. (2020). *Since January 2020 Elsevier has created a COVID-19 resource centre with free information in English and Mandarin on the novel coronavirus COVID- 19.* Elsevier.

Vujovic, S. M., Ćurčić, N. V., & Miletić, V. S. (2016). The influence of tourism on the circular flow of an economic process. *Economics of Agriculture*, *1*, 323–337.

Wahga, A. I., Blundel, R., & Schaefer, A. (2018). Understanding the drivers of sustainable entrepreneurial practices in Pakistan's leather industry. *International Journal of Entrepreneurial Behaviour & Research*, *24*(2), 382–407. doi:10.1108/IJEBR-11-2015-0263

Waleghwa, B., Heldt, T., Kati, V., & Niemelä, T. (2021). Public participation GIS in sustainable tourism planning; experiences from Sweden and Finland. In *Proceedings of 29th Nordic Symposium on Tourism and Hospitality Research (Akureyri)* (pp. 107-111). Academic Press.

Walker, H. V., Jones, J. E., Swarts, N. D., & Kerslake, F. (2021). Manipulating nitrogen and water resources for improved cool climate vine to wine quality. *American Journal of Enology and Viticulture*, *73*(1), 11–25. doi:10.5344/ajev.2021.21004

Walsh, B. (2011). Today's smart choice: Don't own. Share. *Times International*, *1*(3), 49.

Walter, P., Regmi, K. D., & Khanal, P. R. (2018). Host learning in community-based ecotourism in Nepal: The case of Sirubari and Ghalegaun homestays. *Tourism Management Perspectives*, *26*(February), 49–58. doi:10.1016/j.tmp.2018.02.002

Walters, L., Wade, T., & Suttles, S. (2020). Food and agricultural transportation challenges amid the COVID-19 Pandemic. *Choices Magazine*, *35*(3), 1–8.

Wang, C., & Hu, Q. (2020). Knowledge sharing in supply chain networks: Effects of collaborative innovation activities and capability on innovation performance. *Technovation*, *94*, 102010. doi:10.1016/j.technovation.2017.12.002

Wang, C., Liu, J., Wei, L., & Zhang, T. (2020). Impact of tourist experience on memorability and authenticity: A study of creative tourism. *Journal of Travel & Tourism Marketing*, *37*(1), 48–63. doi:10.1080/10548408.2020.1711846

Wang, H., & Hao, N. (2020). Panic buying? Food hoarding during the pandemic period with city lockdown. *Journal of Integrative Agriculture*, *9*(12), 2916–2925. doi:10.1016/S2095-3119(20)63448-7

Wang, L., & Yotsumoto, Y. (2019). Conflict in tourism development in rural China. *Tourism Management*, *70*, 188–200. doi:10.1016/j.tourman.2018.08.012

Wang, T. C., Cheng, J. S., Shih, H. Y., Tsai, C. L., Tang, T. W., Tseng, M. L., & Yao, Y. S. (2019). Environmental sustainability on tourist hotels' image development. *Sustainability*, *11*(8), 2378. doi:10.3390u11082378

Wang, X., Huang, S., Zou, T., & Yan, H. (2012). Effects of the high speed rail network on China's Regional Tourism Development. *Tourism Management Perspectives*, *1*, 34–38. doi:10.1016/j.tmp.2011.10.001

Wang, X., Li, X., Zhen, F., & Zhang, J. (2016). How smart is your tourist attraction?: Measuring tourist preferences of smart tourism attractions via a FCEM-AHP and IPA approach. *Tourism Management*, *54*, 309–320. doi:10.1016/j.tourman.2015.12.003

Wang, X., Peng, L., Huang, K., & Deng, W. (2022). Identifying the influence of disaster education on the risk perception of rural residents in geohazard-prone areas: A propensity score-matched study. *International Journal of Disaster Risk Reduction*, *71*, 102795. doi:10.1016/j.ijdrr.2022.102795

Wang, Y. F., Chen, S. P., Lee, Y. C., & Tsai, C. T. S. (2013). Developing green management standards for restaurants: An application of green supply chain management. *International Journal of Hospitality Management*, *34*, 263–273. doi:10.1016/j.ijhm.2013.04.001

Wang, Y. S. (2009). The impact of crisis events and macroeconomic activity on Taiwan's international inbound tourism demand. *Tourism Management*, *30*(1), 75–82. doi:10.1016/j.tourman.2008.04.010 PMID:32287727

Wan, Y. K. P., & Li, X. (2013). Sustainability of tourism development in Macao, China. *International Journal of Tourism Research*, *15*(1), 52–65. doi:10.1002/jtr.873

Ward, C., Raue, M., Lee, C., D'Ambrosio, L., & Coughlin, J. F. (2017, July). Acceptance of automated driving across generations: The role of risk and benefit perception, knowledge, and trust. In *International Conference on Human-Computer Interaction* (pp. 254-266). Cham, Switzerland: Springer. 10.1007/978-3-319-58071-5_20

Ward, M. P., Xiao, S., & Zhang, Z. (2020). The role of climate during the COVID-19 epidemic in New South Wales, Australia. *Transboundary and Emerging Diseases*, *67*(6), 2313–2317. doi:10.1111/tbed.13631 PMID:32438520

Wattanacharoensil, W., & Schuckert, M. (2016). Reviewing Thailand's master plans and policies: Implications for creative tourism? *Current Issues in Tourism*, *19*(10), 1045–1070. doi:10.1080/13683500.2014.882295

Waugh, N. C., & Norman, D. A. (1965). Primary memory. *Psychological Review*, *72*(2), 89–104. doi:10.1037/h0021797 PMID:14282677

Week, L. (2012). I am not a tourist: Aims and implications of "traveling". *Tourist Studies*, *12*(2), 186–203.

Wei, C., Zhao, W., Zhang, C., & Huang, K. (2019). Psychological factors affecting memorable tourism experiences. *Asia Pacific Journal of Tourism Research*, *24*(7), 619–632. doi:10.1080/10941665.2019.1611611

Weidenfeld, A. (2018). Tourism diversification and its implications for smart specialisation. *Sustainability*, *10*(2), 319. doi:10.3390u10020319

Weigel, R., & Weigel, J. (1978). Environmental concern: The development of a measure. *Environment and Behavior*, *10*(1), 3–15. doi:10.1177/0013916578101001

Weinberg, B. D., & Pehlivan, E. (2011). Social spending: Managing the social media mix. *Business Horizons*, *54*(3), 275–282. doi:10.1016/j.bushor.2011.01.008

Weinberg, T. (2009). *The New Community Rules: Marketing on the Social Web*. Emerald Group Publishing Limited. doi:10.1108/dlo.2011.08125cae.002

Wei, W. (2012). Research on the application of geographic information system in tourism management. *Procedia Environmental Sciences*, *12*, 1104–1109. doi:10.1016/j.proenv.2012.01.394

Wellman, M. L., Stoldt, R., Tully, M., & Ekdale, B. (2020). Ethics of authenticity: Social media influencers and the production of sponsored content. *Journal of Media Ethics, 35*(2), 68-82. doi:10.1080/23736992.2020.1736078

Wen, J., & Huang, S. (2021). The effects of fashion lifestyle, perceived value of luxury consumption, and tourist–destination identification on visit intention: A study of Chinese cigar aficionados. *Journal of Destination Marketing & Management, 22*, 100664. doi:10.1016/j.jdmm.2021.100664

What Is Sustainability and Why Is It So Important ? (2022). https://www.twi-global.com/technical-knowledge/faqs/faq-what-is-sustainability

White-Davis, T., Edgoose, J., Brown Speights, J. S., Fraser, K., Ring, J. M., Guh, J., & Saba, G. W. (2018). Addressing racism in medical education: An interactive training module. *Family Medicine, 50*(5), 364–368. doi:10.22454/FamMed.2018.875510 PMID:29762795

WHO. (2020). *COVID-19 and food safety: Guidance for food businesses: interim guidance.* Retrieved on April 24, 2022, from: https://www.who.int/publications/i/item/COVID-19-and-food-safety-guidance-for-food-businesses

WHO. (2021). *Ageing*. Retrieved on January 13, 2022, from: https://www.who.int/health-topics/ageing#tab=tab_1

Wiastuti, R. D., Adiati, M. P., & Lestari, N. S. (2018). Implementation of accessible tourism concept at museums in Jakarta. *IOP Conference Series: Earth and Environmental Science, 126*(1), 1-9.

Wiedmann, K. P., & Mettenheim, W. (2021). Attractiveness, trustworthiness and expertise – social influencers' winning formula? *Journal of Product and Brand Management, 30*(5), 707–725. doi:10.1108/JPBM-06-2019-2442

Williams, C. C., & Kayaoğlu, A. (2020). COVID-19 and undeclared work: Impacts and policy responses in Europe. *The Service Industries Journal*, 1–18. .1080/02642069.2020.1757073. doi:https://doi.org/10

Willoughby, K., & Galvin, P. (2005). Inter-organizational collaboration, knowledge intensity, and the sources of innovation in the bioscience-technology industries. *Knowledge, Technology & Policy, 18*(3), 56–73. doi:10.100712130-005-1005-z

Wilson, E., & Harris, C. (2006). Meaningful travel: Women, independent travel and the search for self and meaning. *Tourism: An International Interdisciplinary Journal, 54*(2), 161–172.

Wilson, E., & Little, D. E. (2005). A "relative escape"? The impact of constraints on women who travel solo. *Tourism Review International, 9*(2), 155–175. doi:10.3727/154427205774791672

Wimmler, C., Hejazi, G., Fernandes, E., Moreira, C., & Connors, S. (2015). Multi-criteria decision support methods for renewable energy systems on islands. *Journal of Clean Energy Technologies, 3*(3), 185–195. doi:10.7763/JOCET.2015.V3.193

Wisansing, J. (2019). *Creative Tourism Initiatives in Thailand : DASTA Model.* https://www.academia.edu/39983241/Title_Creative_Tourism_Initiatives_in_Thailand_DASTA_Model

Wnag, Y. (2011). Ageing travel market and accessibility requirements. In S. Buhalis & S. Darcy (Eds.), *Accessible Tourism: Concepts and Issues* (pp. 1–20). Channel View Publications Ltd.

Wolcott, H. F. (1994). *Transforming qualitative data: Description, analysis, and interpretation.* Sage Publications.

Wolff, C., Uppink, L., & Malhotra, S. G. (2021, June 10). How India can become a leader in sustainable aviation fuel. *World Economic Forum.* Retrieved on August 19, 2021, from: https://www.weforum.org/agenda/2021/06/how-india-can-become-a-leader-in-sustainable-aviation-fuel-saf-carbon-emissions-transportation-air-quality-pollution-covid/

Wong, A., & Sohal, A. (2002). An examination of the relationship between trust, commitment and relationship quality. *International Journal of Retail & Distribution Management, 30*(1), 34–50. doi:10.1108/09590550210415248

Wood, E. H. (2020). I remember how we all felt: Perceived emotional synchrony through tourist memory sharing. *Journal of Travel Research, 59*(8), 1339–1352. doi:10.1177/0047287519888290

Woods, M., & Deegan, J. (2006). The impact of training on interfirm dynamics within a destination quality network: The Case of the Fuchsia Brand, Ireland. In J. S. Chen (Ed.), *Advances in Hospitality and Leisure* (pp. 25–50). Emerald Group Publishing Limited. doi:10.1016/S1745-3542(05)02002-3

World Commission on Environment and Development. (1987). *The Brundtland report, our common future*. Oxford University Press.

World Economic Forum. (2017). *Travel and Tourism Competitiveness Report*. Retrieved on August 20, 2018, from: https://reports.weforum.org/travel-and-tourism-competitiveness-report-2017/

World Economic Forum. (2019). *The Travel and Tourism Competitiveness Report 2019* [El Informe de Competitividad de Viajes y Turismo 2019]. https://www3.weforum.org/docs/WEF_TTCR_2019.pdf

World Health Organizastion (WHO). (2020a). *Resources Publications*. https://www.who.int/csr/resources/publications/WHO_CDS_EPR_GIP_2007 _2c.pdf

World Health Organization (WHO). (2020b). *Sars Country Table*. https://www.who.int/csr/sars/country/table2004_04_21/en/

World Tourism Organisation (WTO). (2013). *Sustainable Tourism for Development, European Commission*. Retrieved on August 16, 2018, from: https://www.e-unwto.org/doi/pdf/10.18111/9789284415496

World Tourism Organization (UNWTO). (2021). UNWTO Inclusive Recovery Guide – Sociocultural Impacts of Covid-19, Issue 2: Cultural Tourism (Issue 2). doi:10.18111/9789284422579

World Tourism Organization. (2020b). *International tourism growth continues to outpace the global economy*. UNWTO. Retrieved on July 6, 2022, from: https://www.unwto.org/international-tourism-growth-continues-to-outpace-the-economy

World Tourism Organization. UNWTO. (n.d.). https://www.unwto.org/sustainable-development

World Travel and Tourism Council. (2007). *United States: The 2007 travel & tourism economic research*. Retrieved on May 19, 2021, from: http://www.wttc.travel/bin/pdf/original_pdf_file/1unitedstates.pdf

Wright, D., & Sharpley, R. (2018). Local community perceptions of disaster tourism: The case of L'Aquila, Italy. *Current Issues in Tourism*, *21*(14), 1569–1585. doi:10.1080/13683500.2016.1157141

WTTC. (2021). *WTTC global summit: Uniting the world for recovery*. WTTC.

Wu, K. (2016). *YouTube Marketing: Legality of Sponsorship and Endorsement in Advertising*. Academic Press.

Wut, T. M., Xu, J., & Wong, S.-M. (2021). Crisis management research (1985–2020) in the hospitality and tourism industry: A review and research agenda. *Tourism Management*, *85*, 85. doi:10.1016/j.tourman.2021.104307

Xia, J. C., Zeephongsekul, P., & Packer, D. (2011). Spatial and temporal modelling of tourist movements using Semi-Markov processes. *Tourism Management*, *32*(4), 844–851. doi:10.1016/j.tourman.2010.07.009

Xiang, Z., & Gretzel, U. (2010). Role of social media in online travel information search. *Tourism Management*, *31*(2), 179-188. doi:10.1016/j.tourman.2009.02.016

Xiang, Z. (2018). From digitization to the age of acceleration: On information technology and tourism. *Tourism Management Perspectives*, *25*, 147–150. doi:10.1016/j.tmp.2017.11.023

Xie, C., Yu, J., Huang, S., & Zhang, J. (2022). Tourism e-commerce live streaming: Identifying and testing a value-based marketing framework from the Live Streamer Perspective. *Tourism Management*, *91*, 104513. doi:10.1016/j.tourman.2022.104513

Compilation of References

Xu, C., Zhong, S., Li, P., & Xiao, X. (2021). Tourist memory and childhood landscape. *Journal of Tourism and Cultural Change*, 1–21. doi:10.1080/14766825.2021.2015358

Xu, J., & Grunewald, A. (2009). What Have We Learned? A Critical Review of Tourism Disaster Management. *Journal of China Tourism Research*, 5(1), 102–130. doi:10.1080/19388160802711444

Xu, J., Guo, S., Xie, D., & Yan, Y. (2020). Blockchain: A new safeguard for agri-foods. *Artificial Intelligence in Agriculture*, 4, 153–161. doi:10.1016/j.aiia.2020.08.002

Xu, M., Cui, Y., Hu, M., Xu, X., Zhang, Z., Liang, S., & Qu, S. (2019). Supply chain sustainability risk and assessment. *Journal of Cleaner Production*, 225, 857–867. doi:10.1016/j.jclepro.2019.03.307

Xu, X., & Pratt, S. (2018). Social media influencers as endorsers to promote travel destinations: An application of self-congruence theory to the Chinese Generation Y. *Journal of Travel & Tourism Marketing*, 35(7), 958–972. doi:10.1080/10548408.2018.1468851

Xu, Y., & Jeong, E. (2019). The effect of message framings and green practices on customers' attitudes and behavior intentions toward green restaurants. *International Journal of Contemporary Hospitality Management*, 31(6), 2270–2296. doi:10.1108/IJCHM-05-2018-0386

Xu, Z., Elomri, A., Kerbache, L., & El Omri, A. (2020). Impacts of COVID-19 on global supply chains: Facts and perspectives. *IEEE Engineering Management Review*, 48(3), 153–166.

Yacoub, L., & ElHajjar, S. (2021). How do hotels in developing countries manage the impact of COVID-19? The case of Lebanese hotels. *Int. J. Contemp. Hospit. Manag.*

Yadav, N., Gupta, K., Rani, L., & Rawat, D. (2018). Drivers of Sustainability Practices and SMEs: A Systematic Literature Review. *European Journal of Sustainable Development*, 7(4), 531–544. doi:10.14207/ejsd.2018.v7n4p531

Yamak, S., Ergur, A., Karatas-Ozkan, M., & Tatli, A. (2019). CSR and Leadership Approaches and Practices: A Comparative Inquiry of Owners and Professional Executives. *European Management Review*, 16(4), 1097–1114. doi:10.1111/emre.12318

Yang, Y., Zhang, H., & Chen, X. (2020). Coronavirus pandemic and tourism: Dynamic stochastic general equilibrium modeling of infectious disease outbreak. *Annals of Tourism Research*. https://www.ncbi.nlm.nih.gov/pmc/articles/PMC7147856/

Yang, B. (2016). GIS based 3-D landscape visualization for promoting citizen's awareness of coastal hazard scenarios in flood prone tourism towns. *Applied Geography (Sevenoaks, England)*, 76, 85–97. doi:10.1016/j.apgeog.2016.09.006

Yang, E. C. L., & Khoo-Lattimore, C. (2017). Constructing Space and Self through Risk Taking: A Case of Asian Solo Female Travelers. *Journal of Travel Research*, 57(4), 1–43.

Yang, S.-Y., & Chen, K.-Y. (2020). Development of a cloud tourism supported platform with friendly interfaces based on linked open data and Big Data Analysis Techniques. *2020 International Symposium on Computer, Consumer and Control (IS3C)*. 10.1109/IS3C50286.2020.00102

Yan, L., Gao, B. W., & Zhang, M. (2017). A mathematical model for tourism potential assessment. *Tourism Management*, 63, 355–365. doi:10.1016/j.tourman.2017.07.003

Yavuz, H. (2007). *Yiyecek-içecek hizmetlerinde nitelikli işgören istihdamını etkileyen faktörler: Sakarya örneği* [Unpublished master's thesis]. University of Sakarya, Sakarya, Turkey.

Yaylı, H. (2012). Çevre Etiği Bağlamında Kalkınma, Çevre ve Nüfus [Development, Environment and Population in the Context of Environmental Ethics]. *Süleyman Demirel Üniversitesi Sosyal Bilimler Enstitüsü Dergisi*, *1*(15), 151–169.

Yeh, S. S. (2021). Tourism recovery strategy against COVID-19 pandemic. *Tourism Recreation Research*, *46*(2), 188–194. doi:10.1080/02508281.2020.1805933

Yıldırım, A., & Şimşek, H. (2013). *Sosyal Bilimlerde Nitel Araştırma Yöntemleri* [Qualitative research methods in the social sciences]. Seçkin Yayıncılık.

Yıldırım, A., & Şimsek, H. (2016). *Qualitative Research Methods in the Social Sciences* [Sosyal Bilimlerde Nitel Araştırma Yöntemleri]. Seçkin Publishing.

Yılmazer, A., Kalpaklıoğlu, N. Ü., & Yılmaz, S. (2020). A research on the expectations of disabled individuals from hospitality enterprises for tourism participation and current situation determination [Engelli Bireylerin Turizme Katılımına Yönelik Konaklama İşletmelerinden Beklentileri ve Mevcut Durum Tespitine İlişkin Bir Araştırma]. *Türk Turizm Araştırmaları Dergisi*, *4*(3), 2821–2839.

Yılmaz, İ., & Beyter, N. (2021). Changes in the measures taken in food and beverage units for food safety after covid-19. *Journal of Tourism and Gastronomy Studies*, *5*(Special Issue), 321–346.

Yılmaz, M., & Şahin, M. K. (2021). Parents' willingness and attitudes concerning the COVID-19 vaccine: A cross-sectional study. *International Journal of Clinical Practice*, *75*, e14364.

Yılmaz, Y. (2007). *Otel ve yiyecek içecek işletmelerinde ziyafet organizasyonu ve yönetimi*. Detay Yayıncılık.

York, J. G. (2009). Pragmatic Sustainability: Translating Environmental Ethics into Competitive Advantage. *Journal of Business Ethics*, *85*(S1), 97–109. doi:10.100710551-008-9950-6

Young, A. (2021, May 6). *Premiumisation of Australia's wine exports continues*. National Liquor News. Retrieved July 20, 2022, from https://theshout.com.au/national-liquor-news/premiumisation-of-australias-wine-exports-continues/

Young, L. (2013). *Growing your business - A report on growing micro businesses*. Retrieved on June 11, 2019, from: https://assets.publishing.service.gov.uk/government/uploads/system/uploads/attachment_data/file/198165/growing-your-business-lord-young.pdf

Yu, C. P., Chang, W. C., & Ramanpong, J. (2019). Assessing visitors' memorable tourism experiences (MTEs) in forest recreation destination: A case study in Xitou nature education area. *Forests*, *10*(8), 636. doi:10.3390/f10080636

Yücel, H. A. (2020). *Platon State [Devlet]*. Türkiye İş Bankası Kültür Yayınları.

Yücel, M., & Ekmekçiler, Ü. S. (2008). Çevre dostu ürün kavramına bütünsel yaklaşım; Temiz üretim sistemi, eko-etiket, yeşil pazarlama. *Elektronik Sosyal Bilimler Dergisi*, *7*(26), 320–333.

Yue, Y., Li, X., Zhang, D., & Wang, S. (2021). How cryptocurrency affects economy? A network analysis using bibliometric methods. *International Review of Financial Analysis*, *77*, 77. doi:10.1016/j.irfa.2021.101869

Yu, M., Li, Z., Yu, Z., He, J., & Zhou, J. (2021). Communication related health crisis on social media: A case of COVID-19 outbreak. *Current Issues in Tourism*, *24*(19), 2699–2705. doi:10.1080/13683500.2020.1752632

Zadjafar, M. A., & Gholamian, M. R. (2018). A sustainable inventory model by considering environmental ergonomics and environmental pollution, case study: Pulp and paper mills. *Journal of Cleaner Production*, *199*, 444–458. Advance online publication. doi:10.1016/j.jclepro.2018.07.175

Zaman, K., Bashir, S., Afaq, Z., & Khan, N. (2022). Covid-19 Risk Perception of Travel Destination Development and Validation of a Scale. *SAGE Open*, *12*(1). doi:10.1177/21582440221079622

Compilation of References

Zanella, M. (2020). On the challenges of making a sustainable kitchen: Experimenting with sustainable food principles for restaurants. *Research in Hospitality Management, 10*(1), 29–41. doi:10.1080/22243534.2020.1790207

Zatori, A., Smith, M. K., & Puczko, L. (2018). Experience-involvement, memorability and authenticity: The service provider's effect on tourist experience. *Tourism Management, 67*, 111–126. doi:10.1016/j.tourman.2017.12.013

Zencirkıran, M. (2017). *Sociology [Sosyoloji]. Dora Yayıncılık, 6.*

Zerihun, M. E. (2017). Web based GIS for tourism development using effective free and open source software case study: Gondor town and its surrounding area, Ethiopia. *Journal of Geographic Information System, 9*(1), 47–58. doi:10.4236/jgis.2017.91004

Zhang, C. X., Fong, L. H. N., & Li, S. N. (2019). Co-creation experience and place attachment: Festival evaluation. *International Journal of Hospitality Management, 81*(May), 193–204. doi:10.1016/j.ijhm.2019.04.013

Zhang, C. X., Wang, L., & Rickly, J. M. (2021). Non-interaction and identity change in Covid-19 tourism. *Annals of Tourism Research, 89*, 103211. doi:10.1016/j.annals.2021.103211

Zhang, H. F., Cheng, X. J., & Shi, Y. T. (2012). Study on 3D modeling for history building and precision analyzing. *Advanced Materials Research, 443-444*, 471–476. doi:10.4028/www.scientific.net/AMR.443-444.471

Zhang, J., & Dong, L. (2021). Image Monitoring and Management of Hot Tourism Destination Based on Data Mining Technology in Big Data Environment. *Microprocessors and Microsystems, 80*, 80. doi:10.1016/j.micpro.2020.103515

Zhang, J., & Zhang, Y. (2020). Tourism and gender equality: An Asian perspective. *Annals of Tourism Research, 85*, 103067. doi:10.1016/j.annals.2020.103067

Zhang, K., Hou, Y., & Li, G. (2020). Threat of infectious disease during an outbreak: Influence on tourists' emotional responses to disadvantaged price inequality. *Annals of Tourism Research, 84*, 102993.

Zhang, M., & Bell, P. (2010). Price fencing in the practice of revenue management: An overview and taxonomy. *Journal of Revenue and Pricing Management, 11*(2), 146–159. doi:10.1057/rpm.2009.25

Zhang, S., Wu, Z., Ma, Z., Liu, X., & Wu, J. (2021). Wasserstein distance-based probabilistic linguistic TODIM method with application to the evaluation of sustainable rural tourism potential. *Economic Research-Ekonomska Istraživanja, 35*(1), 409–437. doi:10.1080/1331677X.2021.1894198

Zhang, X., Chen, Z., & Jin, H. (2021). The effect of tourists' autobiographical memory on revisit intention: Does nostalgia promote revisiting? *Asia Pacific Journal of Tourism Research, 26*(2), 147–166. doi:10.1080/10941665.2020.1718171

Zhang, X., & Tang, J. (2021). A Study of Emotional Solidarity in the Homestay Industry between Hosts and Tourists in the Post-Pandemic Era. *Sustainability, 13*(13), 7458. doi:10.3390u13137458

Zhang, Y., Qu, H., & Tavitiyaman, P. (2009). The determinants of the travel demand on international tourist arrivals to Thailand. *Asia Pacific Journal of Tourism Research, 14*(1), 77–92. doi:10.1080/10941660902728080

Zhang, Y., Washington, W. M., Weatherly, J. W., Meehl, G. A., Semtner, A. J., Bettge, T. W., Craig, A. P., Strand, W. G., Arblaster, J., Wayland, V. B., & James, R. (2000). Parallel climate model (PCM) control and transient simulations. *Climate Dynamics, 16*(10–11), 755–774. doi:10.100700382000007

Zhang, Y., & Xie, P. F. (2019). Motivational determinates of creative tourism: A case study of Albergue art space in Macau. *Current Issues in Tourism, 22*(20), 2538–2549. doi:10.1080/13683500.2018.1517733

Zhao, Y., Chau, K. Y., Shen, H., & Duan, X. (2022). Relationship between perceived value, satisfaction and behavioral intention of homestays in the experience economy of mainland China. *Anatolia*, 1-12.

Zheng, G. H., Jiang, D. F., Luan, Y. F., & Yao, Y. (2022). GIS-based spatial differentiation of ethnic minority villages in Guizhou Province, China. *Journal of Mountain Science*, *19*(4), 1–14. doi:10.100711629-020-6627-9

Zivkovic, R., Gajic, J., & Brdar, I. (2014). The impact of social media on tourism. *Singidunum Journal of Applied Sciences*, 758-761. doi:10.15308/sinteza-2014-758-761

Zobel, A. K., Lokshin, B., & Hagedoorn, J. (2017). Formal and informal appropriation mechanisms: The role of openness and innovativeness. *Technovation*, *59*, 44–54. doi:10.1016/j.technovation.2016.10.001

Zou, Y., & Meng, F. (2020). Chinese tourists' sense of safety: Perceptions of expected and experienced destination safety. *Current Issues in Tourism*, *23*(15), 1886–1899. doi:10.1080/13683500.2019.1681382

About the Contributors

Hakan Sezerel is a faculty member at Anadolu University, Faculty of Tourism, Department of Tourism Management. He is also a creative drama instructor. His research interests include tourism education, creative drama, process drama, tourist guidance, intercultural competence, and diversity management.

Bryan Christiansen is the President and Founder of Impruve, LLC, an enterprise reinvention organization based in Salt Lake City, Utah. A 30-year veteran of the management consulting industry, Christiansen has worked in over 30 nations in multiple industries. Fluent in Chinese, Japanese, and Spanish, he has given guest lectures at universities on three continents on topics related to business, cultural studies, marketing, project management, and psychology.

* * *

Öznur Akgiş İlhan is a faculty member at Kırşehir Ahi Evran University, Department of Geography. Her research interests are economic geography, tourism geography, sustainable development and poverty, fieldwork, and experiential learning.

Sakib Amin is an Associate Professor in the Department of Economics, and the Director of the Accreditation Project Team (APT) at North South University, Bangladesh. He holds a Ph.D. in Economics from Durham University (UK). Dr. Amin was also the receiver of the Commonwealth Rutherford Fellowship (2017-2018) for conducting his postdoctoral research at Durham University (UK). He is a fellow of the Higher Education Academy (HEA). His research focuses on Energy and Tourism Policy in the Developing Countries.

Mehmet Halit Akin graduated from Akdeniz University, School of Tourism and Hotel Management, Department of Hospitality Management (2009). He received his master's degree from Akdeniz University, Department of Tourism Management (2013), and his doctoral degree from Gazi University, Department of Tourism Management (2020). He started working at Gümüşhane University (2014). He is still working at Erciyes University, Faculty of Tourism as an Associate Professor. His research interests include tourism management, tourism marketing, sustainable tourism, green computing and health tourism.

Ali Avan is the vice dean of Faculty of Tourism at Afyon Kocatepe University. He received his bachelor's degree in hospitality and tourism management at Mersin University, his master's degree in tourism management from Afyon Kocatepe University and his Ph.D. in business administration from Afyon Kocatepe University. He is assistant professor in Tourism Management department now, and his areas of research include consumer behavior in tourism, services marketing, tourism marketing and sustainability in tourism.

Feridun Aydınlı graduated from Selçuk University, Department of Tourism Management. He is doing his master's degree in Tourism Management at Selcuk University (TR). He has worked on local delicacies. He is currently participating in research on food safety. Areas of interest in the Department of Tourism Management are Food Safety in Service Services, Local Tastes, Destination Marketing. Research Subject: Food Safety, Traditional Foods.

Gonca Babadağ is a Research Assistant of Institute of Education Sciences at Celal Bayar University in Manisa, Turkey. She received her MBA from Celal Bayar University. She received her PhD from Anadolu University She specializes ecological art. Her current research interests include visual arts, environmental education, and art education.

Mahmut Barakazı is an Assistant Professor at Harran University. He has studies on gastronomy, sustainable tourism, and technology.

Francesco Maria Barbini is Assistant Professor of Organizational Behavior at the Department of Management of the University of Bologna, where he teaches Human resource management and Organization of tourism enterprises. He is Vice director of the Center for Advanced Studies in Tourism of the University of Bologna. His main research interests are related to the subjects of organizational change, occupational health and safety, and organization in the tourism and cultural heritage industry.

Ahmet Baytok is the head of department at the Tourism Management department at Afyon Kocatepe University and has received his associate professorship in Tourism. He currently interests in the research of leadership in hospitality, organizational behavior, management and sustainability in tourism.

Birsen Bulut-Solak graduated from Ankara University with a BSc in Dairy Technology. She obtained a MSc and a PhD in Food Engineering from Selcuk University (TR). She was awarded an International Post Doctoral Research Fellowship by the Scientific and Technical Research Council of Turkey (TUBITAK). She fulfilled her post-doctoral research in Food and Nutrition Sciences at University College Cork (IRL) under the supervision of Dr. James Anthony O'Mahony between 2013 and 2015. She was a university lecturer in the Programme of Dairy Technology at Selcuk University between 2002 and 2013. Dr. Bulut-Solak is currently an Associate Professor in the Department of Gastronomy and Culinary Arts at Selcuk University, Konya (TR). She has also been an ambassador in Global Harmonization Initiative for Turkey since 2016.She is currently involved in three significant researches that are concerned with food safety, consumer acceptance of traditional foods and the determinant of food choice. She also works closely with others internationally (e.g., University College Cork and University of Illinois).

About the Contributors

Jessica Cattabiani graduated in 2019 in Marketing and Business Organization at the University of Modena and Reggio Emilia. In 2021 Jessica graduated with honors in Tourism Economics and Management at the University of Bologna. During the academic years, Jessica worked on several projects aimed at developing, implementing, and analyzing in a theoretical and creative way the tourism sector, thus leading her to specialize, after graduation, in outdoor and en plein air tourism.

Patrick Cohendet is full professor at HEC Montréal in the International Business Department. His research interests include Theory of the firm, Economics of Innovation, Economics of Knowledge, Economics of Creativity and Knowledge Management. He is the author of 20 books and over 120 articles in refereed journals, such as Research Policy, Organization Science, Industrial and corporate Change, Journal of Economic Geography, Long Range Planning, etc. He was the supervisor of more than 80 Ph.D. He conducted a series of economic studies on the economics of innovation for different international organisations such as the European Commission, the Council of Europe, the European Space Agency or the Canadian Space Agency. He is co-director of the research group Mosaic at HEC Montréal on the management of innovation and creativity, and co-editor of the academic journal "International Management".

Niranjan Devkota is an economist with the special focus on cross border activities and climate change related issues focusing adaptation. He has over 10 years of experience in the field of economics related research with varietal dynamics. His recent research focuses ranges from development economics especially in cross-border activities and agriculture. He received his PhD degree from Tribhuvan University Nepal. He has experience in impact analysis and model building. He has worked in terms to prepare strategic and implementation plans of several economic issues as a research associates. He has received high level training and capacity building workshop on international co-operation, natural resource management and trade related activities from several international agencies like SANDEE (ICIMOD), NDRC (China), Hi-Aware (ICIMOD), SANEM (Bangladesh) and from esteemed organizations and universities (online mode). He has command over STATA and basic knowledge of R.

Ljubomir Drakulevski is full-time Professor at Faculty of Economics, Ss. Cyril and Methodius University, Skopje, Republic of Macedonia. Main activities and responsibilities Strategic Management, International Management, International Business and Organizational Behavior.

Sema Ekincek is a Research Assistant of Gastronomy and Culinary Arts at Anadolu University in Eskisehir, Turkey. She received her MBA and her PhD from Anadolu University. She specializes creativity on the gastronomy. Her current research interests include food art, chefs' creativity, local food, and rural development through gastronomy tourism. She has worked in many national and regional projects on the field of gastronomy.

Massimo Ferdinandi, adjunct professor at the University of Bologna since 2010, carries out his research in the field of the influence of cultural anthropology and religions on marketing and human resource management. His other research interests are directed to the symbolic forms of the myth, the rituals of passage and the critique of ethnographic authority. He has written and participated in the drafting of several books on the relationship between cultural anthropology and internationalization processes. He joined the Foreign Service of the Republic of San Marino in 2010 as Ambassador at Large. In 2012 he was appointed as Ambassador to the Socialist Republic of Vietnam and in October 2017 as the Ambassador to ASEAN (Association of South-East Asian Nations). Before 2010, he covered the roles of CEO, member of BOD and General Manager for several multinational and public listed companies."

Silvia Fernandes is Assistant Professor at the Faculty of Economics, University of Algarve. She holds a PhD from this university and is member of Cinturs (Research Centre for Tourism, Sustainability and Well-being). She lectures Information Technology, Innovation and Entrepreneurship in undergraduate and master courses. She has several publications in books, journals, and communications in national/international conferences in themes such as: enterprise information systems, smart tourism, innovation, and governance.

Lawrence Fredendall joined Clemson University, Department of Management, received a Ph.D. from Michigan State University in 1991. Since then, he has taught Undergraduate, Masters, and Ph.D. level supply chain management courses. His research interest is achieving sustainable enterprises through continuous improvement and lean methods. He has published 76 refereed articles, and three books. Lawrence has been an associate editor at the Journal of Operations Management since 2014 and is currently a senior editor at Production Operations Management Journal. He is a past Editor of the Quality Management Journal, from 2013 to 2016. He was a Special Issue Co-Editor for the Journal of Operations Management Special Issue on Healthcare Delivery. He was also a past Vice-President for Awards for the College of Healthcare Operations Management (CHOM) at Production Operations Management Society. He is currently examining how the Theory of Constraints (TOC) facilitates organizational learning and improvement through the applications of its bottleneck management concepts or the Thinking Processes. He received training as a "Jonah" in 1992 from a Goldratt Institute staff member and received further training at the Avraham Y. Goldratt Institute in 1995.

Merve Özgür Göde is an assistant professor the Department of Gastronomy and Culinary Arts, Anadolu University Eskişehir, Turkey. She received her Master's and Doctorate degrees in Anadolu University, Institute of Social Sciences, Department of Tourism Management. She is currently studying on cost control in food and beverages business, gastronomy, sustainability, food and beverage marketing.

Eun Sun Godwin is a senior lecturer and the Master's course leader in International Business at the University of Wolverhampton Business School. Her research interests include FDI, cross-cultural management, influence of institutional environments on international business and emerging market MNEs.

Zekiye Göktekin received her Ph.D. in Disaster Management from Gümüşhane University in 2021 and she has been working as a research assistant at the same university. She gives lectures on the scope of disaster management and conducts scientific studies. She has focused on disaster risk reduction and decision-making in disaster management, which are sub-disciplines of disaster management in her studies. Göktekin graduated ranking first in school from medical vocational high school in 2010 and worked as an emergency medical technician in the 112 EMS for 5 years under the Ministry of Health of the Republic of Turkey. At the same time, she continued her undergraduate education in the Department of Emergency Aid and Disaster Management at Çanakkale Onsekiz Mart University and graduated with a degree in the program. Afterward, she received Pedagogical Formation Education at Çanakkale Onsekiz Mart University and while continuing her graduate education, she continued her career as a research

About the Contributors

assistant at Gümüşhane University in 2016. She studied the English language at Ankara University for 6 months and then received her M.Ed. in Disaster Education and Management from Çanakkale Onsekiz Mart University in 2018.

Güneli Güçlütürk Baran (PhD) received her PhD from Adnan Menderes University. His research interests in the tourism industry include information technologies, entrepreneurship, outsourcing, consumer behavior and types of tourism (accessible tourism and health tourism, etc.). She has also served as a referee for leading international tourism magazines such as Current Issues in Tourism. She works as an Associate Professor at Isparta University of Applied Sciences, Isparta Vocational School, Hotel, Restaurant and Catering Services Department in Turkey.

Emi (Emanuela) Hanes is an independent researcher. Her cooperations include the Vienna University FH BFI Campus Wien, the University of Salzburg and the University of Graz. Her research interests include China-EU business strategies, RegTech, FinTech, Cryptocurrencies, Geopolitics, Chinese Strategic Planning and Development Policies.

Smilka Janeska Sarkanjac, PhD, is associate professor at the Faculty of Computer Science and Engineering University "Ss. Cyril and Methodius" in Skopje, Republic of Macedonia. She is an electrical engineer (Department of Computer Engineering and Automatics) with MSc and PhD degrees at the Faculty of Economics. Her fields of interest are information systems strategy and management in the companies of the private sector and in the public sector and ICT for development.

Sunita Jatav is presently working as Assistant Professor with School of Management (PG), Dr. Vishwanath Karad, MIT World Peace University, Pune. She has a flair for Research and has contributed and presented Research Papers in various National / International Conferences and Journals. Her areas of interest include International Business, Service Marketing and Research Methodology.

Suja John is Associate Professor, School of Business and Management, Christ University, Bangalore, India.

Sasho Josimovski is full-time professor at the Faculty of Economics, University "Ss. Cyril and Methodius" in Skopje and EU expert in the field of research and innovation policy. One of his main research focuses is the usage of ICT in business and economy and the influence of the new technologies on the socio-economic and regional development.

Selin Kama is a Dr. Research Asistant in the Faculty of Tourism Management at Bitlis Eren University. Her research interests include tourist behavior, sustainability, and recreation.

Mine Karatas-Ozkan is a Professor of Strategy and Entrepreneurship at the Southampton Business School, the University of Southampton. Her research focuses on socially inclusive and sustainable entrepreneurship and leadership. She has carried out many internationally and nationally funded projects; and published numerous books and articles in these domains. She serves as a Vice President Talent Development of the EURAM (European Academy of Management).

Kiril Kjiroski, MSc, is working at the Faculty of Computer Science and Engineering University "Ss. Cyril and Methodius" in Skopje, Republic of Macedonia. He is an electrical engineer with MSc in Information Technology. His fields of interest are Virtualization, Cloud Computing, and Electronic Procurement Systems.

Fatima Lampreia-Carvalho is a researcher at Cinturs (Research Centre for Tourism, Sustainability and Well-being). She holds a PhD in Government from the University of Essex and lectured disciplines related with political theory, research methods, sustainability and governance. She currently develops projects on smart cities and has publications in books, journals, and communications in national/international conferences in themes such as: tourism sustainability, governance, citizenship, and educational policy.

Tipparat Laohavichien earned a Ph.D. in Industrial Management from Clemson University in South Carolina, USA. She is currently an Associate Professor in the Technology and Operations Management Department and a chairperson of the Ph.D. curriculum in Business Administration at the Faculty of Business Administration, Kasetsart University in Bangkok, Thailand. She teaches undergraduate, graduate, and doctoral students in the field of operations management and business statistics. Her primary research theme focuses on sustainable development and quality management in a business context.

Ramya Mahendran is the an managed innovation consultant. She is certified in design thinking, business modeling and jobs to be done. She has over 10 years of experience in the fields of managed innovation, startup incubation and acceleration, crowd sources idea management systems, design thinking and sustainability. She works with student entrepreneurs to build their business ideas into a successful business model. She works with some of India's leading Technology and Business Incubators, Institution Innovation Councils and Entrepreneurship Cells. She specializes in setting up innovation strategy, opportunity identification, large scale ideation campaigns and facilitating rapid prototyping events like design service jams and hackathons, organizing large-scale Innovation summits and global idea crowdsourcing events. Her current area of research is: How can empathy be taught with the help of design tools for product, service, and policy designers?

Samia Mahmood is a Senior Lecturer in Accounting and Finance and co-leads the Entrepreneurship and Small Business Management (ESBM) research cluster at Wolverhampton Business School. Her research and publication focus is women entrepreneurship and empowerment, women-led businesses, microfinance and SME financing. She has developed an interest in UN Sustainable Development Goals (SDGs), such as poverty reduction and women's empowerment through microfinance and access to finance. Her broad areas of research in women's entrepreneurship include Constraints to access finance; Contextual embeddedness of women's entrepreneurship, women empowerment and entrepreneurship. Moreover, she is interested in microfinance/SME finance impact on entrepreneurship development/poverty reduction/women's empowerment and microfinance institutions' performance (Efficiency and Outreach of MFIs).

Priyanka Michael is a student, Bachelor of Business Administration in Tourism and Travel Management, Christ (Deemed to be University), Bangalore, India.

About the Contributors

Tuğçe Özoğul Balyali is a faculty member at Van Yüzüncü Yıl University, Faculty of Tourism, Department of Tourism Guidance. She is a creative drama instructor. Her research interests include tourism education, creative drama, process drama, experiential learning, tourism guidance, tourism geography, intercultural competence, experiential learning, and fieldwork.

Manuela Presutti is an Associate Professor of Management at the Department of Management of Bologna. In 2003, she took a Ph.D in General Management at the University of Bologna - Rimini branch, where she teaches Management of Tourism and Tourism Management From 2005 to 2010 she was an Assistant Professor at the Department of Management of Bologna. She participates in the research activities of the Advanced School of Tourism Sciences - Rimini Campus of the University of Bologna. Manuela Presutti's main research activity was originally focused on small firms and internationalisation process. During the last years, her research interests have included the analysis of social networks, entrepreneurship, and tourism management.

Roya Rahimi is a reader in Marketing and Leisure Management. She is the REF coordinator of UoA 17 at the University of Wolverhampton, Business School. Her research interests are Consumer experience, Innovation, Big data, Sharing Economy, CRM, Organisational Culture, Gender Equality and Tourism Higher Education. Roya is the Associate Editor for Journal of Tourism Management Perspectives, book reviews editor for Journal of Hospitality & Tourism Management (JHTM) and book review editor for Journal of Hospitality and Tourism Technology. She sits on the editorial board of different leading journals in her field.

Lakshmi Raj is a research scholar at Christ University, Bangalore with a research focus in Social media marketing, Influencer marketing, and content marketing. Dual NET (National Eligibility Test) in Management. A year of banking experience at Axis Bank ltd.

Mallika Sankar is a research guide, Assistant professor and researcher with 24 years of experience in academia and industry. Her core competencies include management teaching, course development, research, and data analysis. She teaches courses in Ph D, postgraduate and undergraduate levels. She had published research articles and co-authored books on research methodology. She is an invited speaker in many public events and academic institutions.

Branislav Sarkanjac, PhD, is full professor at the Faculty of Philosophy University "Ss. Cyril and Methodius" in Skopje, Republic of Macedonia. He lectures Sociology of Health and Illness, Political Philosophy, Philosophical Anthropology, and Contemporary Theories of Governance.

Erdeniz Sezer completed his associate degree at Bilgi University, Vocational School of Cookery. He completed his undergraduate education in the field of Gastronomy at Eastern Mediterranean University and completed his graduate education from Istanbul Ayvansaray University, Department of Gastronomy and Culinary Arts. She has worked as a cook in hotels, cafes, and restaurants. She continues to work in the private sector.

Ahmet Bahadır Şimşek received his Ph.D. in 2019 from the Hacettepe University Department of Business Administration. He has been working as a lecturer/researcher at the Faculty of Health Sciences at Gumushane University since 2019. He gives lectures within the scope of operations research and conducts thesis consultancy in various undergraduate and graduate programs such as Health Management, Disaster Management and Business Administration. His research interest focuses on mathematical modeling applications in managerial decision-making and includes interdisciplinary collaboration.

Nasrin Sultana is a Ph.D. candidate at HEC Montreal with a specialization in International Business. Her research interests include social network analysis, knowledge and technology transfer, management of innovation, innovation ecosystem, sustainability, foreign direct investment, and international business. She studies how different organizations are linked and the impact of such linkages on organizations, industries, and ecosystems at both local and global levels. She has published in refereed journals including the International Business Review and the Competitiveness Review.

Ekaterina Turkina holds a PhD in Public and International Affairs from the University of Pittsburgh, USA. She is associate professor at HEC Montreal and a holder of Research Chair in Global Innovation Networks. Ekaterina is also an associate editor of Journal of Small Business and Entrepreneurship, as well as a member of International Advisory Board of International Journal of Productivity Management and Assessment Technologies. Her main research areas are social network analysis, innovation and inter-firm networks, industrial clustering, international business and international entrepreneurship. She has published in Journal of Business Venturing, Economic Geography Journal, Journal of Common Market Studies, Journal of Business Research, Applied Energy, Physica A: Statistical Mechanics and its Applications, International Journal of Computer Science and Network and other journals. She has written four books and was a recipient of several awards, including the Highly Commended Paper Award from the Journal of Enterprising Communities, Best Paper from the European Community Studies Association, and other. She was also the finalist for Alan Rugman Award that is given to most talented researchers in international business under 40 years old.

Sahadeb Upretee earned a PhD in Mathematics (Specializations: Actuarial Science; Statistics) from the University of Wisconsin Milwaukee, USA. Dr. Upretee is an assistant professor at the Department of Mathematics, Central Washington University, Ellensburg, WA. He teaches undergraduate courses in Mathematics, Statistics, and Actuarial Science. His research interest includes Data Science, Applied Statistics, Actuarial Science, Loss Data Analytics, Financial Economics, Structural Equations Modeling, Business Analytics, Model Uncertainty, Risk Measures, and Math Education. He collaborates with faculty members and researchers across different countries for scholarly activities.

Heyun Wang is an independent researcher. Her research interests include tourism, Chinese economy, and business analytics.

YuHan Wang is an independent researcher. His research interests include FinTech, Chinese economy and business analytics.

About the Contributors

Sibel Yamak is a professor of management at the University of Wolverhampton Business School. She specialises in governance with a focus on the relationship between business elites and state, contextual antecedents of top management teams, governance and democratisation relationship and sustainability. She received the Emerald Literati Network award for her work on business elites. She has published in peer reviewed journals such as British Journal of Management, Strategic Management Journal, Group and Organization Management, European Management Review, Journal of World Business. She is the former president of European Academy of Management.

Poshan (Sam) Yu is a Lecturer in Accounting and Finance in the International Cooperative Education Program of Soochow University (China). He is also an External Professor of FinTech and Finance at SKEMA Business School (China), a Visiting Professor at Krirk University (Thailand) and a Visiting Researcher at the Australian Studies Centre of Shanghai University (China). Sam leads FasterCapital (Dubai, UAE) as a Regional Partner (China) and serves as a Startup Mentor for AIC RAISE (Coimbatore, India). His research interests include financial technology, regulatory technology, public-private partnerships, mergers and acquisitions, private equity, venture capital, start-ups, intellectual property, art finance, and China's "One Belt One Road" policy.

Özcan Zorlu is the co-head of Tourism Guidance department at faculty of Tourism at Afyon Kocatepe University. He received his bachelor's degree inhospitality and tourism management at Balıkesir University and his master's degree in tourism management from Balıkesir University. He has received his associate professorship in tourism and written widely on specifically organizational behavior, knowledge management and alternative tourism activities in tourism.

Index

A

ABC Inventory 255, 267-268, 275
ABC Inventory System 267, 275
Accessible Tourism 362, 364-365, 367-370, 373, 388-390
Afyonkarahisar 362, 364, 374-375, 387-388
Airlines 107, 258-259, 400, 465, 475-476, 478-480, 482-488, 495, 526, 560-561
Airports 151, 392, 398, 412, 475, 477-478, 481-484, 486, 488
Australian Wine 26-33, 36-37, 39, 46-48, 50, 52-58, 61-62

B

Behavioral Intention 167, 178, 198, 254, 277-279, 282-283, 285-286, 292-293, 295, 527-528, 532
Blockchain 164, 220-221, 225-234
Business Process 82, 523

C

Chinese Tourists 27, 31-32, 37, 39-40, 42-44, 46-49, 51-53, 57-58, 61, 285, 296, 298, 324, 430
Chinese Wine Market 298
Consumer Behaviors 82, 84, 88, 177, 254, 467
Coronavirus 59, 98, 115, 283, 291, 295, 300, 324, 451, 453, 458, 462-463, 466-472, 474
Corporate Social Responsibility 4, 256, 272, 275, 475, 483, 486, 488, 507, 510, 512-514
COVID-19 2, 12, 21-23, 25, 27, 29-31, 33-35, 37, 39, 42, 47, 52, 56-57, 59-62, 64, 79, 82-99, 108, 114-116, 138-140, 156, 167, 175, 179, 268, 274, 277-278, 280, 282-283, 285-287, 289-296, 298-300, 303, 323-324, 331-332, 336, 342, 345, 356, 358, 391-392, 409, 451-474, 488, 529, 531
Creative Tourism 157, 160-161, 277-292, 294-297, 345, 347-348, 357, 359-361

Cultural Heritage 26-27, 31, 33-35, 58, 165-166, 189, 193, 195, 207, 317, 330-331, 336, 344-347, 351-352, 354, 356, 400, 409, 431, 499, 501, 503, 505-507, 519
Cultural Tourism 23, 60, 134, 170, 192, 218, 223, 233, 278, 281, 283-284, 294, 296, 336-337, 344-348, 359-360, 409, 416, 430, 537, 558, 567

D

Dark Tourism 413-415, 430-432
Data Analytics 159, 167, 466, 480
Dematerializatied 135
Developing Countries 154, 158, 211, 224, 233, 332-333, 397, 406-407, 454, 474, 493, 514, 549, 552-553, 566-567
Development Areas 171-172
Digital Tools 27, 33-34, 36, 163-164, 166, 173, 525, 527-528
Disabled Tourists 362-363, 369-370, 373-374, 387-388
Disaster Risk Reduction 427-428, 432
Disaster Tourism 413-417, 421-423, 425-427, 430-432
Disruptive Innovation 549, 552, 568, 570

E

E-Bill 128, 135
Eco-Gastronomy 80, 433-434, 436-437, 439-443, 445-449
Ecological Art 433, 439-446, 448
Economic Order Quantity 255, 257, 272, 275
Economic Order Quantity (ECQ) Model 255, 257, 272, 275
Economic Sustainability 9-10, 12-14, 164, 190, 192, 199, 221, 235, 256, 263, 267, 269, 275, 351, 363, 405-406, 490, 501, 503-506, 510
Elderly Tourists 362, 387
Emerging Country 490-491, 505, 508-509
Environmental Sustainability 10, 12, 20, 22, 61, 69, 166,

Index

173, 181, 194, 201, 224, 251, 255-256, 263-264, 266-267, 269, 275, 394, 480, 483, 486, 488, 494, 497-498, 500-506, 511-512, 514, 541, 544, 546
Environmentally Touristic Product 135
E-Office 128-129, 135
E-Tour Guide 128-130, 135
European Wine Tourism 298, 325, 332-333
Event Management 200, 528

F

Fine Dining Restaurants 65-67, 70, 78-79
Followers 55, 101, 105, 107-113, 558
Food 7, 9-10, 12-13, 27-30, 34-35, 43-44, 47, 60, 62, 65-71, 73-74, 76-77, 79-93, 95-99, 102, 107, 114, 118-121, 126, 130, 135, 151, 170, 184, 189, 191, 220-234, 236-238, 244, 263-264, 266, 273, 285, 287, 292, 299, 301, 305-306, 308, 311-312, 317, 324, 328-329, 336-338, 342, 345, 347, 352, 365, 367, 374, 384, 393, 403, 409, 433-437, 439-440, 445-449, 451-453, 457-474, 478-480, 491, 496-505, 523-526, 530, 533, 552-553, 555, 570-571
Fuzzy-TOPSIS 413, 419, 421, 425, 432

G

Gabhar Valley 235, 238-239, 241-245, 248, 250
Gastronomy 82, 84, 220-224, 226, 228, 230-234, 281, 345, 347, 352, 357-359, 388, 433-436, 439-442, 444-450, 467, 469, 474, 517, 527-528, 530, 558
Gender in Tourism 203, 218
Geographic Information Systems (GIS) 170, 177-179, 429
Global Hyper-competition 298
Green Computing 118-120, 122-126, 128-135
Green Data Center 127, 130, 135
Green Hotel 136, 252, 405, 499, 512
Green Restaurants 65-67, 70, 79-81, 435, 448
Group Decision Making 413, 419, 431

H

Health Risk Perception 285-286, 296
Hedonism 181, 187, 192-194, 202
Homestay Management 235-241, 243-244, 250
Hospitality Sector 119-122, 124, 129, 272, 451, 456, 492, 495, 552, 567
Hotel Industry 28, 255, 257-259, 268-270, 391-393, 400, 469, 493, 531
Human Agency 490, 504-505, 508-510
Hygiene 82-84, 87, 93, 95, 111, 224-225, 249-250, 289, 436, 451-452, 456, 460-461, 464-465, 472, 523, 528

I

Indian Aviation 475, 481, 483, 485, 488
Information System 163, 168-171, 173, 176-179, 429, 522-523
Innovation Capability 137, 139-140, 143, 145-147, 149, 155
Innovation Environment 137-141, 145, 147, 149, 152, 154-155, 159

J

Just-in-Time 255, 264-265, 270, 275

K

Knowledge Intensity 137, 139-141, 143, 145-147, 149, 154-155, 160, 162

L

Lean System 255, 266
Length of Stay Control 255, 260, 262, 273
Little Red Book 26, 48
Local Culture 100, 181, 186-188, 192, 194, 202, 223, 236-237, 280, 346, 492, 539

M

Marginal Revenue 260, 269
Meaningfulness 187, 189, 193-194
Memorable Eperience 181
Memorable Tourism Experience 187, 192, 196, 200, 202
Monitoring the Effects 172
Multi-Criteria Decision-Making 416, 418-419, 432
Multinational Hospitality Companies (MHC) 490

N

Novelty 160, 181, 187-188, 192-194, 198, 200, 202, 279, 287

O

On Demand 528, 553, 570
Overbooking 260, 262

675

P

Pandemic Situation 18, 42, 285, 288, 290, 296-297, 356, 452
Peer-to-Peer 226, 550, 553, 570
Power Mode 129, 136

Q

Qualitative Research 21, 23, 70, 81, 84, 88, 97, 99, 194, 274, 362, 364, 375, 441, 448, 490, 496, 515, 540, 542

R

Remote Sensing 173, 179-180, 484
Republic of Macedonia 549, 552, 554-558, 560, 564-570
Resource Inventory 163, 168-170
Resource Utilization 172, 405

S

SDGs 1-2, 5-6, 9-10, 12, 14, 16, 18-20, 346, 395, 491, 494, 499, 502, 507, 510, 515
Service Providers 150-151, 258, 277, 279, 282-287, 289, 296-297, 408, 478, 519, 522, 525, 551, 562
Sharing Economy 210, 549-555, 557-558, 560, 562-563, 565-570
Smart Destination 180
Smart Tourism 114, 123-124, 163-168, 173, 175-178, 180, 519, 529, 531-533
SME 63, 337, 490-491, 494, 497, 500-502, 504-506, 508-512, 515
Social Media 6, 12, 26-28, 33, 36-40, 46-63, 100-107, 109-117, 124, 154, 209, 239, 250, 278, 294, 296, 354, 356, 406, 411, 496-497, 501, 506, 518, 532-533, 551-552, 557-558, 563, 566-567, 569-570
Social Media Influencer Marketing (SMIM) 100-102, 105, 112
Social Media Influencers (SMI) 100-101
Social Platforms 55, 325, 341, 549
Social Sustainability 1, 11-12, 14, 63, 67, 192-193, 197, 199, 222, 255-256, 263-264, 266, 268-269, 272, 275, 346, 490, 492, 497-506, 508, 510, 512
Stakeholders of Tourism 155
Structural Equation Modelling 235, 251, 279, 295
Sustainable Development 3, 22, 24-25, 27, 58-59, 79, 134, 139, 161, 163-165, 168-169, 171, 173-176, 180, 193, 211, 221, 225, 230, 233, 237, 253, 274-275, 279, 298-300, 305-306, 309, 321, 332, 345-346, 358, 395, 402, 406, 410, 434, 447, 473, 476, 478, 487-488, 491-495, 506-508, 510-513, 515-516, 538, 543-544, 548
Sustainable Medical Tourism 137, 139, 143-145, 152-154, 159-160, 429
Sustainable Tourism 22-25, 27, 58, 62-64, 97, 114, 131, 135, 139-140, 152, 161, 163-165, 168-178, 180, 191-192, 196, 199, 206, 215, 218-219, 234, 237, 252, 271, 273, 281, 289, 292, 294, 299-300, 305-306, 308, 336, 338, 346, 367, 369, 391-397, 399-402, 405-412, 430-431, 434, 445-446, 468, 494, 508, 510-515, 522, 535-540, 543-548

T

TAM 469, 517-531, 533
Thematic Analysis 334, 362, 376, 496, 511
Thermal Hotels 362-364, 371-375, 379, 382-383, 386-387
Threshold Curve 260
TikTok 26, 48, 104, 250
Tourism and Hospitality 23, 28, 35, 56, 60, 62-63, 108, 114-115, 132-133, 161, 177-178, 195, 202, 217, 282, 291, 303, 338, 391, 398, 428, 431, 448, 454, 491-494, 508-509, 511-512, 531, 549, 552-554, 563, 566-567
Tourism Carrying Capacity 180
Tourism Destination 42, 145-146, 158, 161, 167, 175-176, 180, 218, 283, 288-289, 294, 299, 305-306, 335, 339, 343-351, 357, 360, 429-430, 432, 454, 557
Tourism Destinations 114, 117, 138-140, 142, 144, 151, 154, 164-166, 178, 223, 280, 282, 284, 289, 291, 300, 305-306, 309, 315, 335, 337-338, 344-345, 364, 372, 406, 411, 414, 417-418, 426, 429, 432, 455
Tourism Disaster Management 416-417, 429-430, 432
Tourism Management 60, 63-64, 113-114, 117, 157-158, 166, 168-169, 171, 175-176, 178-179, 196-198, 202, 215-218, 239, 241, 252-254, 270, 273, 291, 293-296, 334-339, 344, 348, 359-360, 403, 411-412, 428-432, 466, 469-470, 472, 511, 515, 530, 532, 537
Tourist Behavior Intention 287, 297
Travel Motivation 285, 297, 512
Travel Practices 277, 280, 284, 286-289, 297
Traveler 287, 289, 552, 571
Triple Bottom Line (TBL) 3-4, 22, 230, 255-256, 269, 271-274, 276

Index

U

Urban Development 151, 344

V

Virtual Tour 116, 130, 136
Visitor Management 16, 23, 169, 171-172, 237, 251

W

Wechat 26, 40, 53
Wine Brand Equity 298, 300-303, 306-312, 315, 319-321, 323-325, 327-333, 340
Wine Business 59, 298, 307
Wine Tourism 26-30, 32-39, 46-48, 50, 52-53, 57-61, 63, 298, 300-303, 305-309, 311-312, 315, 317-318, 321, 323-325, 327-343, 557-558
Women and Tourism 203, 207

Y

Yield Management 255, 258-260, 262-263, 268-270, 272-274, 276

Recommended Reference Books

IGI Global's reference books are available in three unique pricing formats:
Print Only, E-Book Only, or Print + E-Book.

Shipping fees may apply.

www.igi-global.com

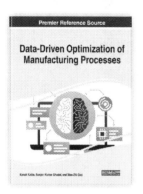

Data-Driven Optimization of Manufacturing Processes

ISBN: 9781799872061
EISBN: 9781799872085
© 2021; 298 pp.
List Price: US$ 225

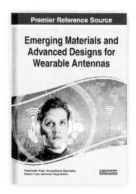

Emerging Materials and Advanced Designs for Wearable Antennas

ISBN: 9781799876113
EISBN: 9781799876120
© 2021; 210 pp.
List Price: US$ 225

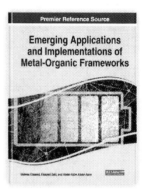

Emerging Applications and Implementations of Metal-Organic Frameworks

ISBN: 9781799847601
EISBN: 9781799847618
© 2021; 254 pp.
List Price: US$ 225

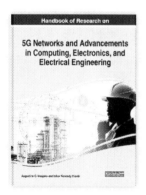

5G Networks and Advancements in Computing, Electronics, and Electrical Engineering

ISBN: 9781799869924
EISBN: 9781799869948
© 2021; 522 pp.
List Price: US$ 295

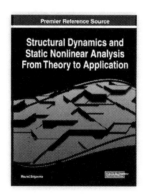

Structural Dynamics and Static Nonlinear Analysis From Theory to Application

ISBN: 9781799843993
EISBN: 9781799844006
© 2021; 347 pp.
List Price: US$ 195

Developing and Monitoring Smart Environments for Intelligent Cities

ISBN: 9781799850625
EISBN: 9781799850632
© 2021; 367 pp.
List Price: US$ 215

Do you want to stay current on the latest research trends, product announcements, news, and special offers?
Join IGI Global's mailing list to receive customized recommendations, exclusive discounts, and more.
Sign up at: **www.igi-global.com/newsletters.**

Publisher of Timely, Peer-Reviewed Inclusive Research Since 1988

Ensure Quality Research is Introduced to the Academic Community

Become an Evaluator for IGI Global Authored Book Projects

 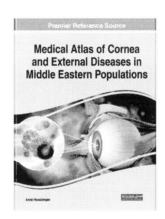 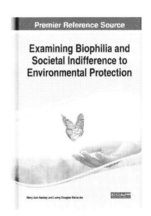 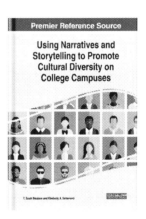

The overall success of an authored book project is dependent on quality and timely manuscript evaluations.

Applications and Inquiries may be sent to:
development@igi-global.com

Applicants must have a doctorate (or equivalent degree) as well as publishing, research, and reviewing experience. Authored Book Evaluators are appointed for one-year terms and are expected to complete at least three evaluations per term. Upon successful completion of this term, evaluators can be considered for an additional term.

If you have a colleague that may be interested in this opportunity, we encourage you to share this information with them.

Easily Identify, Acquire, and Utilize Published Peer-Reviewed Findings in Support of Your Current Research

IGI Global OnDemand

Purchase Individual IGI Global OnDemand Book Chapters and Journal Articles

For More Information:
www.igi-global.com/e-resources/ondemand/

Browse through 150,000+ Articles and Chapters!

Find specific research related to your current studies and projects that have been contributed by international researchers from prestigious institutions, including:

- Accurate and Advanced Search
- Affordably Acquire Research
- Instantly Access Your Content
- Benefit from the InfoSci Platform Features

"It really provides an excellent entry into the research literature of the field. *It presents a manageable number of* highly relevant sources *on topics of interest to a wide range of researchers. The sources are* scholarly, but also accessible *to 'practitioners'."*

- Ms. Lisa Stimatz, MLS, University of North Carolina at Chapel Hill, USA

Interested in Additional Savings?

Subscribe to
IGI Global OnDemand Plus

Learn More

Acquire content from over 128,000+ research-focused book chapters and 33,000+ scholarly journal articles for as low as US$ 5 per article/chapter (original retail price for an article/chapter: US$ 37.50).

6,600+ E-BOOKS. ADVANCED RESEARCH. INCLUSIVE & ACCESSIBLE.

IGI Global e-Book Collection

- Flexible Purchasing Options (Perpetual, Subscription, EBA, etc.)
- Multi-Year Agreements with No Price Increases Guaranteed
- No Additional Charge for Multi-User Licensing
- No Maintenance, Hosting, or Archiving Fees
- Transformative Open Access Options Available

Request More Information, or Recommend the IGI Global e-Book Collection to Your Institution's Librarian

Among Titles Included in the IGI Global e-Book Collection

Research Anthology on Racial Equity, Identity, and Privilege (3 Vols.)
EISBN: 9781668445082
Price: US$ 895

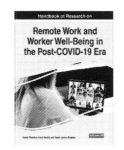

Handbook of Research on Remote Work and Worker Well-Being in the Post-COVID-19 Era
EISBN: 9781799867562
Price: US$ 265

Research Anthology on Big Data Analytics, Architectures, and Applications (4 Vols.)
EISBN: 9781668436639
Price: US$ 1,950

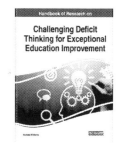

Handbook of Research on Challenging Deficit Thinking for Exceptional Education Improvement
EISBN: 9781799888628
Price: US$ 265

Acquire & Open

When your library acquires an IGI Global e-Book and/or e-Journal Collection, your faculty's published work will be considered for immediate conversion to Open Access *(CC BY License)*, at no additional cost to the library or its faculty *(cost only applies to the e-Collection content being acquired)*, through our popular **Transformative Open Access (Read & Publish) Initiative**.

For More Information or to Request a Free Trial, Contact IGI Global's e-Collections Team: eresources@igi-global.com | 1-866-342-6657 ext. 100 | 717-533-8845 ext. 100